CW00759154

A complete guide to every player 1993-1994

Compiled by

**Barry J. Hugman**

and Alan Platt

Published by Tony Williams Publications



ISBN 1-869833-46-5

Typesetting and Film Origination: Character Graphics, Taunton.
Cover Design: Bob Bickerton.
Illustrations: Empics, Nottingham.
Printed by: J.H. Haynes & Co. Ltd, Sparkford, Nr Yeovil, Somerset BA22 7JJ

Distributed by Little Red Witch Book Distribution,
24a Queen Square, North Curry, Taunton, Somerset TA3 6LE
Tel: 0823 491069 Fax: 0823 490281

# CONTENTS

*Outstanding at the heart of Aston Villa's defence and the cornerstone of the club's exciting, but ultimately abortive Premier League Championship challenge to Manchester United, Paul McGrath, was a popular choice as the PFA's "Player of the Year"*

# ACKNOWLEDGEMENTS

Once again, a tremendous amount of hard work has gone in to making this book irresistible for all those who follow Premier League soccer, a fact I would like to publicly endorse within the pages of the publication.

Firstly, my thanks must go to Rick Parry, Mike Foster, Adrian Cook, Nicola Denham and Jane Scott of the FA Premier League, for allowing Alan Platt and myself to peruse their records and for being extremely helpful over the duration.

Co-author Alan Platt has again been a pillar of strength, especially in the area of player profiles. He is a freelance transport planner whose recent assignments have all been overseas, but as an inveterate statistician he somehow manages to keep up with all the latest information, wherever he is in the world at the time, Unlike many schoolboys, he was never really interested in football until the age of 14, but once involved, he was hooked. From 1960 onwards, he has kept detailed records on all Premier/ Football League clubs and from 1985 to 1986 he contributed to the Chesterfield (where he lives) matchday programme. He and I met, following the publication of my initial Football League Players' Records, when impressed by the depth of research and attention to detail, he volunteered his assistance to all future editions. His expertise has always been gratefully accepted and he has gone on to help me produce many other books, including the Football League Year and the Official Football League Yearbook.

Michael Featherstone has been with me since I first germinated the ideas in 1975 that were to eventually lead to the publishing of Football League Players' Records. A keen sporting statistician, he works in the accounts department of a large public company and first became interested many years ago when he started to collect information on footballers and cricketers. He later became one of the founder members of Ray Spiller's Association of Football Statisticians and is one of the groups' more active recruits, diligently researching many thousands of births and deaths of former players over the last 15 years or more. However, it is when he is given heavy workloads that he comes into his own and apart from four editions of Football League Players' Records, he has worked on many varied publications, including the British Boxing Yearbook, The Olympic Games: Complete Track & Field Results, 1896–1988, the Who's Who of Cricketers and the Official Football League Yearbook and many others.

International appearances for all levels are always difficult to track down with so many games during a season these days and help in this area was forthcoming from Lorraine Kilby (English FA), Malcolm Berry (English Schools FA), Kitty Barlow (FA of Ireland), A. Evans (Welsh FA), R. Simpson (Scottish FA), D. Bowen (Northern Ireland FA), D. Painter (Welsh Schools FA), J. McDonnell (Northern Ireland Schools FA), Marshall Gillespie, Malcolm Stammers and Dave Barber.

Regarding information supplied by the clubs, I am most grateful to David Miles and Gary Lewin (Arsenal), Jim Walker and Dave Richardson (Aston Villa), Jim Furnell and Mike Pettigrew (Blackburn Rovers), Roy Evans and Bert Edwards (Coventry City), Les Helm (Everton), Mike Noye (Ipswich Town), Peter Gunby, Alan Sutton and Phillip Howard (Leeds United), Sheila Watts, Steve Heighway and Sammy Lee (Liverpool), Terry Farrell (Manchester City), Cliff Butler and Eric Harrison (Manchester United), Derek Wright (Newcastle United), Kevan Platt (Norwich City), Billy Urmson and Gordon Lawton (Oldham Athletic), Sheila Marson and Chris Geeler (Q.P.R.), Derek French and Keith Mincher (Sheffield United), Alan Smith (Sheffield Wednesday), Don Taylor (Southampton), John Pollard (Swindon Town), Ashley and John Fennelly (Tottenham Hotspur), Paul Hilton and Steve Bacon (West Ham United), Sharon and Reg Davis (Wimbledon). I would also wish to acknowledge all the anonymous club scouts, without whom the task of producing all 735 required skill factors would have been impossible.

I mentioned last year, that we would have to rely heavily on individual club statisticians and followers, regarding an in depth view on how players performed throughout the season and I am extremely grateful for the expertise provided by Chris Thompson (Arsenal), Denise Allibone, Paul Dann and Dave Hodges (Aston Villa), Harry Berry (Blackburn Rovers), Ron Hockings (Chelsea), Rod Dean (Coventry City), Richard Swift (Everton), Paul Voller (Ipswich Town), Mark Evans (Leeds United), Brian Pead (Liverpool), Dennis Chapman and John Maddocks (Manchester City), Richard Facer (Manchester United), Dave Stewart (Newcastle United), Mike Davage (Norwich City), Gordon Lawton (Oldham Athletic), Keith Westlake (Q.P.R.), Andrew Treharne (Sheffield United), Mick Renshaw (Sheffield Wednesday), John Mason (Southampton), Tony Angell (Swindon Town), Andy Shute (Tottenham Hotspur), John Northcutt (West Ham United), Simon Case (Wimbledon). Their local knowledge made all the difference when it came to elaborating on how the season went for all the players in question. And in many cases, it also explained why certain men who appeared to be replaced in a team because of a lapse of form, were often injured and therefore unavailable. I am sure that you will all agree that the previous season's form guide is an invaluable and most welcome addition to the book.

Virtually all the photographs were once again supplied by Neil Simpson (Empics Photo Agency, 26 Musters Road, West Bridgford, Nottingham, Tel. No. 0602 455885) and I am most grateful to both him and his company for the quality and quantity. Pictures can often make or break a book, but so can bad layout and design. To that end, I am indebted to Mark, Graham and John of Character Graphics (Taunton) Ltd, who with a knowledge of soccer, coupled to their efficiency in typesetting and layout, made the finished product a worthy one.

There were a good many other people who helped along the way and I thank all of them, including Adrian Barber and Michael Williams in the North Curry office and not forgetting the publisher, Tony Williams, who with his customary enthusiasm made the book a pleasure to work on.

Barry J. Hugman

# INTRODUCTION

Now into its second year, along with the FA Premier League and the continuing promise of "a whole new ball game", there is much optimism in this office that the *FA Carling Premiership, The Players* publication, with added improvements, will ultimately be seen as the complete guide on every professional player within the top flight, especially with the support of the FA Carling Premiership. Read by the professionals, the people involved behind the scenes and the fans, there should be almost, if not everything that you need to know about the players who make the game the exciting spectacle that we watch week in and week out. A point of view supported by Joe Royle, a man highly regarded in the game as Oldham Athletic's manager and once of England fame, in his Everton playing days, who personally feels that *FA Carling Premiership, The Players* should be an essential read for all managers and coaches, alike.

The format remains very much the same as last year when, to make it easy to follow, it was decided to split the book into two sections; clubs and players. And, with 735 player profiles and more than 450 photos of your favourite stars, either in pose or action, we hope that it presents not only an informed opinion on the merits of every player, but an attractive one at that.

The club section, which includes a brief history and playing results for 1992-93, also shows the current staff as at 20 July 1993, by position, club League debut and the season's appearances and goals. Players who have left since the beginning of last season are also shown, along with the current trainees. And where a player's name is written in *italic* within the team photo caption, it denotes that he is no longer with that particular club.

The decision to produce career records of all the players in alphabetical order and not within the club section, was made because some of them will almost certainly be transferred within the Premier League during the next 12 months and it will therefore be easier to identify them in this manner. All profiles include full Christian names, birthplaces and birthdates, heights and weights, a summary of all international honours and associated schoolboy, trainee and apprentice dates, where applicable.

When the player profiles were originally put together, the concept was to provide a factual synopsis of each individual career in an objective and neutral manner. Unfortunately, the end result, prior to finalising, was uniformly bland and uninteresting, so it was decided that in order to produce a more "colourful" profile, the authors would highlight both the up and downsides of careers. Therefore, instead of being wholly objective, it became more subjective and thus, arguably, betrayed the authors' biases for and against certain players. It was never the intention to be controversial and if any player, manager, or fan etc, is offended by certain viewpoints, one can only apologise and state that we believe our opinions to be fair comment based on the available information.

I stated last year that it was our intention to ask club experts to kindly provide far more detailed player information for 1992-93, including future aspirations and this has been done at the expense of having to leave out the club captains' articles. We feel that you will agree with that decision, as it acts as a better guide to the players' latest swings of form and also includes details of injuries, where applicable, etc. Every year, the previous season's details will be encapsulated back into the main career part of the profile, which will then be amended with the latest and most up to date information available. This will allow the reader to be able to assess any player's complete career at a glance and at the same time, be able to analyse his most recent form.

This brings me nicely on to the Position/Skill Factor element of the player biographies. Supplied by a senior club scout, who has a love and knowledge of the game, possibly unrivalled and helped by many other former players in a similar position, a description of all playing capabilities are highlighted, along with any suitable background information. This basically portrays playing qualities and attributes, not weaknesses, as it was felt that puting a player under the microscope to that degree would be both negative and ultra-critical.

Regarding the statistical box, the first mentioned club is that of the player in question's initial League side, including Scottish (this edition) and doesn't cover any previous playing details, which can be found amongst the text, while an * denotes his current club at the time of going to press. Due to a lack of information, appearances are not filled in for European clubs and to mix up non-League statistics with that of the Football League, as in the case of Lincoln City, who played both codes in consecutive seasons, for example, would merely lead to confusion. Appearances, plus substitutes and goals are broken down by Premier/Football League, League Cup, FA Cup and others, which includes European competitions, Play-Off games, the Charity Shield, Zenith and Anglo-Italian Cups etc. And the transfer fee shown is the one that would have been reported in the press at the time, but in some cases where player exchanges have taken place, adjustments have been made to take that into account.

Barry J. Hugman

# PREMIER LEAGUE CLUB SECTION

*Steve Bruce (left) and Bryan Robson celebrate Manchester United's Premier League Championship success at the end of a long, hard season*

## ARSENAL

**1886**

**THE GUNNERS**

**Team Manager** George Graham
**Club Address** Arsenal Stadium, Avenell Road, Highbury, London N5 1BU
**Record Attendance** 73,295 v Sunderland Div. 1, 9 March 1935
**Turned Professional** 1891
**Previous Names** Dial Square, Royal Arsenal, Woolwich Arsenal
**Club Honours** Football League: Div. 1 Champions 1930-31, 1932-33, 1933-34, 1934-35, 1937-38, 1947-48, 1952-53, 1970-71, 1988-89, 1990-91. FA Cup: Winners 1930, 1936, 1950, 1971, 1979, 1993. League Cup: Winners 1987, 1993. European Fairs Cup: Winners 1969-70
**League History** 1893-1904 Div. 2; 1904-13 Div 1; 1913-19 Div. 2; 1919-92 Div. 1; 1992- Prem.
**Most League Points in a Season** (2 for a win) 66 in Div. 1 1930-31. (3 for a win) 83 in Div. 1 1990-91
**Most League Goals in a Season** 127 in Div. 1 1930-31
**Record League Victory** 12-0 v Loughborough T. in Div. 2, 12 March 1900
**Record League Defeat** 0-8 v Loughborough T. in Div. 2, 12 December 1896
**Consecutive League Wins** 10 in 1987
**Consecutive League Defeats** 7 in 1977
**Record League Appearances** David O'Leary, 523+35 between 1975-93
**Record League Goalscorer—Career** Cliff Bastin, 150 between 1930-47
**Record League Goalscorer—Season** Ted Drake, 42 in Div. 1 1934-35

### 1992-93 Record

**Premier League** (10th): Played 42, Won 15, Drew 11, Lost 16; Goals For 40, Goals Against 38; Points 56
**FA Cup** Third Round: Yeovil T. (A)3-1; Fourth Round: Leeds U. (H)2-2 (R)3-2; Fifth Round: Nottingham F. (H)2-0; Sixth Round: Ipswich T. (A)4-2; Semi-Final: Tottenham H. (N)1-0; Final: Sheffield Wed. (N)1-1 (R)2-1
**League Cup** Second Round: Millwall (H)1-1 (A)1-1; Third Round: Derby Co. (A)1-1 (R)2-1; Fourth Round: Scarborough (A)1-0; Fifth Round: Nottingham F. (H)2-0; Semi-Final: Crystal Palace (A)3-1 (H)2-0; Final: Sheffield Wed. (N)2-1

**1992-93: Back Row L-R:** Gary Lewin (Physio), Pat Rice (Youth Team Coach), *Perry Groves,* Steve Bould, Alan Miller, *David O'Leary*, Alan Smith, Andy Linighan, *Colin Pates*, David Seaman, Tony Adams, Lee Dixon, Stewart Houston (First Team Coach), George Armstrong (Reserve Team Coach). **Front Row:** Nigel Winterburn, Paul Davis, Kevin Campbell, Pal Lyderson, Ian Wright, Ray Parlour, George Graham (Team Manager), Anders Limpar, Jimmy Carter, Neil Heaney, Paul Merson, John Jensen, David Hillier

## Playing staff for 1993-94 (As at 20 July 1993) — ARSENAL

| PLAYERS | CLUB DEBUT (Premier/Football League) | 1992-93 APPEARANCES | | | | 1992-93 GOALS | | | |
|---|---|---|---|---|---|---|---|---|---|
| | | Lge | FL Cup | FA Cup | Others | Lge | FL Cup | FA Cup | Others |
| **GOALKEEPERS** | | | | | | | | | |
| Miller, Alan | Leed U. (A) 21 November 1992 | 3+1 | | | | | | | |
| Seaman, David | Wimbledon (A) 25 August 1990 | 39 | 9 | 8 | | | | | |
| Will, James | – | | | | | | | | |
| **DEFENDERS** | | | | | | | | | |
| Adams, Tony | Sunderland (H) 5 November 1983 | 33+2 | 9 | 8 | | | | 2 | |
| Bould, Steve | Wimbledon (A) 27 August 1988 | 24 | 5 | 1 | | 1 | | | |
| Campbell, Stuart | – | | | | | | | | |
| Dixon, Lee | Luton T. (H) 13 February 1988 | 29 | 7 | 8 | | | | | |
| Keown, Martin | West Bromwich A. (A) 23 November 1985 | 15+1 | | | | | | | |
| Kirby, Ryan | – | | | | | | | | |
| Linighan, Andy | Chelsea (H) 15 September 1990 | 19+2 | 4 | 7 | | 2 | 1 | 1 | |
| Lyderson, Pal | Norwich C. (A) 8 April 1992 | 7+1 | 1 | | | | | | |
| McGowan, Gavin (Trainee) | Sheffield Wed. (A) 6 May 1993 | 0+2 | | | | | | | |
| Marshall, Scott | Sheffield Wed. (A) 6 May 1993 | 2 | | | | | | | |
| Morrow, Steve | Norwich C. (A) 8 April 1992 | 13+3 | 4+1 | 2+2 | | | 1 | | |
| O'Brien, Roy | – | | | | | | | | |
| Webster, Ken | – | | | | | | | | |
| Winterburn, Nigel | Southampton (H) 21 November 1987 | 29 | 7 | 8 | | 1 | 1 | | |
| **MIDFIELDERS** | | | | | | | | | |
| Davis, Paul | Tottenham H. (A) 7 April 1980 | 6 | 2 | 3 | | | | | |
| Flatts, Mark | Sheffield U. (A) 19 September 1992 | 6+4 | 1 | | | | | | |
| Hillier, David | Leeds U. (A) 29 September 1990 | 27+3 | 7+1 | 4+1 | | 1 | | | |
| Jensen, John | Norwich C. (H) 15 August 1992 | 29+3 | 3 | 4 | | | | | |
| McGoldrick, Eddie | – | | | | | | | | |
| Parlour, Ray | Liverpool (A) 21 January 1992 | 16+5 | 3+1 | 4 | | 1 | | 1 | |
| Selley, Ian | Blackburn Rov. (H) 12 September 1992 | 9 | 1 | 3 | | | | | |
| **FORWARDS** | | | | | | | | | |
| Campbell, Kevin | Everton (A) 7 May 1988 | 32+5 | 5+4 | 4+3 | | 4 | 4 | 1 | |
| Carter, Jimmy | Nottingham F. (A) 8 December 1991 | 11+5 | 1 | 1+1 | | 2 | | | |
| Clarke, Adrian | – | | | | | | | | |
| Connolly, Tony | – | | | | | | | | |
| Dickov, Paul | Southampton (H) 20 March 1993 | 1+2 | | | | 2 | | | |
| Harford, Paul | – | | | | | | | | |
| Heaney, Neil | Sheffield U. (A) 18 April 1992 | 3+2 | | | | | | | |
| Limpar, Anders | Wimbledon (A) 25 August 1990 | 12+11 | 4 | 2 | | 2 | | | |
| Merson, Paul | Manchester C. (H) 22 November 1986 | 32+1 | 9 | 8 | | 6 | 1 | 1 | |
| Read, Paul | – | | | | | | | | |
| Shaw, Paul | – | | | | | | | | |
| Smith, Alan | Liverpool (H) 15 August 1987 | 27+4 | 7 | 5+2 | | 3 | 2 | 1 | |
| Wright, Ian | Southampton (A) 28 September 1991 | 30+1 | 8 | 7 | | 15 | 5 | 10 | |
| Zumruter, Soner | – | | | | | | | | |
| **PLAYERS MAKING APPEARANCES IN 1992-93 (No longer with the club)** | | | | | | | | | |
| **PLAYERS** | **TRANSFERRED TO** | | | | | | | | |
| Groves, Perry | Southampton (August 1992) | 0+1 | | | | | | | |
| O'Leary, David | Leeds U. (June 1993) | 6+5 | 2 | 1+3 | | | | | |
| Pates, Colin | F/T (May 1993) | 2+5 | | | | | | | |

TRAINEES

Michael Black, Jason Brissett, Albert Clarke, Kevin Dennis, Graeme Hall, Jamie Howell, Stephen Hughes, Christopher McDonald, Gavin McGowan, Dafydd Owen, Matthew Rawlins, Matthew Rose, Nicholas Rust, Ross Taylor

# ASTON VILLA

**1874**

**THE VILLANS**

**Team Manager** Ron Atkinson
**Club Address** Villa Park, Trinity Road, Birmingham B6 6HE
**Record Attendance** 76,588 v Derby Co., FA Cup 6th Round, 2 March 1946
**Turned Professional** 1885
**Previous Names** None
**Club Honours** Football League: Div. 1 Champions 1893-94, 1895-96, 1896-97, 1898-99, 1899-1900, 1909-10, 1980-81; Div. 2 Champions 1937-38, 1959-60; Div. 3 Champions 1971-72. FA Cup: Winners 1887, 1895, 1897, 1905, 1913, 1920, 1957. Football League Cup: Winners 1961, 1975, 1977. European Cup: Winners 1982-83. European Super Cup: Winners 1982-83
**League History** 1888-1936 Div. 1; 1936-38 Div. 2; 1938-59 Div. 1; 1959-60 Div. 2; 1960-67 Div. 1; 1967-70 Div. 2; 1970-72 Div. 3; 1972-75 Div. 2; 1975-87 Div. 1; 1987-88 Div. 2; 1988-92 Div. 1; 1992- Prem.
**Most League Points in a Season** (2 for a win) 70 in Div. 3, 1971-72. (3 for a win). 78 in Div. 2, 1987-88
**Most League Goals in a Season** 128 in Div. 1, 1930-31
**Record League Victory** 12-2 v Accrington Stanley in Div. 1, 12 March 1882
**Record League Defeat** 0-7 v Blackburn Rov. in Div. 1, 19 October 1889, v West Bromwich A. in Div. 1, 19 October 1935 and v Manchester U. in Div. 1, 24 October 1964
**Consecutive League Wins** 9 in 1897
**Consecutive League Defeats** 11 in 1910 and 1963
**Record League Appearances** Charlie Aitken, 559+2 between 1961-76
**Record League Goalscorer—Career** Harry Hampton, 213 between 1904-20 and Billy Walker, 213 between 1919-34
**Record League Goalscorer—Season** "Pongo" Waring, 49 in Div. 1, 1930-31

## 1992-93 Record

**Premier League** (2nd): Played 42, Won 21, Drew 11, Lost 10; Goals For 57, Goals Against 40; Points 74
**FA Cup** Third Round: Bristol Rov. (H)1-1 (R)3-0; Fourth Round: Wimbledon (H)1-1 (R)0-0
**League Cup** Second Round: Oxford U. (A)2-1 (H)2-1; Third Round: Manchester U. (H)1-0; Fourth Round: Ipswich T. (H)2-2 (R)0-1

**1992-93: Back Row L-R:** Richard Money (Youth Team Coach), Stefan Beinlich, Matthias Breitkreutz, Mark Cox, Mark Blake, Stephen Froggatt, Bryan Small, Roger Spry (Fitness Consultant). **Middle Row:** Dave Sexton (First Team Coach), Dwight Yorke, Garry Parker, Paul McGrath, *Les Sealey*, Nigel Spink, Martin Carruthers, Ugo Ehiogu, *Cyrille Regis*, Jim Walker (Physio). **Front Row:** Shaun Teale, Earl Barrett, Dariusz Kubicki, Jim Barron (Assistant Team Manager), Ron Atkinson (Team Manager), Kevin Richardson, Dalian Atkinson, Steve Staunton, Tony Daley

## Playing staff for 1993-94 (As at 20 July 1993) — ASTON VILLA

| PLAYERS | CLUB DEBUT (Premier/Football League) | 1992-93 APPEARANCES | | | | 1991-92 GOALS | | | |
|---|---|---|---|---|---|---|---|---|---|
| | | Lge | FL Cup | FA Cup | Others | Lge | FL Cup | FA Cup | Others |
| **GOALKEEPERS** | | | | | | | | | |
| Bosnich, Mark | Luton T. (A) 24 April 1992 | 17 | | 1 | | | | | |
| Oakes, Michael | – | | | | | | | | |
| Spink, Nigel | Nottingham F. (A) 26 December 1979 | 25 | 5 | 3 | | | | | |
| **DEFENDERS** | | | | | | | | | |
| Barrett, Earl | Manchester C. (A) 29 February 1992 | 42 | 5 | 4 | | 1 | | | |
| Boden, Chris | – | | | | | | | | |
| Browne, Paul | – | | | | | | | | |
| Crisp, Richard | – | | | | | | | | |
| Ehiogu, Ugo | Arsenal (H) 24 August 1991 | 1+3 | 1 | | | | | | |
| Evans, Darren | – | | | | | | | | |
| Kubicki, Dariusz | Southampton (A) 31 August 1991 | | 1 | | | | | | |
| McGrath, Paul | Nottingham F. (A) 19 August 1989 | 42 | 4 | 4 | | 4 | 1 | | |
| Small, Bryan | Everton (A) 19 October 1991 | 10+4 | 1 | | | | | | |
| Staunton, Steve | Sheffield Wed. (A) 17 August 1991 | 42 | 5 | 4 | | 2 | | | |
| Teale, Shaun | Sheffield Wed. (A) 17 August 1991 | 39 | 4 | 4 | | 1 | 1 | | |
| **MIDFIELDERS** | | | | | | | | | |
| Berry, Trevor | – | | | | | | | | |
| Blake, Mark | Luton T. (A) 14 October 1989 | 0+1 | | | | | | | |
| Breitkreutz, Matthias | Sheffield Wed. (H) 18 January 1992 | 2+1 | 0+1 | | | | | | |
| Cowans, Gordon | Manchester C. (A) 7 February 1976 | | | | | | | | |
| Cox, Neil | Notts Co. (A) 10 March 1992 | 6+9 | 1+1 | 2+1 | | 1 | | 1 | |
| Farrelly, Gareth | – | | | | | | | | |
| Froggatt, Stephen | West Ham U. (A) 26 December 1991 | 16+1 | 1 | 2+1 | | 1 | | | |
| Houghton, Ray | Ipswich T. (A) 15 August 1992 | 39 | 5 | 4 | | 3 | | 1 | |
| Parker, Garry | Oldham Ath. (A) 30 November 1991 | 37 | 5 | 4 | | 8 | | | |
| Pearce, Dennis | – | | | | | | | | |
| Richardson, Kevin | Sheffield Wed. (A) 17 August 1991 | 42 | 5 | 4 | | 2 | 1 | | |
| Scimeca, Riccardo | – | | | | | | | | |
| Townsend, Andy | – | | | | | | | | |
| Williams, Lee | – | | | | | | | | |
| **FORWARDS** | | | | | | | | | |
| Atkinson, Dalian | Sheffield Wed. (A) 17 August 1991 | 28 | 4 | | | 11 | 2 | | |
| Beinlich, Stefan | Nottingham F. (A) 18 April 1992 | 1+6 | | | | | | | |
| Carruthers, Martin | Wimbledon (A) 8 February 1992 | 0+1 | | | | | | | |
| Cowe, Steven | – | | | | | | | | |
| Daley, Tony | Southampton (A) 20 April 1985 | 8+5 | | | | 2 | | | |
| Davis, Neil | – | | | | | | | | |
| Farrell, David | Oldham Ath. (A) 24 October 1992 | 1+1 | | | | | | | |
| Fenton, Graham | – | | | | | | | | |
| Saunders, Dean | Leeds U. (A) 13 September 1992 | 35 | 5 | 4 | | 13 | 2 | 2 | |
| Yorke, Dwight | Crystal Palace (A) 24 March 1990 | 22+5 | 2+2 | 4 | | 6 | | 1 | |
| **PLAYERS MAKING APPEARANCES IN 1992-93 (No longer with the club)** | | | | | | | | | |
| **PLAYERS** | **TRANSFERRED TO** | | | | | | | | |
| McAvennie, Frank | Glasgow Celtic (October 1992) | 0+3 | | | | | | | |
| Regis, Cyrille | Wolverhampton W. (July 1993) | 7+6 | 1+1 | 0+2 | | 1 | | | |

TRAINEES

Lee Aston, Michael Boxall, Stuart Brock, Ian Brown, Lee Burchell, Darren Byfield, Garry Harrison, Brian Henderson, Lee Hendrie, Leslie Hines, Andrew Mitchell, David Moore, John Murphy, Mark Peters, Adam Rachel, Marc Senior

# BLACKBURN ROVERS
1875

ARTE ET LABORE

THE BLUE & WHITES

**Team Manager** Kenny Dalglish
**Club Address** Ewood Park, Blackburn BB2 4JF
**Record Attendance** 61,783 v Bolton W., FA Cup 6th Round, 2 March 1929
**Turned Professional** 1880
**Previous Names** Blackburn Grammar School OB
**Club Honours** Football League: Div. 1 Champions 1911-12, 1913-14; Div. 2 Champions 1938-39; Div. 3 Champions 1974-75. FA Cup: Winners 1884, 1885, 1886, 1890, 1891, 1928
**League History** 1888-1936 Div. 1; 1936-39 Div. 2; 1946-47 Div. 1; 1947-57 Div. 2; 1957-66 Div. 1; 1966-71 Div. 2; 1971-75 Div. 3; 1975-79 Div. 2; 1979-80 Div. 3; 1980-92 Div. 2; 1992- Prem.
**Most League Points in a Season** (2 for a win) 60 in Div. 3, 1974-75. (3 for a win) 77 in Div. 2, 1988-89
**Most League Goals in a Season** 114 in Div. 2, 1954-55
**Record League Victory** 9-0 v Middlesbrough in Div. 2, 6 November 1954
**Record League Defeat** 0-8 v Arsenal in Div. 1, 25 February 1933
**Consecutive League Wins** 8 in 1980
**Consecutive League Defeats** 7 in 1966
**Record League Appearances** Derek Fazackerley, 593+3 between 1970-86
**Record League Goalscorer—Career** Simon Garner, 168 between 1978-92
**Record League Goalscorer—Season** Ted Harper, 43 in Div. 1, 1925-26

## 1992-93 Record

**Premier League** (4th): Played 42, Won 20, Drew 11, Lost 11; Goals For 68, Goals Against 46; Points 71
**FA Cup** Third Round: Bournemouth (H)3-1; Fourth Round: Crewe Alex. (A)3-0; Fifth Round: Newcastle U. (H)1-0; Sixth Round: Sheffield U. (H)0-0 (R)2-2
**League Cup** Second Round: Huddersfield T. (A)1-1 (H)4-3; Third Round: Norwich C. (H)2-0; Fourth Round: Watford (H)6-1; Fifth Round: Cambridge U. (H)3-2; Semi-Final: Sheffield Wed. (H)2-4 (A)1-2

**1992-93: Back Row L-R:** Nicky Reid, *Craig Skinner*, Wayne Burnett, David May, Frank Talia, Bobby Mimms, Matt Dickins, Darren Collier, *Keith Hill*, Jason Wilcox, Mark Atkins, Peter Thorne. **Middle Row:** Mike Pettigrew (Physio), Ray Harford (Assistant Team Manager), Tim Sherwood, Stuart Ripley, Mike Newell, Colin Hendry, Robert Dewhurst, *Lee Richardson*, Richard Brown, *Steve Agnew*, *Darren Donnelly*, *Stuart Munro*, *Ian McGarry*, *Gordon Cowans*, Tony Parkes (First Team Coach), Asa Hartford (Reserve Team Manager). **Front Row:** Gary Tallon, *Roy Wegerle*, Alan Shearer, *Chris Price*, Alan Wright, *Brendan O'Shaughnessy*, Kenny Dalglish (Team Manager), Kevin Moran, Tony Dobson, *Steve Livingstone*, *John Pickup*, *Scott Lindsay*, Lee Makel

## Playing staff for 1993-94 (As at 20 July 1993) — BLACKBURN ROVERS

| PLAYERS | CLUB DEBUT (Premier/Football League) | 1992-93 APPEARANCES | | | | 1992-93 GOALS | | | |
|---|---|---|---|---|---|---|---|---|---|
| | | Lge | FL Cup | FA Cup | Others | Lge | FL Cup | FA Cup | Others |
| **GOALKEEPERS** | | | | | | | | | |
| Collier, Darren | Ipswich T. (A) 13 May 1989 | | | | | | | | |
| Dickins, Matt | Wolverhampton W. (H) 14 April 1992 | | | | | | | | |
| Mimms, Bobby | Charlton Ath. (A) 1 January 1991 | 42 | 7 | 5 | | | | | |
| Talia, Frank | – | | | | | | | | |
| **DEFENDERS** | | | | | | | | | |
| Andersson, Patrik | Wimbledon (H) 9 January 1993 | 6+5 | 2 | 1 | | | 1 | | |
| Berg, Henning | Crystal Palace (H) 2 February 1993 | 2+2 | 2 | | | | | | |
| Brown, Richard | Port Vale (H) 14 September 1991 | 2 | 1+1 | | | | | | |
| Dewhurst, Robert | Hull C. (H) 28 August 1990 | | | | | | | | |
| Dobson, Tony | Ipswich T. (H) 19 January 1991 | 15+4 | 3 | 2 | | | | | |
| Hendry, Colin | Charlton Ath. (A) 9 November 1991 | 41 | 7 | 5 | | 1 | | | |
| Le Saux, Graham | Liverpool (H) 3 April 1993 | 9 | | | | | | | |
| Marker, Nicky | Oldham Ath. (H) 26 September 1992 | 12+3 | | 2 | | | | | |
| May, David | Swindon T. (A) 1 April 1989 | 34 | 5+1 | 5 | | 1 | 1 | | |
| Moran, Kevin | Stoke C. (H) 27 January 1989 | 36 | 2+1 | 4 | | 4 | | | |
| Scott, Andrew | – | | | | | | | | |
| Wright, Alan | Grimsby T. (H) 26 October 1991 | 24 | 6 | 3 | | | | | |
| **MIDFIELDERS** | | | | | | | | | |
| Ainscough, Paul | – | | | | | | | | |
| Atkins, Mark | Chelsea (A) 27 August 1988 | 24+7 | 5+2 | 2+2 | | 4 | 1 | | |
| Burnett, Wayne | – | | | | | | | | |
| Ireland, Simon | Manchester C. (A) 30 January 1993 | 0+1 | | | | | | | |
| Makel, Lee | Middlesbrough (H) 20 March 1993 | 1 | 0+2 | | | | | | |
| Metcalf, Josh | – | | | | | | | | |
| Sherwood, Tim | Middlesbrough (A) 22 February 1992 | 38+1 | 6 | 4+1 | | 3 | | | |
| **FORWARDS** | | | | | | | | | |
| Gallacher, Kevin | Liverpool (H) 3 April 1993 | 9 | | | | 5 | | | |
| Grunshaw, Steven | – | | | | | | | | |
| Newell, Mike | Barnsley (H) 16 November 1991 | 40 | 6+1 | 5 | | 14 | 5 | 3 | |
| Ripley, Stuart | Crystal Palace (A) 15 August 1992 | 38+2 | 6 | 4 | | 7 | | 2 | |
| Shearer, Alan | Crystal Palace (A) 15 August 1992 | 21 | 5 | | | 16 | 6 | | |
| Tallon, Gary | – | | | | | | | | |
| Thorne, Peter | – | | | | | | | | |
| Wilcox, Jason | Swindon T. (H) 16 April 1990 | 31+2 | 5+1 | 5 | | 4 | | 1 | |
| **PLAYERS MAKING APPEARANCES IN 1992-93 (No longer with the club)** | | | | | | | | | |
| **PLAYERS** | **TRANSFERRED TO** | | | | | | | | |
| Cowans, Gordon | Aston Villa (June 1993) | 23+1 | 4 | 3 | | 1 | | | |
| Hill, Keith | Plymouth Arg. (September 1992) | 0+1 | | | | | | | |
| Livingstone, Steve | Chelsea (March 1993) | 1+1 | 1 | 1 | | | | 1 | |
| Price, Chris | Portsmouth (January 1993) | 2+4 | 1 | | | | | | |
| Wegerle, Roy | Coventry C. (March 1993) | 11+11 | 3+3 | 4+1 | | 4 | 4 | 2 | |

TRAINEES

Christopher Bardsley, Karl Gaston, Andrew Gifford, Wayne Gill, Daniel Goodall, Daren Grassby, Steven Hitchen, Michael Holt, Christopher McCrone, Thomas Morgan, Brett Ormerod, Adam Sinnott, Damian Sweeney, Scott Thornton, Anthony Whealing

**Team Manager** Glenn Hoddle
**Club Address** Stamford Bridge, Fulham Road, London SW6 1HS
**Record Attendance** 82,905 v Arsenal, Div. 1, 12 October 1935
**Turned Professional** 1905
**Previous Names** None
**Club Honours** Football League: Div. 1 Champions 1954-55. Div. 2 Champions 1983-84, 1988-89. FA Cup: Winners 1970. Football League Cup: Winners 1965. European Cup Winners Cup: Winners 1970-71
**League History** 1905-07 Div. 2; 1907-10 Div. 1; 1910-12 Div. 2; 1912-24 Div. 1; 1924-30 Div. 2; 1930-62 Div. 1; 1962-63 Div. 2; 1963-75 Div. 1; 1975-77 Div. 2; 1977-79 Div. 1; 1979-84 Div. 2; 1984-88 Div. 1; 1988-89 Div. 2; 1989-92 Div. 1; 1992- Prem.
**Most League Points in a Season** (2 for a win) 57 in Div. 2, 1906-07. (3 for a win) 99 in Div. 2, 1988-89
**Most League Goals in a Season** 98 in Div. 1, 1960-61
**Record League Victory** 7-0 v Lincoln C. in Div. 2, 29 October 1910, v Walsall in Div. 2, 4 February 1989 and 9-2 v Glossop in Div. 2, 1 September 1906
**Record League Defeat** 1-8 v Wolverhampton W. in Div. 1, 26 September 1953 and 0-7 v Nottingham F. in Div. 1, 20 April 1991
**Consecutive League Wins** 8 in 1927 and 1989
**Consecutive League Defeats** 7 in 1952
**Record League Appearances** Ron Harris, 646+9 between 1962-80
**Record League Goalscorer—Career** Bobby Tambling, 164 between 1958-70
**Record League Goalscorer—Season** Jimmy Greaves, 41 in Div. 1, 1960-61

## 1992-93 Record

**Premier League** (11th): Played 42, Won 14, Drew 14, Lost 14; Goals For 51, Goals Against 54; Points 56
**FA Cup** Third Round: Middlesbrough (A)1-2
**League Cup** Second Round: Walsall (A)3-0 (H)1-0; Third Round: Newcastle U. (H)2-1; Fourth Round: Everton (A)2-2 (R)1-0; Fifth Round: Crystal Palace (A)1-3

**1992-93: Back Row L-R:** Dave Collyer (Youth Development Manager), *Eddie Niedzwiecki* (Reserve Team Manager), David Lee, *Mick Harford*, Paul Elliott, Dave Beasant, *Ken Monkou*, Tony Cascarino, Erland Johnsen, Craig Burley, Gwyn Williams (Assistant Team Manager), *Peter Nicholas* (Youth Team Coach). **Middle Row:** Bob Ward (Physio), Damien Matthew, Darren Barnard, Zeke Rowe, Andy Myers, Ian Pearce, Kevin Hitchcock, *Alan Dickens*, Steve Clarke, *Joe Allon*, *Graeme Le Saux*, *Don Howe* (First Team Coach). **Front Row:** Eddie Newton, Gareth Hall, Graham Stuart, Dennis Wise, *Vinny Jones*, *Ian Porterfield* (Team Manager), *Andy Townsend*, Mal Donaghy, Robert Fleck, John Spencer, Frank Sinclair

## Playing staff for 1993-94 (As at 20 July 1993) — CHELSEA

| PLAYERS | CLUB DEBUT (Premier/Football League) | 1992-93 APPEARANCES | | | | 1992-93 GOALS | | | |
|---|---|---|---|---|---|---|---|---|---|
| | | Lge | FL Cup | FA Cup | Others | Lge | FL Cup | FA Cup | Others |
| **GOALKEEPERS** | | | | | | | | | |
| Beasant, Dave | Crystal Palace (H) 14 January 1989 | 17 | | | | | | | |
| Colgan, Nick | – | | | | | | | | |
| Hitchcock, Kevin | Southampton (H) 26 March 1988 | 20 | 6 | 1 | | | | | |
| Kharine, Dmitri | Q.P.R. (A) 27 January 1993 | 5 | | | | | | | |
| **DEFENDERS** | | | | | | | | | |
| Barness, Anthony | Norwich C. (H) 12 September 1992 | 2 | | | | | | | |
| Clarke, Steve | Norwich C. (A) 24 January 1987 | 18+2 | 1 | 1 | | | | | |
| Donaghy, Mal | Oldham Ath. (H) 15 August 1992 | 39+1 | 5 | 1 | | 2 | | | |
| Dow, Andy | – | | | | | | | | |
| Duberry, Michael | – | | | | | | | | |
| Elliott, Paul | Wimbledon (H) 17 August 1991 | 7 | | | | | | | |
| Hall, Gareth | Wimbledon (A) 5 May 1987 | 36+1 | 4 | | | 2 | | | |
| Hoddle, Glenn | – | | | | | | | | |
| Johnsen, Erland | Q.P.R. (A) 9 December 1989 | 13 | | | | | | | |
| Lee, David | Leicester C. (H) 1 October 1988 | 23+2 | 6 | 1 | | 2 | | | |
| Myers, Andy | Luton T. (H) 6 April 1991 | 3 | 1 | | | | | | |
| Norman, Craig | – | | | | | | | | |
| Pearce, Ian | Aston Villa (A) 11 May 1991 | 0+1 | | | | | | | |
| Sinclair, Frank | Luton T. (H) 6 April 1991 | 32 | 6 | 1 | | | 1 | | |
| Skiverton, Terry | – | | | | | | | | |
| **MIDFIELDERS** | | | | | | | | | |
| Barnard, Darren | West Ham U. (H) 4 April 1992 | 8+5 | 0+1 | | | 1 | | | |
| Burley, Craig | Nottingham F. (A) 20 April 1991 | 1+2 | | 0+1 | | | | | |
| Izzet, Mustafa | – | | | | | | | | |
| Matthew, Damian | Crystal Palace (H) 16 April 1990 | 3+1 | | | | | | | |
| Newton, Eddie | Everton (A) 2 May 1992 | 32+2 | 6 | 1 | | 5 | 1 | | |
| Peacock, Gavin | – | | | | | | | | |
| Spackman, Nigel | Derby Co. (H) 27 August 1983 | 6 | 2 | | | | | | |
| **FORWARDS** | | | | | | | | | |
| Cascarino, Tony | Crystal Palace (H) 8 February 1992 | 8+1 | | | | 2 | | | |
| Fleck, Robert | Oldham Ath. (H) 15 August 1992 | 28+3 | 6 | 1 | | 2 | 1 | | |
| Hopkin, David | Liverpool (H) 10 February 1993 | 2+2 | | | | | | | |
| Livingstone, Steve | Manchester U. (A) 17 April 1993 | 0+1 | | | | | | | |
| Rowe, Zeke | – | | | | | | | | |
| Shipperley, Neil | Southampton (A) 10 April 1993 | 2+1 | | | | 1 | | | |
| Spencer, John | Norwich C. (A) 19 August 1992 | 13+10 | 0+2 | 0+1 | | 7 | | | |
| Stuart, Graham | Crystal Palace (H) 16 August 1990 | 31+8 | 6 | 1 | | 9 | 1 | | |
| Wise, Dennis | Derby Co. (H) 25 August 1990 | 27 | 5 | | | 3 | 1 | | |
| **PLAYERS MAKING APPEARANCES IN 1992-93 (No longer with the club)** | | | | | | | | | |
| **PLAYERS** | **TRANSFERRED TO** | | | | | | | | |
| Allon, Joe | Brentford (November 1992) | 1+2 | | | | | | | |
| Harford, Mick | Sunderland (March 1993) | 27+1 | 5 | 1 | | 9 | 2 | | |
| Jones, Vinny | Wimbledon (September 1992) | 7 | | | | 1 | | | |
| Le Saux, Graham | Blackburn Rov. (March 1993) | 10+4 | 1+3 | 1 | | | | | |
| Peyton, Gerry | Everton (Loan – January 1993) | 0+1 | | | | | | | |
| Townsend, Andy | Aston Villa (July 1993) | 41 | 6 | 1 | | 4 | 3 | | |

TRAINEES

Joseph Baker, Stanley Bowder, Kevin Brown, Lee Carroll, Terence Christie, Allan Cumberbatch, Clinton Ellis, David Hall, Andrew Hughes, Christian McCann, Steven Martin, Hillyard Mendes, Mark Nicholls, Paul Yates

## COVENTRY CITY

**1883**

**THE SKY BLUES**

**Team Manager** Bobby Gould
**Club Address** Highfield Road Stadium, King Richard Street, Coventry CV2 4FW
**Record Attendance** 51,455 v Wolverhampton W., Div. 2, 29 April 1967
**Turned Professional** 1893
**Previous Names** Singers
**Club Honours** Football League: Div. 2 Champions 1966-67; Div. 3 Champions 1963-64; Div. 3(S) Champions 1935-36. FA Cup: Winners 1987
**League History** 1919-25 Div. 2; 1925-26 Div. 3(N); 1926-36 Div. 3(S); 1936-52 Div. 2; 1952-58 Div. 3(S); 1958-59 Div. 4; 1959-64 Div. 3; 1964-67 Div. 2; 1967-1992 Div. 1; 1992- Prem.
**Most League Points in a Season** (2 for a win) 60 in Div. 4, 1958-59 and in Div. 3, 1963-64. (3 for a win) 63 in Div. 1, 1986-87
**Most League Goals in a Season** 108 in Div. 3(S), 1931-32
**Record League Victory** 9-0 v Bristol C. in Div. 3(S), 28 April 1934
**Record League Defeat** 2-10 v Norwich C. in Div. 3(S), 15 March 1930
**Consecutive League Wins** 6 in 1964
**Consecutive League Defeats** 9 in 1919
**Record League Appearances** George Curtis, 483+4 between 1956-70
**Record League Goalscorer—Career** Clarrie Bourton, 171 between 1931-37
**Record League Goalscorer—Season** Clarrie Bourton, 49 in Div. 3(S), 1931-32

## 1992-93 Record

**Premier League** (15th): Played 42, Won 10, Drew 13, Lost 16; Goals for 52, Goals Against 57; Points 52

**FA Cup** Third Round: Norwich C. (A)0-1
**League Cup** Second Round: Scarborough (H)2-0 (A)2-3

**1992-93: Back Row L-R:** *Terry Fleming, David Smith, Billy Woods, Paul Edwards*, Stewart Robson, David Busst, John Williams, *Andy Pearce, Robert Rosario*, Phil Babb, *Chris Greenman, Luke Chadwick*, Ray Woods, Martyn Booty. **Middle Row:** *Kevin Gallacher, Stewart Bowen, Barry Crews*, Peter Ndlovu, Sean Flynn, Anthony Sheridan, Lee Hurst, *Martin Davies*, Steve Ogrizovic, Jon Gould, *Peter Billing, Craig Middleton, Gerard Carr, Michael Stephenson, Ricky Smith, Carl Wilson*, Brian Borrows. **Front Row:** *Kenny Sansom*, Lloyd McGrath, John Gowans (Assistant Physio), Tim Exeter (Fitness Coach), Ian Cockerill (Psychologist), Roy Evans (Youth Development Officer), Phil Neal (Assistant Team Manager), Bobby Gould (Team Manager), Brian Roberts (Reserve Team Coach) Bert Edwards (Youth Team Manager), Peter Hill (Kit Manager), George Dalton (Physio), *Micky Gynn*, Peter Atherton

## Playing staff for 1993-94 (As at 20 July 1993) — COVENTRY CITY

| PLAYERS | CLUB DEBUT (Premier/Football League) | 1992-93 APPEARANCES | | | | 1992-93 GOALS | | | |
|---|---|---|---|---|---|---|---|---|---|
| | | Lge | FL Cup | FA Cup | Others | Lge | FL Cup | FA Cup | Others |
| GOALKEEPERS | | | | | | | | | |
| Gould, Jon | Liverpool (H) 19 December 1992 | 9 | | | | | | | |
| Ogrizovic, Steve | Aston Villa (A) 25 August 1984 | 33 | 2 | 1 | | | | | |
| DEFENDERS | | | | | | | | | |
| Atherton, Peter | Q.P.R. (A) 24 August 1991 | 39 | 2 | 1 | | | | | |
| Babb, Phil | Middlesbrough (H) 15 August 1992 | 27+7 | 2 | 1 | | | | | |
| Booty, Martyn | Chelsea (H) 2 November 1991 | | | | | | | | |
| Borrows, Brian | Manchester C. (H) 17 August 1985 | 36+2 | 2 | 1 | | 2 | 1 | | |
| Busst, David | Norwich C. (A) 16 January 1993 | 10 | | 0+1 | | | | | |
| Hirst, Lee | – | | | | | | | | |
| Hurst, Lee | Wimbledon (A) 2 February 1991 | 35 | 1 | | | 2 | | | |
| Morgan, Steve | – | | | | | | | | |
| Rennie, David | Arsenal (H) 13 March 1993 | 9 | | | | | | | |
| Smith, Jason | – | | | | | | | | |
| MIDFIELDERS | | | | | | | | | |
| Boland, Willie | Chelsea (A) 1 May 1993 | 0+1 | | | | | | | |
| Flynn, Sean | Sheffield U. (A) 26 December 1991 | 4+3 | | | | | | | |
| McGrath, Lloyd | Southampton (A) 28 April 1984 | 20+5 | 2 | 1 | | | | | |
| O'Toole, Gavin | – | | | | | | | | |
| Robson, Stewart | Leeds U. (A) 9 March 1991 | 14+1 | | | | | | | |
| Sheridan, Anthony | Leeds U. (A) 31 October 1992 | 1 | | | | | | | |
| FORWARDS | | | | | | | | | |
| Carmichael, David | – | | | | | | | | |
| Harford, Mick | – | | | | | | | | |
| Jenkinson, Leigh | Arsenal (H) 13 March 1993 | 2+3 | | | | | | | |
| Ndlovu, Peter | Q.P.R. (A) 24 August 1991 | 27+5 | 1 | 1 | | 7 | 1 | | |
| Quinn, Mick | Manchester C. (H) 21 November 1992 | 26 | | 1 | | 17 | | | |
| Wegerle, Roy | Southampton (H) 3 April 1993 | 5+1 | | | | | | | |
| Williams, John | Middlesbrough (H) 15 August 1992 | 38+3 | 2 | 1 | | 8 | | | |
| Woods, Ray | Crystal Palace (H) 2 March 1991 | | | | | | | | |
| PLAYERS MAKING APPEARANCES IN 1992-93 (No longer with the club) | | | | | | | | | |
| PLAYERS | TRANSFERRED TO | | | | | | | | |
| Billing, Peter | Port Vale (February 1993) | 3 | | | | | | | |
| Fleming, Terry | Northampton T. (July 1993) | 8+3 | 0+1 | | | | | | |
| Gallacher, Kevin | Blackburn Rov. (March 1993) | 19+1 | 2 | 1 | | 6 | | | |
| Greenman, Chris | Peterborough U. (March 1993) | 1+1 | | | | | | | |
| Gynn, Micky | F/T (May 1993) | 18+2 | | 0+1 | | 2 | | | |
| Middleton, Craig | Cambridge U. (July 1993) | 1 | | | | | | | |
| Pearce, Andy | Sheffield Wed. (June 1993) | 21+3 | 2 | 1 | | 1 | | | |
| Rosario, Robert | Nottingham F. (March 1993) | 28 | 1 | 1 | | 4 | | | |
| Sansom, Kenny | Everton (February 1993) | 21 | 2 | | | | | | |
| Smith, David | Birmingham C. (March 1993) | 6 | 1 | | | 1 | | | |
| Rowland, Keith | Bournemouth (Loan – January 1993) | 0+2 | | | | | | | |
| Williams, Paul | West Bromich A. (Loan – October 1992) | 1+1 | | | | | | | |

TRAINEES

Jamie Barnwell-Edinboro, Timothy Blake, Iyseden Christie, Jamie Cleland, Marcus Hall, Richard Jones, Thomas Keelings, Jamie Lenton, Andrew Lovelock, Paul O'Brien, Lee Rogers, James Williams, Adam Willis, Simon Wood

**EVERTON**

**1878**

**THE TOFFEEMEN**

**Team Manager** Howard Kendall
**Club Address** Goodison Park, Liverpool L4 4EL
**Record Attendance** 78,299 v Liverpool, Div. 1, 18 September 1948
**Turned Professional** 1885
**Previous Names** St Domingo
**Club Honours** Football League: Div. 1 Champions 1890-91, 1914-15, 1927-28, 1931-32, 1938-39, 1962-63, 1969-70, 1984-85, 1986-87; Div. 2 Champions 1930-31. FA Cup: Winners 1906, 1933, 1966, 1984. European Cup Winners Cup: Winners 1984-85
**League History** 1888-1930 Div. 1; 1930-31 Div. 2; 1931-51 Div. 1; 1951-54 Div. 2; 1954-92 Div. 1; 1992- Prem.
**Most League Points in a Season** (2 for a win) 66 in Div. 1, 1969-70. (3 for a win) 90 in Div. 1, 1984-85
**Most League Goals in a Season** 121 in Div. 2, 1930-31
**Record League Victory** 9-1 v Manchester C. in Div. 1, 3 September 1906 and v Plymouth Arg. in Div. 2, 27 December 1930
**Record League Defeat** 4-10 v Tottenham H. in Div. 1, 1984-85
**Consecutive League Wins** 12 in 1894
**Consecutive League Defeats** 6 in 1930, 1958 and 1972
**Record League Appearances** Ted Sagar, 463 between 1929-53
**Record League Goalscorer—Career** "Dixie" Dean, 349 between 1925-37
**Record League Goalscorer—Season** "Dixie" Dean, 60 in Div. 1, 1927-28

## 1992-93 Record

**Premier League** (13th): Played 42, Won 15, Drew 8, Lost 19; Goals For 53, Goals Against 55; Points 53
**FA Cup** Third Round: Wimbledon (A)0-0 (R)1-2
**League Cup** Second Round: Rotherham U. (A)0-1 (H)3-0; Third Round: Wimbledon (H)0-0 (R)1-0; Fourth Round: Chelsea (H)2-2 (R)0-1

**1992-93: Back Row L-R:** *Kevin Ratcliffe*, John Ebbrell, David Unsworth, Jason Kearton, *Gerry Peyton*, Neville Southall, Andy Hinchcliffe, Matthew Jackson, Gary Ablett. **Middle Row:** Jimmy Martin (Kit Manager), Jimmy Gabriel (Reserve Team Coach), *Peter Beardsley*, *Iain Jenkins*, Stuart Barlow, Robert Warzycha, Ian Snodin, *Alan Harper*, Peter Beagrie, Colin Harvey (First Team Coach), Les Helm (Physio). **Front Row:** Barry Horne, Mark Ward, Dave Watson, Howard Kendall (Team Manager), *Martin Keown*, Tony Cottee, Mo Johnston

## Playing staff for 1993-94 (As at 20 July 1993) — EVERTON

| PLAYERS | CLUB DEBUT (Premier/Football League) | 1992-93 APPEARANCES | | | | 1991-92 GOALS | | | |
|---|---|---|---|---|---|---|---|---|---|
| | | Lge | FL Cup | FA Cup | Others | Lge | FL Cup | FA Cup | Others |
| **GOALKEEPERS** | | | | | | | | | |
| Kearton, Jason | Q.P.R. (A) 28 December 1992 | 2+3 | | 1 | | | | | |
| Reeves, Steve | – | | | | | | | | |
| Southall, Neville | Ipswich T. (H) 17 October 1981 | 40 | 6 | 1 | | | | | |
| **DEFENDERS** | | | | | | | | | |
| Ablett, Gary | Nottingham F. (H) 19 January 1992 | 40 | 6 | 2 | | | | | |
| Doolan, John | – | | | | | | | | |
| Hinchcliffe, Andy | Leeds U. (H) 25 August 1990 | 25 | 3+2 | | | 1 | | | |
| Holmes, Paul | Ipswich T. (H) 24 March 1993 | 4 | | | | | | | |
| Jackson, Matthew | Aston Villa (H) 19 October 1991 | 25+2 | 3 | 2 | | 3 | | | |
| Moore, Neil | Sheffield U. (H) 4 May 1993 | 0+1 | 0+1 | | | | | | |
| Powell, Mark | – | | | | | | | | |
| Ruffer, Carl | – | | | | | | | | |
| Unsworth, David | Tottenham H. (A) 25 April 1992 | 3 | 1+1 | | | | | | |
| Watson, Dave | Nottingham F. (H) 23 August 1986 | 40 | 6 | 2 | | 1 | | 1 | |
| **MIDFIELDERS** | | | | | | | | | |
| Ebbrell, John | Wimbledon (H) 4 February 1989 | 24 | 2 | 2 | | 1 | | | |
| Grant, Tony | – | | | | | | | | |
| Horne, Barry | Sheffield Wed. (H) 15 August 1992 | 34 | 5+1 | 0+1 | | 1 | | | |
| Kenny, William | Coventry C. (H) 17 October 1992 | 16+1 | 4 | 2 | | 1 | | | |
| Priest, Chris | – | | | | | | | | |
| Radosavljevic, Preki | Leeds U. (A) 26 September 1992 | 13+10 | 1 | 1 | | 3 | | | |
| Snodin, Ian | Sheffield Wed. (H) 17 January 1986 | 19+1 | 2 | 2 | | 1 | | | |
| Ward, Mark | Nottingham F. (A) 17 August 1991 | 19 | | | | 1 | | | |
| **FORWARDS** | | | | | | | | | |
| Barlow, Stuart | Wimbledon (H) 10 April 1991 | 8+18 | 2+2 | 1+1 | | 5 | 1 | | |
| Beagrie, Peter | Aston Villa (A) 5 November 1989 | 11+11 | 3+1 | | | 3 | | | |
| Cottee, Tony | Newcastle U. (H) 27 August 1988 | 25+1 | 2+1 | | | 12 | 1 | | |
| Johnston, Mo | Notts Co. (H) 23 November 1991 | 7+6 | 1+1 | | | 3 | | | |
| Jones, Terry | – | | | | | | | | |
| Rideout, Paul | Sheffield Wed. (H) 15 August 1992 | 17+7 | 4 | 1 | | 3 | 2 | | |
| Tait, Paul | – | | | | | | | | |
| Warzycha, Robert | Nottingham F. (H) 23 March 1991 | 15+5 | 3+1 | 0+1 | | 1 | | | |
| **PLAYERS MAKING APPEARANCES IN 1992-93 (No longer with the club)** | | | | | | | | | |
| **PLAYERS** | **TRANSFERRED TO** | | | | | | | | |
| Beardsley, Peter | Newcastle U. (June 1993) | 39 | 4 | 2 | | 10 | 2 | | |
| Harper, Alan | F/T (May 1993) | 16+2 | 4 | 1+1 | | | | | |
| Jenkins, Iain | F/T (May 1993) | 1 | 0+1 | | | | | | |
| Keown, Martin | Arsenal (February 1993) | 13 | 4 | 2 | | | | | |
| Sansom, Kenny | Brentford (March 1993) | 6+1 | | | | 1 | | | |

### TRAINEES

Graham Allen, Richard Emery, Phillip Hayes, Gerard Hennigan, Peter Holcroft, Jonathan O'Connor, Christopher Price, James Quigley, Sean Roberts, Benjamin Singleton, Alex Smith, Dean Smith, James Speare, Andrew Weathers, Matthew Woods

**Team Manager** Mick McGiven
**Club Address** Portman Road, Ipswich IP1 2DA
**Record Attendance** 38,010 v Leeds U., FA Cup 6th Round, 8 March 1975
**Turned Professional** 1936
**Previous Names** None
**Club Honours** Football League: Div. 1 Champions 1961-62; Div. 2 Champions 1960-61, 1967-68, 1991-92; Div. 3(S) Champions 1953-54, 1956-57. FA Cup: Winners 1978. UEFA Cup: Winners 1980-81
**League History** 1938-54 Div. 3(S); 1954-55 Div. 2; 1955-57 Div. 3(S); 1957-61 Div. 2; 1961-64 Div. 1; 1964-68 Div. 2; 1968-86 Div. 1; 1986-92 Div. 2; 1992- Prem.
**Most League Points in a Season** (2 for a win) 64 in Div. 3(S), 1953-54 and in 1955-56. (3 for a win) 84 in Div. 2, 1991-92
**Most League Goals in a Season** 106 in Div. 3(S), 1955-56
**Record League Victory** 7-0 v Portsmouth in Div. 2, 7 November 1964, v Southampton in Div. 1, 2 February 1974 and v West Bromwich A. in Div. 1, 6 November 1976
**Record League Defeat** 1-10 v Fulham in Div. 1, 26 December 1963
**Consecutive League Wins** 8 in 1953
**Consecutive League Defeats** 10 in 1954
**Record League Appearances** Mick Mills, 588+3 between 1966-82
**Record League Goalscorer—Career** Ray Crawford, 204 between 1958-69
**Record League Goalscorer—Season** Ted Phillips, 41 in Div. 3(S), 1956-57

## 1992-93 Record

**Premier League** (16th): Played 42, Won 12, Drew 16, Lost 14; Goals For 60, Goals Against 55; Points 52
**FA Cup** Third Round: Plymouth Arg. (H)3-1; Fourth Round: Tranmere Rov. (A)2-1; Fifth Round: Grimsby T. (H)4-0; Sixth Round: Arsenal (H)2-4
**League Cup** Second Round: Wigan Ath. (A)2-0 (H)4-0; Third Round: Portsmouth (A)1-0; Fourth Round: Aston Villa (A)2-2 (R)1-0; Fifth Round: Sheffield Wed. (H)1-1 (R)0-1

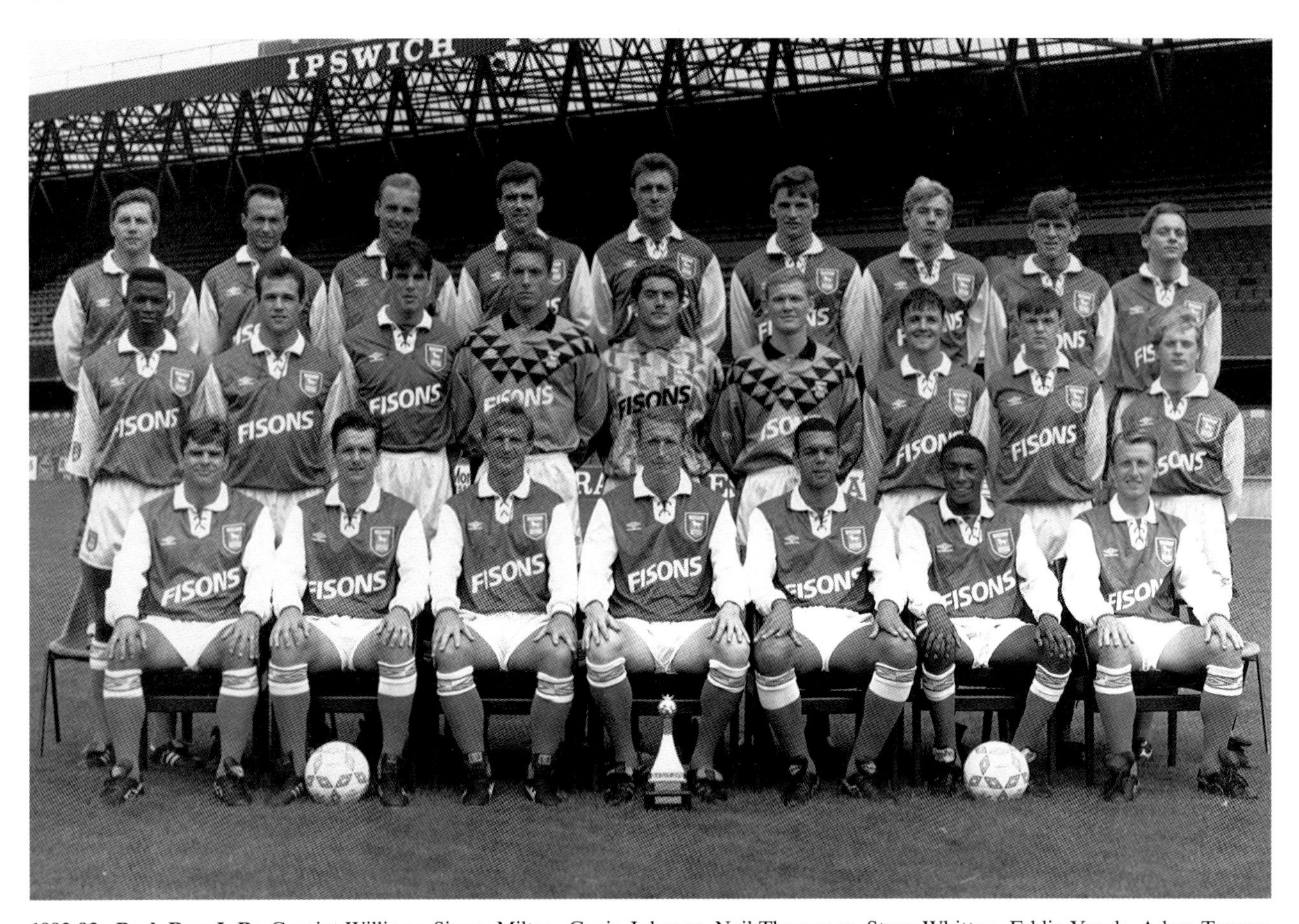


**1992-93: Back Row L-R:** Geraint Williams, Simon Milton, Gavin Johnson, Neil Thompson, Steve Whitton, Eddie Youds, Adam Tanner, *David Lowe*, Lee Honeywood. **Middle Row:** Gary Thompson, Steve Palmer, Phil Whelan, Craig Forrest, *Declan Devine*, *Jason Winters*, David Gregory, Neil Gregory, Lee Durrant. **Front Row:** Mike Stockwell, Frank Yallop, Paul Goddard, David Linighan, Jason Dozzell, Chris Kiwomya, *Glenn Pennyfather*

## Playing staff for 1993-94 (As at 20 July 1993) — IPSWICH TOWN

| PLAYERS | CLUB DEBUT (Premier/Football League) | 1992-93 APPEARANCES | | | | 1992-93 GOALS | | | |
|---|---|---|---|---|---|---|---|---|---|
| | | Lge | FL Cup | FA Cup | Others | Lge | FL Cup | FA Cup | Others |
| GOALKEEPERS | | | | | | | | | |
| Baker, Clive | Sheffield U. (H) 26 September 1992 | 30+1 | 5 | 4 | | | | | |
| Forrest, Craig | Stoke C. (A) 27 August 1988 | 11 | 2 | | | | | | |
| Morgan, Phillip | – | | | | | | | | |
| DEFENDERS | | | | | | | | | |
| Cotterell, Leo | – | | | | | | | | |
| Honeywood, Lee | – | | | | | | | | |
| Linighan, David | Stoke C. (A) 27 August 1988 | 42 | 7 | 3 | | 1 | | | |
| Thompson, Neil | Barnsley (H) 19 August 1989 | 31 | 7 | 4 | | 3 | 1 | 1 | |
| Wark, John | Leicester C. (H) 29 March 1975 | 36+1 | 6+1 | 4 | | 6 | | 1 | |
| Whelan, Phil | Southend U. (A) 4 April 1992 | 28+4 | 5+1 | 2+1 | | | | | |
| Yallop, Frank | Everton (A) 17 March 1984 | 5+1 | 2 | 1+1 | | 2 | | | |
| Youds, Eddie | Derby Co. (A) 16 November 1991 | 10+6 | 1+2 | 0+1 | | | | | |
| MIDFIELDERS | | | | | | | | | |
| Bozinoski, Vlado | Coventry C. (A) 5 December 1992 | 3+6 | 1+1 | 0+1 | | | | | |
| Connell, Graham | – | | | | | | | | |
| Dozzell, Jason | Coventry C. (H) 4 February 1984 | 41 | 7 | 4 | | 7 | | 2 | |
| Durrant, Lee | – | | | | | | | | |
| Gregory, David | Chelsea (A) 26 December 1988 | 1+2 | 0+1 | | | 1 | | | |
| Johnson, Gavin | Barnsley (H) 21 February 1989 | 39+1 | 7 | 4 | | 5 | 2 | | |
| Mason, Paul | – | | | | | | | | |
| Milton, Simon | Swindon T. (A) 28 December 1987 | 7+5 | | | | 2 | | | |
| Palmer, Steve | Oxford U. (A) 23 September 1989 | 4+3 | | | | | | | |
| Stockwell, Mike | Coventry C. (A) 26 December 1985 | 38+1 | 5+1 | 3 | | 4 | | | |
| Tanner, Adam | – | | | | | | | | |
| Williams, Geraint | Aston Villa (H) 15 August 1992 | 37 | 4+1 | 4 | | | | | |
| FORWARDS | | | | | | | | | |
| Goddard, Paul | Millwall (H) 2 February 1991 | 19+6 | 4 | 1+1 | | 3 | | | |
| Gregory, Neil | – | | | | | | | | |
| Guentchev, Bontcho | Manchester C. (H) 12 December 1992 | 19+2 | 2 | 4 | | 3 | | 5 | |
| Kiwomya, Chris | Bradford C. (H) 24 September 1988 | 38 | 7 | 3 | | 10 | 6 | 1 | |
| Pirie, David | – | | | | | | | | |
| Thompson, Gary | – | | | | | | | | |
| Whitton, Steve | West Bromwich A. (H) 12 January 1991 | 20+4 | 4 | 3 | | 3 | 1 | 1 | |
| PLAYERS MAKING APPEARANCES IN 1992-93 (No longer with the club) | | | | | | | | | |
| PLAYERS | TRANSFERRED TO | | | | | | | | |
| Pennyfather, Glenn | Bristol C. (February 1993) | 2+2 | 1 | | | | | | |
| Petterson, Andy | Luton T. (Loan – March 1993) | 1 | | | | | | | |

TRAINEES

Scott Coates, Daniel Eaton, Kevin Ellis, Stephen Graham, Paul Hood, Graham Mansfield, Peter Mortley, Lee Norfolk, Simon Portrey, James Scowcroft, Benjamin Travers, Anthony Vaughan, Kenneth Weston, Matthew Weston

## LEEDS UNITED

**1904**

**THE WHITES**

**Team Manager** Howard Wilkinson
**Club Address** Elland Road, Leeds LS11 0ES
**Record Attendance** 57,892 v Sunderland, FA Cup 5th Round replay, 15 March 1967
**Turned Professional** 1920
**Previous Names** Leeds City
**Club Honours** Football League: Div. 1 Champions 1968-69, 1973-74, 1991-92. Div. 2 Champions 1923-24, 1963-64, 1989-90. FA Cup: Winners 1972. Football League Cup: Winners 1968. European Fairs Cup: Winners 1967-68, 1970-71
**League History** 1920-24 Div. 2: 1924-27 Div. 1; 1927-28 Div. 2; 1928-31 Div. 1; 1931-32 Div. 2; 1932-47 Div. 1; 1947-56 Div. 2; 1956-60 Div. 1; 1960-64 Div. 2; 1964-82 Div. 1; 1982-90 Div. 2; 1990-92 Div. 1; 1992- Prem.
**Most League Points in a Season** (2 for a win) 67 in Div 1, 1968-69. (3 for a win) 85 in Div. 2, 1989-90
**Most League Goals in a Season** 98 in Div. 2, 1927-28
**Record League Victory** 8-0 v Leicester C. in Div. 1, 7 April 1934
**Record League Defeat** 1-8 v Stoke C. in Div. 1, 27 August 1934
**Consecutive League Wins** 9 in 1931
**Consecutive League Defeats** 6 in 1947
**Record League Appearances** Jack Charlton, 628 between 1953-73
**Record League Goalscorer—Career** Peter Lorimer, 168 between 1962-86
**Record League Goalscorer—Season** John Charles, 42 in Div. 2, 1953-54

### 1992-93 Record

**Premier League** (17th): Played 42, Won 12, Drew 15, Lost 15; Goals for 37, Goals Against 62; Points 51
**FA Cup** Third Round: Charlton Ath. (H)1-1 (R)3-1; Fourth Round: Arsenal (A)2-2 (R)2-3
**League Cup** Second Round: Scunthorpe U. (H)4-1 (A)2-2; Third Round: Watford (A)1-2
**Charity Shield** Liverpool (N)4-3
**European Cup** First Round: VFB Stuttgart (A)0-3 (H)4-1 (N)2-1; Second Round: Glasgow R. (A)1-2 (H)1-2

**1992-93: Back Row L-R:** Chris Whyte, Gary McAllister, John Lukic, Lee Chapman, *Mervyn Day*, Jon Newsome, David Wetherall. **Middle Row:** Alan Sutton (Physio), Mel Sterland, Steve Hodge, David Rocastle, Chris Fairclough, Carl Shutt, *Eric Cantona*, Michael Hennigan (Assistant Team Manager). **Front Row:** *Scott Sellars*, Gary Speed, Tony Dorigo, Howard Wilkinson (Team Manager), Gordon Strachan, David Batty, Rod Wallace

## Playing staff for 1993-94 (As at 20 July 1993) LEEDS UNITED

| PLAYERS | CLUB DEBUT (Premier/Football League) | 1992-93 APPEARANCES | | | | 1992-93 GOALS | | | |
|---|---|---|---|---|---|---|---|---|---|
| | | Lge | FL Cup | FA Cup | Others | Lge | FL Cup | FA Cup | Others |
| GOALKEEPERS | | | | | | | | | |
| Beeney, Mark | Coventry C. (A) 8 May 1993 | 1 | | | | | | | |
| Lukic, John | Brighton & H. A. (A) 13 October 1979 | 39 | 3 | 3 | 6 | | | | |
| Pettinger, Paul | – | | | | | | | | |
| DEFENDERS | | | | | | | | | |
| Bowman, Robert | Wimbledon (A) 6 February 1993 | 3+1 | | | | | | | |
| Couzens, Andrew | – | | | | | | | | |
| Dorigo, Tony | Nottingham F. (H) 20 August 1991 | 33 | 1 | 4 | 6 | 1 | | | 1 |
| Fairclough, Chris | Portsmouth (H) 25 March 1989 | 29+1 | 2 | 3+1 | 6 | 4 | | | |
| Humphries, Mark | – | | | | | | | | |
| Kerslake, David | Manchester C. (H) 13 March 1993 | 8 | | | | | | | |
| Newsome, Jon | Wimbledon (A) 2 November 1991 | 30+7 | 2 | 0+1 | 4 | | | | |
| O'Leary, David | – | | | | | | | | |
| Sharp, Kevin | Crystal Palace (H) 17 April 1993 | 4 | | | | | | | |
| Sterland, Mel | Newcastle U. (A) 19 August 1989 | 3 | | 2 | | | | | |
| Wallace, Ray | Nottingham F. (H) 5 December 1992 | 5+1 | | | | | | | |
| Wetherall, David | Arsenal (H) 3 September 1991 | 13 | 2 | 4 | | 1 | | | |
| Whyte, Chris | Everton (A) 25 August 1990 | 34 | 2+1 | 3 | 6 | 1 | | | |
| MIDFIELDERS | | | | | | | | | |
| Batty, David | Swindon T. (H) 21 November 1987 | 30 | 2 | 3 | 5 | 1 | | | |
| Ford, Mark | – | | | | | | | | |
| Hodge, Steve | Sheffield Wed. (H) 24 August 1991 | 9+14 | 0+1 | | 0+3 | 2 | | | |
| McAllister, Gary | Everton (A) 25 August 1990 | 32 | 3 | 4 | 6 | 5 | 1 | 2 | 2 |
| Nicholls, Ryan | – | | | | | | | | |
| Rocastle, David | Ipswich T. (A) 3 October 1992 | 11+7 | 0+2 | 0+3 | 2+1 | 1 | | | |
| Smithard, Matthew | – | | | | | | | | |
| Speed, Gary | Oldham Ath. (H) 6 May 1989 | 39 | 3 | 4 | 6 | 7 | 1 | 3 | 1 |
| Strachan, Gordon | Portsmouth (H) 25 March 1989 | 25+6 | 3 | 4 | 5+1 | 4 | 1 | | 1 |
| Tinkler, Mark | Sheffield U. (A) 6 April 1993 | 5+2 | | | | | | | |
| FORWARDS | | | | | | | | | |
| Chapman, Lee | Blackburn Rov. (A) 13 January 1990 | 36+4 | 3 | 4 | 6 | 14 | 2 | 1 | 1 |
| Deane, Brian | – | | | | | | | | |
| Forrester, Jamie | Nottingham F. (A) 21 March 1993 | 5+1 | | | | | | | |
| Kelly, Garry | Nottingham F. (A) 22 December 1991 | | | | | | | | |
| Shutt, Carl | Bournemouth (H) 1 April 1989 | 6+8 | 1 | 4 | 0+2 | | 1 | 1 | 1 |
| Strandli, Frank | Middlesbrough (H) 30 January 1993 | 5+5 | | | | 2 | | | |
| Wallace, Rod | Nottingham F. (H) 20 August 1991 | 31+1 | 2 | 1+3 | 1+2 | 7 | 1 | | |
| Whelan, Noel | Sheffield Wed. (A) 4 May 1993 | 1 | | | | | | | |
| PLAYERS MAKING APPEARANCES IN 1992-93 (No longer with the club) | | | | | | | | | |
| PLAYERS | TRANSFERRED TO | | | | | | | | |
| Cantona, Eric | Manchester U. (November 1992) | 12+1 | 1 | | 6 | 6 | | | 5 |
| Day, Mervyn | Carlisle U. (July 1993) | 2 | | 1 | | | | | |
| Kerr, Dylan | Reading (July 1993) | 3+2 | 2 | | | | | | |
| Sellars, Scott | Newcastle U. (March 1993) | 6+1 | 1+1 | | 1 | | | | |
| Varadi, Imre | Rotherham U. (March 1993) | 2+2 | | | | 1 | | | |

TRAINEES

Jason Blunt, David Connor, Graham Cross, Kevin Daly, Nicholas Fawell, Anthony Grant, Michael Hoyle, Shaun Kavanagh, Martin Littlewood, Gary Lynam, Jamie Marks, Simon Oliver, Allan O'Shea, Paul Wharton, Harvey Willetts

# LIVERPOOL

**1892**

**THE REDS or POOL**

**Team Manager** Graeme Souness
**Club Address** Anfield Road, Liverpool 4 0TH
**Record Attendance** 61,905 v Wolverhampton W., FA Cup 4th Round, 2 February 1952
**Turned Professional** 1892
**Previous Names** None
**Club Honours** Football League: Div. 1 Champions 1900-01, 1905-06, 1921-22, 1922-23, 1946-47, 1963-64, 1965-66, 1972-73, 1975-76, 1976-77, 1978-79, 1979-80, 1981-82, 1982-83, 1983-84, 1985-86, 1987-88, 1989-90; Div. 2 Champions 1893-94, 1895-96, 1904-05, 1961-62. FA Cup: Winners 1965, 1974, 1986, 1989, 1992. Football League Cup: Winners 1981, 1982, 1983, 1984. League Super Cup: Winners 1985-86. European Cup: Winners 1976-77, 1977-78, 1980-81, 1983-84. UEFA Cup: Winners 1972-73, 1975-76. European Super Cup: Winners 1977
**League History** 1893-94 Div. 2; 1894-95 Div. 1; 1895-96 Div. 2; 1896-1904 Div. 1; 1904-05 Div. 2; 1905-54 Div. 1; 1954-62 Div. 2; 1962-92 Div. 1; 1992- Prem.
**Most League Points in a Season** (2 for a win) 68 in Div. 1, 1978-79. (3 for a win) 90 in Div. 1, 1987-88
**Most League Goals in a Season** 106 in Div. 2, 1895-96
**Record League Victory** 10-1 v Rotherham U. in Div. 2, 18 February 1896
**Record League Defeat** 1-9 v Birmingham C. in Div. 2, 11 December 1954
**Consecutive League Wins** 11 in 1982
**Consecutive League Defeats** 9 in 1899
**Record League Appearances** Ian Callaghan, 637+3 between 1960-78
**Record League Goalscorer—Career** Roger Hunt, 245 between 1959-69
**Record League Goalscorer—Season** Roger Hunt, 41 in Div. 2, 1961-62

## 1992-93 Record

**Premier League** (6th): Played 42, Won 16, Drew 11, Lost 15; Goals For 62, Goals Against 55; Points 59
**FA Cup** Third Round: Bolton W. (A)2-2 (R)0-2
**League Cup** Second Round: Chesterfield (H)4-4 (A)4-1; Third Round: Sheffield U. (A)0-0 (R)3-0; Fourth Round: Crystal Palace (H)1-1 (R)1-2
**Charity Shield** Leeds U. (N)3-4
**European Cup Winners Cup** First Round: Apollon Limassol (H)6-1 (A)2-1; Second Round: Spartak Moscow (A)2-4 (H)0-2

**1992-93: Back Row L-R:** Jan Molby, Nicky Tanner, Mike Hooper, David James, Bruce Grobbelaar, Mark Walters, Rob Jones. **Middle Row:** Ronnie Moran (Assistant Team Manager), David Burrows, Michael Thomas, Istvan Kozma, *Barry Venison*, Ronny Rosenthal, *Ray Houghton*, Steve McManaman, Phil Boersma (First Team Coach), Roy Evans (First Team Coach). **Front Row:** Mike Marsh, *Dean Saunders*, Steve Nicol, Graeme Souness (Team Manager), Mark Wright, Ian Rush, Ronnie Whelan

## Playing staff for 1993-94 (As at 20 July 1993) — LIVERPOOL

| PLAYERS | CLUB DEBUT (Premier/Football League) | 1992-93 APPEARANCES | | | | 1992-93 GOALS | | | |
|---|---|---|---|---|---|---|---|---|---|
| | | Lge | FL Cup | FA Cup | Others | Lge | FL Cup | FA Cup | Others |
| GOALKEEPERS | | | | | | | | | |
| Embleton, Daniel | – | | | | | | | | |
| Grobbelaar, Bruce | Wolverhampton W. (A) 29 August 1981 | 5 | 2 | | 3 | | | | |
| Hooper, Mike | Newcastle U. (A) 23 August 1986 | 8+1 | 3 | 2 | 1 | | | | |
| James, David | Nottingham F. (A) 16 August 1992 | 29 | 1 | | 1 | | | | |
| DEFENDERS | | | | | | | | | |
| Bjornebye, Stig | Coventry C. (A) 19 December 1992 | 11 | | 2 | | | | | |
| Brydon, Lee | – | | | | | | | | |
| Burrows, David | Coventry C. (H) 22 October 1988 | 29+1 | 5 | | 5 | 2 | | | |
| Jones, Rob | Manchester U. (A) 6 October 1991 | 30 | 2+1 | 2 | 2 | | | | |
| Matteo, Dominic | – | | | | | | | | |
| Neal, Ashley | – | | | | | | | | |
| Nicol, Steve | Birmingham C. (A) 31 August 1982 | 32 | 4 | 1 | 2 | | | | |
| Piechnik, Torben | Aston Villa (A) 19 September 1992 | 15+1 | 5 | 2 | | | | | |
| Ruddock, Neil | – | | | | | | | | |
| Scott, John | – | | | | | | | | |
| Stalker, Mark | – | | | | | | | | |
| Tanner, Nicky | Manchester C. (A) 2 December 1989 | 2+2 | 1+2 | | 2+1 | | | | |
| Wright, Mark | Oldham Ath. (H) 17 August 1991 | 32+1 | 2+2 | | 4 | 2 | 1 | | |
| MIDFIELDERS | | | | | | | | | |
| Charnock, Philip | – | | 1 | | 0+1 | | | | |
| Frodsham, Ian | – | | | | | | | | |
| Harkness, Steve | Q.P.R. (H) 27 August 1991 | 9+1 | | | 1+1 | | | | |
| Hutchison, Don | Notts Co. (H) 31 March 1992 | 27+4 | 5 | 1+1 | 3+1 | 7 | 2 | | 1 |
| Kozma, Istvan | Norwich C. (A) 22 February 1992 | 0+1 | 0+1 | | 0+1 | | | | |
| Marsh, Mike | Charlton Ath. (H) 1 March 1988 | 22+6 | 6 | 2 | 5 | 1 | 3 | | |
| McAree, Rodney | – | | | | | | | | |
| Molby, Jan | Norwich C. (A) 25 August 1984 | 8+2 | 1 | | 2 | 3 | | | |
| Nestor, Terry | – | | | | | | | | |
| Paterson, Scott | – | | | | | | | | |
| Redknapp, Jamie | Southampton (A) 7 December 1991 | 27+2 | 6 | 1 | 4 | 2 | 1 | | |
| Stewart, Paul | Nottingham F. (A) 16 August 1992 | 21+3 | 3 | 1 | 3 | 1 | | | 2 |
| Thomas, Michael | Tottenham H. (A) 18 December 1991 | 6+2 | 1 | 2 | 2 | 1 | | | |
| Whelan, Ronnie | Stoke C. (H) 3 April 1981 | 17 | | | 1 | 1 | | | |
| FORWARDS | | | | | | | | | |
| Barnes, John | Arsenal (A) 15 August 1987 | 26+1 | 2 | 2 | | 5 | | | |
| Clough, Nigel | – | | | | | | | | |
| Fallon, Sean | – | | | | | | | | |
| Fowler, Robert | – | | | | | | | | |
| Jones, Lee | – | | | | | | | | |
| McManaman, Steve | Sheffield U. (H) 15 December 1990 | 27+4 | 5 | 1 | 3 | 4 | 2 | | 1 |
| O'Donnell, Paul | – | | | | | | | | |
| Rosenthal, Ronny | Southampton (H) 31 March 1990 | 16+11 | 2+1 | 1+1 | 1+4 | 6 | 1 | | |
| Rush, Ian | Ipswich T. (A) 13 December 1980 | 31+1 | 4 | 1 | 5 | 14 | | 1 | 6 |
| Walters, Mark | Oldham Ath. (H) 17 August 1991 | 26+8 | 5 | 1 | 4 | 11 | 2 | | |
| PLAYERS MAKING APPEARANCES IN 1992-93 (No longer with the club) | | | | | | | | | |
| PLAYERS | TRANSFERRED TO | | | | | | | | |
| Saunders, Dean | Aston Villa (September 1992) | 6 | | | 1 | 1 | | | 1 |

TRAINEES

Scott Brenchley, Iain Brunskill, David Clegg, Andrew Harris, Westley Kinney, Christian Li, Dominic Morley, Stephen Morris, Paul Robinson, Paul Snape, Martin Wilkinson, Stanley Wyke

## MANCHESTER CITY
**1887**

**THE BLUES or CITY**

**Team Manager** Peter Reid
**Club Address** Maine Road, Moss Side, Manchester M14 7WN
**Record Attendance** 84,569 v Stoke C., FA Cup 6th Round, 3 March 1934
**Turned Professional** 1887
**Previous Names** Ardwick
**Club Honours** Football League: Div. 1 Champions 1936-37, 1967-68; Div. 2 Champions 1898-99, 1902-03, 1909-10, 1927-28, 1946-47, 1965-66. FA Cup: Winners 1904, 1934, 1956, 1969. Football League Cup: Winners 1970, 1976. European Cup Winners Cup: Winners 1969-70
**League History** 1892-99 Div. 2; 1899-1902 Div. 1; 1902-03 Div. 2; 1903-09 Div. 1; 1909-10 Div. 2; 1910-26 Div. 1; 1926-28 Div. 2; 1928-38 Div. 1; 1938-47 Div. 2; 1947-50 Div. 1; 1950-51 Div. 2; 1951-63 Div. 1; 1963-66 Div. 2, 1966-83 Div. 1; 1983-85 Div. 2; 1985-87 Div. 1; 1987-89 Div 2; 1989-92 Div. 1; 1992- Prem.
**Most League Points in a Season** (2 for a win) 62 in Div. 2, 1946-47. (3 for a win) 82 in Div. 2, 1988-89
**Most League Goals in a Season** 108 in Div. 2, 1926-27
**Record League Victory** 11-3 v Lincoln C., in Div. 2, 23 March 1895
**Record League Defeat** 1-9 v Everton in Div. 1, 3 September 1906
**Consecutive League Wins** 9 in 1912
**Consecutive League Defeats** 6 in 1910 and 1960
**Record League Appearances** Alan Oakes, 561+3 between 1959-76
**Record League Goalscorer—Career** Eric Brook, 159 between 1927-39
**Record League Goalscorer—Season** Tommy Johnson, 38 in Div. 1, 1928-29

## 1992-93 Record

**Premier League** (9th): Played 42, Won 15, Drew 12, Lost 15; Goals For 56, Goals Against 51; Points 57
**FA Cup** Third Round: Reading (H)1-1 (R)4-0; Fourth Round: Q.P.R. (A)2-1; Fifth Round: Barnsley (H)2-0; Sixth Round: Tottenham H. (H)2-4
**League Cup** Second Round: Bristol Rov. (H)0-0 (A)2-1; Third Round: Tottenham H. (H)0-1

**1992-93: Back Row L-R:** David White, David Brightwell, Martyn Margetson, Tony Coton, Andy Hill, *Mark Brennan*. **Middle Row:** Eamonn Salmon (Physio), Tony Book (First Team Coach), Rick Holden, Garry Flitcroft, Michel Vonk, Niall Quinn, Paul Lake, Adrian Mike, Sam Ellis (Assistant Team Manager). **Front Row:** Ian Brightwell, Steve McMahon, Keith Curle, Peter Reid (Player/Team Manager), Fitzroy Simpson, Mike Quigley, Mike Sheron

## **Playing staff for 1993-94** (As at 20 July 1993) **MANCHESTER CITY**

| PLAYERS | CLUB DEBUT (Premier/Football League) | 1992-93 APPEARANCES | | | | 1992-93 GOALS | | | |
|---|---|---|---|---|---|---|---|---|---|
| | | Lge | FL Cup | FA Cup | Others | Lge | FL Cup | FA Cup | Others |
| GOALKEEPERS | | | | | | | | | |
| Coton, Tony | Tottenham H. (A) 25 August 1990 | 40 | 3 | 5 | | | | | |
| Dibble, Andy | Hull C. (A) 27 August 1988 | 1+1 | | | | | | | |
| Margetson, Martyn | Manchester U. (A) 4 May 1991 | 1 | | | | | | | |
| DEFENDERS | | | | | | | | | |
| Bentley, Jim | – | | | | | | | | |
| Curle, Keith | Coventry C. (A) 17 August 1991 | 39 | 3 | 4 | | 3 | | | |
| Edghill, Richard | – | | | | | | | | |
| Foster, John | – | | | | | | | | |
| Harkin, Joe | – | | | | | | | | |
| Hill, Andy | Luton T. (H) 5 March 1991 | 23+1 | 3 | 2+1 | | 1 | | | |
| Ingram, Rae | – | | | | | | | | |
| Limber, Nicky | – | | | | | | | | |
| Phelan, Terry | Norwich C. (H) 26 August 1992 | 37 | 3 | 5 | | | | 1 | |
| Vonk, Michel | Nottingham F. (A) 21 March 1992 | 26 | | 3+1 | | 3 | | 1 | |
| MIDFIELDERS | | | | | | | | | |
| Brightwell, David | Wimbledon (A) 22 February 1992 | 4+4 | | 1+1 | | | | | |
| Brightwell, Ian | Wimbledon (H) 23 August 1986 | 21 | 3 | 1 | | 1 | | | |
| Flitcroft, Garry | Oldham Ath. (H) 29 August 1992 | 28+4 | 1+1 | 5 | | 5 | | 1 | |
| Holden, Rick | Q.P.R. (H) 17 August 1992 | 40+1 | 3 | 5 | | 3 | 1 | 1 | |
| Ingebrigsten, Kaare | Blackburn Rov. (H) 30 January 1993 | 2+5 | | | | | | | |
| Kerr, David | Crystal Palace (H) 5 May 1993 | 0+1 | | | | | | | |
| Lake, Paul | Wimbledon (A) 24 January 1987 | 2 | | | | | | | |
| Lomas, Steve | – | | | | | | | | |
| McMahon, Steve | Norwich C. (H) 26 December 1991 | 24+3 | 2 | 2 | | 1 | | | |
| Quigley, Mike | Aston Villa (A) 7 December 1991 | 1+4 | | | | | | | |
| Reid, Peter | Everton (A) 17 December 1989 | 14+6 | 1+1 | 2 | | | | | |
| Sharpe, John | – | | | | | | | | |
| Simpson, Fitzroy | Q.P.R. (A) 7 March 1992 | 27+2 | 3 | 4 | | 2 | | | |
| Thomas, Scott | – | | | | | | | | |
| Thomson, Greg | – | | | | | | | | |
| FORWARDS | | | | | | | | | |
| Beech, Chris | – | | | | | | | | |
| Finney, Stephen | – | | | | | | | | |
| Mike, Adrian | Notts Co. (H) 25 April 1992 | 1+2 | | | | | | | |
| Quinn, Niall | Chelsea (H) 21 March 1990 | 39 | 3 | 5 | | 8 | | 1 | |
| Sheron, Mike | Everton (H) 17 September 1991 | 33+5 | 2 | 5 | | 11 | | 3 | |
| White, David | Luton T. (A) 27 September 1986 | 42 | 3 | 5 | | 16 | | 3 | |
| PLAYERS MAKING APPEARANCES IN 1992-93 (No longer with the club) | | | | | | | | | |
| PLAYERS | TRANSFERRED TO | | | | | | | | |
| Ranson, Ray | Reading (July 1993) | 17 | | 1 | | | | | |

TRAINEES

Steven Brennan, Michael Brown, David Crawley, Gareth Evans, Gerald, Kielty, John McDonnell, Mathew Morgan, Phillip Owen, David Roe, Gavin Samuel, Ian Smith, Gerald Tarpey, David Turner, David Walker

**MANCHESTER UNITED**
**1878**

**THE RED DEVILS**

**Team Manager** Alex Ferguson
**Club Address** Old Trafford, Manchester M16 0RA
**Record Attendance** 76,962 Wolverhampton W. v Grimsby T., FA Cup Semi-Final, 25 March 1939
**Turned Professional** 1885
**Previous Names** Newton Heath
**Club Honours** Premier League: Champions 1992-93; Football League: Div. 1 Champions 1907-08, 1910-11, 1951-52, 1955-56, 1956-57, 1964-65, 1966-67; Div. 2 Champions 1935-36, 1974-75. FA Cup: Winners 1909, 1948, 1963, 1977, 1983, 1985, 1990. Football League Cup: Winners 1992. European Cup: Winners 1967-68. European Cup Winners Cup: Winners 1990-91
**League History** 1892-94 Div. 1; 1894-1906 Div. 2; 1906-22 Div. 1; 1922-25 Div. 2; 1925-31 Div. 1; 1931-36 Div. 2; 1936-37 Div. 1; 1937-38 Div. 2; 1938-74 Div. 1; 1974-75 Div. 2; 1975-92 Div. 1; 1992- Prem.
**Most League Points in a Season** (2 for a win) 64 in Div. 1, 1956-57. (3 for a win) 84 in Prem., 1992-93
**Most League Goals in a Season** 103 in Div. 1, 1956-57 and in 1958-59
**Record League Victory** 10-1 v Wolverhampton W. in Div. 2, 15 October 1892
**Record League Defeat** 0-7 v Blackburn Rov. in Div. 1, 10 April 1926, v Aston Villa in Div. 1, 27 December 1930 and v Wolverhampton W. in Div. 2, 26 December 1931
**Consecutive League Wins** 14 in 1904-05
**Consecutive League Defeats** 14 in 1930
**Record League Appearances** Bobby Charlton, 604+2 between 1956-73
**Record League Goalscorer—Career** Bobby Charlton, 198 between 1956-73
**Record League Goalscorer—Season** Dennis Viollet, 32 in Div. 1, 1959-60

## 1992-93 Record

**Premier League** (1st): Played 42, Won 24, Drew 12, Lost 6; Goals For 67, Goals Against 31; Points 84
**FA Cup** Third Round: Bury (H)2-0; Fourth Round: Brighton & H.A. (H)1-0; Fifth Round: Sheffield U. (A)1-2
**League Cup** Second Round: Brighton & H.A. (A)1-0 (H)1-0; Third Round: Aston Villa (A)0-1
**UEFA Cup** First Round: Torpedo Moscow (H)0-0 (A)0-0

**1992-93: Back Row L-R:** *Russell Beardsmore*, Lee Martin, Lee Sharpe, Darren Ferguson, Ryan Giggs, Andrei Kantchelskis, Mike Phelan, *Neil Webb.* **Middle Row:** Jim McGregor (Physio), *Mark Robins*, Brian McClair, Peter Schmeichel, Brian Kidd (Assistant Team Manager), Gary Walsh, Clayton Blackmore, Mark Hughes, Norman Davies (Kit Manager). **Front Row:** Paul Parker, Dennis Irwin, Paul Ince, Alex Ferguson (Team Manager), Bryan Robson, Gary Pallister, Steve Bruce, Danny Wallace

## Playing staff for 1993-94 (As at 20 July 1993) — MANCHESTER UNITED

| PLAYERS | CLUB DEBUT (Premier/Football League) | 1992-93 APPEARANCES | | | | 1992-93 GOALS | | | |
|---|---|---|---|---|---|---|---|---|---|
| | | Lge | FL Cup | FA Cup | Others | Lge | FL Cup | FA Cup | Others |
| **GOALKEEPERS** | | | | | | | | | |
| Pilkington, Kevin | – | | | | | | | | |
| Schmeichel, Peter | Notts Co. (H) 17 August 1991 | 42 | 2 | 3 | 1 | | | | |
| Sealey, Les | Q.P.R. (A) 14 April 1990 | | | | | | | | |
| Walsh, Gary | Aston Villa (A) 13 December 1986 | | 1 | | 1 | | | | |
| **DEFENDERS** | | | | | | | | | |
| Blackmore, Clayton | Nottingham F. (A) 16 May 1984 | 12+2 | 1 | 0+1 | 1 | | | | |
| Bruce, Steve | Portsmouth (A) 19 December 1987 | 42 | 3 | 3 | 2 | 5 | | | |
| Carey, Brian | – | | | | | | | | |
| Casper, Chris | – | | | | | | | | |
| Irwin, Dennis | Coventry C. (H) 25 August 1990 | 40 | 3 | 3 | 2 | 5 | | | |
| McGibbon, Pat | – | | | | | | | | |
| Martin, Lee | Wimbledon (H) 9 May 1988 | | 1 | | 1 | | | | |
| Murdock, Colin | – | | | | | | | | |
| Neville, Gary | – | | | | 0+1 | | | | |
| O'Kane, John | – | | | | | | | | |
| Pallister, Gary | Norwich C. (H) 30 August 1989 | 42 | 3 | 3 | 2 | 1 | | | |
| Parker, Paul | Notts Co. (H) 17 August 1991 | 31 | 2 | 3 | 0+1 | 1 | | | |
| Riley, Steven | – | | | | | | | | |
| Whitworth, Neil | Southampton (A) 13 March 1991 | | | | | | | | |
| **MIDFIELDERS** | | | | | | | | | |
| Beckham, David | – | | 0+1 | | | | | | |
| Brown, Karl | – | | | | | | | | |
| Butt, Nicky | Oldham Ath. (H) 21 November 1992 | 0+1 | | | | | | | |
| Davies, Simon | – | | | | | | | | |
| Dean, Craig | – | | | | | | | | |
| Ferguson, Darren | Sheffield U. (A) 26 February 1991 | 15 | 1 | | | | | | |
| Ince, Paul | Millwall (H) 16 September 1989 | 41 | 3 | 2 | 1 | 6 | | | |
| Keane, Roy | – | | | | | | | | |
| Lawton, Craig | – | | | | | | | | |
| Phelan, Mike | Arsenal (H) 19 August 1989 | 5+6 | | 2 | 1 | | | 1 | |
| Rawlinson, Mark | – | | | | | | | | |
| Robson, Bryan | Manchester C. (A) 10 October 1981 | 5+9 | 1 | 0+1 | 0+1 | 1 | | | |
| Scholes, Paul | – | | | | | | | | |
| Sharpe, Lee | West Ham U. (H) 24 September 1988 | 27 | | 3 | | 1 | | | |
| **FORWARDS** | | | | | | | | | |
| Cantona, Eric | Manchester C. (H) 6 December 1992 | 21+1 | | 1 | | 9 | | | |
| Dublin, Dion | Sheffield U. (A) 15 August 1992 | 3+4 | | | | 1 | | | |
| Giggs, Ryan | Everton (H) 2 March 1991 | 40+1 | 2 | 2 | 1 | 9 | | 2 | |
| Gillespie, Keith | – | | | | | | | | |
| Hughes, Mark | Southampton (H) 21 January 1984 | 41 | 3 | 2 | 2 | 15 | 1 | | |
| Irving, Richard | – | | | | | | | | |
| Kantchelskis, Andrei | Crystal Palace (A) 11 May 1991 | 14+13 | 2+1 | 1 | 1 | 3 | | | |
| McClair, Brian | Southampton (A) 15 August 1987 | 41+1 | 3 | 3 | 2 | 9 | | | |
| McKee, Colin | – | | | | | | | | |
| Roberts, Joseph | – | | | | | | | | |
| Savage, Robert | – | | | | | | | | |
| Thornley, Ben | – | | | | | | | | |
| Wallace, Danny | Manchester C. (A) 23 September 1989 | 0+2 | 1 | 1 | 2 | | 1 | | |
| **PLAYERS MAKING APPEARANCES IN 1992-93 (No longer with club)** | | | | | | | | | |
| **PLAYERS** | **TRANSFERRED TO** | | | | | | | | |
| Webb, Neil | Nottingham Forest (November 1992) | 0+1 | 1 | | 2 | | | | |

### TRAINEES

Michael Appleton, Desmond Baker, Lee Barnes, Mike Clegg, Richard Flash, David Gardner, Paul Gibson, Daniel Hall, Stephen Hall, Ian Hart, Paul Heckingbottom, Vincent Hudson, David Johnson, Paul Lyons, Robert McDonald, Paul Mitten, Matthew Monaghan, Neil Mustoe, Philip Neville, Daniel Parkin, David Pierce, Mark Ryan, Gary Twynham, Ashley Westwood, Philip Whittam

## NEWCASTLE UNITED
## 1882

THE MAGPIES

**Team Manager** Kevin Keegan
**Club Address** St James' Park, Newcastle upon Tyne NE1 4ST
**Record Attendance** 68,386 v Chelsea, Div. 1, 3 September 1930
**Turned Professional** 1889
**Previous Names** Newcastle East End
**Club Honours** Football League: Div. 1 Champions 1904-05, 1906-07, 1908-09, 1926-27; Div. 2 Champions 1964-65, 1992-93. FA Cup: Winners 1910, 1924, 1932, 1951, 1952, 1955. European Fairs Cup: Winners 1968-69
**League History** 1893-98 Div. 2; 1889-1934 Div. 1; 1934-48 Div. 2; 1948-61 Div. 1; 1961-65 Div. 2; 1965-78 Div. 1; 1978-84 Div. 2; 1984-89 Div. 1; 1989-92 Div. 2; 1992-93 Div. 1; 1993- Prem.

**Most League Points in a Season** (2 for a win) 57 in Div. 2, 1964-65. (3 for a win) 96 in Div. 1, 1992-93
**Most League Goals in a Season** 98 in Div. 1, 1951-52
**Record League Victory** 13-0 v Newport Co. in Div. 2, 5 October 1946
**Record League Defeat** 0-9 v Burton W. in Div. 2, 15 April 1895
**Consecutive League Wins** 11 in 1992
**Consecutive League Defeats** 10 in 1977
**Record League Appearances** Jim Lawrence, 432 between 1904-22
**Record League Goalscorer—Career** Jackie Milburn, 177 between 1946-57
**Record League Goalscorer—Season** Hughie Gallacher, 36 in Div. 1, 1926-27

### 1992-93 Record

**Football League** First Division (1st): Played 46, Won 29, Drew 9, Lost 8; Goals For 92, Goals Against 38; Points 96
**FA Cup** Third Round: Port Vale (H)4-0; Fourth Round: Rotherham U. (A)1-1 (R)2-0; Fifth Round: Blackburn Rov. (A)0-1
**League Cup** First Round: Mansfield T. (H)2-1 (A)0-0; Second Round: Middlesbrough (H)0-0 (A)3-1; Third Round: Chelsea (A)1-2
**Anglo-Italian Cup** Prelims: Grimsby T. (A)2-2, Leicester C. (H)4-0; Group "A": Lucchese (A)1-1, Ascoli (H)0-1, Bari (A)0-3, Cesena (H)2-2

**1992-93: Back Row L-R:** David Roche, *Andy Hunt*, Alan Neilson, Darron McDonough, Robert Elliott, Matty Appleby, Barry Venison, *David Kelly*, *Mick Quinn*, *Peter Garland*, *John Watson*, *Phil Mason*. **Middle Row:** Derek Fazackerley (First Team Coach), Colin Suggett (Youth Team Coach), Pavel Srnicek, *Bjorn Kristensen*, Peter Cormack, Liam O'Brien, Steve Howey, Steve Watson, Kevin Scott, Alan Thompson, Tommy Wright, Derek Wright (Physio), Chris Guthrie (Kit Manager). **Front Row:** Mark Stimson, *Kevin Sheedy*, *Franz Carr*, Kevin Brock, Lee Clark, Terry McDermott (Assistant Team Manager), Kevin Keegan (Team Manager), Brian Kilcline, *Gavin Peacock*, *Ray Ranson*, Paul Bracewell, John Beresford

## Playing staff for 1993-94 (As at 20 July 1993)

## NEWCASTLE UNITED

| PLAYERS | CLUB DEBUT (Premier/Football League) | 1992-93 APPEARANCES | | | | 1992-93 GOALS | | | |
|---|---|---|---|---|---|---|---|---|---|
| | | Lge | FL Cup | FA Cup | Others | Lge | FL Cup | FA Cup | Others |
| **GOALKEEPERS** | | | | | | | | | |
| Harper, Steve | – | | | | | | | | |
| Srnicek, Pavel | Sheffield Wed. (H) 17 April 1991 | 32 | | 4 | 5 | | | | |
| Wright, Tommy | Aston Villa (A) 14 January 1989 | 14 | 5 | | 1 | | | | |
| **DEFENDERS** | | | | | | | | | |
| Appleby, Matty | West Bromwich A. (H) 27 October 1990 | | | | 2+1 | | | | |
| Beresford, John | Southend U. (H) 15 August 1992 | 42 | 4 | 4 | 2 | 1 | | | |
| Cormack, Peter | – | | | | | | | | |
| Elliott, Robert | Middlesbrough (A) 12 March 1991 | | | | | | | | |
| Howey, Steve | Manchester U. (A) 13 May 1989 | 41 | 5 | 3 | 4 | 2 | | | |
| Kilcline, Brian | Barnsley (H) 22 February 1992 | 7+12 | 2 | 1+2 | 5 | | | | |
| Murray, Nathan | – | | | | | | | | |
| Neilson, Alan | Watford (A) 9 March 1991 | 2+1 | 1 | | 3 | | | | |
| Scott, Kevin | Sheffield Wed. (H) 6 September 1986 | 45 | 5 | 4 | 2 | 2 | | | |
| Stimson, Mark | Leicester C. (A) 26 August 1989 | 1+1 | | | 2 | | | | |
| Venison, Barry | Southend U. (H) 15 August 1992 | 44 | 4 | 4 | 3 | | | | |
| **MIDFIELDERS** | | | | | | | | | |
| Appleby, Richard (Trainee) | – | | | | 2 | | | | |
| Bracewell, Paul | Southend U. (H) 15 August 1992 | 19+6 | | 2+2 | 2 | 2 | | | |
| Brock, Kevin | Wimbledon (H) 10 December 1988 | 4+3 | 2 | | 2+1 | 1 | | | 1 |
| Clark, Lee | Bristol C. (A) 29 September 1990 | 46 | 5 | 4 | 3 | 9 | | 1 | |
| Lee, Robert | Peterborough U. (A) 26 September 1992 | 36 | 3 | 4 | | 10 | 1 | 2 | |
| McDonough, Darron | Grimsby T. (A) 21 March 1992 | | | | | | | | |
| O'Brien, Liam | Millwall (A) 19 November 1988 | 33 | 3 | 4 | 3 | 6 | 1 | | |
| Papavassiliou, Nicki | – | | | | | | | | |
| Robinson, Mark | Charlton Ath. (H) 10 March 1993 | 2+7 | | | | | | | |
| Roche, David | Arsenal (A) 15 April 1988 | | | | 0+1 | | | | |
| Sellars, Scott | Charlton Ath. (H) 10 March 1993 | 13 | | | | 2 | | | |
| Thompson, Alan | Swindon T. (A) 2 November 1991 | 1+1 | | | 3 | | | | |
| Watson, Steve | Wolverhampton W. (A) 10 November 1990 | 1+1 | | | 2+1 | | | | |
| **FORWARDS** | | | | | | | | | |
| Beardsley, Peter | Barnsley (A) 24 September 1983 | | | | | | | | |
| Cole, Andy | Swindon T. (A) 13 March 1993 | 11+1 | | | | 12 | | | |
| **PLAYERS MAKING APPEARANCES IN 1992-93 (No longer with the club)** | | | | | | | | | |
| **PLAYERS** | **TRANSFERRED TO** | | | | | | | | |
| Carr, Franz | Sheffield U. (January 1993) | 8+2 | 1+2 | | 3+1 | 1 | | | |
| Garland, Peter | Charlton Ath. (December 1992) | | | | 0+1 | | | | |
| Hunt, Andy | West Bromwich A. (March 1993) | | | | 2 | | | | |
| Kelly, David | Woverhampton W. (June 1993) | 45 | 4 | 4 | 4 | 24 | 2 | 1 | 1 |
| Kristensen, Bjorn | Portsmouth (March 1993) | | | | 3+1 | | | | 1 |
| Peacock, Gavin | Chelsea (July 1993) | 29+3 | 4 | 4 | 2 | 12 | 2 | 2 | 2 |
| Quinn, Mick | Coventry C. (December 1992) | 4+1 | 2+2 | | 2+1 | 2 | | | 3 |
| Ranson, Ray | Manchester C. (January 1993) | 3 | 1 | | 0+1 | | | | |
| Sheedy, Kevin | Blackpool (July 1993) | 23+1 | 4 | 2+1 | 4 | 3 | | 1 | 1 |
| Watson, John | Scunthorpe U. (July 1993) | | | | 0+1 | | | | |

TRAINEES

Daniel Anderson, Richard Appleby, Shaun Baldwin, Stuart Elliott, Peter Keen, Gareth McAlindon, Joseph McGivern, Graham Pepper, Alan Pouton, Graham Stokoe, Mark Thornton

## NORWICH CITY
**1905**

**THE CANARIES**

**Team Manager** Mike Walker
**Club Address** Carrow Road, Norwich NR1 1JE
**Record Attendance** 43,984 v Leicester C., FA Cup 6th Round, 30 March 1963
**Turned Professional** 1905
**Previous Names** None
**Club Honours** Football League: Div. 2 Champions 1971-72, 1985-86; Div. 3(S) Champions 1933-34. Football League Cup: Winners 1962, 1985
**League History** 1920-34 Div. 3(S); 1934-39 Div. 2;1939-58 Div. 3(S); 1958-60 Div. 3; 1960-72 Div. 2; 1972-74 Div. 1; 1974-75 Div. 2; 1975-81 Div. 1; 1981-82 Div. 2; 1982-85 Div. 1; 1985-86 Div. 2; 1986-92 Div. 1; 1992- Prem.
**Most League Points in a Season** (2 for a win) 64 in Div. 3(S), 1950-51. (3 for a win) 84 in Div. 2, 1985-86
**Most League Goals in a Season** 99 in Div. 3(S), 1952-53
**Record League Victory** 10-2 v Coventry C. in Div. 3(S), 15 March 1930
**Record League Defeat** 0-7 v Walsall in Div. 3(S), 13 September 1930 and v Sheffield Wed. in Div. 2, 19 November 1931
**Consecutive League Wins** 9 in 1985-86
**Consecutive League Defeats** 7 in 1935 and 1957
**Record League Appearances** Ron Ashman, 592 between 1947-64
**Record League Goalscorer—Career** Johnny Gavin, 122 between 1948-58
**Record League Goalscorer—Season** Ralph Hunt, 31 in Div. 3(S), 1955-56

### 1992-93 Record

**Premier League** (3rd): Played 42, Won 21, Drew 9, Lost 12; Goals For 61, Goals Against 65; Points 72
**FA Cup** Third Round: Coventry C. (H)1-0; Fourth Round: Tottenham H. (H)0-2
**League Cup** Second Round: Carlisle U. (A)2-2 (H)2-0; Third Round: Blackburn Rov. (A)0-2

**1992-93: Back Row L-R:** *Darren Beckford*, Colin Woodthorpe, Ian Culverhouse, Bryan Gunn, Chris Sutton, Mark Walton, Rob Newman, John Polston, Andrew Johnson. **Middle Row:** Tim Sheppard (Physio), *Sean Collins*, *Tim Wooding*, *Jason Minett*, Daryl Sutch, *Paul Blades*, Gary Megson, David Smith, David Phillips, Lee Power, John Faulkner (Reserve Team Manager). **Front Row:** Ian Crook, Jeremy Goss, Ian Butterworth, Mike Walker (Team Manager), John Deehan (Assistant Team Manager), Ruel Fox, Mark Bowen, Robert Ullathorne

## **Playing staff for 1993-94** (As at 20 July 1993) — **NORWICH CITY**

| PLAYERS | CLUB DEBUT (Premier/Football League) | 1992-93 APPEARANCES | | | | 1992-93 GOALS | | | |
|---|---|---|---|---|---|---|---|---|---|
| | | Lge | FL Cup | FA Cup | Others | Lge | FL Cup | FA Cup | Others |
| GOALKEEPERS | | | | | | | | | |
| Gunn, Bryan | Tottenham H. (H) 8 November 1986 | 42 | 2 | 2 | | | | | |
| Marshall, Andrew | – | | | | | | | | |
| Walton, Mark | Aston Villa (A) 28 April 1990 | | 1 | | | | | | |
| DEFENDERS | | | | | | | | | |
| Bowen, Mark | Southampton (H) 19 August 1987 | 42 | 3 | 2 | | 2 | | | |
| Brace, Deryn | – | | | | | | | | |
| Butterworth, Ian | Aston Villa (A) 20 September 1986 | 26 | 2 | 2 | | 1 | | | |
| Culverhouse, Ian | Carlisle U. (A) 12 October 1985 | 41 | 3 | 2 | | | | | |
| Johnson, Andrew | Sheffield Wed. (A) 20 April 1992 | 1+1 | | | | 1 | | | |
| Newman, Rob | Sheffield U. (H) 17 August 1991 | 16+2 | 3 | | | 2 | | | |
| Polston, John | Sunderland (H) 25 August 1990 | 34 | 3 | 2 | | 1 | | | |
| Prior, Spencer | – | | | | | | | | |
| Ullathorne, Robert | Nottingham F. (A) 24 April 1991 | | | | | | | | |
| Woodthorpe, Colin | Sheffield U. (A) 11 May 1991 | 5+2 | | | | | | | |
| MIDFIELDERS | | | | | | | | | |
| Crook, Ian | Chelsea (A) 23 August 1986 | 32+2 | 3 | 1 | | 3 | | | |
| Eadie, Darren | – | | | | | | | | |
| Goss, Jeremy | Coventry C. (A) 12 May 1984 | 25 | 3 | 1+1 | | 1 | 1 | | |
| Megson, Gary | Arsenal (A) 15 August 1992 | 20+3 | | 2 | | 1 | | | |
| Phillips, David | Sheffield Wed. (A) 19 August 1989 | 42 | 2 | 2 | | 8 | | | |
| Smith, David | Derby Co. (A) 21 April 1990 | 5+1 | | | | | | | |
| Sutch, Daryl | Manchester U. (A) 26 December 1990 | 14+8 | 3 | | | 2 | | | |
| FORWARDS | | | | | | | | | |
| Akinbiyi, Ade | – | | | | | | | | |
| Cureton, Jamie | – | | | | | | | | |
| Ekoku, Efan | Manchester U. (H) 5 April 1993 | 1+3 | | | | 3 | | | |
| Fox, Ruel | Oxford U. (H) 29 November 1986 | 32+2 | 0+1 | 2 | | 4 | | | |
| Power, Lee | Aston Villa (A) 28 April 1990 | 11+7 | | 0+1 | | 6 | | | |
| Robins, Mark | Arsenal (A) 15 August 1992 | 34+3 | 2+1 | | | 15 | 1 | | |
| Sutton, Chris | Q.P.R. (H) 4 May 1991 | 32+6 | 3 | 2 | | 8 | 2 | | |
| PLAYERS MAKING APPEARANCES IN 1991-92 (No longer with the club) | | | | | | | | | |
| PLAYERS | TRANSFERRED TO | | | | | | | | |
| Beckford, Darren | Oldham Ath. (March 1993) | 7+1 | | 2 | | 1 | | 1 | |
| Minett, Jason | Exeter C. (July 1993) | 0+1 | | | | | | | |

TRAINEES

Shaun Carey, Joshua Carus, Darren Crawfoot, Alistair Gibb, Justin Harrington, Stacey Kreft, Gavin Levin, Neil Liffen, Richard Mellon, Christopher Morgan, Marcus Oldbury, James Simpson, Gary Weston, Clayton Woodman, Jonathan Wright

**Team Manager** Joe Royle
**Club Address** Boundary Park, Oldham OL1 2PA
**Record Attendance** 47,671 v Sheffield Wed., FA Cup 4th Round, 25 January 1930
**Turned Professional** 1899
**Previous Names** Pine Villa
**Club Honours** Football League: Div. 2 Champions 1990-91; Div. 3(N) Champions 1952-53; Div. 3 Champions 1973-74
**League History** 1907-10 Div. 2; 1910-23 Div. 1; 1923-35 Div. 2; 1935-53 Div. 3(N); 1953-54 Div. 2; 1954-58 Div. 3; 1958-63 Div. 4; 1963-69 Div. 3; 1969-71 Div. 4; 1971-74 Div. 3; 1974-91 Div. 2; 1991-92 Div. 1; 1992- Prem.
**Most League Points in a Season** (2 for a win) 62 in Div. 3, 1973-74. (3 for a win) 88 in Div. 2, 1990-91
**Most League Goals in a Season** 95 in Div. 4, 1962-63
**Record League Victory** 11-0 v Southport in Div. 4, 26 December 1962
**Record League Defeat** 4-13 v Tranmere Rov. in Div. 3(N), 26 December 1935
**Consecutive League Wins** 10 in 1974
**Consecutive League Defeats** 8 in 1932-33 and 1934-35
**Record League Appearances** Ian Wood, 517 between 1966-80
**Record League Goalscorer—Career** Roger Palmer, 141 between 1980-93
**Record League Goalscorer—Season** Tom Davis, 33 in Div. 3(N), 1936-37

## 1992-93 Record

**Premier League** (19th): Played 42, Won 13, Drew 10, Lost 19; Goals For 63, Goals Against 74; Points 49
**FA Cup** Third Round: Tranmere Rov. (H)2-2 (R)0-3
**League Cup** Second Round: Exeter C. (A)1-0 (H)0-0; Third Round: Swindon T. (A)1-0; Fourth Round: Cambridge U. (A)0-1

**1992-93: Back Row L-R:** *Paul Moulden*, Gunnar Halle, Ian Olney, *John Keeley*, Neil Tolson, Jon Hallworth, Andy Holden (Reserve Team Manager/Coach), *Rick Holden*, Willie Donachie (Assistant Team Manager). **Middle Row:** Billy Urmson (Youth Team Coach), Jim Cassell (Chief Scout), Graeme Sharp, Neil McDonald, Craig Fleming, Paul Bernard, Andy Barlow, Neil Adams, Ronnie Evans (Kit Manager), Ian Liversedge (Physio). **Front Row:** Roger Palmer, Ian Marshall, Richard Jobson, Joe Royle (Team Manager), Andie Ritchie, Nicky Henry, Mike Milligan

## **Playing staff for 1993-94** (As at 20 July 1993) **OLDHAM ATHLETIC**

| PLAYERS | CLUB DEBUT (Premier/Football League) | 1992-93 APPEARANCES | | | | 1992-93 GOALS | | | |
|---|---|---|---|---|---|---|---|---|---|
| | | Lge | FL Cup | FA Cup | Others | Lge | FL Cup | FA Cup | Others |
| GOALKEEPERS | | | | | | | | | |
| Gerrard, Paul | Q.P.R. (A) 5 December 1992 | 25 | | 2 | | | | | |
| Gray, Ian | – | | | | | | | | |
| Hallworth, Jon | Leicester C. (H) 30 September 1989 | 16 | 3 | | | | | | |
| DEFENDERS | | | | | | | | | |
| Barlow, Andy | Birmingham C. (H) 25 August 1984 | 6 | | 2 | | | | | |
| Fleming, Craig | Norwich C. (H) 24 August 1991 | 23+1 | 1 | 2 | | | | | |
| Hall, David | – | | | | | | | | |
| Halle, Gunnar | Port Vale (H) 16 February 1991 | 41 | 1 | 2 | | 5 | | | |
| Jobson, Richard | Portsmouth (H) 1 September 1990 | 40 | 4 | 2 | | 2 | | | |
| McDonald, Neil | Southampton (H) 5 October 1991 | 2+2 | 1 | | | | | | |
| Marshall, Ian | Swindon T. (H) 12 March 1988 | 26+1 | 3 | 1 | | 2 | | | |
| Pointon, Neil | Crystal Palace (H) 19 August 1992 | 34 | 4 | | | 3 | | | |
| Redmond, Steve | Chelsea (A) 15 August 1992 | 28+3 | 4 | 0+1 | | | | | |
| MIDFIELDERS | | | | | | | | | |
| Bernard, Paul | Middlesbrough (H) 7 May 1991 | 32+1 | 3 | 2 | | 4 | 1 | 1 | |
| Brennan, Mark | Middlesbrough (H) 28 November 1992 | 14 | 1 | 2 | | 3 | | | |
| Graham, Richard | – | | | | | | | | |
| Henry, Nicky | Hull C. (H) 19 September 1987 | 32 | 4 | 1 | | 6 | 1 | | |
| Makin, Chris | – | | | | | | | | |
| Milligan, Mike | Sheffield U. (A) 12 April 1986 | 42 | 4 | 2 | | 3 | | | |
| Price, Steve | – | | | | | | | | |
| Rickers, Paul | – | | | | | | | | |
| FORWARDS | | | | | | | | | |
| Adams, Neil | Manchester C. (H) 14 January 1989 | 26+6 | 3+1 | 1 | | 9 | | | |
| Beckford, Darren | Wimbledon (H) 3 April 1993 | 6+1 | | | | 3 | | | |
| Eyre, John | – | | | | | | | | |
| Olney, Ian | Arsenal (A) 26 August 1992 | 32+2 | 3 | 2 | | 12 | | 1 | |
| Palmer, Roger | Leyton Orient (H) 22 November 1980 | 5+12 | 0+1 | | | | | | |
| Ritchie, Andy | West Bromwich A. (A) 15 August 1987 | 10+2 | | | | 3 | | | |
| Sharp, Graeme | Liverpool (A) 17 August 1991 | 20+1 | 4 | 1+1 | | 7 | | | |
| Tolson, Neil | Chelsea (A) 15 August 1992 | 0+3 | | | | | | | |
| PLAYERS MAKING APPEARANCES IN 1992-93 (No longer with the club) | | | | | | | | | |
| PLAYERS | TRANSFERRED TO | | | | | | | | |
| Keeley, John | Colchester U. (July 1993) | 1 | 1 | | | | | | |
| Keizeweed, Orpheo | Rodez (Trial – April 1993) | 0+1 | | | | | | | |
| Moulden, Paul | Birmingham C. (March 1993) | 1+3 | | | | | | | |

TRAINEES

David Beresford, Matthew Berry, Liam Boden, Matthew Booth, Richard Evans, Paul Feltham, Darren Gorman, Robert Hilton, Simon Kay, Martin Pemberton, Dean Quinn, Carl Serrant, Howard Smith, Matthew Speak

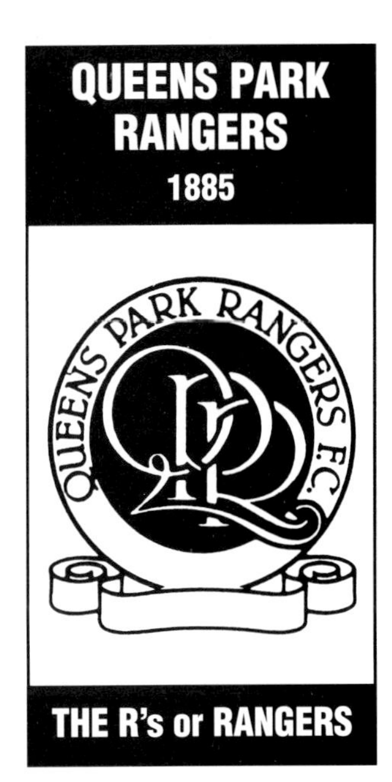


**Team Manager** Gerry Francis
**Club Address** Rangers Stadium, Shepherds Bush, London W12 7PA
**Record Attendance** 34,353 v Leeds U., Div. 1, 27 April 1974
**Turned Professional** 1898
**Previous Names** St Jude's Institute
**Club Honours** Football League: Div. 2 Champions 1982-83; Div. 3(S) Champions 1947-48; Div. 3 Champions 1966-67. Football League Cup: Winners 1967
**League History** 1920-48 Div. 3(S); 1948-52 Div. 2; 1952-58 Div. 3(S); 1958-67 Div. 3; 1967-68 Div. 2; 1968-69 Div. 1; 1969-73 Div. 2; 1973-79 Div. 1; 1979-83 Div. 2; 1983-92 Div. 1; 1992-Prem.
**Most League Points in a Season** (2 for a win) 67 in Div 3, 1966-67. (3 for a win) 85 in Div. 2, 1982-83
**Most League Goals in a Season** 111 in Div. 3, 1961-62
**Record League Victory** 9-2 v Tranmere Rov. in Div. 3, 3 December 1960
**Record League Defeat** 1-8 v Mansfield T. in Div. 3, 15 March 1965 and v Manchester U. in Div. 1, 19 March 1969
**Consecutive League Wins** 8 in 1931
**Consecutive League Defeats** 9 in 1969
**Record League Appearances** Tony Ingham, 514 between 1950-63
**Record League Goalscorer —Career** George Goddard, 172 between 1926-34
**Record League Goalscorer—Season** George Goddard, 37 in Div. 3(S), 1929-30

## 1992-93 Record

**Premier League** (5th): Played 42, Won 17, Drew 12, Lost 13; Goals For 63, Goals Against 55; Points 63
**FA Cup** Third Round: Swindon T. (H)3-0; Fourth Round: Manchester C. (H)1-2
**League Cup** Second Round: Grimsby T. (H)2-1 (A)1-2; Third Round: Bury (A)2-0; Fourth Round: Sheffield Wed. (A)0-4

**1992-93: Back Row L-R:** Les Ferdinand, Stephen Gallen, *Garry Thompson*, Michael Meaker, Jan Stejskal, Tony Witter, Alan McDonald, Peter Caldwell, Karl Ready, Darren Peacock, Danny Maddix, Gary Penrice. **Middle Row:** Des Bulpin (Youth Team Manager), Ron Berry (Kit Manager), Ian Holloway, Dennis Bailey, *David McEnroe*, Maurice Doyle, Bradley Allen, Tony Roberts, *Andy Tillson*, Alan McCarthy, Douglas Freedman, *Garry Waddock*, Roger Cross (Reserve Team Manager), Les Boyle (Youth Team Coach), Brian Morris (Physio). **Front Row:** Clive Wilson, David Bardsley, Rufus Brevett, Andy Sinton, Ray Wilkins, Frank Sibley (Assistant Team Manager), Gerry Francis (Team Manager), Simon Barker, Darren Finlay, Andy Impey, *Justin Channing*, Roberto Herrera

## Playing staff for 1993-94 (As at 20 July 1993) — QUEENS PARK RANGERS

| PLAYERS | CLUB DEBUT (Premier/Football League) | 1992-93 APPEARANCES | | | | 1992-93 GOALS | | | |
|---|---|---|---|---|---|---|---|---|---|
| | | Lge | FL Cup | FA Cup | Others | Lge | FL Cup | FA Cup | Others |
| GOALKEEPERS | | | | | | | | | |
| Caldwell, Peter | – | | | | | | | | |
| Roberts, Tony | Coventry C. (H) 18 December 1987 | 28 | 2 | 2 | | | | | |
| Stejskal, Jan | Leeds U. (A) 20 October 1990 | 14+1 | 2 | | | | | | |
| DEFENDERS | | | | | | | | | |
| Bardsley, David | Derby Co. (H) 16 September 1989 | 40 | 3 | 2 | | 3 | | | |
| Brevett, Rufus | Tottenham H. (A) 23 March 1991 | 14+1 | 1 | 1 | | | | | |
| Gallen, Stephen | – | | | | | | | | |
| Herrera, Roberto | Liverpool (A) 28 April 1990 | | | | | | | | |
| McCarthy, Alan | Arsenal (H) 24 November 1990 | | | | | | | | |
| McDonald, Alan | Wolverhampton W. (A) 24 September 1983 | 39 | 3 | 2 | | | | | |
| Maddix, Danny | Sheffield Wed. (A) 28 November 1987 | 9+5 | 1 | 1 | | | | | |
| Peacock, Darren | Derby Co. (A) 23 December 1990 | 35+3 | 4 | 1 | | 2 | 1 | | |
| Ready, Karl | Wimbledon (H) 1 February 1992 | 2+1 | | | | | | | |
| Wilson, Clive | Nottingham F. (A) 25 August 1990 | 41 | 3 | 2 | | 3 | | | |
| Witter, Tony | – | | | | | | | | |
| MIDFIELDERS | | | | | | | | | |
| Barker, Simon | Manchester U. (A) 27 August 1988 | 21+4 | 1 | 2 | | 1 | | | |
| Croft, Brian | – | | | | | | | | |
| Doyle, Maurice | Ipswich T. (A) 9 February 1993 | 5 | | | | | | | |
| Finlay, Darren | – | | | | | | | | |
| Holloway, Ian | Arsenal (A) 17 August 1991 | 23+1 | 4 | 2 | | 2 | | 1 | |
| Impey, Andy | Coventry C. (A) 11 January 1992 | 39+1 | 3 | 0+1 | | 2 | | | |
| Meaker, Michael | Manchester C. (A) 1 December 1990 | 3 | | | | | | | |
| Sinton, Andy | Sheffield Wed. (A) 25 March 1989 | 36 | 4 | 2 | | 7 | | | |
| Wilkins, Ray | Crystal Palace (A) 2 December 1989 | 27 | 4 | 1 | | 2 | | | |
| FORWARDS | | | | | | | | | |
| Allen, Bradley | Wimbledon (A) 14 January 1989 | 21+4 | 1+1 | 1 | | 10 | 1 | | |
| Bailey, Dennis | Arsenal (A) 17 August 1991 | 13+2 | 2 | 0+1 | | 1 | 1 | | |
| Bryan, Marvin | – | | | | | | | | |
| Dichio, Daniel | – | | | | | | | | |
| Ferdinand, Les | Coventry C. (A) 20 April 1987 | 37 | 3 | 2 | | 20 | 2 | 2 | |
| Freedman, Douglas | – | | | | | | | | |
| Gallen, Kevin | – | | | | | | | | |
| Graham, Mark | – | | | | | | | | |
| Penrice, Gary | Aston Villa (H) 2 November 1991 | 10+5 | 2+1 | 1 | | 6 | | 1 | |
| White, Devon | Chelsea (H) 27 January 1993 | 3+4 | | | | 2 | | | |
| PLAYERS MAKING APPEARANCES IN 1992-93 (No longer with the club) | | | | | | | | | |
| PLAYERS | TRANSFERRED TO | | | | | | | | |
| Channing, Justin | Bristol Rov. (October 1992) | 2 | 1 | | | 1 | | | |
| Thompson, Garry | F/T (May 1993) | 0+4 | 0+2 | | | | | | |

TRAINEES

Matthew Brazier, Trevor Challis, John Cross, Lee Goodwin, Paul Goodwin, Richard Hurst, Billy McCarthy, Michael Mahoney-Johnson, Jonathan Monteath, Christopher Plummer, Graeme Power, Dene White, Kristian Wood

## SHEFFIELD UNITED

**1889**

**THE BLADES**

**Team Manager** Dave Bassett
**Club Address** Bramall Lane Ground, Sheffield S2 4SU
**Record Attendance** 68,287 v Leeds U., FA Cup 5th Round, 15 February 1936
**Turned Professional** 1889
**Previous Names** None
**Club Honours** Football League: Div. 1 Champions 1897-98; Div. 2 Champions 1952-53; Div. 4 Champions 1981-82. FA Cup: Winners 1899, 1902, 1915, 1925
**League History** 1892-93 Div. 2., 1893-1934 Div. 1; 1934-39 Div. 2; 1946-49 Div. 1; 1949-53 Div. 2; 1953-56 Div. 1; 1956-61 Div. 2; 1961-68 Div. 1; 1968-71 Div. 2; 1971-76 Div. 1; 1976-79 Div. 2; 1979-81 Div. 3; 1981-82 Div. 4; 1982-84 Div. 3; 1984-88 Div. 2; 1988-89 Div. 3; 1989-90 Div. 2; 1990-92 Div. 1; 1992- Prem.

**Most League Points in a Season** (2 for a win) 60 in Div. 2, 1952-53. (3 for a win) 96 in Div. 4, 1981-82
**Most League Goals in A Season** 102 in Div. 1, 1925-26
**Record League Victory** 10-0 v Port Vale in Div. 2, 10 December 1892 and v Burnley in Div. 1, 19 January 1929
**Record League Defeat** 3-10 v Middlesbrough in Div. 1, 18 November 1937
**Consecutive League Wins** 8 in 1893, 1903, 1958 and 1960
**Consecutive League Defeats** 7 in 1975
**Record League Appearances** Joe Shaw, 631 between 1948-66
**Record League Goalscorer—Career** Harry Johnson, 205 between 1919-30
**Record League Goalscorer—Season** Jimmy Dunne, 41 in Div. 1, 1930-31

### 1992-93 Record

**Premier League** (14th): Played 42, Won 14, Drew 10, Lost 18; Goals For 54, Goals Against 53; Points 52
**FA Cup** Third Round: Burnley (H)2-2 (R)4-2; Fourth Round: Hartlepool U. (H)1-0; Fifth Round: Manchester U. (H)2-1; Sixth Round: Blackburn Rov. (A)0-0 (R)2-2; Semi-Final: Sheffield Wed. (N)1-2
**League Cup** Second Round: Bristol C. (A)1-2 (H)4-1; Third Round: Liverpool (H)0-0 (R)0-3

**1992-93: Back Row L-R:** John Pemberton, Paul Rogers, *Michael Lake*, Jamie Hoyland, Brian Gayle, *Mel Rees*, *Brian Deane*, Glyn Hodges, Paul Beesley, Alan Cork, Ian Bryson. **Middle Row:** Derek French (Physio), Dane Whitehouse, Carl Bradshaw, David Barnes, Simon Tracey, Nathan Peel, Alan Kelly, Charlie Hartfield, Kevin Gage, John Gannon, Geoff Taylor (Assistant Team Manager). **Front Row:** *Brian Marwood*, Tom Cowan, Andy Gale (Sports Psychologist), John Reed, Dave Bassett (Team Manager), *Richard Lucas*, John Greaves (Kit Manager), Mitch Ward, Adrian Littlejohn

## **Playing staff for 1993-94** (As at 20 July 1993) — **SHEFFIELD UNITED**

| PLAYERS | CLUB DEBUT (Premier/Football League) | 1992-93 APPEARANCES | | | | 1992-93 GOALS | | | |
|---|---|---|---|---|---|---|---|---|---|
| | | Lge | FL Cup | FA Cup | Others | Lge | FL Cup | FA Cup | Others |
| GOALKEEPERS | | | | | | | | | |
| Kelly, Alan | Tottenham H. (A) 2 September 1992 | 32+1 | 3 | 7 | | | | | |
| Kite, Phil | Derby Co. (A) 29 August 1990 | | | | | | | | |
| Tracey, Simon | HuddersfieldT. (H) 11 March 1989 | 10 | 1 | | | | | | |
| DEFENDERS | | | | | | | | | |
| Barnes, David | West Bromwich A. (A) 19 August 1989 | 13 | 1 | 3 | | | | | |
| Beesley, Paul | Derby Co. (A) 29 August 1990 | 39 | 4 | 4+2 | | 2 | | 1 | |
| Cowan, Tom | Norwich C. (A) 17 August 1991 | 21 | 3 | 1 | | | | | |
| Fickling, Ashley | – | | | | | | | | |
| Gage, Kevin | Tottenham H. (A) 23 November 1991 | 27 | 3 | 6 | | | | | |
| Gayle, Brian | Notts Co. (H) 17 September 1991 | 31 | 4 | 6 | | 2 | | | |
| Pemberton, John | Liverpool (H) 25 August 1990 | 19 | | 4 | | | | | |
| Thomson, Martin | – | | | | | | | | |
| Wainwright, Lee | – | | | | | | | | |
| Walton, David | – | | | | | | | | |
| MIDFIELDERS | | | | | | | | | |
| Anthony, Graham | – | | | | | | | | |
| Butterfield, Timothy | – | | | | | | | | |
| Foreman, Matthew | – | | | | | | | | |
| Gannon, John | Blackpool (H) 25 February 1988 | 26+1 | 4 | 2 | | 1 | | | |
| Hartfield, Charlie | Crystal Palace (A) 31 August 1991 | 12+5 | 0+1 | 3 | | | | | |
| Hellewell, Craig | – | | | | | | | | |
| Hoyland, Jamie | Liverpool (H) 25 August 1990 | 15+7 | 0+1 | 5+2 | | 2 | | 1 | |
| Littlejohn, Adrian | Southampton (H) 24 August 1991 | 18+9 | 3 | 3+2 | | 8 | | 1 | |
| Rogers, Paul | LutonT. (A) 22 February 1992 | 26+1 | 4 | 3 | | 3 | 1 | | |
| Smith, Danny | – | | | | | | | | |
| Whitehouse, Dane | Blackpool (A) 15 October 1988 | 14 | 1 | 3 | | 5 | 1 | | |
| FORWARDS | | | | | | | | | |
| Battersby, Tony | – | | | | | | | | |
| Bradshaw, Carl | Plymouth Arg. (A) 16 September 1989 | 24+8 | 4 | 1+1 | | 1 | 1 | | |
| Brocklehurst, David | – | | | | | | | | |
| Bryson, Ian | Reading (A) 27 August 1988 | 9+7 | 1+2 | 3+1 | | 3 | | | |
| Carr, Franz | Ipswich T. (H) 16 January 1993 | 8 | | 4 | | 3 | | | |
| Cork, Alan | Sheffield Wed. (A) 11 March 1991 | 11+16 | 1+2 | 5+1 | | 2 | | 2 | |
| Duffield, Peter | Leicester C. (H) 17 October 1987 | | | | | | | | |
| Hodges, Glyn | Manchester C. (A) 19 January 1991 | 28+3 | 2+1 | 7 | | 4 | | 2 | |
| Peel, Nathan | Tottenham H. (A) 23 November 1991 | | | | | | | | |
| Reed, John | Wimbledon (A) 2 May 1992 | | | | | | | | |
| Scott, Andrew | Sheffield Wed. (A) 21 April 1993 | 1+1 | | | | 1 | | | |
| Ward, Mitch | Manchester C. (H) 8 September 1990 | 22+4 | 1 | 2+2 | | | | 2 | |
| PLAYERS MAKING APPEARANCES IN 1992-93 (No longer with the club) | | | | | | | | | |
| PLAYERS | TRANSFERRED TO | | | | | | | | |
| Deane, Brian | Leeds U. (July 1993) | 41 | 4 | 5+1 | | 15 | 2 | 3 | |
| Kamara, Chris | LutonT. (Loan – November 1992) | 6+2 | | | | | | | |
| Lake, Michael | Wrexham (November 1992) | 6 | | | | | | | |
| McLeary, Alan | Millwall (Loan – July 1992) | 3 | | | | | | | |

TRAINEES

David Anane, Gary Andison, Neil Beech, Eric Collins, Lewis Dickman, Thomas Evans, Matthew Hill, Craig Holt, Lee Innes, Steven Kennedy, Simon Letts, Gary Pearson, Gregory Pearson, Craig Powell, Wayne Quinn, James Rixon, Brett Storey, Jason Tee, Andrew Thorpe, Darren Vine, Barry Zivkovic

**Team Manager:** Trevor Francis
**Club Address** Hillsborough, Sheffield S6 1SW
**Record Attendance** 72,841 v Manchester C., FA Cup 5th Round, 17 February 1934
**Turned Professional** 1887
**Previous Names** The Wednesday
**Club Honours** Football League: Div. 1 Champions 1902-03, 1903-04, 1928-29, 1929-30; Div. 2 Champions 1899-1900, 1925-26, 1951-52, 1955-56, 1958-59. FA Cup: Winners 1896, 1907, 1935. Football League Cup: Winners 1991
**League History** 1892-99 Div. 1; 1899-1900 Div. 2; 1900-20 Div. 1; 1920-26 Div. 2; 1926-37 Div. 1; 1937-50 Div. 2; 1950-51 Div. 1; 1951-52 Div. 2; 1952-55 Div. 1; 1955-56 Div. 2; 1956-58 Div.1; 1958-59 Div. 2; 1959-70 Div. 1; 1970-75 Div. 2; 1975-80 Div. 3; 1980-84 Div. 2; 1984-90 Div. 1; 1990-91 Div. 2; 1991-92 Div. 1; 1992- Prem.
**Most League Points in a Season** (2 for a win) 62 in Div. 2, 1958-59. (3 for a win) 88 in Div. 2, 1983-84
**Most League Goals in a Season** 106 in Div. 2, 1958-59
**Record League Victory** 9-1 v Birmingham C. in Div. 1, 13 December 1930
**Record League Defeat** 0-10 v Aston Villa in Div. 1, 5 October 1912
**Consecutive League Wins** 9 in 1903-04 and 1904-05
**Consecutive League Defeats** 7 in 1893
**Record League Appearances** Andy Wilson, 502 between 1900-20
**Record League Goalscorer—Career** Andy Wilson, 200 between 1900-20
**Record League Goalscorer—Season** Derek Dooley, 46 in Div. 2, 1951-52

## 1992-93 Record

**Premier League** (7th): Played 42, Won 15, Drew 14, Lost 13; Goals For 55, Goals Against 51; Points 59
**FA Cup** Third Round: Cambridge U. (A)2-1; Fourth Round: Sunderland (H)1-0; Fifth Round: Southend U. (H)2-0; Sixth Round: Derby Co. (A)3-3 (R)1-0; Semi-Final: Sheffield U. (N)2-1; Final: Arsenal (N)1-1 (R)1-2
**League Cup** Second Round: Hartlepool U. (H)3-0 (A)2-2; Third Round: Leicester C. (H)7-1; Fourth Round: Q.P.R. (H)4-0; Fifth Round: Ipswich T. (A)1-1 (R)1-0; Semi-Final: Blackburn Rov. (A)4-2 (H)2-1; Final: Arsenal (N)1-2
**UEFA Cup** First Round: Spora Luxembourg (H)8-1 (A)2-1; Second Round: Kaiserslautern (A)1-3 (H)2-2

**1992-93: Back Row L-R:** David Johnson, Peter Shirtliff, Kevin Pressman, *Viv Anderson*, Paul Warhurst, Chris Woods, Julian Watts, Carlton Palmer. **Middle Row:** Richie Barker (Assistant Team Manager), Phil King, John Harkes, Gordon Watson, Chris Bart-Williams, Roland Nilsson, Nigel Worthington, Chris Waddle, Nigel Jemson, Alan Smith (Physio). **Front Row:** John Sheridan, *Danny Wilson*, Nigel Pearson, Trevor Francis (Team Manager), David Hirst, Graham Hyde, Mark Bright

## Playing staff for 1993-94 (As at 20 July 1993) — SHEFFIELD WEDNESDAY

| PLAYERS | CLUB DEBUT (Premier/Football League) | 1992-93 APPEARANCES | | | | 1992-93 GOALS | | | |
|---|---|---|---|---|---|---|---|---|---|
| | | Lge | FL Cup | FA Cup | Others | Lge | FL Cup | FA Cup | Others |
| GOALKEEPERS | | | | | | | | | |
| Key, Lance | – | | | | | | | | |
| Pressman, Kevin | Southampton (A) 5 September 1987 | 3 | 2 | | 1 | | | | |
| Woods, Chris | Aston Villa (H) 17 August 1991 | 39 | 7 | 8 | 3 | | | | |
| DEFENDERS | | | | | | | | | |
| Faulkner, David | – | | | | | | | | |
| King, Phil | Nottingham F. (A) 4 November 1989 | 11+1 | 2 | 1 | | 1 | | | |
| Linighan, Brian | – | | | | | | | | |
| Linighan, John | – | | | | | | | | |
| Nilsson, Roland | Luton T. (H) 9 December 1989 | 32 | 5 | 8 | 1+1 | 1 | 1 | | |
| Palmer, Carlton | Wimbledon (A) 25 February 1989 | 33+1 | 8 | 6+1 | 3+1 | 1 | 1 | | |
| Pearce, Andy | – | | | | | | | | |
| Pearson, Nigel | Nottingham F. (A) 17 October 1987 | 13+3 | 3+2 | 2 | 3 | 1 | | | |
| Shirtliff, Peter | Peterborough U. (A) 19 August 1978 | 20 | 5 | 3 | 1 | | | | |
| Stewart, Simon | Ipswich T. (A) 10 March 1993 | 6 | 0+1 | | | | | | |
| Walker, Des | – | | | | | | | | |
| Warhurst, Paul | Aston Villa (H) 17 August 1991 | 25+4 | 7 | 6+1 | 4 | 6 | 4 | 5 | 3 |
| Watts, Julian | Coventry C. (A) 3 March 1993 | 2+2 | | | 1 | | | | |
| MIDFIELDERS | | | | | | | | | |
| Bart-Williams, Chris | Arsenal (H) 23 November 1991 | 21+13 | 3+4 | 1+3 | 1+2 | 6 | 1 | | 2 |
| Harkes, John | Oldham Ath. (H) 3 November 1990 | 23+6 | 7 | 7 | 4 | 2 | 2 | 1 | |
| Holmes, Darren | – | | | | | | | | |
| Hyde, Graham | Manchester C. (A) 14 September 1991 | 14+6 | 2+1 | 0+4 | 3 | 1 | | | |
| Jones, Ryan | Coventry C. (A) 3 March 1993 | 9 | | | | | | | |
| Sheridan, John | Nottingham F. (A) 4 November 1989 | 25 | 7 | 8 | 1 | 3 | 2 | 1 | 1 |
| Simpson, Ronald | – | | | | | | | | |
| Williams, Mike | Southampton (H) 12 April 1993 | 2+1 | | | 1 | | | | |
| Worthington, Nigel | Brighton & H.A. (H) 25 February 1984 | 40 | 7 | 8 | 3 | 1 | 1 | | 1 |
| FORWARDS | | | | | | | | | |
| Bright, Mark | Nottingham F. (A) 12 September 1992 | 28+2 | 7 | 7 | | 11 | 6 | 3 | |
| Chambers, Leroy | – | | | | | | | | |
| Hirst, David | Charlton Ath. (A) 23 August 1986 | 22 | 3+2 | 3+2 | 1 | 11 | 3 | 1 | 1 |
| Jemson, Nigel | Norwich C. (A) 18 September 1991 | 5+8 | 0+1 | 0+2 | 1+1 | | | | |
| Johnson, David | Aston Villa (A) 18 January 1992 | | | | | | | | |
| Rowntree, Michael | – | | | | | | | | |
| Waddle, Chris | Everton (A) 15 August 1992 | 32+1 | 9 | 8 | 3+1 | 1 | | 2 | 1 |
| Watson, Gordon | Notts Co. (A) 2 March 1991 | 4+7 | 1+2 | 1 | 2+1 | 1 | 3 | | 1 |
| PLAYERS MAKING APPEARANCES IN 1992-93 (No longer with the club) | | | | | | | | | |
| PLAYERS | TRANSFERRED TO | | | | | | | | |
| Anderson, Viv | Barnsley (July 1993) | 24+2 | 5 | 4+1 | 3 | 3 | | | 2 |
| Francis, Trevor | Retired | 1+4 | 1 | | 1 | | | | |
| Williams, Paul | Crystal Palace (September 1992) | 7 | | | | 1 | | | |
| Wilson, Danny | Barnsley (July 1993) | 21+5 | 8 | 7 | 3+1 | 2 | 1 | | 1 |

TRAINEES

Gavin Bailey, Lee Briscoe, Matthew Burkill, Marc Burrows, Simon Carter, Mark Guest, Daniel Jacks, Craig Ludlam, Steven Pass, Jonathan Skargill, Paul Sykes

## SOUTHAMPTON

**1885**

**THE SAINTS**

**Team Manager** Ian Branfoot
**Club Address** The Dell, Milton Road, Southampton SO9 4XX
**Record Attendance** 31,044 v Manchester U., Div. 1, 8 October 1969
**Turned Professional** 1894
**Previous Names** Southampton St Marys
**Club Honours** Football League: Div 3(S) Champions 1921-22; Div. 3 Champions 1959-60. FA Cup: Winners 1976
**League History** 1920-22 Div. 3(S); 1922-53 Div. 2; 1953-58 Div. 3(S); 1958-60 Div. 3; 1960-66 Div 2; 1966-74 Div. 1; 1974-78 Div. 2; 1978-92 Div. 1; 1992- Prem.
**Most League Points in a Season** (2 for a win) 61 in Div. 3(S), 1921-22 and in Div. 3, 1959-60. (3 for a win). 77 in Div. 1, 1983-84
**Most League Goals in a Season** 112 in Div. 3(S), 1957-58
**Record League Victory** 9-3 v Wolverhampton W. in Div. 2, 8 September 1965 and 8-2 v Coventry C. in Div. 1, 28 April 1984
**Record League Defeat** 0-8 v Tottenham H. in Div. 2, 28 March 1936 and v Everton in Div. 1, 20 November 1971
**Consecutive League Wins** 6 in 1964 and 1992
**Consecutive League Defeats** 5 in 1927, 1957, 1967-68 and 1988-89
**Record League Appearances** Terry Paine, 709+4 between 1956-74
**Record League Goalscorer–Career** Mike Channon, 185 between 1966-82
**Record League Goalscorer–Season** Derek Reeves, 39 in Div. 3, 1959-60

### 1992-93 Record

**Premier League** (18th): Played 42, Won 13, Drew 11, Lost 18; Goals For 54, Goals Against 61; Points 50

**FA Cup** Third Round: Nottingham F. (A)1-2
**League Cup** Second Round: Gillingham (A)0-0 (H)3-0; Third Round: Crystal Palace (H)0-2

**1992-93: Back Row L-R:** Jason Dodd, Jeff Kenna, Francis Benali, Neil Maddison, Tommy Widdrington, *David Lee*. **Middle Row:** Lew Chatterley (First Team Coach), *David Speedie*, Richard Hall, Tim Flowers, Kerry Dixon, Ian Andrews, Iain Dowie, Matthew Le Tissier, Don Taylor (Physio). **Front Row:** Stuart Gray, Micky Adams, Glenn Cockerill, Ian Branfoot (Team Manager), Kevin Moore, Steve Wood, Terry Hurlock

## Playing staff for 1993-94 (As at 20 July 1993) — SOUTHAMPTON

| PLAYERS | CLUB DEBUT (Premier/Football League) | 1992-93 APPEARANCES | | | | 1992-93 GOALS | | | |
|---|---|---|---|---|---|---|---|---|---|
| | | Lge | FL Cup | FA Cup | Others | Lge | FL Cup | FA Cup | Others |
| GOALKEEPERS | | | | | | | | | |
| Andrews, Ian | Derby Co. (H) 10 March 1990 | | | | | | | | |
| Flowers, Tim | Manchester U. (A) 13 September 1986 | 42 | 3 | 1 | | | | | |
| DEFENDERS | | | | | | | | | |
| Adams, Micky | Arsenal (H) 25 March 1989 | 38 | 3 | 1 | | 4 | | | |
| Allan, Derek | Manchester C. (H) 1 May 1993 | 0+1 | | | | | | | |
| Benali, Francis | Derby Co. (H) 1 October 1988 | 31+2 | 1+2 | 1 | | | | | |
| Bound, Matthew | Oldham Ath. (H) 25 April 1992 | 1+2 | | | | | | | |
| Charlton, Simon | – | | | | | | | | |
| Dodd, Jason | Q.P.R. (A) 14 October 1989 | 27+3 | 3 | 1 | | 1 | | | |
| Ferguson, Gary | – | | | | | | | | |
| Hall, Richard | Wimbledon (H) 11 May 1991 | 28 | 1 | 1 | | 4 | | | |
| Kenna, Jeff | Derby Co. (A) 4 May 1991 | 27+2 | | 1 | | 2 | | | |
| Monkou, Ken | Manchester U. (H) 24 August 1992 | 33 | 3 | 1 | | 1 | | | |
| Moore, Kevin | Manchester U. (H) 15 August 1987 | 18 | 1 | | | 2 | | | |
| Pickering, Chris | – | | | | | | | | |
| Thomas, Martin | – | | | | | | | | |
| Wood, Steve | Norwich C. (H) 19 October 1991 | 4 | 1 | | | | | | |
| MIDFIELDERS | | | | | | | | | |
| Bartlett, Neal (Trainee) | Manchester C. (H) 1 May 1993 | 0+1 | | | | | | | |
| Cockerill, Glenn | Luton T. (A) 19 October 1985 | 21+2 | 2 | 1 | | | | | |
| Gray, Stuart | Arsenal (H) 28 September 1991 | | | | | | | | |
| Hughes, David | – | | | | | | | | |
| Hurlock, Terry | Manchester U. (H) 14 September 1991 | 30 | 3 | | | | | | |
| Maddison, Neil | Tottenham H. (A) 25 October 1988 | 33+4 | 1 | 1 | | 4 | | | |
| Powell, Lee | Luton T. (H) 21 March 1992 | 0+2 | | | | | | | |
| Robinson, Matthew | – | | | | | | | | |
| Tisdale, Paul | – | | | | | | | | |
| Widdrington, Tommy | Everton (A) 1 April 1992 | 11+1 | 0+1 | | | | | | |
| FORWARDS | | | | | | | | | |
| Banger, Nicky | Norwich C. (A) 8 December 1990 | 10+17 | 1 | 0+1 | | 6 | | | |
| Bennett, Frank | – | | | | | | | | |
| Cramb, Colin | – | | | | | | | | |
| Dixon, Kerry | Tottenham H. (H) 15 August 1992 | 8+1 | 2 | 1 | | 2 | | | |
| Dowie, Iain | Luton T. (A) 4 September 1991 | 34+2 | 2 | | | 11 | 1 | | |
| Groves, Perry | Middlesbrough (H) 29 August 1992 | 13+2 | 2 | 0+1 | | 2 | | | |
| Le Tissier, Matthew | Norwich C. (A) 30 August 1986 | 40 | 3 | 1 | | 15 | 2 | 1 | |
| McDonald, Paul | – | | | | | | | | |
| Moody, Paul | Tottenham H. (H) 17 August 1991 | 2+1 | | | | | | | |
| Sheerin, Paul | – | | | | | | | | |
| PLAYERS MAKING APPEARANCES IN 1992-93 (No longer with the club) | | | | | | | | | |
| PLAYERS | TRANSFERRED TO | | | | | | | | |
| Lee, David | Bolton W. (November 1992) | 0+1 | | | | | | | |
| Speedie, David | Leicester C. (July 1993) | 11 | 1 | | | | | | |

TRAINEES

Nathan Blamey, Neil Carr, James Cole, Kevin Doherty, Lee Elliott, Anthony Everest, Rory Hamill, Paul Harper, John Hooks, Neil Hopper, Nicholas Jensen, Urias Joseph, Andrew Liney, Aron McNally, Daniel Phillips, Richard Rowe

## SWINDON TOWN

**1881**

**THE ROBINS**

**Team Manager** John Gorman
**Club Address** County Ground, Swindon, Wiltshire SN1 2ED
**Record Attendance** 32,000 v Arsenal, FA Cup 3rd Round, 15 January 1972
**Turned Professional** 1894
**Previous Names** None
**Club Honours** Football League: Div. 4 Champions 1985-86. Football League Cup: Winners 1969
**League History** 1920-58 Div. 3(S); 1958-63 Div 3; 1963-65 Div. 2; 1965-69 Div. 3; 1969-74 Div. 2; 1974-82 Div. 3; 1982-86 Div. 4; 1986-87 Div. 3; 1987-92 Div. 2; 1992-93 Div. 1; 1993- Prem.
**Most League Points in a Season** (2 for a win) 64 in Div. 3, 1968-69. (3 for a win) 102 in Div. 4, 1985-86
**Most League Goals in a Season** 100 in Div. 3(S), 1926-27
**Record League Victory** 9-1 v Luton T. in Div. 3(S), 28 April 1921
**Record League Defeat** 0-9 v Torquay U. in Div. 3(S), 8 March 1952
**Consecutive League Wins** 8 in 1926 and 1986
**Consecutive League Defeats** 6 in 1967 and 1980
**Record League Appearances** John Trollope, 767+3 between 1960-80
**Record League Goalscorer–Career** Harry Morris, 216 between 1926-33
**Record League Goalscorer–Season** Harry Morris, 47 in Div. 3(S), 1926-27

### 1992-93 Record

**Football League** First Division (5th): Played 46, Won 21, Drew 13, Lost 12; Goals For 74, Goals Against 59; Points 76
**Play-Offs** Semi-Final: Tranmere Rov. (H)3-1 (A)2-3; Final: Leicester C. (N)4-3
**FA Cup** Third Round: Q.P.R. (A)0-3
**League Cup** Second Round: Torquay U. (A)6-0 (H)3-2; Third Round: Oldham Ath. (H)0-1
**Anglo-Italian Cup** Prelims: Oxford U. (A)3-1, Brentford (H)1-2

**1992-93: Back Row L-R:** John Moncur, *Darren Hall*, Fraser Digby, *Paul Hunt*, Nicky Hammond, *Dave Bennett*, Craig Maskell, Steve White. **Middle Row:** John Trollope (Youth Team Manager) Ross MacLaren, Nicky Summerbee, *Colin Calderwood*, Shaun Taylor, Adrian Viveash, Dave Mitchell, Andrew Thomson, Kevin Horlock, Andy Rowland (Reserve Team Coach). **Front Row:** Kevin Morris (Physio), Martin Ling, *David Kerslake*, Wayne O'Sullivan, *Glenn Hoddle* (Player/Team Manager), John Gorman (Assistant Team Manager), Paul Bodin, *Shaun Close*, Mickey Hazard, Eddie Buckley (Kit Manager)

# Playing staff for 1993-94 (As at 20 July 1993) — SWINDON TOWN

| PLAYERS | CLUB DEBUT (Premier Football League) | 1992-93 APPEARANCES | | | | 1992-93 GOALS | | | |
|---|---|---|---|---|---|---|---|---|---|
| | | Lge | FL Cup | FA Cup | Others | Lge | FL Cup | FA Cup | Others |
| GOALKEEPERS | | | | | | | | | |
| Digby, Fraser | Rotherham U. (H) 27 September 1986 | 33 | 1 | | 5 | | | | |
| Hammond, Nicky | Manchester C. (H) 31 October 1987 | 13 | 2 | 1 | | | | | |
| DEFENDERS | | | | | | | | | |
| Bodin, Paul | Oldham Ath. (A) 12 March 1988 | 34+1 | 1 | 1 | 5 | 11 | | | 1 |
| Horlock, Kevin | Portsmouth (A) 10 October 1992 | 13+1 | 2 | 1 | | 1 | | | |
| MacLaren, Ross | Barnsley (A) 29 August 1988 | 22 | | | 3 | | | | |
| Middleton, Lee | – | | | | | | | | |
| Murray, Edwin | Oxford U. (H) 5 March 1991 | | | 0+1 | | | | | |
| Nijholt, Luc | – | | | | | | | | |
| O'Sullivan, Wayne | – | | | | 1 | | | | |
| Summerbee, Nicky | Woverhampton W. (H) 3 September 1989 | 36+3 | 2+1 | 0+1 | 5 | 3 | | | 1 |
| Taylor, Shaun | Leicester C. (H) 17 August 1991 | 46 | 3 | 1 | 5 | 11 | 1 | | 1 |
| Thomson, Andrew | – | | | | | | | | |
| Viveash, Adrian | Middlesbrough (H) 15 September 1990 | 5 | | | 1 | | | | |
| MIDFIELDERS | | | | | | | | | |
| Berkley, Austin | – | | | | 1 | | | | 1 |
| Hazard, Mickey | Millwall (H) 30 September 1990 | 30+2 | 3 | 1 | 0+2 | 3 | | | |
| Ling, Martin | Port Vale (A) 11 May 1991 | 43 | 3 | 1 | 5 | 3 | 1 | | |
| Marwood, Brian (N/C) | Newcastle U. (H) 13 March 1993 | 6+5 | | | | 1 | | | |
| Moncur, John | Port Vale (H) 4 April 1992 | 11+3 | 1 | | 4 | 1 | | | 1 |
| Phillips, Marcus | – | | 0+1 | | | | | | |
| FORWARDS | | | | | | | | | |
| Fjortoft, Jan | – | | | | | | | | |
| Hamon, Chris | Luton T. (H) 10 April 1993 | 1+1 | | | | | | | |
| Maskell, Craig | Sunderland (H) 15 August 1992 | 32+1 | 2 | 1 | 4+1 | 18 | 1 | | 4 |
| Mitchell, Dave | Leicester C. (H) 17 August 1991 | 37+4 | 3 | 1 | 4 | 11 | 3 | | 3 |
| White, Steve | Notts. Co. (H) 31 August 1986 | 20+14 | 1+2 | 1 | 1+4 | 7 | 2 | | |
| PLAYERS MAKING APPEARANCES IN 1992-93 (No longer with the club) | | | | | | | | | |
| PLAYERS | TRANSFERRED TO | | | | | | | | |
| Calderwood, Colin | Tottenham H. (July 1993) | 46 | 3 | | 5 | 2 | | | |
| Close, Shaun | F/T (May 1993) | 1+6 | 0+1 | | 1 | | | | |
| Gray, Andy | Tottenham H. (Loan – December 1992) | 3 | | | | | | | |
| Hoddle, Glenn | Chelsea (July 1993) | 41+1 | 3 | 1 | 3 | 1 | 1 | | 1 |
| Hunt, Paul | F/T (May 1993) | 3+2 | | | 1 | | | | |
| Kerslake, David | Leeds U. (March 1993) | 30+1 | 3 | 1 | 1 | | | | |

TRAINEES

Shane Cook, David Elsey, James Fraser, Christopher Hamblin, Jonathan Holloway, Stuart James, Mark Jordon, Andrew Kearns, Steven Lane, Scott Medcroft, James Phillips, Jamie Pitman, Stephen Reeves, Gary Thorne, Mark Walter, Benjamin Worrell

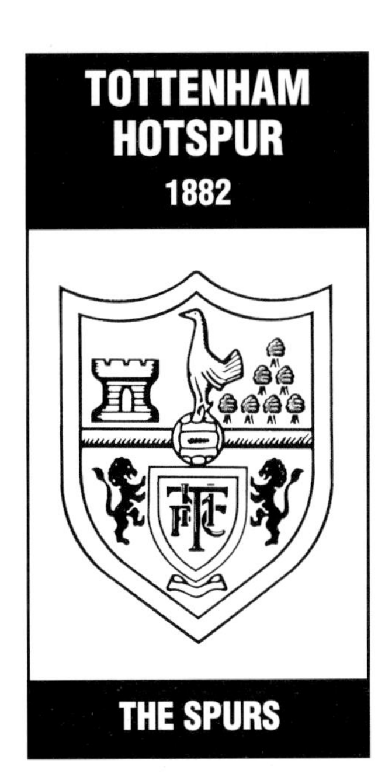


**Team Manager** Ossie Ardiles
**Club Address** White Hart Lane Ground, 748 High Road, Tottenham, London N17 0AP
**Record Attendance** 75,038 v Sunderland, FA Cup 6th Round, 5 March, 1938
**Turned Professional** 1895
**Previous Names** Hotspur
**Club Honours** Football League: Div. 1 Champions 1950-51, 1960-61; Div 2 Champions 1919-20, 1949-50. FA Cup: Winners 1901, 1921, 1961, 1962, 1967, 1981, 1982, 1991. Football League Cup: Winners 1971, 1973. European Cup Winners Cup: Winners 1962-63. EUFA Cup: Winners 1971-72, 1983-84
**League History** 1908-09 Div. 2; 1909-15 Div. 1; 1919-20 Div. 2; 1920-28 Div. 1; 1928-33 Div. 2; 1933-35 Div. 1; 1935-50 Div. 2; 1950-77 Div. 1; 1977-78 Div. 2; 1978-92 Div. 1; 1992- Prem.
**Most League Points in a Season** (2 for a win) 70 in Div. 2, 1919-20. (3 for a win) 77 in Div. 1, 1984-85
**Most League Goals in a Season** 115 in Div. 1, 1960-61
**Record League Victory** 9-0 v Bristol Rov. in Div. 2, 22 October 1977
**Record League Defeat** 0-7 v Liverpool in Div. 1, 2 September 1978
**Consecutive League Wins** 13 in 1960
**Consecutive League Defeats** 5 in 1912, 1955 and 1975
**Record League Appearances** Steve Perryman, 653+2 between 1969-86
**Record League Goalscorer–Career** Jimmy Greaves, 220 between 1961-70
**Record League Goalscorer–Season** Jimmy Greaves, 37 in Div. 1, 1962-63

## 1992-93 Record

**Premier League** (8th): Played 42, Won 16, Drew 11, Lost 15; Goals For 60, Goals Against 66; Points 59
**FA Cup** Third Round: Marlow (H)5-1; Fourth Round: Norwich C. (A)2-0; Fifth Round: Wimbledon (H)3-2; Sixth Round: Manchester C. (A)4-2; Semi-Final: Arsenal (N)0-1
**League Cup** Second Round: Brentford (H)3-1 (A)4-2; Third Round: Manchester C. (A)1-0; Fourth Round: Nottingham F. (A)0-2

**1992-93: Back Row L-R:** Jason Cundy, Darren Anderton, Peter Beadle, Ian Walker, David Tuttle, Erik Thorstvedt, Steve Sedgley, David Howells, Ian Hendon. **Middle Row:** John Sheridan (Physio), David Butler (Physio), Scott Houghton, Andy Gray, Gordon Durie, *Mohamed Nayim*, Vinny Samways, Paul Moran, Keith Waldon (Reserve Team Manager), Roy Reyland (Kit Manager). **Front Row:** Doug Livermore (First Team Coach), Justin Edinburgh, Paul Allen, *Neil Ruddock*, Gary Mabbutt, Dean Austin, *Terry Fenwick*, John Hendry, *Ray Clemence* (Assistant First Team Coach)

## **Playing staff for 1993-94** (As at 20 July 1993) — **TOTTENHAM HOTSPUR**

| PLAYERS | CLUB DEBUT (Premier/Football League) | 1992-93 APPEARANCES | | | | 1992-93 GOALS | | | |
|---|---|---|---|---|---|---|---|---|---|
| | | Lge | FL Cup | FA Cup | Others | Lge | FL Cup | FA Cup | Others |
| GOALKEEPERS | | | | | | | | | |
| Day, Chris | – | | | | | | | | |
| Dearden, Kevin | Nottingham F. (A) 12 April 1993 | 0+1 | | | | | | | |
| Thorstvedt, Erik | Nottingham F. (H) 15 January 1989 | 25+2 | 2 | 5 | | | | | |
| Walker, Ian | Norwich C. (A) 10 April 1991 | 17 | 2 | | | | | | |
| DEFENDERS | | | | | | | | | |
| Austin, Dean | Crystal Palace (H) 22 August 1992 | 33+1 | 2+1 | 5 | | | | | |
| Bergsson, Gudni | Luton T. (H) 26 December 1988 | 0+5 | | 0+1 | | | | | |
| Calderwood, Colin | – | | | | | | | | |
| Culverhouse, David | – | | | | | | | | |
| Cundy, Jason | Coventry C. (H) 28 March 1992 | 13+2 | 2 | | | 1 | | | |
| Edinburgh, Justin | Wimbledon (H) 10 November 1990 | 31+1 | 3+1 | 5 | | | | | |
| Hendon, Ian | Aston Villa (A) 16 March 1991 | | | | | | | | |
| Landon, Chris | – | | | | | | | | |
| Mabbutt, Gary | Luton T. (H) 28 August 1982 | 29 | 2 | 5 | | 2 | | | |
| McDonald, David | Liverpool (A) 8 May 1993 | 2 | | | | | | | |
| Mahorn, Paul | – | | | | | | | | |
| Marlowe, Andrew | – | | | | | | | | |
| Nethercott, Stuart | Chelsea (A) 20 March 1993 | 3+2 | | | | | | | |
| Sedgley, Steve | Luton T. (H) 19 August 1989 | 20+2 | 3 | 2 | | 3 | | 1 | |
| Tuttle, David | Chelsea (A) 1 December 1990 | 4+1 | 2 | | | | | | |
| Van den Hauwe, Pat | Aston Villa (A) 9 September 1989 | 13+5 | 2 | | | | | | |
| Young Neil | – | | | | | | | | |
| MIDFIELDERS | | | | | | | | | |
| Allen, Paul | Watford (H) 17 August 1985 | 38 | 4 | 5 | | 3 | | | |
| Campbell, Sol | Chelsea (H) 5 December 1992 | 0+1 | | | | 1 | | | |
| Caskey, Darren | – | | | | | | | | |
| Gray, Andy | Leeds U. (H) 7 March 1992 | 9+8 | | | | 1 | | | |
| Grogan, Darren | – | | | | | | | | |
| Hill, Danny | Chelsea (A) 20 March 1993 | 2+2 | | | | | | | |
| Howells, David | Sheffield Wed. (A) 22 February 1986 | 16+2 | 0+1 | 2+1 | | 1 | | | |
| McMahon, Gerard | – | | | | | | | | |
| Minton, Jeffrey | Everton (H) 25 April 1992 | | 0+1 | | | | | | |
| Samways, Vinny | Nottingham F. (A) 2 May 1987 | 34 | 3 | 5 | | | 1 | 2 | |
| Turner, Andrew | Southampton (A) 15 August 1992 | 7+11 | 0+2 | 0+1 | | 3 | 1 | | |
| Watson, Kevin | Sheffield Wed. (A) 27 September 1992 | 4+1 | 1+1 | 0+1 | | | 1 | | |
| FORWARDS | | | | | | | | | |
| Anderton, Darren | Southampton (A) 15 August 1992 | 32+2 | 2 | 4+1 | | 6 | 1 | 1 | |
| Barmby, Nicky | Sheffield Wed. (A) 27 September 1992 | 17+5 | 2+1 | 3+1 | | 6 | | 3 | |
| Beadle, Peter | – | | | | | | | | |
| Durie, Gordon | Southampton (A) 17 August 1991 | 17 | 2 | 1 | | 3 | 1 | | |
| Hendry, John | Norwich C. (A) 10 April 1991 | 2+3 | | | | 2 | | | |
| Hodges, Lee | Wimbledon (H) 1 May 1993 | 0+4 | | | | | | | |
| Houghton, Scott | Manchester U. (H) 28 September 1991 | | | | | | | | |
| McDougald, Junior | – | | | | | | | | |
| Moran, Paul | Everton (A) 11 May 1987 | 0+3 | | | | | | | |
| Robinson, Steve | – | | | | | | | | |
| Sheringham, Teddy | Ipswich T. (A) 30 August 1992 | 38 | 4 | 5 | | 21 | 3 | 4 | |
| PLAYERS MAKING APPEARANCES IN 1992-93 (No longer with the club) | | | | | | | | | |
| PLAYERS | TRANSFERRED TO | | | | | | | | |
| Fenwick, Terry | F/T (May 1993) | 3+2 | | | | | | | |
| Nayim, Mohamed | Real Zaragoza (May 1993) | 15+3 | 2 | 3 | | 3 | | 3 | |
| Ruddock, Neil | Liverpool (July 1993) | 38 | 4 | 5 | | 3 | | | |

TRAINEES

Ijah Anderson, Gary Brady, Dean Callcut, Stephen Carr, James Clapham, Daniel Foot, Peter Gain, Darren Gosnell, Junior Haynes, William Hudson, Glynn Hurst, Gareth Knott, Neil Le Bihan, Kevin Maher, Andrew Quy, Robert Simpson, Steven Slade, Simon Spencer, Leon Townley, Richard Williams, Simon Wormull

# WEST HAM UNITED

1895

THE HAMMERS

**Team Manager** Billy Bonds, MBE
**Club Address** Boleyn Ground, Green Street, Upton Park, London E13 9AZ
**Record Attendance** 42,322 v Tottenham H., Div. 1, 17 October 1970
**Turned Professional** 1900
**Previous Names** Thames Ironworks
**Club Honours** Football League: Div. 2 Champions 1957-58, 1980-81. FA Cup: Winners 1964, 1975, 1980. European Cup-Winners Cup: Winners 1964-65.
**League History** 1919-23 Div. 2; 1923-32 Div. 1; 1932-58 Div. 2; 1958-78 Div. 1; 1978-81 Div. 2; 1981-89 Div. 1; 1989-91 Div. 2; 1991-93 Div. 1; 1993- Prem.
**Most League Points in a Season** (2 for a win) 66 in Div. 2, 1980-81. (3 for a win) 88 in Div. 1, 1992-93
**Most League Goals in a Season** 101 in Div. 2, 1957-58
**Record League Victory** 8-0 v Rotherham U. in Div. 2, 8 March 1958 and v Sunderland in Div. 1, 19 October 1968
**Record League Defeat** 2-8 v Blackburn Rov. in Div. 1, 26 December 1963
**Consecutive League Wins** 9 in 1985
**Consecutive League Defeats** 9 in 1932
**Record League Appearances** Billy Bonds, 655+8 between 1967-88
**Record League Goalscorer–Career** Vic Watson, 306 between 1920-35
**Record League Goalscorer–Season** Vic Watson, 42 in Div. 1, 1929-30

## 1992-93 Record

**Football League** First Division (2nd): Played 46, Won 26, Drew 10, Lost 10; Goals for 81, Goals Against 41; Points 88
**FA Cup** Third Round: West Bromwich A. (A)2-0; Fourth Round: Barnsley (A)1-4
**League Cup** Second Round: Crewe Alex. (H)0-0 (A)0-2
**Anglo-Italian Cup** Prelims: Bristol Rov. (H)2-2, Southend U. (A)3-0; Group "B": Cremonese (A)0-2, Reggiana (H)2-0, Cosenza (A)1-0, Pisa (H)0-0

**1992-93: Back Row L-R:** Tim Breacker, Tony Gale, *Steve Banks*, Alvin Martin, Mike Small, Ludo Miklosko, Colin Foster, Martin Allen. **Middle Row:** Trevor Morley, *Simon Clarke*, Kenny Brown, *George Parris*, Steve Potts, Matthew Rush, Clive Allen. **Front Row:** *Kevin Keen*, Mark Robson, Dean Martin, Julian Dicks, Ian Bishop, Peter Butler, Matthew Holmes

## Playing staff for 1993-94 (As at 20 July 1993) — WEST HAM UNITED

| PLAYERS | CLUB DEBUT (Premier/Football League) | 1992-93 APPEARANCES | | | | 1992-93 GOALS | | | |
|---|---|---|---|---|---|---|---|---|---|
| | | Lge | FL Cup | FA Cup | Others | Lge | FL Cup | FA Cup | Others |
| GOALKEEPERS | | | | | | | | | |
| Miklosko, Ludo | Swindon T. (A) 18 February 1990 | 46 | 2 | 2 | 5 | | | | |
| Peyton, Gerry | – | | | | | | | | |
| DEFENDERS | | | | | | | | | |
| Basham, Michael | – | | | | | | | | |
| Breacker, Tim | Swindon T. (A) 20 October 1990 | 39 | 2 | 2 | 4 | 2 | | | |
| Brown, Kenny | Luton T. (H) 17 August 1991 | 13+2 | | 1 | 1+2 | 2 | | | |
| Dicks, Julian | Sheffield Wed. (A) 2 April 1988 | 34 | 1 | 1 | 6 | 11 | | | 3 |
| Foster, Colin | Watford (H) 23 September 1989 | 3+3 | | 1 | 0+1 | 1 | | | |
| Gale, Tony | Ipswich T. (H) 25 August 1984 | 21+2 | | | 1 | 1 | | | |
| Marquis, Paul | – | | | | | | | | |
| Martin, Alvin | Aston Villa (A) 18 March 1978 | 23 | 2 | 1 | 6 | 1 | | | |
| Potts, Steve | Q.P.R. (H) 1 January 1985 | 46 | 2 | 2 | 6 | | | | |
| Thomas, Mitchell | Luton T. (H) 17 August 1991 | 3 | 1 | | | | | | |
| Webster, Simon | – | | | | | | | | |
| MIDFIELDERS | | | | | | | | | |
| Allen, Martin | Plymouth Arg. (H) 26 August 1989 | 33+1 | 2 | 2 | 6 | 4 | | | |
| Bishop, Ian | Leicester C. (A) 30 December 1989 | 15+7 | | | 1+1 | 1 | | | |
| Butler, Peter | Barnsley (A) 16 August 1992 | 39 | 2 | 2 | 1 | 2 | | | |
| Canham, Scott | – | | | | | | | | |
| Currie, Darren | – | | | | | | | | |
| Holland, Matthew | – | | | | | | | | |
| Holmes, Matthew | Newcastle U. (A) 29 August 1992 | 6+12 | | 1 | 3 | 1 | | | 1 |
| Rush, Matthew | Hull C. (H) 6 October 1990 | | | | 2+1 | | | | |
| Williamson, Daniel | – | | | | | | | | |
| FORWARDS | | | | | | | | | |
| Allen, Clive | Chelsea (A) 4 April 1992 | 25+2 | 2 | 1 | 6 | 14 | | 1 | 3 |
| Bunbury, Alex | Brentford (A) 20 December 1992 | 2+2 | | 0+1 | 1 | | | | |
| Gordon, Dale | – | | | | | | | | |
| Jones, Steve | Leicester C. (A) 30 January 1993 | 4+2 | | | 1+1 | 2 | | | |
| Martin, Dean | Coventry C. (A) 25 April 1992 | | | | | | | | |
| Morley, Trevor | Leicester C. (A) 30 December 1989 | 41 | 2 | 2 | 4 | 20 | | 1 | 1 |
| Robson, Mark | Barnsley (A) 16 August 1992 | 41+3 | 2 | 2 | 4+1 | 8 | | 1 | |
| Small, Mike | Luton T. (H) 17 August 1991 | 5+4 | 0+1 | | | | | | |
| Whitmarsh, Paul | – | | | | | | | | |
| PLAYERS MAKING APPEARANCES IN 1992-93 (No longer with the club) | | | | | | | | | |
| PLAYERS | TRANSFERRED TO | | | | | | | | |
| Banks, Steve | Gillingham (June 1993) | | | | 1 | | | | |
| Clarke, Simon | F/T (May 1993) | 0+1 | | | | | | | |
| Keen, Kevin | Wolverhampton W. (July 1993) | 46 | 2 | 2 | 5+1 | 7 | | | |
| Parris, George | Birmingham C. (March 1993) | 10+6 | | | 2 | | | | |
| Speedie, David | Southampton (Loan – March 1993) | 11 | | | | 4 | | | |

TRAINEES

Jonathan Bates, Steven Blaney, Anthony Browne, Jason Geraghty, Jerome John, Roy Johnson, Wayne Josceyline, Darren Maeer, Scott Moore, Christopher Moors, Warren Oakley, Martin Peat, Stuart Richardson, Christopher Rose, Daniel Shipp, Jamie Victory, Gary Waters

## WIMBLEDON

1889

THE DONS

**Team Manager** Joe Kinnear
**Club Address** Selhurst Park, London SE25 6PU
**Record Attendance** 18,000 v HMS Victory, FA Amateur Cup 3rd Round, 1934-35
**Turned Professional** 1964
**Previous Names** Wimbledon Old Centrals
**Club Honours** Football League: Div. 4 Champions 1982-83. FA Cup: Winners 1988
**League History** 1977-79 Div. 4; 1979-80 Div 3; 1980-81 Div. 4; 1981-82 Div. 3; 1982-83 Div. 4; 1983-84 Div. 3; 1984-86 Div. 2; 1986-92 Div. 1; 1992- Prem.
**Most League Points in a Season** (2 for a win) 61 in Div. 4, 1978-79. (3 for a win) 98 in Div. 4, 1982-83
**Most League Goals in a Season** 97 in Div. 3, 1983-84
**Record League Victory** 6-0 v Newport Co. in Div. 3, 3 September 1983
**Record League Defeat** 1-6 v Carlisle U. in Div. 2, 23 March 1985 and v Gillingham in Div. 2, 13 February 1982
**Consecutive League Wins** 7 in 1983
**Consecutive League Defeats** 4 in 1982
**Record League Appearances** Alan Cork, 352+78 between 1978-92
**Record League Goalscorer–Career** Alan Cork, 145 between 1978-92
**Record League Goalscorer–Season** Alan Cork, 29 in Div. 3, 1983-84

## 1992-93 Record

**Premier League** (12th): Played 42, Won 14, Drew 12, Lost 16; Goals For 56, Goals Against 55; Points 54
**FA Cup** Third Round: Everton (H)0-0 (R)2-1; Fourth Round: Aston Villa (A)1-1 (R)0-0; Fifth Round: Tottenham H. (A)2-3
**League Cup** Second Round: Bolton W. (A)3-1 (H)0-1; Third Round: Everton (A)0-0 (R)0-1

**1992-93: Back Row L-R:** Joe Dillon (Assistant Kit manager), Neal Ardley, Chris Perry, Paul Miller, Dean Blackwell, Neil Sullivan, Leighton Allen, Hans Segers, Stewart Castledine, Aiden Newhouse, Brian McAllister, Warren Barton, Ron Suart (Chief Scout). **Middle Row:** Syd Neal (Kit Manager), Peter Fear, Steven Talboys, Scott Fitzgerald, *Carlton Fairweather*, John Scales, Steve Anthrobus, Lawrie Sanchez, John Fashanu, Dean Holdsworth, Roger Joseph, *Steve Cotterill*, *Paul Jennings*, *Vaughan Ryan*, Roger Smith (Youth Development Officer). **Front Row:** Ernie Tippett (Youth Team Manager), Grant Payne, Paul McGee, Gerald Dobbs, Terry Burton (Assistant Team Manager), Robbie Earle, Gary Elkins, Joe Kinnear (Team Manager), *Terry Gibson*, Andy Clarke, Brian Sparrow (Reserve Team Manager), Justin Skinner, *Lee Fiori*, Steve Allen (Physio)

## Playing staff for 1993-94 (As at 20 July 1993) — WIMBLEDON

| PLAYERS | CLUB DEBUT (Premier/Football League) | 1992-93 APPEARANCES Lge | FL Cup | FA Cup | Others | 1992-93 GOALS Lge | FL Cup | FA Cup | Others |
|---|---|---|---|---|---|---|---|---|---|
| GOALKEEPERS | | | | | | | | | |
| Fairbairn, Neil | – | | | | | | | | |
| Segers, Hans | Everton (H) 1 October 1988 | 41 | 4 | 5 | | | | | |
| Sullivan, Neil | Aston Villa (A) 20 April 1991 | 1 | | | | | | | |
| DEFENDERS | | | | | | | | | |
| Barton, Warren | Arsenal (H) 25 August 1990 | 23 | 4 | | | 2 | | | |
| Blackwell, Dean | Manchester C. (H) 16 September 1989 | 19+5 | | 4 | | | | | |
| Cable, Marc | – | | | | | | | | |
| Elkins, Gary | Chelsea (H) 17 November 1990 | 17+1 | 2 | 3 | | | | 1 | |
| Fitzgerald, Scott | Tottenham H. (H) 28 April 1990 | 18+2 | 2 | | | | | | |
| Joseph, Roger | Arsenal (H) 27 August 1988 | 31+1 | 2+1 | 5 | | | | | |
| Kimble, Alan | – | | | | | | | | |
| McAllister, Brian | Arsenal (H) 13 January 1990 | 26+1 | 2 | 3 | | | | | |
| Perry, Chris | – | | | | | | | | |
| Scales, John | Watford (A) 15 August 1987 | 32 | 2 | 5 | | 1 | | | |
| Skinner, Justin | Liverpool (A) 26 September 1992 | 1 | | | | | | | |
| Thomas, Mark | – | | | | | | | | |
| MIDFIELDERS | | | | | | | | | |
| Anthrobus, Steve | Aston Villa (A) 24 February 1990 | 4+1 | 1 | | | | | | |
| Ardley, Neal | Aston Villa (A) 20 April 1991 | 24+2 | 2 | 4 | | 4 | 1 | | |
| Castledine, Stewart | Norwich C. (A) 25 April 1992 | | | | | | | | |
| Dobbs, Gerald | Nottingham F. (H) 2 April 1992 | 16+3 | 2 | 1+1 | | 1 | | 1 | |
| Earle, Robbie | Chelsea (A) 17 August 1991 | 42 | 4 | 5 | | 7 | | 1 | |
| Fear, Peter | Arsenal (A) 10 February 1993 | 2+2 | | | | | | | |
| Jones, Vinny | Nottingham F. (A) 22 November 1986 | 27 | 3 | 4 | | 1 | 1 | | |
| McGee, Paul | Arsenal (A) 17 May 1989 | 1+2 | | | | | | | |
| Sanchez, Lawrie | Birmingham C. (H) 22 December 1984 | 23+4 | 1 | 3 | | 4 | | | |
| Talboys, Steven | Norwich C. (A) 5 December 1992 | 3+4 | 0+1 | 0+1 | | | | | |
| FORWARDS | | | | | | | | | |
| Allen, Leighton | – | | | | | | | | |
| Berry, Greg | Ipswich T. (H) 18 August 1992 | 2+1 | | 0+1 | | | | | |
| Clarke, Andy | Norwich C. (H) 2 March 1991 | 23+10 | 3 | 3 | | 5 | | | |
| Fashanu, John | Portsmouth (A) 29 March 1986 | 27+2 | 2+1 | 5 | | 6 | 1 | 1 | |
| Holdsworth, Dean | Leeds U. (A) 15 August 1992 | 34+2 | 2+1 | 2+1 | | 19 | | | |
| Miller, Paul | Watford (A) 15 August 1987 | 11+8 | 1+1 | 1 | | 2 | | | |
| Newhouse, Aiden | Charlton Ath. (A) 17 April 1990 | 0+1 | 1 | | | | | | |
| Payne, Grant | – | | | | | | | | |
| PLAYERS MAKING APPEARANCES IN 1991-92 (No longer with the club) | | | | | | | | | |
| PLAYERS | TRANSFERRED TO | | | | | | | | |
| Gibson, Terry | F/T (May 1993) | 6+2 | 2 | | | 1 | | | |
| McLeary, Alan | Millwall (Loan – October 1992) | 4 | 2 | | | | | | |
| Cotterill, Steve | Bournemouth (July 1993) | 4+3 | | 2+1 | | 3 | | 1 | |

TRAINEES

Kevin Board, Simon Cobb, Jason Cunningham, Franco Di Rubbo, Jason Evell, Gavin Fell, Leon Finegan, Shaun Fleming, Leonard Griffiths, Daniel Hodges, Vincent John, Iain Laidlaw, Steven Mumford, Clement Owusu, Leonard Piper

*Blackburn Rovers must hope that Alan Shearer can recover his sparkle, following his operation*

**1 August 1993**

Transfers into the Premier League: Gary BLISSETT £350,000 (Brentford – Wimbledon), David CRAWLEY £25,000 (Dundalk – Manchester City), Ross DAVIDSON (Walton & Hersham – Sheffield United), Alphonso GROENEADIJK £500,000 (Ajax – Manchester City), Chris KAMARA (Luton Town – Sheffield United), Alec MATHIE £250,000 (Morton – Newcastle United), Paul MITCHELL £40,000 (Bournemouth – West Ham United), Andy MORRISON £500,000 (Plymouth Argyle – Blackburn Rovers), Keith ROWLANDS £110,000 (Bournemouth – West Ham United), Adrian WHITBREAD £500,000 (Leyton Orient – Swindon Town), Guy WHITTINGHAM £1,200,000 (Portsmouth – Aston Villa), Jonas WIRMOLA £50,000 (Sparvagens – Sheffield United).

Transfers within the Premier League: Jason DOZZELL (Ipswich Town – Tottenham Hotspur). Fee to be decided by tribunal. David TUTTLE £350,000 (Tottenham Hotspur – Sheffield United).

Re-signed after being released: Giuliano MAIORANA (Manchester United).

Trainee/Junior signings: Richard BARKER (Sheffield Wednesday), Steven BROWN (Sheffield Wednesday), Matthew HARDWICK (Sheffield Wednesday), Michael McVEIGH (Sheffield Wednesday), David PRATT (West Ham United), James WHITLEY (Manchester City).

Transferred outside the Premier League: Mark BLAKE (Aston Villa – Portsmouth), Wayne BURNETT (Blackburn Rovers – Plymouth Argyle), Brian CAREY (Manchester United – Leicester City), Martin CARRUTHERS (Aston Villa – Stoke City), Lee CHAPMAN (Leeds United – Portsmouth), Darren COLLIER (Blackburn Rovers – Darlington), Ian HENDON (Tottenham Hotspur – Leyton Orient), Kaare INGEBRIGSTEN (Manchester City – Rosenborg Trondheim), Phil KITE (Sheffield United – Cardiff City), Istvan KOZMA (Liverpool – Ujpest Dozsa), Brian MARWOOD (Swindon Town – Barnet), Dave MITCHELL (Swindon Town – Altay Izmir), Mark STIMSON (Newcastle United – Portsmouth), Alan THOMPSON (Newcastle United – Bolton Wanderers).

## **ABLETT Gary** Ian

Born: Liverpool, 19 November 1965

Height: 6'0"

Weight: 11.4

International Honours: E "U21"-1, E"B"

**Position/Skill Factor:** Natural left footed player, adept at "one-twos" and a great passer of the ball. Joins up in the attack at every opportunity as a provider, rather than scorer. Principally a central defender, he is versatile enough to play anywhere along the back four.

**Career History:** Liverpool born and bred, he signed associated schoolboy forms for the "Reds" in October 1981 and apprentice forms in June 1982. He actually made his FL debut for Derby County, while on loan, at home to Bournemouth on 30 January 1985 and also had further FL experience on loan to Hull City before playing his first League match for Liverpool in December 1986, deputising for Alan Hansen. He established a regular place in the Liverpool team from February 1988, alternating between left-back and central defence until the 1989 close season. However, his progress was retarded by the signings of David Burrows (left-back) and Glenn Hysen (central defence) and although playing quite frequently in 1989-90 and 1990-91, it was as cover for the four defensive positions and not as first choice. A member of the Liverpool side that lifted the FA Cup in 1989 when beating Everton 3-2, he also won two League Championship medals with the club in 1987-88 and 1989-90. Had a golden opportunity to re-establish himself in the heart of the Liverpool defence in 1991-92, following the departure of Gary Gillespie and injuries to Glen Hysen and new signing Mark Wright. Although he formed a partnership with the previously untried Nicky Tanner, he was lacking in confidence and it was he and not Tanner, who made way when Wright returned. His transfer from Anfield was perhaps inevitable, although it was a surprise when he moved to city rivals, Everton. Settled down well at Goodison Park, however, playing both at left-back and in central defence. Virtually ever-present throughout **1992-93,** he began at centre-half due to the long term injury of Keown, but switched to left-back on his return. Adapted well to the change of personnel when injuries decimated the back four and he continued to produce excellent displays, which made him a favourite with the crowd, as his confidence at the back began to flow through the team. The combination of Ablett and Dave Watson would appear to be the best central defensive partnership available at the club for the coming season.

| | | | APPEARANCES | | | | GOALS | | | |
|---|---|---|---|---|---|---|---|---|---|---|
| Clubs | Signing Date | Transfer Fee | Lge | FL Cup | FA Cup | Others | Lge | FL Cup | FA Cup | Others |
| Liverpool | 11.83 | – | 103+6 | 10+1 | 16+2 | 9 | 1 | | | |
| Derby County | 1.85 | Loan | 3+3 | | | 2 | | | | |
| Hull City | 9.86 | Loan | 5 | | | | | | | |
| Everton* | 1.92 | £750,000 | 57 | 6 | 3 | | 1 | | | |

## **ADAMS Anthony (Tony)** Alexander

Born: Romford, 10 October 1966

Height: 6'1" Weight: 12.1

International Honours: E Yth, E "U21"-5, E"B", E-26

**Position/Skill Factor:** Key, commanding central defender, who is exceptional in the air inside both six yard boxes. Also specialises in striking good long balls behind an opponent's defence.

**Career History:** Came through Arsenal's junior ranks, signing associated schoolboy forms in November 1980, before becoming an apprentice in April 1983. After making his FL debut at Highbury against Sunderland on 5 November 1983, two months prior to turning professional, he eventually graduated as the club's youngest ever captain. Recognised at full international level, he made his England debut against Spain in Madrid on 18 February 1987 and, two months later, was at Wembley, playing in Arsenal's 2-1 League Cup Final win over Liverpool. And at the end of that season he was honoured by the PFA as their "Young Player of the Year". He was a regular choice for his country for two years, participating in England's ill-fated appearance in the European Championships in West Germany, June 1988, until losing his place to Des Walker. Scaled the heights in 1988-89, when he led the "Gunners" to the League Championship, following a famous last match of the season victory over Liverpool at Anfield. But two years later he was disgraced, when he was absent from the team for three months, following a well publicised jail conviction for a drink driving offence. However, he was soon back in charge, leading Arsenal to yet another League Championship title, the tenth in the club's history and, perhaps surprisingly, winning two more England caps, both against the Republic of Ireland, after being overlooked for two years by the England management. After playing in all but seven games of Arsenal's League campaign in 1991-92 he entered the **1992-93** season with renewed optimism. It was another solid and consistent season for him and he ended it as a fixture in the England side and as the first captain ever to lift the League and FA Cups in one season when, the "Gunners" twice beat Sheffield Wednesday in Wembley Finals.

| | | | APPEARANCES | | | | GOALS | | | |
|---|---|---|---|---|---|---|---|---|---|---|
| Clubs | Signing Date | Transfer Fee | Lge | FL Cup | FA Cup | Others | Lge | FL Cup | FA Cup | Others |
| Arsenal* | 1.84 | - | 281+3 | 42+1 | 26 | 9 | 20 | 2 | 3 | 1 |

## ADAMS Michael (Micky) Richard

Born: Sheffield, 8 November 1961

Height: 5'6" Weight: 10.4

International Honours: E Yth

**Position/Skill Factor:** Versatile player who can operate at left-back or in defensive left-sided midfield positions. Can go past defenders to create chances and crosses well. A willing worker, he is always prepared to help team-mates in trouble.

**Career History:** Signed as a Gillingham apprentice in August 1978 and made his FL debut at Swindon Town on 19 April 1980 when coming on as a substitute. After four seasons with the Kent side, he moved into the First Division with Coventry City and became an instant hit with the fans when he scored on his home debut. Yorkshire-born, he spent little more than three years at Highfield Road before returning to his home county with Leeds United. Proved to be a shrewd acquisition when helping the club to the 1987 FA Cup Semi-Final, but following the arrival of Glyn Snodin, he found it difficult to hold down a first team place. Moved south to Southampton, settling into the left-back berth, until forced to miss a huge chunk of the 1989-90 season due to injury. Came back as strong as ever, sharing the position with young Francis Benali. A consistent first choice at left-back in 1991-92, apart from a spell out of the team from February to April 1992 and missed only three matches throughout **1992-93.** However, a dislocated shoulder, whilst taking a full coaching badge at Lilleshall during the summer threatened to wreck his start, but fortunately it healed in time for him to begin the season in a left-sided midfield role. Sent off in the second match of the campaign for lashing out at an opponent at Queens Park Rangers, he was man enough to admit his guilt and publicly apologise to club and supporters. Made further amends by striking the equalizing goal in the very next game at Aston Villa and in November scored the winner at Nottingham Forest. Gained practical experience as he helped coach associated schoolboys at the club and during the latter part of the season was once again preferred to Benali in the left-back position.

| | | | APPEARANCES | | | | GOALS | | | |
|---|---|---|---|---|---|---|---|---|---|---|
| Clubs | Signing Date | Transfer Fee | Lge | FL Cup | FA Cup | Others | Lge | FL Cup | FA Cup | Others |
| Gillingham | 11.79 | - | 85+7 | 5 | 6 | | 5 | | | |
| Coventry City | 7.83 | £75,000 | 85+5 | 9 | 7 | 2 | 9 | 1 | | |
| Leeds United | 1.87 | £110,000 | 72+1 | 4 | 6 | 6 | 2 | | 1 | |
| Southampton* | 3.89 | £250,000 | 124+1 | 15 | 7 | 6 | 7 | | | |

## ADAMS Neil James

Born: Stoke, 23 November 1965

Height: 5'8"

Weight: 10.1

International Honours: E "U21"-1

**Position/Skill Factor:** Right-winger with plenty of pace and enthusiasm. Runs at defenders and often drives balls in from crossing positions.

**Career History:** Stoke City plucked him out of local junior football and he made his FL debut away at Charlton Athletic in the number three shirt on 21 September 1985 and held his place for the remainder of the season. Everton moved in smartly for him, but after three years at Goodison and only limited appearances, he signed for Oldham Athletic in the summer of 1989, after impressing manager Joe Royle during a spell on loan in 1988-89. However, he was unable to command a regular place, often selected as substitute, but proved a valuable member of the squad that won the Second Division title in 1990-91. In and out of the team during Oldham's first campaign in Division One for 68 years, sharing the number seven shirt with Roger Palmer, his appearances were restricted by frequent tactical team changes. Still very much the in-and-out man of the team in **1992-93,** although his goals per game ratio were quite high for a winger and on his day he ran some of the best defenders ragged. Came very much into the reckoning on the run in, scoring both goals in a 2-2 draw at Everton in the last three minutes of the game. Next time out, he headed past Peter Schmeichel for the winner over Champions elect, Manchester United and two games later, after having a fine effort turned over the bar, he beat Queen's Park Rangers' goalie, Tony Roberts, for a late equaliser in a 2-2 home draw. Lost his place for the last three critical matches and while having had his best season yet, he still lacks the consistency to become a regular.

| | | | APPEARANCES | | | | GOALS | | | |
|---|---|---|---|---|---|---|---|---|---|---|
| Clubs | Signing Date | Transfer Fee | Lge | FL Cup | FA Cup | Others | Lge | FL Cup | FA Cup | Others |
| Stoke City | 7.85 | - | 31+1 | 3 | 1 | 3 | 4 | | | |
| Everton | 7.86 | £150,000 | 17+3 | 4+1 | | 5+1 | | 1 | | |
| Oldham Athletic | 1.89 | Loan | 9 | | | | | | | |
| Oldham Athletic* | 6.89 | £100,000 | 86+30 | 10+2 | 9+2 | 1+1 | 23 | 1 | 2 | |

## AINSCOUGH Paul Brian

Born: Blackburn, 22 August 1975

Height: 5'11" Weight: 10.9

**Position/Skill Factor:** A neat passing midfielder who is always looking to receive the ball and can play good 'one-twos'.

**Career History:** A local born player, who started at Blackburn Rovers as an associated schoolboy (September 1989), before graduating as a trainee (July 1991) through the youth team, he was given a reserve team outing at the end of **1992-93**, immediately prior to turning professional.

| | | | APPEARANCES | | | | GOALS | | | |
|---|---|---|---|---|---|---|---|---|---|---|
| Clubs | Signing Date | Transfer Fee | Lge | FL Cup | FA Cup | Others | Lge | FL Cup | FA Cup | Others |
| Blackburn Rovers* | 7.93 | – | | | | | | | | |

## AKINBIYI Adeola (Ade) Peter

Born: Hackney, 10 October 1974

Height: 6'1" Weight: 11.10

**Position/Skill Factor:** Striker with good balance and two useful feet, who twists and turns on chances around the box.

**Career History:** A product of Hackney and inner London schools, he signed associated schoolboy forms for Norwich City in March 1989 and had already played for the "Canaries' " youth team before signing on as trainee in July 1991. Has three hat-tricks amongst his 50 youth and reserve team goals from 90 appearances to date, but needs to curb a poor disciplinary record. Turned professional at the the beginning of 1993 and his end of **1992-93** season exploits in both FA Youth Cup Semi-Final legs against the eventual winners, Leeds United, make him a candidate for a first team debut in 1993-94. Definitely one for the future.

| | | | APPEARANCES | | | | GOALS | | | |
|---|---|---|---|---|---|---|---|---|---|---|
| Clubs | Signing Date | Transfer Fee | Lge | FL Cup | FA Cup | Others | Lge | FL Cup | FA Cup | Others |
| Norwich City* | 2.93 | – | | | | | | | | |

## ALLAN Derek Thomas

Born: Irvine, 24 December 1974

Height: 6'0" Weight: 10.13

**Position/Skill Factor:** Central defender who is good in the air and very quick on the ground. Only sees the ball and wants to win it.

**Career History:** One of several youngsters signed by Southampton manager, Ian Branfoot, from Scottish First and Second Division clubs during **1992-93,** in this case, Ayr United, managed by former Ipswich Town full back, George Burley. With only five Scottish League appearances behind him and still a trainee, he was purchased for an initial £75,000 fee, but future installments could eventually take it over £150,000. Starting in "Saints' " youth team, by early April he had been promoted to the reserves and included in Scotland's under 21 squad to play Iceland. The meteoric rise to stardom continued when he was promoted to the first team bench for the penultimate game of the season and made his PL debut at the Dell as a substitute against Manchester City on 1 May 1993. Replacing Matthew Bound with just eight minutes remaining, he looked calm and assured and although he needs to fill out physically, he didn't look out of place. Definitely a smart buy.

| | | | APPEARANCES | | | | GOALS | | | |
|---|---|---|---|---|---|---|---|---|---|---|
| Clubs | Signing Date | Transfer Fee | Lge | FL Cup | FA Cup | Others | Lge | FL Cup | FA Cup | Others |
| Ayr United | – | – | 5 | | | | | | | |
| Southampton* | 3.93 | £75,000 | 0+1 | | | | | | | |

## ALLEN Bradley James

Born: Romford, 13 September 1971

Height: 5'7"

Weight: 10.0

International Honours: E Yth, E "U21"-7

**Position/Skill Factor:** Up and coming striker who is very skilful. Turns quickly and looks to get his shots in, he will almost certainly be another goalscorer in the family mould.

**Career History:** Another member of the Allen footballing family who have succeeded at the top level, starting with his father, Les. Was an associated schoolboy (March 1987) at Loftus Road before turning pro and making his FL debut for Queens Park Rangers at Wimbledon on 14 January 1989, the only first team match he played that season. After three seasons of only occasional appearances he finally earned an extended run in QPR's first team in the closing weeks of 1991-92, scoring five goals in ten games and was rewarded with a call up to the England Under 21 squad for the annual end of season tournament in Toulon, France. Came into the side on a more regular basis in **1992-93** after Gary Penrice broke his leg at Middlesbrough, having already played eight (including three substitute) games and scored three goals earlier in the season. A natural goalscorer, like elder brother Clive, quick and always a danger around the box, he was the hero of the fans after a late equaliser in the derby match against Chelsea at Loftus Road. Finished the season with 11 goals, while scoring three in the final two matches and should be an automatic choice during the coming season.

| | | | APPEARANCES | | | | GOALS | | | |
|---|---|---|---|---|---|---|---|---|---|---|
| Clubs | Signing Date | Transfer Fee | Lge | FL Cup | FA Cup | Others | Lge | FL Cup | FA Cup | Others |
| Q.P.R.* | 9.88 | – | 35+12 | 1+2 | 1+1 | 1 | 17 | 1 | | |

## ALLEN Clive Darren

Born: Stepney, 20 May 1961

Height: 5'10" Weight: 12.3

International Honours: E Sch, E Yth, E "U21"-3, FL Rep, E-5

**Position/Skill Factor:** One of the most prolific goalscorers of recent years, he has the uncanny knack of being in the right place at the right time. Composure in the penalty area is his hallmark.

**Career History:** From a famous football family, his father, Les, played for Chelsea, Tottenham Hotspur and Queens Park Rangers, he is currently with his sixth London club. Starting out with Queens Park Rangers as an associated schoolboy in May 1976, having already played for England boys, it therefore came as no surprise when he graduated as an apprentice (June 1977) to the clubs professional ranks early in 1978-79. He made his FL debut, coming on for Peter Eastoe at Loftus Road against Chelsea on 4 November 1978 and after scoring in his fourth substitute appearance, he grabbed a hat-trick in his first full match, a 5-1 victory at Coventry City on 28 April 1979. The following season he was a sensation at the age of 18, top scoring for Rangers with a remarkable 28 FL goals from 39 games in Division Two, making him the leading scorer in the entire Football League, and an achievement only matched by Jimmy Greaves at a similar age. There then followed the most bizarre transfer saga of the century. Signed by Arsenal in June 1980, he was passed on to Crystal Palace before the new season even started, in part exchange for Kenny Sansom. It was not a good move for either club or player. Despite a good start at Selhurst Park, with a hat-trick in his third game, the "Eagles" struggled and he was dropped from the team in October. He played intermittently thereafter, but Palace were doomed to relegation long befor the end of the season. Although he finished top scorer with nine FL goals it was a disappointing return on a huge investment and unable to justify his First Division salary he was sold back to Queens Park Rangers in the summer of 1981 at a considerable loss (on paper) of half a million pounds. Back at Loftus Road, he struggled to recapture his prolific goal scoring form of 1978-80 and his first season ended in disappointment when, although Rangers reached the FA Cup Final of 1982, he was substituted in the first game which ended in a 1-1 draw and not selected for the replay which they lost 1-0 to Tottenham Hotspur. The following season, when Rangers won promotion back to the top flight as Second Division Champions, he was not an automatic choice, although he scored a respectable 13 FL goals and in 1983-84 he lost his place in November. Returning in March, he finished the season in a blaze of glory with ten goals from 13 games. This form was sufficient to impress Bobby Robson, who included him in England's squad for the end of season South American tour in 1984. After coming on as a substitute in England's historic 2-0 victory over Brazil in the Maracana Stadium on 10 June 1984, he started the games against Uruguay and Chile. Sadly, he missed easy chances in both games and his international career seemed to end as soon as it began. In the summer of 1984, with his goalscoring credentials re-established, he joined Tottenham, but in each of his first two seasons at White Hart Lane his appearances were restricted by injury, although when available, he showed he had not lost his scoring touch. 1986-87 was his "annus mirabilis" when, operating as a lone striker, he scored an amazing total of 49 goals (33 FL, plus 16 in the two cup competitions) as "Spurs" finished third in the League and reached the FA Cup Final, where, despite his early opening goal, they lost 3-2 in extra-time to Coventry City. Unsurprisingly, Allen was voted "Player of the Year" in the annual PFA awards and "Footballer of the Year" by the Football Writers Association. He also won a brief recall to the international scene, but failed to impress in a 0-0 draw in Turkey. By contrast, 1987-88 was an anti-climax for both club and player and at the end of his contract he elected to join the perennial exodus of top British players to the continent of Europe, by signing for French Champions, Bordeaux. However, he struggled to make an impact in the ultra-defensive French League and after only one season he returned to England, signed by Howard Kendall for Manchester City. Failed to impress in his first year at Maine Road and when Kendall was succeeded by Peter Reid, he was left out in the cold, before being rescued by Chelsea. He was an immediate favourite with Chelsea fans, hitting nine FL and Two FA Cup goals in short order, but not with Chelsea manager, Ian Porterfield, who sold him on to West Ham United after only four months at Stanford Bridge, presumably for lack of "work rate". Despite scoring on his debut for the "Hammers", as he had done for most of his previous clubs, his arrival came too late to save the club from the drop into the new First Division. Made a great start to **1992-93**, with a classic winner on the opening day of the campaign at Barnsley and was ever present until 16 January when he limped off at Upton Park during the game against Portsmouth, suffering from a calf injury. At that stage of the season, he had scored 18 goals in 34 first team matches. Not match fit again until early May, he missed 19 League matches and although the "Hammers" gained promotion to the Premier League as runners-up to Newcastle United, they may well have arrived as First Division Champions had they had the constant availability of Allen. As it was, he joined the promotion battle just in time, as a substitute for the last two games and scored twice. The goal in a 3-1 win at Swindon Town was particularly warming as, not only did it put "Hammers" in the automatic promotion second place, a position they didn't relinquish, but it also represented another smack in the face for a club who in 1974 had sacked his father, Les, as their manager.

| | | | APPEARANCES | | | | GOALS | | | |
|---|---|---|---|---|---|---|---|---|---|---|
| Clubs | Signing Date | Transfer Fee | Lge | FL Cup | FA Cup | Others | Lge | FL Cup | FA Cup | Others |
| Q.P.R. | 9.78 | - | 43+6 | 5 | 1 | | 32 | 2 | | |
| Arsenal | 6.80 | £1,250,000 | | | | | | | | |
| Crystal Palace | 8.80 | £1,250,000 | 25 | 4 | | | 9 | 2 | | |
| Q.P.R. | 6.81 | £700,000 | 83+4 | 7 | 8 | | 40 | 2 | 7 | |
| Tottenham Hotspur | 8.84 | £750,000 | 97+8 | 13+1 | 12+1 | 9 | 60 | 13 | 9 | 3 |
| Bordeaux | 5.88 | £1,000,000 | | | | | | | | |
| Manchester City | 8.89 | £1,100,000 | 31+22 | 5+2 | 4+2 | 2 | 16 | 4 | 1 | |
| Chelsea | 12.91 | £250,000 | 15+1 | | 4+1 | 3 | 7 | | 2 | |
| West Ham United* | 3.92 | £275,000 | 29+2 | 2 | 1 | 6 | 15 | | 1 | 3 |

## ALLEN Leighton

Born: Brighton, 22 November 1973

Height: 6'0" Weight: 12.11

**Position/Skill Factor:** Striker does well in the air and has a good work rate.

**Career History:** Signed on the dotted line for Wimbledon during the summer of 1992, having first come to the club as a trainee in July 1990. No first team experience as yet, but the former leading scorer for the youth team played for the reserves in **1992-93** and could make a breakthrough this season if he maintains his current level of progress.

| Clubs | Signing Date | Transfer Fee | APPEARANCES Lge | FL Cup | FA Cup | Others | GOALS Lge | FL Cup | FA Cup | Others |
|---|---|---|---|---|---|---|---|---|---|---|
| Wimbledon* | 6.92 | - | | | | | | | | |

## ALLEN Martin James

Born: Reading, 14 August 1965

Height: 5'10"

Weight: 11.0

International Honours: E Yth, E "U21"-2

**Position/Skill Factor:** Midfield player who is always involved in the game. Drives himself to the limit and although very physical, he is also very constructive.

**Career History:** Another from the footballing Allen family, his father, Dennis, played for Charlton Athletic, Reading and Bournmouth, he followed his cousin, Clive, to Queens Park Rangers as an associated schoolboy (January 1980), before becoming an apprentice in July 1981 after leaving school. Signed as a professional at the end of 1982-83, but had to wait over two years for his FL debut, a 2-2 draw at Loftus Road against Norwich City on 2 March 1985. Earned a regular first team place in midfield in 1985-86 and played in his only Wembley Final to date, later in the season, when Rangers surprisingly lost 3-0 to Oxford United in the League Cup Final. Called into the England Under 21 squad in 1986-87, he was only selected for two games (both as substitute). Remained an automatic choice at Loftus Road until 1988-89, when he was embroiled in a dispute with manager, Trevor Francis, over chosing to stay with his wife for the birth of their first child, instead of travelling with the team for an away game, for which he was disciplined. Although public sympathy was with him, it was the end of the road for him at Loftus Road and he was transferred to West Ham United in the summer. Quickly settled in at Upton Park and in his second season with the "Hammers", assisted them to promotion back to Division One and also to the Semi-Final of the FA Cup where they were easily beaten by Nottingham Forrest after being reduced to ten men, following the sending off of Tony Gale. In 1991-92, the "Hammers" slipped out of the top bracket once again, with Allen out of favour for much of the season and his one highlight, two spectacular long range goals against Sunderland in an FA Cup Replay, proved worthless, as Sunderland won the match 3-2. Stepped out for **1992-93** full of vim and vigour and celebrated his 100th League game for the "Hammers" with a superb low shot inside an upright from 30 yards for the winner, in a 2-1 victory at Upton Park. Known as either "physco" or "mad-dog" by the supporters, for his reckless tackling which gained him too many bookings, he has now settled down with his robust approach to the game well in control, making him an even better player. His good form, also saw him picked as captain of the Football League side and scoring in a 3-1 triumph over the Italian League at Ashton Gate last October. A fairly regular choice for the club, although he did occasionally share the number six shirt with Ian Bishop, he can look forward to playing Premier League soccer this season, following the "Hammers' " promotion to the top flight as runners-up to Newcastle United.

| Clubs | Signing Date | Transfer Fee | APPEARANCES Lge | FL Cup | FA Cup | Others | GOALS Lge | FL Cup | FA Cup | Others |
|---|---|---|---|---|---|---|---|---|---|---|
| Q.P.R. | 5.83 | - | 128+8 | 15+3 | 9 | 2 | 16 | 1 | 1 | 1 |
| West Ham United* | 8.89 | £675,000 | 114+18 | 12+1 | 7 | 10 | 16 | 4 | 2 | |

## ALLEN Paul Kevin

Born: Aveley, 28 August 1962

Height: 5'7"

Weight: 9.12

International Honours: E Yth, E "U21"-3, E"B"

**Position/Skill Factor:** Very under-rated wide midfield player with a tremendous workrate. Can produce crosses at one end of the park and in the next minute be seen making tackles in a defensive role.

**Career History:** From a famous footballing family, uncles Les and Dennis, cousins Martin, Bradley and Clive, have all played League soccer. Learnt his trade at the West Ham United "Academy" where he came up through the junior ranks, first as an associated schoolboy (March 1977) and later as an apprentice (July 1978). Made FL debut at home to Burnley as the youngest player ever to turn out for the "Hammers" on 29 September 1979. He went on to play 31 matches that term as well as making history as the youngest player to appear in an FA Cup Final, when helping West Ham to a 1-0 win over Arsenal, at 17 years and nine months of age. His appearances were restricted the following season as the "Hammers" concentrated on promotion back to the First Division, but from then on he matured in the first team under the guidance of players like Billy Bonds and Trevor Brooking. He was sold in the 1985 close season to Tottenham Hotspur and among his new team mates was his cousin, Clive. Has held down a first team place since that day, despite several challenges. Played in his second FA Cup Final, albeit a losing one, when turning out for "Spurs" against Coventry City in 1987 and was ever present in 1991 when Tottenham beat Nottingham Forest 2-1 in extra-time to win the trophy for the eighth time. In what was a generally disappointing season for the club he was as consistent as ever, while missing only three games in 1991-92 and making 46 first team appearances for "Spurs" in **1992-93,** the opening Premier League campaign and once again underlined his great value to the side. Always seems to pop up with the odd goal or two and the three he scored last season were all decisive in terms of three points finding their way to White Hart Lane. He blasted in the first of a 2-1 home win against Everton, scored the only goal of the game to send visiting north London rivals, Arsenal, back to Highbury pointless and hooked the ball in from close range at Everton to secure a 2-1 victory. Has been a regular at Tottenham for eight years now, but shows no signs of slowing down as yet.

| | | | APPEARANCES | | | | GOALS | | | |
|---|---|---|---|---|---|---|---|---|---|---|
| Clubs | Signing Date | Transfer Fee | Lge | FL Cup | FA Cup | Others | Lge | FL Cup | FA Cup | Others |
| West Ham United | 8.79 | - | 149+3 | 20+4 | 15+3 | 2+1 | 6 | 2 | 3 | |
| Tottenham Hotspur* | 6.85 | £400,000 | 276+15 | 42+2 | 26+1 | 12+2 | 23 | 4 | 1 | |

## ANDERSSON Patrik Jonas

Born: Sweden,
18 August 1971

Height: 6'0¾"

Weight: 13.11

International Honours:
Swedish Int

**Position/Skill Factor:** Central defender who can also play in midfield. A typical continental, he passes the ball at every opportunity and is an excellent footballer.

**Career History:** Signed by Blackburn Rovers' manager Kenny Dalglish in January 1993 from Swedish club Malmö FF, six months after starring for Sweden in the European Championships of 1992. Rated a world class player back home, he struggled to come to grips with the pace and power of the English game in **1992-93**, after making his PL debut as a substitute at home to Wimbledon on 9 January 1993. Although he feels most comfortable at centre-half, he was completely lost in the League Cup-tie against Sheffield Wednesday and was later used to bolster the midfield. Often had difficulty lasting 90 minutes, but once settled he should be a fine acquisition.

| | | | APPEARANCES | | | | GOALS | | | |
|---|---|---|---|---|---|---|---|---|---|---|
| Clubs | Signing Date | Transfer Fee | Lge | FL Cup | FA Cup | Others | Lge | FL Cup | FA Cup | Others |
| Blackburn Rovers* | 1.93 | £800,000 | 6+5 | 2 | 1 | | | 1 | | |

## ANDERTON Darren Robert

Born: Southampton,
3 March 1972

Height: 6'0"

Weight: 11.7

International Honours:
E Yth, E"U21"-9

**Position/Skill Factor:** Excellent left-winger with lovely skill and control. Has the ability to go past defenders to cross good early balls into the danger zone. Scores goals as well.

**Career History:** Potentially brilliant left winger who hit the headlines during Portsmouth's long FA Cup run during 1991-92. Came to Fratton Park, first as an associated schoolboy in September 1986, before moving through the ranks as a trainee in February 1988 to professional status at the beginning of 1990. After showing early promise, he made his FL debut at home to Wolverhampton Wanderers on 3 November 1990 and towards the end of 1990-91 was challenging strongly for a first team place. During 1991-92 he established himself firmly in the "Pompey" team from the start of the season and showed such good form that he was the subject of transfer speculation even before the club started its FA Cup run, during which he came into the national spotlight. Scored both goals in "Pompey's" Fourth Round victory over Leyton Orient and another brace in the astonishing 4-2 Fifth Round victory over Middlesbrough at Ayresome Park – a ground where 20 previous visitors had managed to score only 11 goals between them. In the Semi-Final, he scored a breakaway goal in the 20th minute of extra time against Liverpool – a goal which seemed certain to take Portsmouth to Wembley for the first time since 1939 until the "Reds'" last last equaliser. The dream was ended in the replay, but only after a penalty "shoot out" at the end of extra time. With so much attention, it was inevitable that Portsmouth would lose their prize asset and he signed for Tottenham Hotspur soon after the end of the season. Made his Premier League bow for "Spurs" at Southampton on the opening day of the **1992-93** season and after playing in 13 matches it was clear that he was struggling to regain the form that prompted the club to buy him. Missed a number of games, while recovering from an operation, but returned to full first team duty on Boxing Day and has not been absent from the team since. His excellent performances also warranted a call-up to the England under 21 squad, scoring three goals in as many games and now that he has settled down in his new surroundings, much is expected of him this coming season.

| | | | APPEARANCES | | | | GOALS | | | |
|---|---|---|---|---|---|---|---|---|---|---|
| Clubs | Signing Date | Transfer Fee | Lge | FL Cup | FA Cup | Others | Lge | FL Cup | FA Cup | Others |
| Portsmouth | 2.90 | - | 53+9 | 3+2 | 7+1 | 2 | 7 | 1 | 5 | |
| Tottenham Hotspur* | 5.92 | £1,750,000 | 32+2 | 2 | 4+1 | | 6 | 1 | 1 | |

## **ANDREWS Ian** Edmund

Born: Nottingham, 1 December 1964

Height: 6'2" Weight: 12.2

International Honours: E Yth, E "U21"-1

**Position/Skill factor:** Goalkeeper who always cuts an imposing figure. Very agile, he always comes for crosses. Recognised for his strong left foot volley kicking, which can reach the opposition's box.

**Career History:** Was an associated schoolboy with Nottingham Forest (March 1980), before being released to start an apprenticeship at Mansfield Town. However, Leicester City who were looking for a long-term replacement for Mark Wallington, were sufficiently impressed for him to complete his apprenticeship at Filbert Street and snapped him up in June 1981. Was loaned out to Swindon Town to gain experience and made his FL debut there against Bristol City on 24 January 1984. Once he had taken over the 'keeper's jersey permanently from Wallington during 1984-85, he missed only three games in just under three seasons. But in 1986-87, although ever present, the club was relegated into the Second Division and he began to lose confidence. On losing his place to Paul Cooper, he was sold to Celtic where he became understudy to Pat Bonner, but after spending just over a year at Parkhead, Southampton signed him as cover for Tim Flowers. Made only one appearance in 1991-92 and spent **1992-93** sitting on the bench throughout the campaign as Tim Flowers was ever present. However, at the end of the season he was offered a further one year contract. Gave consistent displays for the reserves as he continued to benefit from the specialist tuition given by the former England coach, Mike Kelly and once again showed an exemplary attitude to the game, while waiting in the wings.

| | | | APPEARANCES | | | | GOALS | | | |
|---|---|---|---|---|---|---|---|---|---|---|
| Clubs | Signing Date | Transfer Fee | Lge | FL Cup | FA Cup | Others | Lge | FL Cup | FA Cup | Others |
| Leicester City | 12.82 | - | 126 | 6 | 7 | | | | | |
| Swindon Town | 1.84 | Loan | 1 | | | | | | | |
| Glasgow Celtic | 7.88 | £300,000 | 5 | 2 | | 1 | | | | |
| Leeds United | 12.88 | Loan | 1 | | | | | | | |
| Southampton* | 12.89 | £200,000 | 5 | | | 1 | | | | |

## **ANTHONY Graham** John

Born: South Shields, 9 August 1975

Height: 5'8" Weight: 9.10

**Position/Skill Factor:** Can play on either side of midfield. Has lots of vision, an excellent first touch and good passing ability.

**Career History:** A skilful youngster who has recently signed professional forms at Sheffield United, he first came to the club as an associated schoolboy in November 1990, before graduating through the youth team as a trainee (July 1991). Played in the last two reserve games of the **1992-93** season and should be given every chance.

| | | | APPEARANCES | | | | GOALS | | | |
|---|---|---|---|---|---|---|---|---|---|---|
| Clubs | Signing Date | Transfer Fee | Lge | FL Cup | FA Cup | Others | Lge | FL Cup | FA Cup | Others |
| Sheffield United* | 7.93 | - | | | | | | | | |

## **ANTHROBUS Stephen (Steve)** Anthony

Born: Lewisham, 10 November 1968

Height: 6'2" Weight: 12.13

**Position/Skill Factor:** Winger who is very strong physically and difficult to knock off the ball. Useful in the air, with a good left foot, he is extremely dangerous at the far post.

**Career History:** Came up through Millwall's junior ranks and made his FL debut for the club away to Plymouth Argyle wearing the number 11 shirt on 20 October 1987. After playing a further couple of games, he was replaced by Jimmy Carter, but the following season when the latter switched flanks, he got back into the side again. Created such a good impression that he was snapped up by Wimbledon, initially replacing Michael Bennett, but has made only limited League appearances for the "Dons" and had another frustrating season in **1992-93.** he only made six (including one substitute) appearances throughout the campaign and although providing some useful runs and crosses he was not in the reckoning for a first team place, following the Third Round League Cup replay against Everton in November. In his quest for League football and with inconsistency still a problem, it would appear that his future lies away from Selhurst Park.

| | | | APPEARANCES | | | | GOALS | | | |
|---|---|---|---|---|---|---|---|---|---|---|
| Clubs | Signing Date | Transfer Fee | Lge | FL Cup | FA Cup | Others | Lge | FL Cup | FA Cup | Others |
| Millwall | 8.86 | - | 19+2 | 3 | | 1 | 4 | | | |
| Wimbledon* | 2.90 | £150,000 | 27+1 | 1 | 2 | | | | | |

## **APPLEBY Matthew (Matty)** Wilfred

Born: Middlesbrough, 16 April 1972

Height: 5'10" Weight: 11.0

**Position/Skill Factor:** Defender who is a good passer and an intelligent reader of the game. Likes to float around picking up the pieces and getting the attack on the move.

**Career History:** Born on Teeside, but instead of joining his local team at Ayresome Park, he signed on as an associated schoolboy with north-east rivals, Newcastle United, in March 1988. Becoming a full-time professional in the 1990 close season, having been a trainee since July 1988, he made his FL debut for the "Magpies" in a 1-1 draw at home to West Bromwich Albion on 27 October 1990, standing in for the injured Roy Aitken. In 1991-92, he was given an extended run in the first team by manager, Ossie Ardiles, along with several other outstanding teenagers at St James' Park. The gambles misfired tragically, some brilliant football being undermined by a fragile defence. Following a traumatic game at home to Charlton Athletic in January 1992, which the "Magpies" lost 4-3 after racing to an early 3-0 lead, he lost his place, Ardiles lost his job and new manager, Kevin Keegan, brought in Brian Kilcline to stiffen the defence. It proved to be the right decision for the club, as United staved off relegation in the final match. Has continued to find it difficult to break into the side since the arrival of Keegan. And in **1992-93,** apart from regular reserve football, he was confined to just three first team games, all in the Anglo-Italian Cup, against Leicester City, Bari and Cesena. Booked in the third match, his opportunities at the club now look distinctly limited and he is currently on the transfer list. His younger brother Richard, who also played in the matches against Bari and Cesena, is a promising young trainee on United's books.

| | | | APPEARANCES | | | | GOALS | | | |
|---|---|---|---|---|---|---|---|---|---|---|
| Clubs | Signing Date | Transfer Fee | Lge | FL Cup | FA Cup | Others | Lge | FL Cup | FA Cup | Others |
| Newcastle United* | 5.90 | - | 17+2 | 2+1 | 2 | 2+2 | | | | |

## APPLEBY Richard Dean

Born: Middlesbrough, 18 September 1975

Height: 5'8½" Weight: 10.6

**Position/Skill Factor:** Midfielder with pace and a strong runner. An excellent link between defence and attack, he has good mobility.

**Career History:** The younger brother of Matty, also of Newcastle United, he first came to St James' Park as an associated schoolboy in November 1989. In **1992-93**, after several impressive junior displays, he was given a run out as a trainee (July 1992) with the club's first team in Anglo-Italian Cup games against Bari and Cesena. Still not a professional, he could be on the verge of playing in the Premier League, following United's First Division Championship triumph. Very highly thought of at the club.

| | | | APPEARANCES | | | | GOALS | | | |
|---|---|---|---|---|---|---|---|---|---|---|
| Clubs | Signing Date | Transfer Fee | Lge | FL Cup | FA Cup | Others | Lge | FL Cup | FA Cup | Others |
| Newcastle United* | - | - | | | | 2 | | | | |

## ARDLEY Neal Christopher

Born: Epsom, 1 September 1972

Height: 5'11"

Weight: 11.9

International Honours: E"U21"-6

**Position/Skill Factor:** A strong tackling midfielder who is not easily beaten. He is also a good passer of the ball and gets forward eagerly when the opportunity presents itself.

**Career History:** Joined Wimbledon while still at school when signing associated schoolboy forms in January 1988, before graduating to trainee status in July 1989. His FL debut, his one and only match in 1990-91, came in a 2-1 victory for the "Dons" at Aston Villa on 20 April 1991. Given further first team opportunities in 1991-92, both in midfield and at full-back, he was unable to establish a regular place, but following some excellent displays early in **1992-93,** he became a fixture in the Premier League after Christmas. Scored in his first two full games, before losing out to Paul Miller and Terry Gibson in the battle for the number seven shirt. However, he returned to play in 26 of the "Dons'" last 29 matches, scoring a double in the 5-2 destruction of Oldham Athletic at Selhurst Park and his good form was an important factor in the team's change of fortunes. Most certainly a star of the future, he was called up to the England under 21 squad and made his debut against Poland last May.

| | | | APPEARANCES | | | | GOALS | | | |
|---|---|---|---|---|---|---|---|---|---|---|
| Clubs | Signing Date | Transfer Fee | Lge | FL Cup | FA Cup | Others | Lge | FL Cup | FA Cup | Others |
| Wimbledon* | 7.91 | - | 32+3 | 2 | 4 | | 4 | 1 | | |

## ATHERTON Peter

Born: Orrell, 6 April 1970

Height: 5'11" Weight: 12.3

International Honours: E Sch, E"U21"-1

**Position/Skill Factor:** Consistent centre-back who can defend tenaciously and should improve with experience.

**Career History:** He first came through Wigan Athletic's junior ranks as an associated schoolboy (October 1984), before signing as a trainee in July 1986. Prior to turning professional, he made his FL debut at Blackpool on 24 October 1987 in a 0-0 draw and played a further 14 League games during 1987-88. Since claiming a regular place the following season, apart from one appearance as a substitute, he has not missed a match and was twice voted Wigan's "Player of the Year". Obviously impressed Coventry City manager Terry Butcher, in two FA Cup ties between Wigan and the "Sky Blues" in January 1991 and moved to Highfield Road in the first week of the 1991-92 season. Quickly established a place in the heart of the City defence and earned an England Under 21 cap in October 1991. Voted "Player of the Year" by the supporters' club on the conclusion of **1992-93,** he again had a very consistent season, only missing three games through injury. The unsung and unseen hero of the "Sky Blues' " defence read the game extremely well, didn't go in for fancy footwork and when danger threatened it was usually his boot that came to the rescue. He accepted a great deal of responsibility, having five different defensive partners throughout the campaign and at 23, with well over 200 League appearances behind him, a bright future remains assured.

| | | | APPEARANCES | | | | GOALS | | | |
|---|---|---|---|---|---|---|---|---|---|---|
| Clubs | Signing Date | Transfer Fee | Lge | FL Cup | FA Cup | Others | Lge | FL Cup | FA Cup | Others |
| Wigan Athletic | 2.88 | - | 145+4 | 8 | 7 | 12+1 | 1 | | | |
| Coventry City* | 8.91 | £300,000 | 74 | 2 | 1 | | | | | |

## **ATKINS Mark** Nigel

Born: Doncaster, 14 August 1968

Height: 6'1" Weight: 12.0

International Honours: E Sch

**Position/Skill Factor:** A tireless midfield worker who seems to cover acres of ground in an effort to plug any gaps. Very competitive, he is also useful in the air.

**Career History:** Came through the Scunthorpe United junior sides to make his FL debut as a substitute at Wrexham on 27 April 1985, whilst still a schoolboy, three and a half months short of his 17th birthday and yet to sign professional forms. Had to wait until October 1986 for his next taste of action, but became a regular selection in a variety of positions, including both full-back slots, central defence and midfield. In 1987-88 he continued his role as a utility player until December, but lost his place and played little further part in the campaign. It was therefore a surprise when Second Division Blackburn Rovers signed him in the summer of 1988, presumably as an investment for the future. It was an even bigger surprise and a great feather in the cap of Rovers' manager, Don Mackay, that he started the 1988-89 at right-back and held his place throughout the campaign, not missing a single game and scoring six goals from open play into the bargain – a tremendous achievement for a young player in his first season with a new club. It was almost a promotion season as Blackburn reached the Play-Off Final only to be denied by a goal in the 27th minute of extra-time which sent Crystal Palace up at Rovers' expense. It was the same story the following term, with Rovers failing in the Play-Offs, as he enjoyed another excellent season with 41 FL appearances and seven goals. 1990-91 by contrast, was almost disastrous as Rovers just staved off relegation and he lost his place for a while. In 1991-91 he was switched from right-back to midfield early in the season to cover for injuries to other players. He remained in this role for most of the season at the end of which, Rovers achieved their ambition of Premier League football the hard way, through the Play-Offs, after appearing to be runaway Second Division Champions in February. Started **1992-93** in midfield, but lost his place when more constructiveness was required and became the regular substitute, due to his ability to play either at full back, midfield, or in central defence. Still displayed a fair degree of flair in sticking away the unexpected chances that came his way, as Rovers looked to cement their high PL position, never being out of the top six all season.

| | | | APPEARANCES | | | | GOALS | | | |
|---|---|---|---|---|---|---|---|---|---|---|
| Clubs | Signing Date | Transfer Fee | Lge | FL Cup | FA Cup | Others | Lge | FL Cup | FA Cup | Others |
| Scunthorpe United | 7.86 | – | 45+5 | 3+1 | 5 | 6+1 | 2 | | | |
| Blackburn Rovers* | 6.88 | £45,000 | 186+18 | 16+2 | 9+2 | 14 | 26 | 4 | | 1 |

## **ATKINSON Dalian** Robert

Born: Shrewsbury, 21 March 1968

Height: 5'11"

Weight: 11.7

International Honours: E "B"

**Position/Skill Factor:** Physically strong, striker, who is not easy to dispossess, especially when in full flow. Extremely quick, he often commits defenders by running straight at them. Also, dangerous in the air.

**Career History:** Began with Ipswich Town, signing as an associated schoolboy in December 1982, before becoming an apprentice in July 1984. Made his FL debut as a substitute for Town away to Newcastle United on 15 March 1986 and impressed. After only occasional appearances for Ipswich, he finally established a first team place in February 1988, scoring eight goals in only 13 full appearances to the end of the season, including a magnificent hat-trick of "solo" goals against promotion bound Middlesbrough and the maturing Gary Pallister. Transferred to Sheffield Wednesday, he immediately became a favourite with the Hillsborough faithful. Only stayed for 12 months, before being sold to the Spanish side, Real Sociedad, with the "Owls" pocketing well over £1 million profit on the transaction. After one year in Spain, where he scored 12 League goals in 29 games in partnership with John Aldridge for the San Sebastian team, he was re-signed in the 1991 close season by his former manager at Hillsborough, Ron Atkinson, who by then had taken over at Aston Villa. Scored on his debut for Villa, by a remarkable coincidence at Hillsborough, in an opening day 3-2 victory over Wednesday. Sadly, it was to prove his only first team goal of the season, as a constant succession of niggling injuries prevented him from winning a regular place in the team. Made a good start to **1992-93,** scoring in the opening game and then struck up a very good partnership with Dean Saunders, netting 19 goals between them from 15 games, following the latter's transfer from Liverpool. It was during this period that he scored a goal that will remain etched in the memory by all who were either there or who saw it on television. Playing at Wimbledon, a 70 yard run from his own half of the field, which ended with a chip over the goalie, won the "Match of the Day – Goal of the Season" competition. He was unfortunate to sustain a stomach muscle injury, which forced him out of the game for a vast number of weeks and after making a few comebacks, an operation was inevitable. He finally regained his place in the side for the remaining seven games of the season, but was unable to score as the club's goals dried up and with it went their Championship winning hopes.

| | | | APPEARANCES | | | | GOALS | | | |
|---|---|---|---|---|---|---|---|---|---|---|
| Clubs | Signing Date | Transfer Fee | Lge | FL Cup | FA Cup | Others | Lge | FL Cup | FA Cup | Others |
| Ipswich Town | 6.85 | – | 49+11 | 5+1 | | 2+1 | 18 | 3 | | |
| Sheffield Wednesday | 6.89 | £450,000 | 38 | 3 | 2 | 2 | 10 | 3 | 1 | 1 |
| Real Sociedad (Spain) | 8.90 | £1,700,000 | | | | | | | | |
| Aston Villa* | 7.91 | £1,600,000 | 39+3 | 5 | 1 | 1 | 12 | 2 | | |

# **AUSTIN Dean** Barry

Born: Hemel Hempstead, 26 April 1970

Height: 6'0"

Weight: 12.4

**Position/Skill Factor:** Strong right-back who is very quick into the tackle. Also has the ability to pass the ball and join in.

**Career History:** Signed by Southend United from Vauxhall League club, St Albans City, after previous experience with Hendon in the same league, he slotted straight into the club's Third Division promotion winning side, making his FL debut as a right-back at Burnley on 10 April, 1990 and holding his place till the end of the season. Made 44 FL appearances in 1990-91 as the "Shrimpers" achieved promotion to Division Two for the first time in their history, finishing second in the Third Division, after heading the table for most of the season. Played 45 FL games in Southend's debut season in Division Two, during which they reached second place in January, only to "tail-off" disappointingly to finish in mid-table. For much of the season, he was the subject of transfer speculation and soon afterwards, was signed by Tottenham Hotspur. The fee of £375,000, plus an additional £150,000 for club appearances and an international cap, fixed by the Transfer Tribunal, seemed a reasonable one in the circumstances, but the Southend chairman, in a fit of pique, stated that no more Southend players would be sold to "Spurs" in future. Made his "Spurs' " debut in the third game of the **1992-93** Premier League season when he came on as a substitute during the home match against Crystal Palace and performed well enough to make the right-back position his own. Had an outstanding season, while making over 40 full first team appearances, until injury forced him out of the side for the remaining four matches and struck up a good understanding with full-back partner, Justin Edinburgh, also an ex-Southend United man.

| | | | APPEARANCES | | | | GOALS | | | |
|---|---|---|---|---|---|---|---|---|---|---|
| Clubs | Signing Date | Transfer Fee | Lge | FL Cup | FA Cup | Others | Lge | FL Cup | FA Cup | Others |
| Southend United | 3.90 | £12,000 | 96 | 4 | 2 | 7 | 2 | 1 | | |
| Tottenham Hotspur* | 5.92 | £375,000 | 33+1 | 2+1 | 5 | | | | | |

# **BABB Philip (Phil)** Andrew

Born: Lambeth, 30 November 1970

Height: 6'0" Weight: 12.0

**Position/Skill Factor:** Utility player, mainly defensive who has pace and strength. Loves to attack and is capable of delivering quality crosses from a superb left foot.

**Career History:** Unable to get a game with Millwall, having been at the club since joining as a trainee in June 1987, he was signed by former "Lions' " manager John Docherty for his new club Bradford City, on being freed during the 1990 close season. After making a scoring debut as a substitute at Valley Parade against Reading on 8 September 1990, he found a temporary niche at left-back. In February 1991, he was recalled to the first team, but as a forward, finishing the season as second top scorer with ten FL goals. He continued as a forward at the start of 1991-92, but was moved to central defence in November by new manager, Frank Stapleton, where he remained for the rest of the season, being ever present. Although clearly a talented and versatile player, it was still a surprise when Coventry City's new manager paid a massive fee to take him to Highfield Road in the 1992 close season. Mainly used as a substitute in the early part of **1992-93,** filling in for a number of positions, but never really impressing. His big chance came in the match at Sheffield United in November when the experienced Kenny Sansom was left out. Coming in to the side at left-back, he was ever present for the rest of the season, occasionally standing in as a centre-half, where his mobility was a major advantage. He is a very good athlete, who can outpace John Williams over 40 yards and is very competitive, also. Although he showed real quality in the centre of the defence, it has yet to be decided where he will eventually end up. Named as the Radio Mercia "Player of the Year", following a phone-in survey, was just another accolade to go with several "Man of the Match" awards. And when he was selected for the Republic of Ireland squad for the end of season friendly against Hungary, it only went to prove that when it comes to spotting talent in the lower divisions, Bobby Gould is one of the best.

| | | | APPEARANCES | | | | GOALS | | | |
|---|---|---|---|---|---|---|---|---|---|---|
| Clubs | Signing Date | Transfer Fee | Lge | FL Cup | FA Cup | Others | Lge | FL Cup | FA Cup | Others |
| Millwall | 4.89 | – | | | | | | | | |
| Bradford City | 8.90 | – | 73+7 | 5+1 | 3 | 3+1 | 14 | | | |
| Coventry City* | 7.92 | £500,000 | 27+7 | 2 | 1 | | | | | |

## **BAILEY Dennis** Lincoln

Born: Lambeth, 13 November 1965

Height: 5'10" Weight: 11.6

**Position/Skill Factor:** Striker, or winger, who is quick off the mark with lovely skills to match. Is extremely dangerous, either with his back to goal, or when he runs at the opposing defence.

**Career History:** Joined Fulham as a non-contract player from Barking in 1986, before moving on to Farnborough Town of the then Vauxhall Opel League, without making a FL appearance. However, Crystal Palace signed him and he made his FL debut at Hull City on 19 December 1987. After a few sporadic appearances at Selhurst Park, he got an opportunity to show what he could do when going on loan to Bristol Rovers, then managed by Gerry Francis. During the 1989 close season he was transferred to Birmingham City and after topping their goalscoring charts in his first season with 18 League goals, he dried up the following season and was allowed to return to Bristol Rovers on loan. It was assumed that Gerry Francis would sign him permanently for the "Pirates". In fact, Francis did sign him, but for his new club, Queens Park Rangers, a remarkable change in his fortunes. Although presumably signed as cover for the forward positions at Loftus Road, he started the season in the first team and was a fairly regular selection through the first half of 1991-92. On New Years Day he achieved a personal "high water mark" in his career with a hat-trick at Old Trafford against the League leaders and Championship favourites, Manchester United. Rangers' 4-1 victory inflicted United's first home defeat and was one of the "turn-ups" of the season. Perhaps the attendant publicity affected him as one month later he lost his place to Les Ferdinand and played no part in the remainder of the campaign. Started **1992-93** as a first team regular, but after losing his place to Gary Penrice and succumbing to the challenge of Bradley Allen, he drifted almost out of sight. In 18 (including 4 substitute) games, he scored only two goals, the winner in a 3-2 home Premier League victory over Sheffield United in August and the overall equaliser in a second leg, League Cup-tie at Grimsby Town, that was eventually won by Rangers following a penalty shoot-out. Will be keen to re-establish himself at Loftus Road in 1993-94.

| | | | APPEARANCES | | | | GOALS | | | |
|---|---|---|---|---|---|---|---|---|---|---|
| Clubs | Signing Date | Transfer Fee | Lge | FL Cup | FA Cup | Others | Lge | FL Cup | FA Cup | Others |
| Crystal Palace | 12.87 | £10,000 | 0+5 | | | | 1 | | | |
| Bristol Rovers | 2.89 | Loan | 17 | | | 1+1 | 9 | | | 1 |
| Birmingham City | 8.89 | £80,000 | 65+10 | 6 | 6 | 3+3 | 23 | 2 | | |
| Bristol Rovers | 3.91 | Loan | 6 | | | | 1 | | | |
| Q.P.R.* | 7.91 | £175,000 | 32+7 | 5 | 1+1 | 1 | 10 | 3 | | |

## **BAKER Clive** Edward

Born: North Walsham, 14 March 1959

Height: 5'9" Weight: 11.0

**Position/Skill Factor:** Very experienced goalkeeper with safe hands and a good shot stopper. Renowned for finding his forwards with wonderful half volleys.

**Career History:** Goalkeeper, who made an amazing "fairy-tale" return to top flight football at the age of 33 when his career seemed to be over. On the small side for a goalkeeper, he had a trial with the Norwich City junior team after leaving school and impressed enough to join the club's professional ranks during the 1977 close season. With both Kevin Keelan and Roger Hansbury unavailable, he got a first team opportunity earlier than expected when making his FL debut in a 2-2 draw at Newcastle United on 26 April 1978. However, despite spending seven years as a professional at Carrow Road, his first team opportunities, often as third choice 'keeper were extremely rare. Indeed, from the arrival of Chris Woods in 1981, he did not get a single "look-in" until his release on a free transfer in 1984. He signed for Second Division Barnsley and quickly displaced Andy Rhodes as the "Tykes' " first choice 'keeper. Remaining number one at Oakwell for the next seven seasons, he missed only 17 games during that period and was ever-present in 1985-86, 1987-88, 1988-89 and 1990-91. Strangely, after a highly successful latter season when Barnsley just missed qualification for the Play-Offs, conceding only 48 goals (in 46 games), while Baker kept 13 "clean sheets", Barnsley manager, Mel Machin, went out to purchase another expensive 'keeper in the summer in Lee Butler from Aston Villa, having previously bought Philip Whitehead from Halifax two years earlier for £150,000. As a result he was released on a "free" transfer on the eve of the 1991-92 season. Maybe there were difficulties in agreeing a new contract, but it seemed that Baker had been treated very shabbily by a club he had served so well. With most clubs having already assembled their playing staff by August, the best offer he could find at such a late stage was a one year contract with Coventry City as short term cover for Steve Ogrizovic. Although he played once for the "Sky Blues" in a League Cup-tie, he sadly missed his only chance of a return to First Division football after Ogrizovic was injured in March 1992 when he also was unavailable through injury and Coventry were forced to sign two 'keepers on loan from other clubs. On being "freed" in the summer of 1992, he seemed a forgotten man, until the eve of the new **1992-93** season when newly promoted Ipswich Town signed him as cover for Craig Forrest. This time his luck was in. He became the first substitute 'keeper under the new Premier League rules when he replaced the injured Forrest in only the third minute of a game against Sheffield United on 26 September 1992 and kept a clean sheet. Three weeks later, when Forrest suffered a recurrence of his previous injury, he started his first match in the top flight since

1981, away to Chelsea on 17 October and subsequently performed with such safety and consistency that he held his place even when Forrest was available again. And after signing a new two and a half year contract with the club in February, history was made when he became the first Town 'keeper ever to keep a clean sheet at Anfield.

| | | | APPEARANCES | | | | GOALS | | | |
|---|---|---|---|---|---|---|---|---|---|---|
| Clubs | Signing Date | Transfer Fee | Lge | FL Cup | FA Cup | Others | Lge | FL Cup | FA Cup | Others |
| Norwich City | 7.77 | - | 14 | | 2 | | | | | |
| Barnsley | 8.84 | - | 291 | 15 | 18 | 8 | | | | |
| Coventry City | 8.91 | - | | 1 | | | | | | |
| Ipswich Town* | 8.92 | - | 30+1 | 5 | 4 | | | | | |

## BANGER Nicholas (Nicky) Lee

Born: Southampton, 25 February 1971

Height: 5'8" Weight: 10.6

**Position/Skill Factor:** Winger who can play up front, he twists and turns well on the edge of the box. Always causing defenders problems with quick darting runs.

**Career History:** Locally born and bred, he was an associated schoolboy (September 1985) and then a trainee (July 1987) before turning pro for Southampton and making his FL debut at Norwich City on 8 December 1990. Although yet to score in a League match, the first time he played for "Saints" was in the second round of the League Cup on 9 October 1990 and he marked that occasion with a hat-trick in the 5-0 home defeat of Rochdale. Made a few substitute appearances in 1991-92, but with Alan Shearer and Iain Dowie holding down the strikers' role, he was unable to make a first team breakthrough. Came on as a substitute at home to Middlesbrough for his first match in **1992-93** and scored, but after starting two games in September, he spent much of the first half of the season in the reserves. However, after netting 13 goals in 12 appearances for the "stiffs", including all four against Portsmouth, he was promoted to the first team again. Scored on his recall and completed a spell of four goals in five matches, impressing as a surprise element when coming off the bench 18 times in all during the season. Learning with every game, he is an important member of the first team squad.

| | | | APPEARANCES | | | | GOALS | | | |
|---|---|---|---|---|---|---|---|---|---|---|
| Clubs | Signing Date | Transfer Fee | Lge | FL Cup | FA Cup | Others | Lge | FL Cup | FA Cup | Others |
| Southampton* | 4.89 | - | 10+27 | 2+1 | 0+1 | 1 | 6 | 3 | | |

## BARDSLEY David John

Born: Manchester, 11 September 1964

Height: 5'10" Weight: 10.0

International Honours: E Yth, E-2

**Position/Skill Factor:** Attacking right-back, with a wonderful right-foot, who is brilliant at striking long balls behind the opposing full-backs. Very effective when he gets forward and is a intelligent crosser of the ball.

**Career History:** Began his career at Blackpool where he was an associated schoolboy (May 1981) and an apprentice (July 1981). He made his FL debut at Bury on 18 May 1982, signing professional forms four months later. Immediately becoming a regular, it wasn't long before other clubs were casting envious eyes in his direction and he eventually moved to Watford. In his first season at Vicarage Road, he helped the club to their first ever Wembley appearance where they were beaten 2-0 by Everton in the 1984 FA Cup Final. Three years later, Oxford United, looking for a replacement for David Langan, were surprised to find him available and signed him for a club record fee. His time there proved disappointing as the club were relegated to the Second Division, although they had earlier reached the Semi-Finals of the League Cup. After beginning the 1989-90 season in United's colours, he joined Queens Park Rangers for a substantial fee, plus striker Mark Stein and after making his debut in a right sided midfield role, he reverted to his favoured defensive position later in the season. A consistent defender, he has missed only five League matches in four seasons at Loftus Road and was awarded his first England cap as a substitute against Spain early in **1992-93.** Was unfortunate to pick up an injury in that game, which kept him out of Rangers' side for three matches, but on coming back he quickly settled into his normal routine and was not absent again during the campaign. At the end of a season, which saw Rangers finish in fifth place, his fellow professionals showed what they thought of him when they selected him for the PFA Premier League team award and his outstanding form gained him a further England cap in a World Cup qualifier in Poland. He was one of the successes of a poor England side and although making way for Lee Dixon in the disastrous defeat in Norway, he should be an England regular on current form.

| | | | APPEARANCES | | | | GOALS | | | |
|---|---|---|---|---|---|---|---|---|---|---|
| Clubs | Signing Date | Transfer Fee | Lge | FL Cup | FA Cup | Others | Lge | FL Cup | FA Cup | Others |
| Blackpool | 11.82 | - | 45 | 2 | 2 | | | 1 | | |
| Watford | 11.83 | £150,000 | 97+3 | 6 | 13+1 | 1 | 7 | 1 | 1 | |
| Oxford United | 9.87 | £265,000 | 74 | 12 | 5 | 3 | 7 | | | |
| Q.P.R* | 9.89 | £500,000 | 150 | 11 | 13 | 3 | 4 | 1 | | 1 |

## BARKER Simon

Born: Farnworth, 4 November 1964

Height: 5'9"

Weight: 11.0

International Honours: E "U21"-4

**Position/Skill Factor:** An attacking midfield player with a good football brain. Directs passes, short and long, very early and is quite capable of opening up the tightest of defences.

**Career History:** Spent six years as a pro with Blackburn Rovers, having been at the club as an associated schoolboy (July 1980) and an apprentice (July 1981). Made his FL debut away to Swansea City on 29 October 1983 and immediately established himself as a regular in the side. He went from strength to strength and was soon regarded as one of the best midfield players in the Second Division. It came as no surprise when he finally left Rovers, when they failed to win promotion to Division One in 1988, following their defeat by Chelsea in the end of season Play-Offs. Although unable to establish himself at Queens Park Rangers in his first season, after the arrival of Ray Wilkins he settled down to play some good football and was a major influence in Q.P.R.'s bid to stave off relegation in 1990-91. A consistent performer in 1991-92, partnering Ian Holloway and Ray Wilkins in midfield, he did not miss a game until February 1992, but thereafter was mainly used as substitute. Had a slightly disappointing **1992-93,** when he was troubled by a long term back injury and was in-and-out of the side. Always a reliable player who never lets Rangers down, he finally got his place back for the remaining four games of the season and although substituted during the match at Arsenal, he was on song for the games against Aston Villa and Sheffield Wednesday. Finishing strongly, Rangers beat the Premier League runners-up and the FA and League Cup finalists to go fifth in the table and he had a hand in several of the goals.

| | | | APPEARANCES | | | | GOALS | | | |
|---|---|---|---|---|---|---|---|---|---|---|
| Clubs | Signing Date | Transfer Fee | Lge | FL Cup | FA Cup | Others | Lge | FL Cup | FA Cup | Others |
| Blackburn Rovers | 11.82 | - | 180+2 | 11 | 12 | 8 | 35 | 4 | | 2 |
| Q.P.R.* | 7.88 | £400,000 | 128+19 | 14+2 | 15+1 | 7 | 12 | 3 | 2 | |

## BARLOW Andrew (Andy) John

Born: Oldham, 24 November 1965

Height: 5'9" Weight: 11.1

**Position/Skill Factor:** Left-back with two good feet and a lovely striker of the ball. Alway prepared to support the attack, he will go all the way at times. Often spells danger with his long throws.

**Career History:** A one club man, he signed as an associated schoolboy for Oldham Athletic in November 1982, while at Hulme Grammar School and made his FL debut, one month after turning pro, at home to Birmingham City on 25 August 1984. In his first five seasons, he struggled to hold down a regular first team place, alternating between midfield and the full-back slots. Since 1989-90, however, he has been automatic first choice at left-back and although Oldham failed to gain promotion that season they achieved miracles in the two cup competitions, reaching the Semi-Final of the FA Cup, before going out after a replay to Manchester United and then losing 1-0 in the League Cup Final to Nottingham Forest. It paved the way to the "Lactics" joining the elite and in 1990-91 he was ever present, winning a Second Division Championship medal as the club finally realised its ambition of First Division football. Absent through injury at the start of 1991-92, he returned to the team in October, holding his place till the end of the season. Instead of building his career, he had a dreadful time in **1992-93**, playing only eight first team games and being restricted by injuries. Broke down at the beginning of the season with cruciate ligament damage and although coming back for the game at Sheffield Wednesday, he was substituted after just 38 minutes and was out of action for a further nine games. Returned in late December to play four matches in place of new signing, Neil Pointon, but a back injury then sidelined him for nearly three months. Took over the number four shirt from Nick Henry for a couple of games, before a groin injury effectively ended his season and he will probably struggle to be match fit in time for 1993-94.

| | | | APPEARANCES | | | | GOALS | | | |
|---|---|---|---|---|---|---|---|---|---|---|
| Clubs | Signing Date | Transfer Fee | Lge | FL Cup | FA Cup | Others | Lge | FL Cup | FA Cup | Others |
| Oldham Athletic* | 7.84 | - | 240+13 | 20 | 19 | 6 | 5 | | | |

## BARLOW Stuart

Born: Liverpool, 16 July 1968

Height: 5'10"

Weight: 11.0

**Position/Skill Factor:** A hard working young striker who is still making his way in the game. Has good pace and runs well off the ball.

**Career History:** Signed from Sherwood Park of the Liverpool Sunday League in the Summer of 1990, he made the gigantic leap from junior club soccer to the First Division inside 12 months when making his FL debut for Everton at home to Wimbledon on 10 April 1991. Joined Rotherham on loan in 1991-92, but his one League appearance as substitute for the "Millers" was cancelled out when Aldershot resigned from the Football League. Returned to Goodison Park and enjoyed a short run in the first team at the end of the season in place of Mo

Johnston. Following the signing of Paul Rideout during the summer, he was unable to find a first team place at the beginning of **1992-93,** but a goal drought at the club saw him brought into the squad of 13, although mainly used as a substitute. He continued as Everton's "super sub" right through to the end of the campaign and shows great promise for the future.

| Clubs | Signing Date | Transfer Fee | APPEARANCES Lge | FL Cup | FA Cup | Others | GOALS Lge | FL Cup | FA Cup | Others |
|---|---|---|---|---|---|---|---|---|---|---|
| Everton* | 6.90 | - | 11+24 | 2+2 | 1+1 | | 5 | 1 | | |
| Rotherham United | 1.92 | Loan | | | | 0+1 | | | | |

## BARMBY Nicholas (Nicky) Jonathan

Born: Hull, 11 February 1974

Height: 5'6" Weight: 11.3

International Honours: E Sch, E Yth

**Position/Skill Factor:** Very skilful striker who holds the ball up well and is adept at bringing his supporting players into the game.

**Career History:** The son of the old Hull City player, Jeff, he joined Tottenham Hotspur as an associated schoolboy in March 1990, before accepting trainee status on leaving school in August 1990. Turned professional early in 1991, having spent some time at the Lilleshall Centre of Excellence and made good progress with the "Spurs' " reserve side. Started **1992-93** in "Spurs' " youth team, but after being promoted to the reserves, he was quickly given a first team "blooding". Made his PL debut at Sheffield Wednesday on 27 September 1992 and coming on as a substitute against Middlesbrough in his first home game, he scored a late equaliser. He soon became a permanent fixture in the side, after alternating between playing and being substitute and scored eight goals in his first 20 games. Caused a club versus country row when he was selected for the England youth side competing in the World Cup Finals in Australia. Tottenham didn't want to release him as they felt he was too valuable to lose during their FA Cup campaign, whilst the FA insisted on his being in Australia. The FA got their way and he helped England to third place in the tournament, before returning to "Spurs" in time for their losing FA Cup Semi-Final against Arsenal. Second in the "Young Player of the Year" awards, much is expected of him as the fans look forward to him renewing his exciting partnership with Teddy Sheringham in 1993-94.

| Clubs | Signing Date | Transfer Fee | APPEARANCES Lge | FL Cup | FA Cup | Others | GOALS Lge | FL Cup | FA Cup | Others |
|---|---|---|---|---|---|---|---|---|---|---|
| Tottenham Hotspur* | 2.91 | - | 17+5 | 2+1 | 3+1 | | 6 | | 3 | |

## BARNARD Darren Sean

Born: Rinteln, Germany, 30 November 1971

Height: 5'10"

Weight: 11.0

International Honours: E Sch

**Position/Skill Factor:** Predominately a winger, he has an excellent left foot and is a lovely crosser of the ball. Also has the ability and skill to go past defenders in order to create goalscoring chances.

**Career History:** Son of an armed forces serviceman, hence his foreign birthplace. Signed by Chelsea from Wokingham Town of the Vauxhall (now Diadora) League in the 1990 close season. His talent was recognised early by the FA, who selected him for the England Schoolboys under 18 side in 1989-90. After waiting patiently for a first team chance, he made his FL debut at Stamford Bridge, when he came on as a substitute against West Ham United on 4 April 1992. Selected for the next three games, he played his first full game at Aston Villa on 20 April. Began to establish a first team place in the latter stages of **1992-93** when he re-appeared as a substitute at fog-shrouded Oldham Athletic, having played at Coventry City earlier in the season. He made a further 11 (four substitute) appearances from the last 16 games, at times being quite outstanding and other times fairly anonymous. Has all the hallmarks of a very good player, but needs an extended run in the side.

| Clubs | Signing Date | Transfer Fee | APPEARANCES Lge | FL Cup | FA Cup | Others | GOALS Lge | FL Cup | FA Cup | Others |
|---|---|---|---|---|---|---|---|---|---|---|
| Chelsea* | 7.90 | £50,000 | 9+8 | 0+1 | | | 1 | | | |

## BARNES David

Born: Paddington, 1
6 November 1961

Height: 5'10"

Weight: 11.4

International Honours:
E Yth

**Position/Skill Factor:** A very experienced left-back who knows just when to tackle, he is a more than capable defender. Has a good left foot and makes excellent use of the ball, with either short or long passes. A player with plenty of nice touches.

**Career History:** Served as an apprentice with Coventry City (August 1978), before turning pro and making his FL debut at Bolton Wanderers on 15 April 1980. Only played the odd match at Highfield Road and signed for Ipswich Town on a free, but again infrequent appearances were the order of the day. On moving to Wolverhampton Wanderers, he managed to hold down a regular place, but the team were struggling and during his three years at Molineux, they dropped from the Second to the Fourth Division. Following that, he had a spell with Aldershot, but after two years at the foot of Division Four, Dave Bassett surprisingly took him to Sheffield United where he shared the left-back spot with Wilf Rostron. In his first season, the club were promoted from the Second Division as runners-up and he certainly didn't look out of place when playing 28 First Division matches in 1990-91. Displaced by the signing of Tom Cowan in the first half of 1991-92, he won his place back in January 1992 and held it till the end of the season, assisting the "Blades' " remarkable rise from the foot of the table to a final placing of ninth. Injuries, including a dislocated shoulder, meant that he only played 13 Premier League games in **1992-93.** After starting as first choice left-back, an ankle injury sustained on the pre-season tour flared up after just three games and lead to a season of frustration. At least on two occasions he probably returned too early in order to help the club out in an injury crisis. On the second occasion, whilst assisting United to their biggest win of the season, a 6-0 victory over Tottenham Hotspur, a recurring groin strain meant that his season was over. Always a model of consistency, he will once again be involved in the battle to hold down the full-back spot during the coming season.

| | | | APPEARANCES | | | | GOALS | | | |
|---|---|---|---|---|---|---|---|---|---|---|
| Clubs | Signing Date | Transfer Fee | Lge | FL Cup | FA Cup | Others | Lge | FL Cup | FA Cup | Others |
| Coventry City | 5.79 | - | 9 | | 4 | | | | | |
| Ipswich Town | 4.82 | - | 16+1 | | | | | | | |
| Wolverhampton W. | 10.84 | £35,000 | 86+2 | 7 | 6 | 6 | 4 | | | |
| Aldershot | 8.87 | £25,000 | 68+1 | 2 | 2+2 | 4 | 1 | | | |
| Sheffield United* | 7.89 | £50,000 | 80 | 5 | 14 | 4 | 1 | | | |

## BARNES John Charles

Born: Jamaica, West Indies, 7 November 1963

Height: 5'11" Weight: 11.10

International Honours: E"U21"-2, FL Rep, E-73

**Position/Skill Factor:** Can play in any position up front, but most frequently appears on the left flank. He has wonderful natural skill, with the ball seemingly tied to his foot at times. Very quick from a standing start, where his pace and strength takes him past defenders as if they didn't exist.

**Career History:** Came out of local junior football with Sudbury Court to turn professional at Watford and made an immediate impact. he made his FL debut for the "Hornets" at home on 5 September 1981 against Oldham Athletic and has rarely looked back. Was soon collecting international honours, making his full England debut against Northern Ireland in Belfast in 1983 when coming on as a substitute in a 0-0 draw, but the lasting international memory of him will surely include the marvellous solo goal he scored in England's 2-0 victory over Brazil in Rio de Janeiro, June 1984, proving that he could live with the best. Was an instant success at Anfield, scoring 15 times in 38 FL matches in his first season, 1987-88, helping the club to the League Championship in the process. Another League Championship medal came his way at the end of the 1989-90 season, with the club looking for the "Double" until losing 4-3 to Crystal Palace in the semi-final of the FA Cup. He was voted "Footballer of the Year" by the FWA in both 1988 and 1990 and the PFA's "Player of the Year" in 1988. His consistently brilliant performances for Liverpool since 1987, mark him out as the outstanding forward of his generation. Sadly it seems that at international level he will forever remain an enigma, the majority of his performances being merely competent rather than inspired. Often alleged to have a desire to play in the warmer climes of Italian Football, he was persuaded to sign a one year contract to remain with Liverpool for 1991-92. It proved a highly expensive decision for the club, as due to a succession of injuries, starting from the second game of the season, he played only 12 League games and in those he was clearly below par and not 100 per cent fit. In fairness to Barnes, his contributions in the FA Cup rescued Liverpool's season from total disaster, but sadly, another thigh injury sustained in the last game of the season, cost him a place in the Cup Final team and ultimately excluded him from the England squad for the 1992 European Championship in Sweden. Returned to League action on 23 November at Queens Park Rangers in a live televised game and celebrated his first match of the **1992-93** season when he set up the winner with a great through ball to Rosenthal. Despite looking close to his best in his early games for Liverpool, he struggled for form and fitness for the remainder of the season, even though he took over the captaincy in the New Year after Steve Nichol relinquished the job. Scored his first goal of the campaign when he curled a shot from the left hand corner of the penalty area into the far corner of Aston Villa's net in a 2-1 defeat at Anfield. But his luck wasn't always in as a free-kick disallowed at Sheffield Wednesday would imply and he even shot wide from the penalty spot in the home game against Queens Park Rangers, after Mike Marsh had failed with an earlier attempt. Gave a magnificent last day of the season display, while scoring two and setting up Ian Rush's 300th goal for the club, in a 6-2 home thrashing of Tottenham Hotspur. Played six times for England during the season, after being surprisingly recalled by Graham Taylor for the

*John Barnes*

match against San Marino in February, where he was booed by the Wembley crowd following another indifferent display. However, he redeemed himself, somewhat, with a better performance versus Holland when he scored with a superb free-kick in the opening minutes.

| | | | APPEARANCES | | | | GOALS | | | |
|---|---|---|---|---|---|---|---|---|---|---|
| Clubs | Signing Date | Transfer Fee | Lge | FL Cup | FA Cup | Others | Lge | FL Cup | FA Cup | Others |
| Watford | 7.81 | – | 232+1 | 21 | 31 | 7 | 65 | 7 | 11 | |
| Liverpool* | 6.87 | £900,000 | 178+1 | 12 | 34 | 5 | 67 | 3 | 14 | 2 |

## BARNESS Anthony

Born: Lewisham, 25 March 1973

Height: 5'10" Weight: 11.0

**Position/Skill Factor:** Left-back with two good feet who can pass both long and short to turn defence into attack. Quite quick, but needs more experience.

**Career History:** This exciting young player first came to Charlton Athletic as a 15-year-old associated schoolboy in January 1988, before signing on as a trainee in July 1989. After making the necessary progress he turned pro on his 18th birthday and was given his FL debut as a substitution for the current club manager, Steve Gritt, at home to Sunderland on 17 September 1991. From December 1991 to March 1992 he enjoyed an extended run at left-back for the "Valiants" at the expense of current England under 21 international, Scott Minto. And again he was preferred to the latter at the start of the **1992-93** season, until snapped up the London neighbours Chelsea in September 1992. With two talented young players competing for the same slot, Charlton were doubtless happy to receive a substantial fee for one of them. Perhaps, unwisely, Chelsea manager, Ian Porterfield, immediately pitched the 19-year-old into battle. Unfortunately, his Premier League debut at home to Norwich coincided with a defensive debacle, as the "Pensioners" let slip a 2-0 lead to lose 2-3 and he was immediately replaced by Frank Sinclair. Was a regular in the reserves, while making only one further Premier League appearance at Blackburn in a 2-0 defeat.

| | | | APPEARANCES | | | | GOALS | | | |
|---|---|---|---|---|---|---|---|---|---|---|
| Clubs | Signing Date | Transfer Fee | Lge | FL Cup | FA Cup | Others | Lge | FL Cup | FA Cup | Others |
| Charlton Athletic | 3.91 | – | 21+6 | 2 | 3 | 1+1 | 1 | | | 1 |
| Chelsea* | 9.92 | £350,000 | 2 | | | | | | | |

## BARRETT Earl Delisser

Born: Rochdale, 28 April 1967

Height: 5'10" Weight: 11.2

International Honours: E "U21"-4, FL Rep, E"B", E-3

**Position/Skill Factor:** An extremely athletic central defender, who can also play at full-back. Has tremendous pace and can change up a gear. Gets forward well, he is a difficult defender to get the better of.

**Career History:** Began as an apprentice with Manchester City, signing in April 1984, but made his FL debut whilst on loan with Chester City at Mansfield Town on 4 March 1986, before his City debut at home against Luton Town on 3 May 1986. Did not make progress at Maine Road and was transferred to Oldham Athletic. Made a good start at Boundary Park until sidelined through injury for a spell during his first season, but was soon back on regular duty at left-back. In 1989-90 he exchanged his number three shirt for that of centre-back and was ever present as the club were losing League Cup Finalists and progressed to the Semi-Final of the FA Cup. The following season again saw him at the heart of "Latics' " defence and for the second successive term he played in every match and hardly put a foot wrong as the club won the Second Division title. Rewarded for his fine displays at club level, he was selected for the international tour of Australasia in the summer of 1991 and made his England debut against New Zealand. In his first season in the First Division, he struggled a little in the heart of the leakiest defence at that level, but held his place, whilst his defensive partners were chopped and changed. it was a great disappointment to "Latics' " fans when he was transferred to Aston Villa in February 1992, immediately slotting in at right-back, but it was for a fee that a small club such as Oldham could hardly refuse. As an ever present in **1992-93,** he went from strength to strength, gaining an excellent understanding with Ray Houghton and even looking a possible replacement for Paul McGrath at a future date. His good form also saw him called into the England squad on a couple of occasions and it was only a matter of time before he added to his single cap. A key player in the charge for Championship honours, with the club never out of the top three throughout 1993, it was a bitter disappointment to lose out to Manchester United as Villa's end of season form slumped, with only four wins in the last 11 games.

| | | | APPEARANCES | | | | GOALS | | | |
|---|---|---|---|---|---|---|---|---|---|---|
| Clubs | Signing Date | Transfer Fee | Lge | FL Cup | FA Cup | Others | Lge | FL Cup | FA Cup | Others |
| Manchester City | 4.85 | – | 2+1 | 1 | | | | | | |
| Chester City | 3.86 | Loan | 12 | | | | | | | |
| Oldham Athletic | 11.87 | £35,000 | 181+2 | 20 | 14 | 4 | 7 | 1 | 1 | |
| Aston Villa* | 2.92 | £1,700,000 | 55 | 5 | 4 | | 1 | | | |

## BART-WILLIAMS Christopher (Chris) Gerald

Born: Sierra Leone, 16 June 1974

Height: 5'10" Weight: 11.0

International Honours: E Yth, E"U21"-3

**Position/Skill Factor:** Midfield player with plenty of stamina, he keeps his passing simple and is not afraid to get his foot in. Progressing all the time.

**Career History:** Began with Leyton-Orient as an associated schoolboy in October 1988 and progressed to trainee status in July 1990. A teenage footballing prodigy, he made his FL debut at the age of 16 years and 4 months, as Orient's youngest ever debutant as a substitute at Grimsby Town on 23 October 1990 and later scored for the "O's" after only ten minutes of his full FL debut at home to Tranmere Rovers on 2 February. Thereafter he was established in midfield for the remainder of the season, still at the tender age of 16, as First Division scouts became alerted to his talent. An automatic first choice for Orient in 1991-92, he was signed up by Sheffield Wednesday manager Trevor Francis in November 1991, a few weeks after the two teams had met twice in a League Cup tie. Francis announced cautiously that he was "one for the future" and that he didn't intend pitching him into First Division action immediately. One week later, Bart-Williams was playing with the composure of a veteran on his Wednesday debut against League Champions, Arsenal, holding his place until January before being rested and making occasional appearances thereafter. Played in a fair proportion of the **1992-93** Premier League programme and has now made more first team appearances than was first forecast at this stage of his career. An extremely popular player, the added bonus has been his ability to score goals. Although most of his games have come in midfield, when the injury crisis pushed him up front, he scored a hat-trick in a 5-2 home victory over Southampton and joined the band of 11 other players who had done likewise in the Premier League this season. Played a vital role for England in the World Youth Cup in Australia, having earlier broken into the under 21 side for three matches. Not selected for the League Cup Final team, he came on as a substitute in both FA Cup Final games at Wembley, before having to settle for a losers medal, following a 2-1 defeat at the hands of Arsenal.

| | | | APPEARANCES | | | | GOALS | | | |
|---|---|---|---|---|---|---|---|---|---|---|
| Clubs | Signing Date | Transfer Fee | Lge | FL Cup | FA Cup | Others | Lge | FL Cup | FA Cup | Others |
| Leyton Orient | 7.91 | - | 34+2 | 4 | | 2 | 2 | | | |
| Sheffield Wednesday* | 11.91 | £275,000 | 33+16 | 3+4 | 2+3 | 1+3 | 6 | 1 | 1 | 2 |

## BARTLETT Neal

Born: Southampton, 7 April 1975

Height: 5'8½" Weight:12.2

International Honours: E Sch

**Position/Skill Factor:** Midfielder converted from striker. Strong tackling and hard working, he is also good in the air. No frills, with simple, but accurate passes.

**Career History:** former Southampton boys player, who initially came to the Dell as an associated schoolboy (June 1990), until making his stay more permanent as a trainee in July 1991. Made two early reserve appearances for Southampton in **1992-93**, before continuing his apprenticeship in the youth team. With the youth programme completed, he played four more reserve games and on giving impressive displays, was called to the first team squad. Acted as an inspiration to all the local school kids when he made his FL debut at the Dell, coming on as a substitute against Manchester City on 1 May 1993, with just 18 minutes left on the clock. One of three second year trainees to turn professional for the club during the summer.

| | | | APPEARANCES | | | | GOALS | | | |
|---|---|---|---|---|---|---|---|---|---|---|
| Clubs | Signing Date | Transfer Fee | Lge | FL Cup | FA Cup | Others | Lge | FL Cup | FA Cup | Others |
| Southampton* | 7.93 | - | 0+1 | | | | | | | |

## BARTON Warren Dean

Born: Stoke Newington, 19 March 1969

Height: 6'0"

Weight: 11.0

International Honours: E"B"

**Position/Skill Factor:** Excellent attacking full-back who is very much suited to the sweeper system, but can play equally well in midfield. Will attack at every opportunity and is a lovely crosser of the ball.

**Career History:** Signed for Maidstone United from Vauxhall League side, Leytonstone & Ilford, prior to the club embarking on their first Football League campaign. He made his FL League debut at Peterborough United on 19 August 1989 and after a difficult introduction to League football, Warren, who had started his career as a Leyton Orient trainee (August 1986), won a permanent place at right-back and helped the "Stones" to reach a Play-Off position. Wimbledon had been suitably impressed with his displays and he was signed for a £300,000 fee, of which £30,000 went to Leytonstone & Ilford. His first game for the "Dons" saw him substituted against Arsenal at Highbury, but that was only a temporary setback as he firmly established himself in midfield, missing only one League match in 1990-91 and 1991-92. A spectacular 35 yard lob over Leeds United's 'keeper, John Lukic, was Wimbledon's first **1992-93** Premier League goal and showed the inventiveness that "Dons' " fans have come to expect from one of their key players. Started the season in midfield, but on the arrival of Vinny Jones from Chelsea, he moved to right-back and continued to show the good form that had won him an England "B" cap the previous season. Unfortunately, a nasty injury put him out of action in November and it wasn't until early April that he was fully match fit. Made his comeback in a 4-0 win over the club's landlords, Crystal Palace and by the end of the season he was back to his best and still one of Wimbledon's hottest properties.

| | | | APPEARANCES | | | | GOALS | | | |
|---|---|---|---|---|---|---|---|---|---|---|
| Clubs | Signing Date | Transfer Fee | Lge | FL Cup | FA Cup | Others | Lge | FL Cup | FA Cup | Others |
| Maidstone United | 7.89 | £10,000 | 41+1 | 0+2 | 3 | 7 | | | 1 | |
| Wimbledon* | 6.90 | £300,000 | 102 | 8 | 5 | 2 | 6 | | | |

## BASHAM Michael

Born: Barking, 27 September 1973

Height: 6'3" Weight: 12.12

International Honours: E Sch, E Yth

**Position/Skill Factor:** Central defender who is strong in the tackle, gives nothing away on the ground and is more than useful in the air.

**Career History:** A former England schoolboy international, who has since progressed to the national team at youth level, he first arrived at West Ham United as an associated schoolboy (November 1987), before signing on as a trainee in July 1990. Made the professional ranks prior to the start of the **1992-93** season and although not called up for first team duty, was a regular in the reserve side by the end of the season.

| | | | APPEARANCES | | | | GOALS | | | |
|---|---|---|---|---|---|---|---|---|---|---|
| Clubs | Signing Date | Transfer Fee | Lge | FL Cup | FA Cup | Others | Lge | FL Cup | FA Cup | Others |
| West Hame United* | 8.92 | - | | | | | | | | |

## BATTERSBY Anthony (Tony)

Born: Doncaster, 30 August 1975

Height: 6'1" Weight: 12.8

**Position/Skill Factor:** Striker. A goalscorer with either foot, he is capable of holding up play, or going it alone. Very quick, with good feet and a hard worker.

**Career History:** Started with Sheffield United as an associated schoolboy in October 1989, before graduating to trainee status in August 1991 and turning professional last summer. Played the odd reserve match in **1992-93**, but was unfortunate to be hampered by a hernia problem, which now appears to have been sorted out.

| | | | APPEARANCES | | | | GOALS | | | |
|---|---|---|---|---|---|---|---|---|---|---|
| Clubs | Signing Date | Transfer Fee | Lge | FL Cup | FA Cup | Others | Lge | FL Cup | FA Cup | Others |
| Sheffield United* | 7.93 | - | | | | | | | | |

## BATTY David

Born: Leeds, 2 December 1968

Height: 5'5" Weight: 10.0

International Honours: E Yth, E "U21"-7, E"B", E-14

**Position/Skill Factor:** Great midfield competitor and a very strong tackler and ball winner in the Norman Hunter mould, who is also a constructive passer of the ball. Causes many opposing defences problems, especially in their penalty area, with his long throws.

**Career History:** Has been at Leeds since signing as an associated schoolboy in November 1983. Becoming an apprentice footballer in August 1985, he went on to make his FL debut against Swindon Town at Elland Road on 21 November 1987. Despite turning out regularly for the club and playing well over 100 FL games, he had only scored two League goals in five seasons coincidentally both against Manchester City. Was a driving force, collecting a Second Division Championship medal while playing 39 times, in Leeds' surge back to the First Division in 1989-90. Towards the end of his first season of First Division football, his fine displays brought him a place in the England squad and he made his debut against the USSR at Wembley on 21 May 1991, coming on as a substitute. Despite his paucity of goals, he is hugely popular with the Elland Road faithful for his non-stop energy and aggression and his work-rate and ball winning tenacity, was a major factor in Leeds United's first League Championship triumph since 1974. After playing in England's first two internationals of 1991-92, he was "rested", while England manager Graham Taylor examined the credentials of Geoff Thomas and Carlton Palmer. His place seemed in doubt, but he was included in the squad of 20 for the European Championship Finals in Sweden and made two appearances, one of them, surprisingly in the the right-back position as England gave way to the host country, Sweden. Currently the only Leeds' born first team player. For a long period of **1992-93** he was played out of position at right-back and was sorely missed in the "engine room", where his pivotal role between defence and midfield had been essential to the club during their Championship winning season. Took over the captaincy when Gary McAllister was injured, but had two spells out of action himself. The first one, for two months, following a tackle by Coventry City's Stewart Robson at Elland Road in October and the second when he missed five games in April due to a tendon problem, normally associated with long distance runners. Returned as skipper for the last two games and although appearing for England a couple of times during the season, will hope for better fortune in 1993-94.

| | | | APPEARANCES | | | | GOALS | | | |
|---|---|---|---|---|---|---|---|---|---|---|
| Clubs | Signing Date | Transfer Fee | Lge | FL Cup | FA Cup | Others | Lge | FL Cup | FA Cup | Others |
| Leeds United* | 8.87 | - | 193+9 | 17 | 12 | 17 | 4 | | | |

## BEADLE Peter Clifford

Born: Lambeth, 13 May 1972

Height: 6'0" Weight: 11.12

**Position/Skill Factor:** Big striker who leads the line well and is useful in the air.

**Career History:** Made his FL debut for Gillingham as a 16-year-old junior at home to Cardiff City on 11 March 1989, when he came on as substitute. Initially, he joined the club as an associated schoolboy in December 1986, later signing on as a trainee in July 1988. Made ten more appearances at the start and end of the 1989-90 season, before turning professional. Played both in midfield and up front during 1990-91, demonstrating his goal scoring potential with seven FL goals in 12 full appearances, plus ten as substitute. Started 1991-92 as a forward, but found goals hard to come by and finished the season in midfield. Increasingly the subject of transfer speculation, he was signed by Tottenham Hotspur at the end of the season. With all the competition at "Spurs" for attacking positions, he spent much of **1992-93** battling for a place in the reserves. However, he was given the opportunity to taste first team football in a loan spell with Bournemouth during the last couple of months of the season. Took the chance well, scoring two goals in nine games to help keep the "Cherries" in Division Two and now back at White Hart Lane, he will be pushing for a place this coming season.

| | | | APPEARANCES | | | | GOALS | | | |
|---|---|---|---|---|---|---|---|---|---|---|
| Clubs | Signing Date | Transfer Fee | Lge | FL Cup | FA Cup | Others | Lge | FL Cup | FA Cup | Others |
| Gillingham | 5.90 | - | 42+25 | 2+4 | 1+1 | 1 | 14 | 2 | | |
| Tottenham Hotspur• | 5.92 | £300,000 | | | | | | | | |
| Bournemouth | 3.93 | Loan | 9 | | | | 2 | | | |

## BEAGRIE Peter Sydney

Born: Middlesbrough, 29 November 1965

Height: 5'8" Weight: 9.10

International Honours: E "U21"-2, E"B"

**Position/Skill Factor:** Clever left sided wingman who deceives opponents with a various array of trickery. Often feinting to cross and then going on with the ball, checking from one foot to the other, he has great balance.

**Career History:** Was an associated schoolboy with Hartlepool United, signing forms in January 1980, before going to Ayresome Park. Made his FL debut for Middlesbrough at Oldham Athletic on 2 October 1984. Signed for Sheffield United prior to the start of the 1986-87 season, establishing himself as joint leading goalscorer with nine to his credit that term and won his first and only international honours at under 21 level. Transferred to Stoke City following the "Blades'" relegation to the Third Division. His displays for the "Potters" attracted the attention of several First Division clubs, before Everton moved in for him in an effort to revive their declining fortunes. Not performing consistently at the highest level with the "Toffees" during his first two years at Goodison, he was in and out of the side. Indeed, for the first two months of 1991-92, was ignored for selection behind Pat Nevin, Mark Ward and Robert Warzycha for the wing slots. When loaned to Sunderland in September, a permanent transfer out of Goodison seemed imminent. However, he was recalled and reinstated in the first team squad, although frequently relegated to substitute. Began **1992-93** as he finished the previous term, with below-par performances, often going unnoticed for long periods of a match. His inconsistency meant that only glimpses of his true talent were ever displayed and following a disastrous run of defeats he was not picked again for 17 matches, apart from one substitute appearance. However, the final match of 1992-93 saw him play a significant role in a 5-2 win over Manchester City, his performance highlighted with two goals.

| | | | APPEARANCES | | | | GOALS | | | |
|---|---|---|---|---|---|---|---|---|---|---|
| Clubs | Signing Date | Transfer Fee | Lge | FL Cup | FA Cup | Others | Lge | FL Cup | FA Cup | Others |
| Middlesbrough | 9.83 | - | 24+8 | 1 | | 1+1 | 2 | | | |
| Sheffield United | 8.86 | £35,000 | 81+3 | 5 | 5 | 4 | 11 | | | |
| Stoke City | 6.88 | £210,000 | 54 | 4 | 3 | | 7 | | 1 | |
| Everton* | 11.89 | £750,000 | 59+26 | 4+2 | 5+2 | 5+1 | 8 | 2 | | 1 |
| Sunderland | 9.91 | Loan | 5 | | | | 1 | | | |

## **BEARDSLEY Peter** Andrew

Born: Newcastle, 18 January 1961

Height: 5'8" Weight: 11.7

International Honours: FL Rep, E "B", E-49

**Position/Skill Factor:** Quick thinking, skilful striker, who is a veritable box of tricks. Very good on the ball, he always looks dangerous when he runs at defenders, or when coming from deep positions.

**Career History:** Carlisle United picked him up as an 18-year-old, when he was playing for a Wallsend Boys Club in his native Tyneside. Made his FL debut at home to Blackburn Rovers on 21 August 1979 and spent three years at Brunton Park before trying his luck in North America with Vancouver Whitecaps. Beardsley's success in the States, alerted Manchester United and they brought him back to Britain, but within six months he was back in Vancouver, without playing a single game for the first team. A year later, Arthur Cox, then manager of Newcastle United, signed him as a striking partner for Kevin Keegan and in his first season, 1983-84, the club were promoted to the First Division in third place when he scored 20 League goals to complement Keegan's 27. Following Keegan's retirement, he was leading scorer in the next two First Division campaigns and although the goals dried up in 1986-87 it came as a great shock to the Geordie faithful when he was allowed to leave for Liverpool. While at Newcastle, he had won 18 full England caps after making his debut against Egypt in Cairo on 29 January 1986, when coming on as a substitute. A late and surprise inclusion for England's World Cup squad for the Finals in Mexico in 1986, his partnership with Gary Lineker revived a flagging campaign and helped establish the latter as one of the world's great strikers with six goals in the tournament. He was subsequently a regular international performer until 1990, but a lack of goals (only eight in 49 games for England) ended his England career somewhat prematurely. Along with John Barnes he inspired another golden era for the "Reds", winning a League Championship medal in his first season at Anfield, which was followed by an FA Cup Winners medal in 1989 and another League title triumph in 1989-90. As much a creator, as scorer, he was never prolific for Liverpool until 1990-91, when he netted 11 goals in his first 11 games, including a hat-trick against deadly rivals, Manchester United. Surprisingly, it was the beginning of the end of his Anfield career. Losing his place through injury, he was then ignored by manager Kenny Daglish, when fit again. Although restored to first team duty after Daglish's amazing departure, he seemed to have lost his zest and failed to recapture his early season form as Liverpool faded out of the championship race. It was still a major shock when new manager Graham Souness discarded him during the summer of 1991 to make way for Dean Saunders and he moved to local rivals, Everton. It was also a questionable decision, as Beardsley was undoubtedly the star of a generally disappointing and lack lustre campaign by the "Toffees", top scoring with 15 League goals, plus four in cup competitions. For the second successive season since joining the club, he finished leading scorer and was the highlight of an almost forgettable **1992-93,** with his immense skill providing some relief from the doom and gloom hanging over Goodison Park. Had a short absence early on in the season, due to injury, but on coming back didn't miss a game and reached a career milestone of 500 full games played in all competitions since starting out at Carlisle back in 1979. But with Everton desperately needing money to rebuild the team, he was sold to Newcastle United during the 1993 close season, thus returning to St James' Park after a ten year break.

| | | | APPEARANCES | | | | GOALS | | | |
|---|---|---|---|---|---|---|---|---|---|---|
| Clubs | Signing Date | Transfer Fee | Lge | FL Cup | FA Cup | Others | Lge | FL Cup | FA Cup | Others |
| Carlisle United | 8.79 | – | 93+11 | 6+1 | 15 | | 22 | | 7 | |
| Vancouver (NASL) | 4.81 | £275,000 | | | | | | | | |
| Manchester United | 9.82 | £300,000 | | 1 | | | | | | |
| Vancouver (NASL) | 3.83 | – | | | | | | | | |
| Newcastle United | 9.83 | £150,000 | 146+1 | 10 | 6 | 1 | 61 | | | |
| Liverpool | 7.87 | £1,900,000 | 120+11 | 13+1 | 22+3 | 5 | 46 | 1 | 11 | 1 |
| Everton | 8.91 | £1,000,000 | 81 | 8 | 4 | 2 | 25 | 5 | 1 | 1 |
| Newcastle United* | 6.93 | £1,500,000 | | | | | | | | |

## **BEASANT David (Dave)** John

Born: Willesden, 20 March 1959

Height: 6'3" Weight: 13.0

International Honours: E "B", E-2

**Position/Skill Factor:** Big, strong, brave goalkeeper, who never stops talking to his defenders. One of the first goalies to run the ball out of his own penalty area in an effort to increase his distance. Also, sets up attacks with good throws.

**Career History:** Discovered by Wimbledon while playing for non-League Edgware Town, he made his FL debut at home to Blackpool on 12 January 1979. Became a regular for the "Dons", not missing a League match from the beginning of 1981-82, until he left for Newcastle United, a total of 304 consecutive FL matches. During that time he won both Division Four and Division Two Championship medals as the club moved up to Division One. His last game for the club was the sensational 1988 FA Cup Final against Liverpool, which saw him save John Aldridge's penalty. The first spot kick saved in Cup Final history at Wembley as Wimbledon held on to take the trophy back to south London. It was not a great surprise when he was sold at the end of that season to Newcastle United, but it was perhaps not a good move for either the player or his new club. The "Magpies" struggled at the foot of the First Division during his short stay and he had little opportunity to further his reputation or become accepted by their fans. No doubt unsettled by his move from his native London, he was "rescued" by Chelsea after only six months on Tyneside for a slightly reduced fee and assisted them to the Second Division Championship. In the summer of 1990, his consistent displays were finally recognised at international level when coming on as a substitute for England against Italy on 7 July 1990, but after appearing in the first 10 games for Chelsea in 1990-91, his incredible run of 394 consecutive FL games came to a halt when he was ruled out with an injured hand. In 1991-92 he was no longer automatic first choice 'keeper for the "Blues", swapping first team duties with Kevin Hitchcock throughout the season. After starting **1992-93** ahead of Hitchcock a large question mark appeared regarding his career, after the home League match against Norwich City on 12 September 1992. He was publicly slated by the then Chelsea manager, Ian Porterfield, following two disastrous errors which ultimately cost the "Blues" the match. Told that he would never play for the club again, he went on loan to Grimsby Town and Wolverhampton Wanderers, where he conceded only eight goals in ten League games and was treated as a hero. Returned to the Bridge when Dave Webb was appointed manager and performed reasonably well until a nightmare 3-0 defeat at Manchester United, cost him his place to Dmitri Kharine. A real "Jekyll and Hyde" character, it is difficult to know where he goes from here, especially under new manager, Glenn Hoddle.

| | | | APPEARANCES | | | | GOALS | | | |
|---|---|---|---|---|---|---|---|---|---|---|
| Clubs | Signing Date | Transfer Fee | Lge | FL Cup | FA Cup | Others | Lge | FL Cup | FA Cup | Others |
| Wimbledon | 8.79 | £1,000 | 340 | 21 | 27 | 3 | | | | |
| Newcastle United | 6.88 | £800,000 | 20 | 2 | 2 | 1 | | | | |
| Chelsea* | 1.89 | £725,000 | 133 | 11 | 5 | 8 | | | | |
| Grimsby Town | 10.92 | Loan | 6 | | | | | | | |
| Wolverhampton W. | 1.93 | Loan | 4 | | 1 | | | | | |

# BECKFORD Darren Richard Lorenzo

Born: Manchester, 12 May 1967

Height: 6'1"

Weight: 11.1

International Honours: E Sch, E Yth

**Position/Skill Factor:** Free scoring striker, who should be suited to the Premier Division. Has good skills for a big lad and is very good in the air.

**Career History:** Started his career with Manchester City as an associated schoolboy (November 1981) and graduated as an apprentice (April 1984), before making his FL debut at Middlesbrough on 20 October 1984. After nearly seven years at Maine Road and limited opportunities, he was transferred to Port Vale. Earlier, he had given a glimpse of what he was capable of when on loan at Third Division Bury. Became an automatic choice for Vale and topped the club's goalscoring lists every season from 1987-88. His 20 League goals were also an important factor when the club climbed out of Division Three in 1988-89 and included a cracking hat-trick in a 4-1 win at Notts County. Transferred to First Division Norwich City for a massive club record fee in the summer of 1991, considered excessive by some. He struggled to justify the amount and was in and out of the side all season, scoring only seven FL goals, plus four more in cup competitions and played only a minor role in the "Canaries' " FA Cup run. Continued to have an unfortunate time at Carrow Road in **1992-93,** with his medical history beginning to read like a script from the TV series Casualty. He had surgery on an old shoulder injury and achilles tendon trouble amongst his ailments. Although showing flashes of what he was capable of (nine goals in 15 reserve games), he only scored twice in nine full games and was transferred to Oldham Athletic just before the March deadline for a sum that showed the "Canaries" losing over £600,000 on the deal. Looking ten pounds overweight, following his barren spell in East Anglia, he made an immediate impact at Boundary Park with three goals in seven outings, including a vital one at home to Liverpool. The club has high hopes on him forming a lethal partnership with Graeme Sharp during the 1993-94 campaign. Has two younger brothers in the game, Jason and Andy.

| | | | APPEARANCES | | | | GOALS | | | |
|---|---|---|---|---|---|---|---|---|---|---|
| Clubs | Signing Date | Transfer Fee | Lge | FL Cup | FA Cup | Others | Lge | FL Cup | FA Cup | Others |
| Manchester City | 8.84 | – | 7+4 | 0+1 | | | | | | |
| Bury | 10.85 | Loan | 12 | | | | 5 | | | |
| Port Vale | 3.87 | £15,000 | 169+9 | 12 | 14 | 9+1 | 71 | 3 | 4 | 3 |
| Norwich City | 6.91 | £925,000 | 32+6 | 3+2 | 4+1 | 1 | 8 | 3 | 1 | 1 |
| Oldham Athletic* | 3.93 | £300,000 | 6+1 | | | | 3 | | | |

## **BECKHAM David** Robert

Born: Leytonstone, 2 May 1975

Height: 5'11"

Weight: 10.7

**Position/Skill Factor:** Midfielder with terrific vision, who can hit great long passes to turn defence into attack. Also known for his workrate.

**Career History:** One of the stars of Manchester United's victorious FA Youth Cup run in 1991-92, culminating in a 6-3 aggregate victory over Crystal Palace in the Final, scoring in the first-leg. First came to Old Trafford as an associated schoolboy in June 1989, graduating to trainee status in July 1991 and signing a professional contract in January 1993. Prior to turning professional, he had already made the first team (as a substitute) in a League Cup-tie at Brighton in September 1992 and come the end of **1992-93** he had played his part as a member of the United "A" team that romped away with the Lancashire League Division One title. He had also helped the youth side to the FA Youth Cup Final for the second year in succession, albeit collecting a losers medal this time around.

| | | | APPEARANCES | | | | GOALS | | | |
|---|---|---|---|---|---|---|---|---|---|---|
| Clubs | Signing Date | Transfer Fee | Lge | FL Cup | FA Cup | Others | Lge | FL Cup | FA Cup | Others |
| Manchester United* | 1.93 | - | | 0+1 | | | | | | |

## **BEECH Christopher (Chris)**

Born: Congleton, 5 November 1975

Height: 5'9" Weight: 11.0

International Honours: E Sch, E Yth

**Position/Skill Factor:** Striker with lots of pace and two good feet.

**Career History:** An England schoolboy international, he signed associated schoolboy forms (February 1990) for Manchester City, having already had a taste of the atmosphere at Maine Road as a ball boy. On leaving school, he became a trainee with the club in July 1992 and quickly caught the eyes of the coaching staff, turning professional on his 17th birthday and going on to establish himself in the reserves in **1992-93.** Recovering well from a bad knee injury during the season, he showed he had the commitment and temperament, as well as the skill, to succeed at the highest level.

| | | | APPEARANCES | | | | GOALS | | | |
|---|---|---|---|---|---|---|---|---|---|---|
| Clubs | Signing Date | Transfer Fee | Lge | FL Cup | FA Cup | Others | Lge | FL Cup | FA Cup | Others |
| Manchester City* | 11.92 | - | | | | | | | | |

## **BEENEY Mark** Raymond

Born: Tunbridge Wells, 30 December 1967

Height: 6'4"

Weight: 14.7

International Honours: E Semi-Pro Int

**Position/Skill Factor:** Goalkeeper who comes out well for crosses and commands his box. Is a tremendous kicker, especially out of his hands.

**Career History:** First came to Gillingham as a 15-year-old associated schoolboy (September 1983), before signing as a non-contract professional during the 1985 close season. But with long serving Ron Hillyard safely esconced between the posts and ever present throughout 1985-86, the prospect of making the first team seemed limited. However, following a League Cup outing early the following season, he eventually made his FL debut in a 4-0 win at home to Walsall on 1 January 1987 and two days later played at Notts County in a 3-1 defeat. Surprisingly, after Hillyard returned to League duty, he was released a few weeks later to join ambitious Maidstone United of the Vauxhall Conference. Two and a half years later he was back in the Football League when the "Stones" won promotion from the Conference in 1988-89. However, in his two FL seasons with the Kent Club (by now exiled to Dartford), he had to share 'keeping duties with the veteran, Nicky Johns and spent two months on loan to struggling Aldershot. There was no hint of his future progress, before his surprise move to Third Division Brighton & Hove Albion in March 1991 as cover for Perry Digweed. When Digweed was injured in the pre-match warm up for a game at Millwall in September 1991, Beeney was urgently summoned to the ground and took the field as a substitute, remaining in place until the latter's return in February 1992. Started **1992-93** as first choice 'keeper at the Goldstone Ground and soon began to attract the interest of higher division clubs, as Brighton hovered on the edge of the "Play-Off" zone throughout the season. It was still a surprise, though, when Howard Wilkinson signed him for Leeds United as cover for John Lukic after the March transfer deadline. The initial payment of £350,000 helped to stave off immediate financial difficulties for the south coast club and with the fee linked to club appearances and international honours, it could eventually rise as high as £750,000. Despite this, Leeds received special dispensation from the Premier League to introduce him in their final match of the season, following another much publicised error by Lukic at Sheffield Wednesday, which presented the "Owls" with an 89th minute equaliser.

| | | | APPEARANCES | | | | GOALS | | | |
|---|---|---|---|---|---|---|---|---|---|---|
| Clubs | Signing Date | Transfer Fee | Lge | FL Cup | FA Cup | Others | Lge | FL Cup | FA Cup | Others |
| Gillingham | 8.86 | - | 2 | 1 | | | | | | |
| Maidstone United | 2.87 | - | 50 | 3 | 11 | 6 | | | | |
| Aldershot | 3.90 | Loan | 7 | | | | | | | |
| Brighton & H.A. | 3.91 | £30,000 | 68+1 | 6 | 7 | 6 | | | | |
| Leeds United* | 4.93 | £350,000 | 1 | | | | | | | |

## BEESLEY Paul

Born: Liverpool, 21 July 1965

Height: 6'1" Weight: 11.5

**Position/Skill Factor:** Footballing central defender who passes the ball, rather than clearing his lines. Intercepts through balls well and is always looking to get his own attack moving.

**Career History:** Was playing for Marine, in the Northern Premier League, before signing pro with near neighbours, Wigan Athletic. Made his FL debut at Reading on 3 October 1984, but only appeared once more that term. Gradually established himself at the heart of the Wigan defence, before being transferred to Leyton Orient, who paid a club record fee to get their man. Although he only played 32 League matches in his first season 1989-90, the Orient players voted him their "Player of the Year". Moved to Sheffield United during the 1990 close season and proved a shrewd investment as he established a regular place in their defence. Struggled at the start of 1991-92 as the "Blades" made their customary disastrous start, but then formed a highly effective defensive partnership with Brian Gayle, newly signed from Ipswich, which stabilised the back four and assisted United to a remarkable recovery, culminating in a final placing of tenth in the First Division. Once again proved a model of consistency in **1992-93.** With a number of different partners during the season he was ever present until being rested, but later showed his versatility by playing the final few games at left-back. Scored what was probably the most vital goal of the season, when notching the FA Cup Third Round equaliser against Burnley, after the "Blades" had been two down with just nine minutes to go. Now approaching the peak of his career, he was deservedly voted the supporters' "Player of the Year".

| | | | APPEARANCES | | | | GOALS | | | |
|---|---|---|---|---|---|---|---|---|---|---|
| Clubs | Signing Date | Transfer Fee | Lge | FL Cup | FA Cup | Others | Lge | FL Cup | FA Cup | Others |
| Wigan Athletic | 9.84 | – | 153+2 | 13 | 6 | 11 | 3 | | | |
| Leyton Orient | 10.89 | £175,000 | 32 | | 1 | 2 | 1 | | | 1 |
| Sheffield United* | 7.90 | £300,000 | 114+2 | 10 | 8+2 | 3 | 5 | | 1 | 1 |

## BEINLICH Stefan

Born: Berlin, Germany, 13 January 1972

Height: 5'11"

Weight: 11.2

**Position/Skill Factor:** A quality striker with very good first touch, his skilful twists and turns, create goalscoring chances for both himself and others.

**Career History:** Signed along with Matthias Breitkreutz from an obscure regional club in East Berlin by the name of Bergmann Borsig in October 1991 for a combined fee of £200,000. He made less impact than his German colleague, with only two first team appearances as a substitute at the end of the season, the first being his FL debut at Nottingham Forest on 18 April 1992. Only called up for first team duty on seven occasions in **1992-93,** he nevertheless had an outstanding season with Villa's reserve side in the Pontins League. He is still very much a young player in the learning mode, as he looks to gain more experience. Definitely one to watch for in the future.

| | | | APPEARANCES | | | | GOALS | | | |
|---|---|---|---|---|---|---|---|---|---|---|
| Clubs | Signing Date | Transfer Fee | Lge | FL Cup | FA Cup | Others | Lge | FL Cup | FA Cup | Others |
| Aston Villa* | 10.91 | £100,000 | 1+8 | | | 0+1 | | | | |

## BENALI Francis Vincent

Born: Southampton, 30 December 1968

Height: 5'9"

Weight: 11.0

International Honours: E Sch

**Position/Skill Factor:** Very determined left-back, who is aggressive in the tackle. With a lovely left foot, he strikes the ball well and is an excellent crosser.

**Career History:** Locally born and bred, he signed associated schoolboy forms for Southampton in January 1983 and graduated as an apprentice in July 1985, before turning pro and making his FL debut as a substitute at home to Derby County on 1 October 1988. After a further couple of appearances as a substitute, he got a chance to impress, following a long term injury to Micky Adams. Originally a left-winger, he was given an extended run at left-back in 1989-90, along with Jason Dodd, another youngster playing at right-back during an injury crisis at the Dell. Subsequently, played second fiddle to Micky Adams until January 1992 when recalled to the "Saints' " team on the left flank and held his place until the end of the season. Started as first choice left-back in **1992-93,** despite being sent off in a pre-season friendly, with Adams playing in a more advanced role. His comittment shone through in the game against Leeds United at the Dell when central defender, Richard Hall, was injured, earning him the "Man of the Match" award. Sent off at Tottenham Hotspur for a rash tackle, he collected a four match ban and with additional personnel coming in to fill the midfield places, he finally lost his first team place to Adams again as the season ended.

| | | | APPEARANCES | | | | GOALS | | | |
|---|---|---|---|---|---|---|---|---|---|---|
| Clubs | Signing Date | Transfer Fee | Lge | FL Cup | FA Cup | Others | Lge | FL Cup | FA Cup | Others |
| Southampton* | 1.87 | - | 85+16 | 8+6 | 12 | 3+1 | | | | |

## BENNETT Frank

Born: Birmingham, 3 January 1969

Height: 5'7" Weight: 11.8

**Position/Skill Factor:** Striker with tremendous strength and pace, which takes him away from defenders and into scoring positions.

**Career History:** Became the eighth player in three years to be recruited by FL and PL clubs from the West Midlands based Beazer Homes League club, Halesowen Town, when he signed for Southampton in **1992-93.** Introduced to "Saints' " reserve side in February as a trialist, while combining his football with night shifts at a Birmingham hotel, he impressed and after scoring in his second outing, was offered a two year contract at the Dell. Before the move, he had spent three years at Halesowen after joining from local soccer and is anxious to make up for any lost time.

| | | | APPEARANCES | | | | GOALS | | | |
|---|---|---|---|---|---|---|---|---|---|---|
| Clubs | Signing Date | Transfer Fee | Lge | FL Cup | FA Cup | Others | Lge | FL Cup | FA Cup | Others |
| Southampton* | 2.93 | £5,000 | | | | | | | | |

## BENTLEY James (Jim) Graham

Born: Liverpool, 11 June 1976

Height: 6'1" Weight: 12.7

**Position/Skill Factor:** Central defender who is good in the air and a strong tackler on the ground. Clears his lines effectively.

**Career History:** The son of John, who played for Everton and Stockport County in the early 1960s, he first came to Manchester City as a trainee in July 1992 and while predominately playing for the youth side in **1992-93**, he was also given a few games in the Central League. Signed professional during the summer, having impressed in a first team testimonial match at Bolton Wanderers last season.

| | | | APPEARANCES | | | | GOALS | | | |
|---|---|---|---|---|---|---|---|---|---|---|
| Clubs | Signing Date | Transfer Fee | Lge | FL Cup | FA Cup | Others | Lge | FL Cup | FA Cup | Others |
| Manchester City* | 7.93 | - | | | | | | | | |

## BERESFORD John

Born: Sheffield, 4 September 1966

Height: 5'6"

Weight: 10.12

International Honours: E Yth

**Position/Skill Factor:** Left-back with the skills and pace of a winger. Has a lovely left foot and enjoys attacking down the flank to provide pin-point crosses.

**Career History:** A young man who created quite a stir during Portsmouth's 1991-92 FA Cup run to the Semi-Finals, he began his career at Manchester City, first as an associated schoolboy (December 1981), before becoming an apprentice (April 1983) and then a professional (September 1983). After three years without a first-team opportunity, however, he was snapped up on a free transfer by Second Division, Barnsley, in the 1986 close season and made his FL debut in the first game of 1986-87 at home to Crystal Palace on 23 August 1986. Originally a midfield player, he was in and out of the team in his first two seasons at Oakwell, before manager Allan Clarke converted him to left-back, where he held down his place in 1988-89. In March 1989 he was transferred to Portsmouth for a fee that Clark claimed he could not refuse, because it was far higher than his own valuation of the player. Subsequent events suggest that John Gregory's judgement for "Pompey" was better than Clarks. In three seasons at Fratton Park, Beresford was generally first choice left-back, although losing his place for a short periods to Gary Stevens and Ray Daniel. At the end of his contract, in the summer of 1992, Liverpool showed an interest in him, but he delayed fatally, hoping for an offer from his home town club, Sheffield Wednesday, thus prompting Graham Souness to pull out of the deal. In the event, he joined Newcastle United and had an outstanding first season on Tyneside in **1992-93**, where his good form saw him called-up to join the England squad for the World Cup fixture in Turkey. Became a terrific favourite with the crowd, with his "never say die spirit" and surging runs out of defence, there being a buzz of anticipation every time he got the ball. Reckoned by many to be the best left-back in the country, he was one of the missing pieces of the jigsaw required by manager, Kevin Keegan, in his bid for promotion. And he only missed four League games, as United stormed to the top of the First Division in September and stayed there throughout the season, to win the title by eight clear points and achieve Premier

League status for 1993-94. If he had a fault, then it was his inability to score more goals, when you consider how many times his skill and fitness got him forward, but if he can rectify that department this season, then the big boys better watch out.

| Clubs | Signing Date | Transfer Fee | APPEARANCES Lge | FL Cup | FA Cup | Others | GOALS Lge | FL Cup | FA Cup | Others |
|---|---|---|---|---|---|---|---|---|---|---|
| Manchester City | 9.83 | – | | | | | | | | |
| Barnsley | 8.86 | – | | 79+9 | 5+2 | 5 | | 5 | 2 | 1 |
| Portsmouth | 3.89 | £300,000 | 102+5 | 12 | 11 | 2 | 8 | 2 | | |
| Newcastle United* | 7.92 | £650,000 | 42 | 4 | 4 | 2 | 1 | | | |

# BERG Henning

Born: Norway, 1 September 1969

Height: 6'0" Weight: 11.9

International Honours: Norwegian Int

**Position/Skill Factor:** Full-back with good skills who likes to get forward and join in with the attack. Also an excellent passer.

**Career History:** Signed by Kenny Dalglish for Blackburn Rovers in January 1993 from Norwegian club, SK Lillestrom, the same club from which Oldham recruited Gunnar Halle, soon after making his international debut for Norway. He came on as substitute in Norway's surprising 1-1 draw at Wembley against England in October 1992, which established their credentials as a strong threat to England's qualification for the World Cup Finals in 1994. Expected to push David May from the right-back position in **1992-93,** he had a tough time accustoming himself to the English game. Although he has many fine qualities, he was not able to perform the covering role that May supplies and found himself unable to dislodge his rival permanently. Made his PL debut as a substitute at home to Crystal Palace on 2 February 1993, but played in only five more games as a late season injury cost him the chance of being included in the final matches. His best performance came when unexpectedly asked to mark Chris Waddle in the League Cup Semi-Final, a job he performed well, although out of position.

| Clubs | Signing Date | Transfer Fee | APPEARANCES Lge | FL Cup | FA Cup | Others | GOALS Lge | FL Cup | FA Cup | Others |
|---|---|---|---|---|---|---|---|---|---|---|
| Blackburn Rovers* | 1.93 | £400,000 | 2+2 | 2 | | | | | | |

# BERGSSON Gudni

Born: Iceland, 21 July 1965

Height: 5'10"

Weight: 10.7

International Honours: Iceland Int

**Position/Skill Factor:** Predominately a right-back, he can play fittingly as well in a centre-back role, where his main strength is in defending. His great pace makes him difficult to beat and he loves to get forward.

**Career History:** First played in his native country for Valur, before having a spell on trial with Aston Villa in October 1985, but returned home having failed to impress. Came back to Britain in November 1988, this time at the invitation of Tottenham Hotspur and after a brief trial period he made his FL debut at home to Luton Town on 26 December 1988. Unable to secure a regular place at "Spurs", he became a vital member of the first team squad. Played more FL games in 1991-92 than in his previous three seasons, in a variety of different shirt numbers, but operating nearly always at right-back, but was unable to hold his place after the turn of the year, with Justin Edinburgh and Pat van den Hauwe firmly established. Following the arrival of Dean Austin at White Hart Lane, the position in **1992-93** became even more tenuous and he was only called upon to sit on the bench on ten occasions, while making just six substitute appearances. And with the foreign player ruling being tightened up, it seems likely that his future now lies away from Tottenham.

| Clubs | Signing Date | Transfer Fee | APPEARANCES Lge | FL Cup | FA Cup | Others | GOALS Lge | FL Cup | FA Cup | Others |
|---|---|---|---|---|---|---|---|---|---|---|
| Tottenham Hotspur* | 12.88 | £100,000 | 51+20 | 4+2 | 2+2 | 5+1 | 3 | | | |

## **BERKLEY Austin** James

Born: Dartford, 28 January 1973

Height: 5'9" Weight: 10.10

**Position/Skill Factor:** Midfielder with a good football brain, who uses the ball intelligently and doesn't lose possession too often. On a good day he is capable of making things happen.

**Career History:** Suprisingly freed by Gillingham after just one year as a professional and six first team appearances, all as a substitute, he had started with the Kent club as a trainee in October 1989, before making his FL debut on Boxing Day 1991 in a 2-1 win over Hereford United at the Priestfield Stadium. Snaped up by Swindon Town during the summer of 1992, his progress has been somewhat hampered in **1992-93** by injury, following an early outing at Oxford United in the Anglo-Italian Cup, when he scored one of the Town's goals in a 3-1 win. Apart from that, he sat on the first team bench a couple of times without playing, but could prove to be a useful long term signing, if given the opportunity.

| | | | APPEARANCES | | | | GOALS | | | |
|---|---|---|---|---|---|---|---|---|---|---|
| Clubs | Signing Date | Transfer Fee | Lge | FL Cup | FA Cup | Others | Lge | FL Cup | FA Cup | Others |
| Gillingham | 5.91 | - | 0+3 | | | 0+3 | | | | |
| Swindon Town* | 5.92 | - | | | | 1 | | | | 1 |

## **BERNARD Paul** Robert James

Born: Edinburgh, 30 December 1972

Height: 5'9"

Weight: 11.0

International Honours: S"U21" - 9

**Position/Skill Factor:** Very positive midfielder, he trains all day long and has a marvellous attitude to the game. With two great feet, and good passing ability and physical toughness, he is a manager's dream.

**Career History:** An associated schoolboy (January 1987) and a trainee (November 1989), before turning pro in the summer of 1991 with Oldham Athletic, he made his FL debut in the penultimate match of the season, a 2-0 win, at home to Middlesbrough on 7 May 1991, whilst still a trainee. He retained his place for the final match of the season at home to Sheffield Wednesday, remarkably scoring the equaliser after Oldham had been losing 2-0 and when Neal Redfearn converted a penalty in injury time, the club were promoted as Second Division Champions. It was amazing that manager Joe Royle should "blood" an untried youngster at such a critical stage of the season. Played in Oldham's first match in Division One for 68 years against Liverpool at Anfield, but did not win a regular place until the New Year when again, remarkably, he scored four goals in consecutive League games and a fifth after seven matches. Meanwhile, he was called into the Scottish Under 21 squad, making one full appearance and two as substitute. Had another excellent season in **1992-93,** as his aggressive approach helped him to hold his place in the team. Continued to play regularly for his country's under 21 side, but was unfortunate to suffer a shin fracture while on international duty, which meant him missing five games during January and February. Scored six goals during the campaign, several of them invaluable and his spectacular 30 yard chip in a 5-3 home win over Nottingham Forest was a prelude of what was to follow. Rated by manager Joe Royle at over £750,000.

| | | | APPEARANCES | | | | GOALS | | | |
|---|---|---|---|---|---|---|---|---|---|---|
| Clubs | Signing Date | Transfer Fee | Lge | FL Cup | FA Cup | Others | Lge | FL Cup | FA Cup | Others |
| Oldham Athletic* | 7.91 | - | 50+6 | 4+1 | 4 | 0+1 | 10 | 1 | 1 | |

## **BERRY Gregory (Greg)** John

Born: Grays, 5 March 1971

Height: 5'11" Weight: 12.0

**Position/Skill Factor:** Left-winger with good skills and two good feet. Tries to commit defenders and gets early crosses into the penalty area.

**Career History:** Yet another non-League discovery made by Leyton Orient, who signed him from East Thurrock United during the 1989 close season. Made his FL debut when he appeared as a substitute at Brisbane Road against Blackpool on 14 October 1989 and in his first full game for the club a week later, he scored in a 4-1 win over Reading. After a short run in the team he went back to the reserves, but started the 1990-91 as a first choice and held the number 11 shirt for most of the season. In 1991-92 he lost his place early in the season, but returned in November and stayed until the closing weeks, recording a personal landmark with a "hat-trick" of goals against Bury in March 1992. During the summer he was signed by Wimbledon for a large fee. Had a disappointing first season in the top flight after making an early Premier League debut at home to Ipswich on 18 August 1992, as selection problems and a nasty back injury kept him out for most of **1992-93.** He didn't play again for five months, re-emerging as a substitute in the Third Round of the FA Cup against Everton and only making two further appearances before the season came to a close. However, he did enough to suggest that when fully fit and with more experience, he should become a useful asset to the "Dons".

| | | | APPEARANCES | | | | GOALS | | | |
|---|---|---|---|---|---|---|---|---|---|---|
| Clubs | Signing Date | Transfer Fee | Lge | FL Cup | FA Cup | Others | Lge | FL Cup | FA Cup | Others |
| Leyton Orient | 7.89 | £2,000 | 68+12 | 6 | 8+2 | 5+3 | 14 | 3 | 2 | 1 |
| Wimbledon* | 8.92 | £250,000 | 2+1 | | 0+1 | | | | | |

## **BERRY Trevor** John

Born: Haslemere, 1 August 1974

Height: 5'7" Weight: 10.8

International Honours: E Yth

**Position/Skill Factor:** Right sided midfield player with two good feet and full of tricks. Has great stamina and is an excellent crosser on the run.

**Career History:** A recent Aston Villa professional signing, in return for a small fee, he had initially joined Bournemouth as an associated schoolboy in February 1989 and at the time of the move, he had been on the club's books as a trainee since September 1990. Yet to make his first team debut, he played in most of Villa's reserve games in **1992-93** and looks to be a player with a future.

| | | | APPEARANCES | | | | GOALS | | | |
|---|---|---|---|---|---|---|---|---|---|---|
| Clubs | Signing Date | Transfer Fee | Lge | FL Cup | FA Cup | Others | Lge | FL Cup | FA Cup | Others |
| Aston Villa* | 4.92 | £50,000 | | | | | | | | |

## **BISHOP Ian** William

Born: Liverpool, 29 May 1965

Height: 5'9"

Weight: 10.12

**Position/Skill Factor:** Midfield player with great vision. A brilliant passer, he can hit 50 yard targets and can also split defences with short passes as well, in order to find a way through.

**Career History:** Started out with his home town club, Everton, as an associated schoolboy in July 1980, before moving up to apprentice (June 1981) status on leaving school and eventually signing professional forms for the "Toffees" at the end of the 1982-83 season. Made his FL debut on loan to Crewe Alexandra on 27 March 1984, away to Darlington. On his return to Goodison Park, manager Howard Kendall gave him an outing as substitute against Manchester United in May, but that was the limit of his first team opportunities, before he was allowed to leave for Fourth Division, Carlisle United. As a ball playing midfielder, he was Carlisle's star player for the next four seasons, but with the Cumbrian team constantly struggling at the foot of the Fourth Division, he was overlooked by the rest of the football world until the summer of 1988 when he was signed by Bournemouth, newly promoted to Division Two, for a modest fee. After an outstanding first season at Dean Court, he returned to the First Division with Manchester City, giving Bournemouth an enormous profit on their investment. Soon became a favourite with City fans, especially after a 5-1 thrashing of Manchester United, but soon afterwards Mel Machin was sacked and replaced by Bishops former manager at Everton, Howard Kendall. It is alleged that Kendall was prejudiced against him because of his long hair and, to the dismay of City fans, within weeks of his arrival, Bishop, along with Trevor Morley, was traded to West Ham United in exchange for Mark Ward, in a deal worth about £1 million. After an uncertain start at Upton Park, he soon became a regular, assisting the "Hammers" to promotion back to Division One and to the FA Cup Semi-Final in 1990-91. And although the team slipped out of the top flight a year later, he was their most consistant player, missing only one FL game. Failed to establish a regular first team place in **1992-93,** after being out for quite a while, recovering from a cartilege operation in the early part of the season and had to be content with reserve football in order to get match fit. Towards the end of the campaign, with the "Hammers" in second place, one of the two automatic promotion spots, he came back into the side, playing in 14 (including four as a substitute) of the last 17 games. And his only League goal of the season, couldn't have come at a more important time, a last minute winner at Birmingham City in April, maintaining the promotion challenge. That goal proved vital when, in the final count, it was West Ham who were promoted to the Premier League and not Portsmouth, when both teams finished on 88 points.

| | | | APPEARANCES | | | | GOALS | | | |
|---|---|---|---|---|---|---|---|---|---|---|
| Clubs | Signing Date | Transfer Fee | Lge | FL Cup | FA Cup | Others | Lge | FL Cup | FA Cup | Others |
| Everton | 5.83 | – | 0+1 | | | | | | | |
| Crewe Alexandra | 3.84 | Loan | 4 | | | | | | | |
| Carlisle United | 10.84 | £15,000 | 131+1 | 8 | 5 | 4 | 14 | 1 | 1 | |
| Bournemouth | 7.88 | £35,000 | 44 | 4 | 5 | 1 | 2 | | | |
| Manchester City | 8.89 | £465,000 | 18+1 | 4 | | 1 | 2 | 1 | | |
| West Ham United* | 12.89 | £500,000 | 109+11 | 7 | 9+1 | 4+1 | 8 | | 2 | 1 |

## **BJORNEBYE Stig** Inge

Born: Norway, 11 December 1969

Height: 5'10" Weight: 11.10

International Honours: Norwegian Int

**Position/Skill Factor:** Left-sided defender who can also play in midfield. Very sound in defence and strong in the tackle,conversely, he can use his great speed to overlap to great effect.

**Career History:** Signed by Liverpool manager Graeme Souness to replenish his diminishing stock of fit and available defenders, from Norwegian First club, Rosenburg Trondheim. A Norwegian international for the past three years, although not an automatic selection, he played in Norway's outstanding 1-1 draw at Wembley against England in October 1992, in a World Cup qualifying group match. He only played half a season for Rosenberg before joining Liverpool, having previously been with Elverum, Strommen and Kongsvinger IL. His introduction to the **1992-93** Premier League season was nothing less than traumatic. Due to Liverpool's injury crisis, he made his PL debut when pitched straight into the fray at Coventry on 19 December 1992 at left-back. With a "patched-up" and unfamiliar looking team, Liverpool crashed to a 5-1 defeat and the next two months proved to

be the nadir of the "Reds' " history since their return to Division One in 1962. Their defence fell apart, whilst the midfield and attack was unable to conjure up sufficient goals to relieve the pressure. His short-lived partnership with Torben Piechnik in the heart of defence, proved a disaster, as first the "Reds" lost at home to Aston Villa and, more alarmingly, were totally overwhelmed by Second Division, Bolton Wanderers, in an FA Cup replay at Anfield in January, when a 2-0 defeat flattered the home team's actual performance. However, for lack of players, Bjornebye held his place at left-back until the return of David Burrows in March.

| | | | APPEARANCES | | | | GOALS | | | |
|---|---|---|---|---|---|---|---|---|---|---|
| Clubs | Signing Date | Transfer Fee | Lge | FL Cup | FA Cup | Others | Lge | FL Cup | FA Cup | Others |
| Liverpool* | 12.92 | £600,000 | 11 | | 2 | | | | | |

## BLACKMORE Clayton Graham

Born: Neath, 23 September 1964

Height: 5'9" Weight: 11.3

International Honours: W Sch, W Yth, W "U21"-3, W-35

**Position/Skill Factor:** Full-back who can play in midfield, he is a great striker of the ball with either foot and is quite capable of scoring from free kicks and 30 yard shots. A great competitor, he enjoys the physical side of the game.

**Career History:** First signed for Manchester United as an associated schoolboy (November 1978), then as an apprentice (June 1981), before joining the professional ranks and making his FL debut at left-back at Nottingham Forest on 16 May 1984. And after only two appearances for United, he made his full international debut for Wales against Norway, when coming on as a substitute for Jeff Hopkins on 5 June 1985 in Bergen. Since then he has been a regular first choice for his country. In most of his early games for United, he played in midfield, usually on the flanks, but in a defensive capacity rather than as a traditional winger. Since 1988 he has been deployed more frequently as a full-back. His versatility has perhaps handicapped his career, as he has been used as cover for both defensive and midfield places, but rarely able to claim one position as his own. Not until 1990-91 was he selected consistently throughout the season. Prior to then, he was frequently chosen as substitute. Despite his defensive role in the team, he is not afraid to go forward and has frequently scored vital goals for United as the record shows. In 1989-90, he popped up to net the winner in a Fourth Round FA Cup tie at Hereford United and on reaching Wembley, he came on as a sub during the drawn match with Crystal Palace. He didn't play in the replay, but still picked up a FA Cup winners medal when United won 1-0. Also, after scoring the first goal for the club on their return to Europe, in the European Cup Winners Cup, he played in every round right through to the Final, when Barcelona were defeated 2-1. On a less euphoric note, however, he was a member of the United side that lost 1-0 in the League Cup Final against Sheffield Wednesday. In 1991-92 he reverted to his role of squad man, alternating between occasional outings at full-back and midfield and frequent appearances as substitute. Thus he played less of a part in United's unsuccessful Championship bid than he would have wished and perhaps surprisingly was excluded from the team which defeated Nottingham Forest 1-0 in the 1992 League Cup Final. Started **1992-93** as a regular, playing 14 full games and showing off his versatility in a number of positions, including left and right-back and midfield, until the signing of Eric Cantona and the return to fitness of Lee Sharpe and Paul Parker kept him on the sidelines after early November. A frustrating second half of the season saw him confined merely to Central League football, apart from one further substitute appearance in the Third Round FA Cup-tie against Bury. However, his season wasn't all disappointment, having participated in enough games to warrant a Championship medal, as United came home clear of Aston Villa to bring the title back to Old Trafford after an absence of 26 years.

| Clubs | Signing Date | Transfer Fee | APPEARANCES Lge | FL Cup | FA Cup | Others | GOALS Lge | FL Cup | FA Cup | Others |
|---|---|---|---|---|---|---|---|---|---|---|
| Manchester United* | 9.82 | - | 150+36 | 23+2 | 15+6 | 19 | 19 | 3 | 1 | 4 |

## BLACKWELL Dean Robert

Born: Camden, 5 December 1969

Height: 6'1"

Weight: 12.10

International Honours: E "U21"-6

**Position/Skill Factor:** Central defender who is good in the air, attacks the ball and has plenty of pace.

**Career History:** Was a Wimbledon associated schoolboy (May 1985) and then a trainee (July 1986), prior to turning pro with the club and making his FL debut, when coming on as a substitute, at home to Manchester City on 16 September 1989. Made two more substitute appearances that season and had a spell on loan with Second Division Plymouth Argyle. Started 1990-91 on the bench, but following a reshuffle, he was given the number five shirt at the end of September and made the position his own, missing just one match throughout the rest of the season. He was also selected for the England Under 21 squad, making five full appearances, plus one, as a substitute. Well established in the heart of the "Dons' " defence, he was most unfortunate to suffer a hernia type injury before 1991-92 was properly underway and on coming back into the side for a few first team games in October, he sustained a leg injury which then put him out for the rest of the season. Started **1992-93** as a substitute at Leeds United in the opening game of the season, before coming into the side as a replacement for the injured John Scales and playing in the next eight games. Formed a good partnership with Scott Fitzgerald and a fit again Scales, until succumbing to injury himself at home to Blackburn Rovers. He returned to the side for the visit of Sheffield Wednesday and played 14 consecutive games, before receiving a further injury setback in the FA Cup Fourth Round replay at home to Aston Villa. A most frustrating season saw him make only one more full appearance, apart from coming off the bench four times and "Dons' " fans can only hope that he remains injury free in 1993-94.

| Clubs | Signing Date | Transfer Fee | APPEARANCES Lge | FL Cup | FA Cup | Others | GOALS Lge | FL Cup | FA Cup | Others |
|---|---|---|---|---|---|---|---|---|---|---|
| Wimbledon* | 7.88 | - | 51+15 | 2 | 7 | 1 | 1 | | | |
| Plymouth Argyle | 3.90 | Loan | 5+2 | | | | | | | |

## BLAKE Mark Anthony

Born: Nottingham, 16 December 1970

Height: 5'11"

Weight: 12.3

International Honours: E Sch, E Yth, E "U21"-8

**Position/Skill Factor:** Constructively skilful midfielder who is capable of beating opponents to create chances.

**Career History:** Joined Villa while still at school, signing associated forms in March 1986, before going on to become a trainee in July 1987. Made his FL debut for the club at Luton Town on 14 October 1989 and was called up for the England Under 21 squad in 1990 after only a handful of first team appearances. Enjoyed an extended run in the team from October 1991, following the departure of Gordon Cowans, to January 1992 and later deputised on two occasions for Dariusz Kubicki at right-back. Unfortunately injured in the early part of **1992-93,** with a hamstring problem, he made his one and only League appearance, when coming on for Garry Parker at Middlesbrough. Having to be extremely patient, he was again hit by injuries in December, which, this time, necessitated a three month lay-off following operations to his calf and knee. In between times he played quite well for Villa's reserve side in the Pontins League.

| Clubs | Signing Date | Transfer Fee | APPEARANCES Lge | FL Cup | FA Cup | Others | GOALS Lge | FL Cup | FA Cup | Others |
|---|---|---|---|---|---|---|---|---|---|---|
| Aston Villa* | 7.89 | - | 26+5 | 1+1 | 2 | 2 | 2 | | | |
| Wolverhampton W. | 1.91 | Loan | 2 | | | | | | | |

## BODEN Christopher (Chris) Desmond

Born: Wolverhampton, 13 October 1973

Height: 5'9" Weight: 11.0

**Position/Skill Factor:** Left-back with a very good left foot, he also has a great attitude to the game. Prepared to battle for possession.

**Career History:** He first came to Aston Villa as an associated schoolboy in February 1988, before graduating as a trainee on leaving school in July 1990 and becoming a professional at the end of 1991. Yet to receive a first team call-up, he performed most capably in **1992-93** as a regular member of Villa's reserve side and looks a promising player for the future.

| Clubs | Signing Date | Transfer Fee | APPEARANCES Lge | FL Cup | FA Cup | Others | GOALS Lge | FL Cup | FA Cup | Others |
|---|---|---|---|---|---|---|---|---|---|---|
| Aston Villa* | 12.91 | - | | | | | | | | |

# BODIN Paul John

Born: Cardiff, 13 September 1964

Height: 5'10" Weight: 10.11

International Honours: W Yth, W "U21" -1, W-19

**Position/Skill Factor:** Excellent attacking left-back with a terrific left foot, who loves to get forward to get his crosses over. Equally adept at dropping balls into the path of his front men.

**Career History:** One of the stars of the unheralded Swindon Town team that gained promotion to the Premier League, via the Play-Offs, scoring the winning goal, a penalty, in a magnificent 4-3 victory at Wembley, he had started his career as an associated schoolboy with Chelsea in January 1980. Not offered terms as an apprentice on leaving school two years later, he joined Newport County, but was freed during the 1982 close season, without making a first team appearance. He then joined his hometown club, Cardiff City, and immediately won a place in the side at left-back, making his FL debut on the opening day of the season on 28 August 1982 at home to Wrexham in a south versus north of Wales clash. After three seasons at Ninian Park, during which he was selected once for the Welsh under 21 team, he was released when Cardiff were relegated from the Second Division. In the absence of any offers from FL clubs, he joined Bath City of the then Gola League (new Vauxhall Conference) and stayed five and a half years at Twerton Park before, ironically, being offered a fresh start in League football by Fourth Division Newport County, the club which discarded him six years earlier. However, by this time the Gwent club were in their death throes, soon to fall out of the League and being subsequently wound up and after only two months he was sold on to Swindon Town, to help pay off their debts. At Swindon he was principally used as a midfield cover player, until the transfer of Phil King to Sheffield Wednesday in November 1989, when he took over the left-back slot and made it his own. At the end of the season, Swindon reached the Play-Offs and "qualified" for the First Division by defeating Sunderland in the Final, only for the Football League Management Committee to declare that Swindon were demoted to Division Three for financial irregularities committed three years earlier! On appeal, the FA commuted the penalty to Swindon retaining their existing status in Division Two, but Bodin, along with his Swindon team-mates, lost the chance of top flight football. But as a consolation prize, he received his first full international cap for Wales in a friendly with Costa Rica on 20 May 1990 and went on to become Wales' first choice left-back, displacing Norwich's Mark Bowen. Although 1990-91 was an anti-climax for Swindon, he was rewarded for his consistent displays by joining the elite, when Steve Coppell signed him for Crystal Palace in March 1991. Sadly, it was a short-lived elevation when, after only a handful of games for Palace, Coppell apparently decided that he did not fit in with the "Eagles'" abrasive style of play. He briefly re-united with his former Swindon manager, Ossie Ardiles, at Newcastle on loan, but as the latter lost his job soon afterwards, no permanent transfer was arranged. Instead, he moved back to Swindon, only ten months after he left, for a fee which was only 40% of that which Palace paid for him, a strange error of judgement by Coppell, who, it should be said in mitigation, earned millions of pounds for Palace with his signings from non-League football. Since returning, he has contributed much to Town's fortunes and also reclaimed his place in the Welsh national side. He came back into the side in January 1992 and played in the last 23 games of the season to get himself in trim for the **1992-93** assault on the Premier League. His 11 League goals, including four penalties, came largely during a period when the club's recognised strikers were experiencing a lean period and on no less than seven occasions, his strike proved to be the winning goal. It was very fitting, therefore, that he should score the vital penalty in the Play-Off Final against Leicester City at Wembley, a game that ended with Town achieving their goal to play in the top flight for the first time. Although now an established defender, he was only really converted to that role during his first spell at the County Ground, having previously played in midfield. Apart from promotion, his season culminated in him being voted the supporter's "Player of the Year" and coming third, behind Ryan Giggs and Mark Hughes, in a poll of Welsh footballers.

| | | | APPEARANCES | | | | GOALS | | | |
|---|---|---|---|---|---|---|---|---|---|---|
| Clubs | Signing Date | Transfer Fee | Lge | FL Cup | FA Cup | Others | Lge | FL Cup | FA Cup | Others |
| Newport County | 1.82 | - | | | | | | | | |
| Cardiff City | 8.82 | - | 68+7 | 11 | 4 | | 4 | | | |
| Bath City | 8.85 | - | | | | | | | | |
| Newport County | 1.88 | £15,000 | 6 | | | | 1 | | | |
| Swindon Town | 3.88 | £30,000 | 87+6 | 12 | 6 | 8 | 9 | | | 1 |
| Crystal Palace | 3.91 | £550,000 | 8+1 | 1 | | | | | | |
| Newcastle United | 12.91 | Loan | 6 | | | | | | | |
| Swindon Town* | 1.92 | £225,000 | 55+1 | 1 | 3 | 5 | 13 | | | 1 |

## BOLAND William (Willie) John

Born: Ennis, Ireland, 6 August 1975

Height: 5'8½" Weight: 10.9

**Position/Skill Factor:** Pacey right-winger with very good skills, who works hard up and down the touchline.

**Career History:** Another in the growing contingent of Irish youngsters signed by Coventry City in the past two years, he made his FL debut when he came on as a substitute in the penultimate game of the **1992-93** season against Chelsea at Stamford Bridge on 1 May 1993. After starting the season in the youth team he had graduated to the reserve side, but an attitude problem held him back for a while. Once he had changed that aspect of his personality he looked a totally different player. Has been compared to a young Ronnie Whelan and looks to have a bright future in the game.

| | | | APPEARANCES | | | | GOALS | | | |
|---|---|---|---|---|---|---|---|---|---|---|
| Clubs | Signing Date | Transfer Fee | Lge | FL Cup | FA Cup | Others | Lge | FL Cup | FA Cup | Others |
| Coventry City* | 11.92 | - | 0+1 | | | | | | | |

## BOOTY Martyn James

Born: Kirby Muxloe, 30 May 1971

Height: 5'10" Weight: 11.13

**Position/Skill Factor:** Adventurous full-back, who likes to get forward and link up with the attack. Reluctant to just clear his lines, he is always looking to pass and is very comfortable on the ball.

**Career History:** Signed professional forms for Coventry City during the 1989 close season, having been at the club as a trainee since July 1987. Made his first appearance at right-back in the League Cup, versus Arsenal when the "Sky Blues" surprisingly eliminated the "Gunners" from the competition, following up with his FL debut three days later at home to Chelsea on 2 November 1991. Also made two FA Cup appearances against Cambridge United, being carried off during the replay with cruciate ligament damage, following a heavy tackle by the United defender, Liam Daish. It took him a long time to recover and it wasn't until last October that he was back in action for the reserves in the Pontins Central League. He found **1992-93** heavy going and while achieving full fitness by the end of the season, he never once threatened to win his first team place back, mainly due to the consistency of Brian Borrows. Offered a one year contract, you can rest assured that he will give it all he's got this coming season.

| | | | APPEARANCES | | | | GOALS | | | |
|---|---|---|---|---|---|---|---|---|---|---|
| Clubs | Signing Date | Transfer Fee | Lge | FL Cup | FA Cup | Others | Lge | FL Cup | FA Cup | Others |
| Coventry City* | 5.89 | - | 2+1 | 1 | 2 | | | | | |

## BORROWS Brian

Born: Liverpool, 20 December 1960

Height: 5'10"

Weight: 10.12

International Honours: E"B"

**Position/Skill Factor:** Right-back with a good range of passing skills, both short and long. A very good player, he likes to get forward and is extremely comfortable on the ball.

**Career History:** Started his career with local club Everton where he was an associated schoolboy (October 1975) and an apprentice (July 1977), before turning pro. After nearly two years in the wings, he made his FL debut at Goodison Park against Stoke City on 13 February 1982. However, unable to establish a regular first team place, he was allowed to join Bolton Wanderers, who were then struggling at the foot of the Second Division. He was too good a player to remain in the Third Division for long and after just over two years at Burnden Park he signed for Coventry City in the 1985 close season. Immediately establishing himself in the number two shirt, he was unfortunate to lose the opportunity of a FA Cup winners medal in 1987, when an injury sustained in the last League game of the season ruled him out of the Final against Tottenham Hotspur. Has since had the consolation of being voted City's "Player of the Year" and has been a model of consistency since his arrival at Highfield Road. Remained first choice at right-back in 1991-92 and although officially on the transfer list at the beginning of **1992-93,** had another good season and only missed the first four games, due to a chest infection. Is now tenth in the club's all-time appearance charts and after patching up his differences with City and signing a new contract, he again proved to be the most effective player in the side, especially around the Christmas period. Unfortunately, after being appointed club captain in March, his form tailed off towards the end of the capaign and if he is to be in contention this coming season he will have to recapture some of his earlier successes.

| | | | APPEARANCES | | | | GOALS | | | |
|---|---|---|---|---|---|---|---|---|---|---|
| Clubs | Signing Date | Transfer Fee | Lge | FL Cup | FA Cup | Others | Lge | FL Cup | FA Cup | Others |
| Everton | 4.80 | - | 27 | 2 | | | | | | |
| Bolton Wanderers | 3.83 | £10,000 | 95 | 7 | 4 | 4 | | | | |
| Coventry City* | 6.85 | £80,000 | 297+4 | 33 | 17 | 10+1 | 11 | 1 | 1 | |

# BOSNICH Mark John

Born: Sydney, Australia, 13 January 1972

Height: 6'2"

Weight: 13.7

International Honours: Australian Int

**Position/Skill Factor:** Brave goalkeeper who is not afraid to come for crosses, not as a catcher, but as a puncher. Active between the posts at all times. Good left footed kicker.

**Career History:** Joined Manchester United as a 17-year-old non-contract player from the Australian side, Sydney Croatia and made three appearances in two years with the "Reds", keeping a clean sheet on his FL debut at home to Wimbledon on 30 April 1990. United were hoping to sign him on contract, but problems in obtaining a work permit forced him to return home to Australia in the summer of 1991. It was therefore something of a surprise and exasperation to Manchester United, when Aston Villa announced his signing, out of the blue, in February 1992; the work permit problem apparently resolved. Made his debut for Villa at Luton in April, but although impressing, he started **1992-93** in the reserves as Nigel Spink's number two. From October, however, he began to appear on the substitutes' bench, but apart from one game in December he didn't get another first team opportunity until February when Spink was unavailable for the FA Cup Fourth Round replay at Wimbledon. In a real test for the young 'keeper, the game was lost 6-5 on penalties. A regular for the rest of the season, on merit, he had an outstanding game in a 1-1 draw against his old club and Championship rivals, Manchester United, making save after save to deny them. Eventually, Villa faltered and had to be satisfied with the runners-up spot, but Bosnich could not be faulted and duly received the club's "Young Player of the Year" award.

| | | | APPEARANCES | | | | GOALS | | | |
|---|---|---|---|---|---|---|---|---|---|---|
| Clubs | Signing Date | Transfer Fee | Lge | FL Cup | FA Cup | Others | Lge | FL Cup | FA Cup | Others |
| Manchester United | 6.89 | - | 3 | | | | | | | |
| Sydney Croatia (Aust) | 8.91 | - | | | | | | | | |
| Aston Villa* | 2.92 | - | 18 | | 1 | | | | | |

# BOULD Stephen (Steve) Andrew

Born: Stoke, 16 November 1962

Height: 6'2" Weight: 11.13

**Position/Skill Factor:** Reliable centre-back, who is extremely good in the air and is always likely to pop up with important goals from set pieces. Not afraid to come out of defence with the ball looking to make a constructive pass.

**Career History:** Came to Stoke City at the age of 15, signing associated schoolboy forms in September 1978, before becoming an apprentice in June 1979. Made his FL debut at Middlesbrough on 26 September 1981 and had a spell on loan with Torquay United while still trying to establish himself with the "Potters". In his first four seasons, he played at right-back, but was converted to central defender with great success, after the departure of Paul Dyson to West Bromwich Albion. Followed former team mate Lee Dixon to Highbury in the Summer of 1988 and was prominent at the heart of Arsenal's defence in their League Championship winning sides of 1988-89 and 1990-91, being ever present in the latter. Surprisingly never considered for international honours, many judges feel he was a key element in Arsenal's impregnable defence of 1990-91, which equalled a Football League record of only 18 goals conceded in 38 games. This judgement appeared to be confirmed in the early months of 1991-92, when in his absence through injury, Arsenal had conceded 18 goals in only 12 games and were falling behind in the Championship race. However, his return in November failed to halt the slump and, perhaps not fully fit, he was rested again. His second comeback heralded a remarkable improvement in the "Gunners' " performances. Unbeaten in their last 16 games, winning ten and drawing six, scoring 41 goals to only 15 against, Arsenal re-established their credentials to be considered the strongest team in the country. Scored Arsenal's first ever Premier League goal against Norwich City in **1992-93,** but ultimately had a disappointing season. Captained the side a couple of times in mid-season, but unfortunately picked up an injury in January and being a traditionally slow healer he didn't return to first team duty until May, missing Arsenal's great triumphs in both the FA and League Cups.

| | | | APPEARANCES | | | | GOALS | | | |
|---|---|---|---|---|---|---|---|---|---|---|
| Clubs | Signing Date | Transfer Fee | Lge | FL Cup | FA Cup | Others | Lge | FL Cup | FA Cup | Others |
| Stoke City | 11.80 | - | 179+4 | 13 | 10 | 5 | 6 | 1 | | |
| Torquay United | 10.82 | Loan | 9 | | 2 | | | | | |
| Arsenal* | 6.88 | £390,000 | 131+5 | 14 | 13 | 1+1 | 4 | | | |

## BOUND Matthew Terence

Born: Melksham, 9 November 1972

Height: 6'2" Weight: 14.0

**Position/Skill Factor:** Centre-back with a great attitude. Attacks the ball both on the ground and in the air. Also a good left footed passer long into the channels.

**Career History:** First came to Southampton as an associated schoolboy in November 1986, before progressing through the club as a trainee (July 1989) to become a full-time professional during the 1991 close season. Following several impressive reserve displays, he stepped up to make his FL debut as a substitute in the last home game of the season against Oldham Athletic on 25 April 1992. As the mainstay of the reserve side in **1992-93,** he regularly caught the eye with assured displays, but with Ken Monkou firmly settled in at the club, first team opportunities were slow in coming. However, with four experienced central defenders ahead of him at the time, his confidence was bolstered when signing a new two and a half year contract just before Christmas. After being on the bench for seven of the previous ten first team matches, making two substitute appearances, he was given his full League debut in the last home game of the season against Manchester City, before giving way to another youngster, Derek Allan, with eight minutes remaining.

| | | | APPEARANCES | | | | GOALS | | | |
|---|---|---|---|---|---|---|---|---|---|---|
| Clubs | Signing Date | Transfer Fee | Lge | FL Cup | FA Cup | Others | Lge | FL Cup | FA Cup | Others |
| Southampton* | 5.91 | - | 1+3 | | | | | | | |

## BOWEN Mark Rosslyn

Born: Neath, 7 December 1963

Height: 5'8" Weight: 11.6

International Honours: W Sch, W Yth, W "U21"-3, FL Rep, W-24

**Position/Skill Factor:** A reliable left-back who favours his right foot. Very dangerous when going forward, especially in playing the ball up front and getting the return of pass within shooting range.

**Career History:** Came to Tottenham Hotspur while still at school, signing associated schoolboy forms in October 1978 and becoming an apprentice in June 1980. After turning professional he made his FL debut at home to Coventry City on 29 August 1983. However, during his time at White Hart Lane, he could never quite lay claim to a regular place in the side, due to a surfeit of established stars always being available and in the summer of 1987 he signed for Norwich City. Had a short run on the left side of midfield, before making his mark at left-back from where he made a huge contribution to the side during 1988-89, when City topped the First Division for most of the early part of the season, eventually finishing fourth. Likes to get forward and the following season he actually finished as the club's joint leading League goalscorer with seven to his credit. Won his first international cap for Wales in 1986 and has been a regular Welsh squad member since joining Norwich, although until 1991 most of his games were as substitute. He remained first choice left-back in 1991-92, until February, when he surprisingly lost his place to Colin Woodthorpe. He was restored to the team later in the season in a variety of positions and took part in the FA Cup Semi-Final versus Sunderland when the "Canaries" missed a golden opportunity to reach their first ever Final. The only ever present in **1992-93,** playing in all 47 senior matches and scoring once from the spot. A disappointing tally, considering that he was joint top scorer in 1989-90. A worrying factor, though, is that he is the club's second highest scorer amongst the current staff. He even missed a penalty at Anfield with the score at 0-0 and promptly lost the job as Liverpool went on the rampage in a 4-1 win. Has hardly missed a game during the last five seasons and has now made over 250 first team appearances for Norwich, placing him 18th in the all-time list. The Bowen/Culverhouse partnership continues to defy all comers as the "Canaries" finished third in the new Premier League, their highest ever placing.

| | | | APPEARANCES | | | | GOALS | | | |
|---|---|---|---|---|---|---|---|---|---|---|
| Clubs | Signing Date | Transfer Fee | Lge | FL Cup | FA Cup | Others | Lge | FL Cup | FA Cup | Others |
| Tottenham Hotspur | 12.81 | - | 14+3 | | 3 | 0+1 | 2 | | | |
| Norwich City* | 7.87 | £90,000 | 210+2 | 19 | 22 | 11 | 16 | 1 | 1 | |

## BOWMAN Robert

Born: Durham City, 6 August 1975

Height: 6'0½"

Weight: 11.3

International Honours: E Yth

**Position/Skill Factor:** Full-back who can also play in central defence. A very good passer with excellent control, he loves to break forward..

**Career History:** Although he first joined Leeds as an associated schoolboy in January 1990, it was not until August 1992 that he was upgraded to trainee status and developed quickly to be offered a professional contract three months later. Within a further three month period, he was called up to the **1992-93** first team squad, making his PL debut, as a substitute, away to Wimbledon on 6 February 1993 and two days later his first full appearance in the problem right-back slot at home to League leaders, Manchester United. He did well to hold his own against the mercurial Lee Sharpe as struggling Leeds held out for a 0-0 draw. His competent performances were all the more pleasing as he filled a position he had never previously occupied. Predominantly a central defender for the youth and reserve sides, but never a right-back, he was the first member of Leeds' successful FA Youth Cup side to break into the first team and should have a big future in the game.

| | | | APPEARANCES | | | | GOALS | | | |
|---|---|---|---|---|---|---|---|---|---|---|
| Clubs | Signing Date | Transfer Fee | Lge | FL Cup | FA Cup | Others | Lge | FL Cup | FA Cup | Others |
| Leeds United* | 11.92 | - | 3+1 | | | | | | | |

## BOZINOWSKI Vlado

Born: Macedonia, Yugoslavia, 30 March 1964

Height: 5'10"

Weight: 11.3

International Honours: Australian Int

**Position/Skill Factor:** Midfield player with great touch and vision, he picks his team-mates out with a whole range of passes.

**Career History:** Yugoslavian born midfielder recommended to Ipswich Town by former Ipswich and England manager, Bobby Robson, now manager of Portuguese club, Sporting Lisbon, along with Bulgarian, Bontcho Guentchev. In fact, Bozinowski was not a regular performer for the Lisbon club, making only 11 appearances (seven as substitute) in 1990-91 and spending 1991-92 on loan to SC Beira Mar, where he made 23 appearances. He made his debut as substitute away to Coventry City on 5 December 1992, but was unable to break into the first team on a regular basis, although a regular resident on the substitutes bench in **1992-93.** May have a future at Portman Road once he settles into the pace of the English game.

| | | | APPEARANCES | | | | GOALS | | | |
|---|---|---|---|---|---|---|---|---|---|---|
| Clubs | Signing Date | Transfer Fee | Lge | FL Cup | FA Cup | Others | Lge | FL Cup | FA Cup | Others |
| Ipswich Town* | 12.92 | £100,000 | 3+6 | 1+1 | 0+1 | | | | | |

## BRACE Deryn Paul John

Born: Haverfordwest, 15 March 1975

Height: 5'7" Weight: 10.5

International Honours: W Yth

**Position/Skill Factor:** An aggressive left-back who loves a tackle and is hard to beat, with excellent recuperative powers

**Career History:** Spotted by a Norwich City scout when playing as a 12-year-old for Tenby United, on leaving school, he came to Carrow Road as a trainee in July 1991 and made good progress to reach the professional ranks during the 1993 close season. Has already shown great determination to succeed this far, in recovering from two avulsion fractures to leg and hip when a schoolboy. A first class competitor, he has the potential to become a fine player and has already made 12 appearances for City reserves in **1992-93.**

| | | | APPEARANCES | | | | GOALS | | | |
|---|---|---|---|---|---|---|---|---|---|---|
| Clubs | Signing Date | Transfer Fee | Lge | FL Cup | FA Cup | Others | Lge | FL Cup | FA Cup | Others |
| Norwich City* | 7.93 | - | | | | | | | | |

## BRACEWELL Paul William

Born: Heswall, 19 July 1962

Height: 5'8" Weight: 10.9

International Honours: E "U21"-13, E-3

**Position/Skill Factor:** Experienced, competitive midfielder, who has a little bit of everything. With two good feet and great vision, he can pass accurately, both short and long.

**Career History:** A player who was later destined to win some of the games' major honours, he started out as an apprentice at Stoke City in September 1978, before signing professional forms some 15 months later and making his FL debut as a substitute at Wolverhampton Wanderers on 22 March 1980. In 1980-81, he won a regular place in Stoke's line-up at the age of 18 and was absent in only three FL matches over the next three seasons. Called up to the England Under 21 squad in 1982-83, he became a regular selection for the next two years. However, at the end of his contract he elected to join Sunderland in the summer of 1983, but after only one year at Roker Park he was signed by Howard Kendall for Everton, thus returning to his native Merseyside. His first season at Goodison Park was probably the zenith of his career, as he orchestrated Everton's first League Championship for 15 years, played in the 1985 FA Cup Final (only to lose in extra-time to Manchester United) and won the first of his three England caps, whilst on a summer tour in North America. He came on as substitute against West Germany in Mexico June, 1985 and followed a few days later with a full game against the USA in Los Angeles. Equally outstanding in 1985-86, his season ended in heartache, as Everton found the "double" snatched from their grasp by deadly rivals, Liverpool, who first took the League Championship with an incredible late surge as the "Toffees" stumbled and also the 1986 FA

Cup Final with a second half "turnaround" to win 3-1. Even more tragically for Bracewell, he was struck down by a serious injury at the height of his career and did not play first team football again for two and a half years, only returning in December 1988. Although he played for the remainder of the season, including the 1989 FA Cup Final, where he received a loser's medal for the third time, as his team once again succumbed to Liverpool, he was a shadow of his former self and in the summer he was allowed to leave and returned to Sunderland. In his first season back at Roker Park, he assisted the "Rokerites" to a fortuitous and undeserved promotion after the team finished sixth and lost the Play-Off Final to Swindon Town, only for the Football League to award them promotion when Swindon were penalised for financial irregularities, committed three years earlier. Unsurprisingly, the team which had not "earned" promotion was unable to compete in the top flight and slid back to Division Two one year later. In 1991-92, the team, although barely escaping a second consecutive relagation, remarkably reached the FA Cup Final with victories over three First Division opponents, West Ham United, Chelsea and Norwich City. Thus, the unlucky Bracewell played in his fourth FA Cup Final and finished with a losers medal for the fourth time, as his team bowed to seemingly inevitable defeat against Liverpool. His transfer to Newcastle United during the summer caused quite a stir, especially among the rival fans, but he certainly got off to a good start with a superb goal from 25 yards to open "Magpies'" **1992-93** account in a 3-2 home win over Southend United. After that, however, things turned sour, with a succession of injuries to ankle and toe, which caused him to miss a large part of the season. In fact, he didn't get a proper run in the side until the beginning of March, when he played in 13 of the last 14 games. But that was good enough for him to win a First Division Championship medal, as United collected the title, having led almost from start to finish. Manager, Kevin Keegan, has gone on record to say that Paul is the bravest player he has ever seen. Recently, he had an operation to correct the damaged toe and looks forward with optimism to playing in the Premier League.

| | | | APPEARANCES | | | | GOALS | | | |
|---|---|---|---|---|---|---|---|---|---|---|
| Clubs | Signing Date | Transfer Fee | Lge | FL Cup | FA Cup | Others | Lge | FL Cup | FA Cup | Others |
| Stoke City | 2.80 | - | 123+6 | 6 | 6 | | 5 | | 1 | |
| Sunderland | 7.83 | £250,000 | 38 | 4 | 2 | | 4 | | | |
| Everton | 5.84 | £425,000 | 95 | 11 | 19+2 | 17+2 | 7 | 2 | | 1 |
| Sunderland | 8.89 | £250,000 | 112+1 | 9 | 10 | 6 | 2 | | | |
| Newcastle United* | 6.92 | £250,000 | 19+6 | | 2+2 | 2 | 2 | | | |

## BRADSHAW Carl

Born: Sheffield,
2 October 1968

Height: 6'0"

Weight: 11.0

International Honours:
E Yth

**Position/Skill Factor:** Quick, darting right-winger, cum striker, who uses his pace to unsettle defenders. Roams across the front line with great enthusiasm, often creating chances for others.

**Career History:** Brother of Darren who has played for Chesterfield, York City, Newcastle United and Peterborough United and Sheffield born and bred, he started as an associated schoolboy with Sheffield Wednesday in March 1983, graduating to apprentice status in April 1985, before turning pro just before his 18th birthday. Made his FL debut the same month whilst on loan to Barnsley at home to Crystal Palace on 23 August 1986 and despite scoring, the "Tykes" lost 3-2. Played his first game for Wednesday later that year and scored in a 2-2 draw at Queens Park Rangers. Being very much in the shadow of Carl Shutt, his first team chances were limited and at the beginning of the 1988-89 season he moved to Manchester City in exchange for Imre Varadi. Only played one full match while at Maine Road, before returning to Sheffield one year later and signing for United. Settled down immediately, helping the club gain promotion to the First Division as runners-up in his first season. Proved a willing partner for Brian Deane, in the absence of Tony Agana, but his scoring record is unimpressive for a forward, although in fairness it must be noted that most of his appearances for United have been on the flanks rather than in the middle. In and out of the team during 1991-92, he spent most of **1992-93** playing wide on the right and only managed to score his first goal in the penultimate game of the season. Due to the injury crisis surrounding Bramall Lane at the end of last year he was called upon to try his hand at full-back and succeeded at being sent off first time out in the position against Coventry City, for exhuberant tackling. Came back strongly after the signing of Franz Carr and played the final eight games of the season in the number seven shirt.

| | | | APPEARANCES | | | | GOALS | | | |
|---|---|---|---|---|---|---|---|---|---|---|
| Clubs | Signing Date | Transfer Fee | Lge | FL Cup | FA Cup | Others | Lge | FL Cup | FA Cup | Others |
| Sheffield Wednesday | 8.86 | - | 16+16 | 2+2 | 6+1 | 1 | 4 | | 3 | |
| Barnsley | 8.86 | Loan | 6 | | | | 1 | | | |
| Manchester City | 9.88 | £50,000 | 1+4 | | 0+1 | 0+1 | | | | |
| Sheffield United* | 9.89 | £50,000 | 83+24 | 8+1 | 11+1 | 4 | 6 | 2 | 3 | |

## BREACKER Timothy (Tim) Sean

Born: Bicester,
2 July 1965

Height: 6'0"

Weight: 12.6

International Honours:
E "U21" -2

**Position/Skill Factor:** Right-back, who makes very important interceptions and last ditch tackles. A lovely striker of the ball, with good feet, he also excels on forward runs, but can recover well if required.

**Career History:** After joining Luton Town as an apprentice on leaving school in July 1981, he progressed to the club's professional ranks during the 1983 close season and received an early first team opportunity in midfield, making his FL debut at Ipswitch Town on 31 March 1984. In 1984-85, after starting the season in midfield, he replaced Mitchell Thomas as substitute right-back in one game in October and so impressed manager, David Pleat, that he retained the position for the remainder of the season and indeed, for the rest of his career at Kenilworth Road. The mid 1980s were the zenith of Luton's history in the football League and he shared in their triumphs of reaching the FA Cup Semi-Finals in 1985 and 1988, the Quarter-Final of 1986 and winning their first ever trophy, the League Cup, in 1988, when the "Hatters" thrillingly defeated Arsenal 3-2 with virtually the last kick of the game. In 1985-86 he was also selected twice for the England Under 21 team, but that was the limit of his international career. He lost his place, temporarily, to Rob Johnson in 1988-89, but returned for the second half of the season and was ever present in 1989-90. However, Luton were finding it difficult to compete at the highest level in front of attendances of 10,000 or less (a self-inflicted handicap due to their ban on away supporters and reduced ground capacity) and when the income from cup runs dried up, they were forced to accept all offers for their best players. In October 1990, he moved to West Ham United for a handsome fee and assisted the "Hammers" to promotion by the end of the season. Sadly, their return to the top level was short lived, as they slid back the following season, with Breacker sharing the right-back slot with Kenny Brown and also turning out on occasions in central defence. Continuing his roller coaster ride at Upton Park in **1992-93**, his third season with the "Hammers", he was one of the mainstays of a defence that was sound enough to keep 17 clean sheets in a tough campaign, which ultimately saw the club promoted to the Premier League as runners-up to Newcastle United. Apart from a hernia operaiton, which forced him to miss seven games, he was ever present in the right-back slot and never looked likely to give way. His high spot of an excellent season for both club and player – excluding promotion – was in scoring against his old club, Luton, albeit with a sizzling daisy cutter in a 2-2 draw at Upton Park.

| | | | APPEARANCES | | | | GOALS | | | |
|---|---|---|---|---|---|---|---|---|---|---|
| Clubs | Signing Date | Transfer Fee | Lge | FL Cup | FA Cup | Others | Lge | FL Cup | FA Cup | Others |
| Luton Town | 5.83 | - | 204+6 | 22+2 | 21 | 7 | 3 | | | |
| West Ham United* | 10.90 | £600,000 | 95+2 | 6 | 14 | 7 | 5 | | | |

## BREITKREUTZ Matthias

Born: Berlin, Germany, 12 May 1971

Height: 5'9" Weight: 11.3

**Position/Skill Factor:** Highly skilled midfield player with great vision who makes telling early passes. Very dangerous around the box with bending free kicks..

**Career History:** Signed from Bergmann Borsig, a former East German club based in Berlin, along with Stefan Beinlich for a combined fee of £200,000. Made faster progress than his colleague, being selected for several games at the end of the season, after making his FL debut as a substitute at Villa Park against Sheffield Wednesday on 18 January 1992. Struggled to make an impact in **1992-93,** playing only four (two substitute) first team games, although a regular in the reserve side. A player to watch out for, at present he is still coming to terms with the English game.

| | | | APPEARANCES | | | | GOALS | | | |
|---|---|---|---|---|---|---|---|---|---|---|
| Clubs | Signing Date | Transfer Fee | Lge | FL Cup | FA Cup | Others | Lge | FL Cup | FA Cup | Others |
| Aston Villa* | 11.91 | £100,000 | 9+2 | 0+1 | | | | | | |

## BRENNAN Mark Robert

Born: Rossendale, 4 October 1965

Height: 5'9"

Weight: 11.1

International Honours: E Yth, E "U21"-5

**Position/Skill Factor:** Very skillful midfielder with a lovely left foot and good vision, who provides chances for others.

**Career History:** Although Lancashire born, he was an associated schoolboy (June 1982) and an apprentice (July 1982) with Ipswich Town, before turning pro with the Suffolk club and making his FL debut at home to Arsenal on 12 November 1983. Won a regular midfield place by the end of the season and became a fixture at Portman Road over the next four years. Was transferred to Middlesbrough in the 1988 close season and settled well on Teeside, but after two seasons, which saw the club continually struggling in the lower reaches of the Second Division, he moved on to Manchester City. Found it difficult to win a regular place in City's midfield and endured another disappointing season at Maine Road in 1991-92, after being in the starting line-up for the first eight games of the season. Reportedly on trial with French First Division club Metz in March 1992, but was soon back in the City team near the end of the season. After failing to make a start in **1992-93** with City, he was transferred to Oldham Athletic, joining up with his old team-mates, Neil Pointon and Steve Redmond, who had made the journey some three and a half months earlier. Having a fine left foot, he was thought to be the ideal replacement for Holden, but after a good opening spell of eight games he twisted an ankle in the FA Cup replay at Tranmere Rovers and was forced to miss three matches. Two games into his second spell he scored a most unusual goal after Chelsea's Kevin Hitchcock came to the edge of the penalty area to clear a poor back pass and only succeeded in hacking the ball as far as the halfway line. With the ball dropping at Brennan's feet and knowing the 'keeper was "miles" off his line, he lifted a shot over him from fully 60 yards for the third goal in a 3-1 home victory. Substituted with torn ligaments at home to Queens Park Rangers, coupled with loss of form, saw his season come to an end.

| | | | APPEARANCES | | | | GOALS | | | |
|---|---|---|---|---|---|---|---|---|---|---|
| Clubs | Signing Date | Transfer Fee | Lge | FL Cup | FA Cup | Others | Lge | FL Cup | FA Cup | Others |
| Ipswich Town | 4.83 | - | 165+3 | 21+1 | 12 | 11 | 19 | 2 | 3 | 1 |
| Middlesbrough | 7.88 | £375,000 | 61+4 | 6 | 4 | 8 | 6 | | | 1 |
| Manchester City | 7.90 | £500,000 | 25+4 | 4 | 1 | 2 | 6 | 1 | | |
| Oldham Athletic* | 11.92 | £200,000 | 14 | 1 | 2 | | 3 | | | |

## **BREVETT Rufus** Emanuel

Born: Derby, 24 September 1969

Height: 5'8"

Weight: 11.0

**Position/Skill Factor:** Strong left footed full-back who is quick into the tackle and defends well. However, when the occasion demands, he can play an overlapping role ending with a telling cross into the penalty area.

**Career History:** After being released as a junior by his home town club, he joined Doncaster Rovers as an associated schoolboy (July 1987) and a month later he signed trainee forms. Almost immediately made his FL debut at home to Sunderland on 29 August 1987 and appeared a further 15 times that season, before the club were relegated to the Fourth Division. Played an important part in Rovers' outstanding youth team of 1987-88, which amazingly reached the FA Youth Cup Final, knocking out Manchester City, Sheffield Wednesday and "Spurs", before capitulating to Arsenal. After joining the professional ranks he soon earned a regular slot at left back, missing only eight League games from a possible 96, before his transfer to Queens Park Rangers in February 1991. When Kenny Sansom moved to Coventry City, he was given his chance in the side immediately and played in the last 10 games of the season. Although signed by Don Howe as Kenny Sansom's replacement, he apparently did not impress new manager Gerry Francis and lost his place to Clive Wilson soon into the 1991-92 season, languishing in the reserves thereafter. Too good a player to remain in the reserves, he finally got a run in **1992-93** when the excellent Clive Wilson was pushed up into midfield. Had deputised for Wilson earlier in the season and jumped at the opportunity of further games, starting in 14 out of a possible 16 and impressing many good judges with his classy play. Would be a regular in many other sides, but will probably have to be content with the occasional game in the Premier League.

| | | | APPEARANCES | | | | GOALS | | | |
|---|---|---|---|---|---|---|---|---|---|---|
| Clubs | Signing Date | Transfer Fee | Lge | FL Cup | FA Cup | Others | Lge | FL Cup | FA Cup | Others |
| Doncaster Rovers | 7.88 | - | 106+3 | 5 | 4 | 10+1 | 3 | | | |
| Q.P.R.* | 2.91 | £250,000 | 30+2 | 2 | 1 | | | | | |

## **BRIGHT Mark** Abraham

Born: Stoke, 6 June 1962

Height: 6'0" Weight: 11.0

**Position/Skill Factor:** Unselfish striker who plays for his team. Very fast with wonderful touch, he controls the ball with all parts of his body, head, chest, thighs and feet and is a good finisher.

**Career History:** Signed by Port Vale from near neighbours Leek Town of the former Cheshire League, he made his FL debut at home to York City on 1 May 1982 in a 0-0 draw. Although he failed to command a regular place at Vale Park, he did enough to impress Leicester City manager Gordon Milne and moved to Filbert Street, following Port Vale's relegation to Division Four in 1984. However, at Leicester, Mark was very much in the shadows of Alan Smith and Gary Lineker and after only two seasons he was signed by Steve Coppell, the Crystal Palace manager. It proved to be a bargain signing as he formed a lethal striking partnership with Ian Wright, which assisted the club's return to the First Division in 1989 and even more remarkably to the 1990 FA Cup Final when Palace succumbed narrowly in a replay to Manchester United, after a thrilling 3-3 draw in the first game. His partnership with Wright lasted almost five years and only ended when the latter was transferred to Arsenal in September 1991. Although the club had still to find an effective replacement for Wright, Bright remained one of Palace's most consistent performers in 1991-92 in a rather disappointing season, playing in every game (54 in all competitions) and finishing leading scorer for the third time with 16 FL goals, plus four in cup games. After a lot of close season transfer talk, he lined up for Palace in the opening game of **1992-93** against Blackburn Rovers and scored the club's first Premier League goal in a 3-3 draw. However, after just four more appearances, he was transferred to Sheffield Wednesday in exchange for Paul Williams, plus cash and immediately settled in at Hillsborough to become "Owls' " leading scorer. His longest spell out of the side came after Christmas when he missed six games due to an injured knee and just as a point of interest, Wednesday completed six victories in his absence. Played in both the League Cup and FA Cup Finals against Arsenal, but showed disappointing form as Wednesday lost out on each occasion.

| | | | APPEARANCES | | | | GOALS | | | |
|---|---|---|---|---|---|---|---|---|---|---|
| Clubs | Signing Date | Transfer Fee | Lge | FL Cup | FA Cup | Others | Lge | FL Cup | FA Cup | Others |
| Port Vale | 10.81 | - | 18+11 | 1+1 | 0+1 | 2 | 10 | | 1 | |
| Leicester City | 7.84 | £33,000 | 26+16 | 3+1 | 1 | | 6 | | | |
| Crystal Palace | 11.86 | £75,000 | 224+3 | 22 | 13+1 | 23 | 90 | 11 | 2 | 9 |
| Sheffield Wednesday* | 9.92 | £1,375,000 | 28+2 | 7 | 7 | | 11 | 6 | 3 | |

## BRIGHTWELL David John

Born: Lutterworth, 7 January 1971

Height: 6'2"

Weight: 12.7

**Position/Skill Factor:** Midfield player who can also play in the centre of the defence. Very good in the air and quick on the ground, he needs to build up his strength for the rigours of First Division football.

**Career History:** The son of the famous 1964 British Olympic track medalists, Ann Packer and Robbie Brightwell and younger brother of Ian, also at Manchester City, he signed professional forms for the club, immediately after finishing his school education. Later he was loaned out to Third Division Chester City in order to gain experience and made his FL debut at home to Cambridge United on 25 March 1991. After waiting nearly four years for his City FL debut, he finally made the breakthrough with a substitute's appearance at Wimbledon on 22 February 1992, followed by his full debut at home to Aston Villa, the week after, replacing Steve Redmond. It seemed that he might keep his place, but was then sidelined in favour of Dutch trialist, Michel Vonk. After a consistent run of 13 games in the reserve side in **1992-93** he was brought forward to the substitute's bench where, with his added height, he could be used either in central defence or as an alternative, support the forwards with equal confidence. Came on twice for his brother, Ian, during the season, but was hampered by an injured right knee received in the game at Arsenal, after playing three first team games in a row. Should improve steadily and challenge for a first team place before too long.

| | | | APPEARANCES | | | | GOALS | | | |
|---|---|---|---|---|---|---|---|---|---|---|
| Clubs | Signing Date | Transfer Fee | Lge | FL Cup | FA Cup | Others | Lge | FL Cup | FA Cup | Others |
| Manchester City* | 4.88 | - | 7+5 | | 1+1 | | | | | |
| Chester City | 3.91 | Loan | 6 | | | | | | | |

## BRIGHTWELL Ian Robert

Born: Lutterworth, 9 April 1968

Height: 5'10" Weight: 11.7

International Honours: E Sch, E Yth, E "U21"-4

**Position/Skill Factor:** Midfielder, who often plays at full-back and is a very useful man to have in your team. Has great stamina.

**Career History:** Son of the famous Olympic athletes, Ann Packer and Robbie Brightwell, Ian has a younger brother David, who is also at Maine Road. Came up through the Manchester City junior ranks as an associated schoolboy (September 1982) and won a FA Youth Cup winners medal before making his FL debut at home to Wimbledon on 23 August 1986. One of a batch of potentially brilliant youngsters who broke into City's first team almost simultaneously during 1987-88, the others being Andy Hinchcliffe, Paul Lake, Steve Redmond, Ian Scott and David White. Initially a midfielder, he was surprisingly discarded midway through the successful 1988-89 promotion campaign, in favour of new signing Gary Megson. In 1989-90, he was an occasional performer in midfield, appearing as substitute as often as first choice, but was given a new role in 1990-91 at right-back, at least until the arrival of Andy Hill from Bury. An infrequent scorer, his equalising goal - a rasping 35 yard drive - against United in the Manchester "derby" game in February 1990 will long remain part of City folklore. Although he re-established himself in midfield in 1991-92, he seemed to be regarded as a utility player, switching to full-back every time Hill or Pointon was unavailable. With Andy Hill moving into midfield, he looked to have found his best position in the side, after settling down at right-back in **1992-93**. Scored just the one goal, but it was a beauty from the edge of the box at home to Leeds United and with added confidence these days, he enjoys nothing better than running at the opposition's defence. Received a bad knee injury during the Third Round FA Cup-tie at home to Reading, which turned out to be quite serious and brought his season to a halt. Although back in training in March, he was not expected to be fully fit until the start of the new season.

| | | | APPEARANCES | | | | GOALS | | | |
|---|---|---|---|---|---|---|---|---|---|---|
| Clubs | Signing Date | Transfer Fee | Lge | FL Cup | FA Cup | Others | Lge | FL Cup | FA Cup | Others |
| Manchester City* | 5.86 | - | 169+28 | 19+2 | 9+4 | 4+3 | 16 | | 1 | |

## BROCK Kevin Stanley

Born: Bicester, 9 September 1962

Height: 5'9"

Weight: 10.12

International Honours: E Sch, E "U21"-4

**Position/Skill Factor:** Midfield player with a good brain and a lovely feel for the ball. Has a great delivery at corners and free-kicks. Tell him where you want it and he will provide it.

**Career History:** Already an England schoolboy international, he signed associated schoolboy forms for Oxford United in May 1978, becoming an apprentice in May 1979. Having had the experience of regular football in the football combination side the previous season, he made his FL debut as a substitute against Barnsley on 3 September 1979. He won a regular place in midfield the following season and was a nearly automatic choice for seven years.

In the early 1980s, Oxford were a "run of the mill" Third Division team, but following the takeover of the club by millionaire publisher, Robert Maxwell and the astute management of Jim Smith, the team embarked on a three year run of success, probably without parallel for a small unfashionable club. With players of the calibre of John Aldridge and Ray Houghton, in addition to Brock himself, Oxford were Third Division Champions in 1983-84 and even more remarkably, followed up with the Second Division Championship in 1984-85 and won the League Cup in 1986, defeating a more experienced Queens Park Rangers' team, 3-0. In the summer of 1987, he followed his former mentor Jim Smith to Queens Park Rangers, but never really established himself at Loftus Road. Soon after Smith had departed to take over Newcastle United, he signed Brock once again for his new team, but neither player, nor manager, could do much to arrest the "Magpies'" slide out of Division One. In 1989-90, the team almost regained their premier status, but lost heartbreakingly to Sunderland in the Play-Offs, after finishing third in Division Two, with Brock playing in all but two games. He remained a regular selection for the next two seasons, under new manager Ossie Ardiles, but with the team in a state of transition they were disappointing times for the Geordie fans. In most other sides he would have been an automatic selection, but found his opportunities restricted in **1992-93**, due to the strength of the squad. Made very few appearances, not enough even to warrant a First Division Championship medal, in a season that saw United win the title. However, he had a remarkable experience at Birmingham City. With United leading 3-2 at half-time and goalkeeper Tommy Wright unable to continue, due to injury, Kevin took over his duties and somehow managed to preserve the lead. It was all the more remarkable when it was later discovered he had spent most of the period suffering from concussion, after being kicked in the head. Now on the transfer list, it could be that he will start the new season with another club.

| | | | APPEARANCES | | | | GOALS | | | |
|---|---|---|---|---|---|---|---|---|---|---|
| Clubs | Signing Date | Transfer Fee | Lge | FL Cup | FA Cup | Others | Lge | FL Cup | FA Cup | Others |
| Oxford United | 9.79 | - | 229+17 | 30+2 | 17+1 | 3 | 26 | 5 | 1 | |
| Q.P.R. | 8.87 | £260,000 | 38+2 | 6 | 4 | 1 | 2 | | 1 | |
| Newcastle United* | 12.88 | £300,000 | 135+10 | 7 | 11 | 9+1 | 8 | | | 2 |

## BROCKLEHURST David

Born: Chesterfield, 7 March 1974

Height: 5'10" Weight: 11.0

International Honours: E Sch

**Position/Skill Factor:** Striker, or wide player, who can play on either side. Deceptive, with good control and a smart change of pace, he has the ability to take defenders on and to score goals.

**Career History:** Signed professional forms for Sheffield United during the summer of 1992, having previously been at Bramall Lane as an associated schoolboy (April 1988) and as a trainee (July 1990). Still awaiting a call-up to the first team squad, he spent **1992-93** playing in the "Blades' " reserve side.

| | | | APPEARANCES | | | | GOALS | | | |
|---|---|---|---|---|---|---|---|---|---|---|
| Clubs | Signing Date | Transfer Fee | Lge | FL Cup | FA Cup | Others | Lge | FL Cup | FA Cup | Others |
| Sheffield United* | 6.92 | - | | | | | | | | |

## BROWN Karl David

Born: Bury, 7 February 1975

Height: 5'5" Weight: 9.9

**Position/Skill Factor:** Midfielder who can also fill in at full-back. A tenacious little battler, he will fight for every ball.

**Career History:** First came to Manchester United as an associated schoolboy (June 1989), before graduating through the youth team as a trainee (July 1991) to the professional ranks. A member of United's FA Youth Cup runners-up squad in **1992-93**, he spent most of the season troubled by long term injury and will be given every chance this coming term.

| | | | APPEARANCES | | | | GOALS | | | |
|---|---|---|---|---|---|---|---|---|---|---|
| Clubs | Signing Date | Transfer Fee | Lge | FL Cup | FA Cup | Others | Lge | FL Cup | FA Cup | Others |
| Manchester United* | 7.93 | - | | | | | | | | |

## BROWN Kenneth (Kenny) James

Born: Upminster, 11 July 1967

Height: 5'8"

Weight: 11.6

**Position/Skill Factor:** Very experienced full-back who is comfortable on either flank. A good passer of the ball, he intercepts well and likes to get forward in order to join in.

**Career History:** The son of Ken, the former West Ham United and England centre-half and Norwich City manager, 1980-87, he signed professional forms for the "Canaries" during the 1985 close season, having previously been on the club's books as a junior. Made his FL debut for Norwich City, substituting for Wayne Biggins at home to Oxford United on 29 November 1986 and by the end of the season was a regular in the right-back position, playing in the last 17 League matches. However, he failed to make the progress expected of him and was allowed to leave at the end of the following season to re-unite with his father, then manager of Plymouth Argyle. Although Ken senior left Home Park in 1990, he remained first choice right-back for the "Pilgrims" for three years, missing only a handful of games during that period. At the end of his contract with Plymouth he looked for a return to his native city and joined West Ham United in August 1991, on loan for two months, before a transfer was arranged, the fee being set by the Transfer Tribunal. Despite the "Hammers'" relegation, he enjoyed a reasonable first season at Upton Park, playing in a variety of strange shirt numbers, but nearly always in defence. He scored with a stunning 30 yard drive in his fourth match against Aston Villa and later in the season struck the only goal in a defeat of Manchester United, which effectively ended their Championship aspirations. It was not a goal that required much effort – Gary Pallister's clearance hitting him on the boot and rebounding into the net! As an excellent stand in for both Tim Breaker and Julian Dicks, while only playing 19 (including four as substitute) games, he proved the ideal clubman for "Hammers" in **1992-93**. Not noted as a goalscorer, he notched two very important ones, the first in a 2-1 win at Birmingham City and the "killer" third, his first touch after coming on as a substitute, in a 3-1 victory at Swindon Town in the penultimate game of the season. The defeat of Swindon, effectively put West Ham in the Premier League as runners-up to Newcastle United, with Portsmouth, who shared the same number of points, pipped on goal difference. He can now look forward to playing in the top flight again after a break of five years.

| | | | APPEARANCES | | | | GOALS | | | |
|---|---|---|---|---|---|---|---|---|---|---|
| Clubs | Signing Date | Transfer Fee | Lge | FL Cup | FA Cup | Others | Lge | FL Cup | FA Cup | Others |
| Norwich City | 7.85 | - | 24+1 | | | 3 | | | | |
| Plymouth Argyle | 8.88 | - | 126 | 9 | 6 | 3 | 4 | | | |
| West Ham United* | 8.91 | £175,000 | 38+4 | 1 | 5 | 2+2 | 5 | | | |

## BROWN Richard Anthony

Born: Nottingham, 13 January 1967

Height: 5'10½"

Weight: 12.12

**Position/Skill Factor:** A full-back who can play on both sides of the park, although basically right footed. Distributes the ball well and will look to pass short and join in.

**Career History:** An ex-Nottingham Forest associated schoolboy (June 1981), he turned professional with Sheffield Wednesday in December 1984, following a spell with Ilkeston Town. Released without a first team appearance, he found his way back into the Football League with Blackburn Rovers, via non-League clubs, Ilkeston Town, Grantham, Boston United and Kettering Town. Having signed for Rovers early in 1990-91, he was loaned out to Maidstone United in order to gain experience and made his FL debut at Hereford United on 23 February 1991. Finally made his Rovers' debut, one year after signing, on 14 September 1991 at home to Port Vale at right-back and played a few games before being rested. Recalled by new manager Kenny Dalglish in November, he held his place until February, when he gave way to new signing Chris Price. Later had a few outings in midfield, before being recalled for the four vital end of season games in the Second Division from which Rovers grabbed eight priceless points and scraped into the Play-Offs . Surprisingly lost his place to previously out of favour David May, as Rovers finally achieved their ambition to play Premier League football. Captain of the successful Blackburn Rover's reserve side in **1992-93,** he was only required for first team duty on four (including one substitute) occasions. The only times he was required for PL duty was when playing in the side that handed out a 7-1 thrashing to Norwich City at Ewood Park and later in the season being part of a 3-0 victory at Queens Park Rangers.

| | | | APPEARANCES | | | | GOALS | | | |
|---|---|---|---|---|---|---|---|---|---|---|
| Clubs | Signing Date | Transfer Fee | Lge | FL Cup | FA Cup | Others | Lge | FL Cup | FA Cup | Others |
| Sheffield Wednesday | 1.85 | £10,000 | | | | | | | | |
| Ilkeston Town | 7.86 | - | | | | | | | | |
| Grantham | 1.87 | - | | | | | | | | |
| Boston United | 7.87 | - | | | | | | | | |
| Kettering Town | 7.88 | £500 | | | | | | | | |
| Blackburn Rovers* | 9.90 | £15,000 | 26+2 | 1+1 | 2 | 1 | | | | |
| Maidstone United | 2.91 | Loan | 3 | | | | | | | |

## BROWNE Paul

Born: Glasgow, 12 February 1975

Height: 6'1" Weight: 12.0

**Position/Skill Factor:** Central defender who loves to tackle and has a good recovery rate.

**Career History:** A summer professional signing for Aston Villa, having been a trainee at Villa Park since August 1991, his only experience to date, apart from a handful of reserve games in **1992-93**, has been confined to the youth team. Very honest and an excellent leader, he is captain material.

| | | | APPEARANCES | | | | GOALS | | | |
|---|---|---|---|---|---|---|---|---|---|---|
| Clubs | Signing Date | Transfer Fee | Lge | FL Cup | FA Cup | Others | Lge | FL Cup | FA Cup | Others |
| Aston Villa* | 7.93 | - | | | | | | | | |

## BRUCE Stephen (Steve) Roger

Born: Corbridge, 31 December 1960

Height: 6'0" Weight: 12.6

International Honours: E Yth, E"B", FL Rep

**Position/Skill Factor:** A very consistent central defender. Good in the air, he competes for everything and has a great approach to the game. Often scores vital goals from corners and penalties.

**Career History:** Born in Northumberland, he was introduced to League football by Gillingham, first signing apprentice forms in July 1977 before making his FL debut at Blackpool on 18 August 1979. He missed just six matches that season as a midfield player, but soon switched to a defensive role, becoming an outstanding Third Division player. Norwich City then signed him for a record fee (For Gillingham) and it wasn't too long before he and Dave Watson were forming a fine central defensive partnership at Carrow Road. However, at the end of his first season, 1984-

85, the club were relegated from Division One, although there was to be some solace in the shape of a League Cup winners medal, following City's 1-0 victory over Sunderland in the Final. The following season, he battled away to help Norwich win the Second Division Championship and became the backbone of the side as they established themselves in the First Division. Since joining Manchester United, he has missed very few games and over the last two seasons has teamed up well with Gary Pallister at the heart of the defence. Played in the losing League Cup final against Sheffield Wednesday in 1991, but hasn't been short of honours while at United, having won an FA Cup Winners medal in 1990 and a European Cup Winners Cup medal in 1991. Always a dangerous presence at corners and free kicks, he puts some First Division forwards to shame. In 1990-91, he was actually United's leading scorer with 13 FL goals, two League Cup goals and an amazing five goals in the European Cup Winners Cup, including United's opener in the Final against Barcelona (incorrectly credited to Hughes by some sources). A grand total of 20 goals is an astonishing total for a defender, although it should be qualified by noting that over half of them were penalties. Played a prominent role in United's Championship bid of 1991-92, ultimately unsuccessful, but had the consolation of another League Cup winners medal after a narrow win over Nottingham Forest, making up for the disappointment of a losers medal the previous year. Appointed team captain in the absence of Bryan Robson, he remained ever present in **1992-93** and ultimately achieved his proudest moment in football, as the League title came back to Old Trafford after a break of 26 years. As he proudly held the Championship trophy aloft with Robson in front of the cheering fans, his mind might well have cast him back some 15 years earlier when his career had kicked off rather inauspiciously in the Third Division. How well he has done, with much of it attributed to sheer hard work. Has scored some important goals in his time, but none more vital than the two headers at home to Sheffield Wednesday, after the "Reds" had been trailing 1-0 with just ten minutes left, while neck and neck with Aston Villa in the title race. With just five matches remaining, that could well have been the "killer" blow, but United with their heads now in front, left nothing to chance and took a maximum 15 points to clinch the title.

| | | | APPEARANCES | | | | GOALS | | | |
|---|---|---|---|---|---|---|---|---|---|---|
| Clubs | Signing Date | Transfer Fee | Lge | FL Cup | FA Cup | Others | Lge | FL Cup | FA Cup | Others |
| Gillingham | 10.78 | - | 203+2 | 15 | 14 | | 29 | 6 | 1 | |
| Norwich City | 8.84 | £125,000 | 141 | 20 | 9 | 10 | 14 | 5 | 1 | |
| Manchester United* | 12.87 | £800,000 | 203 | 22 | 24 | 19 | 31 | 4 | 1 | 5 |

## BRYAN Marvin Lee

Born: Paddington, 2 August 1975

Height: 6'0" Weight: 12.7

**Position/Skill Factor:** Outside-right who is very quick and strong and always looking to run at defenders and cross.

**Career History:** A promising young player who turned professional for Queens Park Rangers at the beginning of **1992-93,** he started out at Loftus Road as an associated schoolboy (November 1989), before graduating as a trainee (September 1991) on leaving school. Yet to play in the first team, before too long he will be looking to use a regular reserve slot as a springboard to the Premier League side.

| | | | APPEARANCES | | | | GOALS | | | |
|---|---|---|---|---|---|---|---|---|---|---|
| Clubs | Signing Date | Transfer Fee | Lge | FL Cup | FA Cup | Others | Lge | FL Cup | FA Cup | Others |
| Q.P.R.* | 8.92 | - | | | | | | | | |

## BRYDON Lee

Born: Stockton, 15 November 1974

Height: 5'11¾" Weight: 11.4

International Honours: E Sch

**Position/Skill Factor:** Central defender who is very fast in recovery. Elegant and cool, he is composed on the ball and is always looking to find his midfield players.

**Career History:** Turned professional for Liverpool during the 1992 close season, having been at the club since first coming to Anfield as an associated schoolboy in January 1991, before progressing through the ranks as a trainee on leaving school in July 1991. No first team experience as yet as he struggled to hold down a reserve slot in **1992-93** and is probably best remembered for conceding an own goal against Manchester United in a Central League match. However, he is still well thought of at Anfield.

| | | | APPEARANCES | | | | GOALS | | | |
|---|---|---|---|---|---|---|---|---|---|---|
| Clubs | Signing Date | Transfer Fee | Lge | FL Cup | FA Cup | Others | Lge | FL Cup | FA Cup | Others |
| Liverpool* | 6.92 | - | | | | | | | | |

## BRYSON James Ian Cook

Born: Kilmarnock, 26 November 1962

Height: 5'11"

Weight: 11.11

**Position/Skill Factor:** Winger who can play on both flanks and is capable of taking defenders on and then beating them. Always a danger around the box, he is very quick off the mark.

**Career History:** Commenced his career with his home town club Kilmarnock, who signed him in 1981 from local junior team Hurlford, he made 220 appearances and scored 44 goals in seven seasons. He was signed by manager Dave Bassett for Sheffield United, following the club's relegation to Division Three in 1988. A fairly typical Bassett signing, in that he cost a modest fee, he was unknown south of the border before his arrival and performed beyond all reasonable expectations, raising his game as the "Blades" became upwardly mobile. Made his FL debut at Reading on 27 August 1988 and got a flying start with his new club, scoring five goals in his first five matches. His aggressive play was a significant factor in helping United out of the Third Division that term and in 1989-90 he missed just seven matches as the team gained promotion for the second season running as Second Division runners-up. As United struggled to get away from the bottom rungs of the First Division for the most part of 1990-91, he made some vital strikes, including winning goals against Sunderland and Chelsea. Enjoyed another good season in 1991-92, although not always first choice and finished as second top scorer with nine FL goals, most of them match winners or savers, which considerably assisted the "Blades'" remarkable recovery from bottom place in November to ninth position by the end of the season. Had a most frustrating season in **1992-93,** playing alongside Brian Deane and also out wide and only managed three goals all season, these coming in the space of 35 playing minutes in two matches against Southampton and Tottenham Hotspur. Was always trying and the coming season will surely be more successful for him.

| | | | APPEARANCES | | | | GOALS | | | |
|---|---|---|---|---|---|---|---|---|---|---|
| Clubs | Signing Date | Transfer Fee | Lge | FL Cup | FA Cup | Others | Lge | FL Cup | FA Cup | Others |
| Kilmarnock | .81 | - | 194+21 | 12+7 | 14+2 | | 40 | 1 | 3 | |
| Sheffield United* | 8.88 | £40,000 | 138+17 | 11+2 | 18+4 | 7 | 36 | 1 | 4 | 3 |

## BUNBURY Alexander (Alex)

Born: Canada, 18 June 1967

Height: 5'11"

Weight: 13.0

International Honours: Canadian Int

**Position/Skill Factor:** A striker, who is both quick and strong and a real threat anywhere near the penalty area.

**Career History:** Signed from the Canadian club, Supra, during **1992-93**, he received an early opportunity to show what he could do when chosen for the Anglo-Italian Cup game against Pisa at Upton Park. That was followed four days later on 20 December 1992 when he came on as a substitute at Brentford for his FL debut and he went on to make six (including three substitute) appearances by the end of the season. Found the pace of the English game very hectic, although scoring five goals in eight reserve games and will do better once he has settled down. Went back home in April to represent Canada in their six World Cup qualifying matches, but will be back looking for a taste of Premier League action on his return.

| | | | APPEARANCES | | | | GOALS | | | |
|---|---|---|---|---|---|---|---|---|---|---|
| Clubs | Signing Date | Transfer Fee | Lge | FL Cup | FA Cup | Others | Lge | FL Cup | FA Cup | Others |
| West Ham United* | 11.92 | £20,000 | 2+2 | | 0+1 | 1 | | | | |

## BURLEY Craig William

Born: Irvine, 24 September 1971

Height: 6'1" Weight: 11.7

International Honours: S Sch, S Yth, S."U21"-4

**Position/Skill Factor:** Non-stop working midfielder who covers a lot of ground. A good passer of the ball, he also has great vision.

**Career History:** A nephew of George Burley, the former Ipswich star, he joined Chelsea as a trainee in December 1987 and made his FL debut when coming on as a substitute in Chelsea's 7-0 thrashing away to Nottingham Forest on 20 April 1991. After making further substitute appearances in 1991-92, he made his full FL debut at right-back at home to Southampton on 12 February 1992. Remarkably, one week later, he was selected for the Scotland Under 21 match versus Denmark and completed five further appearances for Chelsea in his more customary midfield role. Expected to move solidly into first team contention in **1992-93,** he found himself mainly on the outside looking in. Having been capped several times for Scotland's under 21's early on in the season, he put in some solid displays in the Chelsea reserve side, where he is affectionately known as "Mr Angry" among the players and would have surely got a chance under Dave Webb had he not been laid low with a double hernia at the time.

| | | | APPEARANCES | | | | GOALS | | | |
|---|---|---|---|---|---|---|---|---|---|---|
| Clubs | Signing Date | Transfer Fee | Lge | FL Cup | FA Cup | Others | Lge | FL Cup | FA Cup | Others |
| Chelsea* | 9.89 | - | 7+5 | | 0+1 | 2 | | | | |

## BURNETT Wayne

Born: Lambeth, 4 September 1971

Height: 6'0" Weight: 12.6

International honours: E Yth

**Position/Skill Factor:** Midfield player with a good assortment of skills. Excellent on the ball and a passer, he also does quite well in the air.

**Career History:** A south-Londoner by birth, he became an Orient trainee in August 1988 and joined the club's professional ranks two months after his 18th birthday. Later that season, following some promising displays in the reserves, he made his FL debut as a substitute at Crewe

Alexandra on 24 April 1990, before being given a chance at right-back in the final game of 1989-90. After a single appearance (as substitute) in 1990-91, he firmly established himself in Orient's midfield department from the start of 1991-92. It was something of a surprise, however, when Kenny Dalglish signed him for ambitious Blackburn Rovers in the summer of 1992, presumably as an investment for the future, since his first team opportunities seem limited at present in Rovers' star-studded line up. Forgotten in the publicity given to the other acquisitions in **1992-93,** he plugged away steadily in the reserves without ever being in serious contention for a place in the first team squad.

| | | | APPEARANCES | | | | GOALS | | | |
|---|---|---|---|---|---|---|---|---|---|---|
| Clubs | Signing Date | Transfer Fee | Lge | FL Cup | FA Cup | Others | Lge | FL Cup | FA Cup | Others |
| Leyton Orient | 11.89 | - | 34+6 | 3+1 | 3+1 | 4 | 1 | 1 | | |
| Blackburn Rovers* | 8.92 | £90,000 | | | | | | | | |

# BURROWS David

Born: Dudley, 25 October 1968

Height: 5'8" Weight: 11.0

International Honours: E "U21"-7, E"B", FL Rep

**Position/Skill Factor:** Hard tackling left-back who can also play in central defence and midfield when called on. Likes nothing more than a 50-50 tackle and doesn't lose many. Has a good left foot and is always on the lookout for shooting opportunities when getting forward down the left flank.

**Career History:** Started his football career as an associated schoolboy with West Bromwich Albion in January 1983, eventually becoming an apprentice in April 1985. After making his FL debut for Albion at home to Sheffield Wednesday on 22 April 1986, he went on to play a further 36 League matches, before Liverpool recognised his potential and signed him. He quickly laid claim to a regular place at Anfield and played 23 full games in Liverpool's 1989-90 League Championship winning team, alternating with Steve Staunton in the left-back slot, before finally establishing a firm hold on the position in 1990-91. Owing to Liverpool's chronic injury problems in 1991-92, he was often detailed to play in central defence, or midfield, to cover the absence of other players. Less adventurous than previous Liverpool left-backs, he didn't score his first goal for the club until August 1991, when his first minute volley against local rivals, Everton, set the "Reds" up for a 3-1 victory. He finished the season on a high, winning an FA Cup winners medal, playing alongside Mark Wright in the heart of the defence, during Liverpool's 2-0 defeat of Sunderland. Started **1992-93** in good form and actually replaced Bruce Grobbelaar in goal when the latter was sent off during the European Cup Winners Cup-tie at Spartak Moscow, but was unable to save the resulting penalty in a 4-2 defeat. Was the only ever present in the squad until early December when he sustained a bad knee injury at Anfield against Crystal Palace and was carried off after just eight minutes. Came back as a substitute in the home match against Manchester United, having been out of action for 15 games and played so well from thereon that he was put on standby for the England squad at the end of the season. Scored two goals during the campaign, both fierce drives and both from outside the box at Anfield against Norwich City and Coventry City and can always be relied on to pick up the odd long range shot.

| | | | APPEARANCES | | | | GOALS | | | |
|---|---|---|---|---|---|---|---|---|---|---|
| Clubs | Signing Date | Transfer Fee | Lge | FL Cup | FA Cup | Others | Lge | FL Cup | FA Cup | Others |
| West Bromwich Albion | 11.86 | - | 37+9 | 3+1 | 2 | 1 | 1 | | | |
| Liverpool* | 10.88 | £550,000 | 132+10 | 16 | 16+1 | 14 | 3 | | | |

# BUSST David John

Born: Birmingham, 30 June 1967

Height: 6'1"

Weight: 12.7

**Position/Skill Factor:** Centre-back who is a good competitor and is useful in the air in both penalty boxes.

**Career History:** Previously with Kings Heath and Solihull Borough, he was signed by Coventry City from non-League Moor Green early in 1992. Born into a family of Aston Villa supporters, he spent eight years in the insurance business before turning professional and after spending a 12 month apprenticeship in the Central League side sharpening his skills, he finally received his baptism in **1992-93** when coming on as a substitute against Norwich City in the Third round of the FA Cup, after both Andy Pearce and Lloyd McGrath had picked up injuries. Despite City losing 1-0 at Carrow Road, he made his PL debut on 16 January 1993 in the very next match, again at Norwich, only this time it was a 1-1 draw. More or less shared the number five shirt with Phil Babb and Pearce for the rest of the season, making ten Premier League appearances in all. Asked to play as a stopper centre-half, he has done very well and with a good attitude there is no reason why he shouldn't become the number one player in the club in that position.

| | | | APPEARANCES | | | | GOALS | | | |
|---|---|---|---|---|---|---|---|---|---|---|
| Clubs | Signing Date | Transfer Fee | Lge | FL Cup | FA Cup | Others | Lge | FL Cup | FA Cup | Others |
| Coventry City* | 1.92 | - | 10 | | 0+1 | | | | | |

# **BUTLER** Peter James

Born: Halifax, 27 August 1966

Height: 5'9"

Weight: 11.1

**Position/Skill Factor:** Midfield player with great stamina, who is always "snapping" at opponents as soon as they are in possession. Covers every blade of grass.

**Career History:** After nine years, mainly in the lower divisions, this busy midfield player now embarks on his first season in the Premier League, having initially joined Huddersfield Town as an associated schoolboy in May 1981. After signing as an apprentice (July 1982) on leaving school and making good progress to "Town's" professional ranks at the start of 1984-85, he celebrated by making his FL debut as a substitute in the first game of the season at home to Oxford United on 25 August 1984. However, he never started a game for the "Terriers" and after an impressive loan spell with Cambridge United in 1985-86, he joined Bury for a small fee in the summer of 1986. After only four months with the "Shakers", he was re-signed by Cambridge manager, Chris Turner, this time on a permanent basis. Quickly made an impression as a hard working right sided midfield player and within 14 months he moved on to Southend United. Although a struggling Fourth Division side when he joined them, under manager David Webb, the "Shrimpers" suddenly shot up the League to Division Two, with consecutive promotions in 1989-90 and 1990-91, with Butler playing a sterling role in midfield. Strangely, he was almost totally out of favour with the manger for 1991-92 and ended the season back on loan with his first club, Huddersfield Town. A permanent move back to his native Yorkshire seemed the next logical step and it came as a considerable surprise to many when Billy Bonds stepped in to bring him to West Ham United, just before the commencement of **1992-93.** Hardly putting a foot wrong all season, he proved an inspired signing and was sorely missed during the eight weeks leading up to Christmas when he was out of action with a groin injury. Apart from that spell of seven games, he was ever present for the rest of the campaign and was one of the key players in the promotion challenge. At the end of an often tense season, with Newcastle United going clear as First Division Champions, the "Hammers" pipped Portsmouth for the other automatic promotion place on goal difference.

| | | | APPEARANCES | | | | GOALS | | | |
|---|---|---|---|---|---|---|---|---|---|---|
| Clubs | Signing Date | Transfer Fee | Lge | FL Cup | FA Cup | Others | Lge | FL Cup | FA Cup | Others |
| Huddersfield Town | 8.84 | - | 0+5 | | | | | | | |
| Cambridge United | 1.86 | Loan | 14 | | | 1 | 1 | | | |
| Bury | 7.86 | - | 9+2 | 2 | 1 | | | | 1 | |
| Cambridge United | 12.86 | - | 55 | 4 | 2 | 2 | 9 | | | |
| Southend United | 2.88 | £75,000 | 135+7 | 12 | 2 | 11 | 9 | 1 | | 2 |
| Huddersfield Town | 3.92 | Loan | 7 | | | | | | | |
| West Ham United* | 8.92 | £125,000 | 39 | 2 | 2 | 1 | 2 | | | |

# **BUTT Nicholas (Nicky)**

Born: Manchester, 21 January 1975

Height: 5'9½"

Weight: 10.10

International Honours: E Sch, E Yth

**Position/Skill Factor:** Plays in the centre of midfield and is a good communicator. A thinking player, he often pops up in great positions to score vital goals. Has much ability.

**Career History:** Another of Manchester United's brilliant youngsters who helped the club to lift the FA Youth Cup in 1991-92, defeating Crystal Palace 6-3 over two legs, scoring twice in the first-leg victory at Selhurst Park. First signed on at Old Trafford as an associated schoolboy in July 1989, upgrading to trainee in July 1991 and joining the professional ranks in January 1993. Even before this, he had made his PL debut in **1992-93** as substitute in a 3-0 home victory over Oldham Athletic on 21 November 1992 and yet again was an influential member of the United youth side that reached the FA Youth Cup Final, albeit this time round he recieved a losers medal. Scored a lot of "A" team goals during the season and was a member of the England under 19 team that perfomed so well in the World Cup in Australia.

| | | | APPEARANCES | | | | GOALS | | | |
|---|---|---|---|---|---|---|---|---|---|---|
| Clubs | Signing Date | Transfer Fee | Lge | FL Cup | FA Cup | Others | Lge | FL Cup | FA Cup | Others |
| Manchester United* | 1.93 | - | 0+1 | | | | | | | |

## BUTTERFIELD Timothy

Born: Sheffield, 18 October 1974

Height: 6'0" Weight: 11.6

**Position/Skill Factor:** A midfielder who can play at right-back. An athlete, he works hard up and down the pitch and has good control and passing ability.

**Career History:** A steady young player who has recently signed professional for Sheffield United, he first came to the club as an associated schoolboy in April 1989, before progressing through the youth team as a trainee (July 1991). Played in the last two reserve outings of the **1992-93** season and as with the other five upgraded juniors, has a year to prove himself.

| | | | APPEARANCES | | | | GOALS | | | |
|---|---|---|---|---|---|---|---|---|---|---|
| Clubs | Signing Date | Transfer Fee | Lge | FL Cup | FA Cup | Others | Lge | FL Cup | FA Cup | Others |
| Sheffield United* | 7.93 | - | | | | | | | | |

## BUTTERWORTH Ian Stuart

Born: Crewe, 25 January 1964

Height: 6'1" Weight: 12.6

International Honours: E "U21"- 8

**Position/Skill Factor:** Good footballing centre-back, strong and more than useful in the air, he is an influential figure at the back. Not content to boot the ball out of defence and will look to pass at every opportunity.

**Career History:** First joined Coventry City as a 14-year-old when signing as an associated schoolboy player in April 1978, before becoming an apprentice in June 1980. Had been a pro for little more than six months when he made his FL debut for the club at Swansea City on 13 March 1982. Quickly won a regular place at the heart of the "Sky Blues' " defence where his form soon attracted considerable attention. After four seasons at Highfield Road, he moved to Nottingham Forest in a £450,000 deal which also included Stuart Pearce. His stay at Forest lasted just 18 months and after spending a month on loan at Norwich City, the deal was made permanent a short while later. Has proved to be an influential figure in the "Canaries' " side and although he suffered from an illness which forced him to miss much of the 1989-90 season, he is now back to his best. A regular choice in central defence in 1991-92, he missed some games in mid-season through injury but returned in February to play a sterling role in the "Canaries' " F A Cup run to the Semi-Final. As the club captain in **1992-93,** he played his part in taking City to an eight point lead in December, but unfortunately had his worse season ever for injuries. He later missed ten consecutive games with a hamstring injury and was one of seven first teamers absent during a difficult spell in March. Norwich, however, got on with the business in hand, without complaining and topped the Premier League for 18 weeks, eventually finishing third. And courtesy of Arsenal's exploits in the domestic cup scene, the club qualified for European competition. His only goal during the season came at Anfield in reply to a four goal drubbing at the hands of Liverpool and for such a fine header of the ball, it is most surprising that he has scored only four in nearly seven years at Carrow Road.

| | | | APPEARANCES | | | | GOALS | | | |
|---|---|---|---|---|---|---|---|---|---|---|
| Clubs | Signing Date | Transfer Fee | Lge | FL Cup | FA Cup | Others | Lge | FL Cup | FA Cup | Others |
| Coventry City | 8.81 | - | 80+10 | 5 | 5+1 | | | | | |
| Nottingham Forest | 6.85 | £250,000 | 26+1 | 6 | 1 | | | | | |
| Norwich City | 9.86 | Loan | 4 | | | | | | | |
| Norwich City* | 12.86 | £160,000 | 203+3 | 15+1 | 24 | 10+1 | 4 | | | |

## CABLE Marc Brian

Born: Dartford, 18 September 1974

Height: 6'1" Weight: 11.5

**Position/Skill Factor:** Central defender who is useful in the air and a very good passer of the ball.

**Career History:** Released by Brighton and Hove Albion, where he had been an associated schoolboy (December 1989), he joined Wimbledon as a trainee in October 1991 and had graduated to the professional ranks by the 1993 close season. A regular in the youth side in **1992-93**, he also had three run outs with the reserves and showed enough good form to have an excellent future in the game, especially if he can maintain his current rate of progress.

| | | | APPEARANCES | | | | GOALS | | | |
|---|---|---|---|---|---|---|---|---|---|---|
| Clubs | Signing Date | Transfer Fee | Lge | FL Cup | FA Cup | Others | Lge | FL Cup | FA Cup | Others |
| Wimbledon* | 7.93 | - | | | | | | | | |

# CALDERWOOD Colin

Born: Stranraer, 20 January 1965

Height: 6'0" Weight: 12.0

International Honours: FL Rep

**Position/Skill Factor:** A very reliable centre-back who is always around to snuff out danger. Strong and uncompromising, both in the air and on the ground, he is feared by most attackers.

**Career History:** Made his FL debut for Mansfield Town in the most unusual of circumstances, just 52 days after his 17th birthday, at Crewe Alexandra on 13 March 1981, having been signed by the "Stags" from Scottish junior football only days earlier. Unfortunately, the registration forms, although received at the FA, did not reach the Football League in time and the club had two points deducted for playing an unregistered player. Already in the midst of a very poor season and further damaged by the loss of two points, Mansfield finally survived the need to seek re-election to the Fourth Division by a single point. Established himself as a strong central defender in 1982-83 and although Mansfield were a struggling Fourth Division club at the time, he was impressing the scouts from bigger clubs. At the end of his contract he was, however, signed by another Fourth Division club, Swindon Town, with the transfer fee fixed by the Transfer Tribunal. Even at the time, it appeared to be a massive undervaluation and in the light of his subsequent career, absurdly so. He was appointed club captain by manager Lou Macari on his arrival – an amazing vote of confidence in a 20 year old – and led the club to the Fourth Division Championship in his first season when he was ever present. He was also ever present the following season when Swindon won their second consecutive promotion, via the Play-Offs after finishing third in Division Three. Following 121 consecutive FL appearances for Swindon, he finally succumbed to injury in February 1988. In 1989-90, he was again ever present, leading the club to the Second Division Play-Offs and victory in the Final, only for the Football League to deny them the promotion they had earned. Also ever present in FL games in 1991-92 and **1992-93**, for the fifth time in eight seasons, a remarkable level of consistency, probably without parallel in the Football League. Throughout his time at the club, he formed good partnerships with a succession of other central defenders and won recognition when appearing for the Football League against the Italian Serie "B" side over the past two seasons. Known as the "fridge" for his coolness on the field, his one low point in 1992-93 was his sending off – for two bookable offences – at Leicester City. Captaining Town to victory in the Play-Off Final against Leicester will have more than made up for that and as the longest serving member of the side he looked forward with relish to playing in the Premier League. However, the thought of playing at the highest level had hardly had time to sink in, before he was on his way to Tottenham Hotspur as the replacement for Neil Ruddock. His former manager, Ossie Ardiles, moved in quickly for him when it became apparent that he was going to lose Ruddock and he now welcomes the opportunity of shining in a "big time" club.

| | | | APPEARANCES | | | | GOALS | | | |
|---|---|---|---|---|---|---|---|---|---|---|
| Clubs | Signing Date | Transfer Fee | Lge | FL Cup | FA Cup | Others | Lge | FL Cup | FA Cup | Others |
| Mansfield Town | 3.82 | - | 97+3 | 4 | 6 | 7 | 1 | | 1 | |
| Swindon Town | 7.85 | £30,000 | 328+2 | 35 | 17 | 32 | 20 | | 1 | |
| Tottenham Hotspur* | 7.93 | Tribunal | | | | | | | | |

# CALDWELL Peter James

Born: Weymouth, 5 June 1972

Height: 6'1" Weight: 11.7

**Position/Skill Factor:** Goalkeeper with very safe hands who will improve given experience. Good long drop kicks.

**Career History:** A professional since the end of the 1989-90 season, he first came to Queens Park Rangers as an associated schoolboy in December 1986, before becoming a trainee in June 1988. Third in line at Rangers, behind internationals, Jan Stejskal and Tony Roberts, he has battled back from a career threatened by injury to the fringe of the first team. Sat on the bench three times in **1992-93**, without being required to make an appearance, but plugged away in the reserves and will be ready when the time comes.

| | | | APPEARANCES | | | | GOALS | | | |
|---|---|---|---|---|---|---|---|---|---|---|
| Clubs | Signing Date | Transfer Fee | Lge | FL Cup | FA Cup | Others | Lge | FL Cup | FA Cup | Others |
| Q.P.R.* | 3.90 | - | | | | | | | | |

# CAMPBELL **Kevin** Joseph

Born: Lambeth, 4 February 1970

Height: 6'0"

Weight: 13.1

International Honours: E "U21"-4, E "B"

**Position/Skill Factor:** This young striker with strength and pace, two useful feet and who is also good in the air, has every chance of becoming a leading light in the game. He is just as capable of setting up others as well as scoring himself.

**Career History:** Has been at Highbury since signing on as an associated schoolboy in October 1985. In July 1986 he joined the trainee ranks, before turning pro and making his FL debut for Arsenal at Everton on 7 May 1988, when coming on as a substitute during the last game of the 1987-88 season. This followed his part in Arsenal's FA Youth Cup Final victory over Doncaster Rovers, when his place left opposition defenders for dead in a brilliant first half hat-trick of solo goals in the first leg. With Alan Smith and Paul Merson holding down the two strikers' roles at Highbury, first team opportunities were limited and to provide him with more experience, he had long spells on loan at Leyton Orient in 1988-89 and Leicester City in 1990-91, where he was a consistent scorer. 1990-91 saw him win a Championship medal with Arsenal, when, after several appearances as a substitute, he became a regular on the title run-in, scoring seven valuable goals in 14 full League outings. Despite his splendid form he was still not established in 1991-92, even after Paul Merson was switched to the flank, because manager George Graham then signed Ian Wright from Crystal Palace. Not until the end of the season did he win a regular place at the expense of Alan Smith, following an electrifying performance as a substitute against Sheffield Wednesday when he transformed a pedestrian 1-1 draw into a 7-1 rout. His superb strike in the 70th minute opened the floodgates and inspired his forward colleagues to five more breathtaking goals. Despite starting only 22 games, he finished the season as second top scorer with 13 FL goals. It is statistically interesting to note that in the 31 FL games that he played, Arsenal collected 62 points, whilst in the 11 games that he was not required, Arsenal picked up only ten points. One may only speculate therefore that if he had played in every game the "Gunners" might still be Champions! Four goals in the new **1992-93** Premier League was scant return for a striker who had previously scored at the rate of one every two games played and he generally had a fairly miserable time in front of goal. Nevertheless, he scored some very important goals in other competitions and it was his late strikes against Millwall and Derby County that kept Arsenal in the League Cup. Picked up cup winners medals following FA Cup and League Cup victories over Sheffield Wednesday and the sight of his former Arsenal youth team successor, Andy Cole, in full flight for Newcastle United this coming season, maybe just the spur he needs.

| | | | APPEARANCES | | | | GOALS | | | |
|---|---|---|---|---|---|---|---|---|---|---|
| Clubs | Signing Date | Transfer Fee | Lge | FL Cup | FA Cup | Others | Lge | FL Cup | FA Cup | Others |
| Arsenal* | 2.88 | - | 77+29 | 7+8 | 9+5 | 5 | 28 | 4 | 2 | 1 |
| Leyton Orient | 1.89 | Loan | 16 | | | | 9 | | | |
| Leicester City | 11.89 | Loan | 11 | | | 1 | 5 | | | 1 |

# CAMPBELL **Stuart** James

Born: Bexley, 2 January 1975

Height: 5'7" Weight: 11.2

**Position/Skill Factor:** Left-Back with a great left foot. A thinking player, who is always aware of what is going on around him.

**Career History:** A professional signing for Arsenal during the 1993 close season, he first came to Highbury as a trainee in July 1991 and successfully graduated through the club's youth team. Made a handful of appearances for the reserves in **1992-93** and is a promising young player.

| | | | APPEARANCES | | | | GOALS | | | |
|---|---|---|---|---|---|---|---|---|---|---|
| Clubs | Signing Date | Transfer Fee | Lge | FL Cup | FA Cup | Others | Lge | FL Cup | FA Cup | Others |
| Arsenal* | 7.93 | - | | | | | | | | |

# CAMPBELL **Sulzeer (Sol)** Jeremiah

Born: Newham, 18 September 1974

Height: 6'1"

Weight: 12.10

International Honours: E Yth

**Position/Skill Factor:** Midfielder who can also play in central defence. A good athlete with excellent skills, he creates chances for others.

**Career History:** Another of Spurs' young starlets who have earned a surprisingly early first team call up. Campbell joined Tottenham as an associated schoolboy in February 1989, became a trainee on leaving school in August 1991 and signed a three year contract as a professional at the beginning of the **1992-93** season. Within three months he had made his PL debut, as a substitute at Chelsea on 5 December 1992, replacing Nick Barmby midway through the second half and scoring a very late consolation goal in Spurs 2-1 defeat. This was his only first team appearance of the season, but he is most definitely one for the future.

| | | | APPEARANCES | | | | GOALS | | | |
|---|---|---|---|---|---|---|---|---|---|---|
| Clubs | Signing Date | Transfer Fee | Lge | FL Cup | FA Cup | Others | Lge | FL Cup | FA Cup | Others |
| Tottenham Hotspur* | 9.92 | - | 0+1 | | | | 1 | | | |

## **CANHAM Scott** Walter

Born: Newham, 5 November 1974

Height: 5'8" Weight: 10.5

**Position/Skill Factor:** Very skilful little midfielder who passes and moves well.

**Career History:** Locally born youngster, who as a regular in the West Ham United youth team in **1992-93**, was promising enough to be given several outings with the reserves. Started at Upton Park as an associated schoolboy in February 1989, before progressing as a trainee (July 1991) to sign professional forms during the 1993 close season.

| | | | APPEARANCES | | | | GOALS | | | |
|---|---|---|---|---|---|---|---|---|---|---|
| Clubs | Signing Date | Transfer Fee | Lge | FL Cup | FA Cup | Others | Lge | FL Cup | FA Cup | Others |
| West Ham United* | 7.93 | - | | | | | | | | |

## **CANTONA Eric**

Born: Paris, France, 24 May 1966

Height: 6'1½" Weight: 13.7

International Honours: French Int

**Position/Skill Factor:** An extremely skilful striker with a good footballing brain. Very quick in possession, he has fast feet and knows where the goal is.

**Career History:** Mercurial French international forward who joined Leeds United in February 1992, following his voluntary "retirement" from French League football and who added some flair to Leeds's improbable, but well earned, League Championship triumph. Arrived at Elland Road after spells with French First Division Clubs', Auxerre, Bordeaux, Montpellier, Marseille and Nimes Olympique. His record at international level for France is outstanding (14 goals in 20 games), even surpassing his more celebrated partner — Jean Marie Papin of Marseille, but at club level he was not an automatic first choice with Marseille — only 18 games out of 38 in 1990-91 scoring 8 goals — and following his £1 million transfer to newly promoted Nimes in the summer of 1991, he struggled to score in an ultra-defensive set up with, only one goal from 20 games. Saddled with a "bad boy" image in France, following a sending off and a two month suspension after insulting the disciplinary panel, he then announced he would never play for a French club again. His agent arranged an introduction to Sheffield Wednesday, but a "contretemps" in the arrangements caused him to walk out before manager Trevor Francis had seen him in action. He then joined Leeds on loan for a £100,000 initial fee, making his FL debut as a substitute debut at Oldham Athletic on 8 February 1992. Given the background to his signing, it seemed improbable that he would adapt easily to the hurly-burly of English football and it is to his credit that he soon established a "rapport" with the Elland Road faithful with his arrogant and supremely confident forward runs. Manager Howard Wilkinson was unwilling to disturb his existing forward partnership of Chapman and Wallace and most of his appearances were as substitute, but one goal was sufficient to seal the marriage. In the closing minutes of the home game with Chelsea, he collected an airborne pass on his instep, whilst tightly marked by two defenders, flicked the ball between them and wrong footing them in the same movement, smashed the ball on the half volley from an acute angle into the roof of the net. It not only brought the house down, but was rightly selected as "Goal of the Season" by the ITV panel of judges. At the end of the 1991-92 season his transfer from Nimes was finalised and he then played in all three games during France's unsuccessful European Championship sojourn in Sweden during the summer. If 1991-92 was an amazing season for him, then **1992-93** was even more so. Started the new campaign with a hat-trick against Liverpool in the 4-3 Charity Shield victory over Liverpool and before falling out with Howard Wilkinson and leaving Elland Road bound for Manchester United, he had scored eight more goals, including a further hat-trick in a 5-0 win over Tottenham Hotspur. Unable to secure a regular place in the Leeds' side, for whatever reasons, he came to Old Trafford and excelled throughout the remaining games as his subtle flicks, deft touches and vision, apart from vital goals, were seen by many to have been the difference between winning and losing the Championship. As Leeds sunk further and further down the table, his new club went from strength to strength to win the League title after a break of 26 years. And in doing so, he became the first man ever to win a Championship medal two seasons running, with two different clubs. While continuing to play well for his country, scoring two goals in a game on one occasion last season, the burning question at club level, is whether his love affair with Manchester is going to be long or short term.

| | | | APPEARANCES | | | | GOALS | | | |
|---|---|---|---|---|---|---|---|---|---|---|
| Clubs | Signing Date | Transfer Fee | Lge | FL Cup | FA Cup | Others | Lge | FL Cup | FA Cup | Others |
| Leeds United | 2.92 | £900,0000 | 18+10 | 1 | | 6 | 9 | | | 5 |
| Manchester United* | 11.92 | £1,200,000 | 21+1 | | 1 | | 9 | | | |

## CAREY Brian Patrick

Born: Cork,
31 May 1968

Height: 6'3"

Weight: 11.13

International Honours:
IR "U21"-1, 1R-2

**Position/Skill Factor:** A tall central defender who uses his height to good advantage in both penalty areas.

**Career History:** Came to Manchester United from Cork City, but before making an appearance for the "Reds", he was loaned out to Wrexham and made his FL debut at Peterborough United on 19 January 1991. He had an even longer (three month) stay with Wrexham in 1991-92, during which, he starred in their historic FA Cup victory over reigning League Champions, Arsenal and the two epic games with West Ham in the Fourth Round. The Welsh club had hoped to sign him permanently, but United manager Alex Ferguson considered he still had a future at Old Trafford and recalled him. However, he was selected for the Irish Republic national squad at the end of the season and made a brief appearance as substitute in the friendly match against the USA. Still very much a fringe player in **1992-93**, he has yet to make a first team appearance for the "Reds", although included on the bench during the losing Fifth Round FA Cup-tie at Sheffield United in February. An important member of United's Central League side, he also added to his international reputation when making his full debut for the Republic against Wales and must hope for a breakthrough in 1993-94.

| | | | APPEARANCES | | | | GOALS | | | |
|---|---|---|---|---|---|---|---|---|---|---|
| Clubs | Signing Date | Transfer Fee | Lge | FL Cup | FA Cup | Others | Lge | FL Cup | FA Cup | Others |
| Manchester United* | 9.89 | £100,000 | | | | | | | | |
| Wrexham | 1.91 | Loan | 3 | | | | | | | |
| Wrexham | 12.91 | Loan | 13 | | 3 | 3 | 1 | | | |

## CARMICHAEL David

Born: Immingham, 15 March 1975

Height: 5'8" Weight: 10.6

**Position/Skill Factor:** Striker. Very quick around the box, "sniffing" out half chances to get on the end of.

**Career History:** A recent professional signing for Coventry City, having been at the club as an associated schoolboy (March 1990) and as a trainee (July 1991), he was given a run out in a couple of reserve team games towards the end of **1992-93**. Spent the summer in the Finnish Second Division in order to sharpen up for 1993-94 and scored four goals in eight matches.

| | | | APPEARANCES | | | | GOALS | | | |
|---|---|---|---|---|---|---|---|---|---|---|
| Clubs | Signing Date | Transfer Fee | Lge | FL Cup | FA Cup | Others | Lge | FL Cup | FA Cup | Others |
| Coventry City* | 7.93 | - | | | | | | | | |

## CARR Franz Alexander

Born: Preston,
24 September 1966

Height: 5'7"

Weight: 10.12

International Honours:
E Yth, E "U21"-9

**Position/Skill Factor:** Right-winger with electrifying pace who, on his day, can leave defenders for "dead". Inconsistency has been a problem and he often needs to put more quality into his crossing.

**Career History:** Nicknamed the "flying machine", even before his 17th birthday he had the scouts flocking to Blackburn Rovers and only a few days after signing a professional contract in the 1984 close season, was the subject of a large purchase by Nottingham Forest's Brian Clough. He had first come to Ewood Park as an associated schoolboy (April 1981), before becoming an apprentice on leaving school in March 1983. Made his FL debut for Nottingham Forest at Aston Villa on 12 October 1985 and by the end of that season had consolidated his place in the side. In the early months of 1986-87, he was a sensation on the right-wing as Forest set the pace and led the First Division up until November. Already capped by England at all levels up to the 21 mark, he seemed certain to be an international star of the future. Sadly, a hamstring injury, first sustained in November 1987, was to trouble him intermittently over the next few years and sapped his confidence. He showed his best form only in patches and became increasingly marginalised at the City Ground and was often passed over by Clough in favour of Gary Crosby. Two spells on loan to Sheffield Wednesday and West Ham United did little to lift him out of the rut until he was offered a fresh start with Newcastle United in the summer of 1991. Made little impact at St James' Park, with only 13 full first team appearances in 1991-92 as United struggled in the relegation zone for most of the season and in **1992-93** it wasn't much better. After scoring only one goal in 17 games, he was sent out on loan to Sheffield United, a move that was eventually firmed up, and in his first match provided an inch perfect cross for the first goal of a Brian Deane hat-trick in a 3-0 win over Ipswich Town at Brammall. Lane. Not noted as a prolific scorer since his days with Nottingham Forest, he nonetheless managed three spectacular goals in eight Premier League appearances for the "Blades". Played in four FA Cup games and helped United into the Semi-Final, where he made the side's only goal in a 2-1 defeat against local rivals, Sheffield Wednesday, at Wembley. However, his form had already begun to dip and following a calf injury picked up in the Semi-Final, his season came to an abrupt halt.

| Clubs | Signing Date | Transfer Fee | APPEARANCES Lge | FL Cup | FA Cup | Others | GOALS Lge | FL Cup | FA Cup | Others |
|---|---|---|---|---|---|---|---|---|---|---|
| Blackburn Rovers | 7.84 | - | | | | | | | | |
| Nottingham Forest | 8.84 | £100,000 | 122+9 | 16+2 | 4 | 5+2 | 17 | 5 | | 1 |
| Sheffield Wednesday | 12.89 | Loan | 9+3 | | 2 | | | | | |
| West Ham United | 3.91 | Loan | 1+2 | | | | | | | |
| Newcastle United | 6.91 | £250,000 | 20+5 | 2+2 | | 3+1 | 3 | | | |
| Sheffield United* | 1.93 | £120,000 | 8 | | 4 | | 3 | | | |

## CARRUTHERS Martin George

Born: Nottingham, 7 August 1972

Height: 5'11" Weight: 11.9

**Position/Skill Factor:** Striker who is very useful in the air and is always looking to get on the end of far-post opportunities.

**Career History:** Signed trainee forms for Aston Villa in July 1988, before turning professional two years later. His first two appearances in the Villa first team were as substitute in a Zenith Cup game in November 1991 and a FA Cup game at Derby County just before his FL debut at Wimbledon on 8 February 1992. Kicked off the **1992-93** season with Villa's reserve side, before having a three month spell on loan with Hull City. Scored six goals in 16 first team games during his stay with the "Tigers" and gained invaluable experience. Back at Villa Park, he failed to make a first team appearance until the last game of the season, a 2-1 defeat at Queens Park Rangers. A young prospect who is still at the learning stage.

| Clubs | Signing Date | Transfer Fee | APPEARANCES Lge | FL Cup | FA Cup | Others | GOALS Lge | FL Cup | FA Cup | Others |
|---|---|---|---|---|---|---|---|---|---|---|
| Aston Villa* | 7.90 | - | 2+2 | | 0+1 | 0+1 | | | | |
| Hull City | 10.92 | Loan | 13 | | | 3 | 6 | | | |

## CARTER James (Jimmy) William Charles

Born: Hammersmith, 9 November 1965

Height: 5'10"

Weight: 10.4

**Position/Skill Factor:** Tricky right-winger who, on his day, is as good as anyone. With a real turn of pace, he will knock the ball past defenders in order to get in telling crosses.

**Career History:** Signed associated schoolboy forms for Crystal Palace in January 1980, before beginning an apprenticeship with the club in July 1982. After turning pro with the "Eagles" and without getting a game, he was given a free transfer to Queens Park Rangers, where he suffered the same fate before signing for Millwall. Made his FL debut at home to Oldham Athletic on 14 March 1987 and was a regular on the wing for the rest of the season. The following season, he assisted Millwall to the Second Division Championship and became a great crowd favourite at the Den. Nevertheless, he was not always an automatic first choice and it was the cause of great puzzlement when Kenny Dalglish signed him for Liverpool in January 1991 for a massive fee. It was a strange signing since it was unclear which player he was intended to replace and many judges considered that however good he might be in the Second Division, he was hardly Liverpool standard. The question was never answered. After two games for the "Reds", he was replaced by another new signing, David Speedie and one month after he arrived at Anfield, his manager Kenny Dalglish had left mysteriously, thus leaving his two new signings with uncertain futures. It was soon clear that he had no future under new manager Graham Souness in 1991-92 and in any case injury ruled him out of contention for selection. Ironically, had he been fit, he would almost certainly have received another opportunity to show his mettle, such was the injury crisis at Anfield. In the event, once fit again, he was "rescued" from obscurity by Arsenal manager George Graham. Unfortunately, his initial appearances for the "Gunners" coincided with their mid-season slump and he soon found himself in the same position as previously at Anfield — out of contention for a first team place. Disappointed not to figure in George Graham's **1992-93** cup winning sides, having played three games in earlier rounds, after coming into the first team reckoning in the second half of the season. Performed well against his former club, Liverpool, at Highbury in January and this seemed to give him just the confidence he required. He later scored his first goals for the "Gunners" with a pair, which included the winner in a 4-3 League victory over Southampton.

| Clubs | Signing Date | Transfer Fee | APPEARANCES Lge | FL Cup | FA Cup | Others | GOALS Lge | FL Cup | FA Cup | Others |
|---|---|---|---|---|---|---|---|---|---|---|
| Crystal Palace | 11.83 | - | | | | | | | | |
| Q.P.R. | 9.85 | - | | | | | | | | |
| Millwall | 3.87 | £15,000 | 99+11 | 6+1 | 6+1 | 5+1 | 11 | | 2 | |
| Liverpool | 1.91 | £800,000 | 2+3 | | 2 | 0+1 | | | | |
| Arsenal* | 10.91 | £500,000 | 16+6 | 1 | 1+1 | | 2 | | | |

## CASCARINO Anthony (Tony) Guy

Born: Orpington, 1 September 1962

Height: 6'2" Weight: 11.10

International Honours: IR-42

**Position/Skill Factor:** Striker who is one of the best headers of the ball in the game, using his height to maximum advantage and is very dangerous on crosses. He is not just an aerial player, also having a strong left foot.

**Career History:** Signed for Gillingham from Kent League side, Crockenhill, in exchange for a team kit and made his FL debut away to Burnley on 2 February 1982. His

goalscoring exploits in the Third Division over the next five seasons, during which he consistently topped the "Gills'" scoring lists, earned him his first international cap for the Republic of Ireland against Switzerland on 11 September 1985 and led to Millwall parting with their record transfer fee. In his first term at the Den, he formed a deadly partnership with Teddy Sheringham, where their goals helped Millwall to win the Second Division title and carried the "Lions" into the top flight for the first time in their history. Moved to Aston Villa when Millwall were clearly doomed to relegation, but struggled to make an impact and after only 16 months and 11 FL goals for Villa, he was transferred to Glasgow Celtic in the 1991 close season. He was unable to settle in Glasgow either, not scoring his first Scottish League goal until October and was frequently relegated to substitute. Finally, Celtic manager Liam Brady decided to cut his losses and allowed him to return to London, signing for Chelsea, in February 1992. Despite scoring on his Chelsea debut — a late equaliser against Crystal Palace — he was frequently omitted from the team in the remaining games of the season and netted only once more in 12 games. In international football, however, with the Irish Republic, he has looked well capable of holding his own at the highest level. Plagued by injury throughout **1992-93**, he didn't get a first team game until Mick Harford was sold to Sunderland and Dave Webb arrived as caretaker manager. Sent off at Leeds United a few days after he had scored the equaliser against "Spurs", he came back from a three match suspension to hit the winner in the home game, versus Coventry City. He also added to his Republic of Ireland caps, with three (two substitute) more appearances towards the end of the season, but will have to wait and see whether he has a future at Stamford Bridge under new player/manager, Glenn Hoddle.

| | | | APPEARANCES | | | | GOALS | | | |
|---|---|---|---|---|---|---|---|---|---|---|
| Clubs | Signing Date | Transfer Fee | Lge | FL Cup | FA Cup | Others | Lge | FL Cup | FA Cup | Others |
| Gillingham | 1.82 | - | 209+10 | 18 | 15+2 | 15 | 78 | 11 | 9 | 12 |
| Millwall | 6.87 | £200,000 | 105 | 10 | 8 | 5 | 42 | 1 | 2 | 3 |
| Aston Villa | 3.90 | £1,500,000 | 43+3 | 2+1 | 2 | 3 | 11 | 1 | | |
| Glasgow Celtic | 7.91 | £1,100,00 | 13+11 | 1 | 0+1 | 2+2 | 4 | | | |
| Chelsea* | 2.92 | £750,000 | 19+2 | | 2 | | 4 | | | |

## **CASKEY Darren** Mark

Born: Basildon, 21 August 1974

Height: 5'8" Weight: 11.9

International Honours: E Sch, E Yth

**Position/Skill Factor:** Midfield player who is a good competitor and a strong tackler.

**Career History:** The current captain of the England youth team, he signed professional forms for Tottenham Hotspur at the latter end of 1991-92, having been at the club as an associated schoolboy (December 1988) and as a trainee (August 1990). Led the England team to third place in the 1993 World Youth Cup, held in Australia, but although progressing well in the "Spurs'" reserve side in **1992-93**, he has yet to make a Premier League debut.

| | | | APPEARANCES | | | | GOALS | | | |
|---|---|---|---|---|---|---|---|---|---|---|
| Clubs | Signing Date | Transfer Fee | Lge | FL Cup | FA Cup | Others | Lge | FL Cup | FA Cup | Others |
| Tottenham Hotspur* | 3.92 | - | | | | | | | | |

## **CASPER Christopher (Chris)** Martin

Born: Burnley, 28 April 1975

Height: 5'11½"

Weight: 10.7

International Honours: E Yth

**Position/Skill Factor:** An elegant central defender who is a good passer of the ball and likes to come out from the back to set up attacks. He is an excellent reader of the game for one so young.

**Career History:** Son of Frank, who played for Rotherham United and Burnley, he arrived at Manchester United as a trainee in July 1991 and is a recent professional acquisition for the club. A talented youngster, he turned out regularly for the "A" team in **1992-93** and occasionally made the reserves. Also played a leading role in the side that were runners-up to Leeds United in the FA Youth Cup Final and was probably disappointed not to make the first team squad. His chance could come in 1993-94.

| | | | APPEARANCES | | | | GOALS | | | |
|---|---|---|---|---|---|---|---|---|---|---|
| Clubs | Signing Date | Transfer Fee | Lge | FL Cup | FA Cup | Others | Lge | FL Cup | FA Cup | Others |
| Manchester United* | 2.93 | - | | | | | | | | |

## CASTLEDINE Stewart Mark

Born: Wandsworth, 22 January 1973

Height: 6'1" Weight: 12.13

**Position/Skill Factor:** Aggressive midfield player with a tremendous work rate who never gives the opposition a moments peace.

**Career History:** Made his FL debut for Wimbledon as a substitute in the penultimate game of the 1991-92 season at Norwich City on 25 April 1992, having been a professional since the summer of 1991. First came to Plough Lane as an associated schoolboy in May 1987 and showed enough promise for the "Dons" to sign him on as a trainee in July 1989 when he reached school leaving age. A regular in the reserve team in **1992-93**, he made no further first team appearances, but is another young player who looks set for a bright future.

| | | | APPEARANCES | | | | GOALS | | | |
|---|---|---|---|---|---|---|---|---|---|---|
| Clubs | Signing Date | Transfer Fee | Lge | FL Cup | FA Cup | Others | Lge | FL Cup | FA Cup | Others |
| Wimbledon* | 7.91 | - | 0+2 | | | | | | | |

## CHAMBERS Leroy Dean

Born: Sheffield, 25 October 1972

Height: 5'8¾" Weight: 11.4

**Position/Skill Factor:** Strong and aggressive striker, who works hard and gets himself into good positions, but needs to find the net more often.

**Career History:** A promising youngster who has recently turned professional for Sheffield Wednesday, he first came to Hillsborough as an associated schoolboy (November 1986), before progressing to trainee status, on leaving school in July 1989. Yet to make the step up to the first team squad, he showed promise in **1992-93** with the reserve team and was offered a new contract by manager, Trevor Francis. Looks set to challenge for a place this coming season.

| | | | APPEARANCES | | | | GOALS | | | |
|---|---|---|---|---|---|---|---|---|---|---|
| Clubs | Signing Date | Transfer Fee | Lge | FL Cup | FA Cup | Others | Lge | FL Cup | FA Cup | Others |
| Sheffield Wednesday* | 6.91 | - | | | | | | | | |

## CHAPMAN Lee Roy

Born: Lincoln, 5 December 1959

Height: 6'2" Weight: 13.0

International Honours: E "U21"-1, E"B"

**Position/Skill Factor:** An old-fashioned centre-forward, who is one of the best headers in the game today, when the ball is in the penalty area. Also gets in front of defenders to great advantage.

**Career History:** The son of Roy, who was an inside forward with several Midland clubs in the '50s and '60s, he

signed associated schoolboy forms for Stoke City in February, 1977. His FL debut was actually for Plymouth Argyle at home to Watford on 9 December 1978, whilst on loan from the "Potters". Spent three seasons at Stoke before signing for Arsenal, but due to a cartilage operation he was unable to establish a niche at Highbury, finding himself in and out of the side. Moved on to Sunderland, but it was at his next club, Sheffield Wednesday, where he finally came good, scoring 19 goals in his first season and also was leading scorer in 1986-87 and 1987-88. After four good seasons at Hillsborough, he strangely chose to sign for an obscure Second Division French club, Niort, but the move turned sour when the French club were unable even to honour the modest transfer fee. He was "rescued" by Nottingham Forest, and repaid manager Brian Clough's faith in him with 16 League and cup goals, helping the club into third place in the First Division and a League Cup — Simod Cup double. It was a big surprise when Forest allowed him to join Leeds United in order to reinforce their bid for First Division status. The money was well spent as he scored 12 FL goals, including the winner in the final game at Bournemouth, which clinched the Second Division Championship for the club. Scored 21 goals from 38 First Division matches as United claimed fourth position in 1990-91, and established themselves amongst the elite. Playing at the peak of his career, he spearheaded Leeds' successful bid for the 1991-92 League Championship, top scoring once again with 16 FL goals, plus four cup goals, which included two hat-tricks — away to Sheffield Wednesday and at home to Wimbledon. Normally a slow starter, he burst onto the **1992-93** stage with two goals on the opening Saturday at home to Wimbledon and continued his run of good form, including a superb performance against VFB Stuttgart in the second leg, European Cup-tie, while giving the German international, Guido Buchwald, a torrid time. Once again, he finished as the club's top scorer with 18 goals and although many came from inside the six yard box, there were also memorable volleys against Wimbledon and Oldham Athletic and a brilliant headed goal against his old club, Arsenal.

However, he rarely scored away from home and was dropped for three games in February, before returning to forge fruitful partnerships with Rob Wallace and Jamie Forrester. Surprisingly placed on the transfer list at the end of the season, he may not start 1993-94 at Elland Road.

| | | | APPEARANCES | | | | GOALS | | | |
|---|---|---|---|---|---|---|---|---|---|---|
| Clubs | Signing Date | Transfer Fee | Lge | FL Cup | FA Cup | Others | Lge | FL Cup | FA Cup | Others |
| Stoke City | 6.78 | - | 95+4 | 5 | 3 | | 34 | 3 | 1 | |
| Plymouth Argyle | 12.78 | Loan | 3+1 | | | | | | | |
| Arsenal | 8.82 | £500,000 | 15+8 | 0+2 | 0+1 | 2 | 4 | | | 2 |
| Sunderland | 12.83 | £200,000 | 14+1 | | 2 | | 3 | | 1 | |
| Sheffield Wednesday | 8.84 | £100,000 | 147+2 | 17 | 17+1 | 2+1 | 63 | 6 | 10 | |
| Niort (France) | 6.88 | £350,000 | | | | | | | | |
| Nottingham Forest | 10.88 | £350,000 | 48 | 12 | 5 | 6 | 15 | 6 | 3 | 3 |
| Leeds United* | 1.90 | £400,000 | 133+4 | 15 | 11 | 10 | 63 | 10 | 4 | 4 |

## CHARLTON Simon Thomas

Born: Huddersfield, 25 October 1971

Height: 5'6" Weight: 11.1

International Honours: E Sch, E Yth

**Position/Skill Factor:** A footballing left-back, with a lovely left foot. Likes nothing better than joining up with the attack to get good early crosses over. Also the possesor of a long throw.

**Career History:** A former graduate of the FA School of Excellence, he was a 1993 close season signing by Southampton, from his hometown club, Huddersfield Town. Started his career at Leeds Road as an associated schoolboy in March 1986 and won ten England FA schoolboy caps in 1987-88, before joining the club as a trainee (July 1988). After turning professional a year later and making his FL debut as a substitute at home to Crewe Alexandra on 3 March 1990, he gained a regular place in the side the following season, with 34 (one substitute) first team appearances. Ever present in Town's defence during **1992-93**, having been absent just once the previous season, his reputation as one of the best full-backs in the division grew and he began to attract the scouts to Leeds Road. It was not a great surprise, therefore, when he was signed up by a Premier League club, for a downpayment of £350,000, which may increase to £500,000 with appearances and international selection.

| | | | APPEARANCES | | | | GOALS | | | |
|---|---|---|---|---|---|---|---|---|---|---|
| Clubs | Signing Date | Transfer Fee | Lge | FL Cup | FA Cup | Others | Lge | FL Cup | FA Cup | Others |
| Huddersfield Town | 7.89 | - | 121+3 | 9 | 10 | 14 | 1 | 1 | | |
| Southampton* | 6.93 | £350,000 | | | | | | | | |

## CHARNOCK Philip Anthony

Born: Southport, 14 February 1975

Height: 5'9¾" Weight: 11.3

**Position/Skill Factor:** Left sided midfield player. Elegant and in the "Ray Kennedy" mould, he is always looking to set up the attack. Is also an excellent striker of the ball.

**Career History:** Signed professional forms for Liverpool during the 1992 close season, having been at the club since leaving school and coming to Anfield at a trainee in July 1991. Although not making his League debut in **1992-93**, he became Liverpool's youngest ever player to appear in a European competition when he came off the bench at Anfield in the European Cup Winners Cup-tie against Apollon Limassol. Made one further first team appearance when playing in the first leg of the League Cup match against Chesterfield, before being substituted and going back to reserve team football. Very much a player for the future.

| | | | APPEARANCES | | | | GOALS | | | |
|---|---|---|---|---|---|---|---|---|---|---|
| Clubs | Signing Date | Transfer Fee | Lge | FL Cup | FA Cup | Others | Lge | FL Cup | FA Cup | Others |
| Liverpool* | 6.92 | - | | 1 | | 0+1 | | | | |

## CLARK Lee Robert

Born: Wallsend, 27 October 1972

Height: 5'7"

Weight: 11.7

International Honours: E Yth, E "U21"-10

**Position/Skill Factor:** Quality midfield player, who has great ability on the on the ball. Orchestrates the play with good one-twos around the box and spots openings quickly.

**Career History:** Without doubt, the most talented of Newcastle United's current crop of youngsters and a likely England international of the future, he is well placed to take over the mantle of Paul Gascoigne. And if he can avoid the media hype and adulation, which threatens to destroy his Geordie counter part, he may prove to be an even better player. Came up through the club's ranks, first as an associated schoolboy (December 1986) and then as a trainee (July 1989), before signing professional forms at the end of 1989. Made his FL debut as a substitute at Bristol City on 29 September 1990 and was later selected by new manager, Ossie Ardiles, for the last nine games of the season. Started the 1991-92 season as a first choice player in midfield, but although he played well the balance of the team was wrong, with too many youthful and inexperienced players. And while the team played some of the most attractive football in the Second Division, it was constantly undermined by a brittle defence. Eventually, with the "Magpies" struggling at the foot of the table, Ardiles paid the penalty by losing his job. New manager, Kevin Keegan, replaced the youngsters, including Clark, with more experienced new signings which saved United from relegation by the skin of their teeth in the final match of the season. Voted the north-east's "Footballer of the Year" in **1992-93**, an award he deserved for his outstanding performances in helping United win back its pride and, at the same time, become First Division Champions. With his head shaven, he is now something of a cult figure, but it was his ability on the pitch that started the ball rolling. The only ever present in the side, he played 58 competitive games and scored an invaluable ten goals. The winner in a 2-1 victory at Derby County, ranked right up there with the best of them. Collecting the ball on the right touchline, he cut inside, riding tackle after tackle, before scoring with a tremendous left footed shot. As if all that wasn't enough, he created 15 goals for his team-mates and proved to have a marvellous temperament to go with his ability, not being booked all season. Added eight more England under 21 caps to his collection and with the Premier League as his stage this season, he will be looking to move up to the senior squad.

| | | | APPEARANCES | | | | GOALS | | | |
|---|---|---|---|---|---|---|---|---|---|---|
| Clubs | Signing Date | Transfer Fee | Lge | FL Cup | FA Cup | Others | Lge | FL Cup | FA Cup | Others |
| Newcastle United* | 12.89 | - | 84+10 | 8 | 6 | 4 | 16 | | 1 | 1 |

# CLARKE Adrian James

Born: Cambridge, 28 September 1974

Height: 5'9½" Weight: 11.0

International Honours: E Sch

**Position/Skill Factor:** Winger/striker, who can play on either side, with two good feet. Clever on the ball and a superb crosser.

**Career History:** An associated schoolboy (November 1988) at Arsenal, before he won an England Boys cap, he made good progress through the youth team as a trainee (July 1991) and towards the end of **1992-93**, the reserves, to sign professional forms during the close season.

| | | | APPEARANCES | | | | GOALS | | | |
|---|---|---|---|---|---|---|---|---|---|---|
| Clubs | Signing Date | Transfer Fee | Lge | FL Cup | FA Cup | Others | Lge | FL Cup | FA Cup | Others |
| Arsenal* | 7.93 | - | | | | | | | | |

# CLARKE Andrew (Andy) Weston

Born: Islington, 22 July 1967

Height: 5'10"

Weight: 11.7

International Honours: E Semi-Pro Int

**Position/Skill Factor:** Can operate either up front, or as a goalscoring winger. Combines great pace with skill and scores frequently, because he is always looking for shooting positions.

**Career History:** First made his name when playing for Barnet when they were still members of the Vauxhall Conference. Manager Barry Fry has earned a fortune for the north London club by finding young talent, grooming it in the highly successful Barnet team, and then looking for likely buyers. In 1990-91 alone, he had sold Regis and Harding to Notts County for £65,000 and Gridelet to Barnsley for £175,000, but regarded Clarke as his prize asset, after he scored 17 Conference goals in 35 games. He circulated a video of Clarke's finest moments to various FL clubs, but although many showed an interest, including Manchester United, all shied away from the £300,000 asking fee. Eventually, Barnet accepted Wimbledon's reduced offer of £250,000, a record fee paid to a non-League club. Made his FL debut as a sub at home to Norwich City on 2 March 1991 and after three more similar appearances, he claimed a regular place through to the end of the season. During 1991-92, strangely, having invested so much money, Wimbledon seemed reluctant to try him in partnership with John Fashanu and 21 of his 34 appearances during 1991-92 were as substitute. Again, in-and-out of the side in **1992-93**, he made 29 full first team appearances and came off the bench on a further ten occasions. Started the season in the side at Leeds United, before being substituted and then being used from the bench for the next five matches. However, he then had a run of nine full games, scoring a great solo goal against Aston Villa, before a bust-up with boss, Joe Kinear, saw him removed from the first team squad until all was quickly sorted out and he was restored. Of his five League goals, two came against Nottingham Forest; the equaliser at the City Ground and the winner at home. It would appear that consistency is his biggest failing, but if he can overcome this, he could become a major threat for Wimbledon.

| | | | APPEARANCES | | | | GOALS | | | |
|---|---|---|---|---|---|---|---|---|---|---|
| Clubs | Signing Date | Transfer Fee | Lge | FL Cup | FA Cup | Others | Lge | FL Cup | FA Cup | Others |
| Wimbledon* | 2.91 | £250,000 | 43+36 | 4+1 | 3+1 | | 11 | 1 | | |

# CLARKE Stephen (Steve)

Born: Saltcoats, 29 August 1963

Height: 5'9"

Weight: 11.10

International Honours: S Yth, S "U21"-8, S L Rep, S "B", S-5

**Position/Skill Factor:** Intelligent full-back, used mainly on the right hand side, who is adept at hitting long passes into "channels". A good defender, he is not afraid to tackle and is also quick to intercept and start up attacks.

**Career History:** Began in Scottish junior soccer with Beith, before signing for St Mirren and making his debut against Hibernian in September 1982. Transferring south of the border to Chelsea, he had played in more than 150 League games for St Mirren. Made his FL debut as a substitute at Norwich City on 24 January 1987 and had his best season in 1987-88 when making 38 FL appearances. It was also in 1987-88 that he won the first of his full international caps when selected to play for Scotland against Hungary at Hampden Park on 9 September 1987. Since 1989, however, he has had to share the right-back slot with Welsh international, Gareth Hall, but neither player has established a lasting hold on the position. In 1991-92, he started the season as first choice and held his place until December, before making way for Hall. Returned in March for the closing weeks of the campaign. Out of action from September until January in **1992-93**, having his second hernia operation inside a year, he struggled to find any kind of form afterwards, although he came back to reclaim the right-back spot from his rival, Gareth Hall, for the last 11 matches of the season. His early season displays, however, were outstanding and had the older supporters claiming him to be one of the best in that position since the war. Still has a future at the club if he can really get match fit during the summer.

| | | | APPEARANCES | | | | GOALS | | | |
|---|---|---|---|---|---|---|---|---|---|---|
| Clubs | Signing Date | Transfer Fee | Lge | FL Cup | FA Cup | Others | Lge | FL Cup | FA Cup | Others |
| St Mirren | .81 | – | 151 | 21 | 19 | 6 | 6 | | 1 | |
| Chelsea* | 1.87 | £422,000 | 179+4 | 11 | 9 | 16 | 6 | 1 | 1 | 1 |

# **CLOUGH Nigel** Howard

Born: Sunderland, 19 March 1966

Height: 5'9" Weight: 11.4

International Honours: E "U21"-15, FL Rep, E"B", E-14

**Position/Skill Factor:** A deep-lying centre-forward who creates as many goals as he scores with his subtle touches and penetrating passes. His much publicised lack of pace probably hindered his international career, but his unconventional role — half midfield, half forward, is also perhaps difficult to blend with more stereotyped players.

**Career History:** The son of the famous footballer and former manager, Brian Clough, he was playing with Heanor Town in the Northern Counties (East) League and AC Hunters, a Sunday league team in Derby, before joining his father at Nottingham Forest as a non-contract player in 1984. Signed a professional contract a year later, after he had already made his FL debut at home to Ipswich Town on 26 December 1984. He established a regular first team place in his first season as a professional and was leading scorer with 15 goals. Although not a prolific goalscorer, he has topped the Forest charts in most subsequent seasons. Instrumental in helping Forest to win the League Cup in successive years, when scoring twice in the 3-1 victory over Luton Town in 1989 and in laying on the pass for Nigel Jemson to net the only goal of the 1990 Final against Oldham Athletic. Earlier, he had emulated his father, who had played twice for England during 1959-60 and was the club's leading scorer with 14, but although he was a member of the side that reached the FA Cup Final, he was unable to change the course of the match as Tottenham Hotspur won 2-1. Significantly, the FA Cup is the only major trophy that Brian Clough has yet to win, either as a player or manager. 1991-92 was his least productive season for goals (only five FL and three in cup games) and for the first time in his Forest career he suffered the indignity of being dropped from the team. And at the end of the season he even played in central defence to cover for injuries. Despite these upheavals, he was still held in high regard by the England manager and was recalled for the matches against France, Czechoslovakia and the CIS and was also included in the squad of 20 for the European Championships in Sweden, although he didn't get a game. Had the most disappointing season of his life at club level in **1992-93**, while his international career prospered and although he was the only ever present and top scored at Forest, the club were relegated after having just a taste of the new Premier League. To cap it all, his father decided to quit the manager's job at the end of the campaign and once that was confirmed it appeared obvious to many that Nigel would soon be on his way too. After making four more England appearances, in World Cup qualifiers and prior to going on tour for the USA Cup matches, he joined Liverpool at the beginning of June in a £2 million transfer deal. His new manager, Graeme Souness, said of him: "Playing under such a dominating and forceful character as Brian Clough, with such high standards, shows Nigel to have a strong personality. That appeals to me and is the kind of character you need if you're going to play for Liverpool".

| | | | APPEARANCES | | | | GOALS | | | |
|---|---|---|---|---|---|---|---|---|---|---|
| Clubs | Signing Date | Transfer Fee | Lge | FL Cup | FA Cup | Others | Lge | FL Cup | FA Cup | Others |
| Nottingham Forest | 9.84 | – | 307+4 | 46 | 28 | 11+3 | 101 | 22 | 6 | 1 |
| Liverpool* | 6.93 | £2.275.000 | | | | | | | | |

## COCKERILL Glenn

Born: Grimsby,
25 August 1959

Height: 6'0"

Weight: 12.4

**Position/Skill Factor:** Hard working midfield player with strong engines, who is always on hand to help team-mates out of a hole. Often makes forward runs, finishing with an accurate shot, he is useful in the air and a good tackler on the ground.

**Career History:** The son of Ron, who played for Huddersfield Town (1952-58) and Grimsby Town (1958-68), his younger brother, John, is currently at Grimsby. Signed for Lincoln City, having played for non-League Louth United and made his FL debut in an eventful 5-4 win at home to Northampton Town on 5 February 1977. After some good performances, he was transferred to Swindon Town, but when Lincoln decided that they wanted him back 18 months later, in a drive for promotion to the Second Division, they had to part with nearly £30,000 more than they sold him for in the first place, despite the fact that his career had not been advanced to any degree. In all, played over 200 League games during his two spells at City, before transferring to Sheffield United in March 1984, and helping the "Blades" secure promotion to the Second Division. Still utterly dependable, even while United teetered precariously close to the brink, Chris Nicholl made Glenn his first signing when he was appointed manager of Southampton. Soon settled into the side and played a significant part in the "Saints" reaching the FA Cup Semi-Final in 1986. Since then he has missed very few matches, forming a strong midfield partnership with Jimmy Case and Barry Horne and enjoyed another consistent season in 1991-92, missing only six FL games as the team struggled to maintain a place in the First Division, although reaching the Final of the Zenith Cup. Unfortunately, a calf injury sustained in training early in **1992-93**, exiled him to his longest ever spell on the sidelines and allowed Neil Maddison to seize the chance of a first team place. Then, after coming back, another calf strain in the home game against Arsenal in December, forced him off the field yet again and he only started ten more games before the end of the season. However, he was back to his best during the last four games, having proved his value to the team as a second-half substitute against Nottingham Forest at the Dell.

| | | | APPEARANCES | | | | GOALS | | | |
|---|---|---|---|---|---|---|---|---|---|---|
| Clubs | Signing Date | Transfer Fee | Lge | FL Cup | FA Cup | Others | Lge | FL Cup | FA Cup | Others |
| Lincoln City | 11.76 | - | 65+6 | 2 | 2 | | 10 | | | |
| Swindon Town | 12.79 | £11,000 | 23+3 | 3 | | | 1 | | | |
| Lincoln City | 8.81 | £40,000 | 114+1 | 16 | 7 | 1 | 25 | 1 | | |
| Sheffield Wednesday | 3.84 | £125,000 | 62 | 6 | 1 | | 10 | 1 | | |
| Southampton* | 10.85 | £225,000 | 260+13 | 34+1 | 20+2 | 12 | 32 | 5 | 2 | |

## COLE Andrew Alexander

Born: Nottingham, 15 October 1971

Height: 5'11" Weight: 11.2

International Honours: E Sch, E Yth, E."U21"-6

**Position/Skill Factor:** A striker with great potential who is quick and elusive with good skills to match.

**Career History:** First signed for Arsenal as an associated schoolboy in December 1985 and later graduated as a trainee in August 1988. Made his FL debut at Highbury against Sheffield United on 29 December 1990 when coming on as a replacement for Perry Groves. During 1991-92 he made no further appearances for Arsenal, but gained more FL experience in two extended loan spells with Fulham and Bristol City. He proved to be a sensation at Ashton Gate with eight goals from 12 games, which undoubtedly saved the "Robins" from relegation to Division Three. When he joined City they were lying in 23rd place, but his goals inspired a run of five victories and three draws in eight games, which lifted the team well clear of the bottom four. Having come back from a successful England under 21 tournament in France, where he won three caps, he signed for Bristol City on a more permanent basis and scored in a 3-3 draw at home to Portsmouth on the opening day of **1992-93**. Going from strength to strength, he struck 16 goals in 33 games, but when Newcastle United came in with an offer that gave City a £1,250,000 profit margin on their investment of less than eight months, the bait was too large not to swallow. And much to the chagrin of the fans at Ashton Gate, he became United's record signing and made the best goalscoring start at the club since the legendary Hughie Gallacher in 1925-26. Nicknamed Andy "Goal", he has averaged one a game since his arrival and with his ability to turn defenders in the box, coupled with exceptional pace, has scored two hat-tricks in his tally and also created four goals for his team-mates. A brilliant effort at home to Oxford United summed up his appeal when, having received the ball in the penalty area with his back to goal and tightly marked, he turned quickly and lashed the ball into the roof of the net. Played three more times for the under 21s and given a bit of luck with injuries, he is expected to become Tyneside's new "Malcolm McDonald" in the charge for Premier League honours.

| | | | APPEARANCES | | | | GOALS | | | |
|---|---|---|---|---|---|---|---|---|---|---|
| Clubs | Signing Date | Transfer Fee | Lge | FL Cup | FA Cup | Others | Lge | FL Cup | FA Cup | Others |
| Arsenal | 10.89 | - | 0+1 | | | 0+1 | | | | |
| Fulham | 9.91 | Loan | 13 | | | 2 | 3 | | | 1 |
| Bristol City | 3.92 | Loan | 12 | | | | 8 | | | |
| Bristol City | 7.92 | £500,000 | 29 | 3 | 1 | 4 | 12 | 4 | | |
| Newcastle United* | 3.93 | £1,750,000 | 11+1 | | | | 12 | | | |

## COLGAN Nicholas (Nick) Vincent

Born: Drogheda, Ireland, 19 October 1973

Height: 6'1" Weight: 12.10

International Honours: IR "U21"-4

**Position/Skill Factor:** Goalkeeper who reads the game well and is competent in his handling of the ball. Also has excellent kicking ability.

**Career History:** Joined Chelsea as a trainee in October 1990 and signed a professional contract two years later, but only until the end of 1992-93. Started **1992-93** as third choice 'keeper, but frequently sat on the bench as substitute goalie when Hitchoock was injured and subsequently when Dave Beasant fell from grace. Unlucky with a serious hand injury sustained during training that required to be pinned and in plaster for a couple of months. Played regularly for the reserves after recovery and looks a good prospect for the future. Made his debut for the Republic of Ireland's under 21 side in October 1992 and played as a regular from then on, although never being on the winning side and suffering an 8-0 hammering at the hands of Germany.

| | | | APPEARANCES | | | | GOALS | | | |
|---|---|---|---|---|---|---|---|---|---|---|
| Clubs | Signing Date | Transfer Fee | Lge | FL Cup | FA Cup | Others | Lge | FL Cup | FA Cup | Others |
| Chelsea* | 10.92 | - | | | | | | | | |

## COLLIER Darren James

Born: Stockton, 1 December 1967

Height: 6'0" Weight: 12.6

**Position/Skill Factor:** Goalkeeper. Very quick off his line and a good shot stopper.

**Career History:** Turned professional with Blackburn Rovers during 1987-88, having been a non-contract player on Middlesbrough's books and made his FL debut in a 2-0 defeat at Ipswich Town on 13 May 1989, the last match of the season, deputising for Terry Gennoe. Also deputised for Gennoe in 16 FL games in 1989-90 and again at the start of 1990-91, but apparently did not satisfy Rovers' manager, Don Mackay, who then signed Mark Grew on loan from Port Vale and later Bobby Mimms from Tottenham to take over as first choice. Made no first team appearances in either 1991-92 or **1992-93**, losing his substitute 'keeper's place first to Matt Dickins and latterly to the Australian, Frank Talia. In between time he regained the secondary position when Dickins went out on loan to Blackpool, sitting on the bench on 21 occasions, while never having to be called onto the field of play.

| | | | APPEARANCES | | | | GOALS | | | |
|---|---|---|---|---|---|---|---|---|---|---|
| Clubs | Signing Date | Transfer Fee | Lge | FL Cup | FA Cup | Others | Lge | FL Cup | FA Cup | Others |
| Blackburn Rovers* | 12.87 | - | 27 | 3 | | 1 | | | | |

## CONNELL Graham

Born: Glasgow, 31 October 1974

Height: 5'10" Weight: 11.5

**Position/Skill Factor:** Strong tackling midfielder, who can play at right-back. Has great stamina and covers a tremendous amount of ground.

**Career History:** Came down from Scotland, on leaving school, to join Ipswich Town as a trainee in September 1991 and was a regular member and captain of the youth team in **1992-93**, before signing professional during the 1993 close season. A fiery player, he will need to channel his aggression constructively, if he is to progress at a steady rate, a point highlighted when he was sent off early last season for two bookable offences.

| | | | APPEARANCES | | | | GOALS | | | |
|---|---|---|---|---|---|---|---|---|---|---|
| Clubs | Signing Date | Transfer Fee | Lge | FL Cup | FA Cup | Others | Lge | FL Cup | FA Cup | Others |
| Ipswich Town* | 7.93 | - | | | | | | | | |

## CONNOLLY Francis Anthony (Tony)

Born: Cork, 17 June 1975

Height: 5'8" Weight: 11.0

**Position/Skill Factor:** Very strong striker, who goes in "where Angels fear to tread" and is a regular scorer.

**Career History:** Came over from Ireland and passed through Arsenal's junior ranks as a trainee (August 1991), before turning professional for the "Gunners" last summer. A knee injury kept him out of action for much of **1992-93**, until able to return to the youth team in February, but he should be match fit well in time for the start of the new season.

| | | | APPEARANCES | | | | GOALS | | | |
|---|---|---|---|---|---|---|---|---|---|---|
| Clubs | Signing Date | Transfer Fee | Lge | FL Cup | FA Cup | Others | Lge | FL Cup | FA Cup | Others |
| Arsenal* | 7.93 | - | | | | | | | | |

## CORK Alan Graham

Born: Derby, 4 March 1959

Height: 6'0"

Weight: 12.0

**Position/Skill Factor:** Very experienced striker who is one of the cleverest headers of a ball in the game. Always manages to get his head to crosses.

**Career History:** Came through the Derby County junior ranks, prior to turning pro for the "Rams" in the 1977-78 close season. Never picked for the first team, while at the Baseball Ground, he made his FL debut on loan with Lincoln City at Oxford United on 14 September 1977, before being snapped up on a free transfer by Football League newcomers, Wimbledon. He scored his first goal for his new club in a 3-1 win against Bournemouth and in 14 years at Wimbledon, "Corky" as he is affectionately known has extended the "Dons" goalscoring record to more than 150 in all matches. Top scored in 1978-79 with 22 FL goals, 23 in 1980-81, and 29 in 1983-84 when Wimbledon won promotion to the Second Division. A broken leg sustained in September 1981 kept him sidelined for nearly two years, but he returned as sharp as ever in April 1983, scoring five goals in seven games to assist the "Dons" push for the Fourth Division Championship. Has played in every Division with the club during their climb to First Division status and was also a member of the side that unexpectedly defeated Liverpool 1-0 in the 1988 FA Cup Final. In recent years he has been a valuable squad player, playing in a number of different positions and frequently deployed as substitute. For a player who spent all of his career in the lower divisions, he has adapted well to the First Division and when he was given a free transfer by Wimbledon in February 1992, his former manager Dave Bassett, gave him another opportunity to extend his First Division life with Sheffield United. **1992-93**, saw him become United's latest hero of the Kop, where he enjoyed cult status, although being mainly used as a substitute to be thrown into the fray when required. He managed only two Premier League goals all season, but will be remembered for the ones he scored in the FA Cup; the winner against Hartlepool United in the Fourth Round and the equaliser at Wembley in the Semi-Final versus the old enemy, Sheffield Wednesday. During the cup run he grew a beard which was not shaved off until United were defeated. Offered a further one year contract with the "Blades", although he would be released if the right coaching or manager's job came along.

| | | | APPEARANCES | | | | GOALS | | | |
|---|---|---|---|---|---|---|---|---|---|---|
| Clubs | Signing Date | Transfer Fee | Lge | FL Cup | FA Cup | Others | Lge | FL Cup | FA Cup | Others |
| Derby County | 7.77 | - | | | | | | | | |
| Lincoln City | 9.77 | Loan | 5 | | | | | | | |
| Wimbledon | 2.78 | - | 352+78 | 29+7 | 30+7 | 3+4 | 145 | 14 | 8 | 1 |
| Sheffield United* | 3.92 | - | 18+17 | 1+2 | 5+1 | | 4 | | 2 | |

## CORMACK Peter

Born: Southport, 8 June 1974

Height: 6'0" Weight: 12.0

**Position/Skill Factor:** Strong tackling central defender, who can play at left-back and in midfield. Very enthusiastic, he has a wonderful attitude to the game.

**Career History:** Son of the former Nottingham Forest, Liverpool and Scotland player, Peter, he was signed by Newcastle United manager, Kevin Keegan, from Edinburgh based Scottish League Division One team, Meadowbank Thistle, after only one appearance (as substitute) in their last match of 1991-92. Clearly an investment for the future, the only taste of first team action he had in **1992-93** was as a non-playing substitute against Bari in the Anglo-Italian Cup and he spent much of the season getting acclimatised in the reserve side. However, with United back in the top flight, he will be looking for a taste of Premier League action and an early opportunity to emulate his father.

| | | | APPEARANCES | | | | GOALS | | | |
|---|---|---|---|---|---|---|---|---|---|---|
| Clubs | Signing Date | Transfer Fee | Lge | FL Cup | FA Cup | Others | Lge | FL Cup | FA Cup | Others |
| Meadowbank Thistle | 6.92 | - | 0+1 | | | | | | | |
| Newcastle United* | 8.92 | £10,000 | | | | | | | | |

## COTON Anthony (Tony) Philip

Born: Tamworth, 19 May 1961

Height 6'2"

Weight: 13.7

International Honours: E"B"

**Position/Skill Factor:** One of the best goalkeepers in the country. Has a keen positional sense and marshals his defences well. Brave, with very good hands, he is not afraid to come for crosses.

**Career History:** Joined Birmingham City from local non-League side, Mile Oak Rovers of Tamworth and made a sensational start in his FL debut at home to Sunderland on 27 December 1980 when he saved a penalty after less than a minute. Became a regular early in 1982-83 after contesting the goalkeepers jersey, first with Jeff Wealands and then Jim Blyth. Signed for First Division Watford early into the 1984-85 season, when the club having played seven games without a win, had conceded 15 goals. He immediately replaced Steve Sherwood and soon became a big favourite at Vicarage Road, being voted "Player of the Year" on three separate occasions. He was only transferred to Manchester City when the club, needing money desperately, was forced to sell one of its major assets. Only missed four games in his first season at Maine

Road, after he replaced Andy Dibble and confidence spread throughout the side as they finished in fifth place for 1990-91. Regarded by some judges as the safest 'keeper in the First Division during 1991-92, following lapses in form by Chris Woods and David Seaman, he was the backbone of a City side that finished in fifth place. Had another very consistent season in **1992-93**, if not as eye catching as in 1991-92 and only missed one match when keeping 14 clean sheets, two of them on the same Selhurst Park pitch against Crystal Palace and Wimbledon. Among his many great saves during the campaign was a memorable stop from Eric Cantona in the home match against the Champions elect, Manchester United, which kept the score at 1-1. Passed a major milestone when he made his 400th League appearance at Blackburn Rovers on 22 August 1992 and it is amazing that his only international honour to date was as a substitute in an England "B" match in 1991-92.

| | | | APPEARANCES | | | | GOALS | | | |
|---|---|---|---|---|---|---|---|---|---|---|
| Clubs | Signing Date | Transfer Fee | Lge | FL Cup | FA Cup | Others | Lge | FL Cup | FA Cup | Others |
| Birmingham City | 10.78 | - | 94 | 10 | 10 | | | | | |
| Watford | 9.84 | £300,000 | 233 | 18 | 32 | 8 | | | | |
| Manchester City* | 7.90 | £1,000,000 | 110 | 11 | 9 | 3 | | | | |

## COTTEE Anthony (Tony) Richard

Born: West Ham, 11 July 1965

Height: 5'8" Weight: 11.5

International Honours: E Yth, E "U21"-8, E-7

**Position/Skill Factor:** Live wire striker with good pace, who hits the ball well. Often capable of losing his marker in the box, he has a knack of getting in on the end of chances.

**Career History:** Went to West Ham United, signing associated schoolboy forms in November 1979 and later became an apprentice in May 1981. He took the First Division by storm in his FL debut at Upton Park on New Years Day, 1983, marking the occasion with the opening goal in a 3-0 win over Tottenham Hotspur and followed up with another strike at Luton just three days later. Forming good strike partnerships with Paul Goddard and later with Frank McAvennie, he consistently topped the club's goalscoring charts and on 10 September 1986 his good club form was rewarded when he made his full England debut against Sweden, coming on as a substitute. The following two seasons saw him miss only one League game, while scoring 36 goals and Everton were forced to part with a club record fee when they signed him in the 1988 close season. Despite scoring a hat-trick against Newcastle United in his debut for the "Toffees", he has never established an automatic first team slot even though he has been the club's leading goalscorer every season. In 1991-92 followed a similar pattern to his three previous seasons at Goddison Park. In and out of the team, an early hat-trick against Spurs in October was another false dawn. Despite the departure of Mike Newell to Blackburn, his opportunities became fewer and fewer, following the signing of Mo Johnston. Unable to find a place in the side for the first seven matches of **1992-93**, which at the time appeared to signal the end of his Everton career, he was recalled and scored twice at Blackburn Rovers. This proved a false alarm, however, as he was dropped again and didn't return for a sustained period until mid-January. It was then he grabbed his chance, scoring four times in two matches and with renewed confidence the goals continued to flow. Since rewarded with a new three year contract, something that seemed impossible at the beginning of the season.

| | | | APPEARANCES | | | | GOALS | | | |
|---|---|---|---|---|---|---|---|---|---|---|
| Clubs | Signing Date | Transfer Fee | Lge | FL Cup | FA Cup | Others | Lge | FL Cup | FA Cup | Others |
| West Ham United | 9.82 | - | 203+9 | 19 | 24 | 1 | 92 | 14 | 11 | 1 |
| Everton* | 8.88 | £2,300,000 | 122+20 | 14+4 | 13+6 | 11+2 | 56 | 8 | 4 | 12 |

## COTTERELL Leo Spencer

Born: Cambridge, 2 September 1974

Height: 5'9" Weight: 10.0

International Honours: E Sch, E Yth

**Position/Skill Factor:** Very quick right-back who gets forward well. Enjoys his game and can run all day.

**Career History:** An England schoolboy international and Ipswich Town's first player from the FA School of Excellence, he first came to Portman Road as an associated schoolboy in October 1988 and signed on as a trainee (August 1991) on leaving school. After making great strides with Town's youth side in **1992-93**, he turned professional during the 1993 close season.

| | | | APPEARANCES | | | | GOALS | | | |
|---|---|---|---|---|---|---|---|---|---|---|
| Clubs | Signing Date | Transfer Fee | Lge | FL Cup | FA Cup | Others | Lge | FL Cup | FA Cup | Others |
| Ipswich Town* | 7.93 | - | | | | | | | | |

## COUZENS Andrew

Born: Shipley,
4 June 1975

Height: 5'10"

Weight: 11.11

**Position/Skill Factor:** Right-back who likes to get forward. A good passer, he likes nothing better than hitting long balls into his strikers.

**Career History:** A member of the Leeds United FA Youth Cup winning side, he has yet to make a first team appearance, having been at the club since July 1989 when he signed on as an associated schoolboy player. Later joined the staff at Elland Road as a trainee (August 1991) on leaving school and made the requisite progress to join the professional ranks towards the end of **1992-93** season.

| | | | APPEARANCES | | | | GOALS | | | |
|---|---|---|---|---|---|---|---|---|---|---|
| Clubs | Signing Date | Transfer Fee | Lge | FL Cup | FA Cup | Others | Lge | FL Cup | FA Cup | Others |
| Leeds United* | 3.93 | - | | | | | | | | |

## COWAN Thomas (Tom)

Born: Bellshill,
28 August 1969

Height: 5'8½"

Weight: 11.6

**Position/Skill Factor:** A naturally left footed left-back who is a very good passer, both long and short.

**Career History:** Joined Sheffield United from Glasgow Rangers for a surprisingly large fee, considering his limited experience. Started his career with Clyde FC who signed him in 1988 from Netherdale Boys Club, he quickly found his way into the "Bully Wee" team. After only seven months and 16 games with Clyde, he was snapped up by Rangers. However, competition for places is always fierce at Ibrox Park and most of his 12 first team appearances in three seasons were as substitute. Made his FL debut for Sheffield United at Norwich City on 17 August 1991 and although creating a good impression with the supporters at Bramall Lane in the first-half of the season, he was dropped in January 1992 in favour of David Barnes, before reappearing at the end of the season. Although once again involved in the battle for the left-back spot with David Barnes in **1992-93**, he still managed to play in half of United's Premier League games. A player who gives full commitment to the team, he is justifiably popular for his hard, but fair tackling. Another of United's players whose season was spoiled by injury, he has yet to score for the club, but has been unlucky with several good attempts smacking against the woodwork.

| | | | APPEARANCES | | | | GOALS | | | |
|---|---|---|---|---|---|---|---|---|---|---|
| Clubs | Signing Date | Transfer Fee | Lge | FL Cup | FA Cup | Others | Lge | FL Cup | FA Cup | Others |
| Sheffield United* | 8.91 | £350,000 | 41 | 5 | 2 | 1 | | | | |

## COWANS Gordon Sidney

Born: Cornforth, 27 October 1958

Height: 5'9" Weight: 10.7

International Honours: E Yth, E "U21"-5, E"B", E-10

**Position/Skill Factor:** Top class midfield general who can make a side tick. One of the most skilful players in the country, he has good vision and is a great passer, both short and long.

**Career History:** Known as "Sid" to his friends and colleagues, he first came to Aston Villa as an associated schoolboy in July 1973, before signing as an apprentice on leaving school April 1975. Made his FL debut as a substitute at Manchester City on 7 February 1976, while still an apprentice and by the end of the following season was a regular in a side that finished fourth in the First Division and won the League Cup, defeating Everton 3-2 at the third attempt after two dreary drawn games. Remained an automatic first choice in midfield for the next six years. Indeed, he was ever present in FL games for four seasons from 1979 to 1983 – 168 consecutive matches and a remarkable record for a midfield player which could not be equalled in the increasingly physical environment and tactical switches of the 1980s. Voted "Young Player of the Year" in 1980, he inspired Villa to an improbable League Championship in 1980-81 and an even more amazing European Cup triumph in 1982. After winning England Under 21 caps between 1978 and 1980 and a "B" cap in 1980-81, he graduated to full England honours when he made his debut against Wales on 23 February 1983. Seemed well set to be a regular England selection when he broke his leg in a pre-season game in August 1983 which kept him sidelined for the whole of 1983-84. Returned in 1984-85, but could not recapture his pre-injury form and at the end of the season he moved to Italian First Division club, Bari, along with team-mate Paul Rideout. It seemed to be the swansong of his career, but he made a surprise and brief England comeback in 1985-86 with two more caps against Egypt and the Soviet Union. After three not entirely successful years in Italy (two in the Second Division), he returned to Aston Villa in the summer of 1988. Seemed to be well past his best and when he was dropped at the start of the 1989-90 season the "writing was on the wall". To his and Graham Taylor's credit, he came back with renewed vigour to inspire Villa to second place, their best performance since 1980-81. Ever present, for the fifth time, in 1990-91, he amazingly made a second England comeback when Graham Taylor selected him against the Irish Republic in November 1990. The gamble did not pay off, however, as England failed to come to terms with the Irish tactics and the game passed him by. He finally lost his place in the Villa team in October 1991 and transferred soon afterwards to ambitious Blackburn Rovers whom he assisted to promotion, via the Play-Offs after a roller-coaster season. Never a regular in **1992-93**, he was initially omitted for Mark Atkins and on regaining the midfield role he quickly lost it to Patrik Andersson. However, he was never willing to accept demotion and by the end of the season was back in the side. Although his passing, which had been such a great influence the previous season, was not seen to its best effect, he worked tremendously hard to pick up any loose balls and tackled tigerishly. His one outstanding game came against his old team-mates, Aston Villa, which effectively ended their chances of winning the Premier League title and at the end of the season he rejoined his old club, having been released by Rovers.

| | | | APPEARANCES | | | | GOALS | | | |
|---|---|---|---|---|---|---|---|---|---|---|
| Clubs | Signing Date | Transfer Fee | Lge | FL Cup | FA Cup | Others | Lge | FL Cup | FA Cup | Others |
| Aston Villa | 9.76 | - | 276+10 | 23+4 | 19+1 | 23+1 | 42 | 5 | 3 | 2 |
| Bari (Italy) | 7.85 | £500,000 | | | | | | | | |
| Aston Villa | 7.88 | £250,000 | 114+3 | 15 | 9 | 11+1 | 7 | | | |
| Blackburn Rovers | 11.91 | £200,000 | 49+1 | 4 | 5 | 3 | 2 | | 1 | |
| Aston Villa* | 6.93 | - | | | | | | | | |

## COWE Steven Mark

Born: Gloucester, 29 September 1974

Height: 5'8" Weight: 10.2

**Position/Skill Factor:** Striker with a good appreciation of players around him. With two smart feet and a lovely touch, he shields the ball well and brings his team-mates into the game.

**Career History:** An Aston Villa professional signing during the summer, having been at Villa Park as an associated schoolboy (March 1990) and as a trainee (July 1991), his football in **1992-93** was confined merely to the youth team. Will be given every chance to make the step up in grade.

| | | | APPEARANCES | | | | GOALS | | | |
|---|---|---|---|---|---|---|---|---|---|---|
| Clubs | Signing Date | Transfer Fee | Lge | FL Cup | FA Cup | Others | Lge | FL Cup | FA Cup | Others |
| Aston Villa* | 7.93 | - | | | | | | | | |

## COX Neil James

Born: Scunthorpe, 8 October 1971

Height: 5'11" Weight: 13.0

International Honours: E "U21"-4

**Position/Skill Factor:** Right-back who reads the game well for one so young and has a lovely right foot.

**Career History:** Came through the Scunthorpe United junior ranks, first as an associated schoolboy (February 1986) and then as a trainee (July 1988), before turning pro with his local side. Soon afterwards he was pushed into the first team, making his FL debut at Halifax Town on 6 October 1990 at right-back, although misleadingly wearing the number seven shirt. After only 17 FL games for the "Irons", he was signed by Aston Villa manager Josef Venglos, on the recommendation of Villa Youth Coach,

Richard Money, who knew of Cox's potential, when previously a coach with Scunthorpe. Villa paid an astonishing fee for a player with less than six months FL experience. Obviously signed with a view to the future, than the present, his situation became "cloudy" under new manager Ron Atkinson, who made a point of clearing out nearly all of his two predecessors' purchases. Fortunately Cox was young and untried and survived the purge. Made the breakthrough into Villa's first team away to Notts County on 10 March 1992, and made several more appearances, all in midfield. Used either as cover for Earl Barrett when the latter was pushed into midfield, or as a substitute, he wasn't required for first team duty in **1992-93** until December. Progressed well with the England Under 21 side during the season and when picked for Villa he never let the side down, showing plenty of commitment to the cause. His biggest disappointment, apart from not becoming a regular first teamer, was his miss at Wimbledon in an FA Cup Fourth Round 6-5 penalty shoot-out defeat. Most certainly a player with an excellent future, he should become a fixture in the side before too long.

| | | | APPEARANCES | | | | GOALS | | | |
|---|---|---|---|---|---|---|---|---|---|---|
| Clubs | Signing Date | Transfer Fee | Lge | FL Cup | FA Cup | Others | Lge | FL Cup | FA Cup | Others |
| Scunthorpe United | 3.90 | - | 17 | | 4 | 4+1 | 1 | | | |
| Aston Villa* | 2.91 | £400,000 | 10+12 | 1+1 | 2+1 | 1 | 1 | | 1 | |

## CRAMB Colin

Born: Lanark, 23 June 1974

Height: 5'11" Weight: 11.13

**Position/Skill Factor:** Striker with good touch, who scores goals and can hold the ball up well for others.

**Career History:** Summer signing by Southampton manager, Ian Branfoot, from Scottish First Division club, Hamilton Academicals, following excellent displays in **1992-93**, along with team mate, Paul McDonald. One of the growing contingent of young Scots at The Dell, he made his Scottish League debut for the "Accies" in April 1991, but is still relatively inexperienced (at 19) and may have to wait longer than his fellow Scot for a Premier League debut. A player for the future, though.

| | | | APPEARANCES | | | | GOALS | | | |
|---|---|---|---|---|---|---|---|---|---|---|
| Clubs | Signing Date | Transfer Fee | Lge | FL Cup | FA Cup | Others | Lge | FL Cup | FA Cup | Others |
| Hamilton Acad. | 6.93 | - | 27+20 | | | 1 | 1+3 | 10 | | |
| Southampton* | 4.91 | £75,000 | | | | | | | | |

## CRISP Richard Ian

Born: Wordsley, 23 May 1972

Height: 5'6" Weight: 10.6

**Position/Skill Factor:** Hard tackling right-back, who can also play in midfield, he is prepared to work and run for the full 90 minutes. Has a wonderful attitude.

**Career History:** Signed professional in the 1990 close season for Aston Villa, having been on the club's books previously as an associated schoolboy (November 1986) and as a trainee (July 1988). Yet to make a first team appearance with Villa, he was a regular in the reserve side during **1992-93**, until being sidelined for four months with an ankle injury. On regaining full fitness, however, he had a spell on loan with Scunthorpe United, making seven (two substitute) first team appearances, including his FL debut at home to Chesterfield on 6 March 1993, before returning to Villa Park in April.

| | | | APPEARANCES | | | | GOALS | | | |
|---|---|---|---|---|---|---|---|---|---|---|
| Clubs | Signing Date | Transfer Fee | Lge | FL Cup | FA Cup | Others | Lge | FL Cup | FA Cup | Others |
| Aston Villa* | 7.90 | - | | | | | | | | |
| Scunthorpe United | 3.93 | Loan | 6+2 | | | | | | | |

## CROFT Brian Graham

Born: Chester, 27 September 1967

Height: 5'9"

Weight: 11.6

**Position/Skill Factor:** Left-winger with two good feet. Has the pace to go past defenders and makes excellent use of his crossing ability.

**Career History:** Locally born, he first joined Chester City as an associated schoolboy in November 1982, later becoming a YTS player, until signing professional forms during the 1986 close season. Prior to becoming a full-timer, however, he had already made his FL debut as a substitute at Peterborough United in a 3-0 defeat on 24 August 1985. After making occasional appearances in 1986-87, he won a semi-regular place in 1987-88, although frequently selected as substitute. Following a dispute with the manager, he was transferred to Fourth Division Cambridge United in October 1988, but after breaking into their team, quickly lost his place in February 1989 and saw out the season in their reserves. Given the circumstances of his departure from Chester, it was a surprise when manager Harry McNally re-signed him the following summer and with more experience under his belt he played in all but two games in 1989-90. He remained a regular performer until January 1992, when he once again fell out of favour with the manager. Amazingly, in view of his absence from Chester's first team, he was signed by Queens Park Rangers in the summer of 1992, thus finding the opportunity of playing in the Premier League when he might more realistically have faced the prospect of non-league football. However, he showed little sign of breaking into Rangers' first team in **1992-93**, spending the whole season playing in the reserves and will be hoping for an opportunity during the coming campaign.

| | | | APPEARANCES | | | | GOALS | | | |
|---|---|---|---|---|---|---|---|---|---|---|
| Clubs | Signing Date | Transfer Fee | Lge | FL Cup | FA Cup | Others | Lge | FL Cup | FA Cup | Others |
| Chester City | 7.86 | - | 36+23 | 1 | 2+3 | 7+3 | 3 | | 1 | |
| Cambridge United | 10.88 | £10,000 | 12+5 | | 3 | 3 | 2 | | 2 | 1 |
| Chester City | 8.89 | £3,000 | 90+24 | 7+1 | 9 | 9+1 | 3 | 2 | 3 | |
| Q.P.R.* | 8.92 | £60,000 | | | | | | | | |

## **CROOK** **Ian** Stuart

Born: Romford, 18 January 1963

Height: 5'8"

Weight: 10.6

International Honours: E"B"

**Position/Skill Factor:** Can dictate the game from midfield with his vision, flair and passing ability. Great long passer of the ball, who can unlock a defence when the game is tight.

**Career History:** Made his FL debut for Tottenham Hotspur at Coventry City on 1 May 1982, after being earlier signed by the club as an associated schoolboy (September 1977) and as an apprentice (May 1979). Unable to win a permanent place at White Hart Lane due to the vast array of talent available, after six seasons he was transferred to Norwich City. Following his arrival he had spells in and out of the side, but soon became a regular as he blossomed while playing in a good footballing side. Once regarded as a key player in the "Canaries'" passing style, he lost his first team place in October 1991 to the more prosaic Jeremy Goss and made only occasional appearances thereafter, playing little part in Norwich's FA Cup run. Back as a regular in **1992-93**, having come into the side at Manchester City following two substitute appearances, he missed only one more game, apart from a seven match spell between January and March, due to a calf injury. But begging to ask the question of what might have been had City's midfielders scored more goals last season and allowing for the fact that he netted in both matches against Nottingham Forest, for such a curling free-kick specialist, he has a feeble record, with only 17 in seven years. That is not to detract from his all-round value to the team, as he is usually at the heart of any attacking move and as one of the survivors of the last City team to seriously challenge for the title, you will rarely hear a bad word at the club about him.

| | | | APPEARANCES | | | | GOALS | | | |
|---|---|---|---|---|---|---|---|---|---|---|
| Clubs | Signing Date | Transfer Fee | Lge | FL Cup | FA Cup | Others | Lge | FL Cup | FA Cup | Others |
| Tottenham Hotspur | 8.80 | - | 10+10 | 1 | 0+1 | 1+1 | 1 | | | |
| Norwich City* | 6.86 | £80,000 | 183+21 | 17+3 | 14+4 | 11+1 | 14 | 2 | | 1 |

## **CULVERHOUSE** **David** Paul

Born: Harlow, 9 September 1973

Height: 6'0" Weight: 11.6

**Position/Skill Factor:** Centre-back who is very good in the air. Reads the game well and often comes out of defence with the ball.

**Career History:** A 1992 close season professional signing for Tottenham Hotspur, having been at the club since first joining as an associated schoolboy in March 1988, before graduating as a trainee in August 1990. Brother of Ian who plays for Norwich City, he made just five reserve team appearances for "Spurs" in **1992-93**, but will be pushing hard for a regular place this season as a springboard to the Premier League side.

| | | | APPEARANCES | | | | GOALS | | | |
|---|---|---|---|---|---|---|---|---|---|---|
| Clubs | Signing Date | Transfer Fee | Lge | FL Cup | FA Cup | Others | Lge | FL Cup | FA Cup | Others |
| Tottenham Hotspur* | 5.92 | - | | | | | | | | |

## **CULVERHOUSE** **Ian** Brett

Born: Bishops Stortford, 22 September 1964

Height: 5'10"

Weight: 11.2

International Honours: E Yth

**Position/Skill Factor:** Skilful right-back, cum sweeper. Good all rounder who reads the game well and intercepts well. A good passer, he loves to get forward and join in attacking play when the time is right.

**Career History:** Another of the former Tottenham Hotspur connection now at Norwich City, he was an apprentice at White Hart Lane (May 1981), before turning professional and making his FL debut at Notts County as a substitute on 21 February 1984. He had only appeared in one full League game for the "Spurs", but after signing for the "Canaries", he went straight into the first team, playing 18 matches, before he finished on the losing side and ended his first season, 1985-86, with a Second Division Championship medal. At the end of 1990-91 he had played more games for Norwich than any other member of the current squad and was justifiably honoured as City's "Player of the Year". Lost his place through injury in September 1991, but returned in February 1992 to play a part in Norwich's ultimately disappointing FA Cup run. In **1992-93**, while only absent on one occasion, he celebrated his 250th City League game against his old club, Tottenham and also became only the 14th player in "Canaries'" history to make over 300 first team appearances. And he has now played more outfield games for the club in the top flight than any other player. He also became the fifth captain of the season, during City's memorable challenge for the title, when the previous four encumbents, Ian Butterworth, Gary Megson, Ian Crook and John Polston, were all injured and although Norwich slipped to third in the Premier League, having been in the driving seat for much of the time, it was still their highest ever position. His younger brother David is a professional with Tottenham Hotspur.

| | | | APPEARANCES | | | | GOALS | | | |
|---|---|---|---|---|---|---|---|---|---|---|
| Clubs | Signing Date | Transfer Fee | Lge | FL Cup | FA Cup | Others | Lge | FL Cup | FA Cup | Others |
| Tottenham Hotspur | 9.82 | - | 1+1 | | | | | | | |
| Norwich City* | 10.85 | £50,000 | 253+1 | 19 | 26 | 17 | | | | 1 |

## CUNDY Jason Victor

Born: Wandsworth, 12 November 1969

Height: 6'1" Weight: 13.7

International Honours: E Yth, E "U21"-3

**Position/Skill Factor:** A powerfully built centre-back and one of the best young defenders in the country. Strong in the air and aggressive, he has a good turn of pace, which is sometimes used to good effect in an attacking role.

**Career History:** After signing associated schoolboy forms for Chelsea in March 1985, he became a trainee in July 1986. Made his FL debut for the "Blues" in the number five shirt at Queens Park Rangers on 1 September 1990 and showed a lot of early promise. Later that season, he had assured his place in Chelsea's defence, playing alongside Kenneth Monkou and producing some staggering displays in helping to secure a highly suspect defence. Lost his place to new signing Paul Elliott in 1991-92, but returned to first team duty in January 1992 in place of Kenneth Monkou. Somewhat surprisingly, was loaned to Tottenham Hotspur just before the transfer deadline and impressed enough to make the transfer permanent in the summer of 1992. Began **1992-93** partnering new signing, Neil Ruddock, at the heart of "Spurs'" defence, but after just 11 games he lost his place in the side to club captain, Gary Mabbutt. Has since only made six (including two substitute) appearances for the first team as cover for injuries and suspensions and may have to bide his time for a taste of regular football. Remembered mainly by fans for the 50 yard freak goal he scored in a 1-1 draw at Ipswich Town last August. Standing just inside Town's half, while clearing a throw-in aimed for Jason Dozzell, he was as amazed as anyone when the ball became wind assisted and flew goalwards over, out of position 'Keeper, Craig Forrest's head and into the top corner of the net.

| | | | APPEARANCES | | | | GOALS | | | |
|---|---|---|---|---|---|---|---|---|---|---|
| Clubs | Signing Date | Transfer Fee | Lge | FL Cup | FA Cup | Others | Lge | FL Cup | FA Cup | Others |
| Chelsea | 8.88 | - | 40+1 | 6 | 6 | 4 | 2 | | | |
| Tottenham Hotspur* | 3.92 | £750,000 | 23+2 | 2 | | | 1 | | | |

## CURETON Jamie

Born: Chippenham, 28 August 1975

Height: 5'8" Weight: 9.7

**Position/Skill Factor:** Striker. A real good poacher who is extremely quick and dangerous around the box. Always looking to shoot.

**Career History:** A recent Norwich City professional signing, he initially came to the club as an associated schoolboy (May 1990), before progressing as a trainee (October 1991). The first coaching he received was from former "Canary", David Williams, when he was a seven-year-old on a Pontins' holiday camp in north Wales and he has been hooked ever since. Yet to play for the first team, he has scored 87 goals in 108 appearances for other City sides. He set a club record at youth level with 39 goals in 1991-92 and created another with a double hat-trick against Leyton Orient in **1992-93**. And as part of the Norwich youth side's dynamic duo, alongside Ade Akinbiyi, he was invited to join the England under 17 squad and is definitely one to watch out for in the future.

| | | | APPEARANCES | | | | GOALS | | | |
|---|---|---|---|---|---|---|---|---|---|---|
| Clubs | Signing Date | Transfer Fee | Lge | FL Cup | FA Cup | Others | Lge | FL Cup | FA Cup | Others |
| Norwich City* | 5.93 | - | | | | | | | | |

## CURLE Keith

Born: Bristol, 14 November 1963

Height: 6'0" Weight: 12.0

International Honours: E"B", FL Rep, E-3

**Position/Skill Factor:** Central defender with the skills of a winger. Has great pace and is quite capable of coming out of defence with the ball to set up chances. Reads the game well.

**Career History:** Has had a tough soccer education, plying his trade around a variety of west country clubs from the lower reaches, before eventually reaching the top level with Wimbledon. Started as an associated schoolboy with Bristol City in December 1977, but then switched his allegiance to Bristol Rovers, firstly as an apprentice (July 1980) and later as a pro. Made his FL debut in a 2-2 draw at home to Chester City on 29 August 1981 and scored the equaliser for a Rovers side that included Gary Mabbutt and the player-manager, Terry Cooper. After failing to command a regular place, he was transferred to Torquay United, but four months later the club doubled their money when Terry Cooper re-signed him for Bristol City. As a midfielder he was unexceptional, despite his tremendous pace, but in October 1984, Cooper switched him to central defence, in which position he gradually excelled. After three seasons, he moved to Reading and although the club were relegated to the Third Division at the end of 1987-88, his outstanding displays in the "Royals'" defence, prompted Wimbledon to sign him. There, he teamed up with Eric Young, to form a formidable defensive partnership and captained the side with distinction. It was still a major surprise when Peter Reid signed him for Manchester City in the summer of 1991, for a massive fee, considering his lack of honours, except at "B" level. On

*Keith Curle*

the fringe of international selection, he finally made his England debut as substitute in April 1992 against the CIS in Mexico, following up with his full debut in Hungary two weeks later. Originally not included in the England squad for the European Championship Finals in Sweden, he was called up as a last minute replacement for the injured Gary Stevens and played at right-back in the 0-0 draw against the eventual champions, Denmark. A captain who leads by example, he had a very good first Premier League season in **1992-93** and nobody appreciated him more than his player-manager, Peter Reid. Only missing four games all season, his ice cool approach was ably demonstrated as he slotted home the three penalties awarded during the campaign, two of them being vital. Has developed a great understanding with his 'keeper, Tony Coton and his ability to close down opposing forwards is his prime asset and one that would pay the England management to reappraise, especially in the wake of the current defensive problems caused by lack of pace.

| | | | APPEARANCES | | | | GOALS | | | |
|---|---|---|---|---|---|---|---|---|---|---|
| Clubs | Signing Date | Transfer Fee | Lge | FL Cup | FA Cup | Others | Lge | FL Cup | FA Cup | Others |
| Bristol Rovers | 11.81 | - | 21 + 11 | 3 | 1 | | 4 | | | |
| Torquay United | 11.83 | £5,000 | 16 | | 1 | 1 | 5 | | 1 | |
| Bristol City | 3.84 | £10,000 | 113 + 8 | 7 + 1 | 5 | 14 + 1 | 1 | | | |
| Reading | 10.87 | £150,000 | 40 | 8 | | 5 | | | | |
| Wimbledon | 10.88 | £500,000 | 91 + 2 | 7 | 5 | 6 | 3 | | | 1 |
| Manchester City* | 8.91 | £2,500,000 | 79 | 7 | 5 | 1 | 8 | | | |

## CURRIE Darren

Born: Hampstead, 29 November 1974

Height: 5'9" Weight: 10.10

**Position/Skill Factor:** Left-winger with good skills, who has the ability to go past defenders and cross with either foot.

**Career History:** A recent professional signing for West Ham United, having first arrived at Upton Park as a trainee in July 1991, he impressed with his good play in the youth team and the occasional reserve outing during **1992-93** and looks to be an excellent prospect.

| | | | APPEARANCES | | | | GOALS | | | |
|---|---|---|---|---|---|---|---|---|---|---|
| Clubs | Signing Date | Transfer Fee | Lge | FL Cup | FA Cup | Others | Lge | FL Cup | FA Cup | Others |
| West Ham United* | 7.93 | - | | | | | | | | |

## DALEY Anthony (Tony) Mark

Born: Birmingham, 18 October 1967

Height: 5'7"

Weight: 10.8

International Honours: E Yth, E "B", E-6

**Position/Skill Factor:** Predominantly a right-winger, although comfortable on both flanks, he is very quick off the mark, has great pace and leaves defenders trailing when he runs at them. On his day the most exciting winger in the League, but prone to inconsistency and often wastes his superb runs on the ball with weak crosses.

**Career History:** Signed for Aston Villa as an associated schoolboy in April 1983, later becoming an apprentice in July 1984. Made his FL debut for Aston Villa away at Southampton on 20 April 1985 and was an instant hit with the fans. In 1985-86 he suffered the disappointment of relegation with Villa to the Second Division and the following season injury and loss of form kept him out of the side. However, he eventually won back his place in January 1988, making ten appearances and scoring three vital goals as Villa went back to the First Division as runners-up. Over the past few seasons he has missed several matches, mainly due to injury and the 1990-91 season saw him play only three more games after being carried off at Manchester United in December 1990, a sad loss for the Villa faithful. 1991-92 was probably his best season to date, holding down a regular place in the Villa team and winning his first England cap as substitute in the vital European Championship qualifying game in Poland, which England drew 1-1. Later in the season, he made his full international debut in Moscow against the CIS and was retained for the subsequent games against Hungary and Brazil. Used as a substitute in the opening match of the 1992 European Championship Finals in Sweden, a 0-0 draw against Denmark, he later played in what was ultimately the final game for England, against Sweden and had two good chances of scoring. Although he did not score and England went out of the competition, he was a danger to the Swedish defence every time he got the ball wide on the right and proved one of the few successes of a disappointing squad. Expected to shine in **1992-93**, he had a terribly disappointing season and had only played three games before a knee injury and the consequent operation sidelined him until March. Came back into a side who were battling it out with Manchester United at the top of the Premier League, but was obviously not match fit. And following the 0-0 draw at Tottenham Hotspur, he was used as a substitute for several games until starting a crucial match against Arsenal at Highbury and scoring the only goal of the game with a fine header. Also scored in the last game of the season, a 2-1 defeat at Queens Park Rangers, but by that time Villa had already conceded the Championship to United.

| | | | APPEARANCES | | | | GOALS | | | |
|---|---|---|---|---|---|---|---|---|---|---|
| Clubs | Signing Date | Transfer Fee | Lge | FL Cup | FA Cup | Others | Lge | FL Cup | FA Cup | Others |
| Aston Villa* | 5.85 | - | 170+36 | 17+1 | 13+1 | 13+2 | 30 | 4 | 2 | 1 |

## DAVIES Simon Ithel

Born: Winsford, 23 April 1974

Height: 5'11" Weight: 10.2

**Position/Skill Factor:** Midfield player who can run all day and is skilful on the ball.

**Career History:** Joined the Manchester United professional staff during the 1992 close season, having previously been at Old Trafford as an associated schoolboy (June 1988) and as a trainee (July 1990). No first team experience as yet, he only just made United's Central

League side in **1992-93**, although a regular in the "A" team that ran away with the Lancashire League Division One title. Still a young player with promise.

| Clubs | Signing Date | Transfer Fee | APPEARANCES Lge | FL Cup | FA Cup | Others | GOALS Lge | FL Cup | FA Cup | Others |
|---|---|---|---|---|---|---|---|---|---|---|
| Manchester United* | 6.92 | - | | | | | | | | |

# DAVIS Neil

Born: Bloxwich, 15 August 1973

Height: 5'8" Weight: 11.0

**Position/Skill Factor:** Striker who is very quick off the mark and can finish strongly.

**Career History:** Signed from non-League Redditch United in the 1991 close season, he has yet to make a first team appearance for Aston Villa. Played in the reserve side during **1992-93** and while a bit inconsistent at times he forged a good partnership with Graham Fenton. Should be one to watch out for.

| Clubs | Signing Date | Transfer Fee | APPEARANCES Lge | FL Cup | FA Cup | Others | GOALS Lge | FL Cup | FA Cup | Others |
|---|---|---|---|---|---|---|---|---|---|---|
| Aston Villa* | 5.91 | £25,000 | | | | | | | | |

# DAVIS Paul Vincent

Born: Dulwich, 9 December 1961

Height: 5'8"

Weight: 9.7

International Honours: E "U21"-11, E"B", FL Rep

**Position/Skill Factor:** Cultured midfielder with a magical left foot. Always appearing to have plenty of time, the sign of a top player, he is a lovely passer of the ball and has great vision.

**Career History:** Spotted by Arsenal as a 15-year-old, he came to Highbury on associated schoolboy forms in October 1977 and on leaving school he signed as an apprentice (June 1978). Making great progress he turned professional during the 1979 close season and went on to make his FL debut in the 2-1 win over the local rivals, Tottenham, at White Hart Lane on 7 April 1980. Over the next two seasons he battled to establish himself in a talented Arsenal midfield and gained representative honours when doing so. Although winning a League Cup winners medal in 1987 and a runners-up medal the following year, a lengthy suspension imposed early in 1988-89 meant he was unable to regain his place and was forced to spend most of the club's League Championship winning season in the reserves. His suspension for a well publicised off the ball incident, probably cost him an international career and subsequent injury problems left him out in the cold for nearly two years. Made up for that with a League Championship medal in 1990-91, only missing one match in the campaign. However, in 1991-92, after starting the season as first choice, he fell out of favour with manager George Graham following Arsenal's surprise elimination from the European Cup by Benefica, and lost his place to David Hillier. After 18 months in the wilderness at Highbury, he returned in **1992-93** to first team action at Norwich City in early March and retained his place for the remainder of the season, except when injured. Achieved a milestone of 400 first team appearances during a season that also saw him collect two cup winners medals following Arsenal's victories over Sheffield Wednesday in both the FA and League Cups. Had a superb game in the League Cup Final and was the architect of Paul Merson's opening goal.

| Clubs | Signing Date | Transfer Fee | APPEARANCES Lge | FL Cup | FA Cup | Others | GOALS Lge | FL Cup | FA Cup | Others |
|---|---|---|---|---|---|---|---|---|---|---|
| Arsenal* | 7.79 | - | 307+18 | 44+3 | 22+5 | 9+1 | 29 | 4 | 3 | 1 |

# DAY Christopher (Chris) Nicholas

Born: Waltham Cross, 28 July 1975

Height: 6'2"

Weight: 12.4

International Honours: E Yth

**Position/Skill Factor:** Agile goalkeeper and a good shot stopper. Also an excellent dead ball kicker.

**Career History:** A Tottenham Hotspur professional signing in **1992-93** after graduating as a trainee (August 1991) and yet to appear in the first team, he has been at White Hart Lane since first joining the club as an associated schoolboy in November 1989. Recently earned rave reviews for his displays in the successful England youth team.

| Clubs | Signing Date | Transfer Fee | APPEARANCES Lge | FL Cup | FA Cup | Others | GOALS Lge | FL Cup | FA Cup | Others |
|---|---|---|---|---|---|---|---|---|---|---|
| Tottenham Hotspur* | 4.93 | - | | | | | | | | |

## DEAN Craig

Born: Nuneaton, 1 July 1975

Height: 5'10" Weight: 11.7

International Honours: E Yth

**Position/Skill Factor:** Excellent midfield ball player, with creative ability and the skills to go with it. Has a great left foot and looks to hit the target as often as he can.

**Career History:** Started at Manchester United as an associated schoolboy in May 1990, before moving up the ladder as a trainee (July 1991) to sign professional forms during last summer. A promising young player, he has been given every chance by Alex Ferguson, having been injured for most of **1992-93** and playing in less than a handful of youth games.

| | | | APPEARANCES | | | | GOALS | | | |
|---|---|---|---|---|---|---|---|---|---|---|
| Clubs | Signing Date | Transfer Fee | Lge | FL Cup | FA Cup | Others | Lge | FL Cup | FA Cup | Others |
| Manchester United* | 7.93 | - | | | | | | | | |

## DEANE Brian Christopher

Born: Leeds, 7 February 1968

Height: 6'3" Weight: 12.7

International Honours: E"B", E-3

**Position/Skill Factor:** Powerful striker who leads the line well. Quick off the mark, brave and good in the air, he is always good for 20 plus goals a season.

**Career History:** Came through the junior ranks at Doncaster Rovers, making his FL debut at home to Swansea City on 4 February 1986 and spent little more than two seasons at the Belle Vue Ground before Dave Bassett, recognising his potential, signed him for Sheffield United in the 1988 close season. It was another typical "coup" by Dave Bassett as his scoring record for Doncaster was unimpressive, yet he was an instant success at Bramall Lane. Scored on his League debut for United, a 3-1 win at Reading in the opening game of the season and immediately formed a lethal striking partnership with Tony Agana as the club gained promotion to the Second Division that term. The following season, hopes were high of a United return to the First Division after a 15 year absence and Deane's 21 League goals played a big part in helping the "Blades" achieve their ambition. Despite his partner being continually dogged by injury, he continued to find the net regularly, even with United struggling at the foot of Division One. His impressive club form was finally translated into international status when he was selected for England's summer tour of 1991 and played twice against New Zealand. Although dogged by injury in the opening months of 1991-92, he returned in November to enjoy another successful season even without a regular partner and once again finished top scorer with 12 FL goals, plus four cup goals. United's leading scorer for the fourth season running in **1992-93**, he had the distinction of netting the first ever Premier League goal after just four minutes of the opener at home to Manchester United. Almost ever present, he only missed two games (due to suspension on reaching 20 points) and started another on the bench. Registered a hat-trick of headers in the FA Cup Third Round replay at Burnley and scored a second four days later at Ipswich Town. He was once again on the fringe of international honours, being on standby for most of the season and will surely be used by Graham Taylor this coming season. The subject of much transfer activity during the summer, with the United board split as to his worth, he was finally signed by local rivals, Leeds United, for a fee that was apparently £800,000 light of manager, Dave Bassett's valuation.

| | | | APPEARANCES | | | | GOALS | | | |
|---|---|---|---|---|---|---|---|---|---|---|
| Clubs | Signing Date | Transfer Fee | Lge | FL Cup | FA Cup | Others | Lge | FL Cup | FA Cup | Others |
| Doncaster Rovers | 12.85 | - | 59+7 | 3 | 2+1 | 2+2 | 12 | | 1 | |
| Sheffield United | 7.88 | £30,000 | 197 | 16 | 23+1 | 2 | 83 | 11 | 11 | 2 |
| Leeds United* | 7.93 | £2,700,000 | | | | | | | | |

## DEARDEN Kevin Charles

Born: Luton, 8 March 1970

Height: 5'11" Weight: 12.8

**Position/Skill Factor:** Very agile goalkeeper who is a good shot stopper. Also impresses with his early use of the ball.

**Career History:** Has been at Tottenham Hotspur since his early teens, first signing as an associated schoolboy in December 1984 and later graduating to trainee in July 1986. However, goalkeeping opportunities at White Hart Lane, with Erik Thorstvedt and Ian Walker on the staff, have almost been non-existent, apart from an appearance in the League Cup, a 2-1 victory over Hartlepool United in 1990-91. His FL debut came while on loan to

Cambridge United at Exeter City on 11 March 1989 and he kept a clean sheet in a 3-0 win. Has since been loaned out to Hartlepool United, Swindon Town, Peterborough United, Hull City, Rochdale and Birmingham City as he gains valuable experience. Finally made his League debut for Tottenham in **1992-93**, having been waiting in the wings for close on five seasons. While sitting on the bench under the new goalkeeping substitute ruling, he had been unused on seven occasions, but was finally required at half-time during the game at Nottingham Forest, following an injury to the Norwegian international, Thorstvedt. Conceded no further goals in a 2-1 defeat, but was back on the bench for the remainder of the season, as Walker took over as first team 'keeper.

| | | | APPEARANCES | | | | GOALS | | | |
|---|---|---|---|---|---|---|---|---|---|---|
| Clubs | Signing Date | Transfer Fee | Lge | FL Cup | FA Cup | Others | Lge | FL Cup | FA Cup | Others |
| Tottenham Hotspur* | 7.88 | - | 0+1 | 1 | | | | | | |
| Cambridge United | 3.89 | Loan | 15 | | | | | | | |
| Hartlepool United | 8.89 | Loan | 10 | | | | | | | |
| Swindon Town | 3.90 | Loan | 1 | | | | | | | |
| Peterborough United | 8.90 | Loan | 7 | | | | | | | |
| Hull City | 1.91 | Loan | 3 | | | | | | | |
| Rochdale | 8.91 | Loan | 2 | | | | | | | |
| Birmingham City | 3.92 | Loan | 12 | | | | | | | |

# DEWHURST Robert Matthew

Born: Keighley, 10 September 1971

Height: 6'3" Weight: 13.1

**Position/Skill Factor:** Central defender with a great attitude, who is good in the air and has a nice left foot.

**Career History:** Signed as a trainee for Blackburn Rovers in February 1989 and made his FL debut in a 2-1 win at Ewood Park against Hull City on 28 August 1990, a month before turning professional. Enjoyed a brief run in central defence and again at right-back, before returning to reserve team football in January 1991. During 1991-92 he didn't even get a "look-in", but had a two month loan spell with Third Division Darlington where he played 12 games in the number 11 shirt as an auxiliary defender. As in the previous season, **1992-93** brought him no first team opportunities with Rovers and he was loaned out to Huddersfield Town and non-League Wycombe Wanderers, who have since been promoted to the Football League as Champions of the GM Vauxhall Conference. By coincidence, he was at Huddersfield, although made unavailable for the match, when the "Terriers" knocked Blackburn out of the League Cup and on returning from his loan spell he impressed with the "stiffs".

| | | | APPEARANCES | | | | GOALS | | | |
|---|---|---|---|---|---|---|---|---|---|---|
| Clubs | Signing Date | Transfer Fee | Lge | FL Cup | FA Cup | Others | Lge | FL Cup | FA Cup | Others |
| Blackburn Rovers* | 10.90 | - | 13 | 2 | | 1 | | | | |
| Darlington | 12.91 | Loan | 11 | | | 1 | 1 | | | |
| Huddersfield Town | 10.92 | Loan | 7 | | | | | | | |

# DIBBLE Andrew (Andy) Gerald

Born: Cwmbran, 8 May 1965

Height: 6'2" Weight: 13.7

International Honours: W Sch, W Yth, W "U21"-3, W-3

**Position/Skill Factor:** Good all-round experienced goalkeeper who is strong on crosses and gets his angles right. A sound last line of defence.

**Career History:** He started his career with Cardiff City as an associated schoolboy in June 1979, before becoming an apprentice in July 1981. Made his FL debut while still an apprentice at home to Crystal Palace on 8 May 1982, at the end of a season which saw the club relegated to the Third Division. The following term, he was one of five goalies used by City, making 20 League appearances and helping the club back to the Second Division at their first attempt, as runners-up. After a further season at Ninian Park, he moved to Luton Town, but unfortunately, for him, he spent most of his time there as understudy to Les Sealey and was loaned out to Sunderland and Huddersfield Town, despite being capped twice by the full Welsh side against Canada in May 1986. However, he played a few games for the "Hatters" at the end of 1987-88, one of which included the League Cup Final against Arsenal. His 70th minute save from Nigel Winterburn's penalty when Luton were reeling at 2-1 down, was the turning point of the match. Amazingly, Luton found fresh legs to come back to win 3-2, thus collecting their first ever major football trophy. Despite this change of fortunes, three months later he was on his way to Manchester City, where he played a part in the club's successful challenge for promotion back to the First Division. Was a regular between the City posts during the following season, but in 1990-91 and 1991-92, found himself understudying Tony Cotton and was loaned out to Middlesbrough, Bolton Wanderers and West Bromwich Albion. After recovering from a hamstring injury at the end of 1991-92, he then broke his leg in a pre-**1992-93** season friendly against the Irish League. The new back pass rule may have been a contributory factor, as he had to run out to clear and collided with an oncoming forward. Out of action during 1992, he was loaned to Oldham Athletic in February, being promised a game against Chelsea, but was recalled two days later to be a substitute at Queens Park Rangers and found himself playing when Tony Coton was taken ill in the dressing room. Very popular with the fans, he received a great ovation when coming out for the second-half of the last game of the season against Everton.

| | | | APPEARANCES | | | | GOALS | | | |
|---|---|---|---|---|---|---|---|---|---|---|
| Clubs | Signing Date | Transfer Fee | Lge | FL Cup | FA Cup | Others | Lge | FL Cup | FA Cup | Others |
| Cardiff | 8.82 | - | 62 | 4 | 4 | | | | | |
| Luton Town | 7.84 | £125,000 | 30 | 4 | 1 | 1 | | | | |
| Sunderland | 2.86 | Loan | 12 | | | | | | | |
| Huddersfield Town | 3.87 | Loan | 5 | | | | | | | |
| Manchester City* | 7.88 | £240,000 | 75+1 | 6 | 5 | 2 | | | | |
| Middlesbrough | 2.91 | Loan | 19 | | | 2 | | | | |
| Bolton Wanderers | 9.91 | Loan | 13 | | | 1 | | | | |
| West Bromwich Albion | 2.92 | Loan | 9 | | | | | | | |

# DICHIO Daniel

Born: Hammersmith, 19 October 1974

Height: 6'2" Weight: 11.7

International Honours: E Sch

**Position/Skill Factor:** A striker who is very good in the air. Has nice touches and brings his team-mates into the game well.

**Career History:** A recent professional signing and yet another England schoolboy international on Queens Park Rangers' books, he first came to Loftus Road as an associated schoolboy (March 1989), before coming on board as a trainee in July 1991. An outstanding youth team skipper in **1992-93**, he is certainly one to watch out for.

| | | | APPEARANCES | | | | GOALS | | | |
|---|---|---|---|---|---|---|---|---|---|---|
| Clubs | Signing Date | Transfer Fee | Lge | FL Cup | FA Cup | Others | Lge | FL Cup | FA Cup | Others |
| Q.P.R.* | 5.93 | - | | | | | | | | |

# DICKINS Matthew (Matt) James

Born: Sheffield, 3 September 1970

Height: 6'4"

Weight: 14.0

**Position/Skill Factor:** Self assured goalkeeper with a good pair of hands who cuts a commanding figure between the posts.

**Career History:** Started out with his local club, Sheffield United, as an associated schoolboy in October 1986, before progressing as a trainee (July 1987) to professional status in the 1989 close season. After spending 18 months without a first team appearance at Bramall Lane, he received a free transfer and signed for Lincoln City towards the end of 1990-91. Made his FL debut in a 1-1 draw at Darlington on 9 April 1991 and went on to play in the remaining six games of the season, keeping two clean sheets. Created a big impression in 1991-92, despite missing three months of the season to injury, which cost him a move to Burnley. It all worked out well for him, when he was signed by Second Division Blackburn Rovers just before the transfer deadline as a potential replacement for Bobby Mimms. Sadly, for him, a misjudgment in the last minute of his debut game for Rovers at home to Wolverhampton Wanderers on 14 April 1992, allowed a long range shot from Paul Birch to creep into the net and cost his team a vital point. Mimms was recalled for the remaining League games and the Play-Offs. Yet to break back into Rovers' first team in **1992–93**, although he sat on the bench during the early season games, his opportunity seems to have gone with both Frank Talia and Darren Collier apparently now above him in the pecking order under Bobby Mimms. In an effort to keep him busy, he was loaned out to Blackpool where he spent three months with great success and his future may well lie outside the Premier League.

| | | | APPEARANCES | | | | GOALS | | | |
|---|---|---|---|---|---|---|---|---|---|---|
| Clubs | Signing Date | Transfer Fee | Lge | FL Cup | FA Cup | Others | Lge | FL Cup | FA Cup | Others |
| Sheffield United | 7.89 | - | | | | | | | | |
| Lincoln City | 2.91 | - | 27 | 1 | 1 | 2 | | | | |
| Blackburn Rovers* | 3.92 | £250,000 | 1 | | | | | | | |
| Blackpool | 1.93 | Loan | 19 | | | | | | | |

# DICKOV Paul

Born: Livingston, 1 November 1972

Height: 5'5½"

Weight: 11.5

International Honours: S Sch, S Yth, S "U21"-2

**Position/Skill Factor:** A skilful striker who has the ability to go a long way in the game and is a real competitor.

**Career History:** Came down south at the beginning of 1989 to sign on as a trainee at Arsenal and, after making good progress, he graduated to the professional ranks a year later and represented the Scottish Under 21 side during the 1992 close season. Made his PL debut in **1992-93** when he came on as substitute at home to Southampton on 20 March 1993 and in two further League appearances, he scored against Crystal Palace, after coming off the bench and again at Tottenham Hotspur in his first full game. A striker in the Tony Cottee mould, much is expected of the young Scot in the future.

| | | | APPEARANCES | | | | GOALS | | | |
|---|---|---|---|---|---|---|---|---|---|---|
| Clubs | Signing Date | Transfer Fee | Lge | FL Cup | FA Cup | Others | Lge | FL Cup | FA Cup | Others |
| Arsenal* | 12.90 | - | 1+2 | | | | 2 | | | |

# DICKS Julian Andrew

Born: Bristol, 8 August 1968

Height: 5'7" Weight: 11.7

International Honours: E "U21"-4, E "B"

**Position/Skill Factor:** Fierce tackling left-back, who can turn defence into attack with overlapping runs and a ferocious shooting ability, which brings him spectacular goals from free-kicks – also a deadly converter of penalties.

**Career History:** One of the architects of West Ham United's promotion to the Premier League last season, he first came into League football with Birmingham City as an associated schoolboy in September 1982, later becoming an apprentice (July 1984) on leaving school. Made his FL debut for Birmingham City as a substitute at Chelsea on 24 August 1985, while still a second year apprentice and followed a long line of good left-backs at St Andrews, in holding down a regular place by the end of the season, when he was awarded a professional contract. An automatic first choice at the age of 18-19, for the next two seasons, it was no great surprise when he was picked up by a First Division club, West Ham United in March 1988. At the end of the season he was selected for the Under 21 squad to compete in the annual summer tournament in the south of France, where he played four games, but somewhat, surprisingly, was never picked again. Soon became a popular player with supporters at Upton Park and was their "Player of the Year" in 1989-90 when he scored nine FL goals (seven from penalties). Sadly, he missed most of the "Hammers'" promotion season in 1990-91 with a serious knee injury sustained in October 1990. After 14 months out of action, he returned to first team duty in December 1991, scoring the equaliser with a penalty in a 1-1 draw with Sheffield United. However, he could do little to lift the "Hammers" from their position at the foot of the table and they gently subsided out of the top flight. The darling of the fans at Upton Park in **1992-93**, he could little wrong even if he was sent off in matches at Newcastle United, Wolverhampton Wanderers and Derby County and missed 11 games due to suspension. He was a tremendous influence on the team, but really must control his temper, especially under the microscope of the Premier League. Unfortunately, his appalling disciplinary record, with frequent bookings and occasional dismissals, may well prevent him from winning further international honours. Scored 11 (including six penalties) League goals, with only Tony Morley (20) and Clive Allen (14) in the charts ahead of him, an exceptional record for the club's left-back, even if he is of the maruading ilk. Penalties apart, two superb efforts in the 5-3 win at home against Oxford United, summed him up. The first was a thunderous shot into the top corner from outside the box and the second, a free-kick rocket, which went in off the wall. He also scored another brace in a 2-1 Upton Park win over Grimsby Town in March. With "Hammers" pipping Portsmouth on the post for the First Division runners-up tag, he can look forward to being one of the Premier League's stars this season, but only if he contains himself. His elder brother, Grantley, is also a footballer and also a left-back, with Bath City of the Vauxhall Conference.

| | | | APPEARANCES | | | | GOALS | | | |
|---|---|---|---|---|---|---|---|---|---|---|
| Clubs | Signing Date | Transfer Fee | Lge | FL Cup | FA Cup | Others | Lge | FL Cup | FA Cup | Others |
| Birmingham City | 4.86 | - | 83+6 | 5+1 | 5 | 2 | 1 | | | |
| West Ham United* | 3.88 | £300,000 | 152 | 19 | 14 | 11 | 29 | 5 | 2 | 4 |

## **DIGBY Fraser** Charles

Born: Sheffield, 23 April 1967

Height: 6'1"

Weight 12.12

International Honours: E Yth, E "U21"-5

**Position/Skill Factor:** Goalkeeper who is very agile and a great shot stopper. Uses good early throws to set up attacks and is a great long kicker with his left foot.

**Career History:** As an England schoolboy international, he was on Manchester United's books as an associated schoolboy (February 1982), before moving up, via the apprentice ranks (May 1983), to full-time professional towards the end of the 1984-85 season. Although making further progress as an England youth international, he was unable to break into United's first team squad and was transferred to Swindon Town in December 1986, having earlier made his FL debut, whilst on loan, against Rotherham United on 27 September 1986. Since joining the "Robins", he has been first choice up to 1991-92, assisting his team to promotion to Division Two, in his first season and to the Second Division Play-Offs in 1989-90 when, despite winning the Final against Sunderland, Swindon were denied promotion by Football League decree. He won five English under 21 caps in 1986-87 and 1987-88 and as an over age player in 1989-90. In 1991-92 his place came under threat from long time reserve, Nicky Hammond and he was out of the side for a long period in mid-season. However, by the end of 1991-92 he was back in favour and started **1992-93** as first choice. Again he lost his place, due to some indifferent performances on his part and the good form of Hammond in the reserves. His future in the club appeared to be in some doubt, especially when he was allowed out on loan for two months to Manchester United, as cover for Peter Schmeichel. However, his spell at Old Trafford obviously sorted out many of his problems, even though he wasn't called upon to play and with Hammond suffering his own loss of form, he returned to reclaim his place with far greater confidence than he had shown earlier. Playing in the last 27 games, he kept 12 clean sheets and although letting in three goals in a 4-3 thriller, he excelled himself in the Play-Off Final against Leicester City and can look forward to Premier League soccer with some confidence.

| | | | APPEARANCES | | | | GOALS | | | |
|---|---|---|---|---|---|---|---|---|---|---|
| Clubs | Signing Date | Transfer Fee | Lge | FL Cup | FA Cup | Others | Lge | FL Cup | FA Cup | Others |
| Manchester United | 4.85 | - | | | | | | | | |
| Swindon Town* | 9.86 | £32,000 | 256 | 22 | 13 | 28 | | | | |

## DIXON **Kerry** Michael

Born: Luton, 24 July 1961

Height: 6'0"

Weight: 13.10

International Honours: E "U21"-1, E-8

**Position/Skill Factor:** An old fashioned striker with an outstanding scoring record. Good in the air, strong on the ball with a good turn of pace, he also creates goals from wide positions with early crosses.

**Career History:** Son of a former pro, Mike, who turned out for Luton Town and Coventry City, he first played in Tottenham Hotspur's youth team as a centre-forward. No doubt to "Spurs'" later embarrassment, he was released after one year and joined Dunstable Town of the Southern League, where he built a reputation as a prolific goalscorer, before joining Reading. Made his FL debut at home to Walsall on 16 August 1980 and finished the campaign as the club's leading goalscorer. The next season, despite Reading being relegated, he still managed to top the Third Division scoring list with 26 League goals. Joining Chelsea, he quickly made his mark with two strikes in his first match and began to form a lethal partnership with David Speedie, notching 28 goals as the club won the Second Division title in 1983-84. Topped the First Division scoring chart in his first season in the top flight with 24 and despite a great start at international level, he was never given an extended run. This, after making his England debut as a sub against Mexico on 9 June 1985 and playing in the next two full internationals against West Germany and the USA and scoring four goals. Unfortunately for him, his arrival on the international scene coincided with that of Gary Lineker, a very similar player. In 1988-89, after just one season in the Second Division, Dixon's 25 goals were a major factor in the club gaining promotion and the Second Division Championship. His long reign as Chelsea's undisputed first choice centre forward seemed to be drawing to a close in 1991-92 as the goals dried up (only five in 34 FL games) and he lost his place in January to Graham Stuart and new signing, Tony Cascarino. Transferred to Southampton during the summer to replace Alan Shearer, he immediately linked up again with David Speedie in **1992-93** and scored his first goal for the club at Liverpool on 1 September. After injuring his ankle he was out of the side for a couple of matches and briefly won his place back from Ian Dowie, until being sidelined by injuries again. And with Speedie transfer listed soon afterwards, the "dream partnership" was broken. Had just two more full games, while scoring his 200th League goal, before being loaned out to Luton Town for the remainder of the season and helping the "Hatters" to save their First Division status.

| | | | APPEARANCES | | | | GOALS | | | |
|---|---|---|---|---|---|---|---|---|---|---|
| Clubs | Signing Date | Transfer Fee | Lge | FL Cup | FA Cup | Others | Lge | FL Cup | FA Cup | Others |
| Tottenham Hotspur | 7.78 | - | | | | | | | | |
| Reading | 7.80 | £20,000 | 110+6 | 6+1 | 2+1 | | 51 | | | |
| Chelsea | 8.83 | £175,000 | 331+4 | 40+1 | 18+2 | 25 | 147 | 24 | 8 | 12 |
| Southampton* | 7.92 | £575,000 | 8+1 | 2 | 1 | | 2 | | | |
| Luton Town | 2.93 | Loan | 16+1 | | | | 3 | | | |

## DIXON **Lee** Michael

Born: Manchester, 17 March 1964

Height: 5'9" Weight: 10.12

International Honours: E"B", FL Rep, E-20

**Position/Skill Factor:** One of the best attacking full-backs in the country, who gets forward and delivers telling crosses. His coolness under pressure has also proved invaluable in his role of penalty taker.

**Career History:** Broke into League football with Burnley after coming through the club's junior ranks, making his FL debut at home to Queens Park Rangers on 10 May 1983 and played in a handful of games before moving to

Chester City. He spent the best part of two seasons at Sealand Road until signing for Bury, but after just one season he was sold to Stoke City. Proved to be a most reliable defender and was soon transferred to Arsenal in return for a healthy profit margin. However, it wasn't until the beginning of 1988-89 that he won a regular place in the "Gunners'" defence at right-back, when he made the position his own and was rewarded for his consistency with a League Championship medal that season. And on 25 April 1990, he realised another ambition when he made his full England debut against Czechoslovakia at Wembley, sharing the spoils of a 4-2 victory. Was an ever present in 1990-91, scoring five penalties, as Arsenal stormed to their second League Championship in three seasons. His form dipped during 1991-92, but he recovered his poise and assisted the "Gunners" to a superb end of season run, following their mid-season slump. He lost his international place first to Rob Jones and then to Gary Stevens and perhaps was relieved to be recalled for the squad of 20 to compete in the 1992 European Championship Finals in Sweden. Tragically for him, he was then forced to withdraw through injury. **1992-93** saw him returning to his best form and reclaiming his England shirt, although the season was not without its disappointments. Following a poor run of spot-kicks, he lost the job to Ian Wright and after being sent off in the FA Cup Semi-Final against "Spurs", his subsequent suspension meant that he missed playing in the League Cup Final. Captained the team in the latter part of the season when Tony Adams was absent and nobody was stronger at the end of two gruelling FA Cup Final matches, the second of which the "Gunners" won 2-1 to lift the trophy.

| | | | APPEARANCES | | | | GOALS | | | |
|---|---|---|---|---|---|---|---|---|---|---|
| Clubs | Signing Date | Transfer Fee | Lge | FL Cup | FA Cup | Others | Lge | FL Cup | FA Cup | Others |
| Burnley | 7.82 | - | 4 | 1 | | | | | | |
| Chester City | 2.84 | - | 56+1 | 2 | 1 | 3 | 1 | | | |
| Bury | 7.85 | - | 45 | 4 | 8 | 1 | 6 | | 1 | |
| Stoke City | 7.86 | £40,000 | 71 | 6 | 7 | 4 | 5 | | | |
| Arsenal* | 1.88 | £400,000 | 180+2 | 23 | 21 | 8 | 15 | | 1 | |

## DOBBS Gerald Francis

Born: Lambeth, 24 January 1971

Height: 5'8" Weight: 11.7

**Position/Skill Factor:** Enthusiastic midfielder. Always gets his foot in, moves about well and has the ability to take on defenders and beat them.

**Career History:** Came to Wimbledon straight from school as a trainee in September 1989 and following good progress, he signed professional forms during the 1989 close season. After a long wait, he finally made his FL debut on 2 April 1992 at home to Nottingham Forest, appearing three more times before the end of the 1991-92 season. Followed up the previous season with some consistent displays in **1992-93**, appearing 23 (including four substitute) times for the first team and generally creating a good impression, especially with his ability to cross the ball from the left touchline. Although substituted in nine of those full matches and being sent off at Oldham Athletic towards the end of the season, he showed enough form to suggest that he could become a regular this season.

| | | | APPEARANCES | | | | GOALS | | | |
|---|---|---|---|---|---|---|---|---|---|---|
| Clubs | Signing Date | Transfer Fee | Lge | FL Cup | FA Cup | Others | Lge | FL Cup | FA Cup | Others |
| Wimbledon* | 7.89 | - | 18+5 | 2 | 1+1 | | 1 | | 1 | |

## DOBSON Anthony (Tony) John

Born: Coventry, 5 February 1969

Height: 6'1" Weight: 12.10

International Honours: E "U21"-4

**Position/Skill Factor:** Big, strong tackling left-back, or central defender, with a great left foot.

**Career History:** Locally born and bred, he signed for Coventry City as an apprentice in June 1985, graduating to the professional ranks a year later and after making good progress in the reserve side, he made his FL debut as a substitute at home to Leicester City on 6 December, 1986. Established himself at left-back from February 1989 to the end of the season when he won his four England Under 21 caps. Lost his place in October 1989 and when he returned it was more in central defence than his favoured position of left-back. Eclipsed by Paul Edwards from the start of 1990-91, he only played a handful of games, before deciding to further his career with ambitious Blackburn Rovers. At Ewood Park, he took up a position in central defence and assisted Rovers to stave off relegation in the closing weeks of the season. Dropped after only four games of 1991-92, he took little further part in the club's ultimately successful promotion campaign, but started **1992-93** in the left-back slot to allow Alan Wright to move into midfield. Unfortunate to lose his place, following a rather harsh dismissal at Wimbledon, he played steadily whenever required and was extremely unlucky that Wright's absence was covered by the signing of Le Saux from Chelsea. Although he currently appears to be surplus to requirements, he nevertheless had a good season.

| | | | APPEARANCES | | | | GOALS | | | |
|---|---|---|---|---|---|---|---|---|---|---|
| Clubs | Signing Date | Transfer Fee | Lge | FL Cup | FA Cup | Others | Lge | FL Cup | FA Cup | Others |
| Coventry City | 7.86 | - | 51+3 | 5+3 | | 0+1 | 1 | | | |
| Blackburn Rovers* | 1.91 | £300,000 | 36+5 | 5 | 2 | 1 | | | | |

## DODD Jason Robert

Born: Bath,
2 November 1970

Height: 5'10"

Weight: 11.10

International Honours:
E "U21"-8

**Position/Skill Factor:** Very useful right-back. All-round player who can defend, pass the ball well and is better than average in the air. Often comes forward to join up with the attack.

**Career History:** Joined Southampton as an 18-year-old from the Beazer Homes League side, Bath City, at the end of 1988-89. Made his FL debut the following season at Queens Park Rangers on 14 October 1989, when the "Saints" won 4-1 and in the next game, his first home appearance, Liverpool were trounced by the same scoreline. Had a good initial season, making 21 League appearances in all, but had to share the number two shirt with Alexei Cherednik during 1990-91. In 1991-92, he seemed to have established himself as the undisputed right-back at The Dell, only to lose his place to Jeff Kenna in the second-half of the season. Started **1992-93** as first choice right-back until a groin injury in the second match kept him out for two games. Later thrust into the unaccustomed role of substitute, after losing his place to Jeff Kenna, following the home League Cup-tie defeat at the hands of Crystal Palace, he came on for the injured Perry Groves at Chelsea and did so well that he began the next game in the number eight shirt. Briefly won back his full-back slot from Kenna, until making the remainder of his appearances in his new found midfield position in front of Kenna and scoring his first goal for the club on Easter Monday at Sheffield Wednesday.

| | | | APPEARANCES | | | | GOALS | | | |
|---|---|---|---|---|---|---|---|---|---|---|
| Clubs | Signing Date | Transfer Fee | Lge | FL Cup | FA Cup | Others | Lge | FL Cup | FA Cup | Others |
| Southampton* | 3.89 | £50,000 | 90+9 | 17+1 | 11 | 5 | 1 | | | |

## DONAGHY Malachy (Mal) Martin

Born: Belfast, 13 September 1957

Height: 5'10" Weight: 12.7

International Honours: NI "U21"-1, NI-81

**Position/Skill Factor:** Full-back, cum central defender, who does the job without any fuss. A good positional player, he is not easy to beat and passes the ball simply, but effectively.

**Career History:** Joined Luton Town from the Irish League side, Larne, in the 1978 close season and made his FL debut at home in a 6-1 thrashing of Oldham Athletic on 19 August 1978. Settled into the side as a regular and was an ever present in 1979-80, 1980-81, 1981-82, 1984-85, 1985-56 and 1986-87 and during his ten years at Kenilworth Road, he only missed 16 League games, a remarkable record of consistency. Won the first of many international caps when he played for Northern Ireland against Scotland at Windsor Park on 16 May 1980 and shared the spoils of a 1-0 victory. Originally played at left-back, but was switched to central defence in 1981-82, following the transfer of Paul Price to Tottenham. Although not noted as a goalscorer, he scored nine in 1981-82 when the club won the Second Division title. Prior to signing for Manchester United, he also won a League Cup winners medal when Luton beat Arsenal 3-2 in 1988. At United, he initially played alongside Steve Bruce at the centre of the defence, but on the arrival of Gary Pallister he was switched to right-back. Following a lay off through injury in 1989-90, he was loaned back to Luton in an effort to speed up match fitness, before returning to Old Trafford. In 1990-91 he wore five different shirts, although nearly always operating in central defence and was on the bench for the European Cup Winners Cup Final win over Barcelona. Remained a valuable squad player in 1991-92, covering for Steve Bruce and Gary Pallister and for both full-back positions as required. Unlucky to miss out on United's League Cup Final victory over Nottingham Forest, as he had played regularly in the preceding weeks. Transferred to Chelsea at the beginning of **1992-93** for a fee of £100,000, plus £5,000 per game up to 50, he was a revelation, missing only three matches during the term. And at today's inflated prices for inferior quality players, he turned out to be one of the bargains of the first Premier League season where his intelligent reading of the game, compensating for his lack of pace, often delighted "Blues'" supporters. At the age of 35 he could still have a part to play with Chelsea, as the "Blues" prepare for the coming season under new player/manager, Glenn Hoddle.

| | | | APPEARANCES | | | | GOALS | | | |
|---|---|---|---|---|---|---|---|---|---|---|
| Clubs | Signing Date | Transfer Fee | Lge | FL Cup | FA Cup | Others | Lge | FL Cup | FA Cup | Others |
| Luton Town | 6.78 | £20,000 | 410 | 34 | 36 | 3 | 16 | 2 | 3 | |
| Manchester United | 10.88 | £650,000 | 76+13 | 9+5 | 10 | 3+3 | | | | |
| Luton Town | 12.89 | Loan | 5 | | | | | | | |
| Chelsea* | 8.92 | £100,000 | 39+1 | 5 | 1 | | 2 | | | |

## DOOLAN John

Born: Liverpool, 7 May 1974

Height: 5'11½" Weight: 12.4

**Position/Skill Factor:** Right-back, who can play in central defence. Excellent right foot and uses the ball well, both short and long.

**Career History:** A local discovery, he joined the Everton professional staff during the 1992 close season, having previously been at Goodison as an associated schoolboy (February 1989) and as a trainee (June 1990). Didn't make the breakthrough to the first team squad in **1992-93**, but he is a promising player with plenty of time on his side and should achieve this aim in the very near future as he progresses through the reserves.

| | | | APPEARANCES | | | | GOALS | | | |
|---|---|---|---|---|---|---|---|---|---|---|
| Clubs | Signing Date | Transfer Fee | Lge | FL Cup | FA Cup | Others | Lge | FL Cup | FA Cup | Others |
| Everton* | 6.92 | - | | | | | | | | |

## DORIGO Anthony (Tony) Robert

Born: Melbourne, Australia, 31 December 1965

Height: 5'8" Weight: 10.7

International Honours: E "U21"-11, E"B", E-14

**Position/Skill Factor:** Attacking left-back with a lovely left foot. Plays like a midfielder when in possession. Likes nothing better than surging upfield with the ball and his deep crosses have created many goal scoring opportunities. Also packs a fierce shot from free-kicks.

**Career History:** Emigrated from Australia to sign associated schoolboy forms for Aston Villa in January 1982, before being apprenticed in September of the same year. made his FL debut away to Ipswich Town on 12 May 1984 and claimed a regular place over the next two seasons. Joined Chelsea when Villa were relegated from the First Division, but saw his new club suffer the same fate at the end of his first season there. However, the "Blues" bounced straight back as Second Division Champions in 1988-89, with Dorigo's raids down the left flank helping to make goals for both Kerry Dixon and Gordon Durie. Also scored the only goal of the game when Chelsea beat Middlesbrough in the 1989-90 Zenith Data Cup Final at Wembley. Now a regular in the England squad, he made his full international debut against Yugoslavia at Wembley on 6 September 1989, when coming off the sub's bench. Transferred to Leeds in the summer of 1991, his signing perhaps was the final piece of the jigsaw for Howard Wilkinson, in creating a perfectly balanced team with experienced quality players in each position. Reached the zenith of his career to date, playing an outstanding role in Leeds' unexpected, but well merited League Championship triumph. At international level he is unlucky to understudy one of England's (and Europe's) finest players in Stuart Pearce. Nevertheless, he won four more caps in 1991-92 and was included in Graham Taylor's squad of 20 for the 1992 European Championship Finals in Sweden, although he did not make an appearance. Added several more international caps to his collection in **1992-93**, when standing in for Stuart Pearce

and with the latter not available for the World Cup qualifiers at the end of the season, he played in the 1-1 draw against Poland, before travelling to America for the USA Cup games during the summer. Earlier, as 1992-93 got underway, he scored a brilliant free-kick to help clinch the Charity Shield match against Liverpool and in a season of Leeds' inconsistent performances, he was outstanding throughout. Sustained an injury at Chelsea in March, which forced him to miss seven games, before returning at Coventry City on the last day of the campaign. An extremely valuable member of the team and arguably the best left-back in the country, he was selected by his fellow professionals for the PFA Premier League side award.

| | | | APPEARANCES | | | | GOALS | | | |
|---|---|---|---|---|---|---|---|---|---|---|
| Clubs | Signing Date | Transfer Fee | Lge | FL Cup | FA Cup | Others | Lge | FL Cup | FA Cup | Others |
| Aston Villa | 7.83 | - | 106+5 | 14+1 | 7 | 2 | 1 | | | |
| Chelsea | 7.87 | £475,000 | 146 | 14 | 4 | 16 | 11 | | | 1 |
| Leeds United* | 6.91 | £1,300,000 | 71 | 6 | 5 | 7 | 4 | | | 1 |

## DOW Andrew (Andy) James

Born: Dundee, 7 February 1973

Height: 5'9" Weight: 10.7

International Honours: S "U21"-2

**Position/Skill Factor:** Left-back who can also play on the left side of midfield. An athlete with good skills and a sweet left foot, he is a passer rather than an out and out defender.

**Career History:** A talented young Scottish player who became Glenn Hoddle's first signing for Chelsea when coming south during the summer. Started with the Scottish Premier League side, Dundee, having been spotted in local junior football with Sporting Club 85 and following just four substitute appearances in 1991-92, he began to make people sit up and take notice in **1992-93**. In playing a further 15 (including six as substitute) games and showing excellent form, he was awarded a Scottish under 21 cap for the game against Malta at Tannadice Park. Predominantly bought by Chelsea as an investment for the future, it would not surprise anyone who has seen him in action if he came through much earlier than anticipated.

| | | | APPEARANCES | | | | GOALS | | | |
|---|---|---|---|---|---|---|---|---|---|---|
| Clubs | Signing Date | Transfer Fee | Lge | FL Cup | FA Cup | Others | Lge | FL Cup | FA Cup | Others |
| Dundee | 11.90 | - | 8+10 | | 1 | | 1 | | | |
| Chelsea* | 7.93 | Tribunal | | | | | | | | |

## DOWIE Iain

Born: Hatfield, 9 January 1965

Height: 6'1" Weight: 12.12

International Honours: NI "U21"-1, NI-16

**Position/Skill Factor:** Big powerful striker who is an excellent header of the ball, particularly at the far post. A good target man, he brings his team-mates into the game with clever flicks and headers.

**Career History:** Was a relatively late arrival to League football at the age of 23, joining Luton Town from non-League Hendon, having previously played with St Albans City, Hertford Town and Cheshunt. Made his FL debut at Charlton Athletic on 14 January 1989 as a substitute and only played in one full game that season. Finally, won a regular place up front in November 1989, after Roy Wegerle had departed to Queens Park Rangers and his four goals in the final five matches, helped Luton claw themselves away from the foot of the First Division to avoid relegation on goal difference. His good form did not go unnoticed at international level, either and he made his debut as a sub for Northern Ireland against Norway on 27 March 1990 in Belfast. In 1990-91, after scoring twice in the 3-1 win over Liverpool and getting the winner against Nottingham Forest, he was transferred to West Ham United, who were looking to bolster their First Division prospects. Promotion was duly attained, with Iain playing in the final 12 matches and scoring four goals. Surprisingly, in view of the "Hammers'" subsequent inability to score, he was transferred to Southampton in the early weeks of 1991-92 and played a significant role in the "Saints'" ultimately successful struggle against relegation. Whilst goal scoring opportunities were scarce in the club's essentially negative style of play, all of his nine FL goals were either match winners, or point savers. With the new signings of Kerry Dixon and David Speedie, he was expected to act as understudy as the **1992-93** season commenced, but after six matches and only one goal from the pair, he was restored up front to partner Dixon, with Speedie dropping behind. And when both newcomers were dropped from favour, he played virtually every game to the end of the season as lone striker, with Matthew Le Tissier and Nicky Banger feeding off him. Also won his international place back and scored the only goal in the World Cup qualifier in Lithuania.

| | | | APPEARANCES | | | | GOALS | | | |
|---|---|---|---|---|---|---|---|---|---|---|
| Clubs | Signing Date | Transfer Fee | Lge | FL Cup | FA Cup | Others | Lge | FL Cup | FA Cup | Others |
| Luton Town | 12.88 | £30,000 | 53+13 | 3+1 | 1+2 | 5 | 15 | | | 4 |
| Fulham | 9.89 | Loan | 5 | | | | 1 | | | |
| West Ham United | 3.91 | £480,000 | 12 | | | | 4 | | | |
| Southampton* | 9.91 | £500,000 | 59+7 | 3+3 | 4 | 4 | 20 | 1 | | |

## DOYLE Maurice

Born: Ellesmere Port, 17 October 1969

Height: 5'8" Weight: 10.7

**Position/Skill Factor:** A midfielder with very good engines who loves to battle for the ball, he has the right ingredients to become a good player, but needs more experience.

**Career History:** Made his FL debut for Crewe Alexandra, while still a trainee, at Tranmere Rovers on 25 April 1988 in a 2-2 draw. Started life at Gresty Road as an associated schoolboy (December 1985), before becoming a trainee in July 1986 and turning pro with the club in the 1988 close season. Had appeared in only three full League games, although scoring twice, in 1988-89, when Queens Park Rangers signed him as a player for the future. While still awaiting a game for the "Rs", he was loaned back to Crewe for a spell during 1990-91 and on his return, continued to make no first team appearances during the following season. However, as captain of the successful reserve side he kept busy and finally made his Premier League debut for the club in **1992-93**. Standing in for Simon Barker at Ipswich Town, he was substituted, but came back to play four games in a row before stepping back into the reserves.

| | | | APPEARANCES | | | | GOALS | | | |
|---|---|---|---|---|---|---|---|---|---|---|
| Clubs | Signing Date | Transfer Fee | Lge | FL Cup | FA Cup | Others | Lge | FL Cup | FA Cup | Others |
| Crewe Alexandra | 7.88 | - | 6+2 | | | | 2 | | | |
| Q.P.R.* | 4.89 | £120,000 | 5 | | | | | | | |
| Crewe Alexandra | 1.91 | Loan | 6+1 | | 2 | | 2 | | | |

## DOZZELL Jason Alvin Winans

Born: Ipswich, 9 December 1967

Height: 6'2"

Weight: 12.0

International Honours: E Yth, E "U21"-9

**Position/Skill Factor:** Midfield player with lovely skills, whose first touch gives him both time and space. Good in the air, he is also highly capable of scoring with late runs into the box.

**Career History:** Local boy who has come through the ranks with Ipswich Town, firstly as an associated schoolboy (February 1982) and then as an apprentice (April 1984), before turning pro. Actually made his FL debut while still an associated schools player, coming on as a sub at home to Coventry City on 4 February 1984 and scoring in a 3-1 victory. At 16 years and 56 days, he is the youngest player ever to have appeared in a League match for Ipswich. In 1985-86 he won a regular place in the side, but it was not enough to save them from relegation to the Second Division. Was ever present in Town's team the following season and yet again in 1989-90, when he was a key team player in midfield. Lost his place at the beginning of 1990-91 and when John Lyall restored him to the first team in November it was in a forward position. He continued in this role during Ipswich's Second Division Championship campaign of 1991-92 in partnership with Chris Kiwomya. Although not a prolific scorer (11 goals in 45 FL games), his deft touches create scoring opportunities for his colleagues. Also scored four goals in five FA Cup games, including one in extra-time at Anfield in a Fifth Round replay, which seemed certain to give Ipswich a historic victory — never having won there in 25 visits. On this, as on so many other occasions, Liverpool "came back from the dead" to win the tie. Missed just one game in **1992-93**, as Town concentrated on consolidating their newly won Premier League place, playing in a variety of positions — midfield, striker and even central defence. The attack was more potent when he lead the line, but on those occasions his passing skills in midfield were sorely missed. Made his 400th appearance for the club during the season, only the eighth player in Town's history to reach the milestone. The local derby against Norwich City at home brought the best from him, with two goals, one in either half and the second a truly magnificent effort, following a run from the halfway line, which ended with crisp shot from 25 yards to set up a 3-1 victory. Offered a long term contract in February, at the time of going to press he had yet to sign.

| | | | APPEARANCES | | | | GOALS | | | |
|---|---|---|---|---|---|---|---|---|---|---|
| Clubs | Signing Date | Transfer Fee | Lge | FL Cup | FA Cup | Others | Lge | FL Cup | FA Cup | Others |
| Ipswich Town* | 12.84 | - | 312+20 | 29+1 | 22 | 22 | 52 | 3 | 12 | 4 |

## DUBERRY Michael Wayne

Born: London, 14 October 1975

Height: 6'1" Weight: 13.4

**Position/Skill Factor:** Very strong and quick central defender, who is already a excellent reader of the game.

**Career History:** A young player who has made rapid progress recently, he first came to Chelsea as an associated schoolboy in December 1989. After signing on as a trainee in August 1992, he turned professional during the 1993 close season, having impressed in 33 youth and 19 reserve team matches in **1992-93** and has all the makings of a good un.

| | | | APPEARANCES | | | | GOALS | | | |
|---|---|---|---|---|---|---|---|---|---|---|
| Clubs | Signing Date | Transfer Fee | Lge | FL Cup | FA Cup | Others | Lge | FL Cup | FA Cup | Others |
| Chelsea* | 6.93 | - | | | | | | | | |

## DUBLIN Dion

Born: Leicester, 22 April 1969

Height: 6'0" Weight: 12.4

**Position/Skill Factor:** Big, powerful striker who is strong in the air and not short of skill on the ground.

**Career History:** Tall and rangy, he was playing for non-League Oakham United, a works team based in Sutton in Ashfield and competing in the Central Midlands League, when spotted by Norwich City during the latter part of 1987–88. However, after signing pro forms for the "Canaries", he was released during the 1988 close season without receiving a reasonable opportunity and joined Fourth Division Cambridge United on a non-contract basis. Following a trial period, during which, he made his FL debut as a substitute for George Reilly at Wrexham on 16 December 1988, he signed on for the club as full-time

professional and in only his second full appearance, scored a hat-trick in a 5-1 victory at Peterborough. In 1989-90 he played in every FL game, including nine as substitute, forming a highly effective striking partnership with John Taylor and finished joint top scorer with 15 FL goals, plus six in cup competitions. During the season, Cambridge enjoyed their best ever FA Cup run, reaching the Sixth Round after victories over First Division Millwall and Second Division, Bristol City, before falling to Crystal Palace. Making up the backlog of League games, the team rose from 15th to sixth position in the closing months, thus qualifying for the Play-Offs, where they eventually won promotion to the Third Division after defeating Chesterfield 1-0 at Wembley, with Dublin scoring the only goal. Despite scraping into a promotion place, in 1990-91, Cambridge won the Third Division Championship on the last day of the season with Dublin once again playing every game and top scoring with 16 FL goals, plus five in the cups. For the second consecutive season they reached the Sixth Round of the FA Cup, defeating three Second Division teams en-route, Wolves (1-0) Middlesbrough (2-0) and most notably the League Cup winners, Sheffield Wednesday (4-0), before succumbing to Arsenal. In 1991-92 they seemed certain to go all the way to Division One in the shortest possible time, before fading in the closing weeks and being eliminated by Leicester City, who routed them 5-1 in the Play-Offs. For the third consecutive season, Dublin was top scorer with 15 FL goals, plus four cup goals. By this time the secret of Cambridge's success under manager John Beck was "rumbled" and it was not based on good football, but following the egregious style of Wimbledon, with constant high balls into the penalty area, long throw-ins, plus various acts of gamesmanship, both on and off the pitch. The height and strength of Dublin in creating "knock downs" was vital to this strategy. If he was disappointed at failing to reach the Premier League, he did not remain so for long as in a surprise move, Alex Ferguson signed him for Manchester United, before the start of **1992-93**, apparently as a consolation for missing out on Alan Shearer. He made an eventful start at Old Trafford, substitute in the first three games, scoring the winning goal in the last minute of his full debut at Southampton and then breaking his leg in the sixth game at home to Crystal Palace, bringing his season to a premature end. Towards the end of the campaign he recovered enough to make it back into the United squad, but following the arrival of Eric Cantona and with so many talented forwards available, he will find it difficult to gain a regular place in 1993-94.

| | | | APPEARANCES | | | | GOALS | | | |
|---|---|---|---|---|---|---|---|---|---|---|
| Clubs | Signing Date | Transfer Fee | Lge | FL Cup | FA Cup | Others | Lge | FL Cup | FA Cup | Others |
| Norwich City | 3.88 | – | | | | | | | | |
| Cambridge United | 8.88 | – | 133+23 | 8+2 | 21 | 14+1 | 53 | 5 | 11 | 5 |
| Manchester United* | 7.92 | £1,000,000 | 3+4 | | | | 1 | | | |

## DUFFIELD Peter

Born: Middlesbrough, 4 February 1969

Height: 5'6"

Weight: 10.7

**Position/Skill Factor:** Hard working forward who can also play in midfield when required. Often capable of scoring vital goals.

**Career History:** Began his career with his home town club, Middlesbrough, where he signed as an associated schoolboy in September 1984 and as a trainee in August 1985, before going pro. He was released at a time when Middlesbrough were facing bankruptcy, cutting and cut their playing staff to a mere 14 and signed for Sheffield United in the summer of 1987. Made his FL debut as a sub at home to Leicester City on 17 October 1987, but after only a handful of games in his first year, he was loaned out to Fourth Division Halifax Town. Had better fortune there and in his first League game, a 2-2 draw against Scunthorpe United, he scored in the opening minute and followed that up with a second goal, 12 minutes later. After scoring at the rate of a goal every two games during the loan period, he arrived back at Bramall Lane and following a run of subs' appearances and with United losing their way in the Third Division promotion battle, he got the chance he had been waiting for. Having taken on the job of penalty king, he helped himself to a dozen goals as United returned to the Second Division as runners-up. Out in the cold again, his first match of the 1989-90 campaign was when he came on as a substitute against Portsmouth to score twice in a 2-1 win. Six weeks later, he suffered a broken leg, sustained while scoring against Swindon Town. Since that injury, he has only managed a few appearances from the bench as he looks to fight his way back into first team reckoning. Following two substitute appearances for the "Blades" early in 1991-92, he fell out of favour and had an unsuccessful spell on trial at St. Mirren during the latter half of the season, before arriving back at Bramall Lane. Failed to make a single first team appearance for the "Blades" in **1992-93** and on occasion even struggled to make the reserve side. Had loan spells with both Crewe Alexandra and Stockport County, which culminated in making a losing Wembley appearance for the latter in the Play-Off Semi-Final.

| | | | APPEARANCES | | | | GOALS | | | |
|---|---|---|---|---|---|---|---|---|---|---|
| Clubs | Signing Date | Transfer Fee | Lge | FL Cup | FA Cup | Others | Lge | FL Cup | FA Cup | Others |
| Middlesbrough | 11.86 | - | | | | | | | | |
| Sheffield United* | 8.87 | - | 34+24 | 3+5 | 6+2 | 3+2 | 16 | 2 | 1 | 3 |
| Halifax Town | 3.88 | Loan | 12 | | | 1 | 6 | | | |
| Rotherham United | 3.91 | Loan | 17 | | | | 5 | | | |
| Blackpool | 7.92 | Loan | 3+2 | 0+1 | | | 1 | | | |
| Crewe Alexandra | 1.93 | Loan | 0+2 | | 0+1 | | | | | |
| Stockport County | 3.93 | Loan | 6+1 | | | 2+1 | 4 | | | |

## DURIE Gordon Scott

Born: Paisley, 6 December 1965

Height: 5'10" Weight: 13.0

International Honours: S "U21"-4, S"B", S-21

**Position/Skill Factor:** A skilful, strong running striker who is capable of scoring spectacular goals. Has the ability to ghost past defenders and makes good runs off the ball. Always looking to score when inside the box.

**Career History:** Began his soccer career with Scottish junior side, Hill O'Beath, before signing for East Fife and then Hibernian. After scoring 40 goals in 111 matches, he was soon attracting scouts from south of the border and Chelsea moved in quickly for him. He made his FL debut at Stamford Bridge against Watford on 5 May 1986 in the last game of the 1985-86 season and the "Blues" were beaten 5-1. Found it difficult to win a first team place initially, but once David Speedie had left for Coventry City, he became a regular up front, alongside Kerry Dixon. Although unfortunate to be dogged by injuries, he has still managed to score over 50 League goals for Chelsea, including five in a 7-0 win at Walsall during 1988-89, the season that the "Blues" ran away with the Second Division Championship. Earlier, after winning Under-21 honours, he finally made his debut for the full Scottish side as a substitute in a European Championship qualifying round in Bulgaria on 11 November 1987. Struggled with injuries in 1990-91, but still finished as Chelsea's top scorer with 12 goals from 24 League outings. On the eve of the 1991-92 season, he was transferred to Tottenham Hotspur for a massive fee and by comparison with his time at Chelsea, he remained relatively injury free in his first season at White Hart Lane, playing in 31 League games. Unfortunately, his scoring touch deserted him, going 17 League games without a goal between September 1991 and late March 1992, before ending his "drought" with a hat-trick against Coventry City. Six FL goals, plus four in cup matches, was hardly the return "Spurs" were expecting on their investment. Despite his disappointing tally at club level, he remained first choice for Scotland's national team and was included in Andy Roxburgh's squad for the European Championship Finals in Sweden where he played against both Holland and Germany with some distinction. Began **1992-93** with a solitary goal from four matches, before teaming up with new signing, Teddy Sheringham and scoring three more in his next six appearances. At that stage, what had looked to be a winning partnership, was disrupted through injuries sustained by the Scot and he only played a further ten games during the season. Talk of a transfer and an FA enquiry over an alleged "feigning" injury incident during the home game against Coventry City, did not help matters. The incident, which brought a booking for both players, had occured after tempers had become frayed, when a "flare-up" involving City defender, Andy Pearce, had left the "Spurs'" man on the floor. He was accused of trying to get a fellow professional into trouble and was later banned for three matches by the FA, until a court of appeal eventually overruled the judgement.

| | | | APPEARANCES | | | | GOALS | | | |
|---|---|---|---|---|---|---|---|---|---|---|
| Clubs | Signing Date | Transfer Fee | Lge | FL Cup | FA Cup | Others | Lge | FL Cup | FA Cup | Others |
| East Fife | .81 | - | 66+15 | 8+1 | 5+1 | | 26 | | 1 | |
| Hibernian | 10.84 | £65,000 | 45+2 | 6 | 5 | | 14 | 8 | | |
| Chelsea | 4.86 | £380,000 | 115+8 | 11 | 6 | 12 | 51 | 7 | 1 | 3 |
| Tottenham Hotspur* | 8.91 | £2,200,000 | 48 | 8 | 2 | 8 | 10 | 3 | | 3 |

## DURRANT Lee Roger

Born: Great Yarmouth, 18 December 1973

Height: 5'7" Weight: 10.10

International Honours: E Sch

**Position/Skill Factor:** Left sided midfield player who has good skills on the ball and a sweet left foot.

**Career History:** Signed professional forms for Ipswich Town during the 1992 close season, having come to Portman Road as a trainee in July 1990 and although a regular member of the reserve side in **1992-93**, he has yet to play a first team game.

| Clubs | Signing Date | Transfer Fee | APPEARANCES | | | | GOALS | | | |
|---|---|---|---|---|---|---|---|---|---|---|
| | | | Lge | FL Cup | FA Cup | Others | Lge | FL Cup | FA Cup | Others |
| Ipswich Town* | 6.92 | - | | | | | | | | |

# EADIE Darren Malcolm

Born: Chippenham, 10 June 1975

Height: 5'7" Weight: 9.12

**Position/Skill Factor:** Left-winger with terrific pace. Will run at defenders and looks to get the ball in behind the opposing full-back.

**Career History:** Having benefitted from special coaching at Southampton at the tender age of 11, he signed associated schoolboy forms for Norwich City in March 1990, before becoming a trainee at the club in July 1991. After many impressive appearances for the youth team, he turned professional early in 1993 and played 22 games for the reserves in **1992-93**. Had earlier won the most promising City "Player of the Year" award and has since confirmed that promise. Was invited to join the England Under 18 squad for summer training during the 1993 close season.

| Clubs | Signing Date | Transfer Fee | APPEARANCES | | | | GOALS | | | |
|---|---|---|---|---|---|---|---|---|---|---|
| | | | Lge | FL Cup | FA Cup | Others | Lge | FL Cup | FA Cup | Others |
| Norwich City* | 2.93 | - | | | | | | | | |

# EARLE Robert (Robbie) Gerald

Born: Newcastle-under-Lyme, 27 January 1965

Height: 5'9" Weight: 10.10

**Position/Skill Factor:** Attacking midfield player with great energy and excellent in the air. Times his runs into the box to score valuable goals with great precision.

**Career History:** Made his FL debut for Port Vale, after playing in their junior sides, at Swindon Town on 28 August 1982 in a 1-0 defeat. However, it wasn't until 1984-85 that he gained a regular place in the team and was an ever present (including subs' appearances), scoring 15 goals. When he came into soccer with the club, Vale were in the Fourth Division and although promoted shortly after, they were soon relegated. His play was instrumental in raising them to Second Division status by 1988-89 and injuries apart, his appearances were guaranteed. Prior to Vale gaining promotion from the Third Division for the first time since 1953-54, he had formed an effective partnership with Andy Jones. Since Jones' departure to Charlton Athletic in September 1988, he has played in midfield, but with no perceptible reduction in his strike rate (one goal per 3.4 games) which is probably better than any other regular midfielder in the Football League. It is perhaps surprising that no first Division club had

made a move for him before Wimbledon's massive offer in the 1991 close season. Adjusted to First Division football without a tremor, scoring in his first three games for the "Dons" and ending the season as second top scorer with 14 goals from 40 games — clearly a very sound investment. Had another very consistent season in **1992-93** as Wimbledon's only ever present, playing in all 51 matches and scoring eight goals. The dynamic central midfielder notched his first goal in the Premier League at home to Arsenal, securing the "Dons'" 3-2 victory and followed it up with two more in a super 3-2 win at Liverpool, three weeks later. He continued to prove he was the "main" man, scoring winning goals at Everton in the FA Cup Third Round replay and at Queens Park Rangers and an equaliser at Tottenham Hotspur. Also one of the top goal makers in the PL, he finished with 11 assists and if he continues in this vein, an England call-up cannot be too far away.

| Clubs | Signing Date | Transfer Fee | APPEARANCES | | | | GOALS | | | |
|---|---|---|---|---|---|---|---|---|---|---|
| | | | Lge | FL Cup | FA Cup | Others | Lge | FL Cup | FA Cup | Others |
| Port Vale | 7.82 | - | 284+10 | 21+2 | 20+1 | 18+1 | 77 | 4 | 4 | 5 |
| Wimbledon* | 7.91 | £775,000 | 82 | 6 | 7 | 1 | 21 | | 1 | 1 |

# EBBRELL John Keith

Born: Bromborough, 1 October 1969

Height: 5'7"

Weight: 9.12

International Honours: E Sch, E Yth, E "U21"-14, E"B"

**Position/Skill Factor:** Talented midfielder with two good feet and lovely balance. Sprays passes all over the park and is always looking to create chances for others.

**Career History:** From the Lilleshall School of Excellence, he joined Everton as an associated schoolboy in November 1983 and graduated to trainee status in July 1986. His FL debut came as a substitute at home to Wimbledon on 4 February 1989 and he had played a further 13 full League matches by the end of the following season. 1990-91 saw him open his scoring account with the club on the very first day against Leeds United and he went on to play in 34 League matches, while proving a major influence in turning Everton's season around, following their dismal start. Played in all but three end of season games for Everton in 1991-92 and was again expected to be a rock in the "Toffees'" midfield during **1992-93**, but an injury received in early October prevented this and he only really recovered full fitness at the end of the season. Reached the milestone of 100 League games for Everton in January and could be forgiven for not scoring more often, due to the great amount of work he gets through. Having won many England under 21 caps, he still awaits a full international call-up as he looks forward to a more fruitful 1993-94.

| | | | APPEARANCES | | | | GOALS | | | |
|---|---|---|---|---|---|---|---|---|---|---|
| Clubs | Signing Date | Transfer Fee | Lge | FL Cup | FA Cup | Others | Lge | FL Cup | FA Cup | Others |
| Everton* | 11.86 | - | 111+9 | 11 | 12 | 6+2 | 5 | 1 | 2 | 1 |

# EDGHILL Richard Arlon

Born: Oldham, 23 September 1974

Height: 5'8½" Weight: 11.2

**Position/Skill Factor:** Right-back who is very quick and likes getting forward. Also, a very good passer of the ball.

**Career History:** Joined the Manchester City professional staff during the 1992 close season, having previously been at the club as an associated schoolboy (November 1988) and as a trainee (July 1991). After an impressive start to **1992-93** in the reserves he was called to Lilleshall in preparation for the World Youth Cup and was unfortunate not to be selected for the final party. Played in a couple of first team testimonial friendlies, plus 20 reserve team matches, at full-back or midfield. Models himself on Steve McMahon for work rate and should continue to make good progress this season.

| | | | APPEARANCES | | | | GOALS | | | |
|---|---|---|---|---|---|---|---|---|---|---|
| Clubs | Signing Date | Transfer Fee | Lge | FL Cup | FA Cup | Others | Lge | FL Cup | FA Cup | Others |
| Manchester City* | 6.92 | - | | | | | | | | |

# EDINBURGH Justin Charles

Born: Brentwood, 18 December 1969

Height: 5'9" Weight: 11.6

**Position/Skill Factor:** Full-back with a good left foot, who will join up with the attack at every opportunity.

**Career History:** Discovered by Southend United, he signed as a trainee in July 1986 before turning pro and making his FL debut at home to Cardiff City on 23 September 1988. Although yet to become a regular at Roots Hall, he had shown such early promise in the number three shirt that London giants, Tottenham Hotspur, were suitably convinced that he was a star of the future and moved for him in the 1990 close season, after taking a close look at him during a loan period at White Hart Lane from January to March 1990. Having played a few games before Christmas during his first term, he was then alternating with Pat van den Hauwe and Mitchell Thomas in either of the full-back positions, right through to the end of the season. His year was complete, when after being selected for the "Spurs'" FA Cup Final team against Nottingham Forest, he received a winners medal following a 2-1 victory. He started 1991-92 in the reserves, regained his place in October, but lost it again in November. Restored to favour in March 1992, he stayed in the side until the end of the season. Began **1992-93** in possession of the number three shirt, but after just five matches he was displaced by Pat van den Hauwe. However, he was soon back in contention and following two substitute appearances, he regained his place and went on to form a very successful full-back pairing with another ex-Southend player, Dean Austin. A classy player, he should continue to improve.

| | | | APPEARANCES | | | | GOALS | | | |
|---|---|---|---|---|---|---|---|---|---|---|
| Clubs | Signing Date | Transfer Fee | Lge | FL Cup | FA Cup | Others | Lge | FL Cup | FA Cup | Others |
| Southend United | 8.88 | - | 36+1 | 2+1 | 2 | 4+1 | | | | 1 |
| Tottenham Hotspur* | 7.90 | £150,000 | 67+4 | 9+3 | 10 | 3 | 1 | | | |

# EHIOGU Ugochuku (Ugo)

Born: Hackney, 3 November 1972

Height: 6'1"

Weight: 12.0

International Honours: E "U21"-12

**Position/Skill Factor:** A good defender with great pace who is more than capable of man to man marking. Reads the game well.

**Career History:** Came through the West Bromwich Albion junior ranks as a trainee (July 1989) and made his FL debut wearing the number 14 shirt at Hull City on 22 September 1990, appearing once more as a substitute in 1990-91. Normally, clubs with trainees on contract have first option on their services, but before formalities could be completed, Aston Villa stepped in and signed him during 1991-92, creating considerable ill feeling between the two clubs, not assuaged by the modest fee decided upon by the tribunal. Clearly it was a good move for Ugo, who was included in the Villa first team squad from the start of the season, making his debut at right-back at home to Arsenal on 24 August, 1991. Remained on the fringe of the first team all season, making nine further appearances. Called up to the England Under 21 squad, he made his international debut at the end of the season, before participating in the annual Under 21 tournament in Toulon, France. Didn't get many first team opportunities at all in **1992-93**, with the Paul McGrath — Shaun Teale partnership going strong during Villa's Championship chasing season and he subsequently only made the starting line-up on two occasions, having a nightmare game against Norwich City in one of them. However, his consistent displays with the reserves, where he played a major part in their Pontins' League Championship success, saw him captain the England under 21 side. Still has a great future in the game, but will have to be patient.

| | | | APPEARANCES | | | | GOALS | | | |
|---|---|---|---|---|---|---|---|---|---|---|
| Clubs | Signing Date | Transfer Fee | Lge | FL Cup | FA Cup | Others | Lge | FL Cup | FA Cup | Others |
| West Bromwich Albion | - | - | 0+2 | | | | | | | |
| Aston Villa* | 7.91 | £40,000 | 5+7 | 1 | 0+1 | 1 | | | | |

## EKOKU Efangwu (Efan) Goziem

Born: Manchester, 8 June 1967

Height: 6'1"

Weight: 12.0

**Position/Skill Factor:** Striker who combines well with team-mates in the build up. Has very quick feet and his terrific pace will always give him goalscoring opportunities.

**Career History:** A tall, gangling forward, with much potential, he was playing for non-League, Sutton United, having previously been with Merton, before signing for Bournemouth during the 1990 close season. Scored 30 goals in 54 appearances with Sutton and was a non playing substitute for the England semi-pro side, before joining the "Cherries", having already had a trial with Charlton Athletic and turned Sheffield United down. Immediately given the chance to play Third Division football, he made his FL debut at Brentford on 25 August 1990 and by the end of the season had proved to be a more than useful acquisition, with 23 (18 as substitute) appearances and three goals to his credit. Missed the opening months of 1991-92, due to injury, but established a regular place in the second half of the season, scoring 11 FL goals, as the club just missed out on a Play-Off position. Once again, an injury, this time to the ankle, ruled him out of contention in **1992-93**, until January, but he marked his return to first team duty with five goals in four games and added another couple before signing for Norwich City in a transfer deadline purchase. Thrown in at the deep end, as a substitute against Manchester United, he came on again in the next game and scored City's only goal in a 5-1 defeat at Tottenham Hotspur. Those two matches spelt the end of Norwich's outside Championship hopes, but they maintained third position, the highest in their history, as Efan playing his first full match, the last of the season, hammered in two goals during a 3-3 draw at Middlesbrough. Hailing from an outstanding sporting family, his brother Abi is currently the number one shot putter in the United Kingdom and Efan, no mean sprinter himself, is a player you are going to hear a lot more of.

| | | | APPEARANCES | | | | GOALS | | | |
|---|---|---|---|---|---|---|---|---|---|---|
| Clubs | Signing Date | Transfer Fee | Lge | FL Cup | FA Cup | Others | Lge | FL Cup | FA Cup | Others |
| Bournemouth | 5.90 | £100,000 | 43+19 | 0+2 | 5+2 | 3+1 | 21 | | 2 | 2 |
| Norwich City* | 3.93 | £500,000 | 1+3 | | | | 3 | | | |

## ELKINS Gary

Born: Wallingford, 4 May 1966

Height: 5'9"

Weight: 11.13

International Honours: E Yth

**Position/Skill Factor:** Attacking full-back with a smart left foot and a good enough range of passes that allow him to play in midfield when required.

**Career History:** Became a Fulham apprentice in July 1982 and within a year of turning pro he had made his FL debut in a 2-1 win at home against Middlesbrough on 22 September 1984. Unfortunately, just as he was beginning to work his way into the team, he suffered a broken leg in February 1986. Out of the side for over a year, he came back, appearing on and off, mainly in the number three shirt, until transferred to Wimbledon following a loan period at Exeter City. Playing only sporadically in 1990-91, he spent most of his first season at Plough Lane, deputising for Terry Phelan, when required. Whilst still a cover player, he made 17 full appearances in 1991-92, often in midfield and proved a useful man to have in the wings. With Terry Phelan on his way to Manchester City, he started **1992-93** as first choice left-back and despite Wimbledon losing the opening three games he played quite well, before being dispossessed by Brian McAllister. Regained his place a few weeks later, but an injury put him out of action till after Christmas. Came back to play in 15 matches out of a possible 17 and scoring the equaliser in the Fourth Round of the FA Cup at Aston Villa, but following an injury, which saw him substituted at Sheffield Wednesday, he remained out of action for the rest of the season.

| | | | APPEARANCES | | | | GOALS | | | |
|---|---|---|---|---|---|---|---|---|---|---|
| Clubs | Signing Date | Transfer Fee | Lge | FL Cup | FA Cup | Others | Lge | FL Cup | FA Cup | Others |
| Fulham | 12.83 | - | 100+4 | 6 | 2+2 | 7+1 | 2 | | | |
| Exeter City | 12.89 | Loan | 5 | | | | | | | |
| Wimbledon* | 8.90 | £20,000 | 42+4 | 3 | 3 | 1+1 | 1 | | 1 | |

## **ELLIOTT** **Paul** Marcellus

Born: Lewisham, 18 March 1964

Height: 6'2" Weight: 14.1

International Honours: E Yth, E "U21"-3, E "B"

| | | | APPEARANCES | | | | GOALS | | | |
|---|---|---|---|---|---|---|---|---|---|---|
| Clubs | Signing Date | Transfer Fee | Lge | FL Cup | FA Cup | Others | Lge | FL Cup | FA Cup | Others |
| Charlton Athletic | 3.81 | - | 61+2 | 5 | 1+1 | | 1 | 1 | | |
| Luton Town | 3.83 | £95,000 | 63+3 | 5 | 2 | | 4 | | | |
| Aston Villa | 12.85 | £400,000 | 56+1 | 7 | 4 | 1 | 7 | | | |
| Pisa (Italy) | 7.87 | £400,000 | | | | | | | | |
| Glasgow Celtic | 7.89 | £600,000 | 52 | 5 | 8 | 1 | 2 | 3 | | |
| Chelsea* | 7.91 | £1,400,000 | 42 | 2 | 5 | 5 | 3 | | | |

**Position/Skill Factor:** Centre-back who reads the game well. Dangerous from set pieces, he is very quick and often saves the day with last ditch tackles.

**Career History:** Was an associated schoolboy with Charlton Athletic (April 1980), before becoming an apprentice a few months later in July 1980. His FL debut was in an away match against Crystal Palace on 12 September 1981 and, injuries apart, stayed in the team until transferred to Luton Town when the club were under severe financial pressures. Had two full seasons at Kenilworth Road before Aston Villa decided that he was the man they needed as a replacement for Brendan Ormsby, who was injured. Was lured to Italy in the summer of 1987, playing with Pisa for two years. At the end of his contract he returned not to England, but to Scotland, signing for Celtic and played for his new club in the Scottish Cup Final against Aberdeen in 1990, collecting a runners-up medal. During 1991-92, after two years with the "Bhoys", he returned to London, signing for Chelsea. Although performing well personally, his defensive partners were constantly changing in a shaky defence, and it was another disappointing season for the "Blues". Badly injured in the seventh game of **1992-93**, following a clash with Liverpool's Dean Saunders, he was stretchered off, not to play again all season. Whether he will make a full recovery from such a serious operation remains to be seen and he has since served notice of a court action due to be taken against the player involved. Chelsea used 32 players throughout 1992-93, of which 14 suffered injuries of varying degrees, but it is doubtful whether any were more serious to either player or team. Sorely lacking his height and pace at the heart of their defence, the "Blues" were often exposed, until the advent of Erland Johnsen gave them a more stable look.

## **ELLIOTT** **Robert** James

Born: Newcastle, 25 December 1973

Height: 5'10" Weight 11.6

**Position/Skill Factor:** Left-back with a good left foot and bags of skill, who loves to get forward.

**Career History:** Locally born and bred, he signed associated schoolboy forms for Newcastle United in May 1988. After showing the necessary promise, he joined the club as a trainee on leaving school in June 1990 and turned professional ten months later. Prior to that, he had already been blooded in the first team, making his FL debut at Middlesbrough as a substitute on 12 March 1991 and later played in the last five matches at left-back. Started 1991-92 as first choice left-back, but was badly injured in mid-season with cruciate ligament damage that required immediate surgery. A similar injury to the one suffered by the former United idol, Paul Gascoigne, he was out for 14 months. Came back in the latter part of **1992-93**, playing reserve team football, in an effort to regain match fitness and with United now promoted to the Premier League, hopes to be ready in time for the new season.

| | | | APPEARANCES | | | | GOALS | | | |
|---|---|---|---|---|---|---|---|---|---|---|
| Clubs | Signing Date | Transfer Fee | Lge | FL Cup | FA Cup | Others | Lge | FL Cup | FA Cup | Others |
| Newcastle United* | 4.91 | - | 14+1 | 1 | | 1 | | | | |

## **EMBLETON** **Daniel** Charles

Born: Liverpool, 27 March 1975

Height: 5'11" Weight: 12.7

**Position/Skill Factor:** Goalkeeper. Agile and a reflex saver, he stands up as long as possible.

**Career History:** Yet another local, he first came to Anfield as an associated schoolboy (May 1990), before progressing through the Liverpool ranks as a trainee (August 1991) and signing professional forms at the end of **1992-93**.

| | | | APPEARANCES | | | | GOALS | | | |
|---|---|---|---|---|---|---|---|---|---|---|
| Clubs | Signing Date | Transfer Fee | Lge | FL Cup | FA Cup | Others | Lge | FL Cup | FA Cup | Others |
| Liverpool* | 4.93 | - | | | | | | | | |

## EVANS Darren

Born: Wolverhampton, 30 September 1974

Height: 5'10" Weight: 10.12

**Position/Skill Factor:** Right-back who can also play in midfield. Very quick and loves to join in, he links up well to get to the byeline to deliver quality crosses.

**Career History:** Started out with Aston Villa as an associated schoolboy in November 1988, before graduating to trainee status in July 1991 and turning professional last summer. Given two reserve outings at the end of **1992-93**, he showed good skill and will be given every chance.

| | | | APPEARANCES | | | | GOALS | | | |
|---|---|---|---|---|---|---|---|---|---|---|
| Clubs | Signing Date | Transfer Fee | Lge | FL Cup | FA Cup | Others | Lge | FL Cup | FA Cup | Others |
| Aston Villa* | 7.93 | - | | | | | | | | |

## EYRE John Robert

Born: Hull, 9 October 1974

Height: 6'0" Weight: 11.1

**Position/Skill Factor:** Forward who plays on the wide right. Two footed, although stronger on his right, he is both fast and skilful.

**Career History:** Potentially good enough for the first team right now, was the assessment of Oldham Athletic's reserve team coach at the end of **1992-93**. First came to Boundary Park as an associated schoolboy (January 1989), before moving up to trainee in August 1991, he signed professional forms last summer and looks for an early start in 1993-94.

| | | | APPEARANCES | | | | GOALS | | | |
|---|---|---|---|---|---|---|---|---|---|---|
| Clubs | Signing Date | Transfer Fee | Lge | FL Cup | FA Cup | Others | Lge | FL Cup | FA Cup | Others |
| Oldham Athletic* | 7.93 | - | | | | | | | | |

## FAIRBAIRN Neil

Born: Ashington, 4 October 1974

Height: 5'11" Weight: 11.2

**Position/Skill Factor:** Very brave and agile goalkeeper who is extremely quick off his line.

**Career History:** A 1993 close season professional signing for Wimbledon, he goes third choice behind Hans Segers and Neil Sullivan, but with the Premier League substitute goalkeeper ruling in place he may receive an earlier opportunity than one would have normally expected. First came to the club as an associated schoolboy in March 1990, before progressing as a trainee (July 1991), he showed good ability in the youth side in **1992-93** and actually played in a first team friendly at Brighton.

| | | | APPEARANCES | | | | GOALS | | | |
|---|---|---|---|---|---|---|---|---|---|---|
| Clubs | Signing Date | Transfer Fee | Lge | FL Cup | FA Cup | Others | Lge | FL Cup | FA Cup | Others |
| Wimbledon* | 7.93 | - | | | | | | | | |

## FAIRCLOUGH Courtney (Chris) Huw

Born: Nottingham, 12 April 1964

Height: 5'11" Weight: 11.2

International Honours: E "U21"-7, E"B"

**Position/Skill Factor:** Good, reliable centre-back who clears his lines with the minimum fuss. Does well in the air, sticking his head in even when he is likely to get injured.

**Career History:** The elder brother of Mansfield Town's Wayne, he was a Nottingham Forest associated schools player (November 1978) and apprentice (July 1980), before making his FL debut at Anfield on 4 September 1982 when Liverpool won 4-3. Played over 100 games at Forest, despite missing the entire 1985-86 season through injury. Joined Tottenham in the summer of 1987 and was an ever present in his first season at White Hart Lane. Leeds signed him just before the March 1989 transfer deadline in order to stiffen their defence and in helping the club to become the Second Division Champions in 1989-90, he formed a solid defensive partnership with Peter Haddock, while also making a valuable contribution at the other end with eight goals. Back in the top flight for 1990-91, his new partner was Chris Whyte and between them they missed only six games all season as the side finished fourth in the table. After dropping out of the team with injury early into 1991-92, he returned in October to resume his partnership with Whyte, which was the bedrock on which Leeds' eventual League Championship triumph was based. Had an in-and-out time of it in **1992-93**, largely due to the number of goals the team conceded before Christmas and the fact that he played a number of games in the club's problem position of right-back. Due to that, he was unable to continue his partnership with Chris Whyte, which had been the cornerstone of the defence that won the Championship. In fact he was dropped in February and eventually turned down a swap deal to his old club, Nottingham Forest, in return for Gary Charles, preferring to stay and fight for his first team spot. Always dangerous at set pieces, he again weighed in with crucial goals, including a glorious header against Arsenal at Elland Road in November.

| | | | APPEARANCES | | | | GOALS | | | |
|---|---|---|---|---|---|---|---|---|---|---|
| Clubs | Signing Date | Transfer Fee | Lge | FL Cup | FA Cup | Others | Lge | FL Cup | FA Cup | Others |
| Nottingham Forest | 10.81 | - | 102+5 | 9+1 | 6 | 9+2 | 1 | 1 | | |
| Tottenham Hotspur | 7.87 | £387,000 | 60 | 7 | 3 | | 5 | | | |
| Leeds United* | 3.89 | £500,000 | 146+2 | 13+2 | 11+1 | 14 | 19 | 2 | | |

## FALLON Sean Peter

Born: Nelson, 11 May 1976

Height: 5'11" Weight: 13.0

**Position/Skill Factor:** Big, strong, bustling, old fashioned centre-forward, who looks to get on the end of any chances going begging in the penalty area.

**Career History:** After being spotted in local schools football, he came to Liverpool as a trainee (December 1991) and made good enough progress in **1992-93** to be asked to sign professional forms during the 1993 close season.

| | | | APPEARANCES | | | | GOALS | | | |
|---|---|---|---|---|---|---|---|---|---|---|
| Clubs | Signing Date | Transfer Fee | Lge | FL Cup | FA Cup | Others | Lge | FL Cup | FA Cup | Others |
| Liverpool* | 5.93 | - | | | | | | | | |

## FARRELL David William

Born: Birmingham, 11 November 1971

Height: 5'11" Weight: 11.2

**Position/Skill Factor:** Left-winger with tremendous pace, he has a good left foot and is a lovely crosser of the ball.

**Career History:** Signed by Aston Villa from non-League side, Redditch United, early in 1992, he is a most promising young player and began to make good progress in **1992-93**, being elevated to the first team squad after scoring twice and having a particularly fine match for the reserves against Manchester City. Immediately following his PL debut at Oldham Athletic on 24 October 1992, when he came off the bench for the last 15 minutes, he played his first full game for the League side in the live televised game at home to Queens Park Rangers. Later in the season, in order to further his experience, he had a loan spell at Scunthorpe United, making seven first team appearances, before coming back to Villa Park.

| | | | APPEARANCES | | | | GOALS | | | |
|---|---|---|---|---|---|---|---|---|---|---|
| Clubs | Signing Date | Transfer Fee | Lge | FL Cup | FA Cup | Others | Lge | FL Cup | FA Cup | Others |
| Aston Villa* | 1.92 | £45,000 | 1+1 | | | | | | | |
| Scunthorpe United | 1.93 | Loan | 4+1 | | | 2 | 1 | | | |

## FARRELLY Gareth

Born: Dublin, 28 August 1975

Height: 6'1" Weight: 12.4

**Position/Skill Factor:** Central midfield player with great ability. Has an excellent left foot, enjoys the passing game and is always looking for a shooting opportunity.

**Career History:** Highly rated youngster from Ireland, who was upgraded to the professional ranks at Villa Park with a three year contract, barely one month after signing a two year contract as a trainee (August 1992). Yet to make the first team, he made a handful of appearances for the reserves in **1992-93**, but spent a six week period on the sidelines, due to a recurring back problem.

| | | | APPEARANCES | | | | GOALS | | | |
|---|---|---|---|---|---|---|---|---|---|---|
| Clubs | Signing Date | Transfer Fee | Lge | FL Cup | FA Cup | Others | Lge | FL Cup | FA Cup | Others |
| Aston Villa* | 9.92 | - | | | | | | | | |

## FASHANU John

Born: Kensington, 18 September 1962

Height: 6'1"

Weight: 11.2

International Honours: E-2

**Position/Skill Factor:** A great target man. Dangerous and brave in the air, he can hold the ball up until support is forthcoming. Is an unusual penalty taker, with just two or three steps.

**Career History:** Nicknamed "Fash the Bash" in honour of his combative style and the younger brother of Justin, who played for Norwich City and Nottingham Forest, during the 1980s, he turned pro with Norwich City, having previously been an associated schoolboy at Cambridge United (February 1979). He had to wait two years to make his FL debut at home to Shrewsbury Town on 17 October 1981, by which time Justin had moved on and after receiving few opportunities in four years at Carrow Road, which included a spell on loan to Crystal Palace, he was transferred to Lincoln City. Made an immediate impact with City, before being signed by Millwall, where he teamed up with Steve Lovell. Their goalscoring partnership was a major factor in the "Lions" attaining promotion to the Second Division and reaching the Quarter-Finals of the FA Cup. The following season, Dave Bassett saw him as the man to seal Wimbledon's promotion to the First Division and four goals from the final nine League matches proved his judgement correct. In 1988, he collected an FA Cup winners medal after Wimbledon defeated Liverpool 1-0 and his sterling displays were rewarded when he was selected to play for

England against Chile at Wembley on 23 May 1989. Despite suffering more than his fair share of injuries, he has been the club's leading scorer from 1986-87 to 1991-92. That all changed in **1992-93** when he could only finish third in the club's goal charts. However, he reached the new Premier League's Top 20 assists charts with over eight, to go with six League strikes, while forming a good understanding with new partner, Dean Holdsworth. The season had started badly for him, when an injury sustained while practising his martial arts, kept him out of the opening five matches, but back to first team duty, he put a run of seven games together, scoring three goals. He was then unfortunate to pick up a niggling injury which kept him in-and-out of the side for the next few months. But following a settled run of 21 consecutive games, he received a three match suspension after being sent off at Sheffield Wednesday, having already been injured in a clash with Viv Anderson. One of the few remaining members of the 1988 FA Cup winning team, Wimbledon owner Sam Hammam has made great efforts to persuade him to see his football career out with the "Dons", even offering him the club Presidency and a bonus for each goal scored. Off the field, belying his aggressive image on it, he is charming and articulate with a budding career as a media personality ahead of him. His business interests also include a colourful range of football boots and he has many charitable interests in the poorest parts of Africa.

| | | | APPEARANCES | | | | GOALS | | | |
|---|---|---|---|---|---|---|---|---|---|---|
| Clubs | Signing Date | Transfer Fee | Lge | FL Cup | FA Cup | Others | Lge | FL Cup | FA Cup | Others |
| Norwich City | 10.79 | - | 6+1 | | | | 1 | | | |
| Crystal Palace | 8.83 | Loan | 1 | 1 | | | | | | |
| Lincoln City | 9.83 | - | 31+5 | 2 | 2+1 | 1 | 11 | | | |
| Millwall | 11.84 | £55,000 | 50 | 4 | 9 | 2 | 12 | 2 | 4 | 1 |
| Wimbledon* | 3.86 | £125,000 | 236+4 | 15+2 | 24 | 5 | 96 | 9 | 10 | 2 |

## FAULKNER David Peter

Born: Sheffield, 8 October 1975

Height: 6'2" Weight 11.0

International Honours: E Sch, E Yth

**Position/Skill Factor:** Central defender who is a good tackler and loves the physical side of the game.

**Career History:** A Sheffield Wednesday professional signing, mid-way through **1992-93**, he originally came to Hillsborough as an associated schoolboy (November 1989), prior to winning six England schoolboy international caps and graduating to the trainee ranks in July 1992. Played mainly in the junior side throughout 1992-93 and made two reserve appearances, but has yet to make a first team start. Has excellent potential.

| | | | APPEARANCES | | | | GOALS | | | |
|---|---|---|---|---|---|---|---|---|---|---|
| Clubs | Signing Date | Transfer Fee | Lge | FL Cup | FA Cup | Others | Lge | FL Cup | FA Cup | Others |
| Sheffield Wednesday* | 12.92 | - | | | | | | | | |

## FEAR Peter

Born: Sutton, 10 September 1973

Height: 5'10" Weight: 10.8

**Position/Skill Factor:** Useful midfielder who can also play in defence. Capable of creating chances for others, he tackles and cuts down opponents' space well.

**Career History:** Signed professional forms for Wimbledon during the 1992 close season, having previously been at the club as an associated schoolboy (November 1987) and as a trainee (July 1990). Another of Wimbledon's impressive youngsters, he followed up good displays with the reserve side when he came on as a substitute in **1992-93** to make his PL debut in a 1-0 win at Arsenal on 10 February 1993. Appeared on the left-hand side of midfield in his first full match at Oldham Athletic and gave a good account of himself, despite the "Dons" receiving a 6-2 trouncing. Made two further appearances before the season ended and could break through regularly in 1993-94.

| | | | APPEARANCES | | | | GOALS | | | |
|---|---|---|---|---|---|---|---|---|---|---|
| Clubs | Signing Date | Transfer Fee | Lge | FL Cup | FA Cup | Others | Lge | FL Cup | FA Cup | Others |
| Wimbledon* | 6.92 | - | 2+2 | | | | | | | |

## FENTON Graham Anthony

Born: Wallsend, 22 May 1974

Height: 5'10" Weight: 11.3

**Position/Skill Factor:** Can play either up front, or in midfield and for a physical player, he has a good touch.

**Career History:** Started out at Villa Park as an associated schoolboy in May 1989, before joining the club as a trainee on leaving school in July 1990 and turned professional towards the end of the 1991-92 season. Yet to make a first team appearance, he spent **1992-93** as a regular reserve team player, striking up a good partnership with Neil Davis and looks to knock on the first team door this season.

| | | | APPEARANCES | | | | GOALS | | | |
|---|---|---|---|---|---|---|---|---|---|---|
| Clubs | Signing Date | Transfer Fee | Lge | FL Cup | FA Cup | Others | Lge | FL Cup | FA Cup | Others |
| Aston Villa* | 2.92 | - | | | | | | | | |

## FERDINAND Leslie (Les)

Born: Acton, 18 December 1966

Height: 5'11" Weight: 13.5

International Honours: E-4

**Position/Skill Factor:** Good all-round striker. With his aerial strength and pace to match, he cannot be treated lightly by opposing defences.

**Career History:** Was snapped up by Queens Park Rangers after he was spotted playing in the Vauxhall-Opel League with Hayes and was immediately given his FL debut, coming on as a sub at Coventry City on 20 April 1987. With opportunities scarce at Loftus Road, he was loaned out to Brentford and then, more exotically, for one year to the Istanbul-based Turkish team, Besiktas, managed by Gordon Milne, the former Leicester City manager. On his return, he still found it difficult to win a regular place and was kept out of the side by the likes of Trevor Francis, Colin Clarke and Mark Falco and more recently, Roy Wegerle. In 1990-91, he finally began to make an impact as injuries depleted the club's ranks and during Q.P.R.'s fight to get away from the bottom of the First Division table he scored some priceless goals, including winners against Luton Town, Southampton, Manchester City and Coventry City. Under new manager Gerry Francis, he started 1991-92 as first choice, but soon lost his place to new signing Garry Thompson. Returned to favour in March and ended the season in impressive style with eight goals from the last 13 games. Nicknamed "Sir Les" by the fans, he had his best ever season in **1992-93**, finishing as the club's top scorer, their "Player of the Year" and winning four England caps. Started as he meant to carry on with two goals in the club's first home game against Southampton and also scored a pair in home games against Grimsby Town, Oldham Athletic, Swindon Town and Norwich City. However, he saved the best for the end of the season, with two hat-tricks in a row, a 4-3 win at Loftus Road against Nottingham Forest and a 5-3 victory at Everton. His club captain, Ray Wilkins, paid him a glowing compliment when he said of him: "If you put quality balls into the box then Ferdinand will be a real pain, he is a tremendous leaper and a great header of the ball". Scored on his England debut against San Marino and throughout the season has been the subject of much transfer speculation as his career takes off.

| | | | APPEARANCES | | | | GOALS | | | |
|---|---|---|---|---|---|---|---|---|---|---|
| Clubs | Signing Date | Transfer Fee | Lge | FL Cup | FA Cup | Others | Lge | FL Cup | FA Cup | Others |
| Q.P.R.* | 3.87 | £15,000 | 80+10 | 6+2 | 2+1 | 1 | 40 | 4 | 2 | |
| Brentford | 3.88 | Loan | 3 | | | | | | | |
| Besiktas (Turkey) | 6.88 | Loan | | | | | | | | |

# FERGUSON Darren

Born: Glasgow, 9 February 1972

Height: 5'10"

Weight: 10.4

International Honours: S Yth, S "U21"-6

**Position/Skill Factor:** Midfield player. Good passer, both short and long, he comes forward well and should eventually get among the goals.

**Career History:** Son of the Manchester United manager, Alex, he came through the United ranks after signing as a trainee in July 1988 and made his FL debut at Sheffield United on 26 February 1991. In five appearances, including subs, was not once on the winning side in 1990-91. Selected for the first game of 1991-92, he then went back to the reserves, before making a couple of appearances in the closing games of the season. Made his debut for the Scotland Under 21 side in February 1992 and was called up for the annual end of season tournament in Toulon, France. Came on by leaps and bounds in **1992-93**, when starting the season as a regular first teamer in the absence of Lee Sharpe and playing a valuable role in the first 15 Premier League games. Lost his place when he was unfortunate to pull a hamstring in the game at Aston Villa, coupled with the return of Sharpe. And with United fielding a settled side when he finally came back to full fitness, he spent the rest of the season in the reserves. While displaying a great deal of promise, he also showed inexperience in losing his temper on occasion and will be a very good player indeed when that part of his game is remedied. His season was made up when he received a Championship medal as United raced away to win the League title and it could well be the first time that a player has won the award while playing for a team managed by his father.

| | | | APPEARANCES | | | | GOALS | | | |
|---|---|---|---|---|---|---|---|---|---|---|
| Clubs | Signing Date | Transfer Fee | Lge | FL Cup | FA Cup | Others | Lge | FL Cup | FA Cup | Others |
| Manchester United* | 7.90 | - | 19+5 | 1 | | | | | | |

# FERGUSON Gary

Born: Belfast, 16 September 1974

Height: 5'11" Weight: 10.11½

International Honours: NI Yth

**Position/Skill Factor:** Central defender who can also play at left-back. Very aggressive and strong in the air and a good tackler.

**Career History:** After gaining a bit of a "bad-boy" reputation last season as a first year trainee, being sent off several times whilst playing for the Reading youth team, he joined his old boss, Ian Branfoot, when signing professional forms at Southampton in the 1992 close season in return for a small fee. Originally taken on during Branfoot's stewardship at Reading as an associated schoolboy in May 1989, he became a trainee in August 1991 on leaving school and showed signs of making a good player. Having been sent off four times for the youth team the previous season, he started **1992-93** with a six match ban. Comfortable on the ball, he made his reserve debut in September and moved into midfield for the youth team on occasion, before settling down with the "stiffs" on the left side of defence.

| | | | APPEARANCES | | | | GOALS | | | |
|---|---|---|---|---|---|---|---|---|---|---|
| Clubs | Signing Date | Transfer Fee | Lge | FL Cup | FA Cup | Others | Lge | FL Cup | FA Cup | Others |
| Southampton* | 6.92 | £20,000 | | | | | | | | |

## FICKLING Ashley

Born: Sheffield, 15 November 1972

Height: 5'11"

Weight: 11.3

International Honours: E Sch

**Position/Skill Factor:** Full-back who is strong in the tackle and has a tremendous amount of enthusiasm.

**Career History:** Picked up on Sheffield United's doorstep, he signed as an associated schoolboy in December 1987, before progressing to the club's professional ranks in the 1991 close season. Although yet to play a League match, he was "blooded" in a League Cup tie at Bramall Lane against Wigan Athletic on 8 October 1991. Still waiting in the wings for a League opportunity with the "Blades", he continued his footballing education in the reserves in **1992-93**, together with a loan spell at Third Division Darlington. While with the "Quakers", he made his FL debut at home to Barnet on 28 November 1992 and played a further 13 games before returning to Bramall Lane.

| | | | APPEARANCES | | | | GOALS | | | |
|---|---|---|---|---|---|---|---|---|---|---|
| Clubs | Signing Date | Transfer Fee | Lge | FL Cup | FA Cup | Others | Lge | FL Cup | FA Cup | Others |
| Sheffield United* | 7.91 | - | | 1 | | | | | | |
| Darlington | 11.92 | Loan | 14 | | | 1 | | | | |

## FINLAY Darren Jonathan

Born: Belfast, 19 December 1973

Height: 5'4" Weight: 10.0

International Honours: NI Yth

**Position/Skill Factor:** Skilful left-winger with good touch and a lovely left foot.

**Career History:** Signed professional forms for Queens Park Rangers during the 1992 close season, having previously been at Loftus Road as an associated schoolboy (May 1989) and as a trainee (August 1990). No first team experience as yet, but a regular in the reserves throughout **1992-93**, he will be seeking to breakthrough this season, but needs more strength to go with his natural ability.

| | | | APPEARANCES | | | | GOALS | | | |
|---|---|---|---|---|---|---|---|---|---|---|
| Clubs | Signing Date | Transfer Fee | Lge | FL Cup | FA Cup | Others | Lge | FL Cup | FA Cup | Others |
| Q.P.R.* | 5.92 | - | | | | | | | | |

## FINNEY Stephen Kenneth

Born: Hexham, 31 October 1973

Height: 5'10" Weight: 12.0

**Position/Skill Factor:** Striker who makes intelligent runs off the ball and produces excellent crosses from wide positions.

**Career History:** No relation to Tom Finney, he started out as an associated schoolboy (December 1987) at Preston North End and after moving up as a trainee (July 1990), he progressed to the professional ranks at the end of the 1991-92 season. Still a trainee and just four days after coming on as a substitute in the Autoglass trophy at home to Hull City, he made his FL debut from the bench on 18 January 1992 at Deepdale, against Exeter City. Released by North End in **1992-93** after five more appearances, he followed former manager, Les Chapman, who had recently joined the Manchester City coaching staff. Came through a trial period with flying colours in City's "A" team and soon progressed to the reserves, becoming a regular player by the end of the season. If he makes the giant leap to Premier League status, Preston may well rue the day he was freed.

| | | | APPEARANCES | | | | GOALS | | | |
|---|---|---|---|---|---|---|---|---|---|---|
| Clubs | Signing Date | Transfer Fee | Lge | FL Cup | FA Cup | Others | Lge | FL Cup | FA Cup | Others |
| Preston North End | 5.92 | - | 1+5 | | 0+1 | 1+1 | 1 | | | |
| Manchester City* | 2.93 | - | | | | | | | | |

## FITZGERALD Scott Brian

Born: Westminster, 13 August 1969

Height: 6'0"

Weight: 12.2

International Honours: IR "B", IR "U21"-2

**Position/Skill Factor:** Very useful centre-back. Can pass long and short, reads the game well, takes up good covering positions and defends well. Is also a good kicker of the ball.

**Career History:** Starting life at Wimbledon as a trainee in July 1986, he later turned pro and made his FL debut when coming off the subs' bench at Plough Lane against Tottenham Hotspur on 28 April 1990. After four years as a professional with the "Dons" this was his only first team experience and it was therefore a surprise, when he started 1991-92 in the first team, replacing the injured Dean Blackwell. To his credit, he grabbed the opportunity with both hands and remained a first team regular throughout the season. Started **1992-93** as first choice centre-half, alongside John Scales and continued to show his good form of the previous season. However, a bad tempered match at home to Arsenal saw him clash several times with Ian Wright and spend the next two games on the bench. Came back at Bolton Wanderers in the Second Round of the League Cup and stayed for five matches, until a nasty injury robbed Wimbledon of his services for the next four months. He returned for the League match at Arsenal, but a recurrence of the injury kept him out of action until the last six games of the season. Now fully fit and playing strongly, he faces a battle with Dean Blackwell and Brian McAllister to decide who partners John Scales at the heart of the "Dons'" defence in 1993-94.

| | | | APPEARANCES | | | | GOALS | | | |
|---|---|---|---|---|---|---|---|---|---|---|
| Clubs | Signing Date | Transfer Fee | Lge | FL Cup | FA Cup | Others | Lge | FL Cup | FA Cup | Others |
| Wimbledon* | 7.87 | - | 52+5 | 4 | 2 | 1 | 1 | | | |

## FJORTOFT Jan Aage

Born: Norway, 10 January 1967

Height: 6'4½" Weight: 13.6

International Honours: Norwegian Int

**Position/Skill Factor:** Extremely skilful striker who can score goals at the highest level. A very athletic player, he holds up play well until his team-mates are ready to join in.

**Career History:** One of the stars of Norway's 2-0 triumph over England last June in a World Cup qualifying group game, which may prove to be the death knell to the latter's chances, Fjortoft was signed by Swindon Town's new manager John Gorman in the summer, to bolster an attack force light on top level experience. Prior to joining Swindon, he played four seasons in Austria with SK Rapid Wien (Vienna), whom he joined in 1989 from his native Norwegian club, Hamar Kameratene. Played some of his best football ever in **1992-93** and has an excellent scoring record, with ten goals in 34 internationals for Norway, while notching five from ten European Cup appearances with Rapid. A class player, he will add infinitely to Swindon's chances of consolidating in the Premier League.

| | | | APPEARANCES | | | | GOALS | | | |
|---|---|---|---|---|---|---|---|---|---|---|
| Clubs | Signing Date | Transfer Fee | Lge | FL Cup | FA Cup | Others | Lge | FL Cup | FA Cup | Others |
| Swindon Town* | 7.93 | £500,000 | | | | | | | | |

## FLATTS Mark Michael

Born: Islington, 14 October 1972

Height: 5'6"

Weight: 9.8

International Honours: E Yth

**Position/Skill Factor:** A wingman, who can tackle, he has terrific pace, two good feet and is a lovely crosser of the ball.

**Career History:** One for the future, he initially came to Arsenal as an associated schoolboy in January 1987, before signing on as a trainee in July 1989 when he left school and turned professional at the end of 1990, having been a graduate of the FA School of Excellence. Made his PL debut in **1992-93** with a substitute appearance at Sheffield United on 19 September 1992 and followed it up with ten (three substitute) more first team appearances during the season. His most telling contribution was at Maine Road, when he set up Paul Merson for the winner and his pace and tricky runs will probably spell trouble for a few defences in 1993-94

| | | | APPEARANCES | | | | GOALS | | | |
|---|---|---|---|---|---|---|---|---|---|---|
| Clubs | Signing Date | Transfer Fee | Lge | FL Cup | FA Cup | Others | Lge | FL Cup | FA Cup | Others |
| Arsenal* | 12.90 | - | 6+4 | 1 | | | | | | |

## FLECK Robert

Born: Glasgow, 11 August 1965

Height: 5'7" Weight: 10.8

International Honours: S Yth, S "U21"-6, S-4

**Position/Skill Factor:** Stocky, bustling striker, who is a natural goalscorer. Quick and aggressive, he unsettles defenders and when hitting balls early, often catches goalkeepers on the wrong foot.

**Career History:** Began his soccer career with Glasgow Rangers, but first played in a senior match when on loan to Partick Thistle. Won a Scottish Championship medal with Rangers in 1986-87, scoring 19 times in 40 League matches and halfway through the following term, Norwich paid a then club record fee to bring him south. In all games, whilst at Ibrox, he had made 68 full appearances, 34 substitutions and scored 34 goals. He made his FL debut at Wimbledon on 18 December 1987 and despite being unlucky with injuries has found the net fairly consistently at Carrow Road. His unselfish running was duly rewarded when Scotland selected him for the game against Argentina in March 1990 and he went on to play in the World Cup Finals. After missing several games at the start of 1990-91, he rekindled the form he is more than capable of producing on the big occasion. During 1991-92, he enjoyed another good season at Carrow Road, top scoring with 11 FL, plus eight cup goals. Unfortunately injured in the bruising FA Cup Quarter-Final replay with Southampton, he was recalled for the Semi-Final against Sunderland, but was subdued and seemed to be less than 100 per cent fit as the "Canaries" succumbed almost tamely to the "Wearsiders". Signed for Chelsea at the start of **1992-93**, with a goalscoring record that was equal to Mark Hughes and Dean Saunders at the time, but only netted three in 38 first team appearances. A major disappointment at the Bridge, he often came close to scoring, especially in the earlier games, but as he began to snatch at chances, his confidence just evaporated. He contributed quite well to the team in other areas, but was eventually relegated to the reserves where he was still looking for that elusive goalscoring touch when 1992-93 came to a close. Although last season's form showed him to be an expensive miss-fit, the Stamford Bridge faithful know what he is capable of and will look for him to flourish now that Glen Hoddle is in charge of the playing staff.

| | | | APPEARANCES | | | | GOALS | | | |
|---|---|---|---|---|---|---|---|---|---|---|
| Clubs | Signing Date | Transfer Fee | Lge | FL Cup | FA Cup | Others | Lge | FL Cup | FA Cup | Others |
| Glasgow Rangers | .83 | – | 61+24 | 3+5 | 1+1 | 3+4 | 29 | 2 | | 3 |
| Partick Thistle | 11.83 | Loan | 1+1 | | | | | | | |
| Norwich City | 12.87 | £580,000 | 130+13 | 13 | 16+2 | 7 | 40 | 11 | 11 | 4 |
| Chelsea* | 8.92 | £2,100,000 | 28+3 | 6 | 1 | | 2 | 1 | | |

## FLEMING Craig

Born: Halifax, 6 October 1971

Height: 6'0"

Weight: 11.7

**Position/Skill Factor:** Right-back, who can also play in the centre of the defence. A confident player, he is always prepared to have the ball and is very difficult to disposess. Also takes up good positions.

**Career History:** Younger brother of Paul, who played for Halifax Town and Mansfield Town, he Made his FL debut for Halifax Town, while still a trainee, at home to Scunthorpe United on 2 January 1989, coming on as a sub. Started out at the Shay as an associated schoolboy (December 1986) and graduated to trainee status in July 1988, before signing pro forms, 18 months later. Established himself in the number five shirt towards the end of 1989-90 and was the club's only ever present the following season, when despite Halifax's struggles, he showed maturity beyond his years. Signed for Oldham Athletic, newly promoted to the First Division, in the 1991 close season and was soon in action, mainly at full-back. Although in and out of the team up to January, he took a firm hold on the right-back slot by the end of the season. Also scored his first ever FL goal at Everton in March, but it was not enough for the "Latics" to avoid defeat. Used as a permanent substitute for the early part of **1992-93**, but after winning the number six shirt for the home League game against Tottenham Hotspur, he remained in the side for the rest of the campaign. With his terrific turn of pace, he never gave Ryan Giggs a "kick" during the 1-0 win over Manchester United at Boundary Park, a game he rates as his best ever performance. Matured no end in 1993 and as a ferocious tackler, football may have at last found a successor to Norman "bite your legs" Hunter. If he has a fault, it would be that he tends to go to sleep when not involved, but Athletic seem to have unearthed another star in the making.

| | | | APPEARANCES | | | | GOALS | | | |
|---|---|---|---|---|---|---|---|---|---|---|
| Clubs | Signing Date | Transfer Fee | Lge | FL Cup | FA Cup | Others | Lge | FL Cup | FA Cup | Others |
| Halifax Town | 3.90 | - | 56+1 | 4 | 3 | 3+2 | | | | |
| Oldham Athletic* | 8.91 | £80,000 | 51+5 | 3+1 | 4 | 1 | 1 | | | |

## FLITCROFT Garry William

Born: Bolton, 6 November 1972

Height: 6'0"

Weight: 11.7

International Honours: E Sch, E Yth, E "U21"-7

**Position/Skill Factor:** Midfielder who can play in defence. Has a bit of everything, good skills, strong in the tackle and comfortable on the ball.

**Career History:** Initially an associated schoolboy (February 1987) at Maine Road, he joined Manchester City as a trainee in July 1989, on leaving school and progressed to the club's paid ranks by the 1991 close season. As a first year junior professional, he was not called upon by City manager, Peter Reid, but was loaned out to Third Division neighbours, Bury, for experience in late season, making his FL debut at Chester City on 7 March 1992. Although impressing during his 12 match run, playing in both midfield and central defence, he could not help the "Shakers" from sliding back into the Fourth Division. Had a tremendous **1992-93**, making the transition from reserve to first team player in his stride and being voted "Player of the Year", ahead of all the big names. Also, became a regular England under 21 international, scoring on his debut, while making 39 (including five substitute) first team appearances for City and ending a highly successful first season with six goals. His form was so impressive that he was voted the Barclays' "Young Eagle" for January, often switching between right-back and midfield with an ease that surprised and astounded team-mates and fans alike. Everything points to him making even more progress during the coming season.

| | | | APPEARANCES | | | | GOALS | | | |
|---|---|---|---|---|---|---|---|---|---|---|
| Clubs | Signing Date | Transfer Fee | Lge | FL Cup | FA Cup | Others | Lge | FL Cup | FA Cup | Others |
| Manchester City* | 7.91 | - | 28+4 | 1+1 | 5 | | 5 | | 1 | |
| Bury | 3.92 | Loan | 12 | | | | | | | |

## FLOWERS Timothy (Tim) David

Born: Kenilworth, 3 February 1967

Height: 6'2"

Weight: 14.0

International Honours: E Yth, E "U21"-3, E-1

**Position/Skill Factor:** Very consistent goalkeeper, who comes for crosses with confidence and sweeps up well behind his defence. Kicks very long from his hands.

**Career History:** Joined "Wolves" as an associated schoolboy (March 1981) and then as an apprentice (August 1983), before signing pro forms at Molineux. Made his FL debut at home to Sheffield United on 25 August 1984 and though conceding two goals in a 2-2 draw, showed great potential and went on to play 38 League matches that season. The club, however, were relegated to the Third Division and in 1985-86 he shared the goalkeeping duties with Scott Barrett as "Wolves" were relegated yet again, this time to the Fourth Division. Had a spell on loan at Southampton without playing a match, before signing for the "Saints" as Peter Shilton's understudy. He made a less than auspicious start with his new club when on the wrong end of a five goal mauling on his debut and then fractured a cheekbone in his second game. Remained in the shadows of Shilton and then John Burridge, spending a couple of loan periods at Swindon Town, before finally breaking through, following the latter's transfer to Newcastle United in the summer of 1989. Now firmly established as a first choice 'keeper at the club, he missed only five FL games between 1989-90 and 1991-92. Ever present in **1992-93**, he consistently presented a formidable barrier, especially in one-to-one situations, which was highlighted with a penalty save from Stuart Pearce to secure three valuable points at Nottingham Forest. Kept 12 clean sheets during a season that saw the "Saints" finish 18th in the new Premier League and came closer to realising his ambition to play for England when named in the party for the World Cup qualifiers and the tour of the USA during the summer. Following the disaster in Norway, he replaced Chris Woods in the England goal and gave an extremely confident display in a 1-1 draw against a good Brazilian side in the USA Cup match.

| | | | APPEARANCES | | | | GOALS | | | |
|---|---|---|---|---|---|---|---|---|---|---|
| Clubs | Signing Date | Transfer Fee | Lge | FL Cup | FA Cup | Others | Lge | FL Cup | FA Cup | Others |
| Wolverhampton W. | 8.84 | - | 63 | 5 | 2 | 2 | | | | |
| Southampton* | 6.86 | £70,000 | 180 | 24 | 16 | 8 | | | | |
| Swindon Town | 3.67 | Loan | 2 | | | | | | | |
| Swindon Town | 11.87 | Loan | 5 | | | | | | | |

## FLYNN Sean Michael

Born: Birmingham, 13 March 1968

Height: 5'7"

Weight: 11.2

**Position/Skill Factor:** Enthusiastic and robust midfielder, cum striker, with a great work rate, who will only get better with experience. Great in the air.

**Career History:** Formerly an associated schoolboy with West Bromwich Albion (May 1982), he established a growing reputation in local West Midlands football with Beazer Homes League teams, Bromsgrove Rovers and Halesowen Town, before joining Coventry City in December 1991, for an initial fee of £20,000, thus following in the footsteps of Tim Clarke and Andy Pearce,who also joined the "Sky Blues" from Halesowen. Most non-league players joining First Division clubs can expect to serve some time in the reserves before graduating to the first team. Instead, manager Terry Butcher pitched him into action almost immediately on the right side of midfield. He made a fairy tale FL debut away to Sheffield United on Boxing Day 1991, scoring a stupendous goal from 30 yards in City's remarkable 3-0 victory. Although it proved to be his only goal to date, he held his place to the end of the season and after ten games, Halesowen received an additional £10,000 with more to follow if he makes further progress. After doing so well in his first season of top flight soccer, **1992-93** was almost certain to be an anti-climax. He had to effectively start from scratch and perhaps come down to earth with a bump and following a couple of early appearances he disappeared from view to learn the game in the Pontins Central League side. Although he was not rated highly by manager, Bobby Gould, in the first half of the season, he worked very hard at his fitness and all-round game to get back in contention for first team places and came back to play five (including two substitute) League matches before the season came to a halt. Although he scored seven goals in the reserves, he needs to polish up his finishing as he missed twice as many, tending to panic inside the six yard box. Could turn into a super player.

| | | | APPEARANCES | | | | GOALS | | | |
|---|---|---|---|---|---|---|---|---|---|---|
| Clubs | Signing Date | Transfer Fee | Lge | FL Cup | FA Cup | Others | Lge | FL Cup | FA Cup | Others |
| Coventry City* | 12.91 | £30,000 | 25+4 | | | | 2 | | | |

## FORD Mark

Born: Pontefract, 10 October 1975

Height: 5'7" Weight: 9.3

**Position/Skill Factor:** Midfielder. Very good footballer with vision and a lovely passer of the ball.

**Career History:** Yet another of the successful **1992-93** Leeds United FA Youth Cup winning side to turn professional, having been at Elland Road as an associated schoolboy (November 1990) and as a trainee (July 1992), he will be knocking on the first team door before long.

| | | | APPEARANCES | | | | GOALS | | | |
|---|---|---|---|---|---|---|---|---|---|---|
| Clubs | Signing Date | Transfer Fee | Lge | FL Cup | FA Cup | Others | Lge | FL Cup | FA Cup | Others |
| Leeds United* | 3.93 | - | | | | | | | | |

## FOREMAN Matthew

Born: Newcastle, 15 February 1975

Height: 6'1" Weight: 12.5

**Position/Skill Factor:** Versatile midfielder who can also play in defence or attack. Has two good feet and tremendous stamina and is always in the thick of it.

**Career History:** First came to Sheffield United as an associated schoolboy in May 1989, before upgrading to trainee in July 1991 and turning professional last summer. Selected for "Blade's" reserve side at Anfield when still a first year trainee, he played a handful of reserve matches in **1992-93**, two of them against Liverpool. A very promising young player, indeed.

| | | | APPEARANCES | | | | GOALS | | | |
|---|---|---|---|---|---|---|---|---|---|---|
| Clubs | Signing Date | Transfer Fee | Lge | FL Cup | FA Cup | Others | Lge | FL Cup | FA Cup | Others |
| Sheffield United* | 7.93 | - | | | | | | | | |

## FORREST Craig Lorne

Born: Vancouver, Canada, 20 September 1967

Height: 6'4"

Weight: 14.4

International Honours: Canadian Int

**Position/Skill Factor:** Goalkeeper who comes for crosses and is very quick off his line to collect balls played in behind his defenders.

**Career History:** Joined Ipswich Town as an apprentice in September 1984, signing pro forms just under a year later, but when unable to claim a first team place was loaned out to Colchester United and made his FL debut there against Wrexham on 4 March 1988. The following season, he started for Town in the first 22 matches, but after a particularly bad defeat at Chelsea, Ron Fearon displaced him. He eventually got his place back and was an ever present in 1989-90. In 1990-91 he kept eight clean sheets in League games and continued to improve as he reaped the benefit of the club's specialist goalkeeping coaching, provided by Phil Parkes, the former England 'keeper. Played in all 56 League and cup games for Ipswich in 1991-92, which saw the Town carry off the Second Division Championship and earn automatic promotion to the new Premier League. Also selected for the Canadian national team after the season ended. Started **1992-93** as the first team's regular 'keeper, before suspension and then injury put paid to his season and gave Clive Baker the opportunity to prove his value. Had earlier conceded a freak goal in a 1-1 draw at home to Tottenham Hotspur, when a long upfield clearance from Jason Cundy got caught in a strong wind and sailed over his head, before making his 200th appearance for the club at Queens Park Rangers. His suspension came following being sent off in the second minute of the home game against Sheffield United for "serious foul play" against the "Blades'", Adrian Littlejohn. He thus became the first Ipswich goalkeeper ever to be sent off. Then, after playing for Canada in a World Cup qualifier in Jamaica, he picked up a ruptured stomach muscle, which ruled him out of action until the following summer, at least.

| | | | APPEARANCES | | | | GOALS | | | |
|---|---|---|---|---|---|---|---|---|---|---|
| Clubs | Signing Date | Transfer Fee | Lge | FL Cup | FA Cup | Others | Lge | FL Cup | FA Cup | Others |
| Ipswich Town* | 8.85 | – | 173 | 13 | 8 | 11 | | | | |
| Colchester United | 3.88 | Loan | 11 | | | | | | | |

## FORRESTER Jamie Mark

Born: Bradford, 1 November 1974

Height: 5'5½"

Weight: 10.4

International Honours: E Sch, E Yth

**Position/Skill Factor:** Striker who twists and turns around the box. Has great ability and with added control and balance, he is a real threat.

**Career History:** A talented young forward signed by Leeds United in a joint £120,000 deal, along with Kevin Sharp, having both been released by French First Division club, Auxerre, at the beginning of **1992-93**. Remarkably, both players had been offered the French equivalent of trainee contracts at the age of 16 in 1990, which they accepted in preference to joining an English club. But eventually, home-sickness, or lack of progress, prompted their return to native soil. After notching 26 goals in 25 games for the club's successful youth team, including five hat-tricks, he was included in the first team squad and made his PL debut as a substitute at Nottingham Forest on 21 March 1993 and maintained his place in the side for five games. He scored in each of the two legged FA Youth Cup Final, helping the club to lift the trophy for the first time in their history and was capped by England at under 18 level.

| | | | APPEARANCES | | | | GOALS | | | |
|---|---|---|---|---|---|---|---|---|---|---|
| Clubs | Signing Date | Transfer Fee | Lge | FL Cup | FA Cup | Others | Lge | FL Cup | FA Cup | Others |
| Leeds United* | 10.92 | £60,000 | 5+1 | | | | | | | |

## FOSTER Colin John

Born: Chislehurst, 16 July 1964

Height: 6'4" Weight: 13.10

**Position/Skill Factor:** Central defender who is very good in the air, either defensively, or at set plays. Excellent feet for a big man, he is always looking for the ball to find the right pass.

**Career History:** Due to an excellent physique, coupled with natural ability, he broke into the Leyton Orient side prior to turning professional, having been at the club as an associated schoolboy (September 1978) and as an apprentice (July 1980). He first appeared in a Third Round FA Cup-tie at home to Charlton Athletic, before making his FL debut a few days later at Grimsby Town on 9 January 1982. Quickly establishing himself at right-back, he finished the season as a regular with 23 League appearances, plus five in the FA Cup, to his credit. In 1982-83, he became a regular selection in central defence and though missing most of 1983-84 through injury, he re-established himself the following season. After five seasons as a pro. at Brisbane Road he was signed by Nottingham Forest manager, Brian Clough (a close friend of Orient's manager, Frank Clark), for a surprisingly modest fee (£50,000 plus Mark Smalley in exchange). Soon made his mark at the City Ground and was Des Walker's central defensive partner throughout 1987-88. It was Forest's best season since the late 1970s, finishing third in the League and reaching the FA Cup Semi-Final, before losing to Champions, Liverpool. Strangely, Foster lost his place the following season to converted midfielder Terry Wilson and out of favour, was transferred to West Ham United early in 1989-90. After a patchy first season at Upton Park under Lou Macari, he firmly established himself in the "Hammers'" defence in 1990-91, which conceded only 34 goals in 46 games, when winning promotion back to Division One. The following season was less successful for him, however, alternating with several players as Billy Bonds rang the changes to stave off relegation, unsuccessfully. Only played eight (including four as a substitute) games in **1992-93**, but proved the ideal man to have in reserve. Came in for the injured Alvin Martin and had great games at Upton Park against Birmingham City and Portsmouth, scoring the second goal in a 2-0 win against "Pompey". Unfortunate, himself with injuries, he was sidelined with back trouble, before coming back into the side in an away game towards the end of the season at centre-forward, where his height created real problems for the opposing defenders. With West Ham going into the Premier League as runners-up to Newcastle United, he could still have a part to play, especially when you note he is six years younger than Alvin Martin.

| | | | APPEARANCES | | | | GOALS | | | |
|---|---|---|---|---|---|---|---|---|---|---|
| Clubs | Signing Date | Transfer Fee | Lge | FL Cup | FA Cup | Others | Lge | FL Cup | FA Cup | Others |
| Leyton Orient | 2.82 | | 173+1 | 12 | 19 | 5 | 10 | | 5 | 1 |
| Nottingham Forest | 2.87 | £70,000 | 68+4 | 8 | 5 | 2 | 5 | 1 | | |
| West Ham United* | 9.89 | £750,000 | 83+5 | 5 | 9 | 2+2 | 5 | | 2 | |

## **FOSTER John** Colin

Born: Manchester, 19 September 1973

Height: 5'11" Weight: 11.4

International Honours: E Sch

**Position/Skill Factor:** Right-back, who can play in a number of defensive positions. Likes the robust side of the game, but is a good passer as well.

**Career History:** Joined the Manchester City professional staff during the 1992 close season, having previously been at Maine Road as an associated schoolboy (February 1988) and as a trainee (July 1990). Yet to play for the first team, he appeared in about half of the reserve fixtures during **1992-93**, but was unfortunate to receive several hard knocks which kept him out of action on occasion. A strapping lad, who gets on with the game without too much publicity, he had a creditable season and will hope to make a strong impact in the reserve side in 1993-94.

| | | | APPEARANCES | | | | GOALS | | | |
|---|---|---|---|---|---|---|---|---|---|---|
| Clubs | Signing Date | Transfer Fee | Lge | FL Cup | FA Cup | Others | Lge | FL Cup | FA Cup | Others |
| Manchester City* | 6.92 | - | | | | | | | | |

## **FOWLER Robert** Bernard

Born: Liverpool, 9 April 1975

Height: 5'7¾" Weight: 10.3

International Honours: E Yth

**Position/Skill Factor:** Centre-forward. An out and out goalscorer who is comfortable on the ball and has great technique. Has much guile and has the ability to hold up the ball, or go it alone.

**Career History:** Signed professional forms for Liverpool during the summer, having previously been at Anfield as an associated schoolboy (November 1990) and as a trainee (July 1991). No first team experience as yet, although his performances as the top marksman for the reserve side during **1992-93**, were promising enough to earn him a call-up as a named substitute for the last game of the season, a 6-2 thrashing of Tottenham Hotspur at Anfield, even though he was not pressed into action.

| | | | APPEARANCES | | | | GOALS | | | |
|---|---|---|---|---|---|---|---|---|---|---|
| Clubs | Signing Date | Transfer Fee | Lge | FL Cup | FA Cup | Others | Lge | FL Cup | FA Cup | Others |
| Liverpool* | 4.92 | - | | | | | | | | |

## **FOX Ruel** Adrian

Born: Ipswich, 14 January 1968

Height: 5'6"

Weight: 10.0

**Position/Skill Factor:** A winger who is very quick, he favours his right foot, but can go both ways. A real "box of tricks", he loves taking defenders on. Does extremely well in the air for his size.

**Career History:** Progressing through the Norwich City junior ranks, initially as an associated schoolboy (October 1983) and then as an apprentice (August 1984), he signed pro forms early in 1986. Made his FL debut at Carrow Road against Oxford United on 29 November 1986, but, apart from 1987-88, has found it difficult to hold down a regular place in facing fierce competition from Dale Gordon and Ian Crook. However, he finished 1989-90 on a high note with three goals in as many matches and kept his place at the beginning of the next season, eventually playing 23 League games, as the club yet again put the emphasis on good football. A regular performer for the "Canaries" in 1991-92, he occasionally played as a striking partner for Robert Fleck, but did not score often enough to justify continuation of that role. When Dale Gordon departed to Glasgow Rangers in November 1991, he was at last able to claim the right-wing slot as his own. On his day, his sparkling speed, footwork and trickery, render him almost untouchable and in several spells during **1992-93** he showed outstanding form, but yet again he did not always convert that into goals, as evidenced by only another four being added to his career total. He scored on the opening day of the campaign at Arsenal, in a sensational recovery from being 0-2 down to a 4-2 victory and in home draws against Everton and Arsenal, again, but he saved his best for last, a superb winner at Sheffield United, following a typical Norwich passing move. Had a ten match absence early on in the season with a pulled hamstring, an injury which turned out to be caused by a long standing back problem, but on coming back to the side he played in the remaining 30 games as an integral part of arguably, the best every City side.

| Clubs | Signing Date | Transfer Fee | APPEARANCES Lge | FL Cup | FA Cup | Others | GOALS Lge | FL Cup | FA Cup | Others |
|---|---|---|---|---|---|---|---|---|---|---|
| Norwich City* | 1.86 | - | 123+24 | 9+3 | 9+4 | 6+4 | 15 | | | |

## FREEDMAN **Douglas** Alan

Born: Glasgow, 21 January 1974

Height: 5'10" Weight: 10.7

International Honours: S Sch

**Position/Skill Factor:** Striker who is good around the box, always looking for a shot at goal.

**Career History:** Signed professional forms for Queens Park Rangers during the 1992 close season, having been at Loftus Road as a trainee since August 1990. With an eye for goal, he is another youngster who will be looking for some first team action before too long, having experienced reserve football in **1992-93**.

| Clubs | Signing Date | Transfer Fee | APPEARANCES Lge | FL Cup | FA Cup | Others | GOALS Lge | FL Cup | FA Cup | Others |
|---|---|---|---|---|---|---|---|---|---|---|
| Q.P.R.* | 5.92 | - | | | | | | | | |

## FRODSHAM **Ian** Timothy

Born: Liverpool, 22 December 1974

Height: 5'9½" Weight: 10.3

**Position/Skill Factor:** Attacking midfield player with good vision and distribution. An aggressive tackler, he also likes to get forward at every opportunity.

**Career History:** Locally born and bred, he came through the Liverpool ranks as an associated schoolboy (March 1990) and as a trainee (July 1992), before signing professional forms during the 1993 close season, having impressed in the youth side during **1992-93**.

| Clubs | Signing Date | Transfer Fee | APPEARANCES Lge | FL Cup | FA Cup | Others | GOALS Lge | FL Cup | FA Cup | Others |
|---|---|---|---|---|---|---|---|---|---|---|
| Liverpool* | 5.93 | - | | | | | | | | |

## FROGGATT **Stephen** Junior

Born: Lincoln, 9 March 1973

Height: 5'10"

Weight: 11.0

International Honours: E "U21"-4

**Position/Skill Factor:** Exciting young left-winger, who has pace, skill and a lovely left foot. He is capable of both scoring and creating goals. Takes dangerous corner kicks.

**Career History:** First joined Aston Villa as an associated schoolboy in March 1988 and then as a trainee in July 1989, before turning professional 18 months later. Although, as a first year professional, he was not expecting a first team outing so soon, he made his FL debut as a substitute on Boxing Day 1991 at home to West Ham United and subsequently enjoyed a short run in the first team from February to March. Capped by the England under 21 side during **1992-93**, he started the season well as a regular first teamer and appeared in almost every game until sustaining an ankle injury at Wimbledon. Unfortunately, this was followed by a mysterious knee problem, which kept him out of the side for three months. He came back in February for a couple of games and played well, before the injury got the better of him again and left him languishing on the sidelines. Another great young player for the future, he created a lot of scoring chances for Dean Saunders, prior to his injuries.

| Clubs | Signing Date | Transfer Fee | APPEARANCES Lge | FL Cup | FA Cup | Others | GOALS Lge | FL Cup | FA Cup | Others |
|---|---|---|---|---|---|---|---|---|---|---|
| Aston Villa* | 1.91 | - | 22+4 | 1 | 4+2 | | 1 | | 1 | |

## GAGE **Kevin** William

Born: Chiswick, 21 April 1964

Height: 5'9"

Weight: 11.2

International Honours: E Yth

**Position/Skill Factor:** Strong tackling aggressive full-back who gives his opponent no time to settle on the ball and likes to join up with the attack when the opportunity presents itself.

**Career History:** Made his FL debut at Plough Lane for Wimbledon as the club's youngest ever player, while still an apprentice, against Bury on 2 May 1981 in the last game of the 1980-81 season and although the "Dons" were beaten 4-2, they were still able to celebrate promotion to the Third Division. Had previously been an associated schoolboy (January 1980) before becoming an apprentice in July 1980. Made 21 appearances the following term as Wimbledon dropped back into the Fourth Division, but from then on it was success all the way as the little south London side marched to the First Division in four seasons. After helping to establish the "Dons" in the "top bracket", he was transferred to Aston Villa and was an ever present in the side that was promoted to the First Division in 1987-88. While Villa became the League Championship runners-up in 1989-90, he struggled to maintain his form and was in and out of the side from then on. He clearly had no future at Villa Park under new manager Ron Atkinson and was rescued from obscurity by his former manager, Dave Bassett, who took him on loan to Sheffield United in November 1991 and then sealed the transfer two months later. He settled in at right-back and had the satisfaction of scoring against his former club at Villa Park in a 1-1 draw late in the season. Another player to experience an in-and-out season in **1992-93**, after starting as first choice right-back, when injuries later in the year led to him being challenged for his place by Mitch Ward. He also failed to add to his single goal of the previous season, despite frequent forays into the opposition's half. This has, however, shown up a distinct lack of pace in regaining a defensive position, which has occasionally been exploited by the opposition.

| | | | APPEARANCES | | | | GOALS | | | |
|---|---|---|---|---|---|---|---|---|---|---|
| Clubs | Signing Date | Transfer Fee | Lge | FL Cup | FA Cup | Others | Lge | FL Cup | FA Cup | Others |
| Wimbledon | 1.82 | - | 135+33 | 7+2 | 8+3 | 0+1 | 15 | 1 | 1 | |
| Aston Villa | 7.87 | £100,000 | 113+2 | 13 | 9 | 8 | 8 | 3 | 1 | |
| Sheffield United* | 11.91 | £150,000 | 49 | 3 | 8+2 | | 1 | | | |

## GALE **Anthony (Tony)** Peter

Born: Westminster, 19 November 1959

Height: 6'1"

Weight: 12.4

International Honours: E Yth, E "U21"-1

**Position/Skill Factor:** Central defender with wonderful balance for a big man. Good feet and an excellent passer, both short and long, he loves to come out of defence to set up the attack.

**Career History:** When the legendary Bobby Moore retired at the end of 1976-77, Tony Gale, 16-years-old and not yet a professional, became his replacement at the heart of Fulham's defence. He had been at the club since joining as an associated schoolboy in November 1974, before graduating as an apprentice (June 1976) and styled his game on the great man. Making his Fl debut in the first match of 1977-78 at Craven Cottage against Charlton Athletic on 20 August 1977, he quickly settled in, scoring eight goals and missing only four games all season and was a natural choice to captain the England youth side. He remained a regular in the heart of Fulham's defence for seven seasons, suffering the pain of relegation to Division Three in 1979-80, but enjoying the triumph of promotion in 1981-82 and going to the very brink of promotion to Division One in 1982-83. In the summer of 1984, he was signed by West Ham United and helped solidify their frequently suspect defence, in partnership with Alvin Martin. In 1985-86 he assisted the "Hammers" to their best ever League placing, third, only four points behind Champions, Liverpool and with only 40 goals conceded. Sadly, they were unable to sustain that great effort and in subsequent seasons have struggled and "yo-yoed" between the two divisions. In 1990-91, although assisting the "Hammers" to promotion and the FA Cup Semi-Final, he suffered the trauma of being sent off (the first dismissal of his career and almost universally condemned as a bad decision) for an alleged professional foul in the Semi-Final, after only 25 minutes. As a result, Forest went on to win 4-0. 1991-92 was not much better, with the "Hammers" being relegated after just one season in the top flight and although when fit, he remained first choice, at 33 his better days seemed to be behind him. Apart from a couple of substitute appearances early in **1992-93**, he was out of contention until the end of January, when both Martin and Colin Foster were injured. It was then that he proved his great value to West Ham, being on the losing side just four times in 21 matches and soldiering the continuing promotion challenge. Only scored one goal all season, but it was a valuable one, at that, a powerful header taking three points at Leicester City in his second game. Continued to play an important role, as the "Hammers" moved inexorably towards an automatic promotion place and was outstanding in a 3-1 victory at Swindon Town, when the team took full advantage of Portsmouth's slip-up a day earlier, to jump into second position. That was effectively it, as "Hammers" achieved promotion to the Premier League as runners-up to Newcastle United and a further opportunity for him to play in the top flight, yet again.

| | | | APPEARANCES | | | | GOALS | | | |
|---|---|---|---|---|---|---|---|---|---|---|
| Clubs | Signing Date | Transfer Fee | Lge | FL Cup | FA Cup | Others | Lge | FL Cup | FA Cup | Others |
| Fulham | 8.77 | - | 277 | 22 | 16 | | 19 | 2 | | |
| West Ham United* | 8.84 | £150,000 | 262+6 | 26+2 | 28 | 9 | 5 | 1 | 1 | |

## GALLACHER **Kevin** William

Born: Clydebank, 23 November 1966

Height: 5'7" Weight: 9.11

International Honours: S Yth, S "U21"-7, S "B", S-17

**Position/Skill Factor:** Winger cum striker, with great pace, who can go past defenders to get his crosses in, or can cut inside to score. When playing up front, he is very composed in the box and always looks likely to get a goal.

**Career History:** Made his name in the Scottish Premier Division with Dundee United, having been signed from Duntocher BC and scored 27 goals in 131 matches before signing for Coventry City. In four seasons at United, the club went to successive losing Scottish Cup Finals against

St Mirren (1987) and Celtic (1988) and were runners-up in the UEFA Cup Final against IFK Gothenburg in 1987. First capped by Scotland in a Rous Cup match on 17 May 1988, he came south to Coventry for a club record fee and made his FL debut in a 3-2 home win against Chelsea on 3 February 1990. Topped the club's League goalscoring charts in 1990-91 with 11 from 32 appearances and scored a hat-trick in the Fourth Round of the League Cup against Nottingham Forest, in an astonishing 5-4 victory. Undoubtedly Coventry's most talented player and their only forward capable of scoring consistently, he was switched from the wing to central striker in March 1991, scoring six goals in 13 games. He continued in this role for 1991-92 and his absence through injury from March to April 1992 was a major factor in Coventry's slide into the relegation zone. Although he won three more caps for Scotland during the season, they were all as substitute, and he seemed likely to miss out on Scotland's European Championship squad, until called up as a last minute replacement for the injured John Robertson of Hearts. Scotland went out of the tournament after losing to Holland (1-0) and Germany (2-0), although they beat the CIS (3-0) and he enhanced his reputation playing in a side that performed well above expectation. Had several spells out of the "Sky Blues'" side with injuries of one sort or another in **1992-93** and with the transfer deadline looming, the club allowed him to move on to Blackburn Rovers in exchange for Roy Wegerle and £500,000. He struck up an immediate rapport with Mike Newell, that almost had the fans forgetting Alan Shearer, as he used his great speed to good effect and constantly worried defences with challenges. Scored five goals in his nine appearances and greatly contributed to 21 points from a possible 27, as Rovers maintained fourth place in the Premier League.

| | | | APPEARANCES | | | | GOALS | | | |
|---|---|---|---|---|---|---|---|---|---|---|
| Clubs | Signing Date | Transfer Fee | Lge | FL Cup | FA Cup | Others | Lge | FL Cup | FA Cup | Others |
| Dundee United | 11.83 | – | 118+13 | 13 | 20+3 | 15+6 | 27 | 5 | 5 | 3 |
| Coventry City | 1.90 | £900,000 | 99+1 | 11 | 4 | 2 | 28 | 7 | | |
| Blackburn Rovers* | 3.93 | £1,500,000 | 9 | | | | 5 | | | |

## GALLEN **Kevin** Andrew

Born: Chiswick, 21 September 1975

Height: 6'0" Weight: 12.0

International Honours: E Sch, E Yth

**Position/Skill Factor:** Striker with very good skills. An excellent runner off the ball, he is more than capable of causing problems in the penalty area.

**Career History:** An England schoolboy international, he came to Queens Park Rangers as an associated schoolboy player in December 1989 and turned professional on his 17th birthday, not having been a trainee. Had a great first season in **1992-93**, scoring over 60 youth team goals to break Jimmy Greaves longstanding record and won England youth honours to boot. Needs a wee more time to develop and then just watch him go. His brothers, Steve (Q.P.R.) and Joe (Watford), both elected to play for the Irish Republic at youth and under 21 level, having qualified through their parents' birthright.

| | | | APPEARANCES | | | | GOALS | | | |
|---|---|---|---|---|---|---|---|---|---|---|
| Clubs | Signing Date | Transfer Fee | Lge | FL Cup | FA Cup | Others | Lge | FL Cup | FA Cup | Others |
| Q.P.R.* | 9.92 | – | | | | | | | | |

## GALLEN **Stephen** James

Born: Ealing, 21 November 1973

Height: 6'0" Weight: 11.0

International Honours: IR Yth, IR "U21"-2

**Position/Skill Factor:** Centre-back. Strong in the air and tackles well. Adept at knocking long ball into his strikers.

**Career History:** Signed professional forms for Queens Park Rangers during the 1992 close season, having been at Loftus Road as a trainee since June 1990. Already a Republic of Ireland youth international, he won under 21 caps in **1992-93** and is making great progress as he comes through the ranks. A good prospect, his younger brother Kevin is also at Rangers.

| | | | APPEARANCES | | | | GOALS | | | |
|---|---|---|---|---|---|---|---|---|---|---|
| Clubs | Signing Date | Transfer Fee | Lge | FL Cup | FA Cup | Others | Lge | FL Cup | FA Cup | Others |
| Q.P.R.* | 5.92 | – | | | | | | | | |

## GANNON John Spencer

Born: Wimbledon, 18 December 1966

Height: 5'8"

Weight: 10.10

**Position/Skill Factor:** Creative midfielder who is always involved in the game. A confident player, he has a lovely left foot and some nice touches.

**Career History:** Signed for Wimbledon as an associated schoolboy in January 1981 and then as an apprentice in July 1983, but before joining the pro ranks, he made his FL debut at Bradford City on 2 May 1981, scoring in a 1-1 draw. Played a couple of times for Wimbledon in the First Division the following term, but found it difficult to win a regular place and was loaned out to Crewe Alexandra for three months. Still unable to establish himself at Plough Lane on his return, he later spent a period on loan to Sheffield United, managed by his old Wimbledon boss, Dave Bassett. Entering the fray as a sub, he scored in a 4-1 win against Blackpool and stayed on to help United gain promotion to the Second Division at the end of that season, 1988-89. The move was made permanent during the close season and he quickly won a regular place in the "Blades'" midfield, missing only seven matches, as the club went back to the First Division as runners-up. Considering his lack of achievement at Wimbledon, his progress at Bramall Lane has been remarkable and typical of Dave Bassett's talent of transforming apparently undistinguished players into First Division stalwarts. Left out at the beginning of 1991-92, he was restored to the first team in late September and played in every game for the "Blades" thereafter, assisting their remarkable rise from bottom position in November to ninth in May. Restored as first choice in midfield for the start of **1992-93**, he played 26 times during the first Premier League season. Goalscoring once again proved to be a problem and he managed only one, against Oldham Athletic, after coming on as a substitute. Injury and loss of form at the turn of the year, plus competition from Charlie Hartfield, meant that a recall was only forthcoming when suspension ruled the former out and the return was short lived, ending the season out of the side.

| | | | APPEARANCES | | | | GOALS | | | |
|---|---|---|---|---|---|---|---|---|---|---|
| Clubs | Signing Date | Transfer Fee | Lge | FL Cup | FA Cup | Others | Lge | FL Cup | FA Cup | Others |
| Wimbledon | 12.84 | - | 13+3 | 1+1 | | 1 | 2 | | | |
| Crewe Alexandra | 12.86 | Loan | 14+1 | | | 1 | | | | |
| Sheffield United* | 2.89 | - | 124+12 | 11 | 13 | 4 | 6 | | | |

## GAYLE Brian Wilbert

Born: Kingston, 6 March 1965

Height: 6'1" Weight: 12.7

**Position/Skill Factor:** Quick and aggressive centre-back who defends well and is good in the air.

**Career History:** Discovered as a 16-year-old by Wimbledon, he was apprenticed in July 1981, turning pro three years later after having a spell on loan with local Vauxhall League team, Tooting & Mitcham. Made his FL debut in the number five shirt at home to Shrewsbury Town on 27 March 1985 and kept his place for the rest of the season. During 1985-86, the season the "Dons" were promoted to the First Division, he was displaced by Mick Smith during October and didn't regain his position in the side until the following season. Was transferred to Manchester City in the 1988-89 close season, after not being selected for the 1988 Wimbledon FA Cup winning team and immediately helped City back to the First Division, while missing only five games. Dropped when Howard Kendall took over at Maine Road, he signed for Ipswich Town and apart from a short spell in 1990-91, he held down a regular place with the Suffolk club. Signed by his former manager at Wimbledon, Dave Bassett, for Sheffield United soon into the 1991-92 season, his debut was delayed for two weeks as the "Blades'" directors struggled to raise the transfer fee. Made a nervous start with his new club, whose defence was leaking goals in abundance. However, after scoring twice in a 3-2 defeat away to Manchester City, he settled down to form a highly effective central defensive partnership with Paul Beesley, which assisted the "Blades" to rise from the foot of the table to a final ninth place. United's captain started **1992-93** out of the side, replaced by the on-loan, Alan McLeary, from Millwall and after returning to the heart of the defence, his season was again interrupted, this time by a knee operation in November. Following this, he was not able to train regularly, but soldiered on through the remainder of the campaign, until rested for the last match when the team were mathematically safe from relegation. During the close season, a further knee operation is likely to be required and it is hoped that this will enable him to return to his best form.

| | | | APPEARANCES | | | | GOALS | | | |
|---|---|---|---|---|---|---|---|---|---|---|
| Clubs | Signing Date | Transfer Fee | Lge | FL Cup | FA Cup | Others | Lge | FL Cup | FA Cup | Others |
| Wimbledon | 10.84 | - | 76+7 | 7 | 8 | 2 | 3 | 1 | 1 | |
| Manchester City | 7.88 | £325,000 | 55 | 8 | 2 | 1 | 3 | | | |
| Ipswich Town | 1.90 | £330,000 | 58 | 3 | 0+1 | | 4 | | | |
| Sheffield United* | 9.91 | £750,000 | 64 | 7 | 9 | 1 | 6 | | 1 | 1 |

## GERRARD Paul William

Born: Heywood, 22 January 1973

Height: 6'2"

Weight: 11.2

International Honours: E"U21"-8

**Position/Skill Factor:** Brave young goalkeeper, who cuts a commanding figure and kicks long and hard. Has a brilliant attitude to the game.

**Career History:** On leaving school, he joined Oldham Athletic as a trainee in August 1989 and had progressed to the club's professional ranks in the 1991 close season. Almost down and out and ready to quit soccer after two operations on an horrifically injured knee, he was sent out to Crewe Alexandra on loan, in order to gain experience, only to dislocate the same knee the day before his debut. On arriving back, he had talks with Joe Royle about his future and was persuaded to give it one last go and after visiting a leading specialist he was given the all-clear to start training. In the "rags to riches" story of **1992-93**, just two games into the comeback with the reserves and with both Jon Hallworth and John Keeley injured, he was selected to make his PL debut at Queens Park Rangers on 5 December 1992. Although Athletic lost 3-2, he hasn't looked back and is now not only first choice for his club, but also for the England under 21 side, having been capped eight times so far. Continued to make stunning saves throughout the rest of the season and Joe Royle is confident that he will go on to be England's number one 'keeper within three years.

| | | | APPEARANCES | | | | GOALS | | | |
|---|---|---|---|---|---|---|---|---|---|---|
| Clubs | Signing Date | Transfer Fee | Lge | FL Cup | FA Cup | Others | Lge | FL Cup | FA Cup | Others |
| Oldham Athletic* | 7.91 | - | 25 | | 2 | | | | | |

## GIGGS Ryan Joseph

Born: Cardiff, 29 November 1973

Height: 5'11" Weight: 9.9

International Honours: W Yth, W "U21"-1, W-8

**Position/Skill Factor:** Left-winger with lovely skills, who delights in taking defenders on. Has a beautiful left foot and uses it to advantage at set plays. Is also capable of scoring spectacular goals.

**Career History:** The son of the former Rugby League international, Brian Wilson, he has since taken his mother's name and despite his prodigious talent threatening to break Duncan Edwards' record as the youngest ever Manchester United player, he had to wait until he was 17 years and three months for the honour of playing in the first team. He first came to Old Trafford as an associated schoolboy (February 1988), before graduating to trainee (July 1990) and eventually turning pro following his 17th birthday. Made his FL debut when coming on as a sub at home to Everton on 2 March 1991 and in his first full match, the local "derby" against Manchester City, he scored the only goal of the game. Even before his United debut he was tipped as a future football star, but his progress in 1991-92, under the tutelage of the normally ultra-cautious Alex Ferguson, was positively electrifying. Included in the first team squad from the start of the season, his sparkling wing play and supremely confident, audacious goal scoring, soon earned him a regular place and rave reviews in the media. The combination of Giggs on one wing and Kantschelskis on the other, gave the "Reds" a new attacking dimension, missing for years at Old Trafford and for a while it seemed that United would be League Champions with a combination of flair and efficiency. It was not to be, however and although he was a member of the team which brought the League Cup to Old Trafford for the first time, the League Championship prize slipped away in a welter of draws and ultimately, defeats. His contribution to the season's entertainment was recognised by his fellow professionals when he was voted "Young Player of the Year" in the PFA Awards in April — the youngest player ever to receive the accolade. He was also selected by Wales, becoming their youngest full international in October 1991, at 17 years 11 months of age. **1992-93** was another brilliant season for the Welsh "wonder boy" and it came as no surprise when he was honoured as the "Young Eagle of the Year" and for the second year running, the PFA "Young Player of the Year". His season was made complete when he won a Championship medal as the League title came back to Old Trafford after a break of 26 years. Scored 11 goals during the campaign, many of real quality, but to be selective one would not forget too easily the strike from an acute angle in a 1-1 draw at Tottenham Hotspur, that rightly won the "Goal of the Month" award, the stunning free-kick in the last home game against Blackburn Rovers and two in the last eight minutes to beat Southampton 2-1 at Old Trafford. As if all that wasn't enough, he became a permanent member of the Welsh side in 1992-93 and celebrated with a marvellous free-kick in a 2-0 victory over Belgium on his full debut at Arms Park. Already a Premier League star, he is widely tipped to make a name for himself on the world stage.

| | | | APPEARANCES | | | | GOALS | | | |
|---|---|---|---|---|---|---|---|---|---|---|
| Clubs | Signing Date | Transfer Fee | Lge | FL Cup | FA Cup | Others | Lge | FL Cup | FA Cup | Others |
| Manchester United* | 12.90 | - | 73+8 | 8+2 | 4+1 | 2+1 | 13 | 3 | 2 | |

*Ryan Giggs*

# GILLESPIE Keith Robert

Born: Bangor, Northern Ireland, 18 February 1975

Height: 5'10"

Weight: 10.11

International Honours: NI Yth

**Position/Skill Factor:** Old fashioned right-winger, fast raiding and a lovely crosser. Big and strong, he likes to take defenders on, down the touchline.

**Career History:** A key member of the successful Manchester United youth side that reached the FA Youth Cup Final two years running, winning it the first time round, he first came to Old Trafford as an associated schoolboy in June 1989, before becoming more permanent as a trainee (August 1991) on leaving school. Turned professional in **1992-93**, having already made an astonishingly early and successful first team debut for the "Reds", in the Third Round FA Cup-tie at home to Bury on 5 January 1993, laying on the cross for the first goal and scoring the second in a 2-0 victory.

| | | | APPEARANCES | | | | GOALS | | | |
|---|---|---|---|---|---|---|---|---|---|---|
| Clubs | Signing Date | Transfer Fee | Lge | FL Cup | FA Cup | Others | Lge | FL Cup | FA Cup | Others |
| Manchester United* | 2.93 | - | | | 1+1 | | | | 1 | |

# GODDARD Paul

Born: Harlington, 12 October 1959

Height: 5'8" Weight: 11.8

International Honours: E "U21"-8, E-1

**Position/Skill Factor:** A striker who can hold the ball up, he has an excellent touch and a very good brain. Is at his most dangerous when balls are played into him on the edge of the penalty area.

**Career History:** First came to Queens Park Rangers as a 15-year-old when he signed associated schoolboy forms in November 1974. Became an apprentice in July 1976, before turning pro in the Summer of 1977 and going on to make his FL debut at home to Arsenal on 11 April 1978, when introduced as a sub. In his first full game he scored against Coventry City and although claiming a regular place shortly afterwards, it was not until 1979-80 that he really came to the fore, scoring 16 League goals in a great partnership with Clive Allen. On the basis of that form, West Ham United parted with a large fee for him to act as the foil for David Cross. In his first season at Upton Park, he won a Second Division Championship medal and reached the League Cup Final and although he scored in the replay, the "Hammers" were beaten 2-1 by Liverpool. Only missed a handful of games for the club prior to 1985-86 and was honoured by England when he came on as a sub against Iceland on 2 June 1982, but suffered a serious injury in August 1985 and when returned to full fitness again, could not dislodge Terry Cottee and Frank McAvennie, languishing in the reserves before being transferred to Newcastle United. Although highly regarded on Tyneside, he and his family were homesick for the south and after topping United's goalscoring charts, he was allowed to move to Derby County in the 1988 close season. Quickly formed a good partnership with Dean Saunders, but with the side going well, Millwall made an offer for the 30-year-old player that Derby could hardly refuse. It was a desperation signing by the "Lions", struggling in vain for First Division survival and a disastrous move for both club and player. New "Lions'" manager Bruce Rioch had no interest in him and one year later Millwall wrote off their over hasty £800,000 investment and granted him a free transfer. His former manager at Upton Park, John Lyall, then signed him for Ipswich Town and he showed a brief glimpse of his previous form with six goals in ten games, before injury ended his season. Bizarrely, he was listed in the "Lions'" programme on 1 January 1990 as turning out for the opposing side, Derby, but overnight he had signed for the home side and played for them instead. In 1991-92, he played only a minor role in Ipswich's Second Division Championship campaign after losing his place in September and when drafted back into the side in late season it was in midfield. Had a most disappointing season in **1992-93**, when it had been felt that his experience would be invaluable to the younger members of the side, as the club tried to cement its place in the Premier League. Although playing fairly regularly, earlier on, once Bontcho Guentchev established himself in the side at the end of December, his form fell away and he was required only eight more (including four substitute) times.

| | | | APPEARANCES | | | | GOALS | | | |
|---|---|---|---|---|---|---|---|---|---|---|
| Clubs | Signing Date | Transfer Fee | Lge | FL Cup | FA Cup | Others | Lge | FL Cup | FA Cup | Others |
| Q.P.R. | 7.77 | - | 63+7 | 4+1 | | | 23 | | | |
| West Ham United | 8.80 | £800,000 | 159+11 | 26 | 10+1 | 6 | 54 | 12 | 3 | 2 |
| Newcastle United | 11.86 | £415,000 | 61 | 3 | 6 | | 19 | 1 | 3 | |
| Derby County | 8.88 | £425,000 | 49 | 7 | 1+1 | 5 | 15 | 2 | | 1 |
| Millwall | 12.89 | £800,000 | 17+3 | | 4+1 | | 1 | | 1 | |
| Ipswich Town* | 1.91 | - | 56+12 | 5 | 2+2 | 2 | 13 | | | |

## **GORDON Dale** Andrew

Born: Great Yarmouth, 9 January 1967

Height: 5'10" Weight: 11.8

International Honours: E Sch, E Yth, E "U21"-4, E"B"

**Position/Skill Factor:** Very skilful and talented right-winger with great pace and the additional ingredient to score vital goals.

**Career History:** Already an England schoolboy international, he turned down Manchester United to sign for his local club, Norwich City, instead, as an associated schoolboy (January 1981) and moved up the ranks to apprentice (May 1983) on leaving school. Made his FL debut on the opening day of 1984-85 in a 3-3 draw at home to Liverpool on 25 August 1984 and played 27 (including two Substitute) games that first season. Despite making an excellent impression, he was rested towards the end of the season, as the "Canaries" turned to experience in their unsuccessful battle against relegation and played little part in the following campaign when the club swept back to the top flight as Second Division Champions. Finally established himself in 1986-87, when he played in every FL game, bar one and was also selected for the England Under 21 team. However, the following season was a frustrating one, being out of favour, both at the beginning and end of 1987-88. Voted "Player of the Year" in 1988-89, after assisting the club to their highest ever FL placing of fourth, having led the Championship race over the first four months and reaching the FA Cup Semi-Final, before losing out to Everton. He continued to be a key player in the "Canaries'" attack, but as always, Norwich were unable to resist the overtures of predatory wealthy clubs for their star performers and in November 1991 he was snapped up by Glasgow Rangers, paradoxically, at a time that the Scottish Champions were unloading their English imports. Made a dream debut for the "Gers", scoring twice in a 5-0 drubbing of Dunfermline and was a regular selection to the end of the season. However, he was surprisingly omitted from the starting line up for the Scottish FA Cup Final, coming on as a 86th minute substitute, as Rangers narrowly defeated Airdrieonians 2-1. Perhaps this was an omen for **1992-93**, as he became increasingly peripheral in Rangers' team selection — again being substitute in their Skol Cup Final victory over Aberdeen and overlooked for the end of the season, Scottish Cup Final. It was not a great surprise, therefore, that he returned south of the border in the summer, signing for newly promoted West Ham as a replacement for Kevin Keen (a recent departure to Wolves)

| | | | APPEARANCES | | | | GOALS | | | |
|---|---|---|---|---|---|---|---|---|---|---|
| Clubs | Signing Date | Transfer Fee | Lge | FL Cup | FA Cup | Others | Lge | FL Cup | FA Cup | Others |
| Norwich City | 1.84 | - | 194+12 | 21 | 19 | 14+2 | 31 | 3 | 6 | 3 |
| Glasgow Rangers | 11.91 | £1,200,000 | 40+4 | 1+1 | 6+1 | 1 | 6 | 1 | | |
| West Ham United* | 7.93 | £750,000 | | | | | | | | |

## **GOSS Jeremy**

Born: Cyprus, 11 May 1965

Height: 5'9"

Weight: 10.9

International Honours: E Yth, W-3

**Position/Skill Factor:** Non-stop defensive midfield player, who is a real team man. Pressures opponents into mistakes and is good on the ball. Loves to keep the game flowing with quick passing movements.

**Career History:** A member of Norwich City's FA Youth Cup Final team against Everton in 1983, he joined the club on a manpower work experience scheme, before turning to the pro ranks and making his FL debut as a sub, when coming on for Tony Spearing at Coventry City on 12 May 1984. Was selected for an England Under 19 team in 1984, which for statistical purposes is treated as a youth international. In a remarkable story of patience and perseverance by both player and his club, he had to wait until December 1987 before winning a regular place with the "Canaries". Then a knee injury ruled him out of the reckoning in 1988-89 and a hernia operation in the summer of 1989 reduced his chances in 1989-90. He made a comeback in the latter half of 1990-91 and did enough to prompt Wales' manager Terry Yorath to select him for two games at the end of the season, making his international debut against Iceland in April 1991, thus becoming an oddity of a Cyprus born player (albeit of English parentage) turning out for both England and Wales! Started 1991-92 on the bench, but displaced Ian Crook in October and, more than eight years after signing professional, finally won a regular place, holding it until the end of the season. Also won a further cap for Wales in April 1992. Into his tenth season with the club in **1992-93**, before playing his 100th League game, if you include substitute appearances, he enjoyed an unbroken run in the side as City stormed to the top of the new Premier League. However, in November, he made way for the return of Ruel Fox, until an injury to Ian Crook let him back into the team some ten games later. Formed a good understanding in the middle of the park with Gary Megson and received an incredible standing ovation when substituted (wrongly according to the crowd) during the losing Fourth Round FA Cup-tie at home to Tottenham Hotspur. Again substituted, this time when he pulled a hamstring during the match against Manchester City at Carrow Road in mid-February, he didn't come back until playing in six of the last seven games of a memorable season for the "Canaries".

| | | | APPEARANCES | | | | GOALS | | | |
|---|---|---|---|---|---|---|---|---|---|---|
| Clubs | Signing Date | Transfer Fee | Lge | FL Cup | FA Cup | Others | Lge | FL Cup | FA Cup | Others |
| Norwich City* | 3.83 | - | 93+20 | 8 | 11+2 | 9 | 5 | 3 | | 3 |

## GOULD Jonathan (Jon) Alan

Born: Paddington, 18 July 1968

Height: 6'1"

Weight: 12.6

**Position/Skill Factor:** Goalkeeper. Brave and very agile and a good long kicker.

**Career History:** The son of Bobby Gould, the current Coventry City manager, he started his career in non-League football, playing for Clevedon Town of the Western League, prior to signing for Fourth Division Halifax Town in the 1990 close season. A long term back injury to the club's regular 'keeper, David Brown, meant that he did not have to wait too long for his FL debut, a 5-3 win in a thriller at home to Blackpool on 27 October 1990. Unfortunately, after performing admirably in over 20 appearances, he received a facial injury in a match against Walsall and had to be substituted. But he was back for the remaining seven matches of the season and was one of the bright spots during a dismal season for the 'Shaymen". Started the 1991-92 season as first choice, but after losing his place to Lee Bracey from Swansea in October, he was released soon afterwards and was signed by his father for West Bromwich Albion, as second choice 'keeper, but was not called upon for first team duty. When Bobby was dismised from the Hawthorns, he was immediately offered the assistant managership by his former club, Coventry City. Within a month he was manager (after Don Howe resigned) and one of his first signings for Coventry was his son Jonathan to provide **1992-93** cover for Steve Ogrizovic. His first FL game, 14 months after being sacked by Halifax, came when Steve Ogrizovic injured his neck and he was called up to play against Liverpool. Made a brilliant debut for the "Sky Blues" in a 5-1 home victory, but after two more games he was back to the reserves. Later, when Ogrizovic was having a poor spell, he was recalled to play in the last six matches of the season. Although he had a mixed time, he is still in the learning process and is sure to spend the summer break ironing out certain aspects of his game.

| | | | APPEARANCES | | | | GOALS | | | |
|---|---|---|---|---|---|---|---|---|---|---|
| Clubs | Signing Date | Transfer Fee | Lge | FL Cup | FA Cup | Others | Lge | FL Cup | FA Cup | Others |
| Halifax Town | 7.90 | - | 32 | 2 | 5 | 5 | | | | |
| West Bromwich Albion | 1.92 | - | | | | | | | | |
| Coventry City* | 7.92 | - | 9 | | | | | | | |

## GRAHAM Mark Roland

Born: Newry, Northern Ireland, 24 October 1974

Height: 5'7" Weight: 9.9

International Honours: NI Sch, NI Yth

**Position/Skill Factor:** Skilful left winger with good ability and one who causes defenders problems when he runs at them.

**Career History:** A Northern Ireland schoolboy and youth international, he signed associated schoolboy forms with Queens Park Rangers in May 1989, while playing as an amateur with Glenavon. Came to Loftus Road as a trainee (July 1991) on leaving school and made good progress during **1992-93** to join the professional ranks in the close season and looks to be a useful prospect.

| | | | APPEARANCES | | | | GOALS | | | |
|---|---|---|---|---|---|---|---|---|---|---|
| Clubs | Signing Date | Transfer Fee | Lge | FL Cup | FA Cup | Others | Lge | FL Cup | FA Cup | Others |
| Q.P.R.* | 5.93 | - | | | | | | | | |

## GRAHAM Richard Ean

Born: Dewsbury, 28 November 1974

Height: 5'11" Weight: 11.7

**Position/Skill Factor:** Skilful central midfield player with great vision and touch. With a quick brain and much awareness, he is extremely comfortable on the ball.

**Career History:** Another recent Oldham Athletic professional signing that the club have high hopes for in the future and a player who has only been at Boundary Park for two years, having joined as a trainee (August 1991) on leaving school. In **1992-93**, after showing excellent form in the juniors, he was upgraded to the reserve side after Christmas and impressed with mature performances.

| | | | APPEARANCES | | | | GOALS | | | |
|---|---|---|---|---|---|---|---|---|---|---|
| Clubs | Signing Date | Transfer Fee | Lge | FL Cup | FA Cup | Others | Lge | FL Cup | FA Cup | Others |
| Oldham Athletic* | 7.93 | - | | | | | | | | |

## **GRANT Anthony (Tony)** James

Born: Liverpool, 14 November 1974

Height: 5'10" Weight: 10.2

**Position/Skill Factor:** Very skilful midfielder with good vision and superb touch. He can pick the passes out that will create goalscoring chances.

**Career History:** Liverpool born and bred, he initially came to Everton as an associated schoolboy in January 1989 and graduated as a trainee (August 1991) to professional status during the 1993 close season. Made ten reserve team appearances over the last two or three months of **1992-93** and showed enough promise to suggest that he has a future in the game.

| | | | APPEARANCES | | | | GOALS | | | |
|---|---|---|---|---|---|---|---|---|---|---|
| Clubs | Signing Date | Transfer Fee | Lge | FL Cup | FA Cup | Others | Lge | FL Cup | FA Cup | Others |
| Everton* | 7.93 | - | | | | | | | | |

## **GRAY Andrew (Andy)** Arthur

Born: Lambeth, 22 February 1964

Height: 5'10" Weight: 10.2

International Honours: E "U21"-2, E-1

**Position/Skill Factor:** Tremendously powerful midfielder, always in the heat of the action and a strong tackler. Packing a terrific shot in his right foot, he is also respected by opposing defences for his long throws.

**Career History:** Before signing for Crystal Palace, he played non-League soccer first for Corinthian Casuals and then with Dulwich Hamlet of the Vauxhall League where he was observed by Palace manager, Steve Coppell. Made his FL debut at home to Cardiff City on 9 December 1984, coming on as a sub in a 1-1 draw at Grimsby Town. He then began to establish himself in the Palace midfield, taking over from Peter Nicholas, who moved to Luton Town. After three years at Selhurst Park, he joined Second Division Aston Villa, helping the club to promotion as runners-up, but soon found himself back in London with Queens Park Rangers, who were struggling in 16th place in the First Division. In helping the club to climb to mid-table respectability, he finished on the losing side only twice in 11 matches. However, his former club, Palace, having just won promotion from the Second Division decided to take him back to Selhurst Park and he started 1989-90 in midfield against his previous club at Loftus Road. He was influential in helping Palace to their first ever FA Cup Final, scoring the late equaliser which took the epic Semi-Final with Liverpool into extra-time. He was a consistent performer in 1991-92 and was called up, along with club colleague, Geoff Thomas, by England manager Graham Taylor (his boss at Villa) for the vital European Championship qualifier in Poland in November 1991, in which England scraped a 1-1 draw and qualified by the skin of their teeth. Unfortunately, his England debut seemed to turn his head and his attitude so infuriated his manager, Steve Coppell, that he was dropped from the Palace team in January and transfer listed. He was then loaned to Tottenham Hotspur for the remainder of the season with a view to a permanent transfer, eventually firmed up. Began **1992-93** on the bench, being used in five of the opening six matches, until given the chance to start a game. Made three appearances, before sustaining an injury in the home fixture against Manchester United and after struggling to get back in the side, his next taste of first team football came in a spell on loan to Swindon Town. Played just three times for the "Robins", before returning to White Hart Lane and selection for the match at Crystal Palace, scoring in a 3-1 win over his old team-mates. Was then involved in a further eight games, but again lost his place, this time to Steve Sedgley. The coming season may well see him involved in a transfer move, but with the departure of Nayim to Spain, the opportunity is still there for him to win his place back.

| | | | APPEARANCES | | | | GOALS | | | |
|---|---|---|---|---|---|---|---|---|---|---|
| Clubs | Signing Date | Transfer Fee | Lge | FL Cup | FA Cup | Others | Lge | FL Cup | FA Cup | Others |
| Crystal Palace | 11.84 | £2,000 | 91+7 | 9+1 | 3 | 0+1 | 27 | 2 | | |
| Aston Villa | 11.87 | £150,000 | 34+3 | 3 | 3+1 | 0+2 | 4 | 1 | 1 | |
| Q.P.R. | 2.89 | £425,000 | 11 | | | | 2 | | | |
| Crystal Palace | 8.89 | £500,000 | 87+3 | 15 | 11 | 14 | 12 | 4 | 2 | 4 |
| Tottenham Hotspur* | 2.92 | £900,000 | 23+8 | | | | 2 | | | |
| Swindon Town | 12.92 | Loan | 3 | | | | | | | |

## **GRAY Ian** James

Born: Manchester, 25 February 1975

Height: 6'1" Weight: 11.11

**Position/Skill Factor:** Agile goalkeeper, with good hands, who is competent on crosses. Brave when coming for the ball, he also stands up well to make things difficult for oncoming forwards.

**Career History:** A recent Oldham Athletic professional signing, having first come to Boundary Park as a trainee in August 1991, he is currently the club's third choice 'keeper behind Paul Gerrard and Jon Hallworth. However, when John Keeley was out of action for a considerable time in **1992-93**, he was blooded in the reserve side for 15 games and under the substitute goal-keeper ruling, he could get an early first team chance.

| Clubs | Signing Date | Transfer Fee | APPEARANCES | | | | GOALS | | | |
|---|---|---|---|---|---|---|---|---|---|---|
| | | | Lge | FL Cup | FA Cup | Others | Lge | FL Cup | FA Cup | Others |
| Oldham Athletic* | 7.93 | - | | | | | | | | |

## GRAY Stuart

Born: Withernsea, 19 April 1960

Height: 5'10"

Weight: 11.10

**Position/Skill Factor:** Left sided player who can operate either in midfield or at full-back. A steady passer, with a lovely left foot, he specialises in hitting his front men with the long ball.

**Career History:** Signed for Nottingham Forest from Withernsea YC as an 18-year-old in 1978, but had to wait until 7 February 1981, before making his FL debut at Manchester City. Despite only missing a few games in 1981-82, he struggled to command a regular place in the following campaign and had a spell on loan at Bolton Wanderers. Signed for Barnsley that summer and played over 100 games for the club prior to his move to Aston Villa during 1987-88. He quickly fitted in to the Villa midfield and scored five valuable goals in 19 appearances as the club gained promotion to the First Division as runners-up. Since then, he played regularly until losing the left-back slot he had occupied since November 1988, in the closing weeks of 1990-91. Out in the cold under new manager Ron Atkinson, he signed for Southampton after two months of 1991-92, appearing first at left-back and then in midfield. He struggled to hold his place, however and following the Fifth Round FA Cup replay against Bolton Wanderers in late February, which the "Saints" all but lost, he played no further part in the campaign. Had a second operation on a troublesome achilles tendon injury during the summer and a third in September, before he could return to action. Unfortunately, after only two reserve team appearances in **1992-93**, he was told by a specialist that it was a heel injury that had forced a change in stride pattern, which had brought on the achilles tendon problem in the first place. Following a fourth operation, he played in a testimonial game at the end of the season and looks to be fully match fit in time for 1993-94.

| Clubs | Signing Date | Transfer Fee | APPEARANCES | | | | GOALS | | | |
|---|---|---|---|---|---|---|---|---|---|---|
| | | | Lge | FL Cup | FA Cup | Others | Lge | FL Cup | FA Cup | Others |
| Nottingham Forest | 3.78 | - | 48+1 | 5+1 | 3 | 1 | 3 | | | |
| Bolton Wanderers | 3.83 | Loan | 10 | | | | | | | |
| Barnsley | 8.83 | £40,000 | 117+3 | 7 | 6+1 | 2 | 23 | 3 | | 1 |
| Aston Villa | 11.87 | £150,000 | 102+4 | 11 | 5+1 | 7+2 | 9 | 1 | 3 | 2 |
| Southampton* | 9.91 | £200,000 | 10+2 | 5 | 4 | 1 | | | 1 | |

## GREGORY David Spencer

Born: Sudbury, 23 January 1970

Height: 5'11" Weight: 11.6

**Position/Skill Factor:** Useful midfield player who makes good runs into the opposition's penalty area. Sees passes quickly, he makes them and moves into space for the return ball.

**Career History:** Brother of team-mate, Neil, he has been at Ipswich Town since signing associated schoolboy forms for the club in November 1985. Became a trainee in July 1986 and finally made his FL debut at Chelsea on 22 December 1988, nearly two years after signing professional. Prior to 1990-91, he had made only one full League appearance, but temporarily claimed a place in midfield when David Lowe had a spell out of the side early on in the season. Expected to progress in 1991-92, he fell back, making only fleeting appearances in Ipswich's Second Division Championship triumph and automatic promotion to the new Premier League. As in the previous term, he rarely appeared in **1992-93** after breaking a finger in training and then picking up a groin strain during a reserve match against Portsmouth. However, he stood in for Eddie Youds in the penultimate League game of the season and scored Town's only goal in a 3-1 defeat at Crystal Palace.

| Clubs | Signing Date | Transfer Fee | APPEARANCES | | | | GOALS | | | |
|---|---|---|---|---|---|---|---|---|---|---|
| | | | Lge | FL Cup | FA Cup | Others | Lge | FL Cup | FA Cup | Others |
| Ipswich Town* | 3.87 | - | 16+15 | 3+2 | 1 | 3+2 | 2 | | | 4 |

## GREGORY Neil Richard

Born: Ndola, Zambia, 7 October 1972

Height: 5'11" Weight: 12.4

**Position/Skill Factor:** Hard running striker who causes defenders problems in and around the box and has the ability to latch on to half chances.

**Career History:** Younger brother of David, despite the vast geographical disparity of their birthplaces! First joined Ipswich Town as an associated schoolboy in November 1986 and signed on as a trainee in July 1989, after leaving school. At the conclusion of his two year training period, he was retained on a non-contract basis and eventually became a full time professional during the 1992 close season. Selected as a substitute for the Premier League game at home to Wimbledon in **1992-93** and although he didn't play, was part of the most inexperienced bench ever, as not one of the three men had played first team football. Finished the season as the reserves' leading scorer and looks sure to step forward this season.

| Clubs | Signing Date | Transfer Fee | APPEARANCES | | | | GOALS | | | |
|---|---|---|---|---|---|---|---|---|---|---|
| | | | Lge | FL Cup | FA Cup | Others | Lge | FL Cup | FA Cup | Others |
| Ipswich Town* | 7.92 | - | | | | | | | | |

## GROBBELAAR Bruce David

Born: Durban, South Africa, 16 October 1957

Height: 6'1" Weight: 13.0

International Honours: FL Rep, Zimbabwe Int

**Position/Skill Factor:** Highly underrated, perhaps over confident goalkeeper. Comes for crosses anywhere in the box and has superb reflexes. An entertainer, extrovert in the extreme, he loves to leave his box and dribble with the ball and enjoys every minute.

**Career History:** Served in the Zimbabwean army during the civil war before seeking a football career abroad, firstly with Vancouver Whitecaps, in the North American Soccer League. Had a spell as a non-contract player with Crewe Alexandra in the late 1970s, making his FL debut at Wigan Athletic on 21 December 1979. Became the regular choice, playing on to the end of the season and actually scoring from the penalty spot against York City in his last game for the club before returning to Vancouver. A year later, Bob Paisley, the Liverpool manager, having noted his potential at Crewe brought him to Anfield as understudy to Ray Clemence. Instead, after Clemence's abrupt and mysterious, departure to Tottenham, he found himself first choice 'keeper and made his debut at Wolverhampton Wanderers on the opening day of 1981-82. That first season, he was an ever present as Liverpool completed a League Championship — League Cup "double" and during the last nine seasons he has been an integral part of the Liverpool side that has won a further five League Championships, two FA Cup trophies, two League Cups, the European Cup and the Super Cup. Has been an ever present in six of the ten seasons spent at Anfield, a remarkable record. The 1991-92 season was typical for Bruce, brilliant one moment, fallible the next. His place in the team was under threat all season, both from the reserve Mike Hooper and a much speculated new signing. But he held on, only giving way through injury, or (in the case of the UEFA Cup) the bizarre "foreigners" ruling. Injured late in the season, he was restored to first team duty for the FA Cup final against Sunderland when, doubtless to his chagrin, he had little to do, other than collecting his FA Cup winners medal at the end of the match. Replaced by David James at the start of **1992-93**, when he elected to play for Zimbabwe, it seemed to many that his Liverpool career was nearly over. However, he was recalled in place of the jittery James in September and remained first choice until late October, before another bizarre display saw him sent off in a European Cup Winners Cup-tie at Spartak Moscow, after bringing a player down in the area. He had, by then, effectively cost Liverpool the match with too many failed excursions and bad kicking, resulting in three goals in a 4-2 defeat and two games later it came as no surprise when he once again lost his first team place to David James. Later, with Hooper and James continuing to hold down the 'keeper's spot, he was loaned out to Stoke City, before returning to Anfield for the final match of the season, a sparkling 6-2 defeat of Tottenham Hotspur. He was in great form and delighted the crowd with two brilliant saves and a penalty stop. Also helped Zimbabwe in World Cup qualifiers on several occasions in 1992-93.

| | | | APPEARANCES | | | | GOALS | | | |
|---|---|---|---|---|---|---|---|---|---|---|
| Clubs | Signing Date | Transfer Fee | Lge | FL Cup | FA Cup | Others | Lge | FL Cup | FA Cup | Others |
| Crewe Alexandra | 12.79 | - | 24 | | | | 1 | | | |
| Vancouver (NASL) | 5.80 | - | | | | | | | | |
| Liverpool* | 3.81 | £250,000 | 411 | 65 | 60 | 56 | | | | |
| Stoke City | 3.93 | Loan | 4 | | | | | | | |

## GROGAN Darren Michael

Born: Dublin, 16 December 1974

Height: 5'7" Weight: 10.7

**Position/Skill Factor:** Skilful midfield player with good touch and vision. Very comfortable with either foot.

**Career History:** Young Irish born player from the Rivermount Boys' Club, who signed as a trainee with Tottenham Hotspur on leaving school in September 1991 and graduated to the professional ranks during last summer. Made a couple of reserve team appearances in **1992-93** as a substitute and showed promising ability.

| | | | APPEARANCES | | | | GOALS | | | |
|---|---|---|---|---|---|---|---|---|---|---|
| Clubs | Signing Date | Transfer Fee | Lge | FL Cup | FA Cup | Others | Lge | FL Cup | FA Cup | Others |
| Tottenham Hotspur* | 7.93 | - | | | | | | | | |

## GROVES Perry

Born: Bow, 19 April 1965

Height: 5'11" Weight: 11.12

**Position/Skill Factor:** A thrusting unselfish winger whose pace and two useful feet make him a constant threat to defences. Capable of getting among the goals when coming in on his right foot.

**Career History:** The nephew of Vic Groves, who played for Arsenal between 1955 and 1963, he started soccer life as an associated schoolboy (May 1980) at Wolverhampton Wanderers, before becoming an apprentice at Colchester United in September 1981. He made his FL debut at Layer Road against Bournemouth on 10 April 1982, while still an apprentice and spent four good seasons with the Essex club until signing for Arsenal for a surprisingly modest fee at the start of 1986-87. Despite struggling to become a regular in the "Gunners'" line-up, he was frequently employed as a substitute and often popped up to score valuable goals. After coming on as a sub for Arsenal in the 1987 League Cup Final against Liverpool, he set up the winning goal and has since won League Championship medals with the club in 1988-89 and 1990-91. A useful squad player who can cover for both forward and wide positions, his appearances in 1991-92, mainly as substitute, became more sporadic with such a wealth of talent at manager George Graham's disposal and he joined Southampton after making just one substitute appearance for the "Gunners", early in **1992-93**. Played just 18 (including three substitute) games for the "Saints", before being injured at Middlesbrough when a heavy tackle ruptured an achilles tendon. On having the plaster removed, following an operation, he wrecked any chance of a comback when putting too much weight on the injured foot. Another operation to repair the damage was undertaken and with the plaster not to be taken off until July, he has been advised that a comback is unlikely before October 1993.

| | | | APPEARANCES | | | | GOALS | | | |
|---|---|---|---|---|---|---|---|---|---|---|
| Clubs | Signing Date | Transfer Fee | Lge | FL Cup | FA Cup | Others | Lge | FL Cup | FA Cup | Others |
| Colchester United | 6.82 | - | 142+14 | 9+1 | 6 | 6 | 26 | 1 | 1 | 2 |
| Arsenal | 9.86 | £50,000 | 91+65 | 18+8 | 11+6 | 2+4 | 21 | 5 | 1 | 1 |
| Southampton* | 8.92 | £750,000 | 13+2 | 2 | 0+1 | | 2 | | | |

## GRUNSHAW Steven John

Born: Blackburn, 7 January 1975

Height: 5'9" Weight: 11.10

**Position/Skill Factor:** Very strong striker who is a single minded goalscorer. Excellent at holding the ball up and turning defenders in the box.

**Career History:** Started at Blackburn Rovers as an associated schoolboy in March 1989, before moving up the ladder as a trainee (July 1991) to sign professional forms last summer. An unknown quantity, apart from one reserve match in **1992-93**, he has played mainly youth team soccer, but will be given every chance.

| | | | APPEARANCES | | | | GOALS | | | |
|---|---|---|---|---|---|---|---|---|---|---|
| Clubs | Signing Date | Transfer Fee | Lge | FL Cup | FA Cup | Others | Lge | FL Cup | FA Cup | Others |
| Blackburn Rovers* | 7.93 | - | | | | | | | | |

## GUENTCHEV Bontcho

Born: Bulgaria, 7 July 1964

Height: 5'10"

Weight: 11.7

International Honours: Bulgarian Int

**Position/Skill Factor:** A striker with excellent skills. Controls the ball instantly and knows exactly where to find his team-mates. Always takes up intelligent positions for crosses.

**Career History:** Bulgarian striker, signed by Ipswich Town from the Portugese club, Sporting Lisbon, midway through the **1992-93** season, along with Austrian, Vlado Bozinowski, who would act as his interpreter. Both men were recommended by the former Ipswich and England manager, Bobby Robson, then managing the Portugese club. Guentchev had earlier joined Lisbon from the unlikely Bulgarian League Champions of 1990-91, provincial team, Etar Veliko Tarnova, for whom he was leading scorer with 15 goals from 27 games. His first season with Sporting was hardly a roaring success, as he made but just two first team appearances in 1991-92. Of all the numerous Scandinavian and Eastern European players signed in droves by Premier League managers during 1992-93, which provoked an understandable protest by the PFA, Guentchev's credentials appeared the least impressive. On arriving at Portman Road, however, a dispute arose over his international record. Two reputable soccer publications credited him with just one international appearance, whereas Ipswich had a letter from the Bulgarian FA stating that he had played 12 times for Bulgaria. Although the FA launched an enquiry, they eventually decided to leave things as they were. It was ironic, therefore, that his early performances for Ipswich showed far more promise than any of the other more qualified imports. After making his PL debut at home to Manchester City on 12 December 1992, he scored in his third game against front runners, Blackburn Rovers and held his place with five goals in three FA Cup matches, which included a hat-trick against Grimsby Town. Quickly built up a rapport with the fans because of ball skills, but perhaps a bit lightweight for English football, especially on heavy grounds and tended to be a luxury away from home.

| Clubs | Signing Date | Transfer Fee | APPEARANCES Lge | FL Cup | FA Cup | Others | GOALS Lge | FL Cup | FA Cup | Others |
|---|---|---|---|---|---|---|---|---|---|---|
| Ipswich Town* | 12.92 | £250,000 | 19+2 | 2 | 4 | | 3 | | 5 | |

## GUNN Bryan James

Born: Thurso, 22 December 1963

Height: 6'2" Weight: 13.13

International Honours: S Sch, S Yth, S "U21"-9, S "B", S-3

**Position/Skill Factor:** Consistent goalkeeper who cuts a commanding figure in the penalty area. Very good when coming for crosses, he gives an air of confidence to the defence. Has a very long drop kick that can turn defence into attack in an instant.

**Career History:** Was at Aberdeen for six years, after signing from Invergordon BC as understudy to Jim Leighton, but only made 15 appearances. Luckily, when Norwich City were looking for a replacement for Chris Woods, his name sprang readily to mind and he moved south to Carrow Road. Made his FL debut at home to Tottenham Hotspur on 8 November 1986 and his fine performances for the remainder of that season were vital in ensuring the club's fifth place in the First Division. Since joining the "Canaries", he has missed a mere handful of games and his consistency was rewarded at international level when Scotland picked him for a home friendly match with Egypt on 16 May 1990 and included him in their World Cup squad. It was a well merited call-up, but tragically he committed errors which cost two goals in an all-round feeble Scottish performance, ending in a humiliating 1-3 defeat and has not been considered since. His undisputed hold on the 'keepers jersey at Carrow Road came to an end in January 1992 when he suffered a back injury in a match against Sheffield and was forced to retire at half-time. In his absence, his deputy, Mark Walton, staked a formidable claim to the position. Once again back on song, most of the **1992-93** season's accolades went to Bryan, despite the side finishing third in the new Premier League with a negative goal difference, the first time this century that had occured. At times he performed wonders, and his save during the Everton match from a Tony Cottee close range bicycle kick, could rank alongside the often quoted and often shown Pele — Banks confrontation of yesteryear. And in a season of broken records, such as Norwich City's highest ever League placing, he became the club's "Player of the Year" for the second time, played his 300th first team game at Middlesbrough and deservedly won a second Scottish cap in a 3-0 win over Estonia in May. However, it wasn't roses all the way and after missing his only game all season, a League Cup-tie at home to Carlisle United, due to the sad death of his two-year-old daughter, from Leukaemia, he showed remarkable courage when immediately coming back to first team duty.

| Clubs | Signing Date | Transfer Fee | APPEARANCES Lge | FL Cup | FA Cup | Others | GOALS Lge | FL Cup | FA Cup | Others |
|---|---|---|---|---|---|---|---|---|---|---|
| Aberdeen | .81 | - | 15 | 4 | 1 | 1 | | | | |
| Norwich City* | 10.86 | £150,000 | 242 | 20 | 22 | 16 | | | | |

## HALL David Terence

Born: Manchester, 19 October 1973

Height: 6'1" Weight: 11.10

International Honours: E Sch, E Yth

**Position/Skill Factor:** Central defender who is a good footballer. Aggressive, with good distribution, he is an organiser and reads the game well.

**Career History:** Joined the Oldham Athletic professional staff during the summer of 1992, having previously been at the club as an associated schoolboy (December 1987) and as a trainee (July 1990). No first team experience as yet, although he played regularly for the reserves in **1992-93**, he remains undecided about his future in the game.

| Clubs | Signing Date | Transfer Fee | APPEARANCES Lge | FL Cup | FA Cup | Others | GOALS Lge | FL Cup | FA Cup | Others |
|---|---|---|---|---|---|---|---|---|---|---|
| Oldham Athletic* | 6.92 | - | | | | | | | | |

## HALL Gareth David

Born: Croydon, 20 March 1969

Height: 5'8"

Weight: 10.7

International Honours: E Sch, W "U21"-1, W-9

**Position/Skill Factor:** Strong tackling right-back who likes to get forward in support of his forwards. Good shooting capability from long range.

**Career History:** Came up through the Chelsea junior ranks, first as an associated schoolboy (September 1984) and then as an apprentice (July 1985), before turning pro. Made his FL debut at Wimbledon, while still a trainee, on 5 May 1987 and although finding it hard to establish himself in the "Blues'" defence, his performances were good enough for him to be called up to play for Wales, winning his first cap when coming on as a sub against Yugoslavia on 23 March 1988. Was a member of the Chelsea squad that won the Second Division title in 1989-90 and finally earned a regular place towards the end of the following term. Out of contention for a first team place in 1991-92, until January 1992 when he replaced Steve Clarke, he held the right-back slot only until March when the latter returned. His limited first team involvement also hampered his international progress, with only one substitute appearance for Wales to add to his previous caps. **1992-93** turned out to be his best season by far, playing in both full-back positions, before being moved into a midfield slot for the last six games of the season and scoring in the 4-2 home win over Wimbledon. Adding stability to an often poor Chelsea side got him back into the Welsh squad, when his good form was recognised at international level, but possibly more important to him personally was the fact that "Blues'" supporters finally warmed to him.

| | | | APPEARANCES | | | | GOALS | | | |
|---|---|---|---|---|---|---|---|---|---|---|
| Clubs | Signing Date | Transfer Fee | Lge | FL Cup | FA Cup | Others | Lge | FL Cup | FA Cup | Others |
| Chelsea* | 4.86 | - | 107+13 | 11 | 6 | 9+3 | 3 | | | 1 |

## HALL Richard Anthony

Born: Ipswich, 14 March 1972

Height: 6'1"

Weight: 13.0

International Honours: E Yth, "U21"-10

**Position/Skill Factor:** Big strong central defender who enjoys the physical side of the game, both on the ground and in the air. Also good in the air at set plays.

**Career History:** Signed as an associated schoolboy (June 1987) for his local club, Ipswich Town, but was allowed to leave without furthering his career. Became a trainee with Scunthorpe United in July 1988 and showed so much promise that he was deemed good enough to make his FL debut at home to Grimsby Town on 26 December 1989, while still a junior. That was his only League appearance during the season, but in 1990-91 he started as a regular first team choice and after only 21 appearances, he was sold to Southampton in the same week as another promising "Irons'" youngster, Neil Cox, was transferred to Aston Villa. Definitely one for the future, the "Saints" gave him a chance to show his paces at the Dell in the last match of the season against Wimbledon, when he came on for Neil Ruddock. He started 1991-92 as a first choice central defender for the "Saints", scoring on his first full appearance and although in and out of the team during the season he could feel pleased with his progress. At the end of the season he was called up for the England Under 21 squad to compete in the annual tournament in Toulon, France, making one appearance. Struggled to hold down a regular place in the team at the beginning of **1992-93**, but came back strongly to win a Barclays "Young Eagle" award in February and to regain his England under 21 place, scoring his first international goal against San Marino. Had a continuous run of 21 first team games in mid-season, alongside new signing, Kenny Monkou and looks a good long term bet. Asked to sign a three and a half year contract last December, would appear to substantiate that viewpoint.

| | | | APPEARANCES | | | | GOALS | | | |
|---|---|---|---|---|---|---|---|---|---|---|
| Clubs | Signing Date | Transfer Fee | Lge | FL Cup | FA Cup | Others | Lge | FL Cup | FA Cup | Others |
| Scunthorpe United | 3.90 | - | 22 | 2 | 3 | 4 | 3 | | | |
| Southampton* | 2.91 | £200,000 | 49+6 | 5+1 | 6 | 3 | 7 | | 2 | |

## HALLE Gunnar

Born: Oslo, Norway, 11 August 1965

Height: 5'11" Weight: 11.2

International Honours: Norwegian Int

**Position/Skill Factor:** Very quick right-back who is a fitness fanatic. A good passer of the ball, he loves getting forward with the attack.

**Career History:** An established Norwegian international with many caps to his credit, he was signed by Joe Royle in February 1991 from Norwegian League side, Lillestrom, with a view to stiffening the "Latics" defence, following a drubbing at Oxford. He immediately replaced Paul Warhurst in the right-back position, making his FL debut in a 2-0 win at home to Port Vale on 16 February 1991. Needed little time to settle into the English game and after just 17 League matches he was the proud owner of a Second Division Championship medal. In 1991-92 he started the "Latics'" First Division campaign as first choice right-back, but sustained an injury in late September from which he apparently failed to recover full fitness, playing in only two further games to the end of the season. Only missed one Premier League game in **1992-93**, being used both in defence and as an attacking midfielder. Very dependable and influentual, he is one of the few players you can rely on week in and week out, while his continental style of defending tends to frustrate most attackers. Now Oldham's most capped player, he even scored a hat-trick for Norway against San Marino last season and starred in the recent 2-0 World Cup victory over England in Oslo. Also scored five times for the "Latics", the equaliser in a 3-3 draw at Manchester City and the vital fourth goal in the 4-3 win over Southampton at Boundary Park on the last day of the season, being the pick. If the score had remained at 3-3, it would have meant Oldham being relegated to the First Division instead of Crystal Palace.

| Clubs | Signing Date | Transfer Fee | APPEARANCES Lge | FL Cup | FA Cup | Others | GOALS Lge | FL Cup | FA Cup | Others |
|---|---|---|---|---|---|---|---|---|---|---|
| Oldham Athletic* | 2.91 | £280,000 | 68 | 2 | 2 | | 5 | | | |

# HALLWORTH Jonathan (Jon) Geoffrey

Born: Stockport, 26 October 1965

Height: 6'2"

Weight: 12.10

**Position/Skill Factor:** Confident goalkeeper who presents a commanding figure and comes off his line quickly for crosses. He often starts attacks with quick throws and long kicks.

**Career History:** Developed by Ipswich Town after signing as an associated schoolboy in November 1980, he progressed to an apprenticeship in July 1982, before turning pro. He made his FL debut while on loan to Bristol Rovers at Reading on 26 January 1985, conceding three goals in a 3-2 defeat, before his first game for Ipswich in November 1985. Prior to 1987-88, he spent most of his time at Portman Road deputising for Paul Cooper, but started that season as first choice and played 31 consecutive games, before making way for Ron Fearon and Craig Forrest. Never played again for Town's first team and one year later was transferred to Oldham Athletic where he immediately took over the goalkeeping duties from Andy Rhodes. Lost his place temporarily to Rhodes the following term and when the latter was transferred to Dunfermline Athletic in the 1990 close season, Oldham manager Joe Royle signed John Keeley from Brighton for a large fee, presumably to be the "Latics'" number one 'keeper, with Hallworth as cover. Instead, he started the 1990-91 season as first choice and putting his previous erratic form behind him, performed superbly, appearing in all 46 games of Oldham's Second Division Championship season. In Oldham's first season back in Division One, he was again consistent to a fault, missing only the final game of 1991-92, whilst poor John Keeley languished in the reserves. Started **1992-93** where he left off the previous season, as the "Latics'" first choice 'keeper. A keep fit fanatic and a goalie that you could bank on in one to one situations, he was firmly established in the side until a badly damaged right wrist in a freak accident, during a 3-0 defeat at Manchester United, brought his season crashing to an end. Injured while diving at the feet of Mark Hughes, with the score at 1-0, he carried on playing, not realising his wrist was broken in three places. Should be fit and ready for 1993-94, but faces a real battle to win his place back from the brilliant Paul Gerrard.

| Clubs | Signing Date | Transfer Fee | APPEARANCES Lge | FL Cup | FA Cup | Others | GOALS Lge | FL Cup | FA Cup | Others |
|---|---|---|---|---|---|---|---|---|---|---|
| Ipswich Town | 5.83 | - | 45 | 4 | 1 | 6 | | | | |
| Bristol Rovers | 1.85 | Loan | 2 | | | 1 | | | | |
| Oldham Athletic* | 2.89 | £75,000 | 134 | 15 | 13 | 1 | | | | |

# HAMMOND Nicholas (Nicky) David

Born: Hornchurch, 7 September 1967

Height: 6'0"

Weight: 11.13

**Position/Skill Factor:** Agile goalkeeper with good hands, who comes out well for crosses, often choosing to punch clear. In possession, he uses the ball well and has a very long kick.

**Career History:** An Arsenal professional signing during the 1985 close season, after joining the club as a trainee in August 1984, he found opportunities hard to come by with the "Gunners" and made his FL debut against Blackpool on 27 September 1986, while out on loan to Bristol Rovers. During a seven day period with the "Pirates", he played three times and conceded seven goals, before returning to Highbury. Released in the summer of 1987, he was signed by Lou Macari, manager of Swindon Town, as cover for Fraser Digby, making his Swindon debut in

October 1987 and playing four FL games. He was not called upon the following two seasons and did not earn a run in the first team until Glenn Hoddle's reign in 1991-92. Displacing Digby early in the season, he remained first choice 'keeper until March 1992, when the latter returned to favour. It is probably fair to say that, at his best, he is a good 'keeper as is Digby, but overall the latter appears to be the more consistent of the two. When his opportunity came early in **1992-93**, he held his place on merit, but following a dreadful mistake in a 3-3 draw at Peterborough, which cost Town victory, his confidence suffered and Digby's recall after the 3-0 Third Round FA Cup defeat at Queens Park Rangers, came as no great surprise. Certainly, Swindon are fortunate to have someone as capable as Hammond to call upon and his display at West Ham, in preserving a 1-0 lead last September, was one of the finest by any Town 'keeper for many a year. He made 16 first team appearances last season and although not called upon for the Play-Offs, when the club gained access to the top flight, via the dramatic 4-3 victory over Leicester City, maybe he can look forward to an early taste of the Premier League.

| | | | APPEARANCES | | | | GOALS | | | |
|---|---|---|---|---|---|---|---|---|---|---|
| Clubs | Signing Date | Transfer Fee | Lge | FL Cup | FA Cup | Others | Lge | FL Cup | FA Cup | Others |
| Arsenal | 7.85 | - | | | | | | | | |
| Bristol Rovers | 8.86 | Loan | 3 | | | | | | | |
| Swindon Town* | 7.87 | - | 47 | 8 | 6 | 4 | | | | |

## HAMON Christopher (Chris) Anthony

Born: Jersey, 27 April 1970

Height: 6'2" Weight: 12.6

**Position/Skill Factor:** Striker. Big strong target man, who holds the ball up well and brings his midfield players into the game.

**Career History:** One of a select band of Channel Islanders in the Premier League (the others being Graham Le Saux and Matthew Le Tissier), he was playing for the Jersey club, St Peters, when picked up by Swindon in the summer of 1992. After spending most of **1992-93** on monthly contracts, plus a short spell out on loan to Beazer Homes club, Cheltenham Town, he signed a two year contract in March 1993 and made his FL debut as a substitute at the County Ground against Luton Town on 10 April 1993. Although given a full outing in the last game of the season at Barnsley, largely due to injuries, it is too early to form an opinion, but the club obviously feel that he is a player for the future.

| | | | APPEARANCES | | | | GOALS | | | |
|---|---|---|---|---|---|---|---|---|---|---|
| Clubs | Signing Date | Transfer Fee | Lge | FL Cup | FA Cup | Others | Lge | FL Cup | FA Cup | Others |
| Swindon Town* | 8.92 | - | 1+1 | | | | | | | |

## HARFORD Michael (Mick) Gordon

Born: Sunderland, 12 February 1959

Height: 6'2" Weight: 13.12

International Honours: E "B", E-2

**Position/Skill Factor:** One of the great "target men" of the last decade, his strength in the air is legendary, but unlike most of his ilk, he is not only a header of the ball, but also shows great skill on the ground, with an explosive shot in his boots and his scoring ratio is higher than average for a target player.

**Career History:** Started his career with Lincoln City, who invited him for a trial after spotting him playing for Lambton Street Boys Club in his native Sunderland. Signed professional forms in the summer of 1977 and after making his FL debut at Sincil Bank against Gillingham on 10 December 1977, he quickly got among the goals, finishing joint top scorer with nine in the League that season. Top scored again in 1979-80 with 16 FL goals and half way through the following campaign he returned to the north-east, snapped up by Newcastle United, for what remains a record fee received by the "Imps". Unfortunately, he joined the "Magpies" during their "dog days" in the Second Division and unable to end the goal drought at St James Park, he was allowed to join Bristol City the following summer. It was a case of "out of the frying pan, into the fire" for Harford as the "Robins" were on the verge of bankruptcy and could not meet the installments on his transfer fee. Newcastle appealed to the Football League, who ordered Bristol City to return Harford to Newcastle on a "free transfer". City immediately sold him to Birmingham City, the transfer fee of £100,000 being paid to Newcastle, rather than his current club. He was an immediate success at St Andrews, his nine goals in 12 games at the end of 1981-82, earning priceless points, which undoubtedly saved the "Blues" from relegation to Division Two. The following season was generally disappointing, but once again City staved off almost certain relegation by winning five and drawing one of their last six games, with Harford scoring match winning goals in three of them. However, relegation was only delayed until the following season and in 1984-85 he was transferred to Luton Town where he was to enjoy the best years of his football career and become a "household name". When he joined the "Hatters", they were languishing in 21st place in the First Division, but his arrival galvanised the attack, his 16 goals (in only 22 games) lifting the team into mid-table and sparking off a run in the FA Cup, which ended most unluckily in the Semi-Finals at the hands of Everton. He maintained he prolific scoring rate in 1985-86, with 22 FL goals (plus three in the FA Cup) when Luton achieved their then highest FL placing, ninth. In 1988, he won his only major club honour in the game, a League Cup Winners medal, when the "Hatters" defeated Arsenal 3-2 in a remarkable "see-saw" Final. Surprisingly, he was allowed to leave for Derby County in January 1990, soon after returning to the side, following a long absence through injury. Despite forming a useful partnership with Dean Saunders, they could not halt the "Rams'" slide to relegation in 1991 and in the summer he returned to Luton Town, re-signed by David Pleat as a "lucky talisman". Sadly for both, the magic had worn off and although Harford was top scorer with 12 FL goals, he suffered a second consecutive relegation season. Remarkably, at the age of 33, Ian Porterfield of Chelsea, thought Harford still had a future in the Premier League when he signed him before the start of **1992-93**, apparently to set up goal scoring chances for another newcomer, Robert Fleck. Ironically, it was Harford, not Fleck, who proved to be the man of the moment, striking a number of spectacular long range shots, starting with a 30 yard special on the opening day of the season, a 1-1 draw against Oldham Athletic at Stamford Bridge. Having scored ten in his first 21 games, he then could only manage one more in 13 outings, when he was nowhere near as sharp as previous, due to time out on suspension and injury. In the event, he moved on to Sunderland, his hometown club, just before the transfer deadline in March. The move was not to be permanent, however. After just 11 (including one substitute) games and only two goals, with the "Wearsiders" safe from relegation, he was a surprise signing for Coventry City during the 1993 close season. Presumably, he will be asked to do the job that Robert Rosario did before moving to Nottingham Forest, with the added bonus of scoring goals as well.

| | | | APPEARANCES | | | | GOALS | | | |
|---|---|---|---|---|---|---|---|---|---|---|
| Clubs | Signing Date | Transfer Fee | Lge | FL Cup | FA Cup | Others | Lge | FL Cup | FA Cup | Others |
| Lincoln City | 7.77 | - | 109+6 | 8 | 3 | | 41 | 5 | | |
| Newcastle United | 12.80 | £180,000 | 18+1 | | | | 4 | | | |
| Bristol City | 8.81 | £160,000 | 30 | 5 | 5 | | 11 | 1 | 2 | |
| Birmingham City | 3.82 | £100,000 | 92 | 10 | 7 | | 25 | 6 | 2 | |
| Luton Town | 12.84 | £250,000 | 135+4 | 16 | 27 | 4 | 57 | 10 | 11 | 3 |
| Derby County | 1.90 | £450,000 | 58 | 7 | 1 | 2 | 15 | 3 | | |
| Luton Town | 9.91 | £325,000 | 29 | 1 | | 1 | 12 | | | |
| Chelsea | 8.92 | £300,000 | 27+1 | 5 | 1 | | 9 | 2 | | |
| Sunderland | 3.93 | £250,000 | 10+1 | | | | 2 | | | |
| Coventry City* | 7.93 | £200,000 | | | | | | | | |

## **HARFORD Paul** Raymond Thomas

Born: Chelmsford, 21 October 1974

Height: 6'3½" Weight: 14.0

**Position/Skill Factor:** Striker who can play in central defence. Great awareness and a good passer of the ball, he has a lovely touch for a big lad.

**Career History:** Son of Ray, who played for six League clubs between 1964-1974, starting with Charlton Athletic, and one of seven juniors to turn professional for Arsenal during the summer, having been at Highbury as an associated schoolboy (November 1990) and as a trainee (July 1991). Looks to follow in the "Gunners'" tradition of developing good young players through to the League side. A regular in the youth team in **1992-93**, he was given a couple of runs with the reserves towards the end of the season.

| | | | APPEARANCES | | | | GOALS | | | |
|---|---|---|---|---|---|---|---|---|---|---|
| Clubs | Signing Date | Transfer Fee | Lge | FL Cup | FA Cup | Others | Lge | FL Cup | FA Cup | Others |
| Arsenal* | 7.93 | - | | | | | | | | |

## **HARKES John** Andrew

Born: New Jersey, USA, 8 March 1967

Height: 5'10"

Weight: 11.10

International Honours: USA Int

**Position/Skill Factor:** A midfield player who can also play as an attacking right-back. Passes the ball well, is aggressive and a good crosser when getting forward in a wide position.

**Career History:** Spotted by Second Division Sheffield Wednesday, while playing for the University of North Carolina and the USA national side, he was a bargain signing and despite being a natural midfielder, he took over the number two shirt when Roland Nilsson was injured and filled in admirably. He made his FL debut at Hillsborough against Oldham Athletic on 3 November 1990 and in only his tenth first team game, his run and 30 yard dipping volley in a League Cup Fourth Round replay at Derby, with Peter Shilton in goal, not only sealed his acceptance by "Owls'" fans, but was considered by many to be "goal of the season". He completed his first season, assisting the club to gain promotion to the First Division in third place and also collected a League Cup winners medal for his part in the "Owls'" surprise 1-0 victory over Manchester United. During 1991-92 he provided cover right across midfield and was a frequent performer in several different positions, including right-back and central defence. Came good in **1992-93** as his enthusiasm and love of the game bubbled over whenever he played. In a series of firsts, he became the only American to score at Wembley, when he fired past a helpless David Seaman after just nine minutes of the League Cup Final against Arsenal. Unfortunately for him, it wasn't enough to beat the "Gunners", who replied with two of their own. And for the first time ever, the same two teams went back to Wembley for the FA Cup Final, but following a replay defeat, he had to settle for another losers medal. Scored only five goals last season and although he should probably chance his arm more with his lethal shooting, he has matured to become a highly valued member of the squad. Climaxed his season with a great display in the 2-0 defeat of England in the USA Cup during the summer.

| Clubs | Signing Date | Transfer Fee | APPEARANCES Lge | FL Cup | FA Cup | Others | GOALS Lge | FL Cup | FA Cup | Others |
|---|---|---|---|---|---|---|---|---|---|---|
| Sheffield Wednesday* | 10.90 | £70,000 | 59+22 | 17 | 12+1 | 7 | 7 | 3 | 1 | |

## HARKIN Joseph (Joe) Finbarr

Born: Londonderry, 9 December 1975

Height: 5'11" Weight: 11.7

International Honours: NI Sch

**Position/Skill Factor:** Right-back, who can also play in central midfield. A very good passer of the ball, he likes to join in and get forward down the flank.

**Career History:** Joined Manchester City as an associated schoolboy in November 1991, after being recommended by the club's scout, Peter Neal, following brilliant performances in Irish junior soccer. Came to Maine Road as a trainee (August 1992) on leaving school, signing professional mid-way through **1992-93**, but spent most of the season with the "A" and "B" teams. Played a couple of times for the reserves, including a game against an experienced Manchester United side and looked confident on the ball.

| Clubs | Signing Date | Transfer Fee | APPEARANCES Lge | FL Cup | FA Cup | Others | GOALS Lge | FL Cup | FA Cup | Others |
|---|---|---|---|---|---|---|---|---|---|---|
| Manchester City* | 12.92 | - | | | | | | | | |

## HARKNESS Steven (Steve)

Born: Carlisle, 27 August 1971

Height: 5'9"

Weight: 10.11

International Honours: E Yth

**Position/Skill Factor:** Strong tackling midfielder with a good left foot. Very aggressive, he can also play at left-back if required.

**Career History:** Joined his local team Carlisle United as an associated schoolboy in March 1987 and after accepting a trainee contract in September 1987, he made his FL debut at Brunton Park in the 3-0 win over Hereford United on 18 February 1989, shortly before he turned professional. Remaining in the first team until the end of the season, his early development was obviously noted at Anfield and after only four months as a pro at Brunton Park he was signed by Liverpool. Spent his first two season with the "Reds" in the reserve team, although a regular choice for the England youth team. He was called up for his Liverpool debut at right-back early in 1991-92, when Liverpool's injury crisis ruled out five regulars simultaneously and made occasional appearances throughout the season in both full-back positions. Made 12 appearances in **1992-93**, while standing in for a number of players and impressed enough to be called up to join the England under 21 squad, although not playing. Yet to score for the "Reds", the closest he came was in the last game of the season, a 6-2 home defeat of Tottenham Hotspur, when an angled drive following a corner was deflected past the "Spurs'" goalie by one of his own defenders. Still making good progress.

| Clubs | Signing Date | Transfer Fee | APPEARANCES Lge | FL Cup | FA Cup | Others | GOALS Lge | FL Cup | FA Cup | Others |
|---|---|---|---|---|---|---|---|---|---|---|
| Carlisle United | 3.89 | - | 12+1 | | | | | | | |
| Liverpool* | 7.89 | £75,000 | 16+5 | 2+1 | 1 | 4+2 | | | | |

## HARPER Stephen (Steve) Alan

Born: Easington, 14 March 1975

Height: 6'1½" Weight: 13.0

**Position/Skill Factor:** Goalkeeper. Tall and commanding, with good hands, he comes out well for crosses and will continue to improve on all other aspects of his game.

**Career History:** Still at school in **1992-93**, he was spotted by Newcastle United, while giving promising displays in goal for the Durham County youth side and occasionally turning out for Seaham Red Star in the Northern League. Expected to be third choice behind Pavel Srnicek and Tommy Wright, he signed professional forms during the 1993 close season and with the expert tuition readily available from the club's specialist goalkeeping coach, Jim Montgomery, United will look for dramatic improvement.

| Clubs | Signing Date | Transfer Fee | APPEARANCES Lge | FL Cup | FA Cup | Others | GOALS Lge | FL Cup | FA Cup | Others |
|---|---|---|---|---|---|---|---|---|---|---|
| Newcastle United* | 7.93 | - | | | | | | | | |

## HARTFIELD Charles (Charlie)

Born: Lambeth, 4 September 1971

Height: 6'0"

Weight: 12.0

International Honours: E Yth

**Position/Skill Factor:** Strong midfield player who loves a tackle. Displaying a lovely left foot, he also has very good technique.

**Career History:** Joined Arsenal as a trainee in July 1988, having been an associated schoolboy at Aston Villa (July 1986) and turned professional 14 months later. After two years as a professional at Highbury, without a "sniff" of first team action, he was granted a free transfer and Dave Bassett signed him up for Sheffield United in the 1991 close season. Surprisingly, but perhaps, typically for Bassett, he was plunged into first team duty almost immediately, making his FL debut away to Crystal Palace on 31 August 1991. Was perhaps unfortunate to be sent off for an apparently innocuous offence in his third match (at Oldham Athletic) when the "Blades" with only nine men on the field, reduced a 2-0 half time deficit to 2-1. After a handful of games in midfield and at full-back he was then rested and played almost no part in the rest of the campaign. Spent the first few weeks of the **1992-93** season on the bench and after one full appearance and six as a substitute in the first month, he didn't feature in the squad again until a surprise call-up at Villa Park in January. He then had a successful run in midfield and would have played in the FA Cup Semi-Final against Sheffield Wednesday at Wembley if he had not been ruled out by suspension. This hurt him deeply, but he bounced back for the last four games of the season, as United clung precariously on to their Premier League status and has every prospect of going from strength to strength this coming season.

| | | | APPEARANCES | | | | GOALS | | | |
|---|---|---|---|---|---|---|---|---|---|---|
| Clubs | Signing Date | Transfer Fee | Lge | FL Cup | FA Cup | Others | Lge | FL Cup | FA Cup | Others |
| Arsenal | 9.89 | - | | | | | | | | |
| Sheffield United* | 8.91 | - | 18+6 | 1+1 | 3 | | | | | |

## HAZARD Michael (Mickey)

Born: Sunderland, 5 February 1960

Height: 5'7" Weight: 10.5

**Position/Skill Factor:** Midfield player with wonderful ability on the ball. Excellent skill and vision make him one of the most creative men in the game.

**Career History:** A talented player, very much in the Glenn Hoddle mould, he spent most of his time at Tottenham Hotspur, in the shadow of his illustrious colleague. An associated schoolboy player (January 1975), before becoming an apprentice (June 1976), he turned professional early in 1978, but had to wait until 19 April 1980 to make his Fl debut in a 3-0 win over Everton at White Hart Lane. Appeared to make a breakthrough in 1981-82, when he played in 28 FL games and won his first major honour, an FA Cup Winners medal, when he played in both games of the replayed 1982 Cup Final, which was eventually retained by Spurs for a second consecutive year, after defeating Queens Park Rangers 1-0, thanks to a Glenn Hoddle penalty, for the remainder of his stay at White Hart Lane, however, he remained a fringe first team player, deputising for Hoddle, but rarely in partnership with him, although many judges felt that he would be an automatic selection with most First Division clubs. Finally, he moved away to Chelsea in September 1985 and it seemed that at last he had found a stage on which to make his mark. Sadly, it was not to be and for two seasons he was in and out of the team and although he won a regular place in 1987-88, when Chelsea were relegated, he also played in their triumphant return as Second Division Champions, the following season. After four disappointing seasons, he departed Stamford Bridge to join Portsmouth, then struggling at the foot of Division Two, but lost his place at Fratton Park after only two months. His career was rescued by erstwhile "Spurs" colleague, Ossie Ardiles, who signed him for Swindon Town early in 1990-91. And after an uncertain start at the County Ground, he finally found the consistency which had eluded him for ten years and in the twilight of his career, showed his real capabilities. He missed only three games in 1991-92 and built up a good relationship on the field with Glenn Hoddle, who arrived at Town a year later. Started **1992-93** as first choice and apart from one game, he played in every League fixture until being injured against Wolverhampton Wanderers at the end of January. Won his place back in the side for the last five games of the season, but was used only as a substitute in the two Play-Off victories, that saw Swindon reach the top flight for the first time in its history. With the return to fitness of John Moncur it was felt that there was little chance of him holding down a regular place, but with Hoddle departing for Chelsea, he has now signed on for a further year. Strange to think that he nearly left last season, but turned down a move to Sunderland after both clubs had agreed terms and now looks forward to playing in the Premier League.

| | | | APPEARANCES | | | | GOALS | | | |
|---|---|---|---|---|---|---|---|---|---|---|
| Clubs | Signing Date | Transfer Fee | Lge | FL Cup | FA Cup | Others | Lge | FL Cup | FA Cup | Others |
| Tottenham Hotspur | 2.78 | - | 73+18 | 11+3 | 7+3 | 23 | 13 | 5 | 2 | 3 |
| Chelsea | 9.85 | £310,000 | 78+3 | 7+3 | 4+2 | 5+1 | 9 | 1 | 1 | 2 |
| Portsmouth | 1.90 | £100,000 | 8 | | | | 1 | | | |
| Swindon Town* | 9.90 | £130,000 | 105+5 | 10 | 7 | 2+2 | 17 | 1 | | |

## **HEANEY Neil** Andrew

Born: Middlesbrough, 3 November 1971

Height: 5'9"

Weight: 11.1

International Honours: E Yth, E "U21"-6

**Position/Skill Factor:** Skilful left-winger who can get down the flank and is a lovely crosser of the ball.

**Career History:** A full time professional player with Arsenal, having come through the junior ranks first as an associated schoolboy (January 1987) and then as a trainee (July 1988). He first played in the Football League, whilst on loan to Fourth Division Hartlepool in 1990-91, making his FL debut when coming on as a sub at home to Chesterfield on 19 January 1991. During the 1991-92 season, he enjoyed a successful two month loan period with Cambridge United from January to March 1992, scoring on his debut and playing a prominent role in the club's ultimately unsuccessful Second Division promotion challenge. After returning to Highbury, he made his Arsenal debut as a sub away to Sheffield United in April. He was a regular in the England youth teams of 1989 and 1990, before graduating to the England Under 21 squad for the end of season games in May 1992, playing four times. Made five (two substitute) Premier League appearances for Arsenal in **1992-93**, but appeared to have been overtaken at Highbury by Mark Flatts. However, he still turned out for the England under 21 side and should become a valuable member of the "Gunners'" first team squad this coming season.

| | | | APPEARANCES | | | | GOALS | | | |
|---|---|---|---|---|---|---|---|---|---|---|
| Clubs | Signing Date | Transfer Fee | Lge | FL Cup | FA Cup | Others | Lge | FL Cup | FA Cup | Others |
| Arsenal* | 11.89 | - | 3+3 | | | | | | | |
| Hartlepool United | 1.91 | Loan | 2+1 | | | | | | | |
| Cambridge United | 1.92 | Loan | 9+4 | | 1 | | 2 | | | |

## **HELLEWELL Craig**

Born: Doncaster, 19 July 1975

Height: 5'9½" Weight: 11.8

**Position/Skill Factor:** Plays on the left side of midfield. Great enthusiasm and reasonable vision, linked to good touch and passing qualities, are his main assets.

**Career History:** A recent Sheffield United professional signing, having spent **1992-93** playing with the youth team, after joining the club from Nottingham Forest. An associated schoolboy (September 1989) at Forest, prior to signing on as a trainee in August 1991, he was just one year at the City Ground, before an agreement was reached between both clubs for him to spend the second half of his training period at United.

| | | | APPEARANCES | | | | GOALS | | | |
|---|---|---|---|---|---|---|---|---|---|---|
| Clubs | Signing Date | Transfer Fee | Lge | FL Cup | FA Cup | Others | Lge | FL Cup | FA Cup | Others |
| Sheffield United* | 7.93 | - | | | | | | | | |

## **HENDON Ian** Michael

Born: Ilford, 5 December 1971

Height: 6'0"

Weight: 12.10

International Honours: E Yth, E "U21"-7

**Position/Skill Factor:** Highly rated defender cum midfielder, who is a lovely striker of the long ball with his right foot. Useful in the air, he makes a very strong defender.

**Career History:** Signed for Tottenham Hotspur as an associated schoolboy in January 1986, he graduated to trainee status in August 1988, before joining the pro ranks and made his FL debut at Aston Villa on 16 March 1991, when coming on as a sub in a 3-2 defeat. Made further appearances as sub in 1991-92, plus a full game at Swansea in the League Cup when Spurs were surprisingly defeated 1-0 (but easily winning the second leg) and was later farmed out to Portsmouth and Leyton Orient on short loans during the season to increase his experience. After playing many games for the England Youth team, he progressed to the Under 21 squad in May 1992 and made four appearances in central defence. The **1992-93** season promised much, but the only first team experience he got was when going out on loan to Barnsley for six matches during March and April. Other than that, he had to make do with reserve team football and the coming season should see him pushing hard for Premier League action.

| | | | APPEARANCES | | | | GOALS | | | |
|---|---|---|---|---|---|---|---|---|---|---|
| Clubs | Signing Date | Transfer Fee | Lge | FL Cup | FA Cup | Others | Lge | FL Cup | FA Cup | Others |
| Tottenham Hotspur* | 12.89 | - | 0+4 | 1 | | 0+2 | | | | |
| Portsmouth | 1.92 | Loan | 1+3 | | | | | | | |
| Leyton Orient | 3.92 | Loan | 5+1 | | | | | | | |
| Barnsley | 3.93 | Loan | 6 | | | | | | | |

## **HENDRY** Edward **Colin** James

Born: Keith, 7 December 1965

Height: 6'1" Weight: 12.2

International Honours: S "B", S-2

**Position/Skill Factor:** Big, imposing central defender, who does well in the air and is useful on the ground. Often pushed up-front to try and snatch a goal when all seems lost.

**Career History:** Now in his second spell with Blackburn Rovers, he originally came to Ewood Park from the Scottish Premier Division club, Dundee, near the end of 1986-87. Made his FL debut at home to Stoke City on 14 March, 1987 at centre-forward and scored in his next two games, at Derby County and West Bromwich Albion. His fifth game for Rovers was at Wembley in the Final of the then Full Members (now Zenith) Cup and he scored the only goal in their victory over Charlton Athletic. The following season he played exclusively in central defence, struck a remarkable 12 goals from open play and was also ever present. Scored seven goals from 38 games in 1988-89 and in both seasons, Rovers' hopes of promotion were thwarted at the Play-Off stage. Seeking a transfer at the start of 1989-90, he was dropped controversially for a few weeks and soon after his return was transferred to Manchester City. Went straight into the City team and held his place to the end of 1990-91, although his impressive goal scoring ratio was sharply reduced. In 1991-92 he lost his place to new signing Keith Curle at the start of the season and made only a few appearances as substitute, before returning to Ewood Park two years after he left. Apart from losing his place for one month in January, he played a vital role in Rovers' promotion campaign and the Play-Offs, making a quick return to the top flight. Had an outstanding **1992-93**, winning his first cap for Scotland and the consensus choice made him "Player of the Year". A formidable competitor and an embodiment of the club's spirit, he played to a very high degree of consistency as Rovers stayed among the top six throughout the season. His only bad moment came in the last few minutes of extra-time, during the FA Cup Quarter-Final replay at Sheffield United, when tired legs allowed Alan Cork to get behind him to carve out the equaliser and for the "Blades" to go on to win the match on penalties. It was virtually his only mistake all season and was undoubtedly caused by the inanity of the club's fixture list at the time.

| | | | APPEARANCES | | | | GOALS | | | |
|---|---|---|---|---|---|---|---|---|---|---|
| Clubs | Signing Date | Transfer Fee | Lge | FL Cup | FA Cup | Others | Lge | FL Cup | FA Cup | Others |
| Dundee | .83 | - | 17+24 | 2+3 | 2 | 1 | | | | |
| Blackburn Rovers | 3.87 | £30.000 | 99+3 | 4 | 3 | 7 | 22 | | | 1 |
| Manchester City | 11.89 | £700.000 | 57+6 | 4+1 | 5 | 4 | 5 | 1 | 2 | 2 |
| Blackburn Rovers* | 11.91 | £700.000 | 67+4 | 7 | 5+1 | 3 | 5 | | | |

# HENDRY John

Born: Glasgow, 6 January 1970

Height: 5'11"

Weight: 10.0

International Honours: S "U21"-1

**Position/Skill Factor:** Striker who has lovely skills and a very good first touch. Is learning all the time, but already has the ability to make something out of nothing.

**Career History:** Spotted by Scottish League side, Dundee, playing in junior soccer with Hillington YC, he played two games for the club and was loaned out to Forfar Athletic, where he scored six goals in ten matches, before coming south to join Tottenham Hotspur in the 1990 close season. Made his FL debut at Norwich City on 10 April 1991, scoring in a 2-1 defeat and in his only other full game for "Spurs", he got the equaliser in the last game of the season at Manchester United. During 1991-92 he appeared only occasionally as a substitute for "Spurs" and had a spell on loan to Charlton Athletic, late in the season. Started his first full "Spurs'" game for 15 months when selected for the home **1992-93** fixture against Crystal Palace, but with the score standing at 1-1, he was substituted after 63 minutes to make way for former "Eagle", Andy Gray. Made three further appearances from the bench, before being recalled for the final game of the season and scoring two goals in a 3-1 win at Arsenal. Should be given further opportunities to display his goalscoring talent in 1993-94

| | | | APPEARANCES | | | | GOALS | | | |
|---|---|---|---|---|---|---|---|---|---|---|
| Clubs | Signing Date | Transfer Fee | Lge | FL Cup | FA Cup | Others | Lge | FL Cup | FA Cup | Others |
| Dundee | .88 | - | 0+2 | | | | | | | |
| Forfar Athletic | 3.90 | Loan | 10 | | | | 6 | | | |
| Tottenham Hotspur* | 7.90 | £50,000 | 5+9 | 0+1 | | | 5 | | | |
| Charlton Athletic | 2.92 | Loan | 1+4 | | | | 1 | | | |

# HENRY Nicholas (Nicky) Ian

Born: Liverpool, 21 February 1969

Height: 5'6" Weight: 9.8

**Position/Skill Factor:** Keeps things ticking over in midfield. Holds up the ball well, he is a good passer and is always available when team mates get into trouble.

**Career History:** Slipped through the Liverpool net when signing as an associated schoolboy (January 1985) with Oldham Athletic and later progressing to trainee status (July 1986). Illness and injuries severely restricted his progress at first and it was feared at one time that he would not stand up to the rigours of League soccer. On recovering full fitness, however, he made his FL debut at Hull City on 19 September 1987 and by March 1989 was a regular in midfield after spending the summer and autumn of 1988 with Swedish club Halmstad for top level experience. Since then, has only missed a handful of games. A member of the "Latics'" 1989-90 team which created history by reaching the Semi-Finals of the two major cup competitions and contesting the League Cup Final with Nottingham Forest, before losing narrowly 1-0. In the FA Cup, Oldham knocked out both Aston Villa and Everton, before fighting out a thrilling 3-3 draw with Manchester United in the Semi-Final. At a critical stage of the replay, a fierce 25 yard shot from Henry hit the United bar and bounced down on the goal line. Had it counted as a goal it is probable that Oldham would have contested both Finals. Happily, the disappointments of 1990 were soon forgotten when he won a Second Division Championship medal the following season. During 1991-92 he was ever present in Oldham's first season in the top flight for 69 years and scored six vital FL goals to help the "Latics" stay just clear of the relegation battle and preserve their status in the new Premier League. Had another brilliant season in **1992-93**, although he was unfortunate to miss 11 first team games due to an ankle injury and then suffering from a mystery virus. Combined with Mike Milligan to form a tigerish midfield, which earned the pair the nickname of "the hound dogs", coined by Manchester City's, Jimmy Frizzell. If his finishing improved, he would be one of "Latics'" top scorers and of the seven he netted in 1992-93, four were either match winners or savers. The most bizarre goal of his season, however, came at Boundary Park against Chelsea, after the club had gone nine hours without scoring. Andy Ritchie had aimed his cross for the "Blues'" penalty area, but the ball struck the referee on the back and fell nicely for Henry to beat the goalie from all of ten yards. Unfortunate never to be considered for the England under 21 squad.

| | | | APPEARANCES | | | | GOALS | | | |
|---|---|---|---|---|---|---|---|---|---|---|
| Clubs | Signing Date | Transfer Fee | Lge | FL Cup | FA Cup | Others | Lge | FL Cup | FA Cup | Others |
| Oldham Athletic* | 7.87 | – | 174+7 | 20+3 | 15 | 4 | 16 | 3 | | |

## HERRERA Roberto

Born: Torquay, 12 June 1970

Height: 5'7" Weight: 10.6

**Position/Skill Factor:** A full-back with a good left foot. Very quick on his feet in defence, he can get himself out of trouble when the need be. Also, likes to get forward to link up with the attack.

**Career History:** Signed for Queens Park Rangers as a 16-year-old trainee in June 1986, before progressing to the pro ranks and although getting a run out in the first team as a sub in the League Cup in 1988-89, he had to wait until the end of the following season before he was selected for a League match. His FL debut came at Anfield, against Liverpool on 28 April 1990 and he made three more appearances in central defence in 1990-91 during an injury crisis at Loftus Road — unfortunately, all three games were lost. The signing of Rufus Brevett in March 1991 reduced his chances of staking a regular claim to the left-back spot at Loftus Road and in 1991-92 he made only a single appearance as a sub for Rangers in a League Cup tie, before joining his home town club, Torquay United, on loan for the closing weeks of the season. Although he played 11 games for the "Gulls" in the Third Division, he could do little to stop their slide back into the Fourth Division. With Clive Wilson and Brevett consistently ahead of him in the queue for the left-back slot, he was again loaned out to his hometown side in **1992-93** and played five games before returning to Loftus Road. Although a regular in the reserve side, he doesn't appear to have much of a future with the club in terms of first team places.

| | | | APPEARANCES | | | | GOALS | | | |
|---|---|---|---|---|---|---|---|---|---|---|
| Clubs | Signing Date | Transfer Fee | Lge | FL Cup | FA Cup | Others | Lge | FL Cup | FA Cup | Others |
| Q.P.R.* | 3.88 | – | 4+2 | 1+2 | | 1+1 | | | | |
| Torquay United | 3.92 | Loan | 11 | | | | | | | |
| Torquay United | 10.92 | Loan | 5 | | | | | | | |

## HILL Andrew (Andy) Rowland

Born: Maltby, 20 January 1965

Height: 5'11"

Weight: 12.0

International Honours: E Yth

**Position/Skill Factor:** A very experienced right-back for his age, he looks good when breaking out of defence with the ball. Rarely misses a passing opportunity.

**Career History:** Started his soccer career at Old Trafford when signing as an associated schoolboy for Manchester United in October 1979, before graduating as an apprentice (May 1981). Turned pro almost two years later, but after a season in the reserve side he was released and signed for Bury and it was here that he blossomed. He made his FL debut in the number two shirt at Darlington on 25 August 1984 and by the end of his first season at Gigg Lane, 1984-85, the club had gained promotion from the Fourth Division in fourth place. Following many outstanding performances with the "Shakers" and being recognised as one of the best defenders outside the First Division, he was later made club captain. Unfortunately, during 1990-91, Bury FC was hit by financial difficulties and in order for the club to balance its books, he signed for Manchester City on the recommendation of Sam Ellis, City's assistant manager, and previously Hill's manager at Bury, following a short loan period. In 1991-92 he established himself as first choice right-back at Maine Road, scoring four vital FL goals from open play and started **1992-93** where he left off. Replaced by new signing, Terry Phelan, after just three games, he returned wearing the number six shirt when Michel Vonk was injured and excelled with weekly consistent performances during a run of 14 games, until being diagnosed as having a hernia problem, which required an operation. Made a swift return to first team soccer, coming on against Barnsley in the Fifth Round of the FA Cup, before being sidelined again during April. A true clubman, a measure of his game is the quiet way he goes about his work, relatively unnoticed, but then being selected within the club for having "star" games.

| | | | APPEARANCES | | | | GOALS | | | |
|---|---|---|---|---|---|---|---|---|---|---|
| Clubs | Signing Date | Transfer Fee | Lge | FL Cup | FA Cup | Others | Lge | FL Cup | FA Cup | Others |
| Manchester United | 1.83 | - | | | | | | | | |
| Bury | 7.84 | - | 264 | 22 | 12 | 19 | 10 | 1 | | 1 |
| Manchester City* | 12.90 | £200,000 | 66+2 | 8 | 2+1 | 1 | 6 | | | |

## HILL Daniel (Danny) Ronald

Born: Enfield, 1 October 1974

Height: 5'9" Weight: 11.3

International Honours: E Yth

**Position/Skill Factor:** Very skilful midfielder with two useful feet. Has good touch and sprays the ball about all over the field.

**Career History:** A Tottenham Hotspur home grown talent, he turned professional at the beginning of **1992-93**, having been at the club as an associated schoolboy (November 1988) and as a trainee (August 1991). He made rapid strides after joining "Spurs'" first team Squad, coming on as a substitute for Paul Allen at Chelsea on 20 March 1993 for his FL debut. Three more appearances followed, before the season ended, including a full debut in a 6-2 defeat at Liverpool and a creditable game at Highbury against north London rivals, Arsenal. Definitely one for the future.

| | | | APPEARANCES | | | | GOALS | | | |
|---|---|---|---|---|---|---|---|---|---|---|
| Clubs | Signing Date | Transfer Fee | Lge | FL Cup | FA Cup | Others | Lge | FL Cup | FA Cup | Others |
| Tottenham Hotspur* | 9.92 | - | 2+2 | | | | | | | |

## HILLIER David

Born: Blackheath, 19 December 1969

Height: 5'10"

Weight: 11.6

International Honours: E "U21"-1

**Position/Skill Factor:** Impressive midfield player. Has plenty of stamina and is a strong tackler and above all else, he gives everything for the team.

**Career History:** Began his career with Arsenal as an associated schoolboy in January 1984 and was later upgraded to trainee status in July 1986. He was blooded in the League Cup at Chester City in the number four shirt and just four days later, made his FL debut away to Leeds United on 29 September 1990, when coming on as a sub for Nigel Winterburn. Played in most of the final matches of the 1990-91 season, with Michael Thomas on the sidelines and did not look out of place as the "Gunners" won the League Championship. Also won his first and only England Under 21 cap in April 1991. In 1991-92 he started in the first team line-up, but only won a regular place in the "Gunners'" team after their elimination from the European Cup by Benfica in November. With Paul Davis out of favour, Michael Thomas on his way to Liverpool and Siggi Jonsson retired, a lot of responsibility lay on his shoulders, but he came through with flying colours, his place in the team established beyond doubt. Partnered John Jensen for most of **1992-93** in the centre of midfield, but as a pair they were probably too similar in style and, given the potency of the Arsenal front line, the team's sparse amount of goals generally stemmed from a lack of creativity in midfield. Struck a rare goal with a superb volley to save the home PL match against Sheffield United, his only goal throughout the campaign and must look to get on the score-sheet more often in the future. Unfortunately, an injury picked up in a meaningless (for Arsenal) League game at Ayresome Park, meant that he missed both the FA and League Cup Finals and thus lost the opportunity to be a part of the history making "Gunners".

| | | | APPEARANCES | | | | GOALS | | | |
|---|---|---|---|---|---|---|---|---|---|---|
| Clubs | Signing Date | Transfer Fee | Lge | FL Cup | FA Cup | Others | Lge | FL Cup | FA Cup | Others |
| Arsenal* | 2.88 | - | 63+10 | 9+1 | 8+2 | 1 | 2 | | | |

## HINCHCLIFFE Andrew (Andy) George

Born: Manchester, 5 February 1969

Height: 5'10" Weight: 12.10

International Honours: E Yth, E "U21"-1

**Position/Skill Factor:** Full-back with a wonderful left foot. Can strike 60 yard crossfield passes with ease and loves to get forward to deliver quality crosses to the target men.

**Career History:** Joined Manchester City as an associated schoolboy in May 1983, before becoming an apprentice in July 1985. Made his FL debut for City in a 2-1 home win over Plymouth Argyle on 15 August 1987 and missed just two matches that first season. Played a prominent part in the club's promotion to the First Division during the following year, scoring five times from the left-back position. And proved consistent in the top flight before injury forced an early end to his season in 1989-90. During the 1990 close season, however, he was transferred to Everton in exchange for Neil Pointon and a large cash adjustment in City's favour, making his debut at Goodison against Leeds United on 25 August 1990, the opening day of 1990-91. Although injured early on, he recovered well enough to play in 30 matches, including the losing Zenith Data Cup Final against Crystal Palace. It has not proved to be a happy move for him. Once regarded as one of the most promising left-backs in the country, he is now only an occasional performer for Everton. Apparently not highly regarded by manager Howard Kendall, hence his

transfer from City, he found his former manager following him to Goodison Park only a few months later. In 1991-92 he had a run in the team at left-back up to December, but following the arrival of Gary Ablett, his only appearances were on the left side of midfield. After the personal disappointment of the previous season, he began **1992-93** promisingly, in his favoured left-back position. Unfortunately, he suffered yet another set-back to his blighted Everton career when a pelvic injury put him on the side-lines for two months. Following a successful operation and Keown's transfer to Arsenal, came changing fortunes. With over 150 League games behind him, he signed off the season with a string of consistent performances, as he attempted to book a regular place in the side once and for all.

| | | | APPEARANCES | | | | GOALS | | | |
|---|---|---|---|---|---|---|---|---|---|---|
| Clubs | Signing Date | Transfer Fee | Lge | FL Cup | FA Cup | Others | Lge | FL Cup | FA Cup | Others |
| Manchester City | 6.86 | – | 107+5 | 11 | 12 | 4 | 8 | 1 | 1 | 1 |
| Everton* | 7.90 | £800,000 | 61+3 | 8+2 | 5 | 4 | 2 | | | |

## **HIRST David** Eric

Born: Cudworth, 7 December 1967

Height: 5'11" Weight: 12.5

International Honours: E Yth, E "U21"-7, E"B", E-3

**Position/Skill Factor:** One of that rare breed of strikers who can run with the ball and finish with devastating power and accuracy, normally with a strong left foot shot. Also, brave in the air.

**Career History:** Started his career with Barnsley as an apprentice in July 1984, making his FL debut, three months prior to turning professional, at Charlton Athletic on 17 August 1985 and by the end of that first season he had scored nine goals in 27 full matches. His first goal for Barnsley, against Leeds United in October 1985, is still recalled with awe by Oakwell regulars — a 50 yard run, followed by a blistering shot — but down the years it has become his trademark. He soon showed that his first FL goal was no fluke, with eight more in a run of ten games, before being rested. Clearly a "Wonderkind", he was snapped up by neighbouring Sheffield Wednesday at the end of his first season as a professional. Somewhat surprisingly, his first three seasons with the "Owls" were comparatively disappointing, considering his meteoric start with Barnsley and he found himself in and out of the side. Eventually began to make his mark at Hillsborough in 1989-90 when scoring 14 goals, but unfortunately for both him and the fans, the club was relegated to the Second Division. However, he fairly exploded on the scene in 1990-91, with his 24 goals good enough to see Wednesday promoted back to the First Division at the first time of asking and as the proud possessor of a League Cup winners medal, following the club's thrilling victory over Manchester United. At the end of the season, he was called up by Graham Taylor for the England summer tour of Australasia, making his international debut against Australia and then playing in the New Zealand match. He started the 1991-92 season with a magnificent strike in the third minute of the first match against Aston Villa and continued in similar vein. Despite two short absences through injury, he finished the season once again as leading scorer with 18 FL goals, plus three in cup ties. Selected once more for England against France in February, he was withdrawn at half-time to make way for Gary Lineker and was unlucky to be excluded from the England squad for the European Championship finals in

Sweden. Only managed to play half of the **1992-93** Premier League campaign, having first succumbed to injury after notching five goals in five appearances. Injured in the act of scoring at Arsenal, he was forced to miss the next ten matches and because of it he was unable to add to his total of England caps. On his return to the team, however, he put together another run, until a thigh strain at Ipswich Town early in the New Year saw him absent for a further 11 games. After coming on as a substitute during the losing League Cup Final against Arsenal, he scored his 100th goal for Wednesday to take the FA Cup Final against the same team to a replay. Unfortunately for the "Owls", he couldn't manage a repeat of the dose in the second game and had to be satisfied with another losers medal. Much admired by Manchester United, although Wednesday rebuffed all enquiries, the only thing on his mind at present is in getting match fit in time for the coming season.

| | | | APPEARANCES | | | | GOALS | | | |
|---|---|---|---|---|---|---|---|---|---|---|
| Clubs | Signing Date | Transfer Fee | Lge | FL Cup | FA Cup | Others | Lge | FL Cup | FA Cup | Others |
| Barnsley | 11.85 | - | 26+2 | 1 | | | 9 | | | |
| Sheffield Wednesday* | 8.86 | £200,000 | 190+21 | 20+7 | 11+4 | 8 | 83 | 10 | 6 | 5 |

## **HIRST Lee** William

Born: Sheffield, 26 January 1969

Height: 6'2" Weight: 12.7

**Position/Skill Factor:** No frills central defender who gets the job done. Good heading ability and strong in the tackle, he is a "stopper" in the old fashioned mould.

**Career History:** Plucked from a Sheffield parks' side by Scarborough, early in 1990, within two months he had made his FL debut in the centre of "Boro's" defence at Carlisle United on 31 March 1990, following an injury to their regular pivot, Steve Richards. Performed well enough to stay in place for the remaining nine games, but with the latter fit again for the start of 1990-91, Hirst made way. However, when injury robbed Scarborough of the services of Adrian Meyer, he stepped up to form a sound defensive partnership with Richards that stayed in place for virtually the rest of the season. That all changed, when Richards transferred to Halifax Town during the summer and he slotted in creditably alongside, first Meyer and then Chris Curran, to prevail during 1991-92. With 72 League appearances already behind him, he was ever present for the first 19 games of **1992-93** and although he played in another 17 (including one as substitute), it appeared he had somehow lost his way. It was still a surprise to many, that with his contract up for renewal, he was freed at the beginning of May. For a small club to release a young player with plenty of scope for improvement and one who was only recently reckoned to be a hot prospect, it seemed a weird decision. And the point was not lost on Coventry City, of the Premier League, who signed him in time for the 1993-94 season. He had already been noted by the "Sky Blues", after scoring the goal that put them out of last season's Second Round League Cup-tie. With Coventry winning the first leg match by 2-0 and Scarborough having pegged back both goals, Hirst powered in an injury time header, following a free-kick, to take the Yorkshiremen into the next round.

| | | | APPEARANCES | | | | GOALS | | | |
|---|---|---|---|---|---|---|---|---|---|---|
| Clubs | Signing Date | Transfer Fee | Lge | FL Cup | FA Cup | Others | Lge | FL Cup | FA Cup | Others |
| Scarborough | 2.90 | - | 107+1 | 9 | 3 | 6+1 | 6 | 3 | | |
| Coventry City* | 7.93 | - | | | | | | | | |

## **HITCHCOCK Kevin** Joseph

Born: Canning Town, 5 October 1962

Height: 6'1"

Weight: 12.2

**Position/Skill Factor:** All action goalkeeper who is very agile and quick off his line. Is also a good kicker, particularly from his hands.

**Career History:** A former Chelsea associated schoolboy (February 1978), he was released by the club and Nottingham Forest later spotted him playing for Isthmian League team, Barking and moved in smartly for him. Could not immediately break in to the Forest side and was signed by Mansfield Town in a loan deal and made his FL debut at Colchester United on 10 March 1984. Played out the rest of the season at the Field Mill Ground and during the summer the transfer was made permanent. Missed just three matches over the next three seasons, assisting the "Stags'" promotion run to the Third Division in 1985-86, before John Hollins signed him for Chelsea, with half of the large fee going to Forest, according to the terms of his previous transfer. However, Chelsea were struggling at the wrong end of the First Division at the time and his efforts were not enough to prevent defeat by Middlesbrough over two legs of the Play-Off final. Began the next season as second choice to Roger Freestone and following the signing of Dave Beasant his first team prospects seemed even more remote. After playing just four games in 1990-91, he spent some time on loan at Northampton Town during their vain Third Division promotion bid. After three years at Stamford Bridge with little first team action, he made a breakthrough in 1991-92 as Dave Beasant lost form and Roger Freestone departed to Swansea. Called up for the third game of the season, he alternated with Beasant throughout the season, making 21 FL appearances. Started **1992-93** in the reserves, but was recalled after the Dave Beasant "public sacking" and held the job down until a disastrous performance under new manager, Dave Webb, at Blackburn Rovers, saw him dropped. His form was often brilliant, but there was also a tendency to make mistakes, the like of which occurred in games against Middlesbrough in the FA Cup and Sheffield United at home in the League, when he lost possession of the ball and was punished. Following the game at Ewood Park he went on loan to West Ham United, but only as cover for Ludek Miklosko and didn't make a first team appearance.

| | | | APPEARANCES | | | | GOALS | | | |
|---|---|---|---|---|---|---|---|---|---|---|
| Clubs | Signing Date | Transfer Fee | Lge | FL Cup | FA Cup | Others | Lge | FL Cup | FA Cup | Others |
| Nottingham Forest | 8.83 | £15,000 | | | | | | | | |
| Mansfield Town | 2.84 | Loan | 14 | | | | | | | |
| Mansfield Town | 6.84 | £140,000 | 168 | 12 | 10 | 20 | | | | |
| Chelsea* | 3.88 | £250,000 | 55 | 8 | 5 | 9 | | | | |
| Northampton Town | 12.90 | Loan | 17 | | | 1 | | | | |

# HODDLE Glenn

Born: Hayes, 27 October 1957

Height: 6'0" Weight: 11.6

International Honours: E Yth, E "U21"-12, E "B", E-53

**Position/Skill Factor:** Arguably the most gifted midfield player of his generation, with excellent ball control, scorer of long range goals, both fiercely struck and cunning lobs and chips and the best provider of accurate and perfectly weighted long (50 yards or more) passes since Johnny Haynes.

**Career History:** As the new manager of Chelsea, after superbly piloting Swindon Town to the Premier League, via the Play-Offs, it will be interesting to see whether he will continue to make an impression on the pitch in 1993-94 as well as in his managers role. One of the most talented and gifted footballers of modern times, he was at Tottenham Hotspur as an associated schoolboy (April 1973) and as an apprentice (April 1974), prior to signing professional forms towards the end of 1974-75. Winning England youth caps was a step in the right direction and he made his FL debut at White Hart Lane as a substitute on 30 August 1975 against Norwich City and then scored in his first full match, in February 1976 at Stoke City. In 1976-77 he won a regular place in the Tottenham line-up at the age of 18 and although his first full season was marred by relegation, he was the architect of "Spurs'" quick return to the top flight the following year. He enjoyed his best season at White Hart Lane in 1979-80, although a poor one for the team overall, when he scored 19 FL goals from 41 games, far and away "Spurs'" top scorer and a remarkable achievement for a goal-maker, rather than taker. He was promoted by the media and fans alike for international stardom long before his England debut in November 1979, when he scored in a 2-0 victory over Bulgaria. But living in the shadow of Ray Wilkins and Brian Robson, it was not until 1985-86 that he earned an automatic place, much to the chargin of the media who constantly championed his cause. For "Spurs", he won FA Cup Winners medals in 1981, scoring with a free-kick in the first game against Manchester City (although commonly described as own goal by Tommy Hutchison, owing to a wicked deflection) and again in 1982 when he scored in both games against Queens Park Rangers, firstly in a 1-1 draw and then with a penalty in the replay, which gave "Spurs" a 1-0 victory. He also played on the losing side in the 1982 League Cup Final against Liverpool and in the 1987 FA Cup Final against Coventry – a sad end to his "Spurs'" career, which in its latter stages was dogged by injury. In the summer of 1987, feeling unappreciated in this country, he joined French club, AS Monaco, and enjoyed a successful first season, assisting them to the League Championship of France. He became increasingly peripheral as an England player, however, and although playing in all three games in the 1988 European Championship Finals in West Germany, all was lost, with Hoddle largely anonymous. The third match against the USSR was his last for England, as England manager, Bobby Robson, finally lost patience with him, although the media continued to clamour for his recall over the next two years. In truth, Hoddle never revealed his true talents consistently in an England shirt. Although criticised by England managers for lack of "work rate", this would have been irrelevant if he had reproduced the goal-making and goal scoring ability he showed for "Spurs", in an England shirt. Instead, he flattered to deceive, starring in unimportant games against weak opposition, but failing to deliver in the ones that really mattered. After four years in France, which were again dogged by injury in their latter stages, he returned to England in March 1991, signing for Chelsea as a non-contract player, in a bid to regain fitness and resurrect his career. Soon afterwards, he was appointed manager of Swindon Town, by popular demand, in succession to Ossie Ardiles. Although considered by some to be too "laid back" to be a successful manager, he quickly proved himself, by piloting the Wiltshire club to eighth place, narrowly missing out on the Play-Offs. He also made a successful come back as a player, operating in a "Sweeper" or "libero" role behind, or just in front of the back four and exploiting his exceptional passing ability. Every time he was clattered to the ground, or seen rubbing his knee in **1992-93**, Swindon fans held their breath, for seldom can one man have been so influential on one team. He occasionally made mistakes, much to the delight of opposing fans and will probably remember forever his slip at Millwall, which handed the initiative to the home side. He scored only three goals for Town, but contributed the first, a magnificent strike from the edge of the box at Wembley in the Play-Off Final against Leicester City, a game that proved to be his last for the club. In one of the best displays of open football seen for years, Swindon finally beat Leicester 4-3, to reach the Premier League and the whole country enthused at the way they achieved it. The latter part of the season was rife with speculation about his departure for Chelsea. No-one at Swindon wanted him to leave, but if, as everyone believes, he is the future manager of England, his move to a bigger club was inevitable. As the new player/manager of a club with a great tradition of having skilful players, but not many recently, his first task will be to kick start the "Blues" into action and the stage has been set for a new era of exciting football at the Bridge.

| | | | APPEARANCES | | | | GOALS | | | |
|---|---|---|---|---|---|---|---|---|---|---|
| Clubs | Signing Date | Transfer Fee | Lge | FL Cup | FA Cup | Others | Lge | FL Cup | FA Cup | Others |
| Tottenham Hotspur | 4.75 | - | 371+7 | 44 | 47+1 | 21+4 | 88 | 10 | 11 | 1 |
| Monaco | 7.87 | £800,000 | | | | | | | | |
| Swindon Town | 8.91 | - | 63+1 | 6 | 1 | 3+1 | 1 | 1 | | 1 |
| Chelsea* | 7.93 | £175,000 | | | | | | | | |

# HODGE Stephen (Steve) Brian

Born: Nottingham, 25 October 1962

Height: 5'7" Weight: 9.12

International Honours: E "U21"-8, E"B", E-24

**Position/Skill Factor:** Left footed midfield player who is very quick and can get his foot in when required. Often scores goals with late runs into the opponents penalty box.

**Career History:** Was first noticed by Nottingham Forest as a 14-year-old and signed on associated schoolboy forms in July 1977. Later became an apprentice (July 1979), before joining the professional ranks and making his FL debut at Ipswich Town on 15 May 1982. He only missed a handful of games over the next three full seasons and figured prominently in Brian Clough's plans. Was surprisingly allowed to join Aston Villa after just two games in 1985-86 and he impressed enough to warrant a full England call up when coming on for Gordon Cowans during a 1-0 win over the USSR on 26 March 1986 in Tbilisi. After replacing the injured Brian Robson for five matches in the World Cup in Mexico that year, another large fee exchanged hands when Tottenham Hotspur signed him as a replacement for Glasgow Rangers bound Graham Roberts. Helped "Spurs" to the losing FA Cup Final against Coventry City that season, but never settled in London and eventually moved back to Nottingham Forest in the summer of 1988. Since being back at the City Ground, he has won League Cup winners medals in 1989 and 1990 and came on as a sub during the losing 1991 FA Cup Final against his old team, Tottenham. Impatient with his frequent non-availability through injury, Brian Clough sold him to Leeds United in the summer of 1991 and although not an automatic first team choice, he played enough games to qualify for a League Championship medal, while his seven FL goals were vital to United's cause. After being unable to gain a regular first team place in **1992-93** and always appearing to be suffering from small, niggling injuries, the position was made clearer in February when it was announced to the media that he had only just fully recovered from the M.E. virus that had plagued him all season. A valuable squad member, he consistently appeared in the club's final 13 and could count himself unlucky not to be first choice on many occasions, while appearing in nearly twice as many games played, as substitute.

| | | | APPEARANCES | | | | GOALS | | | |
|---|---|---|---|---|---|---|---|---|---|---|
| Clubs | Signing Date | Transfer Fee | Lge | FL Cup | FA Cup | Others | Lge | FL Cup | FA Cup | Others |
| Nottingham Forest | 10.80 | - | 122+1 | 10 | 6 | 11 | 30 | 2 | | 4 |
| Aston Villa | 8.85 | £450,000 | 53 | 12 | 4 | 1 | 12 | 3 | 1 | |
| Tottenham Hotspur | 12.86 | £650,000 | 44+1 | 2 | 7 | | 7 | | 2 | |
| Nottingham Forest | 8.88 | £550,000 | 79+3 | 20+1 | 11+1 | 9 | 20 | 6 | 2 | 2 |
| Leeds United* | 7.91 | £900,000 | 21+25 | 3+3 | 1 | 0+3 | 9 | | | |

# HODGES Glyn Peter

Born: Streatham, 30 April 1963

Height: 6'0" Weight: 12.3

International Honours: W Yth, W "U21"-5, W "B", W-16

**Position/Skill Factor:** Left-winger with lovely skill. By crossing great early balls, he doesn't need to beat defenders and causes all sorts of problems.

**Career History:** After starting his career at Wimbledon as an associated schoolboy in February 1979, he showed enough early promise to be taken on as an apprentice (July 1979) just five months later. He then proceeded to make his FL debut, while still an apprentice, at Halifax Town on 27 September 1980, when coming on as a sub. Played 27 full League games that season as the club were promoted to the Third Division in fourth place and although they were relegated the following year, he won a Fourth Division Championships medal in 1982-83 as the "Dons" came straight back. In 1983-84 he played in 39 League matches when Wimbledon moved into the Second Division as runners-up and at the end of the season he won his first full Welsh cap when he came on as a sub against Norway on 6 June 1984. The fairy story was completed in 1985-86 when the little south Londoners marched into the First Division in third place. He had now played in all four divisions with the same club, an amazing feat and having accomplished that, he signed for Newcastle United in the 1987 close season. After only three months and seven games and unable to settle in the north-east, he joined Watford, a team doomed to relegation to the Second Division at the end of that season. Spent almost three years at Vicarage Road, before moving back to south London with Crystal Palace in the 1990 close season. The move was not a success. Making only a handful of appearances, his career was rescued by his former manager at Wimbledon and Watford, Dave Bassett, who signed him for Sheffield United in January 1991. Scored three vital goals in his first four games for the "Blades" and played a significant role in their remarkable escape from relegation trouble when winning seven consecutive games from January to March. Suffered a rather indifferent season in 1991-92, losing his left-wing slot to the emerging Dane Whitehouse, but reappearing later, on the right side of midfield, without making a great impression. In **1992-93**, he again proved to be the enigma of Bramall Lane. Undoubtedly the most skilful player in the squad, a persistent toe injury and the lack of competition for the left sided berth, meant that his performances were sometimes below par. However, a switch to a central striking role towards the end of the season led to a flurry of goals, although his first attempt as a penalty taker against Everton brought about a save by Neville Southall, from which he slotted home the rebound. He let his temperament get the better of him from time to time and some needless bookings were supplemented by a dismissal at Sheffield Wednesday for injudicious use of the elbow against John Harkes. Due to that offence, he will start the new season under suspension.

| | | | APPEARANCES | | | | GOALS | | | |
|---|---|---|---|---|---|---|---|---|---|---|
| Clubs | Signing Date | Transfer Fee | Lge | FL Cup | FA Cup | Others | Lge | FL Cup | FA Cup | Others |
| Wimbledon | 2.81 | - | 200+32 | 14+2 | 13+2 | 0+1 | 49 | 3 | 2 | |
| Newcastle United | 7.87 | £200,000 | 7 | | | | | | | |
| Watford | 10.87 | £300,000 | 82+4 | 5 | 8 | 2+1 | 15 | 2 | 1 | 1 |
| Crystal Palace | 7.90 | £410,000 | 5+2 | 2+2 | | | | 1 | | |
| Sheffield United* | 1.91 | £450,000 | 62+7 | 2+1 | 10+1 | | 10 | | 3 | |

## **HODGES Lee** Leslie

Born: Epping, 4 September 1973

Height: 5'9" Weight: 11.6

International Honours: E Yth

**Position/Skill Factor:** A natural goal scoring forward with a good first touch.

**Career History:** Another of Tottenham Hotspur's bright youngsters, he first came to White Hart Lane as an associated schoolboy in March 1988, before signing on as a trainee in August 1990 and graduating to the professional ranks early in 1992. Gained valuable experience in a **1992-93** loan spell with Plymouth Argyle, making his FL debut at Chester City on 27 February 1993 and scoring the winning goal in a 2-1 victory. Played a further six (including one substitute) matches and scored another goal, before being recalled to White Hart Lane to take part in the Fiorucci Trophy matches against Real Madrid and Inter Milan. Following that, he stepped up to make substitute appearances for "Spurs" in the last four games of the season and looks certain to be a regular Premier League player in the not too distant future.

| | | | APPEARANCES | | | | GOALS | | | |
|---|---|---|---|---|---|---|---|---|---|---|
| Clubs | Signing Date | Transfer Fee | Lge | FL Cup | FA Cup | Others | Lge | FL Cup | FA Cup | Others |
| Tottenham Hotspur* | 2.92 | - | 0+4 | | | | | | | |
| Plymouth Argyle | 2.93 | Loan | 6+1 | | | | 2 | | | |

## **HOLDEN Richard (Rick)** William

Born: Skipton, 9 September 1964

Height: 5'11" Weight: 12.7

**Position/Skill Factor:** A lively left-winger who can not only score goals, but creates many others with accurate crosses from either foot. Often he will pick the ball up deep and run at the full-back, giving himself the option of crossing early or going past his rival.

**Career History:** Spotted by Burnley playing for Carnegie Teachers Training College in Leeds, he made just one subs' appearance for the club, whilst on trial, for his FL debut at Leyton Orient on 3 May 1986. Not offered a contract by the "Clarets", he joined Halifax Town in September 1986 on a non-contract basis and after winning a regular place, he abandoned any ambitions as a teacher and signed a professional contract in January 1987. His impressive play on the left flank soon had the scouts turning up at the Shay, but with Town almost safe from relegation in March 1988 , he signed for Watford. Went straight into a side that was doomed for the Second Division and stayed at Vicarage Road until the end of the following season when the club failed at the Play-Off stage to regain its First Division status. Was transferred to Oldham Athletic at the start of the 1989-90 season and sparkled as an ever present in 65 matches as the "Latics" reached the FA Cup Semi-Final and the League Cup Final. 1990-91 was even better and he missed only four League matches and won a Second Division Championship medal as the club attained promotion to the top flight for the first time since 1923. He enjoyed another excellent season for the "Latics", on their return to Division One in 1991-92, playing in every single game, although on four occasions as substitute. Now recognised as one of the most effective left-wingers in the country, it is probably now too late for him to start an international career at the age of 28. An in-depth statistical analysis of First Division goals in 1991-92, revealed that his crosses had "created" no fewer than 19 goals for his team mates, more "assists" than by any other top level player. Surprisingly transferred to Manchester City, before the start of the **1992-93** season, he took a while to settle into his new club's style of play, often tending to have a run of good games, before becoming ineffective, particularly when not feeding forwards who were better placed. However, he only missed one game and that through injury and developed a very good understanding with

Terry Phelan, when holding the ball to allow the full-back to overlap. Always noted for his "assists", his accurate crosses brought the best out of Niall Quinn and Garry Flitcroft in the air and the coming season should see City making even better use of that capability.

| | | | APPEARANCES | | | | GOALS | | | |
|---|---|---|---|---|---|---|---|---|---|---|
| Clubs | Signing Date | Transfer Fee | Lge | FL Cup | FA Cup | Others | Lge | FL Cup | FA Cup | Others |
| Burnley | 3.86 | - | 0+1 | | | | | | | |
| Halifax Town | 9.86 | - | 66+1 | 2 | 7 | 8 | 12 | | | |
| Watford | 3.88 | £125,000 | 42 | 2 | 6 | 3+1 | 8 | | 1 | 1 |
| Oldham Athletic | 8.89 | £165,000 | 125+4 | 15+1 | 13 | 3 | 19 | 4 | 2 | 1 |
| Manchester City* | 8.92 | £900,000 | 40+1 | 3 | 5 | | 3 | 1 | 1 | |

## HOLDSWORTH Dean
Christopher

Born: Walthamstow, 8 November 1968

Height: 5'11" Weight: 12.0

**Position/Skill Factor:** A natural goalscorer who invariably arrives in the box at the right time. Pulls away to the far post well to get his headers in.

**Career History:** Along with his twin brother, David, he joined Watford as an associated schoolboy in May 1984, prior to becoming an apprentice on leaving school (May 1985). After progressing to the "Hornets'" professional ranks, he made his FL debut as a substitution for Trevor Senior at Vicarage Road against Luton Town on 12 December 1987, before being loaned out to Carlisle United and Port Vale to gain experience. In 1988-89, he had two further spells out on loan to Swansea City and Brentford. Ironically, his twin brother David, who broke into the "Hornets'" team nearly two years after Dean, was the first to establish himself at Vicarage Road. In fact, Dean remained a fringe first-team player until his departure to Brentford in September 1989 for a large fee, a transfer Watford surely lived to regret. He was an immediate success at Griffin Park, scoring on his debut and consistently throughout the season, to end with 24 FL goals, the highest total by a "Bees'" player since 1978. By contrast, the 1990-91 season was an anti-climax for him as, plagued by injury, he could only score five goals in 30 FL games. Despite the dearth of goals, Brentford qualified for the Third Division Play-Offs, before being eliminated by Tranmere Rovers. However, promotion was not long delayed, Holdsworth leading the way in 1991-92 with 24 FL goals (plus ten more in cup competitions) as the "Bees" stole the Third Division Championship on the last day of the season and thus returned to Division Two after an absence of 38 years. Sadly for "Bees'" fans, he did not stay around to assist their Second Division campaign, although few would begrudge him the opportunity of Premier League football with London neighbours, Wimbledon. Brentford received a massive fee and two players (Mickey Bennett and Detsi Kruszynski) in compensation. At the end of his first season with the "Dons", he proved to be one of the bargain buys of **1992-93**. Two goals in his first four Premier League matches made for a good start, but following an excellent strike at Ipswich Town, he had a run of 13 games without a goal, including a spell out to recover from a hernia operation. The goal touch returned with a pair against Oldham Athletic in an emphatic 5-2 win, but he then had another spell out of the side. However, he could do little wrong in the second half of the season, bagging an incredible 14 goals from Wimbledon's last 19 matches. His tally of 19 goals, saw him finish as third top scorer in the Premier League and was a huge factor in securing the "Dons'" future in the top flight, with a respectable 12th position in the League table.

| Clubs | Signing Date | Transfer Fee | APPEARANCES Lge | FL Cup | FA Cup | Others | GOALS Lge | FL Cup | FA Cup | Others |
|---|---|---|---|---|---|---|---|---|---|---|
| Watford | 11.86 | - | 2+14 | | | 0+4 | 3 | | | |
| Carlisle United | 2.88 | Loan | 4 | | | | 1 | | | |
| Port Vale | 3.88 | Loan | 6 | | | | 2 | | | |
| Swansea City | 8.88 | Loan | 4+1 | | | | 1 | | | |
| Brentford | 10.88 | Loan | 2+5 | | | | 1 | | | |
| Brentford | 9.89 | £125,000 | 106+4 | 7+1 | 6 | 12+1 | 53 | 6 | 7 | 9 |
| Wimbledon* | 7.92 | £750,000 | 34+2 | 2+1 | 2+1 | | 19 | | | |

## HOLLAND Matthew Rhys

Born: Bury, 11 April 1974

Height: 5'9" Weight: 11.4

**Position/Skill Factor:** A midfield player with balance and skill in abundance. A good passer, he will often make excellent runs into the opposition's penalty area.

**Career History:** The son of Pat, the old West Ham United favourite, who made 245 League appearances for the "Hammers" not that long ago, he first came to Upton Park as a trainee in July 1990. Turned professional at the start of **1992-93** and appeared fairly regularly with the reserves, being loaned out to Farnborough and playing 26 games as part of the learning experience.

| Clubs | Signing Date | Transfer Fee | APPEARANCES Lge | FL Cup | FA Cup | Others | GOALS Lge | FL Cup | FA Cup | Others |
|---|---|---|---|---|---|---|---|---|---|---|
| West Ham United* | 8.92 | - | | | | | | | | |

## HOLLOWAY Ian Scott

Born: Kingswood, 12 March 1963

Height: 5'7"

Weight: 9.12

**Position/Skill Factor:** The ideal midfield type who can also play on the right-wing. Has a good footballing brain and works hard to get into good positions in order to receive the ball. Also, he doesn't give the ball away easily.

**Career History:** Locally born and bred, he first came to Bristol Rovers as an associated schoolboy in July 1977 and graduated to apprentice status in July 1979. Made his FL debut a month after turning pro at Wrexham on 25 April 1981, but it wasn't until 1983-84 that he began to hold down a regular place. His promising displays alerted Wimbledon, who were looking to tighten up in midfield for their second season in Division Two. He signed for the "Dons" in the 1985 close season, but spent less than a year at Plough Lane, before being on the move across London, to Brentford. had previously had a spell on loan at Griffin Park in March 1986 and this deal was made permanent in time for the new season. However, the move was not wholly successful and he had another period on loan, this time with Torquay United. The prodigal son finally returned home, re-signing for Bristol Rovers and in 1989-90, as an ever present, he enjoyed his best-ever season, winning a Third Division Championship medal into the bargain. He was ever present yet again in 1990-91 as the club consolidated itself in Division Two and scored winning goals on three separate occasions, albeit two of them being penalties. After ten years playing in the lower divisions, it seemed that any chance of performing at the top level had long since passed him by, but when "Pirates'" manager Gerry Francis moved to Queens Park Rangers in the summer of 1991, one of his first signings for the "R's" was Holloway. He started the season in the first team squad and following Ray Wilkins' injury in the first game, deputised capably in the unfamiliar role of central midfield. On Wilkins' return in November, he switched back to the right-wing, only to move inside again from February until the end of the season in place of Simon Barker. Started **1992-93** in charge of the number eight shirt, playing in the first three games, before his part in the match against Sheffield United was cut short when he had to come off the field with a damaged eye. At first it was feared that he may have suffered a detached retina, but after taking time out, he was fit enough to return to Rangers' midfield for the League Cup-tie against Grimsby Town, having been used as a substitute a few days earlier. Scored three goals during the season, including a late winner at Sheffield United, before being put out of action for six weeks with a groin injury. The unsung hero of the side, he came back until being ruled out yet again, for the final four games of the season.

| Clubs | Signing Date | Transfer Fee | APPEARANCES Lge | FL Cup | FA Cup | Others | GOALS Lge | FL Cup | FA Cup | Others |
|---|---|---|---|---|---|---|---|---|---|---|
| Bristol Rovers | 3.81 | - | 104+7 | 10 | 8 | 5 | 14 | 1 | 2 | |
| Wimbledon | 7.85 | £35,000 | 19 | 3 | 1 | | 2 | | | |
| Brentford | 3.86 | £25,000 | 27+3 | 2 | 3 | 0+1 | 2 | | | |
| Torquay United | 1.87 | Loan | 5 | | | | | | | |
| Bristol Rovers | 8.87 | £10,000 | 179 | 5 | 10 | 20 | 26 | | 1 | 3 |
| Q.P.R.* | 8.91 | £230,000 | 57+7 | 7 | 3 | 1+1 | 2 | | 1 | |

## HOLMES Darren Peter

Born: Sheffield, 30 January 1975

Height: 5'9" Weight: 10.7

**Position/Skill Factor:** Left sided midfield player, with a keen left foot. Has good skill to match his vision and is an excellent passer of the ball.

**Career History:** Locally born and bred, he came through the Sheffield Wednesday ranks as an associated schoolboy (March 1989) and as a trainee (August 1991), to sign professional forms during the 1993 close season. With plenty of youth team experience behind him, he also broke into the Central League side towards the end of **1992-93**, making ten appearances. Looks to be a good player in the making.

| Clubs | Signing Date | Transfer Fee | APPEARANCES Lge | FL Cup | FA Cup | Others | GOALS Lge | FL Cup | FA Cup | Others |
|---|---|---|---|---|---|---|---|---|---|---|
| Sheffield Wednesday* | 7.93 | - | | | | | | | | |

## HOLMES Matthew Jason

Born: Luton,
1 August 1969

Height: 5'7"

Weight: 10.7

**Position/Skill Factor:** Good footballing midfielder in the West Ham tradition, who passes and moves well. Always dangerous at set plays, with a great left foot.

**Career History:** Started his football career down on the south coast with Bournemouth as a trainee in September 1986, before signing as a professional for the "Cherries" at the beginning of 1988-89. Later, having been given a run out in the Simod Cup at Derby County, he made his FL debut whilst on loan to Cardiff City, coming on as a substitute in their home game with Aldershot on 25 March 1989. On his return to Dean Court, at the end of the season, he made his debut for Bournemouth on 29 April 1989 and held his place for the remaining three games, scoring his first senior goal in a remarkable 3-3 draw at Maine Road (after trailing 0-3 at half time), which almost cost Manchester City automatic promotion. He won a regular place in the "Cherries'" line-up from January 1990, although sadly that season ended in the club's demotion, following a chronic injury crisis which deprived them of most of their regular defenders. Thereafter, the team became a "run of the mill" Third Division outfit and at the end of 1991-92, a season in which he appeared in every FL game, he expressed a wish to find a new club. Eventually, he followed recently resigned Harry Redknapp to West Ham United, for a Tribunal determined tranfer fee that Bournemouth felt, not unreasonably, was a "give away". Proved to be an excellent signing for the "Hammers", but was unfortunate to break his nose on his **1992-93** debut at Newcastle United in the third game of the season. Apart from a few substitute appearances, his next full match was at Millwall, when he deputised for the injured Peter Butler and gave a quite brilliant display. Very unlucky not to have become a regular, he was also an impressive substitute when required and will challenge strongly for a Premier League place this season, following West Ham's promotion to the top flight as runners-up to Newcastle United. His brother Danny, who was a non-contract player with Bournemouth in 1991, now plays for Farnborough Town, recently relegated from the Vauxhall Conference League.

| | | | APPEARANCES | | | | GOALS | | | |
|---|---|---|---|---|---|---|---|---|---|---|
| Clubs | Signing Date | Transfer Fee | Lge | FL Cup | FA Cup | Others | Lge | FL Cup | FA Cup | Others |
| Bournemouth | 8.88 | – | 105+9 | 7 | 8+2 | 5 | 8 | | | |
| Cardiff City | 3.89 | Loan | 0+1 | | | | | | | |
| West Ham United* | 8.92 | £40,000 | 6+12 | | 1 | 3 | 1 | | | 1 |

## HOLMES Paul

Born: Stocksbridge, 18 February 1968

Height: 5'10" Weight: 11.0

**Position/Skill Factor:** Right-back. A good athlete, with plenty of pace, he loves to get forward. Has two good feet and is an excellent passer of the ball.

**Career History:** Son of Albert, who made 460 appearances as a full-back for Chesterfield between 1961 and 1976, he seemed certain to see out his career in the lower divisions, but in two surprising moves, climbed up the ladder to the Premier League. Made his FL debut for Third Division Doncaster Rovers, while still an apprentice (having signed in May 1984), at home to Wigan Athletic on 5 November 1985, playing three more games for the club prior to turning professional. By 1987-88, he had won a regular slot with the Belle Vue club and it was something of a surprise that he opted to join Torquay United at the end of his contract, rather than re-sign for Rovers. He spent four years at Plainmoor, mostly as first choice right-back, assisting the Devon club to promotion, via the Play-Offs, to Division Three in 1990-91. However, the team was ill-equipped to survive in the higher grade and fell back to the basement one year later. He was more fortunate, being elevated to the re-designated First Division, when joining newly promoted Birmingham City. He was unable to win regular selection for the "Blues'" struggling team in **1992-93** and it was a minor sensation when he transferred to Everton in March 1993, apparently after impressing "Toffees'" manager, Howard Kendall, in a reserve match. Not expected to appear in the first team, having been bought as cover, he found himself playing in three of the last four matches of the season, after making his Premier League debut at Goodison Park against Ipswich Town. Quickly adapted to the extra class and skill of the top flight and gave steady performances, but is unlikely to figure too heavily in the coming proceedings, unless Matthew Jackson is injured and appears a likely candidate for a regular reserve spot.

| | | | APPEARANCES | | | | GOALS | | | |
|---|---|---|---|---|---|---|---|---|---|---|
| Clubs | Signing Date | Transfer Fee | Lge | FL Cup | FA Cup | Others | Lge | FL Cup | FA Cup | Others |
| Doncaster Rovers | 2.86 | – | 42+5 | | 3+1 | 1 | 1 | | 1 | |
| Torquay United | 8.88 | £6,000 | 127+11 | 9 | 9+2 | 13+3 | 4 | | | |
| Birmingham City | 6.92 | £40,000 | 12 | | 1 | | | | | |
| Everton* | 3.93 | £100,000 | 4 | | | | | | | |

## HONEYWOOD Lee Brian

Born: Chelmsford, 3 August 1971

Height: 5'8" Weight: 10.10

International Honours: E Yth

**Position/Skill Factor:** Young defender who has good ability on the ball. Spots openings quickly and doesn't elaborate when passing.

**Career History:** Joined Ipswich Town as a trainee on leaving school in July 1987 and progressed to the club's professional staff during the summer of 1989. With the new **1992-93** Premier League season looming up and looking to break into the first team squad, he picked up a virus, while on holiday, which ultimately caused further problems, including a blood disorder. Unfortunately, having to attend hospital for regular tests, with plenty of rest required, decimated his season, but he will hopefully be back to full match fitness in time for 1993-94

| Clubs | Signing Date | Transfer Fee | APPEARANCES | | | | GOALS | | | |
|---|---|---|---|---|---|---|---|---|---|---|
| | | | Lge | FL Cup | FA Cup | Others | Lge | FL Cup | FA Cup | Others |
| Ipswich Town* | 5.89 | - | | | | | | | | |

# HOOPER Michael (Mike) Dudley

Born: Bristol, 10 February 1964

Height: 6'2"

Weight: 13.5

**Position/Skill Factor:** Agile goalkeeper. Very brave in coming for the ball and strong on crosses, he will not be intimidated. Also has good kicking ability.

**Career History:** Came to Bristol City from non-League side, Mangotsfield, whom he played for while completing his studies at Bristol University. Earlier, he had been on City's books as a 14-year-old associated schoolboy, signing in November 1978. Made his FL debut, his one and only game for the club, at Ashton Gate against Lincoln City on 1 December 1984, before joining Fourth Division Wrexham on a free transfer. He immediately replaced Stuart Parker as the "Robins'" custodian and showed such potential, having appeared in less than 40 League matches, that Liverpool signed him as cover for Bruce Grobbelaar. Playing as the reserve custodian at Anfield is usually a 'keepers' graveyard, as his predecessors, Ian Wardle and Bob Bolder, left the club without making a single first team appearance. He was more fortunate and made his Liverpool debut in the opening game of 1986-87, deputising for seven FL games until Grobbelaar's return, also playing in the last four matches of the season. He later enjoyed an extended first team run of 17 consecutive games in 1988-89, until two errors at Sheffield Wednesday led to him being dropped. Sidelined in 1989-90, he was loaned to Leicester City in September 1990 and although conceding ten goals in his first two games, it was acknowledged at the time, that it was due more to Leicester's defensive disorganisation, than the hapless 'keeper. After returning to Anfield, he played seven more League games in late season during Grobbelaar's absence through injury. Although a less flamboyant 'keeper than Grobbelaar, many shrewd judges considered that he deserved an extended run in the side and when the latter was dropped "officially" for the first time, in October 1991, he received another chance, but after only two games he was injured. Came back to play four matches at the end of the season when Grobbelaar suffered a hand injury, although the latter was recalled for the 1992 FA Cup Final against Sunderland. With Grobbelaar suspended, he made his first appearance of the **1992-93** season in the European Cup Winners Cup home-tie against Spartak Moscow, in preference to David James and although Liverpool lost 2-0, he was powerless to stop the goals and performed well. Played another 13 consecutive games before giving way to James, following the disastrous FA Cup defeat at the hands of Bolton Wanderers. However, having sat on the first team bench since being demoted, he came on as the substitute at Norwich in May, with half an hour of the game remaining, after James had been sent off. His first job, therefore, was to face the resultant spot kick and as he plunged to his right, David Phillips eased the ball into the opposite corner for the only goal of the game. His future at Anfield must be uncertain if Grobbelaar remains and after eight years as an almost permanent reserve, he deserves the chance of a regular spot somewhere.

| Clubs | Signing Date | Transfer Fee | APPEARANCES | | | | GOALS | | | |
|---|---|---|---|---|---|---|---|---|---|---|
| | | | Lge | FL Cup | FA Cup | Others | Lge | FL Cup | FA Cup | Others |
| Bristol City | 11.83 | _ | 1 | | 1 | 1 | | | | |
| Wrexham | 2.85 | - | 34 | 4 | | | | | | |
| Liverpool* | 10.85 | £40,000 | 50+1 | 10 | 5 | 6+1 | | | | |
| Leicester City | 9.90 | Loan | 14 | | | 1 | | | | |

# HOPKIN David

Born: Greenock, 21 August 1970

Height 6'0" Weight: 13.0

**Position/Skill Factor:** Powerful wide, or front player. Strong in the air, with an excellent right foot, he is a good early crosser of the ball.

**Career History:** Signed by Chelsea in **1992-93**, as an investment for the future, from his home town club, Morton, of the Scottish League First Division, for whom he had played three seasons after joining them from local junior club, Port Glasgow Rangers. He impressed while playing for the reserves and looked very much like he would become a first team regular before too long. However, he picked up a thigh strain, which took him quite a while to recover from and subsequently, his good form suffered. Given his PL debut at home to Liverpool on 10 February 1993, he made three (two substitute) further appearances before the end of the season.

| Clubs | Signing Date | Transfer Fee | APPEARANCES | | | | GOALS | | | |
|---|---|---|---|---|---|---|---|---|---|---|
| | | | Lge | FL Cup | FA Cup | Others | Lge | FL Cup | FA Cup | Others |
| Morton | 7.89 | - | 33+15 | 2 | 2 | | 4 | 2 | 1 | |
| Chelsea* | 9.92 | £300,000 | 2+2 | | | | | | | |

# HORLOCK Kevin

Born: Bexley, 1 November 1972

Height: 5'10" Weight: 11.0

**Position/Skill Factor:** Left-back, or central defender, who has a very cultured left foot. Quite capable at getting forward and creating goal scoring chances and is always dangerous at set plays.

**Career History:** With opportunities scarce and with no first team games under his belt, he was transferred from West Ham United to Swindon Town at the start of the **1992-93** season, having been at Upton Park both as an associated schoolboy (December 1986) and as a trainee (July 1989), prior to turning professional in the 1991 close season. Not expected to feature quickly in first team action, an injury crisis in September pitched him into service as an excellent stand-in for Paul Bodin in a 3-2 League Cup win over Torquay United at the County Ground, four days before making his FL debut at Portsmouth on 10 October 1992. In 17 (including one as a substitute) matches played, the highlight of his season came when he appeared in a winning Town side at West Ham United in only his third full game. With Bodin fit and well, he wasn't selected for either of the Play-Off matches, but can look forward with some confidence at the thought of playing in the Premier League this season.

| | | | APPEARANCES | | | | GOALS | | | |
|---|---|---|---|---|---|---|---|---|---|---|
| Clubs | Signing Date | Transfer Fee | Lge | FL Cup | FA Cup | Others | Lge | FL Cup | FA Cup | Others |
| West Ham United | 7.91 | - | | | | | | | | |
| Swindon Town* | 8.92 | - | 13+1 | 2 | 1 | | 1 | | | |

## HORNE Barry

Born: St Asaph, 18 May 1962

Height: 5'10" Weight: 11.6

International Honours: W-38

**Position/Skill Factor:** Competitive, hard tackling midfield player, who keeps his passing simple and is quite capable of scoring spectacular goals.

**Career History:** A late starter to League football, he completed a chemistry degree at Liverpool University, while playing as a part-timer for Rhyl in the Northern Premier League. On leaving university, he signed for Fourth Division Wrexham and made his FL debut at Swindon Town on 24 August 1984. Showed great promise and consistency during his three years at the Racecourse Ground, missing only two League games and it came as no surprise when he moved to a bigger club, when signing for Portsmouth. Played his first game for "Pompey" at Oxford on the opening day of the 1987-88 season and a month later, made his first appearance for the Welsh national team, coming on as a sub in the 88th minute of a European Championship qualifier against Denmark. Since then he has been an automatic first choice in the Welsh team. Only missed two League matches that season and although the club were relegated to the Second Division, he had firmly established himself in midfield. The following year, Southampton's manager, Chris Nicholl, looking to strengthen his midfield, brought the Welshman to the Dell as the club's most expensive signing. Very quickly settled down in the side and apart from a spell out injured at the end of 1989, very rarely missed a match. While playing a sterling role in the "Saints'" successful battle against relegation in 1991-92, he also became a hero to the club's supporters (if he wasn't before) with two goals in a FA Cup Fifth Round replay at home to Bolton Wanderers in late February. After another consistent season with Southampton, he was unexpectedly snapped up by Everton during the summer and began **1992-93** well, scoring on his debut against Sheffield Wednesday and adding steel to the midfield. Became a key member in trying to stop the rot, as the side's performances worsened, but unfortunately, injuries prevented him from playing throughout after Christmas. With spirited performances and great leadership qualities, he has proved to be an astute buy.

| | | | APPEARANCES | | | | GOALS | | | |
|---|---|---|---|---|---|---|---|---|---|---|
| Clubs | Signing Date | Transfer Fee | Lge | FL Cup | FA Cup | Others | Lge | FL Cup | FA Cup | Others |
| Wrexham | 6.84 | - | 136 | 10 | 7 | 15 | 17 | 1 | 2 | 3 |
| Portsmouth | 7.87 | £60,000 | 66+4 | 3 | 6 | | 7 | | | |
| Southampton | 3.89 | £700,000 | 111+1 | 15+2 | 15 | 7 | 6 | 3 | 3 | 1 |
| Everton* | 7.92 | £675,000 | 34 | 5+1 | 0+1 | | 1 | | | |

## HOUGHTON Raymond (Ray) James

Born: Glasgow, 9 January 1962

Height: 5'8" Weight: 11.4

International Honours: IR-52

**Position/Skill Factor:** Industrious midfield player with wonderful vision, who can unlock the best of defences. Can see the whole pitch and instinctively knows where his team mates are and weights his passes perfectly.

**Career History:** Worked his way through West Ham United's junior ranks, before making his FL debut when coming on as a sub at Arsenal on 1 May 1982. That was to be his only opportunity with the "Hammers" and on being freed, he joined Fulham. Only missed a handful of games in three seasons at Craven Cottage, before signing for Oxford United, newly promoted to the First Division and looking for midfield creativity. In his first season with the club, he collected a League Cup winners medal, scoring

the second goal in the 3-0 victory over Queens Park Rangers and was selected for the Republic of Ireland against Wales in Dublin on 26 March 1986. Although born in Scotland, he qualified for the Irish team, by virtue of his father and went on to become one of the cornerstones of Jack Charlton's team. His unanswered goal for Ireland in the seventh minute of the match against England during the 1988 European Championships in Germany, was the first nail in England's coffin for that competition. Signed by Liverpool in October 1987, he quickly displaced the unfortunate Craig Johnston from the right midfield slot. The move also subtly altered the "Reds'" style of play as Johnston was happy to perform in an orthodox right-wing role, whilst Houghton was preferred in the middle of the pitch. He played 28 FL games in 1987-88, finding the net five times and was good value for his League Championship medal that season. The following term, he played in every game, winning an FA Cup winners medal as Liverpool beat their local rivals, Everton, 3-2 at Wembley, but lost out on another League Championship medal a week later when Arsenal denied the "Reds" in the final minute of the last match. Unfortunately, in 1989-90, he missed half of the season through injury, making only 16 appearances, although enough to qualify him for another League Championship medal. Played consistently during 1990-91 when, after a marvellous start to the season, the "Reds" capsized somewhat, following Kenny Dalglish's dramatic resignation. In 1991-92 he was one of the few Liverpool regulars to avoid serious long term injury and his seven League strikes kept the team afloat at a time when goals were in short supply. Finished the season with an FA Cup winners medal, following Liverpool's 2-0 victory over Sunderland in the Final. Became a surprise signing for Aston Villa during the summer of 1992 and missed only three games throughout **1992-93** as the club, never out of the top three after Christmas, relentlessly kept up their ultimately doomed challenge for the Championship. Still a regular member of the Republic's international side, it proved an excellent move for both player and club and salt was further rubbed into the wound for Liverpool, when Villa did the League "double" over them. Never a great goalscorer, although striking the goal in a 1-0 win at Chelsea was invaluable at the time, he scored a memorable goal in a 3-1 win at home to Manchester City, when a long run ended with him chipping the goalie in the dying seconds of the game.

| | | | APPEARANCES | | | | GOALS | | | |
|---|---|---|---|---|---|---|---|---|---|---|
| Clubs | Signing Date | Transfer Fee | Lge | FL Cup | FA Cup | Others | Lge | FL Cup | FA Cup | Others |
| West Ham United | 7.79 | - | 0+1 | | | | | | | |
| Fulham | 7.82 | - | 129 | 12 | 4 | | 16 | 2 | 3 | |
| Oxford United | 9.85 | £147,000 | 83 | 13 | 3 | 6 | 10 | 3 | | 1 |
| Liverpool | 10.87 | £825,000 | 147+6 | 14 | 26+1 | 8 | 28 | 3 | 4 | 3 |
| Aston Villa* | 7.92 | £900,000 | 39 | 5 | 4 | | 3 | | 1 | |

## HOUGHTON Scott Aaron

Born: Hitchin, 22 October 1971

Height: 5'5" Weight: 11.6

International Honours: E Sch, E Yth

**Position/Skill Factor:** Small tricky winger with good pace, who is quite capable of scoring goals. With two good feet, he is a lovely early crosser of the ball.

**Career History:** A young forward with Tottenham Hotspur, having come through the ranks as an associated schoolboy (June 1986), then a trainee (August 1988), before signing as a professional, he was loaned out to Second Division Ipswich Town in 1990-91 in order to acclimatise him to League football. Made his FL debut at Portman Road against Portsmouth on 2 April 1991, coming on as a sub for Romeo Zondervan and staying until the end of the season. During 1991-92 he frequently appeared as substitute for Tottenham and in one game scored twice, after an interruption due to floodlight failure, when "Spurs" overturned a 0-1 deficit to record a remarkable 4-1 victory over Luton Town. Had a most frustrating time of it in **1992-93**, with three hamstring operations severely disrupting his season. In between times, however, he managed to fit in a couple of loan spells with Gillingham and Charlton Athletic and hopes to be fully fit for the coming campaign.

| | | | APPEARANCES | | | | GOALS | | | |
|---|---|---|---|---|---|---|---|---|---|---|
| Clubs | Signing Date | Transfer Fee | Lge | FL Cup | FA Cup | Others | Lge | FL Cup | FA Cup | Others |
| Tottenham Hotspur* | 8.90 | - | 0+10 | 0+2 | | | 2 | | | |
| Ipswich Town | 3.91 | Loan | 7+1 | | | | 1 | | | |
| Gillingham | 12.92 | Loan | 3 | | | | | | | |
| Charlton Athletic | 2.93 | Loan | 6 | | | | | | | |

## HOWELLS David

Born: Guildford, 15 December 1967

Height: 5'11"

Weight: 11.1

International Honours: E Yth, FL Rep

**Position/Skill Factor:** Good team player who is very adaptable. Has appeared mainly in midfield, but is capable of man-to-man marking, or playing in an attacking role.

**Career History:** Joined Tottenham Hotspur in July 1984 on a YTS scheme and signed full professional forms just six months later. Waited over a year for his FL debut, but it was worth waiting for as he scored the winning goal in a 2-1 victory at Sheffield Wednesday on 22 February 1986. One of the best of a good crop of youngsters who have worked their way into the "Spurs'" side over the last few years, he started his career as a forward, but has now settled into the team in a defensive midfield role. Consolidated his position in 1990-91 when making 29 League appearances and collecting an FA Cup winners medal, following the 2-1 victory over Nottingham Forest. Played through most of 1991-92, but tended to be sacrificed whenever "Spurs" changed their tactical formation and although he started the **1992-93** Premier League campaign in possession of the number four shirt, he was injured after just three games. Returned to the side at Blackburn Rovers, following a couple of substitute runs and scored in a 2-0 win. He then played a further 16 (including two substitute) games before breaking a toe in the home match against Leeds United, which ruled him out for the rest of the season. Coincidentally, he also broke a foot bone in the match at Leeds, earlier in the campaign.

| | | | APPEARANCES | | | | GOALS | | | |
|---|---|---|---|---|---|---|---|---|---|---|
| Clubs | Signing Date | Transfer Fee | Lge | FL Cup | FA Cup | Others | Lge | FL Cup | FA Cup | Others |
| Tottenham Hotspur* | 1.85 | - | 122+30 | 17+3 | 8+3 | 7 | 15 | 2 | 1 | |

## HOWEY Stephen (Steve) Norman

Born: Sunderland, 26 October 1971

Height: 6'1"

Weight: 10.9

**Position/Skill Factor:** Central defender. Successfully converted from a forward, he is very powerful in the air, in both boxes. Always looking to hit the strikers with long, early balls.

**Career History**: With Newcastle United already relegated to the Second Division, he was given the experience of a first team run out, while still a trainee, coming on as a substitute at Manchester United on 13 May 1989 in the last game of the season. First came to St James' Park as an associated schoolboy in June 1986, before joining the club as a trainee on leaving school in July 1988. Was given several opportunities by manager, Ossie Ardiles, mostly as substitute in 1990-91 and enjoyed an extended run in the first team from October to December when Micky Quinn was injured, without suggesting that he was an answer to Newcastle's forward problems. Later in the season, new manager, Kevin Keegan, experimented with him in defence, but as all three matches he played in were lost, it seemed doomed to failure. To the credit of both manager and player, they persevered in the summer, to the point where Keegan felt confident enough to install him in central defence from the start of the season. The move was a resounding success, as Howey, dubbed the new "Alan Hansen" by his manager, turned out to be one of the finds of **1992-93** and forced his way into the England under 21 squad. He missed only five games all season and was a major influence in a side who remained unbeaten in their first 11 League games and romped away to win the First Division Championship. Given a new three year contract in October, as a reward for his excellent start, he created several goals for his team-mates, following great long distance passes and was a constant source of danger to opposing defences at corners and free-kicks. An opperation during the summer to cure a groin problem, that often restricted him to playing more than one game a week, should see him back and raring to go straight into Premier League action on the opening day of the new season.

| | | | APPEARANCES | | | | GOALS | | | |
|---|---|---|---|---|---|---|---|---|---|---|
| Clubs | Signing Date | Transfer Fee | Lge | FL Cup | FA Cup | Others | Lge | FL Cup | FA Cup | Others |
| Newcastle United* | 12.89 | - | 57+17 | 6+2 | 3+2 | 5 | 3 | 1 | | |

## HOYLAND Jamie William

Born: Sheffield, 23 January 1966

Height: 6'0"

Weight: 12.8

International Honours: E Yth

**Position/Skill Factor:** Has all the essential ingredients of the modern midfield player. With plenty of stamina, he makes good forward runs and does well in the air.

**Career History:** Son of Tommy, a wing-half with Bradford City and Sheffield United between 1949 and 1961, he started his career at Manchester City, first as an associated schoolboy (July 1981), then as an apprentice (July 1982), before signing as a fully fledged pro. Introduced at Maine Road for his FL debut against Derby County on 26 November 1983, he only made one further appearance in two years with City and was released during the 1986 close season. On leaving, found his niche in the Third Division with Bury and was ever present in both 1988-89 and 1989-90, when he finished up as the club's top scorer with 16 goals. The time was right for him to move up a grade, but on signing for Sheffield United, one of his father's old clubs, he found it difficult to immediately adjust to the pressures of the First Division. In a side that struggled for most of the season, he appeared in only 17 League games, as the team was continually chopped and changed. Seemed to establish himself in the "Blades'" midfield in 1991-92, playing in every game until the FA Cup Third Round tie with Luton Town in January when he was withdrawn with an injury. After regaining fitness, he surprisingly played only twice more and then only briefly as substitute, as his place went first to Michael Lake and then to new signing, Paul Rogers. Started **1992-93** as a long term casualty, following an operation and was only fit to resume in October. He then returned to a midfield role and scored some vital goals for the club, including the FA Fifth Round equaliser against Manchester United and another equaliser, this time at Oldham Athletic, which played its part in the end of season revival. Yet again, he proved his versatility, when used in a "sweeper" role, whenever manager, Dave Bassett, decided on a change of tactics.

| | | | APPEARANCES | | | | GOALS | | | |
|---|---|---|---|---|---|---|---|---|---|---|
| Clubs | Signing Date | Transfer Fee | Lge | FL Cup | FA Cup | Others | Lge | FL Cup | FA Cup | Others |
| Manchester City | 11.83 | - | 2 | 0+1 | | | | | | |
| Bury | 7.86 | - | 169+3 | 14+1 | 6 | 12 | 35 | 5 | | 2 |
| Sheffield United* | 7.90 | £250,000 | 55+14 | 3+2 | 7+2 | 2 | 6 | 1 | 1 | 1 |

## HUGHES David Robert

Born: St Albans, 30 December 1972

Height: 5'10½" Weight: 10.9

International Honours: E Sch

**Position/Skill Factor:** Hard working midfield player who tackles back. Looks confident with the ball and he passes and moves well.

**Career History**: Signed by Southampton on associated schoolboy terms in March 1991 at the relatively late age of 18, he turned professional during the 1991 close season, on leaving school. Unfortunately, his **1992-93** season came to an abrupt halt on 16 September when he was stretchered off in the second-half of a reserve game against Wimbledon, with a broken left ankle. After returning to reserve team action in February, he played a few more games before being loaned out to the Swedish Second Division side, Karlstad BK, where he will stay throughout the summer in order to boost his fitness in time for the new season.

| | | | APPEARANCES | | | | GOALS | | | |
|---|---|---|---|---|---|---|---|---|---|---|
| Clubs | Signing Date | Transfer Fee | Lge | FL Cup | FA Cup | Others | Lge | FL Cup | FA Cup | Others |
| Southampton* | 7.91 | - | | | | | | | | |

## HUGHES Leslie Mark

Born: Wrexham, 1 November 1963

Height: 5'8" Weight: 12.5

International Honours: W Sch, W Yth, W "U21"-5, W-50

**Position/Skill Factor:** Striker who is as strong as an ox, but skillful as well. Brings maximum pressure to bear in opponents' penalty areas, when tackling defenders, he makes chances for others as well as being a proficient goalscorer himself. A lovely volleyer of the ball.

**Career History:** Came to Manchester United as a 14-year-old, signing as an associated schoolboy in March 1978 and then, on leaving school, becoming an apprentice in June 1980. Turned pro and made his FL debut when coming on as a sub at Old Trafford against Southampton on 21 January 1984. Earlier in the season, however, he had been introduced to the Old Trafford faithful during a League Cup tie against Port Vale and he later played his first full game at Oxford United in the Fourth Round of the competition, marking the occasion with a goal. By the end of 1983-84 he was a regular front runner and his progress was recognised internationally when he was selected to play for Wales against England in May 1984. In a dream debut for his country, he scored the only goal of the game at his hometown ground, Wrexham. In 1984-85, his first full season, he was the club's leading scorer with 24 League goals and was prominent as United triumphed 1-0 in the FA Cup Final against Everton. Although finding goals harder to come by, the following season, he was still the subject of a £2.5 million bid from the Spanish giants, Barcelona, managed by Terry Venables, who eventually signed him to link up with Gary Lineker. However, while Lineker was feted for his goals, the Spanish fans didn't seem to appreciate the Welshman's ability to make space for other players with his unselfish running off the ball. His stay in Spain was less than successful and following a brief spell in Germany on loan with Bayern Munich he returned to Old Trafford in the 1988 close season. More than 46,000 fans welcomed him back for the game against Queens Park Rangers, but the season was generally a disappointing one for both him and United. However, there was consolation in 1989-90 when United beat Crystal Palace 1-0 in a replay to win the FA Cup Final, after the teams had drawn 3-3 in the first match. The six goal thriller had been a personal triumph, when he put United ahead on the hour and then equalised with just seven minutes of extra-time remaining. With that victory, United returned to European competition when the ban on English clubs was finally lifted. After rather nervy progress in the UEFA Cup against inferior opposition,

United reached the final in Rotterdam to face Hughes' former club, Barcelona, as marginal "underdogs". In fact, the "Reds" fully deserved their 2-1 victory and his goal, a tremendous shot on the run from a tight angle, clinched the victory. He is also credited by some sources with scoring the first goal, although he only touched Bruce's already goalbound header over the line. A UEFA Cup winners medal was consolation for defeat by Sheffield Wednesday in the League Cup Final three weeks earlier, as was being voted by his fellow professionals as the 1991 PFA "Player of the Year", an award he had previously won in 1989. During 1991-92 he helped United win the League Cup for the first time, but the club failed at the final hurdle to win the League Championship, having promised to do so all season. More than made up for the disappointment of losing out to Leeds United, when top scoring for the "Reds" in **1992-93**, a season that saw the League title return to Old Trafford for the first time since 1966-67. Seven times he either saved or won matches and as a player, who is always expected to score spectacular goals, he weighed in with a cracking volley at Crystal Palace for the first in a 2-0 win, which virtually sealed the Championship and took his United League tally to 100. Always consistent, missing only two games for United throughout the term and always guaranteed to give of his best, he also had another excellent international season as Wales moved towards the World Cup Finals.

| | | | APPEARANCES | | | | GOALS | | | |
|---|---|---|---|---|---|---|---|---|---|---|
| Clubs | Signing Date | Transfer Fee | Lge | FL Cup | FA Cup | Others | Lge | FL Cup | FA Cup | Others |
| Manchester United | 11.80 | - | 85+4 | 5+1 | 10 | 14+2 | 37 | 4 | 4 | 2 |
| Barcelona (Spain) | 7.86 | £2,500,000 | | | | | | | | |
| Bayern Munich (Germ) | 10.87 | Loan | | | | | | | | |
| Manchester United* | 7.88 | £1,500,000 | 182+4 | 24 | 22+1 | 18+1 | 62 | 7 | 7 | 5 |

# HUMPHRIES Mark

Born: Glasgow, 23 December 1971

Height: 5'11" Weight: 12.0

**Position/Skill Factor:** Left-back who can play in midfield. Tough tackling and defensively sound, with a good recovery rate, he is probably better suited as a full-back. However, he enjoys moving up on the overlap where his pace can again be seen to advantage.

**Career History**: Signed by Aberdeen from Cove Rangers towards the end of 1989-90, he made his Scottish League debut for the "Dons" at Dunfermline Athletic in April 1992 and played against St Johnstone four days later, before making way for the regular left-back, Dave Winnie. Made no headway at all in **1992-93** and with no first team games to his credit during the season, he was freed in order to give him an opportunity of finding a regular place elsewhere. In the event, rather surprisingly, he was snapped up by Leeds United during the summer to understudy Tony Dorigo in competition with young Kevin Sharp.

| | | | APPEARANCES | | | | GOALS | | | |
|---|---|---|---|---|---|---|---|---|---|---|
| Clubs | Signing Date | Transfer Fee | Lge | FL Cup | FA Cup | Others | Lge | FL Cup | FA Cup | Others |
| Aberdeen | 5.90 | - | 2 | | | | | | | |
| Leeds United* | 6.93 | - | | | | | | | | |

# HURLOCK Terence (Terry) Alan

Born: Hackney, 22 September 1958

Height: 5'9" Weight: 13.2

International Honours: E"B"

**Position/Skill Factor:** Very under-rated competitive midfield player who loves a tackle and doesn't lose many. He sees passes very quickly and is a good one-touch player.

**Career History:** Began as an associated schoolboy with West Ham United in October 1974, before signing as an apprentice for the club in April 1975. When his apprenticeship expired he was not offered a professional contract and went into non-League soccer. Was spotted by Third Division Brentford when playing for Leytonstone and Ilford of the then Isthmian League and after signing was pushed straight into the team, making his FL debut at Walsall on 30 August, 1980. Retained his place and proved extremely reliable over the next six seasons at Griffin Park, earning a reputation as the best midfield player in the Third Division. When he moved to promotion chasing Reading in February 1986, the transfer fee was a record for both clubs. Although Reading achieved their objective and Hurlock won a Third Division Championship medal, he never lived up to his reputation at Elm Park and after losing his place, within a year of joining the "Royals", he had signed for Second Division rivals, Millwall. The following season his decision to join Millwall was vindicated as he won a Second Division Championship medal and the "Lions" reached the top flight for the first time in their long history. When the club was relegated at the end of 1989-90, he surprisingly moved north of the border, signing for Scottish League side, Glasgow Rangers. In an outstanding first season at Ibrox, he only missed seven games and won Scottish Championship and Scottish League Cup winners medals. However, with Rangers seeking to reduce their contingent of English players, following the bizarre UEFA ruling on "foreigners", he was sold to Southampton for a profit soon into the 1991-92 season and was an integral part of the "Saints'" team which struggled successfully against relegation and enjoyed good runs in three cup competitions, reaching the Final of the Zenith Cup. Made 30 Premier League appearances in **1992-93**, during a season which saw him inter-changing the number four shirt with young Tommy Widdrington. Considering his role in the team is to stop the other side from playing, it surprised many to learn that when he was sent off with Willie Falconer during the match at Middlesbrough in January, it was his first red card in a "Saints'" shirt. Generally thought to be a harsh decision, it prompted Southampton to take the unusual step of filing an official complaint. The ban that followed, allowed Widdrington to enjoy a run in the side, before Hurlock was recalled for the game at Arsenal in March.

| | | | APPEARANCES | | | | GOALS | | | |
|---|---|---|---|---|---|---|---|---|---|---|
| Clubs | Signing Date | Transfer Fee | Lge | FL Cup | FA Cup | Others | Lge | FL Cup | FA Cup | Others |
| Brentford | 8.80 | £6,000 | 220 | 17 | 17 | 9 | 18 | 2 | 4 | |
| Reading | 2.86 | £82,000 | 29 | 3 | 1 | 2 | | | | |
| Millwall | 2.87 | £95,000 | 103+1 | 9 | 5 | 5 | 8 | 2 | | |
| Glasgow Rangers | 8.90 | £325,000 | 29 | 3+1 | 2 | | 2 | | | |
| Southampton* | 9.91 | £400,000 | 57+2 | 7 | 5 | 6 | | | | 1 |

## HURST Lee Jason

Born: Nuneaton, 21 September 1970

Height: 6'0"

Weight: 11.9

**Position/Skill Factor:** Left-back, who can also play on the wing, with good skill and plenty of pace. Has the ability to beat defenders and get in telling crosses.

**Career History:** Local talent who started with Coventry City as an associated schoolboy (October 1985) and graduated to trainee status in July 1987, before signing as a pro just under two years later. Made his FL debut at Wimbledon on 2 February 1991, following an injury to Paul Edwards and showed promise, playing three more games. Enjoyed a short run at left-back in the "Sky Blues'" team from late October to late December 1991, before giving way to Kenny Sansom, returning after injury. From an occasional left-back, he developed as a left sided midfield anchor man in **1992-93**, having an excellent season and making 35 Premier League appearances. It is alleged that the change of position came about when an old school friend mentioned to Bobby Gould, at a pre-season friendly against Moor Green, that Lee had always played there as a youngster and it was by far his best position. His best form was probably during the first half of the season, when he won "Man of the Match" awards in home games against Tottenham Hotspur, Leeds United and Nottingham Forest. Should score more goals this coming season, following the two brilliant strikes in the first Premier League campaign, when he should have the opportunity to drive forward more often. One of the few local players in the side, he is set to become a mainstay for years to come and much is expected of him.

| | | | APPEARANCES | | | | GOALS | | | |
|---|---|---|---|---|---|---|---|---|---|---|
| Clubs | Signing Date | Transfer Fee | Lge | FL Cup | FA Cup | Others | Lge | FL Cup | FA Cup | Others |
| Coventry City* | 5.89 | - | 46+3 | 3+1 | 1+1 | | 2 | | | |

## HUTCHISON Donald (Don)

Born: Gateshead, 9 May 1971

Height: 6'2"

Weight: 11.4

**Position/Skill Factor:** Midfield player who gets forward well and has the ability to score goals.

**Career History:** Made his FL debut for Hartlepool United, while still a trainee, at home to Scunthorpe United on 7 October 1989 and impressed, scoring twice in his first five League games. First came to the club as a trainee in June 1989 and within seven months of signing pro forms, Hartlepool being desperate for cash, had sold him to Liverpool after videos showing his abilities had been sent to all the leading clubs. With Liverpool's chronic injury crisis in 1991-92, he might have expected to make more progress, but had to wait until late March 1992, before making his Anfield debut as a sub at home to Notts County. Stepped out of the reserves for the **1992-93** Aston Villa away game in September, initially as a replacement for the injured Ian Rush, but was allowed to settle in and become a regular member of the first team squad, thereafter. Scored six goals in his first nine games as he looked to be an exciting young player, who was not afraid to strike the ball when in sight of the posts. Spectacular efforts from outside the area in that spell, included the winner against Apollon Limassol in the away leg of the European Cup Winners Cup, the only goal of the game at Anfield against Sheffield Wednesday and the first in a 2-2 draw at Manchester United. The only real black mark in his first season of regular football in the top flight, came in the penultimate game of the season at Oldham Athletic, when he became the sixth Liverpool player to be sent off in 1992-93. Must look to build on an excellent season.

| | | | APPEARANCES | | | | GOALS | | | |
|---|---|---|---|---|---|---|---|---|---|---|
| Clubs | Signing Date | Transfer Fee | Lge | FL Cup | FA Cup | Others | Lge | FL Cup | FA Cup | Others |
| Hartlepool United | 3.90 | - | 19+5 | 1+1 | 2 | 1 | 3 | | | |
| Liverpool* | 11.90 | £175,000 | 27+7 | 5 | 1+1 | 3+1 | 7 | 2 | | 1 |

## HYDE Graham

Born: Doncaster, 10 November 1970

Height: 5'7"

Weight: 11.7

**Position/Skill Factor:** Midfield player with vision and excellent passing ability. Has a good footballing brain and knows when to release the ball and when not.

**Career History:** Joined Sheffield Wednesday as a trainee in June 1987, having been an associated schoolboy since January 1985 and turned professional one year later. Had to wait over three years for his FL debut, finally turning out in midfield at Manchester City on 14 September 1991, in place of the injured John Sheridan and making further appearances later during the season. After being selected for the opening game of **1992-93**, he went on to consolidate his place as a vital first team fringe player, who never let the side down and an essential part of "Owls'" future plans. Although still viewed as a substitute, rather than a starter, he received valuable big match experience in UEFA Cup games and when coming off the bench for both the League and FA Cup Final matches, including the replay. Scored the winner at Nottingham Forest last term, his only goal for the club to date and with his tremendous endeavour and insatiable workrate, he could be on the verge of a regular first team place fairly shortly.

| | | | APPEARANCES | | | | GOALS | | | |
|---|---|---|---|---|---|---|---|---|---|---|
| Clubs | Signing Date | Transfer Fee | Lge | FL Cup | FA Cup | Others | Lge | FL Cup | FA Cup | Others |
| Sheffield Wednesday* | 5.88 | - | 23+10 | 3+1 | 1+5 | 4 | 1 | | | 1 |

## IMPEY Andrew (Andy) Rodney

Born: Hammersmith, 30 September 1971

Height: 5'8"

Weight: 10.6

International Honours: E "U21"-1

**Position/Skill Factor:** Winger with plenty of ability and two good feet. Very pacy, he will take on and beat defenders to get telling crosses in.

**Career History:** Started his football career as a trainee with Wimbledon in July 1988, but his contract was terminated after only one month and he joined Yeading of the Vauxhall League Division Two South. In 1989-90, Yeading not only won promotion to Division One, as Champions of the League, but they also reached Wembley for the Final of the FA Vase and defeated Bridlington after a replay, with Impey a key player in the team at the age of 18. Soon after the Final, he was signed up by Queens Park Rangers. Had to wait a little time for some first team action, but after three subs' appearances in the League and Zenith Cups in October 1991, he made his FL debut at Coventry City on 11 January 1992, deputising for the injured Andy Sinton. Later, in March, he returned to the team on the right-wing and held his place till the end of the season. A first team regular in **1992-93**, he only missed three matches and had a fine season, as his speed and skill left many left-backs for dead. While not scoring many himself, although he did get the winner at Coventry that put Rangers on top of the table at the beginning of the season, he provided good opportunities for others, especially Les Ferdinand. Played his 50th League game at Arsenal and is getting better and better, a fact highlighted when he won his first England under 21 cap against Turkey in November.

| | | | APPEARANCES | | | | GOALS | | | |
|---|---|---|---|---|---|---|---|---|---|---|
| Clubs | Signing Date | Transfer Fee | Lge | FL Cup | FA Cup | Others | Lge | FL Cup | FA Cup | Others |
| Q.P.R.* | 6.90 | 35,000 | 52+1 | 3+1 | 0+1 | 0+2 | 2 | | | 1 |

## INCE Paul Emerson Carlyle

Born: Ilford, 21 October 1967

Height: 5'11" Weight: 11. 6

International Honours: E Yth, E "U21"-2, E"B", E-9

**Position/Skill Factor:** A midfield bundle of energy, he is both destructive and constructive in breaking up attacks and setting counter-attacks in motion. Capable of scoring spectacular goals.

**Career History:** Came to West Ham United as a 14-year-old associated schoolboy in December 1981, graduating through the YTS scheme, before signing as a professional during the 1985 close season. Made his FL debut when coming on as a sub at Newcastle United on 30 November 1986 and kept his place for the next match, at Upton Park against Southampton. Although scoring in a 3-1 win, he found himself out of the side a few weeks later. Had a better season in 1987-88, but really came to the fore the following year, during West Ham's run to the League Cup Semi-Finals. He scored two spectacular goals in a 4-1 win over Liverpool and another in a 2-1 victory against Aston Villa. However, it ultimately proved a disappointing season for the club as they slipped into the Second Division. Having declared a wish to leave Upton Park, he finally signed for Manchester United after playing the opening game of the 1989-90 season for West Ham. Made his United debut in a 5-1 win against Millwall and then scored twice in a League Cup tie at Portsmouth for a great start to his new career. Unfortunately, he struggled to settle in after that, with the club showing indifferent League form. But United's run in the FA Cup offered respite and he won an FA Cup winners medal, following the eventual 1-0 replay win over Crystal Palace in 1990. Played 31 League games in 1990-91 as the team improved to sixth place in the First Division and was in the side that was beaten 1-0 by Sheffield Wednesday in the League Cup Final. But the highlight of the season was reserved for the penultimate game when he won a European Cup Winners Cup medal, following United's great 2-1 victory over Barcelona in Amsterdam. Played in most of the 1991-92 campaign, earning a League Cup winners medal, after United's 1-0 victory over Nottingham Forest, but missing out on the more coveted League Championship, after the "Reds" had been favourites all season. Another very consistent player for United in **1992-93**, missing only one Premier League game and winning his first ever Championship medal, as the club brought the title back to Old Trafford after a break of 26 years. Has also improved tremendously over the last year or so to become, not only one of the most influential members of the team, having matured and curbed his temper, but one of the finds of the season and is currently first choice for England. A firm favourite with the crowd, he runs United's midfield and has also added goalscoring to his repertoire, as he looks to shoot on sight. Scored in the last three League games and his cracking drive into the far corner at Crystal Palace, after a 30 yard run which took him past two defenders, all but sealed the Championship. The greatest compliment one can pay him is that he has made United fans forget about Bryan Robson.

| | | | APPEARANCES | | | | GOALS | | | |
|---|---|---|---|---|---|---|---|---|---|---|
| Clubs | Signing Date | Transfer Fee | Lge | FL Cup | FA Cup | Others | Lge | FL Cup | FA Cup | Others |
| West Ham United | 7.85 | – | 66+6 | 9 | 8+2 | 4 | 7 | 3 | 1 | 1 |
| Manchester United* | 9.89 | £1,250,000 | 128+3 | 18+1 | 13+1 | 14 | 22 | 3 | | |

## INGEBRIGSTEN Kaare

Born: Trondheim, Norway, 11 November 1965

Height: 5'9" Weight: 11.0

International Honours: Norwegian Int

**Position/Skill Factor:** Right-winger, or midfield player, with good skills and passing ability. Always looking to have a crack from anywhere near the box.

**Career History:** Signed by Peter Reid for Manchester City from Norwegian First Division club, Rosenborg Trondheim (who also provided Stig Bjornebye to Liverpool), in January 1993, having earlier trained with the club in November and come through a one month trial period. Had been a member of the Norwegian national team squad since his international debut in November 1990 and played in Norway's surprising 1-1 draw against England at Wembley in October 1992, a World Cup qualifying group match. He made his **1992-93** PL debut as a substitute at home to Blackburn Rovers on 30 January 1993 and his first full appearance at Norwich on 20 February 1993, but found the style and pace of football in England difficult to settle into. Towards the end of the season, he began to show a more positive approach and will have benefitted from the experience.

| | | | APPEARANCES | | | | GOALS | | | |
|---|---|---|---|---|---|---|---|---|---|---|
| Clubs | Signing Date | Transfer Fee | Lge | FL Cup | FA Cup | Others | Lge | FL Cup | FA Cup | Others |
| Manchester City* | 1.93 | £600,000 | 2+5 | | | | | | | |

## INGRAM Rae

Born: Manchester, 6 December 1974

Height: 5'11" Weight: 11.7

International Honours:

**Position/Skill Factor:** Left-back. An attacking player who is good on the overlap and an excellent crosser of the ball.

**Career History:** A product of Manchester boys, he first joined Manchester City as an assosiated schoolboy in January 1989, before coming to Maine Road as a trainee (August 1991). Played 11 times for the Central League side in **1992-93** and at the end of the season came on as a substituts during a first team friendly in Japan. Signed professional during the 1993 close season.

| Clubs | Signing Date | Transfer Fee | APPEARANCES Lge | FL Cup | FA Cup | Others | GOALS Lge | FL Cup | FA Cup | Others |
|---|---|---|---|---|---|---|---|---|---|---|
| Manchester City | 7.93 | - | | | | | | | | |

## **IRELAND Simon** Piers

Born: Barnstaple, 23 November 1971

Height: 5'11" Weight 11.12

International Honours: E Sch

**Position/Skill Factor:** Winger with two good feet and lots of pace, who goes past defenders to get quality crosses in to the front men.

**Career History:** Born in Devon, he signed on the dotted line for Huddersfield Town on leaving school and made his FL debut just eight months later, as a substitute, in a 3-1 win at home against Crewe Alexandra on 9 March 1991. Made three further full appearances in 1991-92, before going on one months loan to Fourth Division, Wrexham, without making much impact. Deputising for Iffy Onuora in October 1992, he starred in a remarkable **1992-93** League Cup-tie, when Huddersfield, then bottom of the Second Division, overturned a 2-0 deficit, with three goals in the space of ten minutes, to lead the Premier League leaders, Blackburn Rovers, 3-2 on their own ground, although the "Blues and Whites" eventually prevailed in extra-time. He had scored the "Terriers'" third goal when Rovers' 'keeper, Bobby Mimms, comically miskicked a clearance straight to his feet and did enough to impress Kenny Dalglish to sign him one month later, as an investment for the future, even though he had already lost his place in Huddersfield's first team. With Stuart Ripley and Jason Wilcox holding down the wing slots in Rovers line up, he was just starting to become involved with the first team, when he broke a foot and had to miss the last part of the season.

| Clubs | Signing Date | Transfer Fee | APPEARANCES Lge | FL Cup | FA Cup | Others | GOALS Lge | FL Cup | FA Cup | Others |
|---|---|---|---|---|---|---|---|---|---|---|
| Huddersfield Town | 7.90 | - | 10+9 | 1 | 0+1 | 1+1 | | 1 | | |
| Wrexham | 3.92 | Loan | 2+3 | | | | | | | |
| Blackburn Rovers* | 11.92 | £200,000 | 0+1 | | | | | | | |

## **IRVING Richard** James

Born: Halifax,
10 September 1975

Height: 5'7"

Weight: 10.6

International Honours:
E Sch, E Yth

**Position/Skill Factor:** A striker who is very quick and confident on the ball and can twist and turn around the box to unsettle defences.

**Career History:** Another member of Manchester United's successful youth team to turn professional, he first came to Old Trafford as an associated schoolboy in September 1990. He had earlier won five England schoolboy international caps and went on to collect another six, before joining the staff as a trainee July 1992, after leaving school. Not part of United's first team squad in **1992-93,** playing mainly with the "B" and youth sides, he is certain to move up during this coming season.

| Clubs | Signing Date | Transfer Fee | APPEARANCES Lge | FL Cup | FA Cup | Others | GOALS Lge | FL Cup | FA Cup | Others |
|---|---|---|---|---|---|---|---|---|---|---|
| Manchester United* | 10.92 | - | | | | | | | | |

## **IRWIN Dennis** Joseph

Born: Cork, 31 October 1965

Height: 5'7" Weight: 9.7

International Honours: IR Sch, IR Yth,
IR "U21"-3, IR-20

**Position/Skill Factor:** Full-back who can play either side and loves to get forward. A lovely striker of the ball, he takes most of the right sided corners and free-kicks around the penalty area.

**Career History:** Came to Leeds United from his native Ireland to sign as an apprentice in March 1982 and three months after turning pro, he made his FL debut at Elland Road against Fulham on 21 January 1984. The following season he missed only one League game, but after starting out as a regular in 1985-86, he lost his place to Neil Aspin and at the end of the season was amazingly given a free transfer. Was quickly snapped up by Second Division Oldham Athletic, replacing Willie Donachie in the number two shirt for the opening match of 1986-87 and playing in all but one game during a season that saw the club only miss out on promotion at the Play-Off stage. Stayed four years with the "Latics", the highlights coming in 1989-90, his last season at Boundary Park. Oldham reached the League Cup Final, going down 1-0 to Nottingham Forest and were involved in two thrilling FA Cup Semi-Finals against Manchester United, before losing out to a Mark Robins goal in extra-time. He so impressed Alex Ferguson, the United manager, that during the 1990 close season he moved to Old Trafford in exchange for a large fee. Missed very few matches in 1990-91 and although a member of the side that lost 1-0 to Sheffield Wednesday in the League Cup Final, that experience was well and truly pushed into the background a few weeks later when United beat Barcelona 2-1 to win the European Cup Winners Cup. Certainly a season to remember, for he also won his first full cap for the Republic when playing in the 1-0 victory over Morocco in Dublin on 12 September 1990 and has remained an automatic choice since. Switched to left-back in 1991-92, he played a full part in United's tantalising season, missing only seven games through injury during the campaign and won a League Cup medal to make up for the disappointments of 1990 and 1991. An automatic choice for the Republic of Ireland and Manchester United in **1992-93**, he had an excellent season with both. As with all Championship winning sides, consistency is a major feature and he was no exception to the rule, missing just two games, while winning a Championship medal, as the trophy returned to Old Trafford after a 26 year gap. As well as serving up several brilliant free-kicks, he scored some vital goals, none more so than the curling 20 yarder that gave United all three points at Coventry City and a tremendous drive from the edge of the box at Old Trafford, which equalised an Ipswich Town goal scored just a minute earlier. And according to many good judges, he is the most improved left-back in the country today, having been long underrated by the vast majority, who fail to notice good work when done quietly and efficiently.

| | | | APPEARANCES | | | | GOALS | | | |
|---|---|---|---|---|---|---|---|---|---|---|
| Clubs | Signing Date | Transfer Fee | Lge | FL Cup | FA Cup | Others | Lge | FL Cup | FA Cup | Others |
| Leeds United | 11.83 | - | 72 | 5 | 3 | 2 | 1 | | | |
| Oldham Athletic | 5.86 | - | 166+1 | 19 | 13 | 5 | 4 | 3 | | |
| Manchester United* | 6.90 | £625,000 | 110+2 | 17+1 | 9 | 12 | 9 | | | |

## IZZET Mustafa Kemel

Born: Hackney, 31 October 1974

Height: 5'10" Weight: 11.0

**Position/Skill Factor:** All-action midfielder who likes a tackle, but is also very capable in his use of the ball.

**Career History:** A professional signing for Chelsea during the 1993 close season, he first came to Stamford Bridge as an associated schoolboy in November 1989, before progressing through the trainee ranks (August 1991). He showed a great deal of determination to succeed in **1992-93**, a facet of his make-up that wasn't entirely lost on the Chelsea management when they offered him a three year contract and he will be looking for an early opportunity to impress the new manager, Glenn Hoddle.

| | | | APPEARANCES | | | | GOALS | | | |
|---|---|---|---|---|---|---|---|---|---|---|
| Clubs | Signing Date | Transfer Fee | Lge | FL Cup | FA Cup | Others | Lge | FL Cup | FA Cup | Others |
| Chelsea* | 5.91 | - | | | | | | | | |

## JACKSON Matthew Alan

Born: Leeds, 19 October 1971

Height: 6'1"

Weight: 12.12

International Honours: E Sch, E "U21"-9

**Position/Skill Factor:** Right-back who can play at centre-back. Oozing class, he is a lovely striker of the ball. Very confident when in possession.

**Career History:** Played for Luton Town as a junior, signing associated schoolboy forms in November 1986, before turning professional and although making an appearance for the "Hatters" in a Zenith Data Cup match, he was loaned out to Preston North End where he made his FL debut at Deepdale when coming on as a sub against Crewe Alexandra on 30 March 1991. Made his Luton debut as a sub at Arsenal on 27 August 1991 and his first full League game at right-back at home to Southampton on 4 September. After only 11 first team games for Luton, he was transferred to Everton for a massive fee, considering his limited experience. Settled in easily at Goodison Park in the right-back position and held his place to the end of the season, being called into the England Under 21 squad and making four appearances. Made only one appearance in **1992-93**, before being struck by injury and didn't return to full fitness until the New Year. He recovered, to win back his full-back spot and even switched to central defence as he once again demonstrated his amazing versatility for one so young. In maintaining his consistency level, he struck up a great partnership with Gary Ablett and barring injury he will be an integral part of the "Toffees'" campaign this coming season.

| | | | APPEARANCES | | | | GOALS | | | |
|---|---|---|---|---|---|---|---|---|---|---|
| Clubs | Signing Date | Transfer Fee | Lge | FL Cup | FA Cup | Others | Lge | FL Cup | FA Cup | Others |
| Luton Town | 7.90 | - | 7+2 | 2 | | 0+1 | | | | |
| Preston North End | 3.91 | Loan | 3+1 | | | 1 | | | | |
| Everton* | 10.91 | £600,000 | 55+2 | 3 | 4 | 1 | 4 | | | |

## JAMES David Benjamin

Born: Welwyn Garden City, 1 August 1970

Height: 6'4" Weight: 14.7

International Honours: E "U21"-10

**Position/Skill Factor:** Tall young goalkeeper who will continue to improve with experience. Has good positional sense and is very agile for such a big man.

**Career History:** A young England Under 21 international goalkeeper who first hit the headlines last season when surrounded by much transfer speculation, he initially joined Watford as an associated schoolboy in November 1984, before graduating from trainee status in July 1986 to the professional ranks during the summer of 1988. He spent two years in the shadow of Tony Cotton, but when the latter moved to Manchester City in the 1990 close season, he got the break that he had been looking for. Made his FL debut at home to Millwall on 25 August 1990 and at the end of 1990-91, except for one Zenith Cup game, he was ever present. His form was so outstanding that he was soon called up to the England Under 21 squad and was regular first choice throughout the season. During 1991-92 he turned out in all but three FL games, conceding a mere 42 goals in 43 appearances and playing a large part in Watford's recovery from a relegation position to mid-table security. His name was constantly linked with Liverpool and other First Division clubs throughout the season and his eventual departure to Anfield in the 1992 close season was hardly unexpected. Had a disappointing **1992-93**, losing his place three times and showing a great deal of uncertainty in dealing with crosses and corners. Made his Premier League start for Liverpool on the opening day of the season at Nottingham Forest, putting on a good display in a 1-0 defeat, but his Anfield debut, a 2-1 defeat of Sheffield United, was inauspicious to say the least, although he did ultimately manage to protect the lead. After playing in the first 11 games, he gave way to a returning Bruce Grobbelaar and made only one more first team appearance before the following January. Reclaimed his place and seemed to have established himself as first choice, when putting a run of 19 games together, but at Norwich a moment of sheer madness proved most costly. After collecting a corner, he mindlessly kicked John Polston and was shown the red card, having already received a yellow for up-ending Chris Sutton outside his area in the first half. Norwich duly obliged with the only goal of the game from the spot, when David Phillips beat substitute, Mike Hooper. Another disastrous display a few days later at Oldham Athletic, prompted the recall of Grobbelaar for the final game of the season. Still has a lot to prove in order to justify Liverpool's investment in him and will probably start 1993-94 behind Grobbelaar.

| | | | APPEARANCES | | | | GOALS | | | |
|---|---|---|---|---|---|---|---|---|---|---|
| Clubs | Signing Date | Transfer Fee | Lge | FL Cup | FA Cup | Others | Lge | FL Cup | FA Cup | Others |
| Watford | 7.88 | – | 89 | 6 | 2 | 1 | | | | |
| Liverpool* | 6.92 | £1,000,000 | 29 | 1 | | 1 | | | | |

# JEMSON Nigel Bradley

Born: Preston, 10 August 1969

Height: 5'10" Weight: 11.10

International Honours: E "U21"-1

**Position/Skill Factor:** Striker with a good first touch, who passes and moves well, he will always create scoring chances. Very good at playing one-twos on the edge of the penalty area.

**Career History:** Started out with his local team Preston North End as an associated schoolboy in August 1984, before signing on as a trainee on leaving school in August 1986. And he was still only a trainee when he made his FL debut at Aldershot on 3 May 1986. Played in just four games the following season and scored in three of them, but didn't really break into the side until 1987-88, his first year as a full professional. Showing a precocious talent for one so young, he was signed by Nottingham Forest, but before making an appearance for the club, he was loaned out to Bolton Wanderers and back to Preston in order to gain more experience. After nearly two years at the City Ground he finally made his Forest debut on Boxing Day, 1989, at Luton Town, replacing Lee Chapman who had moved on to Leeds United and later in the season scored the only goal of the game against Oldham Athletic in the League Cup Final at Wembley. Made a good start to the 1990-91 season, playing in the first 23 matches, but lost his way after being sidelined through injury and was not selected for the FA Cup Final side that lost 2-1 to Tottenham Hotspur, even though he had earlier scored a hat-trick in the 3-1 Fifth Round replay victory over Southampton. With the signing of Teddy Sheringham in the summer of 1991, his future with Forest seemed bleak and although starting the season wide on the left, he was replaced by another new player, Kingsley Black and transferred shortly afterwards to Sheffield Wednesday. Struggled to make an impact at Hillsborough, despite scoring a brace of goals against Manchester United, when

coming on as substitute in an early game for Wednesday and after January played little part in "Owls'" impressive season. Made more appearances as a substitute, than when starting a match in **1992-93** and having to carry a few niggling injuries hardly helped. Unable to add to his Wednesday goal tally last season, although he scored eight in 24 reserve matches it would be no surprise if he tried to resurrect his flagging career somewhere else.

| | | | APPEARANCES | | | | GOALS | | | |
|---|---|---|---|---|---|---|---|---|---|---|
| Clubs | Signing Date | Transfer Fee | Lge | FL Cup | FA Cup | Others | Lge | FL Cup | FA Cup | Others |
| Preston North End | 7.87 | – | 28+4 | | 2 | 5+1 | 8 | | 1 | 5 |
| Nottingham Forest | 3.88 | £150,000 | 45+2 | 9 | 3+1 | 1 | 13 | 4 | 3 | |
| Bolton Wanderers | 12.88 | Loan | 4+1 | | | | | | | |
| Preston North End | 3.89 | Loan | 6+3 | | | 2 | 2 | | | 1 |
| Sheffield Wednesday* | 9.91 | £800,000 | 16+17 | 1+3 | 1+2 | 2+2 | 4 | | | 1 |

## JENKINSON Leigh

Born: Thorne, 9 July 1969

Height: 6'0" Weight: 12.5

**Position/Skill Factor:** Left-winger with a good turn of pace, that takes him past defenders to provide excellent crosses for the forward players.

**Career History:** First came to Hull City as an associated schoolboy (December 1984), before signing trainee forms on leaving school in July 1986 and graduating to the club's professional ranks during the 1987 close season. His FL debut came in the big Yorkshire clash at home to Sheffield United on 27 February 1988 and following on from that, he scored City's only goal in his next full match, a 4-1 home defeat at the hands of Swindon Town. For the next three seasons he was a useful squad member, rather than a regular performer, appearing more often as a substitute than as first choice. Indeed, he nearly moved to Rotherham in 1990, following a short loan period, but the two clubs could not agree on a transfer fee. Happily for both club and player, he started to realise his early potential in 1991-92, when he held down a regular place on the left-wing and was joint top scorer, albeit with only eight FL goals. Some of those goals were crucial in the "Tigers'" fight against relegation to the basement division. Made a decent start in **1992-93**, before injuries forced him out of seven games and was the subject of a September transfer enquiry by Bobby Gould of Coventry City. Quoted £450,000, Gould bided his time and after going back with a more realistic offer, shortly before the transfer deadline in March, he finally got his man. Jenkinson had earlier challenged John Williams in the final of Rumbelows sprint challenge and now they were on the same side and with Peter Ndlovu, City had three of the fastest men in football on their books. Made a rather ordinary debut at Highfield Road against Arsenal, looking less than match fit and after picking up a slight injury, he came off the bench three times, before having a fine full 90 minutes during the last game of the season, at home to Leeds United. With great things expected of him this season, he looks to improve considerably during the summer training regime.

| | | | APPEARANCES | | | | GOALS | | | |
|---|---|---|---|---|---|---|---|---|---|---|
| Clubs | Signing Date | Transfer Fee | Lge | FL Cup | FA Cup | Others | Lge | FL Cup | FA Cup | Others |
| Hull City | 6.87 | – | 95+35 | 7+2 | 6 | 9+2 | 13 | 1 | | 1 |
| Rotherham United | 9.90 | Loan | 5+2 | | | | | | | |
| Coventry City* | 3.93 | £300,000 | 2+3 | | | | | | | |

## JENSEN John

Born: Copenhagen, Denmark, 3 May 1965

Height: 5'8" Weight: 12.7

International Honours: Danish Int

**Position/Skill Factor:** Central midfielder. A strong and willing worker, with great stamina, who keeps his passing simple and enjoys the tackling game.

**Career History:** One of the stars of Denmark's stunning and wholly unexpected triumph in the European Championship Finals of 1992 held in Sweden, he scored the opening goal in the Final against Germany with a 25 yard drive which formed the springboard for their improbable 2-0 victory. One month later he was signed by Arsenal manager, George Graham, ostensibly as a replacement for David Rocastle, who was sold to Leeds during the summer. Made his PL debut in the opening match of the **1992-93** season at Highbury against Norwich City on 15 August 1992, but struggled to make any sort of impression in the English game. A combination of coming to terms with the frenetic pace and playing without a break for 18 months, were major factors. Dropped in the latter part of the season, he missed the League Cup Final, but returned for the FA Cup Final games against Sheffield Wednesday. Arguably his best performance in an Arsenal shirt came in those games, when he nulified the threat of Chris Waddle, on his way to a winners medal, following the "Gunners'" 2-1 victory in the Wembley replay.

| | | | APPEARANCES | | | | GOALS | | | |
|---|---|---|---|---|---|---|---|---|---|---|
| Clubs | Signing Date | Transfer Fee | Lge | FL Cup | FA Cup | Others | Lge | FL Cup | FA Cup | Others |
| Arsenal* | 8.92 | £1,100,000 | 29+3 | 3 | 4 | | | | | |

# JOBSON Richard Ian

Born: Holderness, 9 May 1963

Height: 6'1"

Weight: 12.2

International Honours: E"B"

**Position/Skill Factor:** Footballing central defender who has the skill of a midfielder. Has some delightful touches and passes the ball well. Reads situations and likes to bring the ball out of defence, rather than just clear his lines.

**Career History:** Came out of non-League football with Burton Albion to sign for Watford during 1982-83 and made his FL debut at home to Ipswich Town on 18 December 1982, before playing a further 13 League games as the club gained promotion to the First Division. The following season he made a good start, but soon lost his place to Les Taylor and on getting back to fitness after recovering from a spell out injured, he was transferred to promotion chasing Hull City. Played just six matches that season as the club were promoted to the Second Division in third place, but soon settled into the side first at right-back and later in central defence as one of the more consistent players and was ever present in 1987-88 and 1988-89, while missing only one game in 1989-90. At the beginning of 1990-91, Oldham Athletic, who were aiming to reach Division One after an absence of nearly 70 years, moved quickly for him when Andy Holden was injured in the second game of the season. Apart from one match on the subs' bench, he didn't miss a game and with the club never out of the top three all season, was good value for his Second Division Championship medal. Injured in the third match of the "Latics'" First Division campaign, he returned one month later and remained in the side for the rest of the campaign. Had another outstanding season in **1992-93**, missing only two games due to a broken nose and was usually the first name on Joe Royle's teamsheet. Rarely beaten in the air and brilliant on the ground, he was the obstacle that opposing attackers had to overcome and for many, he was Oldham's "Player of the Season". Always a danger at set plays, he scored twice, both in the Premier League and both clinical headers, resulting in a 3-3 draw at Manchester City and the only goal of the game at home to Everton. Included in numerous England squads without getting the nod for a full cap, although playing twice for the "B" side in 1991-92, he seems destined to miss the games' highest honours.

| | | | APPEARANCES | | | | GOALS | | | |
|---|---|---|---|---|---|---|---|---|---|---|
| Clubs | Signing Date | Transfer Fee | Lge | FL Cup | FA Cup | Others | Lge | FL Cup | FA Cup | Others |
| Watford | 11.82 | £22,000 | 26+2 | 2 | 0+1 | 5+1 | 4 | | | |
| Hull City | 2.85 | £40,000 | 219+2 | 12 | 13 | 9 | 17 | | 1 | |
| Oldham Athletic* | 8.90 | £460,000 | 119+1 | 10 | 6 | 2 | 5 | 1 | | |

# JOHNSEN Erland

Born: Fredrikstad, Norway, 5 April 1967

Height: 6'0" Weight: 12.10

International Honours: Norwegian Int

**Position/Skill Factor:** Very composed centre-back who never looks to be in a hurry. Useful in the air, he is a confident passer of the ball out of defence.

**Career History:** Signed by Chelsea from Bayern Munich in 1989-90, after winning a Bundesliga Championship medal, he soon established himself in the side when replacing David Lee and making 18 League appearances, following his FL debut at Queens Park Rangers on 9 December 1989. However, on recovering from injuries received at the beginning of the 1990-91 season, he was unable to win back his place in the side after Ken Monkou and young Jason Cundy had struck up such a good understanding at the heart of the Chelsea defence. His first team opportunities were further limited by the signing of Paul Elliott and he made only seven first team appearances in 1991-92. Out of favour throughout **1992-93**, until caretaker manager, Dave Webb, arrived, he was brought back into the squad following the 2-0 defeat at Blackburn Rovers and proved solid and reliable in the old fashioned centre-half mould, while playing in the last 12 games of the season.

| | | | APPEARANCES | | | | GOALS | | | |
|---|---|---|---|---|---|---|---|---|---|---|
| Clubs | Signing Date | Transfer Fee | Lge | FL Cup | FA Cup | Others | Lge | FL Cup | FA Cup | Others |
| Chelsea* | 12.89 | £306,000 | 43+1 | | 4 | 4 | | | | |

# JOHNSON Andrew James

Born: Bristol, 2 May 1974

Height: 6'0" Weight: 12.0

International Honours: E Yth

**Position/Skill Factor:** Very quick defender, who can play in midfield, he loves to bring the ball out of defence and link up with the attack. Is a good passer.

**Career History:** Joined Norwich City as a trainee in July 1990, turning professional in March 1992. One month later, he made his FL debut at Sheffield Wednesday on 20 April 1992 and was promising enough to be selected for the final game of the season against Leeds United. Won his first England youth cap against Egypt, where he impressed on the ball, but had to sit on the bench throughout the **1992-93** World Youth Cup tournament in Australia. On coming home, he followed up an earlier substitute appearance, when he started in the last game of the season at Middlesbrough. He scored City's third in a 3-3 draw with a fine right foot volley, a goal that ultimately clinched third place for the club in the new Premier League. Has the same birthday as Gary Megson, although 15 years younger and appears to have all the attributes required to make it to the top of his profession.

| | | | APPEARANCES | | | | GOALS | | | |
|---|---|---|---|---|---|---|---|---|---|---|
| Clubs | Signing Date | Transfer Fee | Lge | FL Cup | FA Cup | Others | Lge | FL Cup | FA Cup | Others |
| Norwich City* | 3.92 | – | 3+1 | | | | 1 | | | |

## JOHNSON David Alan

Born: Dinnington, 29 October 1970

Height: 6'2" Weight: 13.8

**Position/Skill Factor:** Strong running striker with a good left foot, he also runs well off the ball.

**Career History:** From a mining village east of Sheffield, he first joined Wednesday as an associated schoolboy in November 1985, graduating to trainee in June 1987 and to full professional status two years later. After waiting patiently in the reserves for over two years for a first team opportunity, he made his FL debut whilst on loan to Third Division Hartlepool United on 2 October 1991 at Darlington. Impressed sufficiently during his two month loan to be "blooded" by Wednesday soon after his return, away to Aston Villa in January 1992, making occasional appearances thereafter. Somehow, he was unable to build on his form of the previous season, possibly due to a mix of injuries and fierce competition and was loaned out for a second spell with Hartlepool United during **1992-93**. Back at Hillsborough though, it was a diet of reserve team football, with 24 games for the "stiffs", but his resolve to become a regular has not been broken and he will give it another shot in 1993-94.

| | | | APPEARANCES | | | | GOALS | | | |
|---|---|---|---|---|---|---|---|---|---|---|
| Clubs | Signing Date | Transfer Fee | Lge | FL Cup | FA Cup | Others | Lge | FL Cup | FA Cup | Others |
| Sheffield Wednesday* | 7.89 | - | 5+1 | | | | | | | |
| Hartlepool United | 10.91 | Loan | 7 | | 2 | | 2 | | 1 | |
| Hartlepool United | 11.92 | Loan | 3 | | | 2 | | | | 1 |

## JOHNSON Gavin

Born: Eye, 10 October 1970

Height: 6'0"

Weight: 11.1

**Position/Skill Factor:** Hard working midfielder who can fill any position down the left hand side of the field. With a nice left foot and good skill, he creates chances for others.

**Career History:** Locally born and bred player who first came to Ipswich Town as an associated schoolboy in March 1985, before graduating to trainee status in July 1987. Was given his chance in 1988-89, making his FL debut at Portman Road in the number three shirt against Barnsley on 21 February 1989, just a few days after signing professional. Played only sporadically over the next two seasons, but performed well when required. Finally came to the fore in 1991-92, appearing in most of the games during Ipswich's Second Division Championship campaign. Originally a central defender, where his chances were limited by Brian Gayle and David Linighan, he was switched to the left side of midfield and it was his goals in the last two games of the season which clinched the Championship for Ipswich. Made a great start to the **1992-93** season, when he scored the club's first goal in the new Premier League with a rasping 30 yard shot high into the roof of the Aston Villa net, a strike, incidentally, which was named by the supporters' club, the following May, as their "Goal of the Season". Only missed two games in 1992-93, but was unfortunate to pick up a knee injury during the final match against Nottingham Forest, when his foot got caught in a hole on the Portman Road pitch and necessitated an operation during the summer. Likely to miss the beginning of the new season.

| | | | APPEARANCES | | | | GOALS | | | |
|---|---|---|---|---|---|---|---|---|---|---|
| Clubs | Signing Date | Transfer Fee | Lge | FL Cup | FA Cup | Others | Lge | FL Cup | FA Cup | Others |
| Ipswich Town* | 3.89 | - | 84+15 | 8+1 | 9 | 3+1 | 10 | 2 | 1 | 1 |

## JOHNSTON Maurice (Mo)

Born: Glasgow, 30 April 1963

Height: 5'9" Weight: 10.6

International Honours: S "U21"-3, S-38

**Position/Skill Factor:** A striker with good control who has the ability to turn either way to get his shots in. Always scores goals and is never far away when crosses come in.

**Career History:** Started out with junior side, Milton Battlefield, before being snapped up by Scottish First Division team, Partick Thistle, in July 1980 and scoring 41 goals from 85 games in just over three years. He proved to be an inspired signing by Watford, following the departure of their leading marksman, Luther Blissett, to AC Milan. Prior to him joining Watford, the club had only won two matches out of 15 played. Made his FL debut at Manchester United on 19 November 1983 and quickly made his mark on the scoresheet in his third game when he scored a hat-trick against Wolverhampton Wanderers at Molineux in only eight minutes. At the end of the League programme his tally was 20 goals from 29 matches and the team had surged up the table to 11th place and had reached the FA Cup Final for the first time in the club's history. Although there was to be no fairy tale ending for Watford as they lost 2-0 against Everton, Mo had already had the satisfaction of winning his first full cap for Scotland, when coming on against Wales on 28 February 1984. However, he was unable to settle in the south and during the summer requested a transfer. After playing in Watford's first nine League games in 1984-85, he had his wishes granted when allowed to return home with Glasgow Celtic. Scored 52 goals in 99 games and winning Scottish Premier League (1985-86) and Scottish Cup (1985) medals in three seasons at Celtic, before signing for the French club, Nantes. Returning to Britain two years later, he made headline news when becoming the first Catholic player to play for Glasgow Rangers, after turning down a move to Celtic. In two seasons at Ibrox, he played 65 League games, while scoring 26 goals and won two Scottish Cup medals and a Scottish Premier League Championship medal in 1989-90. From 1985 to 1990, he was a regular selection for Scotland and his six goals from eight games in the qualifying group were a major factor in Scotland reaching the 1990 World Cup Finals in Italy. Sadly, an embarrassing defeat by Costa Rica in their first game, effectively put an end to any further progress and some unfavourable post match publicity prompted Johnston to announce his premature retirement from international football. After one year out, however, he was persuaded to revoke his decision. In another surprising twist to his career, he joined Everton in November 1991. It seemed like a shrewd move to boost the "Toffees'" declining fortunes, but sadly he was unable to provide any spark to the team who finished a disappointing 12th. It was hoped that **1992-93** would see a change of fortune for him after last term's disappointments, but the pre-season signing of Paul Rideout meant that he had limited chances to prove himself. Apart from three early appearances and three more in December, he was out of favour with the management and with time not on his side, a transfer could be an option that he would seriously consider.

| | | | APPEARANCES | | | | GOALS | | | |
|---|---|---|---|---|---|---|---|---|---|---|
| Clubs | Signing Date | Transfer Fee | Lge | FL Cup | FA Cup | Others | Lge | FL Cup | FA Cup | Others |
| Partick Thistle | 7.80 | - | 83+2 | 11+1 | 9 | | 40 | 6 | 7 | |
| Watford | 11.83 | £200,000 | 37+1 | 1 | 7 | | 23 | | 4 | |
| Glasgow Celtic | 11.84 | £400,000 | 97+2 | 8 | 14 | 6 | 52 | 9 | 6 | 4 |
| Nantes (France) | 6.87 | £1,000,000 | | | | | | | | |
| Glasgow Rangers | 7.89 | £1,500,000 | 75+1 | 13 | 4+1 | 6 | 31 | 9 | 1 | 5 |
| Everton* | 11.91 | £1,500,000 | 28+6 | 2+1 | 1 | 1 | 10 | | | |

## JONES Philip Lee

Born: Wrexham, 29 May 1973

Height: 5'8" Weight: 9.7

International Honours: W Yth, W "U21"-4

**Position/Skill Factor:** Very quick striker with a good goal scoring record who will improve greatly with further experience.

**Career History:** Very few 17-year-olds make their first team debut watched by a television audience of millions, but this is what happened to Lee who, due to the UEFA "foreigners" rule, was selected by Wrexham manager Brian Flynn for a second-leg European Cup Winners Cup tie at home to Manchester United on 7 November 1990. What is more, apparently unabashed by the enormity of the occasion, he embarrassed the United defence at least twice with his forward runs. Having earlier signed for the club in July 1990, he made his FL debut two days later as a sub at Northampton Town on 9 November 1990. By the end of the 1990-91 season, he had almost become a regular in the side and had shown tremendous promise of things to come, signing professional forms in the summer. Started the 1991-92 season in Wrexham's first team, but lost his place in September when goals eluded him. He didn't take part in the club's historic FA Cup Third Round victory over League Champions, Arsenal, but in the Fourth Round tie against West Ham at Upton Park, he came on as substitute and in the 80th minute and Wrexham's amazing second equaliser in a 2-2 draw. Sadly, there were to be no more heroics in the replay, but Lee won his place back and shortly after a scoring burst of six goals in six games, he was signed by Liverpool manager Graham Souness for £300,000 with an equivalent amount to follow if he makes the grade. Made a belated end of September start at Liverpool in **1992-93**, having only just recovered from an achilles tendon operation and to allow him a full recovery, he was nursed along gently in the reserve side throughout the season. Remained a regular selection for the Welsh under 21 side and should be raring to go in 1993-94.

| | | | APPEARANCES | | | | GOALS | | | |
|---|---|---|---|---|---|---|---|---|---|---|
| Clubs | Signing Date | Transfer Fee | Lge | FL Cup | FA Cup | Others | Lge | FL Cup | FA Cup | Others |
| Wrexham | 7.91 | - | 24+15 | 2 | 1+2 | 4+1 | 9 | | 1 | 2 |
| Liverpool* | 3.92 | £300,000 | | | | | | | | |

## JONES Robert (Rob) Marc

Born: Wrexham, 5 November 1971

Height: 5'11" Weight: 11.0

International Honours: W Sch, E Yth, E "U21"-2, E-1

**Position/Skill Factor:** He is the complete full-back, decisive in the tackle and winning balls cleanly without fouling. His passing is quick and accurate over both short and long distances and he is not afraid to race down the wing like a traditional winger and cross decisively. He can also play on either flank. In addition to his natural ability his coolness and composure under pressure is astonishing in one so young.

**Career History:** The grandson of Billy Jones who played left-half for Liverpool when they lost 2-0 to Arsenal in the 1950 FA Cup Final, he started as an associated schoolboy with Crewe Alexandra in September 1987 and actually made his FL debut at Gresty Road against Darlington on 9 April 1988, before signing as a trainee in July 1988. The following season, he played 12 times as the club gained promotion to the Third Division in third place, but it wasn't until 1990-91 that he regularly began to hold down the right-back spot and although the club were relegated, his performances were often outstanding. In September 1991, he was simply one of a number of promising youngsters with Crewe. By the end of the season he was undisputed first choice right-back for Liverpool with a FA Cup Winners medal and his first cap for England under his belt and was being hailed as England's future right-back for the next generation — a "fairy tale" almost without parallel in the modern game. When Graham Souness signed him in early October, it was surely intended to bring him on slowly. Instead, because of Liverpool's injury crisis, he was introduced to the first team immediately, in traditionally the toughest game of the season, away to Manchester United at Old Trafford and faced by United's teenage prodigy Ryan Giggs. Rob passed his initial test with flying colours, not putting a foot wrong and except for injuries and cup disqualifications, remained part of the Liverpool team for the rest of the season. In February, England manager Graham Taylor took an enormous gamble by selecting him for the friendly game with France, but as ever he rose to the occasion. Unafraid to go forward, he had a goal chance after only ten minutes, but blasted wide. Otherwise his performance in England's 2-0 victory was impeccable, showing touches and a composure worthy of a veteran. Because of injury and then Liverpool's FA Cup commitments, he was not selected for England's squad for the European Championship Finals in Sweden. After a truly outstanding first season for the "Reds", **1992-93** was an anti-climax. Picked up a virus on Liverpool's pre-season tour, which caused him to miss the opening game of 1992-93 and then after appearing in just six matches, the shin splints repair prevented him from playing in all but three of the next 16 games. Made his comeback at Queens Park Rangers and produced a timely clearance off the line to keep Liverpool ahead, something he repeated at Sheffield Wednesday in the second half of the season. After returning to full fitness, he was switched to left-back in place of the injured David Burrows and only recaptured his previous season's form when the return of the latter allowed him to revert to his natural right-back slot. Made his debut for the England under 21's after Christmas and must still be regarded as a future international player.

| | | | APPEARANCES | | | | GOALS | | | |
|---|---|---|---|---|---|---|---|---|---|---|
| Clubs | Signing Date | Transfer Fee | Lge | FL Cup | FA Cup | Others | Lge | FL Cup | FA Cup | Others |
| Crewe Alexandra | 12.88 | - | 59+16 | 9 | 0+3 | 3 | 2 | | | |
| Liverpool* | 10.91 | £300,000 | 58 | 2+1 | 11 | 4 | | | | |

## JONES Ryan Anthony

Born: Sheffield, 23 July 1973

Height: 6'1¼" Weight: 12.5

**Position/Skill Factor:** At present playing either in midfield or at left-back, he is very strong and athletic and has a sweet left foot.

**Career History:** A local discovery, he first joined Sheffield Wednesday as an associated schoolboy in September 1987. Signed as a trainee in July 1989, on leaving school and progressed to the professional ranks in the 1991 close season. Came on in leaps and bounds from being an occasional member of the reserves in 1991-92, to becoming a regular in the first team squad, towards the end of **1992-93**. Having signed a two year contract during the 1992 close season, he made his PL debut at Coventry City on 3 March 1993 and impressed in eight more games, before the campaign ended. A player who is rated very highly by the club and one who should continue to make further progress.

| | | | APPEARANCES | | | | GOALS | | | |
|---|---|---|---|---|---|---|---|---|---|---|
| Clubs | Signing Date | Transfer Fee | Lge | FL Cup | FA Cup | Others | Lge | FL Cup | FA Cup | Others |
| Sheffield Wednesday* | 6.91 | - | 9 | | | | | | | |

## JONES Stephen (Steve) Gary

Born: Cambridge, 17 March 1970

Height: 6'0" Weight 12.12

**Position/Skill Factor:** A striker with great pace, who is also more than useful in aerial combat.

**Career History:** After starting out with Basildon United, of the Essex Senior League, he joined near neighbours, Billericay Town, in the Diadora League, Second Division. He first came to attention as a prolific goal scorer in 1991-92, when his 46 goals lifted the team to promotion and he had scored another 24 goals in only 17 games in **1992-93** when, out of the blue, Billy Bonds signed him for West Ham United in November 1992. Given an early run out, he set up the winning goal for Clive Allen in an Anglo-Italian Cup game in Italy against Cosenza, in December and impressed enough to make his FL debut at Leicester City on 30 January 1993, when coming on as a substitute. A week later, he stepped out for his first full League game and scored in a 1-1 draw at home to Barnsley, a feat he repeated in the next game at Upton Park, when netting the winner in a 2-1 win over Peterborough United. Played just three more times in the League side that ultimately achieved promotion to the Premier League, as runners-up to Newcastle United, before going back to the reserves, where he finished the season as the leading scorer.

| | | | APPEARANCES | | | | GOALS | | | |
|---|---|---|---|---|---|---|---|---|---|---|
| Clubs | Signing Date | Transfer Fee | Lge | FL Cup | FA Cup | Others | Lge | FL Cup | FA Cup | Others |
| West Ham United* | 11.92 | £22,000 | 4+2 | | | 1+1 | 2 | | | |

## JONES Terence (Terry) Patrick

Born: Liverpool, 3 December 1974

Height: 5'7" Weight: 12.8

**Position/Skill Factor:** Left-winger, with a good turn of pace, who can hit the target with his crosses. Has a great left foot.

**Career History:** Came to Everton as an associated schoolboy (March 1989), before going on to play for Liverpool boys and becoming a trainee (August 1991) on leaving school. A regular for the youth team in **1992-93**, he turned professional during the summer, having been a member of the England youth squad earlier and is a promising young player who should go on to better things.

| | | | APPEARANCES | | | | GOALS | | | |
|---|---|---|---|---|---|---|---|---|---|---|
| Clubs | Signing Date | Transfer Fee | Lge | FL Cup | FA Cup | Others | Lge | FL Cup | FA Cup | Others |
| Everton* | 7.93 | - | | | | | | | | |

## JONES Vincent (Vinny) Peter

Born: Watford, 5 January 1965

Height: 5'11" Weight: 11.10

**Position/Skill Factor:** Midfielder who is a great motivator on the field and hates to lose, always giving 100 per cent Infamous for his intimidatory style, he is perhaps a better player than given credit for and is dangerous from set pieces and his long throws.

**Career History:** One of the most remarkable rises to fame in Football League history. Jones was a bricklayer playing part-time football for Wealdstone of the then Gola League (now Vauxhall Conference), when Dave Bassett signed him for Wimbledon. Unknown and unrated in non-League football, he had played only 28 games in two seasons (1984-86) and none at all in 1986-87 for Wealdstone before the move. Yet Bassett plunged him straight into the First Division, making his FL debut at Nottingham Forest on 22 November 1986 and scoring the winning goal against Manchester United in only his second game and scoring again in his third, fourth and eighth games. Four First Division goals in eight games, all from midfield and yet two months earlier he could not get a game with Wealdstone! Although making only 24 League appearances the following season and sharing the number four shirt with Vaughan Ryan, he played in all the FA Cup rounds, culminating in the 1-0 win over Liverpool in the Final. Continuously dogged by disciplinary problems, he couldn't manage a full set of appearances in 1988-89, but it was still something of a shock when Bobby Gould, the new manager at Wimbledon, allowed him to depart in the close season to Leeds United. Played in all but the club's first three League matches and won a Second Division Championship medal as Leeds pipped Sheffield United for the title in 1989-90, his first season at Elland Road. However, having reached Division One, manager Howard Wilkinson decided to replace midfield muscle with midfield finesse, by signing Gary McAllister from Leicester City and he made only one more appearance for Leeds, before his former Wimbledon manager, Dave Bassett, signed him for Sheffield United in a bid to arrest the club's poor start in the First Division. In order to secure his services, United had to part with a club record fee and he was immediately appointed team captain, a move which surprised many, but was sound, as the "Blades" gradually proved their mettle and moved up the table away from the danger zone. Since he was both successful and popular at Bramall Lane, it was puzzling that Bassett agreed to sell him at a financial loss to Chelsea, in the second week of 1991-92. As with his previous clubs, he quickly became an integral part of the Chelsea team in a disappointing season for the "Blues", but after just seven Premier League games and one goal in **1992-93**, he was transferred to his old club, Wimbledon. Arriving in a cloud of controversy, involving the "Soccer's Hard Men" video, he was later fined £20,000 by the FA for bringing the game into disrepute. His home debut was a real "blood and thunder" match against Blackburn Rovers and was marred by three sendings off, Jones being one of them. Following this, he settled down quite well in the "Dons'" midfield, adding bite and restoring the old "crazy gang" spirit, but was again hauled up before the FA after collecting ten yellow cards and a red one. A misunderstanding over the time of the hearing, saw him arriving 80 minutes late and being suspended indefinitely, before the FA lifted the ban, allowing him to return to action in Wimbledon's last three matches.

| | | | APPEARANCES | | | | GOALS | | | |
|---|---|---|---|---|---|---|---|---|---|---|
| Clubs | Signing Date | Transfer Fee | Lge | FL Cup | FA Cup | Others | Lge | FL Cup | FA Cup | Others |
| Wimbledon | 11.86 | £10,000 | 77 | 6+2 | 11+2 | 3 | 9 | | 1 | |
| Leeds United | 6.89 | £650,000 | 44+2 | 2 | 1 | 4 | 5 | | | |
| Sheffield United | 9.90 | £700,000 | 35 | 4 | 1 | 1 | 2 | | | |
| Chelsea | 8.91 | £575,000 | 42 | 1 | 4 | 5 | 4 | | 1 | 2 |
| Wimbledon* | 9.92 | £700,000 | 27 | 3 | 4 | | 1 | 1 | | |

## JOSEPH Roger Anthony

Born: Paddington, 24 December 1965

Height: 5'11"

Weight: 11.13

International Honours: E"B"

**Position/Skill Factor:** Right-back with tremendous pace, he has a great build for a defender and is lean and hungry. Good at striking long passes in behind the opposing full-back.

**Career History:** Starting in non-League football with Southall, before joining Brentford in 1984-85, he made his FL debut at Griffin Park against Millwall on 19 May 1985 and by the end of the following term had established himself in the right-back position. Had four years with the

"Bees", before Wimbledon, who had carefully been noting his progress, signed him in time for the start of 1988-89 and he went straight into the team, only missing a handful of games in the middle of the season due to injury. After a difficult season in 1989-90, again disrupted by injury, he finally settled down in 1990-91 as an ever present and had his best season yet. His elder brother Francis, now retired from League football, also played for Wimbledon and Brentford in a career which embraced ten different clubs. Injuries again plagued him in 1991-92 and although performing regularly in the first half of the season, he only played in five more games after the New Year. He was in-and-out of the side in the early part of **1992-93**, with inconsistency being the main problem and although restored to the team, at left-back in mid-October, he only recaptured his best form after switching to the other flank, following an injury to Warren Barton in November. Once back in his more familiar position, he came into his own and was a big plus factor on the "Dons'" right side, with his speed and tackling of great importance, either in defence, or when going forward. Injuries kept him out of the last four games, apart from a substitute appearance in the final match and he looks forward to once again making the right-back position his own in 1993-94.

| | | | APPEARANCES | | | | GOALS | | | |
|---|---|---|---|---|---|---|---|---|---|---|
| Clubs | Signing Date | Transfer Fee | Lge | FL Cup | FA Cup | Others | Lge | FL Cup | FA Cup | Others |
| Brentford | 10.84 | - | 103+1 | 7 | 1 | 8 | 2 | | | |
| Wimbledon* | 8.88 | £150,000 | 139+7 | 14+1 | 10+1 | 6 | | | | |

## KANTCHELSKIS Andrei

Born: Kirovograd, USSR, 23 January 1969

Height: 5'10" Weight: 12.4

International Honours: USSR Int

**Position/Skill Factor:** Very direct right-winger, he uses his pace to go past defenders. Presents goal scoring opportunities for his strike-force with good early crosses.

**Career History:** A Soviet Union international before the disintegration of that country, he came to Britain in order to advance his career. Signed for Manchester United as a non-contract player from top Russian side, Shakhtyor Donetsk and made his FL debut at Crystal Palace on 11 May 1991. Alex Ferguson was sufficiently impressed to offer him a contract in the summer of 1991 and in the first game of the new season and his first at Old Trafford, at home to Notts County, he was an instant sensation on the right-wing with United's fans. Although he remained part of the first team scene throughout the season, he was not an automatic first choice and was frequently demoted to substitute. Scored several vital goals during the season, most of them spectacular and won his first honour when he was a member of the United team which defeated Nottingham Forest 1-0 in the League Cup Final. A disappointing season for the Ukranian in **1992-93**, even though he won a Championship medal, as he always appeared to be on the fringe of the Premier League side that eventually won the title. However, on the occasions he did managed to fight his way into the team, he impressed and important goals against Queens Park Rangers and Leeds United helped him to stake a claim, but generally he was kept on the sidelines by the excellent form of Lee Sharpe and Ryan Giggs. Had a good year for the CIS, assisting them in their World Cup campaign by scoring and setting up several vital goals.

| | | | APPEARANCES | | | | GOALS | | | |
|---|---|---|---|---|---|---|---|---|---|---|
| Clubs | Signing Date | Transfer Fee | Lge | FL Cup | FA Cup | Others | Lge | FL Cup | FA Cup | Others |
| Manchester United* | 3.91 | £650,000 | 43+19 | 6+1 | 3 | 3 | 8 | 2 | 1 | |

## KEANE Roy Maurice

Born: Cork, 10 August 1971

Height: 5'10" Weight: 11.3

International Honours: IR Yth, IR "U21"-4, IR-15

**Position/Skill Factor:** A midfield player with plenty of stamina, who comes from deep positions to score valuable goals. Always prepared to play his way out of trouble, he is a good passer of the ball.

**Career History:** Turned out to be one of the finds of 1990-91 after being signed by Nottingham Forest from Cobh Ramblers, in the Republic of Ireland, during the 1990 close season. Typically, Brian Clough plunged him straight into first team action and against the then League Champions! He made his FL debut at Liverpool on 28 August 1990 and finished the season playing in the FA Cup Final side that lost 2-1 to Tottenham Hotspur. In a season where it was generally expected that he would initially have difficulties getting into Forest's reserve side, he made 35 League appearances and was also recognised fully at international level when playing for the Irish Republic against Chile on 22 May 1991 in Dublin. He confirmed the progress made in his initial term with another excellent season in 1991-92 when Forest reached the Finals for two cup competitions, defeating Southampton

3-2 in the Zenith Cup Final, but falling to Manchester United in the League Cup Final. His goal in extra-time of the second-leg of the Semi-Final at White Hart Lane against "Spurs", clinched Forest's place at Wembley. Having established himself in the Irish national team, he was easily Forest's best performer in **1992-93** and arguably, the leading midfielder of his kind in Britain. A very consistent player, he only missed two games all season and that due to him being sent off at Middlesbrough at a time when it was becoming clear that Forest's days in the top flight were numbered. Once the drop to the First Division was confirmed, he made it quite clear that he intended to stay in the Premier League, an announcement which immediately alerted the country's big spenders. At one stage it seemed certain that he would go to Blackburn Rovers, especially when Kenny Dalglish freed Gordon Cowans, a move he would possibly later regret. But from the moment Manchester United joined the chase there was only one club in it. United originally offered £3.5 million and refused to increase the bid, while Forest insisted on a sale figure of £4 million for any transfer to go through before Keane's contract expired in October. The period of intransigency was broken when Alex Ferguson increased his offer by a further £250,000 as it became clear that Blackburn were in the process of tabling an improved bid. Moving to Old Trafford in a record English transfer deal in time for 1993-94, meant that Keane would be joining a squad that cost Alex Ferguson £23 million to assemble.

| | | | APPEARANCES | | | | GOALS | | | |
|---|---|---|---|---|---|---|---|---|---|---|
| Clubs | Signing Date | Transfer Fee | Lge | FL Cup | FA Cup | Others | Lge | FL Cup | FA Cup | Others |
| Nottingham Forest | 6.90 | £10,000 | 114 | 17 | 18 | 5 | 22 | 6 | 3 | 2 |
| Manchester United* | 7.93 | £3,750,000 | | | | | | | | |

## **KEARTON** **Jason** Brett

Born: Ipswich, Australia, 9 July 1969

Height: 6'1"

Weight: 11.10

**Position/Skill Factor:** Very consistent young goalkeeper. A good stopper, he also comes out well for crosses.

**Career History:** Came to England in 1988 seeking to further his football career, after gaining experience in his native country with Brisbane Lions. Signed by Everton, he started as third choice behind Neville Southall and Mike Stowell, but following the latter's departure to "Wolves" in the summer of 1990, he became reserve 'keeper. However, one year later, he was back to third choice when Everton signed Irish international Gerry Peyton as cover for Southall. He was able to advance his career with two extended three month loans, in 1991-92, firstly with Stoke City, where he made his FL debut at Bradford City on 17 August 1991 and later with Blackpool, who won promotion to the Third Division through the Play Offs, after he returned to Goodison Park. Hoping for a first team opportunity in **1992-93**, he spent all season on the bench, following the rule change that allows a 'keeper to be in reserve, as Neville Southall played in all but two League games. However, he made two substitute appearances when Southall was sent off for committing so called "professional" fouls and took his chance well, but lost his place when the former returned from suspension.

| | | | APPEARANCES | | | | GOALS | | | |
|---|---|---|---|---|---|---|---|---|---|---|
| Clubs | Signing Date | Transfer Fee | Lge | FL Cup | FA Cup | Others | Lge | FL Cup | FA Cup | Others |
| Everton* | 10.88 | – | 2+3 | | 1 | | | | | |
| Stoke City | 8.91 | Loan | 16 | | | 1 | | | | |
| Blackpool | 1.92 | Loan | 14 | | | | | | | |

## **KELLY** **Alan** Thomas

Born: Preston, 11 August 1968

Height: 6'2"

Weight: 12.6

International Honours: IR Yth, IR "U21"-3, IR-1

**Position/Skill Factor:** Extremely agile goalkeeper and an excellent shot stopper. Knows all the angles and rarely gets it wrong.

**Career History:** The son of Alan, who played in goal for Drumcondra, Preston North End and the Irish Republic, his brother Gary is also a goalkeeper, currently with Bury, after starting with Newcastle. Following in his father's footsteps, when he joined Preston as a trainee in August 1984, he soon graduated to the professional ranks and made his FL debut at Deepdale against Crewe Alexandra on 8 March 1986, holding his place to the end of the season, when Preston reached the nadir of their history — 23rd place in the Fourth Division. In 1986-87, he shared goalkeeping duties with David Brown, as Preston, in a remarkable turn-around, won promotion to Division Three, after finishing in second place. He again swapped the 'keeper's jersey with Brown in 1987-88, but was forced to sit out the 1988-89 campaign with a long term injury. He finally established himself as first-choice 'keeper at Deepdale in 1989-90, when he played in all but four games. However, he was displaced by new 'keeper Simon Farnworth at the start of 1990-91, before fighting his way back to favour in the second-half of the season. Again he chopped and changed with Farnworth in 1991-92, but ended the season as second choice. After such a "stop-start" career with a struggling Third Division club, when he was automatic first choice in only one of seven seasons at Deepdale, it came as surprise when Dave Bassett signed him for Premier League, Sheffield United, as cover for Simon Tracey in the summer of 1992. However, Bassett has an amazing track record of transforming previously unknown or underrated players into stars and it happened again in **1992-93** with Kelly. He became the first ever substitute goalkeeper under new Premier League rules, when he replaced Tracey for the last ten minutes of a game at Tottenham on 2 September 1992 and stood in for Tracey when the latter was injured again a few weeks later. When Tracey was eventually ruled out for the remainder of the season in November, he acquitted himself so well that he he was called up by Jack Charlton for the Republic of Ireland national squad as reserve to Pat Bonner and made his international debut on 17 February 1993, replacing Bonner at half-time in a "friendly" game against Wales, which the Republic won 2-1. It can only be a matter of time before he replaces Pat Bonner as first choice in the Republic goal. Deservedly voted the Sheffield United Executive Club's "Player of the Year".

| | | | APPEARANCES | | | | GOALS | | | |
|---|---|---|---|---|---|---|---|---|---|---|
| Clubs | Signing Date | Transfer Fee | Lge | FL Cup | FA Cup | Others | Lge | FL Cup | FA Cup | Others |
| Preston North End | 9.85 | - | 142 | 1 | 8 | 13 | | | | |
| Sheffield United* | 7.92 | £150,000 | 32+1 | 3 | 7 | | | | | |

## KELLY Garry

Born: Drogheda, 9 July 1974

Height: 5'9" Weight: 10.0

International Honours: IR Yth, IR "U21"-3

**Position/Skill Factor:** Skillful winger with two good feet, he has some lovely touches and can produce measured crosses.

**Career History:** A young Irish forward who joined Leeds United as a professional soon after his 17th birthday. Amazingly, given the competition for places at Elland Road, he made a first team appearance only one month after joining the club, as a substitute in a League Cup-tie against Scunthorpe and made his FL debut, again as a substitute, away to Nottingham Forest on 22 December 1991. For a 17 year-old to be included in the first team squad, clearly indicated a great deal of potential for the future, but although representing the Republic of Ireland several times at under 21 level during **1992-93**, he failed to make the Premier League side, spending most of his time trying to secure a regular reserve place, instead. Still very young, 1993-94 could be his season.

| | | | APPEARANCES | | | | GOALS | | | |
|---|---|---|---|---|---|---|---|---|---|---|
| Clubs | Signing Date | Transfer Fee | Lge | FL Cup | FA Cup | Others | Lge | FL Cup | FA Cup | Others |
| Leeds United* | 9.91 | - | 0+2 | 0+1 | | | | | | |

## KENNA Jeffrey (Jeff) Jude

Born: Dublin, 27 August 1970

Height: 5'11"

Weight: 11.9

International Honours: IR "U21"-8

**Position/Skill Factor:** Favours his right foot, but can play in both full-back positions. Gets his foot in well and is not afraid to move up field with the ball.

**Career History:** Irish born full-back who joined Southampton as a trainee in June 1987, turning professional two years later. He had to wait another two years for his FL debut, turning out as a substitute in the penultimate game of 1990-91, away to Derby County on 4 May 1991 and made his full debut at right-back one week later. Before his "Saints'" debut, he had already been selected three times for the Irish Republic Under 21 team. In 1991-92 he played second fiddle to Jason Dodd until January, but once in the team he held his place, apart from one brief hiatus, until the end of the season and was a member of the "Saints'" team which lost 2-3 to Nottingham Forest in the Zenith Cup Final. Started **1992-93** as second choice right-back, until an injury to Jason Dodd in the second game allowed him a brief spell of first team action. Lost his place when Dodd recovered, until recalled on 31 October for the visit of Oldham Athletic and remained in the side for 11 consecutive matches. Replaced by Dodd once again, he came back for the rest of the season, after missing four games, with his rival moving into midfield in front of him. Scored his first goal for the club at the Dell against Sheffield United and repeated the feat four games later. Joined a nucleus of promising youngsters pledging their future to the club, when he signed a three year contract in March.

| | | | APPEARANCES | | | | GOALS | | | |
|---|---|---|---|---|---|---|---|---|---|---|
| Clubs | Signing Date | Transfer Fee | Lge | FL Cup | FA Cup | Others | Lge | FL Cup | FA Cup | Others |
| Southampton* | 4.89 | - | 42+3 | | 4+1 | 3 | 2 | | | |

## **KENNY William** Aidan

Born: Liverpool, 19 September 1973

Height: 5'10" Weight: 12.0

International Honours: E "U21"-1

**Position/Skill Factor:** Midfielder with two good feet. Switches play well, using long raking passes and always takes up good positions.

**Career History:** Joined the Everton professional staff during the 1992 close season, having previously been at Goodison as an associated schoolboy (November 1989) and as a trainee (June 1990). His first team opportunity came earlier than expected. Following an injury to John Ebbrell, early into the **1992-93** season and having already had a run with the League Cup side a week earlier, he held off all opposition for the key midfield role to make his PL debut at home to Coventry City on 17 October 1992. A consistent performer, belying his lack of years, he was rewarded with regular appearances in mid-season and a call up for the England under 23 side that played Turkey in March, but ended it being used in more of a substitute role. If his great potential can be fulfilled, he will no doubt be an integral part of the Everton line-up for years to come.

| | | | APPEARANCES | | | | GOALS | | | |
|---|---|---|---|---|---|---|---|---|---|---|
| Clubs | Signing Date | Transfer Fee | Lge | FL Cup | FA Cup | Others | Lge | FL Cup | FA Cup | Others |
| Everton* | 6.92 | – | 16+1 | 4 | 2 | | 1 | | | |

## **KEOWN Martin** Raymond

Born: Oxford, 24 July 1966

Height: 6'1" Weight: 12.4

International Honours: E Yth, E "U21"-8, E "B", E-11

**Position/Skill Factor:** Commanding centre-back who reads situations well. A very good defender with plenty of pace, he is a strong tackler and dominant in the air.

**Career History:** Came to Arsenal as a 14-year-old, signing as an associated schoolboy in October 1980 and moving up to apprentice in June 1982, before turning professional. However, chances were limited at Highbury and he made his FL debut for Brighton & Hove Albion at Manchester City on 23 February 1985, whilst on loan. He remained at the Goldstone Ground on loan for the opening weeks of 1985-86, but after returning to Arsenal, he finally won a place at the heart of the defence, playing through the latter half of the season. During the summer break, though, Aston Villa signed him and after starting out in the number two shirt, he reverted to a more central role, but although he played well, the club were relegated to the Second Division at the end of the season. Was a major influence for Villa during 1987-88 as they regained their First Division status at the first attempt, but once their position had been secured at the end of the following season, he moved on to Everton. Initially, it seemed as if he would be used as cover for Dave Watson and Kevin Ratcliffe, but when both players suffered injuries during the season, he got an extended run in the side, which has continued into 1990-91, with him being used as a full-back and third central defender. He was firmly established in the heart of Everton's defence in 1991-92 as Kevin Ratcliffe's long reign came to an end and missed only three games through injury. At the age of 25 it seemed that an international career had passed him by. However, his Everton form was so impressive that England manager Graham Taylor gave him a chance in the friendly against France in February 1992. He quickly developed an understanding with Des Walker and was retained for the remainder of England's programme, with the bonus of scoring a goal in his second match against Czechoslovakia. By May he had become an automatic selection for the European Championship Finals and played in all three games as England were ultimately sunk without trace by the host nation, Sweden. Missed the first 13 matches of the **1992-93** season, due to injury, but came back strongly to give renewed confidence to a side that were struggling, somewhat. It was therefore something of a surprise when he was transferred to Arsenal in March 1993 and became the first player in living memory to return to the club, having left Highbury seven years earlier. Cup-tied at Everton, he was unable to participate in the "Gunners'" great cup run, but in the League he settled in mainly at full-back and reclaimed his England spot, effectively marking Holland's Ruud Gullitt at Wembley. Eventually, it is expected that he will resume his partnership with Tony Adams, that goes back to their youth team days.

| | | | APPEARANCES | | | | GOALS | | | |
|---|---|---|---|---|---|---|---|---|---|---|
| Clubs | Signing Date | Transfer Fee | Lge | FL Cup | FA Cup | Others | Lge | FL Cup | FA Cup | Others |
| Arsenal | 2.84 | – | 22 | | 5 | | | | | |
| Brighton & H.A. | 2.85 | Loan | 21+2 | 2 | | 2 | 1 | 1 | | 1 |
| Aston Villa | 6.86 | £200,000 | 109+3 | 12+1 | 6 | 2 | 3 | | | |
| Everton | 8.89 | £750,000 | 92+4 | 11 | 12+1 | 6 | | | | |
| Arsenal* | 2.93 | £2,000,000 | 15+1 | | | | | | | |

## KERR David William

Born: Dumfries, 6 September 1974

Height: 5'11" Weight: 11.4

**Position/Skill Factor:** Strong tackling midfield player who covers every blade of grass.

**Career History**: Came down from Scotland on leaving school to sign as a trainee for Manchester City in September 1990 and a year later had progressed to the club's professional ranks. A good grounding with the reserves in **1992-93**, following on from the previous season, saw him making his PL debut as a substitute at home to Crystal Palace on 5 May 1993. He gave a more than useful display and was voted the "Young Player of the Year", showing the same potential as did Gary Flitcroft at a similar age. There are marked signs of a promising future, as manager, Peter Reid, enthuses over his potential. Is one to watch out for in 1993-94.

| | | | APPEARANCES | | | | GOALS | | | |
|---|---|---|---|---|---|---|---|---|---|---|
| Clubs | Signing Date | Transfer Fee | Lge | FL Cup | FA Cup | Others | Lge | FL Cup | FA Cup | Others |
| Manchester City* | 9.91 | - | 0+1 | | | | | | | |

## KERSLAKE David

Born: Stepney, 19 June 1966

Height: 5'8" Weight: 11.0

International Honours: E Sch, E Yth, E "U21"-1

**Position/Skill Factor:** Right-back, who can play in midfield and likes nothing more than getting forward down the flank to deliver quality crosses to the front men, after his pace has taken him clear.

**Career History:** A notable player at England schoolboy international level, when he signed for Queens Park Rangers, first as an associated schoolboy (February 1981) and then as an apprentice in June 1982, he was viewed by many good judges to be the "new Duncan Edwards". However, on turning professional in the 1983 close season, he had to wait nearly two years before making his FL debut as a substitute at Newcastle United on 13 April 1985. Originally a midfield player, he was never able to hold down a regular slot at Loftus Road, despite his impressive pedigree. Eventually, after six and a half years as a professional, he was allowed to join Swindon Town, then managed by Ossie Ardiles. He immediately slotted in at right-back and assisted the Second Division team to fourth place and the end of season Play-Offs. These were reduced to pure farce by a Football League management decision to allow Swindon, then under investigation for financial irregularities committed by a previous regime, three years earlier, to participate. The FLMC then waited until the club had won the Play-Off Final against Sunderland, before announcing that, far from being promoted to Division One, for the first time ever, they would be demoted to the Third Division! Some semblance of justice and sanity prevailed when, on appeal, the FA intervened to restore Swindon to the Second Division. Although Kerslake continued to shine at right-back, the next two seasons were something of an anti-climax for Town's supporters. Then, with Swindon once again heading for the First Division Play-Offs in **1992-93**, he was signed by Howard Wilkinson for Leeds United in March 1993, to fill their problem right-back slot, unresolved since the decline of Mel Sterland. Swindon supporters are by now accustomed to the annual eve of transfer deadline sale of at least one key player. This time it was Kerslake and his departure sparked an outcry which, at the time, threatened to have more serious repercussions within the club. To rub salt into the wound, immediately prior to him signing for the Yorkshire club, he received the accolade of being named in the PFA First Division team awards. He made an immediate debut against Manchester City at Elland Road and gave a solid performance in a 1-0 win. With a classy, natural attacking style, he appeared to be the ideal replacement for Sterland, until injury caused him to miss the last three games of the season.

| | | | APPEARANCES | | | | GOALS | | | |
|---|---|---|---|---|---|---|---|---|---|---|
| Clubs | Signing Date | Transfer Fee | Lge | FL Cup | FA Cup | Others | Lge | FL Cup | FA Cup | Others |
| Q.P.R. | 6.83 | - | 38+20 | 6+2 | 2+2 | 2+2 | 6 | 4 | | |
| Swindon Town | 11.89 | £110,000 | 103+1 | 9 | 7 | 10 | 1 | | | |
| Leeds United* | 3.93 | £500,000 | | | | | | | | |

## KEY Lance

Born: Kettering, 13 May 1968

Height: 6'2" Weight: 14.6

**Position/Skill Factor:** Goalkeeper. Good shot stopper, he is both agile and brave.

**Career History:** Joined Sheffield Wednesday at the tail-end of 1989-90 from non-Leaguers, Histon, only to find himself fourth choice behind England's Chris Woods,

Chris Turner and Kevin Pressman. Still to make a first team appearance for Wednesday, he was loaned out to York City in April 1992 and looked sure to make his FL debut at Bootham Crescent, until picking up an injury which unluckily put him out of action for the rest of the season. Although sitting on the bench twice in **1992-93**, under the new Premier League's substitute goalkeeper ruling, he was not called upon and remains without a first team appearance to his name. Earlier in the season, however, he was loaned out to Portadown and his smart performances helped them win the Irish Cup. Continues to show lots of dedication and ability and can only hope that it will be his turn soon.

| | | | APPEARANCES | | | | GOALS | | | |
|---|---|---|---|---|---|---|---|---|---|---|
| Clubs | Signing Date | Transfer Fee | Lge | FL Cup | FA Cup | Others | Lge | FL Cup | FA Cup | Others |
| Sheffield Wednesday* | 4.90 | £10,000 | | | | | | | | |

# KHARINE Dmitri

Born: Moscow, USSR, 16 August 1968

Height: 6'1"

Weight: 10.2

International Honours: USSR/CIS Int

**Position/Skill Factor:** Agile goalkeeper. Very safe, with good positional sense, he throws well from both hands and also kicks long distances with both feet.

**Career History:** Russian international goalkeeper, who played in all three of the CIS games in the European Championship Finals held in Sweden, June 1992. Midway through **1992-93**, following many weeks of indecision, regarding a work permit, he was signed by Chelsea from the Russian Champions, CSKA Moscow, in order to solve a goalkeeping crisis at Stamford Bridge. After sitting on the bench a couple of times, he made his PL debut at Queens Park Rangers on 27 January 1993 and played well in a 1-1 draw. He then had the strange experience of being substituted in his second game (a 2-0 defeat at the hands of Sheffield Wednesday) at half-time, with the score at 1-0 and being replaced by Gerry Peyton, who was on loan from Everton and also making his home Chelsea debut. Once he settles down in England and begins to master the language and communication problems he has at present, the "Blues" should have themselves a very fine 'keeper indeed.

| | | | APPEARANCES | | | | GOALS | | | |
|---|---|---|---|---|---|---|---|---|---|---|
| Clubs | Signing Date | Transfer Fee | Lge | FL Cup | FA Cup | Others | Lge | FL Cup | FA Cup | Others |
| Chelsea* | 12.92 | £200,000 | 5 | | | | | | | |

# KILCLINE Brian

Born: Nottingham, 7 May 1962

Height: 6'2"

Weight: 12.0

International Honours: E "U21"-2

**Position/Skill Factor:** Big and powerful central defender, who is as brave as a lion, but scrupulously fair. Even hardened defenders cringe when he throws himself at corner kicks.

**Career History:** An associated schoolboy with his hometown club, Notts County, in October 1976, he made the transition to that of apprentice on leaving school in May 1978 and before turning professional two years later, had already been blooded in the first team, having made his FL debut in central defence in a 3-2 win at Bristol Rovers on 6 October 1979. He soon became a fixture in the heart of County's defence and was ever present in 1980-81, when the club won promotion back to Division One, competing at the highest level for the first time since 1926. In 1982-83, he was selected twice for the England Under 21 team, but that was the beginning and end of his international career. When County were relegated back to Division Two in 1984, after three seasons of struggle, he was transferred to Coventry City for a surprisingly modest fee. He formed an effective partnership with Trevor Peake at Highfield Road and for five years was first choice, barring injuries and suspensions. He also proved to be a prolific goalscorer for a central defender, both from set pieces and as penalty converter. In 1989-90 he was usurped by Peter Billing and his appearances more intermittent, until the 1991 close season, when he was signed by Oldham Athletic manager, Joe Royle, to bolster the "Latics'" defence in their first season back in the top flight since 1922-23. However, he found himself playing second fiddle to Earl Barrett and Richard Jobson and after only six months at Boundary Park, he moved on to Newcastle United, as one of new manager Kevin Keegan's first signings, firstly on loan and then permanently. He brought some much needed stability to the "Magpies'" and assisted the club to escape relegation to Division Three on the last day of the season. Started **1992-93** alongside Steve Howey, but pulled a muscle in the fourth game of the season at Mansfield Town in the second leg of the League Cup. And with the team performing so well, he found it difficult to get back into the side, appearing so many times on the substitute's bench (35 times in all competitions) that he became known as the "judge". Whenever he did manage to get on the field he never let the team down, but with United on course for the First Division title, he was philosophical to state that you must never change a winning team. A player who will always perform to his full capability, he qualified for a First Division Championship medal as United marched into the Premier League and will be relied upon to step into the breach this season, if required.

| Clubs | Signing Date | Transfer Fee | APPEARANCES Lge | FL Cup | FA Cup | Others | GOALS Lge | FL Cup | FA Cup | Others |
|---|---|---|---|---|---|---|---|---|---|---|
| Notts County | 4.80 | - | 156+2 | 16 | 10 | | 9 | 1 | 2 | |
| Coventry City | 6.84 | £60,000 | 173 | 16+1 | 15 | 8 | 28 | 4 | 3 | |
| Oldham Athletic | 8.91 | £400,000 | 8 | 2 | | | | | | |
| Newcastle United* | 2.92 | £250,000 | 19+12 | 2 | 1+2 | 5 | | | | |

# KIMBLE Alan Frank

Born: Dagenham, 6 August 1966

Height: 5'10" Weight: 12.4

**Position/Skill Factor:** An attacking left-back, with a superb left foot, who is noted for his long kicks into the channels and throws to match. Always looking to get forward to deliver quality crosses into his forwards.

**Career History:** Although his family home was Dagenham, he was actually born in Poole, along with his twin brother, Gary, while his parents were there on holiday. Both boys started as juniors with Charlton Athletic and eventually turned professional during the 1984 close season, making their FL debuts at the Valley against Sheffield United on 16 April 1985. They even went on loan together to Exeter City, playing in one match, before being freed by Charlton and joining Fourth Division, Cambridge United, in the summer of 1986. Their careers parted ways in 1987-88, when Gary moved on in quick succession to Doncaster Rovers, Fulham, Maidstone United, Gillingham, Peterborough United and is currently with Dagenham & Redbridge, while working as a money broker in the city. Alan, however, stayed put with Cambridge, missing just ten games in nearly four seasons and was an integral part of the side that won promotion to the Third Division, via the Play-Offs in 1989-90, when Chesterfield bit the dust in the Final. 1990-91 was even better and he missed just three games, as United were promoted as Champions and the following season, 1991-92, saw the club reach its highest ever League placing, fifth in the Second Division. He was almost ever present, being absent just once, but any pleasure in viewing the League table had to be tempered with the fact that United failed the "acid" test when they lost 6-1 over both legs of the Play-Off Semi-Final against Leicester City. As the Cambridge penalty "king", he scored four goals in **1992-93** and finally finished a season as an ever present, but with results going badly and manager, John Beck, departing, the club dropped out of the "new" First Division in 23rd place. It was hardly a great surprise, however, having sold their leading goalscorer, Dion Dublin, to Manchester United before the season got underway, a transfer that merely underlined the fact that United would ultimately struggle at that level. Although the team had generally played below par, he had not and had actually enhanced his reputation as one of the better players outside of the Premier League. The point was not lost on Wimbledon, who were similar in style to Cambridge under Beck and they moved in to sign Kimble during the 1993 close season.

| Clubs | Signing Date | Transfer Fee | APPEARANCES Lge | FL Cup | FA Cup | Others | GOALS Lge | FL Cup | FA Cup | Others |
|---|---|---|---|---|---|---|---|---|---|---|
| Charlton Athletic | 8.84 | - | 6 | | | | | | | |
| Exeter City | 8.85 | Loan | 1 | 1 | | | | | | |
| Cambridge United | 8.86 | - | 295+4 | 23+1 | 29 | 22 | 24 | | 1 | |
| Wimbledon* | 7.93 | £175,000 | | | | | | | | |

# KING Philip (Phil) Geoffrey

Born: Bristol, 28 December 1967

Height: 5'10"

Weight: 12.0

International Honours: E"B"

**Position/Skill Factor:** As an attacking left-back, he can often be used as an extra forward when the occasion demands. Has a superb left foot and is capable of delivering quality passes and crosses.

**Career History:** Joined Exeter City as an associated schoolboy in February 1982 and on leaving school, became an apprentice in May 1984. Within a month of turning professional, he had made his FL debut at St James' Park against Halifax Town on 23 February 1985. Created a good impression when in the side, but remained in the shadow of the long serving Keith Viney and was allowed to join Torquay United in the 1986 close season. Slotting into the number three shirt immediately, he showed such promise that Third Division Swindon Town moved for him in mid-season to bolster their promotion hopes. Second Division status was duly attained and he continued to star for the "Robins", being ever present in 1987-88 and very rarely missing a game. It was only a matter of time before he joined the "elite" and it came as no surprise when he signed for Sheffield Wednesday during 1989-90. Sadly for him, Wednesday were relegated at the end of his first season at Hillsborough, but the following term he missed only three League games as the club responded magnificently to the challenge and returned to the First Division at the first time of asking, in third place. He also had the added bonus of receiving a League Cup winners medal, following the great 1-0 victory over Manchester United at Wembley. An unsung hero of the Wednesday team, he played in all but four games of the 1991-92 campaign when the "Owls" achieved their highest placing (third) for 31 years and qualified for the 1992-93 UEFA Cup. Started **1992-93** where he left off the previous season, as the club's first choice left-back, but after playing in the initial four matches, he suffered a cruciate ligament injury in late August, which forced him onto the sidelines for several months. Came back in January, but had to play himself back to match fitness in the reserves and then found his first team opportunities limited, due to the "Owls'" great spell of form. However, he got back in the side just prior to the League Cup Final and after retaining his place for the big game, it was from his half cleared cross that John Harkes scored Wednesday's goal in a 2-1 defeat. Played in three of the remaining eight games of the campaign, sharing duties with Nigel Worthington and is expected back in full swing this coming season.

| Clubs | Signing Date | Transfer Fee | APPEARANCES Lge | FL Cup | FA Cup | Others | GOALS Lge | FL Cup | FA Cup | Others |
|---|---|---|---|---|---|---|---|---|---|---|
| Exeter City | 1.85 | - | 24+3 | 1 | | 1+2 | | | | |
| Torquay United | 7.86 | £3,000 | 24 | 2 | 1 | 2 | 3 | | | |
| Swindon Town | 2.87 | £155,000 | 112+4 | 11 | 5 | 13 | 4 | | | |
| Sheffield Wednesday* | 11.89 | £400,000 | 117+2 | 15 | 9 | 4 | 2 | | | |

## KIRBY Ryan Mark

Born: Redbridge, 6 September 1974

Height: 5'11" Weight: 12.0

**Position/Skill Factor:** Central defender, or full-back, who has a great attitude to the game. A strong tackler and sound in defence, he could settle in a number of positions.

**Career History:** One of a batch of several promising youngsters at Arsenal, he made steady progress through the junior side as a trainee (July 1991), before turning over to the professional ranks last summer. He also made several reserve team appearances towards the end of **1992-93** and will be looking to extend that this coming season.

| | | | APPEARANCES | | | | GOALS | | | |
|---|---|---|---|---|---|---|---|---|---|---|
| Clubs | Signing Date | Transfer Fee | Lge | FL Cup | FA Cup | Others | Lge | FL Cup | FA Cup | Others |
| Arsenal* | 7.93 | - | | | | | | | | |

## KITE Philip (Phil) David

Born: Bristol, 26 October 1962

Height: 6'1"

Weight: 14.7

International Honours: E Sch, E Yth

**Position/Skill Factor:** A very strong and fit goalkeeper, he comes out well for crosses. He is a good shot stopper and extremely agile for such a big man.

**Career History:** Locally born and bred, he signed for Bristol Rovers as an associated schoolboy in January 1978, before taking out a football apprenticeship on leaving school in July 1979. Made his FL debut at Derby County on 10 January 1981, where a Don Gillies own goal was the deciding factor in a 2-1 defeat. In 1982-83 he gained a regular place in the side and was ever present and the following season, impressed Southampton enough to sign him as cover for Peter Shilton. The move, however, was not a great success and he was loaned out to both Middlesbrough and Gillingham. When freed by the "Saints", during the 1987 close season, he remained without a club for eight months, while he recovered from an injury. Eventually, he signed for Gillingham, alternating with the long serving Ron Hillyard, who held the most appearances record for the club. After little more than two years with the "Gills", he moved to Bournemouth to understudy the Eire international, Gerry Peyton. After one year at Dean Court, he was signed by Dave Bassett for Sheffield United as cover for Simon Tracey and received an immediate first team opportunity when the latter was injured during the "Blades'" first game back in Division One. He performed well, despite United's disastrous start to the season, but had to give way to Tracey when fit again towards the end of October. After coming into the side for eight games early in 1991-92, he spent an extended three month loan with Fourth Division Mansfield Town, but was unlucky to be injured in March, when Tracey was also absent, forcing Dave Bassett to sign a third 'keeper, the ill-fated Mel Rees. Made no first team appearances for United in **1992-93**, although sitting on the bench no less than 15 times under the substitute goalkeeper ruling. The "Blades'" loan signings of Kenny Veysey and Jim Leighton during the season, probably meant that his days at Bramall Lane are numbered, while, at the same time, he went in the opposite direction on loan to Plymouth Argyle, Rotherham United, Crewe Alexandra and Stockport County. And indeed, projected transfers to Burnley and Cambridge United, only fell through at the last moment. With Alan Kelly and Simon Tracey currently in front of him, his chances of playing first team soccer next season must be viewed as limited.

| | | | APPEARANCES | | | | GOALS | | | |
|---|---|---|---|---|---|---|---|---|---|---|
| Clubs | Signing Date | Transfer Fee | Lge | FL Cup | FA Cup | Others | Lge | FL Cup | FA Cup | Others |
| Bristol Rovers | 10.80 | - | 96 | 12 | 8 | 2 | | | | |
| Southampton | 8.84 | £50,000 | 4 | | | 1 | | | | |
| Middlesbrough | 3.86 | Loan | 2 | | | | | | | |
| Gillingham | 2.87 | - | 70 | 5 | 4 | 10 | | | | |
| Bournemouth | 8.89 | £20,000 | 7 | 1 | | | | | | |
| Sheffield United* | 8.90 | £25,000 | 11 | 5 | 1 | 1 | | | | |
| Mansfield Town | 11.91 | Loan | 11 | | | 1 | | | | |
| Plymouth Argyle | 9.92 | Loan | 2 | | | | | | | |
| Rotherham United | 10.92 | Loan | 1 | | | | | | | |
| Crewe Alexandra | 11.92 | Loan | 5 | | 1 | 2 | | | | |
| Stockport County | 3.93 | Loan | 5 | | | | | | | |

## KIWOMYA Christopher (Chris) Mark

Born: Huddersfield, 2 December 1969

Height: 5'10"

Weight: 10.5

**Position/Skill Factor:** Athletic striker with great pace. Runs at defenders and twists and turns, making him a difficult player to mark.

**Career History:** Followed his brother Andy, the former Barnsley player, into League soccer, when he joined Ipswich Town as a trainee in July 1986. On turning professional, he had to wait a further 19 months before making his FL debut as a sub at Portman Road against Bradford City on 24 September 1988. Showed early promise, but didn't really become a regular until 1990-91 when he played 34 matches and topped the club's goal scoring charts. Originally a winger, he was converted by Town manager John Lyall into a central striker and responded brilliantly with a burst of seven goals from eight games at the end of the season. Surprisingly overlooked for England Youth and Under 21 honours, he was a regular performer in 1991-92, as Ipswich won the Second Division Championship, leading the way with 16 FL goals, plus three cup goals. Made quite an impact in the new **1992-93** Premier League with his pace, but his form suffered as the team dropped down the table and he only scored three times in the second-half of the season. Earlier, however, he plundered his first ever hat-trick in a 4-0 thrashing of Wigan Athletic in the Second Round of the League Cup and a goal at home to Blackburn Rovers at the end of 1992 notched up his 50th for the club. Must look to be more consistent if he is to shine in the Premier League.

| | | | APPEARANCES | | | | GOALS | | | |
|---|---|---|---|---|---|---|---|---|---|---|
| Clubs | Signing Date | Transfer Fee | Lge | FL Cup | FA Cup | Others | Lge | FL Cup | FA Cup | Others |
| Ipswich Town* | 3.87 | - | 150+23 | 13 | 11 | 5+1 | 42 | 7 | 2 | 3 |

## KOZMA Istvan

Born: Pazto, Hungary, 3 December 1964

Height: 6'0" Weight: 12.6

International Honours: Hungarian "U21" & Full Int

**Position/Skill Factor:** A typically skillful continental midfield player who passes and moves well.

**Career History:** A Hungarian International, who first came to these shores in September 1989 when he joined Scottish Premier Division club Dunfermline Athletic from the famous French club, Girondins de Bordeaux. After nearly three seasons at East End Park as a first team regular, he was signed by Liverpool manager Graham Souness in February 1992 to bolster a first team squad ravaged by injuries. He made his FL debut away to Norwich City on 22 February 1992 and made occasional appearances subsequently, although not in the reckoning for a FA Cup Final place. Apart from holding down a regular reserve spot in **1992-93**, he wasn't required for first team duty, other than being used as a substitute on just three occasions, in the Charity Shield, the Premier League and the League Cup. Played a significant role in Liverpool's amazing League Cup-tie against Chesterfield at Anfield in September. Coming on as a second half substitute, with the "Reds" 3-0 down, he laid on passes or crosses for three goals, which enabled them to level the match at 4-4 and stave off a humiliating defeat.

| | | | APPEARANCES | | | | GOALS | | | |
|---|---|---|---|---|---|---|---|---|---|---|
| Clubs | Signing Date | Transfer Fee | Lge | FL Cup | FA Cup | Others | Lge | FL Cup | FA Cup | Others |
| Dunfermline Athletic | 9.89 | £540,000 | 82+8 | 7 | 6 | | 8 | 1 | | |
| Liverpool* | 2.92 | £300,000 | 3+3 | 0+1 | 0+2 | 0+1 | | | | |

## KUBICKI Dariusz

Born: Warsaw, Poland, 6 June 1963

Height: 5'10"

Weight: 11.7

International Honours: Polish Int

**Position/Skill Factor:** Right-back. A very good defender who is not easily beaten, he also has a constructive side and is an excellent passer of the ball.

**Career History:** Polish international full-back who signed for Aston Villa at the start of the 1991-92 season from Legia Warsaw and made his FL debut at Southampton on 31 August 1991. An automatic first choice at right-back until February 1992, he lost his place to new signing Earl Barrett and took little part in the remaining proceedings. Expected to challenge strongly for a first team place in **1992-93**, he made only one appearance for the first team, when standing in for Shaun Teale and had to settle for the reserves. A consistent player at that level, he will hope for more opportunities this coming season.

| | | | APPEARANCES | | | | GOALS | | | |
|---|---|---|---|---|---|---|---|---|---|---|
| Clubs | Signing Date | Transfer Fee | Lge | FL Cup | FA Cup | Others | Lge | FL Cup | FA Cup | Others |
| Aston Villa* | 8.91 | £200,000 | 23 | 3 | 4+1 | 1 | | | | |

## LAKE Paul Andrew

Born: Denton, 28 October 1968

Height: 6'0"

Weight: 12.2

International Honours: E "U21"-5, E"B"

**Position/Skill Factor:** Hard working midfield player with good passing techniques, who can also play at full-back.

**Career History:** It was only natural that he would sign for Manchester City as an associated schoolboy (February 1983) and later as an apprentice (July 1985). Made his FL debut at Wimbledon on 24 January 1987, while still a trainee and the following season he had become a regular, playing in 37 League matches, as City were promoted to the First Division as runners-up. Originally a midfielder, he was switched to right-back during 1988-89 by manager Mel Machin and alternated between the two positions in 1989-90. Being treated as a utility player did not do much to advance his career and 1990-91 turned into a nightmare for him when he was carried off with a serious knee injury during the third match against Aston Villa. And following an operation to rectify the problem, he didn't play again that season. After a long lay off, re-habilitating, he made an impressive return to first team duty on the opening day of **1992-93**, at home to Queens Park Rangers, having previously appeared in the pre-season friendlies against Brescia and Cremonese in Italy. Although substituted in the last 15 minutes, after tiring in his first League game for two years, he was selected for the next match at Middlesbrough. Unfortunately, a strong tackle in the eighth minute, saw an end to his season, when he was carried off yet again. Following another operation, which was performed in Los Angeles, it will not be known until the new season gets underway whether or not it has been a success and once again the player has to bear an agonising wait.

| | | | APPEARANCES | | | | GOALS | | | |
|---|---|---|---|---|---|---|---|---|---|---|
| Clubs | Signing Date | Transfer Fee | Lge | FL Cup | FA Cup | Others | Lge | FL Cup | FA Cup | Others |
| Manchester City* | 6.87 | - | 106+4 | 10 | 9 | 5 | 7 | 1 | 2 | 1 |

## LANDON Christopher (Chris) Stephen

Born: Epsom, 20 October 1974

Height: 5'7" Weight: 9.7

**Position/Skill Factor:** Athletic full-back who is very quick in recovery. A good tackler, he also likes to link up with play.

**Career History:** Started at Tottenham Hotspur as an associated schoolboy in January 1990, before moving up the ladder as a trainee (August 1991) to sign professional forms during the 1993 close season. Apart from five reserve matches in **1992-93**, he has played mainly youth team soccer, but looks a promising player.

| | | | APPEARANCES | | | | GOALS | | | |
|---|---|---|---|---|---|---|---|---|---|---|
| Clubs | Signing Date | Transfer Fee | Lge | FL Cup | FA Cup | Others | Lge | FL Cup | FA Cup | Others |
| Tottenham Hotspur* | 7.93 | - | | | | | | | | |

## LAWTON Craig Thomas

Born: Hawarden, 5 January 1972

Height: 5'7" Weight: 10.3

International Honours: W Sch, W Yth, W "B"

**Position/Skill Factor:** Midfield player, cum striker, he is a good goal scorer. Has a lovely left foot, can both pass and move and is also a strong tackler.

**Career History:** First came to Manchester United as an associated schoolboy player in September 1987 and on leaving school he joined the club as a trainee in July 1988. Had progressed to the professional ranks by the 1990 close season, but with nearly 40 full-time pros at Old Trafford, competition for places was fierce and an early first team opportunity was not forthcoming. Although plagued with injuries during 1991-92, he impressed enough to make the Welsh "B" team and moved into contention for United's first team in **1992-93**, when he was an unused substitute for the Premier League match at Queens Park Rangers in January. However, as a regular member of the Central League side, he consistently rates good reviews and should make the breakthrough before too long.

| | | | APPEARANCES | | | | GOALS | | | |
|---|---|---|---|---|---|---|---|---|---|---|
| Clubs | Signing Date | Transfer Fee | Lge | FL Cup | FA Cup | Others | Lge | FL Cup | FA Cup | Others |
| Manchester United* | 7.90 | - | | | | | | | | |

## LEE David John

Born: Kingswood, 26 November 1969

Height: 6'3"

Weight: 14.0

International Honours: E Yth, E "U21"-10

**Position/Skill Factor:** Can play at centre-back and in midfield and has lovely skill for such a big man. Has two good feet and a footballing brain. Brings the ball out of defence and is quite capable of scoring goals.

**Career History:** From the Bristol area, he began his career at Chelsea as an associated schoolboy in March 1984, progressing to the professional ranks as a trainee and made his FL debut at Stamford Bridge against Leicester City on 1 October 1988. He came on as a sub and scored in a 2-1 victory and went on to make 20 appearances that first season, mostly in central defence including eight as a substitute as Chelsea won promotion back to the First Division at their first attempt, as Champions. Played in the first 23 games of 1989-90, before injury restricted him to a handful of subs' appearances for the remainder of the season and found it difficult to re-establish himself in the side during 1990-91. In 1991-92 with his future at Stamford Bridge uncertain, he was loaned out to Third Division Reading and Second Division Plymouth Argyle. For Reading he scored a remarkable five goals in five appearances, apparently from central defence! With Plymouth he saw out the season, but was unable to prevent their slide to relegation. Took over the number five shirt in **1992-93** when Paul Elliott was incapacitated and for long periods was the lynch pin of the defence, until being injured in the delayed Third Round of the FA Cup-tie at

Middlesbrough. He only made seven further appearances and appeared to be out of favour with caretaker manager, Dave Webb. Some doubts may remain over his future at Stamford Bridge, but it seems clear that his best position is in front of the back four where his lack of pace is not so important.

| Clubs | Signing Date | Transfer Fee | APPEARANCES | | | | GOALS | | | |
|---|---|---|---|---|---|---|---|---|---|---|
| | | | Lge | FL Cup | FA Cup | Others | Lge | FL Cup | FA Cup | Others |
| Chelsea* | 7.88 | - | 76+21 | 12+1 | 2+4 | 5+1 | 8 | 1 | | 1 |
| Reading | 1.92 | Loan | 5 | | | | 5 | | | |
| Plymouth Argyle | 3.92 | Loan | 9 | | | | 1 | | | |

## LEE Robert Martin

Born: West Ham, 1 February 1966

Height: 5'10" Weight: 11.6

International Honours: E "U21"-2

**Position/Skill Factor:** Right-winger with pace who runs at full-backs in order to commit them. A good crosser, he can finish equally as well and is always looking to get into the box.

**Career History:** Discovered by Charlton Athletic, whilst playing for non-League Hornchurch of the then Isthmian League, he turned professional for the "Valiants" during the summer of 1983 and made his FL debut as a forward later that season at home to Grimsby Town on 10 March 1984, scoring Charlton's second in a 3-3 draw, followed up by three more goals before the end of the season. Established a regular place in 1984-85, finishing second top scorer with ten FL goals and assisted the "Valiants" to promotion to Division One in 1985-86, although sadly, by this time, Charlton had abandoned "The Valley" and moved to the ground of Crystal Palace. Charlton's four years in Division One were a constant struggle against relegation and he seemed at times out of his depth, until manager, Lennie Lawrence, switched him to the right-wing in 1988-89, where he grew in confidence. When the "Addicks" returned to Division Two in 1990, he was undoubtedly their star player, top scoring with 13 FL goals in 1990-91 and 12 in the League in 1991-92, all from a wide position. Since Charlton were forced to sell all their promising youngsters in order to survive (home attendances at Selhurst Park were only about one third of those that might have been available at the Valley), it was perhaps surprising that they held on to him for so long, but when Newcastle United made them an offer they couldn't refuse at the beginning of **1992-93**, the club finally lost their prime asset. The transfer was a great source of embarrassment and disappointment for local rivals, Middlesbrough, who thought they had Lee in the bag, until Kevin Keegan moved in. From the moment he joined United, he missed only three games, while scoring 13 goals in all competitions and managing to create 14 more for his team-mates. He turned out to be another important cog in Keegan's wheel, when collecting a First Division Championship medal, as Newcastle stayed at the top of the table for most of the season to romp home eight points clear of West Ham United. Had several outstanding moments, but one that remains vivid in the memory was when he drove the Brentford 'Keeper's clearance straight into the net from 65 yards, only for the goal to be disallowed for offside. There had been rumours that he was keen to return to London, but these have since been denied and he is looking forward to Premier League action with the "Magpies".

| Clubs | Signing Date | Transfer Fee | APPEARANCES | | | | GOALS | | | |
|---|---|---|---|---|---|---|---|---|---|---|
| | | | Lge | FL Cup | FA Cup | Others | Lge | FL Cup | FA Cup | Others |
| Charlton Athletic | 7.83 | - | 274+24 | 16+3 | 14 | 10+2 | 59 | 1 | 2 | 3 |
| Newcastle United* | 9.92 | £700,000 | 36 | 3 | 4 | | 10 | 1 | 2 | |

## LE SAUX Graeme Pierre

Born: Harrow, 17 October 1968

Height: 5'10"

Weight: 11.2

International Honours: E "U21"-4, E"B"

**Position/Skill Factor:** Left-back or midfield player who is capable of playing anywhere on the left side. Skilful, very quick and a good crosser of the ball, he creates chances wherever he plays.

**Career History:** Spotted by Chelsea when playing for a local Jersey side, St Pauls, he signed professional forms without any further ado and within 18 months had made his FL debut as a sub at Portsmouth on 13 May 1989, the "Blues" having already been confirmed as the 1988-89 Second Division Champions. Had to wait until Boxing Day, 1989, to make his second appearance, again as a sub, but he scored to earn Chelsea a 2-2 draw at Selhurst Park. Even though the club shelled out £3 million for Andy Townsend and Dennis Wise at the start of the 1990-91 season, it did not unduly hinder his progress in the first team as he made 24 League appearances and proved to be one of the most exciting young players in the country. Won a regular place in 1991-92 mostly on the flank, but occasionally at left-back and was one of the few successes that season. Had a disappointing start to **1992-93**, not being selected for first team duty until having a run in mid-season. Following a fairly dreadful game at Blackburn Rovers in February, he was dropped by Dave Webb and was sold to Blackburn shortly before the transfer deadline, in exchange for Steve Livingstone, plus cash. He immediately took over from the injured Alan Wright and quickly became a huge favourite with his forceful forward running, aggressive tackling and sheer enthusiasm. Although he only played during the last nine matches, the club has been provided with the headache of having two extremely capable left-backs.

| | | | APPEARANCES | | | | GOALS | | | |
|---|---|---|---|---|---|---|---|---|---|---|
| Clubs | Signing Date | Transfer Fee | Lge | FL Cup | FA Cup | Others | Lge | FL Cup | FA Cup | Others |
| Chelsea | 12.87 | - | 77+13 | 7+6 | 7+1 | 8+1 | 8 | 1 | | |
| Blackburn Rovers* | 3.93 | £500,000 | 9 | | | | | | | |

## LE TISSIER Matthew Paul

Born: Guernsey,
14 October 1968

Height: 6'0"

Weight: 11.6

International Honours:
E Yth, E"B"

**Position/Skill Factor:** Winger cum striker, with pace, who is brilliant with the ball at his feet, often beating defenders for fun. Can both score and create and opens the door when others can't find the key.

**Career History:** First came to Southampton as an associated schoolboy in September 1984, before graduating as an apprentice in July 1985 and scoring 56 goals for the "Saints'" team that coming season. made his FL debut as a sub at Norwich City on 30 August 1986, two months prior to turning professional and during that first season he scored eight League and cup goals, including a hat-trick in a 4-0 win over Leicester City. The youngest player ever to score a hat-trick for the Club, he was taken along slowly and didn't become a regular until 1989-90, although he had netted nine goals in 21 starts in the previous campaign. Twenty strikes in 35 League matches that term was further testimony to his ability as he linked up well with two more of the club's young stars, Rod Wallace and Alan Shearer. Topping the Southampton scoring charts again in 1990-91 with 27 in all games and netting the winning goal on five separate occasions, he had earlier declined an offer to become part of the French international set-up, preferring to take his chances with England. One of the most exciting young players of his generation, it is astonishing that he was never played at Under 21 level. By comparison with the two previous season, 1991-92 was rather mundane as Southampton changed their playing style under new manager Ian Branfoot and goals became very scarce in their struggle against relegation. Scored only six FL goals, of which two were penalties, but netted nine in the various cup competitions (Rumbelows, Zenith and FA) in all of which the "Saints" enjoyed a long run. He played (and scored) in the Zenith Cup Final his first Wembley appearance, but was on the losing side against Nottingham Forest. Took over the mantle of leading goalscorer at the club in **1992-93**, following the transfer of Alan Shearer to Blackburn Rovers and signed a two and a half year contract in January to curtail any speculation that he would be leaving. Played his 200th League game against Liverpool in January and after scoring at Arsenal in March, he needed one goal going into the Nottingham Forest game to net his 100th for the club. With a spot kick being awarded to "Saints", he stepped up to register his 21st consecutive penalty goal and was thwarted, as Mark Crossley pulled off an incredible save. However, in the 72nd minute, he hit a screaming left-foot volley across the goalie into the far corner of the net, to win their personal argument. And, on the final day of the season, with Oldham Athletic seemingly cruising to victory, he single-handedly brought the game to a thrilling climax with a hat-trick, scoring direct from a free-kick, then a header and finally a volley.

| | | | APPEARANCES | | | | GOALS | | | |
|---|---|---|---|---|---|---|---|---|---|---|
| Clubs | Signing Date | Transfer Fee | Lge | FL Cup | FA Cup | Others | Lge | FL Cup | FA Cup | Others |
| Southampton* | 10.86 | - | 183+30 | 23+6 | 16+1 | 11+1 | 75 | 13 | 6 | 9 |

## LIMBER Nicholas (Nicky)

Born: Doncaster, 23 January 1974

Height: 5'10" Weight: 11.2

**Position/Skill Factor:** A full-back with two useful feet and a nice feel for the ball. Good long thrower.

**Career History:** One of the many promising young players discovered by Doncaster Rovers in recent years, he signed as an associated schoolboy for the club in June 1988, before becoming a trainee on leaving school in July 1990. Made his FL debut at Gillingham on 11 May 1991, the last day of the 1990-91 season, still eight months short of the 18th birthday. Selected for the first match of the new season, he was then rested until October. On his return to the team he scored a brilliant 88th minute equaliser against Gillingham in only his fourth game. Only three weeks after signing professional for Doncaster, he was transferred to Manchester City, as the Fourth Division club were forced to sell their most promising players for modest fees simply to stay in business. At least in Limber's case there may be further payments to a maximum of £300,000, if he makes the grade with City. Had an extremely disappointing time of it in **1992-93**, after making a promising start with the reserve side. Loaned out to Peterborough United in October and playing against Brentford, he damaged a ligament, which was severe enough to put him out of action for five months. And on recovering and playing in a couple of matches for the "A" and reserve sides, a further injury, this time suffered in training, saw his season summarily brought to a close. Still only 19-years-old, he has time on his side in his battle to regain full fitness.

| Clubs | Signing Date | Transfer Fee | APPEARANCES Lge | FL Cup | FA Cup | Others | GOALS Lge | FL Cup | FA Cup | Others |
|---|---|---|---|---|---|---|---|---|---|---|
| Doncaster Rovers | 1.92 | - | 13 | | | 1+1 | 1 | | | 1 |
| Manchester City* | 1.92 | £75,000 | | | | | | | | |
| Peterborough United | 10.92 | Loan | 2 | | | | | | | |

## LIMPAR Anders

Born: Sweden, 24 August 1965

Height: 5'8" Weight: 11.5

International Honours: Swedish Int, FL Rep

**Position/Skill Factor:** Left-winger with wonderful natural ability. Has great balance, with two good feet and can wrong foot defenders with ease. Capable of both scoring and creating goals.

**Career History:** Signed by Arsenal from the Italian club, Cremonese, following his exciting performances for Sweden in the 1990 World Cup Finals, he added a new dimension to the "Gunners'" attack during 1990-91. Following his FL debut at Wimbledon on 25 August 1990, the club was rarely out of the top two all season and he celebrated winning a League Championship medal by scoring a hat-trick in the last match, a 6-1 victory at Highbury over Coventry City. Earlier in the season, he had scored the only goal of the infamous game against Manchester United at Old Trafford when 21 players were booked and both teams heavily fined for bringing the game into disrepute. Finished his first season in English football with a tally of 11 League goals, several of them match winners and delighted the Highbury legions as he showed the art of popping up in the penalty area to pounce on half chances. Prior to his spell in Italy, he played for a leading Swiss team, Young Boys of Berne. His second season at Highbury was a strange affair. In and out of the team throughout, he only started 23 FL games, yet at the end of 1991-92 was credited with 15 goal "assists", more than all but two First Division players, who both played the full season. Ended his disappointing English season with strangely subdued performances for Sweden in the European Championships. He played in all four matches as the host country finally went out 3-2 to Germany in the Semi-Final. A great favourite with the fans, he didn't appear to figure in George Graham's plans in **1992-93**, being a peripheral figure for most of the season. However, he scored a typical "Limpar" goal in the "Gunners'" League win at Liverpool in August, but an injury sustained while on international duty and an ongoing bone of contention between player and manager, ruled him out of possible appearances in both the FA and League Cup Finals.

| Clubs | Signing Date | Transfer Fee | APPEARANCES Lge | FL Cup | FA Cup | Others | GOALS Lge | FL Cup | FA Cup | Others |
|---|---|---|---|---|---|---|---|---|---|---|
| Arsenal* | 8.90 | £1,000,000 | 67+19 | 7 | 7 | 3 | 18 | | 2 | 1 |

## LING Martin

Born: West Ham, 15 July 1966

Height: 5'8"

Weight: 10.2

**Position/Skill Factor:** Midfield player with great balance and the ability to beat defenders. Has an excellent football brain and when he gets in good positions, usually choses the right pass.

**Career History:** Played over 100 League games for Exeter City before moving to Swindon Town, Southend United, Mansfield Town and back to the "Robins" as a key player in the club's promotion to the Premier League. Earlier, he had been spotted playing in junior soccer and first arrived at St James' Park as an associated schoolboy in October 1981. Became an apprentice (July 1982) on leaving school and prior to turning professional in early 1984, he was already a regular performer for the "Grecians", having made his FL debut as a substitute at Sheffield United on 5 March 1983, at the age of 16 years and 8 months. After playing in all but five games from 1984 to 1986, he was transferred to Swindon Town in the summer of 1986, but was discarded by "Robins'" manager, Lou Macari, almost as soon as he arrived at the County Ground and was moved on to Southend United within three months. He assisted the "Shrimpers" to promotion from Division Four in his first season at Roots Hall and was a regular performer for the next two seasons, although the club returned to the basement division in 1988-89. Despite scoring ten FL goals in 1989-90, when Southend continued their "yo-yo" existence in the lower divisions, with promotion back to Division Three, he was left completely out in the cold the following season, as the club reached Division Two, after their second consecutive promotion. A short loan period to Mansfield was followed by another loan back to his former club, Swindon, then managerless. Although he only made one appearance during this space, he did enough to impress newly appointed "Robins'" manager, Glenn Hoddle, to sign him on a permanent basis. He had to wait until December 1991 for a first team breakthrough, but since then has more than repaid Hoddle's confidence in him and in **1992-93**, he missed only three games all season. Small of stature and extremely energetic, although he didn't score himself after November, time and time again he threaded his way through crowded defences to set up chances for his team-mates. As an integral member of the side, the "Man of the Match" award in the 4-3 Wembley Play-Off victory over Leicester City, merely emphasised his value and his capabilities could well be even more pronounced on the Premier League stage this coming season.

| | | | APPEARANCES | | | | GOALS | | | |
|---|---|---|---|---|---|---|---|---|---|---|
| Clubs | Signing Date | Transfer Fee | Lge | FL Cup | FA Cup | Others | Lge | FL Cup | FA Cup | Others |
| Exeter City | 1.84 | - | 109+8 | 8 | 4 | 5 | 14 | | | |
| Swindon Town | 7.86 | £25,000 | 2 | 1+1 | | | | | | |
| Southend United | 10.86 | £15,000 | 126+12 | 8 | 7 | 11+1 | 30 | 2 | 1 | 3 |
| Mansfield Town | 1.91 | Loan | 3 | | | | | | | |
| Swindon Town* | 3.91 | £15,000 | 60+5 | 3 | 4 | 6 | 6 | 1 | | |

## LINIGHAN Andrew (Andy)

Born: Hartlepool, 18 June 1962

Height: 6'3" Weight: 12.6

International Honours: E"B"

**Position/Skill Factor:** Tough tackling, consistent centre-back who is very good in the air and more than adaptable on the ground. Very good at hitting long diagonal balls to the front men.

**Career History:** Elder brother of David, currently of Ipswich Town and the son of Brian, who played a single game for Darlington back in 1958, he began his career with Hartlepool United after coming out of local junior football with Smiths Dock and made his FL debut at home to Stockport County on 28 March 1981. Went on to make over 100 appearances for the "Pool", before moving on to Leeds United in the 1984 close season and was ever present for them until transferring to Oldham Athletic some 18 months later. Quickly established himself at the heart of the "Latics'"defence, where his consistency was noted by several First Division clubs. Norwich City won the race for his signature as they bid to become a force to be reckoned with and he went straight into the side as the replacement for Steve Bruce, who had been transferred to Manchester United four months earlier. he proved as reliable as ever as City made an unprecedented push for the League title in 1988-89, only to falter on the run-in to finish in fourth place, their highest position ever. During a two year spell at Carrow Road, he missed just two games, but was on the move again in the 1990 close season as Arsenal, seeking to strengthen their squad, made the "Canaries" an offer they couldn't refuse. Proved a capable deputy in the absence of club skipper, Tony Adams, but with such a strong squad available at Highbury, he played very few games as the League Championship came back to north London. It was strange that Arsenal should pay such a large fee for a player who only provided cover for Adams and Bould. With Bould injured for the first three months of the 1991-92 season he had the chance to establish himself, but although he played on and off until the New Year, once both Adams and Bould were fit he played no further part in the campaign. Became a first team regular in **1992-93**, after an injury put Steve Bould out of action in January, while earlier, the Boxing Day match against an Ipswich Town side captained by David Linighan, marked the first time brothers had opposed each other in the Premier League. Arguably the most consistent Arsenal player during the latter months of the season, he picked up both League and FA Cup winners medals, following the victories over Sheffield Wednesday at Wembley. His danger value at set pieces was never more appropriate than when scoring the winning goal of the dramatic FA Cup Final replay win in the dying seconds of the game.

| | | | APPEARANCES | | | | GOALS | | | |
|---|---|---|---|---|---|---|---|---|---|---|
| Clubs | Signing Date | Transfer Fee | Lge | FL Cup | FA Cup | Others | Lge | FL Cup | FA Cup | Others |
| Hartlepool United | 9.80 | - | 110 | 7+1 | 8 | 1 | 4 | 1 | | 1 |
| Leeds United | 5.84 | £200,000 | 66 | 6 | 2 | 2 | 3 | 1 | | |
| Oldham Athletic | 1.86 | £65,000 | 87 | 8 | 3 | 4 | 6 | 2 | | |
| Norwich City | 3.88 | £350,000 | 86 | 6 | 10 | 4 | 8 | | | |
| Arsenal* | 7.90 | £1,250,000 | 41+7 | 5+1 | 10+1 | 2 | 2 | 1 | 1 | 1 |

## LINIGHAN Brian

Born: Hartlepool, 2 November 1973

Height: 6'0" Weight: 10.3

**Position/Skill Factor:** Right-back, or central defender, who is solid and reliable in everything he does, especially in the air.

**Career History:** With his twin brother, John, he is the latest of the Linighan family to turn professional. Their father, Brian snr, played for Darlington in the 1950s, while brothers Andy and David are currently defenders with

Arsenal and Ipswich Town, respectively. Having been at the club as an associated schoolboy since June 1988 and a trainee since July 1990, he signed on the dotted line during the 1992 close season. No first team experience as yet, but both he and his brother were regulars with the reserve side in **1992-93** and he can possibly expect to further his experience from the bench this season.

| | | | APPEARANCES | | | | GOALS | | | |
|---|---|---|---|---|---|---|---|---|---|---|
| Clubs | Signing Date | Transfer Fee | Lge | FL Cup | FA Cup | Others | Lge | FL Cup | FA Cup | Others |
| Sheffield Wednesday* | 6.92 | – | | | | | | | | |

## LINIGHAN David

Born: Hartlepool, 9 January 1965

Height: 6'2" Weight: 10.12

International Honours: FL Rep

**Position/Skill Factor:** Strong central defender who is very good in the air and is especially dangerous at set plays. With his excellent left foot, he is adept at hitting long balls in behind the opposing full-backs.

**Career History:** Son of Brian, who played for Darlington in 1958 and like his brother Andy, who also joined Hartlepool United from Smiths Dock, he made his FL debut at home to Bradford City on 27 March 1982. Played mainly in the shadow of Andy for a long while and it wasn't until 1985-86 that he finally held down a regular place, missing just eight matches throughout the campaign. Impressed Arthur Cox enough for Derby County to move for him during the summer, but after just four months and no first team appearances, he was transferred to Shrewsbury Town. Finally getting a chance to prove his worth in League football, he missed only three matches in 18 months at Gay Meadow and alerted Ipswich Town, who were looking to replace Ian Cranson, following his move to Sheffield Wednesday. In three seasons at Portman Road, since signing for the "Town", he has become a fixture in central defence and in 1990-91 he had an outstanding season as the club captain, which was recognised by the fans when he picked up their "Player of the Year" award. Played a sterling role in Ipswich's Second Division Championship campaign in 1991-92, at least until the end of March when an injury sustained in the home game against Barnsley ruled him out for the rest of the season. However, the hard work had already been done, with Ipswich coasting home to promotion. Once again he was the rock that Town built their performances around and was a Premier League ever present in **1992-93**. Recovering from a knee injury sustained in a pre-season friendly at Reading, he led the team out for their first game in the top flight since 1985-86 and throughout the campaign, as you would have expected from such an experienced player, he maintained a high level of defensive consistency. Made his 200th appearance for the club at Oldham Athletic earlier in the season and there seems plenty more left in the tank.

| | | | APPEARANCES | | | | GOALS | | | |
|---|---|---|---|---|---|---|---|---|---|---|
| Clubs | Signing Date | Transfer Fee | Lge | FL Cup | FA Cup | Others | Lge | FL Cup | FA Cup | Others |
| Hartlepool United | 3.82 | – | 84+7 | 3+1 | 4 | 2 | 5 | 1 | | |
| Derby County | 8.86 | £25,000 | | | | | | | | |
| Shrewsbury Town | 12.86 | £30,000 | 65 | 5 | 3 | 1 | 1 | | | |
| Ipswich Town* | 6.88 | £300,000 | 204+1 | 16 | 12 | 10 | 9 | | | |

## LINIGHAN John

Born: Hartlepool, 2 November 1973

Height: 5'8¾" Weight: 8.9

**Position/Skill Factor:** Left-back with a good left foot, who is also very skilful and loves going forward.

**Career History:** Signed professional forms for Sheffield Wednesday during the summer, along with his twin brother Brian, having previously been at Hillsborough as an associated schoolboy (June 1988) and as a trainee (July 1990). Father Brian (Darlington) and brothers Andy and David, currently playing, have all made FL appearances. A regular reserve team player in **1992-93**, he will be hoping to emulate his more famous brothers in the very near future.

| | | | APPEARANCES | | | | GOALS | | | |
|---|---|---|---|---|---|---|---|---|---|---|
| Clubs | Signing Date | Transfer Fee | Lge | FL Cup | FA Cup | Others | Lge | FL Cup | FA Cup | Others |
| Sheffield Wednesday* | 6.92 | – | | | | | | | | |

## LITTLEJOHN Adrian Sylvester

Born: Wolverhampton, 26 September 1970

Height: 5'10"

Weight: 10.4

International Honours: E Yth

**Position/Skill Factor:** Very quick winger, with a natural left foot, who goes past defenders looking to hit the front men.

**Career History:** On being released by West Bromwich Albion during the 1989 close season, after a period at the Hawthorns as an associated schoolboy (November 1984) and later as a trainee (July 1987), he signed for nearby Walsall. Made his FL debut at Huddersfield Town on 13 January 1990 and proved a useful player to have around, both in midfield or on the subs' bench. A graduate from the FA School of Excellence. During the 1991 close season, after two years at Fellows Park, he was given a free transfer and was surprisingly picked up by Dave Bassett for Sheffield United — a curious reversal of the usual trend for First Division free transfers to sign for lower division clubs. Made his debut for the "Blades" in the third match as substitute and his full debut in the fifth game of the season. Was not selected again until December when he was given a short run as Brian Deane's forward partner, but without success and he played no further part in the campaign. Due to the lack of goals from Brian Deane's partners in **1992-93**, he was given further first team opportunities. A skilfully taken winner against Liverpool, his first goal for the club, led to an extended run in the team. However, a "wrestling match" with Burnley's Adrian Heath in a Third Round FA Cup-tie, saw him sent off and the forthcoming suspension cost him his regular place. His conversion from an out-and-out winger to a central role looks to be paying off and the coming season should see further developments.

| | | | APPEARANCES | | | | GOALS | | | |
|---|---|---|---|---|---|---|---|---|---|---|
| Clubs | Signing Date | Transfer Fee | Lge | FL Cup | FA Cup | Others | Lge | FL Cup | FA Cup | Others |
| Walsall | 5.89 | – | 26+18 | 2+1 | 1+1 | 4+1 | 1 | | | |
| Sheffield United* | 8.91 | – | 23+11 | 3 | 3+2 | 1 | 8 | | 1 | |

## LIVINGSTONE Stephen (Steve)

Born: Middlesbrough, 8 September 1967

Height: 6'1" Weight: 12.7

**Position/Skill Factor:** Big striker. Acting as a target man, he is strong in possession and holds the ball up well. Extremely dangerous at the far post with his aerial power.

**Career History:** The son of Joe, who played for Middlesbrough, Carlisle United and Hartlepool United between 1960-1967, he joined Coventry City on a YTS scheme in August 1985, before turning professional just under a year later. After making his FL debut as a substitute at Luton Town on 18 April 1987, he made his full debut in the last match of the season at home to Southampton. Hardly got a look-in for the next two seasons, but caused a sensation in 1989-90 when standing in for Kevin Drinkell in January 1990. In a team which could not even average a goal a game, he scored four in a Fifth Round League Cup replay against Sunderland, who were thrashed 5-0. He then scored three times in the next two League games, plus another in the League Cup Semi-Final against Nottingham Forest, although it was not enough to avoid defeat. Eight goals in four consecutive games, then he was inexplicably dropped from the team, being accused of lacking pace by the Coventry management. Scored twice in an early season game in 1990-91, but clearly his face did not fit at Highfield Road and he was transferred to Blackburn Rovers midway through the term. Made a good start at Ewood Park with seven goals in his first ten games and his final tally of nine was second only to Frank Stapleton with ten. Surprisingly passed over for selection in 1991-92, both by Don Mackay and subsequently by Kenny Dalglish, even when Rovers suffered simultaneous injuries to their main strikers Mike Newell and Dave Speedie, he was again ignored in **1992-93**, until the final acts of both cup competitions. However, shortly after the losing FA Cup Quarter-Final replay against Sheffield United, where he headed the goal that put Rovers into the lead, before the match was ultimately decided on penalties, he figured in an exchange deal, plus cash, for Chelsea's Graham Le Saux. Only made a brief League appearance for his new club at Manchester United, before being substituted because of injury on his reserve debut and then being sent off during their next match, an act which was followed by a three match suspension.

| | | | APPEARANCES | | | | GOALS | | | |
|---|---|---|---|---|---|---|---|---|---|---|
| Clubs | Signing Date | Transfer Fee | Lge | FL Cup | FA Cup | Others | Lge | FL Cup | FA Cup | Others |
| Coventry City | 7.86 | – | 17+14 | 8+2 | | 0+1 | 5 | 10 | | |
| Blackburn Rovers | 1.91 | £450,000 | 25+5 | 2 | 1 | | 10 | | 1 | |
| Chelsea* | 3.93 | £350,000 | 0+1 | | | | | | | |

## LOMAS Stephen (Steve) Martin

Born: Hanover, Germany, 18 January 1974

Height: 6'0" Weight: 11.7

International Honours: NI Yth

**Position/Skill Factor:** Midfield player. Good passer with a lovely touch, he is adept at making long runs upfield into the opposing penalty area.

**Career History:** Turned professional for Manchester City on his 17th birthday, having been at Maine Road, first as an associated schoolboy (May 1988) and then as a trainee (July 1990). Although he has yet to play for City's first team, he actually turned out for the Irish League side, Coleraine, while he was still at school. A regular member of the reserves in **1992-93**, he enjoyed a progressive season, playing 29 games and is strongly tipped to break into the PL side within the next year or two.

| | | | APPEARANCES | | | | GOALS | | | |
|---|---|---|---|---|---|---|---|---|---|---|
| Clubs | Signing Date | Transfer Fee | Lge | FL Cup | FA Cup | Others | Lge | FL Cup | FA Cup | Others |
| Manchester City* | 1.91 | – | | | | | | | | |

## LUKIC Jovan (John)

Born: Chesterfield, 11 December 1960

Height: 6'4" Weight: 13.7

International Honours: E Yth, E "U21"-7, E"B"

**Position/Skill Factor:** Like many goalkeepers, he improves with age, being very consistent and making few mistakes. Extremely agile for a big man, he has safe hands and deals well with crosses. Also, has great kicking ability.

**Career History:** First started out as an associated schoolboy at Leeds United in October 1975 under the watchful eye of David Harvey, before signing as an apprentice in May 1977, on leaving school and later turning pro. Actually played his opening senior match against Valletta in the UEFA Cup and ten days later made his FL debut at Brighton & Hove Albion on 13 October 1979, keeping clean sheets in both games. Went on to play 146 successive League matches for United, a club record, but after asking for a transfer, he was dropped and missed the second half of the 1982-83 season. Transferred to Arsenal, as cover for Pat Jennings in the 1983 close season, he eventually took over the number one jersey at Highbury in 1985 and was soon recognised as one of the top 'keepers in Britain. And in 1986-87 he collected his first club honour when Arsenal beat Liverpool 2-1 to take the League Cup. Later, as an ever present in 1988-89, he won a League Championship medal, when conceding only 36 goals all season, as the "Gunners" stormed to the title. But at the end of the following term, he moved back to Leeds, after Arsenal purchased David Seaman from Queens Park Rangers. With United finishing in fourth place on their return to the First Division, he was a major influence in organising their defence into one of the best in the country. Ever present in Leeds' League Championship triumph of 1991-92, he conceded only 37 goals in 42 games and confirmed his reputation as one of the top 'keepers in the country. Began **1992-93** in the same high standard that he has always set for himself, but unfortunately, a bad mistake in the European Cup, when he conceded Glasgow Rangers' first goal at Ibrox, set him up for a lot of media criticism. This seemed to affect his confidence and a loss of form led to him being dropped for two games in January. Still highly regarded by the management and his team-mates, he was recalled for the FA Cup Fourth Round tie at Arsenal and kept his place until the last game of the season. The highlighting of the "own goal" against Rangers, tended to overshadow all else, including three world class stops against VFB Stuttgart in the European Cup, second leg and the superb diving save to prevent a deflected 25 yarder from Brian McClair at Elland Road.

| | | | APPEARANCES | | | | GOALS | | | |
|---|---|---|---|---|---|---|---|---|---|---|
| Clubs | Signing Date | Transfer Fee | Lge | FL Cup | FA Cup | Others | Lge | FL Cup | FA Cup | Others |
| Leeds United | 12.78 | - | 146 | 7 | 9 | 3 | | | | |
| Arsenal | 7.83 | £75,000 | 223 | 32 | 21 | 4 | | | | |
| Leeds United* | 6.90 | £1,000,000 | 119 | 14 | 10 | 11 | | | | |

## LYDERSON Pal

Born: Norway, 10 September 1965

Height: 6'0½" Weight: 14.1

International Honours: Norwegian Int

**Position/Skill Factor:** A right-footed full-back. Very much a passer, he prefers to play the ball out of defence, rather than to simply clear it.

**Career History:** A Norwegian international, he was signed by Arsenal early in the 1991-92 season from Norwegian club IK Start of Kristiansand. With Lee Dixon and Nigel Winterburn holding firm to the full-back slots at Highbury, first team opportunities were slow in coming. However, he enjoyed a little run at the end of the season, making his FL debut at Norwich City on 8 April 1992 and then deputising for Dixon in the next three games. The **1992-93** season saw him again acting as cover for either full-back, while playing nine (including one substitute) first team games. Versatile and capable of slotting in anywhere across the back four, he would have been used more during the last few weeks of the season had he not been recovering from injury.

| | | | APPEARANCES | | | | GOALS | | | |
|---|---|---|---|---|---|---|---|---|---|---|
| Clubs | Signing Date | Transfer Fee | Lge | FL Cup | FA Cup | Others | Lge | FL Cup | FA Cup | Others |
| Arsenal* | 11.91 | £500,000 | 12+3 | 1 | | | | | | |

## MABBUTT Gary Vincent

Born: Bristol, 23 August 1961

Height: 5'9" Weight: 10.10

International Honours: E Yth, E "U21"-7, E"B", E-16

**Position/Skill Factor:** Cool commanding central defender with a tremendous attitude and a captain who leads by example. A great enthusiast, he has a good football brain and despite a lack of inches, is excellent in the air.

**Career History:** One of a footballing family, his father Ray turned out for Bristol Rovers and Newport County between 1956-71 and elder brother Kevin played first team soccer at Bristol City and Crystal Palace between 1976-85. He followed in his father's footsteps when signing as an associated schoolboy at Bristol Rovers in October 1976, later becoming an apprentice in July 1977, before taking the plunge in the professional ranks. Actually made his FL debut at Burnley, while still an apprentice, on 16 December 1978 and during his four years at Eastville showed his character as well as his great ability, when managing to keep his much discussed diabetes condition under control. Signed for Tottenham Hotspur and made his debut in midfield in the opening game of the 1982-83 season at Luton Town, marking the event with a goal and eventually finished the season as the club's second highest League goal scorer, with ten to his credit. Made his first full England appearance against West Germany on 13 October 1982 at Wembley in the right-back slot, later playing for his country, just like his club, in a variety of positions. Won a UEFA Cup winners medal in 1984, following Tottenham's penalty victory over Anderlecht and as club captain, led "Spurs" to the FA Cup Final against Coventry City in 1987, when after putting his side 2-1 up in the first half, he then deflected a speculative cross from Lloyd McGrath into his own goal for Coventry's winner. Four years later in 1991, he again led Tottenham out at Wembley for an FA Cup Final, against Nottingham Forest, this time he ended with a winners medal, following "Spurs'" 2-1 victory. As consistent as ever in 1991-92, he missed only three games in "Spurs'" disappointing campaign. Also made a surprise comeback to the international scene when Graham Taylor found himself short of available central defenders. But although winning three more caps, he was not included in the squad for the European Championship Finals. Spent the pre-**1992-93** season having operations to a knee, shoulder and wrist, before returning to action at Wimbledon by the end of October. He immediately formed a formidable partnership with new boy, Neil Ruddock, steadying what had previously been a shaky defence. Re-instated as captain, apart from the game at Chelsea in March, he remained ever present for the rest of the season and was soon back to his calm and resolute best. Only scored two goals all season, both in the Premier League; the winner against Nottingham Forest in a 2-1 win at White Hart Lane and the first in a 2-1 victory at Everton.

| | | | APPEARANCES | | | | GOALS | | | |
|---|---|---|---|---|---|---|---|---|---|---|
| Clubs | Signing Date | Transfer Fee | Lge | FL Cup | FA Cup | Others | Lge | FL Cup | FA Cup | Others |
| Bristol Rovers | 1.79 | – | 122+9 | 10 | 5+1 | | 10 | 1 | 1 | |
| Tottenham Hotspur* | 8.82 | £105,000 | 355+13 | 51+2 | 33+2 | 29+4 | 27 | 2 | 3 | 4 |

## McALLISTER Brian

Born: Glasgow,
30 November 1970

Height: 5'11"

Weight: 12.5

**Position/Skill Factor:** Central defender. Good in the air and with a strong left foot, he is capable at hitting wonderful long passes behind the opposing team's full-backs.

**Career History:** Came to Wimbledon as a trainee in September 1987 and later, on turning pro, had to wait almost a year to make a first team appearance. After playing in a Zenith Data Cup match against Portsmouth, he made his FL debut at home to Arsenal on 13 January 1990 and was loaned out to Plymouth Argyle for a short spell in 1990-91. Increased his experience with nine more FL appearances for the "Dons" in the second half of the 1991-92 season, mostly in central defence and improved on that performance substantially in **1992-93** when playing 31 full first team games. He broke into the side, replacing Gary Elkins at left-back in the fourth game of the season at Sheffield United and impressed, until falling victim to injury against Arsenal at Selhurst Park. Came back in October to play 12 consecutive matches, following a substitute appearance, before a sending off at Crystal Palace cost him his place when he was suspended. Returned in late January, consistently performing well at either centre-half or left-back and played in most of the remaining games. Unfortunately, a further sending off in the penultimate game of the season at Tottenham Hotspur, meant that he will start 1993-94 with a suspension and it would be a shame if a promising career was wrecked by a bad disciplinary record.

| | | | APPEARANCES | | | | GOALS | | | |
|---|---|---|---|---|---|---|---|---|---|---|
| Clubs | Signing Date | Transfer Fee | Lge | FL Cup | FA Cup | Others | Lge | FL Cup | FA Cup | Others |
| Wimbledon* | 3.89 | – | 36+4 | 2 | 3 | 1 | | | | |
| Plymouth Argyle | 12.90 | Loan | 7+1 | | | | | | | |

## McALLISTER Gary

Born: Motherwell, 25 December 1964

Height: 5'10" Weight: 9.6

International Honours: S "U21"-1, S"B", S-22

**Position/Skill Factor:** One of the best midfield players in the country. Capable of scoring goals, he has good vision and is able to switch play with long diagonal passes. Very dangerous at free-kicks.

**Career History:** Started out with Fir Park BC, before signing for his home town side, Motherwell. After playing 52 League games and winning a Scottish First Division Championship medal in 1984-85, he came south to join Leicester City during the 1985 close season. Easily adjusting to the pace of the Lnglish First Division, he made his FL debut at home to Ipswich Town on 28 September 1985 and marked his first term at Filbert Street with seven League goals. Unfortunately, his nine goals the following season, when only Alan Smith scored more, couldn't prevent City from making the drop into Division Two. Over the next three seasons, he was Leicester's leading goal scorer twice and his brilliant form was eventually recognised when he was capped by Scotland, making his full international debut against East Germany on 25 April 1990 in Glasgow. It was inevitable that a bigger club would make a move for him and during the 1990 close season, Leeds United, seeking more craft in their midfield on their return to the First Division, forked out a large fee to bring him to Elland Road. Made an immediate impact in midfield and was ever present throughout the 1990-91 campaign as the club finished in fourth position. Played a major role in Leeds' League Championship triumph of 1991-92, vindicating Howard Wilkinson's decision to sign him. Also a vital member of the Scottish national team and an automatic selection for the squad for the 1992 European Championship Finals in Sweden where he performed with distinction, scoring in the 3-0 win over CIS. Took over the job of team captain during **1992-93** and held it throughout the campaign, even after Gordon Strachan's return to the side. Produced many outstanding performances during the season and scored some wonderful goals, particularly against Liverpool and Glasgow Rangers. Also scored with superb long range free-kicks in the FA Cup against both Charlton Athletic and Arsenal. A regular in the Scottish side before Christmas, he was unfortunate to sustain a broken arm in a League game at Arsenal and picked up another injury on his return, causing him to miss ten PL matches in all, as well as being unavailable for the international squad. In fact, he ended the season with his right foot in plaster, owing to a hairline fracture, but in a genuine show of the club's ambition, he signed a new contract, pledging himself to Elland Road for a further three years and ending all the press speculation, linking him at home and abroad with a number of other clubs.

| | | | APPEARANCES | | | | GOALS | | | |
|---|---|---|---|---|---|---|---|---|---|---|
| Clubs | Signing Date | Transfer Fee | Lge | FL Cup | FA Cup | Others | Lge | FL Cup | FA Cup | Others |
| Motherwell | 1.82 | – | 52+7 | 3+1 | 7 | | 6 | | 2 | |
| Leicester City | 8.85 | £125,000 | 199+2 | 14+1 | 5 | 4 | 46 | 3 | 2 | |
| Leeds United* | 7.90 | £1,000,000 | 111+1 | 14 | 11 | 10 | 12 | 3 | 3 | 3 |

## McAREE Rodney Joseph

Born: Dungannon, 19 August 1974

Height: 5'7½" Weight: 10.0

International Honours: NI Yth

**Position/Skill Factor:** An attacking midfielder who likes to be involved, he is very constructive when in possession.

**Career History:** Signed as a Liverpool professional during the 1991 close season, having been with the club as a trainee since June 1990, he has yet to progress beyond the club's youth and "A" teams. Was a regular goalscorer for both in **1992-93** and is a promising youngster.

| | | | APPEARANCES | | | | GOALS | | | |
|---|---|---|---|---|---|---|---|---|---|---|
| Clubs | Signing Date | Transfer Fee | Lge | FL Cup | FA Cup | Others | Lge | FL Cup | FA Cup | Others |
| Liverpool* | 8.91 | – | | | | | | | | |

## McCARTHY Alan James

Born: Wandsworth, 11 January 1972

Height: 5'11" Weight: 12.10

International Honours: E Yth

**Position/Skill Factor:** Central defender who reads situations well enough to stop attacks before they properly develop. Never appearing hurried, he has a good left foot and uses the ball well.

**Career History:** Joined Queens Park Rangers as an associated schoolboy in February 1986, before progressing to trainee status in June 1988 and later turning professional. Made his FL debut at Loftus Road against Arsenal on 24 November 1990, during an injury crisis when Rangers lost both first choice central defenders and three days after appearing in a Zenith Data Cup match at Southampton. Played three games for Rangers in November and December 1991 as a third central defender in the number seven shirt, from which the "Rs" collected seven points. With Alan McDonald and Darren Peacock in outstanding form at the heart of Rangers' defence in **1992-93**, apart from sitting out one Premier League game from the bench, he had no further opportunities and remained a regular in the club's successful reserve side, instead. But while things have not been going so well for him at club level, as a multi-qualified player, he recently chose to represent Wales, if required, and has already broken into their under 21 squad. A very useful player for Rangers to have in hand, if he doesn't get the opportunity to play first team football soon, he may quite justifiably decide that his future lies away from Loftus Road.

| | | | APPEARANCES | | | | GOALS | | | |
|---|---|---|---|---|---|---|---|---|---|---|
| Clubs | Signing Date | Transfer Fee | Lge | FL Cup | FA Cup | Others | Lge | FL Cup | FA Cup | Others |
| Q.P.R.* | 12.89 | – | 4+1 | | 0+1 | 1 | | | | |

*Gary McAllister*

## **McCLAIR Brian** John

Born: Bellshill, 8 December 1963

Height: 5'9" Weight: 12.2

International Honours: S "U21"-8, S"B", S-30

**Position/Skill Factor:** Striker. A wonderful team player who always makes himself available. Timing his forward runs to perfection, he gets into the penalty area to score many goals on the blind side of defenders.

**Career History:** Came down south to sign as an apprentice with Aston Villa in July 1980, but was not offered a professional contract and returned to Scotland to join his local club Motherwell when just 18. On getting into the "Bairns'" first team at the beginning of 1981-82, four goals in 11 games helped the club into the Premier Division and the following season a further 11 strikes, prompted Billy McNeill to sign him for Celtic in July 1983. His first season at Celtic Park saw him find the net 23 times in 35 League matches and in a total of 175 games for the club, he scored 121 goals. Also won a Scottish Cup medal in 1985 and a Premier Division Championship medal in 1985-86 and his fine club performances were finally recognised at international level, when he was picked to play for Scotland against Luxembourg at Hampden Park in November 1986. Desperate to re-establish themselves at the forefront of English soccer and to replace Mark Hughes, Manchester United signed him during the 1987 close season. Made his FL debut at Southampton on 15 August 1987 and became the first United player since George Best in 1967-68 to notch up more than 20 FL goals in a season, with a remarkable haul of 24 League goals, including a hat-trick in a 4-1 victory over Derby County. The following season, his goal ratio dropped as he linked up with the returning Mark Hughes, but eventually the partnership began to bear fruit in terms of club honours, culminating in an FA Cup Final victory over Crystal Palace in 1990. A disappointed member of the side that lost 1-0 in the 1991 League Cup Final to Sheffield Wednesday, his sorrow was short lived when three weeks later he won a European Cup Winners Cup medal, following United's 2-1 defeat of Barcelona. Has shown remarkable consistency during four seasons at Old Trafford, only missing five League matches and in manager Alex Ferguson's frequent tactical manoeuvres, often played in a wide midfield role, leaving Hughes as a lone striker. Ever present in 1991-92, he enjoyed his best season since his initial one at Old Trafford, top scoring with 18 FL goals, plus six cup goals, including the winner in the League Cup Final against Nottingham Forest which brought the trophy to Old Trafford for the first time. For much of the season he appeared certain to add a League Championship medal to his collection of trophies, but United's challenge collapsed in the closing week. A regular member of the Scottish national team and included in the squad for the 1992 European Championship Finals in Sweden and after failing to score for Scotland after 23 games, he broke his "duck" with a goal in the 3-0 demolition of CIS. Unfortunately, despite that great win, Scotland went out of the tournament after earlier losing to Holland and Germany. Missed only one game during **1992-93**, playing almost the entire Championship winning season in midfield, instead of in his normal attacking role, but as always he could be relied upon to score goals when most needed. It was McClair who saw United out of their four match goalscoring drought last November, with a brace at home to Oldham Athletic and he grabbed another pair to bring about a dramatic late recovery from a 3-0 deficit at Sheffield Wednesday on Boxing Day. And by putting the disappointment of last year firmly behind them, the "Reds" marched on to win the League title for the first time since 1966-67. His renewed good form also earned him a recall to the Scottish World Cup side at the end of a tough campaign, that had earlier seen him dropped after the first two international matches. Although the possessor of much vision and an excellent footballing brain, he is often underrated by fans and media, but the opposition only do so at their peril.

| | | | APPEARANCES | | | | GOALS | | | |
|---|---|---|---|---|---|---|---|---|---|---|
| Clubs | Signing Date | Transfer Fee | Lge | FL Cup | FA Cup | Others | Lge | FL Cup | FA Cup | Others |
| Motherwell | 6.81 | - | 33+7 | 9+1 | 2 | | 15 | 4 | 1 | |
| Glasgow Celtic | 6.83 | £100,000 | 129+16 | 19+1 | 14+4 | 13+2 | 99 | 9 | 11 | 3 |
| Manchester United* | 7.87 | £850,000 | 231+4 | 31 | 27 | 20 | 79 | 14 | 11 | 7 |

## **McDONALD Alan**

Born: Belfast,
12 October 1963

Height: 6'2"

Weight: 12.7

International Honours:
NI Sch, NI Yth, NI-39

**Position/Skill Factor:** A rugged and uncompromising, strong tackling central defender, who is difficult to get the better of. Very good in the air, he is extremely dangerous in the opposing box from dead ball situations.

**Career History:** An associated schoolboy (March 1980) and an apprentice (July 1980), before turning professional with Queens Park Rangers, he actually made his FL debut, whilst on loan to Charlton Athletic at the Valley against Crystal Palace on 4 April 1983. Played his first League game for Rangers the following season in a 4-0 win at Wolverhampton Wanderers and scored his first goal for the club two games later, in a resounding League Cup win over Crewe Alexandra. Made way for Steve Wicks during the latter half of the campaign, but over the next few seasons, he established himself as one of the best central defenders in the First Division. In October 1985, he won the first of many international caps when he played for Northern Ireland in a 1-0 win over Romania in Bucharest and a month later was one of the stars of a brave performance against England at Wembley, a 0-0 draw sealing Northern Ireland's place in the 1986 World Cup Finals. That season, he was a key player as Queens Park Rangers reached the League Cup Final against Oxford United, but a winners medal eluded him as Rangers went down 3-0. Very consistent over several years, he struggled with injuries during 1990-91 and missed a large part of the club's programme as they hovered at the bottom of the First Division, before climbing to safety during the last two months of the season. With a surfeit of central defenders at Loftus Road, he played second fiddle to Danny Maddix and Darren Peacock in the first three months of 1991-92. However, after displacing Maddix in November, he held his place till the end of the season and assisted the "Rs" to climb from 21st place to mid-table, following an impressive run of 19 FL games with only one defeat. Rock solid and reliable, he held centre stage for Rangers in **1992-93**, missing only four first team matches through injury and taking his tally of Northern Ireland caps to 39. Would dearly love a goal to his name, having now gone two and a half seasons without one, but it is for his great defensive ability that he is selected time and again, while giving every striker he comes up against a tough time. Now in his 14th year at the club, a vice captain last season, he stepped up to captain the side for 16 matches, while Ray Wilkins recovered from injury and did a fine job in leading by example.

| | | | APPEARANCES | | | | GOALS | | | |
|---|---|---|---|---|---|---|---|---|---|---|
| Clubs | Signing Date | Transfer Fee | Lge | FL Cup | FA Cup | Others | Lge | FL Cup | FA Cup | Others |
| Q.P.R.* | 8.81 | – | 281+5 | 31 | 24 | 5 | 8 | 2 | 1 | |
| Charlton Athletic | 3.83 | Loan | 9 | | | | | | | |

## McDONALD **David** Hugh

Born: Dublin, 2 January 1971

Height: 5'10" Weight: 11.0

International Honours: IR Yth, IR "U21"-3, IR "B"

**Position/Skill Factor:** Strong tackling right-back who uses the ball well from deep positions with long passes into the front players.

**Career History:** After leaving school, he joined Tottenham Hotspur as a trainee in May 1987, before turning professional in the 1988 close season. Was loaned out to Fourth Division Gillingham for a two month spell in 1990-91, making his FL debut wearing the number two shirt at York City on 29 September 1990. And following a blank spell in 1991-92, apart from winning a Republic of Ireland "B" cap against Denmark and two more under 21 caps to go with the one he had won the previous season, he went out for two further loan periods in **1992-93** with Bradford City and Reading. On coming back from a lengthy spell at Elm Park, he was immediately called up to make his "Spurs'" debut in a 6-2 defeat at Liverpool on 8 May and just three days later he was a member of the side that recorded a 3-1 victory at Arsenal.

| | | | APPEARANCES | | | | GOALS | | | |
|---|---|---|---|---|---|---|---|---|---|---|
| Clubs | Signing Date | Transfer Fee | Lge | FL Cup | FA Cup | Others | Lge | FL Cup | FA Cup | Others |
| Tottenham Hotspur* | 8.88 | – | 2 | | | | | | | |
| Gillingham | 9.90 | Loan | 10 | | | 2 | | | | |
| Bradford City | 8.92 | Loan | 7 | | | | | | | |
| Reading | 3.93 | Loan | 11 | | | | | | | |

## McDONALD **Neil** Raymond

Born: Wallsend, 2 November 1965

Height: 5'11"

Weight: 11.4

International Honours: E Sch, E Yth, E "U21"-5

**Position/Skill Factor:** Can play equally well at right-back or in midfield. A great striker of the ball with his right foot, he can hit long crossfield passes with ease. Always looks threatening when he goes forward and is a good crosser of the ball.

**Career History:** On leaving school and having already won English schoolboy honours, he signed as an apprentice for Newcastle United in July 1982 and made his FL debut at St James' Park against Barnsley on 25 September 1982, while still too young to turn professional. Won a permanent place by the end of the season, teaming up in midfield with ex-England star, Terry McDermott, in a side that also included Kevin Keegan and Chris Waddle. Injury restricted his contribution to just 12 matches the following season as United won promotion to the First Division, but he made his mark in the top flight by continuing to churn out consistent performances. Transferred to Everton in the 1988 close season, he was introduced at Goodison Park in the opening match of 1988-89, a 4-0 win over Newcastle, playing in what was a new look, expensive side. Figured most of the season in the right-back position, although missing three months earlier through injury and played in the 3-2 FA Cup Final defeat by near neighbours, Liverpool. Proved a valuable asset to Everton, being able to play in a variety of positions, as the team struggled to find the right balance. Out of favour at the start of 1991-92, he was transferred to newly promoted Oldham Athletic for a large fee. Surprisingly, was mainly unable to claim a regular place either at right-back, where there was a vacancy to be filled, or in midfield and was mainly utilised as a cover player. **1992-93** was even more disappointing than his first season with the club, as a mixture of injuries, which included a badly damaged ankle, lack of motivation and loss of form, accounted for him only playing three full games. Made a couple of appearances at right-back, when Gunnar Halle was pushed forward and played in midfield in a 3-0 defeat by Manchester United. During that match, he was unlucky not to score when hitting the bar, following a Steve Redmond corner and apart from a couple of substitute runs, that was his season. Has now re-located his family and better things are expected in 1993-94.

| | | | APPEARANCES | | | | GOALS | | | |
|---|---|---|---|---|---|---|---|---|---|---|
| Clubs | Signing Date | Transfer Fee | Lge | FL Cup | FA Cup | Others | Lge | FL Cup | FA Cup | Others |
| Newcastle United | 2.83 | - | 163+17 | 12 | 10+1 | 3 | 24 | 3 | 1 | |
| Everton | 8.88 | £525,000 | 76+14 | 7 | 17 | 10+1 | 4 | 3 | | |
| Oldham Athletic* | 10.91 | £500,000 | 16+5 | 3 | | | 1 | | | |

## McDONALD Paul Thomas

Born: Motherwell, 20 April 1968

Height: 5'7" Weight: 9.5

**Position/Skill Factor:** Left-winger with a superb left foot, who goes past defenders in typical Scottish fashion.

**Career History:** Signed by Southampton manager, Ian Branfoot, in the summer from Scottish First Division club, Hamilton Academicals, along with team mate Colin Cramb, having shown impressive form in **1992-93**. Made his Scottish League debut for the "Accies" in October 1986, after being discovered playing for Merry Street boys' club and became a regular choice from 1988 onwards on the left-wing. Having played Scottish League football for so long, he may take a while to adjust to the pace of the English game, but could well end up giving defenders a hard time.

| | | | APPEARANCES | | | | GOALS | | | |
|---|---|---|---|---|---|---|---|---|---|---|
| Clubs | Signing Date | Transfer Fee | Lge | FL Cup | FA Cup | Others | Lge | FL Cup | FA Cup | Others |
| Hamilton Acad. | 6.86 | - | 187+28 | 7+2 | 7+1 | 8 | 26 | 2 | | 3 |
| Southampton* | 6.93 | £75,000 | | | | | | | | |

## McDONOUGH Darron Karl

Born: Antwerp, Belgium, 7 November 1962

Height: 5'11"

Weight: 11.0

**Position/Skill Factor:** Hardworking midfielder, who can play anywhere. Strong in the tackle and good in the air, he is the ideal utility player.

**Career History:** A wholehearted player and the scorer of a great goal on his FL debut for Oldham Athletic in a 2-0 win at Notts County on 13 December 1980, he first came to the club as an associated schoolboy (December 1977), before signing on as an apprentice (July 1979) and then graduating to the professional ranks early in 1980. Played in virtually every position in his seven seasons at Boundary Park, at first as a midfielder, then as a forward, scoring ten FL goals in 1982-83, but later settling down in central defence. He left Oldham in September 1986, following a contractual dispute and stepped up to the First Division with Luton Town. Because of his versatility, he proved to be a valued squad member who could cover several positions, in midfield, central defence, or at full-back, but was rarely given an extended run to establish himself and missed out on the "Hatters'" amazing League Cup Final victory over Arsenal in 1988. Out of favour in 1991-92, he was rescued by Kevin Keegan, who made him one of his first signings after taking over Newcastle United in February 1992. Sadly for him, however, he made only three appearances in the "Magpies'" line-up, before being discarded and played no part in Newcastle's triumphant First Division Championship season in **1992-93**. The closest he got to a first team place was as a non-playing substitute in the Anglo-Italian Cup match against Grimsby Town. And to make matters worse, he suffered a badly damaged ankle while playing in a reserve match towards the end of the season, an injury that stunted any further chance of progress. Appears to have no future at St James' Park!

| | | | APPEARANCES | | | | GOALS | | | |
|---|---|---|---|---|---|---|---|---|---|---|
| Clubs | Signing Date | Transfer Fee | Lge | FL Cup | FA Cup | Others | Lge | FL Cup | FA Cup | Others |
| Oldham Athletic | 1.80 | - | 178+5 | 12 | 5 | | 14 | 3 | | |
| Luton Town | 9.86 | £87,500 | 88+17 | 8+1 | 9+1 | 3 | 5 | 1 | 1 | |
| Newcastle United* | 3.92 | £90,000 | 2+1 | | | | | | | |

## McDOUGALD David Eugene Junior

Born: Texas, USA, 12 January 1975

Height: 5'11" Weight: 10.12

International Honours: E Yth

**Position/Skill Factor:** Striker. Very fast with great skill, he is always looking to score goals.

**Career History:** An excellent prospect, with lots going for him, he first came to Tottenham Hotspur as an associated schoolboy (June 1989), before making good progress through the trainee (August 1991) ranks to sign professional forms last summer. A regular in the South-Eastern Counties side and an England youth selection in **1992-93**, he also had a couple of run outs in "Spurs'" reserves.

| | | | APPEARANCES | | | | GOALS | | | |
|---|---|---|---|---|---|---|---|---|---|---|
| Clubs | Signing Date | Transfer Fee | Lge | FL Cup | FA Cup | Others | Lge | FL Cup | FA Cup | Others |
| Tottenham Hotspur* | 7.93 | - | | | | | | | | |

## McGEE Paul

Born: Dublin, 17 May 1968

Height: 5'6"

Weight: 9.10

International Honours: IR "U21"-4

**Position/Skill Factor:** A live wire winger. Good ability with the ball, with twists and turns, he is well capable of beating defenders. Crosses the ball well with both feet.

**Career History:** Joined Colchester United from the League of Ireland side, Bohemians, early in 1989 and made his FL debut at Layer Road in a 2-2 draw against Burnley on 10 February 1989. After just three games for United, who appeared doomed to relegation to the Vauxhall Conference, but later saved themselves, he was sold to Wimbledon for a massive profit of £85,000. He had to wait until the final game of the season before making his bow for the "Dons", against Championship chasing Arsenal at Highbury and his goal in a 2-2 draw seemed at the time to strike a mortal blow to the "Gunners'" title hopes. Struggled to make an impact after the 1989 summer break, playing just 11 games without finding the net, but regained his place in 1990-91, following a two goal burst away to Crystal Palace in October. In common with the "Dons'" other wingers (Anthrobus, Bennett and Fairweather), he had a hard time in 1991-92, but at least, unlike the others, he broke back into the first team on five occasions for a total of 15 FL games. Injury kept him out for long periods of **1992-93** and even when fit he faced an uphill battle to get into the side, being reduced to three appearances, two of them from the bench. That both his substitute games were in the final three matches of the season, shows him beginning to come back into the selection reckoning and he can be expected to challenge for a first team spot in 1993-94.

| | | | APPEARANCES | | | | GOALS | | | |
|---|---|---|---|---|---|---|---|---|---|---|
| Clubs | Signing Date | Transfer Fee | Lge | FL Cup | FA Cup | Others | Lge | FL Cup | FA Cup | Others |
| Colchester United | 2.89 | £35,000 | 3 | | | 1 | | | | |
| Wimbledon* | 3.89 | £120,000 | 54+6 | 3+1 | 5 | 2 | 9 | 2 | 1 | |

## McGIBBON Patrick

Born: Lurgan, Northern Ireland, 6 September 1973

Height: 6'1½" Weight: 12.12

International Honours: NI Sch

**Position/Skill Factor:** Central defender, who is strong in the air and very aggressive on the ground. Defensively sound, he is also a good passer of the ball.

**Career History:** A schoolboy international while at St Michael's, Lurgan, he signed for Portadown, where his excellent displays soon brought him to the attention of FL scouts and Manchester United moved in quickly at the start of **1992-93**, to secure his services. Although signed as a player for the future, he had a frustrating season, inasmuch that he didn't progress as far as the first team. However, he proved a likely prospect as a regular member of the Central League side and could push hard for a Premier League slot over the next couple of seasons.

| | | | APPEARANCES | | | | GOALS | | | |
|---|---|---|---|---|---|---|---|---|---|---|
| Clubs | Signing Date | Transfer Fee | Lge | FL Cup | FA Cup | Others | Lge | FL Cup | FA Cup | Others |
| Manchester United* | 8.92 | £100,000 | | | | | | | | |

## McGOLDRICK Edward (Eddie) John Paul

Born: Islington, 30 April 1965

Height: 5'10" Weight: 12.0

International Honours: IR "B", IR-8

**Position/Skill Factor:** Originally a winger, he is more than useful as an attacking midfielder, where his pace takes him past defenders. Good early crosser of the ball.

**Career History:** While still at school, he signed associated schoolboy forms with Peterborough United in December 1979, but was allowed to drift away from London Road and joined non-League Kettering Town. Moved on to Gola League rivals, Nuneaton Borough and it was from there that he came into the League with Northampton

Town during the 1986 close season, signed by Graham Carr, his former manager at Nuneaton. Made his FL debut at Scunthorpe United on 23 August 1986 and at the end of his first season had won a Fourth Division Championship medal, with his skilful play being a major contributory factor in the club's success. After two season's at the County Ground, he signed for Second Division Crystal Palace early in 1989 and in his first season at the club he was a member of the team that was promoted to the top flight, via the Play-Offs. Despite being a regular during the early part of 1989-90, he found himself among the long term injured and did not regain his place in time for the FA Cup Final against Manchester United. Eventually won back a place in the team during 1990-91, this time in the number 11 shirt when he made way for John Salako on the right as Palace achieved their highest ever League position, third in the First Division. Played in 36 FL games in 1991-92, all in the number 11 shirt, although his role is primarily defensive these days. Ironically, he scored his first FL goal for Palace after nearly three years "drought". Won his first cap for the Irish Republic against Switzerland in March 1992 and played twice more for the Irish team before the summer break. The only ever present, along with Nigel Martyn in **1992-93**, during a season that promised to be the start of a bright new era for English football with the advent of the Premier League, somehow ended in disaster for him and his team-mates as Palace were relegated. Earlier, after signing a new contract that gave him a bonus of £10,000 if he scored seven League goals, he collected, following the match at Queens Park Rangers, having cracked in two during a 3-1 win and even in a poor season for the club he continued to produce several outstanding performances. Although Palace had a spell in mid-season, when they won six games in a row, they were always trailing for most of the campaign, but it was still a shock when Oldham Athletic and Sheffield United pipped them to avoid the drop. Following the departure of manager, Steve Coppell, it came as no real surprise when McGoldrick was transferred to Arsenal, even though he had two years of his contract left. Quite simply, as a regular with the Republic of Ireland, he wished to retain Premier League status, while the club were probably more than happy to receive a large fee in return.

| | | | APPEARANCES | | | | GOALS | | | |
|---|---|---|---|---|---|---|---|---|---|---|
| Clubs | Signing Date | Transfer Fee | Lge | FL Cup | FA Cup | Others | Lge | FL Cup | FA Cup | Others |
| Northampton Town | 8.86 | £10,000 | 97+10 | 9 | 6+1 | 7 | 9 | | 1 | 1 |
| Crystal Palace | 1.89 | £200,000 | 139+8 | 21+1 | 5 | 13+1 | 11 | | | 3 |
| Arsenal* | 6.93 | £1,000,000 | | | | | | | | |

## **McGOWAN Gavin** Gregory

Born: London, 16 January 1976

Height: 5'9½" Weight: 11.4

International Honours: E Sch

**Position/Skill Factor:** Central defender who can also play at right-back, or in midfield. A strong tackler, he is no mean passer of the ball either.

**Career History:** A former England schoolboy international, he recently became one of a select band of players to have appeared for Arsenal's League side, prior to signing professional forms. An associated schoolboy (November 1990) and only ten months a trainee (July 1992), he made his FL debut in **1992-93** on 6 May 1993 as a substitute at Sheffield Wednesday, against a team that were shortly due to play the "Gunners" in the FA Cup Final. And with Arsenal still very much in the midst of a build up of fixtures, he followed it up with another appearance from the bench in the last game of the season against north London rivals, Tottenham Hotspur. Has an outstanding chance of becoming a very good player.

| | | | APPEARANCES | | | | GOALS | | | |
|---|---|---|---|---|---|---|---|---|---|---|
| Clubs | Signing Date | Transfer Fee | Lge | FL Cup | FA Cup | Others | Lge | FL Cup | FA Cup | Others |
| Arsenal* | - | - | 0+2 | | | | | | | |

## **McGRATH Lloyd** Anthony

Born: Birmingham, 24 February 1965

Height: 5'9"

Weight: 10.6

International Honours: E Yth, E"U21"-1

**Position/Skill Factor:** As a brave, tough tackling, 90 minute midfield player, he is known for his man-to-man marking ability. Always shows great enthusiasm and is useful in the air.

**Career History:** Came up through the Coventry City ranks as an associated schoolboy (January 1980), before signing as an apprentice in June 1981. However, after turning professional, he had to wait more than 18 months to make his first appearance in a "Sky Blue" shirt. Unfortunately, his FL debut at Southampton on 28 April 1984, turned out to be a far from happy occasion as City were thrashed 8-2, their biggest defeat since the war. However, his industry earned him a regular place the following term, even after he had endured another disaster while wearing the number five shirt, a 6-2 defeat at Chelsea. One of the heroes of the Coventry 3-2 FA Cup Final win over Tottenham Hotspur in 1987, he performed an effective marking job on Glenn Hoddle and provided the cross which was deflected by Gary Mabbutt into his own net for the winning goal. Although serious injuries forced him to miss much of the League programme during the last three seasons, he continued to battle away. After nearly ten years at Highfield Road, he finally won a regular place in 1991-92 and was absent for only two games — a remarkable achievement for a utility player who operated in a variety of different positions during the season, playing in both full-back and all four midfield slots. Missed the start of **1992-93** through suspension and was then absent for four separate periods due to injury, while playing 28 (including five substitute) first team games. His best spells came in the early part of the season and around the Christmas period, when he filled what is probably his best position, the midfield man-to-man marking slot. If he can remain relatively injury free, he stands to have a good season in 1993-94, having been awarded a well earned testimonial.

| Clubs | Signing Date | Transfer Fee | APPEARANCES Lge | FL Cup | FA Cup | Others | GOALS Lge | FL Cup | FA Cup | Others |
|---|---|---|---|---|---|---|---|---|---|---|
| Coventry City* | 12.82 | - | 190+13 | 21 | 16 | 6 | 4 | 1 | | |

## McGRATH Paul

Born: Ealing, 4 December 1959

Height: 6'0" Weight: 13.2

International Honours: FL Rep, IR-61

**Position/Skill Factor:** Good all-round player, now settled in central defence after playing in many positions. Strong, good in the air, he has a knack of reading dangerous situations almost before they occur.

**Career History:** Although born in England, he was discovered by Manchester United while playing for St Patricks Athletic in the League of Ireland. Came into the side for his FL debut at Old Trafford against Tottenham Hotspur on 13 November 1982, when deputising for Kevin Moran and eventually gained a regular place. Won an FA Cup winners medal in 1985, following United's 1-0 victory over Everton and earlier that season he had made his international debut for the Republic of Ireland in Dublin, coming on as a substitute against Italy on 5 February 1985. In 1985-86, he was runner-up to Gary Lineker as the PFA "Player of the Year", testament to his outstanding performances and to the fact that he only missed two League matches that season. Spent a long spell out injured in 1987-88, but recovered well and in the summer months, starred in the Irish midfield during the European Championships. Only played 18 League games in 1988-89, as injuries again took their toll and during the close season he was allowed to leave for Aston Villa. Proved an inspired signing as the club rocketed from 17th place the previous term, to First Division runners-up and while they slipped somewhat in 1990-91, he continued to shine as the defensive lynch pin the Villa team depends on. One of the Irish Republic's all-time great players, his performances both in midfield and central defence are perhaps the single most important factor in the establishment of Jack Charlton's team as one of the strongest in Europe and one which qualified for the 1990 World Cup Finals in Italy, the first time ever for the Republic. Another excellent season personally during 1991-92, although a disappointing one for his team. Only missed one FL game and his central defensive partnership with Shaun Teale made the Villa defence one of the tightest in the First Division. Voted the "Player of the Year" by the PFA and also by the Villa supporters in **1992-93**, for the fourth year in succession, he was once again outstanding as the "Villans" finished runners-up to Manchester United in the battle for the first Premier League Championship. Yet again he and Shaun Teale proved totally dominant at the back and were the cornerstone of the club's success. Still a regular for the Republic, as he continues to play on "borrowed" time, with reference to his past injuries, one can't imagine Villa without him.

| Clubs | Signing Date | Transfer Fee | APPEARANCES Lge | FL Cup | FA Cup | Others | GOALS Lge | FL Cup | FA Cup | Others |
|---|---|---|---|---|---|---|---|---|---|---|
| Manchester United | 4.82 | £30,000 | 159+4 | 13 | 15+2 | 9 | 12 | 2 | 2 | |
| Aston Villa* | 8.89 | £400,000 | 153 | 13 | 16 | 7 | 6 | 1 | | |

## McKEE Colin

Born: Glasgow, 22 August 1973

Height: 5'10" Weight: 10.11

International Honours: S Sch

**Position/Skill Factor:** Striker. Very good on the ball, he is quick, skilful and a dangerous finisher.

**Career History:** Signed professional forms for Manchester United in the 1991 close season, having been at Old Trafford as a trainee since June 1989. Played a starring role in United's successful youth squad which defeated Crystal Palace 6-3 on aggregate in the 1992 FA Youth Cup Final and in **1992-93** he became a regular choice for the Central League side. Yet to make a first team appearance for United, he was loaned out to Bury and made his FL debut at home to Walsall on 9 January 1993. Will be expected to push for a place this season.

| Clubs | Signing Date | Transfer Fee | APPEARANCES Lge | FL Cup | FA Cup | Others | GOALS Lge | FL Cup | FA Cup | Others |
|---|---|---|---|---|---|---|---|---|---|---|
| Manchester United* | 6.91 | - | | | | | | | | |
| Bury | 1.93 | Loan | 2 | | | 0+1 | | | | |

## MacLAREN Ross

Born: Edinburgh, 14 April 1962

Height: 5'10"

Weight: 12.12

**Position/Skill Factor:** Midfielder, or central defender, who is a lovely striker of the ball and can be very dangerous when on the edge of the box. Adept at breaking up attacks and setting his team in motion with long, raking passes.

**Career History:** Not offered professional terms by Glasgow Rangers, after a period in their youth team, he came south in the 1980 close season to try his luck in the Football League with Shrewsbury Town. Took a while to settle down, before making his FL debut at Chelsea on 31 January 1981, but quickly became a first team regular in his second season at Gay Meadow, after adjusting to the English game. He became an automatic choice in central defence for the "Shrews", helping them to maintain their previously unfamiliar status in the Second Division. After missing just four games in three seasons and ever present in 1984-85, he then stepped down a division to join ambitious Derby County. He was ever present in his first two seasons with the "Rams" and assisted them back to the top flight with two consecutive promotions, the first in 1985-86 as a nervous third place in Division Three and the second, in 1986-87, more convincingly, as Second Division Champions. With the arrival of Mark Wright in the summer of 1987, competition for central defensive places became more fierce and towards the end of Derby's difficult first season back in the top flight he lost his place to Rob Hindmarch. "Rams'" manager, Arthur Cox, may have felt that he was not sufficiently high calibre for the First Division and therefore accepted a sizeable fee from Lou Macari to take him to Swindon Town in the summer of 1988. However, Swindon had a surfeit of central defenders and for most of his first season at the County Ground he was deployed as a defensive midfield player. When Ossie Ardiles took over the reins in the summer of 1989, he continued in this role and clocked up his fourth ever present season, leading his team to fourth place and victory over Sunderland in the Play-Off Final. Tragically, promotion was denied to the club by Football League decree, but after an appeal to the FA, the club were reinstated in Division Two. After ten seasons of amazing consistency, he was struck down by injury in February 1992, which kept him out of action for almost a year and although severe financial difficulties prohibited the signing of any new players, his return in **1992-93**, after Christmas, was as good as having a new player at the club. To many supporters he has never quite recaptured his best form since that injury, but it is known that he was still suffering pain right up until the end of the season. Speed has never been one of his main assets, but he is a vital member of the team and since coming back he has not missed a match. Due to the defensive nature of his role in the current side, he contributes few goals, but he possesses a fierce shot and it was his 20 yarder that brought about Town's second in a 3-1 Play-Off Semi-Final victory, when Dave Mitchell pounced on an opening, after Tranmere Rover's 'keeper had failed to hold the ball. With the club finally in the top flight for the first time in their history, he can look forward with justification to playing Premier League soccer this season in his 13th year as a professional.

| | | | APPEARANCES | | | | GOALS | | | |
|---|---|---|---|---|---|---|---|---|---|---|
| Clubs | Signing Date | Transfer Fee | Lge | FL Cup | FA Cup | Others | Lge | FL Cup | FA Cup | Others |
| Shrewsbury Town | 8.80 | - | 158+3 | 11 | 7+1 | | 18 | 3 | 1 | |
| Derby County | 7.85 | £67,000 | 113+9 | 13 | 9 | 5 | 9 | 2 | | 1 |
| Swindon Town* | 8.88 | £165,000 | 182 | 19 | 11 | 15 | 9 | 2 | | 1 |

## McMAHON Gerard Joseph

Born: Belfast, 29 December 1973

Height: 5'11½" Weight: 11.0

International Honours: NI Yth

**Position/Skill Factor:** Right-wing or midfield. Skilful, lots of pace and a good passer.

**Career History:** After showing exciting form for Glenavon in the Irish League the previous season, Tottenham Hotspur moved quickly to sign him during the summer of 1992. Yet to play first team football, having played with the reserves in **1992-93**, "Spurs" still expect great things from this young man in the near future.

| | | | APPEARANCES | | | | GOALS | | | |
|---|---|---|---|---|---|---|---|---|---|---|
| Clubs | Signing Date | Transfer Fee | Lge | FL Cup | FA Cup | Others | Lge | FL Cup | FA Cup | Others |
| Tottenham Hotspur* | 6.92 | £30,000 | | | | | | | | |

## McMAHON Stephen (Steve)

Born: Liverpool, 20 August 1961

Height: 5'9" Weight: 11.8

International Honours: E "U21"-6, FL Rep, E"B", E-17

**Position/Skill Factor:** All-purpose midfielder with a wealth of experience. A strong tackler, who is very competitive, he also has a powerful shot. Shows great vision in picking out telling passes.

**Career History:** Began his soccer career on the Everton side of Stanley Park when becoming an apprentice with the "Toffees" in December 1977 and after turning to the professional ranks, he had to wait a further year before appearing in the first team. Made his FL debut at Sunderland on 16 August 1980 and played for most of the season until an injury slowed him down. A great competitor, it was a surprise when he was allowed to move to Aston Villa and in two full seasons at Villa Park, he showed his worth, albeit that the club was not very successful. Then, just two weeks into the 1985-86 season, with Villa having conceded eight goals in three games and Liverpool looking to add extra bite to their midfield, he

transferred his allegiances to Anfield. At the end of his first season with the "Reds", the club had done the "double", only the fifth side to do so and although he wasn't selected for the FA Cup Final side, he picked up a League Championship medal as his share of the spoils. From then on it was success all the way; two more League Championship medals in 1987-88 and 1989-90 and an FA Cup winners medal in 1989, following the 3-2 victory over local rivals, Everton. Recognition at full international level had to come and it was no surprise when he picked up his first England cap in Tel Aviv in a 0-0 draw against Israel on 17 February 1988. Suffered several injury problems in 1990-91 and following the Fifth Round FA Cup tie at Anfield against Everton, he came off the field, not to play again for the rest of the season. The loss of both McMahon and Whelan dealt a fatal blow to Liverpool's title hopes that season. Played the best football of his career in his first three seasons at Anfield. Suffered a serious knee injury in the second game of the 1988-89 and although he recovered and returned to the team he was not quite as effective as before, although still a very committed player. Started his international career at the relatively late age of 26 and probably just after he had passed his peak and as with Peter Reid, his path to the national team was blocked by Bryan Robson. After the appointment of Graham Souness as Liverpool manager, it was soon clear that his days at Anfield were numbered. Nevertheless, the timing of his departure was a surprise, with Liverpool in the middle of an injury crisis. However, the fee was one Liverpool could hardly refuse for a 30-year-old player. Ironically, his last match for Liverpool was against the club about to sign him — Manchester City. It was assumed that McMahon was signed to replace his new manager Peter Reid in the team, but in fact the two played together for a while, with disappointing results. To his credit, McMahon recovered from his ineffective start and was back to his best, assisting City to finish 1991-92 in fine style with a final placing of fifth. Up until being injured in February, he was having a strong impact on the club's performances in **1992-93**, with consistently solid midfield play. Carried off at Queens Park Rangers with a ruptured groin muscle, sidelined him for 12 weeks and was a major factor in City not finishing in a higher position in the League. Although recovering well, he didn't return to the side until the last three games of the season and was substituted during the 5-1 debacle at home to Everton. At 32, he is still young enough to be a major influence at Maine Road for a few more years yet.

| | | | APPEARANCES | | | | GOALS | | | |
|---|---|---|---|---|---|---|---|---|---|---|
| Clubs | Signing Date | Transfer Fee | Lge | FL Cup | FA Cup | Others | Lge | FL Cup | FA Cup | Others |
| Everton | 8.79 | - | 99+1 | 11 | 9 | | 11 | 3 | | |
| Aston Villa | 5.83 | £175,000 | 74+1 | 9 | 3 | 4 | 7 | | | |
| Liverpool | 9.85 | £375,000 | 202+2 | 27 | 30 | 16 | 29 | 13 | 7 | 1 |
| Manchester City* | 12.91 | £900,000 | 42+3 | 2 | 3 | | 1 | | | |

## McMANAMAN Steven (Steve)

Born: Bootle,
11 February 1972

Height: 5'11"

Weight: 10.2

International Honours:
E Yth, E "U21"-6

**Position/Skill Factor:** An old-fashioned winger who has the ability to deceive and "ghost" past defenders. A good dribbler with close control and great balance, he can stop quickly and then in the same breath, accelerate.

**Career History:** A local discovery who first came to Liverpool as an associated schoolboy in February 1987, he graduated through the club as a trainee (May 1988) to professional status. Introduced as a substitute in front of the Anfield faithful on three occasions in 1990-91, making his FL debut against Sheffield United on 15 December 1990, he impressed many sound judges with his play. Such was his talent that he was chosen to play for the England Under 21 team against Wales on 5 December, even before his FL debut. He was expected to make only occasional appearances in 1991-92, but because of the injury crisis at Anfield, he was retained for most of the season. After appearing in a number of positions, including central striker where, despite his confident running, he was fairly ineffectual, he found himself on the right-wing and was devastating in becoming a key player throughout Liverpool's tortuous, but ultimately successful FA Cup run, which ended with a 2-0 victory against Sunderland in the Final. Another young Liverpool player who fell back in **1992-93** after an outstanding first season. Sparkled in the early stages with an important, but ultimately fruitless, "away" goal in the ECWC tie at Spartak Moscow in September and two outstanding goals against Sheffield United in a League Cup replay in November. Unfortunately, after Christmas, he lost form and confidence, while missing a hatful of chances, especially in the home game against Everton. Eventually had his season cut short when sustaining a back injury at Anfield against Oldham Athletic in the closing weeks and being forced to miss the last six games. Prior to his injury, however, he had added four more England under 21 caps to his total and in captaining the side for the first time against San Marino, celebrated by scoring the last goal in a handsome 6-0 win.

| | | | APPEARANCES | | | | GOALS | | | |
|---|---|---|---|---|---|---|---|---|---|---|
| Clubs | Signing Date | Transfer Fee | Lge | FL Cup | FA Cup | Others | Lge | FL Cup | FA Cup | Others |
| Liverpool* | 2.90 | - | 53+10 | 10 | 9+1 | 11 | 9 | 5 | 3 | 1 |

## MADDISON Neil Stanley

Born: Darlington, 2 October 1969

Height: 5'9"

Weight: 11.8

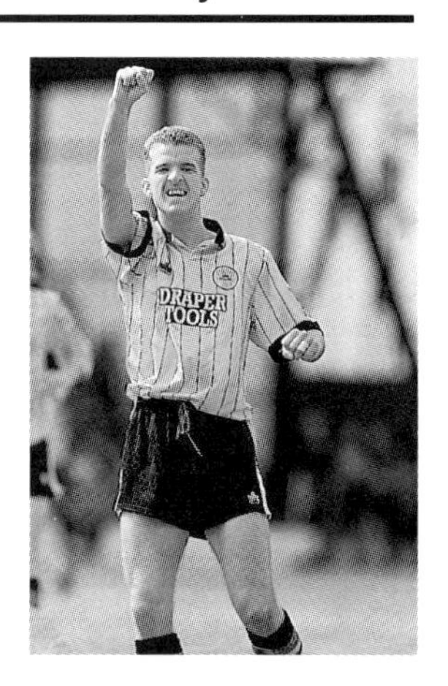


**Position/Skill Factor:** Midfield player who can also play up front. Makes good runs off the ball and gets into the penalty box to score goals. Keeps his passing simple, but effective.

**Career History:** Another north-easterner on Southampton's books, he signed as a 14-year-old associated schoolboy in October 1983, before becoming a trainee, on leaving school, in July 1986. Turned professional and made his FL debut when coming on as a sub at Tottenham Hotspur on 25 October 1988 and in his first two full games during 1988-89, he scored a goal apiece. That form should have accelerated his progress, but he was still waiting for a breakthrough in 1991-92, when making only a handful of appearances in the closing weeks of the campaign. Fully recovered from the knee trouble that resulted in four operations and disrupted his career, he received an early chance in **1992-93** when Glenn Cockerill was injured. Played four matches, before reverting to substitute appearances, but following selection for the Third Round League Cup-tie against Crystal Palace, he remained in the side for the rest of the season. His opening goal in a 2-0 win over Arsenal in December was his first in senior football for four years and three more later on were a reward for his hard running into forward positions. Secured his future by signing a long term contract that will keep him at the Dell until 1996.

| | | | APPEARANCES | | | | GOALS | | | |
|---|---|---|---|---|---|---|---|---|---|---|
| Clubs | Signing Date | Transfer Fee | Lge | FL Cup | FA Cup | Others | Lge | FL Cup | FA Cup | Others |
| Southampton* | 4.88 | - | 41+13 | 1+2 | 1+3 | 1 | 6 | | | |

## MADDIX Daniel (Danny) Shawn

Born: Ashford, Kent, 11 October 1967

Height: 5'11"

Weight: 11.0

**Position/Skill Factor:** Strong tackling central defender who is good in the air and one of the best man-for-man markers around. He sticks like glue to his opponents.

**Career History:** On failing to make an impression at senior level, having been an associated schoolboy (July 1982) and an apprentice (April 1984), before signing professional, he was freed by Tottenham Hotspur in the 1987 close season. This followed a period on loan at Southend United, where he had made his FL debut at Roots Hall against Scunthorpe United on 4 November 1986. Immediately snapped up by west London rivals, Queens Park Rangers, he was introduced to the Rangers' first team as a sub in a 3-1 defeat at Sheffield Wednesday in November 1987, but had to wait until the end of the season for further games. Originally a midfielder, he was converted to central defender by Rangers in 1988-89 with great success and by 1990-91, as an integral part of the Rangers' side, had fitted comfortably into a three man central defence alongside Alan McDonald and Paul Parker. In December 1990, Rangers' manager Don Howe signed two central defenders, Darren Peacock and Andy Tillson, following an injury crisis at Loftus Road. Thereafter, competition for the central defensive slots was intense, especially when new manager Gerry Francis reverted to a conventional flat "back-four". Started 1991-92 as first choice with Peacock, but after losing his place to McDonald in November 1991, he played little part in the remainder of the campaign. Not the best of seasons for him again as he started **1992-93** as third choice centre-back, marginally ahead of Alan McCarthy and Tony Witter. After sitting out six games on the bench, without being required, he made a couple of substitutions, before standing in for the absent Alan McDonald against Grimsby Town and Manchester United. He wasn't required again, apart from three more substitutions, until selected for the home FA Cup-tie against Manchester City and playing in eight of the next nine games, mainly as a replacement for a below form, Darren Peacock. Unfortunate with injuries over the last two years, his season was cut short at Liverpool and he must hope to get lucky in 1993-94.

| | | | APPEARANCES | | | | GOALS | | | |
|---|---|---|---|---|---|---|---|---|---|---|
| Clubs | Signing Date | Transfer Fee | Lge | FL Cup | FA Cup | Others | Lge | FL Cup | FA Cup | Others |
| Tottenham Hotspur | 7.85 | - | | | | | | | | |
| Southend United | 11.86 | Loan | 2 | | | | | | | |
| Q.P.R.* | 7.87 | - | 122+17 | 15 | 14 | 2+3 | 6 | 2 | 1 | |

## MAHORN Paul Gladstone

Born: Leyton, 13 August 1973

Height: 5'8" Weight: 11.6

**Position/Skill Factor:** Young central defender who is very useful in the air and has great speed off the mark.

**Career History:** Signed professional forms for Tottenham Hotspur early in 1992, having been a trainee since May 1990, he has yet to have a taste of first team football, but put ten reserve games under his belt in **1992-93** and will push hard for a breakthrough during the coming season.

| | | | APPEARANCES | | | | GOALS | | | |
|---|---|---|---|---|---|---|---|---|---|---|
| Clubs | Signing Date | Transfer Fee | Lge | FL Cup | FA Cup | Others | Lge | FL Cup | FA Cup | Others |
| Tottenham Hotspur* | 1.92 | - | | | | | | | | |

## MAKEL Lee

Born: Sunderland, 11 January 1973

Height: 5'10" Weight: 9.10

**Position/Skill Factor:** Midfield player. A very confident passer, he sees things early and makes it look easy. Excels at one-twos and is always looking to split defences.

**Career History:** Joined Newcastle United as a trainee in June 1989, having been at St James' Park since February 1987 as an associated schoolboy and played in a Zenith Cup tie in November 1990, before turning professional in February 1991. Made his FL debut as a substitute at West Bromwich Albion on 4 May 1991 and his full debut three days later — one of a deluge of promising youngsters blooded by Ossie Ardiles in 1990-91. Played only a handful of games in 1991-92, mostly in December, for the struggling Tynesiders and he was not selected again, following the arrival of new manager, Kevin Keegan. Clearly unimpressed, Keegan sold him to Blackburn Rovers during the summer of 1992, the fee being decided by tribunal. Still only a youngster, he was tucked away in Rovers' reserve side nearly all of **1992-93** and apart from two substitute League Cup appearances he only played in one full first team game, at home to Middlesbrough on 20 March 1993, where his audacious skills made him the "Man of the Match".

| | | | APPEARANCES | | | | GOALS | | | |
|---|---|---|---|---|---|---|---|---|---|---|
| Clubs | Signing Date | Transfer Fee | Lge | FL Cup | FA Cup | Others | Lge | FL Cup | FA Cup | Others |
| Newcastle United | 2.91 | - | 6+6 | 1 | | 0+1 | 1 | | | |
| Blackburn Rovers* | 7.92 | £160,000 | 1 | 0+2 | | | | | | |

## MAKIN Christopher (Chris)

Born: Manchester, 8 May 1973

Height: 5'11" Weight: 11.0

International Honours: E Sch, E Yth

**Position/Skill Factor:** Midfield player with plenty of stamina who pressures opponents well and has two great feet.

**Career History:** Spotted by Oldham Athletic playing in Manchester schools' football, he came to Boundary Park as an associated schoolboy in June 1987. Signed for the club as a trainee in August 1989 and progressed to the professional ranks during the 1991 close season. No first team appearances for the "Latics" in 1992-92 or **1992-93**, but was loaned out to Wigan Athletic at the beginning of last season and made his FL debut at home to Swansea City on 29 August 1992. After impressing during a 15 match spell and scoring two goals, including the winner against West Bromwich Albion at Springfield Park, Wigan wanted to sign him permanently, but were turned down flat. On his return, he sat on the bench without being required at Coventry City, but is a promising youngster who is highly thought of at the club and could make a breakthrough in 1993-94.

| | | | APPEARANCES | | | | GOALS | | | |
|---|---|---|---|---|---|---|---|---|---|---|
| Clubs | Signing Date | Transfer Fee | Lge | FL Cup | FA Cup | Others | Lge | FL Cup | FA Cup | Others |
| Oldham Athletic* | 7.91 | - | | | | | | | | |
| Wigan Athletic | 8.92 | Loan | 14+1 | | | | 2 | | | |

## MARGETSON Martyn Walter

Born: Neath, 8 September 1971

Height: 6'0"

Weight: 13.10

International Honours: W Sch, W Yth, W "U21"-4, W "B"

**Position/Skill Factor:** Goalkeeper. Still a learner, but a very good shot stopper and a sure kicker.

**Career History:** After joining Manchester City as an associated schoolboy in February 1987, he progressed to trainee status on leaving school in July 1988, before turning professional in the 1990 close season. Made his FL debut in the penultimate game of the 1990-91 season away to Manchester United on 4 May 1991. Standing in for the injured Tony Coton, he was not disgraced when United's Ryan Giggs scored the only goal of the game and a week later turned out against Sunderland. Was regarded as City's number two 'keeper, despite the presence of Andy Dibble, and deputised for Coton in the opening game of 1991-92 and then on three subsequent occasions during the season. Although he was a regular in the Welsh under 21 side in **1992-93**, he spent most of the season sitting on the first team bench as a goalkeeping substitute for Tony Coton and sharing the mid-week reserve spot with Andy Dibble. However, with Coton unavailable, he was selected to make his Premier League bow in the final match of the season, an ultimate 5-1 defeat at home to Everton. Following total defensive disarray in the first 35 minutes, during which he had had to endure a build up of crowd agitation, and with the score at 3-1 against, it was a wise move by the manager to protect his young 'keeper by replacing him at half-time with Dibble. It was a low note to go out of the season on, but it will be well behind him as 1993-94 gets under way.

| Clubs | Signing Date | Transfer Fee | APPEARANCES | | | | GOALS | | | |
|---|---|---|---|---|---|---|---|---|---|---|
| | | | Lge | FL Cup | FA Cup | Others | Lge | FL Cup | FA Cup | Others |
| Manchester City* | 7.90 | - | 6 | 0+1 | | 1 | | | | |

## MARKER Nicholas (Nicky) Robert

Born: Budleigh Salterton, 3 May 1965

Height: 6'1"

Weight: 12.11

**Position/Skill Factor:** Central defender, who can also play in midfield. A good all-rounder, he is capable of doing a marking job at the back, where he is good in the air, or playing further forward, involved in the passing side of the game.

**Career History:** Started his soccer life with his local League club, Exeter City, as an apprentice in July 1981, making his FL debut in the heart of the "Grecian's" defence at Burnley in a 3-3 draw on 17 October 1981 at the age of 16½ years. Prior to turning professional, during the 1983 close season, he had already made 29 full appearances in League matches and had shown much maturity for one so young. Firmly established himself at the heart of Exeter's defence from the start of 1984-85, missing only ten games up to the time of his transfer to Devon neighbours, Plymouth Argyle, in October 1987. He easily made the transition from Fourth to Second Division football and remained a first choice in the "Pilgrim's" central defence for five years. Suffered the disappointment of relegation in 1992, after four years of struggle at Home Park, but early in the **1992-93** his career received a major boost when Kenny Dalglish signed him for ambitious Blackburn Rovers, in a cash plus player deal, which earned the "Pilgrims" £250,000, plus the services of Keith Hill and Craig Skinner. He was presumably signed as a replacement for the veteran Kevin Moran, but the Irish international was playing so well that he is still waiting for a good run in the Premier League team. However, he has been regularly involved with the squad, as either a deputy in the centre of defence, or for the games where midfield bite was required. Without capturing any headlines, he had a quietly proficient first season at Ewood Park and will be a better player for it in 1993-94.

| Clubs | Signing Date | Transfer Fee | APPEARANCES | | | | GOALS | | | |
|---|---|---|---|---|---|---|---|---|---|---|
| | | | Lge | FL Cup | FA Cup | Others | Lge | FL Cup | FA Cup | Others |
| Exeter City | 5.83 | - | 196+6 | 11 | 8 | 8 | 3 | 1 | | 3 |
| Plymouth Argyle | 10.87 | £95,000 | 201+1 | 15 | 9 | 7 | 12 | 3 | 1 | 1 |
| Blackburn Rovers* | 9.92 | £400,000 | 12+3 | | 2 | | | | | |

## MARLOWE Andrew Daniel

Born: Birmingham, 25 September 1973

Height: 5'7" Weight: 11.2

International Honours: E Yth

**Position/Skill Factor:** Very quick and useful when going forward which makes it possible for him to play either wide on the right-wing, or at right-back.

**Career History:** First joining Tottenham Hotspur as an associated schoolboy in November 1987, on leaving school, he came to the club as a trainee in August 1990 and turned professional early in 1992. Yet to make a first team appearance for "Spurs", he played only three reserve matches in **1992-93** and may need a change of clubs if he is to progress further. Still under contract for 12 months.

| Clubs | Signing Date | Transfer Fee | APPEARANCES | | | | GOALS | | | |
|---|---|---|---|---|---|---|---|---|---|---|
| | | | Lge | FL Cup | FA Cup | Others | Lge | FL Cup | FA Cup | Others |
| Tottenham Hotspur* | 2.92 | - | | | | | | | | |

## MARQUIS Paul Raymond

Born: Enfield, 29 August 1972

Height: 6'2" Weight: 12.5

**Position/Skill Factor:** Strong central defender, who is good in the air and favours his left foot.

**Career History:** A West Ham United professional signing in the 1991 close season, having been a trainee at Upton Park since July 1989, he has yet to make a first team appearance. In order to gain more experience, he went out on loan to non-League Dagenham during **1992-93** and on coming back was a fairly regular choice in the Football Combination with the "Hammers'" reserves. Looks to improve on that position in 1993-94.

| Clubs | Signing Date | Transfer Fee | APPEARANCES | | | | GOALS | | | |
|---|---|---|---|---|---|---|---|---|---|---|
| | | | Lge | FL Cup | FA Cup | Others | Lge | FL Cup | FA Cup | Others |
| West Ham United* | 7.91 | - | | | | | | | | |

## MARSH Michael (Mike) Andrew

Born: Liverpool, 21 July 1969

Height: 5'8"

Weight: 11.0

**Position/Skill Factor:** Midfield player who strikes the ball well. His use of the ball is good and he is always looking for the chance of a shot at goal.

**Career History:** Signed from Kirkby Town of the North West Counties League during the 1987 close season, he made his FL debut when coming on for Jan Molby at Anfield against Charlton Athletic on 1 March 1989. Made a breakthrough in 1991-92, largely as a result of Liverpool's chronic injury crisis and remained a useful member of the first team squad throughout the season, playing mostly on the right side of midfield, although occasionally at full-back. He was on the bench, but not required for the 1992 FA Cup Final against Sunderland, but scored a vital goal against Auxerre in the UEFA Cup Second Round second-leg at Anfield which helped the "Reds" to overturn a 2-0 first leg deficit. A useful squad player, he enjoyed an extended run in the first team in **1992-93**, due to injuries to most of the club's first team members. Deputised for Rob Jones at right-back from September onwards and held his place after the latter returned to the side in place of the then injured David Burrows. Eventually lost his place in February when Burrows returned, before joining Liverpool's walking wounded himself, when dislocating a knee during training in April. Earlier, he had showed a suspect temperament when sent off for a brutal and unnecessary tackle against Spartak Moscow in the second leg ECWC tie at Anfield in October, with the game already lost beyond recall. And in the absence of Jan Molby and John Barnes, he temporarily became the club's penalty taker, with three successful conversions in the League Cup, until having one saved by Queens Park Rangers' Tony Roberts in a League match. Awarded two penalties in the same match, John Barnes blasted wide with the other in a 1-0 win.

| | | | APPEARANCES | | | | GOALS | | | |
|---|---|---|---|---|---|---|---|---|---|---|
| Clubs | Signing Date | Transfer Fee | Lge | FL Cup | FA Cup | Others | Lge | FL Cup | FA Cup | Others |
| Liverpool* | 8.87 | - | 42+25 | 10+1 | 6+2 | 12+1 | 1 | 3 | | 1 |

## MARSHALL Andrew John

Born: Bury, 14 April 1975

Height: 6'2" Weight: 12.7

**Position/Skill Factor:** Good young goalkeeper, who is good on crosses and commands his box like a veteran.

**Career History:** A recent Norwich City professional signing, having been at Carrow Road as an associated schoolboy (July 1989) and then as a trainee (July 1991), he was the youth team's regular 'keeper in **1992-93** and did exceptionally well when holding Leeds United at bay at Elland Road in the Semi-Final of the FA Youth Cup. Has only played three reserve matches to date, but under the Premier League substitute goalkeeper ruling, he sat on the bench twice last season, at Manchester United and Middlesbrough, without being called upon. Currently number three choice behind Bryan Gunn and Mark Walton.

| | | | APPEARANCES | | | | GOALS | | | |
|---|---|---|---|---|---|---|---|---|---|---|
| Clubs | Signing Date | Transfer Fee | Lge | FL Cup | FA Cup | Others | Lge | FL Cup | FA Cup | Others |
| Norwich City* | 7.93 | - | | | | | | | | |

## MARSHALL Ian Paul

Born: Liverpool, 20 March 1966

Height: 6'1" Weight: 12.12

**Position/Skill Factor:** Plays equally well either as a central defender or as a striker. As an attacker, he is a chaser of lost causes and his strength and deceptive pace, gives defenders a tough time. He is also a good striker of the ball.

**Career History:** Began with Everton as an associated schoolboy (April 1980), before becoming an apprentice on leaving school in July 1982 and later progressing to the professional ranks. made his FL debut when deputising for the injured Derek Mountfield against West Bromwich Albion at Goodison Park on 20 August 1985, but first team chances were few with Kevin Ratcliffe and Dave Watson holding down the central defensive positions for Everton and he was allowed to sign permanently for Oldham Athletic in March 1987, after just two weeks of a loan period, as a replacement for Andy Linighan. Very consistent at the heart of the Oldham defence in 1988-89, but ever since he'd arrived at Boundary Park he had tried to convince manager Joe Royle that there was a frustrated centre-forward in him trying to get out and when he lost his place to Earl Barrett, Royle did indeed try him up front during Oldham's great twin cup runs of 1989-90 with some success. But after scoring in the first FA Cup Semi-Final against Manchester United in 1990, he was again injured and missed selection for the League Cup final side to play Nottingham Forest. In the opening match of the 1990-91 season away to Wolves he scored a superb hat-trick in a 3-2 victory, including two goals in the last five minutes which turned the game upside down. Afterwards Royle commented ruefully "There'll be no living with him after this"!. Indeed, he proved he could be a natural forward and despite being plagued by injuries, finished the season as top scorer with 17 FL goals from only 26 games as Oldham stormed to the Second Division Championship. He proved he could do it at First Division level as well, by scoring six goals in his first eight games of 1991-92. Thereafter, however, the goals dried up and following a FA Cup disaster away to Leyton Orient when the "Latics" went down 4-2 after extra-time, Royle switched him back to central defence, which became permanent after Earl Barrett's departure to Aston Villa. Started **1992-93** where he left off the previous season, in defence, but in 26 full Premier League appearances, he played 13 times up front and 13 at the back. No one seems to know what his best position is, including himself. Unfortunate with injuries, he suffered a broken finger and a bad bout of flu, before a torn hamstring put him out of the Queens Park Rangers game in March. Returned for a couple of reserve tests, but then pulled a calf muscle which effectively kept him out of action until the last day of the season, when he came off the bench for the last 20 minutes of the vital home game against Southampton. With the score standing at 4-2 to the "Latics", he was sent on to preserve that lead at all costs in a desperate effort to maintain the club's Premier League status. Eventually, the game was won by 4-3 and survival was achieved on goal difference, with Crystal Palace taking the drop, after losing 3-0 at Arsenal.

| | | | APPEARANCES | | | | GOALS | | | |
|---|---|---|---|---|---|---|---|---|---|---|
| Clubs | Signing Date | Transfer Fee | Lge | FL Cup | FA Cup | Others | Lge | FL Cup | FA Cup | Others |
| Everton | 3.84 | - | 9+6 | 1+1 | | 7 | 1 | 1 | | |
| Oldham Athletic* | 3.88 | £100,000 | 165+5 | 17 | 14 | 2+1 | 36 | | | |

## MARSHALL Scott Roderick

Born: Edinburgh, 1 May 1973

Height: 6'1½" Weight: 12.5

International Honours: S Sch, S Yth

**Position/Skill Factor:** Central defender. Very good in the air, he reads the game well and will come out of defence looking to pass the ball, rather than just clear his lines.

**Career History:** Signed professional forms for Arsenal at the end of the 1990-91 season, having been at Highbury as a trainee since July 1989 and eventually made his first team debut in the **1992-93** PL match at Sheffield Wednesday on 6 May 1993. The younger brother of Hearts' 'keeper, Gordon, received another opportunity a few days later against Tottenham Hotspur, as George Graham fully utilised the squad.

| | | | APPEARANCES | | | | GOALS | | | |
|---|---|---|---|---|---|---|---|---|---|---|
| Clubs | Signing Date | Transfer Fee | Lge | FL Cup | FA Cup | Others | Lge | FL Cup | FA Cup | Others |
| Arsenal* | 3.91 | - | 2 | | | | | | | |

## MARTIN Alvin Edward

Born: Bootle, 29 July 1958

Height: 6'1" Weight: 13.9

International Honours: E Yth, E "B", E-17

**Position/Skill Factor:** Vastly experienced central defender, who can almost play with his eyes shut. Reads the game exceptionally well and is very competitive and strong in the air.

**Career History:** Initially an associated schoolboy (December 1972) with his native Everton, on leaving school, he travelled south to sign as an apprentice with West Ham United in August 1974. A star of the "Hammers'" FA Youth Cup side of 1975, that lost in the Final to Ipswich Town, Alvin turned professional during the 1976 close season, but had to wait patiently in the wings before making his FL debut as a substitute at Aston Villa on 18 March 1978. Established himself in the heart of the "Hammers'" defence from January 1979 and remained first choice until 1986. Won his first major honour when West Ham, then in the Second Division, surprisingly defeated Arsenal 1-0 in the 1980 FA Cup Final. The following season he won a Second Division Championship medal, as West Ham stormed back to Division One, conceding only 29 goals and dropping only three points at Upton Park. Shortly afterwards, he won his first international cap against Brazil at Wembley on 12 May 1981. He remained a member of the England squad until 1986 and although never an automatic first choice, he won 16 more caps, including one in the World Cup Finals in Mexico in 1986, when he played against Paraguay. Frequently derided by the media as not up to international standard, the record shows that England lost few of the games in which he played and conceded hardly any goals. His best year was undoubtedly 1985-86, when in partnership with Tony Gale, the "Hammers'" defence conceded only 40 goals and the team finished third, only four points behind Champions, Liverpool. During that season, he scored his one and only "hat-trick", all from open play, in a remarkable 8-1 victory over Newcastle, a scoreline explained partly by an injury to Newcastle's 'keeper and their use of two replacements. Since 1986, his seasonal appearances have usually been restricted by injury, but he remains a valued squad member. Granted a free transfer in June 1992, he opted to remain with West Ham on a one year contract and remarkably (at the age of 34) was first choice from the start of **1992-93**, until unfortunate to suffer a torn calf muscle at Derby County in January, which forced him onto the sidelines for the rest of the season. As the star of successive home games against Watford, Derby County and Sunderland, he had been absent for only one match out of the first 33 and his experience and enthusiasm had proved invaluable. But, although missed, the "Hammers", lucky to have players of the calibre of Tony Gale and Colin Foster waiting in the wings, were still able to sustain their promotion challenge right to the end. With the club returning to the top flight, at the first time of asking, as runners-up to Newcastle United, he can possibly look forward to playing in the Premier League this season, if he decides to carry on.

| | | | APPEARANCES | | | | GOALS | | | |
|---|---|---|---|---|---|---|---|---|---|---|
| Clubs | Signing Date | Transfer Fee | Lge | FL Cup | FA Cup | Others | Lge | FL Cup | FA Cup | Others |
| West Ham United* | 7.76 | - | 422+2 | 66 | 34 | 16 | 25 | 6 | | 1 |

## MARTIN Dean Edward

Born: Islington, 31 August 1972

Height: 5'8" Weight: 11.0

**Position/Skill Factor:** Right-winger, who is very quick and a willing runner off the ball. Always causes defenders problems, as they never quite know where he will "pop-up" next.

**Career History:** A product of non-League football with Docklands club, Fisher Athletic, he was transferred to West Ham United during the 1991 close season, following promising displays in the GM Vauxhall Conference. Quickly adjusted to a higher level of soccer and after coming on as a substitute in the Fourth Round of the FA Cup at Wrexham, during a season that eventually saw the "Hammers" relegated from the First Division, he made his FL debut, again as a substitute, at Coventry City on 25 April 1992. Couldn't add to his West Ham appearances in **1992-93** and had a spell on loan at Colchester United, playing in the number nine shirt and scoring on his debut at Walsall. Earlier, in November, he spent some time with Kettering in the Vauxhall Conference in order to keep match fit and was a regular in "Hammers'" Combination side throughout the remainder of the season. Difficult to ascertain at present whether he has a future at Upton Park, or needs to drop down a rung or two to achieve a regular first team place in a League side.

| | | | APPEARANCES | | | | GOALS | | | |
|---|---|---|---|---|---|---|---|---|---|---|
| Clubs | Signing Date | Transfer Fee | Lge | FL Cup | FA Cup | Others | Lge | FL Cup | FA Cup | Others |
| West Ham United* | 6.91 | £25,000 | 1+1 | | 0+1 | | | | | |
| Colchester United | 12.92 | Loan | 8 | | | | 2 | | | |

## MARTIN Lee Andrew

Born: Hyde,
5 February 1968

Height: 5'11"

Weight: 11.5

International Honours:
E "U21"-2

**Position/Skill Factor:** A very reliable left-back who can also play in the centre of the defence, he is good in the air and not easy to beat. Never misses an opportunity of coming out of defence with the ball to link up with the attack.

**Career History:** First came to Manchester United as an associated schoolboy in February 1982, before joining the YTS scheme on leaving school in June 1985. Turned professional during the 1986 close season and made his FL debut at Old Trafford against Wimbledon on 9 May 1988, when coming on for Remi Moses. Got his chance of a regular first team football in 1988-89, with Viv Anderson injured and made 20 League appearances. But it was during the following season that he really made his mark, as he began to establish himself on the left-hand side of the United defence. His form was such that he was selected for the 1990 FA Cup Final side to play Crystal Palace and he shot to fame in the replay when latching on to a Neil Webb pass to rifle in the only goal of the game. After all the glamour of the previous season, he lost his place in the team at the beginning of 1990-91 and spent most of the time in the shadow of the more experienced Clayton Blackmore. Still recovering from injury, he made only one appearance as sub in the League, plus four other appearances in cup matches during 1991-92. Had another frustrating season in **1992-93**, as he remained on the fringe of first team action throughout the campaign, without making any impact and failed to win a Championship medal when United came on strong to bring the League title back to Old Trafford after an absence of 26 years. Played just two games, in UEFA and League Cup-ties, but with the return to fitness of Paul Parker, he spent much of his time either on the bench or in the Central League side. Will hope for better luck in 1993-94.

| | | | APPEARANCES | | | | GOALS | | | |
|---|---|---|---|---|---|---|---|---|---|---|
| Clubs | Signing Date | Transfer Fee | Lge | FL Cup | FA Cup | Others | Lge | FL Cup | FA Cup | Others |
| Manchester United* | 5.86 | - | 55+17 | 5+2 | 13+1 | 6+5 | 1 | | 1 | |

## MARWOOD Brian

Born: Seaham, 5 February 1960

Height: 5'7" Weight: 11.6

International Honours: E-1

**Position/Skill Factor:** Skilful right-winger with zip and pace and at his best a frequent scorer. More effective in a

wide position where he can get past defenders to either cross the ball accurately for those better placed or to cut inside and shoot.

**Career History:** Came through the ranks at Hull City, first as an associated schoolboy (February 1976) and later, on leaving school, as an apprentice (June 1976). After turning professional, he waited almost two years before making his FL debut at Boothferry Park against Mansfield Town on 12 January 1980. Had a good goal scoring record at Hull and was soon attracting the attention of the bigger clubs. On signing for Sheffield Wednesday during the 1984 close season, he proved to be an excellent acquisition and quickly made his mark in the First Division. Had a spell out of action during the 1986-87 season, which coincided with a lean time for the "Owls", but came back and was just beginning to find his feet when he found himself on his way to Arsenal as part of George Graham's rebuilding process. In just over two seasons at Highbury, he gained his one and only England cap when coming on as a sub against Saudi Arabia on 16 November 1988 and at the end of that same season, celebrated with a League Championship medal, albeit missing the last five games. Found himself in and out of the side as the manager tried various permutations during 1989-90 and then, following the signing of Anders Limpar, was left out in the cold. It was time to move on again and Sheffield United, without a win to their name, came for him at the beginning of 1990-91, in the hope that he could supply the ammunition for Brian Deane and Tony Agana to explode. Although he only made 17 League appearances, he was a valued member of the squad that clawed its way up the First Division table to safety and at the same time successfully managed to combine his football career with his tireless work on behalf of the PFA. Made even fewer appearances in 1991-92 after he had been elected Chairman of the PFA and seemed set to return to his native north-east when he joined Middlesbrough on loan in October 1991, but no permanent deal was arranged. Made no first team appearances for Sheffield United in **1992-93**, but after being granted a free transfer in December, he met Glenn Hoddle purely by chance at a dinner and was invited to sign as a non-contract player with Swindon Town for the rest of the season. Although not claiming a regular place, he became a useful member of the squad, especially in terms of experience and scored a vital goal in a 2-1 win at home to Bristol City. And while not part of the team that reached the Premier League, via the "Play-Offs", he will be a useful man to be able to call on in 1993-94, as Town try to consolidate their place in the top flight.

| | | | APPEARANCES | | | | GOALS | | | |
|---|---|---|---|---|---|---|---|---|---|---|
| Clubs | Signing Date | Transfer Fee | Lge | FL Cup | FA Cup | Others | Lge | FL Cup | FA Cup | Others |
| Hull City | 2.78 | - | 154+4 | 4+1 | 16 | 5 | 51 | | 1 | |
| Sheffield Wednesday | 8.84 | £115,000 | 125+3 | 13 | 19 | 0+1 | 27 | 5 | 3 | |
| Arsenal | 3.88 | £600,000 | 52 | 6 | 2 | 3+1 | 16 | 1 | | 2 |
| Sheffield United | 9.90 | £350,000 | 14+8 | 3 | 0+2 | | 3 | | | |
| Middlesbrough | 10.91 | Loan | 3 | 1 | | 1 | | | | |
| Swindon Town* | 3.93 | - | 6+5 | | | | 1 | | | |

## **MASKELL Craig** Dell

Born: Aldershot, 10 April 1968

Height: 5'10"

Weight: 11.4

**Position/Skill Factor:** Striker with good skill, who twists and turns well to make room for shots at goal. Excellent in wide positions, he is a master of the early cross.

**Career History:** A prolific goalscorer, he started with Southampton as an associated schoolboy in June 1982 and later became an apprentice (July 1984) on leaving school. Made his FL debut immediately after signing professional forms, when substituting for Mark Dennis at Birmingham City on 19 April 1986 and in his next outing, a couple of weeks later, again as a substitute, he scored at Tottenham Hotspur in a 5-3 defeat. But, with little prospect of breaking into the "Saints'" first team on a regular basis, he was sold to Huddersfield Town for a modest fee in the summer of 1988. Although his new team enjoyed only a moderate season in Division Three, he was a tremendous success, playing in every game and breaking the club's post-war scoring record with 28 FL, plus five cup goals. Ironically, his second season with the "Terriers" was more successful for the team, who narrowly missed the Third Division Play-Offs, but less so personally, although after a slow start to the season he again finished top scorer with 19 goals. However, he was homesick for the south and to the dismay of their fans, Huddersfield allowed him to join Reading in the summer of 1990 for a handsome fee. With Trevor Senior and Steve Moran also on their books, Reading seemed certain to challenge for promotion and collect a hatful of goals. But the challenge did not materialise and he had a relatively disappointing season, in and out of the team, with a total of only ten FL goals. Out of favour at the beginning of 1991-92, he returned to first team duty in October and held his place to the end of the campaign, top scoring with 16 FL goals, although it was another mediocre season for his team. Somewhat surprisingly, he was transferred to near neighbours, Swindon Town, in the summer of 1992 in part exchange for Tom Jones and as a replacement for Duncan Shearer, but proved to be a very different type of player, with more skill, but less strength and power. After a couple of quiet games in **1992-93**, he began to hit the net with regular frequency, including a hat-trick in a 4-1 home win against Cambridge United. Had scored 16 goals before being injured at home to Wolverhampton Wanderers, but his season then became disjointed when he attempted to return too early and he was forced to miss 13 games at a crucial stage of the League programme. On coming back, he found it difficult to recapture his early season form, but had an excellent game in the Play-Off Final against Leicester City at Wembley, helping to create the first Town goal for Hoddle and scoring the second in a 4-3 victory, himself. Having once played six (including four substitute) games in the top flight with Southampton, he can now look forward to picking up where he left off this coming season.

| | | | APPEARANCES | | | | GOALS | | | |
|---|---|---|---|---|---|---|---|---|---|---|
| Clubs | Signing Date | Transfer Fee | Lge | FL Cup | FA Cup | Others | Lge | FL Cup | FA Cup | Others |
| Southampton | 4.86 | - | 2+4 | | | | 1 | | | |
| Huddersfield Town | 5.88 | £20,000 | 86+1 | 6 | 8 | 7 | 43 | 4 | 3 | 4 |
| Reading | 8.90 | £250,000 | 60+12 | 2 | 5+1 | 1 | 26 | | | |
| Swindon Town* | 7.92 | £225,000 | 32+1 | 2 | 1 | 4+1 | 18 | 1 | | 4 |

## MASON Paul David

Born: Liverpool, 3 September 1963

Height: 5'9" Weight: 12.1

**Position/Skill Factor:** Midfielder who can also play up front. A good footballer, he can manipulate the ball well to create space and goalscoring opportunities.

**Career History:** An unusual case of an English player starting his football career in mainland Europe and continuing it in Scotland, before entering League football in England ten years later on the verge of 30. In fact, he was signed as an associated schoolboy by Everton in his native city in January 1978, but left Goodison without being offered an apprenticeship by the club. His movements over the next few years are unknown, although it is believed that he played non-league football on Merseyside before going to work in the Netherlands, where he was discovered by Groningen FC, playing for a work's side in 1983. He became an increasingly influential player with the Dutch club and after five seasons he joined the migration of Dutch players to Scotland (although in his case it was a return to native soil), when he signed for Aberdeen in the summer of 1988. He spent five years at Pittodrie with one of Scotland' most powerful clubs, but although his team frequently challenged for the Scottish League Championship, the only honours he won were a Skol Cup winners medal in 1989, when he scored both goals in the "Dons'" 2-1 extra-time victory over Rangers and a Scottish FA Cup Winners medal in 1990, when his team defeated Celtic. He also received a losers medal in the **1992-93** Scottish Cup Final after a 2-1 defeat by Rangers — his last game for Aberdeen before his transfer to Ipswich Town in the summer. Almost unknown hitherto in his native country, he now has a belated chance to forge a reputation in English football.

| | | | APPEARANCES | | | | GOALS | | | |
|---|---|---|---|---|---|---|---|---|---|---|
| Clubs | Signing Date | Transfer Fee | Lge | FL Cup | FA Cup | Others | Lge | FL Cup | FA Cup | Others |
| Aberdeen | 7.88 | £250,000 | 138+19 | 13+2 | 11+1 | 7+1 | 27 | 8 | 1 | 1 |
| Ipswich Town* | 6.93 | £400,000 | | | | | | | | |

## MATTEO Dominic

Born: Dumfries, 28 April 1974

Height: 6'0½" Weight: 11.0

**Position/Skill Factor:** Left-back with very good skill. Can also play on the left-wing, where he runs at defenders in order to express himself in attacking areas.

**Career History:** A 1992 close season professional signing for Liverpool, having been at the club since first coming to Anfield as an associated schoolboy in September 1989, he later progressed through the ranks as a trainee in June 1990. A very promising young player, who was ever present with the reserves in **1992-93** up until February and was called up by the England party to be on World Youth Cup standby. He is very well thought of at Liverpool and may be on the brink of first team action in 1993-94.

| | | | APPEARANCES | | | | GOALS | | | |
|---|---|---|---|---|---|---|---|---|---|---|
| Clubs | Signing Date | Transfer Fee | Lge | FL Cup | FA Cup | Others | Lge | FL Cup | FA Cup | Others |
| Liverpool* | 6.92 | - | | | | | | | | |

## MATTHEW Damian

Born: Islington,
23 September 1970

Height: 5'11"

Weight: 10.10

International Honours:
E "U21"-9

**Position/Skill Factor:** A creative midfield player with great stamina, who passes and moves, always making angles for his team-mates.

**Career History:** Another in a long line of good Chelsea discoveries, he came through as an associated schoolboy (May 1986) and then as a trainee, on leaving school in August 1987. Turned professional during the 1989 close season, making his FL debut at Stamford Bridge against Crystal Palace on 16 April 1990 and followed up with a useful spell in the side during 1990-91 as he tendered his claim for a regular first team place. Expected to make progress in 1991-92, in fact he only made a handful of first team appearances mostly as substitute and although he started the first two Premier League matches of **1992-93** as first choice, following a traumatic experience in Ireland during the summer, he quickly fell by the wayside, mainly due to injuries. After being loaned out to Luton Town and playing in three matches, he returned to Stamford Bridge and put in some good performances with the reserves. It is imperative for him to realise his full potential during the new season if he is to make the progress that was once expected of him.

| | | | APPEARANCES | | | | GOALS | | | |
|---|---|---|---|---|---|---|---|---|---|---|
| Clubs | Signing Date | Transfer Fee | Lge | FL Cup | FA Cup | Others | Lge | FL Cup | FA Cup | Others |
| Chelsea* | 6.89 | - | 13+8 | 5 | | 1 | | | | |
| Luton Town | 9.92 | Loan | 3+2 | | | 1 | | | | |

## MAY David

Born: Oldham,
24 June 1970

Height: 6'0"

Weight: 12.0

**Position/Skill Factor:** Very quick and strong central defender with sound positional sense who is very good in the air and a useful passer of the ball.

**Career History:** Started his soccer career as an associated schoolboy at Blackburn Rovers in October 1984, becoming a trainee in July 1986, on leaving school and eventually graduating to the club's professional ranks in the summer of 1988. Making his FL debut at Swindon Town on 1 April 1989, he had a good run in the side in central defence at the beginning of 1989-90, before sustaining an injury that put him out of first team action until the following November. Once back to full match fitness, he wrested the number five shirt from Andy Hill, only missing one game in 19, until being forced to stand down for three matches near the end of the season. Enjoyed another long run in the first team at the beginning of 1991-92 before making way for Kevin Moran in October. Only played two more Second Division games to the end of the season, but was recalled at right-back for the three Play-Off games against Derby County and Leicester City, a ploy justified by the outcome of Premier League football. Most experts were of the opinion that the club would require a new right-back for their **1992-93** campaign, but he proved them all wrong by performing with distinction. Not at his best, facing a winger head on, he improved until he had few problems and was an immense success with his ability to sweep up behind the central defenders. He became a vital member of the side and was able to keep the Norwegian international, Henning Berg, out of the side. Brought up as a Manchester City fan, it was a huge disappointment to miss the game against Manchester United in the final week of the season, due to suffering whiplash as the result of a car accident.

| | | | APPEARANCES | | | | GOALS | | | |
|---|---|---|---|---|---|---|---|---|---|---|
| Clubs | Signing Date | Transfer Fee | Lge | FL Cup | FA Cup | Others | Lge | FL Cup | FA Cup | Others |
| Blackburn Rovers* | 6.88 | - | 83 | 8+1 | 8 | 5 | 2 | 1 | | |

## MEAKER Michael John

Born: Greenford, 18 August 1971

Height: 5'11" Weight: 11.5

**Position/Skill Factor:** Left-winger who runs well with the ball at his feet and is very quick off the mark. Favours his right foot and loves coming inside the full-back, looking to shoot for goal.

**Career History:** Came to Queens Park Rangers straight from school as a trainee in November 1988 and signed as a professional at the end of 1989. made his FL debut at Manchester City when he came on for Dominic Iorfa on 1 December 1990 and over the remainder of the 1990-91 season appeared a further seven times as a substitute. Only one further selection, again as substitute, for Rangers in 1991-92, but made five full appearances on loan to Plymouth Argyle, in mid season. While still awaiting a breakthrough, he spent most of **1992-93** playing for the reserves and when the chance finally arrived, late in the season, it turned out to be a short lived one, as deputy for the injured Andy Sinton. Came into the side at home to Norwich City and was unlucky to be denied a goal by the goalkeeper's legs in a 3-1 win, before playing in a 1-0 defeat at Liverpool and receiving a yellow card for his part in a "punch-up" at Loftus Road against 2-1 away victors, Wimbledon. Short and not so sweet, it was back to the "stiffs" and hopefully, better opportunities in 1993-94.

| | | | APPEARANCES | | | | GOALS | | | |
|---|---|---|---|---|---|---|---|---|---|---|
| Clubs | Signing Date | Transfer Fee | Lge | FL Cup | FA Cup | Others | Lge | FL Cup | FA Cup | Others |
| Q.P.R.* | 2.90 | - | 3+9 | | | 0+1 | | | | |
| Plymouth Argyle | 11.91 | Loan | 4 | | | 1 | | | | |

## **MEGSON Gary** John

Born: Manchester, 2 May 1959

Height: 5'10" Weight: 11.6

**Position/Skill Factor:** Midfield player who has matured with age and has become a great team man. Always making himself available, he has plenty of stamina which allows him to work all over the pitch.

**Career History:** Started his soccer apprenticeship at Plymouth Argyle in August 1975, with the blessing of his father, Don, the former Sheffield Wednesday and Bristol Rovers full-back (1959-1971) and had progressed to the club's professional ranks by the 1977 close season. Made his FL debut at Home Park against Portsmouth on 29 October 1977 and quickly adjusted to League soccer, showing great verve and spirit. Spent two seasons with the club, before making the giant leap up to the First Division with Everton, for a six figure sum that broke Plymouth's transfer record. Got off to a fair start with the "Toffees", but lost his place to Gary Stanley in 1980-81 and at the end of the season was transferred to his father's former club, Sheffield Wednesday. Missed only three League matches in three years at Hillsborough and after helping Wednesday to promotion to the First Division in 1983-84, he moved down the road to Nottingham Forest. But when suffering the same fate as Asa Harford before him and John Sheridan afterwards, in being rejected by Brian Clough almost as soon as he had signed and after three months without a game, he was sold on to Newcastle United. Unfortunately, his first team chances were also restricted at St James' Park and he only stayed a little over a year before Sheffield Wednesday secured his return to the club for a knock down sum. In his second spell with the "Owls", he again stayed three years and was very consistent, but was allowed to join Manchester City in January 1989 and marked his debut with the only goal of the game at Oldham Athletic. A key figure in midfield as the side won promotion that season, he found himself out in the cold when City found it hard to adjust to the rigours of life in the First Division. However, a change in fortune for the club, coincided with his return to first team duty and in 1990-91 City rose to fifth place in the top flight, as he formed the backbone of the side, playing alongside player-manager, Peter Reid. Started 1991-92 in City's first team and played until October, but only intermittently afterwards, following the arrival of Steve McMahon and Fitzroy Simpson. Given a free transfer during the summer, he became Mike Walker's first signing as Norwich City manager and his gritty displays in **1992-93** helped underpin the club's title challenge every time he took to the pitch. Unfortunately, for both him and the club, his season was interrupted by groin and hamstring injuries, which principally accounted for him playing only 25 games. He certainly belied his age with enthusiastic performances and while only scoring once during the campaign, against his old club, Manchester City, he had a blinder against Aston Villa at Carrow Road in March, when 'keeper Mark Bosnich denied him at least three times, before City won thanks to a John Polston goal. At 34 he is the oldest player on the club's books by four years, but he should be good for a while yet.

| | | | APPEARANCES | | | | GOALS | | | |
|---|---|---|---|---|---|---|---|---|---|---|
| Clubs | Signing Date | Transfer Fee | Lge | FL Cup | FA Cup | Others | Lge | FL Cup | FA Cup | Others |
| Plymouth Argyle | 5.77 | - | 78 | 9 | 5 | | 10 | | | |
| Everton | 12.79 | £250,000 | 20+2 | | 3 | | 2 | | 1 | |
| Sheffield Wednesday | 8.81 | £130,000 | 123 | 13 | 12 | | 13 | 2 | 5 | |
| Nottingham Forest | 8.84 | £175,000 | | | | | | | | |
| Newcastle United | 11.84 | £130,000 | 21+3 | 1+1 | 2 | | 1 | | 1 | |
| Sheffield Wednesday | 12.85 | £60,000 | 107+3 | 10 | 15 | 3 | 12 | | 1 | |
| Manchester City | 1.89 | £250,000 | 78+4 | 5 | 7+1 | 2 | 2 | | | |
| Norwich City* | 8.92 | - | 20+3 | | 2 | | 1 | | | |

## **MERSON Paul** Charles

Born: Harlesden, 20 March 1968

Height: 5'10" Weight: 11.9

International Honours: E Yth, E "U21"-4, E"B", E-12

**Position/Skill Factor:** Top class winger, or forward, who has close control and runs well with the ball. Favours his right foot and will regularly come off the left flank looking for a crack at goal. An exciting player with explosive finishing potential.

**Career History:** Came up through the Arsenal youth system, first as an associated schoolboy (May 1982) and later, on leaving school in July 1984, as an apprentice. Graduated to the professional ranks and made his FL debut at Highbury when coming on for Niall Quinn against Manchester City on 22 November 1986. Marked his first full senior game with a goal in a 2-1 win at Brentford towards the end of that season, following a

| Clubs | Signing Date | Transfer Fee | APPEARANCES Lge | FL Cup | FA Cup | Others | GOALS Lge | FL Cup | FA Cup | Others |
|---|---|---|---|---|---|---|---|---|---|---|
| Arsenal* | 12.85 | - | 171+29 | 22+2 | 21+2 | 7+1 | 55 | 6 | 4 | |
| Brentford | 1.87 | Loan | 6+1 | | | 1+1 | | | | |

brief loan period at Brentford and served notice that it would not be long before he challenged for a regular place in the Arsenal side. Getting his chance in 1988-89, he took it excellently, playing 37 League matches and scoring ten goals, in partnership with Alan Smith, as Arsenal pipped Liverpool in the last game of the season to become League Champions. His progress was acknowledged by his peers when voted the PFA "Young Player of the Year" in 1989. After a disappointing 1989-90, by their high standards, the "Gunners"again went for broke in 1990-91 and he missed only two games when winning his second League Championship medal in three years. His natural combativeness could be explained away by the fact that between 1951-53, his uncle Stan had 13 fights as a professional boxer. With the emergence of Kevin Campbell and the arrival of Ian Wright in 1991-92, he was switched by manager George Graham to a wide role on either flank. It was a very successful move as he not only scored 12 FL goals (including a first ever senior hat-trick against Crystal Palace), but was also credited with 15 assists and played in every game. His form was noted by England manager Graham Taylor who selected him as a substitute for the game against Germany, and played him three more times at the end of the season. He did enough to justify inclusion for the 1992 European Championship Finals and came on for Andy Sinton as England went out of the competition to the host nation, Sweden, following a 2-1 defeat. Like most of the "Gunners" in **1992-93**, he lacked consistency in the new Premier League, but was at his best during important cup matches. However, he scored his usual quota of spectacular goals, a delightful chip in a 2-1 PL victory over Chelsea and a sensational volley to equalise in the first Leeds United FA Cup match and the opener against Sheffield Wednesday in the League Cup Final, being the pick. He was the architect of that performance and collected another winners medal when Arsenal did the cup "double" over Sheffield Wednesday in the FA Cup Final.

## **METCALF Joshua (Josh)** Harold

Born: Dublin, 8 October 1974

Height: 5'9" Weight: 10.12

**Position/Skill Factor:** Midfielder. Very willing, with a great attitude, he is a good passer who is always looking to link up defence and attack.

**Career History:** First came to Blackburn Rovers as an associated schoolboy (November 1988), before graduating through the youth team as a trainee (August 1991) to the professional ranks. Played mainly in the junior side in **1992-93**, but was given a reserve outing right at the end of the season and impressed.

| Clubs | Signing Date | Transfer Fee | APPEARANCES Lge | FL Cup | FA Cup | Others | GOALS Lge | FL Cup | FA Cup | Others |
|---|---|---|---|---|---|---|---|---|---|---|
| Blackburn Rovers* | 7.93 | - | | | | | | | | |

## **MIDDLETON Lee** John

Born: Nuneaton, 10 September 1970

Height: 5'11" Weight: 10.12

**Position/Skill Factor:** Central defender who reads the game and intercepts well. Always looking to make the right pass, he sets up attacks with sensible balls from the back.

**Career History:** He joined Coventry City, along with his twin brother, Craig, as an associated schoolboy in January 1987, eventually becoming a trainee (July 1987) on leaving school. Turned professional two years later and made his FL debut at Sheffield Wednesday on 30 September 1989, playing in one more game, again as a substitute. Suffered a bad back injury in 1990, which eliminated him from any competitive football in 1990-91 and 1991-92 and he was later released. Given trials with Swindon Town during the 1992 close season, he impressed enough to be offered a monthly contract, which was later updated for a year, when it was felt that he wouldn't suffer a recurrence of his old injury. Having been out of competitive football for so long, he was carefully nursed along in Town's reserve side during **1992-93**, making the second highest number of appearances with 29, before suffering from injury towards the end of the season. If match fit, could get a surprise call-up for a taste of Premier League action in 1993-94.

| Clubs | Signing Date | Transfer Fee | APPEARANCES Lge | FL Cup | FA Cup | Others | GOALS Lge | FL Cup | FA Cup | Others |
|---|---|---|---|---|---|---|---|---|---|---|
| Coventry City | 5.89 | - | 0+2 | | | | | | | |
| Swindon Town* | 7.92 | - | | | | | | | | |

## **MIKE Adrian** Roosevelt

Born: Manchester, 16 November 1973

Height: 6'0"

Weight: 11.8

International Honours: E Sch

**Position/Skill Factor:** Very quick striker, who turns well in and around the box and is adept at making good runs off the ball to let his team-mates in. Has an excellent first touch.

**Career History:** An exciting young star of the future, he made his FL debut for Manchester City, while still a trainee, at home to Notts County on 25 April 1992 and in the next match, the last game of the season at Oldham Athletic, he scored the first goal in a 5-2 victory. A 1992 summer professional signing, he first came to Maine Road as an associated schoolboy in January 1988, before joining the trainee ranks in July 1990. After his elation at playing in the last two matches of the previous season, he settled down in **1992-93** to reserve team football, although being called up to make two substitute appearances in the new Premier League. Following his one and only full first team game at home to Sheffield Wednesday on 23 February, he was selected for the England youth team to travel to Australia in March for the World Cup. Played in one match, as England finished third and came home to a spell on loan at Bury. Scored in his opener for the "Shakers" and after seven (including two substitute) games he was recalled to Maine Road to join a City party for a short tour of Japan. Will be challenging strongly for a first team slot in 1993-94..

| | | | APPEARANCES | | | | GOALS | | | |
|---|---|---|---|---|---|---|---|---|---|---|
| Clubs | Signing Date | Transfer Fee | Lge | FL Cup | FA Cup | Others | Lge | FL Cup | FA Cup | Others |
| Manchester City* | 7.92 | - | 3+2 | | | | 1 | | | |
| Bury | 3.93 | Loan | 5+2 | | | | 1 | | | |

## **MIKLOSKO Ludek (Ludo)**

Born: Ostrava, Czechoslovakia, 9 December 1961

Height: 6'5" Weight: 14.0

International Honours: Czech Int

**Position/Skill Factor:** Goalkeeper with a wonderful build, who takes crosses comfortably and makes difficult saves look easy. An excellent kicker, also.

**Career History:** A Czech international, the giant goalie was signed by West Ham United from Banik Ostrava to replace the ageing Phil Parkes and in doing so he joined the growing band of foreign 'keepers to play for English sides. After making his FL debut in a 2-2 draw at Swindon Town on 18 February 1990, he played in the last 19 games of the season, becoming a great favourite with the crowd, while keeping seven clean sheets and was instrumental in helping the "Hammers" climb the Second Division table to a respectable seventh place. In 1990-91, he further enhanced his reputation in West Ham's promotion season, which owed far more to their defence than their attack, being ever present and conceding a mere 34 goals in 46 games, which included no less than 21 "clean sheets". He had no rivals in the voting for "Hammer of the Year" and although West Ham lost their First Division place the following season, no blame was attached to Ludo, who was acknowledged to be one of the safest, if not the best, 'keeper in the entire Football League. Ever present in **1992-93**, he was one of the cornerstones of a side that came roaring back to the top flight at the first time of asking. A huge favourite with the fans, he decided to retire from international football during the season, in order to give his full commitment to West Ham. Saved a penalty at Upton Park against Sunderland, although he needn't have bothered, as six goals without return crashed into the Wearsider's net that afternoon. Kept 17 clean sheets and conceded just 41 goals in 46 League matches, despite a calamitous 5-2 defeat at Tranmere Rovers in December. On a night where almost everything went wrong for the "Hammers", Miklosko "gifted" Rovers' John Aldridge, when he, of all people, set the Republic of Ireland international up for his hat-trick, with a poor clearance. However, all that was forgotten as West Ham finally overhauled Portsmouth to reach the Premier League with a better goal difference, as runners-up to Newcastle United.

| | | | APPEARANCES | | | | GOALS | | | |
|---|---|---|---|---|---|---|---|---|---|---|
| Clubs | Signing Date | Transfer Fee | Lge | FL Cup | FA Cup | Others | Lge | FL Cup | FA Cup | Others |
| West Ham United* | 2.90 | £300,000 | 146 | 10 | 12 | 8 | | | | |

# MILLER Alan John

Born: Epping, 29 March 1970

Height: 6'2"

Weight: 13.8

International Honours: E Yth, E "U21"-4

**Position/Skill Factor:** Good all-round goalkeeper from the FA School of Excellence at Lilleshall. .Possessing a safe pair of hands, he inspires confidence. Is also recognised for his kicking ability.

**Career History:** Started his football life at Highbury as an associated schoolboy in July 1984, becoming a trainee in July 1986. Yet to play for Arsenal's first team since turning professional, mainly due to the consistency of John Lukic and then David Seaman, he was loaned out to Plymouth Argyle in 1988-89 and made his FL debut at Home Park against Oldham Athletic, keeping a clean sheet in a 3-0 win on 26 November 1988. Amazingly made his England Under 21 debut just after signing professional forms and before appearing in the League. Unfortunate to be understudy to David Seaman, as he would probably be a first choice at most clubs, he gained further FL experience on loan with West Bromwich Albion and Birmingham City during 1991-92, spending three months at St Andrews assisting the "Blues'" drive to promotion. Finally made his Arsenal debut in **1992-93**, after coming on as a second-half substitute for the injured David Seaman at Leeds United on 21 November 1992 and later in the season he made three more appearances, as the "Gunners" ran into a fixture "pile-up", due to the cup games.

| | | | APPEARANCES | | | | GOALS | | | |
|---|---|---|---|---|---|---|---|---|---|---|
| Clubs | Signing Date | Transfer Fee | Lge | FL Cup | FA Cup | Others | Lge | FL Cup | FA Cup | Others |
| Arsenal* | 5.88 | – | 3+1 | | | | | | | |
| Plymouth Argyle | 11.88 | Loan | 13 | | 2 | | | | | |
| West Bromwich Albion | 8.91 | Loan | 3 | | | | | | | |
| Birmingham City | 12.91 | Loan | 15 | | | 1 | | | | |

# MILLER Paul Anthony

Born: Woking, 31 January 1968

Height: 6'0" Weight: 11.0

**Position/Skill Factor:** A good runner off the ball, he also does well in the air and always looks to score goals.

**Career History:** Started his soccer career as a Wimbledon associated schoolboy in March 1982, before leaving to play for non-League sides, Wealdstone and Yeovil Town. After coming back to the club as a professional during the summer of 1987, he made his FL debut at Watford on 15 August 1987, but only managed a couple more games during the season and was loaned out for a short while to Newport County. The following season he was given a concerted run in the side, which extended into 1989-90 and although interspersed with another spell on loan, this time to Bristol City, he appeared to be making good progress. Unfortunate to be injured during the first match of 1990-91, against Arsenal, he was unable to play again for the rest of the season. Remained sidelined for 16 months, not returning to first team duty until December 1991. Appropriately his first goal after his return was an equaliser against Arsenal at Highbury. A regular team member in the second half of the season, goals eluded him, however. With John Fashanu injured, he started **1992-93** partnering new signing, Dean Holdsworth, but only one goal and the return to fitness of the former, relegated him to sitting on the bench, or playing in the reserves. Apart from standing in for Fashanu in mid-season, he was forced to wait a further three months, before twice coming off the bench, prior to playing in the home game against Nottingham Forest and at Manchester City. Scrambled the equaliser in a 1-1 draw at Maine Road to register his second goal in the Premier League, before being substituted for Paul McGee and missing the final two games of the season.

| | | | APPEARANCES | | | | GOALS | | | |
|---|---|---|---|---|---|---|---|---|---|---|
| Clubs | Signing Date | Transfer Fee | Lge | FL Cup | FA Cup | Others | Lge | FL Cup | FA Cup | Others |
| Wimbledon* | 8.87 | – | 55+15 | 3+3 | 3 | 1 | 11 | | | |
| Newport County | 10.87 | Loan | 6 | | | | 2 | | | |
| Bristol City | 1.90 | Loan | 0+3 | | | 2 | | | | |

# MILLIGAN Michael (Mike) Joseph

Born: Manchester, 20 February 1967

Height: 5'8" Weight: 11.0

International Honours: IR "U21"-1, IR"B", IR-1

**Position/Skill Factor:** All-action midfield general who is a good competitor and a reliable team player. A tenacious performer, he is a useful man to have on your side, especially in breaking down the oppositions rhythm.

**Career History:** Although starting out as a Manchester City associated schoolboy (April 1981), he was not offered terms by the club when leaving school and joined Oldham Athletic on a YTS scheme in December 1984. After progressing to the club's professional ranks early in 1985, he had to wait a further year before making his FL debut at Sheffield United on 12 April 1986. Very consistent over the next four season, he was inspirational to a side seeking to attain First Division status, but the nearest he came during his time with the "Latics" was when reaching the Play-Offs in 1986-87. Played a significant role in Oldham's wonderful cup runs of 1989-90, winning through to the Semi-Final of the FA Cup, before succumbing in a replay to Manchester United and the Final of the League Cup, losing to Nottingham Forest. Moved to Everton in the 1990 close season, as an aspiring First Division midfield general, but did not fit in at Goodison Park and struggled to win a regular place. His older brother Terry was with Crewe Alexandra in 1986-87, having previously been at Manchester City and Oldham, without getting a game. Returned to Oldham at a knock-down price in the summer of 1991 and played a leading role in consolidating the "Latics'" newly won First Division status. After a long wait, he finally broke into the Irish Republic team in April 1992, although only as substitute in a low priority friendly against the USA team. As team captain, he consistently turned in excellent performances in **1992-93** and was "Latics'" only ever present during a season that was fraught with difficulty, with the club hovering around the danger zone for most of the duration. And as the obvious choice for "Player of the Year", he was seen at his best during the run-in when he led the club to three consecutive victories and eventual Premier League safety. Written off by the media, well in advance, somehow, the team ultimately prevailed and that had a lot to do with the character of the man that Joe Royle had chosen to lead by example. If a fault can be found it is probably in his goal return, especially in the fact that only three clubs in the Premier League bettered Oldham's tally during 1992-93.

| | | | APPEARANCES | | | | GOALS | | | |
|---|---|---|---|---|---|---|---|---|---|---|
| Clubs | Signing Date | Transfer Fee | Lge | FL Cup | FA Cup | Others | Lge | FL Cup | FA Cup | Others |
| Oldham Athletic | 3.85 | - | 161+1 | 19+1 | 12 | 4 | 17 | 1 | 1 | |
| Everton | 8.90 | £1,000,000 | 16+1 | 0+1 | 1 | 4+1 | 1 | | | 1 |
| Oldham Athletic* | 7.91 | £600,000 | 78 | 8 | 2 | 1 | 6 | 1 | | 1 |

## MILTON Simon Charles

Born: Fulham, 23 August 1963

Height: 5'9" Weight: 11.9

**Position/Skill Factor:** Right-winger who is capable of scoring explosive goals after bursting through from midfield. Produces good early crosses and is a sweet striker of the ball.

**Career History:** Joined Ipswich Town from local Eastern Counties League club, Bury Town, in the 1987 close season and made his FL debut while on loan with Exeter City at home to Stockport County on 21 November 1987, scoring two goals, plus another in their next League game at Darlington. He was soon back at Portman Road for a run out and following another spell on loan at Torquay United, he played in Ipswich's last six League games of 1987-88. In the final match of the season, a 3-2 victory over Bradford City, he scored the winner, which lifted Town from 11th to eighth place in the Second Division. Has worked hard to establish himself during the last three season, only missing five League matches in 1989-90, but lost his way temporarily in 1990-91 as he struggled to find his true form. Out of favour at the start of 1991-92, he fought his way back into the first team in October and held his place for the remainder of the season as Town climbed up the table to finish as Second Division Champions with a superb run in the New Year, playing mainly on the right side of midfield. Extremely unfortunate with injuries in **1992-93**, he made a few substitute appearances at the beginning of the season, before being sidelined, when having an operation to his ankle after x-rays had revealed the presence of scar tissue around a joint. On recovering and following a comeback with the reserve side, he was told to rest after having problems with the ankle and later underwent another operation, this time on his knee. With his season disrupted and virtually wiped out, he came back to play in the final seven games and scored two magnificent goals.

| | | | APPEARANCES | | | | GOALS | | | |
|---|---|---|---|---|---|---|---|---|---|---|
| Clubs | Signing Date | Transfer Fee | Lge | FL Cup | FA Cup | Others | Lge | FL Cup | FA Cup | Others |
| Ipswich Town* | 7.87 | £5,500 | 138+23 | 8+2 | 8 | 10+1 | 37 | 1 | 1 | 3 |
| Exeter City | 11.87 | Loan | 2 | | | 1 | 3 | | | |
| Torquay United | 3.88 | Loan | 4 | | | | 1 | | | |

## MIMMS Robert (Bobby) Andrew

Born: York, 12 October 1963

Height: 6'2"

Weight: 12.13

International Honours: E "U21"-3

**Position/Skill Factor:** Very experienced goalkeeper. Extremely agile for such a big man, he commands his lines well. Sets up attacks with good quick throws to his full-backs and kicks long and accurately from his hands.

**Career History:** An associated schoolboy (October 1979) and then an apprentice (April 1980) with Halifax Town, he graduated as a professional in the 1981 close season. With John Kilner and Lee Smelt barring his way at the Shay, he was transferred to Rotherham United after only three months as a professional and eventually made his FL debut at home to Blackburn Rovers on 8 May 1982. Understudy to Ray Mountford and then Alan Stevenson, he became first choice 'keeper at Millmoor from March 1984 and was ever present the following season, when he won two England Under 21 caps, both times as substitute. Transferred to Everton in the summer of 1985 to act as deputy to Neville Southall, he made his debut for the "Toffees" in late October and was hurriedly recalled from a loan spell with Notts County late in the season when the latter was injured. Played in the last nine League games of 1985-86, during which Everton lost the League Championship to Liverpool. No blame can be attached to Mimms, however, who kept a clean sheet in the first six of those games! Also played in the 1986 FA Cup Final, but was powerless to prevent Liverpool overturning a half-time deficit to run out 3-1 winners and complete the "Double". Although getting some first team action in each of his three seasons at Goodison Park, he was frequently loaned out to other clubs to keep in trim. Finally, he welcomed the chance of regular first team football when he was signed by Tottenham Hotspur late in 1987-88. Sadly for him, his reign as first team 'keeper at White Hart Lane lasted slightly less than one year as "Spurs" then signed Norwegian Erik Thorstvedt in January 1989. After two years of understudying Thorstvedt and a short period on loan to Aberdeen, he was sold to Blackburn Rovers. Immediately replaced Mark Grew, who had been on loan from Port Vale and played in the last 22 games of the season, with relegation to the Third Division being averted in the penultimate match, a 1-1 draw at home to Wolverhampton Wanderers. In 1991-92, a season that was fraught with tension, he kept 14 clean sheets as Rovers won their way back to the First Division after an absence of 26 years, despite scraping into the Play-Offs in sixth position. With the club being linked to at least ten other goalkeepers during **1992-93**, he was the only ever present in the team, keeping 23 clean sheets in 54 matches. Struggled a bit with the back pass ruling and gifted Huddersfield Town a goal in the League Cup, when he drove the ball against an oncoming forward, but on many occasions he looked the part. Has always been susceptible in facing long range shots and he endured spells when he could not make up his mind whether to leave his line or not. The high spot of his season came when fully playing his part in a 2-1 win in the penultimate game at Tottenham Hotspur, his former club.

| | | | APPEARANCES | | | | GOALS | | | |
|---|---|---|---|---|---|---|---|---|---|---|
| Clubs | Signing Date | Transfer Fee | Lge | FL Cup | FA Cup | Others | Lge | FL Cup | FA Cup | Others |
| Halifax Town | 8.81 | - | | | | | | | | |
| Rotherham United | 11.81 | £15,000 | 83 | 7 | 3 | 1 | | | | |
| Everton | 5.85 | £150,000 | 29 | 2 | 2 | 4 | | | | |
| Notts County | 3.86 | Loan | 2 | | | 1 | | | | |
| Sunderland | 12.86 | Loan | 4 | | | | | | | |
| Blackburn Rovers | 1.87 | Loan | 6 | | | | | | | |
| Manchester City | 9.87 | Loan | 3 | | | | | | | |
| Tottenham Hotspur | 2.88 | £325,000 | 37 | 5 | 2 | | | | | |
| Aberdeen | 2.90 | Loan | 6 | | 2 | | | | | |
| Blackburn Rovers* | 12.90 | £250,000 | 109 | 9 | 9 | 4 | | | | |

## MINTON Jeffrey Simon Thompson

Born: Hackney, 28 December 1973

Height: 5'5" Weight: 11.7

**Position/Skill Factor:** Skilful midfielder with a lovely touch and good vision. Has much awareness around the box and can make telling passes.

**Career History:** Turned professional with Tottenham Hotspur early in 1992, having first come through the ranks at White Hart Lane as an associated schoolboy (March 1988), before becoming a trainee in August 1990. Soon after signing professional forms, he made his FL debut for "Spurs" in an end of season game at home to Everton on 25 April 1992 and scored in a 3-3 draw. Having promised so much the previous season, it was a surprise to many that he spent **1992-93** playing reserve team soccer, apart from a single substitute outing against Brentford in the first leg of a Second Round League Cup-tie. Will push hard for a first team place this coming season.

| | | | APPEARANCES | | | | GOALS | | | |
|---|---|---|---|---|---|---|---|---|---|---|
| Clubs | Signing Date | Transfer Fee | Lge | FL Cup | FA Cup | Others | Lge | FL Cup | FA Cup | Others |
| Tottenham Hotspur* | 1.92 | - | 2 | 0+1 | | | 1 | | | |

## MITCHELL David (Dave) Stewart

Born: Glasgow, 13 June 1962

Height: 6'1"

Weight: 11.8

International Honours: Australian Int

**Position/Skill Factor:** A striker who runs himself into the ground and is prepared to chase lost causes where his pace can often tell. Also, good in the air.

**Career History:** A widely travelled forward who plays his international football for Australia, he started out with Adelaide City and Sydney City, before signing for hometown club, Glasgow Rangers. After making his debut for Rangers at the beginning of 1983-84, he went on to make 26 appearances in two seasons before joining the exodus to mainland Europe with Eintracht Frankfurt (Germany) and later, Feyenoord (Holland). At the beginning of 1989 he was offered the chance of playing in England with Chelsea, predominately for the purpose of covering Kerry Dixon and Gordon Durie. However, he got an early opportunity to impress when making his FL debut at Stamford Bridge against Crystal Palace on 14 January 1989, but was required to make only five more appearances during a season that ultimately saw the "Blues" return to the top flight as Second Division Champions. For the next two seasons he was ignored by manager, Bobby Campbell and a short loan spell with Newcastle United failed to revive his flagging career. He was rescued from obscurity by Glenn Hoddle who, following his return from France, had spent a short time with Chelsea before being appointed manager of Swindon Town. Even then, he had to wait until mid-season to break into Swindon's team, but after displacing Steve White in January 1992, he held his place for the rest of the campaign. Really earned his place in **1992-93**, with his speed catching a lot of defenders unawares and was a regular, apart from a period of injury and suspension. Sent off at Brentford, he atoned on his return to the side with a hat-trick in a 6-4 victory at Birmingham City. His appearance at Wembley in the Play-Off Final against Leicester City was in considerable doubt at one stage, but thankfully the club was able to obtain his release from the Australian squad, due to meet New Zealand during the same weekend. Although he didn't score in Town's 4-3 victory, he was a constant threat and will certainly worry a good many Premier League defences this season. At the moment, however, it seems certain that he will miss the start of 1993-94, as Australia have a World Cup match against Canada that coincides with the opening games, but Town's supporters can rest assured that he will not be away too long.

| | | | APPEARANCES | | | | GOALS | | | |
|---|---|---|---|---|---|---|---|---|---|---|
| Clubs | Signing Date | Transfer Fee | Lge | FL Cup | FA Cup | Others | Lge | FL Cup | FA Cup | Others |
| Glasgow Rangers | .80 | | 18+8 | 6+5 | 2+1 | 2+3 | 6 | 3 | 1 | 4 |
| Eintracht Frankfurt | .85 | | | | | | | | | |
| Feyenoord | .87 | | | | | | | | | |
| Chelsea | 1.89 | £200,000 | 7 | | | 1 | | | | |
| Newcastle United | 1.91 | Loan | 2 | | | | 1 | | | |
| Swindon Town* | 7.91 | £30,000 | 61+7 | 4 | 4 | 4 | 16 | 4 | 2 | 3 |

## MOLBY Jan

Born: Jutland, Denmark, 4 July 1963

Height: 6'1" Weight: 14.7

International Honours: Danish Int

**Position/Skill Factor:** Midfield player with a wonderful touch and possessing quick feet for such a big man. Great strength in possession and a lovely striker of the ball, he is possibly the best long ball passer in the modern game. Dangerous at free-kicks with a powerful shot and Liverpool's first choice penalty taker.

**Career History:** Signed for Liverpool in the 1984 close season, following a successful stay with the Dutch side, Ajax of Amsterdam and made his FL debut at Norwich City on 25 August 1984. His great influence in midfield minimised the loss of Graeme Souness to Italian soccer, although later, Kenny Dalglish would often use him as a "sweeper". Played 39 League games in 1985-86, as Liverpool did the "double", winning the League Championship and defeating local rivals, Everton 3-1 in the FA Cup Final. But it could have been so different. After Gary Lineker had given Everton the lead at Wembley, it was only Jan's tremendous passing ability that turned the game around as he picked out Ian Rush for the equaliser and Craig Johnston for the second "Reds'" goal. In the following season, almost a failure by Liverpool's standards, he was a key member of the side that finished second in the First Division and were beaten 2-1 by Arsenal in the League Cup Final. Suffered from injury in 1987-88, making only one full League appearance, although coming on as a sub in the losing FA Cup Final against Wimbledon and was absent for a large tract of the following season after being jailed for three months on a drink-driving conviction. Although winning a second League Championship medal in 1989-90, he only made 12 appearances and in recent years lost his way somewhat, with weight and injury problems and had to play second fiddle to Ronnie Whelan and Steve McMahon in Liverpool's midfield. Injured at the start of 1991-92, he returned to the side in October 1991 and was a fairly regular selection for the remainder of the season. Because of his weight problems and his lack of mobility, he is sometimes caught in possession, although he has the strength to shove off most challenges. Given time and space he can direct operations as he showed in the winning 1992 FA Cup Final against Sunderland, when he orchestrated nearly all of Liverpool's second-half offensive, seemingly without moving from the centre circle! Although not selected at the start of **1992-93**, he soon replaced the injured Michael Thomas and was performing well until being carried off with an ankle injury in the vital away clash at Manchester United in October, when Liverpool were leading 2-0. Following his departure, United hit back to level at 2-2. After six months enforced absence, he made his return as a substitute at Anfield in the Everton derby game on 20 March, only to aggravate his hamstring and be sidelined until the end of the season. At the time of going to press a possible move to Tranmere Rovers was being discussed.

| | | | APPEARANCES | | | | GOALS | | | |
|---|---|---|---|---|---|---|---|---|---|---|
| Clubs | Signing Date | Transfer Fee | Lge | FL Cup | FA Cup | Others | Lge | FL Cup | FA Cup | Others |
| Liverpool* | 8.84 | £575,000 | 172+21 | 21+3 | 24+4 | 16+2 | 40 | 8 | 4 | 4 |

## MONCUR John Frederick

Born: Stepney,
22 September 1966

Height: 5'7"

Weight: 9.10

**Position/Skill Factor:** Midfield player who cannot get enough of the ball. Always makes himself available by finding space for himself and with two good feet, is an excellent passer.

**Career History:** As the son of one of the backroom staff at Tottenham Hotspur, it was only natural that he would start his career at White Hart Lane. Made good progress as an associated schoolboy (November 1980) and as an apprentice (April 1983), before moving into the paid ranks, but his first taste of first team football was not with the "Spurs". In order to gain experience, with such a glut of talent available at Tottenham, he was loaned out to Doncaster Rovers, making his FL debut in a Third Division match at home to York City on 27 September 1986. Later the same season, he was also loaned out to Cambridge United, before returning to White Hart Lane and making his debut for "Spurs" away to Everton on 11 May 1987, when the club fielded its reserve team for the last match of the season, immediately prior to the 1987 FA Cup Final. This remained the pattern of his career for the next five years, with occasional first team outings for "Spurs", interspersed with short loans out to lower division clubs, none of which led to the permanent move he needed to progress his career, until former club colleague, Glenn Hoddle, signed him for Swindon Town in March 1992.Unfortunately, appearances have been limited, at first by the presence of Mickey Hazard, but more recently by injury and suspension. However, he finally claimed a regular place in the **1992-93** Play-Off matches and would appear to be lined up as Hazard's long term replacement, being more of a ball winner and the type of player that the side has lacked for too long. Had an excellent game in the Play-Off Final, when he impressed a good many people and was involved in two of the goals in the 4-3 victory over Leicester City. Looks set to start the new term under the Premier League spotlight, but the one question mark still hanging over him is probably his temperament. On several occasions he has shown an inclination to retailiate and was sent off for such an offence during a reserve match, whilst making his comeback last season.

| | | | APPEARANCES | | | | GOALS | | | |
|---|---|---|---|---|---|---|---|---|---|---|
| Clubs | Signing Date | Transfer Fee | Lge | FL Cup | FA Cup | Others | Lge | FL Cup | FA Cup | Others |
| Tottenham Hotspur | 8.84 | - | 10+11 | 1+2 | | | 1 | | | |
| Doncaster Rovers | 9.86 | Loan | 4 | | | | | | | |
| Cambridge United | 3.87 | Loan | 3+1 | | | | | | | |
| Portsmouth | 3.89 | Loan | 7 | | | | | | | |
| Brentford | 10.89 | Loan | 5 | | | 1 | 1 | | | |
| Ipswich Town | 10.91 | Loan | 5+1 | | | | | | | |
| Swindon Town* | 3.92 | £80,000 | 12+5 | 1 | | 4 | 1 | | | 1 |

# MONKOU Kenneth (Ken) John

Born: Necare, Surinam, 29 November 1964

Height: 6'0" Weight: 12.9

International Honours: Dutch "U21" Int

**Position/Skill Factor:** Central defender who is strong in the air and powerful in the tackle, he is also a good athlete. Has good skills on the ball and is capable of hitting quality long balls behind opposing defences.

**Career History:** After being signed by Chelsea from the Dutch club, Feyenoord, at the back end of 1988-89, he was refused permission to play in a match for his former club shortly afterwards and the plane that he would have been travelling on, crashed, killing many of his old team-mates. Made his FL debut at Stamford Bridge in Chelsea's Second Division title winning side against Stoke City on 1 May 1989, coming on for Joe McLaughlin, who

was shortly to leave the club. Soon established himself at the heart of the Chelsea defence, missing just four games in his first full season as the club consolidated its position in the First Division, finishing in the fifth place. In 1990-91, although the "Blues" fared less well than expected, one of the bonuses of a disappointing season was his partnership with promising young Jason Cundy. Partnered new signing Paul Elliott for the first half of 1991-92, until losing his place to Cundy in January, but returned to the Chelsea team in March, following the latter's departure to Tottenham Hotspur. Following the signing of Mal Donaghy from Manchester United, he was transferred to Southampton at the beginning of **1992-93** and was voted "Man of the Match" in each of his first three games at the Dell. Having created a tremendous impression at the club, it was only a series of niggling injuries in the last third of the season that cost him several appearances. Earlier, his finest hour came when Alan Shearer returned to the Dell as a Blackburn Rovers' player in November, only to be completely shackled by the newcomer. After this game, he was widely tipped to get a Dutch full cap and if he continues to turn in performances of that ilk, his time will most certainly come.

| | | | APPEARANCES | | | | GOALS | | | |
|---|---|---|---|---|---|---|---|---|---|---|
| Clubs | Signing Date | Transfer Fee | Lge | FL Cup | FA Cup | Others | Lge | FL Cup | FA Cup | Others |
| Chelsea | 3.89 | £100,000 | 92+2 | 12 | 3 | 10 | 2 | | | |
| Southampton* | 8.92 | £750,000 | 33 | 3 | 1 | | 1 | | | |

# MOODY Paul

Born: Portsmouth, 13 June 1967

Height: 6'3" Weight: 13.12

**Position/Skill Factor:** Tall striker who is obviously a handful in the air and has a strong shot. Pulls away to the far post well when team-mates get into crossing positions.

**Career History:** Signed in the summer of 1991 by Southampton from local Beazer Homes League club, Waterlooville, for whom he was top scorer with 25 goals in 1990-91. Prior to 1988, he played for Fareham Town in the same league. Made his FL debut in the first game of the season at home to Tottenham Hotspur on 17 August

1991 as a substitute and made his full debut two weeks later at home to Aston Villa. Thereafter, first team opportunities were extremely scarce with Iain Dowie and Alan Shearer holding down the strikers' slots at The Dell. After scoring three goals in eight appearances for the reserves in **1992-93**, he got a surprise call to join the first team for the trip to Wimbledon. Having partnered Iain Dowie in a tactical ploy that earned a point, he came off the bench in the next game before going back to the reserves. Went to Reading on loan in December and whilst gaining valuable experience, also scored his first League goal. On his return to the Dell he continued with the "stiffs", until again coming out of the wilderness to replace the suspended Dowie against visiting Everton.

| | | | APPEARANCES | | | | GOALS | | | |
|---|---|---|---|---|---|---|---|---|---|---|
| Clubs | Signing Date | Transfer Fee | Lge | FL Cup | FA Cup | Others | Lge | FL Cup | FA Cup | Others |
| Southampton* | 7.91 | £50,000 | 4+3 | | 0+1 | | | | | |
| Reading | 12.92 | Loan | 5 | | | 1 | 1 | | | |

## MOORE Thomas Kevin

Born: Grimsby, 29 April 1958

Height: 5'11"

Weight: 12.2

International Honours: E Sch

**Position/Skill Factor:** Commanding central defender who is a wonderful professional. Strong in the air, a good defender, with a smashing left foot and a useful scorer of goals from set plays.

**Career History:** One of three footballing sons of Norman, who was a centre-forward with Grimsby Town, Hull City, Blackburn Rovers and Bury between 1946-1952. His younger brothers, Andy and David, also played for Grimsby, among other teams, as did his uncle Roy, soon after the war. Signed as a professional for Grimsby straight from school and after working his way through the junior sides, he made his FL debut at Bury on 21 August 1976. In more than ten seasons at Blundell Park, he was an automatic choice, starting out at left-back, before moving to the centre of the defence and winning a Third Division Championship medal in 1979-80. Joined promotion chasing Oldham Athletic during 1986-87 when his chances of playing in the top flight with Town had all but evaporated and then saw his First Division prospects with his new club disappear at the Play-Off stage. However, got his chance in the First Division when his old team-mate Chris Nicholl, then managing Southampton, brought him to the Dell as a replacement for the outgoing Mark Wright. Settled into the side well as a regular choice for a couple of seasons, but more recently has had to share the central defensive duties with Russell Osman and Neil Ruddock. Released on a free transfer in the summer of 1991, he was subsequently re-signed for one more year by incoming "Saints'" manager, Ian Branfoot. With five other central defenders on the books it seemed a strange decision, especially when he was scarcely used in the first-half of the season. However, after returning to The Dell from a successful loan period with Bristol Rovers, he was restored to the "Saints'" first team in place of Richard Hall and held his place for the remainder of the season. After missing the first game of the **1992-93** season, he quickly teamed up with newcomer, Kenny Monkou, at the expense of Richard Hall and Steve Wood, before losing his place and yet again going on loan to Bristol Rovers. In the process of signing for Rovers, when their manager was sacked, he returned to the Dell and was restored to the first team for the visit to Middlesbrough, where he made his 550th League appearance. At the end of the season he was awarded another one year contract as recognition for producing sterling performances just when it seemed that he is on his way from the club.

| | | | APPEARANCES | | | | GOALS | | | |
|---|---|---|---|---|---|---|---|---|---|---|
| Clubs | Signing Date | Transfer Fee | Lge | FL Cup | FA Cup | Others | Lge | FL Cup | FA Cup | Others |
| Grimsby Town | 7.76 | - | 397+3 | 41 | 25 | 2 | 28 | 3 | 3 | |
| Oldham Athletic | 2.87 | £100,000 | 13 | | | 2 | 1 | | | |
| Southampton* | 8.87 | £125,000 | 130+4 | 16+1 | 12 | 5 | 10 | 1 | | 1 |
| Bristol Rovers | 1.92 | Loan | 7 | | | | | | | |
| Bristol Rovers | 10.92 | Loan | 4 | | | | 1 | | | |

## MOORE Neil

Born: Liverpool, 21 September 1972

Height: 6'0½" Weight: 11.13

**Position/Skill Factor:** A good all-round central defender who is very aggressive and strong in the air.

**Career History:** Came to Everton straight from school as an associated schoolboy in February 1988, before signing on as a trainee in June 1989 and turning professional during the 1991 close season. With no first team appearances in his first year as a professional, he was a regular for the reserves in **1992-93** and pushed hard for a chance at the big-time. Although he didn't manage the starting line-up, on two occasions he was used as a substitute, making his PL debut in the penultimate game of the season at home to Sheffield United on 4 May, 1993. If he continues his present rate of development he could find himself partnering Gary Ablett, or David Watson, in the near future.

| | | | APPEARANCES | | | | GOALS | | | |
|---|---|---|---|---|---|---|---|---|---|---|
| Clubs | Signing Date | Transfer Fee | Lge | FL Cup | FA Cup | Others | Lge | FL Cup | FA Cup | Others |
| Everton* | 6.91 | - | 0+1 | 0+1 | | | | | | |

## MORAN Kevin Bernard

Born: Dublin, 29 April 1956

Height: 5'11" Weight: 12.9

International Honours: IR-65

**Position/Skill Factor:** Very experienced, tough tackling, never-say-die central defender, who will not be beaten. He is never afraid to tackle and has picked up many injuries for his pains.

**Career History:** A former Irish Gaelic footballer with the Pegasus club of Dublin, he signed for Manchester United early in 1978, with only limited experience of soccer. After making his FL debut in a 1-1 draw at Southampton on 30 April 1979, he became a first team regular in 1980-81, replacing Gordon McQueen, having already won his first Republic of Ireland cap against Switzerland on 30 April 1980. won his first major club honour in 1983 when United defeated Brighton & Hove Albion 4-0 in the FA Cup Final replay, after a 2-2 draw. Two years later he again appeared in the FA Cup Final and created a record he would rather forget by becoming the first player in the history of the competition to be sent off. Whilst it was a crude foul on Peter Reid, it was a professional foul and not a vicious one and although the referee was technically correct in his decision, it must be said that worse fouls in previous and subsequent Finals have gone unpunished. Despite his absence, United went on to win 1-0 in extra-time and happily, but belatedly, he eventually received his winners medal. Plagued by injury throughout his United career, he only once came close to completing a full season — in 1983-84. After ten years at Old Trafford, he decided to see out his career overseas, joining Sporting Gijon of the Spanish First Division. However, after 16 months out of the limelight, he returned to League football with Second Division Blackburn Rovers, turning down an offer by Ron Atkinson, who would not guarantee him first team football with Sheffield Wednesday. A mainstay of the Irish Republic team since his debut, the highlight of his international career was undoubtedly playing in all five games in the World Cup Finals in 1990. Remarkably, at the age of 35, he played in no fewer than 41 FL games of Blackburn's tortuous, but ultimately successful promotion campaign of 1991-92, plus the three vital Play-Off games. Those who thought that the **1992-93** Premier League would be too much for his ageing legs were proved wrong as his immense influence and professionalism seldom saw him caught for speed. Proved irreplaceable alongside Hendry, despite suffering a broken nose and several facial cuts and continued his international career. A major player in Rovers' rise up the Premier League to finish in fourth place.

| | | | APPEARANCES | | | | GOALS | | | |
|---|---|---|---|---|---|---|---|---|---|---|
| Clubs | Signing Date | Transfer Fee | Lge | FL Cup | FA Cup | Others | Lge | FL Cup | FA Cup | Others |
| Manchester United | 2.78 | - | 228+3 | 24+1 | 18 | 15+1 | 21 | 2 | 1 | |
| Sporting Gijon (Spain) | 8.88 | - | | | | | | | | |
| Blackburn Rovers* | 1.90 | - | 124+4 | 7+1 | 8 | 6 | 9 | | | |

## MORAN Paul

Born: Enfield, 22 May 1968

Height: 5'10" Weight: 10.0

**Position/Skill Factor:** Speedy winger who likes to run at defenders in order to commit them. A good striker of the ball, he is always looking for a shooting opportunity in and around the penalty area.

**Career History:** Came to Tottenham Hotspur on the YTS scheme on leaving school in July 1984 and two years after signing professional forms, made his FL debut at Everton on 11 May 1987. Has only played sporadically for the "Spurs" since then, having been loaned out to three different teams, Portsmouth (1988-89), Leicester City (1989-90) and Newcastle United (1990-91), while he awaits his chance of a prolonged run at White Hart Lane. Looked to be a potentially brilliant player in a televised game at Derby in December 1987, when after coming on as a second-half substitute, his runs and crosses turned the match in "Spurs'" favour. Since 1989, his career has been at a standstill and after making only one first team appearance, as a substitute, in a European Cup Winners Cup game against Stockerau of Austria in 1991-92, he came off the bench in three Premier League games in **1992-93** without creating an impression. However, he was given some useful experience in the Fiorucci Trophy against Inter Milan and Real Madrid in April 1993, but if he is going to succeed in the top flight, 1993-94 could be his final chance.

| | | | APPEARANCES | | | | GOALS | | | |
|---|---|---|---|---|---|---|---|---|---|---|
| Clubs | Signing Date | Transfer Fee | Lge | FL Cup | FA Cup | Others | Lge | FL Cup | FA Cup | Others |
| Tottenham Hotspur* | 7.85 | - | 14+17 | 1+5 | 3+1 | 0+1 | 2 | | | |
| Portsmouth | 1.89 | Loan | 3 | | | | | | | |
| Leicester City | 11.89 | Loan | 10 | | | | 2 | | | |
| Newcastle United | 2.91 | Loan | 1 | | | | | | | |
| Southend United | 3.91 | Loan | 1 | | | | | | | |

## MORGAN Phillip Jonathan

Born: Stoke, 18 December 1974

Height: 6'1" Weight: 13.0

International Honours: E Sch, E Yth

**Position/Skill Factor:** Goalkeeper. Very brave and a more than useful shot stopper, he also kicks long and accurately with his right foot.

**Career History:** A professional signing for Ipswich Town during the 1993 close season, he first came to Portman Road as a trainee in September 1991, after gaining England schoolboy international honours and successfully graduated through the club's youth team. Made several appearances for the reserves in **1992-93** and will start the new season as the club's third choice 'keeper, behind Craig Forrest and Clive Baker.

| | | | APPEARANCES | | | | GOALS | | | |
|---|---|---|---|---|---|---|---|---|---|---|
| Clubs | Signing Date | Transfer Fee | Lge | FL Cup | FA Cup | Others | Lge | FL Cup | FA Cup | Others |
| Ipswich Town* | 7.93 | - | | | | | | | | |

## MORGAN Stephen (Steve)

Born: Oldham, 19 September 1968

Height: 5'11" Weight: 12.0

International Honours: E Yth

**Position/Skill Factor:** Fast and skilful left-back who can play in midfield if required. Capable of producing excellent crosses after overlapping down the left flank, where his speed can often take him clear of defenders.

**Career History:** A product of Blackpool's youth policy, he first came to Bloomfield Road as an apprentice in September 1985 and following excellent progress with the juniors and reserves, he made his FL debut at Bristol Rovers on 12 April 1986, four months before turning professional, on the left wing, and making four further appearances before the end of the season. He then had to wait until March 1987 for his next first team opportunity when he made a number of appearances in midfield. He started 1987-88 in the left back slot and established himself in this position, playing in every game that season and all but two games in 1988-89. When Blackpool were relegated to Division Four at the end of 1989-90 he elected to join a new club at the end of his contract, signing for Second Division, Plymouth Argyle. After an excellent first term at Home Park, he was switched to midfield in 1991-92, but despite his consistency (missing only one FL game), the "Pilgrims" were relegated to Division Three at the end of the season. Strangely, he was out of favour with new manager Peter Shilton at the start of **1992-93**, but re-established himself at left-back from November onwards. It was not a shock that he left Home Park at the end of his contract during the summer, but more of a surprise that he was then elevated to the Premier League when Bobby Gould signed him for Coventry City. At this point he seems more likely to be a squad player than automatic first team choice, but there is little doubt that he has the talent to establish himself at this level.

| | | | APPEARANCES | | | | GOALS | | | |
|---|---|---|---|---|---|---|---|---|---|---|
| Clubs | Signing Date | Transfer Fee | Lge | FL Cup | FA Cup | Others | Lge | FL Cup | FA Cup | Others |
| Blackpool | 8.86 | – | 135+9 | 13 | 16 | 10+1 | 10 | 2 | 1 | 1 |
| Plymouth Argyle | 7.90 | £115,000 | 120+1 | 7 | 6 | 5 | 6 | | | |
| Coventry City* | 7.93 | £150,000 | | | | | | | | |

## MORLEY Trevor William

Born: Nottingham, 20 March 1961

Height: 5'11"

Weight 12.1

International Honours: E Semi-Pro Int

**Position/Skill Factor:** Striker who holds the ball up well and brings his midfield players into the game. Very strong, he turns defenders to get scoring shots in.

**Career History:** A Derby County apprentice from July 1977, he was allowed to drift away from the Baseball Ground to Southern-League, Corby Town, in 1979 when he was not offered professional terms. His form there was such (28 goals in 78 games), that in early 1981 he was transferred for a fee of £10,000 to Nuneaton Borough of the Alliance League. He remained four and a half years with "Borough", helping them to the Southern League Championship in 1981-82 and second place in the Alliance Premier League in 1983-84 and 1984-85. Never a prolific scorer with the club, sometimes operating in midfield, he laid on plenty of goals for their perennial top scorer, Paul Culpin and also represented the England Semi-Pro side. When Borough manager, Graham Carr, took over Northampton Town in March 1985, he soon went back to his former club to snap up Morley, Richard Hill and Eddie McGoldrick. After making his FL debut and scoring in the opening game of 1985-86 at Burnley on 17 August 1985, he capped a fine season with 51 appearances and 13 goals, only missing the last three matches because of injury. In 1986-87, Northampton ran away with the Fourth Division Championship, amassing 99 points and scoring 103 goals and but for a second half of the season tail-off, both totals would have been much higher. The following season, the "Cobblers" set off as though to run through the Third Division, likewise, but when a second promotion became a fading dream, Morley was sold to Manchester City, then in Division Two, for a large fee. Although a regular selection in their promotion season of 1988-89, when he scored 12 FL goals, his striking ratio was not impressive enough to win over all City fans who were still pining for Paul Stewart (sold to "Spurs" in the summer). After a shaky start in the First Division, manager, Mel Machin, was replaced by Howard Kendall, who quickly traded Morley and Ian Bishop to West Ham United in exchange for Mark Ward, valued at about £1 million. An immediate hit at Upton Park, he scored ten goals in 19 games up to the end 1989-90 and was top scorer with 12 FL (plus five cup) goals in the "Hammers'" promotion season of 1990-91. Sadly, he had a torrid time on his return to the elite, not helped by a domestic incident which put him out of action for two months and without a reliable goalscorer, the "Hammers'" quickly lost their First Division status again. Unavailable for the first three games of **1992-93**, he soon got into the swing of things with 13 goals in his first 17 League matches. And it was that good form that ultimately paved the way for "Hammers" to gain promotion at the first time of asking, when they pipped Portsmouth on goal difference to finish runners-up behind Newcastle United. He ended a highly satisfactory season on both a club and personal level as the side's leading goalscorer with 22. Three times during the season he scored equalising goals, but none were more vital than the one that was chipped over the Swindon Town 'keeper from 18 yards to open "Hammers'" account in the penultimate game, away from home. He can now look forward to playing in the Premier League with some relish.

| | | | APPEARANCES | | | | GOALS | | | |
|---|---|---|---|---|---|---|---|---|---|---|
| Clubs | Signing Date | Transfer Fee | Lge | FL Cup | FA Cup | Others | Lge | FL Cup | FA Cup | Others |
| Northampton Town | 6.85 | £20,000 | 107 | 10 | 6 | 7 | 39 | 4 | 2 | |
| Manchester City | 1.88 | £175,000 | 69+3 | 7 | 1 | 2 | 18 | 3 | | |
| West Ham United* | 12.89 | £500,000 | 110+12 | 7 | 11+3 | 5+1 | 44 | 2 | 7 | 1 |

## **MORROW** Stephen (Steve) Joseph

Born: Bangor, Northern Ireland, 2 July 1970

Height: 6'0"

Weight: 11.3

International Honours: NI Sch, NI Yth, NI "U21"-1, NI-9

**Position/Skill Factor:** A full-back with an educated left foot, he also has a penchant for linking up with the attack.

**Career History:** First spotted by Arsenal as a 14-year-old in Northern Ireland, he signed associated schoolboy forms in May 1985, before coming to Highbury as a trainee on leaving school in July 1987. Although still to play for the "Gunners", his ability was recognised at full international level when he came on as a sub for Northern Ireland against Uruguay in Belfast on 18 May 1990. Has continued to play for Northern Ireland and has also had a spell on loan at Reading where he made his FL debut against Exeter City on 19 January 1991. With his path to the Arsenal first team blocked by Nigel Winterburn, he had three loan periods in 1991-92, with Watford (for two months), Reading (two weeks) and Barnet where he puzzlingly played only one game. Finally called up to the "Gunners'" first team squad in April 1992, he made two appearances as substitute, but found another full-back blocking his way — the Norwegian, Pal Lyderson. Deputised early on in **1992-93** for Winterburn, producing some accomplished solid displays and when the former returned to the side, he moved into midfield, usually with a specific marking job in hand. Rarely has somebody gone from the sublime to the ridiculous quite as quickly as the Ulsterman. Having scored his first goal for the club, the winner in the League Cup Final against Sheffield Wednesday, he accidentally sustained a broken arm in the post-match celebrations and instead of collecting his medal he left the field on a stretcher, requiring an oxygen mask.

| | | | APPEARANCES | | | | GOALS | | | |
|---|---|---|---|---|---|---|---|---|---|---|
| Clubs | Signing Date | Transfer Fee | Lge | FL Cup | FA Cup | Others | Lge | FL Cup | FA Cup | Others |
| Arsenal* | 5.88 | - | 13+5 | 4+1 | 2+2 | | | 1 | | |
| Reading | 1.91 | Loan | 10 | | | | | | | |
| Watford | 8.91 | Loan | 7+1 | | | 1 | | | | |
| Reading | 10.91 | Loan | 3 | | | | | | | |
| Barnet | 3.92 | Loan | 1 | | | | | | | |

## **MURDOCK** Colin James

Born: Ballymena, Northern Ireland, 2 July 1975

Height: 6'1" Weight: 12.0

International Honours: NI Sch, NI Yth

**Position/Skill Factor:** Footballing central-defender who loves to get the ball down in order to pass. A skilful player, not for him the "big boot".

**Career History:** A Manchester United professional signing on his 17th birthday, he had earlier joined the club as a trainee (September 1989), following successes with the Northern Ireland schoolboy and under 16 sides, while on Linfield's books. Yet to make the first team squad, he spent **1992-93** playing for United's "B" team.

| | | | APPEARANCES | | | | GOALS | | | |
|---|---|---|---|---|---|---|---|---|---|---|
| Clubs | Signing Date | Transfer Fee | Lge | FL Cup | FA Cup | Others | Lge | FL Cup | FA Cup | Others |
| Manchester United* | 7.92 | - | | | | | | | | |

## **MURRAY** Edwin John

Born: Ilford, 21 August 1973

Height 5'11" Weight: 12.0

**Position/Skill Factor:** A player who can perform at full-back, or in the centre of the defence where his pace makes him difficult to beat, he is also starting to read the game well.

**Carrer History:** A Londoner by birth, he first came to Swindon Town as an associated schoolboy (May 1988), before progressing through the club's junior ranks as a trainee (July 1989). As a strapping youngster and prior to signing professional forms in the 1991 close season, he was considered promising enough to be given his FL debut, as substitute, at home to Oxford United on 5 March 1991. Made no further FL appearances in **1992-93**, but he came on as substitute in a FA Cup-tie at Queens Park Rangers in January 1993, performing reasonably well and later in the season sat on the bench on two or three occasions without getting the call. Rated a player for the future, he could well get an early opportunity to play in the Premier League.

| | | | APPEARANCES | | | | GOALS | | | |
|---|---|---|---|---|---|---|---|---|---|---|
| Clubs | Signing Date | Transfer Fee | Lge | FL Cup | FA Cup | Others | Lge | FL Cup | FA Cup | Others |
| Swindon Town* | 7.91 | - | 0+1 | | 0+1 | | | | | |

## **MURRAY** Nathan Andrew

Born: South Shields, 10 September 1975

Height: 6'1" Weight: 12.7

International Honours: E Sch, E Yth

**Position/Skill Factor:** Hard working central defender who is strong on the ground and in the air. A tough, tigerish tackler, he can only see the ball.

**Career History:** A recent Newcastle United professional signing, he is highly thought of at St James' Park and although recovering at the present from a broken ankle it didn't stop the club from giving him a three year contract. Captain of England schools, he was already on United's books as an associated schoolboy (November 1989) before becoming a trainee in July 1992. Spent time at the School of Excellence and was named as substitute against

Ascoli and Cesena in the **1992-93** Anglo-Italian Cup, without getting on the pitch. Has a bright future in the game.

| Clubs | Signing Date | Transfer Fee | APPEARANCES Lge | FL Cup | FA Cup | Others | GOALS Lge | FL Cup | FA Cup | Others |
|---|---|---|---|---|---|---|---|---|---|---|
| Newcastle United* | 4.93 | - | | | | | | | | |

## MYERS Andrew (Andy) John

Born: Hounslow, 3 November 1973

Height: 5'9"

Weight: 12.6

International Honours: E Yth

**Position/Skill Factor:** Can play at left-back or along the left side of midfield. A very good competitor, he has great pace and ability.

**Career History:** Only with Chelsea as a trainee since July 1990, he made his FL debut at Stamford Bridge when coming on as a sub for Damian Matthew against Luton Town on 6 April 1991, two months before signing professional forms. The youngest Chelsea debutant since Tommy Langley in 1974, before being superseded by Ian Pearce just over a month later, he was a regular choice for the England Youth team in 1990-91. Made his first full appearance for Chelsea, in place of Dennis Wise, against Liverpool in October 1991 and scored their second goal in a 2-2 draw, before enjoying two short runs at left-back later in the season. Still a good prospect, although appearing only four times for Chelsea in **1992-93**, mainly due to injury problems, he was one of the club's two World Cup representatives who played for the England under 19 side in Australia. Will be looking for a regular place in Glenn Hoddle's new look Chelsea.

| Clubs | Signing Date | Transfer Fee | APPEARANCES Lge | FL Cup | FA Cup | Others | GOALS Lge | FL Cup | FA Cup | Others |
|---|---|---|---|---|---|---|---|---|---|---|
| Chelsea* | 7.91 | - | 12+5 | 1+1 | 2 | 1 | 1 | | | |

## NDLOVU Peter

Born: Bulawayo, Zimbabwe, 25 February 1973

Height: 5'8" Weight: 10.12

International Honours: Zimbabwe Int

**Position/Skill Factor:** A forward with great pace, he shows real skill on the ball and looks to be an exciting player when in full flow.

**Career History:** A Zimbabwe international from the age of 15, he was first noted by Coventry City during their summer tour of that country in 1990. Invited for a trial, he signed a contract the following summer. Soon given a first team opportunity, making his FL debut away to Queens Park Rangers on 24 August 1991, as a substitute. In his fifth game, also as substitute, away to League Champions, Arsenal, he scored a superb breakaway solo goal to clinch the points for Coventry — a remarkable entry to big time football. Scored another spectacular goal — the winner — against Aston Villa a few weeks later. Apart from these highlights he struggled, as did all of Coventry's forwards in 1991-92 and he was rested after December, not returning to first team duty until the closing weeks. Travelled nearly 90,000 air miles in **1992-93** in order to represent Zimbabwe in African Nations Cup matches and to ultimately play 34 (including five substitute) Premier League games for City. The start of the season was disjointed mainly by international calls, but once they were behind him he was at his peak between September and December, scoring more brilliant goals: A glorious header at Sheffield Wednesday, a breathtaking diagonal run, finishing with a super dummy against Norwich City, a thunderbolt at Leeds United and a length of the pitch run at Everton, with a shot over the goalie, being the pick. As in the previous season, the travelling appeared to get him down after Christmas and he had a rather poor spell until the final game against Leeds, when he scored one and made the other. A great new season is expected of him, as he is now tied down to a lengthy contract, with less calls on his services by his country and should be able to concentrate his abilities on the "Sky Blues".

| Clubs | Signing Date | Transfer Fee | APPEARANCES Lge | FL Cup | FA Cup | Others | GOALS Lge | FL Cup | FA Cup | Others |
|---|---|---|---|---|---|---|---|---|---|---|
| Coventry City* | 8.91 | £10,000 | 36+19 | 3 | 1 | 0+1 | 9 | 1 | | |

## NEAL Ashley James

Born: Northampton, 16 December 1974

Height: 5'11" Weight: 13.8

**Position/Skill Factor:** Central defender who is good in the air and one of the best strikers of a "dead" ball at Liverpool. An excellent leader, he marshalls the defence and organises his team-mates well.

**Career History:** The son of Phil, the former Northampton Town, Liverpool, Bolton Wanderers and England full-back, he first came to Anfield as a trainee (July 1991) and signed professional forms for Liverpool at the end of **1992-93**.

| | | | APPEARANCES | | | | GOALS | | | |
|---|---|---|---|---|---|---|---|---|---|---|
| Clubs | Signing Date | Transfer Fee | Lge | FL Cup | FA Cup | Others | Lge | FL Cup | FA Cup | Others |
| Liverpool* | 4.93 | - | | | | | | | | |

## NEILSON Alan Bruce

Born: Wegberg, Germany, 26 September 1972

Height: 5'11" Weight: 12.4

International Honours: W"B", W"U21"-3, W-1

**Position/Skill Factor:** Right-back. A sound passer, who brings confidence to the back third of the field, his main attribute, however, is his ability to get forward.

**Career History:** Born in West Germany to a Welsh soldier based there, he came to Newcastle United as a trainee in August 1989, before graduating to the club's professional ranks early in 1991. A few weeks later he made his FL debut as a substitute in a 2-1 win at Watford on 9 March 1991 and showed enough promise to be selected for the next two League games. Made several appearances in 1991-92, mainly at right-back, as one of Ossie Ardiles' young starlets, but since the arrival of Kevin Keegan as manager and more experienced defenders, such as Barry Venison and John Beresford, he returned to the reserves to await his turn for promotion. Surprisingly, made his full international debut for Wales in February 1992, coming on as a very late substitute in a 1-0 victory over the Republic of Ireland in Dublin, before he had even made his Under 21 debut, which eventually came the following season. Had few opportunities to shine in **1992-93**, a season that ultimately saw Newcastle storm into the Premier League as First Division Champions, having led the way from almost start to finish. Although he played for the first team on six occasions, only two were League appearances, in deputising on both flanks for Barry Venison and John Beresford, but he remained highly rated on Tyneside. It also showed the strength of United's defence when they could afford to leave out an international player of his calibre, but he is still young and will be back.

| | | | APPEARANCES | | | | GOALS | | | |
|---|---|---|---|---|---|---|---|---|---|---|
| Clubs | Signing Date | Transfer Fee | Lge | FL Cup | FA Cup | Others | Lge | FL Cup | FA Cup | Others |
| Newcastle United* | 2.91 | - | 20+2 | 3 | | 4 | 1 | | | |

## NESTOR Terence (Terry)

Born: Warrington, 22 October 1974

Height: 5'8" Weight: 11.3

**Position/Skill Factor:** Tenacious midfielder with plenty of stamina, he can run all day. Aggressive ball winner who can distrubute well, also.

**Career History:** First came to Anfield as a trainee (July 1991) after leaving school and made good enough progress to be asked to sign professional forms for Liverpool at the end of **1992-93**.

| | | | APPEARANCES | | | | GOALS | | | |
|---|---|---|---|---|---|---|---|---|---|---|
| Clubs | Signing Date | Transfer Fee | Lge | FL Cup | FA Cup | Others | Lge | FL Cup | FA Cup | Others |
| Liverpool* | 4.93 | - | | | | | | | | |

## NETHERCOTT Stuart

Born: Ilford, 21 March 1973

Height: 5'9" Weight: 12.4

**Position/Skill Factor:** Extremely competitive central defender who is strong both in the air and on the ground. Specialises in kicking long balls into the areas behind the opposing full-backs.

**Career History:** Joined Tottenham Hotspur as a trainee in July 1989, turning professional two years later. Not expected to make an appearance in "Spurs'" first team for a year or two, he nevertheless had an early baptism in the Football League on loan to Fourth Division Maidstone United, making his FL debut on 7 September 1991 at Scunthorpe United. He remained with the Kent club for three months before returning to White Hart Lane and later had a shorter loan spell with Fourth Division newcomers, Barnet. Finally "blooded" for Tottenham, he made his debut in a **1992-93** Premier League match at Chelsea in March, deputising at centre-back for the indisposed Gary Mabbutt. Then played two matches at right-back at home to Wimbledon and Blackburn Rovers, either side of two substitute PL appearances and gained further experience in a Fiorucci Cup match against Inter Milan in April.

| | | | APPEARANCES | | | | GOALS | | | |
|---|---|---|---|---|---|---|---|---|---|---|
| Clubs | Signing Date | Transfer Fee | Lge | FL Cup | FA Cup | Others | Lge | FL Cup | FA Cup | Others |
| Tottenham Hotspur* | 8.91 | - | 3+2 | | | | | | | |
| Maidstone United | 9.91 | Loan | 13 | | | 1 | 1 | | | |
| Barnet | 2.92 | Loan | 3 | | | | | | | |

# NEVILLE Gary Alexander

Born: Bury,
18 February 1975

Height: 5'10"

Weight: 11.7

International Honours:
E Yth

**Position/Skill Factor:** Central defender who is very committed and leads by example. A natural defender and an excellent tackler, he also has a very long throw-in capability.

**Career History:** Joined Manchester United on associated schoolboy forms in June 1989 and was upgraded to trainee in July 1991 and full professional in January 1993. Captain of United's youth team which won the FA Youth Cup in 1991-92, defeating Crystal Palace 6-3 over two legs. Made his first team debut as a substitute in a **1992-93** UEFA Cup tie against Torpedo Moscow in September 1992, when Alex Ferguson strangely selected three members of the youth team (in preference to reserves) as substitutes to comply with the UEFA ruling on "foreigners" in European competition.

| | | | APPEARANCES | | | | GOALS | | | |
|---|---|---|---|---|---|---|---|---|---|---|
| Clubs | Signing Date | Transfer Fee | Lge | FL Cup | FA Cup | Others | Lge | FL Cup | FA Cup | Others |
| Manchester United* | 1.93 | - | | | | 0+1 | | | | |

# NEWELL Michael (Mike) Colin

Born: Liverpool, 27 January 1965

Height: 6'0" Weight: 11.0

International Honours: E "U21"-4, E"B"

**Position/Skill Factor:** Strong running striker. Good in the air, he competes well on the ground and holds the ball up until others are at hand.

**Career History:** Formerly a Liverpool junior, he was not offered terms at Anfield and made his FL debut, whilst on trial with Crewe Alexandra, at home to Swindon Town on 8 October 1983. Surprisingly, in view of his subsequent progress, he did not impress the "Alex" manager, Dario Gradi, who has probably developed more young talent than any manager in the game today and he moved on for another trial with Wigan Athletic. Did enough to earn a contract, but despite winning a regular place in 1984-85, was not a consistent scorer until 1985-86 when he netted 16 FL goals in 24 games — form which persuaded Luton Town to sign him in mid-season. Took the leap from Third to First Division football in his stride and in 1986-87 he was ever present to joint top score with 12 FL goals. Soon after, he was signed by David Pleat for Second Division Leicester City and scarcely missed a match in his two seasons at Filbert Street, top scoring with 13 FL goals

in 1988-89. By this time he was being talked of as a future England player, although his modest scoring ratio belied his reputation. Returned to the First Division and his native city, in the summer of 1989, when he joined Everton for a massive fee. Although he went straight into the "Toffees'" team at the expense of Tony Cottee, lack of goals resulted in him losing his place to the latter later in the season. 1990-91 also proved to be another "in and out" season for him as manager Howard Kendall alternated between Cottee and Newell, without getting the best from either of them. Returned to the team in September 1991, but without showing any improvement in his scoring form and Everton decided to recoup their investment when Kenny Dalglish made an offer to take him to Blackburn Rovers for the same valuation as when Everton first signed him. Scored on his debut for Rovers and was showing some useful form when injured in February, prompting Dalglish to sign two more strikers, Roy Wegerle and Duncan Shearer. Returned to first team duty in April to assist Rovers through the critical end of season games and the Play-Offs. Scored a vital goal to level the scores in the first-leg match against Derby (which Rovers eventually won 4-2) and in the Play-Off Final against Leicester, he struck the only goal from the penalty spot, to bring top level football back to Ewood Park for the first time since 1966. One of the finest team players ever seen at Ewood Park, with an astounding work rate, his unselfish play contributed greatly to Alan Shearer's astonishing start to **1992-93**. While his scoring record paled by comparison, he still bagged five pairs in his 22 strikes and was even more vital to the team than Colin Hendry, if that was possible. He was prepared to chase back and tackle and was never afraid to go in where it hurt and scored winning goals on no less than six occasions, throughout the term.

| | | | APPEARANCES | | | | GOALS | | | |
|---|---|---|---|---|---|---|---|---|---|---|
| Clubs | Signing Date | Transfer Fee | Lge | FL Cup | FA Cup | Others | Lge | FL Cup | FA Cup | Others |
| Crewe Alexandra | 9.83 | - | 3 | | | | | | | |
| Wigan Athletic | 10.83 | - | 64+8 | 6 | 8 | 5+1 | 25 | 1 | 6 | 3 |
| Luton Town | 1.86 | £100,000 | 62+1 | | 5 | | 18 | | 1 | |
| Leicester City | 9.87 | £350,000 | 81 | 9 | 2 | 4 | 21 | 5 | | |
| Everton | 7.89 | £1,100,000 | 48+20 | 7+3 | 6+4 | 6 | 15 | 4 | | 2 |
| Blackburn Rovers* | 11.91 | £1,100,000 | 58+2 | 6+1 | 7 | 3 | 20 | 5 | 6 | 2 |

## NEWHOUSE Aiden Robert

Born: Wallasey, 23 May 1972

Height: 6'0" Weight: 12.0

International Honours: E Yth

**Position/Skill Factor:** Striker with two useful feet and good ability on the ball. Brings his team-mates into the game with astute passes. Is at his best when he can get into wide positions.

**Career History:** Joined Chester City on associated schoolboy forms in October 1986 and became the club's youngest ever player when he made his FL debut at Bury on 7 May 1988, two months before signing as a trainee on leaving school in July 1988. Something of a sensation in 1988-89, he was a regular member of Chester's first team squad at the age of 16. Turned professional after his 17th birthday and was an automatic selection in the first two months of 1989-90, until rested as his team struggled at the foot of the table. Ironically, he was not in the first team when First Division Wimbledon signed him, although his potential was obvious. Made his debut for the "Dons" at Charlton Athletic as a substitute in April 1990, before coming off the bench once more that season and in 1990-91 he only played one full game in nine first team appearances. Continued to be used sparingly in 1991-92, but no goals was scant return for 14 (including seven substitute) matches played and he spent most of his time in the reserve side. **1992-93** was no different as he struggled to win a place in the Premier League side. Although he came off the bench for the injured John Fashanu in a 3-2 defeat at Aston Villa and then deputised for him in a 1-0 League Cup defeat at home to Bolton Wanderers, despite playing quite well, he was substituted and spent the rest of the season out of contention.

| | | | APPEARANCES | | | | GOALS | | | |
|---|---|---|---|---|---|---|---|---|---|---|
| Clubs | Signing Date | Transfer Fee | Lge | FL Cup | FA Cup | Others | Lge | FL Cup | FA Cup | Others |
| Chester City | 7.89 | - | 29+15 | 5+1 | 0+2 | 2+3 | 6 | | | 1 |
| Wimbledon* | 2.90 | £100,000 | 7+16 | 1+1 | 2 | 0+1 | 2 | | | |

## NEWMAN Robert (Rob) Nigel

Born: Bradford-on-Avon, 13 December 1963

Height: 6'2" Weight: 12.0

**Position/Skill Factor:** Utility player who can play in midfield, centre-back or at full-back. Good in the air and is always dangerous at set plays. Also, a direct free-kick specialist.

**Career History:** Came up through the ranks at Bristol City, first as an associated schoolboy (October 1979) and then as an apprentice (June 1980), before becoming a professional. Made his FL debut at Ashton Gate against Fulham on 6 February 1982, following the departure of eight experienced players whose long term contracts on First Division salaries were threatening the very existence of a club about to drop into the Fourth Division. He immediately settled down as a regular and proved his versatility, playing in five different positions during 1983-84, as the club gained promotion to the Third Division in fourth place. An ever present in 1988-89 and again the following season as the "Robins" moved into the Second Division as runners-up, he increased his reputation for scoring vital goals. At the end of 1990-91, a season that consolidated City's Second Division status, he had played 147 consecutive League games and was by far and away the club's longest serving player. Signed for First Division Norwich City, in the summer of 1991 and although it was a disappointing one for the "Canaries", he enjoyed an excellent first season personally, playing in all but one of his club's 54 match programme and scoring several vital goals from midfield. Had a mixed season in **1992-93**, missing several early games when not completely match fit and then, just two days after playing his 450th League game against Tottenham Hotspur on Boxing Day, he had the great misfortune to fracture an ankle at Leeds United. And with Norwich heading the League table and the Championship race most definitely on, the "Canaries" had to resign themselves to losing him for a fair while. Earlier, he had scored the only goal of the game at home to Sheffield Wednesday, plus a consolation effort in a 7-1 hiding at Blackburn Rovers. With a reputation as a free-kick specialist to maintain, one of his shots had been timed at 85 mph. Back for the last two games of the season, he would like to lose his utility tag and carve out a permanent position for himself, either up front, or in the centre of the defence.

| | | | APPEARANCES | | | | GOALS | | | |
|---|---|---|---|---|---|---|---|---|---|---|
| Clubs | Signing Date | Transfer Fee | Lge | FL Cup | FA Cup | Others | Lge | FL Cup | FA Cup | Others |
| Bristol City | 10.81 | - | 382+12 | 29+1 | 27 | 33 | 52 | 2 | 2 | 5 |
| Norwich City* | 7.91 | £600,000 | 57+2 | 8 | 6 | 1 | 9 | 1 | 1 | |

# NEWSOME Jonathan (Jon)

Born: Sheffield,
6 September 1970

Height: 6'2"

Weight: 13.11

**Position/Skill Factor:** A good all-round full-back. Although capable of using the ball well and supporting the attack, as a defender he is not easy to pass, having a quick recovery rate and being an excellent and decisive tackler.

**Career History:** Home grown talent, he started at Sheffield Wednesday as an associated schoolboy in June 1985 and on leaving school in July 1987, he joined the staff as a trainee, before turning professional. made his FL debut at Arsenal on 9 September 1989, when he was introduced as a sub during a 5-0 drubbing and then had a short run in the number two shirt before the club signed Roland Nilsson. With John Harkes, Viv Anderson and Nilsson all vying for the right-back slot, he made only one League appearance in 1990-91. Surprisingly allowed to leave Hillsborough in the summer of 1991, along with another talented "Owls'" youngster, David Wetherall; they signed for former Wednesday manager Howard Wilkinson at Leeds United as investments for the future. He played little part in United's Championship challenge until March, when he deputised for the injured Mel Sterland. With brilliant last-ditch and scrupulous tackling, he saved his team on several occasions and his headed goal from a free-kick in the vital penultimate fixture away to Sheffield United were a major factor in Leeds' unlikely Championship triumph. His ten FL appearances in 1991-92 were one short of qualification for a Championship medal, but Wilkinson appealed to the Football League and, happily, they agreed that he had richly earned one. Began **1992-93** where he left off in the Championship season, as the right-back replacement for the injured Mel Sterland. Inconsistency led him to being rested from this position, but he was never out of the squad and often used as a substitute. Now that David Kerslake has joined the club from Swindon Town, he should be free to concentrate on a central defender's job, where he showed his real ability during the replay victory over VFB Stuttgart in Barcelona.

| | | | APPEARANCES | | | | GOALS | | | |
|---|---|---|---|---|---|---|---|---|---|---|
| Clubs | Signing Date | Transfer Fee | Lge | FL Cup | FA Cup | Others | Lge | FL Cup | FA Cup | Others |
| Sheffield Wednesday | 7.89 | - | 6+1 | 3 | | | | | | |
| Leeds United* | 6.91 | £150,000 | 37+10 | 2 | 0+1 | 5 | 2 | | | |

# NEWTON Edward (Eddie) John Ikem

Born: Hammersmith,
13 December 1971

Height: 5'11"

Weight: 11.2

International Honours:
E "U21"-1

**Position/Skill Factor:** A midfielder who has already played in a number of different positions, he can use both feet and passes well.

**Career History:** Joined Chelsea as a trainee in August 1988, having been an associated schoolboy since November 1986 and turned professional two years later. Played in a variety of positions in the "Blues'" youth and reserve teams, including central defence, midfield and up front. Loaned out to Fourth Division Cardiff City in January 1992, he made his FL debut at home to Chesterfield on 25 January 1992 and played a major role in launching the "Bluebirds'" challenge for promotion with his dynamic midfield performances, plus four crucial goals. Sadly, it was not quite enough, as the Welsh club finished three points short of a Play-Off place. At the end of his three month loan period he returned to Stamford Bridge and was rewarded with his first call up to the Chelsea team in the last game of the season away to Everton. Coming on as a second-half substitute, he beat Neville Southall with a stunning 35 yard cross shot to reduce the deficit to 2-1. After coming on as a substitute for the first two games of **1992-93**, he went on to make 38 consecutive first team appearances, until being injured in the home League match against Middlesbrough on 3 April 1993. A potential international, at times he was quite brilliant, but often found it difficult to motivate himself over the full 90 minutes and needs to work on that side of his game. He should be one of Chelsea's star players in 1993-94, especially if the new manager, Glenn Hoddle, elects to play.

| | | | APPEARANCES | | | | GOALS | | | |
|---|---|---|---|---|---|---|---|---|---|---|
| Clubs | Signing Date | Transfer Fee | Lge | FL Cup | FA Cup | Others | Lge | FL Cup | FA Cup | Others |
| Chelsea* | 5.90 | - | 32+3 | 6 | 1 | | 6 | 1 | | |
| Cardiff City | 1.92 | Loan | 18 | | | | 4 | | | |

# NICHOLLS Ryan Rhys

Born: Cardiff, 10 May 1973

Height: 5'10" Weight: 11.0

International Honours: W Sch

**Position/Skill Factor:** Midfielder with good ability. A lovely passer of the ball, he can beat defenders to set up goal scoring chances for others.

**Career History:** Former Welsh schoolboy international who first joined Leeds United on associated forms in January 1989, before signing on as a trainee in September 1990. After turning professional during the 1991 close season, he was out injured for most of 1991-92 and spent **1992-93** in the reserve side, trying to get back to match fitness. Unfortunate to suffer further injury problems towards the end of the campaign, he must hope to be ready in time for 1993-94.

| | | | APPEARANCES | | | | GOALS | | | |
|---|---|---|---|---|---|---|---|---|---|---|
| Clubs | Signing Date | Transfer Fee | Lge | FL Cup | FA Cup | Others | Lge | FL Cup | FA Cup | Others |
| Leeds United* | 7.91 | - | | | | | | | | |

## NICOL Stephen (Steve)

Born: Irvine, 11 December 1961

Height: 5'10" Weight: 12.0

International Honours: S "U21"-14, S-27

**Position/Skill Factor:** A versatile player who never lets the side down, whether at full-back, centre-back or in midfield. Very competitive, he is a good passer, both short and long and also likes to get up in support of the attack.

**Career History:** A stalwart of the Liverpool team since 1984, although his career has been punctuated by injuries, particularly in 1986-87 and 1989-90, he has played a full part in the "Reds'" almost unbroken run of success over the last ten years, winning four League Championship medals in 1983-84, 1985-86, 1987-88 and 1989-90, and three FA Cup winners medals in 1986, 1989 and 1992, plus a losers medal in 1988. Before coming south to join Liverpool early in 1981-82, he spent just over two seasons with Ayr United, having impressed at full-back after signing from a local boy's club. Had to wait nearly 12 months for his FL debut at Birmingham City on 31 August 1982 and made only three more appearances, two of them as a substitute, until earning a more permanent place in midfield the following year. Came into the side in 1983-84 when Craig Johnston was injured and ended the season with League Championship and European Cup winners medals. Fortunately for him, his miss in the penalty "shoot out" against Roma did not prove disastrous, as Liverpool won 4-2 to bring the trophy back to England. Played on the right side of midfield until taking over the right-back position from Phil Neal in October 1985, but following the signing of Barry Venison, he alternated between full-back and midfield and scored his first and only senior "hat-trick" away to Newcastle United in September 1987. In 1988-89, he was switched to central defence, following injuries to Gary Gillespie and Alan Hansen and performed so well in this emergency role that he was voted the Football Writers' Association Footballer of the Year in 1989. Made his international debut for Scotland on 12 September 1984 against Yugoslavia at Hampden Park (a remarkable 6-1 victory for the Scots) and has been a fairly regular selection since playing in the 1986 World Cup Finals in Mexico. One of the few senior players at Anfield to escape long-term injury in 1991-92, he appeared in a variety of positions. Starting out at right-back, he switched to midfield after the emergence of Rob Jones and then to central defence to cover the absence of Nicky Tanner, but had reverted to full-back when winning another FA Cup winners medal at the end of the season. An innocent victim of a constant "club versus country" tug of war between Liverpool and Scotland, he made what was probably his last Scottish appearance against Switzerland in September 1991. Troubled by groin and thigh injuries in the early stages of **1992-93**, even Liverpool's most consistent and dependable player was afflicted by the defensive jitters which plagued the "Reds" all season, most notably, when his miscued clearance set up Eric Young's winner for an understrength Crystal Palace and a humiliating League Cup defeat. That and a farcical own goal for Middlesbrough in March which, fortunately for him, did not prove too costly as the "Reds" finally prevailed, were his lowpoints. Apart from these uncharacteristic lapses, however, he was a tower of strength in the heart of the club's beleaguered defence and one of the few Liverpool players who could look back on the season with some pride. Took over the captaincy from Mark Wright between October and the New Year, before relinquishing the responsibility to John Barnes.

| | | | APPEARANCES | | | | GOALS | | | |
|---|---|---|---|---|---|---|---|---|---|---|
| Clubs | Signing Date | Transfer Fee | Lge | FL Cup | FA Cup | Others | Lge | FL Cup | FA Cup | Others |
| Ayr United | .79 | - | 68+2 | 16 | 3 | | 7 | 1 | | |
| Liverpool* | 10.81 | £300,000 | 297+11 | 39 | 48 | 32+2 | 35 | 4 | 3 | 3 |

## NIJHOLT Luc

Born: Zaandam, Holland, 29 July 1961

Height: 5'10" Weight: 12.4

International Honours: Dutch "U21" Int

**Position/Skill Factor:** As a defender, who can play anywhere in the back four, he is extremely comfortable on the ball and is always looking to get a pass on. Reads the game well and with two good feet is a hard, but scrupulously fair tackler.

**Career History:** Following "hot on the heels" of Colin Calderwood's transfer to Tottenham Hotspur and Glenn Hoddle's departure to Chelsea, new Swindon Town manager, John Gorman, moved swiftly to sign Motherwell's stylish "flying Dutchman", Luc Nijholt, presumably in a bid to plug the gaps. On the face of it the "Well's" "Player of the Year" last season, having played 39 League games during **1992-93**, appears an admirable choice in terms of experience. He started his career in Holland with Harlem (1981-1988), making 207 appearances, before moving on in quick succession to AZ67 Alkmaar (1988), Utrecht (1988-1989) and OB Basle (1989-1990). A true utility performer in the Dutch football sense, he joined Motherwell at the start of 1990-91 and soon became a big favourite with the fans, enthralled by his cultured play. In his first season at Fir Park, he was at right-back in the side that won the Scottish Cup, when beating Dundee United 4-3 in the Final and the following campaign, he played in both legs of the European Cup Winners Cup, as Motherwell went out to Katowice, of Poland, in the First Round. May take a while to get adjusted to the speed of the English game, but once he does, expect him to effectively fill the "sweeper" role in Town's defence.

| | | | APPEARANCES | | | | GOALS | | | |
|---|---|---|---|---|---|---|---|---|---|---|
| Clubs | Signing Date | Transfer Fee | Lge | FL Cup | FA Cup | Others | Lge | FL Cup | FA Cup | Others |
| Motherwell | 8.90 | £95,000 | 91+5 | 5 | 9 | 2 | 5 | | 1 | |
| Swindon Town* | 7.93 | £175,000 | | | | | | | | |

## **NILSSON** Nils Lennart **Roland**

Born: Helsingborg, Sweden, 27 November 1963

Height: 6'0" Weight: 11.6

International Honours: Swedish Int

**Position/Skill Factor:** Right-back. Typical continental defender who passes forward and is confident enough to join up with the attack, whether in-field or wide. Great passer of the ball.

**Career History:** Swedish international full-back who was signed by Sheffield Wednesday from IFK Gothenburg to fill the right-back position that had remained unfilled since Mel Sterland joined Glasgow Rangers in February 1989. Made his FL debut at Hillsborough against Luton Town on 9 December 1989 and apart from missing just one match, held his place for the remainder of the season. However, his presence was not enough to save the club from being relegated to the Second Division, following a run of five defeats in the last six games. With the club unbeaten for the first 14 games of 1990-91, he was injured during the next game at Millwall when the "Owls" were leading 2-0. Wednesday were unable to reorganise defensively after his departure and lost 4-2 and the injury was serious enough to keep him out of the team until the following April. Played in ten of the last 11 matches as Wednesday made sure of promotion back to the First Division at the first time of asking and as an added bonus, won a League Cup winners medal, when starring in the "Owls'" 1-0 victory over Manchester United at Wembley. Played in all but five of Wednesday's excellent 1991-92 campaign when they finished in third place and qualified for the UEFA Cup. Starred for Sweden in the European Championship Finals in 1992, appearing in all four matches, as the host nation went out in the Semi-Finals to Germany after earlier beating England. Consolidated his position in the side and with "Owls'" supporters in **1992-93**, as his classy displays, arguably, saw him emerge as the best right-back in the Premier League. Unfortunately picked up a thigh injury early in September, which ruled him out for ten or 11 games, but once he had overcome that there was no stopping him. After collecting a losers medal, following the 2-1 defeat by Arsenal in the League Cup Final and the 1-1 draw in the FA Cup Final against the same team, he was faced by a major club versus country problem. With the replay booked for the night after he'd captained Sweden to a 1-0 victory over Austria in a World Cup qualifier, he flew directly from Stockholm to London and played supremely well, before coming off the field suffering from exhaustion with just four minutes remaining of extra-time and the score standing at 1-1. But with a penalty shoot-out looming and one minute of the game left, Andy Linighan headed the winner for the "Gunners" and it was all he could do to collect his second losers medal in a month.

| | | | APPEARANCES | | | | GOALS | | | |
|---|---|---|---|---|---|---|---|---|---|---|
| Clubs | Signing Date | Transfer Fee | Lge | FL Cup | FA Cup | Others | Lge | FL Cup | FA Cup | Others |
| Sheffield Wednesday* | 12.89 | £375,000 | 113 | 10 | 12 | 3+1 | 2 | 1 | | |

## **NORMAN Craig** Terence

Born: Perivale, 21 March 1975

Height: 5'7" Weight: 10.5

**Position/Skill Factor:** Left-back who can play in midfield and loves to get forward to hit the forwards with quality crosses. With a superb left foot, he is also capable of turning defence into attack in one swift movement.

**Career History:** Signed professional forms for Chelsea during the 1993 close season, having first come to Stamford Bridge as an associated schoolboy in July 1989, before turning to the trainee (August 1991) ranks on leaving school. His excellent form with the youth team in **1992-93** ensured that he would continue to step up the ladder at a club with a history of nurturing talented young players.

| Clubs | Signing Date | Transfer Fee | APPEARANCES Lge | FL Cup | FA Cup | Others | GOALS Lge | FL Cup | FA Cup | Others |
|---|---|---|---|---|---|---|---|---|---|---|
| Chelsea* | 5.93 | - | | | | | | | | |

## **OAKES Michael** Christian

Born: Northwich, 30 October 1973

Height: 6'1" Weight: 12.7

**Position/Skill Factor:** Goalkeeper with lots of potential. He is brave, comes out well for crosses and is a good shot stopper. Also a great kicker.

**Career History:** Son of Alan, the former Manchester City wing-half and record appearance holder, he joined Aston Villa as an associated schoolboy in February 1991, before signing as a professional early in 1992. Started as an outfield player until being converted to goalkeeper. A member of the England under 21 squad, he has yet to make a first team appearance for Villa, but at least was called up four times to sit on the bench in **1992-93**, without having played a single reserve game. Later, was loaned out to Gloucester City and Bromsgrove Rovers to gain more experience of competitive football, prior to being called back to make his debut for the reserve side.

| Clubs | Signing Date | Transfer Fee | APPEARANCES Lge | FL Cup | FA Cup | Others | GOALS Lge | FL Cup | FA Cup | Others |
|---|---|---|---|---|---|---|---|---|---|---|
| Aston Villa* | 2.92 | - | | | | | | | | |

## **O'BRIEN Roy** Joseph

Born: Cork, 27 November 1974

Height: 5'11¾" Weight: 11.5

**Position/Skill Factor:** Quick and determined right-back, or central defender, who is excellent in the air.

**Career History:** Another of the Arsenal Irish youth connection, he first came to Highbury as a trainee (July 1991), before progressing through the ranks to turn professional last summer. A regular in the youth side in **1992-93**, he was also given a taste of reserve team football, making several appearances.

| Clubs | Signing Date | Transfer Fee | APPEARANCES Lge | FL Cup | FA Cup | Others | GOALS Lge | FL Cup | FA Cup | Others |
|---|---|---|---|---|---|---|---|---|---|---|
| Arsenal* | 7.93 | - | | | | | | | | |

## **O'BRIEN William (Liam)** Francis

Born: Dublin, 5 September 1964

Height: 6'1" Weight: 11.10

International Honours: IR Yth, LoI Rep, IR-10

**Position/Skill Factor:** Midfielder who plays in front of the back four to intercept and pick up the pieces. A good striker of the ball, he is dangerous at set plays and can spray 40 yard passes around the park.

**Career History:** Already a star with Shamrock Rovers and the holder of a Republic of Ireland cap, having played against Uruguay in a 1-1 draw on 23 April 1986, he signed for Manchester United the following season and two months later made his FL debut at Old Trafford in a 2-0 win over Leicester City on 20 December 1986. Never seemed likely to be more than a useful squad member in United's star studded line up and after only two years at Old Trafford he moved on to Newcastle United, at a considerable profit to the "Reds". His first season at St James' Park was traumatic, as the "Magpies" slid out of the First Division and so, ultimately, was his second. Although out of favour for much of the campaign, he returned as a substitute for the end of the season and Play-Off games, when Newcastle lost their deserved promotion to deadly rivals, Sunderland. Not until 1991-92 did he re-established a regular place in the "Magpies'" line-up and was unfortunate to be involved in a desperate struggle for the team to hold on to its Second Division status. Although his season was cut short in mid-March of **1992-93**, due to a shin injury, his part in the ultimately successful promotion campaign must not be overlooked. Played in 33 League games and scored six goals, most of them spectacular efforts from outside of the box, with three of them proving to be either match winners or savers and he made five more for his team-mates. In the local derby game at Roker Park, he bent a superb free-kick around the Sunderland wall to send United's fans home ecstatic, following a 2-1 win and scored another glorious goal in the League Cup victory over their other north-east rivals, Middlesbrough. As always, he played with total commitment, but a downside to his game were the five bookings he collected. However, on reflection, a further Republic international cap in the game against Wales and a First Division Championship medal, made for an excellent season.

| | | | APPEARANCES | | | | GOALS | | | |
|---|---|---|---|---|---|---|---|---|---|---|
| Clubs | Signing Date | Transfer Fee | Lge | FL Cup | FA Cup | Others | Lge | FL Cup | FA Cup | Others |
| Manchester United | 10.86 | £60,000 | 16+15 | 1+2 | 0+2 | | 2 | | | |
| Newcastle United* | 11.88 | £250,000 | 127+18 | 9 | 12+2 | 9+2 | 19 | 1 | 1 | 1 |

## O'DONNELL Paul Gerrard

Born: Limerick, Ireland, 6 October 1975

Height: 5'11" Weight: 11.3

International Honours: IR Yth

**Position/Skill Factor:** Right-winger who is good on the ball and an old fashioned dribbler. Likes to run at defenders.

**Career History:** Signed professional on his 17th birthday, one year after joining Liverpool as a trainee (October 1991) and made excellent progress in **1992-93**. An Irish youth international, he promises to be a very good player, indeed.

| | | | APPEARANCES | | | | GOALS | | | |
|---|---|---|---|---|---|---|---|---|---|---|
| Clubs | Signing Date | Transfer Fee | Lge | FL Cup | FA Cup | Others | Lge | FL Cup | FA Cup | Others |
| Liverpool* | 10.92 | - | | | | | | | | |

## OGRIZOVIC Steven (Steve)

Born: Mansfield, 12 September 1957

Height: 6'3"

Weight: 14.7

International Honours: FL Rep

**Position/Skill Factor:** Commanding goalkeeper with good positional sense, who seems to fill the goal. Big and brave, with safe hands, he is not afraid to come for crosses. Can volley-kick the ball into the opponents' box.

**Career History:** The son of an immigrant Yugoslav miner, he was a police cadet playing in a local Mansfield league, before signing professional forms with Chesterfield in the 1977 close season. Made his FL debut in 3-1 win at Port Vale on 20 August 1977 and appeared in the opening 16 matches that season, keeping six clean sheets. His potential was such that he was quickly snapped up by Liverpool to understudy Ray Clemence, but unfortunately, his first game for the club resulted in a 4-2 defeat at Derby County. After only four games in five years at Anfield, he was involved in a straight swap for Bob Wardle, the Shrewsbury Town goalkeeper. Spent two seasons between the posts at Gay Meadow as an ever present and impressed enough for Coventry City to pay a relatively modest sum for his services during the summer of 1984. He made the news on 25 October 1986, as the first City goalkeeper to score a League goal, when his long punt upfield cleared Martin Hodge in the Sheffield Wednesday goal. And it was his grand display in the "Sky Blues'" goal, especially in the first-half, that helped Coventry win the FA Cup for the first time in their history when they beat Tottenham Hotspur 3-2 in 1987. Recognised for his consistency over the years, it was only an injury suffered at Millwall in October 1989 that brought to an end a run of 320 consecutive matches and at the end of 1991-92 he had only been absent on six occasions since joining "Sky Blues". By his own high standards, he had an up-and-down season in **1992-93**. There were the high spots, such as the home match against Arsenal in March when he finally overhauled Bill Glazier's record of 346 goalkeeping appearances and establishing himself as number three in the all-time lists behind George Curtis and Mick Coop. But on the other side of the coin, although still cutting a commanding figure, he suffered a bit behind a back four that regularly changed its composition and found the new back pass rule difficult to "handle". And, for the first time in ten years, he had real competition from Jon Gould. However, the general feeling at Highfield Road is that he will be back in pole position for 1993-94 as he attempts to reach 500 appearances for the club.

| | | | APPEARANCES | | | | GOALS | | | |
|---|---|---|---|---|---|---|---|---|---|---|
| Clubs | Signing Date | Transfer Fee | Lge | FL Cup | FA Cup | Others | Lge | FL Cup | FA Cup | Others |
| Chesterfield | 7.77 | - | 16 | 2 | | | | | | |
| Liverpool | 11.77 | £70,000 | 4 | | | 1 | | | | |
| Shrewsbury Town | 8.82 | £70,000 | 84 | 7 | 5 | | | | | |
| Coventry City* | 6.84 | £72,000 | 349 | 34 | 20 | 11 | 1 | | | |

## O'KANE John Andrew

Born: Nottingham, 15 November 1974

Height: 5'10" Weight: 11.5

**Position/Skill Factor:** Right-back who is a natural athlete. Very good on the ball, he likes to get forward to join in the attack.

**Career History:** Son of Liam, former Nottingham Forest and Northern Ireland defender and currently a coach at the same club. He first signed for Manchester United as an associated schoolboy in June 1989 and was upgraded to trainee in July 1991 and to full professional status in January 1993. He starred in United's youth team which won the FA Youth Cup in 1991- 92 and were runners up a year later, in **1992-93**, also playing for the "A" team and reserves last season.

| | | | APPEARANCES | | | | GOALS | | | |
|---|---|---|---|---|---|---|---|---|---|---|
| Clubs | Signing Date | Transfer Fee | Lge | FL Cup | FA Cup | Others | Lge | FL Cup | FA Cup | Others |
| Manchester United* | 1.93 | - | | | | | | | | |

## **O'LEARY David** Anthony

Born: Stoke Newington, 2 May 1958

Height: 6'1"

Weight: 13.2

International Honours: IR-67

**Position/Skill Factor:** Cool, reliable central defender who makes few mistakes. Very consistent, he takes up good positions when defending, does well in the air and rarely gives the ball away.

**Career History:** First came to Highbury as an apprentice in May 1973 and within a month of turning professional had made his FL debut for Arsenal at Burnley on 16 August 1975. His talents were soon rewarded with the first of more than 50 international caps for Eire, coming against England on 8 September 1976 at Wembley. In 1979, he won his first club honour as a member of the "Gunners'" side that won the FA Cup when beating Manchester United, 3-2, a result that made up for the 1-0 defeat at the hands of Ipswich Town in the Final, the previous year. 1979-80 was less successful as far as trophies were concerned, as Arsenal's European Cup Winners Cup Final team were beaten on penalties by Spain's Valencia only four days after losing 1-0 to West Ham United in the FA Cup Final. But on a personal front, he had played in three successive FA Cup Finals at Wembley. Lost his place in the Irish team for reasons unknown, for two seasons (1986-88) after Jack Charlton's appointment, but was restored to favour in 1988-89. Surprisingly, he had to wait a further eight years for his next club honour as Arsenal almost swept all before them. A 2-1 victory over Liverpool brought him a League Cup winners medal in 1987 and the following season, although missing a large chunk of it due to injury, he won a League Championship medal, after one of the closest finishes for many a day. Although he made only one substitute appearance less than the 11 full games he played in during 1990-91, at the end of the season he won another League Championship medal when Arsenal regained the title that they had lost to Liverpool in 1989-90. Also in 1991-92, he passed another milestone, that of George Armstrong's record of 500 League appearances for Arsenal. In **1992-93**, his last season at Highbury, the final curtain on a great career as a "Gunner" could not have come down in more dramatic circumstances. To tumultuous applause, he came on at Wembley as a substitute in the FA Cup Final replay victory over Sheffield Wednesday, only three days after his farewell testimonial match. Earlier, he had already added to his Arsenal League appearance record and by the end of the season he had also become the club's record holder for FA Cup appearances. Given a free transfer after 20 years of wonderful service, he decided to continue playing for the time being, when he turned down an approach by Chelsea in order to join an ailing Leeds United.

| | | | APPEARANCES | | | | GOALS | | | |
|---|---|---|---|---|---|---|---|---|---|---|
| Clubs | Signing Date | Transfer Fee | Lge | FL Cup | FA Cup | Others | Lge | FL Cup | FA Cup | Others |
| Arsenal | 7.75 | - | 523+35 | 68+2 | 66+4 | 26 | 11 | 2 | 3 | |
| Leeds United* | 6.93 | - | | | | | | | | |

## **OLNEY Ian** Douglas

Born: Luton, 17 December 1969

Height: 6'1"

Weight: 11.3

International Honours: E "U21"-10

**Position/Skill Factor:** Striker. Good in the air, he pulls away to the far post when team-mates are in crossing positions. Always looking to bring the midfield players into the game.

**Career History:** First joined Aston Villa as an associated schoolboy in March 1985 and eventually became a trainee on leaving school in July 1986. Made his FL debut at Charlton Athletic on 15 October 1988, three months after signing professional forms and didn't get a proper run in the side until the end of that season. Won a regular place in the side in 1989-90 and finished second in the Villa scoring lists with nine League goals, as the club achieved a magnificent second place in the First Division. However, with keen competition for places in the Villa forward line under Jozef Venglos, he found it difficult to hold down a regular slot in 1990-91. Made only 14 full appearances under the new manager, Ron Atkinson in 1991-92 and was transferred to Oldham Athletic during the summer when he became Joe Royle's record signing. Got off to a slow start with his new club in **1992-93** and struggled to find the form that had won him ten England under 21 caps at Villa. But as the season progressed, his confidence began to return and following the injury to Graeme Sharp, he took over the leadership of the "Latics'" attack. Teamed up well with Neil Adams in the club's return from "the dead", with three vital goals in the last three games and finished the season as leading scorer with 13 in all competitions. Earlier, he had to overcome the worse bout of flu seen at the club and also missed several games due to a bad knock on the ankle, but he promises that the best is still to come.

| | | | APPEARANCES | | | | GOALS | | | |
|---|---|---|---|---|---|---|---|---|---|---|
| Clubs | Signing Date | Transfer Fee | Lge | FL Cup | FA Cup | Others | Lge | FL Cup | FA Cup | Others |
| Aston Villa | 7.88 | - | 62+26 | 8+2 | 5+1 | 8+2 | 16 | 1 | 2 | 2 |
| Oldham Athletic* | 5.92 | £700,000 | 32+2 | 3 | 2 | | 12 | | 1 | |

## **O'SULLIVAN Wayne** St John

Born: Cyprus, 25 February 1974

Height 5'11" Weight: 11.2

**Position/Skill Factor:** Attacking full-back with good skills, who favours his right foot and will often check back when on the left flank to cross dangerous inswingers.

**Career History:** A local youngster from Pewsey, he started at Swindon Town as an associated schoolboy in March 1988, before becoming a trainee (July 1990) and and eventually progressing to the professional ranks in the 1992 close season. Yet to play in Town's League side, he made just one first team appearance in **1992-93** in the Anglo-Italian Cup at Oxford United on 1 September 1992. Freed towards the end of the season, he was re-instated, following several good performances in the reserve side and was retained for 1993- 94.

| | | | APPEARANCES | | | | GOALS | | | |
|---|---|---|---|---|---|---|---|---|---|---|
| Clubs | Signing Date | Transfer Fee | Lge | FL Cup | FA Cup | Others | Lge | FL Cup | FA Cup | Others |
| Swindon Town* | 7.92 | – | | | | 1 | | | | |

## **O'TOOLE Gavin** Francis

Born: Dublin, 19 September 1975

Height: 5'9" Weight: 10.7

International Honours: IR Yth

**Position/Skill Factor:** Midfielder who is an excellent passer of the ball and has great vision for one so young.

**Career History:** Came across the Irish Sea to sign on as a trainee for Coventry City in November 1991, following in the wake of Anthony Sheridan and turned professional last summer, after being capped at youth level in **1992-93** by the Irish Republic. Captain of City's youth side.

| | | | APPEARANCES | | | | GOALS | | | |
|---|---|---|---|---|---|---|---|---|---|---|
| Clubs | Signing Date | Transfer Fee | Lge | FL Cup | FA Cup | Others | Lge | FL Cup | FA Cup | Others |
| Coventry City* | 7.93 | – | | | | | | | | |

## **PALLISTER Gary** Andrew

Born: Ramsgate, 30 June 1965

Height: 6'4" Weight: 13.0

International Honours: FL Rep, E"B", E-9

**Position/Skill Factor:** Central defender who is a tower of strength in the air and has good pace. A good passer for such a big man, he is comfortable when bringing the ball out of defence and is dangerous at set plays.

**Career History:** Signed by Middlesbrough at the age of 19, after impressing with his performances for Northern League side, Billingham Town. However, he was not introduced to the League side until the beginning of the following season when he made his FL debut at Wimbledon on 17 August 1985. A 3-0 defeat was hardly an auspicious start for an aspiring youngster, especially when "Boro" were beaten 2-0 by Mansfield Town, four days later and he was loaned out to Darlington for a short spell. Middlesbrough were relegated from the Second Division at the end of that season, but bounced straight back again as runners-up in 1986-87. By now a regular, he was a rock at the heart of the defence, making 44 League appearances. The following season, he was again influential as an ever present in helping the club back to the First Division, via the Play-Offs and was rewarded by England

with a full international cap against Hungary in Budapest on 27 April 1988. Unfortunately, his consistent performances couldn't prevent an immediate return to the Second Division and after playing in the first three games of the 1989-90 season for "Boro", he was signed by Manchester United for what was a record transfer fee between two Football League teams and remains one for a defender. With such a large fee and great expectations surrounding him, he took time to settle down with United and his Old Trafford debut was an anti-climax when he conceded a penalty as United went down 2-0 to Norwich City. However, he began to forge a strong partnership with Steve Bruce and was a key player in the "Red Devils'" march to the FA Cup Final and an eventual 1-0 victory over Crystal Palace in 1990. He finished the campaign as United's "Player of the Year" and 1990-91 brought more success, for after being in the side that lost 1-0 in the League Cup Final to Sheffield Wednesday, he won a European Cup Winners Cup medal, following United's 2-1 victory over Barcelona. A mainstay of United's successful, although ultimately disappointing 1991-92 season, he won League Cup Winners medal, but missed out on League Championship honours. Voted "Player of the Year" by his fellow professionals in the PFA Awards of 1992, he was recalled to the England squad and played in England's first game of 1991-92 against West Germany. Had a magnificent **1992-93** season, culminating in him winning a Championship medal, as United took the new Premier League title at the first attempt and playing his way back into an England team that was crying out for extra stability at the back. Dramatic improvement in his concentration made him far more consistent than in the past and his tackling inspired confidence throughout the entire team. While often to be seen producing "Alan Hansen type" runs upfield, it was strange that he only scored once during the campaign, but his real strength was at the back where a "mean" defence conceded only 35 goals in 50 games. Looks to be one of the men England should start building around for the future.

| | | | APPEARANCES | | | | GOALS | | | |
|---|---|---|---|---|---|---|---|---|---|---|
| Clubs | Signing Date | Transfer Fee | Lge | FL Cup | FA Cup | Others | Lge | FL Cup | FA Cup | Others |
| Middlesbrough | 11.84 | – | 156 | 10 | 10 | 13 | 5 | | 1 | |
| Darlington | 10.85 | Loan | 7 | | | | | | | |
| Manchester United* | 8.89 | £2,300,000 | 150+3 | 23 | 17 | 16+1 | 5 | | | 1 |

## **PALMER Carlton** Lloyd

Born: Rowley Regis, 5 December 1965

Height: 6'2" Weight: 11.10

International Honours: E "U21"-4, E"B", E-17

**Position/Skill Factor:** Can play equally as well either at full-back, in central defence or in midfield. His long legs make him a difficult opponent to pass and at the same time, he can run all day. Often produces tremendous runs from midfield into the penalty area.

**Career History:** Came to West Bromwich Albion on a YTS scheme in August 1983, after leaving school and turned professional just before Christmas in 1984. Made his FL debut at Newcastle United on 16 September, 1985, when coming on for Robbie Dennison in a 4-1 defeat. But when Steve Hunt left the club in March 1986, Carlton stepped into his shirt, only to face the prospect of Second Division soccer the following season as Albion found themselves relegated. He continued to hold down a regular place in a struggling side, until signed by his former manager Ron Atkinson for Sheffield Wednesday in February 1989. After settling down well in his first full season, the club, having appeared to have preserved its status, faltered at the last hurdle, losing five of its last six games and were relegated to the Second Division. He only missed two matches during 1990-91 as the "Owls" came back to the First Division at the first time of asking, in third place, but tragically was injured and thus unavailable for Wednesday's surprise League Cup Final victory over Manchester United. At the Hawthorns, he alternated between full-back, central defence and midfield. At Hillsborough, however, he immediately settled into central midfield, forming a partnership with John Sheridan which transformed Wednesday from a typically prosaic and uninspiring First Division side into one of the "classiest" passing teams in the Football League. Confident and composed on the ball, he is not afraid to carry it forward to create penalty box scoring opportunities for his colleagues. An infrequent scorer himself, he caused a sensation in an early season game in 1991-92 by scoring a first-half hat-trick of goals from open play against Queens Park Rangers. It was merely the prelude to his finest season to date, playing in every single game of Wednesday's highly successful season, which was suitably rewarded by a call up to the England squad at the end of the season. Made his international debut against the CIS in Moscow and then played in three subsequent games, performing both in midfield and the unfamiliar role of "sweeper". Included in the England squad for the European Championship Finals, he was one of the few genuine successes of England's generally lack-lustre performances and reinforced that view by playing in ten of the 11 international games held since. Produced some tremendous performances for "Owls" from midfield during **1992-93** and continued in the same vein when switched to centre-back because of forced absenteeism, despite carrying niggling injuries himself. Such was his enthusiasm for the game that he played in the 2-1 FA Cup Semi-Final victory over local rivals, Sheffield United, just three days after having several stitches inserted in a foot wound, following the international match against Turkey. An earlier criticism of him had been his erratic passing, but this has much improved over the last 12 months. Although Wednesday reached both the League and FA Cup Finals, they twice lost to the same opponents, Arsenal, but he at least had the privilege of captaining the replay side at Wembley, in the absence of Viv Anderson. Is much appreciated at Hillsborough by both fans and management and has just signed a new five year contract.

| | | | APPEARANCES | | | | GOALS | | | |
|---|---|---|---|---|---|---|---|---|---|---|
| Clubs | Signing Date | Transfer Fee | Lge | FL Cup | FA Cup | Others | Lge | FL Cup | FA Cup | Others |
| West Bromwich Albion | 12.84 | – | 114+7 | 7+1 | 4 | 6 | 4 | 1 | | |
| Sheffield Wednesday* | 2.89 | £750,000 | 167+1 | 23 | 14+1 | 8+1 | 9 | 1 | | 1 |

## **PALMER Roger** Neil

Born: Manchester, 30 January 1959

Height: 5'10" Weight: 11.0

**Position/Skill Factor:** Striker, who can also star in midfield. An excellent worker, he can play in most attacking positions and will always give a sound performance.

**Career History:** Not only Oldham's all time record goal scorer, he is one of their greatest ever players, playing a major role in their rise from a struggling unfashionable Second Division outfit to one of the most impressive footballing teams in the country. Manchester City first spotted his potential in local schools soccer and signed him on associated schoolboy forms in January 1974. Following a football apprenticeship (May 1975), he turned professional and just under a year later made his FL debut at Middlesbrough on 27 December 1977. Despite showing his ability to score at the top level, he was given little opportunity at Maine Road and during 1980-81, signed for Oldham Athletic, who were seeking a replacement for Simon Stainrod. He proved extremely consistent as Athletic strove for promotion to the First Division throughout the 1980s and during 1989-90 he broke Eric Gemmill's long standing club goal scoring record of 110 League goals. After a marvellous 1989-90, when the club went so close to cup glory, losing in the FA Cup Semi-Final to Manchester United after a replay and then reaching Wembley only to be beaten in the League Cup Final by Nottingham Forest, promotion success was just around the corner. Although he was injured during the West Ham United game at Boundary Park on 29 March 1991 and was not fit enough to play again in 1990-91, he won a Second Division Championship medal as the "Latics" finally made it to the top flight after a wait of nearly 70 years. His goal scoring ratio of one in every three games, is truly remarkable considering that for most of his Boundary Park career he has been deployed not as an "out and out" striker, but on the right flank. After ten years out of the top flight, he richly deserved the opportunity to play there again and happily regained fitness and returned to first team action in October 1991, although no longer an automatic first team choice in view of his advancing years. Playing on the right flank, he continued to demonstrate his ability to score vital goals. Was only used as a stop-gap in **1992-93**, although starting the first two games at number eight and for the first time during his long stint at the club and with Manchester City, previously, he failed to find the net during a season. On the bench for 20 first team games, he came on as a substitute in 13 of them, while making, just five full appearances. A firm favourite with the Boundary Park faithful, his testimonial last year raised £70,000 as a special thank you for 12 years of loyal service and although offered the choice of a free transfer, when he could negotiate his own terms, he accepted a new one year deal with "Latics", instead. Reckoned by the club to still be one of the best finishers in the business, if his legs can get him there.

| | | | APPEARANCES | | | | GOALS | | | |
|---|---|---|---|---|---|---|---|---|---|---|
| Clubs | Signing Date | Transfer Fee | Lge | FL Cup | FA Cup | Others | Lge | FL Cup | FA Cup | Others |
| Manchester City | 3.77 | - | 22+9 | 3+3 | | 4 | 9 | 1 | | 1 |
| Oldham Athletic* | 11.80 | £70,000 | 418+40 | 34+3 | 19+4 | 5+2 | 141 | 10 | 5 | 1 |

## **PALMER** Stephen (Steve) Leonard

Born: Brighton, 31 March 1968

Height: 6'1"

Weight: 12.7

**Position/Skill Factor:** Midfielder who can also play in central defence. Strong and willing, he is an ideal anchor man. He can run all day long, tackles well and wins more than his fair share of balls in the air.

**Career History:** One of very few footballers who have come into professional soccer from Cambridge University. Signed for Ipswich Town in the 1989 close season, following an impressive display in the Varsity match and made his FL debut at Oxford United, ironically, on 23 September 1989. By a strange coincidence, one of his opponents in the 1989 Varsity match, New Zealander, Ceri Evans, also signed professional forms — for Oxford United. Only played two more matches that season, but in 1990-91, after a long period on the bench, he finally got a run from December 1990 until April 1991, firstly deputising for Brian Gayle in central defence and later in midfield. Still not a regular in 1991-92, although he did play a part in Ipswich's Second Division Championship campaign with further first team opportunities from November 1991 through to March 1992, before giving way to Paul Goddard. Another Town player who had a disastrous season with injuries in **1992-93**, he came back from a summer operation to play a handful of games in October and November, before being sidelined yet again with a thigh injury. Unfortunately, after taking quite a while to diagnose the true problem, he was forced to have another operation in March. Came back yet again for the final two matches of the season, but will need the summer to become fully match fit in time for the new season.

| | | | APPEARANCES | | | | GOALS | | | |
|---|---|---|---|---|---|---|---|---|---|---|
| Clubs | Signing Date | Transfer Fee | Lge | FL Cup | FA Cup | Others | Lge | FL Cup | FA Cup | Others |
| Ipswich Town* | 8.89 | - | 41+17 | 2 | 6 | 3+2 | 1 | | | |

## **PAPAVASSILIOU Nicodimos (Nicki )**

Born: Cyprus, 31 August 1970

Height: 5'9" Weight: 11.8

International Honours: Cypriot Int

**Position/Skill Factor:** Very skilful left-winger and quick with it. With a super left foot, he is a great crosser of the ball.

**Career History:** An unusual signing by Newcastle manager, Kevin Keegan, Papavassiliou is a Cypriot international who played on the neighbouring island of Crete for Greek First Division club, OFI of Iraklion, for three years before joining the Geordies, following the **1992-93** season. Described as an attacker, or forward, his scoring record in Greek football was modest with only two goals from 45 games in 1990- 91 and 1991- 92 and he seems more likely to be used as a winger.

| | | | APPEARANCES | | | | GOALS | | | |
|---|---|---|---|---|---|---|---|---|---|---|
| Clubs | Signing Date | Transfer Fee | Lge | FL Cup | FA Cup | Others | Lge | FL Cup | FA Cup | Others |
| Newcastle United* | 6.93 | £125,000 | | | | | | | | |

## **PARKER Garry** Stuart

Born: Oxford, 7 September 1965

Height: 5'10" Weight: 11.0

International Honours: E Yth, E "U21"-6, E"B"

**Position/Skill Factor:** Midfield player, who will not be hurried and hates to give the ball away. A quality passer, he has a lovely touch and is a great striker of the ball.

**Career History:** Was an associated schoolboy with Queens Park Rangers (September 1980), before signing for Luton Town as an apprentice in June 1982, on leaving school.

Turned professional for the "Hatters" and immediately made his FL debut at Manchester United on 9 May 1983, but was never able to win a regular place in the Town's midfield. Looking to play first team football, he joined Second Division Hull City in 1985-86 and missed very few games for the "Tigers" in two years at Boothferry Park, during which time he also won the first of his England Under 21 caps. With the bigger clubs now watching him, he signed for Nottingham Forest at the tail end of 1987-88 and made just one League appearance that term, before breaking into the team midway through 1988-89. After securing a first team place on the left side of midfield, as the club maintained third place in the League, he also won a League Cup winners medal, following the 3-1 victory over his old club, Luton Town. Only missed two games as Neil Webb's replacement in central midfield during 1989-90 and picked up a second successive League Cup winners medal when playing in the Forest team that defeated Oldham Athletic, 1-0. But in 1990-91, as a member of the side that lost 2-1 to Tottenham Hotspur in the FA Cup Final, it proved to be third time unlucky on the famous Wembley turf. In terms of consistency, he was absent on just five occasions from the Forest team during the last 100 League matches through to the end of the 1990-91 season, a record bettered only by Nigel Clough over the same period. Lost his place to Scot Gemmill at the start of 1991-92, but returned to first team duty in September. After losing his place again, however, he was transferred to Aston Villa in November. Although he became a regular first choice with Villa, he had a quiet first season at Villa Park and his team a disappointing one, suffering from a goal drought. Again a first team regular in midfield, missing only five games in **1992-93**, despite being dogged by a torn stomach muscle throughout the season, he was boosted by the signings of Ray Houghton and Dean Saunders. Called up by the England squad in October was just reward for his excellent play and he was a key player in Villa's quest for Premier League Championship honours. Five of his nine goals were scored away from home, with those at Sheffield United, Liverpool and Leeds United, being of the spectacular variety. Lack of pace at the highest level is more than made up for by his quality.

| | | | APPEARANCES | | | | GOALS | | | |
|---|---|---|---|---|---|---|---|---|---|---|
| Clubs | Signing Date | Transfer Fee | Lge | FL Cup | FA Cup | Others | Lge | FL Cup | FA Cup | Others |
| Luton Town | 5.83 | – | 31+11 | 1+3 | 6+2 | | 3 | 1 | | |
| Hull City | 2.86 | £72,000 | 82+2 | 5 | 4 | 2 | 8 | | | 1 |
| Nottingham Forest | 3.88 | £260,000 | 99+4 | 22+1 | 16 | 9 | 17 | 4 | 5 | 3 |
| Aston Villa* | 11.91 | £650,000 | 62 | 5 | 9 | | 9 | | 1 | |

# PARKER Paul Andrew

Born: West Ham, 4 April 1964

Height: 5'7" Weight: 10.9

International Honours: E Yth, E "U21"-8, E"B", E-17

**Position/Skill Factor:** Right-back, or central defender, who climbs very well in the air for his size. With plenty of pace, he has a very fast recovery rate and is difficult to beat. Reads the game well and always appears to have plenty of time on the ball.

**Career History:** Crossed London to sign associated schoolboy forms with Fulham in June 1978 and on leaving school he became an apprentice (May 1980). Progressing through the club's youth side, he made his FL debut at Craven Cottage against Reading on 25 April 1981, following his 17th birthday and while still an apprentice. He duly turned professional a year later and it wasn't until 1983-84 that he began to hold down a regular place in the side. At the end of 1985-86, however, Fulham were relegated to the Third Division and although he remained at the club during the following season, it was patently obvious that he deserved a higher class of football. Neighbours, Queens Park Rangers, finally gave him that opportunity in the 1987 close season and he made an impressive debut for them on the opening day of the 1987-88 campaign in a 3-0 win at West Ham United. Ever present throughout his first season at Loftus Road, he was rewarded the following year by England for continued consistent club displays with his first full cap, when coming on as a sub against Albania. Had an impressive World Cup in 1990, but although scoring his first goal for Rangers after 140 appearances, his 1990-91 season was disrupted by injury problems and he made only 13 League appearances. Transferred to Manchester United in the 1991 close season, he established a niche at right-back. Again troubled by injuries in the second half of the season, he made a comeback for the League Cup Final, leaving with a winners medal after a 1-0 victory over Nottingham Forest. A knee injury ruled him out of United's critical last four games of the season, in which three defeats cost them the Championship and still not fit in time for the start of **1992-93**, he missed the first 14 matches, apart from one substitute appearance, before returning to Premier League duty. Came back into a side that was nicely placed for another title challenge and as he gradually achieved peak fitness, without being further absent, his pace not only made him difficult to pass, but he was often able to get forward along the flanks to create valuable goals with good crosses. The end of a highly successful season, saw him back in contention for an England place and the proud winner of a Championship medal, as United stormed to their first League title since 1966-67, losing just two of their last 27 games.

| | | | APPEARANCES | | | | GOALS | | | |
|---|---|---|---|---|---|---|---|---|---|---|
| Clubs | Signing Date | Transfer Fee | Lge | FL Cup | FA Cup | Others | Lge | FL Cup | FA Cup | Others |
| Fulham | 4.82 | - | 140+13 | 16 | 11 | 2 | 2 | 1 | | |
| Q.P.R. | 6.87 | £300,000 | 121+4 | 14 | 16 | 5 | 1 | | | |
| Manchester United* | 8.91 | £2,000,000 | 55+2 | 8 | 6 | 2+1 | 1 | | | |

## PARLOUR Raymond (Ray)

Born: Romford, 7 March 1973

Height: 5'10½"

Weight: 11.12

International Honours: E "U21"-7

**Position/Skill Factor:** Clever midfield player with an impressive range of passing skills.

**Career History:** Joined Arsenal as a trainee in July 1989, having been an associated schoolboy since January 1988 and turned professional in March 1991. Not expected to make a breakthrough in 1991-92, he benefited from a sudden shortage of midfield players at Highbury and was "thrown in at the deep end" by George Graham when selected to make his FL debut at Anfield, away to Liverpool on 29 January 1992. Impressive in the first-half, he unfortunately conceded a penalty in the second session as the "Gunners" went down 2-0. In his second full game away to Wimbledon he scored in the first minute. Selected for the England Under 21 squad at the end of the season. Returning to Anfield in **1992-93** for his first game in the Premier League, he made amends for his previous visit by setting up chances for Anders Limpar and Ian Wright to give Arsenal their opening victory of the season. Although he appeared in both the League and FA Cup winning Finals against Sheffield Wednesday, before being dropped for the latter replay, he probably didn't make as much progress as expected and often appeared to have a stamina problem.

| | | | APPEARANCES | | | | GOALS | | | |
|---|---|---|---|---|---|---|---|---|---|---|
| Clubs | Signing Date | Transfer Fee | Lge | FL Cup | FA Cup | Others | Lge | FL Cup | FA Cup | Others |
| Arsenal* | 3.91 | - | 18+9 | 3+1 | 4 | | 2 | | 1 | |

## PATERSON Scott

Born: Aberdeen, 13 May 1972

Height: 6'1" Weight: 11.9

**Position/Skill Factor:** A constructive midfield player with skill on the ball and good passing ability.

**Career History:** Young Scottish player signed by Liverpool from Aberdeen-based Highland League club, Cove Rangers in March 1992. Played in the reserve side in **1992-93** and impressed manager, Sammy Lee, with his efforts. Still a youngster in terms of experience, he might get an opportunity during the coming season.

| | | | APPEARANCES | | | | GOALS | | | |
|---|---|---|---|---|---|---|---|---|---|---|
| Clubs | Signing Date | Transfer Fee | Lge | FL Cup | FA Cup | Others | Lge | FL Cup | FA Cup | Others |
| Liverpool* | 3.92 | £25,000 | | | | | | | | |

## PAYNE Grant

Born: Chertsey, 25 December 1973

Height: 5'10" Weight: 12.5

**Position/Skill Factor:** Strong, forceful striker with excellent control. Very good with his back to the goal, he can hold the ball up and bring his team-mates into the game.

**Career History:** Signed professional forms for Wimbledon during the 1992 close season, having previously been at the club as an associated schoolboy (March 1988) and as a trainee (July 1990). No first team experience as yet, he spent **1992-93** with the reserves, but should have a bright future ahead of him according to local sources.

| | | | APPEARANCES | | | | GOALS | | | |
|---|---|---|---|---|---|---|---|---|---|---|
| Clubs | Signing Date | Transfer Fee | Lge | FL Cup | FA Cup | Others | Lge | FL Cup | FA Cup | Others |
| Wimbledon* | 6.92 | - | | | | | | | | |

## PEACOCK Darren

Born: Bristol, 3 February 1968

Height: 6'2"

Weight: 12.6

**Position/Skill Factor:** A central defender, who is both strong in the air and on the ground. Aggressive, but fair, when he tackles he means business.

**Career History:** Was on Bristol Rover's books as an associated schoolboy (September 1983) until leaving school, but joined Newport County on a YTS scheme in August 1984. Made his FL debut, as a substitute at Plymouth Argyle on 14 September 1985 and before turning professional the following February, he already had eight full League appearances to his credit. Suffered a serious injury in October 1986 and did not return to FL action until April 1988, by which time Newport were already doomed to demotion from the Football League. Continued playing with the Welsh club in the Vauxhall Conference in 1988-89. At this stage his FL career seemed over, but he was rescued from obscurity by Hereford United and soon won a regular place in their team. In the opening months of 1989-90, he was actually deployed as a striker with some success, but eventually settled down in central defence. His career took another twist in 1990-91 when he was elevated to the First Division by Queens Park Rangers, who signed him in an emergency following injuries to all their central defenders, along with Andy Tillson from Grimsby Town, with whom he formed a highly effective partnership which assisted Rangers to First Division safety. Held his place in 1991-92, despite the return to fitness of Danny Maddix and Alan McDonald and started **1992-93** as a first team regular, alongside the latter. Played 28 consecutive games, before a loss of form saw him replaced by Danny Maddix, following a 3-1 home defeat against Manchester United. United, who went top of the Premier League after the match, punished bad defensive lapses by Rangers and it was Peacock who took the brunt of the blame, being substituted on 72 minutes. Regained his place in the side when Danny Maddix was injured and appeared in all but one game for the remainder of the season.

| | | | APPEARANCES | | | | GOALS | | | |
|---|---|---|---|---|---|---|---|---|---|---|
| Clubs | Signing Date | Transfer Fee | Lge | FL Cup | FA Cup | Others | Lge | FL Cup | FA Cup | Others |
| Newport County | 2.86 | - | 24+4 | 2 | 1 | 1+1 | | | | |
| Hereford United | 3.89 | - | 56+3 | 6 | 6 | 6 | 5 | | 1 | |
| Q.P.R.* | 12.90 | £200,000 | 93+3 | 8 | 2 | 2 | 3 | 1 | | |

## **PEACOCK Gavin** Keith

Born: Eltham, 18 November 1967

Height: 5'8" Weight: 11.10

International Honours: E Sch, E Yth

**Position/Skill Factor:** Midfielder who can play up front when required. A danger man when behind the front two where his ability to run effortlessly and play one-twos, often take him into scoring positions.

**Career History:** The son of Keith, the former Charlton player between 1962-1978 and the holder of England schoolboy and youth caps, it was not until he left his first club, Queens Park Rangers, that he began to make the expected progress. An associated schoolboy (June 1983) and apprentice (June 1984), prior to turning professional, it was a further two years before he made his FL debut on 29 November 1986 in a 2-2 draw at Loftus Road against Sheffield Wednesday. With 11 more appearances to follow later that season, he seemed to be making a breakthrough and it was surprising, therefore, that the following season he chose to join Third Division, Gillingham, for regular first team action, after a short loan period. When Gillingham were relegated to Division Four at the end of 1988-89, he clearly required a higher level of football and was transferred to Second Division, Bournemouth. Sadly, his first season with the "Cherries" also ended in relegation, when an injury crisis at Dean Court saw them slide from mid-table security to the foot of the table in only two months. His career was rescued from obscurity by Jim Smith, who signed him for Newcastle United a few months before his own departure from the club. Prior to 1991-92, he had always played in midfield, but new manager, Ossie Ardiles, tried him in a new role as a striker and he responded with the best football of his career. In a season where the team stumbled to the very brink of relegation, he was ever present and top scored with 19 goals, which included two hat-tricks, one of them at Crewe Alexandra in a League Cup-tie, which turned a potentially humiliating defeat at 3-1 down into a 4-3 triumph. For Peacock to still be at St James' Park for the start of **1992-93**, was a major boost for United fans, but it took some persuasive talking by new manager, Kevin Keegan, to keep him, with Middlesbrough being just one of the clubs to miss out. Although he was unfortunate with a persistent hamstring injury, which forced him out of 14 League games, he still managed to score 12 vital goals and create 11 more for his team-mates as Newcastle stormed to the First Division title, ahead of West Ham United. However, he was still looking to leave the north-east and during the summer, Chelsea pipped Tottenham Hotspur for his signature and he will start the new season at Stamford Bridge under Glenn Hoddle.

| | | | APPEARANCES | | | | GOALS | | | |
|---|---|---|---|---|---|---|---|---|---|---|
| Clubs | Signing Date | Transfer Fee | Lge | FL Cup | FA Cup | Others | Lge | FL Cup | FA Cup | Others |
| Q.P.R. | 11.84 | - | 7+10 | | 0+1 | | 1 | | | |
| Gillingham | 10.87 | £40,000 | 69+1 | 4 | 2 | 5 | 11 | | | 1 |
| Bournemouth | 8.89 | £250,000 | 56 | 6 | 2 | 2 | 8 | | | |
| Newcastle United | 11.90 | £275,000 | 102+3 | 6 | 6 | 3 | 35 | 5 | 3 | 4 |
| Chelsea* | 7.90 | £1,250,000 | | | | | | | | |

## PEARCE Andrew (Andy) John

Born: Bradford-on-Avon, 20 April 1966

Height: 6'4"

Weight: 13.0

**Position/Skill Factor:** Central defender who is very strong in the air and a good distributor of long passes.

**Career History:** Came to Coventry City from Beazer Homes League team, Halesowen Town, during the 1990 close season after previous experience with West Midland's non-League teams, Wednesbury and Stourbridge. One of three players City have signed from Halesowen, the others being Tim Clarke (now with Huddersfield Town) and Sean Flynn. Made his FL debut deputising for the injured Brian Kilcline at Leeds United on 9 March 1991 and settled in well, keeping his place for the remainder of the season and scoring the winning goal in only his second game at home to Luton Town. Following the departures of Brian Kilcline and Trevor Peake, he established a regular spot in 1991-92 at the heart of one of the "meanest" defences in the First Division, partnering Peter Atherton. Started **1992-93** very well, with a number of impressive performances, particularly in the 1-0 victory at Oldham Athletic and if there had to be a downside to his game it was probably in his lack of aggression. He was also prone to the odd unforced error and became the first City player since George Curtis, 30 years ago, to score two own goals in one season in Premier League games against Sheffield United and Queens Park Rangers. Following that, his appearances became very spotty and he eventually dropped out of the team due to a number of minor injuries and poor form. Ended the season as third choice behind Phil Babb and David Busst and joined Sheffield Wednesday in a £½ million transfer deal during the 1993 close season.

| | | | APPEARANCES | | | | GOALS | | | |
|---|---|---|---|---|---|---|---|---|---|---|
| Clubs | Signing Date | Transfer Fee | Lge | FL Cup | FA Cup | Others | Lge | FL Cup | FA Cup | Others |
| Coventry City | 5.90 | £15,000 | 68+3 | 6 | 3 | 1 | 4 | | | |
| Sheffield Wednesday* | 6.93 | £500,000 | | | | | | | | |

## PEARCE Dennis Anthony

Born: Wolverhampton, 10 September 1974

Height: 5'10" Weight: 10.13

**Position/Skill Factor:** Midfielder who can also play equally well at left-back. With a good left foot, he likes to get involved and packs a powerful shot. Excellent in the air and a strong tackler to boot.

**Career History:** A young player who has recently signed professional for Aston Villa, he first came to the club as an associated schoolboy in February 1989, before progressing as a trainee (July 1991). Apart from regular service in the youth team, he was given a reserve outing during **1992-93** and must look to consolidate in 1993-94.

| | | | APPEARANCES | | | | GOALS | | | |
|---|---|---|---|---|---|---|---|---|---|---|
| Clubs | Signing Date | Transfer Fee | Lge | FL Cup | FA Cup | Others | Lge | FL Cup | FA Cup | Others |
| Aston Villa* | 7.93 | - | | | | | | | | |

## PEARCE Ian Anthony

Born: Bury St Edmunds, 7 May 1974

Height: 6'3" Weight: 14.0

International Honours: E Yth

**Position/Skill Factor:** Yet to settle in a fixed position, he can play anywhere: full-back, central defender or striker. A strong header of the ball and also skilful on the ground.

**Career History:** Joined Chelsea as a 14-year-old associated schoolboy in November 1988 and signed professional forms after leaving school in the 1991 close season. Prior to that, however, he made his FL debut when coming off the bench four days after his 17th birthday, during a 2-2 draw at Aston Villa on 11 May 1991, the last game of the 1990-91 season. Made three further first team appearances as a substitute in October and November 1991, before going back to reserve team football. Surprisingly made only one substitute appearance for Chelsea in **1992-93**, but is still young enough to make a name for himself. Had a good tour with the England under 19 World Cup squad in Australia recently and came back with an enhanced reputation, but needs to build on that with regular first team football.

| | | | APPEARANCES | | | | GOALS | | | |
|---|---|---|---|---|---|---|---|---|---|---|
| Clubs | Signing Date | Transfer Fee | Lge | FL Cup | FA Cup | Others | Lge | FL Cup | FA Cup | Others |
| Chelsea* | 8.91 | - | 0+4 | | | 0+1 | | | | |

## PEARSON Nigel Graham

Born: Nottingham, 21 August 1963

Height: 6'1"

Weight: 13.7

**Position/Skill Factor:** Strong central defender, brave in the air and uncompromising on the ground. A good steady player, he rarely ever gets caught out of position. Inspires by example.

**Career History:** Came out of non-League football with Heanor Town of the Midland Counties League, when he signed for Shrewsbury Town in 1981-82 and had to wait nine months before being selected for the "Shrews'" first team. Eventually made his FL debut at Oldham Athletic on 28 August 1982 and settled down into the side on a regular basis, until being injured towards the end of 1983-84. Out for well over 12 months, he made a great recovery, establishing himself as one of the best centre-backs in the Second Division. Ever present in 1986-87, he so impressed Sheffield Wednesday after playing against them in the Second Round of the League Cup the following season, that they immediately moved for him. Signed to add a touch of steel to the heart of Wednesday's defence, he rarely missed a game, but in 1989-90 the club dropped into the Second Division when, after appearing to be safe, they lost five of the last six games. As club skipper, however, come the end of the 1990-91 season, he had led the side to an historic 1-0 League Cup Final victory over Manchester United and back to the First Division at the first time of asking, scoring no fewer than 12 goals (six FL, plus six cup) mostly from free-kicks and corners. Although frequently rested or absent through injury in 1991-92, he still played a prominent part in the "Owls'" highly successful season as they finished in third place and qualified for the UEFA Cup. Began **1992-93** on a high note when he scored the opening goal of Wednesday's Premier League campaign after 15 minutes at Everton. But then it began to sour for the club captain yet again, as intermittent injuries kept him from stringing a good run of games together. Having made only 13 full appearances, he spent several matches coming off the bench at timely intervals and with a little over half an hour remaining on the clock during the League Cup Semi-Final at Blackburn, he was required once more. Within moments he had to be treated after challenging for the ball, but courageously carried on until being forced to leave the field with just ten minutes remaining. Wednesday won the game 4-2, but it wasn't all joy as it was later discovered that Nigel had suffered a broken leg and would be out for the rest of the season.

| | | | APPEARANCES | | | | GOALS | | | |
|---|---|---|---|---|---|---|---|---|---|---|
| Clubs | Signing Date | Transfer Fee | Lge | FL Cup | FA Cup | Others | Lge | FL Cup | FA Cup | Others |
| Shrewsbury Town | 11.81 | £5,000 | 153 | 19 | 6 | 3 | 5 | | | |
| Sheffield Wednesday* | 10.87 | £250,000 | 172+3 | 17+2 | 15 | 10 | 14 | 5 | 1 | |

## PEEL Nathan James

Born: Blackburn,17 May 1972

Height: 6'1" Weight: 12.7

**Position/Skill Factor:** Big striker with two good feet who is also useful in the air. Has a lovely first touch for a big man.

**Career History:** Joined Preston North End as an associated schoolboy (September 1987) and on leaving school signed on for the club as a trainee in September 1988. Made his FL debut at Deepdale, a month after turning professional, against Grimsby Town on 25 August 1990, when coming off the bench to replace Steve Harper. Scored at Reading, the only time he played for the full 90 minutes during 1990-91. With so little FL experience under his belt, it was a surprise when Dave Bassett signed him for Sheffield United in the summer of 1991, especially when he only made one appearance (as a substitute away to Tottenham Hotspur in November) in 1991-92. Had a most disappointing season and did not feature at all in United's **1992-93** campaign, despite being leading goalscorer for the reserves. Went out for a spell on loan at Halifax Town in February and played three games for the "Shaymen" without getting on the scoresheet, before returning to Bramall Lane.

| | | | APPEARANCES | | | | GOALS | | | |
|---|---|---|---|---|---|---|---|---|---|---|
| Clubs | Signing Date | Transfer Fee | Lge | FL Cup | FA Cup | Others | Lge | FL Cup | FA Cup | Others |
| Preston North End | 7.90 | - | 1+9 | 1 | | 1+1 | 1 | | | |
| Sheffield United* | 8.91 | £50,000 | 0+1 | | | | | | | |
| Halifax Town | 2.93 | Loan | 3 | | | | | | | |

## PEMBERTON John Matthew

Born: Oldham, 18 November 1964

Height: 5'11"

Weight: 12.3

**Position/Skill Factor:** Very experienced right-back who links up well with the attack to deliver useful crosses and is a good passer of the ball. Also a long throw specialist.

**Career History:** Lancashire born defender who was playing with local North West Counties League club Chadderton, when given his FL debut as a trialist for Rochdale at Spotland against Aldershot on 2 October 1984. Following that solitary appearance he continued to play for Chadderton, but towards the end of the season Crewe Alexandra stepped in for him and he immediately went into their League side. He made such good progress that, after three years and over 100 games at Gresty Road, he moved from the Fourth to the Second Division when he signed for Crystal Palace in March 1988. Held down the right-back slot at Selhurst Park throughout the 1988-89 campaign, missing just four games, as Palace gained promotion to the First Division in third place. In 1990, he played a major part in Palace's great FA Cup run and in particular the epic Semi-Final against Liverpool which was won 4-3 after extra-time. His run and cross to set up Mark Bright for Palace's initial goal, first revealed the vulnerability in the heart of the "Reds'" defence, which the "Eagles" exploited to the full. After Manchester United beat Palace 1-0 in the replayed Final, he signed for newly promoted Sheffield United, who were looking to strengthen their squad for an assault on the First Division. He quickly settled into the right-back berth, but injuries interrupted his season as the "Blades" struggled near the foot of the table, before pulling clear to safety. With United having another inconsistent season in 1991-92, he was in and out of the team up to December, but after losing his place to Kevin Gage, he was not selected again until the closing weeks of the campaign. Started **1992-93** out of the team, as Kevin Gage held on to the right-back spot and he had to wait until November before getting the call to replace injury victim, Brian Gayle, in the centre of the defence. Made way for Gayle on his return to fitness and later returned as his partner, when Beesley was unavailable. Scored his first goal for the club when blasting home the decisive penalty in the FA Cup Fifth Round replay "shoot-out" at home to Blackburn Rovers. His undoubted pace proved a major asset when United were desperately trying to avoid relegation and he retained his place through to the end of the season.

| | | | APPEARANCES | | | | GOALS | | | |
|---|---|---|---|---|---|---|---|---|---|---|
| Clubs | Signing Date | Transfer Fee | Lge | FL Cup | FA Cup | Others | Lge | FL Cup | FA Cup | Others |
| Rochdale | 9.84 | - | 1 | | | | | | | |
| Crewe Alexandra | 3.85 | - | 116+5 | 7 | 3 | 7 | 1 | 1 | | |
| Crystal Palace | 3.88 | £80,000 | 76+2 | 6+1 | 8 | 12 | 2 | | | |
| Sheffield United* | 7.90 | £300,000 | 59+1 | 3 | 4 | 1 | | | | |

## PENRICE Gary Kenneth

Born: Bristol, 23 March 1964

Height: 5'7"

Weight: 10.0

**Position/Skill Factor:** A striker who is always on the move, making angles for team-mates in possession. An extremely unselfish player, with good vision.

**Career History:** Became a Bristol Rovers' associated schoolboy player in April 1978, before crossing town on leaving school to sign as an apprentice at Bristol City in June 1980. On being released, he developed his skills with local Western League club, Mangotsfield and impressed Bristol Rovers, one of the clubs who had rejected him as a youngster. Duly signed professional forms for Rovers and made his FL debut when coming on as a sub at Eastville against Leyton Orient on 27 April 1985. He was soon holding down a regular place and as an ever present in 1987-88, he topped the club's scoring charts for the first time with 18 League goals. The following season he scored 20 and in November 1989, Watford, who were lacking in firepower, brought him to Vicarage Road where his 12 goals from 29 League matches proved vital in preserving their Second Division status. Unfortunately, in 1990-91, he suffered from a string of injury problems and only managed to play 13 times for the "Hornets", prior to March. However, once fully fit, Watford doubled their money when they transferred him to Aston Villa as a potential replacement for David Platt, who was due to leave for Italian football during the coming summer. Although playing a few games at the start of 1991-92 under new manager Ron Atkinson, as a signing of previous Czech manager, Josef Venglos, his cards were marked and he soon rejoined his former manager, Gerry Francis, by now installed at Queens Park Rangers. Since joining Rangers, however, he struggled to score, apart from two late goals which saved a point at Coventry and had lost his place by the end of the season. After four substitute appearances in **1992-93**, he was called up for first team duty and in his second full game at home to Middlesbrough, scored a goal in a 3-3 draw. Two weeks later he picked up another couple in a 4-1 win over Tottenham Hotspur, but was substituted at Norwich City after receiving a knock and was absent for the next five matches. Coming back to League duty against Oldham Athletic at Loftus Road, he volleyed home the winner in a 3-2 victory and scored a further three goals in five matches, before hobbling off at Middlesbrough, the end product of a heavy tackle by Jon Gittens, which earned the defender a booking. Diagnosed as a fractured bone in his right leg and having established himself as Les Ferdinand's strike partner, it was a heavy blow and to make matters worse, he suffered another break in a training accident, while preparing for a comeback. How unlucky can you get!

| | | | APPEARANCES | | | | GOALS | | | |
|---|---|---|---|---|---|---|---|---|---|---|
| Clubs | Signing Date | Transfer Fee | Lge | FL Cup | FA Cup | Others | Lge | FL Cup | FA Cup | Others |
| Bristol Rovers | 11.84 | - | 186+2 | 11 | 11 | 13+2 | 53 | 3 | 7 | 2 |
| Watford | 11.89 | £500,000 | 41+2 | | 4 | 1 | 17 | | 1 | 1 |
| Aston Villa | 3.91 | £1,000,000 | 14+6 | | | | 1 | | | |
| Q.P.R.* | 10.91 | £625,000 | 23+11 | 3+1 | 1+1 | 1 | 9 | 1 | 1 | |

## PERRY Christopher (Chris) John

Born: Sutton, 26 April 1973

Height: 5'10" Weight: 10.2

**Position/Skill Factor:** A central defender with plenty of pace. Reads situations well for one so young and is a good competitive tackler.

**Career History:** First came to Wimbledon as an associated schoolboy in December 1987, graduating to trainee status in July 1989 and then to the professional ranks during the 1991 close season. Another member of the successful side that reached the Semi-Final of the 1991-92 FA Youth Cup before going out to neighbours, Crystal Palace, he played for the "Dons'" reserve side in **1992-93** and could be knocking on the door shortly.

| | | | APPEARANCES | | | | GOALS | | | |
|---|---|---|---|---|---|---|---|---|---|---|
| Clubs | Signing Date | Transfer Fee | Lge | FL Cup | FA Cup | Others | Lge | FL Cup | FA Cup | Others |
| Wimbledon* | 7.91 | - | | | | | | | | |

## PETTINGER Paul Allen

Born: Sheffield, 1 October 1975

Height: 6'1"

Weight: 13.4

International Honours: E Sch, E Yth

**Position/Skill Factor:** Goalkeeper with good technique for one so young. Excellent reflexes and good on crosses, he uses the ball sensibly and kicks well.

**Career History:** An England schoolboy international and the goalkeeping star of the most successful Leeds United youth side ever and one that won the FA Youth Cup in **1992-93**, he turned professional a month after first coming to Elland Road as a trainee in September 1992. Yet to play for the first team, the nearest he came was when sitting it out on the bench as Mervyn Day kept goal for the club at Manchester City last November. One for the future, though, as he looks to get ahead of John Lukic, Mark Beeney and Scott Cousin in 1993- 94.

| | | | APPEARANCES | | | | GOALS | | | |
|---|---|---|---|---|---|---|---|---|---|---|
| Clubs | Signing Date | Transfer Fee | Lge | FL Cup | FA Cup | Others | Lge | FL Cup | FA Cup | Others |
| Leeds United* | 10.92 | - | | | | | | | | |

## PEYTON Gerald (Gerry) Joseph

Born: Birmingham, 20 May 1956

Height: 6'2"

Weight: 13.9

International Honours: IR "U21", IR-33

**Position/Skill Factor:** Very experienced goalkeeper, who has good positional and handling skills. Makes difficult saves look easy. Also, a good long kicker.

**Career History:** On leaving school he joined Aston Villa as an apprentice (February 1973), before being released in 1974 and going into non-League football with Atherstone Town of the Southern League for one year. He was signed by Burnley, who were looking for a deputy for Alan Stevenson and on making his FL debut at Turf Moor against Liverpool on 6 December 1975, he kept a clean sheet. At the same time, he replaced Stevenson and although the club were relegated to the Second Division at the end of 1975-76, he did so well that he retained his place in the team until October 1976. Following an injury to Peter Mellor, Fulham, who had noted his steady progress, moved in for him and in just under ten years at Craven Cottage he became the all-time third ranking "Cottagers'" goalkeeper, in terms of appearances. During that period, Fulham fluctuated between the Second and Third Divisions, but his form was such, apart from the odd match and a spell on loan at Southend United, that he was regularly chosen to represent the Irish Republic, on his parents' birthright, after winning his first cap against Spain in Dublin on 9 February 1977. Freed at the end of 1985-86, following a long service testimonial, he joined Bournemouth during the summer and won a Third Division Championship medal as an ever present in his first season with the club. Had very few serious threats to his dominance between the posts, despite Bournemouth suffering relegation to the Third Division in 1989-90, still proving to be a reliable goalkeeper. It was a surprise, nevertheless, when Everton signed him in the summer of 1991 as cover for Neville Southall. However, there was to be no dramatic return to the First Division as the Welsh international 'keeper did not miss a game all season. Instead, Peyton spent the closing months of the season on loan to Bolton Wanderers and Norwich City, but only as cover. He did, however, add four more international caps to his tally, playing in an end of season tournament in the USA. Deemed not to make an appearance for Everton, he was loaned out to Brentford at the beginning of **1992-93** and the move became more permanent following another temporary transfer spell at Chelsea early in the New Year. With Graham Benstead struggling, particularly with clearances because of the new back pass ruling, Brentford were more than pleased to acquire his services. However, with Premier League newcomers, West Ham United, woefully short of experienced cover for Ludek Miklosko, he moved from west to east London during the close season.

| | | | APPEARANCES | | | | GOALS | | | |
|---|---|---|---|---|---|---|---|---|---|---|
| Clubs | Signing Date | Transfer Fee | Lge | FL Cup | FA Cup | Others | Lge | FL Cup | FA Cup | Others |
| Burnley | 5.75 | - | 30 | 1 | 1 | | | | | |
| Fulham | 12.76 | £40,000 | 345 | 26 | 20 | 2 | | | | |
| Southend United | 9.83 | Loan | 10 | | | | | | | |
| Bournemouth | 7.86 | - | 202 | 15 | 13 | 8 | | | | |
| Everton | 7.91 | £80,000 | | | | | | | | |
| Bolton Wanderers | 2.92 | Loan | 1 | | | | | | | |
| Brentford | 9.92 | Loan | 14 | | | | | | | |
| Chelsea | 1.93 | Loan | 0+1 | | | | | | | |
| Brentford | 3.93 | - | 5 | | | 3 | | | | |
| West Ham United* | 6.93 | - | | | | | | | | |

## PHELAN Michael (Mike) Christopher

Born: Nelson, 24 September 1962

Height: 5'11"

Weight: 12.3

International Honours: E Yth, E-1

**Position/Skill Factor:** Steady and reliable midfielder who can also play at full-back. Holds the ball up well and keeps his passing simple. Difficult to pass, he invariably gets a foot in and is ideal for a man-for-man marking exercise.

**Career History:** Joined nearby Burnley on associated schoolboy forms in July 1977, before becoming an apprentice on leaving school in July 1979. Turned professional in the 1980 close season and made his FL debut as a substitute at Chesterfield on 31 January 1981. Won a Third Division Championship medal in 1981-82, but in the very next season, as an ever present, he experienced the misery of relegation as the team slid back into Division Three. And when Burnley descended into Division four at the end of 1984-85, he was obviously too talented to be playing at that level and was transferred to Norwich City in the summer. In his first season at Carrow Road, 1985-86, he was present throughout the campaign, winning a Second Division Championship medal as the club moved into the top flight. Rarely missing a game for the "Canaries" over four seasons, he was never better than when captaining the side to fourth place in the First Division in 1988-89, Norwich's highest ever League position. His consistency attracted the attention of bigger clubs and during the 1989 close season, he followed his former club colleague, Steve Bruce, to Manchester United. Made his debut alongside another big money signing, Neil Webb, against Arsenal at Old Trafford on the opening day of 1989-90 and expectancy was high for the club to mount a challenge for the elusive League Championship that season, after a 4-1 win. However, as the side's League form faltered, it was fortunate that United had a good FA Cup run which ended successfully when Crystal Palace were beaten 1-0 in the Final, following a replay. But the season was memorable for other reasons as well, most of all when winning his first England cap, coming on as a sub against Italy on 15 November 1989 at Wembley. And despite the disappointment of finishing on the losing side in the League Cup Final against Sheffield Wednesday in 1991, he climaxed 1990-91 with a European Cup Winners Cup medal, following United's 2-1 victory over Barcelona. In 1991-92 he took a back seat for most of the season but was recalled for out of favour Neil Webb in the closing months, winning a League Cup winners medal, following the 1-0 victory over Nottingham Forest. Although he qualified for a Championship medal in **1992-93**, as United won the new Premier League title at the first attempt, he had another frustrating season in a playing sense. While still a valuable member of the first team squad, he only appeared occasionally, when injuries dictated, spending most of his time either sitting on the bench, or in the reserve side and with a playing record of 14 games, six were as a substitute, while he was replaced in four of the eight he actually started. During the past two seasons, with stiff competition for the midfield places, he has found himself becoming more and more of a utility player, often sitting in at right-back. However, these days, the role is a vital one in the context of winning titles over a long and arduous campaign and his part in it will have been duly appreciated by the manager

| | | | APPEARANCES | | | | GOALS | | | |
|---|---|---|---|---|---|---|---|---|---|---|
| Clubs | Signing Date | Transfer Fee | Lge | FL Cup | FA Cup | Others | Lge | FL Cup | FA Cup | Others |
| Burnley | 7.80 | – | 166+2 | 16 | 16 | 8 | 9 | 2 | | 2 |
| Norwich City | 7.85 | £60,000 | 155+1 | 14 | 11 | 13 | 9 | | 1 | |
| Manchester United* | 7.89 | £750,000 | 87+13 | 12+2 | 10 | 14 | 2 | | 1 | |

## PHELAN Terence (Terry)

Born: Manchester, 16 March 1967

Height: 5'8" Weight: 10.0

International Honours: IR Yth, IR "U21"-1, IR "U23"-1, IR "B", IR-14

**Position/Skill Factor:** Competitive left-back with electric pace and a good left foot. Loves to run at defenders with the ball.

**Career History:** Started at Leeds United as an associated schoolboy in March 1982, before progressing to the professional ranks, via the YTS scheme (August 1983). Made his FL debut at Shrewsbury Town on 7 September 1985 and although having a good run of ten games in the side, was freed at the end of the season, along with right-back Dennis Irwin, who also went on to fame and fortune with Oldham Athletic, Manchester United and the Irish Republic. Joining Swansea City during the 1986 close season, he missed just one game during 1986-87, before becoming one of Bobby Gould's first signings for Wimbledon. Apart from a period out, due to injury in the middle of 1987-88, he kept his place throughout the campaign and won an FA Cup winners medal, following the "Dons'"surprise 1-0 victory over Liverpool at Wembley. Continuing to make good progress, he was as consistent as ever in 1991-92, missing only five games through injury during the season and making his international debut for the Irish Republic on 11 September 1991. Doubts were raised when Manchester City paid a record fee for a full-back at the beginning of **1992-93** in order to bring him to Maine Road. However, he settled in immediately, giving top class performances throughout the season and his fast running and overlapping with Rick Holden down the left has become a great part of the team's raiding power. A regular for the Republic, he gave his all in every game, while his pace complimented Keith Curle and assisted goalkeeper, Tony Coton, over the new back pass rule. Has been a real success for City.

| | | | APPEARANCES | | | | GOALS | | | |
|---|---|---|---|---|---|---|---|---|---|---|
| Clubs | Signing Date | Transfer Fee | Lge | FL Cup | FA Cup | Others | Lge | FL Cup | FA Cup | Others |
| Leeds United | 8.84 | – | 12+2 | 3 | | 2 | | | | |
| Swansea City | 7.86 | – | 45 | 4 | 5 | 3 | | | | |
| Wimbledon | 7.87 | £100,000 | 155+4 | 13+2 | 16 | 8 | 1 | | 2 | |
| Manchester City* | 8.92 | £2,500,000 | 37 | 3 | 5 | | | | 1 | |

## PHILLIPS David Owen

Born: Wegberg, Germany, 29 July 1963

Height: 5'10" Weight: 11.2

International Honours: W Yth, W "U21"-3, W-46

**Position/Skill Factor:** Left sided midfielder, who is also comfortable at full-back. Has two good feet and is a lovely striker of the ball, especially when around the box. Known for his diagonal passing.

**Career History:** Born in West Germany, where his father was serving in the RAF, his career started at Plymouth Argyle as an apprentice in August 1979 and on turning professional at the beginning of 1981-82, he made his FL debut at Home Park against Oxford United on 29 August 1981. Appearing sporadically at first, he gained a regular place in the side in 1983-84 and helped Argyle to the FA Cup Semi-Finals, as the first Third Division club to reach that stage of the competition since the early 1960s, scoring the goal that won the Quarter-Final tie against Derby County, direct from a corner in injury time. His good form did not go unnoticed at international level, being selected for Wales at right-back against England at Wrexham on 2 May 1984. Manchester City were impressed by his skills and a few months after his international debut, he was on his way to Maine Road. Was ever present in his first season at City, scoring 12 goals as the club were promoted to the First Division as the third placed side and missed only a handful of matches the following year, before moving to Coventry City in part exchange for goalkeeper Perry Suckling in the summer of 1986. In his first season at Highfield Road, he won an FA Cup winners medal, following Coventry's great 3-2 victory over Tottenham Hotspur at Wembley. After three seasons at Highfield Road he was transferred to Norwich City in the 1989 close season, for a fee that was fixed by a tribunal and marked his debut with a goal in a 2-0 win at Sheffield Wednesday on the opening day of 1989-90. Ever present during 1989-90 and 1990-91, he formed a good left-wing partnership with Mark Bowen as the club looked to improve. In 1991-92, he was switched early in the season to right-back to cover for the absence of Ian Culverhouse, but reverted to his usual position in February, until losing his place in the closing stages of the season. Had a good season in **1992-93**, finishing as the club's second highest scorer, after hitting five in the first eight matches and eventually taking over the responsibility for spot kicks, following misses by his colleagues. Some of his goals were "blinders" and his cartwheel celebrating his opening day goal at Highbury will be treasured by all those City followers who saw it. Sadly, however, he had a 22 match spell between December and April when he failed to get on the score-sheet and with the club only winning eight of those games, it was hardly Championship form. Continued to play for Wales, having made more international appearances than any other Norwich player and has now played over 500 first team games since starting out with Plymouth back in 1981.

| | | | APPEARANCES | | | | GOALS | | | |
|---|---|---|---|---|---|---|---|---|---|---|
| Clubs | Signing Date | Transfer Fee | Lge | FL Cup | FA Cup | Others | Lge | FL Cup | FA Cup | Others |
| Plymouth Argyle | 8.81 | - | 65+8 | 2+1 | 12+1 | 4 | 15 | | | 1 |
| Manchester City | 8.84 | £65,000 | 81 | 8 | 5 | 5 | 13 | | | 3 |
| Coventry City | 6.86 | £150,000 | 93+7 | 8 | 9 | 5+1 | 8 | | 1 | 2 |
| Norwich City* | 7.89 | £525,000 | 152 | 12 | 14 | 8 | 17 | | 1 | 1 |

## PHILLIPS Marcus Stuart

Born: Trowbridge, 17 October 1973

Height: 5'10" Weight: 11.4

**Position/Skill Factor:** Midfield player with two good feet and strong shooting ability. Is excellent at wrong footing defenders and setting up attacks.

**Career History:** A young player with bags of potential, he first came to Swindon Town as an associated schoolboy in June 1988 and later became a trainee (July 1990), before joining the professional ranks in the 1992 close season. Although he has yet to make his FL debut, he sat on the bench for the game against Watford in **1992-93** and three days later, came on as a substitute during the second leg of the League Cup-tie at home to Torquay United. A regular reserve, he has a younger brother, Kevin, who, in following in the family footsteps, is currently a trainee at Town.

| | | | APPEARANCES | | | | GOALS | | | |
|---|---|---|---|---|---|---|---|---|---|---|
| Clubs | Signing Date | Transfer Fee | Lge | FL Cup | FA Cup | Others | Lge | FL Cup | FA Cup | Others |
| Swindon Town* | 7.92 | - | | 0+1 | | | | | | |

## PICKERING Christopher Gary

Born: Stockport, 18 December 1974

Height: 5'11" Weight: 12.0

**Position/Skill Factor:** Central defender who can also play at left-back. Very good left foot, strong in the air and an excellent competitor. Has adequate pace and uses the ball well.

**Career History:** A product of Manchester schools football, he first came to Southampton as a trainee in March 1992. Turned professional during the 1993 close season after showing an impressive attitude in 24 youth team matches during **1992-93** and as a reward for making steady improvement.

| | | | APPEARANCES | | | | GOALS | | | |
|---|---|---|---|---|---|---|---|---|---|---|
| Clubs | Signing Date | Transfer Fee | Lge | FL Cup | FA Cup | Others | Lge | FL Cup | FA Cup | Others |
| Southampton* | 7.93 | - | | | | | | | | |

## **PIECHNIK** Torben

Born: Denmark,
21 May 1963

Height: 6'0"

Weight: 12.9

International Honours:
Danish Int

**Position/Skill Factor:** Footballing central defender in the continental style. A good passer of the ball, he likes to join up with the attack.

**Career History:** One of the stars of Denmark's amazing and heroic triumph in the European Championships, held in Sweden in June 1992, he was not a first choice for his country at the start of the Finals. He did not appear until their third match, when he replaced Kent Nielson in the second-half against France, but held his place for the Semi-Final against Holland, which Denmark won on penalties after a 2-2 draw and then the Final when they remarkably defeated the reigning World Cup holders, Germany, 2-0. A late arrival on the international stage, he did not make his debut for Denmark until November 1991, at the age of 28 and it was a surprise when Graeme Souness signed him on a three year contract from Danish First Division club, FC Copenhagen (previously known as B1903), in September 1992. Made his **1992-93** PL debut in a 4-2 defeat at Aston Villa on 19 September 1992, followed by a 3-2 humiliation at Anfield, at the hands of Wimbledon. At the time of his arrival, the Liverpool defence was leaking goals to all comers, but gradually, after displacing Mark Wright, he formed a partnership in central defence with Steve Nicol, which seemed to steady the boat. It was short lived, however, as Liverpool collapsed after a damaging League Cup knock-out by an inexperienced and under strength, Crystal Palace team and stumbled from disaster to disaster. Next came a 5-1 defeat at Coventry, followed by an FA Cup knock-out at Anfield by Bolton Wanderers, when Liverpool's defence allowed the Second Division club's forwards to run riot. After another dismal display at Wimbledon, when he gave away an unnecessary penalty, he lost his place to Mark Wright and his future at Anfield must now be uncertain.

| | | | APPEARANCES | | | | GOALS | | | |
|---|---|---|---|---|---|---|---|---|---|---|
| Clubs | Signing Date | Transfer Fee | Lge | FL Cup | FA Cup | Others | Lge | FL Cup | FA Cup | Others |
| Liverpool* | 9.92 | £500,000 | 15+1 | 5 | 2 | | | | | |

## **PILKINGTON** Kevin William

Born: Hitchin, 8 March 1974

Height: 6'0" Weight: 12.6

International Honours: E Sch

**Position/Skill Factor:** Ideally built for a goalkeeper, he comes out well for crosses and stands up to attackers. Also has a very good kick.

**Career History:** A 1992 summer professional signing for Manchester United, he came to Old Trafford straight from school and has had to take his place in the queue behind Peter Schmeichel, Gary Walsh and more recently, Les Sealey. Called up for the first team squad in **1992-93** as substitute 'keeper for the home leg UEFA Cup-tie against Torpedo Moscow, was a good experience, although he wasn't used and apart from the odd reserve match, it was back to the "A" side that cruised to the Lancashire League title.

| | | | APPEARANCES | | | | GOALS | | | |
|---|---|---|---|---|---|---|---|---|---|---|
| Clubs | Signing Date | Transfer Fee | Lge | FL Cup | FA Cup | Others | Lge | FL Cup | FA Cup | Others |
| Manchester United* | 6.92 | - | | | | | | | | |

## **PIRIE** David Weir

Born: Glasgow, 15 April 1975

Height: 5'9" Weight: 11.5

International Honours: S Sch

**Position/Skill Factor:** Busy striker, who twists and turns around the box to bring chances for himself and his teammates.

**Career History:** A recent Ipswich Town professional signing, he first came to Portman Road as a trainee in September 1991, after starring for Scotland schoolboys and top scored for the club's youth side in **1992-93**.

| | | | APPEARANCES | | | | GOALS | | | |
|---|---|---|---|---|---|---|---|---|---|---|
| Clubs | Signing Date | Transfer Fee | Lge | FL Cup | FA Cup | Others | Lge | FL Cup | FA Cup | Others |
| Ipswich Town* | 7.93 | - | | | | | | | | |

## **POINTON** Neil Geoffrey

Born: Warsop,
28 November 1964

Height: 5'10"

Weight: 11.0

**Position/Skill Factor:** Very experienced left-back, he is a real professional. Has a good left foot and pushes forward at every opportunity to deliver accurate crosses, whilst sound in defence.

**Career History:** Although he signed associated schoolboy forms with Nottingham Forest in June 1979, on leaving school, he became an apprentice with Scunthorpe United in June 1981, before turning to the professional ranks with the "Irons" just over a year later. Prior to that he had made his FL debut in a 2-0 home defeat at the Old Show Ground against Torquay United on 6 February 1982 and the following season as an every present he was an integral member of the side that fought its way out of the Fourth Division in fourth place. That success was short lived, however, as the club were immediately relegated, but he was making his mark in the game and in November 1985, League Champions, Everton, swooped to take him to Goodison Park, following early season injuries that had forced them to move Pat van den Hauwe from left-back to the centre of the defence. Slotted straight into the side, but after 14 games, injury brought a premature end to his season and ruled him out of the FA Cup Final team to play Liverpool. Although he won a League Championship medal in 1986-87, the emergence of Pat van den Hauwe and Neil McDonald, made further opportunities in five years at the club hard to come by and he eventually moved to Manchester City in the 1990 close season as part of the deal which took Andy Hinchcliffe to Everton. Quickly making the left-back position his own as City progressed to fifth place in the First Division, he even got on to the score sheet when scoring a late winner at Aston Villa in his second appearance at Maine Road. He played probably the best football of his career in 1991-92 in a rapidly improving City team and it came as quite a surprise to many when he joined Oldham Athletic, along with Steve Redmond, as part of the deal that took Rick Holden in the opposite direction, prior to the start of the **1992-93** season. Has an extremely aggressive approach to the game and enjoyed an excellent first term at the club, being used as much as a winger as a full-back and his dead ball crosses on certain occasions, proved lethal. He even opened up the scoring in the final game of the season, the game they had to win against Southampton at Boundary Park to ensure Premier League survival, when an inswinging corner beat Tim Flowers as it swirled into the top right hand corner of the net. A month earlier he had done the same to England 'keeper, Chris Woods, in a 1-1 home draw against Sheffield Wednesday and all this after he had been carried off during a televised match against Sheffield United when sustaining a suspected broken leg, which luckily turned out to be just severe bruising. A snip at the price say the Oldham fans.

| | | | APPEARANCES | | | | GOALS | | | |
|---|---|---|---|---|---|---|---|---|---|---|
| Clubs | Signing Date | Transfer Fee | Lge | FL Cup | FA Cup | Others | Lge | FL Cup | FA Cup | Others |
| Scunthorpe United | 8.82 | - | 159 | 9 | 13 | 4 | 2 | 1 | | |
| Everton | 11.85 | £75,000 | 95+7 | 6+2 | 16+2 | 9+3 | 5 | | | |
| Manchester City | 7.90 | £600,000 | 74 | 8 | 4 | 4 | 2 | | | |
| Oldham Athletic* | 8.92 | £300,000 | 34 | 4 | | | 3 | | | |

# POLSTON John David

Born: Walthamstow, 10 June 1968

Height: 5'11"

Weight: 11.0

International Honours: E Yth

**Position/Skill Factor:** Centre-back who is strong both on the ground and in the air. First and foremost, he is a useful defender.

**Career History:** Elder brother of Andy, who also played for Tottenham Hotspur, he stepped out with "Spurs" as an apprentice in June 1984, before joining the club's professional ranks a year later. Made his FL debut in a 1-0 win at White Hart Lane against Coventry City on 15 November 1986, but in four seasons he made very few appearances as competition for places was intense. Followed in the footsteps of former "Spurs", Mark Bowen, Ian Crook and Ian Culverhouse, when he joined Norwich City in the 1990 close season. Settled in immediately at the heart of the "Canaries'" defence as a replacement for Andy Linighan, using his natural ability to make up for what he lacked in height and weight. Out of favour for the first half of 1991-92, he returned to the first team in January 1992 in place of Paul Blades and held his position till the end of the season, playing his part in the "Canaries'" FA Cup run which ended so disappointingly at the Semi-Final stage. Was not found wanting for one moment in **1992-93** and thrived on the responsibility of taking over as captain, following the injury sustained by Ian Butterworth. Showed a tremendous level of commitment, often throwing himself at point blank shots and an unintentional boot in the face from Chelsea's Mick Harford at Carrow Road left him with a broken nose. Carried off in the 43rd minute, he was forced to sit out the next five games, before making a return to first team duty. He only missed three more games as the club kept up their Championship challenge and he showed a rare sense of timing, when his only goal of the season, the winner at home to Aston Villa in March, arrived the day before he became a father for the first time.

| | | | APPEARANCES | | | | GOALS | | | |
|---|---|---|---|---|---|---|---|---|---|---|
| Clubs | Signing Date | Transfer Fee | Lge | FL Cup | FA Cup | Others | Lge | FL Cup | FA Cup | Others |
| Tottenham Hotspur | 7.85 | - | 17+7 | 3+1 | | | 1 | | | |
| Norwich City* | 7.90 | £250,000 | 77+3 | 3+1 | 11+1 | 5 | 6 | | | |

# POTTS Steven (Steve) John

Born: Hartford, USA, 7 May 1967

Height: 5'8"

Weight: 10.5

International Honours: E Yth

**Position/Skill Factor:** Steady and reliable with good qualities for a top class central defender. Not one to take risks, he has good pace and passes the ball simply, but well

**Career History:** One of the mainstays of West Ham United's recent surge back to the top flight, he first came to Upton Park as a 15-year-old associated schoolboy (May 1982), before progressing as an apprentice (July 1983) to the club's professional ranks in 1984 close season.

Although making his FL debut at home to Queens Park Rangers on 1 January 1985, he made only 17 (two substitute) League appearances during the next three seasons, but his patience was eventually rewarded when he won a regular place in the side at the expense of Ray Stewart in 1988-89. He remained at right-back until the signing of Tim Breacker from Luton Town in October 1990, but since then he has demonstrated his versatility by operating as a defensive midfielder, or central defender, as well as covering the right-back slot when required. He assisted the "Hammers" to promotion in 1990-91 and was one of their more consistent performers when the club were relegated one year later. Had a great season in **1992-93**, his best ever, as "Hammers" came back to the top flight at the first time of asking, when they pipped Portsmouth on goal difference to finish runners-up to Newcastle United. Ever present throughout the campaign, he took over as team captain, following Alvin Martin's injury in early January and there were no cries of indignation when he won the club's "Player of the Year" award. Now at his peak, he will be a major influence at Upton Park as West Ham look to consolidate their position in the Premier League this season.

| | | | APPEARANCES | | | | GOALS | | | |
|---|---|---|---|---|---|---|---|---|---|---|
| Clubs | Signing Date | Transfer Fee | Lge | FL Cup | FA Cup | Others | Lge | FL Cup | FA Cup | Others |
| West Ham United* | 5.84 | - | 185+10 | 20+1 | 23 | 14+1 | 1 | | | |

## POWELL Lee

Born: Caerleon, 2 June 1973

Height: 5'5" Weight: 8.10

International Honours: W "U21"-3

**Position/Skill Factor:** Nippy little winger who can play on either flank. Favouring his right foot, he has quick feet and the ability to unbalance defenders.

**Career History:** Joined Southampton as a trainee in July 1989, having been on associated schoolboy forms since December 1987. Turning professional at the end of 1990-91, he won a Welsh Under 21 cap, as a substitute, in Poland. Made an early first team appearance from the bench in a League Cup, Second Round tie, at home to Rochdale in October, but had to wait until the end of the season to make his FL debut as a substitute at the Dell against Luton Town on 21 March 1992. A third operation on a troublesome knee injury in the summer put his **1992-93** season on hold until the last day of September when he turned out for the reserves. Two weeks later he was on the bench for the seniors at Wimbledon and played 35 minutes of the second-half. Back in the reserves he was sent off for a second bookable offence in February. Given a further first team opportunity as a substitute at the Dell in a 0-0 draw against Everton, he created a good impression when producing some excellent crosses from the right touchline. Promises to be a very good player.

| | | | APPEARANCES | | | | GOALS | | | |
|---|---|---|---|---|---|---|---|---|---|---|
| Clubs | Signing Date | Transfer Fee | Lge | FL Cup | FA Cup | Others | Lge | FL Cup | FA Cup | Others |
| Southampton* | 5.91 | - | 1+5 | 0+1 | | 0+1 | | | | |

## POWELL Mark Anthony

Born: Ellesmere Port, 8 May 1975

Height: 5'9" Weight: 11.1

International Honours: E Sch

**Position/Skill Factor:** Right-back. Has a good delivery of the ball and loves to get forward to get his crosses over.

**Career History:** As an England schoolboy international hailing from the home of many an Everton talent, Ellesmere Port and already registered as an associated schoolboy (September 1989) at Goodison Park, he graduated through the club as a trainee (August 1991) to the professional ranks last summer. Given eight reserve outings in **1992-93**, following sound displays with the youth team, he will look to hold down a regular Central League place in 1993-94.

| | | | APPEARANCES | | | | GOALS | | | |
|---|---|---|---|---|---|---|---|---|---|---|
| Clubs | Signing Date | Transfer Fee | Lge | FL Cup | FA Cup | Others | Lge | FL Cup | FA Cup | Others |
| Everton* | 7.93 | - | | | | | | | | |

## POWER Lee Michael

Born: Lewisham, 30 June 1972

Height: 5'11"

Weight: 11.2

International Honours: IR Yth, IR "U21"-11, IR "B"

**Position/Skill Factor:** Striker who spells danger around the box, he is a natural goal scorer and shields the ball well.

**Career History:** A Londoner, he signed associated schoolboy forms with Norwich City in November 1986 and on leaving school he joined the club as a trainee (July 1988), before graduating to their professional ranks two years later. Prior to that, however, he had already made his FL debut at Aston Villa, when substituting for Robert Fleck in a 3-3 thriller on 28 April 1990. Had a couple of runs in the side during 1990-91 and impressed when scoring Norwich's first two goals in a 3-1 victory over Queens Park Rangers at Loftus Road. In 1991-92, he was somewhat eclipsed by the emergence of Chris Sutton, but returned to make a handful of appearances at the end of the season. Voted the Republic of Ireland's "Young Player of the Year" in **1992-93**, he has now amassed a record number of under 21 caps for that country. But with the signing of Mark Robins from Manchester United, although scoring two goals in three matches, his chances were going to be few and far between and after suffering illness and injury he had a handful of games on loan to Charlton Athletic. Came back match fit and refreshed, playing alongside Robins and scored four goals in 12 (including five substitute) matches, helping to secure wins over Crystal Palace, Manchester City and Nottingham Forest. Back in the reserves, however, an interesting aside was his appearance in goal and letting in six at Tottenham Hotspur, after the regular 'keeper was mistakenly not picked up on the motorway.

| | | | APPEARANCES | | | | GOALS | | | |
|---|---|---|---|---|---|---|---|---|---|---|
| Clubs | Signing Date | Transfer Fee | Lge | FL Cup | FA Cup | Others | Lge | FL Cup | FA Cup | Others |
| Norwich City* | 7.90 | - | 26+13 | 1 | 0+1 | | 10 | | | |
| Charlton Athletic | 12.92 | Loan | 5 | | | | | | | |

## PRESSMAN Kevin Paul

Born: Fareham, 6 November 1967

Height: 6'1"

Weight: 13.0

International Honours: E Sch, E Yth, E"U21"-1

**Position/Skill Factor:** Quick off his line for a big man, he doesn't commit himself too often and excels in one-to-one situations. Kicks very long with his left foot.

**Career History:** Born in Hampshire, he was spotted by Sheffield Wednesday playing for England schools and signed associated schoolboy forms in December 1981. He became an apprentice with the club on leaving school in June 1984, joining the paid ranks some 18 months later and made his Fl debut in a 1-1 draw at Southampton, incidentally, only a few miles from his birthplace, on 5 September 1987. Took over from Martin Hodge, who had been sold to Leicester City, towards the end of 1987-88 and did well until the last game of the season when Liverpool exploded five past him at Hillsborough in a 5-1 defeat. He was replaced by the returning Chris Turner and made only five first team appearances the following term. However, on regaining his place in 1989-90, he was unfortunately injured during the home game against Manchester City and was carried off, not to play again in a season that ended with the club being relegated to the Second Division. After recovering and playing in the first 22 matches of 1990-91, he was again replaced by Turner between the posts. Although returning to the side for the final match, with the club already assured of promotion back to the top flight, he missed selection for one of Wednesday's finest ever moments, the 1-0 League Cup Final victory over Manchester United. Highly regarded by the "Owls'" supporters, he was shut out of the Wednesday first team in 1991-92, except for one game, by the arrival of Chris Woods, the England 'keeper and was loaned to Stoke City for a short spell near the end of the season. Remained in the shadows of Woods in **1992-93**, playing only six first team games throughout the season, but when called upon he always gave sound displays and showed why he could well be first choice at a good many other Premier League clubs. Content to sign a contract last December that committed him to the club for a further four years, to keep in trim he made 28 reserve appearances in mid-week matches, while having to sit on the bench under the new Premier League goalkeeper substitute ruling. As part of Wednesday's future, he will grab the chance of a regular place with both hands when the opportunity arises.

| | | | APPEARANCES | | | | GOALS | | | |
|---|---|---|---|---|---|---|---|---|---|---|
| Clubs | Signing Date | Transfer Fee | Lge | FL Cup | FA Cup | Others | Lge | FL Cup | FA Cup | Others |
| Sheffield Wednesday* | 11.85 | - | 62 | 11 | | 4 | | | | |
| Stoke City | 3.92 | Loan | 4 | | | 2 | | | | |

## PRICE Stephen (Steve) John

Born: Rinteln, Germany, 30 November 1974

Height: 5'11" Weight: 11.7

**Position/Skill Factor:** Plays on the wide right of midfield, where he can take opponents on in order to deliver good crosses. Very quick off the mark and tidy in possession.

**Career History:** A recent Oldham Athletic professional signing and the second Premier League player to be born in Rinteln, the other is Darren Barnard of Chelsea, he first came to Boundary Park as a trainee in August 1991. Yet to play in the first team, having only had the occasional run out with the Central League side in **1992-93**, he could be one to watch out for, especially if he continues to develop as an old fashioned "outside-right".

| | | | APPEARANCES | | | | GOALS | | | |
|---|---|---|---|---|---|---|---|---|---|---|
| Clubs | Signing Date | Transfer Fee | Lge | FL Cup | FA Cup | Others | Lge | FL Cup | FA Cup | Others |
| Oldham Athletic* | 7.93 | - | | | | | | | | |

## PRIEST Christopher (Chris)

Born: Leigh, 18 October 1973

Height: 5'10" Weight: 10.10

**Position/Skill Factor:** Right-winger or midfielder. A creative player with plenty of stamina and good tackling ability. ability.

**Career History:** Joined the Everton professional staff during the 1992 close season, having previously been at Goodison as an associated schoolboy (July 1988) and as a trainee (June 1990). Yet to make a League appearance, he held down a regular central midfield spot in the reserve side during **1992-93** and appears to be on the fringe of the first team squad for the coming season.

| | | | APPEARANCES | | | | GOALS | | | |
|---|---|---|---|---|---|---|---|---|---|---|
| Clubs | Signing Date | Transfer Fee | Lge | FL Cup | FA Cup | Others | Lge | FL Cup | FA Cup | Others |
| Everton* | 6.92 | - | | | | | | | | |

## PRIOR Spencer

Born: Southend, 22 April 1971

Height: 6'1" Weight: 12.10

**Position/Skill Factor**: Central defender who is both powerful and mobile. Strong in the air and given time, he passes the ball well.

**Career History**: First signed for his local club in 1987, only a few months after joining as an associated schoolboy (April 1987). He made an early FL debut at the age of 17, when he was blooded at Gillingham on 25 February 1989 and did well enough to play 13 more games to the end of the season, when the "Shrimpers" were relegated to Division Four. Offered a professional contract, he started 1989-90 as a first choice central defender, but a serious injury in November sidelined him for the rest of the season. In his absence, the team maintained their excellent start to the season and earned an early passage to Division Three. He returned to action in September 1990, but though his team were setting the pace at the top of the table, he was displaced by new signing, Pat Scully, from Arsenal in January 1991 and played little further part in the successful promotion campaign. He finally established a regular place in 1991-92, as partner to Scully, when he missed only four games in the season as Southend seemed on course for a third consecutive promotion, or at least a Play-Off place, only to fade away. Only absent for one game in **1992-93**, as his team struggled long and hard, but ultimately successfully, to avoid relegation. Never overawed by an opponents pedigree, he proved the equal and more often than not, the better of many forwards last season. At home in the air and on the ground, he became a fine central defensive prospect at Roots Hall and signed for Norwich City during the summer.

| | | | APPEARANCES | | | | GOALS | | | |
|---|---|---|---|---|---|---|---|---|---|---|
| Clubs | Signing Date | Transfer Fee | Lge | FL Cup | FA Cup | Others | Lge | FL Cup | FA Cup | Others |
| Southend United | 5.89 | - | 135 | 9 | 5 | 7 | 3 | | | 1 |
| Norwich City* | 6.93 | £200,000 | | | | | | | | |

## QUIGLEY Michael (Mike) Anthony

Born: Manchester, 2 October 1970

Height: 5'6"

Weight: 9.4

**Position/Skill Factor:** Hard working midfield player, who sees passes early and constantly puts opponents under pressure. Great team man.

**Career History:** Joined Manchester City as a trainee in July 1987 and turned professional two years later. Has had to show extreme patience for a first team opportunity, which finally arrived in a Zenith Cup tie away to Sheffield Wednesday on 23 October 1991 in the unfamiliar position of right-back. Several weeks later he made his FL debut as a substitute away to Aston Villa on 7 December 1991 and made a few more appearances from the bench before the end of the season. Finally made his full League debut for City in **1992-93** when he played in the home game against Sheffield Wednesday in February and also came off the bench as a substitute on four other occasions. Captained the reserves throughout the season, making 26 appearances, but a niggling back problem interfered with team selection at times and needs to be sorted out before next season gets underway.

| | | | APPEARANCES | | | | GOALS | | | |
|---|---|---|---|---|---|---|---|---|---|---|
| Clubs | Signing Date | Transfer Fee | Lge | FL Cup | FA Cup | Others | Lge | FL Cup | FA Cup | Others |
| Manchester City* | 7.89 | - | 1+9 | | | 1 | | | | |

## QUINN Michael (Mick)

Born: Liverpool, 11 May 1962

Height: 5'10" Weight: 13.4

**Position/Skill Factor:** Striker with a wonderful goal sense. Times his runs to perfection and is always pouncing on defenders' mistakes. His quick brain often takes him clear of the opposition.

**Career History**: An old fashioned striker, who has scored at the rate of at least one in every two matches, nearly everywhere he has played, first came into League football with recently elected , Wigan Athletic in 1979, after being freed by Derby County, following an apprenticeship which started in July 1978. He had to wait to the end of the season for his FL debut, but when it duly came, he scored the first goal for the "Latics" in a 3-1 victory over Halifax Town on 12 April 1980. Became a regular selection in his second season at Springfield Park, finishing top scorer with 14 FL goals, but after a disappointing campaign in 1981-82, scoring only four goals in 29 appearances (despite which, his team were promoted to Division Three), he was released and joined Stockport County. An immediate success at Edgley Park, he became the first County player for 15 years to top 20 goals in a season, finishing with a final tally of 24 in the League. Despite this, his team could only finish 16th. He maintained his prolific scoring rate, with 15 FL goals from 24 games the following season, before he was snapped up by Second Division, Oldham Athletic. At Boundary Park, he was leading scorer in 1984-85 with 18 FL goals and netted another 11 in 1985-86, before his transfer to Portsmouth in March 1986, for a fee, the then struggling "Latics" could not afford to refuse. On his arrival at Fratton Park, Portsmouth were lying second in the Second Division table, but, unfortunately, four defeats in the last seven games left them three points short of a promotion place. They made no mistake the following season, however, even though five defeats in the last nine games cost them the Second Division Championship — Quinn leading the way with 22 FL goals. Sadly, the team was not strong enough to survive in the First Division, after 28 years absence and fell back to the Third Division, despite leading in November, after losing their last six games. However, Quinn enjoyed a good season, personally finishing as leading scorer with 18 FL goals. At the end of his contract, he opted to join Newcastle United, the fee being decided by the Transfer Tribunal. He made a sensational start for his new club, scoring four goals on his debut, versus Leeds in August 1989 and nine in his first five games, quickly becoming an idol of the St James' Park faithful. By the end of the season he had scored 32 FL goals (plus two in the FA Cup) to become the "Magpies'" highest scorer in a season since Hughie Gallagher (36) in 1926-27. Newcastle finished third in the Second Division that season and under the old rules would have qualified for automatic promotion. Instead, they were subjected to the vagaries of the Play Off system and tragically lost out to their north-east rivals, Sunderland, who had finished six points behind them. 1990-91, by contrast, was an anti -climax for both club and player, Newcastle finishing in mid-table and Quinn top scoring again with a mere 18 goals! The following season, Newcastle were struggling at the foot of the table when Quinn suffered a serious injury in October, which sidelined him until February 1992. During this time, Newcastle had signed David Kelly from West Ham to lead the attack and Kevin Keegan had replaced Ossie Ardiles as manager. Quinn never found favour with Keegan, partly because he was considered overweight and with Newcastle starting **1992-93** with consecutive victories in the League and with Kelly and Peacock leading the attack, his days were clearly numbered at St James' Park. Thus, he was loaned to Premier League, Coventry City, in November 1992, only his second taste of top flight football. If anything, his start at Highfield Road was even more sensational than that with Newcastle. After scoring twice on his "Sky Blues " debut, he proceeded to amass ten goals in his first six starts, including two in a 5-1 rout of Liverpool, followed by two more against Championship hopefuls, Aston Villa. Needless to say, the transfer was made permanent for a relatively modest fee! His best spell came early when it seemed he was a certainty to win the "Golden Boot" award, but then he and the club lost their way after Robert Rosario moved to Nottingham Forest. Balls stopped coming to him in the box and goals dried up. After a fairly barren spell, he scored two goals in the final two games of the season and even at the age of 30, big things are expected of him this coming term.

| | | | APPEARANCES | | | | GOALS | | | |
|---|---|---|---|---|---|---|---|---|---|---|
| Clubs | Signing Date | Transfer Fee | Lge | FL Cup | FA Cup | Others | Lge | FL Cup | FA Cup | Others |
| Wigan Athletic | 9.79 | - | 56+13 | 5 | 3 | | 19 | 1 | 1 | |
| Stockport County | 7.82 | - | 62+1 | 5 | 2 | | 39 | 2 | | |
| Oldham Athletic | 1.84 | £52,000 | 78+2 | 4 | 2 | | 34 | 2 | 1 | |
| Portsmouth | 3.86 | £150,000 | 115+6 | 7 | 7 | 4 | 54 | 6 | 7 | 1 |
| Newcastle United | 8.89 | £680,000 | 110+5 | 7+2 | 7 | 8+1 | 59 | | 4 | 8 |
| Coventry City* | 12.92 | £250,000 | 26 | | 1 | | 17 | | | |

## **QUINN Niall** John

Born: Dublin, 6 October 1966

Height: 6'4" Weight: 12.4

International Honours: IR Yth, IR "U21"-1, IR "U23"-1, IR-38

**Position/Skill Factor:** An old fashioned centre-forward who is one of the finest headers in the game. A rare phenomenon as not only is he a "target man", knocking down high balls for his colleagues, but is also a consistent goal scorer himself, with a devastating shot in addition to his aerial power.

**Career History:** Spotted by Arsenal playing junior football in the Republic with Manortown United, he first came to Highbury on leaving school and played with the juniors until signing as a professional towards the end of 1983. Had to wait a further two years for a chance in the first team, before making his FL debut against Liverpool on 14 December 1985 and he celebrated with a goal in a 2-0 home win. Established himself during the next season, as George Graham's young side began to take shape, but after heading the table for a long period, the "Gunners" faded to finish fourth. But compensation came earlier in the form of selection as a sub for the Irish Republic's full international side in Iceland on 25 May 1986 and later, a League Cup winners medal, following Arsenal's 2-1 victory over Liverpool in 1987. However, after the club had signed Alan Smith in the summer of 1987, opportunities became less frequent and he found himself languishing in the reserves. He played just two games during Arsenal's Championship winning season in 1988-89 and made only a handful of appearances in 1989-90, before he was rescued from obscurity when signing for Manchester City in March 1990. Marked his debut at Maine Road with a goal in a 1-1 draw against Chelsea and three more strikes by the end of the season, secured his place in the Irish World Cup squad for Italy. Only missed one game in 1990-91 as City climbed to fifth place in the First Division and he scored freely, with 20 in the League, as well as laying on chances for others. Enjoyed another excellent season in 1991-92, with 12 FL goals from 36 games, plus two goals in cup competitions, but was overshadowed by his striking partner David White, who scored 22 goals. Still an integral part of the Republic of Ireland side, he missed only three games for City in **1992-93**, but while only scoring nine in the new Premier League, initially seems low for a central striker, he had an excellent season overall. As always, he worked hard and created and assisted with openings and goal chances too numerous to mention and remains one of the leading target men in the country. He can score goals with his feet as well as in aerial combat and a great shot on the run in a 3-1 home win over Ipswich Town, testifies to that. It seems impossible to imagine him out of the side.

| | | | APPEARANCES | | | | GOALS | | | |
|---|---|---|---|---|---|---|---|---|---|---|
| Clubs | Signing Date | Transfer Fee | Lge | FL Cup | FA Cup | Others | Lge | FL Cup | FA Cup | Others |
| Arsenal | 11.83 | - | 59+8 | 14+2 | 8+2 | 0+1 | 14 | 4 | 2 | |
| Manchester City* | 3.90 | £800,000 | 121 | 10 | 8 | 3 | 44 | 2 | 2 | 1 |

## RADOSAVLJEVIC Predrag (Preki)

Born: Belgrade, Yugoslavia, 24 June 1963

Height: 5'8"

Weight: 12.1

International Honours: Yugoslavian Int

**Position/Skill Factor:** Left-winger with tremendous ability on the ball and full of tricks. Has a lovely left foot and a tremendous shot.

**Career History:** A former Yugoslav international, who played for his native country before emigrating to the USA. Popularly known as "Preki", for the convenience of journalists and commentators alike, he signed for Everton on the eve of the **1992-93** season, after spending seven years in the North American Indoor Soccer League (MSL), five with Tacoma Stars (1985-1990) and two with St Louis Storm (1990-1992), to whom Everton paid the transfer fee. During that time, he scored over 300 goals in the competition at the rate of nearly one strike per game, although it must be stated that goals are fairly cheap in five-a-side football and several players in the MSL have similar records. Played on the left-wing in a League Cup-tie at Rotherham United and three days later, on 26 September 1992, he made his PL debut against League Champions, Leeds United, at Elland Road. A slow start to his Everton career saw him make few appearances until he settled down into midfield and began to turn out improved and confident displays, following the turn of the year. Most notably, he was responsible, along with Beardsley, for perfectly weighted through balls which were often converted by the forwards. But by the end of the season, he himself had found the goal touch, including the "Toffees'" fourth in an amazing 5-2 win over Manchester City.

| | | | APPEARANCES | | | | GOALS | | | |
|---|---|---|---|---|---|---|---|---|---|---|
| Clubs | Signing Date | Transfer Fee | Lge | FL Cup | FA Cup | Others | Lge | FL Cup | FA Cup | Others |
| Everton* | 8.92 | £100,000 | 13+10 | 1 | 1 | | 3 | | | |

## RAWLINSON Mark David

Born: Bolton, 9 June 1975

Height: 5'8" Weight: 11.11

**Position/Skill Factor:** Midfield player who revels in the man-to-man marking job and is a good tackler. Well disciplined, he sticks to the task at hand

**Career History:** A recent professional signing for Manchester United, having been at the club as an associated schoolboy (November 1989) and as a trainee (July 1991), he was given a run out in a handful of reserve team games towards the end of **1992-93**, after playing mainly with the youth side in "A" and "B" team matches. Also, made infrequent appearances for United in the FA Youth Cup.

| | | | APPEARANCES | | | | GOALS | | | |
|---|---|---|---|---|---|---|---|---|---|---|
| Clubs | Signing Date | Transfer Fee | Lge | FL Cup | FA Cup | Others | Lge | FL Cup | FA Cup | Others |
| Manchester United* | 7.93 | - | | | | | | | | |

## READ Paul Colin

Born: Harlow, 25 September 1973

Height: 5'11" Weight: 12.6

International Honours: E Sch

**Position/Skill Factor:** A young striker who appears to have the knack of being in the right position at the right time.

**Career History:** Snapped up by Arsenal while still at school, he signed associated schoolboy forms in December 1987, before progressing as a trainee (July 1990) to professional status in October 1991. Although he still awaits a first team call-up, he proved his ability in the "Gunners'" youth team, when breaking all previous goal scoring records. Only made limited appearances for the reserves in **1992-93** and the coming season will be an extremely important one for him in his quest to play Premier League soccer.

| | | | APPEARANCES | | | | GOALS | | | |
|---|---|---|---|---|---|---|---|---|---|---|
| Clubs | Signing Date | Transfer Fee | Lge | FL Cup | FA Cup | Others | Lge | FL Cup | FA Cup | Others |
| Arsenal* | 10.91 | - | | | | | | | | |

## **READY** Karl

Born: Neath, 14 August 1972

Height: 6'1" Weight: 12.0

International Honours: W Sch, W "U21"-3, W "B"

**Position/Skill Factor:** Full-back, or central defender, who is good in the air. A steady player, he passes the ball simply and effectively.

**Career History:** After joining Queens Park Rangers as a trainee in May 1989, having been on the club's books as an associated schoolboy since March 1988, he turned professional on his 18th birthday. His first team debut came in a League Cup tie at home to Hull City on 9 October 1991 when he was used as a substitute. Later in the season made his FL debut at home to Wimbledon on 1 February 1992, deputising for David Bardsley at right-back. A member of the Welsh under 21 squad and a great prospect, who can play anywhere across the back four, he came into the side late in the **1992-93** season for two games as a replacement for first Alan McDonald and then Darren Peacock. Had an impressive game in a 2-0 home win over Coventry City, bringing a great save out of Steve Ogrizovic at one end of the park and clearing a shot from Peter Ndlovu off the line at the other. Not so fortunate in the second game, a 3-0 defeat at Loftus Road at the hands of Blackburn Rovers, after coming on as a substitute four days earlier on the same ground against 2-1 winners, Wimbledon. That was the measure of his Premier League performances during the campaign, before making a return to reserve team duties.

| | | | APPEARANCES | | | | GOALS | | | |
|---|---|---|---|---|---|---|---|---|---|---|
| Clubs | Signing Date | Transfer Fee | Lge | FL Cup | FA Cup | Others | Lge | FL Cup | FA Cup | Others |
| Q.P.R.* | 8.90 | - | 3+1 | 0+1 | | | | | | |

## **REDKNAPP Jamie** Frank

Born: Barton-on-Sea, 25 June 1973

Height: 5'11" Weight: 11.8

International Honours: E Sch, E Yth, E "U21"-7

**Position/Skill Factor:** Midfielder with all-round ability. Has excellent close control and is a very good passer of the ball.

**Career History:** The son of Harry, the former West Ham United, Brentford and Bournemouth player between 1964

and 1983, he was courted by Tottenham Hotspur as an associated schoolboy (September 1987). However, on leaving school, he joined his father who was then managing Bournemouth, as a trainee in September 1989 and made his FL debut at Hull City on 13 January 1990 at the age of 16 years and six months and was called up for his full debut later on in the season, before turning professional in the summer on his 17th birthday. Clearly a player of great potential, his name was already being mentioned as a target for bigger clubs and although not a first team regular in 1990-91, he was picked up by Liverpool in January as an investment for the future, one of Kenny Dalglish's last signings before his shock departure from Anfield. He received a first team opportunity earlier than expected due to Liverpool's long injury list and actually made his debut in a critical UEFA Cup tie away to Auxerre of France on 23 October which Liverpool lost 2-0, although overturning the deficit in the second leg. His Liverpool League debut came at Southampton on 7 December when he scored the equaliser after coming on as a substitute. Further opportunities came his way later in the season, but he played no part in the later stages of the "Reds'" FA Cup run. Along with Don Hutchison, he was Liverpool's major discovery of **1992-93**. Replacing the injured Paul Stewart early in the season, he held his place until the return of Ronnie Whelan in March. Having earlier been overshadowed by his goalscoring tyro colleague, he came into his own during November and December, with outstanding displays against Spartak Moscow in the European Cup Winners Cup and Middlesbrough (4-1) and Crystal Palace (5-0) in the League. Faded somewhat in mid-season, as Liverpool collectively disintegrated and was sent off for a second bookable offence in the 5-1 debacle at Coventry City in December, after scoring from a superb free-kick. "Young Eagle of the Month" for October, he made a scoring debut for the England under 21 side against San Marino, before becoming a regular selection. Returned in some style for Liverpool at the end of the season, following a back injury and promises plenty during 1993-94.

| | | | APPEARANCES | | | | GOALS | | | |
|---|---|---|---|---|---|---|---|---|---|---|
| Clubs | Signing Date | Transfer Fee | Lge | FL Cup | FA Cup | Others | Lge | FL Cup | FA Cup | Others |
| Bournemouth | 6.90 | - | 6+7 | 3 | 3 | 2 | | | | |
| Liverpool* | 1.91 | £350,000 | 32+3 | 6 | 3 | 5+1 | 3 | 1 | | |

## **REDMOND** Stephen (Steve)

Born: Liverpool, 2 November 1967

Height: 5'11"

Weight: 12.13

International Honours: E Yth, E "U21"-14

**Position/Skill Factor:** A very experienced central defender for one so young, he reads situations well at the back and is a good striker of the ball.

**Career History:** Although born on Merseyside, he signed as an associated schoolboy player with Manchester City (October 1982), before becoming an apprentice in July 1984, when leaving school. After turning professional he had to wait over 12 months for a chance of first team soccer and while he was learning his trade, he was captaining the City youth side to victory over local rivals Manchester United in the Final of the 1986 FA Youth Cup. By then, he had already made his FL debut at Maine Road against Queens Park Rangers on 8 February 1986 and soon began to hold down a regular place in the side. Played 28 times in the League as City were relegated to the Second Division at the end of 1986-87, but was ever present the following season as the team looked for a quick return and his form and popularity was such, that the fans named him as their "Player of the Year". As the club captain, he led the team back to the First Division as runners-up in 1988-89. A run of 138 consecutive League games was halted at the beginning of 1990-91, but he soon re-established himself and his experience was vital to a side who were challenging for a top three position for most of the season. After playing in all but one of City's first 30 games in 1991-92, he was suddenly dropped in late February, in favour of first David Brightwell and then Dutchman Michel Vonk and demanded a transfer. Moved to Oldham Athletic from City in the 1992 close season, along with Neil Pointon, plus £300,000, as Rick Holden travelled in the opposite direction. Started out with "Latics" on the opening day of **1992-93** and gave strong, determined displays, mixed with good football, which sometimes got him into difficulty at the back. Played in the first 20 games of the campaign, before being dropped following three heavy defeats, when it appeared he was caught out on several occasions while looking for an offside decision. Lost his place to Craig Fleming and apart from intermittent appearances, he didn't return to the side until Neil Adams made way for him in the last three vital games of the season. As the club avoided the drop by the narrowest of margins, he did well with simple, straightforward defending and can now look forward with renewed optimism to playing Premier League Football this season.

| | | | APPEARANCES | | | | GOALS | | | |
|---|---|---|---|---|---|---|---|---|---|---|
| Clubs | Signing Date | Transfer Fee | Lge | FL Cup | FA Cup | Others | Lge | FL Cup | FA Cup | Others |
| Manchester City | 12.84 | - | 231+14 | 24 | 17 | 11 | 7 | | | |
| Oldham Athletic* | 8.92 | £300,000 | 28+3 | 4 | 0+1 | | | | | |

## **REED** John Paul

Born: Rotherham, 27 August 1972

Height: 5'6" Weight: 8.11

**Position/Skill Factor:** Right-winger with good skills and a lot of pace who gets past defenders. A good crosser of the ball, he can also score goals.

**Career History:** First signing as an associated schoolboy (October 1987) and then as a trainee (July 1988), on graduating he turned professional for Sheffield United during the 1990 close season. Yet to play for United, he was loaned out to Fourth Division Scarborough, in order to gain playing experience and made his FL debut at Chesterfield on 12 January 1991. He did very well with five goals in 14 games, including a brace in a 2-0 win at Northampton Town and a late equaliser at Stockport County. He returned to Scarborough for another loan period in 1991-92, before finally making an appearance for the "Blades" as a substitute in their last match of the season away to Wimbledon on 2 May 1992. Although not being required for first team duty at Bramall Lane in **1992-93**, he continued to learn his trade with the reserves and also had a spell on loan to Darlington under old United manager, Billy McEwan.

| | | | APPEARANCES | | | | GOALS | | | |
|---|---|---|---|---|---|---|---|---|---|---|
| Clubs | Signing Date | Transfer Fee | Lge | FL Cup | FA Cup | Others | Lge | FL Cup | FA Cup | Others |
| Sheffield United* | 7.90 | - | 0+1 | | | | | | | |
| Scarborough | 1.91 | Loan | 14 | | | | 5 | | | |
| Scarborough | 9.91 | Loan | 5+1 | 1 | | | | | | |
| Darlington | 3.93 | Loan | 8+2 | | | | 2 | | | |

## **REEVES** Stephen (Steve) Terence

Born: Romford, 24 September 1974

Height: 6'0" Weight: 12.7

International Honours: E Sch

**Position/Skill Factor:** Goalkeeper who is technically sound. A great shot stopper, with good hands, he is also a very good kicker

**Career History:** Spotted as a potential England boys player, he first came to Everton as an associated schoolboy in February 1989, before progressing through the trainee (August 1991) ranks to sign professional forms during the close season. A regular in the youth side in **1992-93**, he also had half a dozen run outs with the reserves and will line up behind Neville Southall and Jason Kearton as "Toffees'" third choice this season.

| | | | APPEARANCES | | | | GOALS | | | |
|---|---|---|---|---|---|---|---|---|---|---|
| Clubs | Signing Date | Transfer Fee | Lge | FL Cup | FA Cup | Others | Lge | FL Cup | FA Cup | Others |
| Everton* | 7.93 | - | | | | | | | | |

## **REID** Peter

Born: Huyton, 20 June 1956

Height: 5'8" Weight: 10.7

International Honours: E "U21"-6, E-13

**Position/Skill Factor:** Indomitable midfield battler who never shirks a tackle and is constructive when in possession. Knows the game inside out, with a great footballing brain, he leads by example. Courage is another hallmark of this gritty player.

**Career History:** Probably the most vital ingredient of Everton's formidable team of the mid 1980s, which won two League Championships in 1984-85 and 1986-87, the FA Cup in 1984 and made three other Cup Final appearances in 1985, 1986 and 1989, he joined Bolton Wanderers straight from school, signing as an apprentice in July 1971, before turning professional three years later. Made his FL debut at Burnden Park when coming on as a substitute against Leyton Orient on 9 October 1974 and by the end of 1974-75 he was holding down a regular place in the side. He missed only three games during the next three seasons and won a Second Division Championship medal as the "Trotters" re-joined the top flight at the end of 1977-78. Suffering an injury at the start of the club's First Division campaign, he recovered to play 14 games, before breaking a leg on New Year's Day 1979 at snowbound Burnden Park, following a collision with George Wood, the Everton goalie, in a League match that was later abandoned. Out for over a year, he came back into a side that would be relegated at the end of the season. He played very few games in 1980-81, mainly due to contractual problems and returning to the team at the beginning of the next season, after just two matches, he had the incredible misfortune to break his right leg again during a League game at Barnsley. On recovering, Everton snapped him up at a basement bargain fee in December 1982, nearly three years after the "Toffees" had originally offered to pay Bolton £600,000 for his services! Injured almost before he got started at Goodison Park, he missed very few games in 1983-84 and won an FA Cup winners medal, following Everton's 2-0 victory over Watford. A member of the side that lost 1-0 to Manchester United in the 1985 FA Cup Final, he was out injured for a large chunk of 1985-86, but was back in time to play in Everton's third successive FA Cup Final, a 3-1 defeat against local rivals, Liverpool. Prior to that, his sterling club displays were finally translated into full international terms, when he was selected to play for England against West Germany in Mexico on 12 June 1985 and another honour followed as the PFA voted him as their "Player of the Year". Injuries were still a major factor in his career and he made only 15 League appearances as Everton won the League title in 1986-87. There was still plenty of spark left when he was allowed a free transfer to Queens Park Rangers during 1988-89 and when Howard Kendall was appointed manager of Manchester City, one of his first tasks was to bring him to Maine Road as player-coach. As inspirational as ever, he played 28 League matches for City in 1990-91, was appointed player-manager, on Kendall's departure in November 1990 and lifted the club into fifth place in the First Division. Continued to play First Division football in 1991-92, but following the signings of Steve McMahon and Fitzroy Simpson, he was expected to take a back seat. However, **1992-93**, the opening Premier League season, saw him play 20 (including four substitute) first team games, mainly due to an injury sustained by McMahon and with his commitment and willingness to chase and harry throughout, he often brought out the best from the younger players. However, at the age of 37, his footballing days must be almost behind him, but he is still a registered professional and who better to rejuvenate inept performances from the bench. Has a younger brother, Shaun, who played for Rochdale and York City.

| | | | APPEARANCES | | | | GOALS | | | |
|---|---|---|---|---|---|---|---|---|---|---|
| Clubs | Signing Date | Transfer Fee | Lge | FL Cup | FA Cup | Others | Lge | FL Cup | FA Cup | Others |
| Bolton Wanderers | 5.74 | – | 222+3 | 18+1 | 17 | | 23 | 1 | 1 | |
| Everton | 12.82 | £60,000 | 155+4 | 23+2 | 35 | 15 | 8 | 1 | 3 | 1 |
| Q.P.R. | 2.89 | – | 29 | 2+1 | | | 1 | | | |
| Manchester City* | 12.89 | – | 89+10 | 4+1 | 7 | | 1 | | 1 | |

## **RENNIE** David

Born: Edinburgh, 29 August 1964

Height: 6'0"

Weight: 12.0

International Honours: S Yth

**Position/Skill Factor:** Journeyman midfielder or Central defender. Experienced player who can sit in front of the back four, pick up the pieces, and spray long crossfield passes about.

**Career History**: A player who showed great promise for the future, while representing the Scotland youth side, he received limited opportunities to shine with his first League club, Leicester City, having first joined them as an apprentice in July 1980. Graduated to the club's professional ranks in May 1982, making his FL debut on 3 September 1983 at West Bromwich Albion and played a further 14 League games in a number of positions that season, as City struggled in the First Division after finishing Fourth in 1982-83. Unable to earn a regular place in the "Foxes'" line up after four seasons at Filbert Street, he was transferred for a modest fee to Leeds United in January 1986, at that time struggling in Division Two and immediately slotted into the centre of their defence. However, in 1986-87, he alternated between defence and midfield, before losing his place in January, thereafter being in and out of a team struggling to recapture its former glories. In the summer of 1989, he was transferred to Bristol City and enjoyed his most consistent season to date, playing mostly in central defence and missing only one match, as the Ashton Gate team stormed to promotion from Division Three. After losing his place midway through 1990-91, he reverted to midfield and was a regular selection up until his surprise move in early 1992 to Birmingham City of the Third Division, whom he assisted to promotion. Unable to show the same consistency of the previous season, mainly due to a series of injuries, he was in-and-out of the team in **1992-93**, as manager, Terry Cooper, strove to find an effective combination. With the season drawing to a close, he was surprisingly traded to Coventry City in exchange for "Sky Blue's" winger, David Smith, in a deal valued at around £100,000. At the age of 28, he probably felt that the opportunity of playing in the Premier League had passed him by, but he took the chance with both feet and although City only won one of the last nine games, he impressed as a player who should do well this coming season.

| | | | APPEARANCES | | | | GOALS | | | |
|---|---|---|---|---|---|---|---|---|---|---|
| Clubs | Signing Date | Transfer Fee | Lge | FL Cup | FA Cup | Others | Lge | FL Cup | FA Cup | Others |
| Leicester City | 5.82 | - | 21 | 2 | | | 1 | | | |
| Leeds United | 1.86 | £50,000 | 95+6 | 7 | 7 | 4 | 5 | | 1 | 1 |
| Bristol City | 7.89 | £175,000 | 101+3 | 8 | 9 | 5 | 8 | | | |
| Birmingham City | 2.92 | £120,000 | 32+3 | 1 | | 1 | 4 | | | |
| Coventry City* | 3.93 | £100,000 | 9 | | | | | | | |

## RICHARDSON Kevin

Born: Newcastle, 4 December 1962

Height: 5'10" Weight: 10.12

**Position/Skill Factor:** Very experienced underrated midfielder. Great competitor and a decisive tackler, he has the ability to swerve the ball and takes a lot of free kicks and corners.

**Career History:** Hailing from the north-east, he first came to Everton on associated schoolboy forms (July 1978) and on leaving school, a year later, he signed as an apprentice (May 1979). After turning professional, he had to wait nearly 12 months before making his FL debut at Goodison against Sunderland on 21 November 1981, but

by the end of 1981-82 he had settled nicely into the number six shirt. The following season he appeared for Everton in both the League Cup and FA Cup Finals. The club were defeated 1-0 by Liverpool in the former, but the "Toffees'" 2-0 victory over Watford in the latter, was recompense enough when collecting an FA Cup winners medal. Never an automatic first choice at Goodison with Paul Bracewell and Peter Reid dictating operations in central midfield, most of his appearances were on the left side of midfield, deputising capably for Kevin Sheedy and scoring several vital goals, but 14 League appearances in 1984-85 assured him of a League Championship medal, as Everton took the title. At the beginning of 1986-87, he moved to Watford and as an influential member of their successful side, his performance in the 3-1 victory over Arsenal in the Sixth Round of the FA Cup that season, impressed the "Gunners" so much that they signed him during the summer. Proving what a versatile player he could be, he replaced the injured Graham Rix and immediately became an important cog in the side that broke the club record with 14 consecutive wins. And following an incredible victory over Liverpool in the last match of 1988-89, having made 32 appearances for Arsenal, he added another League Championship medal to his list of honours. After playing in Arsenal's first 38 games in 1989-90, he suffered an injury towards the end of the season and, on recovering, he signed for the Spanish team Real Sociedad of San Sebastion, linking up with John Aldridge and Dalian Atkinson during the 1990 close season. Ironically, when John Toshack was reappointed manager of the Spanish club, he decided he only wanted native players in his team and the three expatriates returned to England, Richardson joining Dalian Atkinson at Aston Villa. Played in every one of Villa's 51 match programme without being substituted — a remarkable achievement in today's competitive environment, where few players escape injury during a season. As the team captain, he was yet again one of the most consistent players around and as in the previous season, was ever present in **1992-93**, not even being substituted. And, at the end of a tremendous season for both club and player, he just missed out on becoming the first man to win three League Championship medals with three different clubs, as Villa finished runners-up to Manchester United. Suffered his other main disappointment when Villa were knocked out of the FA Cup in a Fourth Round replay at Wimbledon, following his miss in a penalty shoot-out. A great example to the younger players, he tended to adopt a more "holding role" in the centre of the park, while Garry Parker pushed further forward.

| | | | APPEARANCES | | | | GOALS | | | |
|---|---|---|---|---|---|---|---|---|---|---|
| Clubs | Signing Date | Transfer Fee | Lge | FL Cup | FA Cup | Others | Lge | FL Cup | FA Cup | Others |
| Everton | 12.80 | - | 95+14 | 10+3 | 13 | 7+2 | 16 | 3 | 1 | |
| Watford | 9.86 | £225,000 | 39 | 3 | 7 | 1 | 2 | | | |
| Arsenal | 8.87 | £200,000 | 88+8 | 13+3 | 9 | 3 | 5 | 2 | 1 | |
| Real Soceidad (Spain) | 7.90 | £750,000 | | | | | | | | |
| Aston Villa* | 8.91 | £450,000 | 84 | 7 | 9 | 2 | 8 | 1 | | |

## **RICKERS Paul** Steven

Born: Pontefract, 9 May 1975

Height: 5'10" Weight: 10.11

**Position/Skill Factor:** Right sided midfield player. Skilful and comfortable in possession, with a good right foot, he is always looking to start a move. Has great stamina, he can play at both ends and is tidy in possession.

**Career History:** Came to Oldham Athletic as an associated schoolboy (July 1990), before becoming a trainee (August 1991) on leaving school and developing into the professional ranks by last summer. A regular for the youth team in **1992-93**, he was given a run in the last six reserve matches and did enough to convince the management that he might have a future.

| | | | APPEARANCES | | | | GOALS | | | |
|---|---|---|---|---|---|---|---|---|---|---|
| Clubs | Signing Date | Transfer Fee | Lge | FL Cup | FA Cup | Others | Lge | FL Cup | FA Cup | Others |
| Oldham Athletic* | 7.93 | - | | | | | | | | |

## **RIDEOUT Paul** David

Born: Bournemouth, 14 August 1964

Height: 5'11" Weight: 12.0

International Honours: E Sch, E Yth, E "U21"-5

**Position/Skill Factor**: Striker with instant control, who will always be among the goals. Good in the air, with much skill on the ground, he can finish with the best of them.

**Career History**: Nomadic player, who despite commanding many large transfer fees, has rarely lived up to his early promise. A man with a footballing pedigree, he was already an England schoolboy international star, when he signed associated forms for Swindon Town in September 1978. Just under two years later, on leaving school in June 1980, he joined the club as an apprentice and not only scored on his FL debut at the County Ground, in a 3-1 victory over Hull City on 29 November 1980, but at the age of 16 years and 107 days, he became Swindon's

youngest ever player. He played in 15 more games in 1980-81, before signing professional on his 17th birthday, winning a regular place the following season and finishing top scorer with 14 FL goals, although they did not prevent his team dropping into the Fourth Division for the first time. After top scoring again, with 20 FL goals in 1982-83 (which included an unusually high number of nine converted penalties), he was signed by Aston Villa in the summer. Although playing in more than half the number of games possible, he was never entirely sure of his place at Aston Villa, despite top scoring with 14 FL goals in 1984-85, during which he was "capped" several times for the England Under 21 team. It was a considerable surprise when, along with team mate, Gordon Cowans, he was sold to Italian First Division Team, Bari, in the summer of 1985 (a path followed by David Platt six years later). It was not a happy move for either player, as Bari were relegated in their first season in Italy, but to their credit both men "stuck out" their contracts in the obscurity of the Italian Second Division. In the summer of 1988, both returned to England, Cowans to Villa, Rideout to his native Hampshire, signing for Southampton. Despite an excellent start with the "Saints", scoring twice on his debut, he found it difficult to hold his place in competition with the Wallace brothers and the emerging Matthew Le Tissier, and subsequently, Alan Shearer. He briefly returned to Swindon on loan at the end of 1990-91, but no permanent move resulted. Soon into 1991-92, he was signed by newly promoted Notts County, to provide more punch to their limited attacking resources and despite scoring in his first two games, within two months he was out of favour. It came as a shock, therefore, when he was picked up by Glasgow Rangers only four months later, with County pocketing a considerable profit of £200,000 over his purchase price. With such a large playing staff, Rangers' need for another striker was unclear, and in competition with Ali McCoist and Mark Hateley, his opportunities were limited. Nevertheless, he played 11 games for the perennial Scottish Champions and was present for the end of season celebrations, albeit in an unfamiliar defensive role. In the summer of 1992, with Rangers deciding to reduce their colony of English players, he was unloaded to Everton, a move which was surely his last chance to shine at the highest level. Thrown straight into the first team in **1992-93**, he was unable to forge a partnership with Peter Beardsley and this, coupled with injury, saw him in and out of the team and frequently substituted, as Everton struggled near the foot of the table. With Tony Cottee rediscovering his form, competition for places increased. After Christmas he was dropped and only made two more full appearances, along with two as a substitute. Rather a disappointing term, with his lack of goals worrying, he will hope for another chance to "hit it off" with Cottee this coming season.

| | | | APPEARANCES | | | | GOALS | | | |
|---|---|---|---|---|---|---|---|---|---|---|
| Clubs | Signing Date | Transfer Fee | Lge | FL Cup | FA Cup | Others | Lge | FL Cup | FA Cup | Others |
| Swindon Town | 8.81 | - | 90+5 | 3 | 7 | | 38 | 2 | 1 | |
| Aston Villa | 6.83 | £200,000 | 50+4 | 4+2 | 1+1 | 1 | 19 | | | |
| Bari (Italy) | 7.85 | £400,000 | | | | | | | | |
| Southampton | 7.88 | £430,000 | 68+7 | 13 | 5+2 | 1 | 19 | 2 | | |
| Swindon Town | 3.91 | Loan | 9 | | | | 1 | | | |
| Notts County | 9.91 | £250,000 | 9+2 | 2 | 1 | 2 | 3 | | | |
| Glasgow Rangers | 1.92 | £500,000 | 7+5 | 0+1 | 1+1 | | 1 | | | |
| Everton* | 8.92 | £500,000 | 17+7 | 4 | 1 | | 3 | 2 | | |

## RILEY Steven

Born: Manchester, 6 February 1975

Height: 5'9" Weight: 10.9

**Position/Skill Factor**: Full-back who can play on both sides with comfort. A good defensive player, with pace, he is also a telling passer of the ball.

**Career History**: A professional signing for Manchester United during the 1993 close season, he first came to Old Trafford as a trainee in September 1991 and successfully graduated through the club's youth team. Played in the United side that performed with distinction, before losing to Leeds United in the FA Youth Cup Final in **1992-93** and is a promising young player.

| | | | APPEARANCES | | | | GOALS | | | |
|---|---|---|---|---|---|---|---|---|---|---|
| Clubs | Signing Date | Transfer Fee | Lge | FL Cup | FA Cup | Others | Lge | FL Cup | FA Cup | Others |
| Manchester United* | 7.93 | - | | | | | | | | |

## RIPLEY Stuart Edward

Born: Middlesbrough, 20 November 1967

Height: 5'11" Weight: 12.6

International Honours: E Yth, E "U21"-8

**Position/Skill Factor:** A left-winger who is good on the ball and has the ability to go past defenders when using his pace to good effect. Always looking to get into scoring positions.

**Career History:** A member of the local schoolboy team that won the FA schools trophy, it was not surprising that he joined Middlesbrough, first as an associated schoolboy (March 1983), then later as an apprentice (August 1984), before signing professional during 1985-86. Prior to turning professional, however, he had made his FL debut at Ayresome Park when coming on as a substitute against Oldham Athletic on 5 February 1985. After a short loan spell with Bolton, he played a few matches at the tail end of 1986-87 when "Boro" were relegated to the Third Division and became a regular the following season as the side returned to the Second Division as runners-up. Enjoyed an excellent season in 1987-88, playing 40 League games and scoring eight goals, including a hat-trick in a 6-0 home defeat of Sheffield United, which assisted Middlesbrough back into the First Division following the Play-Offs. But after only one season, the club was relegated, only recording one victory in their last 17 matches. Having just escaped further relegation in 1989-90, the "Boro" could consider themselves fortunate to reach the First Division Play-Off stage in 1990-91, before losing to Notts County. But when available for selection, he was one of their few stars in an ultimately disappointing season, scoring in each of the club's last four victories. Played in most of "Boro's" successful 1991-92 campaign, with long runs in the two major cup competitions, before clinching automatic promotion to the Premier League in the last match of the season. Having just helped "Boro" into the top flight, he became a surprise summer signing for the other new boys when he moved across the Pennines to Blackburn Rovers in exchange for a large fee. Started like a world beater in **1992-93**, when his great pace and trickery left defenders floundering in his wake and scored the opening Premier League goal for Rovers on his debut. Later, he struggled for a while as opponents wised up to his trickery, but he again proved his worth when playing in a floating role across the forward line after tactics needed changing. Missed only four matches, as big spending Blackburn stayed among the top six throughout the campaign.

| | | | APPEARANCES | | | | GOALS | | | |
|---|---|---|---|---|---|---|---|---|---|---|
| Clubs | Signing Date | Transfer Fee | Lge | FL Cup | FA Cup | Others | Lge | FL Cup | FA Cup | Others |
| Middlesbrough | 12.85 | - | 210+39 | 21+2 | 17+1 | 20+1 | 26 | 3 | 1 | 1 |
| Bolton Wanderers | 2.86 | Loan | 5 | | | 0+1 | 1 | | | |
| Blackburn Rovers* | 7.92 | £1,300,000 | 38+2 | 6 | 4 | | 7 | | 2 | |

## **RITCHIE** Andrew (Andy) Timothy

Born: Manchester, 28 November 1960

Height: 5'9"

Weight: 11.11

International Honours: E Sch, E Yth, E "U21"-1

**Position/Skill Factor:** A striker who has improved with age and experience. With good skill and a lovely touch, he pulls away from defenders well and gets into excellent scoring positions. Also makes great runs off the ball.

**Career History:** One of the most accomplished forwards in his heyday, he was a major factor in Oldham Athletic's rise to fame. It is interesting to speculate whether, if Manchester United had shown as much faith in him as their expensive imports, he would now enjoy a similar stature in the game to Gary Lineker and Ian Rush. First went to Manchester United as an associated schoolboy in October 1975 and on leaving school, he signed as an apprentice in September 1977. Less than three months later, on turning professional, he made his FL debut in a 6-2 win at Everton on 26 December 1977 and held his place for three more games until Stuart Pearson was fit enough to return to the side. The following season, he got an extended run, playing 16 times and scoring ten goals, including a hat-trick in the League against Leeds United. Not given many more opportunities to shine, although he scored another hat-trick against Tottenham Hotspur in 1979-80, he was allowed to leave for Brighton & Hove Albion early in the 1980-81 season. Never found his best form on the south coast, although as the club's top scorer with 13 League goals in 1981-82, he was exchanged for Terry Connor and signed for Second Division Leeds United at the back end of 1982-83. Spent four full seasons at Elland Road and although he showed glimpses of his talent, he and the club never quite hit it off. Contractual disputes were obviously a problem and he was on a weekly contract for well over a year before finally getting away and signing for Oldham Athletic during the 1987 close season. Despite missing eight games due to injury in his first season at Boundary Park, he delighted the fans with his 19 goals. Consistently finding the net, alongside Roger Palmer and Frankie Bunn, he had a glorious season in 1989-90, scoring 12 times in cup matches as the club reached the League Cup Final, losing 1-0 to Nottingham Forest and the FA Cup Semi-Final, before going out to Manchester United. But the heartaches of the previous season were forgotten in 1990-91, as he won a Second Division Championship medal and could look forward to playing again in the top flight, after an absence of eight years. Plagued by injury in 1991-92, he made only a handful of appearances in the First Division, although showing that his scoring touch had not deserted with four goals in an early season 7-1 thrashing of Torquay in the League Cup. Again his appearances were limited in **1992-93** as he recovered from a major operation to right the long standing back injury, which first laid him low two years earlier. Returned in January for a handful of appearances, but later stood down on suffering some reaction to the back and was forced to rest. However, he was almost back in full swing as the season came to a close and his three goals could not have been more important, as Oldham struggled to avoid the drop into the First Division. He scored the winner at Middlesbrough, the equaliser at home to Sheffield United and the third goal in the dramatic 4-3 victory over Southampton, that preserved the club's Premier League status for another year at least. Now back to his brilliant self, he will be a major force again in 1993-94.

| | | | APPEARANCES | | | | GOALS | | | |
|---|---|---|---|---|---|---|---|---|---|---|
| Clubs | Signing Date | Transfer Fee | Lge | FL Cup | FA Cup | Others | Lge | FL Cup | FA Cup | Others |
| Manchester United | 12.77 | - | 26+7 | 3+2 | 3+1 | | 13 | | | |
| Brighton & H.A. | 10.80 | £500,000 | 82+7 | 3+1 | 9 | | 23 | 1 | 2 | |
| Leeds United | 3.83 | £150,000 | 127+9 | 11 | 9 | 2+1 | 40 | 3 | 1 | |
| Oldham Athletic* | 8.87 | £50,000 | 14+13 | 15 | 6 | 3 | 70 | 17 | 3 | |

## **ROBERTS** Anthony (Tony) Mark

Born: Holyhead, 4 August 1969

Height: 6'0"

Weight: 12.0

International Honours: W Yth, W "U21"-2, W "B", W-1

**Position/Skill Factor:** A good shot stopper, he is a goalkeeper who never stops giving instructions to his defenders. Very good kicker from his hands.

**Career History:** Came to Queens Park Rangers as a trainee in November 1986 and after impressing in the juniors, he was taken on the professional staff during the 1987 close season. Made his FL debut at Loftus Road against Coventry City on 18 December 1987, when deputising for David Seaman and was unfortunate to let in two very late goals during a 2-1 defeat. Stood in for Seaman in 1989-90, keeping two clean sheets in five League games and in 1990-91, after starting the season as first choice, following the England goalie's departure to Arsenal, he was later replaced by the club's new signing, Jan Stejskal. With the consistent Stejskal showing such commanding form in 1991-92, he only made two first team appearances, versus Tottenham Hotspur in the League and Crystal Palace in the Zenith Cup. Finally established himself as the club's number one 'keeper in **1992-93**, not only displacing Stejskal between the sticks, but also winning his first Welsh international cap, albeit as a substitute for Neville Southall in the game against the Republic of Ireland. After appearing in seven games earlier in the season, he came back into the side at Sheffield Wednesday in December and remained from thereon in, as Rangers held their form to finish fifth in the new Premier League. A 1-0 defeat at Anfield, saw Liverpool miss two penalty kicks as Roberts made a brilliant save from Mike Marsh, while John Barnes shot wide from the other attempt. If he can keep free of injuries and steadily improve, he has a great future in the game.

| Clubs | Signing Date | Transfer Fee | APPEARANCES Lge | FL Cup | FA Cup | Others | GOALS Lge | FL Cup | FA Cup | Others |
|---|---|---|---|---|---|---|---|---|---|---|
| Q.P.R.* | 7.87 | - | 47 | 5 | 2 | 2 | | | | |

## ROBERTS Joseph Edward

Born: Congleton, 12 September 1974

Height: 5'8" Weight: 10.10

**Position/Skill Factor:** Goalscoring striker who is at his best in the penalty area. Reads the game well and seems to turn up in the right place at the right time.

**Career History:** First came to Manchester United as an associated schoolboy in November 1988, before progressing up the ladder as a trainee (July 1991) to sign professional forms during the 1993 close season. Impressed in eight reserve team matches in **1992-93** and was a member of the side that were runners-up to Leeds United in the FA Youth Cup.

| Clubs | Signing Date | Transfer Fee | APPEARANCES Lge | FL Cup | FA Cup | Others | GOALS Lge | FL Cup | FA Cup | Others |
|---|---|---|---|---|---|---|---|---|---|---|
| Manchester United* | 7.93 | - | | | | | | | | |

## ROBINS Mark Gordon

Born: Ashton-under-Lyne, 22 December 1969

Height: 5'7" Weight: 10.1

International Honours: E "U21"-6

**Position/Skill Factor:** Very skilful striker who does well with his back to goal, twisting and turning to get his shots in. Always looking to play his team-mates into goal scoring positions.

**Career History:** Came to Manchester United as a trainee on leaving school in July 1986 after being on the club's books as an associated schoolboy player (February 1984). Joined the professional ranks at the end of 1986, but had to wait nearly two years, before coming off the bench for his FL debut at Wimbledon on 22 October 1988. It was during United's FA Cup run in 1990 that he really came to the fore. He netted the only goal of the Third Round tie at Nottingham Forest and then the one that put the club on their way to a 3-2 win at Newcastle United in the Fifth Round. In the Semi-Final, he came on as a substitute to score the winner in the spectacular tie with Oldham Athletic, a goal that finally broke the resistance of the Second Division side. That goal was one of six he scored in six consecutive games. Finished the season with ten League and FA Cup goals and an FA Cup winners medal, following United's 1-0 win over Crystal Palace in the replayed Final. Remained in the shadows of Brian McClair and Mark Hughes in 1990-91, making just 19 appearances, 12 of them from the bench. Almost totally ignored in 1991-92, despite the fact that a shortage of goals in the second half of the season cost United the Championship. In one of his rare outings he scored two goals against Portsmouth in a League Cup tie, after coming on as a substitute. Signed by Norwich City in time for the start of the **1992-93** Premier League season, it would be true to say that Norwich fans forgot all about the transfer of Robert Fleck to Chelsea, following the opening day of the season. He showed all his predatory and uncanny goalscoring instincts, with two that day against Arsenal and went on to score more League goals for the club in a season, since Kevin Drinkell six years previously. His two goals at Chelsea inspired another tremendous comeback by the "Canaries", but the undoubted highlight was the hat-trick at Oldham on 9 November in front of the TV cameras. Disappointingly, for all concerned, he never reached his intended target of 20 goals — being out for a month with an ankle ligament injury and not finding the net after the disastrous home defeat at the hand of Manchester United. Has proved a real asset for City.

| Clubs | Signing Date | Transfer Fee | APPEARANCES Lge | FL Cup | FA Cup | Others | GOALS Lge | FL Cup | FA Cup | Others |
|---|---|---|---|---|---|---|---|---|---|---|
| Manchester United | 12.86 | - | 19+29 | 0+7 | 4+4 | 4+3 | 11 | 2 | 3 | 1 |
| Norwich City* | 8.93 | £800,000 | 34+3 | 2+1 | | | 15 | 1 | | |

## ROBINSON Mark James

Born: Rochdale, 21 November 1968

Height: 5'9" Weight: 10.6

**Position/Skill Factor:** Midfield player who can perform at full-back if required. Defends well and is very good going forward to cross quality balls into the middle. Also strikes excellent long passes from the back.

**Career History:** Signing as an apprentice for West Bromwich Albion on leaving school in June 1985, having earlier created a good impression as an associated schoolboy (March 1983), he was given an early taste of first team soccer. With the "Baggies" already on their way out of the First Division and looking to blood young talent in time for the coming season, he made his FL debut at the

Hawthorns against Sheffield Wednesday on 22 April 1986. Surprisingly, he was not offered a contract when his apprentice period expired at the age of 18, but he remained on the books as a non-contract player until the end of 1986-87, when he was released. Picked up by Barnsley, he had to wait until February 1989 for an extended run in the first team on the right-wing. However, the next two seasons were frustrating for him, still being unable to win automatic selection. Not until manager Mel Machin tried him out at right-back in the latter stages of 1990-91, did he appear to have a future at Oakwell. In 1991-92, he finally established a regular first team place in this position, which he held until his transfer to Newcastle United towards the end of **1992-93**. Made a slow start at St James' Park, with nine (seven as substitute) League appearances, a total that didn't qualify him for a First Division Championship medal, as the "Magpies" waltzed to the Premier League. However, the management have high hopes of him, either at right-back, or in midfield, a view that was supported when he did an excellent marking job on Oxford United's danger man, Chris Allen, in the penultimate game of last season. Expected to progress rapidly in the Premier League.

| | | | APPEARANCES | | | | GOALS | | | |
|---|---|---|---|---|---|---|---|---|---|---|
| Clubs | Signing Date | Transfer Fee | Lge | FL Cup | FA Cup | Others | Lge | FL Cup | FA Cup | Others |
| West Bromwich Albion | 1.87 | - | 2 | 0+1 | | | | | | |
| Barnsley | 6.87 | - | 117+20 | 7+2 | 7+1 | 3+2 | 6 | | | 1 |
| Newcastle United* | 3.93 | £450,000 | 2+7 | | | | | | | |

## ROBINSON Matthew Richard

Born: Exeter, 23 December 1974

Height: 5'10" Weight: 10.8

**Position/Skill Factor:** Left sided midfielder with a good touch and a great left foot. Makes runs that can often take him into the box for scoring chances.

**Career History:** A player with individual flair and a recent professional signing for Southampton, he first came to the club as an associated schoolboy (October 1989), before graduating through the trainee ranks (August 1991). Top scorer for the youth team in **1992-93**, at one stage he had notched eight from his first 13 appearances, but in having to overcome a thigh injury, it was hardly surprising that the goal rate dropped. Selected for the reserves in April, he is one to watch out for.

| | | | APPEARANCES | | | | GOALS | | | |
|---|---|---|---|---|---|---|---|---|---|---|
| Clubs | Signing Date | Transfer Fee | Lge | FL Cup | FA Cup | Others | Lge | FL Cup | FA Cup | Others |
| Southampton* | 7.93 | - | | | | | | | | |

## ROBINSON Stephen (Steve)

Born: Lisburn, Northern Ireland, 10 December 1974

Height: 5'8" Weight: 10.7

International Honours: NI Sch, NI Yth

**Position/Skill Factor:** Small, skilful striker, who is quick with good touch.

**Career History:** The captain of Tottenham Hotspur's recent successful youth team, he turned professional at the beginning of 1993, but has yet to make the first team. Initially came to White Hart Lane as an associated schoolboy (August 1989), before becoming a trainee (August 1991) when leaving school. Played less than a handful of reserve matches in **1992-93**, but seems to be a typical "Spurs'" player and should make further progress this coming season.

| | | | APPEARANCES | | | | GOALS | | | |
|---|---|---|---|---|---|---|---|---|---|---|
| Clubs | Signing Date | Transfer Fee | Lge | FL Cup | FA Cup | Others | Lge | FL Cup | FA Cup | Others |
| Tottenham Hotspur* | 1.93 | - | | | | | | | | |

## ROBSON Bryan

Born: Witton Gilbert, 11 January 1957

Height: 5'11" Weight: 11.12

International Honours: E Yth, E "U21"-7, E"B", FL Rep, E-90

**Position/Skill Factor:** Inspirational midfield player who has all the right ingredients. A strong tackler, he passes the ball well when in possession and is always looking to break into the opposition's penalty area to score vital goals. A great captain, he leads by example.

**Career History:** The outstanding midfield player of his generation, he became an England "icon", whose international displays were, if anything, greater than his club performances and his ability to snatch priceless goals out of nothing helped England to victory on many occasions and on others saved his team from humiliating defeat. His 26 goals from 90 England games, ranks him as England's sixth highest all-time scorer — an astonishing record for a player whose role in the team was as much defensive as attacking. A major influence in every game he plays, his career has been a catalogue of triumphs, mixed with long periods on the sidelines through injury. It is a tribute to his character that he has always come back strongly from each setback. A native of the north-east, he ventured south on leaving school, joining West Bromwich Albion as an apprentice in September 1972, before signing on as a professional in the 1974 close season. He made his FL debut at York City on 12 April 1975 and in his next two games, scored a goal apiece. The following season, he played in 14 League matches as Albion were promoted to the First Division, behind Sunderland and Bristol City, but his progress was hindered when he suffered two broken legs during 1976-77. However, he returned to win his first full England cap against Republic of Ireland at Wembley on 6 February 1980 and in October 1981, he became Britain's costliest player when he signed for Manchester United in a deal that included his team-mate, Remi Moses. He made his United debut in the heat of a Manchester "derby", a goalless draw in front of more than 52,000 fans at Maine Road. Immediately struck up a daunting partnership with Ray Wilkins in United's midfield, showing what a versatile player he was and it came as no surprise when he was appointed club captain and later captain of the England team. Although the League title always eluded the "Reds" prior to 1992-93, he has been more fortunate in the FA Cup and in a hat-trick of Wembley appearances, he has never been on the losing side. In 1983, he scored two goals in the 4-0 defeat of Brighton & Hove Albion, in a replay and later led United

*Bryan Robson*

to victory in 1-0 wins over Everton (1984) and Crystal Palace (1990), a match which also required a replay to settle the result. In both 1989-90 and 1990-91, he spent long periods out of the game and was sometimes used as a sweeper in order to prolong his career. Although only playing 15 League games in 1990-91, after missing the early part of the season, he came back to win a European Cup Winners Cup medal at the end of a pulsating 2-1 victory over Barcelona, following the disappointment of the 1-0 League Cup defeat at the hands of Sheffield Wednesday, just three weeks earlier. Skippered England in the 1982 and 1986 World Cups, although on both occasion, his personal involvement was interrupted by injury and his opening goal after only 27 seconds in England's first game of the 1982 World Cup against France is still the fastest goal ever scored in the tournament. Although a regular member of United's team for the first-half of 1991-92, his absence through injury for much of the second-half of the season was considered to be a major factor in the club's failure to land the League Championship, which appeared to be theirs for the taking until the closing weeks of the campaign. Finally realised his long-standing dream of winning a League Championship medal in **1992-93**, as United brought the title back to Old Trafford after an absence of 26 years, but as the club captain, his playing season had been a frustrating one. Out of action for much of the time, with various injuries, even when fit he struggled to get into the side and appeared in only 17 (including 11 substitute) games. However, when he did play he could always be guaranteed to give of his best and it was befitting that the last goal in the club's Premier League programme, although the title already belonged to them, should fall to him when he got in behind Wimbledon's offside trap for the winner. One of the game's great servants, he must surely now be near the end of a wonderful career, especially having won all the honours on offer and will probably be looking to go into management before too long. His younger brother, Gary, played for West Bromwich Albion in 1992-93, but was freed in the close season and has joined Bradford City.

| | | | APPEARANCES | | | | GOALS | | | |
|---|---|---|---|---|---|---|---|---|---|---|
| Clubs | Signing Date | Transfer Fee | Lge | FL Cup | FA Cup | Others | Lge | FL Cup | FA Cup | Others |
| West Bromwich Albion | 8.74 | – | 194+4 | 17+1 | 10+2 | 12 | 39 | 2 | 2 | 3 |
| Manchester United* | 10.81 | £1,500,000 | 316+14 | 45+1 | 32+1 | 28+1 | 73 | 5 | 9 | 10 |

# ROBSON Mark Andrew

Born: Newham, 22 May 1969

Height: 5'7"

Weight: 10.2

**Position/Skill Factor:** Winger with great skill and balance who, more often than not, beats defenders with ease. With two good feet, he is also a great crosser of the ball.

**Career History:** As a diminutive London born youngster, he started his soccer career with Fourth Division, Exeter City, first as an associated schoolboy (July 1984) and then as an apprentice (August 1985), before signing professional at the end of 1986. Prior to that, however, he had shown such promise that he was introduced to the first team, making his FL debut at home to Lincoln City on 11 October 1986 and scoring the first goal in a 2-0 victory. He held his place up to the end of the season, when he was picked up by David Pleat, then manager of Tottenham Hotspur, as an investment for the future, but had to wait until December 1988 before making his "Spurs'" debut(as a substitute) and February 1989 for his first full appearance. Apparently, he never impressed new manager Terry Venables greatly and with over 40 professionals on the books at White Hart Lane, his opportunities were scarce. Several short term loans to Watford, Plymouth Argyle and his original club, Exeter, did not lead to anything and finally, in the summer of 1992, over two years since his last outing for "Spurs", he was granted a free transfer. Picked up by Billy Bonds for West Ham United, he returned to his roots, having stood on the terraces as a young supporter, but it wasn't his signing for the club that created the surprise in **1992-93,** just his brilliant performances. He turned out to be an outstanding aquisition and for a player, whose career had previously been held back by injury, he was a revelation, missing just two League games and scoring eight goals, as the "Hammers" stormed back to the top flight at the first time of asking, as runners-up to Newcastle United. Scored West Ham's "Goal of the Season" at Millwall when he beat two defenders with ease, before flicking the ball over the 'keeper and not known as one to head the ball, he even picked up one of that variety in a 2-1 win over Leicester City. With Premier League soccer on the menu at Upton Park this coming season, he is sure to offer his old club, "Spurs", a warm welcome.

| | | | APPEARANCES | | | | GOALS | | | |
|---|---|---|---|---|---|---|---|---|---|---|
| Clubs | Signing Date | Transfer Fee | Lge | FL Cup | FA Cup | Others | Lge | FL Cup | FA Cup | Others |
| Exeter City | 12.86 | – | 26 | | 2 | 2 | 7 | | | |
| Tottenham Hotspur | 7.87 | £50,000 | 3+5 | 1 | | | | | | |
| Reading | 3.88 | Loan | 5+2 | | | | | | | |
| Watford | 10.89 | Loan | 1 | | | | | | | |
| Plymouth Argyle | 12.89 | Loan | 7 | | | | | | | |
| Exeter City | 1.92 | Loan | 7+1 | | | 3 | 1 | | | 1 |
| West Ham United* | 8.92 | – | 41+3 | 2 | 2 | 4+1 | 8 | | 1 | |

# ROBSON Stewart Ian

Born: Billericay, 6 November 1964

Height: 5'11" Weight: 11.13

International Honours: E Yth, E "U21"-8

**Position/Skill Factor:** Midfielder with a great attitude to the game, having to overcome terrible injury problems. A tenacious player, who likes to get forward for a shooting opportunity, he is also a good passer of the ball.

**Career History:** One of the few players to come into the professional game after a Public School education, he was discovered by Arsenal while playing at Brentwood and signed associated schoolboy forms in December 1978. On leaving school in May 1981, he joined the club as an apprentice and turned over to the paid ranks just seven months later. At the same time, he made his FL debut at

West Ham United on 5 December 1981 and within a couple of months had settled into the Arsenal midfield. Unfortunately for him, the club were not among the honours during his time with them, but he impressed the fans well enough to become the "Gunners'" "Player of the Year" in 1985. After losing his place in the side to Steve Williams early in 1986-87, he was eventually transferred to West Ham United and immediately slotted into midfield, alongside his old team-mate, Liam Brady. Injured for most of 1988-89, he was powerless to assist the "Hammers" as they struggled against ultimate relegation and on top of that he was then sidelined for most of the following season, managing only seven League games. On returning, midway through 1990-91, for the FA Cup match against Aldershot, he couldn't finish the match and a few weeks later was loaned out to Coventry City, who signed him on a free transfer at the end of the season. Thought by many to be "finished" at the top level, he proved to be one of the "Sky Blues'" few successes in a dismal season, missing only five FL games during the 1991-92 and scoring three goals (worth seven points to his team), which in the final analysis helped the club to avoid relegation by the skin of their teeth. He was justly voted the supporters "Player of the Year". Started the **1992-93** campaign brilliantly, being "Man of the Match" on a couple of occasions, as City stormed to the top of the table. When everyone thought his terrrible injury problems were now behind him, misfortune struck once again. An eye infection that kept him out for six games, returned and on being stripped of the captaincy and coming back for a couple of games at the end of February, a recurrence of the hamstring injury more or less finished his season. Apart from that, continued homesickness, a couple of newspaper articles which brought a reprimand from City and interest from a number of London clubs, further destablised the situation. With a year of his contract to run, he must put last season behind him and hope that he can remain injury free, as City strive to recapture the form they showed they were capable of.

| | | | APPEARANCES | | | | GOALS | | | |
|---|---|---|---|---|---|---|---|---|---|---|
| Clubs | Signing Date | Transfer Fee | Lge | FL Cup | FA Cup | Others | Lge | FL Cup | FA Cup | Others |
| Arsenal | 11.81 | – | 150+1 | 20 | 13 | 2 | 16 | 3 | 1 | 1 |
| West Ham United | 1.87 | £700,000 | 68+1 | 8 | 6 | 1 | 4 | 1 | 1 | |
| Coventry City* | 3.91 | – | 54+2 | 2 | 1 | 1 | 3 | | | |

## **ROCASTLE David** Carlyle

Born: Lewisham, 2 May 1967

Height: 5'9" Weight: 11.12

International Honours: E "U21"-14, E"B", E-14

**Position/Skill Factor:** Skilful right-sided midfield player with good vision and quick feet, who always manages to find space. Is capable of scoring spectacular goals.

**Career History:** First came to Arsenal as an associated schoolboy in May 1982 and on leaving school, signed as an apprentice in August 1983. Made his FL debut, nine months after turning over to the paid ranks, at Highbury, against Newcastle United on 28 September 1985. Soon became a regular on the "Gunners'" right flank, missing only a handful of games during the next couple of seasons and won a League Cup winners medal, following Arsenal's 2-1 victory over Liverpool in 1987. Ever present in 1988-89, as the club won the League Championship, he was rewarded at full international level with an England cap against Denmark on 7 June 1989. The following season saw the club slip to fourth place in the League and this coincided with him suffering a loss of form. Worse was to follow in 1990-91, when after playing in the first ten League games, he lost his place in the side and only made another three appearances as Arsenal won the League Championship for the second time in three years. Made a highly creditable comeback in 1991-92 in a new role in central midfield, playing in all but three games of the campaign and scoring one of the goals of the season in a 1-1 draw away to League leaders, Manchester United in October. Also won a recall to the England squad, playing three times, but was not included in the squad for the European Championship Finals. Having already been the subject of several bids from Leeds United, in a surprise £2 million summer signing, he joined the Yorkshiremen in time for the **1992-93** Premier League season and broke the club transfer fee record into the bargain. Apparently signed as Gordon Strachan's successor, he had to wait patiently, as the Scotsman's injury proved not as serious as first thought and didn't play a full League game until November. His opportunity finally came when David Batty was ruled unfit and he played a midfield pivotal role in orchestrating a fine win over his old mates at Arsenal, which justifiably earned him the "Man of the Match" award. However, following that short lived success, although playing in over half of the remaining games, many of them were as a substitute, while others were in varying roles and he was never given the chance of a settled run. Mainly because of this, he had to endure press speculation all season, linking him to a number of clubs and it can only get better in 1993-94.

| | | | APPEARANCES | | | | GOALS | | | |
|---|---|---|---|---|---|---|---|---|---|---|
| Clubs | Signing Date | Transfer Fee | Lge | FL Cup | FA Cup | Others | Lge | FL Cup | FA Cup | Others |
| Arsenal | 12.84 | - | 204+14 | 32+1 | 18+2 | 9 | 24 | 6 | 4 | |
| Leeds United* | 8.92 | £2,000,000 | 11+7 | 0+2 | 0+3 | 2+1 | 1 | | | |

## ROCHE David

Born: Newcastle, 13 December 1970

Height: 5'11" Weight: 12.1

**Position/Skill Factor:** Full of enthusiasm, he can play equally well at the back or in midfield. A good passer, who is always looking for the return ball in order to get forward into shooting range.

**Career History:** A local discovery and a 1988 close season professional signing for Newcastle United, he first came to the club as an associated schoolboy in June 1986, eventually becoming a trainee (June 1987) under the YTS scheme. Made his FL debut as a substitute in a 1-0 defeat at Highbury against the prospective League Champions, Arsenal on 15 April 1988, playing in a side doomed to relegation to the Second Division. Appeared to have little future at St James' Park, until Ossie Ardiles gave youth its fling at the end of 1990-91 and in a short spell, Roche impressed sufficiently for the new manager to offer him a new three year contract. A regular member of the first team squad in 1991-92, until the dismissal of Ardiles and the arrival of Kevin Keegan as manager in February 1992. In common with most of Ossies' "Young Eagles", he was then discarded in favour of more experienced players and had a disappointing **1992-93**, making only one first team appearance, early on, as a substitute at Bari in the Anglo-Italian Cup and playing no part in the club's First Division Championship win. Went on loan to Gateshead in the Vauxhall Conference and also to Peterborough United, playing in four League games. Interestingly, he played in the side that was beaten 3-0 by Newcastle at St James' Park and was then the subject of some controversy when Peterborough claimed that he had been sent to them clearly overweight and unfit. Currently on the transfer list, he appears to have no future at United.

| | | | APPEARANCES | | | | GOALS | | | |
|---|---|---|---|---|---|---|---|---|---|---|
| Clubs | Signing Date | Transfer Fee | Lge | FL Cup | FA Cup | Others | Lge | FL Cup | FA Cup | Others |
| Newcastle United* | 8.88 | - | 23+13 | 2 | 1 | 1+2 | | | | |
| Peterborough United | 1.93 | Loan | 4 | | | | | | | |

## ROGERS Paul Anthony

Born: Portsmouth, 21 March 1965

Height: 6'0"

Weight: 11.13

International Honours: E Semi-Pro Int

**Position/Skill Factor:** All-round midfield player who can both pass and defend well.

**Career History:** An England semi-professional international from 1989 to 1991 and a stockbroker by profession, he had played nine years for Sutton United in the Isthmian League, Vauxhall-Opel League and Vauxhall Conference when, "out of the blue", Dave Bassett persuaded him to give up his lucrative career and sign professional for Sheffield United at the age of 26. As with many of Bassett's signings it seemed crazy, but it worked! After making his FL debut in midfield away to Luton Town on 22 February 1992 in place of the injured Michael Lake, he took the leap from the Vauxhall League to the First Division in his stride and held his place till the end of the season, helping the "Blades" to rise from 18th place (on his debut) to a final place of ninth. Started **1992-93** out of the team, having lost his place to Lake, but regained it after five games and became a valued member of the squad, with 27 (including one substitute) PL appearances to his credit. Scored his first goal for the club in the Second Round of the League Cup at Bristol City and has undoubtedly benefited from full pre-season training for the first time in his career.

| | | | APPEARANCES | | | | GOALS | | | |
|---|---|---|---|---|---|---|---|---|---|---|
| Clubs | Signing Date | Transfer Fee | Lge | FL Cup | FA Cup | Others | Lge | FL Cup | FA Cup | Others |
| Sheffield United* | 1.92 | £35,000 | 39+1 | 4 | 3 | | 3 | 1 | | |

## ROSENTHAL Ronny

Born: Haifa, Israel, 4 October 1963

Height: 5'10" Weight: 11.12

International Honours: Israeli Int

**Position/Skill Factor:** Excellent striker with pace, skill and a terrific left foot. Always looking to get shots in, he is very quick over the vital first ten yards.

**Career History:** Starting out in his native Israel with Maccabi, Tel Aviv, he arrived at Liverpool in March 1990, following experience with leading Belgian teams, FC Brugge and Standard Liege. Initially at Anfield on loan, the move became permanent during the 1990 close season after he had made a sensational start in English soccer. Came off the bench for his FL debut, in front of the Kop against Southampton on 31 March 1990. Two weeks later, when deputising for the injured Ian Rush at Charlton Athletic, he made a dream start, scoring a remarkable hat-trick, consisting of two breakaway solo goals and a bullet header. He followed that up with a goal in his next match against Nottingham Forest, scoring another against Chelsea and two more in the final game of the season at Coventry City, with Liverpool having already been crowned League Champions. Rosenthal's introduction, galvanised Liverpool's end of season flourish to their 18th League Championship when it appeared to be ending in anti-climax after the "Reds'" shock defeat by Crystal Palace in the FA Cup Semi-Final. An instant hero with Liverpool supporters because of his direct approach, wherever he receives the ball, he has only one thought in mind — to put his head down and charge towards goal until he can get in a shot. Unfortunately, this style is inimical to Liverpool's passing game and in 1991-92 he was used by the management more as a substitute to save games slipping away from Liverpool's grasp, rather than as an integral member of the team. With the departure of Dean Saunders to Aston Villa in September, Rosenthal at last had the opportunity to establish a regular place in the Liverpool line-up in **1992-93**, as a partner to Rush. Sadly, he did not grasp it. In his second full game of the season at Aston Villa he missed a glorious chance to give the "Reds" the lead when he beat the offside trap, rounded the 'keeper and faced with the formality of stroking the ball into a empty net from five yards, elected to finish with a flourish and hit the bar instead of the net! Although he scored later in the game, Liverpool were by then well beaten 4-2 and even when he cracked in two individual goals at Anfield against Middlesbrough in November and a last minute winner versus Everton in March, he remained a peripheral first choice, either in-and-out of the team, a frequent substitute, or replaced after starting the game. Transfer listed at the end of the season, he was expected to join the Turkish club, Besiktas.

| | | | APPEARANCES | | | | GOALS | | | |
|---|---|---|---|---|---|---|---|---|---|---|
| Clubs | Signing Date | Transfer Fee | Lge | FL Cup | FA Cup | Others | Lge | FL Cup | FA Cup | Others |
| Liverpool* | 3.90 | £1,000,000 | 32+39 | 2+7 | 5+3 | 2+5 | 21 | 1 | | |

## **ROWE** **Ezekiel (Zeke)** Bartholomew

Born: Stoke Newington, 30 October 1973

Height: 6'0" Weight: 12.8

**Position/Skill Factor:** Striker with great pace, who is a willing runner into the channels. Puts defenders under pressure and picks up the pieces.

**Career History:** A 1992 close season signing for Chelsea, he first came to Stamford Bridge as an associated schoolboy in April 1989, before advancing as a trainee in July 1990. Yet to make his first team debut, having played his football with the reserves in **1992-93**, he is one of several youngsters who could get the opportunity of doing so under Glenn Hoddle.

| | | | APPEARANCES | | | | GOALS | | | |
|---|---|---|---|---|---|---|---|---|---|---|
| Clubs | Signing Date | Transfer Fee | Lge | FL Cup | FA Cup | Others | Lge | FL Cup | FA Cup | Others |
| Chelsea* | 6.92 | - | | | | | | | | |

## **ROWNTREE** **Michael** Clive

Born: Hartlepool, 18 November 1973

Height: 5'6" Weight: 10.1

**Position/Skill Factor:** Very quick striker who takes defenders on and can finish well.

**Career History:** Signed professional forms for Sheffield Wednesday during the 1992 close season, having previously been at Hillsborough as an associated schoolboy (October 1988) and as a trainee (July 1990). Yet to play first team football, he remained on the fringe of the reserve side in **1992-93**, with only seven appearances and will be expected to "beef" that up this coming season.

| | | | APPEARANCES | | | | GOALS | | | |
|---|---|---|---|---|---|---|---|---|---|---|
| Clubs | Signing Date | Transfer Fee | Lge | FL Cup | FA Cup | Others | Lge | FL Cup | FA Cup | Others |
| Sheffield Wednesday* | 6.92 | - | | | | | | | | |

## **RUDDOCK** **Neil**

Born: Wandsworth, 9 May 1968

Height: 6'2" Weight: 12.6

International Honours: E Yth, E "U21"-4

**Position/Skill Factor:** Very strong central defender, who attacks the ball well in the air and heads bravely. Has a great left foot and can hit 50 yard diagonal balls with no difficulty.

**Career History:** Came through the Millwall junior academy, first as an associated schoolboy (October 1983) and then as an apprentice (June 1984), before turning professional in March 1986. Transferred to Tottenham Hotspur one month later, without a single League appearance at the Den, he made his FL debut at White Hart Lane against Charlton Athletic on 18 April 1987 and played three more times that season. At the end of 1987-88, after just three more full appearances, he returned to his former club, Millwall, who had recently been promoted to the First Division, for a fee six times the original amount. Even stranger, in view of the large transfer fee, was the fact that he spent eight months at Millwall without getting a full 90 minutes on the park in a League match. He was then on the move yet again, this time to Southampton. Replacing Kevin Moore at the heart of the defence, he came into a side that was hovering dangerously close to the bottom of the First Division, having gone 13 games without a win. Played 13 matches in 1988-89, as the "Saints" finished outside the danger zone and apart from a short spell out of the side in 1989-90, he settled down as a regular. An exemplar of Southampton's physical approach, he played for most of the 1991-92 season when not suspended. He was sent off twice and booked in every other game up to Christmas, but seemed to "clean up his act" in the New Year. In another bizarre twist to his career, he returned to Tottenham Hotspur soon after the end of the season as the Londoners looked to shore up a defence that had leaked 63 League goals during the season. Began his second spell at the club as captain, but was sent off against Crystal Palace in the third game of the **1992-93** Premier League season. However, with the return of Gary Mabbutt, he went from strength to strength, missing only four games and having the time to score four goals, one of them a thunderous free-kick against Norwich City on Good Friday. One of the most recent of Terry Venables' signings, he faced a difficult new season ahead in the wake of the "Spurs'" chief executive's dismissal, following the well documented "bust-up" at the club with Alan Sugar. After much soul searching, he told the new manager, Ossie Ardiles, that he no longer wished to play for the club and was extremely happy to get away, when Liverpool met "Spurs'" asking price. Once he puts the events of this summer behind him, he should do very well at Liverpool.

| | | | APPEARANCES | | | | GOALS | | | |
|---|---|---|---|---|---|---|---|---|---|---|
| Clubs | Signing Date | Transfer Fee | Lge | FL Cup | FA Cup | Others | Lge | FL Cup | FA Cup | Others |
| Millwall | 3.86 | - | | | | 3+1 | | | | 1 |
| Tottenham Hotspur | 4.86 | £50,000 | 7+2 | | 1+1 | | | | 1 | |
| Millwall | 6.88 | £300,000 | 0+2 | 2 | | 1+1 | 1 | 3 | | |
| Southampton | 2.89 | £250,000 | 100+7 | 14+1 | 10 | 6 | 9 | 1 | 3 | |
| Tottenham Hotspur | 5.92 | £750,000 | 38 | 4 | 5 | | 3 | | | |
| Liverpool* | 7.93 | £2,500,000 | | | | | | | | |

## RUFFER Carl James

Born: Ellesmere Port, 20 December 1974

Height: 5'11" Weight: 11.10

**Position/Skill Factor:** Central defender who is very cool on the ball and likes to come out of defence, looking to make the right pass.

**Career History:** A player who has shown great improvement over the last year, he first came to Everton as an associated schoolboy (February 1989), before graduating through the trainee (August 1991) ranks to sign professional forms last summer. A regular in the youth side in **1992-93**, he also had half a dozen run outs with the reserves and if he continues to improve at the same rate, could be a good un.

| | | | APPEARANCES | | | | GOALS | | | |
|---|---|---|---|---|---|---|---|---|---|---|
| Clubs | Signing Date | Transfer Fee | Lge | FL Cup | FA Cup | Others | Lge | FL Cup | FA Cup | Others |
| Everton* | 7.93 | - | | | | | | | | |

## RUSH Ian James

Born: St Asaph, 20 October 1961

Height: 6'0" Weight: 12.6

International Honours: W Sch, W "U21"-2, FL Rep, W-60

**Position/Skill Factor:** Striker with phenomenal work rate, who puts defenders under pressure and then picks up the pieces. A snapper up of half chances, he is very quick and scores many goals from good near post runs.

**Career History:** After representing Wales at schoolboy level, he joined Chester City, first as an associated schoolboy (March 1977) and then as an apprentice (August 1978), before signing as a professional at the beginning of 1979-80. Prior to that, he had already made his FL debut at home to Sheffield Wednesday on 28 April 1979 and the following season, he was the club's leading goal scorer with 14. At the tail-end of 1979-80, Liverpool, having noted his potential, moved in to sign him and before he even kicked a ball for the "Reds", he received the first of many Welsh caps when coming on as a substitute during a 1-0 defeat at Hampden Park against Scotland on 21 May 1980. Made no impact in his first season at Anfield, failing to score in seven end of season games. Out of favour at the start of 1981-82, he went to see Bob Paisley about his future at the club and was given the tart answer, "just score goals". Deputising for the injured David Johnson that October, he netted twice in a 3-0 victory over Leeds

United and the rest, so to speak, is history, as he simply burst on the First Division scene with 17 League goals in 32 matches, ending the season with a League Cup winners medal after scoring the third goal in a 3-1 win over Tottenham Hotspur. The next five seasons were honours all the way, except for 1984-85, when the cupboard remained strangely bare, with three League Cup wins (1983 and 1984), a European Cup winners medal (1983-84) and an FA Cup winners medal (1986), after he had scored twice in a 3-1 victory over Everton. It was during this time that his partnership with Kenny Dalglish became legendary and when the latter took over the manager's seat, it was feared that his goal scoring opportunities would suffer, but luckily, Jan Molby also proved to be an expert provider. However, after repeated overtures from the top Italian side, Juventus, he was transferred for a new English record transfer fee during the 1987 close season. He had been the "Reds'" leading scorer in five of his six full seasons at Anfield and seemed to be almost impossible to replace after striking 207 goals in 331 matches (a ratio of one in every 1.6 games, only equalled by Gary Lineker in recent times). Unfortunately, his time at Juventus was not a happy one as the club coach expected him to forage alone. Nevertheless, although he scored eight goals in 29 games, a respectable total for the Italian League, he made no effort to acclimatise and Juventus allowed him to rejoin Liverpool in the summer of 1988. His first term back in England was plagued by injury problems, but he came back with a bang in the FA Cup Final against Everton when, as a substitute, he scored two of Liverpool's goals in a 3-2 extra-time win over their Mersey rivals. In winning his fifth League Championship medal in 1989-90, he found the net 18 times and in 1990-91, he once again headed the club's scoring charts with 16. Endured a miserable time in 1991-92, being absent through injury much of the time. Missing from action at the beginning of the season, he did not appear match fit when returning in September, scoring only four goals in 15 games and apart from playing just three times during February, he was out until late March. Happily, three goals in the closing four games against Nottingham Forest, Manchester United (his first in 24 attempts against the men from Old Trafford) and Sunderland in the FA Cup Final (his fifth in three Finals), demonstrated that he had not lost the "killer instinct". A disappointing **1992-93**, which seemed at one time likely to signal his departure from Anfield, ended in a blaze of glory, with 11 goals from the last 13 games. Early in the season, he scored four goals in the ECWC against Apollon Limassol of Cyprus to beat Roger Hunt's record of 18 in European competition and had netted a hat-trick for Wales against the Faroe Isles a week before to claim the all-time scoring record (24 goals) for his country. In October he made his 500th appearance for Liverpool and struck his 200th FL goal in November. Despite establishing new records every other week, his form in the Premier League was fitful and without Molby, Ray Houghton and Peter Beardsley to supply the ammunition, he appeared disinclined to create his own chances. After scoring only three times in 19 PL games, Graeme Souness finally lost patience and dropped him in late February, for the first time in his Liverpool career. It was one of Souness' better decisions. Stung by the humiliation, Rush returned as a substitute in the following game at home to Manchester United and lashed in a magnificent equaliser, although Liverpool subsequently lost the game. He then scored in six of the next seven games and finished the season with a brace against Oldham Athletic and Tottenham Hotspur, while notching his 300th Liverpool goal in the process.

| | | | APPEARANCES | | | | GOALS | | | |
|---|---|---|---|---|---|---|---|---|---|---|
| Clubs | Signing Date | Transfer Fee | Lge | FL Cup | FA Cup | Others | Lge | FL Cup | FA Cup | Others |
| Chester City | 9.79 | - | 33+1 | | 5 | | 14 | | 3 | |
| Liverpool | 5.80 | £300,000 | 224 | 47 | 25 | 34+1 | 139 | 25 | 20 | 23 |
| Juventus (Italy) | 6.87 | £3,200,000 | | | | | | | | |
| Liverpool* | 8.88 | £2,800,000 | 136+11 | 17 | 21+2 | 14 | 59 | 11 | 16 | 7 |

## RUSH Matthew James

Born: Hackney, 6 August 1971

Height: 5'11" Weight:12.10

International Honours: IR"U21"-3

**Position/Skill Factor:** Right-winger with excellent pace and two good feet. Also, useful in the air.

**Career History:** First came to West Ham United as a young 14-year-old associated schoolboy in October 1985, before signing as a trainee on leaving school (July 1988) and then, as expected, graduating to the senior ranks towards the end of the 1989-90 season. He didn't have to wait long for his FL debut, coming on as a substitute in a 7-1 win over Hull City at Upton Park on 6 October 1990 and by the end of the season he had made a further five (two as substitute) appearances. In 1991-92 he continued to have occasional outings as substitute and late in the season, in a full appearance, scored twice in a 4-0 victory over Norwich City. It was a rare victory in a season of gloom for the "Hammers", which ended in relegation. Did not contribute to the League side at all in **1992-93**, a season that ended with the "Hammers" going back to the top flight after just one year away, as runners-up to First Division Champions, Newcastle United. Apart from playing in three of the Anglo-Italian Cup games and incidentally, being sent off against Pisa, he spent much of his time in the reserve side, with over 20 appearances to his name. However, from mid-March onwards, he had a useful spell out on loan at Cambridge United, but was recalled prior the club visiting Upton Park for the final game of the season. It is difficult to see him breaking into the Premier League side at present and he may well decide to try his luck elsewhere.

| | | | APPEARANCES | | | | GOALS | | | |
|---|---|---|---|---|---|---|---|---|---|---|
| Clubs | Signing Date | Transfer Fee | Lge | FL Cup | FA Cup | Others | Lge | FL Cup | FA Cup | Others |
| West Ham United* | 3.90 | - | 5+10 | 1 | | 2+1 | 2 | | | |
| Cambridge United | 3.93 | Loan | 4+6 | | | | | | | |

## SAMWAYS Vincent (Vinny)

Born: Bethnal Green, 27 October 1968

Height: 5'8"

Weight: 9.0

International Honours: E Yth, E "U21"-5

**Position/Skill Factor:** Midfielder with superb vision. Has a lovely touch and controls the ball with ease. Rarely giving anything away, he is also an outstanding passer.

**Career History:** After a period on Tottenham Hotspur's books as an associated schoolboy, beginning in November 1982, he left school in April 1985 to sign on with the club as an apprentice. Turned professional in 1985-86, but didn't make his FL debut until 2 May 1987, as a substitute during a 2-0 defeat at Nottingham Forest. Made rapid strides during 1987-88, with 21 League appearances, but, although a valuable member of the first team squad, he found it hard to hold down a permanent place. However, with Paul Gascoigne often absent through injury in 1990-91, he was given the chance to exert some influence in "Spurs'" midfield and earned his first club honour when he won an FA Cup winners medal, following Tottenham's 2-1 victory over Nottingham Forest. With Gascoigne out of action during 1991-92, he was at last able to stake a regular claim to a first team slot. Unfortunately, he seemed to be made a "scapegoat" for "Spurs'" disappointing season and was dropped in February 1992, manager Peter Shreeves explaining that the "boggy" White Hart Lane pitch was inimical to his passing game. This did not explain, however, why he was not suitable for away games or why he disappeared from the first team squad for the remainder of the season. After coming off the transfer list during the summer, he began the **1992-93** new Premier League season well, but picked up an ankle injury at Coventry City in September and was forced to miss the next three games. Absent only six more times all season, due to various injuries, he was a major influence in "Spurs'" all-round improvement in the latter half of the campaign and while remaining goalless in the League, notched up three in cup games. Two of them coming in the 5-1 defeat of Marlow in the Third Round of the FA Cup, hailed the start of a good run in the competition that eventually ended in the Semi-Final at the hands of north London rivals, Arsenal.

| | | | APPEARANCES | | | | GOALS | | | |
|---|---|---|---|---|---|---|---|---|---|---|
| Clubs | Signing Date | Transfer Fee | Lge | FL Cup | FA Cup | Others | Lge | FL Cup | FA Cup | Others |
| Tottenham Hotspur* | 9.85 | - | 126+28 | 22+4 | 12+1 | 7+1 | 8 | 4 | 2 | |

## SANCHEZ Lawrence (Lawrie) Philip

Born: Lambeth, 22 October 1959

Height: 5'11"

Weight: 11.7

International Honours: E Sch, NI-3

**Position/Skill Factor:** Midfield player who has a good football brain. Very confident with the ball, he never seems to be hurried and is always looking to create scoring opportunities.

**Career History:** The son of John Sanchez, who played for Arsenal and Watford between 1957-1961, he started his career as an associated schoolboy at Reading in September 1977 and then Thatcham Town, before returning to Reading to make his FL debut in a 2-2 draw at Elm Park, ironically, against Wimbledon on 1 October 1977. Turned professional a year later and spent eight years with the "Royals", winning a Fourth Division Championship medal in 1978-79, making 34 League appearances. Suffered the disappointment of relegation in 1982-83, before experiencing the euphoria of helping the club back to the Third Division at the first time of asking, in third place. During the winter of 1984, he was snapped up by Wimbledon manager, Dave Bassett, as another piece in the jigsaw which would be completed when the "Dons" reached the First Division and then went on to capture the FA Cup. Made his bow at Plough Lane against Notts County on Boxing Day 1984 and the following season, as an ever present, he helped Bassett achieve his objective of First Division football, when the club finished in third place behind Norwich City and Charlton Athletic. His performances for Wimbledon earned him an international call-up for Northern Ireland in November 1986, when he came on as a sub during a European Championship qualifying match in Turkey and he won two more caps in 1988-89. However, the highlight of his career came in the 1988 FA Cup Final against mighty Liverpool, when he headed in Denis Wise's free-kick for the only goal of the game and set up a result that confounded the critics. Still a force to be reckoned with, although the past two seasons have often seen him struggling with injuries and loss of form, before he re-established himself. Out of contention for the first half of 1991-92, he was recalled to the first team in January when the "Dons" were struggling near the foot of the table and his experience proved invaluable as the club climbed to a mid-table position. Starting well enough in **1992-93**, he played in 22 of the opening 32 first team games and worked hard with new signing, Vinny Jones, to strengthen the midfield. Always a scorer of useful goals, the fact was further highlighted when he got the first in a 3-2 home defeat of Arsenal and turned in Terry Gibson's low free-kick for a late winner at Manchester United. However, he was used sparingly in the New Year and made only five full appearances over the last few months of the season. Still an excellent clubman for the "Dons".

| | | | APPEARANCES | | | | GOALS | | | |
|---|---|---|---|---|---|---|---|---|---|---|
| Clubs | Signing Date | Transfer Fee | Lge | FL Cup | FA Cup | Others | Lge | FL Cup | FA Cup | Others |
| Roading | 9.78 | - | 249+13 | 20+1 | 14 | 1 | 28 | | 1 | |
| Wimbledon* | 12.84 | £29,000 | 239+16 | 18 | 26+1 | 7 | 31 | | 2 | |

## **SAUNDERS Dean** Nicholas

Born: Swansea, 21 June 1964

Height: 5'8" Weight: 10.6

International Honours: FL Rep, W-40

**Position/Skill Factor:** Quicksilver striker who often chases lost causes. Loves balls in behind defenders when he can use his pace to maximum effect and is useful in the air for his size.

**Career History:** The son of Roy, who played for Liverpool and Swansea City between 1948-1963, he came into League football with Swansea City as an apprentice in November 1980, before graduating to the professional ranks in the 1982 close season. After waiting nearly 18 months for an opportunity, he made his FL debut as a substitute in a 2-2 draw at Charlton Athletic on 22 October 1983. Not highly regarded by Swansea manager John Bond, he was released on a free transfer, following a spell on loan at Cardiff City and signed for Brighton & Hove Albion during the summer of 1985. Immediately impressing the "Seagulls" with 15 League goals in 1985-86, he was recognised by the Welsh manager and made his international debut against the Irish Republic on 26 March 1986 in Dublin, when coming on as a sub. Towards the end of the following season he was sold to Oxford United, who were struggling at the foot of the First Division and he made an immediate impact, scoring six times in 12 games, including two at Luton Town which effectively safeguarded United's status. However, at the end of 1987-88, Oxford were relegated to the Second Division and despite much bitterness towards the club's directors, which ultimately cost manager Mark Lawrenson his job, he was sold to Derby County in October 1988. The "Rams" received an immediate return on their investment when he hit a brace in a 4-1 win home win over Wimbledon and in three seasons at the Baseball Ground, was the club's leading scorer. His 17 goals from a total of 37 scored in 1990-91, was a remarkable achievement for a team doomed to relegation almost from the start of the season. Scored a hat-trick against relegation companions Sunderland, but even that could only bring a 3-3 draw. Sold to Liverpool during the summer of 1991, for a record transfer fee between two English clubs, along with Mark Wright, he struggled to make an impact at Anfield, despite finishing as the club's leading scorer with 23 goals in all competitions and collecting an FA Cup winners medal. A breakdown of his goals tally reveals the reason why — nine in the UEFA Cup, including four against Kuusysi Lahti of Finland, two in the League Cup, two in the FA Cup, but only ten from 36 First Division games. Made six early season appearances for Liverpool in **1992-93** and scored only one goal, before being transferred to Aston Villa for a sum £600,000 less than they paid for him. Started with Villa at Leeds United and played in every game throughout the rest of the campaign, immediately striking up an excellent partnership with Dalian Atkinson. His first home game was, ironically, against Liverpool, when he scored two of the goals in a 4-2 victory and he went on to become the club's leading goalscorer, with 17 from all first team matches. Even when the goals dried up at the latter end of the season, he was still going flat out and was unfortunate to hit the woodwork six times in the last seven home games. Was left to rue over what might have been, as Villa finished runners-up to Manchester United in the chase for the Premier League Championship.

| | | | APPEARANCES | | | | GOALS | | | |
|---|---|---|---|---|---|---|---|---|---|---|
| Clubs | Signing Date | Transfer Fee | Lge | FL Cup | FA Cup | Others | Lge | FL Cup | FA Cup | Others |
| Swansea City | 6.82 | - | 42+7 | 2+1 | 1 | 1+1 | 12 | | | |
| Cardiff City | 3.85 | Loan | 3+1 | | | | | | | |
| Brighton & H. A. | 8.85 | - | 66+6 | 4 | 7 | 3 | 20 | | 5 | |
| Oxford United | 3.87 | £60,000 | 57+2 | 9+1 | 2 | 2 | 22 | 8 | 2 | 1 |
| Derby County | 10.88 | £1,000,000 | 106 | 12 | 6 | 7 | 42 | 10 | | 5 |
| Liverpool | 7.91 | £2,900,000 | 42 | 5 | 8 | 6 | 11 | 2 | 2 | 10 |
| Aston Villa* | 9.92 | £2,300,00 | 35 | 5 | 4 | | 13 | 2 | 2 | |

## **SAVAGE Robert** William

Born: Wrexham, 18 October 1974

Height: 5'11½" Weight: 10.1

International Honours: W Sch, W Yth

**Position/Skill Factor:** Hard working striker, who holds the ball up well and is always prepared to take defenders out of the penalty area to allow his team-mates into scoring positions.

**Career History:** A 1993 close season professional signing for Manchester United, he first came to Old Trafford as an associated schoolboy (November 1988), before moving up as a trainee (June 1991) on leaving school. Won Welsh youth caps in **1992-93** to go with his schoolboy honours and played an active part in United's run to the FA Youth Cup Final where they lost out to Leeds United. A promising player and one who will look to build on the eight reserve appearances he made prior to the end of last season.

| | | | APPEARANCES | | | | GOALS | | | |
|---|---|---|---|---|---|---|---|---|---|---|
| Clubs | Signing Date | Transfer Fee | Lge | FL Cup | FA Cup | Others | Lge | FL Cup | FA Cup | Others |
| Manchester United* | 7.93 | - | | | | | | | | |

## **SCALES John** Robert

Born: Harrogate, 4 July 1966

Height: 6'0"

Weight: 12.2

**Position/Skill Factor:** Pacey central defender with an athletic build. Can play in most defensive positions, is powerful in the air, has two good feet and is very dangerous at set plays.

**Career History:** Signed for Leeds United on a YTS scheme in August 1984, but was freed during the 1985 close season and joined Bristol Rovers as a professional. Made his FL debut in a 3-0 defeat at Newport County on 7 September 1985 and by the end of the season he was holding down a permanent place at a club that had been forced to part with many of its leading players due to a financial crisis. Spent two years at Rovers, but when Bobby Gould was given the Wimbledon job in the summer of 1987, he was among his former manager's first signings. Turning out for the "Dons" in both full-back positions in 1987-88, he settled down well to make 23 League appearances and won an FA Cup winners medal after coming on for Terry Gibson during the 1-0 victory over Liverpool. Since switching to a more central role to replace Eric Young, he has proved to be one of the club's most consistent players, often scoring invaluable goals, as Wimbledon continue to make their presence felt on the First Division scene. An ever present in 1991-92, apart from the last game of the season, he was unlucky to be injured in the opening **1992-93** Premier League match against Leeds United. Forced to miss six games before returning to the side, he had another spell out of action after playing a handful of games, but from then on he didn't miss a match. He was the rock that Joe Kinnear built his defence around and had outstanding games against the leading strikers in the country, with Ian Wright and Teddy Sheringham, being just two of the men he successfully shackled during the season. Voted Wimbledon's "Player of the Year", he had an outstanding season and international honours may not be far away.

| | | | APPEARANCES | | | | GOALS | | | |
|---|---|---|---|---|---|---|---|---|---|---|
| Clubs | Signing Date | Transfer Fee | Lge | FL Cup | FA Cup | Others | Lge | FL Cup | FA Cup | Others |
| Bristol Rovers | 7.85 | - | 68+4 | 3 | 6 | 3+1 | 2 | | | |
| Wimbledon* | 7.87 | £70,000 | 195+5 | 13+1 | 17+1 | 7+1 | 11 | | | 3 |

## **SCHMEICHEL Peter** Boleslaw

Born: Denmark, 18 November 1968

Height: 6'4" Weight: 14.0

International Honours: Danish Int

**Position/Skill Factor:** Top class goalkeeper with great presence. Extremely agile and very fast off his line, he gives the attacker little to aim at. Sets up attacks with accurate throws.

**Career History:** Danish international goalkeeper who signed for Manchester United from Danish League champions, Brondby IF of Copenhagen. He played in all but four games of United's 57 match programme in 1991-92, following his FL debut at Old Trafford against Notts County on 17 August 1991, winning a League Cup medal, but missing out on a League Championship medal in the closing weeks of the campaign. Apart from occasional lapses in concentration, he proved to be the answer to a problem position for United since Jim Leighton's fall from grace, conceding only 32 goals in 40 FL games, the best statistics in the First Division. Played for Denmark in the 1992 European Championship Finals in Sweden, as last minute participants, following the expulsion of Yugoslavia. Despite being unprepared for the tournament, the Danes confounded everyone by defeating France and the Netherlands to beat Germany in the Final. Quite apart from keeping superbly throughout the tournament, he became a national hero by saving Marco van Basten's penalty in the Semi-Final "shoot-out" against the Dutch, which enabled Denmark to win 5-4 on penalties, after a gripping 2-2 draw. Had another brilliantly consistent season in **1992-93**, as United powered to the Premier League title and when the chips were down it was often his world class ability that was the difference between victory and defeat. To reflect this point, a save at Liverpool, when he somehow palmed away a shot with an incredible reflex action, was memorable and good enough to maintain three points. And in keeping 23 clean sheets in all games throughout the campaign, at one stage he went 626 minutes without conceding a goal. Arguably the best 'keeper in the Premier League, he stands on top of a pile that includes at least ten "foreigners", a moot point among certain discerning critics and is still the obvious first choice for Denmark.

| | | | APPEARANCES | | | | GOALS | | | |
|---|---|---|---|---|---|---|---|---|---|---|
| Clubs | Signing Date | Transfer Fee | Lge | FL Cup | FA Cup | Others | Lge | FL Cup | FA Cup | Others |
| Manchester United* | 8.91 | £550,000 | 82 | 8 | 6 | 5 | | | | |

## SCHOLES Paul

Born: Salford,
16 November 1974

Height: 5'6"

Weight: 10.8

International Honours:
E Yth

**Position/Skill Factor:** Very talented midfield schemer who can also play up front. Has a great through ball and often scores checky goals. Yet another young player with an excellent attitude.

**Career History:** Turned Professional for Manchester United at the beginning of 1993, having scored goals at all levels to date, after coming through the ranks as an associated schoolboy (September 1989) and as a trainee (July 1991). Highly rated at Old Trafford, he appeared in the reserves in **1992-93** and was a valuable member of the United side that reached the FA Youth Cup Final for the second year running.

| | | | APPEARANCES | | | | GOALS | | | |
|---|---|---|---|---|---|---|---|---|---|---|
| Clubs | Signing Date | Transfer Fee | Lge | FL Cup | FA Cup | Others | Lge | FL Cup | FA Cup | Others |
| Manchester United* | 1.93 | - | | | | | | | | |

## SCIMECA Riccardo

Born: Leamington, 13 June 1975

Height: 6'0" Weight: 12.13

**Position/Skill Factor:** Central midfielder who is comfortable on the ball, with lovely skills and tight control. Has an eye for goal and often goes past defenders as if they don't exist.

**Career History:** Of Italian parents, he signed professional for Aston Villa during the summer, having been at Villa Park as an associated schoolboy (June 1990) and as a trainee (July 1991). Yet to have even a taste of reserve football, he was unfortunate to fracture a leg in March 1992 and wasn't back in action until after Christmas in **1992-93**. Will be given every chance to prove himself during this season.

| | | | APPEARANCES | | | | GOALS | | | |
|---|---|---|---|---|---|---|---|---|---|---|
| Clubs | Signing Date | Transfer Fee | Lge | FL Cup | FA Cup | Others | Lge | FL Cup | FA Cup | Others |
| Aston Villa* | 7.93 | - | | | | | | | | |

## SCOTT Andrew

Born: Epsom, 2 August 1972

Height: 6'1" Weight: 12.0

**Position/Skill Factor:** Winger who can play wide on the left, or up front. Has a good left foot and crosses the ball well.

**Career History:** Followed in the footsteps of Paul Rogers, when Sheffield United's Dave Bassett signed him from Diadora League club, Sutton United, in December 1992. Had Joined Sutton in 1989 and established himself in the Surrey based team during 1991-92 and at the time of his departure he was the club's leading scorer in **1992-93**. Having come to Bramall Lane as a winger, it was somewhat of a suprise to the fans when he was named as a substitute for the local derby against Sheffield Wednesday at Hillsborough on 21 April 1993. Came on in the last few seconds for Brian Deane, to make his PL debut and it was even more of a surprise when he was named as strike partner to the latter, for the last match of the season, at home to Chelsea. A goal after only six minutes, plus several near misses, justified the decision and he is most definately one to watch out for in 1993-94.

| | | | APPEARANCES | | | | GOALS | | | |
|---|---|---|---|---|---|---|---|---|---|---|
| Clubs | Signing Date | Transfer Fee | Lge | FL Cup | FA Cup | Others | Lge | FL Cup | FA Cup | Others |
| Sheffield United* | 12.92 | £50,000 | 1+1 | | | | 1 | | | |

## SCOTT Andrew Michael

Born: Manchester, 27 June 1975

Height: 5'11½" Weight: 11.9

**Position/Skill Factor:** Full-back with a very good left foot and plenty of pace. Always looking to pass the ball when in possession, he scores goals as well.

**Career History:** Signed a professional contract committing him to Blackburn Rovers until the end of 1993-94 in January, after initially joining as an associated schoolboy in July 1989 and upgrading to trainee status in July 1991. No first team appearances in **1992-93**, but had a run of eight games in the reserve side.

| | | | APPEARANCES | | | | GOALS | | | |
|---|---|---|---|---|---|---|---|---|---|---|
| Clubs | Signing Date | Transfer Fee | Lge | FL Cup | FA Cup | Others | Lge | FL Cup | FA Cup | Others |
| Blackburn Rovers* | 1.93 | - | | | | | | | | |

## SCOTT John Alan

Born: Aberdeen, 9 March 1975

Height: 5'7¼" Weight: 10.13

International Honours: S Sch

**Position/Skill Factor:** Defensive left-back with an excellent left foot. Cool on the ball, he deliberates when passing, looking to move his team-mates quickly from defence to attack.

**Career History:** Turned professional for Liverpool during the 1992 close season, having been at the club since coming to Anfield as a trainee in August 1991. Already a recognised penalty taker at the club, he spent **1992-93** playing his football in the youth and "A" teams. It is too early at present to tell whether he will make the grade at Anfield.

| | | | APPEARANCES | | | | GOALS | | | |
|---|---|---|---|---|---|---|---|---|---|---|
| Clubs | Signing Date | Transfer Fee | Lge | FL Cup | FA Cup | Others | Lge | FL Cup | FA Cup | Others |
| Liverpool* | 6.92 | - | | | | | | | | |

## SCOTT Kevin Watson

Born: Easington, 17 December 1966

Height: 6'2"

Weight: 11.6

**Position/Skill Factor:** Central defender who is strong in the air and particularly dangerous at set plays. Has a good left foot and likes to come out of defence on the break to provide the final pass.

**Career History:** One of Newcastle United's first YTS players, he signed professional on his 18th birthday, but had to wait nearly two years for his FL debut on 6 September 1986 at home to Sheffield Wednesday. Although it ended in a 2-3 defeat, he marked his debut with a goal, as did Joe Allon, another former YTS player. As understudy to Peter Jackson and Glen Roeder, he had to wait another two years for a regular first team place, until displacing the former in September 1988. Although playing for most of the season alongside Andy Thorn, or Glenn Roeder, it was perhaps too much responsibility for a young player as the team subsided into Division Two without much of a fight. However, in Division Two, he became a tower of strength in the Newcastle defence, missing only ten games in three seasons and holding his place, whilst his defensive partners were chopped and changed and managers came and went. With the arrival of new boss, Kevin Keegan, early in 1992, it was felt that maybe he wouldn't stay at St James' Park, due to contractual problems, but on the eve of **1992-93** everything was resolved. Again the epitome of consistency, he only missed one game all season, due to suspension, as Newcastle charged to the new First Division title, after leading all the way. He was also a tower of strength when opponents tried to intimidate a side that had gone undefeated for the first 11 League games, but with his influence, he and his team-mates gave as good as they got. Currently, United's longest serving player, his downsides during a very successful season were when gifting Millwall a goal in a 1-1 home draw and being booked five times. Should be well suited to Premier League football.

| | | | APPEARANCES | | | | GOALS | | | |
|---|---|---|---|---|---|---|---|---|---|---|
| Clubs | Signing Date | Transfer Fee | Lge | FL Cup | FA Cup | Others | Lge | FL Cup | FA Cup | Others |
| Newcastle United* | 12.84 | - | 209 | 16 | 14+1 | 12+1 | 8 | | 1 | 2 |

## SEALEY Leslie (Les) Jesse

Born: Bethnal Green, 29 September 1957

Height: 6'1"

Weight: 12.8

**Position/Skill Factor:** Brave and agile goalkeeper who makes saves that are worth points. Known in the game as a great talker, he never stops shouting instructions and advice to his defenders.

**Career History:** A great character, he hails from a footballing family, being a cousin of Alan who was prominent for Leyton Orient and West Ham United between 1959-1967. London born, he joined Coventry City as an apprentice in April 1974, before turning professional and making his FL debut at Queens Park Rangers in a 1-1 draw on 11 April 1977. Shared the goalkeeping duties with Jim Blyth until 1982-83, when he only missed three games, but at the end of the season he signed for Luton Town, for whom he was ever present throughout 1983-84. Lost his place to Andy Dibble early in 1984-85, after suffering injury problems and on recovering, he spent some time on loan with Plymouth Argyle. He soon won back a regular place in the "Hatters'" goal and was extremely unlucky in missing the club's 1988 League Cup Final triumph over Arsenal, because of injury. But following the 3-1 League Cup Final defeat at the hands of Nottingham Forest in 1989, he lost his place to Alec Chamberlain. Alex Ferguson took him to Manchester United for two short loan periods, one in December 1989, when he didn't make an appearance and the second time in March 1990 when he played in two League matches. And after United's 3-3 FA Cup Final draw against Crystal Palace, he was called up to replace the unfortunate Jim Leighton for the replay. Returning to the scene of his cousin Alan's 1965 triumph, he made some important saves to ensure a 1-0 victory and was rewarded with a one year contract. Had mixed fortunes in 1990-91. After being left helpless by John Sheridan's strike in the League Cup Final, as United lost 1-0 to Sheffield Wednesday, less than a month later he won a European Cup Winners Cup medal, following the "Red Devils'" brilliant 2-1 victory over Barcelona. Following the signing of Danish 'keeper Peter Schmeichel, he was allowed to leave Old Trafford on a free transfer, signing for Aston Villa as cover for Nigel Spink. From October 1991 to late February 1992, he was actually first choice 'keeper at Villa Park until Spink won his place back. Towards the end of the season he was loaned out to his old club, Coventry City, who had Steve Ogrizovic incapacitated and played two games until the latter was fit to resume. After sitting on the bench under the new Premier League substitute goalkeeper ruling for Aston Villa in the first 11 games of **1992-93**, he was loaned out to Birmingham City in order to give Mark Bosnich more experience. Made 12 appearances at St Andrews, deputising for the injured Andy Gosney, combining brilliant saves with moments of madness and when the latter was back to full fitness, he went straight to his former club, Manchester United, on a free transfer as cover for Peter Schmeichel. Always a good player to have in the dressing room, he covered the big Dane for 19 games, without ever being required, as United stormed to the Championship for the first time since 1966-67.

| | | | APPEARANCES | | | | GOALS | | | |
|---|---|---|---|---|---|---|---|---|---|---|
| Clubs | Signing Date | Transfer Fee | Lge | FL Cup | FA Cup | Others | Lge | FL Cup | FA Cup | Others |
| Coventry City | 3.76 | - | 158 | 11 | 9 | | | | | |
| Luton Town | 8.83 | £100,000 | 207 | 21 | 28 | 3 | | | | |
| Plymouth Argyle | 10.84 | Loan | 6 | | | | | | | |
| Manchester United | 3.90 | Loan | 2 | | 1 | | | | | |
| Manchester United | 6.90 | - | 31 | 8 | 3 | 9 | | | | |
| Aston Villa | 7.91 | - | 18 | | 4 | 2 | | | | |
| Coventry City | 3.92 | Loan | 2 | | | | | | | |
| Birmingham City | 10.92 | Loan | 12 | | | 3 | | | | |
| Manchester United* | 1.93 | - | | | | | | | | |

## SEAMAN David Andrew

Born: Rotherham, 19 September 1963

Height: 6'3" Weight: 13.0

International Honours: E "U21"-10, E"B", E-9

**Position/Skill Factor:** Confident, unspectacular, yet agile goalkeeper, who is always on his toes. Strong hands are his passport. A good kicker, he will run the ball out to gain extra distance.

**Career History:** It seems hard to realise that Leeds United released him before he could make an appearance. He had gone to Elland Road as an apprentice in March 1980 and had graduated to the professional ranks early in 1981-82, but with an abundance of goalies available, including John Lukic, United let him go. Fourth Division Peterborough United snapped him up and he soon established himself as the first team choice at London Road, after making his FL debut at Stockport County on 28 August 1982 in a 1-1 draw. In October 1984, Birmingham City, having just sold Tony Coton to Watford, moved in for him as a replacement and he came straight into the side, keeping 13 clean sheets in 33 League matches to assist the "Blues'" promotion to the First Division behind the Champions, Oxford United. Although ever present, City were relegated first time round and in order to continue playing in the top flight, he signed for Queens Park

Rangers in time for 1986-87. Ironically, the only game he missed in his first season at Rangers was a 7-1 defeat at Sheffield Wednesday and his consistency was finally rewarded at international level on 16 November 1988 when he kept goal for England against Saudi Arabia in a 1-1 draw. Rarely absent during the four years he spent at Loftus Road, his transfer to Arsenal created something of a stir during the 1990 close season when George Graham decided to release John Lukic and parted with the highest transfer fee ever paid for a goalkeeper. He proved superb value for money, making a solid Arsenal defence even more watertight and won his first League Championship medal as the "Gunners" celebrated their second title win in three years. His League statistics as an ever present in 1990-91, which include 24 clean sheets, 540 minutes without a goal being scored against him and just 18 goals conceded, speak for themselves. Ever present in 1991-92, it was not such a good season for Arsenal's defence, which conceded 46 goals. Regarded by Graham Taylor as England's number two, his occasional international appearances were often the subject of unfair media criticism. After a mistake in the game against Czechoslovakia in March, he was dropped so that Taylor could take a look at Nigel Martyn of Crystal Palace. In the event, it was Martyn and not Seaman, who travelled to Sweden as understudy to Chris Woods for the European Championship Finals. It was pleasing to see him back on top form in **1992-93**, a fact borne out early in the season, when he kept Arsenal alive in the League Cup at Millwall with a brilliant performance in the penalty shoot-out. In the FA Cup, a stunning save from Rod Wallace at Highbury allowed Arsenal to haul back a two goal deficit against Leeds United and, again in the League Cup, two quick clearances set up both goals in the win over Derby County. Although he fell foul of the new back pass law and was booked in an FA Cup Fifth Round-tie against Nottingham Forest, generally things went well and he capped a fine season with League and FA Cup winners medals after two victories over Sheffield Wednesday. Hopes to be fit in time for the 1993-94 season, following a double hernia operation in the summer.

| | | | APPEARANCES | | | | GOALS | | | |
|---|---|---|---|---|---|---|---|---|---|---|
| Clubs | Signing Date | Transfer Fee | Lge | FL Cup | FA Cup | Others | Lge | FL Cup | FA Cup | Others |
| Leeds United | 9.81 | - | | | | | | | | |
| Peterborough United | 8.82 | £4,000 | 91 | 10 | 5 | | | | | |
| Birmingham City | 10.84 | £100,000 | 75 | 4 | 5 | | | | | |
| Q.P.R. | 8.86 | £225,000 | 141 | 13 | 17 | 4 | | | | |
| Arsenal* | 5.90 | £1,300,000 | 119 | 16 | 17 | 5 | | | | |

## SEDGLEY Stephen (Steve) Philip

Born: Enfield, 26 May 1968

Height: 6'1" Weight: 12.6

International Honours: E "U21"-11

**Position/Skill Factor:** A central defender, he is a true competitor, who is aggressive and makes decisive tackles. Has an excellent left foot and can hit good diagonal passes. Useful in the air at set pieces.

**Career History:** A Londoner by birth, he signed as an associated schoolboy for Coventry City in February 1984 and on leaving school, he joined the ground staff as an apprentice in June 1984. Made his FL debut in the "Sky Blues'" midfield, three months after turning professional, at Highfield Road against Arsenal on 26 August 1986. Although he appeared in 25 League matches that season, he was considered too inexperienced to be included in the club's 1987 FA Cup Final team which defeated Tottenham Hotspur 3-2. After three years of steady progress at Coventry, he found himself the subject of a substantial offer made by North London's Tottenham Hotspur and during the 1989 close season he joined the club, who four years earlier could have signed him for free. Immediately fitting into the middle of the back four, alongside Gary Mabbutt, he helped "Spurs" overcome a sticky start to finish third in the League. By now a big favourite with the home fans, he missed a handful of matches through niggling injuries early in 1990-91, but recovered well enough to win an FA Cup winners medal, following the 2-1 victory over Nottingham Forest. In and out of the team during the disappointing 1991-92 campaign, he was usually selected as a substitute when not a first choice and lost his place to on-loan Jason Cundy at the end of the season. Back in the side for the third game of the **1992-93** Premier League season, he scored a last minute equaliser in a 2-2 draw at home to Crystal Palace and then set about retaining his place. Unfortunately, he picked up a knee injury from the Liverpool game at White Hart Lane at the end of October and didn't return until being selected for the FA Cup Quarter-Final-tie against Manchester City, having had a run out as a substitute in the first team a few days earlier. Again he scored an important goal and remained in "Spurs'" midfield for the rest of the season.

| | | | APPEARANCES | | | | GOALS | | | |
|---|---|---|---|---|---|---|---|---|---|---|
| Clubs | Signing Date | Transfer Fee | Lge | FL Cup | FA Cup | Others | Lge | FL Cup | FA Cup | Others |
| Coventry City | 6.86 | - | 81+3 | 9 | 2+2 | 5+1 | 3 | 2 | | |
| Tottenham Hotspur* | 7.89 | £750,000 | 105+17 | 19+3 | 9+1 | 5+3 | 3 | 1 | 1 | |

## SEGERS Johannes (Hans)

Born: Eindhoven, Holland, 30 October 1961

Height: 5'11"

Weight: 12.7

**Position/Skill Factor:** Not very big for a goalkeeper, but extremely agile and not easy to beat. A very good kicker, he uses the ball well with early throws.

**Career History:** Dutch goalkeeper who played for PSV Eindhoven, before joining Nottingham Forest in the 1984 close season, in part-exchange for the Dutch international 'keeper, Hans van Breukelen. Made his FL debut in a 3-1 win at Coventry City on 17 November 1984, when replacing Steve Sutton in the Forest goal and kept his place for the rest of the season. Sutton regained the goalkeeping duties during the following term and over the next couple of seasons, he had spells on loan at Stoke City, Sheffield United and Dunfermline Athletic to keep in trim for first team football. After Dave Beasant's surprise move to Newcastle United in the summer of 1988, Wimbledon manager, Bobby Gould, moved to sign him as a replacement, following a run of five defeats at the beginning of 1988-89. He made his debut for the "Dons" in a 2-1 win at Everton and has missed only three matches since being signed — an amazing record of consistency. Has still not given up hope of winning a full Dutch international cap, after having another excellent season in the **1992-93** Premier League as the "Dons'" last line of defence. Absent for just one match, he was often outstanding, keeping 16 clean sheets and even with the influx of foreign 'keepers around at present, it would be difficult to find someone with better credentials.

| | | | APPEARANCES | | | | GOALS | | | |
|---|---|---|---|---|---|---|---|---|---|---|
| Clubs | Signing Date | Transfer Fee | Lge | FL Cup | FA Cup | Others | Lge | FL Cup | FA Cup | Others |
| Nottingham Forest | 8.84 | £50,000 | 58 | 4 | 5 | | | | | |
| Stoke City | 2.87 | Loan | 1 | | | | | | | |
| Sheffield United | 11.87 | Loan | 10 | | | 1 | | | | |
| Dunfermline Athletic | 3.88 | Loan | 4 | | | | | | | |
| Wimbledon* | 9.88 | £180,000 | 190 | 17 | 15 | 7 | | | | |

## SELLARS Scott

Born: Sheffield, 27 November 1965

Height: 5'7" Weight: 9.10

International Honours: E "U21"-3

**Position/Skill Factor:** Very skilful winger with a good brain. Always creating chances for others, he will make things happen around the opposition's penalty area.

**Career History:** Missed by the two big Sheffield clubs, he joined Leeds United as an associated schoolboy in December 1981 and on leaving school in July 1982, he had impressed enough for the club to take him on as an apprentice. Just before turning professional, he was given an early first team opportunity, making his FL debut at Shrewsbury Town on 7 May 1983. Enjoyed a good run in midfield the following season, from December 1983 to April 1984 and fully established himself in 1984-85 when he missed only three games. However, he fell out of favour after Leeds' poor start to 1985-86 and was allowed to join Blackburn Rovers for a surprisingly modest fee in the 1986 close season. He started his Rovers' career in midfield, but was switched late in the season to the left-wing to devastating effect. During the next three seasons, he established a reputation as the most dynamic, exciting left-winger in the Second Division. Ever present in 1988-89 and second top scorer with 14 FL goals in 1989-90, injuries unfortunately curtailed his appearances in 1990-91 to a minimum. Having been strangely out of favour with Rovers' manager, Don Mackay, at the start of 1991-92, the new boss, Kenny Dalglish, immediately restored him to the team as a substitute and after coming on in the 39th minute, he inspired Rovers to a 5-2 victory over Plymouth in October. In the penultimate game of the Second Division campaign, he scored a vital 86th minute equaliser against Sunderland to secure a crucial point and in the first Play-Off game against Derby, he struck Rovers' first goal from a free-kick to set up a thrilling comeback to 4-2 after his team had gone 2-0 down inside the first 14 minutes. With many players at his disposal, Dalglish sold him back to his first club, Leeds United, during the 1992 close season for a sum of £700,000, more than Blackburn paid for him six years earlier. At Elland Road he was used mainly as full-back cover in **1992-93** for Tony Dorigo and Jon Newsome and rarely played in what was rapidly becoming a difficult season for the club. Thus, it came as no surprise when he was transferred to Newcastle United shortly before the transfer deadline and he made a quick debut in a 2-2 draw against Charlton Athletic, playing in his more natural role on the left wing. On his own admission, it took time to adjust to the pace of the First Division, having spent most of his time during the last seven months playing reserve team football, but he soon became a vital member of the team. After scoring in a 6-0 rout of Barnsley, three games later, he bent a superb free-kick around the wall for the vital winner against Sunderland at St James' Park, but more importantly, he created at least five assists in the 13 matches he played. And with Newcastle winning promotion as First Division Champions, he can look forward with some satisfaction to playing against Leeds and Blackburn in the Premier League this season.

| | | | APPEARANCES | | | | GOALS | | | |
|---|---|---|---|---|---|---|---|---|---|---|
| Clubs | Signing Date | Transfer Fee | Lge | FL Cup | FA Cup | Others | Lge | FL Cup | FA Cup | Others |
| Leeds United | 7.83 | – | 72+4 | 4 | 4 | 2 | 12 | 1 | | 1 |
| Blackburn Rovers | 7.86 | £20,000 | 194+8 | 12 | 11 | 20 | 35 | 3 | 1 | 2 |
| Leeds United | 7.92 | £720,000 | 6+1 | 1+1 | | 1 | | | | |
| Newcastle United* | 3.93 | £700,000 | 13 | | | | 2 | | | |

## SELLEY Ian

Born: Chertsey, 14 June 1974

Height: 5'9"

Weight: 10.1

International Honours: E Yth

**Position/Skill Factor:** Very skilful midfield player with good vision and a shot to match. Always looking for an opportunity around the opponents' box, he also has the ability to create good scoring chances for others.

**Career History:** Signed professional forms for Arsenal during the 1992 close season, having been at Highbury as an associated schoolboy since October 1988, before graduating to the trainee ranks in July 1990. Made his PL debut in **1992-93**, when picked for the home match against Blackburn Rovers on 12 September 1992, but surprisingly did not resurface again until a Fourth Round FA Cup replay against Leeds United. Following that, he played in the next five matches, including the 3-1 League Cup Semi-Final victory at Crystal Palace and the home Fifth Round

FA Cup-tie against Nottingham Forest, where he released Ian Wright to score both goals in a 2-0 win. Went to Australia for the World Youth Cup, which seemed to take the edge off his game and although being named as substitute for both the League Cup Final and the FA Cup Final replay, he remained on the bench.

| | | | APPEARANCES | | | | GOALS | | | |
|---|---|---|---|---|---|---|---|---|---|---|
| Clubs | Signing Date | Transfer Fee | Lge | FL Cup | FA Cup | Others | Lge | FL Cup | FA Cup | Others |
| Arsenal* | 5.92 | - | 9 | 1 | 3 | | | | | |

## **SHARP Graeme** Marshall

Born: Glasgow, 16 October 1960

Height: 6'1" Weight: 11.8

International Honours: S "U21"-1, S-12

**Position/Skill Factor:** Tall, powerful striker who is very good in the air and is a difficult opponent to get the better of. Shields the ball excellently and brings his team-mates into the game.

**Career History:** A product of Scottish junior side, Eastercraigs, Dumbarton introduced him as a raw 19-year-old, in a 6-3 victory at Airdrie in November 1978 and less than 18 months later he was on his way to Everton, after scoring 17 times in 40 matches for the Scottish Second Division side. Made his FL debut at Brighton & Hove Albion on 3 May 1980 and following a "settling-in" season, he established himself during 1981-82, finishing as the club's leading goal scorer with 15. In 1983-84, Everton reached both the League Cup and FA Cup Finals. After losing 1-0 against Liverpool in the former, the "Toffees" returned triumphantly to Wembley to defeat Watford in the FA Cup Final, Graeme scoring the opening goal in a 2-0 win. His 21 goals during the next season went a long way to ensuring a League Championship medal, but the club were not so fortunate in the FA Cup this time round, losing 1-0 in the 1985 Final against Manchester United. Scored the "goal of a lifetime" in a rare "Merseyside Derby" victory over eternal rivals, Liverpool, in October 1984. A Grobbelaar goal-kick was played back from the Everton half to Sharp, who received the ball and turned Alan Hansen in one movement, then hit a dipping volley over the goalkeeper from 30 yards. No more than four seconds had elapsed between Grobbelaar's kick into the safety zone and the ball nestling in the Liverpool net! However, consolation for the FA Cup Final defeat at the hands of Manchester United came in the shape of a European Cup Winners Cup medal, following a 3-1 win over Rapid Vienna. When playing alongside Gary Lineker in 1985-86, their partnership brought 49 goals, but after losing out to Liverpool in the League title race, Everton, in their third consecutive FA Cup Final, succumbed 3-1 to the same team, after an inspired second-half display by the men from Anfield. Absent for a lengthy period in 1986-87, he came back to win another League Championship medal, although his goal rate had dried up somewhat and in the 1989 FA Cup Final, Everton's fourth appearance in six years, he remained goalless as Liverpool won 3-2. Between 1988-89 and 1990-91, he scored only 15 League goals, as his value to the team became more as a provider, than a taker of chances. Won the first of his dozen full Scottish caps in Iceland in May 1985, but has not been selected for several years now. Transferred to newly promoted Oldham Athletic in the summer of 1991, he took on a new lease of life, playing in every single game of 1991-92 and leading the "Latics'" scoring charts with 15 goals, including four in an end of season fixture against Luton Town. Started **1992-93** where he left off last season, as the hard working leader of the front line, playing in the first 25 matches and looking set to be an ever present, when he was struck down with a similar back problem that had sidelined Andy Ritchie earlier. After being injured in the Third Round FA Cup draw against Tranmere Rovers, he made a couple of substitute appearances, before it was confirmed that he needed an operation to repair the damage. Badly missed, the good news is that he should be fit in time for the coming season.

| | | | APPEARANCES | | | | GOALS | | | |
|---|---|---|---|---|---|---|---|---|---|---|
| Clubs | Signing Date | Transfer Fee | Lge | FL Cup | FA Cup | Others | Lge | FL Cup | FA Cup | Others |
| Dumbarton | .78 | - | 37+3 | 2 | 3 | | 17 | | 2 | |
| Everton | 4.80 | £125,000 | 306+16 | 46+2 | 52+2 | 21+1 | 111 | 15 | 20 | 11 |
| Oldham Athletic* | 7.91 | £500,000 | 62+1 | 8 | 3+1 | 1 | 19 | 2 | 1 | |

## **SHARP Kevin** Phillip

Born: Canada, 19 September 1974

Height: 5'8"

Weight: 10.12

International Honours: E Yth

**Position/Skill Factor:** Left-back who can step up in midfield. With great technique, a lovely left foot, telling passes and strong running, he can really play.

**Career History:** One of the two youngsters signed by Leeds United, following their release by French First Division club, Auxerre, the other being Jamie Forrester.

Remarkably, both had been recruited as trainee or junior professionals by the French club in 1990 at the age of 16. Had a great first season in **1992-93** at Elland Road, as a prominent member of the FA Cup winning youth team and made a memorable PL debut when deputising for Tony Dorigo at home to Crystal Palace on 17 April 1993. He almost scored with a tremendous shot from all of 30 yards and subsequently earned rave reviews and "Man of the Match" plaudits from the press. Along with Mark Tinkler and Jamie Forrester, he is a member of the England under 18 squad and continued to impress in the next three League games. 1993-94 should see him as Dorigo's understudy now that Dylan Kerr has left the club.

| | | | APPEARANCES | | | | GOALS | | | |
|---|---|---|---|---|---|---|---|---|---|---|
| Clubs | Signing Date | Transfer Fee | Lge | FL Cup | FA Cup | Others | Lge | FL Cup | FA Cup | Others |
| Leeds United* | 10.92 | - | 4 | | | | | | | |

## **SHARPE John** James

Born: Birmingham, 9 August 1975

Height: 5'10" Weight 11.0

**Position/Skill Factor:** Left sided midfielder who goes past defenders as if they don't exist and with a super left foot, is a good crosser of the ball.

**Career History:** A recent professional signing for Manchester City, he was originally spotted playing for Halesowen boys and first came to Maine Road as an associated schoolboy (February 1991), before becoming a trainee a few months later in July 1991. Although mainly confined to the youth side in **1992-93**, he was given a run out in the Central League and impressed.

| | | | APPEARANCES | | | | GOALS | | | |
|---|---|---|---|---|---|---|---|---|---|---|
| Clubs | Signing Date | Transfer Fee | Lge | FL Cup | FA Cup | Others | Lge | FL Cup | FA Cup | Others |
| Manchester City* | 7.93 | - | | | | | | | | |

## **SHARPE Lee** Stuart

Born: Halesowen, 27 May 1971

Height: 5'11" Weight: 11.4

International Honours: E "U21"-8, E"B", E-6

**Position/Skill Factor:** A very skilful player with pace, who is adept either on the left-wing, or at left-back. He is very good when taking defenders on and giving himself the option of shooting or crossing. Strong on the ball.

**Career History:** An associated schoolboy with Birmingham City (July 1986), on leaving school, however, he signed as a trainee with Torquay United in April 1987 and became their youngest ever player when making his FL debut as a sub at Exeter City on 3 October 1987. Four days later, he impressed a television audience with his impudent and confident skills against "Spurs" in a League Cup tie at White Hart Lane, after coming on as a substitute. He signed professional at the end of 1987-88 and was almost immediately transferred to Manchester United, as the impoverished Fourth Division side cashed in their investment. Made his United debut against West Ham United at Old Trafford in September and proved a reliable squad player, filling in mainly at left-back. After making a good start in 1989-90 on the left-wing, he was injured on New Year's Day against Queens Park Rangers and didn't play again that season, thus missing out on United's FA Cup triumph. Came to prominence in 1990-91 with a hat-trick against Arsenal in an amazing Third Round League Cup 6-2 defeat of Arsenal at Highbury, but despite scoring in both legs of the Semi-Final, there was no happy ending as United lost 1-0 at Wembley against Second Division, Sheffield Wednesday. However, it was a different story in Europe as he won a European Cup Winners Cup medal, following United's great 2-1 victory over Barcelona. Earlier, on 27 March 1991, he had made his England debut in the European Championships, when coming on for Tony Adams in a 1-1 draw against Eire at Wembley and at just 20 years of age, he could well consider himself as having arrived. He was also voted "Young Player of the Year" in the PFA Awards. After all the excitement of the previous season, 1991-92 was a terrible anti-climax. Absent through injury in the first-half of the season, when fit again in December, he found another teenage prodigy, Ryan Giggs, had taken his place on the left-wing. He could not force his way back on a regular basis and was only a substitute in the League Cup Final victory over Sheffield Wednesday. Having been struck down with viral meningitis during the summer, he missed the start of the **1992-93** Premier League and was not expected back for quite a while. Made a remarkable recovery, however, and came back for the match at Aston Villa in November, looking like he had never been away. Only missed one more game, as United laid low the disappointment of the previous year and swept to the League title, leaving nearest challengers, Aston Villa, in their wake. Recognised by Alex Ferguson as the club's leading assist player, he only scored one goal, but his value to the team was immense as both he and Ryan Giggs gave added width to the Championship thrust. His good play also excited the England manager, Graham Taylor and following a further substitute appearance in March, he made his full debut in the World Cup qualifier against Norway and played in three more summer games.

| | | | APPEARANCES | | | | GOALS | | | |
|---|---|---|---|---|---|---|---|---|---|---|
| Clubs | Signing Date | Transfer Fee | Lge | FL Cup | FA Cup | Others | Lge | FL Cup | FA Cup | Others |
| Torquay United | 5.88 | - | 9+5 | | | 2+3 | 3 | | | |
| Manchester United* | 6.88 | £185,000 | 87+17 | 11+4 | 11+2 | 8+2 | 5 | 7 | | 1 |

## SHAW Paul

Born: Burnham, 4 September 1973

Height: 5'11" Weight: 12.4

International Honours: E Yth

**Position/Skill Factor:** A striker who can also play in midfield, he has a lovely first touch and is always looking for the chance of a long range shot.

**Career History:** First signing for Arsenal as an associated schoolboy in March 1988, he came to Highbury as a trainee in July 1990 and had progressed to the professional ranks a year later. A very enthusiastic youngster who has yet to make his League debut, he established himself in the reserves during **1992-93** with a healthy goal per game ratio. Will be looking to break into the first team squad in 1993-94.

| | | | APPEARANCES | | | | GOALS | | | |
|---|---|---|---|---|---|---|---|---|---|---|
| Clubs | Signing Date | Transfer Fee | Lge | FL Cup | FA Cup | Others | Lge | FL Cup | FA Cup | Others |
| Arsenal* | 9.91 | - | | | | | | | | |

## SHEARER Alan

Born: Newcastle, 13 August 1970

Height: 5'11" Weight: 11.3

International Honours: E Yth, E "U21"-11, E"B", E-6

**Position/Skill Factor:** One of the best strikers in the country, he has all the right attributes. Brave, strong on the ball, he shields it well and is useful in the air.

**Career History:** Although born in Newcastle, he signed for Southampton, first as an associated schoolboy in September 1984 and then, on leaving school, as a trainee in July 1986. Made his FL debut at Chelsea on 26 March 1988, as a substitute, a month before turning professional. In his first full League game, he caused a sensation, netting a hat-trick in a 4-2 win over Arsenal and becoming the youngest player to score three times in a First Division match. Hit by injuries in 1988-89, he didn't get a run, but by the following season he was beginning to force his way into the side, although he only scored three goals in 19 full League outings. Missed just four games in 1990-91, as he, Matthew le Tissier and Rod Wallace made the "Saints" into one of the most entertaining teams in the First Division. Remarkably, he scored only four goals in 36 FL games, but netted eight times in ten cup games! In 1991-92, incoming manager, Ian Branfoot, changed the "Saints'" style to a physical ultra-defensive one, despite possessing two of the most exciting young forwards in the game and goal chances were at a premium. Nevertheless, he finished as leading scorer with 13 FL goals, plus six in cup games and missed only one match in the club's heavy programme of 60 matches, which included long runs in the League Cup and FA Cup, plus an appearance in the Zenith Cup Final, where the "Saints" were defeated 2-3 by Nottingham Forest after extra-time. Although he has often found goals hard to come by for the "Saints", at international level his record is sensational. 13 goals in 11 England Under 21 games was a prelude to his full international debut against France in February 1992, in which he scored the first and set up the second for Nigel Clough and Gary Lineker in England's 2-0 victory. Included in the England squad for the European Championship Finals in Sweden, he played in one match (again versus France), but in common with his team mates, failed to advance his burgeoning reputation. However, after arriving home from the European tournament, he signed for big spending Blackburn Rovers, as they looked to cement their newly won Premier League status. Many felt that the British record paid for the striker was excessive, but by Boxing Day, **1992-93**, when he had already scored 22 goals in 25 games he was already a bargain. Proved that the size of the fee was no handicap by scoring two sensational goals on his debut and, unusually for such a prolific striker, his goals contained a high number of spectacular efforts, with a stunning shot at Liverpool firmly etched in the mind. Appeared to have overcome England's striking problem until he received the injury at home to Leeds United on 26 December, which necessitated first a cartilage operation and then one to remove ligaments. If he had been able to play all season he might well have rewritten the record books, but he had some form of compensation when finishing third in the "Player of the Year" awards.

| | | | APPEARANCES | | | | GOALS | | | |
|---|---|---|---|---|---|---|---|---|---|---|
| Clubs | Signing Date | Transfer Fee | Lge | FL Cup | FA Cup | Others | Lge | FL Cup | FA Cup | Others |
| Southampton | 4.88 | - | 105+13 | 16+2 | 11+3 | 8 | 23 | 11 | 4 | 5 |
| Blackburn Rovers* | 7.92 | £3,600,000 | 21 | 5 | | | 16 | 6 | | |

## SHEERIN Paul George

Born: Edinburgh, 28 August 1974

Height: 5'10" Weight: 11.1

International Honours: S Yth

**Position/Skill Factor:** Left-winger with plenty of pace and an excellent crosser of the ball.

**Career History:** Signed by Southampton as investment for the future, only three months after he had joined Scottish Second Division side, Alloa Athletic, from junior club, Whitehill Welfare. Slightly built, he slotted into the "Saints'" youth side in midfield during **1992-93** and after three substitute appearances, made his full debut for the reserves in February 1993. A regular for the second string for the remainder of the season, he scored in successive games in April and looks to make the Premier League in 1993-94.

| | | | APPEARANCES | | | | GOALS | | | |
|---|---|---|---|---|---|---|---|---|---|---|
| Clubs | Signing Date | Transfer Fee | Lge | FL Cup | FA Cup | Others | Lge | FL Cup | FA Cup | Others |
| Alloa Athletic | 7.92 | - | 6+2 | 2 | | 1 | | | | |
| Southampton* | 10.92 | £60,000 | | | | | | | | |

## SHERIDAN Anthony Joseph

Born: Dublin, 21 October 1974

Height: 6'0" Weight: 12.4

International Honours: IR Yth, IR"U21"-3

**Position/Skill Factor:** Very skilful left-winger with a lovely left foot who can really play.

**Career History:** On leaving school in the summer of 1991, he came across the Irish Sea to join Coventry City and after signing as a professional on his 17th birthday, immediately began to impress as a member of the "Sky Blues'" youth team. After a prolonged period of homesickness, he finally returned to Highfield Road in time for the start of the **1992-93** season and before long had turned in a wonderful display for the Republic of Ireland's youth team against Romania, earning rave reviews from Maurice Setters. Named the "Young Player of the Year" by the Irish FA, he made his PL debut at Leeds United on 31 October 1992 and was selected for the Republic's under 21 squad in Spain. Unfortunately, he then damaged his ankle ligaments, which restrained his programme somewhat. Played for his countries under 21 side against Germany (twice) and Denmark, but never broke through for City again. However, Bobby Gould is convinced that if his attitude can match his ability, he can be a great player.

| | | | APPEARANCES | | | | GOALS | | | |
|---|---|---|---|---|---|---|---|---|---|---|
| Clubs | Signing Date | Transfer Fee | Lge | FL Cup | FA Cup | Others | Lge | FL Cup | FA Cup | Others |
| Coventry City* | 9.91 | - | 1 | | | | | | | |

## SHERIDAN John Joseph

Born: Manchester, 1 October 1964

Height: 5'9" Weight: 10.8

International Honours: IR Yth, IR "U21"-1, IR-15

**Position/Skill Factor:** Midfield player who oozes confidence. Always prepared to have the ball and always looking to create goal scoring chances for others. Has a great range of passing skills.

**Career History:** Started his football career as an associated schoolboy in November 1978 with Manchester City, but was released and snapped up by Leeds United. Made his FL debut at Elland Road on 20 November 1982 against Middlesbrough and remained in the side until the end of the season. After adjusting so quickly to Second Division football, he had the misfortune to suffer a broken leg at Barnsley in October 1983, but on recovering, he came back brilliantly as an ever present in 1984-85. His form didn't go unnoticed by Jack Charlton and he made his debut for the Irish Republic, through parental qualification, against Romania on 23 March 1988. After seven seasons of Second Division football at Elland Road, he seemed to realise his ambition of playing in the First Division when Brian Clough signed him for Nottingham Forest in the summer of 1989. As with Asa Hartford and Gary Megson in previous season, however, once signed he was totally ignored by Clough until rescued by Ron Atkinson for Sheffield Wednesday after four months at the City ground without a FL appearance to his name. When he arrived at Hillsborough, the "Owls" were bottom of the First Division with only one victory and two goals from 11 games. He immediately formed a midfield partnership with Carlton Palmer, which not only stabilised Wednesday and lifted them to mid-table, but also transformed them into a stylish passing outfit, until a tragic late season collapse condemned the team to relegation. He only missed one game in 1990-91, scoring ten goals, including five penalties, as the club returned to the First Division at the first time of asking, but the goal everybody will remember him for came after 38 minutes of the 1991 League Cup Final against the strong favourites, Manchester United. His powerful shot sped into the net to ultimately give Wednesday a shock 1-0 victory and enabled him to pocket a coveted FA Cup winners medal. Although troubled by injuries in 1991-92, he played a part in Wednesday's best League campaign for 30 years, as they finished in third place and qualified for the 1992-93 UEFA Cup. Made a late start in **1992-93**, as he recovered from a knee operation and wasn't available for first team duty until the end of October. Once back, however, he exerted his usual influence on the game, seeming to have added more grit to his play and signalled his return to match fitness with a wonderful free-kick equaliser in a 2-2 home draw against Kaiserslautern in the return leg of the UEFA Cup. Only missed four more games during the remainder of the campaign and played a leading role in the "Owls'" march to Wembley to contest both the League and FA Cup Finals against Arsenal. Although he had a hand in two of Wednesday's three goals, it wasn't enough to stop the "Gunners" from taking the trophies and "Shezz", as he is known to the fans, had to be satisfied with a matching pair of losers medals. Jack Charlton, the Republic of Ireland manager, continued to rave about him on television, but had largely ignored him for two years until recalling him as a substitute for the Latvia game this summer and if his fitness holds, he should continue to add to his tally of 15 caps.

| | | | APPEARANCES | | | | GOALS | | | |
|---|---|---|---|---|---|---|---|---|---|---|
| Clubs | Signing Date | Transfer Fee | Lge | FL Cup | FA Cup | Others | Lge | FL Cup | FA Cup | Others |
| Leeds United | 3.82 | - | 225+5 | 14 | 11+1 | 11 | 47 | 3 | 1 | 1 |
| Nottingham Forest | 8.89 | £650,000 | | 1 | | | | | | |
| Sheffield Wednesday* | 11.89 | £500,000 | 121+1 | 18 | 15 | 4 | 21 | 3 | 3 | 2 |

## SHERINGHAM Edward (Teddy) Paul

Born: Walthamstow, 2 April 1966

Height: 5'11" Weight: 12.4

International Honours: E Yth, E "U21"-1, E"B", E-2

**Position/Skill Factor:** Striker with nice ball skills who is always looking for a shooting opportunity. Good in the air, on the ground he keeps his passing simple, but effective.

**Career History:** Joined Millwall as an apprentice in June 1982, before graduating through the club's junior sides and making his FL debut at the Den against Brentford on 15 January 1984, after turning professional. Following a spell on loan at Aldershot and the occasional game for the "Lions", he was finally given a run in 1986-87 when he was ever present, scoring 18 goals. He missed only one game in 1987-88 and in Tony Cascarino, he found the perfect foil to support his ability on the ground. Between them, they scored 42 League goals as the "Lions" roared their way into the top flight for the first time in their history as Second Division Champions. During the club's two seasons in the First Division, it was obvious that goals would be more difficult to come by, although in 1988-89, Millwall amazed the critics by finishing tenth in the table. However, after making a good start in 1989-90, at the end of the season the club were relegated with only five wins to their credit. But back in the Second Division, it was a different story for both the club and Teddy. Although the "Lions" failed at the Play-Off stage, he had a quite magnificent season, scoring 33 League goals, including four in a 4-1 win over Plymouth Argyle and three further hat-tricks. He ended the season as the highest goal scorer in the club's history with 111 and his 38 in all games equalled Richard Parker's and Peter Burridge's records set in 1926-27 and 1960-61, respectively. As Millwall lost out on promotion, it was perhaps inevitable that a First Division club should snap him up, but at least the "Lions" were able to extract a massive fee (for a non-international player) from Nottingham Forest for his services. Not an unqualified success in his first season at the City Ground, despite playing in all but three games of Forest's 60 match programme and topping the scoring lists with 12 FL goals and nine cup goals. The highlights of his season were a hat-trick against Crystal Palace in a Fifth Round League Cup tie in February and his first two appearances at Wembley, first as a winner in the Zenith Cup Final against Southampton and then as a loser in the League Cup Final against Manchester United. Kicked off the new **1992-93** Premier League season in a Nottingham Forest shirt, with a goal against Liverpool, but two games later he got his wish to return to London, when signing for Tottenham Hotspur. Impressed in his debut for "Spurs" in a live televised match at Ipswich Town and in his next game, he introduced himself to White Hart Lane when netting the opening goal of a 2-0 win against Sheffield United. Although he scored eight times in his first 20 appearances for the club, he took time to settle, but after Christmas the goals began to flow freely, including six "pairs", a hat-trick in a 4-0 win at home against Leeds United and two penalties in a 4-1 victory over Oldham Athletic, that celebrated his 300th League game. Finishing the season with 29 goals, he won the Premier League "Golden Boot" award and earned himself a call-up to the England squad, preparing for the end of season World Cup qualifying games. After gaining his first cap in a 1-1 draw against Poland, he did enough to be selected for the "debacle" against Norway, but like the rest of his team-mates, disappointed in a lacklustre 2-0 defeat.

| | | | APPEARANCES | | | | GOALS | | | |
|---|---|---|---|---|---|---|---|---|---|---|
| Clubs | Signing Date | Transfer Fee | Lge | FL Cup | FA Cup | Others | Lge | FL Cup | FA Cup | Others |
| Millwall | 1.84 | - | 205+15 | 16+1 | 12 | 11+2 | 93 | 8 | 5 | 5 |
| Aldershot | 2.85 | Loan | 4+1 | | | 1 | | | | |
| Nottingham Forest | 7.91 | £2,000,000 | 42 | 10 | 4 | 6 | 14 | 5 | 2 | 2 |
| Tottenham Hotspur* | 8.92 | £2,100,000 | 38 | 4 | 5 | | 21 | 3 | 4 | |

## **SHERON Michael (Mike)** Nigel

Born: Liverpool,
11 January 1972

Height: 5'9"

Weight: 11.3

International Honours:
E "U21"-12

**Position/Skill Factor:** A striker, who can also play in midfield, he has good vision with plenty of skill and looks to have the makings of a top-class player.

**Career History:** Came through Manchester City's junior ranks, after signing on as a trainee in July 1988, to turn professional during the 1990 close season. Loaned out to Third Division Bury at the end of 1990-91, he made his FL debut at Preston North End on 6 April 1991. Scored the winning goal at Tranmere Rovers in his only full League game, which sent the "Shakers" into the Play-Offs, but was unable to find the net again as Bolton Wanderers ultimately ended Bury's vain hopes of promotion. Made rapid strides in 1991-92, after making his debut for City as a substitute at home to Everton on 17 September. A permanent member of the first team squad thereafter, he established a regular slot on the right side of midfield in the last two months of the campaign, although previously a free scoring striker in City's youth and reserve teams. Called up for the England Under 21 squad at the end of the season. Maintained his excellent rate of progress in **1992-93**, making 38 (including five substitute) first team appearances in the new Premier League and adding to his tally of England under 21 caps. Although having a penchant for the ball being delivered to his feet, he often played quite ingeniously from midfield, laying off for Niall Quinn and David White and slipping forward to score some delightful goals. His season's total of 14, included a few "corkers", but none better than when chasing a headed back pass from a Leeds' defender and flicking the ball over an advancing 'keeper for the first goal in a 4-0 home win.

| | | | APPEARANCES | | | | GOALS | | | |
|---|---|---|---|---|---|---|---|---|---|---|
| Clubs | Signing Date | Transfer Fee | Lge | FL Cup | FA Cup | Others | Lge | FL Cup | FA Cup | Others |
| Manchester City* | 7.90 | - | 53+14 | 4+1 | 5+1 | 1 | 17 | 1 | 3 | |
| Bury | 3.91 | Loan | 1+4 | | | 2 | 1 | | | |

## **SHERWOOD Timothy (Tim)** Alan

Born: St Albans, 6 February 1969

Height: 6'1" Weight: 11.4

International Honours: E Yth, E "U21"-4

**Position/Skill Factor:** An attacking midfielder who likes to get forward to join up in the attack. A very determined competitor, he uses the ball constructively.

**Career History:** Signed for nearby Watford as an apprentice in February 1986, having been at the club as a junior since the summer of 1985. After turning professional, he made his FL debut as a substitute at Sheffield Wednesday on 12 September 1987 and made nine full appearances in midfield during a season that ultimately saw the "Hornets" relegated to the Second Division. Had a brief run in the first team in mid-1988-89, but then played little further part in Watford's ultimately unsuccessful promotion drive. With so little experience under his belt, it was a surprise when First Division Norwich signed him for a handsome fee in the summer of 1989, but it proved to be a shrewd signing. He soon won a place in the "Canaries'" team and proved to be a valuable utility player, turning out at right-back, in midfield and central defence and winning selection for the England Under 21 squad. In 1990-91 he firmly established himself in midfield, replacing the departed Andy Townsend and playing in every FL game, bar the last of the season. At this point his career seemed set fair, but it was set back at the start of 1991-92 when he was fined and suspended for a breach of club discipline. Consequently, he lost his place and although making a brief "comeback" in November and December he was eventually transferred, for a large profit, to ambitious Blackburn Rovers. Yet to settle in Lancashire, he soon lost his place in the Rovers' team and played almost no part in the vital end of season games or the Play-Offs. He soon put the previous season's lamentable form behind him as he became the accepted midfield leader of the team in **1992-93** and proved to be a splendidly mobile, hard working player, who was always on hand to assist the defence. Essentially defensive, he seldom made forward runs, but enjoyed scoring against his old team Norwich City and netted a real beauty in the final game of a very successful first Premier League season, a 1-0 win at home to Sheffield Wednesday.

| | | | APPEARANCES | | | | GOALS | | | |
|---|---|---|---|---|---|---|---|---|---|---|
| Clubs | Signing Date | Transfer Fee | Lge | FL Cup | FA Cup | Others | Lge | FL Cup | FA Cup | Others |
| Watford | 2.87 | - | 23+9 | 4+1 | 9 | 4+1 | 2 | | | |
| Norwich City | 7.89 | £175,000 | 66+5 | 7 | 4 | 5+1 | 10 | 1 | | 2 |
| Blackburn Rovers* | 2.92 | £500,000 | 45+5 | 6 | 4+1 | | 3 | | | |

## SHIPPERLEY Neil Jason

Born: Chatham, 30 October 1974

Height: 6'0" Weight: 12.10

**Position/Skill Factor:** A striker with great workrate, who chases lost causes. Always pressuring defenders and forcing them into errors. Packs a good shot in both feet.

**Career History:** Son of David, a central defender with Charlton, Gillingham and Reading in the 1970s, Neil first joined Chelsea as an associated schoolboy in February 1991, signed a two year trainee contract in July 1991 and was upgraded to full professional status in September 1992. After a good season in the juniors and reserves, scoring over 50 goals, he continued in the same vein in **1992-93** and made his PL debut as a substitute at Southampton on 10 April 1993. Played in the next game at home to Wimbledon and scored the fourth goal in a 4-2 win and looks to have an outstanding career ahead of him at his present rate of progress.

| | | | APPEARANCES | | | | GOALS | | | |
|---|---|---|---|---|---|---|---|---|---|---|
| Clubs | Signing Date | Transfer Fee | Lge | FL Cup | FA Cup | Others | Lge | FL Cup | FA Cup | Others |
| Chelsea* | 9.92 | - | 2+1 | | | | 1 | | | |

## SHIRTLIFF Peter Andrew

Born: Hoyland, 6 April 1961

Height: 6'2"

Weight: 13.4

**Position/Skill Factor:** Very brave central defender, who rarely loses out in the air and is a strong tackler on the ground. Normally clears his lines, but passes the ball well when not under pressure.

**Career History:** The older brother of Paul, who played for Sheffield Wednesday and Northampton Town between 1980-1985, he signed for the "Owls" as an associated schoolboy in October 1975, before graduating as an apprentice in June 1977. He actually made his FL debut for Sheffield Wednesday, two months prior to turning professional, at Peterborough United on 19 August 1978. But it wasn't until the following season that he began to make his mark, although often having to alternate with Mike Pickering. Only missed six games in 1983-84 as Wednesday were promoted to the First Division, behind Chelsea, but later, with much competition for places, he signed for Charlton Athletic in the summer of 1986. In his first season in London, drama unfolded, as Athletic, by dint of their lowly First Division placing, were forced to play-off against Second Division Leeds United to decide which side would compete in the top flight during 1987-88. One nil down in extra-time, with seven minutes to go, he scored the equaliser and with just four minutes left on the clock, he dived in for the winner. Nothing else in his career could ever match that for excitement, but he was very sound and reliable during his three years at the club and was only ever absent, when injured. However, when Sheffield Wednesday manager Ron Atkinson came for him in the 1989 close season, he returned to Hillsborough for a then club record fee. In his first season, the team, after seeming to secure its First Division status, faltered badly in their last seven matches and were relegated. Promotion was duly attained at the first time of asking in 1990-91, as Wednesday went up behind Oldham Athletic and West Ham United and although he missed the last four games of the season through injury, he was very much present when winning a League Cup winners medal as a result of the "Owls'" splendid 1-0 victory over Manchester United. Out of favour in 1991-92, following the signing of Paul Warhurst, he did not get a game until the New Year, but played a more significant role in the second-half of the season as Wednesday achieved a highly creditable third place. Played in slightly less than half the Premier League programme in **1992-93**, as injuries ruined his season. Having already missed a fair chunk of the campaign, he took the opportunity of putting a run of 15 games together, when taking over defensive duties from Paul Warhurst. Was then unfortunate to fracture an arm during the Liverpool game at Hillsborough, which not only kept him out of action for a considerable period, but effectively ruled him out of contention for both the losing League and FA Cup Finals. When he was fit to play, however, he showed all the qualities that have made him such a popular figure during his two spells at the club.

| | | | APPEARANCES | | | | GOALS | | | |
|---|---|---|---|---|---|---|---|---|---|---|
| Clubs | Signing Date | Transfer Fee | Lge | FL Cup | FA Cup | Others | Lge | FL Cup | FA Cup | Others |
| Sheffield Wednesday | 10.78 | - | 188 | 17+1 | 17+1 | | 4 | | 1 | |
| Charlton Athletic | 8.86 | £125,000 | 102+1 | 10 | 5 | 7 | 7 | | | 2 |
| Sheffield Wednesday* | 7.89 | £500,000 | 104 | 18 | 9 | 4 | 4 | 1 | 2 | |

## SHUTT Carl Steven

Born: Sheffield, 10 October 1961

Height: 5'10"

Weight: 11.10

**Position/Skill Factor:** A striker whose pace takes him away from defenders. Very dangerous in the penalty area, he has the ability to pounce on any mistakes.

**Career History:** Sheffield Wednesday introduced him to League football, having snapped him up from Spalding United, of the Northern Counties (East) League, at the end of 1984-85. Ironically, he was previously signed by Wednesday as an associated schoolboy player in April 1978, but had been released. Made his FL debut as a substitute at Oxford United on 31 August 1985 and in his first full League appearance, he struck the equaliser at Hillsborough against Coventry City. Scored nine times in 17 games in his first season. A hero of Wednesday's fine FA Cup run of 1985-86, he netted twice against Derby County in a Fifth Round replay, scored the winner against West Ham United in the Quarter-Final and the first goal in the Semi-Final against Everton, when the "Toffees" came back to win in extra-time. Despite scoring five times in his first ten FL games of 1986-87, he strangely lost his place and thereafter played second fiddle to David Hirst. Therefore it was not too surprising when he was allowed to leave for Bristol City in October 1987. Netted twice in his first game for the "Robins", a 4-2 reversal at Blackpool and scored all four goals in a 4-0 home victory over Fulham, a few weeks later. In 1988-89, however, his scoring rate ground to a halt and he was transferred back to his native Yorkshire, rejoining his former manager, Howard Wilkinson, at Leeds United. Remarkably, he scored a hat-trick against Bournemouth on his Leeds debut and struck again in his second game, but it was not enough to guarantee him a first team place. Due to a glut of forwards at Elland Road, he found it difficult to make his mark during his first term, but had some solace in the shape of a Second Division Championship medal as United once again rejoined the top flight. From November 1990 onwards, he had a good run in a side that eventually finished fourth in the First Division and in settling down alongside Lee Chapman, the pair scored 31 goals between them. Out of favour again in 1991-92, following the signing of Rod Wallace, he made only occasional appearances, but his 14 FL games (eight as a substitute) were enough for him to qualify for a League Championship medal when United won the title. Played only 14 (including eight substitute) games during **1992-93**, while appearing in a midfield role and at the end of a disastrous season for the club, he was considered surplus to requirements and placed on the transfer list. Scored only three goals throughout the campaign, all in cup competitions, with the wonderful winner against VFB Stuttgart in the third match of a First Round European Cup-tie, Being the pick. The low point of his season came when he was stretchered off at Elland Road, having just come on as a replacement for Scott Sellars in the League match against Oldham Athletic. Originally thought to be a punctured lung, he was eventually given the all-clear and was back on the bench after a six week spell out of the game. Always giving 100%, he is consistent to a fault and still has plenty left in the tank.

| | | | APPEARANCES | | | | GOALS | | | |
|---|---|---|---|---|---|---|---|---|---|---|
| Clubs | Signing Date | Transfer Fee | Lge | FL Cup | FA Cup | Others | Lge | FL Cup | FA Cup | Others |
| Sheffield Wednesday | 5.85 | - | 36+4 | 3 | 4+1 | | 16 | 1 | 4 | |
| Bristol City | 10.87 | £55,000 | 39+7 | 5+2 | 7+1 | 10+1 | 10 | 4 | 4 | 4 |
| Leeds United* | 3.89 | £50,000 | 46+33 | 6+2 | 10 | 4+5 | 17 | 2 | 1 | 4 |

## SIMPSON Fitzroy

Born: Bradford-on-Avon, 26 February 1970

Height: 5'8" Weight: 10.7

**Position/Skill Factor:** Powerful left-winger with an excellent left foot, who will often shoot on sight of goal and is not afraid to take defenders on.

**Career History:** Signed as a professional for Swindon Town in the 1988 close season, having been a trainee at the club since July 1987 and made his FL debut as a substitute during the home game against Barnsley on 14 January 1989. Given a couple of good runs in 1989-90, he gradually settled into a side that won the First Division Play-Off place at the end of the season, only to be denied by the League's ruling that the club be demoted due to financial irregularities. The following season saw Swindon avoid the drop into Division Three by a narrow margin, but he did well in a team that only won three of its last 17 League matches. A first team regular on the Town left-wing in 1991-92, he played in nearly every game up to the time of his transfer to Manchester City in March 1992. Slotting in immediately at Maine Road, after replacing Michael Hughes on the left-wing, he played in the last nine League matches, scoring his first goal for the club in a home 2-0 win over Notts County. In and out of the side in **1992-93** with 27, plus two substitute appearances, although he played in the first 18 games until being called off at Manchester United. A fine game at home to Nottingham Forest, saw him at his best, when a five man move ended with him placing a low drive into the corner of the net for City's second in a 2-2 draw. At times he promised more consistent play, but his youthful, fiery approach, will need to be harnessed and turned to his benefit in order that the necessary progress can be made.

| | | | APPEARANCES | | | | GOALS | | | |
|---|---|---|---|---|---|---|---|---|---|---|
| Clubs | Signing Date | Transfer Fee | Lge | FL Cup | FA Cup | Others | Lge | FL Cup | FA Cup | Others |
| Swindon Town | 7.88 | - | 78+27 | 15+2 | 2+1 | 3+2 | 9 | 1 | | |
| Manchester City* | 3.92 | £500,000 | 36+4 | 3 | 4 | | 3 | | | |

## SIMPSON Ronald James

Born: Easington, 12 March 1974

Height: 5'8" Weight: 11.3

**Position/Skill Factor:** Midfield player. Has good all-round ability, coupled with excellent vision and passing skills.

**Career History:** Joined the Sheffield Wednesday professional ranks during the 1992 close season, having previously been at Hillsborough as an associated schoolboy (October 1988) and as a trainee (July 1990). Suffered from various injuries in **1992-93**, but continued to play for the youth side, while having a handful of games for the reserves. Will look to consolidate on that this coming season.

| | | | APPEARANCES | | | | GOALS | | | |
|---|---|---|---|---|---|---|---|---|---|---|
| Clubs | Signing Date | Transfer Fee | Lge | FL Cup | FA Cup | Others | Lge | FL Cup | FA Cup | Others |
| Sheffield Wednesday* | 6.92 | - | | | | | | | | |

## SINCLAIR Frank Mohammed

Born: Lambeth, 3 December 1971

Height: 5'8"

Weight: 11.2

**Position/Skill Factor:** Can play either at full-back or central defence and is very good in the air for his size. Enthusiasm and great pace are his major assets.

**Career History:** Came to Chelsea from the same school that produced Alan Hudson, when signing associated schoolboy forms in January 1986. Became a trainee in July 1988 and turned professional during the 1990 close season, after some impressive displays in the juniors. He was given a taste of big-time soccer at the end of 1990-91, when he stood in at left-back for England's Tony Dorigo and made his FL debut in a 3-3 draw at Stamford Bridge against Luton Town on 6 April 1991. Made an early appearance in 1991-92 as a fifth defender away to Oldham Athletic, to no avail, as Chelsea crashed 3-0. His next FL action was on loan to West Bromwich Albion at Christmas time where he achieved unwanted notoriety for being sent off in a game at Exeter for assaulting a referee — a charge he denied — and was suspended for nine games. Returned to the Chelsea team at left-back late in the season, playing in seven of the last ten League games. Very impressive for most of **1992-93**, having come into the side a couple of games after Paul Elliott's injury, his great pace made him more than a match for any attacker when going for the ball. Recovered well from injury to gradually regain his form and become Chelsea's "Player of the Year" at the end of the very testing season.

| | | | APPEARANCES | | | | GOALS | | | |
|---|---|---|---|---|---|---|---|---|---|---|
| Clubs | Signing Date | Transfer Fee | Lge | FL Cup | FA Cup | Others | Lge | FL Cup | FA Cup | Others |
| Chelsea* | 5.90 | - | 44 | 6 | 2 | | 1 | 1 | | |
| West Bromwich Albion | 12.91 | Loan | 6 | | | | 1 | | | |

## SINTON Andrew (Andy)

Born: Newcastle, 19 March 1966

Height: 5'7" Weight: 10.7

International Honours: E Sch, FL Rep, E"B", E-10

**Position/Skill Factor:** Left-winger with a tremendous work rate, who is the ideal wide player. Has a good footballing brain and will often play the ball early, aiming to get it back.

**Career History:** An England schoolboy international, he joined Cambridge United as an associated schoolboy in September 1980, before signing as an apprentice on leaving school in August 1982. Became United's youngest ever player when he made his FL debut at the Abbey Stadium against Wolverhampton Wanderers on 2 November 1982 and on signing professional forms, towards the end of the season, he was already holding down a regular place. In four seasons at the club, he played over 100 first team games before the age of 20, while United dropped from the Second to Fourth Division. With Cambridge strapped for cash, he signed for Brentford in 1985-86 and in three and a half years at Griffin Park, barely missed a match for the Third Division outfit. His ability and consistency were noted by Brentford's close neighbours, Queens Park Rangers and in March 1989 he made the jump from Third to First Division football. Started by netting the winner against Aston Villa on his home debut and finished the campaign with three goals. Ever present in 1989-90 and 1990-91 and as consistent as ever in 1991-92, he missed only four FL games and was rewarded with a full international call-up for the vital match in Poland, which England drew 1-1 to qualify for the European Championship Finals. In his second international against the CIS in Moscow, he played in the unfamiliar position of left-back and appeared twice more before the Finals. Although not included in the original squad for Sweden, he was called up a late replacement for the injured John Barnes. Played twice in the Finals, once at right-back, but like his colleagues, was unable to provide any inspiration in England's disappointing showing. Rapidly becoming one of the stars of the English game, he added four more England caps to his collection in **1992-93** and was a major influence in Rangers attaining fifth place in the new Premier League. Missed only six games throughout the campaign, due to varying injuries, after scoring the first televised goal in a 1-1 draw at Manchester City on the opening day of the new Premier League season. More of a maker, than taker of chances, he excelled in both departments, scoring seven, including a hat-trick in a 4-2 victory over Everton at Loftus Road in the last game of 1992, while his ability as a play maker led to many of the 72 first team goals. As stated previously he is a player who fits in well to the modern system and one that Rangers will surely be building around in the future.

| | | | APPEARANCES | | | | GOALS | | | |
|---|---|---|---|---|---|---|---|---|---|---|
| Clubs | Signing Date | Transfer Fee | Lge | FL Cup | FA Cup | Others | Lge | FL Cup | FA Cup | Others |
| Cambridge United | 4.83 | - | 90+3 | 6 | 3 | 2 | 13 | 1 | | 1 |
| Brentford | 12.85 | £25,000 | 149 | 8 | 11 | 14 | 28 | 3 | 1 | 2 |
| Q.P.R.* | 3.89 | £350,000 | 160 | 14 | 13 | 3 | 22 | | 2 | 1 |

## SKINNER Justin James

Born: Dorking, 17 September 1972

Height: 5'6" Weight: 11.5

**Position/Skill Factor:** Enthusiastic left-back who is a strong tackler. And with an excellent left foot, he is well capable of hitting good long diagonal passes.

**Career History:** A professional signing for Wimbledon during the 1991 close season, having been at the club as a trainee since July 1989, he was a member of the successful side that reached the FA Youth Cup Semi-Final, before being defeated by Crystal Palace. In **1992-93** he spent all season playing for the reserves, apart from one match, his PL debut at Liverpool on 26 September 1992. With Gary Elkins injured, he came into the first team, showing no apparent nerves and great maturity as he shared in a surprise 3-2 victory, before going back to the "stiffs". Most definitely one for the future.

| | | | APPEARANCES | | | | GOALS | | | |
|---|---|---|---|---|---|---|---|---|---|---|
| Clubs | Signing Date | Transfer Fee | Lge | FL Cup | FA Cup | Others | Lge | FL Cup | FA Cup | Others |
| Wimbledon* | 7.91 | - | 1 | | | | | | | |

## SKIVERTON Terence (Terry) John

Born: Mile End, 26 June 1975

Height: 6'0" Weight: 12.6

**Position/Skill Factor:** Can play in most defensive positions, but favours right-back at present. Useful in the air, he might well end up as a centre-back. Has a trusted right foot and is already noted for hitting super long balls out of defence to set the forwards in motion.

**Career History:** An east-ender, he moved across London to sign as an associated schoolboy for Chelsea in September 1989 and on leaving school, came to Stamford Bridge as a trainee (August 1991). Made good progress in **1992-93**, to be asked to sign professional forms during the summer.

| | | | APPEARANCES | | | | GOALS | | | |
|---|---|---|---|---|---|---|---|---|---|---|
| Clubs | Signing Date | Transfer Fee | Lge | FL Cup | FA Cup | Others | Lge | FL Cup | FA Cup | Others |
| Chelsea* | 5.93 | - | | | | | | | | |

## SMALL Bryan

Born: Birmingham, 15 November 1971

Height: 5'9"

Weight: 11.8

International Honours: E Yth, E "U21"-9

**Position/Skill Factor:** Left-back, or midfielder, he is very strong on the ball and is difficult to dispossess. Has a good left foot and is always keen to get forward.

**Career History:** Joined Aston Villa as a trainee in July 1988, having been at the club as an associated schoolboy since January 1986, he turned professional two years later. Made his FL debut wearing the number three shirt on 19 October 1991 away to Everton and had a number of further games both at left-back and in midfield during the season, usually standing in for Steve Staunton. Became a regular with the England under 21 side in **1992-93** and played in 14 first team games for Villa, always at left-back in place of Staunton, when the latter was pushed forward into midfield. An asset to a side chasing Championship honours, with his man-to-man marking ability, he was also encouraged to get forward as often as possible. A very good player, who could come into his own this coming season, if anything, he needs to improve on his crossing of the ball.

| | | | APPEARANCES | | | | GOALS | | | |
|---|---|---|---|---|---|---|---|---|---|---|
| Clubs | Signing Date | Transfer Fee | Lge | FL Cup | FA Cup | Others | Lge | FL Cup | FA Cup | Others |
| Aston Villa* | 7.90 | - | 18+4 | 1 | 2+1 | 2 | | | | |

## SMALL Michael (Mike) Antony

Born: Birmingham, 2 January 1962

Height: 6'0" Weight: 13.5

International Honours: E Yth

**Position/Skill Factor:** Well built striker, who is strong on the ball and has the physique to withstand challenges and still come through successfully. His good skill often takes him into excellent scoring positions, especially when outwitting defenders.

**Career History:** Came out of local football to join Luton Town, signing professional forms early in 1979-80 and after making excellent progress and winning England youth honours, he made his FL debut as a substitute for the "Hatters" on 5 September 1981 at Bolton Wanderers. He failed to make a real breakthrough at Kenilworth Road and when a short loan period with Peterborough United led to nothing, he left Luton in January 1983 and followed a path taken by many young English professionals in the 1980s, by trying his luck on the continent of Europe, joining Dutch club Go Ahead Eagles of Deventer. Precise details of his subsequent career for the next seven years are not available, but it is understood that he played in turn for Twente Enschede (Holland), Standard Liege (Belgium) and PAOK Salonika (Greece), before returning to England in the summer of 1990. Barry Lloyd, manager of Brighton & Hove Albion, has a good record for resurrecting the careers of English players returning from abroad (John Byrne, Mark Farrington, Raphael Meade and Dean Wilkins, to name just a few), but Small was his greatest coup. For a modest fee, he obtained a player who was a revelation, playing the full season and top scoring with 15 FL, plus six cup goals, which helped to propel the "Seagulls" into the Second Division Play-Offs, where they lost out to Notts County in the Final. Not surprisingly, bigger clubs were interested in him and after only one year at the Goldstone Ground, he was snapped up by Billy Bonds for West Ham, at a considerable profit to Brighton. He was an instant success at Upton Park, scoring 13 goals in his first 18 games for the "Hammers", but sadly, the lack of a consistent and effective striking partner, affected his own confidence and lack of goals from elsewhere cost West Ham their First Division place. Nevertheless, 18 first team goals represented a splendid introduction to top level football. Had a disappointing season in **1992-93**, even though the club won immediate promotion to the Premier League as runners-up to Newcastle United. Being sent off on the opening day at Barnsley, was merely a taste of what was to come and following a handful of games, most of them as substitute, he was out injured for over a month with spinal disc trouble. Never looked properly fit after that, although he played three more first team games towards the end of the season and spent a fair bit of time in the reserves. While many of the other players were out celebrating a return to the top flight, he was at the Lilleshall National Sports Injury Clinic, trying to get in shape for 1993-94.

| | | | APPEARANCES | | | | GOALS | | | |
|---|---|---|---|---|---|---|---|---|---|---|
| Clubs | Signing Date | Transfer Fee | Lge | FL Cup | FA Cup | Others | Lge | FL Cup | FA Cup | Others |
| Luton Town | 10.79 | - | 0+4 | | | | | | | |
| Peterborough United | 10.82 | Loan | 2+2 | | | | 1 | | | |
| GAE Deventer (Neth) | 1.83 | - | | | | | | | | |
| Twente Enschede (Neth) | | | | | | | | | | |
| Standard Liege (Bel) | | | | | | | | | | |
| PAOK Salonika (Greece) | | | | | | | | | | |
| Brighton & H.A. | 8.90 | £70,000 | 39 | 2 | 3 | 6 | 15 | 1 | 2 | 3 |
| West Ham United* | 8.91 | £400,000 | 42+7 | 5+1 | 4+1 | 2 | 13 | 4 | 1 | |

## SMITH Alan Martin

Born: Bromsgrove, 21 November 1962

Height: 6'3" Weight: 12.10

International Honours: E Semi-Pro Int, E"B", FL Rep, E-13

**Position/Skill Factor:** Unselfish striker and a wonderful team player, who often acts as a foil for others. Has a good touch and runs well off the ball. He also uses his height and skill in the air to good effect.

**Career History:** Before signing as a professional with Leicester City, he played with Southern League team, Alvechurch and while at the club, he represented the English semi-pro international side. He made his FL debut at Filbert Street against Charlton Athletic on 28 August 1982 and went on to play 39 games that first season, with his 13 League goals playing a major part in City's promotion to the First Division in third place, a remarkable achievement for a first year professional. Partnering the up-and-coming Gary Lineker, he was the perfect decoy, but after the latter's transfer to Everton in the summer of 1985, he assumed the mantle of the club's leading scorer for the next two years. However, his 17 FL goals in 1986-87 were not enough to save Leicester from relegation back to the Second Division and at the end of the season, he signed for Arsenal. In his first term at Highbury he netted 11 goals, including a hat-trick in his fourth game, a 6-0 victory over Portsmouth, to top the "Gunners'" charts and he also scored in the League Cup Final against Luton Town, but couldn't prevent Arsenal going down 3-2 in a thrilling finish. The following season, 1988-89, he won a League Championship medal, striking 23 times in 36 games and opened the scoring in the final game, the 2-0 victory at Liverpool, which decided the title. During the season his club form was finally recognised by Bobby Robson, who selected him to play as a substitute in England's 1-1 draw against Saudi Arabia on 16 November 1988, which also gave him the opportunity to renew his old partnership with Gary Lineker. The goals dried up somewhat in 1989-90, as Arsenal fell away in the League, but he still headed the club's goal charts with just ten. Arsenal were never out of the top two during 1990-91 and at the end of an eventful season, he had won a second League Championship medal. And at the same time he had yet again proved to be a vital cog in the Highbury machine in scoring 22 League goals and laying on several chances for others. He started 1991-92 in lethal form, with seven goals in the first nine FL games and a personal landmark of four in one match (all scored in the space of 16 minutes) against Austria Vienna in the First Round of the European Cup. Thereafter, the goals dried up as Arsenal went into a mid-season slump and he scored only six more to the end of the season, losing his place to the rapidly developing Kevin Campbell. Had to fight to regain his place at the beginning of **1992-93** and it was mid-October before he netted his first goal. Although joining the elite band who have scored a 100 goals for the club, he had a poor season in goalscoring terms. However, two goals against Crystal Palace in the first leg of the League Cup Semi-Final, virtually ensured the "Gunners'" place in the Final, while the subtle flick-on which sent Ian Wright on his way to open the scoring in the FA Cup Final replay against Sheffield Wednesday, was perfection itself. Incredibly, he received his first ever recorded booking during the latter match. Didn't appear in the League Cup Final, but collected an FA Cup winners medal, following the win over Wednesday.

| | | | APPEARANCES | | | | GOALS | | | |
|---|---|---|---|---|---|---|---|---|---|---|
| Clubs | Signing Date | Transfer Fee | Lge | FL Cup | FA Cup | Others | Lge | FL Cup | FA Cup | Others |
| Leicester City | 6.82 | £22,000 | 190+10 | 8+1 | 8 | | 76 | 4 | 4 | |
| Arsenal* | 3.87 | £800,000 | 204+16 | 29+1 | 21+2 | 9 | 81 | 14 | 5 | 4 |

## SMITH Daniel (Danny) Stuart

Born: Sheffield, 8 January 1975

Height: 5'8" Weight: 11.10

**Position/Skill Factor:** Has played at right-back, but will probably settle on the outer right side of midfield. Strong, with good, quick feet, he can work in tight areas up and down the pitch.

**Career History:** Sheffield born and bred, he elected to start his career in Manchester as an associated schoolboy (September 1989) with City, before moving up to trainee status (July 1991) at Maine Road. However, things didn't quite work out as he expected and an agreement reached between the two clubs, saw him finishing his training period with Sheffield United, playing with the youth side in **1992-93** and signing professional forms during the close season.

| | | | APPEARANCES | | | | GOALS | | | |
|---|---|---|---|---|---|---|---|---|---|---|
| Clubs | Signing Date | Transfer Fee | Lge | FL Cup | FA Cup | Others | Lge | FL Cup | FA Cup | Others |
| Sheffield United* | 7.93 | - | | | | | | | | |

## SMITH David Christopher

Born: Liverpool, 26 December 1970

Height: 5'9" Weight: 11.12

**Position/Skill Factor:** Small, compact midfield man, who passes well and takes up good positions in order to receive the return ball.

**Career History:** Liverpool born, he came to Norwich City as a trainee in November 1987 and progressed enough to be taken on as a professional in the summer of 1989. Made his FL debut as a substitute at Derby County on 21 April 1990, but apart from a handful of games in 1990-91, he was still looking forward to a proper run in the side. After making little headway in 1991-92, with just one appearance, it was hard to see him in contention for a first team place in **1992-93**, especially with the "Canaries" battling away for most of the season as Championship challengers. Although spending most of the time in the reserves, he was called up for six end of season games and acquitted himself well, winning "Man of the Match" awards and praise from his fellow team-mates. He also proved that the club had strength in depth and played a key role in three vital victories and twice came within a whisker of scoring his first senior goal at home to Oldham Athletic in March. Should get further opportunities in 1993-94.

| | | | APPEARANCES | | | | GOALS | | | |
|---|---|---|---|---|---|---|---|---|---|---|
| Clubs | Signing Date | Transfer Fee | Lge | FL Cup | FA Cup | Others | Lge | FL Cup | FA Cup | Others |
| Norwich City* | 7.89 | - | 8+3 | | 2 | 1+1 | | | | |

## SMITH Jason Leslie

Born: Birmingham, 6 September 1974

Height: 6'3" Weight: 13.7

International Honours: E Sch

**Position/Skill Factor:** Central defender. Good in the air and a strong tackler, with plenty of pace, he has excellent powers of recovery. At present, a simple pass will often do, but he likes to come out of defence with the ball on occasion.

**Career History:** Already a **1992-93** England under 18 schoolboy international, he came to attention as a member of the Tiverton Town team from the Great Mills Western League, that reached the Final of the 1993 FA Vase competition, before losing 1-0 to Bridlington Town. Earlier, he had been on Tottenham Hotspur's books as an associated schoolboy (October 1989), but chose to go to college for two years, rather than move to London as a trainee. Signed by Coventry City manager, Bobby Gould, during the summer, as a player for the future, if he makes the grade he will be one of the first to do so from this little publicised League.

| | | | APPEARANCES | | | | GOALS | | | |
|---|---|---|---|---|---|---|---|---|---|---|
| Clubs | Signing Date | Transfer Fee | Lge | FL Cup | FA Cup | Others | Lge | FL Cup | FA Cup | Others |
| Coventry City* | 7.93 | - | | | | | | | | |

## SMITHARD Matthew

Born: Leeds, 13 June 1975

Height: 5'8½" Weight: 9.10

**Position/Skill Factor:** Plays on the wide right of midfield, but can perform with equal ability in any of the forward positions. With good balance and pace, he takes defenders on and passes well with either foot.

**Career History:** Signed professional forms for Leeds United, along with a whole clutch of extremely talented youngsters, who by the end of the **1992-93** season, had performed quite magnificently in helping the Yorkshire club to win the FA Youth Cup for the first time in its history. After arriving at Elland Road as an associated schoolboy in June 1991, he progressed to the ranks of trainee (July 1992) on leaving school and will be knocking on United's first team door this coming season.

| | | | APPEARANCES | | | | GOALS | | | |
|---|---|---|---|---|---|---|---|---|---|---|
| Clubs | Signing Date | Transfer Fee | Lge | FL Cup | FA Cup | Others | Lge | FL Cup | FA Cup | Others |
| Leeds United* | 3.93 | - | | | | | | | | |

## SNODIN Ian

Born: Rotherham, 15 August 1963

Height: 5'7" Weight: 8.12

International Honours: E Yth, E "U21"-4, E"B"

**Position/Skill Factor:** Accomplished midfield player who looks comfortable either defending or further forward. A good competitor, he passes the ball effectively.

**Career History:** Younger brother of Glyn, he followed in his footsteps by joining Doncaster Rovers as an associated schoolboy in February 1989, before becoming an apprentice with the club, in August 1979. Made his FL debut at the Belle Vue Ground as a substitute against Bournemouth on 29 March 1980 and scored a few weeks later at Aldershot, before turning professional during the summer. Spent six years at Rovers as they yo-yoed between the Third and Fourth Divisions, making over 200 appearances, before being transferred to the club's more illustrious Yorkshire neighbours, Leeds United, during the 1985 close season. Immediately appointed as club captain, he was at Elland Road for less than two years before the Everton manager, Howard Kendall, added him to his title chasing side in January 1987. Thrown straight into the "Toffees'" midfield, he played throughout the final four months of the season, making 11 League appearances and winning a League Championship medal, after helping his new club to regain the title they had won two years earlier. Despite keen competition for places at Goodison, injuries apart, he would be a regular first team choice. Unfortunately, an injury received in a League match against Sheffield Wednesday in March 1989, kept him out of both selection for England against Albania and the Everton side that lost 3-2 to Liverpool in the FA Cup Final. Eventually recovering to play 25 League games in 1989-90, he yet again succumbed to injury and made only one appearance in 1990-91 and none at all in 1991-92. Finally made a welcome return from his long-term injury problems in **1992-93** and revitalised the midfield with simple passing and movement. Although he was unable to completely shrug off his injury worries and found it difficult to string more than a few matches together at a time, his presence was certainly appreciated by his manager, Howard Kendall, who said, on his return to first team duty, that it was like signing a £2 million player. A player of his quality would surely be part of the international setup, if only he could escape recurring injuries.

| | | | APPEARANCES | | | | GOALS | | | |
|---|---|---|---|---|---|---|---|---|---|---|
| Clubs | Signing Date | Transfer Fee | Lge | FL Cup | FA Cup | Others | Lge | FL Cup | FA Cup | Others |
| Doncaster Rovers | 8.80 | - | 181+7 | 9 | 11+1 | 3 | 25 | 1 | 1 | |
| Leeds United | 5.85 | £200,000 | 51 | 3 | 1 | | 6 | 2 | | |
| Everton* | 1.87 | £840,000 | 112+4 | 17+1 | 24 | 3 | 3 | 1 | 2 | |

## SOUTHALL Neville

Born: Llandudno, 16 September 1958

Height: 6'1" Weight: 12.1

International Honours: W-68

**Position/Skill Factor:** Very consistent goalkeeper. Never easy to beat, he makes stunning saves when all seems lost. Has tremendous reflexes and is as brave as a lion.

**Career History:** Now regarded by many good judges to be the best goalkeeper in Europe, if not the world, he had a humble beginning to his football career when joining Fourth Division Bury from non-League Winsford United, having previously played for Bangor, in the summer of 1980. Made his FL debut in a 2-1 defeat at Wigan Athletic on 29 March 1980 and on keeping his place in the side, immediately impressed several top clubs, including Everton, who signed him during the 1981 close season. After taking over the goalkeeper's jersey on a regular basis half-way into 1981-82, he was called up to replace Dai Davies in the Welsh goal for the match against Northern Ireland at Wrexham on 27 May 1982. Keeping a clean sheet in a 3-0 win, was a great experience, but the harsh reality of First Division football lay just around the corner when he was replaced by the experienced Jim Arnold, following a 5-0 home defeat by Liverpool in November 1982. After losing his place, he was loaned out to Port Vale where he finished on the losing side just once, before returning to Goodison. Showing great character, he went on to regain his place in the side and became the mainstay in the most successful period of the club's history between 1984-1987, when they won two League Championship medals, the FA Cup and the European Cup Winners Cup. His brilliant displays in 1984-85, when Everton won both the League Championship and the European Cup Winners Cup were personally rewarded by the Football Writers' Association when they named him as their "Footballer of the Year". Since those heady days, he has suffered the pain of a losing FA Cup Final at the hands of deadly rivals, Liverpool and the lengthy rebuilding of a side that has yet to threaten the best. However, he remains a model of consistency, having played in every single League game for Everton since October 1987, an unbroken run of 184 matches. Played an outstanding part in Wales' valiant, but ultimately unsuccessful bid to qualify for the 1992 European Championship Finals, during which they defeated the World Champions, Germany, in Cardiff, only to be eliminated in their final group match in the return game. Missed just two League matches in **1992-93**, when he became the victim of the professional foul ruling and was twice sent off, suffering suspension as the price for his uncertainty. As always, remarkably consistent, he broke the club's first team appearance record, which had stood for 22 years, when playing at Chelsea on 10 March 1993 and still makes difficult saves look easy.

| | | | APPEARANCES | | | | GOALS | | | |
|---|---|---|---|---|---|---|---|---|---|---|
| Clubs | Signing Date | Transfer Fee | Lge | FL Cup | FA Cup | Others | Lge | FL Cup | FA Cup | Others |
| Bury | 6.80 | £6,000 | 39 | | 5 | | | | | |
| Everton* | 7.81 | £150,000 | 411 | 54 | 56 | 32 | | | | |
| Port Vale | 1.83 | Loan | 9 | | | | | | | |

## SPACKMAN Nigel James

Born: Romsey, 2 December 1960

Height: 6'1"

Weight: 13.0

**Position/Skill Factor:** Midfield anchor man. An unspectacular player, who rarely captures the headlines because of his paucity of goals, but one of rare consistency. A ball winner, fetcher and carrier, that every successul team needs, in order to keep "ticking".

**Career History:** Attracted the attention of Bournemouth when starring with Southern-League club, Andover, he was quickly snapped up by the south-coast club during the 1980 close season. After making his FL debut in the opening game of 1980-81, at York City on 16 August 1980, he missed only two League matches during the entire season and was one of the few successes of a side that finished mid-table in the Fourth Division. In his second season, he assisted the "Poppies" to promotion from Division Four and at the end of his third season at Dean Court, he was snapped up by Chelsea, then in Division Two, for a modest fee. He immediately established himself at Stamford Bridge and won his first medal, missing only two games, as the "Blues" swept to the Second Division Championship in 1983-84. His remarkable consistency continued in 1984-85, being ever-present in his first season of First Division football and again in 1985-86, when he was absent in only three games. Somewhat surprisingly, he was allowed to leave Chelsea in February 1987 and even more surprisingly, he signed for Liverpool, who had a surfeit of excellent midfield players. In his early games for the "Reds" he looked a misfit and was sidelined for much of 1987-88, Liverpool's "annus mirabilis", when they went 29 FL games undefeated from the start of the season up to March. However, when Ronnie Whelan was injured in January, Spackman deputised admirably, with no loss of efficiency to the Liverpool midfield. At the end of the season, Liverpool won the Championship by a margin of nine points and a record points haul of 90 (equalling Everton's total of 1984-85). He nearly added a FA Cup winners medal to his Championship medal, but tight marking by Wimbledon, allied to an inexplicably timid performance by the "Reds", denied his team "the double" in the 1988 Cup Final. The following season he found himself behind McMahon, Whelan and Molby in the pecking order for places and towards the end of the season he was signed by Trevor Francis for Queens Park Rangers. His return to London lasted only nine months, however, as following a conflict with Francis' abrasive management style, he was dropped and soon afterwards joined the ever expanding colony of English players recruited by Graeme Souness for Glasgow Rangers, in part exchange for Ray Wilkins. He immediately slotted into Rangers' midfield, missing only three games in three seasons to the end of 1991-92 and collecting three Scottish League Championship medals, one Skol Cup winners medal in 1990-91 and a Scottish FA Cup winners medal in 1992. At the start of **1992-93**, however, he found himself out of favour, as Rangers sought to reduce their contingent of "foreign" born players, in order to prepare a team to compete in the European Cup that complied with UEFA's arcane qualification criteria. Rescued by Chelsea, he returned to Stamford Bridge in September 1992, but after only six games he suffered a serious injury, which required an operation, in an inconsequential Coca Cola (League) Cup-tie against Walsall. Recovered well enough to play in the last two games of the season and hopes to be fully fit for 1993-94 action.

| | | | APPEARANCES | | | | GOALS | | | |
|---|---|---|---|---|---|---|---|---|---|---|
| Clubs | Signing Date | Transfer Fee | Lge | FL Cup | FA Cup | Others | Lge | FL Cup | FA Cup | Others |
| Bournemouth | 5.80 | – | 118+1 | 5 | 7 | 6 | 10 | | | |
| Chelsea | 6.83 | £40,000 | 139+2 | 22+1 | 8 | 7 | 12 | | 1 | 1 |
| Liverpool | 2.87 | £400,000 | 39+12 | 6+1 | 5 | | | | | |
| Q.P.R. | 2.89 | £500,000 | 27+2 | 2 | | 2 | 1 | 1 | | |
| Glasgow Rangers | 11.89 | £500,000 | 100 | 10 | 7 | 5 | 1 | 1 | 1 | |
| Chelsea* | 9.92 | £485,000 | 6 | 2 | | | | | | |

## **SPEED Gary** Andrew

Born: Hawarden, 8 September 1969

Height: 5'9" Weight: 10.6

International Honours: W Yth, W "U21"-3, W-20

**Position/Skill Factor:** Left-winger with a cultured left foot. Can also play in defence, where he is capable of creating and defending well. Also, very powerful in the air.

**Career History:** Promising young player who came through the Leeds United youth system, first as an associated schoolboy (January 1985) and then as a trainee (July 1986), before progressing into the paid ranks in the 1988 close season. Made his FL debut in the penultimate game of 1988-89, a 0-0 draw at Elland Road against Oldham Athletic on 6 May 1989. In 1989-90, he found himself regularly on the subs' bench during the early stages of Leeds' Second Division Championship winning season, before getting a run in the side in March and seizing the opportunity in brilliant style. His form earned him a full Welsh cap against Costa Rica on 20 May 1990 and he went on to make United's left-wing slot his own in 1990-91, missing only three League games as the club consolidated its First Division status. Played in all but one of Leeds' victorious League Championship campaign in 1991-92 and scored several vital goals. Towards the end of the season, he deputised effectively for Tony Dorigo at left-back and for Mel Sterland at right-back. Only missed three games in **1992-93**, playing in a variety of position, other than his own, that included striker, central defender and full-back and was selected by manager, Howard Wilkinson, as his "Player of the Season", as well as having the accolade of being named in the PFA Premier League side awards by his fellow professionals. Praise indeed, for his value to the side. Scores his fair share of goals, including a stunning effort against VFB Stuttgart and put away 12 in all games last season. An automatic choice for the Welsh national side since 1991-92, although yet to reach his peak, he matured throughout an inconsistent season for the club to become a formidable opponent. If he can sustain his current rate of progress, he could become as important to Leeds as was John Charles some 40 years ago.

| | | | APPEARANCES | | | | GOALS | | | |
|---|---|---|---|---|---|---|---|---|---|---|
| Clubs | Signing Date | Transfer Fee | Lge | FL Cup | FA Cup | Others | Lge | FL Cup | FA Cup | Others |
| Leeds United* | 6.88 | – | 128+16 | 14+1 | 11 | 10+3 | 24 | 7 | 3 | 1 |

## **SPENCER** John

Born: Glasgow,
11 September 1970

Height: 5'7"

Weight: 9.10

International Honours:
S "U21"-3

**Position/Skill Factor:** Striker, who is both skilful and quick. Turns defenders well to get his shots in and often turns up in wide positions, creating chances for others.

**Career History"** A Glasgow Rangers reserve, he was signed by Chelsea just before the start of the **1992-93** season to provide cover for their new striking partnership of Robert Fleck and Mick Harford. He first signed for Rangers as a junior in 1987, but after two years, his only first team experience was four games on loan to Morton in 1988-89. And the following season he was farmed out to a club in Hong Kong (Lisbung FC) for experience. He rejoined Rangers in June 1990 and finally made his Scottish League debut in February 1991. Remarkably, for one with no first team experience, he had already been capped at international level, appearing (as substitute) for the Scottish Under 21 team in October 1990. After a handful of first team games and opportunities restricted by the presence of Ally McCoist and Mark Hateley, he was allowed to leave Ibrox to further his career south of the border, in return for a substantial fee. His first nine appearances in Chelsea's first team were all as substitute, including his PL debut at Norwich City on 19 August 1992, but in January 1993 he finally displaced the out of form (and goalless) Robert Fleck and did well enough to hold his place. Often scored important goals, especially when the "Blues" were struggling to keep out of the relegation zone and four of his seven strikes were either match winners, or savers. Very small for a forward, but he made up for his lack of size with great enthusiasm and skill, while attacking Premier League defenders head on. Definitely one of Chelsea's better buys.

| | | | APPEARANCES | | | | GOALS | | | |
|---|---|---|---|---|---|---|---|---|---|---|
| Clubs | Signing Date | Transfer Fee | Lge | FL Cup | FA Cup | Others | Lge | FL Cup | FA Cup | Others |
| Glasgow Rangers | 9.87 | - | 7+6 | 2 | | 1+1 | 2 | | | 1 |
| Morton | 3.89 | Loan | 4 | | | | 1 | | | |
| Chelsea* | 8.92 | £450,000 | 13+10 | 0+2 | 0+1 | | 7 | | | |

## **SPINK Nigel** Philip

Born: Chelmsford, 8 August 1958

Height: 6'1" Weight: 14.6

International Honours: E"B", FL Rep, E-1

**Position/Skill Factor:** Commanding goalkeeper, whose huge build helps him dominate his goal area. Confidently comes for crosses and quickly turns defence into attack with a throw or a long kick.

**Career History:** Joined Aston Villa from his local club, Chelmsford City, in 1976-77, but had to wait nearly three years before making his FL debut at Nottingham Forest on 26 December 1979. Incredibly, his next first team appearance was in the 1982 European Cup Final in Rotterdam, when he came on as a substitute for the injured Jimmy Rimmer after only eight minutes of the game. He played superbly to deny the Bayern Munich forwards, while a Peter Withe goal at the other end won the trophy for Villa. Although he found himself immediately back in the reserves, in 1982-83, he at last usurped Rimmer in December 1982 and grabbed the opportunity with both hands, holding his place for the remainder of the season and impressing enough to be selected for the England trip to Australia in the summer of 1983. It was there that he won his only international cap, coming on at half-time for Peter Shilton during a 0-0 draw on 11 June 1983. Starting 1983-84 as the number one choice for Villa, he had fully established himself when injury struck in a League game at Coventry City in March 1984. He missed the remainder of the season and failed to reclaim his place from Mervyn Day until December 1984. Injuries yet again interrupted his career in each of the next two campaigns, but he was back as an ever present in 1987-88 as Villa were promoted to the First Division, behind Millwall, at the first attempt. And he only missed one League game as Villa became First Division runners-up to Liverpool in 1989-90, when conceding just 38 goals. Automatic first choice 'keeper at Villa Park since 1985, he lost his first team jersey to Les Sealey in October 1991 and his future seemed uncertain. To his credit, he won his place back in March 1992 and held it for the remainder of the season. Started **1992-93** as first choice and played in every game, except one, due to a knee injury, up to the end of January. Unfortunately struck down by a stomach bug, prior to the Fourth Round FA Cup replay at Wimbledon, he was replaced by Mark Bosnich and failed to regain the goalkeeper's jersey. Still a reliable 'keeper, he kept nine clean sheets in 33 first team matches, before being consigned to the bench.

| | | | APPEARANCES | | | | GOALS | | | |
|---|---|---|---|---|---|---|---|---|---|---|
| Clubs | Signing Date | Transfer Fee | Lge | FL Cup | FA Cup | Others | Lge | FL Cup | FA Cup | Others |
| Aston Villa* | 1.77 | £4,000 | 331 | 44 | 27 | 19+1 | | | | |

## SRNICEK Pavel

Born: Ostrava, Czechoslovakia, 10 March 1968

Height: 6'2"

Weight: 14.9

International Honours: Czech Int

**Position/Skill Factor:** Typical continental goalkeeper, who will often take on the attacker when the ball is played back. Confident, with good hands, he is a real shot stopper..

**Career History:** With John Burridge nearing the end of a long career, Newcastle United bought the young Czech international goalie from Banik Ostrava, where he was once understudy to Ludek Miklosko, now at West Ham United, with a view to the future. Made his FL debut in a 1-0 win over Sheffield Wednesday at St James's Park on 17 April 1991, after United had conceded 12 goals in five matches and held his place for the remaining six games of the season. Started 1991-92 as first choice 'keeper, but was regarded with some suspicion by Newcastle fans for his Grobblaar-like excursions from the penalty area and weakness on high crosses. After 12 games, with the "Magpies" rooted to the foot of the table, he lost his place to Tommy Wright for the remainder of the season and when a dream move to Marseille fell through at the beginning of **1992-93**, the future looked bleak. Not content to play second fiddle to Wright, he slapped in a transfer request and seemed condemned to reserve team football, especially when United remained unbeaten in the League for the first 11 matches. His luck changed, however, when Wright was injured at Birmingham City and he grasped the opportunity with both hands. Thanks to personal coaching from the former Sunderland 'keeper, Jim Montgomery, he showed dramatic improvement and had wonderful games at Bristol City, Southend United and Luton Town to keep United on course for promotion. Occasionally he had his problems with crosses and was blamed for letting Charlton's Carl Leaburn in for the equaliser in a 2-2 home draw, but on the other side of the coin, he kept 13 clean sheets in 32 games and proved to be one of the best goalies in the country. A great favourite with the crowd, as United stormed to the First Division title, his brilliant form ensured that the unlucky Wright remained in the reserves, even if he was Northern Ireland's first choice.

| | | | APPEARANCES | | | | GOALS | | | |
|---|---|---|---|---|---|---|---|---|---|---|
| Clubs | Signing Date | Transfer Fee | Lge | FL Cup | FA Cup | Others | Lge | FL Cup | FA Cup | Others |
| Newcastle United* | 2.91 | £350,000 | 52 | 2 | 4 | 6 | | | | |

## STALKER Mark Edward

Born: Liverpool, 24 September 1974

Height: 5'9" Weight: 10.13

**Position/Skill Factor:** Left-back who can both defend and attack well. Good on the ball, he likes to get down the line on the overlap to get his crosses into the front men.

**Career History:** Locally born and bred, he came through the Liverpool ranks as an associated schoolboy (November 1988) and as a trainee (July 1991), before signing professional forms towards the end of **1992-93**.

| | | | APPEARANCES | | | | GOALS | | | |
|---|---|---|---|---|---|---|---|---|---|---|
| Clubs | Signing Date | Transfer Fee | Lge | FL Cup | FA Cup | Others | Lge | FL Cup | FA Cup | Others |
| Liverpool* | 4.93 | - | | | | | | | | |

## STAUNTON Stephen (Steve)

Born: Drogheda, Ireland, 19 January 1969

Height: 5'11" Weight: 11.2

International Honours: IR "U21"-4, IR-40

**Position/Skill Factor:** Left-back, or left sided midfielder, he likes to push forward and is a good crosser of the ball. Also an excellent passer, who always seems to have plenty of time.

**Career History:** Joined Liverpool from the League of Ireland side, Dundalk, early in 1986-87 and after spending his first 14 months at Anfield without first team football, he was loaned out to Bradford City and made his FL debut at Valley Parade against Sheffield United on 14 November 1987. He finally broke into the Liverpool squad in 1988-89, making his debut as a second-half substitute at home to Tottenham Hotspur on 17 September 1988. Eventually wresting the left-back slot in the face of stiff competition from David Burrows, he won an FA Cup winners medal at the end of the season, following Liverpool's 3-2 victory over Everton. His performances also brought him international recognition for the Republic of Ireland and during the season he won his first cap against Tunisia on 19 October 1988. An automatic choice for his country, he found it more difficult to hold down a regular place at Anfield during 1989-90, although his 18 League appearances, mainly in midfield, still entitled him to a League Championship medal when Liverpool won the title for a record breaking 18 times. It was the same story in 1990-91 as he competed in the "Reds'" midfield, wearing at least six different shirt numbers, while making 20 League appearances as Liverpool finished as runners-up to Arsenal in the Championship. Transferred to Aston Villa for a massive fee in the summer of 1991, he made a dream debut for his new club, scoring the winner in an amazing 3-2 turnaround away to Sheffield Wednesday in the first match of the season and remained Villa's first choice left-back for the bulk of a largely disappointing season for the Birmingham club. An ever present in **1992-93**, largely in the left-back position, but occasionally in midfield, he was a great success in Villa's drive for the Premier League Championship, a trophy they ultimately failed to win by ten clear points. A regular taker of corners and free kicks, his set pieces were always a threat to opposing defences, he scored a vital League goal at Manchester United in March which took Villa back to the top of the table. Ultimately, the "Villans" finished as runners-up to United, but it was an important goal at the time. Still a regular for the Republic of Ireland, he is one of three former Liverpool players in the side built by Ron Atkinson, along with Dean Saunders and Ray Houghton.

| | | | APPEARANCES | | | | GOALS | | | |
|---|---|---|---|---|---|---|---|---|---|---|
| Clubs | Signing Date | Transfer Fee | Lge | FL Cup | FA Cup | Others | Lge | FL Cup | FA Cup | Others |
| Liverpool | 9.86 | £20,000 | 55+10 | 6+2 | 14+2 | 1 | | 4 | 1 | 1 |
| Bradford City | 11.87 | Loan | 7+1 | 2 | | 1 | | | | |
| Aston Villa* | 8.91 | £1,100,000 | 79 | 7 | 8 | | 6 | | | |

## STEJSKAL Jan

Born: Czechoslovakia, 15 January 1962

Height: 6'3"

Weight: 12.0

International Honours: Czech Int

**Position/Skill Factor:** Quality goalkeeper who is a good shot stopper and has no fear of coming for crosses. Also a very long kicker with his left foot.

**Career History:** Initially signed by Queens Park Rangers from Sparta Prague in the 1991 close season, as the replacement for David Seaman, he was not released by the Czech side until their elimination from European competition in mid-October 1990. Made his FL debut in a 3-2 win at Leeds United on 20 October 1990, but after conceding 11 goals in his first four matches, he was rested in order for him to re-adjust to the English game. Justifying his reputation, he came back with renewed vigour to play in the last 22 League games of the season, being beaten only 21 times in assisting Rangers to climb from the foot of the First Division to mid-table security. Unfortunately, lost his Czech international place to his great rival, Ludek Miklosko of West Ham United, however. Once again proved to be one of the safest 'keepers in the League during 1991-92, conceding only 45 goals in 41 games and again helping his club to recover from a dreadful start to the season to finish in mid-table. Had a disappointing season in **1992-93**, having seemed settled after earlier teething problems, finally losing his place to Tony Roberts, following the 3-1 home defeat at the hands of Crystal Palace in December. The defeat had been a nightmare for him personally and the third Palace goal just epitomised things in general. With a minute left on the clock, he threw the ball out to Clive Wilson, who seemed unaware at what was going on and Palace's Eddie McGoldrick nipped in to lob the goalie from fully 30 yards. Apart from one more game, when he came on for the injured Roberts against Wimbledon, he was not further required and sat out the rest of the season on the bench. A quality 'keeper, his chance will surely come again.

| | | | APPEARANCES | | | | GOALS | | | |
|---|---|---|---|---|---|---|---|---|---|---|
| Clubs | Signing Date | Transfer Fee | Lge | FL Cup | FA Cup | Others | Lge | FL Cup | FA Cup | Others |
| Q.P.R.* | 10.90 | £600,000 | 81+1 | 6 | 2 | 2 | | | | |

## STERLAND Melvyn (Mel)

Born: Sheffield, 1 October 1961

Height: 5'10"

Weight: 12.10

International Honours: E "U21"-7, FL Rep, E"B", E-1

**Position/Skill Factor:** Brilliant attacking right-back who likes to get forward in order to pick his forwards out with wonderful crosses. Very dangerous with free-kicks around the box.

**Career History:** Came to Sheffield Wednesday as an apprentice in June 1978 and made his FL debut as a substitute at Hillsborough against Blackpool on 17 May 1979, prior to signing as a professional. In his very next game, his first full appearance, he scored against Hull City. After gaining a regular place in the side in 1980-81, he soon earned the nickname of "Zico" because of his tremendous ability at dead ball situations. Originally a midfielder, he was converted successfully to right-back in 1981-82. He made 39 League appearances when the "Owls" gained promotion to the First Division in 1983-84 and by this time had become the club's penalty taker, scoring five that season. Niggling injuries prevented him from completing any season at Hillsborough as an ever present, but he had a good recovery rate and was never absent for long. Eventually recognised by the international selectors, he won his one and only full cap for England against Saudi Arabia on 16 November 1988. He would probably have remained at Hillsborough for the duration of his career, but for an inexplicable decision in late 1988 to relieve him of the captaincy, which unsettled him and he requested a transfer, joining the large contingent of English players at Glasgow Rangers. In his brief stay at Ibrox Park, he scored three goals and assisted Rangers to the Scottish Championship, but, presumably homesick, he was surprisingly allowed to leave in the summer to reunite with his former manager, Howard Wilkinson, at Leeds United. Immediately slotting into a side who were desperate to rekindle former glories, with a blend of youth and experience, he won a Second Division Championship medal as United booked their return to the top flight. Back in the First Division for the first time in eight years, Leeds surprised many when finishing fourth, but for him, 1990-91, was memorable as his first season in League football as an ever present. Won his first major honour in English football in 1991-92 as a member of the team which captured the Football League Championship. Once again, his prodigious free-kicks and penalties were a vital factor in that success, although he was sadly forced to sit out the closing weeks of the campaign with injury. A disastrous **1992-93**, saw him returning from a nine month lay-off in December and playing just five games, before having to have a fourth operation on his ankle. His scoring ratio and ability to get forward was sorely missed, as Leeds slumped from a position of League Champions to 17th place in the new Premier League. Fortunately, amid press "fears for his career", he was reported to have resumed light training in May towards a full comeback.

| | | | APPEARANCES | | | | GOALS | | | |
|---|---|---|---|---|---|---|---|---|---|---|
| Clubs | Signing Date | Transfer Fee | Lge | FL Cup | FA Cup | Others | Lge | FL Cup | FA Cup | Others |
| Sheffield Wednesday | 10.79 | - | 271+8 | 30 | 34+1 | 3 | 37 | 7 | 5 | |
| Glasgow Rangers | 3.89 | £800,000 | 7+2 | | 4 | | 3 | | | |
| Leeds United* | 7.89 | £600,000 | 111+3 | 13 | 10 | 9 | 16 | 1 | 1 | 2 |

## STEWART Paul Andrew

Born: Manchester, 7 October 1964

Height: 5'11" Weight: 11.10

International Honours: E Yth, E "U21"-1, E"B", E-3

**Position/Skill Factor:** A bustling ex-striker who has been recently converted to midfield. Tackles strongly and powerful in the air, he still scores important goals from good forward runs.

**Career History:** Joined Blackpool as an apprentice in April 1981, after being on associated schoolboy forms since December 1978 and turned professional early in 1981-82. A few months later, he made his FL debut at Bloomfield Road as a substitute against Rochdale on 10 February 1982. He soon established a regular first team place and was a key player when the "Seasiders" were

promoted to the Third Division as runners-up in 1984-85. After making rapid progress in 1986-87 as an out-and-out front man and scoring 21 goals in 32 League games, he signed for Manchester City, who were struggling at the foot of the First Division. Arrived too late to prevent a goal shy team from sliding into the Second Division, but was able to rectify the situation in 1987-88. He hit the target 25 times in 40 League games, including two hat-tricks, before Tottenham Hotspur signed him during the 1988 close season, giving City a profit of £1.5 million in just over one year. An injury delayed his "Spurs'" debut until 1 October and he finally appeared as a substitute at White Hart Lane against Manchester United. And with the score standing at 2-2, he had the misfortune of hitting the bar with a late penalty. Recovering his composure, he ended the season with 12 League strikes and despite a patchy 1989-90, when he shared goal scoring duties with Paul Walsh, he still managed to notch some vital goals. However, it was not until 1990-91, when Terry Venables tried him out in the middle of the park, did he meet with lasting success. He ended the season with an FA Cup winners medal, after starting Tottenham's FA Cup run with the only goal of the game against his old club, Blackpool, in the Third Round. And he all but finished it in the Final, when scoring the equaliser against Nottingham Forest, with "Spurs" winning the FA Cup in extra-time. One of the club's few consistent players in a disappointing 1991-92 campaign, he played in all but four FL games and was called up for the England squad for the first time. Made three international appearances, all as a substitute, but was not included in the squad for the European Championship Finals. During the close season, he became perhaps the most questionable of Graeme Souness' signings when he joined Liverpool for a fee well in excess of £2 million. After making a glorious start to **1992-93**, with the winning goal in a 2-1 defeat of Sheffield United, on his home debut, he achieved little of note for the remainder of the campaign and was a great disappointment. Sent off for raising his hand to an opponent in the away leg of the ECWC tie with Apollon Limassol, he was thus suspended for the more important game against Spartak Moscow, at a time when Souness was struggling to find 11 fit men to make up the team. And plagued by a recurring hamstring in the first half of the season, he was in-and-out of the side, until losing his place in March. Recalled for the closing game to partner Ian Rush up front, he was again ineffective and was pulled off three times. Clearly, he is a much better player than last season's performances suggest, but unless he demonstrates it in 1993-94, he would seem to have little future at Anfield.

| Clubs | Signing Date | Transfer Fee | APPEARANCES Lge | FL Cup | FA Cup | Others | GOALS Lge | FL Cup | FA Cup | Others |
|---|---|---|---|---|---|---|---|---|---|---|
| Blackpool | 10.81 | - | 188+13 | 11 | 7 | 6 | 56 | 3 | 2 | 1 |
| Manchester City | 3.87 | £200,000 | 51 | 6 | 4 | 2 | 27 | 2 | 1 | 1 |
| Tottenham Hotspur | 6.88 | £1,700,000 | 126+5 | 23 | 9 | 9 | 28 | 7 | 2 | |
| Liverpool* | 7.92 | £2,300,00 | 21+3 | 3 | 1 | 3 | 1 | | | 2 |

## STEWART Simon

Born: Leeds, 1 November 1973

Height: 6'1" Weight: 12.4

**Position/Skill Factor:** Central defender who attacks the ball well. Has good feet and an ideal temperament.

**Career History:** After impressing in the club's junior side, he joined the Sheffield Wednesday professional staff last summer, having been at Hillsborough as a trainee since July 1990. Had an excellent first season as a professional in **1992-93**, when he made the giant leap from youth and reserve team football to Premier League status. With the club still involved in both cup competitions and struggling through injuries, he was given a PL debut at Ipswich Town on 10 March 1993 in place of the absent Carlton Palmer. He impressed enough to play in a further five League matches and showed a calm and unruffled attitude to the game. Very much a player of the future and one to watch out for, he recently signed a new contract that will keep him at Hillsborough for a further three years.

| Clubs | Signing Date | Transfer Fee | APPEARANCES Lge | FL Cup | FA Cup | Others | GOALS Lge | FL Cup | FA Cup | Others |
|---|---|---|---|---|---|---|---|---|---|---|
| Sheffield Wednesday* | 6.92 | - | 6 | | | | | | | |

## STIMSON Mark

Born: Plaistow, 27 December 1967

Height: 5'11" Weight: 11.0

**Position/Skill Factor:** Left-back with a very good touch, who controls the ball with ease and passes well. Loves to get forward.

**Career History:** After joining Tottenham Hotspur in July 1984 as a trainee, he graduated to the professional ranks in the summer of 1985 and made his FL debut at Everton on 11 May 1987, when deputising for Mitchell Thomas. In four seasons as a pro at White Hart Lane, he received only one more first team outing (as substitute), but gained more FL experience on extended loans with Leyton Orient, and Gillingham, both at Fourth Division level. With no first team opportunities on the horizon with "Spurs", he joined Newcastle United in the summer of 1989 for a surprisingly large fee, given his lack of experience at the top level. He was first choice left-back for the "Magpies" in 1989-90, when Newcastle "earned" promotion by finishing third in Division Two, but lost out to sixth place Sunderland in the Play Offs. However, he lost his way in the next two seasons, sharing the left-back position with a number of players, until totally eclipsed by the signing of John Beresford in the summer of 1992. Made only four first team appearances in **1992-93** — against Leicester City and Bari in the Anglo-Italian Cup and at home in League matches to Charlton Athletic and Brentford, where he layed on a goal in a 5-1 win. With United on their way to the First Division title, he had a short spell at Portsmouth on loan in December and turned down the chance to join his old United team-mate, Mark McGhee, at Reading. Currently on the transfer list, his opportunities at the club are limited, with Beresford and Scott Sellars playing on the left hand side and he appears likely to leave before too long.

| Clubs | Signing Date | Transfer Fee | APPEARANCES Lge | FL Cup | FA Cup | Others | GOALS Lge | FL Cup | FA Cup | Others |
|---|---|---|---|---|---|---|---|---|---|---|
| Tottenham Hotspur | 7.85 | - | 1+1 | | | | | | | |
| Leyton Orient | 3.88 | Loan | 10 | | | | | | | |
| Gillingham | 1.89 | Loan | 18 | | | | | | | |
| Newcastle United* | 6.89 | £150,000 | 82+4 | 5 | 7 | 6 | 2 | | 1 | |
| Portsmouth | 12.92 | Loan | 3+1 | | | 0+1 | | | | |

## STOCKWELL Michael (Micky) Thomas

Born: Chelmsford, 14 February 1965

Height: 5'6"

Weight: 10.2

**Position/Skill Factor:** A versatile player who can play at right-back, central midfield and on the flanks, with equal efficiency. Quick tackling, quick thinking and never easily beaten, he passes and moves well.

**Career History:** After coming to Ipswich Town as an apprentice in June 1981, he graduated to the professional ranks during 1982-83 and then waited three years before making his FL debut in a 1-0 win at Coventry City on 26 December 1985. Played a few more times that season, mainly as a substitute, as the team slid into the Second Division. On winning a regular place on the left side of midfield in 1987-88, he was injured during a match at Walsall in January 1989 and did not win his place back, this time at right-back, until October. In 1990-91, he slotted into Town's midfield and played in all but two FL games in the number four shirt. However, the number on his back is not a reliable guide to the position he takes up in any particular game. Ever present in 1991-92, as Ipswich swept to the Second Division Championship, he rose to the challenge presented by the new Premier League quite magnificently and ended **1992-93** as the supporters' "Player of the Year". Played a few games up front, early on in the season, when Chris Kiwomya dropped out and scored two goals against Wimbledon at Portman Road. What made it an even better day for many supporters, was the fact that Ladbrokes set odds of 14-1 for Stockwell to score the first goal of the game, totally unaware that he was playing as an emergency striker and many fans profited by the bookmaker's generosity that day. Stretchered off at Sheffield United in January with muscular damage to his right leg, he returned three matches later to make his 300th appearance for the club. Proved he could raise the game and should do even better during the coming season.

| | | | APPEARANCES | | | | GOALS | | | |
|---|---|---|---|---|---|---|---|---|---|---|
| Clubs | Signing Date | Transfer Fee | Lge | FL Cup | FA Cup | Others | Lge | FL Cup | FA Cup | Others |
| Ipswich Town* | 12.82 | - | 243+15 | 20+3 | 13+3 | 16+2 | 19 | 2 | | 1 |

## STRACHAN Gordon David

Born: Edinburgh, 9 February 1957

Height: 5'6"

Weight: 10.3

International Honours: S Yth, S "U21"-1, S-50

**Position/Skill Factor:** Fiery right-sided midfielder with a brilliant footballing brain. A tireless goal scoring player, he sees openings quickly and creates goal scoring chances from nothing. Rarely ever gives the ball away, he displays a steely determination and the will to win at all times.

**Career History:** He started his illustrious career with Dundee, after joining them straight from school and kicked off in the Scottish League as a 19-year-old in 1976. After 60 appearances at Dens Park, he moved to Aberdeen for a fee of £50,000 in November 1977 and it was there, during a purple spell, that he would eventually win just about every honour possible; two Premier Division Championship medals in 1979-80 and 1983-84, a hat-trick of Scottish Cup winners medals between 1982 and 1984 and a European Cup Winners Cup medal in 1983. His form was such that at the end of that first successful season with the "Dons" he won a full Scottish cap, the first of many, when selected to play against Northern Ireland on 16 May 1980. Having scored 55 goals in 183 League games for Aberdeen, he signed for Manchester United in the 1984 close season, along with Jesper Olsen. After making his FL debut at Old Trafford against Watford on 28 August 1984, by the end of the season he had won an FA Cup winners medal, following the 1-0 extra-time win over Everton. In nearly five years at United, he had been an automatic choice, injuries apart, so it came as something of a surprise when he was sold to Leeds United just before the transfer deadline in 1989. Showing renewed vigour, on being appointed captain for the coming season, he immediately led Leeds, by example, to the Second Division Championship, as an ever present and as the club's top scorer with 16 League goals, including seven penalties and was honoured as "Footballer of the Year" for 1991. Always inspirational, he missed very few games in 1990-91, while Leeds consolidated their First Division status, in fourth place. Remained a mainstay of the team in 1991-92 as Leeds progressed further to win the League Championship in a remarkable end of season twist of fortune. As enthusiastic as ever, he also held his place in the Scotland team and in a low key international against Northern Ireland in February his effervescent performance at the age of 35 put the other 19 younger outfield players to shame. Sadly, his next international appearance — his 50th cap — was probably his last, as at the end of the season, he announced his unavailability through injury for the European Championship Finals. Still the inspiration of the team at 36, a much publicised diet of bananas and seaweed tablets are a superficial explanation to his success. Was recalled to the side in **1992-93**, after being a substitute for six of the first eight games and brilliantly dismissed close season worries about a back problem. He was a permanent feature of the side, until missing four games in February through injury and being suspended for two further matches, having been sent off in a friendly tournament in Italy. He returned to the team in top form and hit a hat-trick against Blackburn Rovers in a super individual performance, which at the time went a long way to easing relegation worries. Received more "Man of the Match" awards from match sponsors than any other player during the season and it is almost inconceivable that he may not be part of the set-up when his existing contract runs out.

| | | | APPEARANCES | | | | GOALS | | | |
|---|---|---|---|---|---|---|---|---|---|---|
| Clubs | Signing Date | Transfer Fee | Lge | FL Cup | FA Cup | Others | Lge | FL Cup | FA Cup | Others |
| Dundee | 2.74 | - | 56+13 | 10+1 | 7 | | 13 | 1 | 1 | |
| Aberdeen | 11.77 | £50,000 | 165+6 | 43+3 | 25 | 34 | 53 | 20 | 7 | 7 |
| Manchester United | 8.84 | £500,000 | 155+5 | 12+1 | 22 | 10+2 | 33 | 1 | 2 | 3 |
| Leeds United* | 3.89 | £300,000 | 151+7 | 16 | 11 | 14+1 | 34 | 3 | 1 | 3 |

## STRANDLI Frank

Born: Norway, 16 May 1972

Height: 6'1"

Weight: 13.13

International Honours: Norwegian Int

**Position/Skill Factor:** Striker with an excellent touch, who is good in the air and shoots on sight. A natural goalscorer.

**Career History:** Joined the swelling rank of Scandinavian players in the **1992-93** Premier League, when Leeds United's manager, Howard Wilkinson, signed him from Norwegian First Division club, IK Start of Kristiansand, one year after his international debut for Norway. Quickly created a good impression at Elland Road, making his PL debut a day later on 30 January 1993 at home to Middlesbrough and scoring the opening goal in a 3-0 victory, only 11 minutes after coming on as a substitute. The following week, he made his full debut away to Wimbledon and Howard Wilkinson went on record to say "he had been as excited at signing Strandli, as much as he had when he brought David Hirst to Sheffield Wednesday. He replaced Lee Chapman for a short while, but struggled to fit into the pace and fitness of the English game and was dropped in March. A heavy summer training schedule could see him proving his manager's confidence in him during 1993-94.

| | | | APPEARANCES | | | | GOALS | | | |
|---|---|---|---|---|---|---|---|---|---|---|
| Clubs | Signing Date | Transfer Fee | Lge | FL Cup | FA Cup | Others | Lge | FL Cup | FA Cup | Others |
| Leeds United* | 1.93 | £350,000 | 5+5 | | | | 2 | | | |

## STUART Graham Charles

Born: Tooting, 24 October 1970

Height: 5'8" Weight: 11.6

International Honours: E Yth, E "U21"-5

**Position/Skill Factor:** Striker or winger, with good ability on the ball. Having both strength and pace, he can beat defenders to get his shots or crosses in.

**Career History:** First came to Chelsea as a 15-year-old associated schoolboy in March 1985 and on leaving school he joined the club as a trainee in August 1987, before graduating to the professional ranks via the FA School of Excellence in the 1989 close season. Made his FL debut at the end of that season at Stamford Bridge against Crystal Palace on 16 April 1990 and scored the final goal in a 3-0 win. Received further opportunities to shine in 1990-91, making 19 League appearances, including two as a substitute and impressed when scoring against two of the top three sides, Arsenal and Crystal Palace. Out of contention at the start of 1991-92, he came into the first team squad in November and was a regular performer for the rest of the season, sometimes on the flanks and sometimes inside, in place of Kerry Dixon. Surprisingly, scored only one goal, but it was one to remember, the winner in the FA Cup Fifth Round tie against Sheffield United. Must like playing against Sheffield sides, as he scored one of the goals of the season in **1992-93**, this time at Sheffield Wednesday, where a long mazy run saw him beat several defenders before finishing with great aplomb. Unfortunately, he can run up blind alleys on occasion, but when he is on song he is more than a match for any defender in the country.

| | | | APPEARANCES | | | | GOALS | | | |
|---|---|---|---|---|---|---|---|---|---|---|
| Clubs | Signing Date | Transfer Fee | Lge | FL Cup | FA Cup | Others | Lge | FL Cup | FA Cup | Others |
| Chelsea* | 6.89 | - | 70+17 | 11 | 5+2 | 3+2 | 14 | 2 | 1 | 1 |

## SULLIVAN Neil

Born: Sutton, 24 February 1970

Height: 6'0" Weight: 12.1

**Position/Skill Factor:** Brave young goalkeeper who is not afraid to come for crosses. Agile and alert to the dangers of through balls into the penalty area, he is also an excellent long kicker.

**Career History:** After coming to Wimbledon straight from school to sign as a trainee in July 1986, having been on the club's books as an associated schoolboy player since May 1985, he joined the professional ranks in the 1988 close season. Made his FL debut in a 2-1 win at Aston Villa on 20 April 1991 and with the wonderfully consistent Hans Segers missing just one game in three years, he remained in the wings. Continued to wait patiently as understudy to Segers, for his second first team outing, coming by coincidence, exactly one year later at home to Southampton. Then, with Nigel Martyn indisposed and Crystal Palace desperate for a replacement, he signed on a loan transfer and made his debut for the "Eagles" in the last game of the season, a 1-0 defeat at Queens Park Rangers. With the **1992-93** Premier League season underway and with Hans Segers not being fully fit for the trip to Southampton, he was called upon to make his third first team appearance in five seasons, playing reasonably well in a 2-2 draw. He then spent the rest of the season as he had done previously, sitting on the bench and combining those duties with weekly reserve team outings until an injury, sustained in mid-March, kept him out for the rest of the campaign. Must wonder if he is ever going to have an extended run in League football, without having to leave Wimbledon.

| | | | APPEARANCES | | | | GOALS | | | |
|---|---|---|---|---|---|---|---|---|---|---|
| Clubs | Signing Date | Transfer Fee | Lge | FL Cup | FA Cup | Others | Lge | FL Cup | FA Cup | Others |
| Wimbledon* | 7.88 | - | 3 | | | | | | | |
| Crystal Palace | 5.92 | Loan | 1 | | | | | | | |

## SUMMERBEE Nicholas (Nicky) John

Born: Altrincham, 26 August 1971

Height: 5'8"

Weight: 11.8

International Honours: E "U21"-2

**Position/Skill Factor:** A right-back, who is quick and aggressive and loves to get forward to produce telling crosses.

**Career History:** One of the few players to have followed both father and grandfather into League soccer. Father, Mike, was of Swindon Town, Manchester City and England fame, among other clubs, spanning the period 1960-1978, while his grandfather played his League football before and during the war. Arriving at Swindon Town as a trainee in October 1987, he made excellent progress to turn professional during the 1989 close season and in what turned out to be his only first team appearance in 1989-90, made his FL debut as a substitute against Wolverhampton Wanderers on 3 September 1989. He had to wait another year for his next first team opportunity, also as substitute and until the final match of 1990-91 for his first full appearance. Started the 1991-92 season as first choice left-back, but following the signing of Paul Bodin in January, he reverted to his original position as a wide midfield player, although more frequently selected as substitute than as first choice. After previously having difficulty in establishing a regular place, or even a regular position, apart from five substitute appearances, he missed only seven other games in **1992-93**. Has inherited much of his father's attacking flair, but was used by Glenn Hoddle more as a defender, especially after David Kerslake's departure to Leeds United in March. Settling in at right-back, his good form made him a valuable member of the team and saw him capped twice for the England under 21 side. Although the possessor of a powerful shot, he only scored four goals last season, but his excellent crosses paved the way for several of his team-mates and it was from his corner that Shaun Taylor headed Town into a 3-0 lead in the Play-Off Final against Leicester City. A hugely exciting game was eventually won 4-3 by Swindon and as a result, he will have the opportunity of developing his skills in the Premier League this coming season.

| | | | APPEARANCES | | | | GOALS | | | |
|---|---|---|---|---|---|---|---|---|---|---|
| Clubs | Signing Date | Transfer Fee | Lge | FL Cup | FA Cup | Others | Lge | FL Cup | FA Cup | Others |
| Swindon Town* | 7.89 | - | 53+21 | 6+1 | 0+4 | 7 | 3 | 1 | | 1 |

## SUTCH Daryl

Born: Beccles,
11 September 1971

Height: 6'0"

Weight: 12.0

International Honours:
E Yth, E "U21"-4

**Position/Skill Factor:** An attacking midfield player and a good passer of the ball, he likes to join in the play in order to create opportunities for others.

**Career History:** Another good young local player, he first came to Norwich City as an associated schoolboy (January 1986), before joining the club as a trainee in July 1988 and progressing into the paid ranks during the summer of 1990. Made his FL debut, substituting for Lee Power, at Manchester United on 26 December 1990 and sadly his four appearances (two subs) coincided with the "Canaries'" heaviest defeats of the season. He was recalled to the first team squad in January 1992 and made a handful of appearances before the end of season. In view of his limited experience, his end of season call-up to the England Under 21 squad to play in the annual tournament in France, was a little surprising, but presumably was a beneficiary of the policy to ensure continuity from the England Youth set-up to full international level. Fully expected to shine in **1992-93**, he had a frustrating season and although playing 14 full games and coming off the bench on eight occasions, spent much of the time alternating on the left side of midfield with Gary Megson. Described by one pressman as a bits-and-pieces player, he does bits of defending and pieces of attacking, the bulk of his appearances came between September and December and he scored two invaluable goals, an equaliser at Middlesbrough and the winner at Aston Villa. Very impressive at Villa Park, he made the first goal in a 3-2 win with a strong run through three challenges, before scoring the winner when he swept in a low cross-shot from the edge of the box. Made a further appearance for the under 21 side, before a hernia operation ended his season.

| | | | APPEARANCES | | | | GOALS | | | |
|---|---|---|---|---|---|---|---|---|---|---|
| Clubs | Signing Date | Transfer Fee | Lge | FL Cup | FA Cup | Others | Lge | FL Cup | FA Cup | Others |
| Norwich City* | 7.90 | - | 21+14 | 3+1 | 0+1 | 1 | 2 | | | |

## SUTTON Christopher (Chris) Roy

Born: Nottingham,
10 March 1973

Height: 6'2"

Weight: 11.12

International Honours:
E "U21"-8

**Position/Skill Factor:** A tall centre-forward, or central defender, he is strong, direct and more than useful in the air.

**Career History:** The son of the former Norwich City, Chester City and Carlisle United footballer, Mike, who played between 1962-1972, he signed for Norwich City as a trainee in July 1989 on the recommendation of his father, before graduating to the club's paid ranks in the 1991 close season. Prior to that, however, he had already made his FL debut at Carrow Road against Queens Park Rangers on 4 May 1991, when coming off the bench to replace Ian Crook. Made good progress in 1991-92. In his second first team game at home to Coventry City he scored an injury time winner in a 3-2 victory, after coming on as substitute. He then had a two month run in central defence in place of the injured Ian Butterworth, before being switched to the attack where he became an FA Cup hero. Scored twice in the "Canaries'" 3-0 Fifth Round victory over Notts County and headed the winner in extra-time against Southampton in a Sixth Round replay. Unfortunately, his "lucky mascot" tag failed to work in the Semi-Final, when Norwich went out limply to Sunderland. Built on his experiences of the previous season, as he became a fixture in the **1992-93** side, while emulating Paul Warhurst of Sheffield Wednesday. Manager Mike Walker was quoted as saying that he believed his future was at centre-back, but in 15 starts up front, Chris scored ten goals — a better rate than Mark Robins. At the back he was both calm and solid and in attack, brave and purposeful. He scored both goals in the second leg of the League Cup-tie against Carlisle United and banged in a hat-trick in the Premier League at home to Leeds United towards the end of the season, even after missing a penalty. Won the first of eight England under 21 caps against Spain in September and had a superb game against Holland. Is surely a star in the making.

| | | | APPEARANCES | | | | GOALS | | | |
|---|---|---|---|---|---|---|---|---|---|---|
| Clubs | Signing Date | Transfer Fee | Lge | FL Cup | FA Cup | Others | Lge | FL Cup | FA Cup | Others |
| Norwich City* | 7.91 | - | 48+13 | 5 | 8 | | 10 | 2 | 3 | |

## TAIT Paul

Born: Newcastle, 24 October 1974

Height: 6'1" Weight: 11.0

**Position/Skill Factor:** Striker with great feet for such a big lad and and explosive shot to match.

**Career History:** Rejected the opportunity of joining up with his local club, Newcastle United, when he came down to Everton from the north-east, having initially been registered as an associated schoolboy (June 1989) at Goodison Park. Became a trainee (August 1991) at the club on leaving school and progressed to the professional ranks during the close season, having impressed when scoring over 30 goals in youth and reserve matches during **1992-93**.

| | | | APPEARANCES | | | | GOALS | | | |
|---|---|---|---|---|---|---|---|---|---|---|
| Clubs | Signing Date | Transfer Fee | Lge | FL Cup | FA Cup | Others | Lge | FL Cup | FA Cup | Others |
| Everton* | 7.93 | - | | | | | | | | |

## TALIA Francesco (Frank)

Born: Australia, 20 July 1972

Height: 6'1" Weight: 13.0

**Position/Skill Factor:** Goalkeeper. Extremely agile and a good shot stopper, he also comes out well for crosses.

**Career History:** Signed by Blackburn Rovers from Australian soccer, where he starred with Sunshine George X, he was loaned out to Hartlepool United for experience during **1992-93**. Made his FL debut on 9 January 1993 at Leyton Orient and kept a clean sheet in a 0-0 draw. Played in the "Pool's" next 13 League games before returning to Ewood Park, where he appeared to move ahead of Matt Dickins and Darren Collier, when named as substitute goalie, covering Bobby Mimms for the last nine games of the season.

| | | | APPEARANCES | | | | GOALS | | | |
|---|---|---|---|---|---|---|---|---|---|---|
| Clubs | Signing Date | Transfer Fee | Lge | FL Cup | FA Cup | Others | Lge | FL Cup | FA Cup | Others |
| Blackburn Rovers* | 8.92 | - | | | | | | | | |
| Hartlepool United | 2.93 | Loan | 14 | | | 1 | | | | |

## TALBOYS Steven John

Born: Bristol, 18 September 1966

Height: 5'11"

Weight: 11.1

**Position/Skill Factor:** Winger with plenty of stamina who can get into shooting positions and is good in the air.

**Career History:** Started his career as an associated schoolboy with Bristol Rovers in March 1981, before being released and drifting into non-League soccer with Mangotsfield, Bath City and Trowbridge, prior to joining Gloucester City in November 1987. Signed by Wimbledon from a Beazer Homes League club, having played all his football in the west country, he went straight into the club's reserve side and did enough to suggest that he might have a future in the top flight. After coming off the bench in **1992-93**, during the 1-0 League Cup defeat at the hands of Bolton Wanderers, he made his PL debut in the number two shirt at Norwich City on 5 December 1992 and played a further seven (including five substitute) games before the close of the season. Appeared mostly on the left side of midfield and looks set to become a useful member of the squad.

| | | | APPEARANCES | | | | GOALS | | | |
|---|---|---|---|---|---|---|---|---|---|---|
| Clubs | Signing Date | Transfer Fee | Lge | FL Cup | FA Cup | Others | Lge | FL Cup | FA Cup | Others |
| Wimbledon* | 9.92 | £11,000 | 3+4 | 0+1 | 0+1 | | | | | |

## TALLON Gary Thomas

Born: Drogheda, Ireland, 5 September 1973

Height: 5'10" Weight: 11.7

**Position/Skill Factor:** Naturally left footed left-winger, who can play at left-back and is a lovely crosser of the ball. A very skilful player, indeed.

**Career History:** Signed from League of Ireland side Drogheda United towards the end of 1991, he has yet to make his first team bow, having played solely in the club's youth team during 1991-92 and occasionally with the reserves in **1992-93**. Brought to Ewood Park in order to tap his potential, he seemed to be going nowhere until tried at left-back in the reserve side at the very end of the season and finally showed rich promise.

| | | | APPEARANCES | | | | GOALS | | | |
|---|---|---|---|---|---|---|---|---|---|---|
| Clubs | Signing Date | Transfer Fee | Lge | FL Cup | FA Cup | Others | Lge | FL Cup | FA Cup | Others |
| Blackburn Rovers* | 11.91 | £30,000 | | | | | | | | |

## TANNER Adam David

Born: Maldon, 25 October 1973

Height: 6'0" Weight: 11.12

**Position/Skill Factor:** Central midfield player who has good passing ability and touch for one so big. Adept at hitting great long passes to his strikers.

**Career History:** Signed professional forms for Ipswich Town during the 1992 summer, having first come to the club as a trainee in July 1990. Still awaits a first team call-up, although he did get on the bench for the home game against Wimbledon in **1992-93**. A regular reserve, his chance should come shortly.

| Clubs | Signing Date | Transfer Fee | APPEARANCES Lge | FL Cup | FA Cup | Others | GOALS Lge | FL Cup | FA Cup | Others |
|---|---|---|---|---|---|---|---|---|---|---|
| Ipswich Town* | 6.92 | - | | | | | | | | |

## TANNER Nicholas (Nicky)

Born: Kingswood, 24 May 1965

Height: 6'1"

Weight: 13.10

**Position/Skill Factor:** Central defender who is both strong in the air and on the ground. A good tackler, he rarely comes away without the ball.

**Career History:** After playing with the local Western League side, Mangotsfield, he was signed by Bristol Rovers during the summer of 1985 and made his FL debut in a 3-3 draw on the opening day of the 1985-86 season at Darlington on 18 August 1985. A regular first team player in his first two seasons with the "Pirates", he operated in a number of different positions — in midfield, on the flanks and in both full-back positions. At the end of his third season, it was decided to release him for a modest fee and he was faced with a strange choice — regular first team football with Fourth Division strugglers, Torquay United, or as cover for First Division Champions, Liverpool! He elected to join the "Reds", but unsurprisingly found the first team opportunities hard to come by, playing in the reserves as a central defender, a role he had rarely played for Rovers. His first appearance for Liverpool came in December 1989 as substitute, but although he played three more games in 1989-90 it was not enough to qualify for a Championship medal. He then had two loan spells with Norwich City and Swindon Town, respectively, in 1990, but no permanent transfer resulted. After three years at Anfield with only four first team games to his name, it seemed unlikely he would ever break through to regular first team action, but patience is a virtue and when new signing Mark Wright was injured in the second match of 1991-92, Tanner took his place. He grabbed the opportunity splendidly and was a tower of strength in Liverpool's injury-riddled team. So much so, that he held his place when Wright returned to first team duty and in January 1992 manager Graham Souness offered him an improved contract up to 1995. Tragically, after 26 consecutive FL games, he himself was victim of the injury jinx that cursed Liverpool through the season and although he returned to the first team action before the end of the season, he was no longer first choice and missed the FA Cup Final. Despite an impressive breakthrough in 1991-92, he was almost totally ignored by Souness in **1992-93**, making only two full Premier League appearances at the start of the season and two more in the League Cup and European Cup Winners Cup. His disappearance from first team duty was even harder to explain, in view of Wright's disastrous loss of form and the failure of the two Scandinavians, Torben Piechnik and Stig Bjornebye, to adapt to the frenetic English style of play. Will look to make a fresh start this coming season.

| Clubs | Signing Date | Transfer Fee | APPEARANCES Lge | FL Cup | FA Cup | Others | GOALS Lge | FL Cup | FA Cup | Others |
|---|---|---|---|---|---|---|---|---|---|---|
| Bristol Rovers | 6.85 | - | 104+3 | 5 | 10 | 5 | 3 | | | |
| Liverpool* | 7.88 | £20,000 | 36+4 | 6+2 | 2 | 7+2 | 1 | | | |
| Norwich City | 3.90 | Loan | 6 | | | | | | | |
| Swindon Town | 9.90 | Loan | 7 | | | | | | | |

## TAYLOR Shaun

Born: Plymouth, 26 February 1963

Height: 6'1"

Weight: 12.8

**Position/Skill Factor:** Big, strong and brave central defender, who saves difficult situations with his bravery and anticipation. Also scores many important goals.

**Career History:** A late arrival to professional football, Taylor had been playing for several years in the obscurity of the Western League with Bideford before being snapped up by Exeter City midway through 1986-87, following a short trial period. He immediately made his FL debut at Wolverhampton Wanderers on 27 December 1986 as a third centre-back and held his place to the end of the season. Over the next four seasons, he was a fixture in the heart of the "Grecians'" defence, ever present in 1988-89 and missing only a handful of games in the others. Appointed team captain by manager, Terry Cooper, he led them to the Fourth Division Championship in 1989-90, when he was voted their "Player of the Year". Also proved to be a useful goalscorer both from set pieces and open play. Signed by Glenn Hoddle for Swindon Town in the summer of 1991, he immediately formed an effective partnership with Colin Calderwood in the heart of the "Robins'" defence and enjoyed an excellent first season at this higher level of football, as Swindon narrowly missed out on a Second Division Play-Off place. The only ever present for Town during **1992-93**, the big Devonian must be a manager's model professional, whose attitude is an example to everyone. Two incidents late in the season were typical of him. In one, he ignored a head wound which had, minutes earlier, required ten stitches and moved upfield to power in a header that put Swindon back in the game. The other one, saw him flattened by a late, crunching tackle from which many players would have retaliated or rolled in agony. He merely picked himself up, patted his assailant on the shoulder and got on with the game. Amazingly, no less than 22 League goals came from the two back four men, Taylor and Paul Bodin, who finished equal second highest scorers with 11 and both men scored at Wembley too. In a pulsating game by anybody's standards, Town beat Leicester City 4-3 in the

Final of the First Division Play-Offs and will play Premier League soccer this season.

| Clubs | Signing Date | Transfer Fee | APPEARANCES Lge | FL Cup | FA Cup | Others | GOALS Lge | FL Cup | FA Cup | Others |
|---|---|---|---|---|---|---|---|---|---|---|
| Exeter City | 12.86 | - | 200 | 12 | 9 | 12 | 17 | | | |
| Swindon Town* | 7.91 | £200,000 | 88 | 9 | 4 | 7 | 15 | 2 | | 1 |

## **TEALE Shaun**

Born: Southport, 10 March 1964

Height: 6'0" Weight: 13.7

International Honours: E Semi-Pro Int

**Position/Skill Factor:** Combative central defender, who is aggressive both in the air and on the ground and there are no free headers to be had when he is about. Very dangerous at set plays, he has a good left foot.

**Career History:** Discarded by Everton, following a period spent as an associated schoolboy (December 1979) and as an apprentice (June 1980) at Goodison, he played for a number of non-League clubs, including Southport, Ellesmere Port, Northwich Victoria and Burscough, before joining Bournemouth from Weymouth in January 1989. Whilst with Weymouth he was selected for a Semi-Professional international against Wales in 1988. Made his FL debut for the "Cherries" as a substitute at home to West Bromwich on 4 February 1989 and immediately settled into the team in central defence in place of Kevin Bond. Ever present in 1989-90, until injured in March, his absence was a major factor in Bournemouth slipping from 14th to 22nd place and relegation back to Division Three. Recognised as one of the most accomplished central defenders in the lower divisions, he was ever present in 1990-91 and realised an ambition he must have thought had long since passed him by, when he was signed by Aston Villa in the summer of 1991. Went straight into Villa's first team, forming a defensive partnership with Paul McGrath as solid as any in the First Division. Although a disappointing season for Villa, he enjoyed an excellent first year at the top level, missing only one game throughout and contributing greatly to a defence which conceded only 44 FL goals. Had another outstanding season in **1992-93**, when continuing his great defensive partnership with McGrath and was a major factor in the club's prolonged challenge for the Premier League Championship, which only faltered at the "death". Earlier, a tweaked knee ligament suffered at Tottenham Hotspur marked the end of 70 consecutive appearances for Villa, forcing him to miss the next three games and later in the season a suspension incurred, saw him absent for the home game against Manchester City. A must in central defence, if Villa expect to challenge for titular honours this season.

| Clubs | Signing Date | Transfer Fee | APPEARANCES Lge | FL Cup | FA Cup | Others | GOALS Lge | FL Cup | FA Cup | Others |
|---|---|---|---|---|---|---|---|---|---|---|
| Bournemouth | 1.89 | £50,000 | 99+1 | 8 | 5 | 3 | 4 | | 1 | |
| Aston Villa* | 7.91 | £300,000 | 81 | 6 | 9 | 2 | 1 | 2 | | |

## **THOMAS Mark** Leslie

Born: Wandsworth, 22 November 1974

Height: 5'9" Weight: 10.8

**Position/Skill Factor:** Strong tackling left-back, who can also play in midfield. A very confident player, he is useful in the air and has a good left foot.

**Career History:** Registered as an associated schoolboy at Wimbledon in December 1989, he eventually joined the club as a trainee (August 1991), on leaving school and progressed to the professional ranks during last summer. As a regular youth team player in **1992-93** and one who impressed on the left side of the defence, his good form warranted half a dozen reserve outings before the season came to a close. Could be another useful player for the "Dons".

| Clubs | Signing Date | Transfer Fee | APPEARANCES Lge | FL Cup | FA Cup | Others | GOALS Lge | FL Cup | FA Cup | Others |
|---|---|---|---|---|---|---|---|---|---|---|
| Wimbledon* | 7.93 | - | | | | | | | | |

## **THOMAS Martin** Russell

Born: Lymington, 12 September 1973

Height: 5'8" Weight: 10.8

**Position/Skill Factor:** A right-back who makes timely interceptions and tackles to break up attacks. Also a good passer of the ball.

**Career History:** Turned professional for Southampton during the 1992 close season, having previously been at the Dell as an associated schoolboy (December 1987) and as a trainee (August 1990). Although finding himself more in the role of substitute with the reserve side early in **1992-93**, he had established himself as a regular after Christmas and ended the season second in the appearance charts. He will now hope to aspire to the first team squad in 1993-94.

| | | | APPEARANCES | | | | GOALS | | | |
|---|---|---|---|---|---|---|---|---|---|---|
| Clubs | Signing Date | Transfer Fee | Lge | FL Cup | FA Cup | Others | Lge | FL Cup | FA Cup | Others |
| Southampton* | 6.92 | - | | | | | | | | |

## **THOMAS Michael** Lauriston

Born: Lambeth, 24 August 1967

Height: 5'10" Weight: 12.4

International Honours: E Sch, E Yth, E "U21"-12, E"B", E-2

**Position/Skill Factor:** Midfield player with wonderful stamina. Makes great runs, both on and off the ball and has the knack of turning up in the opponent's penalty area and scoring at vital moments.

**Career History:** A schoolboy international, he signed associated schoolboy forms with Arsenal in July 1982, before progressing through the ranks as an apprentice (August 1983) to become a professional at the end of 1984. Had to wait for over two years for his FL debut and when the opportunity finally came, it was whilst on loan to Portsmouth on New Years Day 1987 at home to Reading at left-back. Soon after returning to Highbury, he made his Arsenal debut in February and remained part of the first team squad till the end of the season, playing in both full-back positions and in midfield. He firmly established himself at right-back in 1987-88, only to be switched to midfield in February 1988 in place of the suspended Steve Williams. He also showed his talent for scoring unexpected goals – his total of nine in the League, plus two cup goals, made him second highest scorer for Arsenal that season. Made his first Wembley appearance in the 1988 League Cup Final, but the "Gunners" surprisingly went down to Luton by 3-2. Reached the apex of his career in 1988-89, missing only one game in Arsenal's campaign and winning his first England cap against Saudia Arabia in November. However, the best was saved till last. At one point in the season, Arsenal were runaway leaders of Division One and 19 points ahead of Liverpool, but with one game to go, the Merseysiders, already FA Cup winners, were three points clear with a superior goals difference. By a remarkable twist of fate, Arsenal's last match was at Anfield against their rivals and a 2-0 victory would give them the Championship by the narrowest of margins — equal points, equal goal difference, but superior on goals scored. It is now history that Arsenal achieved this seemingly impossible objective with a goal in the very last minute (if not injury time) by Michael Thomas. Running on to a through ball, he survived an attempted interception by Steve Nicol and went on to steer the ball coolly past Grobbelaar — the most amazing climax to a League Championship in FL history. After this, everything was an anti-climax, although the following season he played in all but two games of a disappointing time for the "Gunners", by their high standards and won a second England cap against Yugoslavia. In 1990-91 he played a large part in Arsenal's stupendous League Championship campaign (losing only once and conceding only 18 goals), but fell out of favour with George Graham, losing his place to David Hillier in the closing weeks of the campaign. No longer an automatic first choice in 1991-92, he was transferred to the scene of his former triumph when Liverpool signed him apparently as a replacement for Steve McMahon. He made a promising start at Anfield, helping the team to climb to third place, before falling victim to the injury jinx which plagued the "Reds" throughout the season. On his return to the team for the vital Fifth Round FA Cup match against Aston Villa, along with three other long term casualties (Barnes, Whelan and Venison), he scored the winning goal after being put clear by Barnes. For the remainder of the season he looked hesitant, unconfident and frequently caught in possession and was perhaps fortunate to be included in the FA Cup Final team against Sunderland, following Ronnie Whelan's withdrawal. All was forgiven and forgotten, however, immediately after half-time when the ball came to him on the corner of the penalty area, after a wonderful run by Steve McManaman and without waiting for it to drop, he smashed a rising volley into the roof of the net. Liverpool then took control of the game and Thomas also had a part in the second goal, teeing up the ball for Ian Rush to steer into the net. Another of Graeme Souness' signings, who has yet to display his best form for Liverpool, but in his defence at least he had the legitimate excuse of carrying serious long term injuries. After damaging his ankle ligaments early in **1992-93**, he returned in October to give his best ever display for the "Reds" in a 4-1 victory over the Premier League leaders, Norwich City, when he first cancelled out the "Canaries'" early lead, before laying on another a few minutes later for Hutchison. Two weeks later, his ankle injury sidelined him again and although he made a brief and unsuccessful comeback in January, he was then ruled out for the remainder of the season. Liverpool supporters are still of the opinion that he has something to offer, if he can shake off the injury jinx that has plagued him since his arrival at Anfield.

| Clubs | Signing Date | Transfer Fee | APPEARANCES Lge | FL Cup | FA Cup | Others | GOALS Lge | FL Cup | FA Cup | Others |
|---|---|---|---|---|---|---|---|---|---|---|
| Arsenal | 12.84 | - | 149+14 | 21+2 | 14+3 | 5+2 | 24 | 5 | 1 | 1 |
| Portsmouth | 12.86 | Loan | 3 | | | | | | | |
| Liverpool* | 12.91 | £1,500,000 | 22+3 | 1 | 7 | 2 | 4 | | 2 | |

# THOMAS Mitchell Antony

Born: Luton, 2 October 1964

Height: 6'0"

Weight: 12.0

International Honours: E Yth, E "U21"-3, E "B"

**Position/Skill Factor:** Adventurous full-back who loves to go forward, sometimes leaving his flank exposed to counter attack. As a result, he is frequently deployed in midfield, with a defender to cover him. He is a good competitor, has two good feet and is useful in the air.

**Career History:** Luton born and bred, he joined the "Hatters" as an apprentice (September 1981), just prior to his 17th birthday and had graduated to the professional ranks early in 1982-83. Later that season, following an injury to left-back, Richard Money, he made his FL debut in a 3-2 win at West Ham United on 4 January 1983 and within a year, with the former, then transferred to Portsmouth, he had gained England youth honours and was holding down a regular place in the side. Part of David Pleat's outstanding Luton team of the mid 1980s, which achieved high placings in Division One and reached the FA Cup Semi-Final in 1984-85 and Quarter-Finals in 1985-86, he also won several international honours in this period. When Pleat was appointed manager of Tottenham Hotspur in 1986, Thomas was one of his first signings at White Hart Lane. He enjoyed a successful start with "Spurs", but was ultimately disappointed, as the team in the running for three trophies, missed out on all of them, finishing third in the League, beaten by Arsenal in the Semi-Final of the League Cup and finally losing to Coventry City in the 1987 FA Cup Final. However, under new manager, Terry Venables, success became even more elusive and Thomas' position came increasingly under pressure from new arrivals, Gudni Bergsson, Justin Edinburgh and Pat van den Hauwe. He was often redeployed in midfield, but not on a consistent basis, so that he had little chance to re-establish himself in a new position. When he was left out of the 1991 FA Cup Final team, which defeated Nottingham Forest 2-1, it was clearly time to move on and he joined West Ham United in the summer of 1991. Although he started the season in occupation of the left-back slot, he was subsequently switched to midfield, following the return of Julian Dicks after injury, but could do little to prevent the "Hammers" sliding out of the top flight, once again. Like Mike Small, his personal **1992-93** was also not in keeping with the celebrations surrounding West Ham, when the club made it to the Premier League at the first time of asking, as runners-up to Newcastle United. Although proving to be an excellent deputy for Julian Dicks in September, a month later, he was out of action himself, following a cartilage operation and was unable to regain full fitness during the remainder of the season, making only nine reserve team appearances. While not a regular first teamer at present, he could well be required to deputise at the back, or in midfield and needs to be match fit in time for the start of the new campaign.

| Clubs | Signing Date | Transfer Fee | APPEARANCES Lge | FL Cup | FA Cup | Others | GOALS Lge | FL Cup | FA Cup | Others |
|---|---|---|---|---|---|---|---|---|---|---|
| Luton Town | 8.82 | - | 106+1 | 5 | 18 | | 1 | | | |
| Tottenham Hotspur | 7.86 | £233,000 | 136+21 | 28+1 | 12 | | 6 | 1 | 1 | |
| West Ham United* | 8.91 | £525,000 | 37+1 | 5 | 4 | 2 | 3 | | | |

# THOMAS Scott Lee

Born: Bury, 30 October 1974

Height: 5'11" Weight: 11.0

**Position/Skill Factor:** Plays on the far right of midfield as an old fashioned outside-right. Adept at taking defenders on and whipping past them to get his crosses over.

**Career History:** A Manchester City professional signing at the end of 1991-92, he first came to Maine Road as an associated schoolboy in December 1988, prior to becoming a trainee on leaving school in July 1991. Came into the reserve side in **1992-93** and settled down, while making frequent appearances and scoring a couple of goals. Yet to make the first team.

| Clubs | Signing Date | Transfer Fee | APPEARANCES Lge | FL Cup | FA Cup | Others | GOALS Lge | FL Cup | FA Cup | Others |
|---|---|---|---|---|---|---|---|---|---|---|
| Manchester City* | 3.92 | - | | | | | | | | |

# THOMPSON Alan

Born: Newcastle, 22 December 1973

Height: 6'0" Weight: 12.5

International Honours: E Yth

**Position/Skill Factor:** Midfielder who can also play up front, or at full-back. Has a cracking left foot, is a good passer and is always looking to take up intelligent positions in order to receive the ball.

**Career History:** A promising young player, his career was almost nipped in the bud when he broke his neck in a car crash, an injury which sidelined him for nearly 12 months, before he courageously recovered. An associated schoolboy (February 1988) and a trainee (June 1990) at Newcastle United, prior to signing professional, he made his FL debut as a substitute at Swindon Town on 2 November 1991 and impressed enough to make a further 14 (including one substitute) first team appearances during the season. With the club racing away to the First Division title, he received few opportunities in **1992-93**, making only two home League appearances, when coming on as a substitute against Portsmouth and being selected for the Cambridge United match. Released for part of the season to play for the England youth side in the World Cup, down under, it is not clear at present whether he will stay at the club for the coming season, having turned down the offer of a new contract.

| | | | APPEARANCES | | | | GOALS | | | |
|---|---|---|---|---|---|---|---|---|---|---|
| Clubs | Signing Date | Transfer Fee | Lge | FL Cup | FA Cup | Others | Lge | FL Cup | FA Cup | Others |
| Newcastle United* | 3.91 | - | 13+3 | | 1 | 3 | | | | |

## THOMPSON Gary McDonald

Born: Ipswich, 7 September 1972

Height: 6'0" Weight: 11.4

International Honours: E Sch, E Yth

**Position/Skill Factor:** Brave young striker, who is very quick, especially in the penalty area and is good in the air.

**Career History:** Locally born and bred, he has been with Ipswich Town since first signing as an associated schoolboy in October 1986 and progressing through the England schools and youth sides to full professional status during the 1990 close season. After breaking a leg in his first season, he fully recovered and performed well in the "stiffs" during 1991-92. A regular reserve, he was not called into the first team squad during **1992-93** and still awaits his debut. Had an ankle operation last March, but should be fully match fit in time for the new season.

| | | | APPEARANCES | | | | GOALS | | | |
|---|---|---|---|---|---|---|---|---|---|---|
| Clubs | Signing Date | Transfer Fee | Lge | FL Cup | FA Cup | Others | Lge | FL Cup | FA Cup | Others |
| Ipswich Town* | 7.90 | - | | | | | | | | |

## THOMPSON Neil

Born: Beverley, 2 October 1963

Height: 6'0"

Weight: 13.7

International Honours: E Semi-Pro Int

**Position/Skill Factor:** Strong tackling left-back. Supports his forwards well, packs a good shot in his left foot and is very dangerous at set plays. Also, a long throw specialist.

**Career History:** A player who is in the second phase of his career, having begun in the Football League, before dropping out and making his reputation in non-League football. Started out with Nottingham Forest as an associated schoolboy (January 1979) and later as an apprentice (July 1980). On not being offered professional terms by Forest, he joined Fourth Division Hull City early in 1981-82 and made his FL debut at Tranmere Rovers on 13 February 1982 at left-back, holding his place for the rest of the season. In 1982-83, he was plagued by injury, making only a handful of appearances in Hull's promotion campaign. Released at the end of the season, he joined Scarborough of the Alliance Premier League. At this point his FL career seemed to be over and so it proved, at least for four years. However, in 1986-87, Scarborough won the Championship of the re-titled Vauxhall Conference and became the first team to be "promoted" (rather than elected) to the Football League. Back in the League, he missed only five FL games in 1987-88 and was ever present in 1988-89, scoring nine FL goals and assisting his team to the Promotion Play-Offs. After being defeated by Leyton Orient, any disappointment for him was short lived, as he moved up the League to join Ipswich Town in the Second Division. In his first season at Portman Road, he played in all but one game in his customary position of left-back and although he lost his place for a while early in 1990-91, he won it back in December. As consistent as ever in 1991-92, he realised an ambition which he must have thought had long since passed him by, as Ipswich swept to the Second Division Championship and with it automatic promotion to the new Premier League. Ever present in **1992-93**, until injured in the second-half of the Sixth Round FA Cup-tie against Arsenal, when he was carried off with an achilles tendon injury that was to force him to miss the rest of the season. It was an unfortunate ending to this first season in the top flight, as he had been the most improved player on Town's books and was sorely missed as the club slipped down the table, only winning two of the remaining 11 games. Twice during the season he scored valuable match winning, or saving goals and his value to the team is immeasurable.

| | | | APPEARANCES | | | | GOALS | | | |
|---|---|---|---|---|---|---|---|---|---|---|
| Clubs | Signing Date | Transfer Fee | Lge | FL Cup | FA Cup | Others | Lge | FL Cup | FA Cup | Others |
| Hull City | 11.81 | - | 29+2 | | | | | | | |
| Scarborough | 8.83 | - | 87 | 8 | 4 | 9 | 15 | 1 | | 1 |
| Ipswich Town* | 6.89 | £100,000 | 153+6 | 11+1 | 12 | 8 | 18 | 1 | 1 | 1 |

## THOMSON Andrew John

Born: Swindon, 28 March 1974

Height: 6'3" Weight: 12.0

**Position/Skill Factor:** Strong, tough tackling central defender, who is also great in the air. A lovely striker of the long ball with his favoured right foot.

**Career History:** A locally born player, he initially came to Swindon Town as a 14-year-old associated schoolboy in December 1988 and graduated through the trainee (July 1990) ranks to professional status during the 1992 close season. Having held down a regular Combination slot in **1992-93**, with 29 appearances, he showed enough promise to suggest that he will be challenging for a place in the first team squad this season.

| | | | APPEARANCES | | | | GOALS | | | |
|---|---|---|---|---|---|---|---|---|---|---|
| Clubs | Signing Date | Transfer Fee | Lge | FL Cup | FA Cup | Others | Lge | FL Cup | FA Cup | Others |
| Swindon Town* | 7.92 | - | | | | | | | | |

## THOMSON Gregory (Greg)

Born: Edinburgh, 13 September 1975

Height: 5'9" Weight: 11.0

**Position/Skill Factor:** Plays in midfield and is a passer. With typical Scottish craft, he is always looking to probe the opposition's defence.

**Career History:** Spotted by Manchester City scout, John Ferguson, while playing for Edinburgh boys and youth, he came to Maine Road as a trainee in August 1992. Turning professional a month later, following his 17th birthday, he was groomed through the club's "A" and "B" teams during **1992-93**, but has yet to make the reserves. Football is in his blood, however, as his father turned out for Motherwell and his uncle, Richard Thomson, played for Preston North End in the 1970s.

| | | | APPEARANCES | | | | GOALS | | | |
|---|---|---|---|---|---|---|---|---|---|---|
| Clubs | Signing Date | Transfer Fee | Lge | FL Cup | FA Cup | Others | Lge | FL Cup | FA Cup | Others |
| Manchester City* | 9.92 | - | | | | | | | | |

## THOMSON Martin

Born: Bradford, 3 October 1974

Height: 5'10" Weight: 11.12

**Position/Skill Factor:** Strong, aggressive right-back, who can defend resolutely, if required. A great competitor, he is good in the air, can tackle and gives nothing away. Will often bring the ball out of defence to start up a quick break.

**Career History:** Given a two year professional contract by Sheffield United during the summer, he first arrived at the club as an associated schoolboy in June 1989, before graduating through the youth team as a trainee (July 1991). Showed up well in a couple of reserve outings in **1992-93** and is promising enough to make an early first team breakthrough.

| | | | APPEARANCES | | | | GOALS | | | |
|---|---|---|---|---|---|---|---|---|---|---|
| Clubs | Signing Date | Transfer Fee | Lge | FL Cup | FA Cup | Others | Lge | FL Cup | FA Cup | Others |
| Sheffield United* | 7.93 | - | | | | | | | | |

## THORNE Peter Lee

Born: Manchester, 21 June 1973

Height: 6'0" Weight: 12.2

**Position/Skill Factor:** Athletic striker with a lovely build. Holds the ball up well in and around the penalty area and looks set to find the net regularly.

**Career History:** A young player who has yet to turn out for the first team, he first signed for Blackburn Rovers as a trainee in July 1989, before progressing to the club's professional ranks in the 1991 close season. At first his chances of making any kind of progress was restricted by the presence of so many players, but once Roy Wegerle and Steve Livingstone had moved on, he began to receive more opportunities and finished **1992-93** as the highest scoring reserve, after Livingstone, with nine goals.

| | | | APPEARANCES | | | | GOALS | | | |
|---|---|---|---|---|---|---|---|---|---|---|
| Clubs | Signing Date | Transfer Fee | Lge | FL Cup | FA Cup | Others | Lge | FL Cup | FA Cup | Others |
| Blackburn Rovers* | 6.91 | - | | | | | | | | |

## THORNLEY Benjamin (Ben) Lindsay

Born: Bury, 21 April 1975

Height: 5'9"

Weight: 10.9

International Honours: E Sch

**Position/Skill Factor:** Left-winger who is basically right footed. A great crosser of the ball, he has good passing ability, coupled to control and looks to take defenders on.

**Career History:** Another of Manchester United's outstanding players and a member of the team which won the FA Youth Cup in 1991-92, defeating Crystal Palace 6-3 on aggregate. He joined United as an associated schoolboy in September 1989, upgraded to trainee in July 1991 and signed professional in January 1993. A former England schoolboy international, he had a good season in **1992-93**, helping the "A" team win the Lancashire League, along with being a member of the side that reached the FA Youth Cup for the second year running and is reckoned by the United staff to have a great future in the game.

| | | | APPEARANCES | | | | GOALS | | | |
|---|---|---|---|---|---|---|---|---|---|---|
| Clubs | Signing Date | Transfer Fee | Lge | FL Cup | FA Cup | Others | Lge | FL Cup | FA Cup | Others |
| Manchester United* | 1.93 | - | | | | | | | | |

## THORSTVEDT Erik

Born: Stavanger, Norway, 28 October 1962

Height: 6'3" Weight: 14.4

International Honours: Norwegian Int

**Position/Skill Factor:** Agile goalkeeper with a wonderful build who seems to fill the goal. A good shot stopper, he is also safe on crosses. Sets up attacks with long drop kicks.

**Career History:** Had trials for Tottenham Hotspur as long ago as December 1984 and also with Queens Park Rangers, Arsenal and Borussia Moechengladbach, during

his time playing with EIK Tonsberg and Viking Stavanger in his native Norway. After joining the Swedish side IFK Gothenburg, he went for a second trial with "Spurs" in the summer of 1987 and later signed on at White Hart Lane in 1988-89. His English career got off to a less than auspicious start when he conceded a "soft" goal during his FL debut at home to Nottingham Forest on 15 January 1989, a 2-1 defeat that was televised live throughout Europe. Despite this disappointing start, he proved to be a safe and reliable 'keeper and an automatic first choice up to the end of 1990-91 when he won an FA Cup winners medal as "Spurs" defeated Nottingham Forest 2-1 after extra-time. Lost his place to promising youngster Ian Walker, soon into the 1991-92 season, but won it back in October. However, after a shaky performance against Coventry City in late March, he once again gave way to Walker. Made his first **1992-93** appearance as the Premier League's first substitute goalkeeper under the new ruling, when coming on at half-time, following an injury to Walker in the second match of the season, a 2-0 home defeat against Coventry City. With "Spurs" already 2-0 down, he saved a Micky Gynn penalty and played well enough to stop the "Sky Blues" from adding to the score. Repeated the feat in the next game against Crystal Palace, but after just one more appearance he made way for Walker, again. However, injury again forced Walker out and Thorstvedt took full advantage to produce some excellent performances for both club and country. Unfortunate to miss the end of the season games, after breaking a finger at Nottingham Forest in April, he came back in time to help Norway to a 2-0 World Cup qualifier win over England in Oslo.

| | | | APPEARANCES | | | | GOALS | | | |
|---|---|---|---|---|---|---|---|---|---|---|
| Clubs | Signing Date | Transfer Fee | Lge | FL Cup | FA Cup | Others | Lge | FL Cup | FA Cup | Others |
| Tottenham Hotspur* | 12.88 | £400,000 | 138+2 | 20 | 13 | 7 | | | | |

## **TINKLER** Mark Roland

Born: Bishop Auckland, 24 October 1974

Height: 5'11½"

Weight: 11.4

International Honours: E Sch, E Yth

**Position/Skill Factor:** Midfield player with very quick feet who runs well with the ball. Also, useful in the air.

**Career History:** He signed professional forms for Leeds United towards the end of 1991, having been on the club's books as an associated schoolboy, since January 1991 and as a trainee from August 1991. A regular in Leeds' reserve side during 1991-92 and **1992-93**, despite outstanding competition in midfield from vastly experienced professionals, such as David Rocastle, Scott Sellars and Steve Hodge. Operating in a central midfield position, he was included in pre-season friendlies and the squad for the Charity Shield match against Liverpool and eventually made his PL debut at Sheffield United on 6 April 1993. After an impressive display, he played in six (including two substitute) of the last seven games of the season and was rewarded with a new three year contract. Looks to have a big future in the game.

| | | | APPEARANCES | | | | GOALS | | | |
|---|---|---|---|---|---|---|---|---|---|---|
| Clubs | Signing Date | Transfer Fee | Lge | FL Cup | FA Cup | Others | Lge | FL Cup | FA Cup | Others |
| Leeds United* | 11.91 | - | 5+2 | | | | | | | |

## **TISDALE** Paul Robert

Born: Malta, 14 January 1973

Height: 5'8" Weight: 10.12

International Honours: E Sch

**Position/Skill Factor:** Midfielder who can also play at right-back. A good footballer, he likes to pass the ball around and is very creative.

**Career History:** An England junior international, he joined Southampton on associated schoolboy forms in February 1987, before progressing to the club's professional ranks in the 1991 close season. A broken toe, which disrupted his pre-season training, healed in time for him to take his place in the reserve midfield for the opening game of **1992-93**. As in the previous term, he was a fixture with the "stiffs", until being offered the opportunity to go on loan to Third Division, Northampton Town, in order to gain first team experience. Made his FL debut at Hereford United on 13 February 1993 and played a further four games for the "Cobblers", impressing the locals with exciting mazy runs, before returning to the Dell. The official view from Northampton was that he was a player with a fine future ahead of him.

| | | | APPEARANCES | | | | GOALS | | | |
|---|---|---|---|---|---|---|---|---|---|---|
| Clubs | Signing Date | Transfer Fee | Lge | FL Cup | FA Cup | Others | Lge | FL Cup | FA Cup | Others |
| Southampton* | 6.91 | - | | | | | | | | |
| Northampton Town | 2.93 | Loan | 5 | | | | | | | |

## **TOLSON** Neil

Born: Wordsley, 25 October 1973

Height: 6'2" Weight: 11.5

**Position/Skill Factor:** Aggressive striker who is extremely quick off the mark. Very good in the air, he is likely to score goals at the higher level and will benefit from added experience.

**Career History:** Joined Walsall as a trainee in July 1990, having been an associated schoolboy since September 1989 and was one of a crop of talented youngsters that manager Kenny Hibbitt introduced to FL action in 1991-92. Made a dramatic entrance as a substitute in a First Round FA Cup tie away to Yeovil Town on 16 November 1991, scoring a late equaliser to force a replay at Bescot — all to no avail as the "Saddlers" eventually lost! He made his FL debut, again as substitute, the following week, at Rotherham United on 22 November 1991, shortly before signing a professional contract. Further substitute appearances followed, before his first full game away to Doncaster in late February. No sooner had "Saddlers" fans caught a glimpse of their budding "star", however, than he was whipped away from them by Oldham Athletic and made his debut for the club as a substitute on the opening day of the new **1992-93** Premier League season. Although he only made two further first team appearances, both from the bench, he impressed with his excellent ball skills and it was no surprise to "Latics'" supporters that he finished the season as top scorer for the reserve side. Still learning, 1993-94 could be his year!

| | | | APPEARANCES | | | | GOALS | | | |
|---|---|---|---|---|---|---|---|---|---|---|
| Clubs | Signing Date | Transfer Fee | Lge | FL Cup | FA Cup | Others | Lge | FL Cup | FA Cup | Others |
| Walsall | 12.91 | - | 3+6 | | 0+1 | 1+2 | 1 | | 1 | |
| Oldham Athletic* | 3.92 | £150,000 | 0+3 | | | | | | | |

## **TOWNSEND Andrew (Andy)** David

Born: Maidstone, 23 July 1963

Height: 5'11" Weight: 12.7

International Honours: IR-38

**Position/Skill Factor:** Hard working midfield player who covers both ends of the park. Very creative, he also is highly capable of scoring spectacular goals with his left foot.

**Career History:** Now recognised as one of the best midfield players around, he followed his father Don, who played for Charlton Athletic and Crystal Palace between 1959-1965, into League soccer, after starting his career in non-League football with Welling United in the Southern League. In the summer of 1984 he joined Weymouth, along with team mate Tony Agana (currently with Notts County), thus stepping up one grade to the Gola League (now Vauxhall Conference). After only half a season with the Dorset club, for whom he made 29 appearances and scored 10 goals, his performances attracted the attention of Southampton who signed him in January 1985. He did not make an immediate impact in the First Division, however and had to wait until the end of the season before making his FL debut as a left-back, when deputising for Mark Dennis, at the Dell against Aston Villa on 20 April 1985. In 1985-86 he played 27 games, alternating between left-back and midfield, but missed the first half of 1986-87 through injury, before establishing himself as a commanding midfielder in 1987-88. Surprisingly sold to Norwich City in the summer of 1988, he helped to establish the "Canaries'" reputation as a classy passing team which achieved its highest ever FL placing (fourth) and reached the FA Cup Semi-Final. He also won international recognition with the Republic of Ireland, making his debut against France in February 1989 and has remained a regular choice every since. After one more season at Carrow Road he was transferred to Chelsea for a fee the "Canaries" could hardly refuse and immediately confirmed his reputation as one of the leading midfield operators in the top flight, despite the "Blues'" inability to recapture their former glories. While only missing seven FL games in 1991-92, he was never really at his best, and carried a groin strain for much of the season. Only absent for one game in **1992-93**, as he recaptured some of his best form and as both the club and team captain he was inspirational to those around him. Scored a fantastic goal at Crystal Palace in a 3-1 League Cup defeat, when he ran from the half-way line, beating several defenders on the way, before finishing with a left-footed shot into the far corner. The subject of outside transfer talk, throughout 1992-93, he was transferred to Aston Villa in the summer, following the arrival of a new manager, Glenn Hoddle, at Stamford Bridge. After signing Gavin Peacock from Newcastle United, Hoddle saw Townsend as surplus to requirements, while Ron Atkinson, Villa's manager, claimed that the new arrival would make competition for midfield places intense during the coming season.

| | | | APPEARANCES | | | | GOALS | | | |
|---|---|---|---|---|---|---|---|---|---|---|
| Clubs | Signing Date | Transfer Fee | Lge | FL Cup | FA Cup | Others | Lge | FL Cup | FA Cup | Others |
| Southampton | 1.85 | £35,000 | 77+6 | 7+1 | 2+3 | 3+2 | 5 | | | |
| Norwich City | 8.88 | £300,000 | 66+5 | 3+1 | 10 | 3 | 8 | | 2 | |
| Chelsea | 7.90 | £1,200,000 | 110 | 17 | 7 | 4 | 12 | 7 | | |
| Aston Villa* | 7.93 | £2,000,000 | | | | | | | | |

# TRACEY Simon Peter

Born: Woolwich,
9 December 1967

Height: 6'0"

Weight: 13.0

**Position/Skill Factor:** An extremely agile goalkeeper who is a good shot stopper. One of the growing band of 'keepers who dribble out of their penalty area in a bid to obtain extra distance on their kicks.

**Career History:** Believed to be the only player to make his first team debut at Wembley — the 1988 FA Charity Shield match against Liverpool on 20 August. Currently recognised among the top flight of goalkeepers, he joined Wimbledon on the YTS scheme in August 1985, but made such excellent progress that he was offered professional terms just six months later. As understudy to the remarkably consistent Dave Beasant, he had to wait two and a half years to make his FL debut against Arsenal at Plough Lane on 27 August 1988, after the latter was transferred to Newcastle United. Tragically, it proved to be a nightmare debut as the "Gunners" fired five goals past him in a 5-1 defeat. He was immediately dropped and after the "Dons" signed Hans Segers in October, he was allowed to rejoin his former manager Dave Bassett at Sheffield United for a modest fee. Signed as cover for Graham Benstead, he had to wait until near the end of 1988-89 to make his debut for the "Blades", playing the last six matches of their Third Division promotion season. Quickly established himself as first choice at Bramall Lane and was ever present in his second season as the club raced through Division Two to their second consecutive promotion. Unluckily injured in a collision with Ian Rush in their first game back in the top flight at home to Liverpool, he returned to October 1990 to assist United to recover from a dreadful start to the season. It was a similar story in 1991-92. Returning from injury in November with the "Blades" anchored to the foot of the table, he brought some defensive stability back to the team, which pulled off another remarkable recovery. Touted as the best 'keeper in the country by "Blades'" supporters and the Sheffield press, it is believed that his tendency to roam far and wide from his goal area did not endear him to England manager, Graham Taylor. Ironically, when Taylor relented and included him in an England squad in April 1992, he was already injured during a game at Chelsea in March and thus unavailable for duty! After starting **1992-93** as the first choice 'keeper, he lost his cool at Tottenham Hotspur and following a booking for kicking the ball away, he received the red card for preventing Andy Gray from taking a quick throw in, having pursued him to the touch line. It was undoubtedly the new back pass law, which caused the initial problem. Later, he regained his place, but a dislocated shoulder sustained in training in early November brought his season to an end. A session at Lilleshall to strengthen the joint should enable him to be fit and fighting for his place at the start of the new season.

| | | | APPEARANCES | | | | GOALS | | | |
|---|---|---|---|---|---|---|---|---|---|---|
| Clubs | Signing Date | Transfer Fee | Lge | FL Cup | FA Cup | Others | Lge | FL Cup | FA Cup | Others |
| Wimbledon | 2.86 | - | 1 | | | 1 | | | | |
| Sheffield United* | 10.88 | £7,500 | 123 | 5 | 10 | 5 | | | | |

# TURNER Andrew Peter

Born: Woolwich,
23 March 1975

Height: 5'9"

Weight: 11.0

International Honours:
E Sch, E Yth,
IR "U21"-1

**Position/Skill Factor:** Very quick and skilful left-winger who has a great left foot and is a lovely crosser of the ball.

**Career History:** A 1992 close season professional signing for Tottenham Hotspur, having been at the club since first joining as an associated schoolboy in July 1990, before graduating as a trainee in August 1991. Made a surprise PL debut on the opening day of the **1992-93** season at Southampton on 15 August 1992 and turned out ten (including seven substitute) more times during the next 16 games, while scoring twice, including a last minute winner at home to Everton, after coming on as a substitute. Did not feature again until March when he came back to figure in ten more games. After coming off the bench in seven of those and scoring two more late goals, although substituted in his last full match, he will be looking for a more permanent role this coming season. Having represented England at school and youth level, in 1992-93 he elected to play for the Irish Republic and made an under 21 debut against Denmark in April.

| | | | APPEARANCES | | | | GOALS | | | |
|---|---|---|---|---|---|---|---|---|---|---|
| Clubs | Signing Date | Transfer Fee | Lge | FL Cup | FA Cup | Others | Lge | FL Cup | FA Cup | Others |
| Tottenham Hotspur* | 4.92 | - | 7+11 | 0+2 | 0+1 | | 3 | 1 | | |

# TUTTLE David Philip

Born: Reading, 6 February 1972

Height: 6'1" Weight: 12.10

International Honours: E Yth

**Position/Skill Factor:** Strong tackling central defender who has the perfect build for the job in hand and loses little in the air. On the ground, he is a lovely striker of the ball with his right foot.

**Career History:** A young player with a promising future, he joined Tottenham Hotspur as an associated schoolboy in April 1986, before signing on as a trainee on leaving school in August 1988. Turned professional early in 1990 and following a substitute appearance in the League Cup, he made his FL debut at Chelsea on 1 December 1990 in a

3-2 defeat, playing a few more times towards the end of the season. Broke back into the "Spurs'" team in October 1991 and in his second game of 1991-92, scored a vital early goal against Hajduk Split in the European Cup Winners Cup, in helping his team to a 2-1 aggregate victory. Tragically, he suffered a serious injury in a League Cup-tie against Swansea City, which ruled him out for the remainder of the season. Having fully recovered from last year's injury, he played seven games in the opening three months of **1992-93** in a variety of defensive positions, before being ruled out with a groin strain during the home match against Middlesbrough in mid-October. However, on his return to fitness he had a spell on loan at Peterborough United early in the New Year, making seven appearances for "Posh" and impressing, until injury struck yet again in the shape of an injured shin. Out of action for the rest of the season, he is sure to be back to match fitness in time for the resumption of 1993-94.

| | | | APPEARANCES | | | | GOALS | | | |
|---|---|---|---|---|---|---|---|---|---|---|
| Clubs | Signing Date | Transfer Fee | Lge | FL Cup | FA Cup | Others | Lge | FL Cup | FA Cup | Others |
| Tottenham Hotspur* | 2.90 | - | 10+3 | 3+1 | | 1 | | | | 1 |
| Peterborough United | 1.93 | Loan | 7 | | | | | | | |

## ULLATHORNE Robert

Born: Wakefield, 11 October 1971

Height: 5'7"

Weight: 10.7

International Honours: E Yth

**Position/Skill Factor:** Left-back who can play anywhere down the left side. Not very big, but full of enthusiasm, he has the ability to beat defenders and get telling crosses over with a lovely left foot.

**Career History:** Born in Yorkshire, he joined Norwich City, first as an associated schoolboy (October 1986) and later on leaving school, as a trainee in July 1988. Making good progress, he turned professional during the 1990 close season and made his FL debut in a 5-0 defeat at Nottingham Forest on 24 April 1991, when he replaced Mark Bowen. Began to establish himself in 1991-92, when called up to the first team in September and held down a regular place in midfield until rested in February. The impressive displays of the previous season seemed to signal that a bright future was just around the corner in **1992-93**. Unfortunately, his dream turned into a nightmare. After a toe operation and a spinal complaint, he appeared to be recovering well and was progressing through the reserves, when he twisted his back in training and was restricted to running in straight lines. If things go to plan, he will look to make a fresh start in 1993-94.

| | | | APPEARANCES | | | | GOALS | | | |
|---|---|---|---|---|---|---|---|---|---|---|
| Clubs | Signing Date | Transfer Fee | Lge | FL Cup | FA Cup | Others | Lge | FL Cup | FA Cup | Others |
| Norwich City* | 7.90 | - | 22 | 4 | 2 | | 3 | | | |

## UNSWORTH David Gerald

Born: Chorley, 16 October 1973

Height: 6'0" Weight: 13.0

International Honours: E Yth

**Position/Skill Factor:** Left-back who can also play in central defence. A well balanced player, he has a lovely left foot and a great first touch of the ball.

**Career History:** An extremely promising youngster, he made his FL debut for Everton, while still a trainee, at Tottenham Hotspur on 25 April 1992 and although substituting at left-back for Andy Hinchcliffe, he scored a stunning equalising goal with a first touch volley from a corner in a 3-3 thriller. Turned professional in the 1992 close season, having been at Goodison as an associated schoolboy since December 1987 and as a trainee since May 1990. Unexpectedly, was not given a real chance in **1992-93**, making only four first team appearances, after impressing many good judges the previous season. With the left-back spot causing problems when injuries set in, instead of being given an extended run, short-term signing, Kenny Sansom, was preferred, before being freed a short while later. It appears that his main chance of holding down a regular place will ultimately arrive due to injuries.

| | | | APPEARANCES | | | | GOALS | | | |
|---|---|---|---|---|---|---|---|---|---|---|
| Clubs | Signing Date | Transfer Fee | Lge | FL Cup | FA Cup | Others | Lge | FL Cup | FA Cup | Others |
| Everton* | 6.92 | - | 4+1 | 1+1 | | | 1 | | | |

## VAN DEN HAUWE Patrick (Pat) William Roger

Born: Dendermonde, Belgium, 16 December 1960

Height: 6'0"

Weight: 10.8

International Honours: W-13

**Position/Skill Factor:** Strong tackling full-back who loves the physical side of the game. Basically right footed, he can play either side. A ball winner, he leaves others to provide the finesse.

**Career History:** The son of a Belgian professional goalkeeper, Rene, he moved to England at an early age, before signing as an apprentice for Birmingham City in June 1977. Turning to the paid ranks just over a year later, he made his FL debut at St Andrews against Manchester City on 7 October 1978 and although he did reasonably well, it took him a further three years to win a permanent place in the "Blues'" line-up. A versatile defender, he alternated between both full-back slots and central defence, until settling down at left-back in 1983-84 as an ever present — a season in which the "Blues" were relegated, although enjoying long runs in the League Cup and FA Cup. Not long into 1984-85, he returned to the First Division, signing for Everton and shared in the "Toffees'" impressive run of success with a League Championship medal and a European Cup Winners Cup medal in his first season, an FA Cup Final runners-up medal in 1986 and another League Championship medal in 1986-87. Despite missing most of that season through injury, his 11 end of season games were just enough to qualify him for a medal. Disqualified from playing for his native country, by opting out of National Service, he was "adopted" by Wales, making his international debut against Spain in Wrexham in April 1985. From 1987 to 1989 he shared the left-back slot with Neil Pointon and also filled in at right-back and central defence when required. His last game for Everton was in the 1989 FA Cup Final against Liverpool, when once again he finished on the losing side. Soon afterwards his international career was brought to an end by Welsh manager Terry Yorath when he failed to show up for a match without prior warning. Transferred to Tottenham Hotspur in the second week of the 1989-90 season, he has been a regular choice at left-back (or right-back when paired with Justin Edinburgh) since arriving at White Hart Lane. Returned to Wembley again for a FA Cup Final in 1991 and was "third time lucky", as "Spurs" prevailed 2-1 over Nottingham Forest. Apart from injuries, was once again a regular in the "Spurs'" rearguard during 1991-92, making 35 FL appearances and even scoring, an unusual occurrence for him, in a 3-0 Third Round League Cup-tie victory at Grimsby Town. He began **1992-93** in the reserves, until winning back the left-back spot in September for a run of nine games. Completed his 100th League appearance for "Spurs" at Everton during this period, but then lost his place in the side and didn't reappear until late January. Came off the bench five times, before playing six further full games as a replacement for Justin Edinburgh and seems certain to push for a more regular place this coming season. Off the field, he made the headlines when he married Mandy Smith, the former teenage wife of rock star, Bill Wyman.

| | | | APPEARANCES | | | | GOALS | | | |
|---|---|---|---|---|---|---|---|---|---|---|
| Clubs | Signing Date | Transfer Fee | Lge | FL Cup | FA Cup | Others | Lge | FL Cup | FA Cup | Others |
| Birmingham City | 8.78 | - | 119+4 | 12 | 5 | | 1 | | | |
| Everton | 9.84 | £100,000 | 134+1 | 20 | 30 | 14+1 | 2 | | 1 | |
| Tottenham Hotspur* | 8.89 | £575,000 | 110+6 | 16 | 7 | 7 | | 1 | | |

## VENISON Barry

Born: Consett, 16 August 1964

Height: 5'10"

Weight: 11.9

International Honours: E Yth, E "U21"-10

**Position/Skill Factor:** Versatile right-back who links well with midfield and is a good passer of the ball.

**Career History:** First came to Sunderland as a 14-year-old associated schoolboy (June 1979), before signing on as an apprentice in July 1980, after leaving school. Made his FL debut, while still a junior, at Notts County on 10 October 1981 and by the time he had turned professional, he had already totted up a further nine League appearances for the club. In his eleventh first team game, he scored a superlative goal to win a close 3-2 encounter with Manchester City after coming on as substitute. His first two seasons as a pro at Roker Park, saw him alternate between right-back and midfield, but from 1983 to 1985, he was firmly established at right-back, missing only four FL games in two years and also becoming a regular choice for the England Under 21 team. Sadly for him, the "Rokermen" were relegated to the Second Division at the end of 1984-85. After one season in Division Two, during which he again switched positions between full-back and midfield, he was transferred to First Division Champions, Liverpool, ostensibly as a replacement for Phil Neal. In six seasons at Anfield, he never truly established himself either in the team, or in the hearts of the supporters. He shared the right-back slot with Steve Nicol, but tended to be selected only when Nicol was required for other duties. Nevertheless, he shared in the apparently never-ending Liverpool success story, winning League Championship medals in 1987-88 and 1989-90, plus an FA Cup Winners medal (as substitute) against Everton in 1989. In 1991-92 he was struck down by injury and by the time he regained fitness a new challenger had claimed the right-back slot in the shape of Rob Jones. Returned to the first team in the vital sixth Round FA Cup tie against Aston Villa in March and played several more games to the end of the season, but was not selected for the Cup Final squad against Sunderland. It came as no great surprise when he moved back to the north-east with Newcastle United during the 1992 close season and at £250,000, the locals thought he was an absolute "steal". And when **1992-93** came to an end, with the club promoted to the Premier League as First Division Champions, not many would argue with manager, Kevin Keegan's, personal choice of Venison as his "Player of the Year". That was easy to understand when he gave quality performances week in and week out, and only one player, Chris Allen, of Oxford United, bothered him all season. However, he wasn't given an easy ride, because he had once captained arch rivals, Sunderland and such is the fierce divided loyalty in that part of the world, he had to first win over Tyneside. That he did, when missing just two League games all season and he can now look forward with pride in playing for a club with such a rich tradition, back where it belongs, in the top flight.

| | | | APPEARANCES | | | | GOALS | | | |
|---|---|---|---|---|---|---|---|---|---|---|
| Clubs | Signing Date | Transfer Fee | Lge | FL Cup | FA Cup | Others | Lge | FL Cup | FA Cup | Others |
| Sunderland | 1.82 | - | 169+4 | 21 | 7+1 | 3 | 2 | | | 1 |
| Liverpool | 7.86 | £200,000 | 103+7 | 14+3 | 16+5 | 6+4 | 1 | | | 2 |
| Newcastle United* | 7.92 | £250,000 | 44 | 4 | 4 | 3 | | | | |

## VIVEASH Adrian Lee

Born: Swindon, 30 September 1969

Height: 6'1" Weight: 11.9

**Position/Skill Factor:** Strong, left footed defender, who is equally adept in the centre, or at left-back. Can defend quite well and makes good use of the ball with long passes from the back third of the field.

**Career History:** A Swindon Town home grown talent, having been an associated schoolboy (December 1984) and a trainee (July 1986) at the club, before signing professional forms in the 1988 close season, he made his FL debut as a substitute at home to Middlesbrough on 15 September 1990. Originally a forward, he made his first full appearance in central defence, one month later and then enjoyed two short run of games in this position, before taking over at left-back in March 1991, following Paul Bodin's transfer to Crystal Palace. While clearly doing enough to impress Ossie Ardiles, he found himself out of favour under new manager Glenn Hoddle, in 1991-92, losing the left-back spot to Nick Summerbee and later to the returning Paul Bodin. Although he can provide cover for the defensive slots, he has never won the confidence of Town supporters and his career at the club has always looked to be with the reserves. He is a player who often starts a little nervously and suffers from any early mistakes, but for all that he has never really let the club down when called upon and towards the end of **1992-93**, with Swindon striving for promotion, he was given five League games as cover for first Hoddle and then Bodin. Earlier, he had been on loan with Reading and it could be that his future lies with another club, especially with Town playing in the Premier League this season.

| | | | APPEARANCES | | | | GOALS | | | |
|---|---|---|---|---|---|---|---|---|---|---|
| Clubs | Signing Date | Transfer Fee | Lge | FL Cup | FA Cup | Others | Lge | FL Cup | FA Cup | Others |
| Swindon Town* | 7.88 | - | 37+3 | 5+1 | 0+1 | 2 | 1 | | | |
| Reading | 1.93 | Loan | 5 | | | 1 | | | | 1 |

## VONK Michel Christian

Born: Netherlands, 28 October 1968

Height: 6'2"

Weight: 11.10

**Position/Skill Factor:** A good solid central defender, who is excellent in the air and excels as a man-to-man marker.

**Career History:** Signed on trial by Manchester City from Dutch First Division club, SVV Dordrecht, towards the end of the 1991-92 season, he immediately made his FL debut, as a substitute at Nottingham Forest on 21 March 1992 and quickly settled into the side, replacing Steve Redmond in central defence. Made a positive start to **1992-93**, until substituted due to an ankle injury in the game at home to Middlesbrough. Out of the team for four months, he had a runout as a substitute in the FA Cup replay at Reading, before coming back for the full 90 minutes and scoring the winner in the next round against Queen Park Rangers. Played consistently well for the last 21 games of the season as he gained in experience and with his athletic style, he proved a perfect foil, alongside Keith Curle.

| | | | APPEARANCES | | | | GOALS | | | |
|---|---|---|---|---|---|---|---|---|---|---|
| Clubs | Signing Date | Transfer Fee | Lge | FL Cup | FA Cup | Others | Lge | FL Cup | FA Cup | Others |
| Manchester City* | 3.92 | £500,000 | 34+1 | | 3+1 | | 3 | | 1 | |

## WADDLE Christopher (Chris) Roland

Born: Felling, 14 December 1960

Height: 6'0" Weight: 11.5

International Honours: E "U21"-1, FL Rep, E-62

**Position/Skill Factor:** One of the most skilful of modern day players, he has the ability to leave defenders trailing in his wake. His superb ball control and deceptive pace are ideal for a wide attacking role, but he is equally adept in midfield.

**Career History:** One of the most exciting players of the last decade, he started his career with Newcastle United who picked him up from local Northern League club, Tow Law Town, in the 1980 close season, having been previously rejected by Sunderland. Quickly found his way into the team after making his FL debut at St James' against Shrewsbury Town on 22 October 1980 as a forward and later in the season he enjoyed a run on the left-wing. Ever present in 1981-82 and missing only five FL games in 1982-83, he was part of perhaps the most star-studded forward line the "Magpies" have ever produced when they won promotion back to Division One in 1983-84 with Waddle scoring 18 FL goals from the left-wing to complement Peter Beardsley's 20 and Kevin Keegan's 27. Called up the same season for his first England cap against the Irish Republic on 26 March 1985, he remained a regular member of the squad for the next six seasons. Following the retirement of Keegan, he reverted to twin striker with Beardsley for Newcastle's first season back in the top flight, scoring 13 goals in a fairly anti-climatic campaign. After a well publicised dispute with "Magpies'" manager, Jack Charlton, he was transferred to Tottenham Hotspur in the summer of 1985 for what appeared, in retrospect, to be a "give away" fee. Accompanied the England squad to the 1986 World Cup Finals, but was dropped in favour of Steve Hodge after the two disappointing opening games against Portugal and Morocco. Enjoyed an excellent second season at White Hart Lane, playing 39 FL games in a campaign when "Spurs" finished third in Division One and reached the 1987 FA Cup Final, only to lose unexpectedly to Coventry City. Plagued by injury and loss of form in 1987-88, he came back strongly the following season in a new creative midfield role to be ever present and top scorer with 14 FL goals, assisting "Spurs" to finish in sixth place, after finding themselves at the foot of the table in November. With "Spurs" facing mounting financial problems, he was sold to French League Champions, Olimpique de Marseille, for a new record fee for an English player. In three seasons with the French club, he won three League Championship honours and reached the Final of the 1991 European Cup when Marseille lost on penalties to Red Star Belgrade after a dreadful 0-0 draw. Cruelly and unjustly derided for his performance in that game, he was the one player on either side actually trying to create and score a goal, narrowly missing the target on two occasions. After speculation linking his name with Newcastle and Leeds United he signed for Sheffield Wednesday in the summer of 1992. Following a series of

*Chris Waddle*

disputes with the England manager concerning his availability, he played probably his last game for the national side against Turkey in October 1991. In truth, he only showed glimpses of his true ability in an England shirt, frequently wasting good approach work with poor crosses and scoring a paltry six goals in his 62 international appearances. While always disappointing on the big occasions such as the 1986 and 1990 World Cup final tournaments and the 1988 European Championships, he remains, like John Barnes and Glenn Hoddle, an enigma doomed never to reproduced his club form at the highest international level. After three years away from the English game, he came back with a bang in **1992-93** to become both the football writers and Wednesday supporters' "Player of the Year" to round off a magnificent season for him and the club. Missing just a handful of games at either end of the term, his skilful promptings in 54 first team appearances made him the star of a side that only just failed to attain a top six Premier League place and were runners-up in both the League and FA Cup Finals. A lack of goals was the only drawback to his play, but that was more than compensated by his ability to lay chances on for others, although the four he did score were absolute crackers. While his FA Cup Final replay equaliser against Arsenal may have kept millions of television viewers on the edge of their seats, his free-kick that opened the scoring in the Semi-Final against the old enemy, Sheffield United, was positively magical. A snip at the price, when you compare him with other less talented players around, Wednesday should continue to benefit further from his silky skills this coming season.

| | | | APPEARANCES | | | | GOALS | | | |
|---|---|---|---|---|---|---|---|---|---|---|
| Clubs | Signing Date | Transfer Fee | Lge | FL Cup | FA Cup | Others | Lge | FL Cup | FA Cup | Others |
| Newcastle United | 7.80 | £1,000 | 169+1 | 8 | 12 | | 46 | 2 | 4 | |
| Tottenham Hotspur | 7.85 | £590,000 | 137+1 | 21 | 14 | 4 | 33 | 4 | 5 | |
| Marseille (France) | 7.89 | £4,250,000 | | | | | | | | |
| Sheffield Wednesday* | 6.92 | £1,000,000 | 32+1 | 9 | 8 | 3+1 | 1 | | 2 | 1 |

## WAINWRIGHT Lee

Born: Sheffield, 9 January 1975

Height: 6'0" Weight: 12.12

**Position/Skill Factor:** Central defender who can also play in midfield. A strong tackler, with reasonable pace, he is good in the air and has excellent control for a big man.

**Career History:** Not related to Danny, another youngster of the same surname at Sheffield United, he first came to Bramall Lane as an associated schoolboy (April 1989), before upgrading to trainee in August 1991. Captain of Sheffield boys, while at school, he turned professional last summer, having impressed in a couple of reserve matches at the end of **1992-93** and earlier, had showed to good advantage when bolstering the attack.

| | | | APPEARANCES | | | | GOALS | | | |
|---|---|---|---|---|---|---|---|---|---|---|
| Clubs | Signing Date | Transfer Fee | Lge | FL Cup | FA Cup | Others | Lge | FL Cup | FA Cup | Others |
| Sheffield United* | 7.93 | - | | | | | | | | |

## WALKER Desmond (Des) Sinclair

Born: Enfield, 26 November 1965

Height: 5'11" Weight: 11.9

International Honours: E "U21"-7, E-58

**Position/Skill Factor:** England's most effective central defender over the last five years and one of the most outstanding "sweepers" of the post war era. Noted both for his tremendous pace and coolness under pressure, his distribution is good and he rarely gives the ball away. Reads attacking situations well and nips them in the bud.

**Career History:** First signed for Nottingham Forest as an apprentice in July 1982, having been an associated schoolboy (March 1980) with Tottenham Hotspur and was offered a professional contract in November 1983. He made his FL debut at right-back at home to Everton on 14 March 1984 in a 1-0 victory, but had to wait until 1985-86 before establishing himself, despite winning his first England Under 21 call-up in 1984-85. After starting 1985-86 in the first team in central defence, he remained an automatic first choice for seven seasons at the City Ground. By 1987-88 he was being described by many judges as the best central defender in England, but it was not until the following season that he was called up by Bobby Robson for the England squad, making his debut as substitute against Denmark at Wembley. His first full game for England came in February 1989 against Greece in Athens, the away side winning 2-1, after which he became an automatic choice when available. He reached the zenith of his international career during the 1990 World Cup Finals in Italy when England won through to the Semi-Final (losing on penalties to Germany) and was hailed as the outstanding player of the tournament in his position. At club level, he assisted the club to a series of great cup runs in both the League Cup and FA Cup, with League Cup Winners medals in 1988-89 (3-1 v. Luton Town) and 1989-90 (1-0 v. Oldham Athletic) and a finalists medal in 1991-92, when Forest lost to Manchester United. In the FA Cup, Forest reached the Semi-Final in 1988 and 1989, only to lose to Liverpool on both occasions, before reaching the Final in 1991, where a lightweight and inexperienced team succumbed to Tottenham Hotspur after extra-time. It was both ironic and tragic that "Spurs'" winning goal should be scored by Walker himself. When attempting to head a dangerous cross out for a corner, he succeeded only in steering the ball into his own net. Prior to this, Walker had never scored a FL goal for Forest, but in his last season at the City Ground he put this right. In the final minute of a match against Luton, he carried the ball forward out of his own half (in the style of Alan Hansen), played a one-two on the edge of Town's box and thundered the return pass into the next. It was a goal fit to win any match, but on this occasion it merely saved a point. At the end of his contract in 1992, after England's ill-starred efforts in the European Championships in Sweden, he exercised his option to move to Italy, signing for Sampdoria for a pre-determined fee well below his true transfer market value. If 1989-90 represented the zenith of his career, then **1992-93** was his nadir. On the occasions that Sampdoria's matches were transmitted on Channel 4's live coverage of Italy's Serie "A" games, he was shown to be uncomfortable and ill at towards the end of the season suffered the indignity of being switched to an unfamiliar left-back slot. Worse was to follow, as in England's vital end of season World Cup qualifying matches against Holland, Poland and Norway, he appeared to have lost his pace, his mistakes, giving away penalties and goals which cost England vital points in all three games. Although he redeemed himself, somewhat, with good performances against Brazil and Germany on the summer tour to the USA, it remains to be seen if he can recapture the dependability and consistency of his early England form. During the summer, his Italian nightmare was brought to a close when Trevor Francis signed him for Sheffield Wednesday. He thus joins a depressing list of top Englishmen who have failed to make the grade in the world's most demanding League, while Dutch, German and Scandinavian players have less problem in adjusting — a sad commentary on the state of English football.

| | | | APPEARANCES | | | | GOALS | | | |
|---|---|---|---|---|---|---|---|---|---|---|
| Clubs | Signing Date | Transfer Fee | Lge | FL Cup | FA Cup | Others | Lge | FL Cup | FA Cup | Others |
| Nottingham Forest | 12.83 | – | 259+5 | 40 | 28 | 14 | 1 | | | |
| Sampdoria (Italy) | 5.92 | £1,500,000 | | | | | | | | |
| Sheffield Wednesday* | 7.93 | £2,700,000 | | | | | | | | |

## WALKER Ian Michael

Born: Watford, 31 October 1971

Height: 6'1"

Weight: 11.9

International Honours: E Yth, E "U21"-8

**Position/Skill Factor:** Very agile goalkeeper who looks confident in everything he does. Has good hands, comes for crosses and uses the ball well. Is also a good drop kicker.

**Career History:** Son of the Norwich City manager, Mike, who used to play in goal for Reading, Shrewsbury Town, York City, Watford, Charlton Athletic and Colchester United between 1963-1983, he aspires to surpass his father at the top level. Started his career at Tottenham Hotspur where he had the advantage of first-hand tutelage from the former England Star, Ray Clemence, first as an associated schoolboy (June 1987) and then as a trainee (August 1988), before turning professional at the end of 1989. Unable to get a game at "Spurs", due to the consistency of Erik Thorstvedt, he was loaned out to Oxford United and made his FL debut in a 1-1 draw at the Manor Ground against Wolverhampton Wanderers on 29 September 1990. Such was his talent, that he made his debut for the England Under 21 team against Wales in December before his "Spurs" debut in an end of season game at Norwich in April 1991. Displaced "Spurs'" 'keeper Erik Thorstvedt after three games of 1991-92, but was rested in October, until being restored to the team in April 1992 and ending the season as first choice. Started the new **1992-93** Premier League in front of Thorstvedt, but after being withdrawn at half-time, suffering from a back strain in the home match against Coventry City, he also missed the next fixture. Then, after coming back to the side, he was injured in a clash with John Fashanu at Wimbledon in October and again lost his place to the Norwegian international. However, he was eventually restored to the team in April when Throstvedt broke a finger, having spent much of the time sitting on the bench. Clearly a player with a future in the game, as he battles to become a regular in the side.

| | | | APPEARANCES | | | | GOALS | | | |
|---|---|---|---|---|---|---|---|---|---|---|
| Clubs | Signing Date | Transfer Fee | Lge | FL Cup | FA Cup | Others | Lge | FL Cup | FA Cup | Others |
| Tottenham Hotspur* | 12.89 | – | 36 | 3 | | 2 | | | | |
| Oxford United | 8.90 | Loan | 2 | 1 | | | | | | |

## WALLACE David (Danny) Lloyd

Born: Greenwich, 21 January 1964

Height: 5'4" Weight: 10.6

International Honours: E Yth, E "U21"-14, E-1

**Position/Skill Factor:** Winger with two good feet who is very quick off the mark. Extremely direct, he runs straight at defenders in order to commit them and is an excellent crosser from the flanks.

**Career History:** At 16 years, 313 days of age, he became Southampton's youngest ever player when he made his FL debut while still an apprentice in a 1-1 draw at Manchester United on 29 November 1980. Elder brother of twins, Raymond and Rodney, who currently play for Leeds United, he joined the "Saints" as an associated schoolboy in February 1978, before becoming an apprentice, on leaving school, in July 1980. He then went on to show such exciting form in the junior and reserve sides that he was "blooded" in the cauldron of Old Trafford, as a deputy for the injured Kevin Keegan, 15 months before he signed professional forms for the "Saints". Won a regular place in the team on the left-wing from October 1982 and finished the season as top scorer with 12 FL goals. In 1983-84 he missed only one game, as the club achieved their highest ever placing (second — only three points behind Champions, Liverpool). First choice on the "Saints'" left-wing for the next five seasons, he never

reached the heights once predicted for him and despite 14 England Under 21 caps between 1982 and 1985, he made only one full international appearance in England's first ever international against Egypt in Cairo on 29 January 1986. He scored once in a 4-0 victory, but was never selected again. By 1988-89, his last full season at the Dell, he was overshadowed by the exploits of his younger brother Rod on the right-wing and when Manchester United signed him early the next season, some cynics suggested that Alex Ferguson had signed the wrong brother! It has not proved a happy move for either player, or club. Although a regular in United's team in 1989-90, he failed to provide a spark to their goal shy attack which recorded only 46 FL goals. However, he had the consolation of receiving an FA Cup Winners medal when United defeated Crystal Palace after a replay. After being upstaged by the brilliance of Lee Sharpe and playing only a peripheral role in 1990-91, he was left completely in the cold in 1991-92, making only two appearances (both in the European Cup Winners Cup). Had a most frustrating time in **1992-93**, as yet again, he found himself out in the cold, making just two substitute appearances in United's Championship winning season, while playing four games in other competitions. Scored an equaliser at Brighton & Hove Albion in the League Cup and was used in both the UEFA Cup games against Torpedo Moscow, before limping off with a pulled hamstring in the second match. Later in the season, when Andrei Kantchelskis pulled out of the home Fourth Round FA Cup-tie, again versus Brighton, he was called up for last minute duty, but limped out of action, this time with a damaged ankle. That was his lot for 1992-93, apart from a spell on loan at Millwall and it is difficult to see where he goes from here, especially with Ryan Giggs and Lee Sharpe in such scintillating form.

| | | | APPEARANCES | | | | GOALS | | | |
|---|---|---|---|---|---|---|---|---|---|---|
| Clubs | Signing Date | Transfer Fee | Lge | FL Cup | FA Cup | Others | Lge | FL Cup | FA Cup | Others |
| Southampton | 1.82 | - | 238+15 | 36 | 21+1 | 10+2 | 64 | 6 | 4 | 5 |
| Manchester United* | 9.89 | £1,200,000 | 36+11 | 4+3 | 7+2 | 6+2 | 6 | 3 | 2 | |
| Millwall | 3.93 | Loan | 3 | | | | | | | |

# WALLACE Raymond (Ray) George

Born: Greenwich, 2 October 1969

Height: 5'6"

Weight: 10.2

International Honours: E "U21"-4

**Position/Skill Factor:** A right-back with great pace, who is extremely difficult to go past. He is also a very aggressive tackler.

**Career History:** Brother of Danny and twin of Rodney, he first joined Southampton as an associated schoolboy in December 1983, before signing as a trainee in July 1986 and later turning professional at the tail end of 1987-88. The following season he made his FL debut in the right-back position at the Dell against Sheffield Wednesday on 22 October 1988, playing alongside his two brothers in a 2-1 defeat and held his place for most of the season. Started the first eight games of 1989-90, but lost his place to Jason Dodd in October and never appeared in first team football for Southampton again, apart from one substitute appearance. Up to that point he was keeping pace with his twin brother Rod, both in the "Saints'" team and the England Under 21 squad. After spending all of 1990-91 in the reserves, he was transferred to Leeds United in a joint deal, more it seems to keep his brother company than because the club needed another right-back. His only FL action in 1991-92 was at the end of the season on loan to Swansea City, but even this turned sour. After two games for the "Swans", it was discovered that his registration forms were not received by FL headquarters before the March transfer deadline. Swansea were fined for the administrative error and Wallace returned sadly to Elland Road. Continued to have a hard time at the club in **1992-93**, especially considering the problems at right-back, where nine players were used to try and plug the gap created by Mel Sterland's long term injury. Eventually made his full League debut in the disastrous 4-1 defeat at home to Nottingham Forest in December and was promptly dropped. Recalled to the side, after playing one full game in February and coming on as a substitute at Liverpool, he retained the right-back spot for the last three matches of the season and with the threat of relegation hanging over the club, produced high quality performances, particularly against Queens Park Rangers and Sheffield Wednesday.

| | | | APPEARANCES | | | | GOALS | | | |
|---|---|---|---|---|---|---|---|---|---|---|
| Clubs | Signing Date | Transfer Fee | Lge | FL Cup | FA Cup | Others | Lge | FL Cup | FA Cup | Others |
| Southampton | 4.88 | - | 33+2 | 8 | 2 | 2 | | | | |
| Leeds United* | 7.91 | £100,000 | 5+1 | | | | | | | |
| Swansea City | 3.92 | Loan | 2 | | | | | | | |

## WALLACE Rodney (Rod) Seymour

Born: Greenwich, 2 October 1969

Height: 5'7" Weight: 10.1

International Honours: E "U21"-11, E "B"

**Position/Skill Factor:** Winger with tremendous pace over the first vital ten yards, which takes him away from defenders and gets him into shooting, or crossing positions.

**Career History:** Brother of Danny, currently with Manchester United, he joined Southampton as an associated schoolboy in December 1983, along with his twin, Ray and on leaving school, both of them signed as trainees in July 1986. Made his FL debut, while still a trainee, when coming on as a substitute at Newcastle United on 26 September 1987 and later celebrated his new professional status with a goal in his second full appearance — a late equaliser against Liverpool at Anfield, a scorching cross shot taken with the aplomb of a veteran. In his first full season, mostly on the right-wing, he was ever present and top scorer with 12 FL goals. At this stage he was arguably a more exciting prospect than his elder brother Danny at the same age. In 1989-90 he enjoyed another superb season and the "Saints'" three "pronged" attack of Wallace, Le Tissier and Shearer, made the team one of the most entertaining in the League. Remarkably, of his 18 FL goals, 14 were scored in "braces" — that is to say, in seven games he scored twice. The following season was more of a struggle for his team, but he still achieved 14 FL goals, second only to Le Tissier. It was inevitable perhaps, but sad, that he should move on to a bigger club and shortly after the end of 1991-92 he joined Leeds United, along with twin brother, Ray. After a slow start at Elland Road, he was dropped from the United team, but on his return in October, a burst of six goals in five games, established him as a crowd favourite and maintained his team's momentum towards the League Championship. In the vital penultimate game of the season away to Sheffield United, he scored (if that is the right word!) the most bizarre goal of the season. A clearance by a United defender cannoned sideways off Gary Speed and ricocheted into the net off Wallace's thigh. It was a vital goal as Leeds went on to win 3-2 and virtually clinch the Championship. In the final game at home to Norwich, he scored a more typical goal to win the game — a dash from the halfway line with a clinical finish. Began **1992-93** where he left off the previous season, in blistering fashion, causing havoc to opposing defences with tremendous pace and skill and creating chances aplenty for his team mates. Rewarded with a first ever call-up to the England squad for the friendly in Spain, he unfortunately received an injury at Manchester United in September and was put out of action for seven weeks, thus losing the opportunity. On coming back, he found it difficult to recapture any sort of form and at the end of December, apart from three games, was dropped from the starting line up until mid-February. He struggled as a goalscorer and was responsible for some glaring misses, but Howard Wilkinson kept faith with him. After scoring United's only goal at Nottingham Forest, he rediscovered the knack, including a superb strike at home to Blackburn Rovers and a solo effort at Norwich City, before rounding the season off with his first ever hat-trick for the club at Coventry City.

| | | | APPEARANCES | | | | GOALS | | | |
|---|---|---|---|---|---|---|---|---|---|---|
| Clubs | Signing Date | Transfer Fee | Lge | FL Cup | FA Cup | Others | Lge | FL Cup | FA Cup | Others |
| Southampton | 4.88 | - | 111+17 | 18+1 | 10 | 3+1 | 44 | 6 | 3 | 2 |
| Leeds United* | 6.91 | £1,600,000 | 65+1 | 5 | 2+3 | 1+3 | 18 | 3 | | 1 |

## WALSH Gary

Born: Wigan, 21 March 1968

Height: 6'1"

Weight: 12.12

International Honours: E "U21"-2

**Position/Skill Factor:** Tall and commanding goalkeeper with good safe hands.

**Career History:** A Manchester United associated schoolboy signing in June 1983, he joined the professional ranks at Old Trafford at the rear end of 1984-85, but due to the form of Gary Bailey and Chris Turner he had to wait until 13 December 1986, before making his FL debut in a 3-3 draw at Aston Villa. By the end of the 1986-87 season he was first choice 'keeper and remained so for the first three months of 1987-88, until Turner returned in December 1987. During this first team run, he won two England

Under 21 caps, but then had to wait over three years until February 1991 for his next game with United, whilst understudying Jim Leighton and Les Sealey. Found himself deputising for Peter Schmeichel in 1991-92, making only four first team appearances and with arguably the world's finest goalkeeper firmly entrenched at Old Trafford, he knew that opportunities in **1992-93** would be thin on the ground. Played in both the UEFA Cup games against Torpedo Moscow and was a regular for the reserves, until an injury brought his season to a halt at the end of October.

| | | | APPEARANCES | | | | GOALS | | | |
|---|---|---|---|---|---|---|---|---|---|---|
| Clubs | Signing Date | Transfer Fee | Lge | FL Cup | FA Cup | Others | Lge | FL Cup | FA Cup | Others |
| Manchester United* | 4.85 | - | 37 | 4 | | 3 | | | | |
| Airdrieonians | 8.88 | Loan | 3 | 1 | | | | | | |

## WALTERS Mark Everton

Born: Birmingham, 2 June 1964

Height: 5'9" Weight: 11.5

International Honours: E Sch, E Yth, E "U21"-9, E "B", E-1

**Position/Skill Factor:** Skilful, speedy left-winger with good balance, who can go both ways. Favours his left side, but commits defenders by running at them.

**Career History:** Aston Villa signed him as a 14-year-old associated schoolboy in July 1978, following exciting displays in local schools football that would lead him to an England junior cap later that year. On leaving school, he signed as an apprentice in July 1980 and progressed to the paid ranks during the 1982 close season, after being a key member of the club's FA Youth Cup winning side. His FL debut came on 28 April 1982 at home to Leeds United when he substituted for Tony Morley — a few days before turning professional. In 1982-83 he shared the left-wing slot with Morley, but fully established himself in 1983-84 when he emerged as one of the most exciting attacking wingers in the country, winning the first of his England Under 21 caps. He continued to thrill the Villa Park faithful for the next two years, scoring several outstanding goals, until it all went sour in 1986-87. Villa were relegated, hardly putting up serious resistance and under new manager, Billy McNeill, he found himself in-and-out of the team. Incensed at his treatment, he demanded a transfer and although his third manager, Graham Taylor, restored him to favour and tried to persuade him to stay, he left halfway through Villa's Second Division promotion campaign to join the large English contingent at Glasgow Rangers. The first black player to sign for the Scottish giants, he had to face the taunts of the bigoted minority, but quickly won over the discerning fans with his thrilling wing play and played a full part in the "Gers'" three consecutive Scottish League Championships from 1988 to 1991, plus winning two Skol League Cup medals in 1988 and 1990. In the summer of 1991, he followed manager Graham Souness to Liverpool, after making his long overdue England debut against New Zealand on the summer tour of Australasia. However, when handed a glorious opportunity to "win his spurs" by the long term injury to John Barnes early in the season, he proved to be a pale shadow of the player that once transfixed Villa and Ibrox Parks. Hesitant, unconfident and seemingly not match fit, he lost his place in November and appeared only occasionally thereafter. Although a vast improvement on his anaemic first season for the "Reds", he was not consistent enough to be an automatic first choice in **1992-93**. After a superlative performance in the thrilling 4-3 Charity Shield defeat against Leeds United in August, there were high hopes that he might at last establish himself, but a recurring groin strain in November reduced his mobility. However, he made a barnstorming return in December, with two late goals to defeat Blackburn Rovers 2-1, after coming on as a substitute, but remained in-and-out until the closing weeks of the season. It was then that he recaptured his best form and scored his first League hat-trick in a 4-0 defeat of Coventry City. And after John Barnes and Mike Marsh missed penalties in the game against Queens Park Rangers, he took over the responsibility, with successful conversions against Coventry City, Leeds United and Tottenham Hotspur in the last five games. If he can stay clear of injury in 1993-94, he may yet prove to be an inspired signing.

| | | | APPEARANCES | | | | GOALS | | | |
|---|---|---|---|---|---|---|---|---|---|---|
| Clubs | Signing Date | Transfer Fee | Lge | FL Cup | FA Cup | Others | Lge | FL Cup | FA Cup | Others |
| Aston Villa | 5.82 | - | 168+13 | 20+1 | 11+1 | 7+3 | 39 | 6 | 1 | 2 |
| Glasgow Rangers | 12.87 | £500,000 | 101+5 | 13 | 14 | 10 | 32 | 11 | 6 | 2 |
| Liverpool* | 8.91 | £1,250,000 | 44+15 | 9 | 3+1 | 8+1 | 14 | 4 | | 1 |

## WALTON David Lee

Born: Ashington, 10 April 1973

Height: 6'2" Weight: 13.4

**Position/Skill Factor:** Dogged and determined central defender, who is good in the air and quite quick on the ground for a big man.

**Career History:** Discovered by Sheffield United while playing non-League football for his hometown club, Ashington, he signed professional forms for the "Blades" during the 1992 close season, thus being given the opportunity of joining many famous former footballing heroes from the town, including Jackie Milburn and Bobby Charlton, who made it to the top. Yet to make a first team appearance, he continued to learn his trade with the reserves in **1992-93** and put in many useful performances.

| Clubs | Signing Date | Transfer Fee | APPEARANCES Lge | FL Cup | FA Cup | Others | GOALS Lge | FL Cup | FA Cup | Others |
|---|---|---|---|---|---|---|---|---|---|---|
| Sheffield United* | 5.92 | - | | | | | | | | |

## **WALTON Mark** Andrew

Born: Merthyr Tydfil,1 June 1969

Height: 6'2" Weight: 13.13

International Honours: W "U21"-1

**Position/Skill Factor:** An all-action goalkeeper who is always issuing instructions to his defence. Very strong when coming out for crosses, he also sets up attacks with great left footed drop kicks.

**Career History:** The son of Ron, who had a varied career as a winger between 1963-1977 in the lower reaches and currently coaches at Swansea City, he joined Luton Town early in 1987, having been a junior on Swansea City's books. Due to the presence of Les Sealey and Alec Chamberlain at Kenilworth Road, first team opportunities were nil and it wasn't long before he signed for Colchester United at first on loan and then permanently. Made his FL debut at Layer Road against Wolverhampton Wanderers on 21 November 1987 and played in 17 League games during 1987-88. Missed half of the 1988-89 season through injury and somewhat surprisingly moved to First Division Norwich City in the summer of 1989 on the recommendation of his former manager at Layer Road, Mike Walker. Signed as cover for Bryan Gunn, he made his First Division debut in April 1990 away to Aston Villa. In deputising for Gunn, when the latter was injured at Bramall Lane in mid-January 1992, he performed so well that he held his place to the end of the season. With Gunn in such tremendous form in **1992-93**, Mark became his perpetual understudy on the first team bench under the new substitute goalkeeper ruling. And apart from making a single appearance in a League Cup-tie against Carlisle United, when he kept a clean sheet after the latter had suffered a family bereavement, he had to keep match fit by playing in the Friday night reserve team matches. Unless Gunn is injured, or transferred, he is in all honesty destined to continue to play a supporting role.

| Clubs | Signing Date | Transfer Fee | APPEARANCES Lge | FL Cup | FA Cup | Others | GOALS Lge | FL Cup | FA Cup | Others |
|---|---|---|---|---|---|---|---|---|---|---|
| Luton Town | 2.87 | - | | | | | | | | |
| Colchester United | 11.87 | £15,000 | 40 | 3 | 8 | 5 | | | | |
| Norwich City* | 8.89 | £75,000 | 22 | 1 | 5 | | | | | |

## **WARD Mark** William

Born: Huyton 10 October 1962

Height: 5'6" Weight: 9.12

International Honours: E Semi-Pro Int

**Position/Skill Factor:** Tiny winger who is a lovely striker of the ball and quite capable of scoring from long range free-kicks. Very competitive, he will tackle full-backs with relish.

**Career History:** A player who has come the full cycle in football terms, having initially been with Everton as an associated schoolboy (September 1977), an apprentice (June 1979) and a professional (September 1980), before being released in the summer of 1981. He didn't let the experience get him down for too long, however, joining Northwich Victoria of the Alliance Premier League and representing the England Semi-Pro side, before Oldham Athletic recognised his potential and gave him another chance of League soccer. Made his FL debut on the opening day of the 1983-84 season and scored the only goal of the game against Brighton and Hove Albion on 27 August 1983 at Boundary Park. In two seasons with the "Latics", playing on the right-wing, he did not miss a single game — a remarkable record of consistency for a young pro — and it was perhaps not surprising he was snapped up by a First Division club, West Ham United. He was again ever present in his first season at Upton Park, assisting the "Hammers" to their highest ever FL placing (third) and in total he played 131 consecutive games from his FL debut, before being absent, which if not a FL record, must be close to one. He stayed over four years at Upton Park, hardly missing a game until injured in November 1988. However, disciplinary problems started to interrupt his appearances and his form and following the "Hammers'" relegation to Division Two in 1989-90, he moved back north in mid-season to join Manchester City. His arrival at Maine Road allowed David White to move inside and become one of the most deadly strikers in the country and in 20 months with City, he missed only two games. In the 1991 close season, he was surprisingly allowed to leave and rejoin the club that discarded him ten years earlier and made a great start at Goodison Park, scoring twice against League Champions Arsenal in his second game. But like most of his team mates, he was generally inconsistent and disappointing. As he had done in the previous season, he made a good start to **1992-93**, but was unfortunate to become the victim of a bad ligament injury picked up at Blackburn Rovers. After returning in March, incidentally, at home to Blackburn, he scored a superb volleyed winner in the next game at Coventry City.

However, his main use to the team was as a winger, supplying ammunition for the forwards, which allied to his close control and skill, added an extra dimension to the team's play and was a welcome addition in their struggle to get away from the foot of the table.

| | | | APPEARANCES | | | | GOALS | | | |
|---|---|---|---|---|---|---|---|---|---|---|
| Clubs | Signing Date | Transfer Fee | Lge | FL Cup | FA Cup | Others | Lge | FL Cup | FA Cup | Others |
| Everton | 9.80 | – | | | | | | | | |
| Northwich Victoria | 8.81 | – | | | | | | | | |
| Oldham Athletic | 7.83 | £10,000 | 84 | 5 | 3 | | 12 | | | |
| West Ham United | 8.85 | £250,000 | 163+2 | 20+1 | 17 | 6 | 12 | 2 | | |
| Manchester City | 12.89 | £1,000,000 | 55 | 3 | 6 | 3 | 14 | | | 2 |
| Everton* | 8.91 | £1,100,000 | 56 | 2 | 2 | 1 | 5 | | | |

## **WARD Mitchum (Mitch)** David

Born: Sheffield,
19 June 1971

Height: 5'8"

Weight: 10.7

**Position/Skill Factor:** Right-winger with two good feet who is an excellent striker of the ball.

**Career History:** Sheffield born and bred, he first joined Sheffield United as an associated schoolboy (July 1985), before progressing through the club as a trainee (July 1987) to professional status in the 1989 close season. With few opportunities available, he had to wait over a year before making his FL debut in a 1-1 draw at home to Manchester City on 8 September 1990. Retained his place the following week at Southampton, before a spell on loan at Crewe Alexandra and two more end of season games. Remained on the fringe of first team action in 1991-92 and scored twice in six occasional FL outings. The new Premier League **1992-93** season started with him putting in a transfer request, as he was desperate for first team football. Indeed, an offer was actually received from Cambridge United, before being turned down. Due to the club's injury situation, he played several times at full-back and although appearing a few times as a wingman, he invariably found himself wearing the number two shirt. Came off the bench to score twice in the FA Cup Sixth Round replay at Blackburn Rovers to force the match into a penalty "shoot-out", the first of which he confidently rammed home as United stormed on to a Semi-Final clash with their great rivals, Sheffield Wednesday. Following that, he was named as the Barclays' "Young Eagle of the Month" and is now a valued member of the first team squad.

| | | | APPEARANCES | | | | GOALS | | | |
|---|---|---|---|---|---|---|---|---|---|---|
| Clubs | Signing Date | Transfer Fee | Lge | FL Cup | FA Cup | Others | Lge | FL Cup | FA Cup | Others |
| Sheffield United* | 7.89 | – | 29+7 | 1+1 | 3+2 | 0+1 | 2 | | 2 | |
| Crewe Alexandra | 11.90 | Loan | 4 | | 1 | 2 | 1 | | 1 | |

## **WARHURST Paul**

Born: Stockport,
26 September 1969

Height: 6'1"

Weight: 14.0

International Honours:
E "U21"-8

**Position/Skill Factor:** Athletic central defender, or full-back, with good recovery, who is equally at home in the attack. Reads situations well at the back and breaks up attacks with timely interceptions. Comes out of defence with the ball, looking to pass, rather than clearing his lines.

**Career History:** Followed in his father Roy's footsteps when he joined Manchester City as an associated schoolboy in November 1983. Roy Warhurst was a tough, uncompromising wing-half, who joined Sheffield United during the last war and went on to play for Birmingham City, Manchester City, Crewe Alexandra and Oldham Athletic, before hanging his boots up in 1961. On leaving school, the younger Warhurst signed on as a trainee at Maine Road in July 1986 and eventually joined the City professional ranks in the 1988 close season. But after only four months and without a chance to prove himself, he was amazingly transferred to Oldham Athletic for a modest fee. Made his FL debut in a 1-1 draw at Portsmouth on 29 October 1988, but spent the rest of the season in the reserves, apart from three other FL outings. Established himself strongly in 1989-90 in central defence, after standing in for the injured Andy Holden, his pace impressed many observers during Oldham's historic double cup runs, when they reached the Final of the League Cup and the Semi-Final of the FA Cup. In 1990-91, he was switched to right-back with great success and became a regular member of the England Under 21 squad. However, he fell out of favour with manager, Joe Royle, following a heavy defeat at Oxford and lost his place to Norwegian, Gunnar Halle. He returned to the team late in the season in the unfamiliar role of striker as the "Latics" stormed to the Second Division Championship and promotion to Division One. He did not stay long enough to see First Division football return to Boundary Park, however, as he was sold for an enormous profit to Sheffield Wednesday in the 1991 close season. Soon established a place in central defence at Hillsborough in 1991-92, but had a mixed season, looking impressive in the first four months, but in-and-out over the second-half. Had a truly amazing season in **1992-93**. After starting out in his natural position at centre-back, he was asked by Trevor Francis if he would move up as a striker due to the club having major injury problems. He reluctantly agreed and in the absence of England striker, David Hirst, astounded everyone in football by knocking in goal after goal, with 12 in cup competitions and six in the League. He scored in his first game up front in a 2-1 win over Nottingham Forest, but on his next appearance, against Spora of Luxemborg and having already got one under his belt, his life was saved only by the quick action of the club's physio, Alan Smith. In scoring his second, he inadvertently collided with the goalie and suffered a fit after swallowing his tongue. Missed three matches following that traumatic experience, but was soon back to his best and during a period in January and February he equalled Derek Dooley's post-war record of scoring in seven successive games for the "Owls". Unable to find the net as Wednesday went down to defeat at the hand of Arsenal in both the League and FA Cup Finals, that was more than compensated by the news of his call up for the England World Cup standby squad.

| | | | APPEARANCES | | | | GOALS | | | |
|---|---|---|---|---|---|---|---|---|---|---|
| Clubs | Signing Date | Transfer Fee | Lge | FL Cup | FA Cup | Others | Lge | FL Cup | FA Cup | Others |
| Manchester City | 7.88 | - | | | | | | | | |
| Oldham Athletic | 10.88 | £10,000 | 60+7 | 8 | 5+4 | 2 | 2 | | | |
| Sheffield Wednesday* | 7.91 | £750,000 | 56+6 | 9 | 7+1 | 5 | 6 | 4 | 5 | 3 |

## WARK John

Born: Glasgow, 4 August 1957

Height: 5'10" Weight: 12.10

International Honours: S "U21"-8, S-29

**Position/Skill Factor:** A very experienced player, who is now playing as a central defender and reads situations like the back of his hand, having seen it all before. Still very good in the air, he is also dangerous at set plays.

**Career History:** A player who has just completed his 17th season of competitive League football and is now back with Ipswich Town, the club with whom he first started out as an apprentice in September 1973. After turning professional with Ipswich during the 1974 close season, he made his FL debut at Portman Road against Leicester City on 29 March 1975, but it was not until 1976-77 that he became a regular in Town's midfield and gave early warning of his goalscoring prowess with ten FL goals from 33 games. In 1977-78 he was absent, injured for the first-half of the season, but returned in January to assist his team to the FA Cup Final against Arsenal. After a wretched League campaign, in which relegation was narrowly averted, Ipswich were definite underdogs, yet they totally outplayed the "Gunners". Paul Mariner headed against the crossbar and Wark hit two tremendous shots against the post. Just when it seemed that the Gods had predetermined that the FA Cup must go to Highbury, Roger Osborne at last scored the winner that Ipswich so richly deserved. Made his international debut for Scotland against Wales on 19 May 1979 and remained a regular selection until 1984, accompanying the squad to the 1982 World Cup finals in Spain, playing in all three games. In total he scored seven goals in his 29 international appearances. In three consecutive seasons from 1979 to 1982, Town came close to winning the League Championship, without clinching it and his goals (12, 18 and 18, respectively) were instrumental in keeping his team at or near the top. Consolation for these near misses was found in their UEFA Cup victory of 1980-81, in which his contribution was astounding. Four goals against Aris Salonika in the First Round, a hat-trick against Widzew Lodz in the Third Round, goals in both legs of the Fourth Round against St. Etienne, a goal in the Semi-Final against Cologne and goals in each leg of the Final against Dutch team, AZ67 of Alkmaar, which Ipswich won narrowly, 5-4 on aggregate. In total, he scored 14 goals from midfield in 12 games of the competition — a record surely without parallel. In 1982-83 he was top scorer with 20 FL goals, but by then Bobby Robson's team was in decline and he became disaffected and moved to Liverpool in March 1984, in time to share in their League Championship triumph, if not to qualify for a medal. Liverpool's top scorer in 1984-85, with 18 FL goals from 40 games, ahead of Ian Rush, who missed one third of the season with injuries, he continued his remarkable record in European competition with five goals in nine European Cup games, including a hat-trick against Lech-Poznan. But the campaign ended in the disaster of Brussels, when Liverpool lost a meaningless Final to Juventus. Plagued by injury in 1985-86, he again missed out on a League Championship medal and never won his place back at Anfield. After four years at Liverpool, mostly out of the team, he moved back to Ipswich and proved he had not lost his goalscoring touch with 13 FL goals in 1988-89 and ten in 1989-90. Surprisingly, he moved to Middlesbrough for the 1990-91 season and held his place until March, although his goal output dropped sharply. In 1991-92 after being released by "Boro", he returned to Ipswich for the third time, as a non-contract player, apparently to help on the coaching side, rather than as a first team player. Remarkably, he returned to the team in October in a new role, as central defender and held his place to the end of the season as Town swept to the Second Division Championship. Had another excellent season in **1992-93**, when he again proved that he was still good enough to play at the highest level. Always an inspiration to those around him, he became the second highest appearance maker of all time for Town, behind Mick Mills. Earlier in the season he had a mixed match at Oldham Athletic, scoring at both ends, while a 2-1 defeat at home to Arsenal on 10 April 1993, became the tale of two penalties. He converted the first in the 27th minute, sending David Seaman the wrong way, but fortunes were reversed in the 50th minute as the goalie guessed right and saved the second. Turned down the Cambridge player/manager post during the season as he wishes to continue to play Premier League football.

| Clubs | Signing Date | Transfer Fee | APPEARANCES | | | | GOALS | | | |
|---|---|---|---|---|---|---|---|---|---|---|
| | | | Lge | FL Cup | FA Cup | Others | Lge | FL Cup | FA Cup | Others |
| Ipswich Town | 8.74 | - | 295+1 | 24+1 | 36+1 | 25 | 94 | 12 | 10 | 18 |
| Liverpool | 3.84 | £450,000 | 64+6 | 6+4 | 11+2 | 13+2 | 28 | 3 | 6 | 5 |
| Ipswich Town | 1.88 | £100,000 | 87+2 | 4 | 3 | 9 | 23 | | | 2 |
| Middlesbrough | 8.90 | £50,000 | 31+1 | 5 | 2 | 1 | 3 | | | |
| Ipswich Town * | 9.91 | - | 72+2 | 7+1 | 9 | 3 | 9 | | 1 | |

## WARZYCHA Robert

Born: Wielun, Poland, 20 August 1963

Height: 5'9"

Weight: 11.9

International Honours: Polish Int

**Position/Skill Factor:** Very fast right-winger, with two good feet, who likes to take full-backs on and looks to get in early crosses or shots at goal.

**Career History:** A 27-year-old Polish international, he signed for Everton from Gornik Zabre and immediately went into the first team, making his FL debut at Goodison against Nottingham Forest on 23 March 1991. Quickly became a favourite of the crowd, playing in 11 of the last 13 end of season games and scoring both goals in a 2-2 draw at Aston Villa. A regular member of the first team squad in 1991-92, but not an automatic first choice, sharing right-wing duties with Mark Ward and Pat Nevin. Nevertheless, he played 26 full FL games, scoring the winner at Luton Town in one of his 11 substitute appearances. Inconsistency yet again dogged his game in **1992-93**, which meant that he was in and out of the side throughout the season. His longest stint came in October when he played seven consecutive matches, but was dropped when Everton failed to score in five of them. His career at Goodison Park appears almost over, especially when you note that he went long periods almost unnoticed during matches and was completely ignored for selection from February onwards and is fast approaching the 30 mark.

| Clubs | Signing Date | Transfer Fee | APPEARANCES | | | | GOALS | | | |
|---|---|---|---|---|---|---|---|---|---|---|
| | | | Lge | FL Cup | FA Cup | Others | Lge | FL Cup | FA Cup | Others |
| Everton* | 3.91 | £300,000 | 48+17 | 4+2 | 1+2 | 4 | 6 | | | 2 |

## WATSON David (Dave)

Born: Liverpool, 20 November 1961

Height: 6'0" Weight: 11.12

International Honours: E "U21"-7, E-12

**Position/Skill Factor:** Very good central defender, who is strong in the air and aggressive in the tackle. Always dangerous from corner kicks, where he plunders many vital goals.

**Career History:** The elder brother of Alex, who also played for Liverpool but is currently with Bournemouth, he started his career at Anfield as an associated schoolboy in October 1976, before turning professional during the summer of 1979. Released by Liverpool 18 months later, without a first team appearance, he joined Norwich City for a six figure sum and went straight into action, making his FL debut at Ipswich Town on 26 December 1980. An instant success at Carrow Road, he became a fixture in the heart of the "Canaries'" defence for the next six years, missing a mere handful of games during that time. After winning Under 21 caps in 1983-84, he was a surprise selection for England's summer tour of South America in 1984, making his full international debut in the historic 2-0 victory over Brazil in the Maracana Stadium on 10 June. One of the successes of the tour, he remained a semi-regular England performer until 1987-88. In the summer of 1986 he returned to his native city, joining his former club's great rivals, Everton. Formed a very effective central defensive partnership with Kevin Ratcliffe, which lasted until 1991 when Ratcliffe gave way to Martin Keown. In his first season at Goodison Park he assisted the "Toffees" to their second League Championship in three years and also won an FA Cup Finalists medal in

1989, when Everton went down to Liverpool. In 1991-92 he played in every game, until injured in March and apart from the final three matches of **1992-93**, he was ever-present, playing a major role in holding together a leaky defence. One of the first names Howard Kendall could put on the team sheet, his consistent performances were even more remarkable considering the number of different players he partnered. As ever, his qualities were not only confined to defensive matters and he was often seen playing a prominent role in the opposition's box, especially on set pieces.

| | | | APPEARANCES | | | | GOALS | | | |
|---|---|---|---|---|---|---|---|---|---|---|
| Clubs | Signing Date | Transfer Fee | Lge | FL Cup | FA Cup | Others | Lge | FL Cup | FA Cup | Others |
| Liverpool | 5.79 | - | | | | | | | | |
| Norwich City | 11.80 | £100,000 | 212 | 21 | 18 | | 11 | 3 | 1 | |
| Everton* | 8.86 | £900,000 | 139+1 | 29 | 32 | 14 | 17 | 2 | 4 | 3 |

## WATSON Gordon William George

Born: Sidcup, 20 March 1971

Height: 6'0"

Weight: 12.0

International Honours: E "U21"-2

**Position/Skill Factor:** Hard working centre-forward, who tackles defenders as he chases lost causes. Useful in the air, he is a good target man.

**Career History:** A local discovery, he came through the Charlton Athletic junior ranks as an associated schoolboy (June 1985) and as a trainee (July 1987), before graduating as a professional towards the end of 1988-89. He was soon into first team action, making his FL debut on the opening day of the following season as a substitute at home to Derby County on 19 August 1989, but spent much of 1989-90 sitting on the bench awaiting further opportunities. Forced his way into the Charlton team early in 1990-91 and was a great success, netting seven goals in 15 games, although his team was struggling at the foot of the table. Rested in December, he was signed by Ron Atkinson in February for Sheffield Wednesday as an investment for the future. Made just one full appearance, plus four from the bench for the "Owls" and at the end of the season was called up for the England Under 21 squad to compete in the annual tournament in France. Made a handful of appearances in 1991-92, the last of them, at home to Leeds in January and did nothing to help his career when he seemingly took a blatant "dive" in the penalty area to earn the "Owls" a penalty. Still very much a fringe player in **1992-93**, he faced stiff opposition in his bid to get a regular berth as a striker. His lack of pace at the highest level appeared to hold up his progress, but his sheer joy and enthusiasm in playing can possibly compensate for this deficiency in the long run. Scored his first goals for the club last season, but was extremely unfortunate to suffer a bad injury in the last three weeks of the campaign, which threatens to keep him out for the start of 1993-94.

| | | | APPEARANCES | | | | GOALS | | | |
|---|---|---|---|---|---|---|---|---|---|---|
| Clubs | Signing Date | Transfer Fee | Lge | FL Cup | FA Cup | Others | Lge | FL Cup | FA Cup | Others |
| Charlton Athletic | 4.89 | - | 20+11 | 2 | 0+1 | 1+1 | 7 | 1 | | |
| Sheffield Wednesday* | 2.91 | £250,000 | 9+11 | 2+2 | 2 | 2+2 | 1 | 3 | | 1 |

## WATSON Kevin Edward

Born: Hackney, 3 January 1974

Height: 5'9"

Weight: 12.6

**Position/Skill Factor:** Skilful midfield player with a lovely touch on the ball. Very creative, passing is his forté.

**Career History:** Turned professional for Tottenham Hotspur at the end of 1991-92, after being at the club since signing as an associated schoolboy in March 1988 and graduating as a trainee in August 1990. Improved in leaps and bounds during **1992-93**, to make his PL debut as a substitute at Sheffield Wednesday on 27 September 1992 after scoring in his first senior action, a 3-1 home win against Brentford in the Second Round of the League Cup. Didn't come out again until November, with four full and two substitute appearances spread over the rest of the season, including away matches at Manchester City, Nottingham Forest, Chelsea and Liverpool. Definitely one for the future.

| | | | APPEARANCES | | | | GOALS | | | |
|---|---|---|---|---|---|---|---|---|---|---|
| Clubs | Signing Date | Transfer Fee | Lge | FL Cup | FA Cup | Others | Lge | FL Cup | FA Cup | Others |
| Tottenham Hotspur* | 5.92 | - | 4+1 | 1+1 | 0+1 | | | 1 | | |

## WATSON Stephen (Steve) Craig

Born: North Shields, 1 April 1974

Height: 6'1" Weight: 13.0

International Honours: E Yth, E "U21"-2

**Position/Skill Factor:** Midfielder who can also operate effectively at right-back. Always looking comfortable on the ball, he has excellent ability and is a great passer.

**Career History:** Once hailed as another "Paul Gascoigne", he came to Newcastle United as an associated schoolboy in September 1989 and moved rapidly through the trainee (June 1990) ranks to full professional status. Earlier, as United's youngest ever player at 16 years and 223 days, he made his FL debut as a substitute for Liam O'Brien at Wolverhampton Wanderers on 10 November 1990 and by the end of that season he had become a fixture in the number two shirt with 28 (including two substitute) first team appearances. Played 23 full League games in 1991-92, but in common with most of the starlets blooded by Ossie Ardiles, he returned to reserve team football under Kevin Keegan. And, with United taking the First Division by storm to win the Championship in **1992-93**, even though he won two England under 21 caps early on in the season, he had very few chances to shine, with only two League appearances, one of them as a substitute. Also missed part of the season to play for the England World Cup youth side in Australia, but with time on his side, he is certain to be challenging for a regular place in the near future.

| | | | APPEARANCES | | | | GOALS | | | |
|---|---|---|---|---|---|---|---|---|---|---|
| Clubs | Signing Date | Transfer Fee | Lge | FL Cup | FA Cup | Others | Lge | FL Cup | FA Cup | Others |
| Newcastle United* | 4.91 | - | 46+8 | | 5 | 3+1 | 1 | | | |

## WATTS Julian

Born: Sheffield, 17 March 1971

Height: 6'3" Weight: 12.1

**Position/Skill Factor:** Central defender. Good in the air, with excellent pace, he is prepared to come out of defence to pass the ball.

**Career History:** Signed by Rotherham United from local Northern Counties (East) League team, Frecheville CA, during the 1990 close season, he was soon "blooded", making his FL debut in a 3-1 defeat at Millmoor against Huddersfield Town on 13 October 1990. Held his place in central defence until December before being rested, but returned for two end of season games. Included in the first team squad at the beginning of 1991-92, he seemed to be establishing himself, until he was dropped from the team in late November. Apparently out of favour at Millmoor, it was something of a surprise when neighbours Sheffield Wednesday swooped for him just before the March transfer deadline. After making his debut for Wednesday in a UEFA Cup-tie in Luxemborg against Spora in **1992-93**, he had a spell on loan at Shrewsbury Town, where he created a good impression in nine Third Division games, before coming back to Hillsborough. Continued to come on in leaps and bounds and following a substitute appearance at Coventry City he was given a full game at Ipswich Town and then gained more useful experience of Premier League football in three further matches, before a broken foot put an end to his season. Look for him to come through in 1993-94.

| | | | APPEARANCES | | | | GOALS | | | |
|---|---|---|---|---|---|---|---|---|---|---|
| Clubs | Signing Date | Transfer Fee | Lge | FL Cup | FA Cup | Others | Lge | FL Cup | FA Cup | Others |
| Rotherham United | 7.90 | - | 17+3 | 1 | 4 | 2 | 1 | | | |
| Sheffield Wednesday* | 3.92 | £80,000 | 2+2 | | | 1 | | | | |
| Shrewsbury Town | 12.92 | Loan | 9 | | | 1 | | | | |

## WEBSTER Kenneth (Ken) Darren

Born: Hammersmith, 2 March 1973

Height: 5'9" Weight: 12.12

International Honours: E Yth

**Position/Skill Factor:** Enthusiastic right-back, who can also play in the centre of the defence. Quick, strong and aggressive, with a very powerful right foot.

**Career History:** Yet to make his FL debut, he has been a professional at Arsenal for just over one year, having earlier come through the ranks as an associated schoolboy (November 1988) and as a trainee (July 1989). Made only limited reserve team appearances in **1992-93** and appears to have a long way to go yet before his dreams are realised at Highbury.

| | | | APPEARANCES | | | | GOALS | | | |
|---|---|---|---|---|---|---|---|---|---|---|
| Clubs | Signing Date | Transfer Fee | Lge | FL Cup | FA Cup | Others | Lge | FL Cup | FA Cup | Others |
| Arsenal* | 3.91 | - | | | | | | | | |

## WEBSTER Simon Paul

Born: Hinckley, 20 January 1964

Height: 6'0" Weight: 11.7

**Position/Skill Factor:** Central defender who is very strong, especially in the air. Wins almost everything from dead ball situations and is a good long kicker.

**Career History:** An enthusiastic and consistent performer, he joined Tottenham Hotspur as an apprentice on leaving school in May 1980 and turned professional on his 17th birthday, having been a member of the successful team that had reached the FA Youth Cup Final the previous season. Made his debut at White Hart Lane against visiting Everton on 3 January 1983 and followed it up with a solitary substitute appearance, before being loaned out to Exeter City to gain further experience. Remained with the Third Division club from November to the end of the season and with little chance of a breakthrough at White Hart Lane, he was allowed to leave less than a year later to join Second Division, Huddersfield Town. Immediately slotted into the heart of their defence and in four seasons at Leeds Road he missed only four games until a calamitous 10-1 defeat by Manchester City in November 1987. After being dropped, although recalled in January, his confidence was shattered in a struggling team and he was allowed to leave for Sheffield United, as one of Dave Bassett's first signings for the "Blades". However, it was "out of the frying pan into the fire" for Webster, as United accompanied the "Terriers" in the drop to Division Three. After starting 1988-89 in an unfamiliar midfield slot, he suffered a serious injury in late October, which sidelined him for over one year. When he returned in November 1989, with the "Blades" back in Division Two and challenging for promotion, he was switched between midfield and defence and unable to establish a regular slot, he played little part in the crucial end of season games, which clinched promotion to Division One. However, his future lay elsewhere, as he remained in Division Two, by moving to London to sign for recently relegated Charlton Athletic in the summer of 1990. After three disappointing years in the north, he returned to top form with the "Valiants" and re-established his credentials as a central defender in one of the tightest defences in the Division. Missed only three games in **1992-93**, having been absent just eight times previously in his time at Charlton and as the captain, he led from the front with great enthusiasm. An extremely consistent performer, his summer transfer to newly promoted West Ham United gave him a well earned chance of Premier League football, which seemed to have passed him by. However, a tragic post-season training accident, involving team-mate, Julian Dicks, saw him break a leg and he is now expected to miss the whole of 1993-94.

| | | | APPEARANCES | | | | GOALS | | | |
|---|---|---|---|---|---|---|---|---|---|---|
| Clubs | Signing Date | Transfer Fee | Lge | FL Cup | FA Cup | Others | Lge | FL Cup | FA Cup | Others |
| Tottenham Hotspur | 12.81 | - | 2+1 | | | | | | | |
| Exeter City | 11.83 | Loan | 26 | | | 3 | | | | |
| Huddersfield Town | 2.85 | £15,000 | 118 | 7 | 7 | 2 | 4 | | | |
| Sheffield United | 3.88 | £35,000 | 26+11 | 5 | 5+1 | 3+1 | 3 | | | |
| Charlton Athletic | 8.90 | £50,000 | 127 | 7 | 6 | 3 | 7 | | | |
| West Ham United* | 6.93 | £525,000 | | | | | | | | |

## WEGERLE Roy Connon

Born: Johannesburg, South Africa, 19 March 1964

Height: 5'8" Weight: 10.2

International Honours: FL Rep, USA Int

**Position/Skill Factor:** Striker with a wonderful talent. Good controlling and passing ability, with silky skills to match. He can twist and turn defenders inside out and is capable of scoring spectacular goals. A natural athlete, he also possesses great pace.

**Career History:** Discovered playing in South Africa by the former Ipswich goalkeeper, Roy Bailey, he had a brief trial with Manchester United before heading for the USA and a university scholarship. After joining NASL side, Tampa Bay Rowdies, he created such a good impression that Chelsea eventually signed him during the 1986 close season, following a successful trial period. Made his FL debut as a substitute for Keith Jones in a 2-2 draw at Everton on 8 November 1986 and played seven full matches that season, scoring against Queens Park Rangers and Wimbledon. Appeared mostly on the wing for Chelsea, but never enjoyed much of a run in two seasons at Stamford Bridge, nor did an end of season loan with Swindon in 1987-88 lead to anything. Transferred to Luton Town in the summer of 1988, he established a regular place as a front runner and started to show glimpses of his true potential, particularly in the team's fine League Cup run, when he scored twice in a 3-1 victory over Manchester City in the Fourth Round and in both legs of the Semi-Final against West Ham. Sadly for Luton, the final was lost 3-1 to Nottingham Forest, despite a half-time lead. After two FL goals in 15 games in 1989-90, he was transferred to Queens Park Rangers for a truly astonishing fee of £1 million — astonishing in view of his limited experience and previous valuations. Although he looked a quality player for Rangers, six goals in 19 FL games did not seem to justify the fee. However, it made more sense in 1990-91 when he was outstanding and finished the season as leading scorer with 18 FL goals. His goals included one at Leeds when he cut in from the right touch line, dribbled round or past six United players, before scoring with a low drive. In truth, the shot was less impressive than the run, but the goal was deservedly chosen as "Goal of the Season" by the ITV panel of experts. In 1991-92 after scoring only five goals in 23 appearances, he was sold to ambitious Blackburn Rovers. Kenny Dalglish signed him to replace the injured Mike Newell and to keep Rovers' promotion campaign on course. The gamble failed, as Rovers lost seven of the first nine games he played in and fell from the first place to outside the Play-Offs zone and after only two goals in 12 games he was dropped. Although Rovers recovered just in time to reach the Play-Offs and eventually win them, he played no further part in the proceedings. However, having taken

USA nationality, he played his first match for the USA national team at the end of the season, after waiting three years to see if he would be selected for the England team. He and team- mate, John Harkes of Sheffield Wednesday, were major factors in the USA's amazing victory in a four team tournament, including Italy, The Republic of Ireland and Portugal. Confined mainly to substitute during the early matches in **1992-93**, due to the impressive partnership of Mike Newell and Alan Shearer, he was only promoted when the latter's season was ended by injury. Conversely, he played well as the team slumped, but was never at home trying to compensate for Shearer. Continued to delight with his wonderful ability, but those around him found great difficulty in anticipating his moves. Scored a memorable goal to dump Newcastle United out of the FA Cup, while in the next round he only came on as a substitute, as Rovers were finally beaten on penalties by Sheffield United. Played just one more game before he joined Coventry City just after the transfer deadline as a makeweight in the deal that took Kevin Gallacher to Ewood Park. Played in the last six matches for the "Sky Blues" and a lot is expected from his partnership with Mick Quinn this coming season, especially in the wake of his great close season display for the USA against the inept England side that were defeated 2-0.

| | | | APPEARANCES | | | | GOALS | | | |
|---|---|---|---|---|---|---|---|---|---|---|
| Clubs | Signing Date | Transfer Fee | Lge | FL Cup | FA Cup | Others | Lge | FL Cup | FA Cup | Others |
| Chelsea | 7.86 | £100,000 | 15+8 | | 1+1 | 2+1 | 3 | | 1 | |
| Swindon Town | 3.88 | Loan | 7 | | | | 1 | | | |
| Luton Town | 7.88 | £75,000 | 39+6 | 10 | 1 | 2+1 | 10 | 8 | | |
| Q.P.R. | 12.89 | £1,000,000 | 71+4 | 5 | 11 | 1 | 29 | 1 | 1 | |
| Blackburn Rovers | 3.92 | £1,200,000 | 20+14 | 3+3 | 4+1 | | 6 | 4 | 2 | |
| Coventry City* | 3.93 | £500,000 | 5+1 | | | | | | | |

## WETHERALL David

Born: Sheffield, 14 March 1971

Height: 6'3"

Weight: 12.0

International Honours: E Sch

**Position/Skill Factor:** Strong tackling central defender who is also very good in the air.

**Career History:** Signed for Sheffield Wednesday as an associated schoolboy in May 1987, having represented England schools, he eventually turned professional at Hillsborough during the 1989 close season. Surprisingly sold to Leeds United two years later for a six figure fee, along with Jon Newsome, another promising "Owls'" youngster and without a first team game to his name, he made his FL debut as a substitute in a 2-2 draw against Arsenal at Elland Road on 3 September 1991, his only appearance during a season in which the club would ultimately win the League Championship. After spending the previous year at university and playing four games early on in **1992-93**, he came into the side over Christmas and helped to bolster a defence that was conceding goals with an alarming regularity. Uncompromising and confident in possession, he played consistently well and had excellent games at Arsenal and Nottingham Forest in the League, while scoring a brilliantly headed goal at Elland Road against Chelsea. Assured and talented, he has a big future at the club.

| | | | APPEARANCES | | | | GOALS | | | |
|---|---|---|---|---|---|---|---|---|---|---|
| Clubs | Signing Date | Transfer Fee | Lge | FL Cup | FA Cup | Others | Lge | FL Cup | FA.Cup | Others |
| Sheffield Wednesday | 7.89 | - | | | | | | | | |
| Leeds United* | 7.91 | £125,000 | 13+1 | 2 | 4 | | 1 | | | |

## WHELAN Noel

Born: Leeds, 30 December 1974

Height: 6'1½"

Weight: 11.3

International Honours: E Yth

**Position/Skill Factor:** Versatile forward with good touch for such a big lad. Covers a lot of ground and always seems to be in the right place at the right time.

**Career History:** Local product and a prolific scorer for Leeds United's FA Cup winning youth team, he turned professional towards the end of the **1992-93** season, signing a three year contract, having been at the club as an associated schoolboy (January 1990) and a trainee since September 1991. Scored six goals in a youth match at Scarborough last season and following reserve team experience, stepped up to make his PL debut at Sheffield Wednesday on 4 May 1993. Another exciting United youngster, who looks set to make things hum at Elland Road in the near future.

| | | | APPEARANCES | | | | GOALS | | | |
|---|---|---|---|---|---|---|---|---|---|---|
| Clubs | Signing Date | Transfer Fee | Lge | FL Cup | FA Cup | Others | Lge | FL Cup | FA Cup | Others |
| Leeds United* | 3.93 | - | 1 | | | | | | | |

## WHELAN Philip (Phil) James

Born: Stockport, 7 March 1972

Height: 6'4" Weight: 14.1

International Honours: E "U21"-2

**Position/Skill Factor:** A central defender who looks the part, he is good in the air and passes the ball with confidence.

**Career History:** Following a successful trial, he signed professional for Ipswich Town straight from school during the 1990 close season. Following an early season Zenith Cup outing in 1991-92, he made his FL debut away to Southend United on 4 April 1992, standing in for the injured Dave Linighan in central defence and remarkably, for a defender, scored a goal in a 2-1 victory. Even more remarkably, he scored again in his second game and showed much composure in his eight end of season games, as Town swept to the Second Division Champion-ship and promotion to the Premier League. Often played out of position during **1992-93**, he was unable to really establish himself, even though he made 41 (including six substitute) first team appearances. However, he impressed enough to be called up by the England under 21 side, playing twice, before being released to concentrate on preparing for his final accountancy exams. Once he settles into Premier League football, he could become one of Town's best ever players.

| | | | APPEARANCES | | | | GOALS | | | |
|---|---|---|---|---|---|---|---|---|---|---|
| Clubs | Signing Date | Transfer Fee | Lge | FL Cup | FA Cup | Others | Lge | FL Cup | FA Cup | Others |
| Ipswich Town* | 7.90 | - | 36+4 | 5+1 | 2+1 | 1 | 2 | | | |

## WHELAN Ronald (Ronnie)

Born: Dublin, 25 September 1961

Height: 5'9" Weight: 10.13

International Honours: IR "U21"-1, IR-45

**Position/Skill Factor:** The anchor man in midfield, his forté is to break up the opposition's attacks with timely interceptions and release the ball quickly to his partners with short passes. Frequently inconspicuous during matches, his value to the team is out of all proportion to the time he spends on the ball and is most noticeable when he is not playing!

**Career History:** Son of a former international, who never played in the Football League, he was spotted by Liverpool, playing for the League of Ireland team, Home Farm and was quickly snapped up and brought to Anfield early in 1979-80. Waited patiently for 18 months to make his FL debut, which came when he was called in to replace the injured Ray Kennedy against Stoke City on 3 April 1981 and he scored in a 3-0 win. Won a regular place in Liverpool's midfield from November 1981 at the expense of Ray Kennedy on the left side and enjoyed an outstanding first season as a regular, scoring ten FL goals and two in the 1982 League Cup Final against Tottenham. The first in the 87th minute taking the match into extra-time and his second with nine minutes remaining, clinching the "Reds'" 3-1 victory. It was the second of Liverpool's four consecutive League Cup triumphs and in the 1983 Final against Manchester United, once again, he popped up to score the winner in extra-time. In addition to his three League Cup winners medals, he has won seven League Championship medals in 1981-82, 1982-83, 1983-84, 1985-86, 1987-88 and 1989-90, two FA Cup winners medals in 1986 and 1989 and a European Cup winners medal in 1984, plus a finalists medal in 1985, despite a career riddled with injury problems which have often restricted his appearances. An infrequent scorer after his early exploits, he has occasionally been deployed as the forward run midfielder, most notably in a match against Coventry in April 1986, when he scored his only senior hat-trick in a 5-0 victory. In 1987-88, he was switched from his traditional left side duties to his present more pivotal role just in front of the back four, in place of the injured Jan Molby and his long term knee injury incurred in a match against Everton in February 1991, coupled with the loss of his midfield partner, Steve McMahon, was a critical factor in Liverpool's late season collapse. An Irish Republic international since his debut as substitute against Czechoslovakia on 29 April 1981 — shortly after his Liverpool debut — his appearances have been limited both by injury and his club commitments. Selected for both the European Championship Finals in West Germany 1988 and World Cup Finals in Italy 1990, he will always be remembered for his bicycle-kick volley against the Soviet Union in the former competition, which was considered to be "goal of the tournament" until van Basten's effort in the Final. Sadly troubled by injury, he played little part in the Republic's remarkable progress to the World Cup Quarter-Finals in

and lose his chance of a third FA Cup Final appearance. After two injury plagued seasons, he started **1992-93** in "good nick" and scored with a magnificent dipping volley at Leeds United in the fifth match of the season. However, two weeks later he was withdrawn with a thigh injury and was out for so long that many "Reds'" supporters feared that it was one setback too many and that he would never play again. Happily, he returned to duty in March and it was a measure of his value to Liverpool that a potentially disastrous season was turned into one of mediocre respectability. Prior to his return, the "Reds" had accumulated a pitiful eight points from 11 games, but in the match against Queens Park Rangers, he re-established the Liverpool tradition of quiet and composed authority, as the side won more convincingly than the 1-0 scoreline suggests. Of his nine end of season games, Liverpool won six and drew twice, to finish in a rather flattering sixth place, instead of being involved in a mad scramble to avoid relegation.

| | | | APPEARANCES | | | | GOALS | | | |
|---|---|---|---|---|---|---|---|---|---|---|
| Clubs | Signing Date | Transfer Fee | Lge | FL Cup | FA Cup | Others | Lge | FL Cup | FA Cup | Others |
| Liverpool* | 10.79 | - | 328+11 | 46+4 | 40+1 | 38+2 | 45 | 14 | 7 | 6 |

# WHITE David

Born: Manchester, 30 October 1967

Height: 6'1"

Weight: 12.9

International Honours: E Yth, E "U21"-6, E"B", E-1

**Position/Skill Factor:** One of the most exciting forwards in the modern game, he loves to run with the ball at defences and scores spectacular goals from prodigious distances and acute angles.

**Career History:** Discovered on Manchester City's doorstep, he signed associated schoolboy forms in December 1981, before joining the club on a YTS scheme in June 1984, on leaving school. After turning professional early in 1985-86, he had to wait nearly a year to make his FL debut as a substitute at Luton Town on 27 September 1986. However, he did well enough to hold down a place on the right-wing for short spells, although the club sank into the Second Division at the end of the season. Sprang to fame in 1987-88, in a City team brimming with brilliant youngsters, which frequently ripped Second Division defences to shreds, most notably in a 10-1 mauling of Huddersfield in November, in which White, along with two colleagues, scored a hat-trick — possibly a unique occurrence in FL history. Sadly, the team lacked the experience to sustain a challenge, finishing eighth, but the following season promotion was achieved, with White playing in all but one game, as he did in 1989-90 when City struggled successfully to hold onto their First Division status. Always noted for his confident surging runs and powerful shooting, he was switched from the wing to central striker by manager Peter Reid in January 1990, following the signing of Mark Ward. It proved to be an inspired move as he formed a dangerous partnership with Niall Quinn which brought him 16 FL goals in 1990-91. Top scorer in 1991-92 with 19 FL goals, his haul included two against Liverpool in an early season 2-1 victory and another brace in the return match at Anfield in December — an achievement possibly without parallel in the last 30 years — and he rounded off the season with a last match hat-trick at Oldham. Got off to a tremendous start in **1992-93** and was going great guns until making his England debut in a 1-0 defeat against Spain on 9 September 1992 at Santander. Although not overawed by the occasion, he had England's best two chances, but was denied both times by good goalkeeping. Ever present throughout the season, his form dipped slightly after the England game, but his 19 goals still made him one of the most prolific scorers around and at Tottenham Hotspur in March he completed 300 full first team appearances for City. Also scored his first FA Cup goal for five years when hammering a brilliant shot into the top corner at Queens Park Rangers for the opener in a 2-1 Fourth Round win.

| | | | APPEARANCES | | | | GOALS | | | |
|---|---|---|---|---|---|---|---|---|---|---|
| Clubs | Signing Date | Transfer Fee | Lge | FL Cup | FA Cup | Others | Lge | FL Cup | FA Cup | Others |
| Manchester City* | 11.85 | - | 272+12 | 20+2 | 22 | 9 | 80 | 9 | 4 | 2 |

# WHITE Devon Winston

Born: Nottingham, 2 March 1964

Height: 6'3"

Weight: 14.0

**Position/Skill Factor:** Big, strong physical striker, with tremendous aerial power on the far post. Provides goals for others with timely knock-downs.

**Career History:** A player who has finally made the Premier League after a chequered career, during which he was discarded by both a Fourth Division and a Vauxhall Conference club. He first came to the attention of Third Division Lincoln City, while playing for non-League Arnold FC, a Nottingham based club in the Northern Counties (East) League and was snapped up during the 1984-85 season. Made his FL debut immediately, as a substitute at home to Gillingham on 15 December 1984 and played in his first full match on 16 February 1985, at home to Wigan. After making 22 appearances in 1985-86, without establishing himself in the "Imps'" team, he was loaned out to Lincolnshire neighbours, Boston United, of the GM Vauxhall Conference, at the start of 1986-87, the transfer being made permanent in October 1986. Ironically, almost as soon as he signed for Boston, he was dropped from the team and spent the closing months of 1986-87 on loan to Shepshed Charterhouse of the Southern League. A free agent in the summer of 1987, he had a short trial with Charlton Athletic, before he was surprisingly offered a contract by Bristol Rovers' manager, Gerry Francis. He was an immediate success with the "Pirates", playing 39 games and scoring 15 FL goals in his first season and forming an effective partnership with Gary Penrice. In his second season, less productive goalwise, Rovers missed promotion after reaching the Play-Offs, but they made no mistake in 1989-90, going up as Third Division Champions, with White playing in all but three games and scoring 12 FL goals. Back in the Second Division, Rovers consolidated their position and he missed only one game during the season. Following the departure of Gerry Francis to Q.P.R. in the summer of 1991, Rovers struggled until new manager, Dennis Rofe, steered them to safety. Once again he was an automatic first choice and it was a surprise when he was transferred on the March transfer deadline to high riding, Cambridge United, in exchange for John Taylor. Curiously, while Taylor was an immediate success with Rovers, White played little part in Cambridge's final games of the season, which ended in disappointment, after being eliminated by Leicester City in the Play-Offs. He never settled in at Cambridge, as the team struggled at the foot of the First Division table and following the departure of manager John Beck in **1992-93** and his eventual replacement by Ian Atkins, he lost his place. In another surprise move, his former manager, Gerry Francis, rescued him from obscurity in January 1993 and he made his Premier League bow as a substitute on 27 January 1993, something he would scarcely have dreamed of six years ago! In his next game, he came off the bench at Ipswich Town and scored the equaliser in a 1-1 draw, before being selected for the match at Tottenham Hotspur and heading a late goal in a 3-2 defeat. But after another two appearances, he made way for the return of Bradley Allen. He then scored a host of goals for the reserves and is sure to come into the reckoning, as Rangers look to consolidate on their fifth placing in the new Premier League.

| | | | APPEARANCES | | | | GOALS | | | |
|---|---|---|---|---|---|---|---|---|---|---|
| Clubs | Signing Date | Transfer Fee | Lge | FL Cup | FA Cup | Others | Lge | FL Cup | FA Cup | Others |
| Lincoln City | 12.84 | - | 21+8 | | | 2+1 | 4 | | | 2 |
| Boston United | 8.86 | £2,000 | | | | | | | | |
| Shepshed Chart. | 3.87 | Loan | | | | | | | | |
| Bristol Rovers | 8.87 | - | 190+12 | 9 | 10 | 19 | 54 | 2 | 3 | 2 |
| Cambridge United | 3.92 | £100,00 | 15+7 | 4 | 1 | | 4 | 1 | | |
| Q.P.R.* | 1.93 | £100,000 | 3+4 | | | | 2 | | | |

## WHITE Stephen (Steve) James

Born: Chipping Sodbury, 2 January 1959

Height: 5'10"

Weight: 11.4

International Honours: E Sch

**Position/Skill Factor:** Striker, who still has that vital burst of pace that takes him clear of defenders. Always likely to be a source of danger because he is prepared to get in where the boots are flying.

**Career History:** An under 18 England schoolboy international, he was spotted by Bristol Rovers, while playing for neighbouring Western League club, Mangotsfield, signing him as a professional during the 1977 close season. After gaining useful experience with the reserves, he made his FL debut at Southampton on 27 March 1978, playing alongside Paul Randall and scored four goals in eight games before the season closed. In two and a half seasons at Eastville, he was not always an automatic first choice and was signed by Luton Town for a substantial fee. He struggled to make an impact at Kenilworth Road until 1981-82, when he enjoyed an excellent season, playing every game and scoring 18 FL goals in assisting the "Hatters" to the Second Division Championship and a triumphant return to the top flight. Sadly, for White, he did not taste the fruits of promotion, as he was inexplicably transferred to Charlton Athletic for a lower fee than Luton paid for him, presumably a much improved and more experienced player. His one season at the Valley was equally bizarre. As a regular scorer, he was dropped in mid season and loaned to Lincoln City and Luton, before returning to favour at the end of the season. He was then transferred back to his first professional club, Bristol Rovers, for an almost token fee, although he could hardly be classed as a failure! The mid 1980s were a difficult time for the "Pirates", both on and off the field and after three seasons back at Eastville he was granted a free transfer. This was probably less an error of judgement by Rovers' management, than an acknowledgement that the club could not afford to offer him improved terms at the end of his contract. He then joined Wiltshire neighbours, Swindon Town and has since proved to be one of the best free transfers of all time. Top scorer with 15 FL goals in his first season with the "Robins", he also struck the two goals which helped to defeat Gillingham 2-0 in the end of season Play-Off Final, which ensured Swindon's elevation to Division Two. Since then, he has been a reliable performer and frequent goalscorer for six seasons, until reaching the veteran stage and losing his place to Dave Mitchell in January 1992. A regular choice as a substitute at the start of **1992-93**, he made an appearance at some stage in almost every match, but in mid-season, with Craig Maskell and Mitchell losing their touch and suffering injuries, he reclaimed his place and held it on merit. His high point of the season — The Play-Off Final at Wembley excluded — was a superb hat-trick in a 4-0 victory at Watford, while the low point came when he was sent off at Brentford for alleged use of the elbow. During the season he reached two personal milestones, the 200th goal of his career and his 200th League appearance for Swindon, while his third strike at Watford — a classic Glenn Hoddle free kick, flicked on by Paul Bodin and volleyed in by White — was chosen by Mark Lawrenson as the "HTV Goal of the Season". A free transfer seven years ago, he now finds himself playing in the Premier League this season. After coming on at Wembley, within six minutes he was adjudged to have been fouled by the Leicester City 'keeper and Bodin converted the penalty for the fourth goal in a 4-3 thriller.

| | | | APPEARANCES | | | | GOALS | | | |
|---|---|---|---|---|---|---|---|---|---|---|
| Clubs | Signing Date | Transfer Fee | Lge | FL Cup | FA Cup | Others | Lge | FL Cup | FA Cup | Others |
| Bristol Rovers | 7.77 | - | 46+4 | 2 | 3 | | 20 | 1 | 3 | |
| Luton Town | 12.79 | £200,000 | 63+9 | 3+1 | 2+1 | | 25 | 1 | | |
| Charlton Athletic | 7.82 | £150,000 | 29 | 2 | | | 12 | | | |
| Lincoln City | 1.83 | Loan | 2+1 | | | | | | | |
| Luton Town | 2.83 | Loan | 4 | | | | | | | |
| Bristol Rovers | 8.83 | £45,000 | 89+12 | 8 | 7+1 | 5+2 | 24 | 2 | 2 | 1 |
| Swindon Town* | 7.86 | - | 198+40 | 20+7 | 9+2 | 22+5 | 83 | 11 | 2 | 15 |

## WHITEHOUSE Dane Lee

Born: Sheffield, 14 October 1970

Height: 5'8" Weight: 10.12

**Position/Skill Factor:** Hard working left sided midfield player, who can also link up well with the attack when required.

**Career History:** Locally born and bred, he first joined Sheffield United as an associated schoolboy in November 1985 and continued to progress through the club as a trainee (July 1987), before turning professional during the 1989 close season. Still a trainee when he stepped out on the left-wing to make his FL debut in a 2-1 win at Blackpool on 15 October 1988, he made only limited progress, however, over the next two seasons. Was a regular member of the first team squad in 1991-92, enjoying an extended run on the left-wing and also showed he had an eye for goal scoring opportunities with seven FL goals, including two in an away win over Chelsea and three cup goals. After missing the start of the **1992-93** season, due to a pre-season practice match injury, he was just coming into a run of form, with three goals from five appearances, when he sustained a cracked shinbone in the League Cup match at home to Bristol City. This put him out of action for five months, before he made a surprise return to first team action at left-back in the FA Cup Sixth Round-tie at Blackburn Rovers. He continued in this role until after the Wembley FA Cup Semi-Final defeat by Sheffield Wednesday, when a move back to the left side of midfield brought further success, including two goals at Chelsea in the last game of the season. Given an injury free 1993-94 he will continue to be a key member of the squad.

| | | | APPEARANCES | | | | GOALS | | | |
|---|---|---|---|---|---|---|---|---|---|---|
| Clubs | Signing Date | Transfer Fee | Lge | FL Cup | FA Cup | Others | Lge | FL Cup | FA Cup | Others |
| Sheffield United* | 7.89 | - | 51+18 | 4+1 | 9+3 | 3 | 13 | 1 | 1 | 2 |

## WHITMARSH Paul

Born: Beckenham, 18 September 1973

Height: 5'8" Weight: 11.0

International Honours: E Sch

**Position/Skill Factor:** Left-winger who is very confident with the ball at his feet and is a good crosser. Also, makes excellent runs off the ball to assist his team-mates.

**Career History:** Joined West Ham United, as a trainee from school in 1991, but as the "Hammers" had already filled their permitted complement of registered trainees, he was registered as a non-contract player, before turning professional in the 1992 close season. Yet to be afforded a first team opportunity, he spent **1992-93** fighting for a regular reserve team slot, a situation that was only partially remedied as the season drew to a close. Still a young and inexperienced player, if he wants a taste of the Premier League, he must continue to make headway in 1993-94.

| | | | APPEARANCES | | | | GOALS | | | |
|---|---|---|---|---|---|---|---|---|---|---|
| Clubs | Signing Date | Transfer Fee | Lge | FL Cup | FA Cup | Others | Lge | FL Cup | FA Cup | Others |
| West Ham United* | 7.92 | - | | | | | | | | |

## WHITTON Stephen (Steve) Paul

Born: East Ham, 4 December 1960

Height: 6'0"

Weight: 12.7

**Position/Skill Factor:** Midfield, winger, or forward, he is a great striker of the ball, especially with the right foot. On the flanks, he can deceive 'keepers with outswinging crosses. Powerful in the air and an expert penalty taker.

**Career History:** One of many east-London youngsters discovered by Coventry City, he signed as an associated schoolboy in June 1976, before moving up as an apprentice (April 1977) and later joining the professional ranks during the 1978 close season. Just over a year later, he made his FL debut in midfield at Highfield Road against Tottenham Hotspur on 29 September 1979 and subsequently made six substitute appearances that season. He did not breakthrough until the beginning of 1981-82 when he started as a forward, before losing his place to Mark Hateley and returning to the team in March on the right-wing. The following term he was a regular choice on the wing and finished the season as the "Sky Blues'" top scorer with 12 FL goals. At the end of 1982-83 he returned to his native east-end to join the "Hammers", but in three seasons at Upton Park, was never able to establish a regular place. Returned to the Midlands in the summer of 1986 to join Birmingham City, recently relegated to Division Two, after spending two months on loan to the "Blues" the previous season. At St Andrews he was converted to a central striker, top scoring with 14 FL goals in his second season. In 1988-89, the club was relegated to the Third Division, but before the axe fell, he surprisingly was back in the First Division with Sheffield Wednesday, although unable to improve the "Owls'" dismal scoring record that season. Tried out in midfield at the beginning of 1989-90, without success, he was replaced by new signing, John Sheridan. And for the remainder of his Hillsborough career, made only occasional appearances as a substitute, until rescued from obscurity by his former West Ham manager, John Lyall, who signed him for Ipswich Town. Scored in his first two games for Town, but then lost form and his place. After several disappointing seasons, he enjoyed probably the best time of his career in 1991-92 while operating in midfield, missing only two FL games and guiding Ipswich to the Second Division Championship. Still recovering from a knee operation at the start of **1992-93**, he didn't come into the side until the match at Chelsea when he came on in the 71st minute for Phil Whelan and scored the winner nine minutes later. Had a disjointed first season in the Premier League, mainly due to a variety of niggling injuries and looks forward to being fully fit for the new season.

| Clubs | Signing Date | Transfer Fee | APPEARANCES Lge | FL Cup | FA Cup | Others | GOALS Lge | FL Cup | FA Cup | Others |
|---|---|---|---|---|---|---|---|---|---|---|
| Coventry City | 9.78 | - | 64+10 | 3+2 | 3 | | 21 | | 2 | |
| West Ham United | 7.83 | £175,000 | 35+4 | 6 | 1 | | 6 | 2 | | |
| Birmingham City | 1.86 | Loan | 8 | | | | 2 | | | |
| Birmingham City | 8.86 | £60,000 | 94+1 | 7+1 | 5 | 3 | 28 | 4 | | 1 |
| Sheffield Wednesday | 3.89 | £275,000 | 22+10 | 3 | 0+1 | 0+1 | 4 | 4 | | |
| Ipswich Town* | 1.91 | £150,000 | 73+4 | 6 | 8 | 4 | 14 | 1 | 2 | |

## WHITWORTH Neil Anthony

Born: Wigan, 12 April 1972

Height: 6'2" Weight: 12.6

International Honours: E Yth.

**Position/Skill Factor:** Strong tackling central defender with plenty of pace, who is also very good in the air.

**Career History:** Signed as a trainee by Wigan Athletic in July 1988, he made his FL debut at Springfield Park against Leyton Orient on 10 February 1990 and following just one more appearance as a substitute, he was transferred to Manchester United during the 1990 close season, before he had signed a professional contract for Wigan. Made his United debut at right-back away to Southampton on 13 March 1991, but has not been required for first team duty since and to gain more experience he was loaned to both Preston North End and Barnsley during 1991-92. Although a regular reserve player in **1992-93**, he was not required for any first team action and at first glance would appear not to have made the expected progress to warrant Premier League status.

| Clubs | Signing Date | Transfer Fee | APPEARANCES Lge | FL Cup | FA Cup | Others | GOALS Lge | FL Cup | FA Cup | Others |
|---|---|---|---|---|---|---|---|---|---|---|
| Wigan Athletic | 7.88 | - | 1+1 | | | | | | | |
| Manchester United* | 7.90 | £45,000 | 1 | | | | | | | |
| Preston North End | 1.92 | Loan | 6 | | | | | | | |
| Barnsley | 2.92 | Loan | 11 | | | | | | | |

## WHYTE Christopher (Chris) Anderson

Born: Islington, 2 September 1961

Height: 6'1"

Weight: 11.10

International Honours: E "U21"-4

**Position/Skill Factor:** Central defender who is strong in the air. Very quick, he likes to intercept balls and make good early passes to his midfield players.

**Career History:** After signing professional forms for Arsenal early in 1979-80, having been an associated schoolboy since May 1977, he made his FL debut two years later at Highbury against Manchester City on 17 October 1981 and held his place throughout the rest of the season, forming a strong central defensive partnership with David O'Leary. A regular choice in 1982-83, he won selection for the England Under 21 team and appeared to have a glittering future. However, in 1983-84, he lost his place first to Colin Hill and then to Tommy Caton and his career went into a tailspin. Loaned to Crystal Palace at the beginning of 1984-85, he did well but no transfer materialised and he spent the rest of the season in the Arsenal reserves. After a handful of appearances in midfield during 1985-86, he was amazingly granted a free transfer. Even more amazingly he received no offer from an English club, or perhaps he chose to start a new career in the USA Indoor Soccer League (MISL), which is more akin to five-a-side football than the real game. Spent two years in the USA, firstly with New York Express and later with Los Angeles Lazers, before returning home. Though many have tried, very few English players have made successful comebacks to League football after playing American indoor soccer. Happily for Whyte, however, he was offered a trial by West Bromwich Albion manager, Ron Atkinson, which he successfully completed and hardly missed a game over the next two seasons. However, 1989-90 was a poor season for the "Baggies", who avoided relegation from the Second Division by a whisker. Therefore, it was something of a surprise when he was signed by newly promoted Leeds United, immediately forming a strong central defensive partnership with Chris Fairclough as an ever present in 1990-91. Absent for only one game in 1991-92, he became the proud winner of a League Championship medal - an honour he could not even have dreamed about five years earlier in the USA. Although he played 34 Premier League games in **1992-93**, it was an inconsistent season by the high standards attained during the Championship winning campaign. In a defence that was leaking goals at a steady rate, he missed two games in December, two in January, one in February and three in March, before returning to form a partnership with David Wetherall, which at least began to stabilise the central defence and contribute to less goals being conceded. However, he was deemed surplus to requirements at the end of the season and placed on the transfer list.

| Clubs | Signing Date | Transfer Fee | APPEARANCES Lge | FL Cup | FA Cup | Others | GOALS Lge | FL Cup | FA Cup | Others |
|---|---|---|---|---|---|---|---|---|---|---|
| Arsenal | 12.79 | - | 86+4 | 14 | 5 | 3+1 | 8 | | | |
| Crystal Palace | 8.84 | Loan | 13 | 4 | | | | | | |
| Los Angeles (NASL) | 7.86 | - | | | | | | | | |
| West Bromwich Albion | 8.88 | - | 83+1 | 5 | 5 | 2 | 7 | 2 | | |
| Leeds United* | 6.90 | £400,000 | 113 | 14+1 | 8 | 11 | 5 | 1 | | |

## WIDDRINGTON Thomas (Tommy)

Born: Newcastle, 1 October 1971

Height: 5'8" Weight: 11.1

**Position/Skill Factor:** Competitive midfield player who likes to battle and looks as though he might develop into a captain. Keeping his passes simple, he doesn't give the ball away often.

**Career History:** Yet another north-easterner on Southampton's books, he first signed as an associated schoolboy in February 1987, before coming south as a trainee on leaving school in July 1988. Making good progress, he joined the "Saints'" professional staff during the 1990 close season, where his abilities were confined to the reserve side in 1990-91. While still awaiting a first team opportunity and in order to gain experience, he had a spell on loan at Wigan Athletic early in 1991-92, making his FL debut for the "Latics" at Springfield Park against Hull City on 14 September 1991. He proved a versatile player, operating at full-back, in central defence and in midfield, during his eight games for the Lancashire club. After returning to the Dell, he made his "Saints'" debut in late season, away to Everton on 1 April, deputising for Alan Shearer, while playing as fifth defender. Began the new **1992-93** Premier League season, helping "Saints" to a 2-1 victory at Crystal Palace in September, but then had to wait until early February before getting another chance in the side. With Terry Hurlock suspended and Glenn Cockerill injured, he renewed his partnership in midfield with the rapidly emerging Neil Maddison. The two Geordie lads had come through youth and reserve sides together and it showed as they helped the team to a 3-0 win over Norwich City at the Dell. He kept his place for a further six games, of which only one was lost, until making way for Hurlock at Highbury. Unfortunately, an injured ankle received in training, kept him out for three weeks, before he returned to the side for the last two games of the campaign.

| | | | APPEARANCES | | | | GOALS | | | |
|---|---|---|---|---|---|---|---|---|---|---|
| Clubs | Signing Date | Transfer Fee | Lge | FL Cup | FA Cup | Others | Lge | FL Cup | FA Cup | Others |
| Southampton* | 5.90 | – | 13+2 | 0+1 | | | | | | |
| Wigan Athletic | 9.91 | Loan | 5+1 | 2 | | | | | | |

## WILCOX Jason Malcolm

Born: Farnworth, 15 July 1971

Height: 5'10" Weight: 11.6

**Position/Skill Factor:** A left-winger with pace and two useful feet, although favouring his left, who can go past defenders in order to produce telling crosses.

**Career History:** Showing great potential, he first joined Blackburn Rovers as an associated schoolboy in June 1986, before progressing through the ranks as a trainee (July 1987) and later as a professional (June 1989). Came out for his FL debut at home to Swindon Town on 16 April 1990, his only appearance in 1989-90, but played 18 times during the following season. Established a regular first team place in 1991-92, playing in 38 FL games, being switched from the left to the right-wing early in the season and although unavailable for the Play-Offs was a valuable member of the side that reached the top flight after 25 years in the wilderness. **1992-93** saw him mature enormously, as a left winger of real pace and skill who delivered wickedly slanting crosses that defenders found difficult to defend against. Devastating on his day and attracting television recognition, it is worth noting that he was less conspicuous against defenders of recognised ability. However, while sometimes spoiling much good work by his inconsistency, his attacks down the left flank were often the club's main method of progress and in missing few matches he had a very successful first season in the top flight.

| | | | APPEARANCES | | | | GOALS | | | |
|---|---|---|---|---|---|---|---|---|---|---|
| Clubs | Signing Date | Transfer Fee | Lge | FL Cup | FA Cup | Others | Lge | FL Cup | FA Cup | Others |
| Blackburn Rovers* | 6.89 | – | 80+10 | 7+1 | 5 | 2 | 8 | | 1 | |

## WILKINS Raymond (Ray) Colin

Born: Hillingdon, 14 September 1956

Height: 5'8" Weight: 11.2

International Honours: E Sch, E Yth, E "U21"-1, E "U23"-2, E-84

**Position/Skill Factor:** One of the most creative midfield players in the country, he sees passes early and invariably picks the right option. Still capable of running a game from central midfield and can still hit great through balls.

**Career History:** The son of George, an inside-forward with Brentford, Nottingham Forest and Leeds United, before and after the war, he also had two brothers playing in recent times. The elder, Graham, played for Chelsea, Brentford and Southend United, while younger brother, Dean, assisted Queens Park Rangers, Leyton Orient and Brighton & Hove Albion. Eventually to become Chelsea's youngest ever captain, Ray first came to Stamford Bridge as an associated schoolboy in September 1970, before making giant steps after signing as an apprentice in July 1972. Made his FL debut as a substitute for David Webb in a 3-0 win at home to Norwich City on 26 October 1973, six days after turning professional and had become a first team regular by the end of 1974-75, coinciding with the club being relegated to the Second Division. Became a great crowd favourite in six seasons at Stamford Bridge with his aggressive midfield play and spectacular goals and captained his team to promotion back to Division One in 1976-77. Sadly, he was unable to stop Chelsea's slide back to Division Two in 1978-79 and it was the cause of much dismay, tinged with resignation, when he moved to Manchester United in the summer of 1979. By then he was already a regular choice for England, after making his international debut against Italy on 25 May 1976 in an end of season tournament in New York, USA. Spent five good years at Old Trafford, but with only an FA Cup winners medal in 1983 to show for it, although United came close to winning the League Championship in his first season (1979-80), two points behind Champions, Liverpool and again in 1981-82 and 1983-84, as well as reaching the League Cup Final in 1983. Much less adventurous at Old Trafford than at Stamford Bridge, he scored remarkably few goals. But one in the first FA Cup Final game against Brighton & Hove Albion in 1983 will be remembered for ever — a curling 30 yard shot, which ranks as one of the greatest Cup Final goals, although it did not bring immediate victory, United winning 4-0 at the second attempt, following a 2-2 draw. Became the subject of controversy in the early 1980s, his admirers claiming that he never gave the ball away and his detractors retorting that this was because he passed the ball sideways! In 1984 he joined the exodus to Italy, although remaining an England regular and team captain, participating in two World Cup Final series in Spain 1982 and Mexico 1986. Sadly, the latter proved to be his "swansong" in an England shirt — sent off in the second disappointing game against Morocco for allegedly remonstrating with the referee (hardly credible for such a composed and disciplined player), he took no further part in the competition. He enjoyed three good years with AC Milan before losing his place and moving to French club, Paris St Germain, in the summer of 1987. However, he hardly got a game in the French team and was rescued by Graham Souness, who signed him for Glasgow Rangers in the November. Hardly missed a game in two years at Ibrox Park and won Scottish League Championship and Skol Cup winners medals in 1988-89. Returning to his native city in November 1989, joining Queens Park Rangers, he did not miss a single game in his first two seasons at Loftus Road — a tribute to his amazing stamina and durability at the age of 35. Injured in the first match of 1991-92, he returned in November with the "R's" at the foot of the First Division and guided them to mid-table respectability. Awarded an OBE in the honours' list for services to soccer, he was again Rangers' "main man" in **1992-93** and was sorely missed when fracturing a shin in a freak accident just before the game at Middlesbrough in early January. The injury, which put him out of the game for 16 matches, came about on the morning of the game during a warm-up, when he caught his studs in the turf as he tried to turn and run. Prior to that, he had made things tick, playing just in front of the back four, where his quality passing had proved to be invaluable. Returning to the side on 10 April for the match at Loftus Road against Nottingham Forest, he led Rangers to a 4-3 victory and a six match unbeaten run, culminating with fifth place in the new Premier League. Almost certain to move into management before too long, Rangers' fans can only hope that he stays on for a while longer.

| | | | APPEARANCES | | | | GOALS | | | |
|---|---|---|---|---|---|---|---|---|---|---|
| Clubs | Signing Date | Transfer Fee | Lge | FL Cup | FA Cup | Others | Lge | FL Cup | FA Cup | Others |
| Chelsea | 10.73 | - | 176+3 | 6+1 | 10+1 | | 30 | 2 | 2 | |
| Manchester United | 8.79 | £825,000 | 158+2 | 14+1 | 10 | 9 | 7 | 1 | 1 | 1 |
| A. C. Milan (Italy) | 7.84 | £1,500,000 | | | | | | | | |
| Paris St. Germain (Fr) | 7.87 | - | | | | | | | | |
| Glasgow Rangers | 11.87 | £250,000 | 69+1 | 10 | 8+1 | 7 | 2 | 1 | | |
| Q.P.R.* | 11.89 | - | 114+1 | 9 | 12 | 2 | 6 | | 2 | 1 |

## WILL James Alexander

Born: Turriff, 7 October 1972

Height: 6'2" Weight: 13.13

International Honours: S Sch, S Yth, S "U21"-4

**Position/Skill Factor:** Goalkeeper with a powerful build, who reacts well to through balls into the penalty area and is a good shot stopper.

**Career History:** After gaining Scottish schoolboy international caps, he joined Arsenal as a trainee in July 1989 and on making the necessary progress, signed as a professional at Highbury early in 1990-91. Although third choice 'keeper, behind David Seaman and Allan Miller, he still awaits a first team appearance, but has already been recognised at Under 21 level by Scotland. Found his progress hampered in **1992-93** by the Premier League ruling that allows a substitute goalie to be named. Alan Miller didn't go out on loan during the season and required regular reserve outings, which restricted Will's opportunities, although he sat on the first team bench himself on four occasion.

| | | | APPEARANCES | | | | GOALS | | | |
|---|---|---|---|---|---|---|---|---|---|---|
| Clubs | Signing Date | Transfer Fee | Lge | FL Cup | FA Cup | Others | Lge | FL Cup | FA Cup | Others |
| Arsenal* | 11.90 | - | | | | | | | | |

## WILLIAMS David Geraint

Born: Treorchy, 5 January 1962

Height: 5'7"

Weight: 10.6

International Honours: W Yth, W "U21"-2, W-12

**Position/Skill Factor:** Hard tackling, competitive midfielder, who is always in the thick of things. Equally good at breaking up attacks as in setting them up with simple passes.

**Career History:** Initially signed by Bristol Rovers on associated schoolboy forms (November 1976), before becoming an apprentice in July 1978, he had graduated to the club's professional ranks by the beginning of 1980. By 1980-81 he was challenging for a first team place and made his FL debut in a 3-3 draw at Eastville against Sheffield Wednesday on 18 October 1980, holding his place for the remainder of the season, despite Rovers' eventual relegation to Division Three. The following season, he was used more sparingly, but in 1982-83 he was back in favour again and remained a regular performer for three seasons, in each of which Rovers "flirted" with promotion, without achieving it, before his transfer to

Derby County for a surprisingly modest fee in March 1985. He quickly established himself in a defensive midfield anchor role at the Baseball Ground, assisting the "Rams" to two consecutive promotion seasons in 1985-86 and 1986-87, the latter as Second Division Champions. He easily adjusted to the demands of First Division football, being ever present in 1987-88 and was rewarded with his first call-up to the Welsh national squad. Made his international debut in Czechoslovakia in November 1987 and remained a regular choice up to 1989. After missing only one game in 1988-89 and ever present again in 1989-90, he was strangely dropped from the Welsh national squad and was not recalled until 1992. His star fell with Derby's inevitable relegation (starved of cash to buy players by chairman Robert Maxwell) in 1990-91 and he missed out on a quick return to the top flight the following season, in the end of season Play-Offs, after a late run of good results had carried the "Rams" into third place. However, he did not have to wait long for a chance to play in the Premier League, as he was signed by Ipswich Town in the summer of 1992 and after winning a regular place in their team during **1992-93**, was recalled to the Welsh national team. Suffered a loss of form in the second half of the season and was left out of the side for a couple of matches. However, on his return, he soon gave a good account of himself and had a brilliant game in the 3-1 local "derby" victory over Norwich City. Back to his best, he gave a tough tackling midfield performance and laid on the opening goal for Jason Dozzell to celebrate.

| | | | APPEARANCES | | | | GOALS | | | |
|---|---|---|---|---|---|---|---|---|---|---|
| Clubs | Signing Date | Transfer Fee | Lge | FL Cup | FA Cup | Others | Lge | FL Cup | FA Cup | Others |
| Bristol Rovers | 1.80 | – | 138+3 | 14 | 9+2 | 5 | 8 | | 2 | |
| Derby County | 3.85 | £40,000 | 276+1 | 26+1 | 17 | 11 | 9 | 1 | | |
| Ipswich Town* | 7.92 | £650,000 | 37 | 4+1 | 4 | | | | | |

## **WILLIAMS John** Nelson

Born: Birmingham, 11 May 1968

Height: 6'2"

Weight: 12.3

**Position/Skill Factor:** Lightning fast striker. Will always give problems to defenders with his willingness to chase lost causes. He can reach balls that defenders accept as "dead".

**Career History:** A relatively late starter in League football at the age of 23, John Williams achieved fame by winning the televised sprints (featured on the "Saint and Greavsie" show) to find the "fastest man in football", in only his first season. A West Midlands postman by trade, he was playing for lowly Cradley Town of the Boddingtons West Midland League, when he was signed up by Swansea City in August 1991, along with team-mate Jon Ford, for a combined fee of £10,000. He made his FL debut at Vetch Field against Bolton Wanderers on 24 August 1991, but failed to impress in his first few games and lost his place. Restored to first team duty in November, he created a minor splash with a "hat-trick" in a remarkable 6-4 victory away to Bradford City, a result and scoreline doubly remarkable for the fact that the "Swans" were struggling at the foot of the table and had previously failed to score in their first six away fixtures of 1991-92! Holding his place in the team, he inspired a mini-revival, which lifted the "Swans" to mid-table safety (although they later slumped to 19th place) and he ended the season as top scorer with 11 FL goals. During the summer, he returned to the West Midlands when newly appointed Coventry City manager, Bobby Gould, signed him for £250,000. Ironically, Gould had considered signing him a year earlier for his previous club, West Bromwich Albion, but while he deliberated, Swansea stepped in! Williams made an electrifying start in the Premier League in **1992-93**, scoring in the ninth minute of his "Sky Blues'" debut against Middlesbrough and four days later, hitting both goals in a 2-0 victory at Tottenham. Having become the 61st player to score for City on their debuts, he levelled out a little later when he seemed to lose confidence, but came back strongly towards the end of the season as he recaptured his goalscoring knack. Picked up the basics well and became a far better all-round player and if the club can match his speed of thought, to his speed of foot, he could become a tremendous asset to the Premier League.

| | | | APPEARANCES | | | | GOALS | | | |
|---|---|---|---|---|---|---|---|---|---|---|
| Clubs | Signing Date | Transfer Fee | Lge | FL Cup | FA Cup | Others | Lge | FL Cup | FA Cup | Others |
| Swansea City | 8.91 | £5,000 | 36+3 | 2+1 | 3 | 1 | 11 | | | |
| Coventry City* | 7.92 | £250,000 | 38+3 | 2 | 1 | | 8 | | | |

## **WILLIAMS Lee**

Born: Birmingham, 3 February 1973

Height: 5'7" Weight: 11.0

International Honours: E Yth

**Position/Skill Factor:** Midfield player. Not very big, but he has good balance, can use both feet well and is a very useful passer of the ball.

**Career History:** Locally born and bred, he first came to Aston Villa as a 15-year-old associated schoolboy in November 1988. On leaving school, he signed as a trainee in July 1989 and had progressed to the club's professional ranks by early 1991. A regular reserve player in **1992-93**, without getting near to making a first team appearance, he was loaned out to Shrewsbury Town to gather more experience. Allowed to become FA Cup-tied, he played in a First Round match at home to Mansfield Town, scoring in a 3-1 win and a week later he made his FL debut at home to Walsall on 21 November 1992, before appearing twice (including one substitute) more and returning to Villa Park.

| | | | APPEARANCES | | | | GOALS | | | |
|---|---|---|---|---|---|---|---|---|---|---|
| Clubs | Signing Date | Transfer Fee | Lge | FL Cup | FA Cup | Others | Lge | FL Cup | FA Cup | Others |
| Aston Villa* | 1.91 | – | | | | | | | | |
| Shrewsbury Town | 11.92 | Loan | 2+1 | | 1+1 | 2 | | | 1 | |

## WILLIAMS Michael (Mike) Anthony

Born: Bradford, 21 November 1969

Height: 5'8"

Weight: 10.6

**Position/Skill Factor:** Hard working right-winger, or midfield player, with plenty of pace. Also has good ability on the ball.

**Career History:** A late starter from non-league football, he was signed by Sheffield Wednesday from local Northern Counties (East) League club, Maltby MW, following trials with a number of clubs. Like Julian Watts, he was given a taste of first team football in Luxemborg in the UEFA Cup-tie against Spora in **1992-93** and to further his experience went out on loan to Halifax Town. Made his FL debut at the Shay Ground against Bury on 19 December 1992 and played in eight more matches before coming back to Hillsborough with renewed confidence. Definitely a player who will challenge for a first team place this coming season, he appeared in three (including one substitute) end of term League games for Wednesday and was rewarded by manager, Trevor Francis, with a three year contract.

| | | | APPEARANCES | | | | GOALS | | | |
|---|---|---|---|---|---|---|---|---|---|---|
| Clubs | Signing Date | Transfer Fee | Lge | FL Cup | FA Cup | Others | Lge | FL Cup | FA Cup | Others |
| Sheffield Wednesday* | 2.91 | – | 2+1 | | | 1 | | | | |
| Halifax Town | 12.92 | Loan | 9 | | | | 1 | | | |

## WILLIAMSON Daniel Alan

Born: Newham, 5 December 1973

Height: 5'11" Weight: 12.3

**Position/Skill Factor:** Midfielder with a good football brain, who shines at the passing game and has plenty of stamina.

**Career History:** A trainee since July 1990, having been an associated schoolboy (January 1988) earlier, he signed professionally for West Ham United at the beginning of **1992-93**. A regular in the "Hammers'" reserve side by the end of last season, he has yet to make a first team appearance. Earlier, he was loaned out to Farnborough Town (Vauxhall Conference) for experience, following in the path of Matthew Holland and played six games before returning to Upton Park in March.

| | | | APPEARANCES | | | | GOALS | | | |
|---|---|---|---|---|---|---|---|---|---|---|
| Clubs | Signing Date | Transfer Fee | Lge | FL Cup | FA Cup | Others | Lge | FL Cup | FA Cup | Others |
| West Ham United* | 8.92 | – | | | | | | | | |

## WILSON Clive

Born: Manchester, 13 November 1961

Height: 5'7"

Weight: 10.0

**Position/Skill Factor:** Predominately a left-back, he can also play in midfield and on the left-wing. Has a cultured left foot and is a lovely passer of the ball. A good attacking player, he is very comfortable when going forward.

**Career History:** Christened Euclid Aklana, he was discovered by Manchester City while playing in local junior soccer and following trials at Maine Road, signed professional forms at the tail-end of 1979. Had to wait two years before making his FL debut, but when the opportunity finally came, he impressed when wearing the number three shirt at home to Wolverhampton Wanderers on 28 December 1981. No further appearances for City in 1982-83, but he gained first team experience in two loan periods with Chester City, the first for one month and the latter for three months. Had to wait until November 1983 for his next City game, but ended the season in possession of the left-back shirt. Made a breakthrough in 1984-85, playing in midfield for the first 27 games of City's promotion season, only to lose his place in February and was in-and-out of the team the following season. Not until 1986-87 did he firmly establish a first team place at left-back, playing in every FL game, only to see his team slide back to the Second Division. And with Andy Hinchcliffe waiting in the wings, City allowed him to join Chelsea at the end of the season. After playing in the first 25 games of 1987-88 on the left-wing, he lost his place and for the remainder of his stay at Stamford Bridge he could never quite nail down a permanent first team slot, although he won a Second Division Championship medal in 1988-89. Transferred to west London neighbours, Queens Park Rangers, in the summer of 1990, he started 1991-92 in a midfield role, but soon lost his place and was passed over for the remainder of the season. After three highly disappointing seasons, he was given a chance at left-back by new manager, Gerry Francis, in the third game of 1991-92 and held his place throughout. Had another very good season in **1992-93**, playing either at left-back, or in midfield, where he switched to, following the unfortunate injury to Ray Wilkins in early January. On the return to fitness of Wilkins, this fine utility player, who a good many clubs would like to have on their books, calmly slotted in at left-back again, as though he had never been away. Missed only two games all season and as the penalty king of Loftus Road, he scored two more from the spot to add to the two he had scored previously, after taking over from Roy Wegerle. Playing better at this late stage of his career than ever before, although international honours now seem to have passed him by.

| | | | APPEARANCES | | | | GOALS | | | |
|---|---|---|---|---|---|---|---|---|---|---|
| Clubs | Signing Date | Transfer Fee | Lge | FL Cup | FA Cup | Others | Lge | FL Cup | FA Cup | Others |
| Manchester City | 12.79 | – | 107+2 | 10 | 2 | 5 | 9 | 2 | | |
| Chester City | 9.82 | Loan | 21 | | | | 2 | | | |
| Chelsea | 3.87 | £250,000 | 68+13 | 3+3 | 4 | 10+2 | 5 | | | |
| Q.P.R.* | 7.90 | £450,000 | 92+2 | 9 | 4 | 2+1 | 7 | | | |

## **WINTERBURN Nigel**

Born: Nuneaton,
11 December 1963

Height: 5'10"

Weight: 10.7

International Honours:
E Yth, E "U21"-1,
E "B", FL Rep, E-2

**Position/Skill Factor:** Tough tackling left-back who likes to get forward to supply accurate crosses to the attack. Has a good left foot, can play short or long passes and is also noted for his very long throws.

**Career History:** Gained England Youth honours while an apprentice (May 1980) with Birmingham City, but in two years as a professional at St Andrews he failed to make the first team and was given a free transfer. Joined Wimbledon, following a unsuccessful trial at Oxford United (August 1983) and immediately made his FL debut at Bolton Wanderers on 27 August 1983, missing only three games throughout the season. In four seasons at Plough Lane he was a fixture at left-back and was absent for only seven FL games in that period, assisting the "Dons" to two promotions, to Division Two in 1983-84 and to the First Division in 1985-86, when he also won an England Under 21 cap. Transferred to Arsenal at the end of 1986-87, he had to play second fiddle to Kenny Sansom at first, but had a good run in the team in both full-back positions in the second-half of the season. Dislodged Sansom from the left-back slot at the start of 1988-89 and played in every game of the "Gunners'" remarkable last gasp League Championship triumph. Won his one and only England cap in November 1989, coming on as substitute against Italy and was ever present again in 1990-91 when winning his second League Championship medal. Although he missed only one League match all season, neither he nor his team enjoyed the best of times in 1991-92, but the terrific end of the season flourish saw Arsenal losing only one of their last 20 League matches. Another solid and consistent season in **1992-93**, saw him force his way back into the England squad and collect League and FA Cup winners medals, following the wins over Sheffield Wednesday. Had his injury problems, however, and also had his nadir when sent off at Highbury for a rash challenge in the game against Liverpool, but on the reverse side of the coin he scored a spectacular goal in the fog at Scarborough to take the "Gunners" into the Quarter-Finals of the League Cup.

| Clubs | Signing Date | Transfer Fee | APPEARANCES Lge | APPEARANCES FL Cup | APPEARANCES FA Cup | APPEARANCES Others | GOALS Lge | GOALS FL Cup | GOALS FA Cup | GOALS Others |
|---|---|---|---|---|---|---|---|---|---|---|
| Birmingham City | 8.81 | – | | | | | | | | |
| Wimbledon | 9.83 | – | 164+1 | 13 | 12 | 2 | 8 | | | |
| Arsenal* | 5.87 | £407,000 | 198+1 | 26 | 25 | 9 | 5 | 3 | | |

## **WISE Dennis** Frank

Born: Kensington,
16 December 1966

Height: 5'6"

Weight: 9.5

International Honours:
E "U21"-1, E"B", E-5

**Position/Skill Factor:** Winger who normally operates on the right flank and is a great crosser of the ball. Always likely to cause goalkeepers problems as he can either drive them in, or bend them away. Top class penalty taker.

**Career History:** Having been an associated schoolboy (January 1981) and an apprentice (July 1983) with Southampton, he was released without being offered professional terms and was snapped up by Wimbledon at the end of 1984-85. Made his FL debut in the final match of the season at Plough Lane as a substitute against Cardiff City on 11 May 1985 and played just four times during the "Dons'" successful promotion campaign in 1985-86, before securing a regular place for himself during the following term. Rose to national fame in 1987-88 during Wimbledon's FA Cup run, scoring the winner against Luton in the Semi-Final and cleverly flighting a free-kick from which Laurie Sanchez headed the only goal to defeat Liverpool in the Cup Final. Also netted ten FL goals that season, second only to John Fashanu in the scoring lists. While most of his Cup Final colleagues then deserted Wimbledon, he remained two more years at Plough Lane, missing only four FL games during that period and demonstrating his ability to snap up vital goals. In the summer of 1990, near neighbours Chelsea made an irresistible offer and he moved to Stamford Bridge where he has enjoyed two good seasons in spite of some disciplinary problems caused by his aggressive temperament. Called up by Graham Taylor for his England debut in a vital European Championship qualifying match in Turkey on 1 May 1991, he scored the only goal to secure two priceless points. Subsequently played against the Soviet Union and gained three further caps on the summer tour of Australasia. Finished 1991-92 as Chelsea's leading scorer with 14 goals, mainly from set plays, while the club's recognised strikers, Clive Allen apart, invariably failed to take full advantage of chances going begging in the penalty area. Missed nearly half of **1992-93**, due to injury, his time off unfortunately coinciding with the "Blues'" bad run after Christmas. Although he is a great crosser of the ball, having a more mobile role behind the front men rather than predominately using the flanks, could suit both him and the club better and it will be interesting to see where he settles into the side under new manager, Glenn Hoddle.

| Clubs | Signing Date | Transfer Fee | APPEARANCES Lge | APPEARANCES FL Cup | APPEARANCES FA Cup | APPEARANCES Others | GOALS Lge | GOALS FL Cup | GOALS FA Cup | GOALS Others |
|---|---|---|---|---|---|---|---|---|---|---|
| Wimbledon | 3.85 | – | 127+8 | 14 | 11 | 5 | 26 | | 3 | |
| Chelsea* | 7.90 | £1,600,000 | 97+1 | 14 | 5 | 5 | 23 | 4 | 2 | 2 |

## WITTER Anthony (Tony) Junior

Born: London, 12 August 1965

Height: 6'1" Weight: 12.7

**Position/Skill Factor:** A central defender whose tremendous pace makes him difficult to beat on the ground, he is also good in the air.

**Career History:** Following some impressive early season displays for the Vauxhall Opel League side, Grays Athletic, having had previous experience with Yeading and Uxbridge, he signed for Crystal Palace in October 1990 and went straight into their reserve side. Ten months later, without ever receiving a first team opportunity, he was transferred along with Garry Thompson, to fellow Londoners, Queens Park Rangers, in the first week of the 1991-92 season. It was a strange signing, since Rangers already possessed six experienced central defenders and seemed to be overstocked in that department. Loaned out to Millwall in November 1991, he did not get a game. However, he was luckier with Plymouth Argyle. When making his FL debut for the "Pilgrims" against Leicester City on 11 January 1992, he scored in the second minute of the game, which would have been remarkable for a forward, but for a defender, it must surely be a record! Played twice more before he returned to Loftus Road. Still awaits a game in the top flight, having sat on the bench twice in **1992-93** without being required for first team duty, although being a backbone of the reserve side that finished third in the Combination League last season. Has now been at Rangers for two years and will hope for a breakthrough in 1993-94.

| | | | APPEARANCES | | | | GOALS | | | |
|---|---|---|---|---|---|---|---|---|---|---|
| Clubs | Signing Date | Transfer Fee | Lge | FL Cup | FA Cup | Others | Lge | FL Cup | FA Cup | Others |
| Crystal Palace | 10.90 | £10,000 | | | | | | | | |
| Q.P.R.* | 8.91 | £125,000 | | | | | | | | |
| Plymouth Argyle | 1.92 | Loan | 3 | | | | 1 | | | |

## WOOD Stephen (Steve) Alan

Born: Bracknell, 2 February 1963

Height: 6'0" Weight: 11.9

**Position/Skill Factor:** Good central defender. With two useful feet, he can pass both short and long. Never seems hurried and when he wins the ball, he invariably comes out of defence looking to make a worthwhile pass.

**Career History:** Came to Reading as an associated schoolboy in May 1979, before signing for the club as an apprentice, just three months later, in August 1979. Made his FL debut while still an apprentice at Southend United on 25 February 1980, deputising for the injured Steve Hetzke and was given one more outing in the side, prior to turning professional. Won a regular place in 1981-82, but was absent injured for the second half of 1982-83 when the "Royals" were relegated to Division Four. Returned in September 1983 to assist his team back to Division Three at the first attempt and was ever present for the next two seasons, winning a Third Division Championship medal in 1985-86 as Reading reached the Second Division for the first time since 1931. After one further season at Elm Park, he joined Millwall in the summer of 1987. Although injured after only seven FL games for the "Lions", he returned in February 1988 to help lift his team from fifth place to the Second Division Championship and Millwall's first ever sojourn in the top flight. A regular in the "Lions'" first season in Division One, but in-and-out the following season as they collapsed in the second half — doomed to relegation long before the end. Back in favour in 1990-91, he was injured in January and played no further part in the Second Division campaign when Millwall lost their chance of promotion in the Play-Offs. Early in 1991-92, he left the Den for the Dell and a second chance of First Division football with Southampton. However, with six central defenders already on the "Saints'" books, competition for the two (or three) first team slots was intense and after losing his place in January, he did not return until the last two games of the season. Started **1992-93** as first choice, having two different partners, Richard Hall and Kevin Moore, in the first two games. Unfortunately, a hamstring injury kept him out of the third game and with Ken Monkou being signed from Chelsea, he had to wait until October before he could displace Moore. He kept his place for just two matches until replaced by Hall. Eventually, an injury to Monkou gave him a final chance and for the rest of the season he had to make do with reserve team soccer.

| | | | APPEARANCES | | | | GOALS | | | |
|---|---|---|---|---|---|---|---|---|---|---|
| Clubs | Signing Date | Transfer Fee | Lge | FL Cup | FA Cup | Others | Lge | FL Cup | FA Cup | Others |
| Reading | 2.81 | - | 216+3 | 10 | 15 | 4 | 9 | | | |
| Millwall | 6.87 | £80,000 | 108+2 | 10 | 10 | 3+1 | | | | |
| Southampton* | 10.91 | £400,000 | 19 | 1 | 1 | 4 | | | 1 | |

## WOODS Christopher (Chris) Charles Eric

Born: Boston, 14 November 1959

Height: 6'2" Weight: 13.5

International Honours: E Yth, E "U21"-6, E-43

**Position/Skill Factor:** Top class, experienced goalkeeper. Technically very sound, he possesses lightning reflexes, is agile, has big safe hands and judges crosses to perfection. Also marshals his defences well.

**Career History:** Currently England's first choice 'keeper, he started out with Nottingham Forest as an associated schoolboy in September 1975, before becoming an apprentice on leaving school in June 1976 and graduating as a professional just six months later. Sprang to fame in 1977-78 when Forest, newly promoted to Division One, ran away with the League Championship. However, he played no part in that particular triumph, but starred in the club's first ever League Cup victory. Early in the season, Brian Clough had signed Peter Shilton from Stoke City and sold previous first choice John Middleton to Derby, leaving him as sole cover. However, Shilton was ineligible for the League Cup, having previously played in the competition for Stoke and he played in every match from the Third Round through to the Cup Final. One of the youngest and certainly least experienced players to appear in a Wembley Cup Final, it was a big test, particularly against the country's strongest team, Liverpool. However, after making a great save from Kenny Dalglish in the first minute, he performed impeccably and thanks to the protection of a well marshalled defence, was rarely troubled in either of the two matches, which saw Forest triumph 1-0 in a replay, after a 0-0 draw at Wembley. The following season he was selected for the England Under 21 team — the first player to be so honoured without a FL appearance to his name. Clearly too good a player to remain as understudy to the indestructible Peter Shilton, he was allowed to join Queens Park Rangers, then in Division Two, in the summer of 1979 and made his FL debut in the first game of the new season at home to Bristol Rovers on 18 August 1979, keeping a clean sheet in a 2-0 victory. An automatic first choice at Loftus Road for one and a half seasons, he inexplicably lost his place to John Burridge in December 1980 and was sold to Norwich City in the summer of 1981, after ending the season on loan at Carrow Road. Ever present in four of his five seasons with the "Canaries", he was absent for only four FL games, all in 1984-85, when winning his second League Cup winners medal after Norwich defeated Sunderland 1-0. At the end of the season, on tour with the England team, he won his first cap against the USA on 16 June 1985 and since that date was recognised as first choice deputy to Peter Shilton until the latter's retirement from international football in 1990. Although relegated in 1984-85, Norwich came back as Second Division Champions at the first attempt, but he did not stay for their next stint of First Division football, being one of the first English internationals to join the exodus to Graham Souness' re-created Glasgow Rangers' team. In five years at Ibrox Park he won four Scottish League Championship medals and four Skol League Cup medals and never lost his place except for injuries. However, in 1991, Rangers reduced their contingent of English players to avoid problems with the UEFA ruling on "foreigners" in European competition and he was sold to newly promoted Sheffield Wednesday. Curiously, his arrival was not universally welcomed by the "Owls'" supporters, some of whom were fans of the displaced Kevin Pressman and perhaps unfairly, he bore the brunt of the criticism for Wednesday's heavy defeats to Leeds (1-6) and Arsenal (1-7) and the two losses to arch-rivals, Sheffield United. Despite these disasters, Wednesday finished third and all but "stole" the League Championship "at the death". Since 1990, he has been England's undisputed first choice 'keeper and continued in that vein in **1992-93** when playing in nine of 11 international matches, while allowing Graham Taylor to experiment in two USA Cup games with Tim Flowers and Nigel Martyn. At club level he kept 13 clean sheets, including three in a row, in 57 first team games and surpassed himself at the beginning of last season when his confident displays helped the team through some sticky patches while results were not going their way. A disappointing season in many respects, having to bend the knee to Arsenal in both the League and FA Cup Finals, but an excellent one when you consider that the club was 17th in the Premier League prior to Christmas and then lost only six from the remaining 23 matches to finish seventh. He had much to do with those performances and with a more settled defence in front of him, Wednesday will do better still.

| | | | APPEARANCES | | | | GOALS | | | |
|---|---|---|---|---|---|---|---|---|---|---|
| Clubs | Signing Date | Transfer Fee | Lge | FL Cup | FA Cup | Others | Lge | FL Cup | FA Cup | Others |
| Nottingham Forest | 12.76 | - | | 7 | | | | | | |
| Q.P.R. | 7.79 | £250,000 | 63 | 8 | 1 | | | | | |
| Norwich City | 3.81 | £225,000 | 216 | 26 | 19 | 6 | | | | |
| Glasgow Rangers | 6.86 | £600,000 | 173 | 21 | 15 | 21 | | | | |
| Sheffield Wednesday* | 8.91 | £1,200,000 | 80 | 11 | 10 | 5 | | | | |

## **WOODS Raymond (Ray)** Guy

Born: Birkenhead, 7 June 1965

Height: 5'11" Weight: 11.0

**Position/Skill Factor:** Old fashioned right-winger who hugs the touchline and likes to have the ball at his feet so he can take defenders on. Has plenty of pace and can produce telling crosses.

**Career History:** A remarkable "rags-to-riches" story, which should serve as an inspiration to all young footballers who are thrown on the scrapheap, he joined Tranmere Rovers as an apprentice in July 1981, having been with the club on associated schoolboy forms since November 1980. Made his FL debut as a substitute at Bristol Rovers on 18 January 1983, while still an apprentice, but found it difficult to hold down a place and only appeared occasionally, before being freed and signing for Bangor City of the Northern Premier League in November 1984. He then had spells with Northwich Victoria and Runcorn both of the Alliance Premier League (Now Vauxhall Conference) and with Caernarfon Town of the NPL, before joining the all-conquering Colne Dynamoes club in 1988. Ironically, because the east Lancashire team carried a squad of no fewer than 25 full time professionals, he could not get a game with them and it was pure chance that his former manager at Tranmere Rovers, Brian Hamilton, invited him for a trial with Wigan Athletic. After eight end of season games in 1988-89, he was offered a contract, but no sooner had he started his FL comeback than it was ended again by a groin injury, which ruled him out for the whole of 1989-90. To his credit, Hamilton kept faith with him and when he shone in two FA Cup games with Coventry City in January 1991, he was immediately signed up by the "Sky Blues'" manager, Terry Butcher. In two years, including one out of action, he had graduated from Colne Dynamoes' reserve team to the First Division! He seized the opportunity gratefully and after making his Coventry debut on 2 March 1991, held his place to the end of the season. Sadly plagued by injuries in 1991-92, he made only a handful of appearances in the first-half of the season and when fit again was ignored in favour of Sean Flynn. Another nightmare season in **1992-93**, restricted his appearances to a few in the Central League side and 17, while out on loan to Wigan Athletic. At least it seems that the long standing pelvic injury has finally been diagnosed as having one leg slightly shorter than the other and that it can hopefully be remedied by special exercises. If all goes well, he could have the opportunity in the close season to prove himself to a manager who has yet to see him in action.

| Clubs | Signing Date | Transfer Fee | APPEARANCES | | | | GOALS | | | |
|---|---|---|---|---|---|---|---|---|---|---|
| | | | Lge | FL Cup | FA Cup | Others | Lge | FL Cup | FA Cup | Others |
| Tranmere Rovers | 6.83 | - | 9+5 | 1 | | 0+1 | 2 | | | |
| Bangor City | 11.84 | - | | | | | | | | |
| Northwich Victoria | 7.85 | - | | | | | | | | |
| Runcorn | .85 | - | | | | | | | | |
| Caernarfon Town | .86 | - | | | | | | | | |
| Colne Dynamoes | .88 | - | | | | | | | | |
| Wigan Athletic | 3.89 | - | 25+3 | 2 | 4 | 2 | 3 | | 1 | |
| Coventry City* | 1.91 | £200,000 | 21 | 1 | 0+1 | | 1 | | | |
| Wigan Athletic | 1.93 | Loan | 12+1 | | | 4 | | | | 3 |

# WOODTHORPE Colin John

Born: Ellesmere Port, 13 January 1969

Height: 5'11"

Weight: 11.8

**Position/Skill Factor:** Left-back who likes to get forward, he is also a good man-for-man marker, if required.

**Career History:** Started his football career in the lower reaches with Chester City as an associated schoolboy in September 1985 and on leaving school he signed for the club as a trainee on 23 August 1986, making his FL debut exactly a week later at Bury in a 1-1 draw. Impressed enough to be taken on as a full professional the following month, by the end of the season he was a first team regular at left-back, with 30 appearances under his belt. Remained first choice left-back at Sealand Road until the end of 1989-90, a season he was an ever present. His form warranted a higher grade of football and during the summer he was signed by Norwich City, as understudy to Mark Bowen, but did not make his FL debut for the "Canaries" until the last match of 1990-91. After occasional first team outings in 1991-92, he forced his way into the team at the expense of Bowen in February 1992 and held his place for most of the remainder of the campaign, playing in the later rounds of the "Canaries'" FA Cup run up to the disappointing Semi-Final "knock-out" by Sunderland. With Bowen an ever present in **1992-93**, as City vainly strove to take the League Championship prize, first team places were thin on the ground and although he remained on the fringe of selection, when he finally got an opportunity to play in March it was out of position as cover for central defenders, John Polston and Ian Butterworth. He made five appearances until the team came a cropper in an awful display at Wimbledon and then it was back to the reserves. Apart from that, he spent 14 games on the bench, while only being used twice and will hope for better fortune in 1993-94

| Clubs | Signing Date | Transfer Fee | APPEARANCES | | | | GOALS | | | |
|---|---|---|---|---|---|---|---|---|---|---|
| | | | Lge | FL Cup | FA Cup | Others | Lge | FL Cup | FA Cup | Others |
| Chester City | 8.86 | - | 154+1 | 10 | 8+1 | 18 | 6 | | | 1 |
| Norwich City* | 7.90 | £175,000 | 18+5 | 0+2 | 4 | 0+1 | 1 | | | |

# WORTHINGTON Nigel

Born: Ballymena, 4 November 1961

Height: 5'10" Weight: 12.6

International Honours: NI Yth, NI-42

**Position/Skill Factor:** Experienced left sided player, used mainly at left-back or in midfield. Supplies quality crosses to the front men when he gets forward and is also corner kick specialist.

**Career History:** Has proved to be a most consistent performer since the then Notts County manager, Jimmy Sirrel, crossed the Irish Sea to sign him from Ballymena United during the 1981 close season. After making his FL debut on 26 September 1981 at Wolverhampton Wanderers, he only played once more that season, but firmly established himself in 1982-83, missing just one match. In February 1984, his former manager at Meadow Lane, Howard Wilkinson, brought him to Hillsborough to join Sheffield Wednesday in order to assist their successful drive to promotion and First Division status for the first time since 1970. At the end of the season on 22 May 1984, he won his first cap for Northern Ireland against Wales in the penultimate match of the ill-fated Home Championship and has been a regular international selection since then, including a visit to Mexico for the World Cup Finals in 1986. Apart from a one year hiatus from September 1985 to September 1986, when eclipsed by

Glynn Snodin and Chris Morris, he has been a regular first choice for the "Owls" and absent only through injury. Since the arrival of Phil King in November 1989, he has switched from left-back to left midfield, although he covers for the absence of his left flank partner and often interchanges with him, so it is difficult to say which is his true position. In 1990-91, he assisted the "Owls" to Division One, after their quite undeserved relegation the previous season and was a member of the team that carried a cup back to Hillsborough for the first time since 1935 — the League Cup after a shock 1-0 victory over favourites, Manchester United. Had a good first season back in the First Division in 1991-92, as the "Owls" finished in third place, playing 34 FL games and scoring five goals. Missed only five games throughout **1992-93** for Wednesday and once again he was most solid and dependant, even though his role in the side was more defensive than in previous seasons, mainly due to the early injury suffered by left-back, Phil King. Stood down for the returning King in the League Cup Final, but was back on duty for the FA Cup Final, only to collect a losers medal, following the "Gunner's" 2-1 victory in the replay. Played five times for Northern Ireland during the season and has now surpassed Ron Springett as "Owls'" most capped player, while also being named as Northern Ireland's "Player of the Year".

| | | | APPEARANCES | | | | GOALS | | | |
|---|---|---|---|---|---|---|---|---|---|---|
| Clubs | Signing Date | Transfer Fee | Lge | FL Cup | FA Cup | Others | Lge | FL Cup | FA Cup | Others |
| Notts County | 7.81 | £100,000 | 62+5 | 11 | 4 | | 4 | | | |
| Sheffield Wednesday* | 2.84 | £125,000 | 304+3 | 38 | 28 | 9 | 11 | 1 | | 1 |

## WRIGHT Alan Geoffrey

Born: Ashton-under-Lyne, 28 September 1971

Height: 5'4"

Weight: 9.4

International Honours: E Sch, E Yth, E "U21"-2

**Position/Skill Factor:** A left-back with the skill and pace of a winger, who uses it when getting forward to produce lovely crosses. Great in the air for his size.

**Career History:** A tremendous prospect who joined Blackpool as a trainee in August 1988, following excellent displays for England schoolboys, he soon graduated to professional status, winning England youth honours on the way. Prior to that, however, he became the youngest player to play for the "Seasiders" when he made his FL debut as a substitute at home to Chesterfield on 2 May 1988 at the tender age of 16 years and 217 days. He made his first team breakthrough in April 1989, on the left-wing and the next season played on both flanks as a full-back and in midfield. Following the departure of Steve Morgan to Plymouth, he established a fixed position at left-back, appearing in all but the opening game of 1990-91. After 57 consecutive FL appearances for the "Seasiders", he became Kenny Dalglish's first signing for Blackburn Rovers early in 1991-92. Looked totally at ease in the Second Division, missing only one game out of 34, before assisting Rovers through the Play-Offs to the Premier League. Asked to play midfield at the start of **1992-93**, he moved back to his natural position of left-back and appeared there until problems with his stomach muscles necessitated an operation. Having become an England under 21 regular and easy on the ball among quality players, he was certainly enhancing his chances of picking up a full cap, when injury struck. Must expect a strenuous challenge for the left-back berth from newcomer, Graham Le Saux, when the new season gets underway.

| | | | APPEARANCES | | | | GOALS | | | |
|---|---|---|---|---|---|---|---|---|---|---|
| Clubs | Signing Date | Transfer Fee | Lge | FL Cup | FA Cup | Others | Lge | FL Cup | FA Cup | Others |
| Blackpool | 4.89 | - | 91+7 | 10+2 | 8 | 11+2 | | | | |
| Blackburn Rovers* | 10.91 | £400,000 | 56+1 | 6 | 5 | 3 | 1 | | | |

## WRIGHT Ian Edward

Born: Woolwich, 3 November 1963

Height: 5'11" Weight: 11.11

International Honours: E"B", E-13

**Position/Skill Factor:** Livewire striker who twists and turns well around the box and shoots early with either foot. Very quick, he loves to run at defenders.

**Career History:** A natural goalscorer who, after signing for Crystal Palace from Greenwich Borough during the

1985 close season, continued to score at a good rate. Was immediately introduced to first team football, making his FL debut as a substitute at Selhurst Park against Huddersfield To'vn on 31 August 1985 and at the end of the season, he had scored nine goals in 32 League appearances (16 as a substitute). In 1986-87 he was joint top scorer with only eight FL goals from 38 games. For ten seasons, Palace had been voted as one of the lowest scoring teams in the Football League, but with a stern defence. All that changed in 1987-88 when they were the highest scoring Second Division team with 86 goals, although the defence "leaked" 59. Was it a change of tactics, or simply the birth of the lethal Mark Bright-Ian Wright partnership? Whatever the case, he scored 20 FL goals (plus three in the cups) to Bright's 24 and the following season the totals were reversed (24 to Wright and 20 to Bright), as Palace swept to promotion through the Play-Offs. He scored the winning goal against Swindon in the Play-Off Semi-Final and two goals, including the winner three minutes from the end of extra-time, against Blackburn in the Final. Unsurprisingly, perhaps, the goals dried up in the First Division as Palace struggled to hold on to their new status, but thanks to a succession of favourable FA Cup draws against lowly opposition the side reached the Semi-Final where they amazingly defeated Liverpool 4-3 after extra-time. Having suffered a broken leg twice during the season, he played little part in the FA Cup run and was hardly match-fit for the Final against Manchester United. Nevertheless, he was selected as a substitute and after coming on in the 69th minute, he turned the match upside-down with two quite brilliant goals. Firstly, he turned the United defence inside-out to score a solo goal which took the match into extra-time and then scored with a magnificent header from a John Salako cross to put Palace 3-2 ahead. United fought back to force a replay and it was a surprise when he was left on the bench again. In a bitter, bruising and bad tempered replay, Palace showed none of the enterprise of the first match and lost 1-0, Wright's introduction coming too late to make any difference to the game. Back to full fitness in 1990-91, he played in every FL game, top scoring with 15 goals as Palace achieved their highest ever FL placing (third). He also won his first England cap against Cameroon on 6 February 1991 and played three more games that season, including the summer tour of Australasia. After scoring five goals in eight FL games at the start of 1991-92, he was transferred to Arsenal for a massive fee. Normally strikers with large transfer fees round their neck take time to settle with a new club. Wright, however, wasted no time, scoring an equaliser at Leicester in the League Cup tie in his first game, a hat-trick at Southampton in his FL debut for Arsenal and further goals in his third and fourth games. A few weeks later, he scored all four Arsenal goals in a 4-2 victory over Everton and continued to score consistently throughout the season, which he rounded off nicely with another hat-trick against Southampton's tough defence in the final match of the season. The final analysis showed that he was Arsenal's leading scorer with 24 FL goals from 30 games, plus two cup goals and that he was the First Division's leading scorer with 29 goals. Another prolific goalscoring season in **1992-93**, saw him reach his 50th goal for Arsenal inside 18 months. On the other side of the coin there were perhaps, inevitably, disciplinary problems — most notably a three match ban for the much publicised David Howells affair. Like many at the club, the cup competitions brought the best out of him and his 15 goals were a vital factor in Arsenal's League and FA Cup Final record "double" successes over Sheffield Wednesday. After getting a goal apiece in both the FA Cup Final and the replay, he scored his first goal for England in the World Cup qualifier in Poland, having come on as a substitute in the latter stages.

| | | | APPEARANCES | | | | GOALS | | | |
|---|---|---|---|---|---|---|---|---|---|---|
| Clubs | Signing Date | Transfer Fee | Lge | FL Cup | FA Cup | Others | Lge | FL Cup | FA Cup | Others |
| Crystal Palace | 8.85 | – | 206+19 | 19 | 9+2 | 19+3 | 90 | 9 | 3 | 16 |
| Arsenal* | 9.91 | £2,500,000 | 60+1 | 11 | 7 | | 39 | 7 | 10 | |

# WRIGHT Mark

Born: Dorchester-on-Thames,
1 August 1963

Height: 6'3" Weight: 12.1

International Honours: E "U21"-4, E-43

**Position/Skill Factor:** Central defender who never seems hurried and always gives himself time on the ball. Attacks the ball in the air in both penalty areas. Extremely constructive, he passes the ball accurately and carries it forward confidently.

**Career History:** Having signed professional for Oxford United on his 17 th birthday, after playing in the youth side, he had to wait a little over a year before making his FL debut at the Manor Ground against Bristol City on 17 October, 1981, deputising for Gary Briggs. After just ten more first team games for Oxford he was used as a "makeweight" in a complicated deal which took him and Keith Cassells to Southampton in exchange for Trevor Hebberd and George Lawrence. It seemed a strange deal at the time, but "Saints'" manager, Lawrie McMenemy, clearly knew what he was doing. While Cassells never made the grade at The Dell, Wright became a fixture in central defence from the start of the 1982-83, after making his "Saints'" debut (as a forward!) in April 1982. He was selected for the England Under 21 side in 1982-83 and graduated to the national team in 1983-84, winning his first cap against Wales at Wrexham on 2 May 1984. Became an England regular the following season, but was unavailable for the 1986 World Cup Finals in Mexico due to a broken leg suffered in the FA Cup Semi-Final against Liverpool. After five good years at the Dell, apart from a well publicised "fracas" with Lawrie McMenemy, he joined Peter Shilton in moving to Derby County as part of owner Robert Maxwell's drive to establish the "Rams" as a First Division force. For a while all went well as Derby reached fifth place in 1988-89, but then Maxwell lost all interest in the club, which "withered on the vine", unable either to buy or sell players. Meanwhile, however, he was a tower of strength in central defence and continued his England career up to the European Championship Finals in West Germany 1988. Although he played well, he could not escape some of the "flak" arising from van Basten's hat-trick for the Netherlands, which knocked England out of the competition and he was not chosen at all in 1988-89. However, he picked up his England career again in 1990 and was one of the heroes of the 1990 World Cup campaign in Italy in which England started as "duffers" and returned as heroes, after reaching the Semi-Final and only losing to eventual World Champions, West Germany, on penalties, with Wright deployed as a sweeper for the first time during the campaign. Back home, the dam finally burst at Derby and the team sank without trace to the foot of the First Division, doomed to relegation long before the end of the season. Even Wright himself wilted under the pressure, most notably in a humiliating 7-1 home defeat by Liverpool which, perhaps fortunately for him, new "Reds'" manager to be, Graham Souness, did not witness. During the summer of 1991 he was sold, along with team-mate Dean Saunders, to Liverpool, to enable Derby to finally pay off Maxwell and start anew. While there was no doubt about his class and ability, there was considerable doubt among "Reds'" fans of his discipline and self-control (after three sending-offs with Derby). These questions were not immediately answered as he was injured in his second game for the "Reds" and missed the first three months of the campaign. However, when he returned to the team in late November, he was magnificent, getting his head, by hook or by crook, to every high ball in the penalty area and bringing an air of authority and confidence to a defence which had been "ball watching" for at least two seasons. Under his influence, the side embarked on a run of seven victories and three draws in ten FL games, which carried them from mid-table to third place. Sadly, further injury in the second leg of the UEFA Cup Quarter-Final, not only cost Liverpool any hope of saving the tie (Genoa scoring the "killer" goal ten minutes after he departed), but also deprived the club of his services for most of the remaining matches. Fortunately he was able to return for the FA Cup Semi-Final games against Portsmouth and the Final against Sunderland. No honour was more richly deserved than when he captained the "Reds" to a 2-0 victory. Sadly, his season ended on a sour note. Having already angered Graham Taylor by joining the Liverpool victory celebrations in their home city instead of the national party for Hungary, he (or his club) failed to inform the England manager in good time of a recurrence of the leg problem aggravated in the match against Finland and did not link up with the team in Malmo. Rarely has a current international player had to endure such an embarrassing and disastrous season as Mark did in **1992-93**. Perhaps, still smarting over his humiliation in the summer, although being selected for England's first game of 1992-93 in Spain, his Liverpool season collapsed in dramatic fashion, following a 4-2 defeat at Aston Villa, a 4-4 draw at home to modest Third Division side, Chesterfield, in the League Cup and another bad home result when losing 3-2 at the hands of Wimbledon. He was dropped from the team and rumours were rife on Merseyside of a rift with Souness and an early departure from Anfield. However, even if he so desired, the manager could hardly afford to part with defenders, in view of the club's long injury list and the failure of the two Scandinavian imports, Torben Piechnik and Stig Bjornebye. As a result he made several comebacks, but on each occasion it coincided with another defensive debacle. Only towards the end of a painful season did he re-establish himself and begin to show some semblance of his best form. Although his England career seems over, he may yet prove to be the commanding central defender that Liverpool need if they are to challenge for top honours again.

| | | | APPEARANCES | | | | GOALS | | | |
|---|---|---|---|---|---|---|---|---|---|---|
| Clubs | Signing Date | Transfer Fee | Lge | FL Cup | FA Cup | Others | Lge | FL Cup | FA Cup | Others |
| Oxford United | 8.80 | - | 8+2 | | 1 | | | | | |
| Southampton | 3.82 | £80,000 | 170 | 25 | 17 | 10 | 7 | 2 | 1 | 1 |
| Derby County | 8.87 | £760,000 | 144 | 15 | 5 | 7 | 10 | | | |
| Liverpool* | 7.91 | £2,200,000 | 53+1 | 3+2 | 9 | 8 | 2 | 1 | | |

## WRIGHT Thomas (Tommy) James

Born: Belfast, 29 August 1963

Height: 6'1" Weight: 12.13

International Honours: NI "U23"-1, NI-13

**Position/Skill Factor:** Experienced, agile goalkeeper, who is a very good kicker from his hands and has the ability to set up smart attacks with swift throws to his full-backs..

**Career History:** Discovered playing for the Irish League side, Linfield, he signed for Newcastle United at the beginning of 1988 as third choice 'keeper, behind Gary Kelly and Martin Thomas. First team opportunities seemed even scarcer the following close season when United parted with a large sum to purchase Wimbledon's Dave Beasant. But when the Londoner failed to settle in the north-east and was transferred to Chelsea early in 1989, Tommy was finally given the chance to show what he was capable of, making a rather less than auspicious FL debut in a 3-1 defeat at Aston Villa on 14 January

1989. However, he held his place for five more games before being displaced by Kelly. At the end of the season he received his first international caps for Northern Ireland in a World Cup group-tie in Malta and then at home to Chile in May. In the next two seasons, with no outstanding 'keeper available, he lost out somewhat to Paul Kee (Oxford United) and Alan Fettis (Hull City), but in 1991-92 he came back to favour as manager Billy Bingham's preferred choice. He started 1990-91 as first choice for the "Magpies", but soon lost his place to veteran, John Burridge. When the Czech 'keeper, Pavel Srnicek, arrived at St James Park, his future seemed very doubtful, but a short loan out to Hull City did not lead to a permanent move. However, after 18 months without a first team game he was restored to first team duty by Ossie Ardiles in place of the erratic Srnicek in October 1991 and held his place for the remainder of the season. Started **1992-93** as first choice and played brilliantly, as United went unbeaten for the first 11 League games. After a 2-1 victory at Bristol Rovers, manager, Kevin Keegan, thought Wright's performance that afternoon had been one of the best goalkeeping displays he had ever seen. Shortly afterwards, however, his season turned sour. Carried off with an injured leg at Birmingham City, he was unable to regain his place from an inspired Srnicek and had to be content with reserve team football for the rest of the campaign. But with 14 League appearances to his name, he was happy to collect a First Division Championship medal when the "Magpies" stormed to the Premier League. Still number one for his country, his international high spot came in a World Cup qualifier, where his penalty save enabled Northern Ireland to win 2-1 in Albania and record their first away victory since September 1991.

| | | | APPEARANCES | | | | GOALS | | | |
|---|---|---|---|---|---|---|---|---|---|---|
| Clubs | Signing Date | Transfer Fee | Lge | FL Cup | FA Cup | Others | Lge | FL Cup | FA Cup | Others |
| Newcastle United* | 1.88 | £30,000 | 70 | 6 | 4 | | | | | |
| Hull City | 2.91 | Loan | 6 | | | | | | | |

## YALLOP Frank Walter

Born: Watford, 4 April 1964

Height: 5'11"

Weight: 11.3

International Honours: E Yth, Canadian Int

**Position/Skill Factor:** Very experienced right-back, who drops off his opponents well and makes himself hard to beat. A good steady passer.

**Career History:** Spotted by Ipswich Town playing in schools football, he initially came to Portman Road as an apprentice in September 1980 and made steady progress into the club's professional ranks. Eventually, after a wait of over two years, he made his FL debut at Everton on 17 March 1984, when deputising for George Burley, but it wasn't until 1985-86 that he won a regular place in the team at full-back. Sadly for him, it coincided with the Town's relegation to Division Two. He became first choice right-back at Portman Road for the next five seasons, although occasionally filling in on the left side, or in central defence. In 1990-91, he was selected for the Canadian national team, presumably qualified by parentage. Coincidentally, the only other Canadian international in the Football League, is his teammate, Craig Forrest. Having appeared in all but one FL match during the previous season, he lost his place early in 1991-92. He remained a member of the first team squad until January, but subsequently played no further part in Ipswich's successful Second Division Championship campaign. Played only sporadically in **1992-93**, but even scoring two super goals in successive matches in January was not enough to guarantee him a regular place in the side. Basically, it was a season that was disrupted by World Cup calls, playing seven times for the international team of his choice, before returning to Canada in March for further qualifying games.

| | | | APPEARANCES | | | | GOALS | | | |
|---|---|---|---|---|---|---|---|---|---|---|
| Clubs | Signing Date | Transfer Fee | Lge | FL Cup | FA Cup | Others | Lge | FL Cup | FA Cup | Others |
| Ipswich Town* | 1.82 | - | 243+18 | 20+1 | 13+3 | 21+2 | 6 | 1 | | |

## YORKE Dwight

Born: Tobago, West Indies, 3 November 1971

Height: 5'10"

Weight: 11.12

International Honours: Trinidad & Tobago Int

**Position/Skill Factor:** Exciting forward who can play on either wing, where he can use his pace to advantage, or up front as a striker. A natural athlete with lovely balance, he has a good left foot.

**Career History:** Created such a good impression when playing for his country against Aston Villa on a summer tour, that Graham Taylor moved in quickly to sign him from his club, Signal Hill, in return for a substantial fee. Following a short period acclimatising at Villa Park, he made his FL debut as a substitute at Crystal Palace on 24 March 1990. Made further appearances in 1990-91 under new manager Jozef Venglos and when the latter was replaced by Ron Atkinson in the summer of 1991, he was the only Taylor signing to escape the "axe". He enjoyed an outstanding season in 1991-92, until "running out of steam" late in the season. Top scored with 11 FL goals, plus five in the cup competitions, including a first-half hat-trick at Derby in the FA Cup, Fourth Round. Had an unpredictable **1992-93**, regarding a first team place, following the signing of Dean Saunders and was not helped when he picked up a groin injury in the early part of the season, which also badly affected his back. However, he played in 34 (including seven substitute) games and while only scoring seven times, all of them in League games, most of them were memorable. Two of them, at home to Sheffield Wednesday, when nine of the Villa players touched the ball before he put it into the next for a goal, which came third in the "Match of the Day" competition and a diving header from a Steve Staunton cross against Ipswich Town, were brilliant by anybody's standards. Regardless of those successes, 1993-94 will see him severely challenged by Dalian Atkinson for the other striker's spot, alongside Dean Saunders.

| | | | APPEARANCES | | | | GOALS | | | |
|---|---|---|---|---|---|---|---|---|---|---|
| Clubs | Signing Date | Transfer Fee | Lge | FL Cup | FA Cup | Others | Lge | FL Cup | FA Cup | Others |
| Aston Villa* | 12.89 | £120,000 | 57+22 | 5+2 | 11 | 1 | 19 | | 5 | 1 |

## YOUDS Edward (Eddie) Paul

Born: Liverpool, 3 May 1970

Height: 6'0" Weight: 11.0

**Position/Skill Factor:** Good looking central defender who is useful in the air and will look to come out from the back in order to pass the ball, rather than clear his lines..

**Career History:** Local born player, he first joined Everton as a 14-year-old associated schoolboy in April 1985. On leaving school, he went to Goodison as a trainee in June 1986 and progressed to the "Toffees'" professional ranks during the 1988 close season. Games were hard to come by and in order to gain experience he had a couple of spells out on loan, making his FL debut as a substitute in his only League appearance for Cardiff City at Bolton Wanderers on 20 January 1990. Later, the same season, he joined Wrexham on loan and played a major role in saving the Welsh club's Football League status. When he joined the "Robins" they were not only bottom of the Fourth Division, but so far behind the 23rd club as to be lost beyond recall. However, nine victories and two draws, in the space of 13 games, hauled the team to safety. Naturally, Brian Flynn, the Wrexham manager, was eager to sign him permanently, but Colin Harvey felt that he still had a future with Everton. The following term he made his Everton FL debut as substitute away to Norwich on 22 December and his full debut at right-back in the next match, finishing the season with six more games under his belt. However, failing to make any further breakthrough in 1991-92, he was transferred to Ipswich Town, debuting at right-back away to Derby County on 16 November. Tragically he broke his leg in that game and missed the rest of the season. After almost a year out recovering, he came back as Town's first Premier League substitute, when he replaced Jason Dozzell after 69 minutes of the opening match of the **1992-93** season at home to Aston Villa. A few weeks later, he himself was taken off after just two minutes, without touching the ball, in order to allow goalkeeper, Clive Baker, to replace Craig Forrest, who had just been sent off in the home match against Sheffield United. Injuries and circumstances stopped him having more than a handful of games in the early part of the season, but he was given a run in the side and appeared in five of the last six games.

| | | | APPEARANCES | | | | GOALS | | | |
|---|---|---|---|---|---|---|---|---|---|---|
| Clubs | Signing Date | Transfer Fee | Lge | FL Cup | FA Cup | Others | Lge | FL Cup | FA Cup | Others |
| Everton | 6.88 | - | 5+3 | 0+1 | | 0+1 | | | | |
| Cardiff City | 12.89 | Loan | 0+1 | | 0+1 | | | | | |
| Wrexham | 2.90 | Loan | 20 | | | | 2 | | | |
| Ipswich Town* | 11.91 | £250,000 | 11+6 | 1+2 | 0+1 | | | | | |

## YOUNG Neil Anthony

Born: Harlow, 31 August 1973

Height: 5'8" Weight: 11.7

**Position/Skill Factor:** Strong tackling full-back who loves getting forward to join up with play.

**Career History:** Signed professional forms for Tottenham Hotspur during the 1991 close season, having been on the club's books as a trainee since August 1989 and has yet to turn out for the first team. Made 24 appearances for "Spurs'" reserve side in **1992-93** and could be knocking at the door before too long.

| | | | APPEARANCES | | | | GOALS | | | |
|---|---|---|---|---|---|---|---|---|---|---|
| Clubs | Signing Date | Transfer Fee | Lge | FL Cup | FA Cup | Others | Lge | FL Cup | FA Cup | Others |
| Tottenham Hotspur* | 7.91 | - | | | | | | | | |

## ZUMRUTEL Soner

Born: Islington, 6 October 1974

Height: 5'5½" Weight: 10.0

**Position/Skill Factor:** Right-winger who is very quick and always on the go. With good all-round ability, he is also a strong player, especially if he has to defend.

**Career History:** A recent professional signing for Arsenal, having been at Highbury as an associated schoolboy (May 1989) and as a trainee (July 1991), he was given a run out in a couple of reserve team games towards the end of **1992-93**, after playing mainly with the youth side.

| | | | APPEARANCES | | | | GOALS | | | |
|---|---|---|---|---|---|---|---|---|---|---|
| Clubs | Signing Date | Transfer Fee | Lge | FL Cup | FA Cup | Others | Lge | FL Cup | FA Cup | Others |
| Arsenal* | 7.93 | - | | | | | | | | |